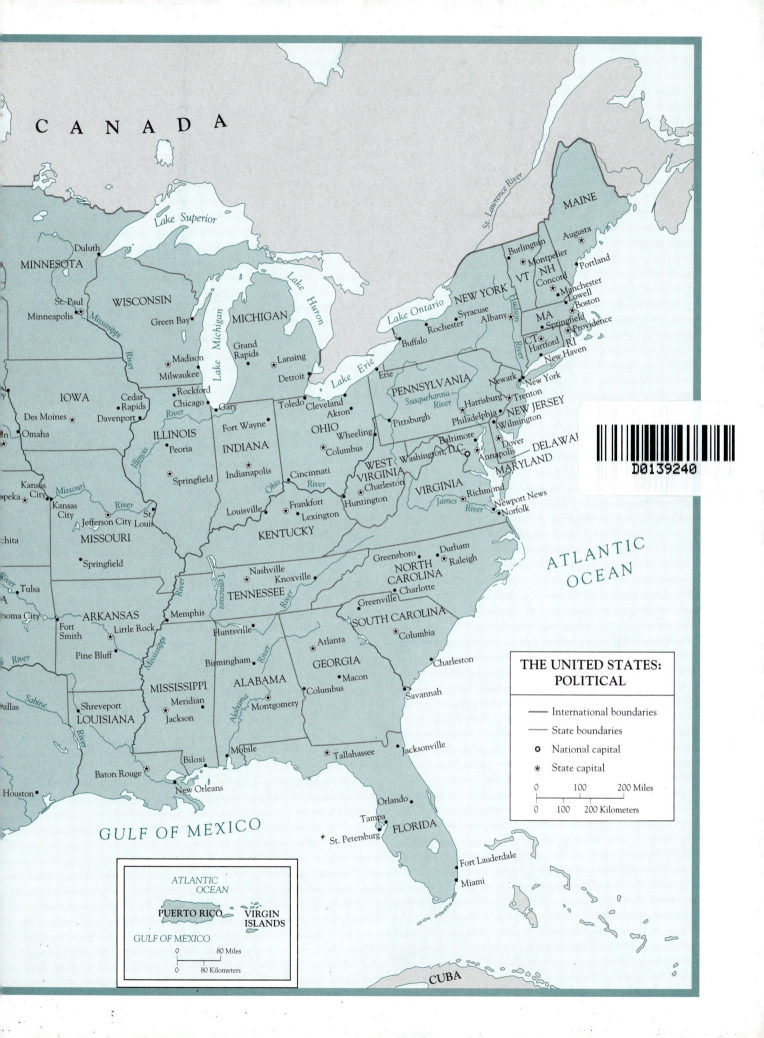

THE AMERICAN PAST

A Survey of American History

THE AMERICAN PAST

A Survey of American History

Volume II

EIGHTH EDITION

Joseph R. Conlin

THOMSON
™
WADSWORTH

Australia • Brazil • Canada • Mexico • Singapore • Spain • United Kingdom • United States

The American Past: A Survey of American History, Volume II
Eighth Edition

Joseph R. Conlin

Publisher: Clark Baxter
Senior Acquisitions Editor: Ashley Dodge
Senior Development Editor: Margaret McAndrew
Assistant Editor: Jessica Kim
Editorial Assistant: Kristen Judy
Technology Project Manager: David Lionetti
Marketing Manager: Lori Grebe Cook
Marketing Assistant: Teresa Jessen
Project Manager, Editorial Production: Katy German
Creative Director: Rob Hugel
Art Director: Maria Epes

Print Buyer: Doreen Suruki
Permissions Editor: Joohee Lee
Production Service: Interactive Composition Corporation/
Matrix Productions
Text Designer: Patricia McDermond
Photo Researcher: Lili Weiner
Copy Editor: Susan Swanson
Cover Designer: William Stanton
Cover Image: © SSPL / The Image Works
Compositor: Interactive Composition Corporation
Printer: Quebecor World-Taunton

Printed in the United States of America
1 2 3 4 5 6 7 10 09 08 07 06

Thomson Higher Education
10 Davis Drive
Belmont, CA 94002-3098
USA

For more information about our products, contact us at:
Thomson Learning Academic Resource Center
1-800-423-0563
For permission to use material from this text or product, submit a request online at
http://www.thomsonrights.com.
Any additional questions about permissions can be submitted by e-mail to
thomsonrights@thomson.com.

Library of Congress Control Number: 2005933159

ISBN 0-495-05059-9

To the memory of
J.R.C. (1917–1985)
L.V.C. (1920–2001)

Brief Contents

Table of Contents

List of Maps

How They Lived

Preface

TO THE PROFESSOR

I prepared this new edition because since the time I wrote its predecessor, recently published books (and some older ones that I read for the first time) convinced me that much of nineteenth-, eighteenth-, and seventeenth-century American history had changed. I have listed some of these areas below.

Because I wrote *The American Past* for young men and women who may be taking history only because it's a requirement, my overriding aspiration has been to produce a reading and learning experience that is pleasurable as well as illuminating. Narrative is the kind of prose that most people find enjoyable to read, so narrative is the way I do it. During the more than two decades that *The American Past* has been in print, I have heard from many professors—perhaps close to 200—who have assigned the text to their classes. It has been gratifying that even some of the annoyed correspondents closed their letters with a comment something like, "My students really like *The American Past*. They actually read it!"

NEW TO THIS EDITION

Topics on which I have focused or about which my understanding has been significantly altered since writing the seventh edition have received fresh treatment in this volume. These include:

- Pre-Columbian America
- The early slave trade in West Africa
- The conquest of Mexico
- Elizabethan era colonization ("the failed colonies")
- Witchcraft in colonial New England
- "The overlooked colonies," especially New Netherlands and New Jersey
- The Eastern Woodlands Indians
- New France and the Anglo-French rivalry
- The military history of the War for Independence
- Evangelical religion and denominations
- Fugitive slaves and the Underground Railroad
- Big city political machines
- Racism, Jim Crow segregation, and lynching
- The Civil Rights Movement in the courts
- Popular culture in the 1890s–1900s and 1950s
- The partisan upheaval of the late twentieth century

The treatment of the Revolutionary, Confederation, Federalist, and Jeffersonian eras, particularly of the great movers and shapers of the era, has been profoundly changed by recent scholarship. Since 1995 George Washington, Alexander Hamilton, John Adams, Thomas Jefferson, and James Madison have each been the subject of at least three biographical studies that range in quality from very good to superb (and there have been biographies of John Jay and Gouverneur Morris in the same league).

For the information of instructors who have previously assigned *The American Past,* chapters in this edition that have been written virtually from scratch or so substantially changed as to be new are Chapters 1, 2, 5, 6, 15, 17, 35, 46, 47, and 48. There are about ten **How They Lived** features new to this edition and several dozen new sidebars. I have discarded all the chapter bibliographies ("Further Reading") of the seventh edition and prepared new, more extensive ones with an emphasis on titles published since about 1980. The **Timelines,** lists of **Key Terms** (defined in an appendix), and the **Online Sources Guides** at the end of each chapter are new to this edition.

Where necessary, I have reorganized chapters for the sake of greater clarity and have polished the prose with an eye on making the book more appealing to survey course students. There are, I think, few paragraphs here that read word for word as they did in the seventh edition. I have added illustrative evidence new to me—data, facts, anecdotes—and fresh interpretations throughout the book.

ACKNOWLEDGMENTS

My publishers, as they prepared this new edition, asked history professors from every part of the country to read from one to three chapters of the book and to write critiques for my guidance during revision: What is done well? What is done not so well? What subjects are inadequately covered or could be better explained? Where are my interpretations dead wrong?

This time around all but a half-dozen of the chapter reviews were invaluable. I have not agreed with every criticism. Deadlines and space limitations prevented me from accommodating some suggestions for improvement with which I was and am in complete agreement. (I have filed them for future reference.) I am grateful for the extraordinary and, in my experience, unprecedented favors done me by the following professors of history and—it is a safe bet—teachers of the first order.

LIST OF REVIEWERS

George Alvergue, *Lane Community College*
Mary Ann Bodayla, *Southwest Tennessee Community College*
Scott Carter, *Shasta College*
Albert Churella, *Southern Polytechnic State University*
Craig R. Coenen, *Mercer County Community College*
Richard H. Condon, *University of Maine at Farmington*
Stacy A. Cordery, *Monmouth College*
Linda Cross, *Tyler Junior College*
Barry A. Crouch, *Gallaudet University*
Brian Dirck, *Anderson University*
William Marvin Dulaney, *College of Charleston*

Carla Falkner, *Northeast Mississippi Community College*
Francis Flavin, *University of Texas—Dallas*
George E. Frakes, *Santa Barbara City College*
Thomas M. Gaskin, *Everett Community College*
Joan E. Gittens, *Southwest State University*
Paula K. Hinton, *Tennessee Technological University*
John E. Hollitz, *Community College of Southern Nevada*
Robert R. Jones, *University of Southwestern Louisiana*
Martha Kirchmer, *Grand Valley State University*
Mary S. Lewis, *Jacksonville College*
Milton Madden, *Lane Community College*
Patricia L. Meador, *Louisiana State University, Shreveport*
Angelo Montante, *Glendale Community College*
Jack Oden, *Enterprise State Junior College*
Martin T. Olliff, *Troy University—Dothan Campus*
John S. Olszowka, *University of Maine—Farmington*
Emmett Panzella, *Point Park College*
Richard H. Peterson, *emeritus, San Diego State University*
Nancy L. Rachels, *Hillsborough Community College*
Michelle Riley, *Del Mar College*
Stephanie Abbot Roper, *West Texas A&M University*
Karen Rubin, *Florida State University*
William Scofield, *Yakima Valley Community College*
Richard S. Sorrell, *Brookdale Community College*
Amos St. Germain, *Wentworth Institute of Technology*
Ronald Story, *University of Massachusetts*
Ruth Suyama, *Los Angeles Mission College*
Daniel C. Vogt, *Jackson State University*
Pamela West, *Jefferson State Community College*
Loy Glenn Westfall, *Hillsborough Brandon Community College*
Donald W. Whisenhunt, *Western Washington University*
Lynn Willoughby, *Winthrop University*
Larry Wright, *Inver Hills Community College*

It has been my astonishingly good fortune to have as friends two remarkable librarians who were willing to put their expertise and time at my disposal.

Susan Kling of Bandon, Oregon organized and administered a massive, customized interlibrary loan program that put into my hands every book I requested of her, certainly more than a hundred over the last six months. The late Marilyn Murphy of Eureka, California did not know everything, as she enjoyed saying, but she knew where to find it out. I posed questions to her about the obscurest of data which, I was certain in many instances, simply did not exist. Instance after instance, often in hours, sometimes after a week with daily progress reports, she had the citation for me. Rest in peace, Marilyn.

For the third time now, Margaret McAndrew Beasley was the developmental editor of *The American Past*. Margaret coordinated me, the chapter reviewers, manuscript, photos, permissions, and a squadron of production people. Margaret remained calm and in control when I fell behind schedule or proclaimed an insurrection because of one or another editorial decision. If, in the end, she usually got her way, when the flare-ups were extinguished, I usually recognized that she had been right. There cannot be too many of Margaret's caliber in this business.

Finally, my thanks to those of the many people who had a hand in making this book whose names are known to me.

Clark Baxter, Publisher
Ashley Dodge, Senior Acquisitions Editor
Katy German, Production Project Manager
Rozi Harris and Merrill Peterson, Project Managers
Lili Weiner, Freelance Photo Researcher
Joohee Lee, Permissions Editor

TO THE STUDENT

"History" and "the past" are two different things. The past does not change, but *history* changes all the time because history is not an account of the past but the story of the past *as we understand it*. What we have in our heads is changeable indeed (or at least it should be).

Our understanding of what happened five hundred or even fifty years ago may change because of additions to the information available to us—the "sources," historians call them (speeches, letters, diaries, photographs, etc.)—or because of an alteration in the way we look at that information.

Documents thought lost forever are discovered, sometimes in far corners of farmhouse attics (it really does happen). Documents we never knew existed turn up, sometimes right in the archives where they belong but on the wrong shelf. The personal papers of important historical figures, sealed for twenty or thirty years by the terms of their last wills and testaments (usually to allow everyone mentioned in them to die off), are legally opened in a reading room crowded with historians. Governments, often grudgingly, eventually publish official documents that had been rubber-stamped "Top Secret."

History is also rewritten when sources of information that had been in full view all the time are suddenly understandable. During the short time (historically speaking) since the first edition of *The American Past* was published, the most momentous example of such a breakthrough was the deciphering of the written language of the ancient Maya. The innumerable carvings on the ruins of Mayan temples in Central America had long been admired for their artistry, and archaeologists knew they were more than decorations. When they were finally able to read most of the inscriptions, they not only revealed a portrait of Mayan civilization very different from what was in every textbook, they pushed back the date American history begins—for history is based on *written* sources—by a thousand years from that starting date known to everyone, 1492. Change indeed!

Technology changes history, too. The number-crunching capacity of the computer means that data that was always available but too vast to be approached—for example, the raw reports that census takers turned into the Census Bureau every ten years—becomes easily-accessible rich sources of social history. Baptismal and marriage registries moldering in thousands of churches, even the names and dates etched in stone in ancient graveyards, previously of interest only to genealogists and antiquarians, become historical goldmines.

Because history is changing all the time, history textbooks like this one are regularly revised. I have not prepared this eighth edition in order to keep *The American Past* up-to-date with coverage of events of the several years that have elapsed since the publication of the seventh. Fastidiously objective summaries of such "current events," at least as good as I could compile, are readily available in almanacs and news magazines.

All of this about the changeability of history will be old hat to research historians, history teachers, graduate students, and even history majors. However, *The American Past* was not written for people who already love history enough to have made it their profession. *The American Past* was written and revised for first- and second-year college students enrolled in United States history survey courses; majors in accounting, botany, mathematics, psychology, zoology, and a dozen other fields for whom the fact that history is always in flux may well be a fresh idea (and one worth knowing).

THE AMERICAN PAST

A Survey of American History

CHAPTER 25

Aftermath

Reconstructing the Union; Failing the Freedmen 1865–1877

National Archives

You say you have emancipated us. You have; and I thank you for it. But what is your emancipation? ... When you turned us loose, you gave us no acres. You turned us loose to the skies, to the storm, to the whirlwind, and, worst of all, you turned us loose to the wrath of our infuriated masters.

Frederick Douglass

When the guns fell silent in 1865, some southern cities—Vicksburg, Atlanta, Columbia, Richmond—were flattened, eerie wastelands of charred timbers, rubble, and free-standing chimneys. Few of the South's railroads could be operated for more than a few miles. Bridges were gone. River commerce had dwindled to a trickle; the only new boats were from the North. Commercial ties with Europe—and with the North—had been snapped. All the South's banks were ruined.

Even the cultivation of the soil had been disrupted. Thousands of small farms owned by the men who served in the Confederate ranks lay fallow. Plantation owners who fled when Union armies advanced discovered that weeds and brambles were more destructive conquerors than Yankees. Many who had labored in their fields for them, the former slaves, were likely to be gone. When southern blacks were told they were free men and women, the first impulse of many was to test their freedom by walking off, even if they had no destination in mind. Ex-slaves who stayed in the only

home they had ever known wondered if the crop they were planting that spring belonged to them or to their old master.

THE RECONSTRUCTION CRISIS

In view of the desolation, *Reconstruction* seems the appropriate word for America's postwar era. In fact, as the word was understood in 1865 and 1866 and for another decade, "Reconstruction" had nothing to do with laying bricks, rehabilitating railroads, or recovering fields. Reconstruction referred to the political procedure by which the eleven rebel states were restored to "a normal constitutional relationship" with the federal government. It was the Union, that great abstraction over which so many had died, that was rebuilt.

Blood was shed during the Reconstruction era too, but little glory was won. Few political reputations—northern, southern, white, black, Republican, Democratic—emerged from Reconstruction unstained. Perhaps Abraham Lincoln

National Archives

Richmond in ruins, more from a fire that got out of control than from bombardment. Atlanta looked worse. The Shenandoah Valley and northeastern Georgia were laid waste. Even areas of the South untouched by war were impoverished, dwellings and fields neglected. This was the condition of many of the states that had to be reconstructed.

had been sainted only because he did not survive the war. Indeed, the Reconstruction procedure Lincoln proposed as early as 1863 was repudiated by Congress, which surely would have fought him over it had he lived and tried to push it through. His successor, Andrew Johnson, adopted Lincoln's Reconstruction plans, and Congress ruined him.

Lincoln foresaw the serious problems that faced him. He described as "pernicious" the constitutional hair-splitting with which both sides began to debate the nation's Reconstruction policy. But when Richmond fell and Lee surrendered, he had offered no alternative to his 1863 plan.

LINCOLN VERSUS CONGRESS

By December 1863, Union armies occupied large chunks of the Confederacy. Ultimate victory in the war, while not yet in the bag, was a reasonable expectation. To provide for the rapid reconciliation of North and South—Lincoln's postwar priority—he proclaimed that as soon as 10 percent of the eligible voters in a former Confederate state took an oath of allegiance to the Union, the people of that state could write a new state constitution, organize a government, and elect representatives to Congress. Immediately, southern states that were mostly occupied—Tennessee, Arkansas, and Louisiana—complied.

But Congress refused to recognize them as Union states, returning them to military command. Republican congressmen had been alarmed from the start of the war by Lincoln's unilateral expansion of presidential powers. No president, not even Andrew Jackson (still vilified by Republicans), had exercised as much authority as Lincoln did. During a war that threatened to destroy the Union, congressmen swallowed their anxieties. But Reconstruction was a postwar issue, and Lincoln's 1863 proposal did not involve Congress. That would not do, particularly inasmuch as Lincoln spoke of prompt elections of senators and representatives; Congress was keenly sensitive to its right to judge the credentials of men who showed up claiming to be duly elected members. That was no pernicious abstraction!

THE WADE–DAVIS BILL

The radicals were a minority of the congressional Republicans in 1864. But they were vociferous and persuasive, and they had additional reasons to reject Lincoln's proposal. They were abolitionists who blamed the slavocracy, the South's great planters, for causing the terrible war. They were determined that the slavocrats be punished—if not hanged then gelded politically. To ensure that the reconstructed southern states be governed differently than they had been before the war, they insisted that the *freedmen*, as the emancipated slaves were called, participate in southern government. (The word freed*men* referred to women—and children, for that matter—not just to adult males; it would not have occurred to Americans of 1865 to speak of "freedpeople" or "freedpersons.")

So in July 1864 Congress enacted the **Wade–Davis Bill.** It provided that only after *50 percent* of the eligible voters of a former Confederate state swore loyalty could the Reconstruction process begin. And Congress—not the president!—would decide when the southern states were again part of the Union. Wade–Davis did not include a comprehensive procedure for Reconstruction. Mainly, it was enacted to slow down a process that, to the radical Republicans, Lincoln seemed to be hell-bent on hastening. If Congress was just buying time, it won the skirmish with the president.

Lincoln killed Wade–Davis with a **pocket veto,** which did not require him to explain his reasons for rejecting it in a veto message that would likely exacerbate the dispute. During the final months of his life, he dropped hints that he would compromise with Congress. He even reached out to the radicals (whom he had never much liked) by saying he had no objection to giving the right to vote to blacks who were "very intelligent and those who have fought gallantly in our ranks." He urged the military governor of Louisiana whom he had appointed to extend suffrage to some blacks. And there things stood when John Wilkes Booth sent history on an unanticipated course.

LINCOLN'S GOALS

Why did Lincoln dodge radical demands that the **freedmen** be granted civil rights equal to those of whites? First, his highest postwar priority was the reconciliation of northern and southern whites, no little thing given the bitterness of the war. He made his intentions eloquently clear in his second inaugural address a few weeks before he was shot. "With malice toward none, with charity for all, . . . let us strive on to finish the work we are in, to bind up the nation's wounds, . . . to do all which may achieve and cherish a just and lasting peace among ourselves."

For Lincoln, the interests of the freedmen were secondary to the interests of American whites, if that. If white southerners' insistence that they would never accept blacks as equals prevented reconciliation with the Union, Lincoln was willing to give way. Radical Senator Ben Wade said that Lincoln's views on black people "could only come of one who was born of poor white trash and educated in a slave state." This was as unfair as it was ugly. Lincoln's racial attitudes changed during the war, slowly and ambivalently. Again, he dodged making any strong statements for which he would be held accountable. But he was impressed by African-American bravery in battle.

As ever, Lincoln the politician was flexible: "Saying that Reconstruction will be accepted if presented in a specified way, it is not said that it will never be accepted in any other way." He was telling the radicals that nothing about Reconstruction, including the future status of the freedmen, was final.

Still, for Lincoln, it all kept coming back to what was best for the goal of sectional reconciliation.

Reconstruction 1863–1877

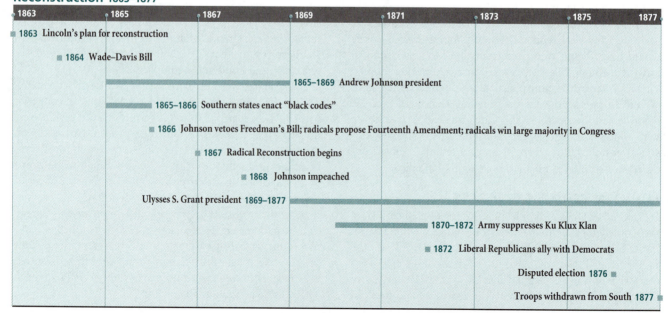

- 1863 Lincoln's plan for reconstruction
- 1864 Wade–Davis Bill
- 1865–1869 Andrew Johnson president
- 1865–1866 Southern states enact "black codes"
- 1866 Johnson vetoes Freedman's Bill; radicals propose Fourteenth Amendment; radicals win large majority in Congress
- 1867 Radical Reconstruction begins
- 1868 Johnson impeached
- Ulysses S. Grant president 1869–1877
- 1870–1872 Army suppresses Ku Klux Klan
- 1872 Liberal Republicans ally with Democrats
- Disputed election 1876
- Troops withdrawn from South 1877

STUBBORN ANDREW JOHNSON

After April 15, 1865, it did not matter what Lincoln thought, and Andrew Johnson was not a flexible politician. Nor had his own "white trash" views on race undergone any changes during the war.

Johnson grew up in stultifying frontier poverty in Tennessee. Unlike Lincoln, who taught himself to read as a boy, Johnson was an illiterate adult when he asked a schoolteacher in Greenville to teach him how to read and write. She did, and married him too, and encouraged her husband to go into politics. Johnson won elective office on every level from town councilman to congressman to senator. He owned a few slaves, but he hated the secessionist cotton planters of western Tennessee. He was the only southern senator to refuse to walk out of Congress in 1861; he called for a ruthless war on the rebels and, when they were defeated, not reconciliation but punishment, the gallows for Jefferson Davis. Lincoln appointed him governor of occupied Tennessee and chose him to run for vice president in 1864 in the hope of winning the votes of other southern Unionists.

Johnson's political experience was extensive, but his personality was ill suited to national politics. Whereas Lincoln was sure of what he could accomplish, Johnson was unsubtle, insensitive, willful, and stubborn. He got off to an unlucky start as vice president. Near collapse with a bad cold on inauguration day, he bolted several glasses of brandy and was visibly drunk when he took the oath of office. Fortunately, only a few people were present, and Lincoln told aides that Johnson was not to speak at the public ceremony outside the Capitol.

Johnson was not, in fact, a "problem drinker." Inauguration day was a fluke. And nothing was made of his gaffe at the time because the likeliest group to jump on Lincoln's vice president, the radical Republicans, rather liked Johnson; they liked him much more than they liked Lincoln because of Johnson's repeated calls for punishing leading rebels. As military governor of Tennessee he had approved some confiscations of rebel estates.

But the radicals misread Johnson's anti-Confederate ardor. Emancipation pleased him only because it hit at the wealth and power of the great planters, not because he thought slavery was a wicked institution or cared about how blacks were treated. Before he was president, there was no call for him to express his views on race or, for that matter, about the differences between Lincoln and Congress on Reconstruction policy.

JOHNSON: THEY ARE ALREADY STATES

In fact, Johnson ignored Lincoln's hints that he would discuss Reconstruction with congressional Republicans. With insignificant changes, he made Lincoln's presidential Reconstruction program of 1863 his own program. Reconciliation would be quick; the president, not Congress, would oversee the procedure and decide when the rebel states were readmitted to the Union. Johnson did not consult with congressional leaders before announcing his plan.

Johnson was a pretty fair student of the Constitution. To him, as to Daniel Webster, the Union of states was permanent. Constitutionally, the Union *could not* be dissolved; states *could not* secede. There had indeed been a rebellion, a war, and an entity known as the Confederate States of America. But, said Johnson, individuals had rebelled, fought against the U.S. government, and created the Confederacy. The states of Virginia, Alabama, and the rest had not seceded because that was constitutionally impossible. Virginia and the rest were still states, constitutional components of the Union. Seating their duly elected representatives in Congress was a purely administrative matter, which made it the responsibility of the executive branch of the government. It was simple and obvious to him.

REBEL CONGRESSMEN, PARDONS, AND BLACK CODES

There was nothing wrong with Johnson's constitutional reasoning. In 1861 every Unionist had said what he said in 1865. Johnson's problem was his refusal to see beyond constitutional propriety to the messy world of human feelings, hatred, resentment, and flesh and blood—especially blood. To real people, what the Preamble to the Constitution, John Marshall, and Daniel Webster might say about Virginia and the rest meant far less in 1865 than the fact that in four years of a war begun by southerners, more than half a million people had been killed.

Now, under Johnson's Reconstruction rules, the white people of the rebel states quickly wrote state constitutions and elected congressmen and senators—including four Confederate generals, six members of Jefferson Davis's cabinet, and as senator from Georgia, the Confederate vice president, Alexander H. Stephens. This did not sit well with northerners, some of whom were still buying tombstones for their menfolk.

Johnson's pardons did not improve the mood in the North. Some Confederate leaders had to be pardoned, of course. Lincoln, in the interests of reconciliation, would surely have pardoned many respected (and cooperative) rebel leaders soon after the war ended. But Johnson was manic in the matter. Before the end of 1865 he signed pardons for 13,000 Confederates, restoring their civil rights. That was a rate of 2,000 per month; few who applied were denied. What was Johnson thinking? Reconciliation required the goodwill of northerners too.

Few white northerners believed in the intrinsic equality of the races. Probably only a minority of congressional radicals did; the same Congress that wrote the Fourteenth Amendment guaranteeing equal civil rights to all voted to segregate schools by race in the District of Columbia. Nevertheless, the war had been fought to abolish slavery, and the *black codes* enacted by the Johnson-approved southern state governments seemed, to many people, to reintroduce slavery without using the word. Indeed, South Carolina refused to repeal its ordinance of secession, and Mississippi refused to ratify the Thirteenth Amendment; Alabama rejected part of it (a neat trick in that its guts consist of thirty-two words).

The **black codes** of some states made it illegal for African Americans to live in towns and cities, a backhanded way of keeping them in the fields. In no state were blacks allowed to vote or to bear arms. South Carolina said that African Americans could not sell goods! Mississippi required freedmen to sign twelve-month labor contracts before January 10 of each year. Those who did not could be arrested, with their labor for the year sold to the highest bidder in a manner strongly reminiscent of the slave auction. Dependent children could be forced to work. Blacks who reneged on their contracts were not paid for the work they already had performed. Mississippi even made it a crime for blacks to insult white people or make insulting "gestures."

THE RADICALS: THE STATES HAVE FORFEITED THEIR RIGHTS

The radical Republicans knew that Johnson's Reconstruction plan and the southern response to it were unpopular in the North. But that did not mean that a majority of northern voters would look favorably on their plan to grant full civil rights to the freedmen. Sixteen of twenty-three Union states did not allow blacks to vote. The radicals needed to win majority support, particularly from the Republicans in Congress who considered themselves moderates.

Different radicals offered different constitutional justifications for rejecting Johnson's stalled Reconstruction program and supporting Congress's right to oversee the process. It

Thaddeus Stevens of Pennsylvania, a longtime abolitionist, was the leader of the Radical Republicans in the House of Representatives. Proslavery southern extremists hated him; a Confederate raiding party went out of its way to burn a factory he owned. He hoped to establish complete civil equality for blacks in both north and south, but settled for less.

might be more accurate to say that they offered different terminologies.

Thaddeus Stevens of Pennsylvania, the radical leader in the House, said that the Confederate states had committed "state suicide" when they seceded. They were not, in 1865, alive. Therefore, it was within the power of Congress alone to admit them as states when they were "reborn." Charles Sumner, a prominent Senate radical, said that the former southern states were "conquered provinces." Their constitutional status was identical to that of territories seized from Mexico in 1848. Congress (not the president) had admitted California as a state in 1850; Congress would admit the former Confederate states when Congress approved of the state constitutions they wrote. Another Republican, Samuel Shellabarger of Ohio, came up with language that was more persuasive to moderates sitting on the fence: when the rebel states seceded, they "forfeited" the rights given states by the Constitution.

Congress's Joint Committee on Reconstruction settled on a plausible formula: "The States lately in rebellion were, at the close of the war, disorganized communities, without civil government, and without constitutions or other forms, by virtue of which political relations could legally exist between them and the federal government." This provided all but a few Republicans loyal to Johnson with grounds for refusing to seat the southerners who came to Washington as the elected representatives of the rebel states.

RADICAL GOALS AND MOTIVES

The radicals were motivated by ideals, passions, and hard-headed politics. Most of them had been abolitionists, morally repelled by the institution of slavery. Thaddeus Stevens, Ben Wade, Charles Sumner, and others believed in racial equality and were determined, if they could carry the day, that African Americans would enjoy full civil rights. Stevens, Wade, and George W. Julian hated the slavocracy, the great planter elite that they blamed for the war.

The planters' power had been maimed by the abolition of slavery, but they still owned the land. Julian proposed to confiscate the estates of the planters, particularly those who had been active Confederates, high-ranking army officers, and government officials. He had a good precedent to point at: the confiscation of Loyalist estates after the War for Independence. Not only would confiscation punish the rebels and destroy their economic power at a strike; but by dividing the plantations into forty-acre farms to be granted to the freedmen, the government would give southern blacks the economic independence that, in the Jeffersonian tradition, was essential to good citizenship.

The radicals had frankly partisan motives too. The Republican party was a sectional party. In 1860, the last election before the rebellion, the southern states did not bother to list Republican candidates on ballots. To the radicals, if the party did not establish itself in the South, it was doomed to be defeated at the polls. The party's precarious political situation was worse in 1865 than it had been before the war when Democrats controlled the Senate and the Republicans held only a slender majority in the House. With slavery gone, the number of southern representatives would increase. The three-fifths compromise was dead. Where slave states had counted three-fifths of the slaves in calculating the number of their congressmen, they were now entitled to count the entire population at face value.

There were white southern Republicans in 1865: Whig Unionists who had sat out the war and small-scale farmers in the mountain counties of Kentucky, Tennessee, Virginia, and North Carolina who had opposed secession. Many of them had fought in Union armies, and they no more wanted to see the return to power of the secessionist Democrats than the radicals did. But white Republicans were a minority in every state, a tiny minority in the cotton South. If the party was to compete with the Democrats in the former Confederacy, it was necessary to ensure that the freedmen voted. Thaddeus Stevens put no pressure on moderate Republicans to work for African-American suffrage in the North, where the idea was not popular. But if southern blacks did not vote, he argued, the Republican party was a dead duck. "I am for Negro suffrage in every rebel state," he told Congress (specifying *rebel states*). "If it be just, it should not be denied; if it be necessary, it should be adopted; if it be a punishment to traitors, they deserve it."

1866: THE CRITICAL YEAR

Stevens and the other radicals had to be accommodating with the moderate Republicans. This was difficult for natural antagonists like Ben Wade. But the radicals were few. If they were to see their programs effected, they had to win over Republicans who were not as sure as they were that the freedmen had to have full citizenship.

Luckily for them, President Johnson was uncompromising. He pushed the Republican moderates into the radicals' arms by trying to destroy a constructive federal agency that was averting starvation and social chaos in the South and, then, by writing off the moderate Republicans and turning to the hated Democrats, including southern Democrats, for political support.

THE FREEDMEN'S BUREAU

The former slaves responded to freedom in different ways. Some, who were bewildered by the announcement or who had been treated decently by their masters, stayed put. Promised wages when their masters found money, they worked in the fields much as they always had (no longer worrying about the blacksnake whip). Other freed slaves took to the roads. Some heard rumors that every slave family would be granted "forty acres and a mule," and they searched for the Union officer who would provide the coveted farm. Some wanderers gathered in ramshackle camps that were often disorderly. Gangs of discharged Confederate soldiers, trudging sometimes hundreds of miles toward their homes, clogged the roads too. There were plenty of racial incidents.

Congress saw more problems coming and acted to avert chaos. In March 1865 Congress established the Bureau of Refugees, Freedmen, and Abandoned Land, to be administered by the army commanded by General O. O. Howard.

Howard's most pressing task was relief: avoiding mass starvation in the South. Just in 1865, the **Freedman's Bureau** distributed rations to 150,000 people, about a third of them whites. When Congress decided not to confiscate land on a large scale, Bureau agents negotiated labor contracts between destitute former slaves and landowners. Because there was little coin in the South and southern banknotes were worthless, many of these arrangements were not unlike what some black codes prescribed. They were sharecropping arrangements: the actual field workers and the landowners taking shares of the crop in varying proportions.

The Bureau set up medical facilities for the inevitable health problems. (Again, whites were served as well as freedmen.) Ultimately the Bureau built and staffed forty-six hospitals and treated more than 400,000 cases of illness and injury.

With the freedmen, the most popular Bureau program was its school system. Freedom released a craving for education among blacks, adults as well as children. Appleton and Company, a publishing house, sold a million copies annually of Noah Webster's *Elementary Spelling Book*—the "Blue-Backed Speller" from which American schoolchildren learned to read for forty years. In 1866 sales jumped to 1.5 million, the 50 percent increase due to sales to freedmen. Teachers from the North, mostly white women, opened multigrade "one-room schoolhouses" throughout the South. Many of the teachers later reminisced that never before or after had they such dedicated pupils.

OPEN CONFLICT

In 1865 Congress gave the Freedmen's Bureau a year to do its job. The assumption was that, by then, reconstructed state governments would take over the schools, hospitals, and Bureau-run institutions. In February 1866, however, Reconstruction was at a standstill. Congress refused to recognize Johnson's state governments but had itself certified none. The South was still occupied territory. So Congress extended the life of the Freedman's Bureau for two years.

Johnson vetoed the bill, insisting that the former rebel states had constitutional governments. A month later, he vetoed another bill that granted citizenship to the freedmen. The Constitution, he said, gave the states the power to decide the terms of citizenship within their borders. Once again he

Discouraging Rebellion

A now forgotten but, at the time, significant provision of the Fourteenth Amendment forbade the former Confederate states to repay "any debt or obligation incurred in aid of insurrection or rebellion against the United States." By punishing banks and individuals, including Europeans and European banks, that had loaned money to the rebel states (the Confederacy no longer existed), the amendment put potential underwriters of future rebellions on notice that such loans had consequences.

The Valentine Museum

The Freedmen's Bureau was the federal government's response to the old proslavery argument that freeing the slaves in the South would cause serious social and economic problems. The Bureau confronted many of those problems, from starvation to African-American illiteracy, with remarkable success. Former slaves gratefully remembered Bureau schools, so great was their hunger to learn. Many Freedmen's Bureau schools were run by northern white women; this class has (far right) a black teacher, probably a northerner.

had the better constitutional argument, and he might have won the political contest had northerners not been appalled by some of the black codes and massive mob attacks on freedmen in several southern cities, including New Orleans.

In June 1866, perceiving the shift in mood in their favor, radical Republicans, now joined by moderates, drew up a constitutional amendment on which to base congressional Reconstruction policy (and to answer Johnson's point about citizenship). The long, complex Fourteenth Amendment banned from federal and state office all high-ranking Confederates unless they were pardoned by Congress. The amendment also established, for the first time, national citizenship. It guaranteed that all "citizens of the United States and of the State wherein they reside" would be treated equally under the laws of all the states.

If ratified, the Fourteenth Amendment would prevent the southern states from passing laws like the black codes. However, the radicals were taking a big chance. The Fourteenth Amendment would also cancel northern state laws that

discriminated against blacks. In that aspect of the amendment Johnson saw his opportunity. Calculating that many northerners, particularly in the Midwest, would rather have ex-Confederates in Washington than grant equal rights to African Americans, he decided to campaign personally against the radicals in the 1866 congressional election.

THE RADICAL TRIUMPH

The first step was to organize a new political party. Just as Lincoln did not want to run as a Republican in 1864, Johnson did not want to be labeled a Democrat in 1866. On his behalf, Secretary of State Seward, a few Republican senators, the governor of Massachusetts, and some prominent Democrats held a "National Union party" convention in Philadelphia. Their message was sectional reconciliation. As a symbol, the convention opened with a procession of northern and southern Johnson men in pairs, a southerner and a northerner, marching arm in arm.

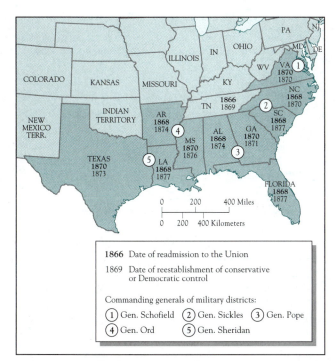

MAP 25:1 Radical Reconstruction

The radicals partitioned the Confederacy into five military districts of manageable size. The Union army supervised the establishment of state governments that guaranteed equal civil rights to freedmen, whence each state was readmitted to the Union (with Republican-dominated governments). Tennessee was not included in the program. Occupied for much of the war by the Union army, Tennessee had a reconstructed state government by 1866 thanks, ironically, to its wartime governor, Andrew Johnson, who, as president, opposed radical Reconstruction.

Unhappily for Johnson, the first couple on the floor was South Carolina Governor James L. Orr, a huge, fleshy man, and Massachusetts Governor John A. Andrew, a little fellow with a way of looking intimidated. When Orr seemed to drag the mousy Andrew down the length of the hall, the radicals had a field day. It would have been worse in the age of television, or even when newspapers were able to reproduce photographs. But Republican cartoonists filled the gap: the National Union party was a rebel's party with northern flunkeys.

In the fall, Johnson himself ensured defeat. He toured the Midwest on what he called a "swing around the circle," delivering dozens of blistering speeches denouncing the Republicans. No president had ever politicked so personally, not even when seeking election for himself. To make things worse, Johnson had learned his oratorical technique in the rough-and-tumble, stump-speaking tradition of eastern Tennessee. Voters there liked a hot debate between politicians scorching each other and ridiculing hecklers—when the issue at stake was selecting the next county sheriff. But the style was disconcerting when the president of the United States snapped at the bait radical hecklers waved in front of him. Drunk again, the radicals said with mock sadness, reminding voters of Johnson's inauguration as vice president.

The result was a landslide. Most of Johnson's candidates were defeated. The Republican party, now firmly in radical

hands, controlled more than two-thirds of the seats in both houses of Congress, enough to override every veto Johnson handed them.

RADICAL RECONSTRUCTION

The radical Reconstruction program was adopted in a series of laws passed by the Fortieth Congress in 1867. They dissolved Johnson's southern state governments and partitioned the Confederacy into five military provinces, each commanded by a major general. The army would maintain order while voters were registered: blacks and those whites not disenfranchised by the Fourteenth Amendment. The constitutional conventions these voters elected were required to ratify the Thirteenth and Fourteenth Amendments and to give the vote to adult black males. After Congress approved their constitutions, the reconstructed states would be admitted to the Union and their senators and representatives to Congress.

RADICALS IN CONTROL

Tennessee complied immediately; the state was never really affected by radical Reconstruction. In 1868, as a result of a large freedman vote, six more states were readmitted. Alabama,

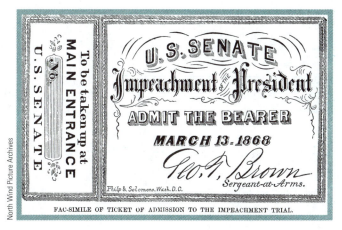

A ticket to the impeachment trial of President Johnson. It was the high point of Washington's social season with the chief justice presiding, the entire Senate sitting as jury, and leading House radicals as prosecutors. The president, however, did not attend; he was acquitted by one vote.

Impeached Presidents

Andrew Johnson was impeached—that is, accused by the House of Representatives of offenses grave enough to warrant his removal from office. Impeachment is the equivalent of indictment in criminal law. At his trial—the Senate is the "jury"—Johnson was acquitted by one vote and remained in office.

President William Clinton was impeached for perjury and obstruction of justice in 1999. He too was acquitted. Articles of impeachment were drawn up against President Richard M. Nixon for lying to Congress in 1974. When impeachment and conviction seemed likely, he resigned the presidency.

Gullah

A *dialect* is a regional variety of a language that is distinctive because of words unique to it, or different rules of grammar, or pronunciation—or a combination of the three. The nonstandard speech of many African Americans today is a dialect.

A *pidgin* is a simplified language that is consciously invented by different peoples in close contact who do not understand each other. Pidgins have evolved everywhere in the world where two different peoples have traded with one another. (The word *pidgin* was how Chinese merchants in South Asia pronounced "business.") Pidgins are usually based on one dominant language, but they reduce its grammar to basics for easy learning and instant communication on a narrow range of subjects such as business. Several English-based, French-based, and Portuguese-based pidgins are spoken by hundreds of thousands of people today. The "Hawaiian accent" is a remnant of what was once a pidgin.

When people adopt a pidgin as their language, elaborating on it so they can speak about a broad range of subjects, linguists call it a *creole*. Creoles sometimes become full-blown languages; Jamaican English, a creole, may be in the process of becoming a language independent of English.

Uncountable creoles developed among the first Africans in America. Their masters spoke English. The other slaves with whom they worked and lived spoke languages just as incomprehensible. So the first generation created a pidgin so they could understand overseers and fellow slaves. Their children—second-generation African Americans—had no use for their parents' mother tongues (who else spoke them?) and they knew more English than their parents had. They transformed the pidgin into a fuller creole.

Almost all slave creoles died out after emancipation. African Americans began to move around the country during Reconstruction and found their localized creoles useless. However, on the "sea islands" off the coast of South Carolina, Georgia, and far northern Florida, Gullah, sometimes called Geechee, flourished and survives to this day. It is still the language of home, church, and social occasions for at least a hundred thousand people. At last count, between 5,000 and 8,000 mostly elderly sea islanders spoke only Gullah.

Because Gullah is not a written language, its history is something of a mystery. Even the origin of the name is disputed. The most obvious explanation is that Gullah is a corruption of Angola, which makes sense. During the final years of the legal African slave trade, 1803–1807, sea island planters imported 24,000 Africans; 60 percent of them were from Angola (present-day Angola and Congo). However, there is some reason to believe that the word *Gullah* was in use by 1750, before Angolans had been imported in great numbers. Some linguists think it derives from Gola, the name of a tribe that lived on the border of modern Liberia and Sierra Leone. Sea island planters favored Africans from that region because they were skilled rice growers. Similarities between Gullah and a creole still spoken in Sierra Leone, Krio, are so striking that Gullah may have first emerged not on the sea islands but in Africa. Another school of linguists sees strong Jamaican and Barbadian creole influences, which is plausible: most slaves destined for North America were "seasoned" on those islands.

Arkansas, Florida, Louisiana, North Carolina, and South Carolina all sent Republican delegations, including some black congressmen, to Washington. In the remaining four states—Georgia, Mississippi, Texas, and Virginia—whites obstructed every attempt to set up a government in which blacks participated. The military continued to govern there until 1870.

In the meantime, Congress effectively took charge of the federal government. Johnson was reduced to vetoing every radical bill and watching as his vetoes were overridden. Congress even took partial control of the army away from Johnson, then struck at his control of his own cabinet. The Tenure of Office Act forbade the president to remove any appointed official who had been confirmed by the Senate without the Senate's approval of his dismissal.

It was obvious to all what was coming. The radicals wanted Johnson to violate the Tenure of Office Act so they could impeach him. Johnson knew it, and in part because of his constitutional scruples, he meant to violate it, certain that it was an infringement on the independence of the executive branch of the government. Moreover, his secretary of war inherited from Lincoln, Edwin P. Stanton, had allied with the radicals. He was, in effect, a not very well-disguised spy within the cabinet. In February 1868 Johnson fired Stanton. The House of Representatives passed articles of impeachment. The chief justice, Salmon B. Chase, sat as judge at the trial. The Senate was the jury. Conviction—and removal of Johnson from office—required a two-thirds vote. Four-fifths of the senators were Republicans. All but a few had dependably voted the radical line. The radicals were confident.

THE IMPEACHMENT TRIAL

All but two of the eleven articles of impeachment dealt with the Tenure of Office Act. As expected, Johnson's defenders argued that even if the act was constitutional, which was

Gullah is quite different from the "southern accent" and from "African American dialect." Its sounds are soft and it is spoken rapidly, not drawled. Well over 90 percent of its vocabulary is English, but pronunciation differs so radically from any other English pronunciation that outsiders cannot understand much more than the shortest, simplest statements. Spelled out phonetically, however, Gullah is easily deciphered. Here is the first sentence of the Lord's Prayer in Gullah:

> Ow'urr Farruh, hu aht in Heh'um, hallowed be dy name, dy kingdom come, dy wil be done on ut as it done in heh'um.

Linguists have traced hundreds of Gullah words, especially the names given to Gullah children, to Mandinka, Yoruba, Iwo, and Ibo, all Nigerian languages. Probably they were introduced to the language by slaves from that country, who were numerous.

How did Gullah thrive when other slave creoles died out? Cultural continuity is part of the reason. Before 1800, when the Angolans began to arrive, most sea island slaves' African roots were in a rather limited area of Sierra Leone. The isolation of the sea islands cut the Gullahs off from mixing with mainland slaves, reinforcing their sense of cohesion. Their creole was adequate for all their communications. Whites were few on the islands. Wealthy planters lived in Charleston. Many plantations were supervised by black slave drivers and sometimes, even at the top, by black plantation managers. When the Civil War began, there were more than 33,000 blacks in the Beaufort district of South Carolina, and 6,700 whites. When Union troops occupied the islands early in the war, virtually every white southerner fled. By 1870, 90 percent of St. Helena Island's population was black.

Because of their isolation, the Gullahs were generally more self-sufficient than most mainland slaves—and likely more confident in themselves. When the Union army put up confiscated sea island plantations for sale, an astonishing number of Gullahs had enough money to buy farms in small parcels, sometimes just ten acres. By 1870 seven of ten Gullah families owned their homes and farms.

African religious practices survived on the sea islands even after the Gullahs became Methodists or Baptists in the early nineteenth century. White missionaries were frustrated to distraction, even anger, when islanders explained that, while a dead person's "soul" went to live with God in heaven, his "spirit" or ghost continued to roam the islands, sometimes helping live descendants, sometimes doing them mischief. Only a century later was it learned that Gullah spirits had West African origins. The word *voodoo* entered the American language through the Gullahs, although on the sea islands it simply meant "magic" with none of the sinister connotations of West Indian voodoo as sensationalized in movies.

African folktales survived longer and closer to the originals on the sea islands than they did elsewhere in the South. Joel Chandler Harris, the white journalist who collected the B'rer Rabbit and other slave stories (now known to have African origins) found the sea islands his most productive hunting grounds. In 1925 DuBose Heyward wrote a play, *Porgy,* better known as the opera based on it, *Porgy and Bess.* It was set among Gullahs who, after the Civil War, moved to Charleston.

dubious, it did not apply to Johnson's dismissal of Stanton because Johnson had not appointed him; Lincoln had. It was a good argument, enough to win the day had the issue been a legal one rather than political. The other two articles condemned Johnson for disrespect of Congress, which was silly. Johnson had indeed insulted Congress: he had neglected only obscenities in the words with which he described congressional radicals. The president's defenders replied that pointed and vulgar language did not qualify as one of the "high crimes and misdemeanors" the Constitution stipulates as grounds for impeachment.

The radicals needed 36 senators' votes to remove Johnson from office. No more than 18 could vote to acquit. The tally was 35 to 19 for conviction. Johnson remained president by a single vote.

Actually, it was not that close. The radicals' case was so flimsy and motivated by such sordid politics that at least six Republican senators who otherwise voted for radical programs were privately disgusted. Each agreed privately that if his vote was needed to acquit, he would vote for acquittal. However, they were practical politicians. If their votes were not essential to win acquittal, they would vote to convict so as to maintain their good standing in the party. It was 1868, an election year. The Republican candidate was General Grant, and he was a sure winner. The "secret six" wanted to enjoy the advantages of belonging to the majority party with a friendly president.

Events proved they had good reasons to vote their careers rather than their consciences. The Republican from Kansas who provided Johnson's margin of victory was kicked out of the party and lost when he ran for reelection.

THE FIFTEENTH AMENDMENT

In the 1868 electoral vote, Grant easily defeated New York Governor Horatio Seymour, 214 to 80. However, the popular vote was very close; Grant won several states' electoral votes by a whisker. In fact, only a minority of white voters chose Grant. His nationwide plurality was 300,000; he got 500,000 black votes in the southern states. Grant lost New York, the largest state, by a thin margin. Had all blacks been able to vote in New York (a few could, under special circumstances), Grant would have carried the state easily. Grant won Indiana by a handful of votes; had African Americans been able to vote in Indiana, Grant would have won by a landslide.

Thaddeus Stevens had argued in 1865 that the Republican party's future depended on the freedmen voting in the southern states. The results of the 1868 election showed that the party's edge in some northern states depended on black men voting there.

Consequently, the Republicans drafted a third "**Civil War Amendment.**" The Fifteenth Amendment forbade states to deny the vote to any person on the basis of "race, color, or previous condition of servitude." Because Republican governments favorable to blacks still controlled most southern states, the amendment was easily ratified.

GRANT AND THE RECONSTRUCTED STATES

At 46 years of age, Ulysses S. Grant was the youngest president yet. A military man most of his adult life, he had never expressed much interest in politics. Certainly he never expressed any strong feelings about slavery or abolition; nor had he shown any particular hostility to or sympathy toward African Americans.

Grant had admired Lincoln and was loyal to him. One of Grant's more attractive personal traits was his loyalty to those who stood by him; after Shiloh and through the carnage before Richmond, Lincoln did just that. But Lincoln was four years dead, and Lincoln's wartime critics, the radicals, were calling the shots for the Republican party that honored Grant by making him president. In things political, Grant deferred to them. Circumstances, not conviction, made him the defender of radical Reconstruction.

The southern states readmitted under the radical program elected Republican majorities in their legislatures and sent mostly Republicans to Congress. In some states, where black people were a majority of the population or nearly so—South Carolina, Mississippi, Louisiana—Republican domination was a matter of course. In other southern states, a bloc

African-American vote plus white Republicans plus the demoralization of Democrats under military occupation, and some intimidation of whites by the army, put Republicans in power.

Blacks were the backbone of the southern party, providing 80 percent of Republican votes. But white men ran the party. No African American was elected governor in any state; there were only two black senators, Blanche K. Bruce and Hiram Revels, both from Mississippi. There were fewer than twenty black Republican congressmen. Indeed, Blacks filled only a fifth of appointed jobs, mostly low-level ones, although the size of the African-American vote justified four times as many. The "black rule" of which Democrats spoke was a myth.

CORRUPTION

Who were the white Republicans in the South? Some were former Whigs who had opposed secession. In the mountain counties, particularly in Tennessee, a majority of ordinary whites voted Republican. A few prominent Confederates decided that any political future they had lay with the Republicans. Democrats called them "scalawags"—scoundrels, reprobates—they betrayed the white race to ignorant, savage former slaves. Northern Republicans who moved South after the war for political purposes or to invest in the redevelopment of the shattered economy, likely to be a high-profit enterprise, were known as "carpetbaggers." Supposedly they had arrived in the South so poor they could fit everything they owned in a carpetbag, the cheapest sort of suitcase; but they were soon rich from looting southern state treasuries along with their scalawag friends and their black stooges.

Lowlife carpetbaggers could be found on the lower levels of the Republican party. But the dozen or so carpetbaggers who rose to high political office were men with money that the South sorely needed. The real "crime" of Reconstruction was the fact that African Americans had a say in government.

There was plenty of corruption, as there inevitably is when governments spend a lot of money quickly. The Republican legislatures voted huge appropriations for legitimate, even essential programs that the prewar southern legislatures had ignored. There was not a single statewide public school system in any former Confederate state until Reconstruction. The first free schools for white as well as black southern children were founded by the Republican legislatures. Programs for relief of the destitute and institutions for the handicapped and the insane were few in the prewar South.

Start-up costs for such institutions were immense, and politicians, all the way to the top, dipped into the flow of money to fill their own purses. The Republican governor of Louisiana, Henry C. Warmoth, banked $100,000 during a year when his salary was $8,000. Favored state contractors padded their bills obscenely and bribed state officials not to examine their invoices closely. In 1869 the state of Florida spent as much on printing as had been spent on every function of the state's government in 1860. The Democrats liked to zero in on petty but open and ludicrous corruption, as when former slaves in the South Carolina legislature appropriated $1,000 to one of their number who had lost that sum at the racetrack.

There was nothing unique to southern Republicans or African Americans in such thievery. The 1860s and 1870s were an era of corruption throughout American society. Civil War contractors had cheated the government. The crooked "Tweed Ring" that looted New York City was Democratic. The champion crooks of the nineteenth-century South were not Reconstruction Republicans but post-Reconstruction Democrats. After a "black Republican" administration in Mississippi ran a nearly corruption-free regime for six years, the first Democratic treasurer of the state absconded with $415,000. This paled compared to the swag E. A. Burke, the first post-Reconstruction treasurer of Louisiana, took with him to Honduras in 1890: $1,777,000.

THE REDEEMERS AND THE KLAN

Nevertheless, political corruption was an effective issue for Democrats out to defeat Republicans at the polls. They persuaded whites who had voted Republican to switch to the Democrats as the only way to avoid ruinous taxes. Race was an even more effective issue. The spectacle of former slaves who had said "yes sir" and "no sir" abjectly to every white man now dressing in frock coats and cravats, making laws, and drinking in hotel bars infuriated many whites. Democratic politicians called themselves "redeemers." They would redeem the prostrate South from thieving **carpetbaggers and scalawags** and redeem white southerners from the degradation the "Damn Yankees" were forcing upon them.

In states where a more or less solid white vote could be mobilized for the Democrats, the solidly Republican black vote could be overcome. Virginia was "redeemed" immediately, North Carolina and Georgia after a brief campaign. Elsewhere, redeemers brought economic pressure on blacks to stay home on election day. Most southern blacks survived as tenant farmers; in only a few small areas, such as the sea islands of South Carolina and Georgia, did a substantial number of black farmers own land. Tenants with families to support were inclined to value their leased cabins and acreage more highly than voting when their landlords told them it was one or the other.

Blacks determined to exercise their rights were met with violence. In 1866 General Nathan Bedford Forrest of Tennessee founded the Ku Klux Klan as a social club for Confederate veterans. Like other men's lodges, the Klan was replete with hocus-pocus, including the wearing of white robes and titles like Kleagle and Grand Wizard. In 1868, with the triumph of the radical Republicans in Congress, the Klan was politicized. Similar organizations, such as the Knights of the White Camellia and dozens of local groups, were formed. Masked and riding only at night to avoid Union army attachments, Klan-type organizations harassed, terrorized, whipped, and murdered not only politically active African Americans but also blacks who were said to be "impudent" or refused to work for whites. The Klan hit the South like a tornado. The federal government estimated that the Klan

The Granger Collection, New York

Ku Klux Klan night riders shoot up the house of an African American who voted or, possibly, merely offended whites by insisting on his dignity as a free man. At the peak of Klan violence in 1868 and 1869, it is estimated that Klan-like terrorists murdered an average of two people a day, almost all of them blacks.

The Grant Scandals

In 1872 newspapers exposed a massive fraud in the construction of the Union Pacific Railroad. Union Pacific officials created a dummy corporation, the Crédit Mobilier, to construct the line on contract. The Crédit Mobilier then overcharged the Union Pacific as much as $20 million. When rumors of the scam prompted talk of a congressional investigation, the Union Pacific sold stock at a big discount to key politicians to quash the investigation. Grant knew nothing of it. But his vice president, Schuyler Colfax, was in the fix up to his neck.

Grant's secretary of war, William W. Belknap, pocketed bribes from a federal contractor who supplied western army units and Indian tribes with goods due them under the terms of treaties with the government. Belknap then shut his eyes when the company delivered less than the contracts required. He was caught red-handed and resigned, but Grant refused to prosecute him. Officials in the Treasury Department, in cahoots with the president's personal secretary, Orville Babcock, provided excise tax stamps to whiskey distillers at a discount. In effect, they stole the stamps as a clerk in a store might steal cigars. No one was punished.

murdered 700 in 1868, all but a few of them blacks. The next year was worse.

And it worked. Rather than invite a Klan visit, African Americans in increasing numbers stopped voting. In 1870 and 1871 Congress passed two Ku Klux Acts, which made it a federal offense "to go in disguise upon the public highway . . . with intent to . . . injure, oppress, threaten, or intimidate [citizens] and to prevent them from enjoying their constitutional rights." The laws were effective. The Union army harassed known or suspected Klansmen and destroyed many "Klaverns." Between 1870 and 1872 Texas arrested 6,000 Klansmen. Still, the greatest single Klan atrocity occurred in April 1873 when 100 blacks were killed.

By then five former rebel states were in redeemer hands, and the Republicans faced powerful Democratic opposition in the others. Just as important, northern support for radical Reconstruction was in rapid decline.

GRANT'S TROUBLED ADMINISTRATION

Grant was lionized after Appomattox. He was showered with gifts, including cold cash. New York City's present to him of $100,000 was the biggest. Wealthy businessmen and bankers, knowing he would be president, treated him well. The Illinois shopkeeper and soldier in dusty, rumpled uniform who whittled sticks during battles was dumbstruck. He took zestfully to the high life, from dining on fancy food to wearing silk top hats and well-tailored suits of the finest fabrics.

The celebrity and money came too fast to a man who had struggled to pay the bills for thirty years—and to his wife Julia Grant, who had struggled to keep a family together. The Grants never quite grasped the fact that their benefactors were not so much appreciating them as they were paying in advance for future favors. There is no evidence that corruption tainted Grant personally. But his administration was shot through with it, and his sense of loyalty was so strong that he never punished or even shunned those of his "friends" who were exposed as crooks.

BLACK FRIDAY: A REPUTATION TARNISHED

Most of the thievery that discredited Grant's presidency was exposed only late in his eight years as president. But there was an odor of corruption in Washington from the start. Henry Adams, the fourth-generation scion of the distinguished Massachusetts family, smelled it in 1869 when, returning from a sojourn in Europe, he visited the city, in part to inquire how the Grant administration might wish to use his services. Adams virtually fled Washington, writing that the capital was filled with men of shady character chasing the fast buck and, to all appearances, catching it. Another writer described the Grant years as "the great barbecue" with the government "supplying the beef."

Grant got off to a bad start as president. He made the mistake of accepting an invitation to visit the yacht of James "Jubilee Jim" Fisk, not a social occasion one could enjoy inconspicuously. Fisk and his associate, Jay Gould, who was also aboard, were already disreputable financial schemers. In the "Erie War" the previous year (see Chapter 27), they had tried to bilk railroader Cornelius Vanderbilt of hundreds of thousands of dollars in a stock fraud. The final acts of the battle were played out in public, chronicled in detail in the newspapers. At one point, to avoid arrest, Gould and Fisk fled New York to New Jersey and holed up in a hotel guarded by underworld toughs.

Their purpose in entertaining Grant on a yacht was that there he would be seen. Gould and Fisk created the illusion that they had a privileged relationship with the president while they secretly schemed with Grant's brother-in-law, Abel R. Corbin. The stakes were high: Gould and Fisk planned to corner the nation's gold supply. Success depended on the federal government keeping its gold holdings—the largest in the country—off the open market. Corbin assured them that, as a trusted relative, he would ensure that Grant would do just that.

The stage set, Gould and Fisk bought up gold futures, commitments to buy gold at an agreed price at a specified future date. By snapping up every future on the market, Gould and Fisk sent the price of gold soaring. By September 1869 it was selling for $162 an ounce. By taking delivery of gold futures they had purchased at $20, $30, $40 less per ounce, they would make a killing in an instant.

Corbin kept the pressure on Grant, but treasury officials, realizing what was happening, persuaded Grant that he would look very bad indeed if he took no action. On their advice, he dumped $4 million of the government's gold on the market on Friday, September 24—**Black Friday.**

Culver Pictures, Inc.

Horace Greeley was one of the country's most influential editors in a day when, with newspapers the sole source of information for common people, editors were powerful political figures. But he was a terrible choice as a presidential candidate. He had backed almost every reform and dabbled in almost every fad, many of them objects of popular ridicule, for forty years. Even if all the corruption in Grant's administration had been known in 1872, it is unlikely Greeley could have defeated General Grant.

The price of gold collapsed. Gould did not make as much money as he had hoped, but he made plenty. Without informing his partner, he had already sold out. Nor did Fisk lose; he simply refused to honor his future commitments and hired thugs to intimidate those with whom he had signed contracts. But businessmen who had purchased gold at bloated prices to pay debts and wages were ruined; thousands of employees of bankrupt companies lost their jobs. And the luster of a great general's reputation was tarnished before he had been president for eight months.

THE ELECTION OF 1872

By 1872 some Republicans like Henry Adams's father, Charles Francis Adams; Senators Carl Schurz of Missouri, Lyman Trumbull of Illinois, and Charles Sumner of Massachusetts; and crusading editors **Horace Greeley** of the *New York Tribune* and E. L. Godkin of *The Nation* concluded that, with Grant's acquiescence, thieves were taking over the party.

They were even more disgusted by the well-publicized thievery in the southern state governments that, they believed, stayed in power only because of Grant's support. Some of them—Sumner was an exception—concluded that the whole idea of entrusting poor and ignorant blacks with the vote was a mistake. Better to allow the redeemers, Democrats that they were, to take over and run clean governments. The dissidents formed the Liberal Republican party and said they would oppose Grant in the presidential election of 1872. Their convention nominated Horace Greeley to run against him.

It was an unwise choice. Greeley was a lifelong eccentric and looked it. During his 61 years he had clambered at least briefly aboard every reform movement and fad that had marched down the street, not only abolitionism and women's rights, but vegetarianism, spiritualism, and phrenology (reading a person's character in the bumps on his or her head). His appearance invited ridicule. He looked like a crackpot with his round, pink face, close-set, beady eyes, and a wispy white fringe of chin whiskers. He wore an ankle-length white overcoat on the hottest days and carried a brightly colored umbrella on the driest. Pro-Grant cartoonists had an easy time making fun of him.

Greeley also seemed to be a poor choice because, on their own, the Liberal Republicans had no chance of winning the election. They needed the support of both northern and southern Democrats. The Horace Greeley of 1872 might call for North and South to "clasp hands across the bloody chasm" and denounce carpetbaggers as "stealing and plucking, many of them with both arms around Negroes, and their hands in their rear pockets." The Horace Greeley of 1841–1869 had roasted northern Democrats daily in the *Tribune* and vilified southern Democrats for their espousal of slavery and rebellion.

Nevertheless, the Democrats nominated Greeley. If the Liberal Republicans could not hope to win without the Democrats, the Democrats could not hope to win without the Liberal Republicans. The ratification of the Fifteenth Amendment in 1870 had added tens of thousands of blacks—all Republicans, and *not* Liberals—to the voters' lists.

In fact, the mismatched two-party coalition could not win anyway. With half the southern states still governed by Republicans, and Grant still a hero in the North despite rumors of scandals, the president won 56 percent of the popular vote and a crushing 286 to 66 victory in the electoral college.

THE TWILIGHT OF RECONSTRUCTION

Poor Greeley died weeks after the election. One by one, dragging their feet, the other Liberals returned to the Republican party. Grant would be gone after the election of 1876, they figured. Perhaps the party would learn its lesson and nominate a reformer. In fact, the exposure of several scandals during Grant's second term guaranteed just that.

Except for Sumner, who was pushing for a federal civil rights law when he died in 1874 (it was enacted in 1875

The Civil Rights Act of 1875

In 1875, the twilight of Reconstruction, Congress enacted the Civil Rights Act. It outlawed racial discrimination in public facilities such as hotels and theaters, and forbade the exclusion of blacks from juries. Another provision forbidding racially segregated schools, which had been in Charles Sumner's draft of the bill, was not included. Although the law was not as thoroughgoing as the historic Civil Rights Act of 1964, its purposes were identical.

The 1875 law had no effect on racial discrimination. Rutherford B. Hayes, president in 1877 because he acquiesced in white Democratic control of the South, did not enforce it. In 1883 a number of lawsuits calling for its enforcement reached the Supreme Court. In the civil rights cases, with only one dissenting vote, the Court ruled the act unconstitutional because it outlawed *social* discrimination, which was beyond the power of Congress. The dissenting justice was John Marshall Harlan, who also stood alone in defending equal rights for blacks in

the more famous case of *Plessy v. Ferguson* in 1896.

In Congress, the last gasp of Republican support for African-American rights was the Force Bill of 1890, designed to guarantee southern blacks the right to vote. (It was the equivalent of the Voting Rights Act of 1965.) The House approved the Force Bill, but it failed passage in the Senate when Republican senators from silver-producing states voted against it in return for southern Democratic support of a law propping up the price of silver.

---

thanks to the regular Grant Republicans in Congress), the Liberals of 1872 were not unhappy when, at the end of 1874, redeemers in Texas, Arkansas, and Mississippi wrested those states back to the Democratic party. By 1876 radical Republicans were in power only in South Carolina, Florida, and Louisiana.

THE DISPUTED ELECTION

The Democratic candidate in 1876, New York Governor Samuel J. Tilden, said he would withdraw the troops from those three states, which would reduce the numbers of black voters there and end Reconstruction. The Republican candidate, Governor Rutherford B. Hayes of Ohio, ran on a platform that guaranteed African Americans rights in the South but weakly. Personally, Hayes was well known to be skeptical of black capabilities, and he was a personal friend of several white southern politicians. Both candidates were honest government reformers. Tilden had helped destroy the Tweed Ring in New York. As governor, Hayes had run a squeaky-clean administration.

When the votes were counted, Hayes's personal opinions about the wisdom of Reconstruction seemed beside the point. Tilden won the popular vote handily, and he appeared to have won the electoral college 204 to 165. However, Tilden's count included the electoral votes of South Carolina, Florida, and Louisiana, where Republicans still controlled the state governments. On telegraphed instructions from Republican party leaders in New York, officials in those three states declared that Hayes had carried their states. According to this set of returns, Hayes eked out a 185 to 184 electoral vote victory.

It was not that easy. When the returns reached Washington, there were two sets of them from each of the three disputed states—one set for Tilden and one for Hayes. Because the Constitution did not provide for such an occurrence, a special commission was established to decide which returns were valid. Five members of each house of Congress and five members of the Supreme Court sat on the panel. Seven of them

were Republicans; seven were Democrats; one, David Davis of Illinois, a Supreme Court justice and once Abraham Lincoln's law partner, was known as an independent. No one else was interested in determining the case on its merits; each commissioner intended to vote for his party's candidate, no matter what documents were set before him. The burden of naming the next president of the United States fell on David Davis.

He did not like the setup. No matter how conscientious and honest Davis was—and he had a good reputation—half the country would call for his scalp. Davis prevailed on friends in Illinois to get him off the hook by naming him to a Senate seat that was vacant. He resigned from the Court and, thereby, from the commission. His replacement was a Republican justice, and the stage was set for the Republicans to steal the election.

THE COMPROMISE OF 1877

The commission voted on strict party lines, eight to seven, to accept the Hayes returns from Louisiana, Florida, and South Carolina—giving Rutherford B. Hayes the presidency by a single electoral vote. Had that been all there was to it, there might well have been violence. At a series of meetings, however, prominent northern and southern politicians and businessmen came to an informal agreement with highly placed southern Republicans with redeemer connections.

The "Compromise of 1877" involved several commitments, not all of them honored, for northern investments in the South. Also not honored was a vague agreement on the part of conservative southerners to build a white Republican party in the South based on the economic and social views that they shared with northern conservatives.

As for the disputed election, Hayes would move into the White House without resistance by either northern or southern Democrats. In return, he would withdraw the troops from South Carolina, Florida, and Louisiana, thus allowing the Democratic party in these states to oust the Republicans and eliminate African-American political power. Those parts of the compromise were honored.

FURTHER READING

General Eric Foner, *Reconstruction: America's Unfinished Revolution,* 1988, and *A Short History of Reconstruction,* 1990; James McPherson, *Ordeal by Fire: The Civil War and Reconstruction,* 1982; Michael Perman, *Emancipation and Reconstruction, 1862–1879,* 2003.

African Americans after Slavery Herman Belz, *Emancipation and Equal Rights,* 1978; Eric Foner, *Nothing but Freedom,* 1983; Leon F. Litwack, *Been in the Storm So Long,* 1979; William McFeeley, *Frederick Douglass,* 1991; James McPherson, *The Struggle for Equality,* 1964; Harold O. Rabnowitz, *Southern Black Leaders of the Reconstruction Era,* 1982; Daniel Sowll, *Rebuilding Zion: The Religious Reconstruction of the South, 1863–1877,* 1998; Joel Williamson, *The Crucible: Black–White Relations in the American South since Emancipation,* 1984.

The Freedmen's Bureau Barry A. Craven, *The Freeman's Bureau and Black Texas,* 1992; Jacqueline Jones, *Soldiers of Light and Love: Northern Teachers and Georgia Blacks,* 1980; Peter Kolchin, *First Freedom,* 1972; Robert C. Morris, *Reading, 'Riting, and Reconstruction: The Education of Freedmen in the South, 1861–1870,* 1981; Donald Nieman, *To Set the Law in Motion: The Freedman's Bureau and the Legal Rights of Blacks, 1865–1868,* 1979.

Politics Michael L. Benedict, *The Impeachment and Trial of Andrew Johnson,* 1973; Dan Carter, *When the War Was Over: The Failure of Self-Reconstruction in the South, 1865–1867,* 1985; LaWanda Cox, *Lincoln and Black Freedom: A Study in Presidential Leadership,* 1981; Laura F. Edwards, *Gendered Strife and Confusions: The Political Culture of Reconstruction,* 1997; Dewey Grantham, *Life and Death of the Solid South,* 1988; Peyton McCrary, *Abraham Lincoln and Reconstruction,* 1978; Roy Morris, *Fraud of the Century: Rutherford B. Hayes, Samuel Tilden, and the Stolen Election of 1876,* 2003; Otto H. Olson, *Reconstruction and Redemption in the South,* 1980; Michael Perman, *The Road to Redemption: Southern Politics 1868–1879,* 1984; George C. Rable, *But There Was No Peace: The Role of Violence in the Politics of Reconstruction,* 1984; L. Seip, *The South Returns to Congress,* 1983; Brooks D. Simpson, *The Reconstruction Presidents,* 1998; Jean E. Smith, *Grant,* 2001; Xi Wang, *The Trial of Democracy: Black Suffrage and Northern Republicans, 1860–1910,* 1997.

The Southern Economy Richard N. Current, *Those Terrible Carpetbaggers,* 1988; Michael Goray, *A Ruined Land: The End of the Civil War,* 1999; Lawrence Powell, *New Masters: Northern Planters during the Civil War and Reconstruction,* 1980; Roger L. Ransom and Richard Sutch, *One Kind of Freedom: The Economic Consequences of Emancipation,* 1977; James Roark, *Masters without Slaves: Southern Planters in the Civil War and Reconstruction,* 1977; Gavin Wright, *Old South, New South: Revolutions in the Southern Economy since the Civil War,* 1986.

KEY TERMS

The following terms are covered in this chapter and can also be found in the list of Key Terms at the back of the book.

black codes	"Civil War Amendment"	Horace Greeley	Wade–Davis Bill
Black Friday	freedmen	pocket veto	
carpetbaggers and scalawags	Freedmen's Bureau		

ONLINE SOURCES GUIDE

Use this listing to find online documents, images, interactive maps, simulations, and other resources related to this chapter:

American History Resource Center
http://history.wadsworth.com/rc/us

Selected Images
Union troops parade in Washington, 1865
Depiction of Andrew Johnson as unsympathetic to South
Black codes

Freedmen in Richmond, Virginia, 1865
Burning of a freedmen's school, 1866

Interactive Time Line (with online readings)
Aftermath: The Reconstruction of the Union, 1865–1877

CHAPTER 26

Parties, Patronage, and Pork

Politics in the Late Nineteenth Century

University of Hartford Collection

That ... a man like Grant should be called—and should actually and truly be—the highest product of the most advanced society, made evolution ludicrous. One must be as commonplace as Grant's own commonplaces to maintain such an absurdity. The progress of evolution from President Washington to President Grant, was alone evidence to upset Darwin.

Henry Adams

The presidents of the late nineteenth century are not an inspiring lot. Their portraits lined up on a wall—Grant, Hayes, Garfield, Arthur, Cleveland, Harrison, Cleveland, McKinley—they might be a line of mourners at a midwestern funeral. They were dignified. They were soberly drab (except for Arthur, who was a clotheshorse), and they were grandly bewhiskered (except McKinley). Their honesty was beyond question (except for a slip by Garfield with the Crédit Mobilier when he was congressman), as were their morals (except for a slip by Cleveland back home in Buffalo). They competently performed their executive duties. But it is difficult to imagine a boy who, on looking up at the portrait gallery, would say to his mother, "I want to be president when I grow up."

None of them could be elected today or even considered for nomination. In our age of ceaseless commercial amusement, the entertainer has the edge in the race for the great American prize. Moreover, Americans have become accustomed to vigorous chief executives who seize the initiative.

The presidents from Grant to William McKinley believed that initiative in government rested with Congress, where laws were made. The president's task was to represent the nation in his person (thus the importance of a grave demeanor), to enforce the laws Congress enacted, and, if necessary, to brake an erring Congress with a veto.

A third reason there were no giants among the presidents of what is sometimes called the Gilded Age is the fact that what was most vital in America in the late nineteenth century—what attracted the most ambitious, energetic men—was not politics but business and, to a lesser extent, the development of what was left of the West.

And yet the politicians of the era cannot be ignored. They were businessmen of a sort themselves. Political parties were themselves a kind of business. From White House to city halls, politicians were "employees" of corporate enterprises with concrete, ultimately economic goals. And more Americans loved politics and elections than in any era since. Party politics was the nation's favorite spectator sport.

Uncle Sam weighs the Republican and Democratic parties and finds them evenly matched. President Grant is in the background (although he was no longer the sloven depicted here). His ally, Republican "Stalwart" Roscoe Conkling (who was mocked for having a "turkey-gobbler strut") is perched at the upper right. The man at the left is holding a pathetic Liberal Republican party bird. The Liberal Republicans joined with the Democrats in 1872.

More than 80 percent of eligible voters voted in 1876; the percentage never fell below 70 before 1900. In the late twentieth and early twenty-first centuries, for comparison, despite more convenient registration procedures and relentless media cheerleading, it is a good year when half the eligible voters bother to go to the polls.

HOW THE SYSTEM WORKED

Presidential elections brought out the most fans. In part this was because, nationally, the two major parties were evenly matched. Between 1875 and 1891, control of the House of Representative changed six times. During those twenty-two years, one of the parties controlled presidency, House, and Senate only four years.

Almost every presidential election provided evidence for the cliché that a single voter (a handful of voters, anyway) did make a difference. Between 1872, when Grant won re-election by 750,000 votes, and 1896, when William McKinley ushered in a new political era of Republican party dominance with an 850,000-vote victory, two of the presidential contests (1880 and 1884) saw the candidates just 40,000 votes apart in a total of 9–10 million. In two other

Yellow Dog Democrats

In eastern Texas, white voters took pride in the name "Yellow Dog Democrat." They meant that they were so loyal to their party that if the Republican candidate for office was Jesus, and the Democratic candidate an old yellow dog, they would vote for the yellow dog.

elections (1876 and 1888), the winning candidates had fewer popular votes than the losers, an outcome that would not be seen again until 2000.

Only one presidential candidate between 1876 and 1896 won more than 50 percent of the popular vote: Samuel J. Tilden in 1876. And he did not move to Washington; he lost the "stolen election" in the ruling of a fifteen-member special commission.

SOLID SOUTH AND REPUBLICAN RESPECTABILITY

The parties were not evenly matched within regions or among identifiable social groups. Except for Connecticut, which was evenly divided between Republicans and Democrats, New England and Pennsylvania were rock-solid Republican. The upper and middle classes of the Northeast and Midwest were largely Republican. They thought of the GOP, the "Grand Old Party," as a bastion of morality and respectability. In the words of Senator George F. Hoar of Massachusetts, Republicans were "the men who do the work of piety and charity in our churches; the men who administer our school systems; the men who own and till their own farms; the men who perform skilled labor in the shops."

Hoar went on to describe Democrats as (among other unattractive things) the "criminal class" and the "ballot-box stuffers" of the great cities. That was true of New York, which was run by Democrats. Philadelphia, however, was in the pocket of a Republican party machine employing the same techniques that kept the Democrats in office in New York. Indeed, Republican machines ran more of the "great cities" during the late nineteenth century than Democrats did.

Southern African Americans who still voted after Reconstruction were staunch Republicans, as were northern blacks. The GOP paid little more than symbolic attention to civil rights issues after 1877, but it was still the party of Lincoln and emancipation.

One-Party Politics

When Judge M. B. Gerry sentenced Alfred E. Packer to death for murdering and eating five companions when trapped by a blizzard in Colorado in 1873, he said, "There were seven Democrats in Hinsdale County, but you, you voracious, man-eating son-of-a-bitch, you ate five of them."

The Democrats built their national totals on the foundation of the "Solid South." Once the last of the former Confederate states was "redeemed" in 1877, none gave the Republicans a majority during the final quarter of the nineteenth century. Nor did the border states that had not been part of the Confederacy: Delaware, Maryland, West Virginia, Kentucky, and Missouri.

SWING STATES

The Democrats could not win a presidential election with the Solid South alone. In 1880, for example, all the former slave states cast 138 electoral votes; 185 electoral votes were needed to win the White House. By 1892 the admission of several western states increased the magic number in the electoral college to 223; the Solid South delivered 155 votes.

To win the presidential election, the Democrats had to carry some northern and western states too. Connecticut was usually dependable but added only six electoral votes. The Democrats' attention (and, of course, the Republicans!) was concentrated on the so-called *swing states,* where the two parties were about equal in strength and could, therefore, go either way. New York, with 35–36 electoral votes, more than any other state, was essential. Between 1880 and 1892, no candidate won the presidency without winning a majority in New York. Which way the state voted depended on whether New York City's Democratic machine—**Tammany Hall**—could roll up a larger plurality than the upstate counties could roll up for the Republicans.

With the Solid South plus Connecticut and New York, Democrats could eke out an electoral college majority by carrying one or two more **swing states.** Indiana was a fair bet, Illinois a realistic possibility. Party strategists considered Ohio a swing state; the Republicans carried Ohio in every presidential election during the Gilded Age but sometimes narrowly (by 72 votes in a total of 810,000 in 1892).

Consequently, a disproportionate number of presidential and vice presidential nominees were from Indiana, New York, Illinois, and Ohio, where they had demonstrated that they were personally popular. In the elections held between 1876 and 1892, the major parties filled twenty presidential and vice presidential slots. Eighteen of the twenty were filled by men from the swing states. Eight (40 percent!) were from New York. There was at least one New Yorker on one of the party tickets in every election; five were from Indiana. Neither party was particularly interested in finding the best man for the job. The idea was to win the election, which meant carrying the swing states.

BOSSES AND CONVENTIONS

Today presidential nominations are made in primary elections. The Republican and Democratic national conventions are holidays for delegates and boring television shows for everyone else. In the late nineteenth century, conventions were the heart of national political party life. There were no primaries. Convention delegates really did choose the nominees. Moreover, state and city political leaders could not consult with one another by picking up a telephone or sending e-mail. In the late nineteenth century, congressmen saw one another in Washington regularly. However, governors and political bosses, who were, with few exceptions, the real powers in party politics, met their counterparts from elsewhere in the country only at conventions.

There they wheeled and dealed, bargained and traded, made and broke political careers. There was no army of television reporters shoving microphones and cameras into the midst of every circle of politicos that gathered on the floor of the barnlike convention halls. There were newspaper reporters, but with no cameras recording the action, they were kept away from the interesting conversations by strong-arm bodyguards, a career opportunity for washed-up prizefighters.

Politics 1873–1897

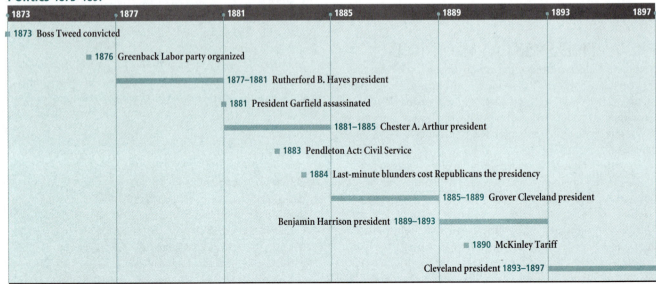

| 1873 | 1877 | 1881 | 1885 | 1889 | 1893 | 1897 |

■ 1873 Boss Tweed convicted

■ 1876 Greenback Labor party organized

1877–1881 Rutherford B. Hayes president

■ 1881 President Garfield assassinated

1881–1885 Chester A. Arthur president

■ 1883 Pendleton Act: Civil Service

■ 1884 Last-minute blunders cost Republicans the presidency

1885–1889 Grover Cleveland president

Benjamin Harrison president 1889–1893

■ 1890 McKinley Tariff

Cleveland president 1893–1897

In the Democratic party, the most important bosses were the head of Tammany Hall and the **Bourbons** of the Solid South—the name given to the redeemers when they had finished their redemptions. They were named after the Bourbon kings of France (for their extreme conservatism), not after Kentucky's famous liquor, much as they might have enjoyed it. The Republican party's key figures were boss Matthew Quay of Republican Pennsylvania and bosses Roscoe Conkling and, later, Thomas C. Platt of New York. The New Yorkers could not always deliver their state's electoral votes, but their support was essential to Republican victory.

Dozens of politicos traded the support of their delegations for the promise of a prestigious cabinet post for a favorite son or a healthy share of the government jobs and contracts that a victorious party had at its disposal. Republican delegations from the southern states, which delivered no electoral votes in November, were nonetheless courted assiduously by rival candidates at conventions for their votes. Party conventions were the only sector of American politics in which African Americans played a significant role.

THE PATRONAGE

The spoils system had come a long way since the days of Andrew Jackson. Jackson had about 5,000 federal jobs to hand out to the party faithful. In 1871, 50,000 federal employees served at President Grant's pleasure. In 1881 President Garfield could fire and hire people in 100,000 positions. (One whom he did not hire was to kill him.)

About three federal jobs in four were with the post office in 1871, half of them in 1881. The second largest federal employer was the Treasury Department; collecting customs generated lots of paperwork in every seaport. Postal and customs employees were scattered throughout the country, as were Indian agents and civilians employed by the army. In 1871 about 6,000 people worked for the government in Washington, 12 percent of the total. (The government had few employees abroad. Ministers and consuls in even the important European countries had little assistance.)

The presidents did not, of course, sift through applications for postmasterships in every town (although a woman acquainted with James Garfield who wanted a job in the Cincinnati post office sat in his home for five hours until he agreed to appoint her). Job seekers made their wishes known to mayors, congressmen, and local bosses who belonged to the president's party. They decided which should be rewarded on the basis of their contributions to the party and

passed their recommendations up the line to the state's senators, if the party had a man in that office. Senators had access to the president; they passed their lists to him, and he usually approved their recommendations.

When President Grant gave Senator Roscoe Conkling a blank check in filling federal positions in New York State, it made Conkling the state's most powerful politician, bar none. The juiciest plum at Conklin's disposal was the customs house in New York City; it had an annual payroll of $2 million. The Collector of Customs in New York was paid a salary of $20,000 (about $400,000 in today's money). And the Collector earned bonuses when importers trying to cheat the government were caught. Conkling's choice for Collector, his top political henchman and close personal friend, Chester A. Arthur, took home $40,000 a year between 1871 and 1874—more than the president.

There were plenty of state employees too. Pennsylvania's Republican machine had 20,000 jobs to hand out. With so many people owing their income to the Republican party, it is a small wonder that Democrats were helpless in Pennsylvania and Philadelphia.

PORK

Government contracts were another means of rewarding friends of the winning party. Usually at the end of each congressional session, when the House and Senate were tying up loose ends at top speed, Congress enacted "pork barrel" bills, so called because, like the barrel of salt pork in brine that sat in the kitchens of most homes, they were not pretty to look into. Pork barrel bills were usually bipartisan because, during the Gilded Age, the two houses of Congress were controlled by different parties more often than not. They collected together for a single vote proposals that most members had for government spending in their districts: construction of post offices or government piers, dredging a river, and so on. The idea was not to get worthwhile work done but to allow congressmen to reward political supporters.

Thus the River and Harbor Bill of August 1886 appropriated $15 million to begin work on more than 100 new projects. Fifty-eight government building projects that had been started two years earlier but were not complete were ignored—forgotten—because they were in the districts of congressmen who had retired or been defeated.

There was not, of course, a job or contract for every voter. To turn out the numbers on election day, the two

The Bloody Shirt in Indiana

Every unregenerate rebel, . . . every man who labored for the rebellion in the field, who murdered Union prisoners by cruelty and starvation calls himself a Democrat. Every wolf in sheep's clothing who pretends to preach the gospel but proclaims the righteousness of man-selling and slavery; every one who shoots down Negroes in the streets, burns up Negro school-houses and meeting-houses, and murders women and children by the light of their own flaming dwellings, calls himself a Democrat. . . . In short, the Democratic party may be described as a common sewer and loathsome receptacle, into which is emptied every element of treason North and South, every element of inhumanity and barbarism which has dishonored the age.

Oliver Morton

parties exploited the emotional politics of memory and, for the Republicans, the decidedly unsentimental politics of pensions.

MEMORIES, MEMORIES

If the Republican party forgot its commitments to African Americans, it remembered the Civil War. Party orators "waved the bloody shirt," reminding northern voters that Democrats had caused the Civil War. Lucius Fairchild, a Wisconsin politician who lost an arm in battle, literally flailed the air with his empty sleeve during campaign speeches. With armless and legless veterans hobbling about every sizable town, it was an effective technique.

The **GAR**—the Grand Army of the Republic, a Union veterans' association founded in 1866—was officially nonpolitical but in practice was an auxiliary of the Republican party that kept the memory of the war alive. Members put on their old uniforms and marched on Independence Day and Memorial Day, a national holiday the GAR established. The GAR's annual "encampments" (conventions under tents) gave Republican politicians their best opportunities to wave the **bloody shirt.** The GAR was powerful: In 1890 it had 400,000 members.

Between 1868 and 1901, every president except the Democrat Grover Cleveland was a former Union officer. (Arthur's military service was brief, even momentary, but he still liked to be addressed as "General.") When Cleveland, believing that sectional bitterness was fading, returned captured

Civil War Pensions

Between 1890, when pensions for Union veterans and their dependents were granted practically for the asking, and 1905, when the practice was prohibited, it was not uncommon for very young women to marry very old veterans to collect widows' pensions after their husbands died. As late as 1983, forty-one Civil War widows were still receiving a monthly check of about $70 from the federal government.

Confederate battle flags to their states for display at museums and war monuments, a northern protest mobilized by the GAR forced him to back down. (An old Confederate soldiers' association, the United Confederate Veterans—Democratic, of course—was founded in 1889, but its peak membership was only 50,000.)

The Republican who defeated Cleveland in 1888, Benjamin Harrison, was still waving the bloody shirt after twenty years. "I would a thousand times rather march under the bloody shirt, stained with the lifeblood of a Union soldier," Harrison told voters, "than march under the black flag of treason or the white flag of cowardly compromise." Dwelling on the past was not constructive, but it helped win elections.

VOTE YOURSELF A PENSION

The Republican party converted the bloody shirt into dollars in the form of pensions for veterans. Late in the war,

Bettmann/Corbis

The 1880 Republican convention in Chicago, which may have seen more scheming than any other in an age of convention bargaining. The delegates deadlocked for more than thirty ballots. On the thirty-fourth ballot, a few cast votes for James A. Garfield of Ohio, whose name was not in nomination. On the thirty-sixth ballot, he was nominated. The blurred figure standing at a podium just right of the center of this photograph is Senator Garfield when, to no avail, he told the delegates he was not a candidate and they should not vote for him. A historic moment!

The Surplus

Many late-nineteenth-century congressmen voted for dubious veterans' pensions and pork barrel bills because spending won votes. However, there was also a sound economic reason to get rid of the government's money during the 1880s. The U.S. Treasury collected about $100 million more in taxes each year than it spent. Each dollar that remained in the treasury was a dollar less fueling the economy. Allowing the surplus to grow meant risking a depression.

Reducing revenue was out of the question. More than half the government's collections came from the tariff, which was backed by powerful interests. So the government spent on pensions, often dubious building projects, and during the 1890s, the construction of a large modern navy.

Even then, it took a major depression and war to wipe out the surplus. In 1899, after the war with Spain, the government had a deficit of $90 million.

Congress had approved federal pensions for Union soldiers who were disabled by wounds or diseases contracted while in the army. The law was strictly worded, and many handicapped veterans failed to qualify for pensions under its terms. In 1879 eligibility was liberalized, but northern congressmen also introduced "special pension" bills that provided monthly stipends to specifically named constituents who had requested them.

By the 1880s the procedure for awarding special pensions was grossly abused. Congressmen took little interest in the worthiness or even the truthfulness of petitions for special pensions. (One applicant was disabled, he said, because he had been thrown from a horse as he was rushing to enlist in the army.) They introduced every request. When virtually all Republican congressmen and many northern Democrats had special pension bills in the hopper, the lot was rushed through by voice vote and passed on to the president. Republican presidents signed them. Instead of declining as old soldiers died off, the cost of the pension program climbed to $56 million in 1885 and $80 million in 1888.

Democrat Grover Cleveland, elected in 1884, closely scrutinized every special pension bill placed on his desk and vetoed those he judged undeserving. In 1888, an election year, Congress put him on the spot by enacting a revised general pension law that granted a small monthly income to every Union army veteran who had served ninety days and was disabled for any reason whatsoever. An old soldier who fell from a stepladder in 1885 qualified, as did his widow when he died. Cleveland vetoed the general pension law, and the Republicans ran their campaign on the slogan "Vote Yourself a Pension."

They won the election, and in 1889 the new president, Benjamin Harrison, signed an even more generous Dependent Pensions Act. Harrison appointed the head of the GAR, James "Corporal" Tanner, to oversee the distribution of pensions. "God help the surplus," Tanner said, referring to the money in the treasury. He meant it. By the end of Harrison's term, Tanner had increased the annual expenditure on Civil War pensions to $160 million. With widows qualifying for pensions too, local wags took notice of the young women of the town who promptly married doddering old Billy Yanks who had an occasional gleam in their eyes and a check in the mail every month.

Northern Democrats posed as men of principle in the bloody shirt and pension controversies. In the South, however, Democrats played the Civil War game too. They orated about the nobility of the Confederate cause, and southern state governments provided some benefits for Confederate veterans.

PROTECTION.
"We will Support the Interests of America."

1840.   1888.
Tippecanoe and
MORTON TOO.

The Smithsonian Institute

What the nineteenth century called a "balloon lamp" (we call it a "Chinese lantern"). Hundreds of them would have been hung at a nighttime rally for presidential candidate Benjamin Harrison. Harrison was the grandson of President William Henry Harrison, thus the reference to "Tippecanoe."

PRESIDENTS AND PERSONALITIES

In 1876 President Grant was rounding out his second term. He was only 55; he was not rich; and he had given up his army pension when he became president. Despite the two-term tradition, he wanted to run for reelection. Roscoe Conkling, whom Grant had made a powerful political boss, wanted him to run too. But too many scandals in his administration had

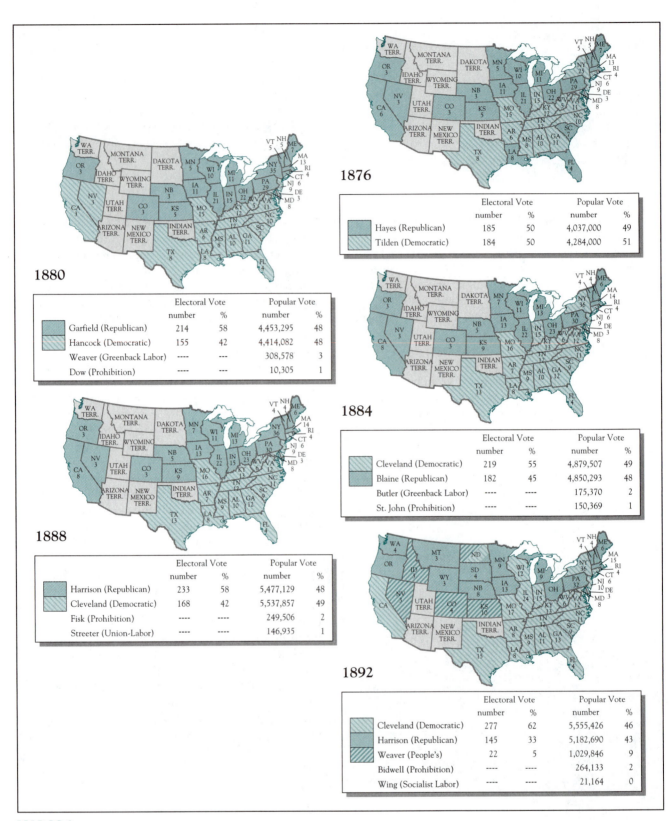

1876

	Electoral Vote		Popular Vote	
	number	%	number	%
Hayes (Republican)	185	50	4,037,000	49
Tilden (Democratic)	184	50	4,284,000	51

1880

	Electoral Vote		Popular Vote	
	number	%	number	%
Garfield (Republican)	214	58	4,453,295	48
Hancock (Democratic)	155	42	4,414,082	48
Weaver (Greenback Labor)	----	---	308,578	3
Dow (Prohibition)	----	---	10,305	1

1884

	Electoral Vote		Popular Vote	
	number	%	number	%
Cleveland (Democratic)	219	55	4,879,507	49
Blaine (Republican)	182	45	4,850,293	48
Butler (Greenback Labor)	----	----	175,370	2
St. John (Prohibition)	----	----	150,369	1

1888

	Electoral Vote		Popular Vote	
	number	%	number	%
Harrison (Republican)	233	58	5,477,129	48
Cleveland (Democratic)	168	42	5,537,857	49
Fisk (Prohibition)	----	----	249,506	2
Streeter (Union-Labor)	----	----	146,935	1

1892

	Electoral Vote		Popular Vote	
	number	%	number	%
Cleveland (Democratic)	277	62	5,555,426	46
Harrison (Republican)	145	33	5,182,690	43
Weaver (People's)	22	5	1,029,846	9
Bidwell (Prohibition)	----	----	264,133	2
Wing (Socialist Labor)	----	----	21,164	0

MAP 26:1

Except for Connecticut, New England was dependably Republican; so was Pennsylvania, and with 29–30 electoral votes, it was a valuable property. After the end of Reconstruction in 1877, the former slave states—including those that did not join the Confederacy—were solidly Democratic. Illinois and Indiana were swing states, fought over fiercely in every election. The key to the election was New York. Except for the "stolen election" of 1876, the winner in every election carried New York. And in every election except 1892, if the winner had not won New York, he would not have been elected.

been exposed. The House of Representatives, by a vote of 233–18, crushed his hopes by endorsing the two-term tradition. The large majority included most Republican congressmen. They knew that to have a chance of electing a Republican, they needed a candidate with a squeaky-clean reputation.

They found him in Governor Rutherford B. Hayes. *The Nation* called Hayes and his running mate "the most respectable men, in the strict sense of the word, the Republican party has ever nominated." So when Hayes was awarded the presidency in the "stolen election" of 1876, Democrats took particular delight in calling him "His Fraudulency" and "Rutherfraud" B. Hayes.

HAYES, INTEGRITY, AND OBLIVION

Hayes had been seriously wounded in the Civil War; he was more an abnormally reckless soldier than a brave one. He was serious and intense but seems to have been luckier than he was bright. He and his wife, "Lemonade Lucy" Hayes, were temperance people. No alcohol was served in the Hayes White House.

President Hayes pleased few people. Democrats called him a fraud. Old radical Republicans were angered by his abandonment of southern blacks to the redeemers. "**Stalwarts,**" as their leader, Roscoe Conkling, called Republicans who resolutely and uncompromisingly backed the party and expected to be rewarded for their loyalty with government jobs, were infuriated when Hayes appointed reformers and even southern Democrats to choice positions. When Hayes fired New York Customs Collector Chester A. Arthur, "the prince of spoilsmen," Conkling went into opposition and began to work to nominate ex-president Grant in 1880.

Even Conkling's chief Republican rival in the Senate, James G. Blaine of Maine (his faction in the party was known as "**Half-Breeds**"), was unhappy with the share of the patronage Hayes allotted to him. He too announced that he would seek the Republican presidential nomination in 1880. So did Hayes's fellow Ohioan, Secretary of the Treasury John Sherman. During the last two years of his presidency, poor Hayes had fewer supporters than John Tyler in 1844. It did not seem to bother him. Hayes loved to travel; he longed to hit the tourist trail.

GARFIELD: A DARK HORSE

At the Republican convention of 1880, neither Grant, Blaine, nor Sherman could win a majority of the delegates, and none would yield to the other. Nor would several favorite son

candidates give up; each hoped that the deadlocked convention would turn to them. After thirty-four ballots, several delegates broke ranks; but instead of switching to a favorite son, they voted for James A. Garfield of Ohio, who was managing John Sherman's campaign. Garfield protested, but on the thirty-fifth ballot, more delegates named him. Because Garfield was a Half-Breed, Blaine released his supporters in favor of Garfield, and on the thirty-sixth ballot, he was nominated.

Garfield was shocked; he had no plans, but he knew he needed the support of the Stalwarts if he was to win. He asked Chester A. Arthur to be his running mate. Conkling was furious and told Arthur to decline. For the only time in their long relationship, Arthur did not obey. To him, the vice presidency was an honor he never imagined possible. Conkling sulked and snubbed Garfield when the candidate came to New York to talk with him. But he got over his anger and did not protest when Arthur mobilized the Stalwart machine in New York.

Arthur won the election for Garfield as surely as Aaron Burr won it for Jefferson in 1800 and Martin Van Buren for Jackson in 1828. Had the Democratic candidate General Winfield Scott Hancock carried New York (he lost the state to Garfield narrowly), he would have been elected.

A LUST FOR PATRONAGE

Garfield was intelligent and scholarly. He read both Latin and Greek; he did a parlor trick in which he simultaneously wrote in Latin with one hand and Greek with the other. He would have graced any university that had him as its president. He had succeeded in politics, however, by being a pliant, party-line regular. Both Conkling and Blaine believed they could use him. The day after the election, Blaine's wife wrote to her daughter, "Your father and I have picked out Garfield's cabinet for him."

Blaine had the inside track. He and Garfield (and their wives) were personally friendly; Garfield picked Blaine as his secretary of state. At first Garfield wanted to placate Conkling too, but Conkling was imperious and bullying; he demanded that Garfield turn the New York patronage over to him as Grant had done. He insulted Garfield once too often, playing into Blaine's hands. Instead of choosing as New York Collector of Customs someone who was neither Stalwart nor Half-Breed, Garfield did Blaine's bidding and named Conkling's worst enemy in the state. In protest, Conkling and

A District Leader's Day

2 A.M.: Aroused from sleep by the ringing of his doorbell; went to the door and found a bartender, who asked him to go to the police station and bail out a saloon-keeper who had been arrested for violating the excise law. Furnished bail and returned to bed at three o'clock.

Thus began a working day in the life of George Washington Plunkitt, sachem of Tammany Hall, the Democratic party machine in New York City, and leader of District Fifteen. Plunkitt was born in 1842 in an Irish slum that was later razed to build Central Park. He worked for a butcher as a teenager, but before he was old enough to vote, he was running errands for Tammany Hall. He was, Plunkitt said, a "statesman" in the making.

As a sachem, he was one of the dozen bosses who ran New York's Democratic party, which usually meant they ran New York City. Like other Tammany men, Plunkitt believed that "politics is as much a regular business as the grocery or the dry-goods . . . business. You've got to be trained up to it or you're sure to fail." Before he was 30, when Boss Tweed ran New York, Plunkitt made money in his business by collecting three city salaries at once. Later he went into real estate speculation. In "Honest Graft," the most famous of the talks on practical politics he gave to a newspaper reporter, Plunkitt explained,

"My party's in power in the city, and it's goin' to undertake a lot of public improvements. Well, I'm tipped off, say, that they're going to lay out a new park at a certain place.

"I see my opportunity and I take it. I go to that place and I buy up all the land I can in the neighborhood. Then the board of this or that makes its plan public, and there is a rush to get my land, which nobody cared particular for before.

"Ain't it perfectly honest to charge a good price and make a profit on my investment and foresight? Of course, it is. Well, that's honest graft."

Plunkitt stayed away from "dirty business"—taking bribes, protecting brothels and illegal gambling houses, and the like—because there was "so much honest graft lyin' around." Probably, for he was a man of high personal morality, he found such business disagreeable too.

6 A.M.: Awakened by fire engines passing his house. Hastened to the scene of the fire, according to the custom of the Tammany district leaders, to give assistance to the fire sufferers, if needed. Met several of his election district captains who are always under orders to look out for fires, which are considered great vote-getters. Found several tenants who had been burned out, took them to a hotel, supplied them with clothes, fed them, and arranged temporary quarters for them until they could rent and furnish new apartments.

8:30 A.M.: Went to the police court to look after his constituents. Found six "drunks." Secured the discharge of four by a timely word with the judge, and paid the fines of two.

9 A.M.: Appeared in the Municipal District Court. Directed one of his district captains to act as counsel for a widow against whom dispossession proceedings had been instituted and obtained an extension of time. Paid the rent of a poor family about to be dispossessed and gave them a dollar for food.

11 A.M.: At home again. Found four men waiting for him. One had been discharged by the Metropolitan Railway Company for neglect of duty and wanted the district leader to fix things. Another wanted a job on the road. The third sought a place on the subway, and the fourth, a plumber, was looking for work with the Consolidated Gas Company. The district leader spent nearly three hours fixing things for the four men, and succeeded in each case.

Although he was 60 when this account of his day was written, Plunkitt still worked long, exhausting days, providing

---

his protégé, Thomas Platt, resigned their Senate seats. They intended to remind Garfield of their political power by having the state legislature reelect them.

The lust for the patronage, from the top to the bottom, had taken over government. "If all the reports are true," *The New York Times* editorialized, "President Garfield's cabinet will contain about 125 persons." The first week after he was nominated, 200 people visited his home, at least half of them putting in bids for jobs. Between election day and his inauguration, Garfield was flooded daily with mail from office seekers. When he moved into the White House, he did little but see one applicant after another; the waiting room outside

his office was crowded every day with people "lying in wait for me like vultures for a wounded bison." He exclaimed to Blaine, "My God! What is there in this place that a man should ever want to get into it!"

ANOTHER MURDERED PRESIDENT

Charles Guiteau sat in the president's waiting room several days each week. He managed to speak to the president several times, at first requesting the consulate in Vienna, then deciding he would rather be consul in Paris. When he was not waiting for Garfield, he was buttonholing Blaine, Arthur, Grant, Senator Benjamin Harrison of Indiana, and other top

personal and practical services to voters with problems. He took little interest in the issues of the day because he knew that ordinary New Yorkers, struggling to stay afloat, took none. "I know every man, woman, and child in the Fifteenth District, except them that's been born this summer and I know some of them, too. I know what they like and what they don't like, what they are strong at and what they are weak in. . . .

"For instance, here's how I gather in the young men. I hear of a young feller that's proud of his voice, thinks that he can sing fine. I ask him to come around to Washington Hall and join our Glee Club. He comes and sings, and he's a follower of Plunkitt for life. Another young feller gains a reputation as a baseball player in a vacant lot. I bring him into our baseball club. That fixes him. You'll find him workin' for my ticket at the polls next election day. . . . I don't trouble them with political arguments. I just study human nature and act accordin'."

> *3 P.M.: Attended the funeral of an Italian as far as the ferry. Hurried back to make his appearance at the funeral of a Hebrew constituent. Went conspicuously to the front in both the Catholic church and the synagogue, and later attended the Hebrew confirmation ceremonies in the synagogue.*
>
> *7 P.M.: Went to district headquarters and presided over a meeting of election district captains. Each captain submitted a list of all the voters in his district, reported on their attitude toward Tammany, suggested who might be won over and how they could be won, and told who were in need and who were in trouble of any kind and the best way to reach them. District leader took notes and gave orders.*
>
> *8 P.M.: Went to a church fair. Took chances on everything, bought ice cream for the young girls and the children. Kissed the little ones, flattered their mothers, and took their fathers out for something down at the corner.*

> *9 P.M.: At the clubhouse again. Spent $10 on tickets for a church excursion and promised a subscription for a new church bell. Bought tickets for a baseball game to be played by two nines from his district. Listened to the complaints of a dozen pushcart peddlers who said they were persecuted by the police and assured them he would go to police headquarters in the morning and see about it.*

Plunkitt got started in politics by bringing "marketable goods"—votes—to the party:

Let me tell you: I had a cousin, a young man who didn't take any particular interest in politics. I went to him and said, "Tommy, I'm goin' to be a politician, and I want to get a followin'; can I count on you?" He said, "Sure, George." That's how I started in business. I got a marketable commodity—one vote. Then I went to the district leader and told him I could command two votes on election day, Tommy's and my own. He smiled on me and told me to go ahead. If I had offered him a speech or a bookful of learnin', he would have said, "Oh, forget it!"

Soon, as Plunkitt told it, he had three votes in his following and, before long, sixty in the George Washington Plunkitt Association. "What did the district leader say then when I called at headquarters? I didn't have to call at headquarters. He came after me and said, 'George, what do you want? If you don't see what you want, ask for it. Wouldn't you like to have a job or two in the departments for your friends?'"

That was how the political machine worked—and how George Washington Plunkitt became a statesman.

> *10:30 P.M.: Attended a Hebrew wedding reception and dance. Had previously sent a handsome wedding present to the bride.*
>
> *12 A.M.: In bed.*

Republicans, asking for their support and letters of recommendation.

Guiteau was deranged. He described himself as an important figure in the Stalwart machine. In fact, he was a penniless ne'er-do-well (he survived in Washington by jumping from one boardinghouse to another without paying) with a history of attaching himself to fringe religious groups. He believed he was entitled to a consular appointment when he did not have the standing in the party to claim a post office job in the Dakotas. When he realized he was going nowhere and decided to kill Garfield, he believed that after a few weeks in jail, he would be freed and honored by the new president,

Chester Arthur. He scouted the accommodations at the Washington jail a week before he acted and told the jailer that they were "excellent."

Guiteau shot Garfield in the back at point-blank range in the Washington railway station on July 2, 1881, shouting, "I am a Stalwart! Arthur is president!" Had it happened today, Garfield would have recovered. But with no means of locating the bullet but probing Garfield's wound, doctors could only guess where it was (they were off by a full foot). Garfield lived in excruciating pain for eleven weeks, wasting away from 200 pounds to 130. He died from infection (and starvation) on September 19.

Culver Pictures, Inc.

President Garfield, who did little as president but interview Republicans asking for government jobs, was shot in the back by one of them in a railroad station in Washington. The man assisting him is Secretary of State James G. Blaine. The assassin, Charles Guiteau, has been seized at the left.

Guiteau should have been acquitted as insane, even under the strict definition of insanity in American law. But the country's shock was too great—two presidents murdered in sixteen years—and Guiteau was hanged, shouting "Bound for glory! I'm bound for glory!"

CIVIL SERVICE REFORM

The shooting wrote an end to Roscoe Conkling's political career. The New York legislature defiantly refused to send him back to the Senate. The backlash to the assassination also resulted in Congress's hurried enactment of the **Pendleton Act** of 1883, a bill that would not have reached the floor

Turkey

Roscoe Conkling was a physical-culture nut. He exercised daily and liked to show off his physique. James G. Blaine, when both were young congressmen, twitted him on the floor of the House by describing Conkling's "haughty disdain, his grandiloquent swell, his majestic, overpowering, turkey-gobbler strut." Blaine's putdown may have had more to do with the men's lifelong enmity than any other factor. They did not differ in their political views.

a year earlier. The Pendleton Act established the Civil Service Commission, a bureau empowered to draw up and administer examinations for applicants for some low-level government positions. Once in these civil service jobs, employees could not be fired simply because the political party to which they belonged lost the presidency.

President Arthur put only 10 percent of 131,000 government workers on the civil service list. However, the Pendleton Act entitled future presidents to add job classifications to the civil service. Because the presidency changed hands between the parties every four years between 1883 and 1897, each outgoing president added jobs to the list to protect government employees they had appointed. By 1897, 41 percent of 256,000 government employees were classified as civil service. (The percentage peaked in 1970 at 90 percent. It has declined since to less than 50 percent chiefly because in 1971 Post Office Department employees became employees of the Postal Service, which is not covered by civil service law.)

The Pendleton Act also abolished assessments. That is, the parties were forbidden to require members in government jobs to donate a percentage of their salaries to political campaign funds. An unforeseen consequence of this reform was that both parties turned to rich businessmen and other special interests to finance them.

Conkling the Idealist

Although he is chiefly remembered for his cynical attitude toward patronage and party loyalty, Roscoe Conkling remained truer to radical Republican ideals than most Republicans. Until his death in 1888, Conkling's top-drawer law firm, on his instructions, took cases from poor African Americans at nominal or no cost.

1884: BLAINE VERSUS CLEVELAND

Chester A. Arthur may have been president illegally. His enemies claimed that he was born not in Fairfield, Vermont, as he said, but in a cabin a few miles north—in Canada. However that may have been, the urbane and elegant Arthur, resplendent in his New York wardrobe compared to the gray look favored by Republican politicians, amazed everyone with his dignity and sense of duty as president. He remained personally loyal to Conkling, twice offering him a seat on the Supreme Court. However, he pushed an investigation into post office frauds that involved Stalwart employees. He tried to woo the Half-Breeds by deferring to Secretary of State James G. Blaine's judgment in foreign affairs and appointing Blaine's supporters to high positions. No other president of the era used the patronage with more integrity. But Blaine rebuffed him. He resigned from the cabinet to compete with Arthur for the Republican presidential nomination in 1884. With Conkling retired to a lucrative law practice and disinterested in Arthur's fate, Blaine won the nomination easily.

New York State was, as in 1880, the key to the election. When the Democrats nominated New York's governor, Grover Cleveland, things did not look good for the Republicans. Republican reformers in the state, genteel and upperclass, announced that they supported Cleveland, who had a spotless record while Blaine had been caught in lies about a dubious railroad deal early in his career. Blaine's supporters sarcastically called them *mugwumps,* supposedly an Algonkian Indian word for "big chief" or "big shot," a reference to their often pompous self-righteousness. (They described themselves as men "who need nothing and want nothing from government except the satisfaction of using their talents.")

But Blaine expected to compensate for the defection and more by cutting into New York City's large Irish Catholic vote, which was usually solidly Democratic. Blaine's mother was Catholic, and his sister was a nun. And he campaigned hard, making several hundred speeches, mostly in New York. Then Republicans broke the news that Cleveland was supporting an illegitimate child he had fathered in Buffalo. "Ma, Ma, Where's my Pa?" Republicans chanted, "Gone to the White House, Ha, ha, ha."

HOW LITTLE THINGS DECIDE GREAT ELECTIONS

Just days before the election, Blaine blundered. Forgetting how Grant damaged himself by consorting with Jim Fisk

A political toy, with Republican candidate Benjamin Harrison (left) and Democrat Grover Cleveland weighed in the balance. It is obviously a Republican toy, with Harrison coming in weightier. (In the flesh, Harrison was a small man and Cleveland tall and, although not quite fat, certainly portly.)

and Jay Gould, Blaine dined with a group of millionaires in Delmonico's, the most elegant and expensive restaurant in New York City. It was not a good idea when he was courting the votes of working-class Irishmen. At another dinner, apparently dozing, he made no comment when a Presbyterian minister, Samuel Burchard, denounced the Democrats as the party of "rum, romanism, and rebellion" (that is, the party of the saloon, the Roman Catholic church, and the Confederacy).

This was common Republican sloganeering in Bangor, Maine, or Moline, Illinois. But it was New York City, and Blaine was wooing Irish Catholic voters. When Democratic newspapers plastered the insult across their front pages, Blaine rushed to express his distaste for Burchard's statement, but the damage was done. Irish voters trundled back into the Democratic column, and upstate blizzards snowed many Republican voters in. New York State gave Cleveland a majority, and its electoral votes gave him the election. (Blaine

Shocking

Electricity was installed in the White House in 1890. But President Harrison and his wife were terrified of the switches; they would not touch them. Servants turned the lights on in the evening. During the day, the entire system was closed down at the president's insistence.

could have won anyway had he carried Indiana and either Connecticut or New Jersey. It was, as usual, a close race.)

In 1888 it was Cleveland who was undone by a trivial incident. A Republican newspaperman, posing as an English-born naturalized American, wrote to the British minister in Washington asking which of the two candidates, Cleveland or Benjamin Harrison of Indiana, would make the better president from the British point of view. Foolishly, the minister replied that Cleveland was better disposed toward British interests. The Republican press immediately labeled Cleveland the British candidate, and thousands of Irish Democrats, reflexively hostile to anything the British favored, voted Republican. Harrison won New York.

ISSUES

Real issues were not unknown in Gilded Age politics. For example, when President Grant tried to annex San Domingo (the Dominican Republic) in 1870, he was frustrated by the resistance of Republican senators. As late as 1890, northeastern Republicans tried to revive the party's commitment to the welfare of southern blacks when southern Democrats, playing to the racism of poor whites, launched a campaign to deny the vote to all African Americans, which the redeemers had never tried to do.

However, both episodes show that differences of principle were as likely to lie within the parties as between them. Even the question of the tariff, the nearest thing to an issue dividing Republicans and Democrats, found members of both parties on both sides. The level at which import duties were set could inspire orators to sweating, thumping, and prancing. But their position on the issue, low tariff or high protective tariff, depended more on the place their constituents occupied in the economy than on the party to which they belonged.

THE TARIFF

Farmers were inclined to favor a low tariff. Corn, wheat, and cotton were so cheaply produced in the United States that

Bettmann/Corbis

The tariff (how high should import duties be?) had been a partisan issue since the Federalists and the Jefferson Republicans first squared off. In the late 19th century, few American manufacturers needed "protection" from foreign competitors. Andrew Carnegie regularly underbid British steelmakers in Great Britain. But manufacturers continued, through the Republican party, to insist that "infant industries" be protected. This cartoon pokes fun at their pleas.

American farmers were able to undersell foreign growers of the same crops in their own countries—if those countries did not levy tariffs on American crops in retaliation for high American duties on their exports. Moreover, low duties on imported manufactured goods allowed consumers (such as farmers) to pay less for them. The interest of agriculturalists in keeping import duties down made the Democratic party, with its powerful southern agrarian contingent, generally the low-tariff party. However, Republican congressmen representing rural areas also voted for low rates.

Most industrialists, who wanted to protect their products from foreign competition, were Republican and set that party's high-tariff tone. However, some equally rich and powerful railroaders and bankers supported lower duties either within the Republican party or as Democrats. Some railroaders wanted a low tariff because they were huge consumers of steel for rails; high tariffs kept such prices artificially high.

In the late nineteenth century, high-tariff interests had their way. After bobbing up and down from a low of 40 percent (by no means a low tariff) to a high of 47 percent, rates were increased to 50 percent by the McKinley Tariff of 1890. That is, on average, imports were slapped with a tax equivalent to half their value.

When a depression ensued after the McKinley Act, Grover Cleveland and the Democrats campaigned against high rates and won the election of 1892. Congress's Wilson–Gorman tariff lowered duties to about 39 percent of the value of imports. Cleveland did not sign the Wilson–Gorman bill, but neither did he veto it; it became law without his signature.

MONEY

The issue that, in the 1890s, shattered the political equilibrium of the Gilded Age was money. The question was whether circulating currency should be backed by gold (all paper money redeemable on demand in gold coins or bullion) or whether the federal government should instead regulate the supply (and therefore the value) of paper money in response to changing economic conditions or in the interests of justice.

The controversy had its roots with the greenbacks issued during the Civil War to help finance the fighting. The greenbacks were not redeemable, at face value, in gold. When the war was going badly, they were discounted; it might take $7 or $8 in greenbacks to buy what a $5 gold piece would buy. Bankers and industrialists were uneasy with a currency that fluctuated, sometimes rapidly, in value. Bankers did not want borrowers paying back loans in greenbacks worth less in real value than the money they had borrowed. President Grant's secretaries of the treasury, who shared the *gold standard* views of the big bankers, began to retire the greenbacks. When the bills flowed into the treasury in payment of taxes, they were destroyed and not replaced by new greenbacks.

The result was deflation: a contraction of the amount of money in circulation. Prices dipped, and so did wages. It took less to buy a sack of flour or a side of bacon than it had when the greenbacks were abundant. And the farmers who grew the wheat and slopped the hogs, of course, received less for their efforts.

This would not have mattered as much if the farmers had not borrowed heavily when the currency was inflated because greenbacks were plentiful. It was unjust, they argued, that they should have to pay off their mortgages in gold. For example, a $1,000 loan taken out during the 1860s represented 1,200 bushels of grain. By the 1880s, when a farmer might still be paying off that debt, $1,000 represented 2,300 bushels. A farmer had to produce twice as much to pay back each dollar borrowed, not to mention the interest owed.

THE GREENBACK LABOR PARTY

In 1876 the Greenback Labor party was founded with mostly farmer support but with hopes of appealing to industrial workers, whose wages (in dollars) had declined since the war. The greenbackers chose as their presidential candidate ancient Peter Cooper, who was 85 years old. He was famous as the builder of the first American steam locomotive, as an exemplary employer in New Jersey, and as a philanthropist. And he favored increasing the money supply by keeping the greenbacks in circulation.

Cooper made a poor showing, but in the congressional race of 1878, the greenbackers elected a dozen congressmen, and some Republicans and Democrats backed their calls for inflation. However, President Hayes's monetary policy was as conservative as Grant's, and retirement of the greenbacks proceeded. In 1880 the Greenback Labor ticket, led by a Civil War general from Iowa, James B. Weaver, won 309,000 votes, but federal policy remained unchanged.

In 1884 Benjamin J. Butler of Massachusetts led the greenbackers one more time, but he received only one-third of the votes Weaver won in 1880. The demand to inflate the currency was not dead. Within a decade American politics would be turned upside down because of it. But by the 1880s the greenbacks were history.

POLITICS IN THE CITIES

By 1896 silver coinage had replaced the greenbacks as the talisman of Americans who wanted to inflate the nation's money supply. Both the Republican and Democratic parties were shaken by a fierce debate in which gold and silver became sacred symbols. (See Chapter 32.) The political atmosphere was religious, evangelical, even fanatical. "Gold bugs"

Citizenship

The New York machine naturalized some newly arrived immigrants almost as soon as they stepped off the boat. The record day was October 14, 1868, when a judge swore in 2,109 new citizens, three a minute. One James Goff attested to the "good moral character" of 669 applicants. Two days later, Goff was arrested for stealing a watch and two diamond rings.

and "free silverites" both believed they were engaged in a holy war in which there could be no compromise. The political equilibrium of the 1870s and 1880s was shattered.

The Democratic party convention of 1896 was the most tumultuous since the party destroyed itself in 1860. Richard Croker, then the leader of Tammany Hall, was bewildered by the fury. He listened to an agitated gold versus silver debate and shook his head. He could not understand what the fuss was about. As far as he was concerned, gold and silver were both money, and he was all for both kinds.

THE POLITICAL MACHINE

Urban politics in the late nineteenth century resembled national politics in some ways. Issues were of secondary importance; what counted was winning elections. The big-city political party existed, like a business, for the benefit of those who "owned" it. The technique of election victory, therefore, was the politician's profession. His skill and willingness to work for "the company," and his productivity in delivering votes, determined how high he rose in an organization as finely tuned as any corporation.

The chairman of the board of the urban political company was "the boss." He was not necessarily the mayor, who was often a respectable front man. The boss coordinated the complex activities of the machine. Voters had to be aroused by the same sort of emotional appeals and hoopla that sustained national political campaigns. The machine was expected to provide material incentives comparable to the GOP's pension program. Party activists (the company's "employees") who worked to get the voters out to the polls and kept them happy between elections were "paid" with patronage and pork courtesy of the city treasury. Control of the municipal treasury was what counted in urban politics, not the service of principles or the implementation of a program.

"You are always working for your pocket, are you not?" an investigator into government corruption asked Richard Croker, thinking to embarrass him. Croker snapped back, "All the time, the same as you." On another occasion Croker told writer Lincoln Steffens, "Politics is business, and reporting—journalism, doctoring—all professions, arts,

sports—everything is business." Candor as blunt as the prow of a ferryboat was one quality that distinguished municipal politicians from national politicians. Another was that the control of cities that many political machines exercised was so nearly absolute that political profiteering sometimes took the form of blatant thievery.

THE PROFIT COLUMN

The political machine in power controlled law enforcement. In return for regular cash payments, politicians winked at the operations of illegal businesses: unlicensed saloons, gambling houses, opium dens, brothels, even strong-arm gangs. "Bathhouse" John Coughlan and "Hinky-Dink" Kenna, Chicago's "Gray Wolves," openly collected tribute from the kings and queens of Chicago vice at an annual ball.

The political machine in power peddled influence to anyone willing to buy. Although he was no lawyer, William Marcy Tweed of New York, the first of the great city bosses, was on Cornelius Vanderbilt's payroll as a legal adviser. What the commodore was hiring was the rulings of judges who belonged to Tweed's organization. In San Francisco after the turn of the century, Boss Abe Ruef held office hours on designated nights at an elegant French restaurant; would-be purchasers of influence filed in between appetizer and entrée, and entrée and roast, and negotiated their deals.

KICKBACKS AND SANDBAGGING

The rapid growth of cities in the late nineteenth century provided rich opportunities for kickbacks on contracts awarded by city governments. In New York, Central Park was a gold mine of padded contracts. The most notorious swindle was the New York County Courthouse, a $600,000 building that cost taxpayers $13 million. Plasterers, carpenters, and plumbers who worked on the building had standing orders to bill the city two to three times what they needed to make a reasonable profit, kicking back half or more of the padding to Tammany Hall, the club that controlled the Democratic party. Forty chairs and three tables cost the city $179,000. "Brooms, etc." cost $41,190.95.

Another technique for getting rich in public office was called "sandbagging." It worked particularly well in dealing with the streetcar lines that needed city permission to lay tracks on public thoroughfares. Getting such contracts in machine-run cities required bribes. The most corrupt aldermen, such as Coughlan and Kenna in Chicago, would grant a line the rights to lay tracks on only a few blocks at a time; thus the Chicago "Traction King," Charles T. Yerkes, would be back for a further franchise at an additional cost. Another variety of sandbagging involved threatening an existing trolley line with competition on a nearby parallel street. Rather than have their traffic decline by half, traction companies coughed up the money to prevent new construction.

It was not necessary to break the law to profit from public office. A well-established member of a political machine could expect to be on the city payroll for jobs that did not really exist but were quite legal. In one district of New York City where there were four water pumps for fighting fires, the city paid the salaries of twenty pump inspectors. Probably none of them ever looked at a pump. Their real job was to keep the political machine in power at taxpayers' expense. It was possible to hold several meaningless city jobs simultaneously. Cornelius Corson, who kept his ward safe for New York's Tweed Ring from an office in his saloon, was on the books as a court clerk at $10,000 a year, as chief of the Board of Elections at $5,000 a year, and as an employee of four other municipal agencies at $2,500 per job.

This was a munificent income in the late nineteenth century, but the bosses at the top of the machine did better. Altogether, the Tweed Ring looted the city treasury of as much as $200 million. Tweed went to jail, but his chief henchman, Controller "Slippery" Dick Connolly, fled abroad with several million dollars. Richard Croker, head of Tammany Hall at the end of the century, retired to Ireland a millionaire. Timothy "Big Tim" Sullivan rose from poverty to riches as well as adulation; when he died as the result of a streetcar accident, 25,000 people attended his funeral.

STAYING IN BUSINESS

Big Tim's sendoff illustrates the fact that despite their profiteering, machine politicians stayed in office. Although few of them were above stuffing ballot boxes or marching gangs of

Tim Sullivan (right), an immensely popular ward boss in New York. His friends sometimes called him "Dry Dollar" Sullivan because, they said, as a young man he was found drunk, drying out the excise stamp from a barrel of whiskey, apparently thinking it was a dollar bill. The debonair gent shown here does not seem the type.

Culver Pictures, Inc.

"repeaters" from one polling place to the next, they won most elections fairly. The majority of city voters usually chose them over candidates pledged to govern honestly.

The machines acted as highly personalized social services among hard-pressed people. During the bitter winter of 1870, Boss Tweed spent $50,000 on coal that was dumped by the hundreds of tons at street corners in the poorest parts of the city. Tim Sullivan gave away 5,000 turkeys every Christmas. It was the duty of every block captain to report when someone died, was born, was making a first holy communion in the Catholic church, or was celebrating a bar mitzvah in the Jewish synagogue. The ward boss had a gift delivered.

Ward bosses brought light into dismal lives by throwing parties. In 1871 Mike Norton treated his constituents to 100 kegs of beer, 50 cases of champagne, 20 gallons of brandy, 10 gallons of gin, 200 gallons of chowder, 50 gallons of turtle soup, 36 hams, 4,000 pounds of corned beef, and 5,000 cigars.

Ward bosses fixed up minor (and sometimes major) scrapes with the law. In control of the municipal government, the machines had jobs at their disposal—not only the phony high-paying sinecures that the bosses carved up among themselves, but jobs that required real work and that unemployed men and women were grateful to have. Boss James McManes of Philadelphia had more than 5,000 positions at his disposal; the New York machine controlled four times that number. It is estimated that 20 percent of New York's voters had a direct financial interest in the outcome of municipal elections. With the votes of appreciative relatives and friends, the machine had a nice political base.

THE FAILURE OF THE GOO-GOOS

Not everyone brimmed with gratitude. Middle-class people, who paid property taxes, periodically raised campaigns for good government (the machines called them "Goo-Goos") and occasionally won elections. The Tweed Ring's fall led to the election of a reform administration; in 1894 even the powerful Richard Croker was ousted. Chicago's "Gray Wolves" were thrown out of city hall, and a major wave of indignation swept Abe Ruef and Mayor Eugene Schmitz out of power in San Francisco in 1906. But until the turn of the century, reform governments were generally short-lived. The machines came back.

One political weakness of the Goo-Goos was that they offered no alternative to the informal social services the machine provided. They believed that honest government was synonymous with inexpensive government. Facing material problems and inclined from their European backgrounds to think of government as an institution that one used or was used by, the immigrants preferred the machines.

ERIN GO BRAGH

"The natural function of the Irishman," said a wit of the period, "is to administer the affairs of the American city." In fact, some bosses had other lineages: Cox of Cincinnati and Crump of Memphis were WASPs; Tweed was of Scottish descent; Ruef was Jewish; and Schmitz was German. But a list of nineteenth-century machine politicians reads like a roll call of marchers in a St. Patrick's Day parade: Richard Connolly, "Honest" John Kelley, Richard Croker, George Plunkitt, Charles Murphy, and Tim Sullivan of New York; James McManes (unlike the New Yorkers, a Republican) of Philadelphia; Christopher Magee and William Finn of Pittsburgh; and Martin Lomasney of Boston.

The Irish were successful in politics in part because they were the first of the large ethnic groups in the cities, and in part because they were highly political in their homeland as a consequence of rule by Great Britain. Moreover, the Irish placed a high premium on oratory, which led naturally to politics. Most important of all, the Irish spoke English (of a particularly lovely pronunciation), a head start in the race to succeed over the other major immigrant groups of the late nineteenth century.

The primacy of the Irish did not mean that later immigrants were shut out of politics. The political machine lacked ethnic prejudice. If a ward became Italian and an Italian ward boss delivered the votes, he was welcomed into the organization and granted a share of the spoils commensurate with his contribution in votes on election day. In many cities, while the police forces retained an Irish complexion, sanitation departments and fire departments often were predominantly Italian.

FURTHER READING

General Robert Cherny, *American Politics in the Gilded Age, 1868–1900,* 1997; Paul Kleppner, *The Third Electoral System, 1852–1892,* 1979; H. Wayne Morgan, *From Hayes to McKinley: National Party Politics, 1877–1896,* 1969; Mark W. Summers, *The Era of Good Stealings,* 1993, and *The Gilded Age or The Hazard of New Functions,* 1997; Alan Trachtenburg, *The Incorporation of America: Culture and Society in the Civil War,* 1988.

Cities Oliver E. Allen, *The Tiger: The Rise and Fall of Tammany Hall,* 1993; Steven P. Eric, *Rainbow's End: Irish Americans and the Dilemmas of Machine Politics, 1840–1945,* 1988; Thomas M. Henderson, *Tammany Hall and the New Immigrants,* 1976;

Peter McCaffery, *When Bosses Ruled Philadelphia: The Emergence of the Republican Machine, 1867–1933,* 1993; William M. Riordan, *Plunkitt of Tammany Hall,* 1994; Daniel R. Roediger, *Working toward Whiteness: How America's Immigrants Became White,* 2005; John Teaford, *The Unheralded Triumph: City Government in America, 1870–1900,* 1984.

Politicians Kenneth D. Ackerman, *Dark Horse: The Surprise Election and Political Murder of President James A. Garfield,* 2003; R. G. Caldwell, *Gentleman Boss: The Life of Chester A. Arthur,* 1975; Charles W. Calhoun, *Benjamin Harrison,* 2005; Edward W. Crapol, *James G. Blaine: Architect of Empire,* 2000; Justus T. Doenecke, *The Presidencies of James A. Garfield and Chester A. Arthur,* 1981; Henry

F. Graff, *Grover Cleveland*, 2002; Ari Hoogenboom, *Rutherford B. Hayes: Warrior and President*, 1995; H. Paul Jeffers, *An Honest President: The Life and Presidencies of Grover Cleveland*, 2002; Jean

Edward Smith, *Grant*, 2001; Mark W. Summers, *Rum, Romanism, and Rebellion: The Making of a President, 1884*, 2000.

KEY TERMS

The following terms are covered in this chapter and can also be found in the list of Key Terms at the back of the book.

bloody shirt	gold standard	Pendleton Act	swing states
Bourbons	"Half-Breeds"	"Stalwarts"	Tammany Hall
GAR	*mugwumps*		

 ## ONLINE SOURCES GUIDE

Use this listing to find online documents, images, interactive maps, simulations, and other resources related to this chapter:

American History Resource Center
http://history.wadsworth.com/rc/us

Selected Documents
Excerpts from William Riordan's Plunkitt of Tammany Hall

Selected Images
McKinley–Roosevelt campaign poster
An attack on Tammany Hall and William "Boss" Tweed

Interactive Time Line (with online readings)
Parties, Patronage, and Pork: Politics in the Late Nineteenth Century

CHAPTER 27

Technology, Industry, and Business

Economic Revolution in the Late Nineteenth Century

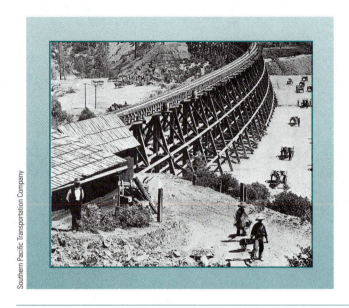

Southern Pacific Transportation Company

This movement was the origin of the whole system of modern economic administration. It has revolutionized the way of doing business all over the world. The time was ripe for it. It had to come, though all we saw at the moment was the need to save ourselves from wasteful conditions. . . . The day of the combination is here to stay. Individualism has gone, never to return.

John D. Rockefeller

In 1876 Americans celebrated a hundred years of independence. The birthday party—the **Centennial Exposition**—was held in Philadelphia where the Declaration of Independence had been signed. It was a roaring success. Sprawling over the hills of Fairmount Park, housed in more than 200 structures, the great show dazzled 10 million visitors with its displays of American history and American products.

The emphasis was on the products and the way they were made. The heart of the fair was not the hallowed Declaration, although it was there, but Machinery Hall, a building that covered twenty acres and housed the latest American inventions and technological improvements from the typewriter and telephone to new kinds of looms and lathes. And there was a dizzying variety of agricultural machines—an American specialty—bewildering to city folk but understood perfectly by the farmers who attended.

The centerpiece of Machinery Hall (it towered over everything, five times the height of a man) was the largest steam engine ever built, the "Giant Corliss." Smoking, hissing, rumbling, clanking, chugging, and gleaming in enamel, nickel plate, brass, chrome, and copper, the monster powered every machine in the building through seventy-five miles of shafts and leather belts spinning on pulleys. When President Grant officially opened the fair by throwing the switch on the Giant Corliss, setting Machinery Hall in motion, he proclaimed without need of a speech not just that Americans were free and independent, but that they had hitched their destiny to machines that made and moved goods quickly, cheaply, and in astonishing quantities. "It is in these things of iron and steel that the national genius most freely speaks."

A LAND MADE FOR INDUSTRY

Between 1865 and 1900 the population of the United States more than doubled from 36 million to 76 million. Wealth grew six times over. At the end of the Civil War, the nation's annual production of goods was valued at $2 billion. It increased to $13 billion in 1900.

Even in 1860 the United States ranked fourth among industrial nations with more than 100,000 factories capitalized at $1 billion. But the United States was not a fraction so industrial and urban as Great Britain, which had to import much of the food its factory workers ate. Over 70 percent of the American population lived on farms or in small towns that serviced farmers. In 1860 just over a million people worked in industrial jobs. Because many of them were women and children who did not vote, factory workers were an inconsequential political force. In 1876 it was still plausible to call the United States "a farmer's country."

By 1900, however, $10 billion was invested in American factories, and 5 million people worked in industrial jobs. Early in the 1890s American industrial production surpassed Great Britain's, making the United States the world's premier industrial power. By 1914 fully 46 percent of the world's industrial and mining economy was American—more than the combined economies of Germany and Great Britain, the second and third largest industrial powers.

AN EMBARRASSMENT OF RICHES

Viewed from the twenty-first century, this success story seems to have been predestined. The ingredients of industrial revolution were heaped upon the United States in an abundance no other country has enjoyed.

In contrast to the plight of undeveloped countries today, Americans were rich in capital and therefore able to welcome foreign investment without fear of losing control of their own economy. Once the Union victory in 1865 assured foreign investors that the federal government was stable and in charge of the whole country, the pounds, guilders, and francs rolled in. By 1900 more than $3.4 billion in foreign investment was fueling the American economy. Americans had to divert only 11 to 14 percent of their national income into industrial growth, compared with 20 percent in Great Britain half a century earlier and in the Soviet Union half a century later. The experience of industrialization was therefore far less painful in America. Americans sacrificed less for the sake of a more abundant future for their descendants than the British or Russians or, for that matter, than the French, the Japanese, and other industrial peoples did.

The United States drew from a labor pool that was literate and skilled at one end and unlimited in numbers at the other. The American farm population provided mechanically inclined young men to fill skilled industrial jobs. Unlike Asian or European peasants suspicious of ways of doing things different from what was handed down to them, American farmers had always been quick to embrace and invent new techniques. In 1854 an Englishman observed, "There is not a working boy of average ability in the New England states, at least, who has not an idea of some mechanical invention or improvement in manufactures." In the final decades of the nineteenth century, the children of those boys packed up in large numbers to fill "mechanical" jobs paying good wages in industrial towns and cities. If their parents were inclined to stay home, even their heads were turned by labor-saving farm machines displayed at county fairs.

During this same half century, Europe's population underwent a spurt of growth with which European agriculture could not keep pace. Cheap American foodstuffs began to

---

Clouded Crystal Balls

It may seem so, but it is not true that incompetent business executives are unique to our times. The fabulous success of American technology can obscure the fact that technological innovators have often faced the disinterest of businessmen and government officials. In 1845 the postmaster general passed on an opportunity to purchase the patent for the telegraph for $100,000 because "under any rate of postage that could be adopted, its revenues could [not] be made equal to its expenditures." Within ten years a private telegraph company, Western Union, was one of the most profitable American businesses. In 1876 Western Union's president turned down Alexander Graham Bell's offer to sell the commercial rights to the telephone. He said, "What use could this company make of an electrical toy?"

In 1907 a businessman told broadcasting pioneer Lee De Forest that "all the radio . . . apparatus that the country will ever need" would fit in a single room. In 1985 there were 500 million radio receivers in the United States. If they were spread out evenly throughout the country, no person, even in northern Alaska, would be more than 233 feet from the ravings of a call-in talk show host. In 1926 De Forest said of television that "commercially and financially I consider it an impossibility, a development on which we need waste little time dreaming." Today Americans buy 50,000 TV sets every day.

The phonograph's inventor, Thomas Edison, said it was "not of any commercial value." In the mid-1980s, before compact disks rendered them obsolete, 574,000 records were manufactured daily. (When Edison belatedly decided to compete in the industry he had made possible, he opted for an inferior technology and was driven out of the business.) David Sarnoff, who seized on radio, the phonograph, and television, tried to sabotage FM radio after he had blundered in refusing to finance the research that developed it.

The president of IBM laughed at the preposterous idea of a "personal computer." Apple, a company in a garage, developed the first one. Valued at $5,309 in 1977, Apple was worth $1.8 billion three years later. Apple permitted a former contractor named Bill Gates to copy some features of its MacIntosh computer in return for a worthless marketing concession. Gates developed the look-alike Windows platform. Today 8 percent of American personal computers are Apples; most of the rest run Windows.

Gates is the richest man in the world thanks to Windows—but only because, when he concluded he had wasted his time developing it and offered the platform to IBM for $1 million (lunch money at IBM), the corporation's top executives turned him down, no doubt congratulating one another that they had "stuck" Gates with Windows.

Persistence

Cyrus Field was a paper manufacturer who, in his early forties, was bored with his business and became intrigued with the idea of laying a telegraph cable across the Atlantic between Great Britain and the United States. The shortest run for such a cable was between Ireland and Newfoundland, which were already connected by wire to London and New York.

The first problem was to design a cable strong enough that it would not break from its own weight when being lowered to the ocean floor, and insulated so that seawater could not penetrate to the transmission wires and short them. In 1857, just three years after conceiving his scheme, Field began laying a cable, but it broke. The next year, with a strengthened design, he made the crossing. The cable worked for three weeks, then went dead. The insulation had failed.

The Civil War put Field's project on hold. Confederate commerce raiders would have singled out Field's cable ship as a target. But he was ready to try again in 1865. Field chartered the largest ship in the world, the British *Great Eastern*. It was an engineering marvel at 700 feet long and 120 feet across the beam. It had never been properly used. With a crew of 2,000 and able to carry 4,000 passengers, it should have been used on long runs such as Britain to Australia. Instead the *Great Eastern*'s owners put it on the Atlantic run, where its operating costs made it a poor competitor with smaller ships.

Cyrus Field wanted it for one transatlantic crossing; he exploited its size to convert it into a cable factory. Instead of laying cable made on land, which required splicings (weak points by definition) each time a reel or cable was played out, the cable was manufactured in one continuous length aboard the *Great Eastern* as it was reeled out. It was not quite one continuous length, as it turned out. The cable broke but, miraculously, in mid-ocean, the loose end was retrieved, hauled aboard, and spliced. In 1866 Old World and New World could communicate instantaneously.

Cyrus Field did not die wealthy. Too trusting of his business associates (among them Jay Gould), he saw his fortune evaporate. Field was the kind of businessman for whom money was less important than the challenge of succeeding.

---

undersell peasant-grown crops in Poland and Italy—all over Europe—contributing to the impoverishment of people whose forebears had lived adequately well on the land. Millions emigrated to the United States to fill low-paying, unskilled jobs that industrialization created in greater numbers than it created skilled, machine-savvy work.

A LAND OF PLENTY

The United States was blessed as no other country with the natural resources essential to industrialization. It had a rich and productive agricultural base producing more cheap food than the population could consume. In the nineteenth century, North America's forests seemed inexhaustible. Wanderers in the mountains and deserts, first by accident, than as professional "prospectors," discovered deposits of gold, silver, semiprecious metals like copper, and plenty of dross like phosphates. Only a few useful minerals were not to be found in abundance in the United States. The most essential in the industrial world were coal and iron and later petroleum.

The gray-green mountains of Pennsylvania, West Virginia, and Kentucky were virtually made of coal, the indispensable fuel of the age of steam. In the Marquette Range of Michigan's upper peninsula, discovered in the 1840s, was a 150-feet-deep vein of ore that was 60 percent iron and ran for 100 miles. In 1890, just as Michigan's iron seemed no longer up to supplying the nation's needs, the Mesabi Range of Minnesota was opened, yielding even richer iron ore in greater quantity than any other iron deposit in the world.

The ever-growing American population was a huge, ready-made market for mass-produced goods. And thanks to the spirit of Alexander Hamilton and Henry Clay as preserved in the Republican party, and the Civil War's triumph over southern agrarianism, industrial entrepreneurs found helpful partners in the federal and state governments.

Inventions and Innovations 1869–1896

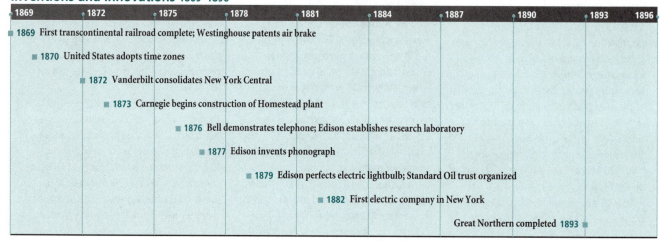

1869	1872	1875	1878	1881	1884	1887	1890	1893	1896

■ 1869 First transcontinental railroad complete; Westinghouse patents air brake

■ 1870 United States adopts time zones

■ 1872 Vanderbilt consolidates New York Central

■ 1873 Carnegie begins construction of Homestead plant

■ 1876 Bell demonstrates telephone; Edison establishes research laboratory

■ 1877 Edison invents phonograph

■ 1879 Edison perfects electric lightbulb; Standard Oil trust organized

■ 1882 First electric company in New York

Great Northern completed 1893 ■

The first telephone operators were teenage boys. Bell fired the lot of them because to amuse one another (a major activity of adolescent boys) they were sarcastic with callers. The result was an unforeseen employment opportunity for young working-class women. They were instructed to say "thank you" no matter what customers said, and they did. They worked twelve-hour shifts.

YANKEE INGENUITY

Abraham Lincoln (who himself owned a patent) observed that Americans have "a perfect rage for the new." An English visitor to the Centennial Exposition wrote, "As the Greek sculpted, as the Venetian painted, the American mechanizes." Actually, the invention that turned the most heads at the fair, the telephone, was the creation of a Scotsman who came to the United States via Canada, Alexander Graham Bell. Visitors to Bell's exhibit at the exposition picked up the odd-looking devices he had set up and, alternately amused and amazed, chatted through them with companions elsewhere in the room. Young men unwittingly dropped a hint of what was to come when they "rang up" young women standing across from them, casually striking up conversations that would have been improper had the young men approached in person.

Bell might easily have had the idea for the telephone in Scotland. Even if he had, it was only in the United States that he could parlay his idea into a gigantic enterprise: the American Telephone and Telegraph Company. As a writer in the *Saturday Evening Post* put it at the end of the century, "The United States is the only country in the world in which inventors form a distinct profession. . . . With us, inventors have grown into a large class. Laboratories . . . have sprung up almost everywhere, and today there is no great manufacturing concern that has not in its employ one or more men of whom nothing is expected except the bringing out of improvements in machinery and methods."

THE TELEPHONE

Bell was a teacher of the deaf who was working on a mechanical hearing aid when he realized that if he linked two of his devices by wire, he could transmit voice over distance. After failing to sell his invention to Western Union, he found the capital to set up a pilot company in New York. Telephones were an immediate success in businesses but also in middle- and upper-class residences. President Hayes installed a telephone in the White House in 1878. By 1880, only four years after Americans first heard of the thing, 50,000 people were paying monthly fees to hear it jangle on their walls and jumping up to chat. By 1890, there were 800,000 phones in the United States; by 1900, 1.5 million people in even small towns knew all about exchanges, party lines, and operators.

The first telephone systems were strictly local, for communication within a city or town. The telegraph remained the medium for long-distance communication. As early as 1892, however, large eastern and midwestern cities were linked by a long-distance network, and proud little western desert communities noted in their thin directories that "you can now talk to San Francisco with ease from our downtown office."

Instantaneous give-and-take communication was invaluable to businessmen. For getting things done, talking on the telephone was as superior to exchanging telegrams as telegrams had been better than an exchange of letters. And phone conversations were safely confidential. They generated no written records of transactions as letters did. They did not have to be put into code as was essential with sensitive telegrams, which passed through the hands of several telegraphers.

THE WIZARD OF MENLO PARK

Bell was lionized. Thomas Alva Edison was a folk hero. Written off in boyhood as a dunce, Edison was, in fact, bewildered by people who pursued knowledge for its own sake. He was the ultimate, practical, money-minded American tinkerer who first looked for a need that people would pay to have filled, and then went to work to fill it. Often preoccupied and abrupt to the point of rudeness, Edison struck some businesspeople as unscrupulous. In 1877 the president of Western Union remarked, "That young man has a vacuum where his conscience ought to be."

To the public, however, Edison was a hero. People admired him not only because of his inventions that changed their lives, but because of his gruff "just folks" anti-intellectual explanations of how he worked. When he was called a genius, he replied that genius was 1 percent inspiration and 99 percent perspiration. Ordinary Americans liked that, and in Edison's case it was largely true. He did not sit in darkened rooms thinking abstractly. He went to work each morning at the world's first research and development laboratory, which he built in Menlo Park, New Jersey, in 1876. It was a factory that manufactured solutions to practical problems. Edison hired "mechanically minded young men" by the dozen to discover by trial-and-error experimentation the solutions to the problems he defined for them. And he was often by their side at the workbench.

U.S. Dept. of the Interior, National Park Service, Edison National Historic Site. Photo taken by Matthew Brady, 1878

Thomas Edison was idolized for his inventions when he was still a young man. He founded the first "R&D" laboratory, but he was not as good a businessman as an inventor. Some of his business decisions resulted in others, who invented nothing, reaping most of the profits of Edison's inspiration and perspiration.

Edison took out more than a thousand patents between 1876 and 1900. Some were seedbeds for entirely new industries, such as the storage battery and the motion picture projector. Most were for improvements to existing machines and processes, commissioned by manufacturers who needed to straighten out kinks in their processes. Alexander Graham Bell himself turned to Edison for help with a problem that stumped him.

At least one of Edison's inventions was, despite his contempt for pointless tinkering, the fruit of just fooling around: the phonograph. Edison dismissed the invention as useless. When others began to exploit the commercial possibilities of

Edison's Oddest Invention

Alexander Graham Bell invented the telephone, but Thomas Edison invented the word Americans say when they answer a call—"Hello!" Bell liked the nautical term "Ahoy!" Others suggested "What is wanted?" and "Are you ready to talk?" Other nations adopted a variety of salutations. In Great Britain people answer the phone by giving their phone number (which disposes of "wrong numbers" right away). In Italy one utters an abrupt but to the point *pronto!*: "Ready!"

Edison, who was hard of hearing, suggested to Bell an archaic English word hunters used to hail others at a distance: "Halloo!" How Edison knew anything about the ways of English hunters is a mystery, but as "Hello!" his nomination was adopted in the summer of 1877. By 1880 it was widely enough known that Mark Twain could use it in a story without fear of confusing readers. In *A Connecticut Yankee in King Arthur's Court*, published in 1889, operators were known as "Hello Girls."

recorded music, Edison set up a company to make and sell phonographs and recordings.

THE LIGHTBULB

Edison's most famous invention, the incandescent lightbulb, was actually a perfection of a patent he had purchased. The object was to convert electricity into stable, safe, controllable illumination. In the 1870s the poor still extended the day with candles. Many Americans were bringing light to the night with kerosene lanterns. (The whale oil lamp was gone; the world's whales had been overhunted before the Civil War.) Cities illuminated their busiest streets by pumping gas to street lamps; the well-to-do had gaslight in their homes, as did some nighttime businesses like hotels. A few cities were experimenting with electric arc lighting on streets.

But arc light was far too harsh for use inside and required extremely high voltage, which was dangerous. Gas lamps on streets had to be individually ignited each evening and extinguished each morning. Inside, gaslight could be dangerous. Malfunctions caused devastating fires—as did carelessness when, because of ignorance, forgetfulness, or too much to drink, someone blew out the flame (as one extinguished a kerosene lamp) instead of turning off the gas valve. Then, half an hour later, the gas having filled the room, someone decided to smoke a cigar. Hotel managers plastered the walls of rooms with reminders that the lights were gas, not kerosene.

It was well known that in a vacuum within a translucent glass ball, an electrically charged filament glowed. The challenge was to find the filament that would burn brightly enough and long enough that people would think the price of the bulb was worth spending. Edison's laboratory tested 6,000 different fibers before it found one that glowed brightly for 40 hours. By the time he patented the incandescent lightbulb, Edison had extended its lifetime to 170 hours.

Financier J. P. Morgan (who loathed the telephone; he shouted at it angrily when he had no choice but to use it) was immediately taken by electric lighting. His home and bank in New York were among the first electrically illuminated buildings in the United States. And Morgan's skill in raising investment capital did not hurt.

The incandescent bulb succeeded as dramatically as the telephone. From a modest start in New York in 1882 (about eighty customers), Edison's invention spread so quickly that by 1900 more than 3,000 towns and cities were electrically illuminated. Within a few more years gaslight was disappearing, and the kerosene lantern survived only on farms or for backup when the power went out.

WESTINGHOUSE AND THE AIR BRAKE

George Westinghouse was not so versatile as Edison, although he proved to be a better businessman. His first important invention was a system for bringing long trains to a safe stop: the air brake. Locomotives and the cars they pulled had brakes, mechanical friction devices on each car that were individually operated by brakemen. (It was a dangerous job.) They worked well enough at scheduled stops. Well before arriving at a depot or water tank, the brakeman, who rode in the caboose at the end of the train, applied its brake, then the brake on the next car forward, and so on. This created a drag on the train so that it was moving at a crawl when the engineer halted the locomotive.

Emergency stops were the problem. When, without any preliminary braking at the rear of the train, the engineer sharply braked the locomotive because there was another train on the track or a herd of cattle (or a bridge was washed out), the momentum of dozens of unbraked cars piled them up in catastrophic wrecks. Thousands of passengers and railroad workers were killed in emergency stops every year.

At age 22, just out of the Union army, Westinghouse solved the problem. Each car on a train was equipped with brakes operated pneumatically by compressed air forced through hoses running the length of the train. Even the most frantic of stops started the braking at the rear so that there was no pile-up. Westinghouse patented the air brake in 1869. By 1880 most of the nation's major railroads had installed them.

AC VERSUS DC

During the 1880s Westinghouse turned his attention to a problem that Edison had left dangling: the efficient transmission of electricity from generator to consumer. Edison's incandescent bulbs ran on direct current. DC did the job at low voltage, so it was safe. However, DC could be transmitted only about three miles, which meant building a great many generating plants—usually coal burning—to electrify a large area. That was expensive.

Alternating current (AC) could be transmitted twenty-five to thirty miles in the 1880s, and potentially many times that distance, making it cheaper to produce than DC; one central generating plant could provide power for more than 2,000 square miles. Westinghouse learned about AC's possibilities from a Serbian immigrant, Nikola Tesla, who had quarreled with Edison in the matter. Westinghouse hired him and bought his patents.

The catch was that AC had to be transmitted at extremely high voltage—too much voltage for safe use. Westinghouse and Tesla solved the problem by stringing transmission wires on inaccessibly high towers and inventing the transformer to step down the voltage for safe use in factories and homes. Edison launched a clever but unsuccessful campaign to frighten the public away from AC. In 1888, to dramatize its dangers, he persuaded New York State to adopt the AC electric chair to execute murderers. Westinghouse countered by refusing to sell the state prison an AC generator. (New York had to go to Argentina to buy one.)

Westinghouse's AC became the standard. He won two big high-profile contracts: electrifying the Columbian Exposition in Chicago in 1893 and, in 1896, the electrification of Buffalo, New York (then one of the country's ten largest cities), with power generated at Niagara Falls twenty miles away.

CONQUERING THE WIDE-OPEN SPACES

The United States was rich in natural resources, capital, labor, and its cultural openness to technological innovation. The impediments to the creation of a national industrial economy were the size of the country and its formidable mountain ranges and deserts. No point in England is farther than twenty miles from a navigable river. The only significant mountains in Great Britain are on the fringes, in Scotland and Wales. In the eighteenth century the British were able to build a network of canals that crisscrossed the country. Cheaply and efficiently, manufacturers could assemble iron, coal, and the other materials needed for manufacture—and dispatch their products to a national market and to ports for shipment abroad. Transportation costs were low. England's compactness was a major reason it was the first country to industrialize so thoroughly.

The railroad was an English invention. But the United States exploited it to the fullest. Within a few years of the first run of the *Rocket* in England, the United States had laid more miles of track than the British had. The railroad was valuable in Great Britain; it was essential in America, where vast distances and a rugged topography limited the utility of canals.

THE EASTERN TRUNK LINES

By the end of the Civil War there were 35,000 miles of railroad track in the United States but only a few integrated systems. In the former Confederacy there had been 400 independent railroad companies with an average track run of forty miles. It was possible to ship a cargo from St. Louis to Atlanta by any of twenty different routes with many interruptions: few railroads linked up with others. Goods shipped long distances—salt pork from Chicago to Boston, for instance—were carried in stages by independent lines. At each point of transfer, the barrels had to be unloaded at one terminal (hand labor added to costs), carted across town by horse and wagon (another bottleneck), and reloaded on another company's cars. Six railroads ran into Richmond; no two shared a depot. Baltimore was a hot spot early in the Civil War because Union soldiers headed for Washington had to detrain and march across the pro-Confederate city to another depot to continue on to the capital. Chicago

Hetty Green

Finance was a man's world, but a few women made their mark. Sisters Victoria Woodhull and Tennessee Claflin did quite well as stockbrokers until they were ruined because of their sexual eccentricities. Hetty Green was eccentric too, but in a different way. She bought and sold stock almost daily—in person, no brokerage fees—dressed in black crepe that was usually soiled and tattered and carrying her shares in an old bag. On one occasion she pulled a revolver on the Southern Pacific's Collis P. Huntington because she believed he was manipulating the price of Southern Pacific stock specifically to injure her. But Hetty had no peers when it came to playing the market. When she died, her estate was worth $100,000,000, as much as Cornelius Vanderbilt's. Hetty owned so much stock in one company that she single-handedly caused a panic when she dumped it.

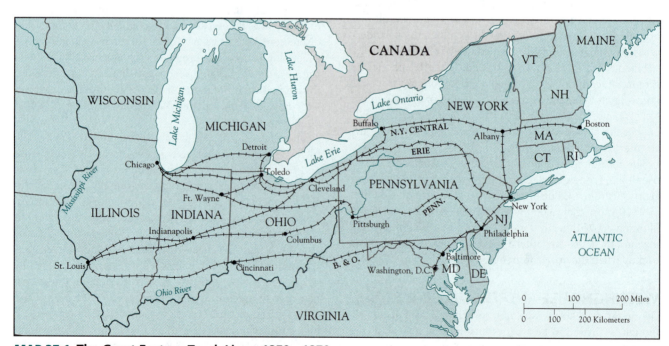

MAP 27:1 The Great Eastern Trunk Lines, 1850s–1870s
Four trunk lines connected the Midwest (and through Chicago and St. Louis, the entire West) to eastern seaports: the New York Central, Erie, Pennsylvania, and Baltimore and Ohio. In the 1890s the Pennsylvania had more employees than any company of any kind.

Standard Gauge

The standard American railroad gauge is 4 feet, 8½ inches. Why this odd figure? Because British builders of trams and trains used wagon jigs to make the first railroad cars. Approximately 4 feet 8 inches was the width of wagon wheel ruts in English roads because the oldest roads in the country were Roman roads. The Romans spaced their chariot wheels at that distance because it was just wide enough to accommodate two horses harnessed side by side. Actually, American gauges varied somewhat after standardization. Wheels on rolling stock were designed to be safe with a variation of an inch or so either way.

Jay Gould. After the Erie War with Vanderbilt, in which he was guilty of outright fraud, his business ethics and methods were probably close to the norm for nineteenth-century big businessmen. But his enemies continued to portray him as, in the words of one former partner, "the worst man on earth since the beginning of the Christian era." Gould responded by, outside of business hours, becoming a hermit. But he had defenders. John D. Rockefeller said Gould was the greatest businessman he knew. Henry Flagler said he was the "fairest, squarest" railroad man in the country.

and New York were linked by rail on maps, but a shipment going the entire distance had to be unloaded and reloaded six times.

There were three east–west trunk lines: long-distance lines designed to haul freight and passengers without such interruptions. The Baltimore and Ohio connected Baltimore with the Ohio River (and to St. Louis in 1857). The Pennsylvania Railroad linked Philadelphia and Pittsburgh; under J. Edgar Thomson, president between 1852 and 1874, it was the best-run American railroad, managed in "sections" by superintendents Thomson picked for their business skills. The Erie Railroad linked the Hudson River just north of New York

City to the Great Lakes. It was the longest railroad in the world but never had a president as constructive as Thomson. Moreover, the Erie was hogtied by its charter, which forbade it to build beyond the borders of New York State. During the Civil War, the Erie was eclipsed by the Pennsylvania, which was better positioned to exploit federal contracts for carrying supplies to the army.

Lincoln appointed the Pennsylvania's vice president, Thomas A. Scott, as undersecretary of war in charge of transporting troops. By becoming, in effect, the federal government's transportation arm, the Pennsylvania gained political influence to the degree that, it was said, the Pennsylvania state legislature did nothing not cleared with the railroad. After the war, Thomson and Scott used the railroad's windfall profits to buy up other railroads in surrounding states, linking their tracks to the Pennsylvania's "main line." After he became president of the railroad in 1874, Scott extended the line to New York City and Chicago; Chicago was the terminal of most western railroads. With 30,000 miles of track in thirteen states by 1890, the Pennsylvania was the nation's largest and richest railroad.

THE ERIE WAR AND THE NEW YORK CENTRAL

The fourth great eastern trunk line, the New York Central, was a postwar creation. It was put together from a dozen short lines in New England and New York by a crusty former ferryboat captain, "Commodore" Cornelius Vanderbilt, who never shook off his salty harbor rat language and rough manners. Vanderbilt was rich from his virtual ferry monopoly in New York Harbor and his steamship lines running to Central America and Europe. But rich as he was, Vanderbilt was never quite respectable. To the chagrin of his children, who wanted to break into New York high society, he befriended Victoria Woodhull and Tennessee Claflin, two sisters who flouted propriety by preaching free love and not shunning its practice. They delighted the Commodore, and he set them up as stockbrokers, sending them clients.

In 1867 the Commodore made a false start toward building the New York Central, a quiet attempt to win control of the 300-mile-long Erie Railroad. Through fronts, so as not to drive up the price of Erie stock because of his interest in the railroad, Vanderbilt began to buy every Erie share on the market. Unfortunately, the "Erie Ring" that had control of the company and was already milking it learned of Vanderbilt's purchases.

The Erie Ring consisted of three scoundrels next to whom Vanderbilt looked virtuous. Daniel Drew, a pious Methodist who knew much of the Bible by heart but put a liberal interpretation on the admonishment in Exodus that "Thou shalt not steal," was the senior member of the ring. James "Jubilee Jim" Fisk, just 33 years old, had no interest in the Bible. He was a stout, jolly extrovert who sported garish clothing, tossed silver dollars to street urchins, and caroused with showgirls. (One of them, Josie Mansfield, was his undoing; in 1872 Fisk was murdered by another one of her suitors.) Fisk openly mocked Vanderbilt by wearing a comic opera naval uniform and commissioning himself "Admiral," a higher rank than Commodore. The third member of the ring was Jay Gould, a man of the shadows who was smarter than Drew or Fisk.

As Vanderbilt bought Erie, the Ring watered the stock. That is, they issued shares far in excess of the railroad's real assets. Gould privately told a friend that "there is no intrinsic value to it, probably." But the face value of Erie stock—there was so much of it—increased from $24 million to $78 million. Vanderbilt bought and bought but was still a minority stockholder. Drew, Fisk, and Gould pocketed the profits on the watered stock and still controlled the Erie.

When the Commodore realized what was going on, he went to New York judges to whom he regularly made cash gifts and indicted the trio. Forewarned they would be arrested, Drew, Fisk, and Gould fled to New Jersey, where they holed up in a hotel guarded by gunmen. (Hostile takeovers in the Gilded Age were very hostile.) Nonetheless, a settlement was arranged. Vanderbilt got most of his money back; the Ring kept the Erie.

Vanderbilt built the New York Central connecting Boston and New York City to Chicago by purchasing smaller lines and building his own track. When his railroad crossed Erie tracks near Lake Erie, he provided that line with its first out-of-state connection.

BRINGING ORDER TO CHAOS

It would be a mistake to call Drew, Gould, and Fisk "railroaders." They took no interest in the Erie's track, locomotives, rolling stock, and the freight and passengers it hauled. They did not care if the railroad showed a profit. (It never did under their ownership.) They were pirates, manipulating Erie paper to enrich themselves. The Erie had the worst accident record of any American railroad because of neglected roadbeds and dilapidated equipment. The company did not pay a dividend to its stockholders for seventy years.

Scott and Vanderbilt were not above playing with company books. But Scott and Vanderbilt operated railroads that were national assets of inestimable value to millions of people. They invested profits in improvements as well as expansion. They perfected their services and were open to

innovation. Railroaders from the West and from Europe examined the Pennsylvania's roadbeds because they were "state of the art." The Pennsylvania was the first railroad to convert from wood to coal for fuel. The New York Central pioneered the use of stronger, safer steel rails and was the first major railroad to equip its trains with the life-saving Westinghouse air brake. Scott and Vanderbilt were builders. It would await a later generation of corporate thieves with none of the colorful rascality of the Erie Ring to loot the Pennsylvania and New York Central into decrepitude.

The Pennsylvania and New York Central also took the lead in establishing **time zones,** which were an American innovation. In 1870 railroads set their clocks, and therefore their schedules, according to local time in the city where their headquarters were located. However, every city and town set its clocks according to local calculations or, just as likely, what the mayor's watch read. In 1870 there were somewhere between 80 and 100 "official" clock settings in the United States. It was all very well when a Chicago businessman wanted to arrange with another to meet at a restaurant at noon. But when it was noon in Chicago, it was 11:27 in Omaha, 11:56 in St. Louis, 12:09 in Louisville, and 12:17 in Toledo.

When it was noon in Washington, D.C., it was 12:24 in Baltimore, seventy miles away. The Baltimorean in Washington who tried to catch a train home might discover that although his watch was correct for his hometown, he was nearly half an hour late for the train that he expected would take him there. In Buffalo's station, which served both the New York Central and the Michigan Southern, there were three clocks: one for each railroad and one for Buffalo time. In Pittsburgh's station there were six clocks. Traveling from Maine to California on the railroad, one passed through twenty time zones. Nor was the mess just a nuisance. Confusion as to what time it was caused wrecks when two trains tried to use the same track at the same "real time."

In 1870 Charles F. Dowd (who was a dead ringer for Abraham Lincoln) proposed bringing order to the chaos by establishing four official *time zones* in the United States. The big railroads immediately adopted Dowd's system—gladly. Many cities and towns resisted, as if Dowd were tampering with the passage of the sun across the sky. Finally, in 1883, Congress legally established the four zones. So obviously sensible was the system that the next year, twenty-five nations meeting in Washington adopted the "universal day": twenty-four worldwide time zones.

MAP 27:2 Transcontinental Railroads, 1862–1900

By 1890 five transcontinental railroads spanned the United States. (Within a few years two more crossed Canada.) Although the southern route's most important eastern termini were New Orleans and St. Louis, it too had connections into Chicago, the major terminus of the other four. The story of Chicago's incredible growth can be read on this map.

Building the Transcontinental

The early business history of the great American railroads is a sorry story. The least rapacious of the men who owned the roads were so preoccupied with the money that stock manipulations, subsidies, and fraud were putting into their pockets that they were oblivious to the fact that the public had an interest in their railroads. Only a few men who made policy for the first railroads considered safety and the long-term financial health of the company to be as important as making big money.

In sharp contrast, the story of the actual construction of the railroads, particularly the first transcontinental—the Union Pacific and the Central Pacific—is an adventure tale of pathbreaking engineering and superb organization of a massive undertaking. In the Sierra Nevada and along the tracks in Nebraska and Wyoming, there were many heroes—thousands of nameless Chinese who, even in winter, missed hardly a day's work pushing the Central Pacific across mountains 8,000 feet above sea level; and Jack Casement of the Union Pacific who, dressed as a Russian Cossack, fought Indians, supervised rail laying in quick-time, and housed and fed thousands of unruly laborers. If necessary, Casement disciplined men who were unruly on company time by knocking them unconscious.

The Central Pacific's starting point was Sacramento. Except for timber, which was abundant, California provided none of the materials needed to build a railroad. Locomotives, rolling stock, rails, spikes, black powder—everything had to be brought from the East by ship around Cape Horn, an 18,000-mile voyage taking five to eight months. Buying

what was needed was hard enough until the Civil War ended; the federal government had first claim on locomotives, rails, and a good many other things. Coordinating shipment so that materials arrived at the right time was a daunting job.

Nor were there nearly enough unemployed men in California for the huge workforce needed to build—it was all hand labor—across the chasms, along the sheer cliffs of the Sierra Nevada, and *through* the granite mountains. By September 1865 the Central Pacific track reached only fifty-four miles to Colfax, and those were the easiest miles on the route. Charles Crocker, in charge of construction, decided to try a gang of Chinese laborers—reluctantly; Crocker shared the anti-Chinese prejudices of gold rush Californians. He soon changed his mind about the "Celestials." He was awed by the efficiency of Chinese workers. Moreover, because they hired on in gangs under a Chinese contractor who provided their meals (and governed them tyranically), Crocker was spared the task of supervision. Eighty percent of the Central Pacific's workforce was Chinese; there were 7,000 on the payroll at one time, 12,000 overall.

They built trestles (one was 1,600 feet long) and carved platforms for the tracks out of perpendicular cliffs, sometimes working while dangling in baskets lowered from above. To blast, they used black powder, as many as 500 kegs a day. Twice the Central Pacific exhausted the black powder supply in California; the price of a keg, normally $2.50, rose to $15. Crocker tried nitroglycerine, a much more powerful explosive; but after a few horrible accidents he forbade the Chinese to use it.

THE TRANSCONTINENTAL LINES

In the East, the creation of integrated railroad systems—trunk lines—was largely a matter of consolidating independent short lines. During the 1880s, the names of 540 railway companies disappeared from the registers. West of Chicago, the hub in which dozens of railroads converged, extensive and integrated railroad systems were constructed from scratch.

PUBLIC FINANCE

The first four transcontinental railroads were built and owned by private companies subsidized by the federal government. (The fifth, James J. Hill's Great Northern, was built without federal subsidies.) Without federal funding, the lines would not have been built. Railroad construction was expensive. Building just a mile of track meant excavating or building up a grade, bedding 3,000 ties in gravel, and attaching 400 iron rails to them by driving 12,000 spikes. Once beyond the environs of Omaha in the East and Sacramento in the West—the termini of the first transcontinental—there was little population, customers who would ship and receive freight.

Few paying customers meant little revenue and no profits—not a prospect that excites investors. The federal government's political and military interests in binding the Pacific Coast to the rest of the Union were the impetus behind the **Pacific Railway Act** of 1862.

The Railway Act gave two companies, the Union Pacific and the Central Pacific, a right of way 200 feet wide between Omaha and Sacramento. For each mile of track that the

Narrow Gauge

Building the narrow-gauge feeder railroads that snaked into canyons and wound around mountains to bring out ore or logs was not the colossal undertaking the great trunk lines were. But the engineering that went into them is impressive. The California Western hauled redwood logs to the mill town and port of Fort Bragg. It was only forty miles long, but its longest straightaway was less than a mile. It crossed 115 bridges (almost three per mile!), and ran through a tunnel 1,122 feet long. It still exists, offering tourist excursions.

The winter of 1866–1867 was one of the worst in California history. There were forty-four snowstorms in the mountains, several dropping six feet of snow. Luckily the Central Pacific had eleven tunnels under way before the Sierra was buried. The Chinese "lived like moles" all winter, blasting and digging from each end of the tunnels and even from the center of some reached via a shaft drilled from above. By spring it was obvious that mountain track not in tunnels would be buried in snow every winter. Central Pacific engineers built snowsheds of huge hewn timbers. The Central Pacific was a "railroad in a barn," running through sheds or tunnels for thirty-four miles.

The Union Pacific, building westward from Omaha, Nebraska, had no difficult mountains to cross. Its challenge was endless distance. Its supply problem was the opposite of the Central Pacific's. Most everything could be brought to the railhead by rail, but there was no source of cheap, good timber on the Plains. After experimenting with cottonwood for ties, the Union Pacific had to import ties from the north woods of Minnesota, Wisconsin, and Michigan.

The Union Pacific had Indian problems the Central Pacific was spared. Survey and grading crews, working well ahead of the thousands of laborers, frequently exchanged gunfire with small bands of Indians. Probably they fired on many friendly groups. The Cheyenne were not friendly and, in August 1867, derailed a train bringing supplies to the workers and killed several men. The army retaliated the next year, killing many more Cheyenne.

The Union Pacific workers were recently discharged Civil War veterans and Irish immigrants. Construction supervisor Jack Casement designed bunkhouses, kitchens, dining halls, and offices on wheels so the "town" could be constantly moved west. Union Pacific camps were not orderly like the Central Pacific Chinese camps. Winter headquarters in 1867–1868 were at Cheyenne, where "the principal pastimes were gambling, drinking villainous rotgut whiskey, and shooting"—and consorting with prostitutes. "Sodom-at-the-end-of-the-line," a visitor called the town.

Once Casement's system was well oiled, Union Pacific workers laid an average two miles of track each day. A newspaper reporter wrote:

> Track laying is a science. A light car, drawn by a single horse, gallops up to the front with its load of rails. Two men seize the end of a [eighteen-foot to twenty-five-foot] rail and start forward, the rest of the gang taking hold by twos. They come forward at a run. At a word of command the rail is dropped in its place, less than thirty seconds to a rail for each gang, and so four rails go down to the minute.

Toward the end of the great project, when the Central Pacific and Union Pacific were racing, a Central Pacific work crew set the record: 10.6 miles of more or less functional railroad in one day. That involved bedding 31,000 ties and pounding 120,000 spikes!

companies built, they were to receive, on either side of the tracks, ten alternate sections (square miles) of the public domain: a belt of land forty miles wide laid out like a checkerboard on which the Union Pacific and Central Pacific owned half the squares.

The railroads were to sell the land to settlers to raise the money for construction (thus creating customers) or to put the real estate up as collateral with which to secure loans from banks. In addition, depending on the nature of the terrain, the government lent the two companies between $16,000 and $48,000 per mile of track at bargain interest rates.

THE ROMANCE OF THE RAILS

These lavish terms attracted men who were less interested in operating railroads than in the money to be made building them. Within twenty years this resulted in the overbuilding of railroads in the West: laying more track than was needed or than the sparsely populated country could support. The government's generosity also encouraged frauds like the Union Pacific's Crédit Mobilier, a construction company

(owned by the same men who owned the Union Pacific) to which the Union Pacific paid grotesquely padded bills. When, during the 1870s, investigators picked their way through the accounts, they concluded that $44 million of the Union Pacific's construction expenditures had been skimmed by the Crédit Mobilier. The extent of fraud in the construction of the Central Pacific was never determined because when the Crédit Mobilier investigation began, the owners of the railroad burned their books.

So central to the project was the government subsidy that when the Union Pacific and Central Pacific approached one another in Utah, they raced to win every mile of land grant and loan they could. The grading crews of the two railroads actually laid out parallel grades within sight of one another for almost 100 miles. A peace meeting of the two companies' directors agreed on Promontory Point, Utah, north of Salt Lake City, as the point where they would actually link up. There, on May 10, 1869, the "golden spike" was driven. (Actually, all sorts of souvenir gold and silver spikes, as well as iron spikes plated in gold and silver, were tapped briefly into place.)

Southern Pacific Transportation Company

■ *Most of the laborers who built the Central Pacific Railroad from Sacramento to Utah were Chinese immigrants, hired in gangs organized by Chinese jobbers. For the few years the railroad was under construction, they enjoyed employment opportunities denied them for racial reasons during the gold rush and after the age of massive construction projects was over in the West.*

RAILROAD MANIA

Seeing the owners of the Union Pacific and Central Pacific become instant multimillionaires, other ambitious men descended on Washington in search of subsidies. In 1864, when the first transcontinental was hardly begun—when it was by no means a sure thing that it would be completed—Congress granted the Northern Pacific, which proposed to build from Lake Superior to Puget Sound, an even more generous grant. In the territories, the Northern Pacific received forty alternate sections of land for every mile of railway. The Atchison, Topeka, and Santa Fe—another land-grant transcontinental—ran from Kansas to (eventually) Los Angeles. The Texas Pacific and Southern Pacific linked New Orleans and San Francisco at El Paso, Texas. In 1884 the Canadians (who were even more generous with government land) completed the Canadian Pacific.

The total costs were astronomical. The federal government gave railroads 131 million acres. To this, state governments added 45 million acres. An area larger than France and Belgium was given to a handful of capitalists. In addition, towns along the proposed routes enticed the builders to choose them over nearby rivals as sites for depots and switching yards by offering town lots, cash bounties, and exemption from taxes.

Some of these gifts were acts of desperation. If a railroad bypassed a town, the town was likely to die. Railroad companies did not hesitate to set communities against one another like roosters in a cockfight. The Union Pacific bypassed Denver, the only city for hundreds of miles in every direction, in part because the perquisites Denver offered were not up to par. The original route of the Atchison, Topeka, and Santa Fe, which was popularly known as "the Santa Fe," did not go near the city of that name. Albuquerque offered a better financial deal and got the tracks.

THE PANIC OF 1873

Money was made in western railroads by building them, not by operating them. Consequently, too much railroad was built too soon. When the lines were done, high operating costs and low revenues meant that it was difficult, if not impossible, to pay off a railroad's loans. In 1872 only one American railroad in three showed a profit.

On September 18, 1873, a Friday, the chickens came home to roost. **Jay Cooke and Company,** a bank that lent heavily to railroads, announced that it was bankrupt. Jay Cooke was not an ordinary bank. It was the most prestigious financial house in the United States; Cooke had been the federal government's chief financial agent during the Civil War. Its

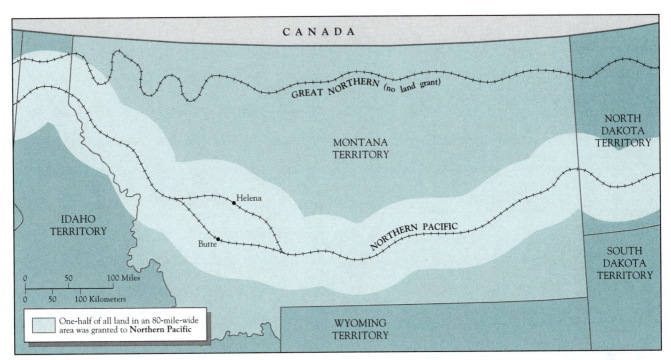

MAP 27:3 Northern Pacific Land Grant, 1864

The Great Northern was the only one of the five transcontinental railroads built without a federal land grant. James J. Hill financed the line by promoting settlement (shippers) along completed sections of the line, then using revenues to build farther west. The Great Northern alone was built by "private enterprise." The others were built by men with the political contacts to win massive federal and state giveaways. The Northern Pacific was the federal government's grandest beneficiary. Half the land in the eighty-mile-wide belt along the railroad was Uncle Sam's gift to the railroad.

failure led to a panic as speculators, fearing other failures, rushed to sell their stocks and depositors at other banks closed their accounts. The market crashed; banks failed. By the end of 1873, 5,000 businesses had declared bankruptcy

Like the depressions of the 1890s and the 1930s, the depression of the 1870s became a financial "panic" on the stock exchange, a "crash" in the values of shares. The Panic of 1873 began with the announcement that Jay Cooke and Company, a bank thought invulnerable, was bankrupt. The bank had too much money tied up in railroads that were producing little or no revenue.

and a half million workers were jobless. The depression of the 1870s was the worst in American history to that time.

It would not be the last. A by-product of fabulous economic growth was a wildly erratic business cycle—the "unprecedented disturbance and depression of trade" in the words of a contemporary. For a time the industrial capitalist economy boomed, luring investment and speculation, encouraging expansion and production. Sooner or later, the capacity of railroads to carry freight, or factories to produce goods, outpaced the capacity of the market to absorb their services and products. When that happened, banks failed, investments and savings were wiped out, factories locked their gates, workers lost their jobs, and the retail shops they frequented went broke.

THE ORGANIZERS

In a free, unregulated, market economy the boom and bust cycle was inevitable; and most Americans regarded the free economy as sacred. Businessmen who reached the top of the economic pyramid, however, ceased to be enchanted with the idea of wide-open competition. To the entrepreneur who was no longer scrambling but was in charge of a commercial or industrial empire in which millions of dollars were invested and which employed thousands of people, stability was what counted: the assurance that supplies of raw materials would be unhindered two, three, or ten years in the future, and that future revenues could be reliably projected. Competition was a threat to stability. In the late

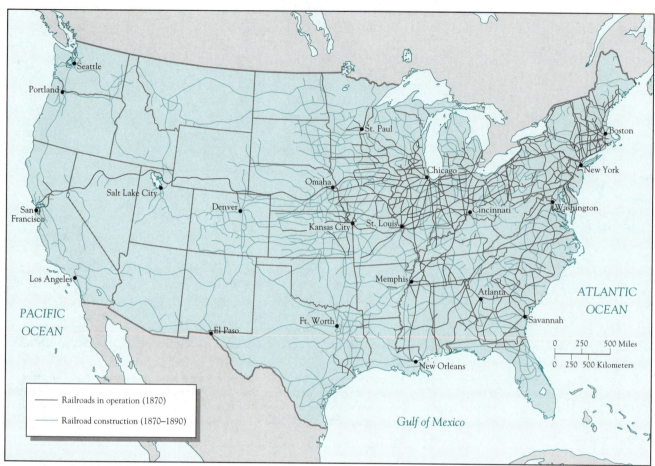

MAP 27:4 Railroad Expansion, 1870–1890
Between 1870 and 1890, much railroad expansion was in the construction of "feeder lines" tying productive parts of the West into one or another of the transcontinentals.

nineteenth century the organizers of big businesses in numerous industries—from sugar refining to the manufacture of cigarettes—strove, in different ways, to minimize or eliminate the uncertainty that competitors brought to their business.

Andrew Carnegie in steel and oilman John D. Rockefeller were the two most famous big businessmen of the era. Carnegie immunized his steel manufacturing empire from the threat of competitors by cutting production costs in his mills so low that he could dictate the market price of steel, keep his factories running at capacity, and let other steel companies pick up what business he could not handle. John D. Rockefeller faced a different kind of problem in the oil business. It was impossible to dominate crude oil production—major new discoveries of crude oil deposits were routine news—and there were too many refineries to undersell at a price Rockefeller needed to stay in business. He solved his problem by persuading most of his competitors to let him take over their refineries.

STEEL: THE BONES OF THE ECONOMY
Steel is the element iron from which all impurities except a carefully controlled amount of carbon have been burned out at extremely high temperatures. Steel is many times stronger

per unit of weight than iron. Its recommendations had been known since antiquity. But it could be made only in small quantities because the process of making steel consumed huge quantities of fuel. Steel was practical only for small, expensive items like (famously) the finest swords of Japan and Toledo in Spain, high-end firearms, bearings in machines, and precision instruments.

During the 1850s, working secretly in the Kentucky woods, William "Pig Iron" Kelly developed a technique for making steel cheaply in large quantities out of **pig iron** (iron ingots sold by iron smelters to makers of finished goods). When he patented his process, he discovered that an Englishman, Henry Bessemer, had independently developed the same process. Although it became known universally as the *Bessemer process,* the Patent Office acknowledged that Kelly had been first by a couple of months.

No one grasped the significance of the **Bessemer process** more quickly than Andrew Carnegie. He had emigrated to the United States with a destitute family when he was a child. He became a telegrapher who caught the eye of Pennsylvania Railroad Vice President Thomas A. Scott, who quickly promoted him to an executive position. In 1865 Carnegie left the railroad to found the Keystone Bridge Company, which built both iron and steel bridges. (Carnegie built the first span

Depressions

The "most noteworthy peculiarity" of the depressions of the industrial age, wrote D. A. Wells in 1889, was their inevitability. There seemed no escaping the inevitable collapses of economic life:

> Depression afflicted nations which have a stable currency based on gold, and those which have an unstable currency, those which live under a system of free exchange of commodities and those whose exchanges are more or less restricted. It has been grievous in old communities like England and Germany, and equally so in Australia, South Africa, and California, which represent the new; it has been a calamity exceeding heavy to be borne alike by the inhabitants of sterile Newfoundland and Labrador, and of the sunny, fruitful sugar islands of the East and West Indies; and It has not enriched those at the centers of the world's exchanges, whose gains are ordinarily greatest when business is most fluctuating and uncertain.

across the Mississippi.) When the depression of the 1870s lowered the prices of materials and labor, Carnegie exploited the opportunity to build the largest steel mill in the world in Braddock, Pennsylvania, outside Pittsburgh. One of his business mottos was "put all your eggs in one basket and then watch that basket."

A HEAD FOR BUSINESS

Carnegie knew apples as well as eggs—how to polish them. He named his factory after J. Edgar Thomson, the president of the Pennsylvania Railroad, his former employer, and because Carnegie would be making the Pennsylvania's rails, a major customer. However, Carnegie sited his great plant outside the city of Pittsburgh. It was a one-railroad city; the Pennsylvania set rates for Pittsburgh without competition. Two other railroads ran through Braddock, where Carnegie built this plant; they would have to bid against one another to get his shipping business. Indeed, from Braddock, Carnegie could legally build his own company railroad to connect the J. Edgar Thomson Works with Erie, Pennsylvania, where iron ore boats docked. In time, he did just that. Carnegie admired Thomson. He was willing to flatter him. But he would not trust the health of Carnegie Steel to his former boss's goodwill.

Carnegie was uninterested in the technology of steelmaking, but he had a keen eye for those who were. He hired the best engineers and bound some of them to his company by making them partners. His most important partner was Henry Clay Frick, a coal and coke magnate as well as an engineer. Not only did Frick supervise day-to-day operations of the company, but he brought mines to Carnegie's company.

"VERTICAL INTEGRATION"

Carnegie's contribution to business organization was his exploitation of the principle of "vertical integration." That is, to get a leg up on competitors, Carnegie expanded his operation from a base of steel manufacture to ownership of the raw materials from which steel was made and the means of assembling them. Bessemer furnaces were fueled by coke (which is to coal what charcoal is to wood: a hotter-burning distillation of the mineral). To avoid having to buy coke from others, Carnegie's (and Frick's) company absorbed Frick's 5,000 acres of coalfields and 1,000 coke ovens. Carnegie and Frick then added Michigan, Wisconsin, and Minnesota iron mines to their holdings.

While never completely independent of trunk line railroads, Carnegie controlled as much of his own shipping as he could. He owned ships and barges that carried iron ore from the Marquette and later the Mesabi Ranges to his own port facilities in Erie, Pennsylvania. He owned a short railroad that brought the ore from Erie to his greatest factory, the Homestead mill. By eliminating from his final product price the profits of independent suppliers, distributors, and carriers, Carnegie could undersell competing companies that had to include the profits of independent suppliers in their final price. In 1870 there were 167 iron and steel firms around Pittsburgh. By the end of the century there were 47; those Carnegie did not control priced their product according to Carnegie's dictates.

Vertical integration served Andrew Carnegie well. In 1890 the company was responsible for a quarter of the nation's steel production. His personal income rose to $25 million a year. He was able to lead an active intellectual life and spend much of his time in a castle in Scotland not far from where his father had worked as a weaver.

In 1901, 66 years old and bored with business, Carnegie agreed to sell all his interests to a syndicate organized by investment banker J. P. Morgan. Carnegie pocketed $500 million, then the largest personal commercial transaction ever, and Morgan created the first billion-dollar corporation,

Smoke Is Good for You

Factory smoke was not called *pollution* in the nineteenth century. It was considered a sign that times were good. The parents of a girl in Pittsburgh, where there were 14,000 factory smokestacks, told her, "We should be grateful for God's goodness in making work, which makes smoke, which makes prosperity."

Let's Do Lunch

Few partners had a more bitter falling-out than Carnegie and Frick had in 1899. Frick called Carnegie a thief, sued him, and won. Twenty years later, both men now ancient, Carnegie contacted Frick through a mutual friend, suggesting that they meet again before they died. "Tell Mr. Carnegie," Frick said, "I will meet him in hell, where we are both going."

Steel at One Cent a Pound

Just as John D. Rockefeller liked to point out that kerosene was cheaper after Standard Oil controlled refining, Andrew Carnegie had a neat justification of vertical integration of steel manufacture:

> Two pounds of iron ore mined in Minnesota Lake Superior and transported on the Great Lakes and by railroad 900 miles to Pittsburgh; a pound and a half of coal, mined and manufactured into coke, and brought to Pittsburgh; a little bit of manganese ore mined in Virginia and brought to Pittsburgh—four pounds of materials transformed into one pound of steel cost the customer one cent.

United States Steel. From birth, U.S. Steel controlled "the destinies of a population nearly as large as that of Maryland or Nebraska" and had a bigger annual budget than all but a handful of the world's nations.

THE CORPORATION'S EDGE

Carnegie was a progressive and innovative businessman. But he organized his empire as a partnership rather than as a corporation, the business structure that was the agent of industrial development and business consolidation in the United States. The corporation—capitalized by selling shares in the company—was advantageous to both investors and business organizers. Dispersed ownership meant dispersed risk. The investor who owned shares in a number of companies did not lose everything if one of those companies failed. American law gave investors in corporations the privilege of limited liability. A corporation's legal liability in the event of bankruptcy was limited to the assets of the corporation. It did not extend to the other assets of shareholders. By way of contrast, if an individually owned business or a partnership went bust, creditors could seize all the property of the bankrupt owners.

Although Carnegie did well enough, corporations generally could amass much more capital than a partnership could. Of course, corporation organizers wanted to ensure that they retained control of their enterprises. Widely dispersed ownership worked in their favor; it was unlikely that 10,000 investors owning a share each would band together to outvote the entrepreneur who owned 9,500 shares. So nineteenth-century corporate organizers took care to reserve key blocks of stock for themselves. The master of the nineteenth-century corporation—or rather the man who

Inc. and Ltd.

In the United States a company with legal liability limited to its assets is distinguished by the word "corporation" in its name or the abbreviations "Corp." or "Inc.," meaning "incorporated." In Great Britain the comparable designation is "Ltd.," meaning "limited."

John Davison Rockefeller at the time he was creating Standard Oil. Rockefeller wanted to be rich, and he became the richest man in the world. He was generous throughout his life to the Baptist Church, to which he was devoted. In his long retirement, he and his son were by far the nation's greatest and most constructive philanthropists.

coordinated the activities of the business innovators and lawyers who were the masters of corporate manipulation—was John D. Rockefeller of Cleveland, Ohio.

JOHN D. ROCKEFELLER AND BLACK GOLD

No corporation of the era was so great or so notorious as Standard Oil. Solemn, muscular, and deeply religious John Davison Rockefeller was the undisputed head of the men who created it: William Rockefeller, Henry Flagler, Maurice B. Clark, Samuel Andrews, and lawyer Johnson Newlon Camden. Starting as a bookkeeper, Rockefeller dodged the Civil War draft by hiring a substitute and made a small fortune selling provisions to the Union army. But Rockefeller calculated—correctly—that when the war ended and government contracts were terminated, the bottom would fall out of the provisions business.

In the meantime, he and his associates invested in oil refineries in Cleveland, which was then the refining center of the infant industry because of its proximity to the first commercial oilfield in western Pennsylvania. Crude oil had seeped to the surface of the earth since before there were human beings to step into it. Ancient Mesopotamians wrote of it. Europeans used it as a lubricant. Jesuit priests in western New York in the seventeenth century reported "a stagnant thick water that ignites like brandy, burning with bubbles of flame when fire is tossed into it." The Seneca ate it for a laxative. Farmers who lived around Titusville, Pennsylvania, hated it. It fouled the soil, polluted streams, and caught fire.

During the 1850s a chemist at Yale University developed a process to break crude oil down into chemical components, one of which was kerosene, a liquid that could be burned safely to heat a house or cookstove or illuminate the night. It was a timely discovery. By then overharvesting had decimated the world's whale population. Whale oil, an illuminant in middle- and upper-class homes (it was always expensive), was no longer available. Kerosene, limitless in supply by comparison, was cheap; even the poor could afford it. In 1859, seeing the opportunity, a former army officer named Edwin Drake went to Titusville, Pennsylvania, and devised a drill-and-pump system by which crude oil could be extracted in commercial quantities.

The Pennsylvania oil rush that followed was as wild as the gold rush of 1849. Drilling for oil, like panning for gold, required only modest capital, so thousands of men dreaming of instant riches descended on western Pennsylvania. Pithole, just four log cabins in 1859, had a population of 12,000 in 1860. Rockefeller came and looked. He did not like the social and moral disorder of the oilfield—Rockefeller was a rigorous Baptist—and he did not like the wild price swings caused by new wells brought into production and the cutthroat competition among drillers. In 1861 the price of crude oil swung from $10 to—very briefly—10 cents a barrel. Even in 1864, when things had settled down, the price of a barrel bobbed up and down from $4 to $12. Drilling for oil was not the conservative Rockefeller's kind of business.

"HORIZONTAL INTEGRATION"

Oil refining was a fragmented business too; there were 250 refiners as late as 1870 (although most were paper companies). However, operating a refinery called for more capital than sinking a drill into the ground and saying a prayer. Rockefeller recognized that unlike drilling, which would always attract "wildcatters" who might get lucky and become competitors overnight, the refining end of the business was manageable. Refining was like a "narrows" on the river of oil that flowed from well to consumers. Like the robber barons of medieval Europe, who built castles at narrows on the Rhine and Danube and charged boats to pass, the company that controlled refining would be able to determine the level of production and the selling price of kerosene. It did not matter how many wild-eyed visionaries roamed the countryside with drilling rigs. If there was one great refiner, they would sell their crude at the price the refiner was willing to pay.

Controlling an entire industry by controlling a key phase of its process is known as *horizontal integration*. Instead of dominating an industry by integrating a portion of the business from top to bottom, from source of raw materials to market (as Carnegie did in steel), horizontal integration meant establishing a stranglehold on an industry at its key point.

In 1870 Rockefeller and his associates, who owned one of twenty-six refineries in Cleveland, accounting for about 10 percent of kerosene production, formed the South Improvement Company, which quickly won control of twenty-two of the city's refineries. They did this by persuading their competitors that by ceasing to compete, they would no longer have to live in fear of a price war that would impoverish the losers and leave the winners with crippled enterprises.

The South Improvement Company evolved into the Standard Oil Trust. Refinery owners turned their properties over to the trust. Standard issued them trust certificates equivalent to the value of their refinery—Rockefeller and his associates retaining control of enough shares to make all corporate decisions. Obsolete, wasteful refineries were razed. Others were improved and new ones constructed. Refiners who refused to cooperate were run out of business in ruthless rate wars. Within twenty years Standard Oil controlled 90 percent of American refining. Former refiners who had played ball with Standard at the start became richer from dividends than they could have imagined when they were slogging around in oil, turning valves at the refineries they had owned outright.

Rockefeller became the richest man in the world (his associates not far behind). When J. P. Morgan died in 1913, leaving an estate of $80 million, Rockefeller was stunned. He said, "and to think he wasn't even a rich man." Indeed, in recent computations assessing personal fortunes as a percentage of gross national product, John D. Rockefeller, with a personal fortune of $3.7 billion when he died in 1937—this after decades of giving away millions—was the richest man in the history of the world. (Bill Gates of Microsoft is only thirty-first on the list.)

FURTHER READING

General Elliott Brownlee, *Dynamics of Ascent: A History of the American Economy,* 1974; Vincent P. DeSantis, *The Shaping of Modern America, 1877–1916,* 1973; John A. Garraty, *The New Commonwealth, 1877–1890,* 1968; Walter Licht, *Industrializing America: The Nineteenth Century,* 1995; David E. Nye, *Electrifying America: Culture and Society in the Gilded Age,* 1982; Carroll Pursell, *The Machine in America: A Social History of Technology,* 1995.

Big Business Ron Chernow, *Titan: The Life of John D. Rockefeller, Sr.,* 1998, and *The House of Morgan: An American Banking Dynasty,* 1990;

Harold C. Livesay, *Andrew Carnegie and the Rise of Big Business,* 1975; Glenn Porter, *The Rise of Big Business, 1860–1900,* 1992; C. J. Schmitz, *The Growth of Big Business in the United Sates and Western Europe, 1850–1939,* 1993; Charles Slack, *Hetty: The Genius and Madness of America's First Female Tycoon,* 2004; J. F. Wall, *Andrew Carnegie,* 1971; David O. Whitten, *The Emergence of Giant Enterprise, 1860–1914,* 1983.

Railroads Robert G. Angevine, *The Railroad and the State: War, Politics, and Technology in Nineteenth Century America,* 2004;

H. Roger Grant, *The Railroad: The Life Story of a Technology,* 2005; John F. Stover, *History of the Baltimore and Ohio Railroad,* 1987, and *The Life and Decline of the American Railroad,* 1970; Claire Strom, *Profiting from the Plains: The Great Northern Railway and Corporate Development of the American West,* 2003; Steven W. Usselman, *Regulating Railroad Innovation: Business, Technology, and Politics in America, 1840–1920,* 2002; James E. Vance, *Capturing the Horizon: The Historical Geography of Transportation since the Transportation Revolution of the Sixteenth Century,* 1986.

Technology and Invention Neil Baldwin, *Edison: Inventing the Century,* 1995; Robert V. Bruce, *Alexander Graham Bell and the Conquest of Solitude,* 1973; Thomas P. Hughes, *American Genesis: A History of Invention and Technological Enthusiasm, 1879–1970,* 1998; A. J. Millard, *Edison and the Business of Innovation,* 1990; Richard Moran, *Executioner's Current: Thomas Edison, George Westinghouse, Thomas Edison, and the Invention of the Electric Chair,* 2002; Elting E. Morison, *From Know-How to Nowhere: The Development of American Technology,* 1974; David F. Noble, *America by Design: Science, Technology, and the Rise of Corporate Capitalism,* 1977.

KEY TERMS

The following terms are covered in this chapter and can also be found in the list of Key Terms at the back of the book.

Bessemer process	**Cyrus Field**	**Pacific Railway Act**	**time zones**
Centennial Exposition	**Jay Cooke and Company**	**pig iron**	**vertical integration**

ONLINE SOURCES GUIDE

Use this listing to find online documents, images, interactive maps, simulations, and other resources related to this chapter:

American History Resource Center
http://history.wadsworth.com/rc/us

Selected Images
Thomas Edison in his Menlo Park, N.J., laboratory
Jay Gould
Collis P. Huntington, railroad entrepreneur

Interactive Time Line (with online readings)
Big Industry, Big Business: Economic Development in the Late Nineteenth Century

CHAPTER 28

Living with Leviathan

Big Business and Great Wealth

Courtesy of the New York Historical Society, New York City

Success is counted sweetest
By those who ne'er succeed.
    Emily Dickinson

A successful man cannot realize how hard an unsuccessful man finds life.
    Edgar Watson Howe

The moral flabbiness of the exclusive worship of the bitch-goddess SUCCESS. That—with the squalid cash interpretation put on the word success—is our national disease.

    William James

In *Democracy in America,* Alexis de Tocqueville was struck by the equity with which wealth was distributed in the United States. In Jackson's America, he observed (always excepting the slaves), few households were so poor as to be without hope of improving their lot; few families were so rich that they could be said to be an aristocracy, a social class permanently established above the masses. Indeed, many of the well-fixed Americans Tocqueville met seemed, to him, to be haunted by the anxiety that a stroke of ill fortune would send them tumbling down into a life of hard work, sore backs, and calloused hands.

Wealth was not so equitably distributed in Jacksonian America as Tocqueville believed. Nevertheless, the gap between the poorest and the richest was much narrower than it became after the Civil War, when money-making opportunities made possible a class of millionaires whose fortunes were so great that it was difficult to imagine them falling into poverty. Indeed, mere investment without further hustling ensured that the largest fortunes continued to grow. Cornelius Vanderbilt amassed $110 million, $5 million more than the U.S. government kept on reserve. His son, William, inherited $90 million from him and doubled it in eight years. In 1900 Andrew Carnegie pocketed $480 million in a single transaction. John D. Rockefeller gave away $550 million while his family grew richer.

It would be remarkable if the emergence, within a single lifetime, of such a super-rich social class—with power to match its millions—had not antagonized ordinary people imbued with the idea that the United States was the country of equality of opportunity. Some reformers thought they should try to reverse or, at least, regulate the concentration of wealth and power in ever fewer big corporations.

They did try, but without much success. When broad popular demand pressured state legislatures and Congress to enact laws regulating big business, the antimonopoly movement was foiled by hostile judges and government reluctance to enforce the laws.

REGULATING RAILROADS AND TRUSTS

The railroads, America's first "big business," had enemies from the beginning, even before they were very big. Poets, painters, philosophers, and other intellectuals recoiled from them on cultural grounds. Their ugly, dirty, noisy locomotives were "machines in the garden," defiling the peace and moral health of pastoral, "natural" America. In cities, railroads faced a different kind of criticism. Ordinary people protested, even rioted against the first railroads to snake as deeply as they could into city centers. On tracks built on streets where only pedestrians and horse-drawn vehicles had moved at a walk, trains running at high speed and unable to stop quickly ran people and wagons down at an alarming rate: 330 Chicagoans were killed by trains in one year (the dead horses were not counted).

But these were weak and passing enemies. Realizing that railroads could not run on busy urban streets, cities required railroads to isolate their tracks by laying them below (or above) ground level and locating their terminals outside the congested heart of the city and their yards on the outskirts. As for the cultural laments that something beautiful and valuable was being destroyed by trains, such sentiments have never won battles against economic progress in the United States. So far as the farmers in the poets' pastoral countryside were concerned, the hissing and whistles of the iron horse meant they could ship their produce to markets anywhere the tracks reached.

THE FARMERS' GRIEVANCES

The farmers' initial enthusiasm for railroads cooled by about 1870. Railroads may have expanded the market for their crops, but as farmers in the midwestern grain belt saw it, the greed and power of the railroad companies ensured that the railroads, not farmers, were the beneficiaries of the new economy.

In the Northeast, where competing small feeder lines ran from cities to their hinterlands like the spokes of a wheel, the tracks of the great trunk lines—the New York Central, the Erie, the Pennsylvania, the Reading, and the Baltimore and Ohio—roughly paralleled one another; sometimes they crossed, in which case they had to attract shippers by lowering freight charges. The Midwest, however, had fewer railroads. Farmers in all but a few areas had one choice when they shipped their wheat, corn, steers, and hogs to processors. The railroads had to consult only their own interests when they set their rates.

Railroad control of storage facilities—stockyards and grain elevators—was particularly galling because the farmers had to pay storage fees until the railroad sent a train to haul their products to market. It was usually in the railroad's interests to delay shipment for no better reason than to collect more storage fees.

THE GRANGER LAWS

In the early 1870s a farmers' social lodge, the Patrons of Husbandry, commonly known as the Grange (see Chapter 32), organized farmer protest in the Midwest. When they turned to politics, the Grangers were a formidable power in Indiana, Illinois, and Iowa. From meager beginnings (in 1869 there were only thirty-nine local chapters in the entire country) the Grange within a few years grew to 20,000 chapters with 800,000 dues-paying members, largely because of the organization's anti-railroad agitation.

The Grangers did not form a political party. In every legislative district they endorsed whichever candidate—Republican, Democrat, or independent—who most persuasively promised to enact laws that bridled the railroads. In Illinois, allied with small businessmen with similar

Business, Wealth, and Protest 1866–1900

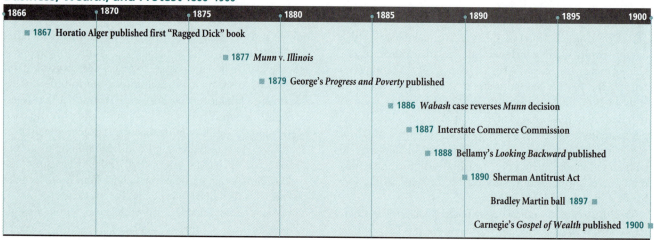

1866   1870   1875   1880   1885   1890   1895   1900

■ 1867 Horatio Alger published first "Ragged Dick" book

■ 1877 *Munn* v. *Illinois*

■ 1879 George's *Progress and Poverty* published

■ 1886 *Wabash* case reverses *Munn* decision

■ 1887 Interstate Commerce Commission

■ 1888 Bellamy's *Looking Backward* published

■ 1890 Sherman Antitrust Act

Bradley Martin ball 1897 ■

Carnegie's *Gospel of Wealth* published 1900 ■

Courtesy of the New York Historical Society, New York City

The Union Pacific, the pride of the nation when it was completed in 1869, was the subject of this cartoon depicting the railroad as a bandit and oppressor a decade later. The thug astride the locomotive is William Vanderbilt, famous for responding to a question about the public's interests in his railroads, "The public be damned."

grievances against the railroads, the Grangers elected a comfortable majority in the state legislature, which promptly enacted a series of "Granger laws" to set maximum fees railroads could charge for storing grain and (for shipments within the state) freight rates.

The railroads challenged the constitutionality of the Granger laws in court. They had two principal arguments. First, they were involved in interstate commerce, which only Congress could regulate. Second, by dictating how much they could charge customers, the state of Illinois had deprived them of their property—how they used their property—in violation of the recently ratified Fourteenth Amendment. In *Munn v. Illinois* in 1877, the Supreme Court ruled against the railroads. By a 7–2 vote, the Court said that the state of Illinois had the right to regulate business transacted within the state, such as storage fees, because when a corporation devoted its "property to a use in which the public has an interest," the corporation granted the public the right to regulate its property "for the common good."

This was a big victory for state regulation, but it was temporary. The railroads hired high-powered, creative business lawyers with political connections like Richard B. Olney (a prominent Democrat) and Senator Roscoe Conkling (the boss of the New York Republican party) who,

at first in several California cases, began to pick away at the Court's reasoning in *Munn* while looking for the right case in which to persuade the Court to reverse itself.

Just as important, five of the nine justices who ruled on *Munn* retired and were replaced by judges with pro-business records. In the *Wabash* case of 1886 (*Wabash, St. Louis, and Pacific Railway Co. v. Illinois*), the Court held that states could not regulate any of the operations of a railroad that crossed state lines because the Constitution reserved the regulation of interstate commerce to Congress. Even a stationary grain elevator, if it was owned by an interstate railroad, was defined as part of interstate commerce. The Supreme Court has, in its history, seen a number of dramatic reversals; its reversal of its own *Munn* decision after just nine years was one of the most dramatic.

THE INTERSTATE COMMERCE COMMISSION

The *Wabash* case did not kill the regulatory movement. Anti-railroad activists—a movement now much broader than the Grange—demanded that if only Congress could bridle the iron horse, Congress had better do it. The regulatory movement was not well organized, but anger with the arrogance of the big railroads was widespread.

In 1887, less than a year after the *Wabash* decision, Congress passed the Interstate Commerce Act. The law seemed to put the railroads on a federal leash. It required railroads to publish their rates and forbade them to depart from their price lists or to pay under-the-table rebates such as John D. Rockefeller had collected. Railroads were no longer allowed to charge less for long hauls along routes where they faced competition than for shorter distances in areas where a company had a monopoly on shipping. (Variable costs per mile were common.) The act also prevented combinations of railroad companies from pooling business to avoid competitive pricing. To enforce the act and to monitor rates and compliance, Congress created the permanent, independent federal **Interstate Commerce Commission** (ICC).

The Interstate Commerce Act calmed anti-railroad protest, but it had little impact on railroad company practices because the ICC had little real power. Commissioner Charles A. Prouty complained, "If the ICC was worth buying, the railroads would try to buy it. The only reason they have not is that the body is valueless in its ability to correct railroad abuses."

The railroads did not have to buy the ICC; for almost fifteen years it was given to them. The Harrison, Cleveland, and McKinley administrations were sympathetic to big business and staffed the commission with railroaders and their lawyers.

RAILROAD CONSOLIDATION

During the early 1890s, due in part to the weakness and amenability of the ICC, most of the nation's largest railroads were linked together in five great systems. By 1900 all five were under the control (or influence just short of control) of two New York–based investment banks, J. P. Morgan and Company and Kuhn, Loeb, and Company—the latter in league with Union Pacific president Edward H. Harriman.

The bankers were called in because the railroads needed capital to lay second, third, and fourth tracks; replace aging locomotives and rolling stock; and build or purchase spur lines. The federal government's construction subsidies were long gone. Revenues from freight charges were inadequate. Issuing new stock was out of the question; although no other railroad was as overvalued as the still tortured Erie, the books of virtually all of them had been cooked to some extent. Every transcontinental line except the Great Northern was in receivership or had been. Then there was the depression of the 1890s. Only the great investment banks commanded the capital the railroads needed.

Investment banks were not "service banks" providing savings accounts for working people depositing a dollar a week and the equivalent of checking accounts for small businesses. The only individuals with whom investment banks dealt directly were those who entrusted them with hundreds of thousands of dollars. They served as sales agents for big corporations like the railroads and city and state and foreign governments—and the federal government—when they needed large infusions of money. The investment banks found buyers for their bonds both privately and on the open market, collecting handsome commissions for their services.

Jay Cooke and Company (twenty years defunct by the 1890s) had sold more than $1.3 billion in federal bonds during the Civil War. The investment banks arranged the finances of corporate mergers, again on commission, and lent their own money.

When J. P. Morgan and Kuhn–Loeb came to the rescue, however, as they did with bankrupt railroads during the 1890s, they insisted that their own representatives sit on the corporations' board of directors to ensure that their money was well used. By 1900, through interlocking directorates, either the Morgan or Kuhn–Loeb bank was coordinating the policies and practices of most big railroads. The banks called a halt to the periodic and ruinous rate wars among the New York Central, Pennsylvania, and Baltimore and Ohio in the eastern states. In 1903 J. P. Morgan engineered a merger of the Northern Pacific and the Great Northern, two systems with parallel lines between the Great Lakes and the Pacific Northwest.

Banker control of the railroads had several benefits. No more did pirates like the Erie Ring ruin transportation systems for the sake of a short-term killing. Coordination of the nation's railways also gradually but significantly lowered freight rates and even fares for passengers. Between 1866 and 1897, the cost of shipping a hundredweight of grain from Chicago to New York dropped from 65 cents to 20 cents, and the rate for shipping beef from 90 cents per hundredweight

North Wind Picture Archives

John Pierpont Morgan, the single most powerful man in the United States in the 1890s and 1900s by virtue of his bank's reorganization of railroads and other major industries. In 1901 Morgan engineered the creation of United States Steel, the first billion-dollar corporation.

to 40 cents. J. P. Morgan's self-justification was identical to John D. Rockefeller's. Competition was wasteful and destructive; consolidation better served the nation as a whole, as well as its capitalists.

J. P. MORGAN

Despite the fact that Morgan could point to improvements in railroad services and a decline in shipping rates, he was no people's hero. He rivaled Rockefeller in the popular mind as the personification of the era's dangerous capitalist consolidation of power. Where was individual freedom and opportunity, people asked, when a secretive, sinister money power could decide the fate of millions of farmers and working people?

Morgan never attempted to deny his power. He reveled in it. He was supremely arrogant in his undisguised contempt for ordinary mortals. He liked to be feared and held in awe. Unlike Rockefeller, he was utterly indifferent to the fact that he was also hated. In the end, he was vulnerable only to ridicule. A skin affliction had swollen his nose to grotesque proportions and colored it bright red when he was angered (which was often). The people with whom he rubbed elbows, fortunately—partners in his bank, industrialists seeking his help, art dealers with paintings or sculptures for sale, and Episcopal bishops, the only class of people in the world to whom he deferred—did not mention his single human weakness.

THE SHERMAN ANTITRUST ACT

The **Sherman Antitrust Act's** early history paralleled the ICC's. It too was enacted—in 1890—only when Congress was alarmed by popular pressure to do something about monopolies. The law stated that "every contract, combination, in the form of trust or otherwise, or conspiracy, in restraint of trade or commerce among the several states . . . is hereby declared to be illegal." The attorney general was authorized to prosecute business combinations powerful enough to control the practices of an industry, and to force them to dismantle into the companies that had joined to end competition.

Congress was treading unfamiliar ground, and some of the wording of the act was careless, creating loopholes and technicalities soon discovered and tested by corporation lawyers. Its effectiveness was also undercut by the fact that both the Democratic Cleveland and the Republican McKinley administrations were friendly to big business; neither was particularly interested in slapping regulations on institutions they regarded as the engines of the national economy. Indeed, Grover Cleveland's attorney general, Richard B. Olney, was a corporation lawyer who had won fame and wealth by fighting and usually foiling state regulatory laws. During the first ten years the Sherman Act was on the books, the government instituted only eighteen prosecutions; four of them were filed against labor unions, which, when they went on strike, could be defined as "conspiracies in restraint of trade."

When the government did prosecute corporations, it fared poorly in the courts. The first major case under the Sherman Act was brought against the most nearly perfect monopoly in the country: the American Sugar Company, which refined 95 percent of the sugar sold in the United States. Conviction looked to be a sure thing. But in *U.S.* v. *E. C. Knight Company* in 1895, the Supreme Court ruled that the sugar monopoly did not violate the Sherman Act because its business was manufacturing, which was not trade or commerce. The Court rejected the argument that because the company monopolized the manufacture of sugar, it set the prices at which sugar was sold. The Court ruled that the price fixing was an *indirect* consequence of American Sugar's monopoly and therefore not subject to commerce law.

The *Knight* decision effectively told business combinations to go right ahead, and they did. Big business got bigger during the 1890s. The number of state-chartered trusts grew from 251 to 290. The money invested in trusts increased from $192 million to $326 million.

SOCIAL CRITICS

The Interstate Commerce and Sherman Antitrust laws were enacted by mainstream politicians who believed that the individual pursuit of wealth was a virtue. They wished to restore competition and the opportunity to succeed that business combinations threatened to destroy. Outside this mainstream, sometimes radical critics of the new industrial capitalism raised their voices and wielded their pens in opposition to the new order itself. At least briefly, some of them won large followings.

HENRY GEORGE AND THE SINGLE TAX

A lively writing style and a knack for simplifying difficult economic ideas made journalist Henry George and his **"single tax"** the center of a short-lived but momentous social movement. In *Progress and Poverty,* published in 1879, George observed what was obvious—but also bewildering to many people. Instead of freedom from onerous labor, as the machine once seemed to promise, the machine had put millions to work at stultifying labor for long hours. Instead of making life easier and fuller for all, mass production of goods had enriched the few in the "House of Have" and impoverished the millions in the "House of Want."

George blamed neither industrialization nor capitalism for the misery. Like most Americans, he believed that the competition for wealth was a wellspring of national energy. The trouble began only when those who were successful in the race—and those who inherited property—were so wealthy that they ceased to be entrepreneurs and became parasites who lived off the income their property generated. George was at his most scathing when he discussed rent, which of course is income based solely on the fact of ownership.

George called income derived from mere ownership of property "unearned increment" because it required no work or ingenuity of its possessors. Property grew more valuable and its owners richer only because other people needed access to it to survive. Such value was spurious, George said, even heinous. Government should confiscate unearned increment by levying a 100 percent tax on it. Because the revenues from this tax would be quite enough to pay all the expenses of government, all other taxes could be abolished. "Single Tax" became the rallying cry of George's movement. It would destroy the idle, parasitic rich as a social class. The entrepreneurship and competition that made the country great would flourish without the handicaps of taxation.

George's gospel was popular enough that in 1886 he narrowly missed being elected mayor of New York, a city where unearned increment from real estate may have been higher than anywhere in the world.

EDWARD BELLAMY LOOKS BACKWARD

Another book that became the Bible of a protest movement was Edward Bellamy's novel of 1888, *Looking Backward, 2000–1887*. Within two years of its publication, the book sold 200,000 copies and led to the founding of 150 Nationalist Clubs of people who shared Bellamy's vision of the future.

The story that moved them was simple, its gimmick conventional. A proper young Bostonian of the 1880s succumbs to a mysterious sleep and awakens in the United States of the twenty-first century. There he discovers that technology has produced not a world of sharp class divisions and widespread misery (as in 1887) but a utopia that provides abundance for all. Like George, Bellamy was not opposed to industrial development.

Capitalism no longer exists in the world of *Looking Backward*. Through a peaceful democratic revolution at the polls, the American people have abolished competitive greed and idle, unproductive living because they were at odds with American ideals. Instead of private ownership of land and industry, the state owns the means of production and administers them for the good of all. Everyone contributes to the common wealth. Everyone lives decently, none miserably or wastefully.

Bellamy's vision was socialistic. However, because he rooted it in American values rather than in Marxism, he called it Nationalism. The patriotic facet of his message made his gospel palatable to middle-class Americans who, while troubled by the growth of fantastic fortunes and of wretched poverty, found Marxist talk of class warfare "foreign" and frightening.

SOCIALISTS AND ANARCHISTS

A few Americans were attracted to the Marxist doctrine of class conflict: that the interests of producers were incompatible with the interests of capitalism and must, inevitably, destroy it. Not many old-stock Americans, however, accepted Marxist teachings, which they associated with Europe. In fact, most American Marxists were immigrants and the children of immigrants, particularly Germans. Briefly after 1872, the General Council of the First International, the official governing body of world socialism founded by Karl Marx, was headquartered in New York, where Marx had sent it to prevent the followers of his anarchist rival, Mikhail Bakunin, from winning control of it.

Most German-American Marxists were social democrats, what revolutionary Marxists called "revisionists." The revolutionaries believed that capitalism would be destroyed in a violent and bloody uprising of the proletariat, the industrial working class. Social democrats held that, in democratic countries like Britain and the United States, socialists could come into power by winning at the polls. Social democratic hopes made less sense in the United States, where the industrial working class was a minority of the population, than in Germany and Great Britain, where workers were a majority. However, the social democratic rejection of violent revolution made it acceptable to more than a few middle-class Americans who were disturbed by the concentration of wealth and power in the great corporations.

In Milwaukee, Wisconsin, the Social Democratic party led by an Austrian immigrant, Victor Berger, grew rapidly during the late 1890s and into the 1900s. Berger's base of support was Milwaukee's large German and German-American population, but he won allies among the non-German middle class as well. Between 1910 and 1960, the Social Democratic party (although progressively less anticapitalist) was Milwaukee's majority party.

Like the revolutionary socialists, the anarchist followers of Mikhail Bakunin regarded the violent destruction of capitalism as inevitable. Anarchists differed from socialists in two ways. First, socialists foresaw a society in which the state would own the "means of production," land and factories; anarchists said that the state was as oppressive as capitalism. Men and women would be free only when the state itself was destroyed. Second, whereas socialists foresaw a long campaign educating the working class before there could be a revolution, Bakuninist anarchists were skeptical that the working class could be weaned from its acquiescence in the capitalist system by rational argument. They believed that the revolution would begin when enlightened individuals—militant anarchists—forced a crisis by the "propaganda of the deed": individual acts of terrorism against capitalism and the state.

The 1880s and 1890s were an era of anarchist assassinations in Europe. Anarchists killed several heads of state, including the Russian czar and the president of France. In 1901 a self-styled anarchist assassinated President William McKinley. Anarchists were never numerous, particularly in the United States. But their numerous and dramatic propagandas of the deed inspired widespread fear and hatred—precisely what the anarchists intended. Anarchists figured prominently in an incident in Chicago in 1886 that caused an overreaction that, when passions cooled, no one justified.

HAYMARKET

In the spring of 1886 workers at the McCormick International Harvester Company, the world's largest manufacturer of farm machinery, went on strike. The Chicago police unabashedly sided with the company, and over several days of picketing and sporadic rioting, they killed four workers. On May 4, a group of anarchists, mostly Germans but including a Confederate Army veteran from a family of some social standing, Albert Parsons, called for a rally in support of the strikers at Haymarket Square, just south of the city center.

© Bettmann/Corbis

There was no need for Chicago police to march into Haymarket Square in May 1886; the demonstration there was peaceful and about to disband. When the police did arrive, an unknown assassin threw a bomb into their midst, killing seven and wounding sixty-seven. Chicago's outrage was so great that the public accepted the railroading of eight anarchists for the crime (four were hanged) despite the lack of evidence that any were involved.

The oratory was red-hot; but the speakers broke no laws, and the crowd was orderly. Indeed, the rally was beginning to break up (a downpour was threatening) when a large formation of police entered the square. Someone threw a bomb into their midst, killing seven policemen and wounding sixty-seven. The police fired a volley, and four workers fell dead.

News of the incident fed an anti-anarchist hysteria in Chicago. Authorities rounded up several dozen individuals who were known to have attended anarchist meetings, and authorities brought eight men to trial for the murder of the officers. Among them was Parsons and a prominent German agitator, August Spies. The trial was a farce. No one on the prosecution team knew or even claimed to know who threw the bomb. (His or her identity remains unknown.) Nor did the prosecution present evidence that tied any of the eight accused to the bombing. One of them, a disturbed young German named Louis Lingg, was infatuated with bombs and had probably made them; but even he had a plausible alibi and may well not have been involved in the incident. Several defendants had not attended the rally. Parsons had been sick in bed for days before the rally was called, conspiring with no one. There was no hard evidence against any of the defendants.

All this was irrelevant. Chicago was in a blind fury and determined to have scapegoats. The charge was murder, but the Haymarket anarchists were tried for being anarchists. Four were hanged. Lingg committed suicide in his cell. Three were sentenced to long prison terms. (Several years later, when the governor of Illinois pardoned them on the grounds there had been no evidence against them, it ruined his career.)

DEFENDERS OF THE FAITH

Industrial capitalism was not without defenders. Like some social critics of the era, the system's apologists drew on both familiar American values and ideas new to the era.

SOCIAL DARWINISM

Intellectuals at peace with the era found a justification for great wealth and even dubious business ethics in a series of books, essays, and lectures by the British philosopher Herbert Spencer. Because Spencer seemed to apply Charles Darwin's celebrated theory of biological evolution to human society, his philosophy is known as *social Darwinism*. (Actually, Spencer did much of his writing before Darwin's *Origin of Species* was published.)

A Survival of the Fittest Sampler

We have unmistakable proof that throughout all past time, there has been a ceaseless devouring of the weak by the strong.

　　　　　　Herbert Spencer

The ultimate result of shielding men from the effects of folly is to fill the world with fools.

　　　　　　Herbert Spencer

Whatever capital you divert to the support of a shiftless and good-for-nothing person is so much diverted from some other employment, and that means from somebody else.

　　　　　　William Graham Sumner

The price which society pays for the law of competition . . . is . . . great; but the advantages of this law are . . . greater still, for it is to this law that we owe our wonderful

material development, which brings improved conditions in its train. But whether the law be benign or not, we must say of it . . . : It is here; we cannot evade it; no substitutes for it have been found; and while the law may be sometimes hard for the individual, it is best for the race, because it ensures the survival of the fittest in every department.

　　　　　　Andrew Carnegie

The Last Dance of the Idle Rich

How They Lived

In the winter of 1896–1897, the depression had hit bottom. Several million people were out of work. Perhaps a hundred thousand people had been evicted from their homes. The treasuries of charitable organizations were dry; some had closed their doors.

At breakfast in his Fifth Avenue mansion, Bradley Martin, one of New York society's adornments, had an idea. "I think it would be a good thing if we got up something," he told his wife and brother, Frederick. "There seems to be a great deal of depression in trade; suppose we send out invitations to a concert."

Mrs. Martin observed that a concert would benefit only foreigners. Most professional musicians were German or Italian; she wanted to do something for Americans. "I've got a far better idea," she said. "Let us give a costume ball at so short notice that our guests won't have time to get their dresses from Paris. That will give an impetus to trade that nothing else will."

The conversation was recorded by Frederick Townshend Martin with no intention of ridiculing his brother and sister-in-law. He justified their curious economic theories by explaining that when the invitations went out, "Many New York shops sold out brocades and silks which had been lying in their stockrooms for years."

The ball was held on February 10, 1897, at the Waldorf-Astoria Hotel. The ballroom was decorated to resemble Louis XIV's palace at Versailles. According to journalists, there was never such a display of jewels in the United States. August Belmont 's gold-inlaid armor cost him $10,000. The costumes of others were inferior only by comparison. One woman said that to help the particularly hard-pressed Indians, she had had Native Americans make her Pocahontas costume. Bradley Martin made a curious selection. As the host at Versailles, he had first claim to be Louis XIV, the Sun King, the most glorious of the French monarchs. But Bradley chose to be his great-grandson, Louis XV; he would not have wanted to be Louis XVI, who was beheaded because of his and his predecessors' extravagance in a country where the poor suffered wretched misery. But Louis XVI was who Bradley turned out to be.

Even before the first waltz, Martin and his friends were vilified from pulpit, editorial desk, and political platform for their callous decadence in difficult times. More than one business leader, including J. P. Morgan, denounced the ball. If idle heirs such as Bradley Martin did not know that such public spending on glitter caused resentment and class hatred, Morgan did. At about the same time he scolded an associate, Charles Schwab, for a well-publicized spending spree in Monte Carlo. When Schwab protested that at least he had not done his high-stakes gambling behind closed doors, Morgan snapped, "That's what doors are for."

In *The Theory of the Leisure Class,* published in 1899, sociologist Thorstein Veblen gave a name to the Bradley Martin lifestyle: "conspicuous consumption." Somewhat later, the historians Charles and Mary Beard called the **Bradley Martin ball** of 1897 the "climax of lavish expenditure" in the United States. "This grand ball of the plutocrats astounded the country, then in the grip of a prolonged business depression with its attendant unemployment, misery, and starvation."

The Bradley Martins carried on as always, but not in New York. The ball was so unpopular that city hall slapped a big tax increase on the Martin mansion on Fifth Avenue. In a huff, the Martins moved to London. Brother Frederick Townshend Martin wrote despondently of their exile; the United States had lost two valuable citizens.

According to **social Darwinism,** as in the world of animals and plants, where species compete and those best adapted survive, the worthiest people rise to the top in the social competition for riches: "survival of the fittest." Eventually, in the dog-eat-dog world, they alone survive. "If they are sufficiently complete to live," Spencer wrote, "they do live, and it is well that they should live. If they are not sufficiently complete to live, they die, and it is best they should die."

This tough-mindedness made Spencer (in popularized dilution) appealing to some American businessmen. Social Darwinism accounted for brutal business practices and underhanded methods with a shrug, justifying them as "natural," the law of the jungle. However, the ruthlessness of the philosophy made it unpalatable to most businessmen who, in their personal lives were, like the Rockefellers, deeply religious. The most important American social Darwinist, William Graham Sumner, was no businessman but a professor. Having no financial stake in business, he could be consistent in applying the principle that government should in no way interfere with the "law of the jungle."

Sumner opposed all government regulation of business: "The men who are competent to organize great enterprises and to handle great amounts of capital must be found by natural selection, not political election." That was all right. But Sumner also opposed government action that favored capitalists, including the protective tariff. Industrialists would hear nothing of that sort of nonsense. And he objected to government intervention in strikes on behalf of employers. Strikes, to Sumner, were legitimate tests of fitness between employers and their employees. Police and even military intervention in industrial disputes was too valuable a tool to employers for them to accept Sumner as their philosopher.

THE SUCCESS GOSPEL

The Gospel of Success had far more influence among late nineteenth-century capitalists than social Darwinism did. The United States was built on the desire to prosper, Success Gospellers said. Therefore, if competition for riches was a virtue, what was wrong with winning? Far from a reason for anxiety or evidence of social immorality, the fabulous fortunes of America's wealthy families were an index of their virtue. The Carnegies and Morgans deserved their money. John D. Rockefeller was quoted as saying of his wealth, "God gave it to me."

Success manuals—books purporting to show would-be Rockefellers and Morgans how to do it—were read as avidly as the works of George and Bellamy, and by far more people. All much the same, the manuals were, of course, not "how to" books like guides to organic gardening and automobile maintenance. They were pious frauds: hard work, honesty, frugality, loyalty to employers, and other virtues would inevitably lead to material success. The undisguised implication was that having succeeded, America's millionaires deserved not resentment but admiration.

A Baptist minister from Philadelphia, Russell B. Conwell, made a fortune delivering a lecture on this theme. In "Acres of Diamonds," which he delivered to paying audiences more than 6,000 times, Conwell said that great wealth was a great blessing. Not only could every American be rich, but every American *should* be rich. If a man failed, the fault lay within himself, not with society. "There is not a poor person in the United States," Conwell said, "who was not made poor by his own shortcomings." The opportunities, the acres of diamonds, were everywhere, in the backyards, waiting to be collected. Those who already were rich were by definition virtuous. "Ninety-eight out of one hundred of the rich men of America are honest. That is why they are rich." Conwell was a popular man in honest circles.

HORATIO ALGER AND RAGGED DICK

In 130 novels written for boys, another minister, Horatio Alger, conveyed the Gospel of Success to the next generation.

Alger was an embarrassingly bad writer. His prose was leaden, his characters cardboard cut-outs; their conversation would have put even their dull fellow characters to sleep. Alger's plots were variations on two or three simple themes. It was a given that the goal of male existence was to make money. God—or America (this was not clear; Alger was neither a Bible-thumper nor a flag-waver)—put wealth within the grasp of all. Most of the heroes of Alger's novels were lads grappling with destitution; many of them were orphans, although there was often a loving, impoverished, widowed mother waiting patiently back home for her boy to make a bundle. Alger's heroes were honest, hard-working, loyal to their employers, and clean-living. Ragged Dick, Alger's first hero and the prototype for Tattered Tom, Lucky Luke, and dozens of others, was insufferably priggish and smarmy.

Curiously, Ragged Dick and most of the others did not get rich penny by penny, putting in fourteen hours a day to save a dollar a week. (This would have made for even duller reading.) At the beginning of the final chapter, the Alger hero was often as badly off as he had been on page one. Then, however—the Horatio Alger touch—he was presented with what amounts to a visitation of grace, a divine gift rewarding him for his virtues. The child of a factory owner falls off the Staten Island Ferry; or the teenaged daughter of a banker stumbles into the path of runaway Clydesdales pulling a brewery wagon, or she slips into the Niagara River just above the falls. Alger's boy hero, luckily, is there; he acts in an instant and rescues the poor girl. And in five or six pages, the heroic lad is rewarded with a job, marriage to the daughter (who has nothing resembling a personality either), and eventually—sometimes after "The End"—the grateful father's fortune.

So the Alger books had, in addition to the American evangelical assumption of a monetized grace, an appeal to the adolescent boy's adventure fantasies. Just as he gave John D. Rockefeller his money, God gave a less munificent fortune to Ragged Dick. Between 1867 and 1899, Alger's books sold 20 million copies! A battalion of imitators accounted for millions more. And yet, with pulp novels about Wild Bill Hickock and Belle Starr, the "Bandit Queen," also on the market and costing only a dime, perhaps the chief purchasers of the Alger books may have been the hopeful parents of adolescent boys.

The Granger Collection, New York

Horatio Alger's "Ragged Dick" books for boys preached that living a virtuous life would lead to material success. His heroes, like this boy, were invariably dirt-poor but virtuous.

Keystone-Mast Collection UCR/California Museum of Photography, UC Riverside

Andrew Carnegie, second from right, with other businessmen–philanthropists at Tuskegee Institute, the most famous African-American college in the United States. Tuskegee president Booker T. Washington is front and center. John D. Rockefeller was also generous with African-American institutions. Spelman College in Georgia was named for his wife.

PHILANTHROPY

The weakness of the Success Gospel as a justification of great wealth was the obvious fact that many of the country's richest men got their money by practicing the opposite of the touted virtues: dishonesty, betrayal of partners and employers, and reckless speculation. And they grew richer while living a life of sumptuous luxury and leisure that was, in some instances, decadent. Rockefeller's business methods were not nearly so unethical as his enemies said, but there was no question that he cut corners. None of the great magnates of the era shied away from ruthless destruction of competitors because it occurred to them that to do so was unseemly. It would be wrong to say that the giants of American industry were all Jacob Marleys and Ebeneezer Scrooges. But there were no Mr. Fezziwigs among them. That was why the more thoughtful among them, like Carnegie, preferred social Darwinism as a justification of their wealth.

This may also be why, perhaps recognizing that many of the dollars were, by their own lights, ill-gotten, many wealthy businessmen of the age became philanthropists. Horatio Alger—no multimillionaire—supported institutions that housed homeless boys in New York City. Russell B. Conwell, another man of modest riches, founded Temple University in Philadelphia, where poor young men could study cheaply

and improve their prospects. Leland Stanford built a new "Harvard of the West" in California (Stanford University). Rockefeller and other industrial millionaires gave huge sums to churches, universities, and other useful institutions. In retirement, Rockefeller took particular interest in helping African Americans. Spelman College in Georgia existed only because of Rockefeller's gifts. (It was named for his wife.) His son, John D. Rockefeller Jr., devoted little time to business; his profession was the distribution of the Rockefeller millions.

Andrew Carnegie devised a coherent theory that justified fabulous fortunes like his own by the concept of stewardship. In a celebrated, often reprinted essay titled "Wealth," he argued that individuals' unrestricted pursuit of riches made American society vital and strong. However, the man who succeeded and amassed millions was merely a steward, a trustee. He had an obligation to distribute his money where it would "do the most good," where it would provide opportunities for poor young men of the next generation to participate in the energizing economic competition. In one of his phrase-coining moods, Carnegie said that the rich man who died rich, died a failure.

Carnegie retired from business in 1901. While not denying himself pleasures—he spent much of each year at his castle in Scotland—he devoted the working hours of the rest of his life, almost twenty years, to giving money to useful social institutions; his specialty was libraries. Despite his generosity, he died a multimillionaire. Carnegie's theory came closer than any other to justifying huge personal and corporate fortunes. However, when those fortunes could not be redistributed, when they were so big that they continued to grow despite massive giveaways, Carnegie's "stewardship" theory did not work any better than the theory that God decided who would be rich and who would be poor.

HOW THE VERY RICH LIVED

No doubt, the philanthropy of Carnegie, Rockefeller, and others changed many people's opinions of them as individuals. Ironically, however, but plausibly, socially responsible multimillionaires like them had less to do with reconciling Americans to the existence of a permanently ensconced

Private Cars

J. P. Morgan was partial to yachts; he never owned a private railroad car. For other millionaires, the custom-made "Palace Car" was one of the ultimate status symbols. In George Gould's private car, guests dressed white-tie for dinner; waiters in livery served the meal on solid gold plates. The Vanderbilt family's car could not always accommodate all the friends they invited to travel with them, so they had a second one built. At Palm Beach, a pleasuring ground of the wealthy at the end of the century, twenty to thirty private cars were sometimes parked in a special section of the train yard. When Morgan decided to go somewhere he could not reach by yacht, he rented an opulent Palace Car from the Pullman Company. On one occasion he paid for an entire train of private cars to transport the nation's Episcopalian bishops to a conference in San Francisco.

social class that was "filthy rich" than the shallowest and least constructive representatives of that class. The very rich who spent their millions on what sociologist Thorstein Veblen called "conspicuous consumption" put on a splendid show for the multitudes. Then, like today, most people were dazzled by a good show.

CONSPICUOUS CONSUMPTION

The very rich competed with one another in spending by hosting lavish parties, by building extravagant homes, by purchasing yachts and private railway cars to get from one home to another, by adorning themselves with costly jewelry and clothing that (in the case of the women) they hoped to wear only once, and—the ultimate one-upmanship of the era—by buying Europeans with titles for their daughters to marry.

"High society" social get-togethers lasting a few hours often cost more than $100,000. At one party hosted by Harry Lehr, who took pride in calling himself the "prince of spenders," a hundred dogs dined on "fricassee of bones" and gulped down shredded dog biscuit prepared by a French chef. The guests at a New York banquet ate their meal while mounted on horses (trays balanced on the withers) while the horses munched oats out of sterling silver feedbags. At a costume ball, guests boasted that they had spent $10,000 on their fancy dress to others who had just boasted they had spent $5,000.

It was a golden age for yachting or, at least, for buying yachts. Cornelius Vanderbilt's *North Star* was 250 feet long. Albert C. Burrage's *Aztec* carried 270 tons of coal; it could steam 5,500 miles without calling at a port for fuel. As on land, J. P. Morgan was champion at sea. He owned

Photograph by Byron. The Byron Collection, Museum of the City of New York

A banquet of wealthy gentlemen in a New York. Women were dining at elegant restaurants by the end of the century, but they were still largely masculine institutions. Actress Lillian Russell, not exactly "high society," was notorious for the size of the meals she put away; it was said that only her longtime companion, James "Diamond Jim" Brady, himself a long way from high society, could outeat her.

Having Her Cake and Eating It Too

One American heiress actually improved her finances by marrying a European aristocrat. Alice Heine, daughter of a New Orleans banker, married the French Duc de Richelieu. When the duke died in 1879, he left her $15 million. The young widow then married Prince Albert of Monaco, thus becoming the wife of a prince who actually ruled a country and was quite wealthy in his own right.

The Grand Tour

It was a social necessity for rich Americans—the women of the family, at least, when the head of household was the gruff meat-and-potatoes type—to tour western Europe and, usually, Egypt. "The Grand Tour" was no two-week race-around; one spent months, even a year or more, sopping up culture and socializing with other tourists at grand hotels. In 1879, when a million tourists visited Switzerland, the first international "vacationland," 200,000 of them were Americans.

three successively larger, faster, and more opulent yachts called *Corsair*. Morgan had a sense of humor: the corsairs were Barbary pirates, infamous for their ruthlessness.

Nowhere was consumption more conspicuous than at upper-class summer resorts, of which the pinnacle was Newport, Rhode Island. An ordinary summer "cottage" of thirty rooms, occupied only three months a year, cost $1 million. Coal baron E. J. Berwind spent $1.5 million to build "The Elms." William K. Vanderbilt outdid everyone with "Marble House." His cottage cost $2 million; to furnish it, Vanderbilt spent $9 million. There was no topping that.

A LORD IN THE FAMILY

A fad of the filthy rich during the 1880s and 1890s was marrying their daughters to titled Europeans, thus ennobling the lucky girls too. It was not difficult to find fortune-hunting earls who were for sale. Accustomed to living well without working, their incomes, based on land, were inadequate by themselves in the age of industrial capitalism. It was a win–win marketplace. American daughter got to be introduced as "Countess" at Newport; her husband got plenty of money. A contemporary student of the phenomenon counted 100 such matches with dowries totaling $100 million.

There were, of course, personal disappointments, even personal tragedies. Heiress Alice Thaw was embarrassed on her honeymoon as Countess of Yarmouth when the count's creditors seized her husband's luggage. She had to wire her father for the money to get it out of hock. Helena Zimmerman, the daughter of a coal and iron millionaire from Cincinnati, married the duke of Manchester. For twenty years their substantial bills were paid by the duchess's father out of the labor of workers living on subsistence wages.

The most famous American aristocrats were the heiresses of two of the greatest robber barons, Jay Gould and Cornelius Vanderbilt. Anna Gould became the Countess Boni de Castellane. Before she divorced him to marry his cousin, the higher-ranking Prince de Sagan, the count extracted more than $5 million from Jay Gould's purse. No American businessman had pocketed a fraction of that sum at Gould's expense. Consuelo Vanderbilt was effectively forced to marry the head of one of England's proudest families, the Churchills; she had to be locked in her room the day before the wedding to "Sunny," the ninth Duke of Marlborough (dowry: $2.5 million), to prevent her from running away. Sunny, who was the cousin of Winston Churchill (the son of an American heiress himself) was not a bad sort, but he was of no substance.

Consuelo was a substantial woman. After she divorced the duke, she devoted her life to social welfare programs.

WOMEN AS DECOR

The role of young heiresses in the game of conspicuous waste (another of Veblen's terms) helps to illustrate the function of the women of the Gilded Age super-rich. They were idler than their businessmen husbands (although not necessarily idler than their sons). With the exception of a few eccentrics

The Granger Collection, New York

Beautiful Consuelo Vanderbilt did not want to marry the Duke of Marlborough. But such a "catch"—no dukes ranked higher than the Marlboroughs—was too much for her mother to entertain her wishes. She buckled under, married the fortune-hunting duke, was miserable from the start, and later divorced him, costing the Vanderbilt family yet more money. The rest of her long life she devoted to worthy causes such as children's hospitals. Living in France when the Nazis invaded in 1940, she fled to the South with several dozen orphans.

You Can Take It with You

At the Vanderbilt family tomb on Staten Island, watchmen punched a time clock every hour around the clock. William Vanderbilt, son of the Commodore, had an obsessive fear of grave robbers.

like brokers Victoria Woodhull and Tennessee Claflin, and the miserly and successful investor Hetty Green, "the witch of Wall Street," there was no place for women in big business. But what were wealthy women to do? They had no domestic duties beyond giving instructions to servants.

They were their husband's adornments, mannequins on which to display wealth. Mrs. George Gould (Jay Gould's daughter-in-law and mother of the Countess Boni de Castellane) went through life best known for the fact that she owned a pearl necklace that cost $500,000. Several portraits of her are, in fact, portraits of the necklace with Mrs. Gould as the model.

High-society fashion emphasized women's idleness. Wealthy women (and middle-class women who imitated them) were laced up tightly in crippling steel and bone corsets, which made it laborious just to move about. They said with their costume that there were other people to perform even the least onerous physical tasks for them—such as lacing up their corsets.

Wealthy women were often their husbands' conspicuous-consumers-in-chief. Although William K. Vanderbilt was not uninterested in building mansions, his wife, a southern belle named Alva Smith, was the family's big spender (and the parent who arranged and forced Consuelo's marriage; William K. was sympathetic with Consuelo's resistance).

AVID WATCHERS

The conspicuous consumers were interested in impressing and exciting the envy of people like them. But because it was by definition display, the lifestyle of the very rich was well known to everyone thanks to journalists who described their yachts, mansions, marriages, balls, and dinners with as much detail as they could discover or, when necessary, imagine. Some journals depicted the rich with the same awe that today's *People* magazine and television programs lavish on movie actors and popular singers.

In popular songs of the day, and in the melodramas favored by working people, the idleness and extravagance of the filthy rich were favorite themes. They were shrewdly calculated to arouse both envy and resentment but, in the end, justified great riches. New York's "Tin Pan Alley," the center of the sheet music business, turned out dozens of songs, a few of them still standards, that preached pity for the "bird in a gilded cage" (the wealthy but unhappy young woman) and the moral that because poor people earned their own way by working, they were more virtuous.

Popular plays with little subtlety of character and predictable plots—melodramas—pitted simple, right-living poor people against unscrupulous rich villains and their arrogant womenfolk. "You are only a shopgirl," said a high-society lady in a typical scene, attempting to put the heroine in her place. "An honest shopgirl," the heroine replied, "as far above a fashionable idler as heaven is above earth!" Before the final curtain fell, however, the shopgirl was, like Horatio Alger's boys, rewarded for her virtue by marriage to a rich young man.

Sensationalist working-class scandal sheets like the *Police Gazette* specialized in upper-class scandals. When the very rich divorced, court proceedings were reported in detail because in the nineteenth century the grounds for most divorces were adultery or lurid, sometimes sexual abuse. In 1872, the dawn of the Gilded Age, Jim Fisk was shot to death by a rival for the affections of his showgirl mistress, Josie Mansfield. Newspaper readers could find a moral in the fact that Fisk's wealth and power could not save him from a violent death at the age of 38. The 1906 murder of high-living architect Stanford White and the trial of his killer, millionaire Harry Thaw, made for even juicier news. Thaw accused White of having seduced his beautiful fiancée, Evelyn Nesbit. Her testimony concerning White's peculiarities behind closed doors simultaneously titillated the public and served Thaw as a moral justification of his act. (He went free.)

FURTHER READING

General Stuart Bruchey, *The Growth of the Modern Economy*, 1975; Vincent P. DeSantis, *The Shaping of Modern America, 1877–1916*, 1973; John A. Garraty, *The New Commonwealth, 1877–1890*, 1968; Alan Trachtenberg, *The Corporation of America: Culture and Society in the Gilded Age*, 1982.

Big Business Saul Engelbourg, *Power and Morality: American Business Ethics, 1840–1914*, 1980; L. Galambos, *The Public Image of Big Business in America*, 1975; Naomi Lamoreaux, *The Great Merger Movement in American Business, 1895–1904*, 1985; Glenn Porter, *The Rise of Big Business, 1860–1910*, 1973; David O. Whitten, *The Emergence of Giant Enterprise, 1860–1914*, 1983; Oliver Zunz, *Making America Corporate, 1870–1930*, 1990.

Magnates, Courtiers, and Critics Ron Chernow, *Titan: The Life of John D. Rockefeller, Sr.*, 1998, and *The House of Morgan: An American Banking Dynasty*, 1990; Harold C. Livesay, *Andrew Carnegie and the Rise of Big Business*, 1975; Barbara Goldsmith, *Other Powers: The Age of Suffrage, Spiritualism, and the Scandalous Victoria Woodhull*, 1998; Andrew Sinclair, *Corsair: The Life of J. Pierpont Morgan*, 1981; Charles Slack, *Hetty: The Genius and Madness of America's First Female Tycoon*, 2004; John L. Thomas, *Alternative America: Henry George, Edward Bellamy, Henry Demarest Lloyd*, 1983; J. F. Wall, *Andrew Carnegie*, 1971.

Railroads and Regulation Robert G. Angevine, *The Railroad and the State: War, Politics, and Technology in Nineteenth Century America*, 2004; David H. Bain, *Empire Express: Building the First Transcontinental Railroad*, 1999; Steven W. Usselman, *Regulating Railroad Innovation: Business, Technology, and Politics in America, 1840–1920*, 2002.

KEY TERMS

The following terms are covered in this chapter and can also be found in the list of Key Terms at the back of the book.

Bradley Martin ball *Looking Backward*   "single tax"   social Darwinism

Interstate Commerce **Sherman Antitrust Act**
Commission

 ## ONLINE SOURCES GUIDE

Use this listing to find online documents, images, interactive maps, simulations, and other resources related to this chapter:

American History Resource Center
http://history.wadsworth.com/rc/us

Selected Documents
Andrew Carnegie's essay, "Wealth"
Frederick Townshend Martin's The Passing of the Idle Rich

Selected Images
Andrew Carnegie
J. P. Morgan

Interactive Time Line (with online readings)
Living with Leviathan: Reactions to Big Business and Great Wealth

CHAPTER 29

We Who Built America

Factories and Immigrants

Reproduced from the Collections of the Library of Congress

So at last I was going to America! Really, really going at last! The boundaries burst! The arch of heaven soared! A million suns shone out for every star. The winds rushed in from outer space, roaring in my ear, "America! America!" . . .

Mary Antin

Leland Stanford and James J. Hill thought of themselves as the men who built the railroads. Journalists called Andrew Carnegie the nation's greatest steelmaker. In the popular mind, industries were associated with individuals, just as battles were identified with generals: Sherman marched across Georgia; Grant took Richmond; Vanderbilt ran the New York Central; John D. Rockefeller was Standard Oil. J. P. Morgan spoke of his hobby, yachting, in personal terms. "You can do business with anyone," he snorted, "but you can only sail a boat with a gentleman."

In reality, Morgan decided when and where the boat was to go. But it took eighty-five grimy stokers and hardhanded sailors to get the *Corsair* out of New York Harbor and safely into Newport or Venice. Stanford, Hill, Rockefeller, Carnegie, Swift, Armour, and other great entrepreneurs supervised the creation of industrial America, but it was built by millions of anonymous men and women who wielded the shovels and tended the machines that whirred and whined in the factories and mills.

A NEW WAY OF LIFE

America's industrial workers could not be kept below decks like the crew of the *Corsair*. They were everywhere. While the population of the United States more than doubled between 1860 and 1900, the size of the working class quadrupled. In 1860, 1.5 million Americans made their living in workshops and mills, another 700,000 in mining and construction. By 1900, 6 million people worked in manufacturing, 2.3 million in mining and construction. Industrial workers, once few in numbers and sometimes, like the "mill girls" of New England, romanticized, had come to constitute a distinct social class second in size only to farmers. And there was little about their lives that lent itself to romance.

BIGGER FACTORIES, BETTER TECHNOLOGY

The size of their workplace grew dramatically, a fact of profound importance to the quality of working-class life. In 1870 the average American workshop employed eight people. It was owned by an individual or by partners who

Andrew Carnegie's Homestead Works, the heart of his steelmaking empire. It was the largest factory in the world for decades. In 1892 it was the scene of a violent strike, during which several hundred guards sent to disperse the strikers were captured and expelled from the town.

their employees. Even Pittsburgh's iron mills, the largest factories in the country at the end of the Civil War, employed on average just ninety workers. The men stoking the furnaces were not apt to chat with the owners of the mill, but they knew them by sight.

By 1900, industrial workers labored in shops averaging twenty-five employees. Plants employing 1,000 men and women were common. The average payroll of Pittsburgh iron and steel plants was 1,600, and a few companies listed 10,000 on the payroll. Carnegie Steel employed 23,000. The men who directed these mammoth concerns might never step on a factory floor; Carnegie never did. He and men in similar positions were interested in wages only in the aggregate—as "costs"—and in the hours in a workday and safety conditions only insofar as they translated into numbers in ledgers.

Improvements in manufacturing machines cut operating costs by reducing the number of highly skilled craftsmen in factories. A few crafts, like the machinist's trade, increased in importance. But in most industries, machines took over from artisans, performing their jobs more quickly and often better, and reducing their numbers.

Many machines were tended by unskilled or semiskilled men and women (and children) who guided or merely watched their operation. Unlike craftsmen, they were interchangeable, easily replaced because the jobs they did required little training. Consequently, they were poorly paid and commanded scant respect from employers, small businessmen, professionals, politicians, and skilled workers. "If I wanted boiler iron," said one industrialist, "I would go out on the market and buy it where I could get it cheapest; and if I wanted to employ men I would do the same." The "mechanic," who commanded respect during the Age of Jackson, was a threatened species and in some trades was almost extinct.

WAGES

In numbers of dollars in pay envelopes, wages declined during the final decades of the century. Real wages, however—actual purchasing power—rose because the cost of food, clothing, and housing dropped faster than hourly pay did. As

personally supervised the business, working at the bench alongside their employees in the smallest shops. Kind, callous, or cruel as the boss might be (*boss* was already an old world, adopted from the Dutch), they were personally involved in their workers' lives. Like it or not, they heard of births of children and deaths of parents. They discussed wages, hours, and conditions in the shop face-to-face with

Labor and Immigration 1866–1900

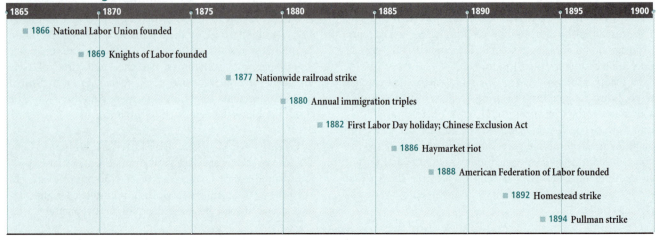

1865	1870	1875	1880	1885	1890	1895	1900

- 1866 National Labor Union founded
- 1869 Knights of Labor founded
- 1877 Nationwide railroad strike
- 1880 Annual immigration triples
- 1882 First Labor Day holiday; Chinese Exclusion Act
- 1886 Haymarket riot
- 1888 American Federation of Labor founded
- 1892 Homestead strike
- 1894 Pullman strike

a whole, industrial workers enjoyed almost 50 percent more purchasing power in 1900 than they did in 1860.

But this statistic can be misleading. The skilled "aristocracy of labor"—locomotive engineers, machinists, master carpenters, printers, and other highly trained artisans—improved their economic situation much more than did the unskilled workers at the bottom of the pile. The average annual wage for all manufacturing workers in 1900 was only $435, or $8.37 a week. Unskilled workers were paid about 10 cents an hour on the average (about $5.50 a week). A girl of 13, tending a loom in a Carolina textile mill, might take home as little as $2 a week after various fines (for being late to work, for example) were deducted from her pay. In 1904 sociologist Robert Hunter estimated that one American in eight lived in poverty.

HOURS

Hours on the job varied. Most government employees enjoyed an eight-hour day, but that was unusual. Skilled workers, especially in the building trades (bricklayers, carpenters, plumbers), worked ten hours. Factory workers and telephone operators worked twelve-hour days. Most mills ran as long as workers could see, from sunup to sundown. During the summer that could mean sixteen-hour days.

The average workweek was sixty-six hours long in 1860, fifty-five hours in 1910. Most employees were on the job five and a half or six days a week. (Half-day Saturdays were considered holidays.) In industries that had to run around the clock, such as iron and steel manufacturing (the furnaces could not be shut down), the workforce was divided into two shifts on seven-day schedules. Each shift worked twelve hours. At the end of two weeks, the day workers switched shifts with the night workers. This meant a holiday of twenty-four hours once a month. The price of that holiday was working twenty-four hours straight two weeks later.

True holidays were few. Christmas and July 4 were almost universally observed, as was Memorial Day in the northern states. Other legal holidays varied from state to state.

However, because of the swings in the business cycle, factory workers had plenty of unwanted time off. Some industries were seasonal. Coal miners could expect to be without wages for weeks, sometimes months, during summer when people did not heat their homes.

CONDITIONS

Although some employers were safety conscious, the number of injuries and deaths on the job are chilling from today's perspective. Between 1870 and 1910, there were 10,000 major boiler explosions in American factories—almost one per workday. Between 1880 and 1900, 35,000 American workers were killed on the job—one every two days. Railroads were particularly dangerous. Every year one railroad worker in 26 was seriously injured, and one in 400 was killed. In 1910, 3,383 railway workers were killed, 95,671 injured.

In many cases, injured workers and the survivors of those who were killed on the job received no compensation. In others, compensation amounted to little more than burial

expenses. In the Pennsylvania coalfields, mine owners were thought generous to a family if they allowed a dead miner's son younger than regulation age to take his dead father's job in the pit.

Employer liability law was stacked against workers. During the nineteenth century, courts held that employers were not liable for an injury on the job unless the employee could prove he or she in no way contributed to the accident. Short of the collapse of a factory roof or the boss's son run amok with a revolver, total lack of responsibility for a mishap was difficult to prove and, in fact, unusual. Courts ruled that even if an employee was hurt because a machine was dangerous but the employee was aware of the danger, the employer was not liable.

Occupational diseases—the coal miner's "black lung," the cotton mill worker's "white lung," and the hard-rock miner's silicosis—were not considered the employer's responsibility. Poisoning resulting from work with toxic chemicals was rarely identified as job-related.

WHO WERE THE WORKERS?

Skilled workers tended to be native-born white males of "old immigrant" stock—that is, of British, Irish, or German ancestry. The term "old immigration" was coined during the 1890s to describe national groups from northern and western Europe that had predominated before 1880. Unskilled jobs were, in general, filled by **new immigrants**—southern and eastern Europeans who were a large majority of new-comers after 1880. In smaller industrial cities, half to three-quarters of the workforce was foreign-born, including Irish newly-arrived "old immigrant" and Germans—nationalities—who continued to arrive in large numbers throughout the "new immigration" period.

CHILD LABOR

In 1900 the socialist writer John Spargo estimated that 1.8 million children under 16 years of age were employed full-time. They did all but the heaviest jobs. Girls as young as 12 tended spinning machines in textile mills. "Bobbin boys" of 10 hauled wooden boxes filled with spindles from spinning rooms to weaving rooms and back again. Children swept filings in machine shops. Boys of 8 worked the "breakers" at coal mines, handpicking slate from anthracite in filthy, frigid wooden sheds.

In sweatshops in city tenements, whole families sewed clothing, rolled cigars, or made small items by hand; children worked as soon as they were able to master the simplest tasks. In cities, children practically monopolized messenger service work, light delivery, and some kinds of huckstering.

In part, child labor was the fruit of greed. On the grounds that children had no dependents to support, employers paid them less than they paid adults, even when the jobs were identical. In southern textile towns, the "Mill Daddy" became a stock figure. Unable to find work because his own children could be hired for less, the Mill Daddy was reduced to carrying lunches to the factory and tossing them over the fence at noon.

Museum of the City of New York, #RiisEE, photograph by Lewis Hine. The Jaco A. Riis Collections.

An oyster cannery in Louisiana. Hardly a factory, it was a shed in which women shucked the oysters by hand, as they might do preparing dinner, except that they prepared the oysters for packing by the thousands. Pay was in pennies. The women here have brought their daughters to work, one not more than 4 years old and already learning the miserable job.

The use of child labor also illustrated a "cultural lag." Children had always worked. It took time for society to recognize that labor in the world of the dynamo and the big factory was qualitatively different from doing chores on a family farm. Relations on the farm or in a small shop were personal. In these settings the limited capacity of children—particularly their fatigue when set to tedious, repetitive tasks—was easy to recognize and to take into account. Placed in a niche in a massive factory, the child laborer was a number on the payroll.

WOMEN WORKERS

The first industrial workers were female. This was true partly because the first modern industry was textiles, and women had been the mainstay of cloth making in Western culture—and partly because the founders of the first American textile mills (like the Lowells) could not imagine factory work as a lifetime career for a male head of household. As factory work became heavier, requiring greater physical strength, the industrial workforce became predominantly male. Nevertheless, the difficulty of supporting a family on one income forced many working-class women to continue to labor for wages even after they married. In 1900 almost 20 percent of the total workforce was female. About half the workers in textiles were women, and the percentage in the needle trades (which were not factory work) was much higher.

With few exceptions, women were paid less than men for performing the same tasks for the same number of hours. Abysmally low pay was particularly characteristic of the largest female occupation. In 1900, 2 million women were employed for subsistence wages or less in domestic service: cooking, cleaning, and tending the vanities and children of the well-off. In an age before household appliances and other mechanical conveniences, even middle-class families on a strict budget had a live-in maid and often a combination gardener–stable hand.

Women in the Workforce

There was at least one woman in every occupation listed by the Census Bureau in 1890. More than 225,000 women were running farms, and 1,143 listed their occupation as "clergyman." Women outnumbered men as teachers and as waiters by five to one. There were twenty-eight female lumberjacks. However, among 12,856 wheelwrights (makers and repairers of wagon wheels), there was only one woman.

A woman and a teenage girl in a southern cotton mill. The girl would not have been the youngest employee in the factory. Younger girls and "bobbin boys" would have been kept out of sight when this posed photograph was taken. Southern mills employed only white people, but employees were told that African Americans would be hired to take their jobs if they were not docile.

NO BLACKS NEED APPLY

Blacks worked in southern turpentine mills and coal mines—dirty, dangerous jobs—and in the most menial factory jobs—sweeping floors, for example. But by custom, most industrial work went to whites. African Americans remained concentrated in agriculture and in low-paying service occupations: domestic servants, waiters, porters, and the like. In 1900 more than 80 percent of the African-American population still lived in the South, most on the land.

The industrial color line, drawn everywhere, was least flexible in the South. When the cotton textile industry moved south toward the end of the century, mill owners drew their workforce from the poor white population. Implicitly, and sometimes explicitly, employees were informed that if they were troublesome (that is, if they complained about wages or hours), the companies would replace them with blacks. Their own racism kept southern mill workers the poorest factory workers in the country. Rather than lose their jobs to the despised blacks, they accepted near-subsistence living with only occasional outbursts of resistance. It was because of the tractability of the southern workforce that the cotton mills had moved from New England to the South.

ORGANIZE!

The majority of workers, most of the time, tacitly accepted the wages they were paid and the hours they had to work. The usual alternative was no job at all. Nevertheless, workers expressed their discontent, desperation, or anger in ways as ancient as civilization. Absenteeism was high, particularly on "Blue Monday" after beery Sunday. In good times, when finding another job was easier, workers needing a holiday for health, sanity, or just plain relaxation quit on a minute's notice. Sabotage was a word yet to be invented, but the practice was well understood. When the pace of work reached the breaking point, or a foreman stepped beyond the bounds of tolerable behavior, it was easy enough to jam or damage a machine so that it could be represented as an accident—and take a break while it was fixed. An angry worker who made up his mind to quit might decide literally to throw a monkey wrench into the works or slash the leather belts that turned the factory's looms, drills, stampers, or lathes.

A HERITAGE OF INDUSTRIAL VIOLENCE

Most, but not all, workplace violence was spontaneous and individual. During the early 1870s, Irish coal miners in northeastern Pennsylvania formed a secret society called the Molly Maguires within a fraternal lodge, the Ancient Order of Hibernians. Knowing the consequences of the campaign of terror they planned, they were few and tight-knit. Only other Mollies knew who members were. They systematically destroyed mine property and murdered supervisors who were exploitative or quick to fire miners.

The frustrated mine owners hired an undercover Irish-American agent, James McParland, from the Pinkerton Agency, a detective bureau that specialized in helping employers to keep their workers in line. Although it took him months of working as a miner and infiltrating the Mollies (dangerous work—he would have been killed if his identity had been discovered) McParland gathered evidence that led to the hanging of nineteen men.

During a nationwide railroad strike in 1877 that had roots in the Panic of 1873, workers by the thousands stormed in mobs into railroad yards and set trains and buildings afire. In a few places they fought pitched gun battles with company guards and, toward the end of the unsuccessful strike, with troops called out to put them down.

At the **Homestead** Works in 1892, Andrew Carnegie's partner, Henry Clay Frick, refused to talk to strikers belonging to the Amalgamated Association of Iron and Steel Workers and told newspapers he would crush the union. Enraged steelworkers and others besieged the giant factory like an army. When Frick brought in 300 armed guards from the Pinkerton Detective Agency on river barges, the strikers attacked them before they could get ashore. Ten were killed before the **Pinkertons** surrendered, whence they were marched to a train that took them out of town. The Homestead strike was war.

THE PULLMAN BOYCOTT

The Pullman Palace Car works just outside Chicago made "bunk-bed" sleeping cars for long-distance trains ("Pullmans") and custom "Palace Cars," luxurious accommodations for millionaires who did not care to sit in public coaches when they traveled. George Pullman, the founder of the company, had built the town of Pullman, Illinois, to house his employees, who were required to live there as a condition of working at the plant.

Until 1894, that requirement had been an attraction. The cottages in Pullman were well-built, and, subsidized by George Pullman, the company town provided a full range of urban services. Pullman was praised as a model paternalistic employer.

However, when the depression of the 1890s caused a decline in Pullman's revenues, the company cut wages by 25 percent but did not reduce rents and utility bills in the town. Some 4,000 employees responded by joining the **American Railway Union** (ARU), a newly formed organization that was rapidly enlisting lower-level railroad workers throughout the Northeast and Midwest. It was headed by Eugene V. Debs, a former fireman who had been disillusioned by both politics and the railway brotherhoods, unions that admitted only the highly skilled and well-paid "aristocracy" of railroad workers: engineers, firemen, and brakemen.

When Pullman's employees went on strike, ARU members working for several of the nation's major railroads voted to support them by boycotting Pullman cars. That is, they refused to hook Pullmans to trains. George Pullman did not sell his sleeping cars to railroads; he retained ownership of the patented cars and rented them. Debs hoped to avoid a conflict with the railroads by keeping the trains running and interfering only with George Pullman's profits.

It did not work. Seeing an opportunity to destroy the ARU before it was strong enough to shut them down, the railroads arranged that U.S. mail cars, which were usually next to the locomotive (they often carried large amounts of money), would be hooked at the end of the train behind the Pullmans. To cut out the Pullmans in railroad yards, the workers had to disconnect the mail cars, push the Pullmans to a sidetrack, and then reconnect the mail cars.

A federal judge defined this as interfering with the U.S. mail and ordered the ARU to desist. Although Illinois Governor John Peter Altgeld protested, blaming the "interference" on the railroads, President Grover Cleveland ordered federal troops into Chicago to crush the boycott. Railroad workers from Oakland, California, to the East Coast went on a rampage, destroying millions in railroad property. Not until mid-July did the trains begin to run again. The ARU was destroyed; Debs was jailed for disobeying the court's order.

THE UNION MAKES US STRONG

Violence, no matter who initiated it, almost always worked to the detriment of industrial workers and to the advantage of employers. Violence alienated middle-class people who might otherwise sympathize with underpaid workers. And violence in labor disputes meant the intervention of the police or even, as in the Pullman boycott, the federal government—on the side of employers.

This was the message of every prominent labor leader who made a mark in the final decades of the late nineteenth century. Workers could force their employers to increase wages or reduce workweeks only by threatening to withdraw their skills or labor, bringing production to a halt. To do this, workers had to organize in unions so that all those who practiced a craft, or every employee in a mill, spoke with one voice.

Delegates to the Knights of Labor national convention in 1886. The Knights were unique among labor organizations in recruiting women and African Americans to the union. The craft unions of the American Federation of Labor had "whites only" provisions in their constitutions.

Unionization was easier for highly skilled craftsmen, the "aristocracy of labor." Their numbers were few, and sharing the same hard-won skills gave them a sense of solidarity. Since medieval times, bakers and carpenters and artisans practicing other trades had organized in guilds. If they were forced to strike to have their demands met, the fact that their employers could not easily replace them gave them an immense and often decisive advantage. That is, if all the brick-layers in a city or all the locomotive engineers on a railroad refused to work, their bosses could not easily dismiss them and hire others to do their highly-skilled work.

The Railway Brotherhoods—of Locomotive Engineers, Locomotive Firemen, and Brakemen—rarely had to go on strike. Having little choice, the railroads met regularly with their representatives and negotiated contracts setting their wages and the number of hours they worked. If building trades unions—of bricklayers, stonemasons, carpenters, and so on—organized all or nearly all members of their craft in a locality, building contractors could not ignore their demands. By the 1870s such skilled workers had organized effective local **crafts unions** in much of the country.

However, skilled craftsmen comprised a small minority of working people in the industrial era. In 1866 William Sylvis, a visionary iron puddler (a man who made iron castings in molds), founded the National Labor Union (NLU), in which he hoped to enlist all industrial workers. He devoted the final three years of his life to traveling—often by foot—throughout the northeastern states, addressing meetings of workers in churches and fraternal lodges.

Sylvis believed that the workers' future depended on political action. He formed alliances with several reform groups, including the woman suffrage movement and farmers' organizations lobbying for cheap currency. The National Labor party put up candidates in the presidential election of 1872 but made so poor a showing that both the party and the NLU folded. From a membership of 400,000 in 1872, the NLU disappeared within two years.

THE KNIGHTS OF LABOR

A different kind of national labor union had already emerged. Organized in 1869 by tailors led by Uriah P. Stephens, the Noble and Holy Order of the Knights of

The Yellow-Dog Contract

Many companies required newly hired employees to sign "yellow-dog contracts" as a condition of starting work. They agreed that "in consideration of my present employment I hereby promise and agree that I will forthwith abandon any and all membership, connection, or affiliation with any organization or society, whether secret or open, which in any way attempts to regulate the conditions of my services or the payment therefore." The penalty for violating the contract (by joining a union) was dismissal.

The yellow-dog contract was effective in discouraging open recruitment by union organizers. It encouraged—it mandated!—that unions work secretly, which could mean a violation of conspiracy laws. If enough of a company workforce to shut a factory down secretly joined a union, the contracts were moot. Their principal purpose was to intimidate.

Good Catholics

James Cardinal Gibbons used several arguments to persuade the pope to overcome his hostility to Catholics fraternizing with Protestants in the Knights of Labor. Gibbons pointed out that while European union activists who were born Catholic were now "misguided and perverted children, looking on their Mother the Church as a hostile stepmother," American Catholics—most of them Irish when Gibbons wrote—were famously devoted to the faith.

One of the most persuasive of Gibbons's arguments was that Catholics were already joining the Knights in such numbers that they dominated the organization in many areas. "It is not in the present case that Catholics are mixed with Protestants," Gibbons wrote, "but rather that Protestants are admitted to the advantages of an association, two-thirds of whose members and the principal officers are Catholics."

Labor spread its message more quietly than Sylvis had. Indeed, the Knights were a secret society at first. Knowing that employers fired union activists, the Knights, when they announced meetings in newspapers, did not reveal their meeting place (that was known to members) or even their name; they identified the group as "******". The Knights of Labor also differed from the NLU in their disinterest in political action as an organization. Members were urged to vote, but Stephens believed that the interests of working people were served by solidarity in the workplace, not at the ballot box.

Some Knights believed in class conflict: irreconcilable differences between producers and parasites—workers and farmers on the one hand, capitalists on the other. But their concept of class lines was not so clear-cut as those drawn by followers of Karl Marx. The Knights barred from membership only saloon keepers, lawyers, and gamblers—parasites, perhaps, but hardly the people who ran industrial America. Stephens himself disliked the idea of class conflict; he looked forward to a day when all men and women of goodwill would abolish the wage system and establish a cooperative commonwealth.

Women were welcome in the Knights; so were African Americans and unskilled workers, who were usually overlooked as union material. However, the Knights had problems appealing to one group that was essential to the success of any American labor organization: Roman Catholics, particularly Irish Americans.

Stephens, a lifelong Mason, had encrusted the Knights of Labor with the mystery, symbolism, ritual, secret handshakes, and other rigmarole of the Masonic Order. And the pope had forbidden Catholics to join the Masons or other secret societies. Many Catholics ignored the ban and joined the Knights; but many more, obeying their priests, refused to join.

ENTER TERENCE POWDERLY

In 1879 Stephens was succeeded as Grand Master Workman by Terence V. Powderly, a Catholic who had joined the Knights. Powderly resolved the conflict between the Knights and the Catholic Church on two fronts. He brought the Knights into the open—no more secrecy—and eliminated or toned down the Masonic flavor of union ceremonies. More important, he persuaded an influential Catholic bishop with working-class sympathies, James Gibbons, to prevail on the pope to remove his prohibition of Catholic membership.

Gibbons succeeded, and the Knights grew at a dazzling rate. With 110,000 members in 1885, the organization claimed 700,000 the next year. Ironically (Powderly opposed strikes), the major impetus for the growth was a victory by the Knights in a strike of Jay Gould's Missouri–Pacific Railroad. Gould had vowed to destroy the union. "I can hire half the working class to kill the other half," he growled. But the Knights closed down the Missouri–Pacific, forcing him to meet with their leaders and agree to their terms.

The dramatic victory and explosive growth of the union proved to be more curse than blessing. Powderly and the union's general assembly were unable to control the new members. Instead of coordinating their activities nationally—the rationale of a national labor organization—they lost control of local leaders, who called strikes, often ill-advised ones, in a dozen locations. Powderly fumed and sputtered and refused to back the rash of strikes in 1885 and 1886. But he could not stop them. Then, in 1886, the Haymarket tragedy (see Chapter 28) was unfairly but effectively imputed to the Knights. Membership plummeted.

SAMUEL GOMPERS AND THE AFL

In the same year as Haymarket, a national labor organization dedicated to union and stability for *some* workers was pieced together by a few dozen existing associations of skilled workers. The American Federation of Labor's (AFL) guiding spirit was a cigar maker born in London of Dutch Jewish parents who emigrated to the United States as a boy.

Samuel Gompers astonished his fellow workers (and their employers) with his intelligence, learning, tough bargaining, and eloquence on the soapbox. He was a homely, even ugly man, squat and thick of body with a broad, coarse-featured face. But this uncomely character had definite ideas about

Labor Day

Today Labor Day means nothing more to anyone than the Monday of the "long weekend" that ends the summer—a day off from school or work as welcome as a day off because of a blizzard, and having no more significance. Until about 1960, it was a day for parades, community picnics, and oratory honoring those who, in the words of one of its founders, "from rude nature have delved and carved all the grandeur we behold." The first Labor Day was celebrated in New York City on September 5, 1882.

In most other industrial nations, labor's holiday is May 1. Curiously, "May Day" also originated in the United States. American unions abandoned it when, in Europe, socialists and then communists made it their annual holiday. Most American unions were not only antisocialist, they were supersensitive to any allusion to socialist sympathies in their practices.

Also, May Day was international; Labor Day was uniquely American.

how labor organizations could not only survive in the United States, but become one of the interlocking institutions that governed the country.

First, Gompers believed that only skilled workers could effectively force employers to negotiate. When bricklayers refused to work, the boss who wanted bricks laid had no choice but to talk. When unskilled hod carriers (men who carried the bricks to the bricklayers) went out on strike, employers had no difficulty in finding others with strong backs and growling stomachs to take their place. Gompers was not without sympathy for hod carriers and other unskilled laborers. But he thought their prospects hopeless. The AFL would admit only skilled workers.

Second, the sole goal of AFL unions was "bread and butter": higher wages, shorter hours, and better working conditions. The National Labor Union and the Knights failed, Gompers believed, because they muddied the workers' interests by mixing them with other reforms. Gompers had no patience with utopian dreamers or socialists. What counted, he said, was the here-and-now, not "pie in the sky." Unions that looked forward to a revolution—peaceful or violent—that would replace capitalism distracted workers from the concrete issues that counted. Moreover, they were easy targets for suppression by bosses, who were able (as in the Haymarket episode) to persuade Americans that labor unions threatened the foundations of society.

Third, although Gompers believed that the strike was the union's best weapon (in that he was more "radical" than Terence Powderly), he made it clear that AFL unions would cooperate with employers who recognized and bargained with them. Make unions partners, he told employers, meaning AFL unions that supported the capitalist system. Their industry would be peaceful and stable; radical anticapitalist unions would wither and die.

FRIENDS OF FRIENDS

Gompers, who lived until 1924, was elected president of the AFL every year but one. With his carrot-and-stick approach

to dealing with employers—striking against those who refused to bargain with the AFL, cooperating with those who accepted unions—he saw the AFL grow from 150,000 members in 1888 to more than a million shortly after the turn of the century.

Most employers, however, continued to hate him and the AFL with the same intensity with which they hated socialists and revolutionary unions. "Can't I do what I want with my own?" Cornelius Vanderbilt had sputtered. The majority of American industrialists believed with him that the wages they paid and the hours their employees worked were no one's business but their own. The worker who did not like his job was free to quit. In 1893 hard-nosed antilabor employers formed the National Association of Manufacturers to fight unions wherever they appeared.

More enlightened manufacturers, led by Frank Easley and Senator Mark Hanna of Ohio, a former Rockefeller associate, concluded that labor unions were a permanent part of American industry. The choice was not between unions and no unions. The choice was (as Gompers had preached for more than a decade) between conservative, procapitalist unions willing to cooperate with employers and desperate, revolutionary unions determined to destroy capitalism. Easley and his associates joined with Gompers in 1900 to form the National Civic Federation. Its purpose was to work for industrial peace through employer–union cooperation.

NATION OF IMMIGRANTS

Increasingly, as the century drew to a close, recent immigrants filled the less skilled jobs in construction, factories, mines, and sweatshops in urban tenements. By 1900, immigrants and their children made up half the population in Philadelphia, Pittsburgh, and Seattle; 60 percent in Buffalo, Detroit, and Minneapolis; and 70 percent in New York, Chicago, and Milwaukee.

THE FLOOD

Immigration had been an intrinsic part of American life from the beginning, of course. The word itself, meaning migration *to* a place, was coined by an American as more appropriate to the United States than *emigration,* movement *from* a place. From 10,000 arrivals in 1825, immigration topped 100,000 in 1845. Except for the first two years of the Civil War, the annual total never dipped below that figure. In 1854 a record 428,000 foreigners stepped ashore. That record fell in 1880, when 457,000 immigrants made landfall in Boston, New York, Philadelphia, Baltimore, New Orleans, and a few smaller ports. Only the crippling depression of the 1890s pushed the annual total below 300,000. For each of six years after the turn of the twentieth century, more than a million people arrived in the United States. On one day in 1907, 11,747 immigrants were processed at a single point of entry, New York's famous Ellis Island. Always a stream, sometimes swollen, immigration became a flood.

Immigration after 1880 differed in character from what had gone before. Before 1880, a large majority of immigrants

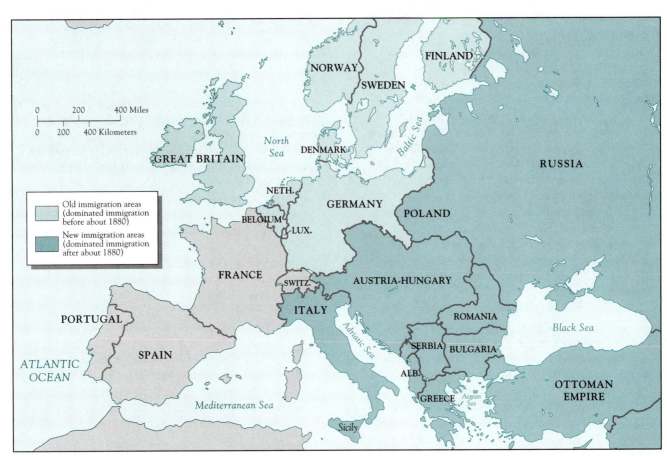

MAP 29:1 European Immigration, 1815–1914

The "old immigrants" originated in northern and western Europe. Only after 1880 did "new immigrants" from southern and eastern Europe begin to come to the United States in large numbers. By 1900 the new immigrants constituted an overwhelming majority of newcomers.

listed the British Isles, Germany, or Scandinavia as their place of birth. Although many of these northern and western Europeans continued to arrive after 1880, an annually increasing proportion of newcomers originated in southern Italy, the Turkish Empire (Turks, Armenians, Bulgarians), Greece, and the Austro-Hungarian Empire (Hungarians, Rumanians, Serbs, Croatians, Slovenes). And from Russia, which then included most of Poland, came both Christian and Jewish Russians, Poles, Lithuanians, Latvians, Estonians, and Finns. From Asia came Japanese.

Before 1880 only about 200,000 people of southern and eastern European origin resided in the United States. Between 1880 and 1910 about 8.4 million arrived. In 1896 this "new immigration" exceeded the "old" for the first time. By 1907 new immigrants were almost the whole of the influx. Of 1,285,349 legal immigrants registered that year, a million began their long journey in southern and eastern Europe.

BIRTH PAINS OF A WORLD ECONOMY

Only parts of Europe, North America, and Japan could be described as "industrialized" in the nineteenth century. However, the effects of the economic and social revolution were felt everywhere but in the remotest cultures. Declining infant mortality and an increase in life expectancy—side effects of technology—resulted in a giant leap in population in agricultural as well as in industrial countries.

World production of foodstuffs soared too, but not uniformly. The biggest gains were made where agriculture was mechanized, as in the United States and Canada. Where peasants with hand tools remained the agricultural workforce, food production lagged behind the increase of population. Peasants growing grain on small parcels of land were undersold in local markets by grain from the American and Canadian prairies. Even a Pole living in Warsaw, at the center of "the granary of eastern Europe," could buy American flour more cheaply than flour milled from grain grown twenty-five miles away.

The bottom fell out of the standard of living in these economic backwaters. During the latter decades of the nineteenth century, southern Italian and Polish farmworkers made between $40 and $60 a year. The cash income of peasants in southern China was too small to be worth calculating. When large landowners in Europe attempted to consolidate and modernize their holdings so they could mechanize American-style, they pushed people off the land even more efficiently than declining incomes did.

Divide and Conquer

A western lumber magnate explained that to have a tractable workforce, an employer should hire from several ethnic groups: "Don't get too great a percentage of any one nationality for your own good, and then mix them up and obliterate clannishness and selfish social prejudices." The reasoning was reminiscent of the Atlantic slave traders' policy of filling a ship with captives from different tribes.

The Jews of the Russian Empire (which included Poland) felt the effects of the worldwide Industrial Revolution in their own way. Forbidden by law to own land, most of them were old-fashioned artisans who handcrafted shoes, clothing, and furniture—anything that might make a kopek. Others were retailers—shopkeepers or wandering peddlers. Both craftsmen and peddlers found their way of life undercut by modernization. The shoes made by a cobbler in a Russian *shtetl* (a Jewish market town) could not compete with cheap, machine-made shoes from England or the United States. The peddler who wandered around Russian Poland trying to sell hats and trousers learned the same lesson.

PROMOTING IMMIGRATION

Industrialists encouraged immigration in various ways. Until the Foran Act of 1885 outlawed the practice, some companies paid immigrants' steamship fares if they signed contracts agreeing to work for their patrons when they arrived in the United States. James J. Hill plastered every sizable town in Sweden with posters describing the richness of the soil along his Great Northern Railroad. (South Dakota got its nickname the "Sunshine State" in such a promotional campaign: One advertisement depicted palm trees swaying in the balmy Dakota breezes.) The American Woolens Company circulated handbills in southern Italy showing a well-dressed immigrant worker with a sleek handlebar mustache carrying a sack of money from the mill to a *banco* across the street. In the West, before 1884, railroaders contracted with Cantonese labor recruiters to import gangs of Chinese "coolies" to do heavy construction work at minuscule wages.

Employers liked immigrant workers because, in general, they accepted lower wages than native-born Americans would and performed menial jobs that Americans shunned. At least at first, immigrants were more docile employees than old-stock Americans. So far from familiar surroundings and customs, they hesitated to complain. Many of them intended to work in America only temporarily—a few months or a few years—and then return to their homelands. They wanted to save; they had little interest in joining a union or going on strike, sacrificing in the short run for the sake of a better life in the long run. For them, the long run was back in Ireland, Italy, or Greece.

Economically, immigrant labor was pure asset. More than 60 percent of arrivals on late nineteenth-century immigrant ships were able-bodied males; the percentage was higher

Going Home

The immigrant ships were not empty when they steamed eastward across the Atlantic. Some carried cargo; most ships that put immigrants ashore in New Orleans were actually designed to haul cotton, which is what they took aboard.

Ships designed specifically to carry passengers returned to Europe with immigrants who had become disillusioned in America. An estimated 370,697 British nationals, mostly Irish, returned during the 1880s. Between 1875 and 1910, 18 percent of Swedish immigrants went home after a year or two. In the depression year of 1875, about half the German immigrants to the United States turned around.

Many Italians were virtual commuters, known as "birds of passage." They shipped to the United States, worked for six months or so, living frugally and saving, then returned to *bell'Italia*, where they and their families lived (frugally) on their earnings until they were gone—whence they commuted once again. After 1900, about one Italian returned to Italy for every three that arrived. Greeks were said to be the most likely to be temporary immigrants. Between 1908 and 1931, about 40 percent of Greek immigrants made the trip back home.

among Italians and Greeks. The "old country" had borne the expense of supporting them during their unproductive childhood years and was still supporting the women and children. In the United States immigrants were producers, pure and simple. It was a profitable arrangement.

ETHNIC AMERICA

In addition to the general pressures at home and the attractions of the United States that influenced all immigrants, some national groups had reasons to leave their ancestral homelands unique to them.

THE IRISH

Immigrants from Great Britain continued to be numerous in the late nineteenth century. Between the Civil War and 1900, 1.9 million of them came to the United States. But they were scarcely noticed as immigrants, in part because they were outnumbered by other national groups and in part because they were more at home in America than immigrants who knew no English.

The story was somewhat different for Irish Catholics, 3.4 million of whom came to the United States between 1845

Irish-American Patriotism

In 1835 John England, the Roman Catholic bishop of Charleston, explained why the Irish took so adeptly to American politics: "The Irish are largely amalgamated with the Americans, their dispositions, their politics, their notions of government; their language and their appearance become American very quickly, and they praise and prefer America to their oppressors at home."

Crossing the Atlantic

The new immigrant's odyssey began with a walk. Most of the people who came to the United States after 1880 were from rural areas far from a seaport or even, for many, a railroad. So they walked—a circumstance that put a stricter limit on the baggage they could carry than did the rules of the steamship companies. Most left with a cheap suitcase or a bundle per person stuffed with clothing; a blanket or down-filled comforter; a treasured keepsake; and sometimes a vial of the soil of the native land that most would never see again.

In Italy they usually walked all the way to the sea: to Genoa in the north, Naples in the south. In Greece, all peninsulas and islands, there would usually be a ferry ride to Piraeus, the port of Athens. From deep within Russia, Lithuania, Poland, and Germany, there would be a train ride. Russians and Poles tried to get to a German port, Bremen or Hamburg. While the czarist government gave both Christians and Jews excellent reasons to leave, it did not help emigrants; German steamship lines built "villages" where emigrants could live while they waited for a ship with room for them.

Tickets were cheap. By the 1890s, heated competition among steamship companies for passengers in steerage (the lowest class of accommodation) pushed the price of

The dining hall at Ellis Island, the most important port of entry for new immigrants. The diners here, of many ethnic groups, would have found the food unfamiliar and perhaps disagreeable. But their chief concern would have been the fact that their entrance to New York City had been delayed for some reason. Immigrants that passed quickly through Ellis Island did not pause to have a meal.

AP/Wide World Photos

transatlantic passage below $20. There were humiliating but important ceremonies on departure day: a rude bath and fumigation for lice, and a close examination by company doctors for contagious diseases (especially tuberculosis), insanity, feeble-mindedness, and trachoma, an inflammation of the eye that leads to blindness and was endemic in Italy and Greece. The United States refused entry to anyone with those diseases, and the ship that brought them over was required to take them back. With paying passengers or a cargo waiting in America for transportation to Europe, captains took care to minimize rejects who would take up space without paying.

The immigrants were crowded in steerage: "It is a congestion so intense, so injurious to the health and morals that there is nothing on land to equal it!" (Emigrating by steamship, however, was not nearly the ordeal it had been during the age of sail.) Large steamships carried as many as a thousand steerage passengers. There were no cabins for emigrants until after 1905; rather, there were large dormitories formed by bulkheads in the hull. Men and women slept in separate compartments; families united only during the

and 1900. Almost all of them spoke English, but they were considered outsiders because of their Catholic religion. The Know-Nothings were gone even before the Civil War; but in 1887 organized anti-Catholicism was revived with the formation of the American Protective Association (APA). Strongest in the Midwest, the APA was on its face a missionary movement; its members swore an oath to "strike the shackles and chains of blind obedience" to the pope from the benighted Catholics. Politically, the APA successfully opposed government financial assistance to Catholic schools.

Informally, the organization encouraged employers to discriminate against Irish Catholics. Newspaper advertisements for jobs commonly ended with **"NINA"**—"No Irish Need

Apply"—as did "Help Wanted" notices in shop windows and even on some factory gates. Anti-Irish prejudice was respectable among the genteel northeastern Republicans who were among the last to resist the oppression of African Americans in the South. People who disapproved of demeaning cartoon stereotypes of blacks were not disturbed by the chimpanzee faces Republican cartoonists employed to identify Irish thugs, maids, and respectable workingmen alike.

Yet Irish Americans took zestfully to America. Sufficiently numerous to insulate their personal lives from prejudice, the Irish parlayed their cohesive sociability and eloquence into a formidable political force. By the time of the Civil War, the Democratic party organizations in heavily Irish cities like

day. Bickering and fistfights were common, although there was not much sexual depredation; there was no privacy! Except when the weather was bad, almost everyone preferred sitting on the open deck to huddling in the hold.

Cooking was prohibited, except the brewing of tea on the open deck. Meals, included in the price of passage (another change from sailing ships), were unsurprisingly cheap, simple, and not very good. (The German and Italian governments tried to regulate the quality of food and cookery.) Meals were taken in shifts: The final breakfast shift was followed immediately by the first dinner shift. Even when meals were decent and prepared in sanitary galleys, the ship's galley could not please every ethnic group's preferences. Immigrant manuals recommended smuggling familiar sausages or cheeses on board, although that was forbidden by most steamship companies.

Between meals the immigrants chatted, sewed, played games, sang, danced, studied English, and read and reread manuals and letters from friends and relatives who were already in the United States. Days could be interminable, but the voyage was not long. Depending on the port of embarkation and the size of the ship, it took from eight days to two weeks to arrive in New York, the chief port of entry.

Actually, a steamer arriving at the same time as others might lie at anchor for almost as long as it had taken to cross the Atlantic. In 1892 the U.S. Immigration Service opened a facility designed specifically for the rapid "processing" of newcomers on Ellis Island, a landfill site in New York Harbor that had been an arsenal. Laid out so a stream of immigrants would flow in controlled lines through corridors and examination rooms to be inspected by physicians, nurses, and officials, Ellis Island, its architects boasted, could handle 8,000 people a day. Fifteen thousand immigrants passed through on some days.

Ellis Island was an experience few immigrants forgot. Crowds milled about and shoved for position before they entered the maze of pipe railings that took them from station to station. Instructions were boomed over loudspeakers in half a dozen languages; infants wailed, anxious parents called for their lost children. The first person to examine the immigrants was a doctor expected to make an instant diagnosis of afflictions for which the newcomers might be denied entry. If he saw a facial rash, he marked a large *F* on the immigrant's clothing with a piece of soft white chalk. People so marked were cut out of the queue and examined more closely. *H* meant suspected heart disease; *L* meant a limp and examination for rickets (children were made to do a little dance); and a circle around an *X* meant feeble-mindedness and immediate return to the ship.

Those who were not chalked were examined for trachoma by a specialist and then interviewed by an immigration officer. Everyone was prepared for the trick question "Do you have a job waiting for you?" Immigrant manuals cautioned in capital letters *NOT* to reply in the affirmative. The Foran Contract Labor Law of 1885 forbade making agreements to work before arriving. Previously, labor contractors had impressed immigrants into jobs under virtually slavelike conditions.

About 80 percent of those who entered Ellis Island were given landing cards that let them board ferries to the Battery, the southern tip of Manhattan Island. The U.S. government was through with them. Now a horde of hustlers who made their living by offering "services" took charge. Again in a babel of languages, previously arrived countrymen shouted that they could offer jobs, provide train tickets, change currency, recommend an excellent boardinghouse. Some (not many) were honest. Every large ethnic group in the United States eventually founded aid societies to provide newcomers with such services, protecting them from being swindled within hours of their arrival in the land of opportunity.

Boston and New York were catering to the interests of the Irish community and reaping the reward of an almost unanimous Irish vote. By the 1880s, Irish immigrants and Irish Americans dominated urban politics in parts of the East and Midwest and in San Francisco. Ironically, it was their considerable power on the West Coast that led to the first American anti-immigrant legislation since the Alien Acts of 1797.

GUESTS OF THE GOLDEN MOUNTAIN

In 1849 seamen brought the news to the Chinese port of Canton that a "Mountain of Gold" had been discovered in California. In a country plagued by overpopulation, flood, famine, epidemic disease, and regional tyrants, the southern Chinese listened avidly to the usual distortions of life across the ocean. "Americans are a very rich people," one promoter explained. "They want the Chinaman to come and will make him welcome."

By the time the Chinese arrived in large numbers, California's rich placer mines were exhausted. Accustomed to working communally at home, they scraped out a living in diggings Caucasians had abandoned as not worth working. Some found employment in menial, low-paying work that few whites were willing to do, as cooks, gardeners, stable hands, and domestic servants. The "Chinese laundry" was so ubiquitous in western towns as to be a fixture, as were, soon enough, cheap Chinese restaurants.

By 1860 there were 35,000 Chinese living in California, almost all of them men who hoped to return to China. There were only 1,800 Chinese women in the state, all but a few of them prostitutes who had, effectively, been "purchased" from their parents. In San Francisco, Sacramento, and Marysville, lively Chinatowns flourished.

Race and a radically different culture kept the Chinese separate. "When I got to San Francisco," wrote Lee Chew, later a wealthy businessman, "I was half-starved because I was afraid to eat the provisions of the barbarians. But a few days living in the Chinese Quarter and I was happy again." Leaders of the Gum Shan Hok—the Guests of the Golden Mountain—encouraged the immigrants to stick to themselves. "We are accustomed to an orderly society," explained a leader of San Francisco's Chinatown, "but it seems as if the Americans are not bound by rules of conduct. It is best, if possible, to avoid any contact with them."

When the construction of the transcontinental railroad began in 1864, Chinese immigration increased. Whereas 3,000 to 6,000 Chinese had entered California each year, after 1868 the annual immigration jumped to 23,000.

KEEPING JOHN CHINAMAN OUT

As long as there was plenty of work in the West, hostility to the Chinese was restrained. In 1873, however, the depression reached California, bringing widespread unemployment. The Chinese were natural targets. In 1877, when the Chinese constituted 17 percent of California's population, a San Francisco teamster named Denis Kearney discovered he had a knack for oratory. On the city's "sandlots"—the local name for empty properties—he blamed the joblessness among his audiences on the willingness of the Chinese to work for less than an American needed to survive. From inflammatory rhetoric, Kearney moved on to leading rampages through

The Chinese were not despised everywhere in the West. In John Day in eastern Oregon, between 800 and 900 Chinese lived peacefully, even cordially, among their white neighbors for decades. Ing Hay was an herbalist many whites "swore by," preferring him to medical doctors. When local physicians tried to prosecute him for practicing medicine, the county prosecutor told them he could not find a jury that would convict him. Lung On got quite rich from a number of enterprises. Ing Hay thought he got along too well with white women of the town; he scolded Lung On harshly for sleeping with them. Not unreasonably, Ing Hay feared that if he were caught, the entire Chinese community would suffer. Markee Tom, shown here, was a cowboy who rode and lived with white cowboys as an equal. In fact, he was highly esteemed for his skills. He joked that he was "an Oriental barbarian."

From the collections of the Kam Wah Chung Museum, Oregon Parks & Recreation Department

San Francisco's large Chinatown, and the violence spread. Once-sizable Chinatowns in Oroville and Marysville disappeared when white mobs literally drove the Chinese out. As late as 1885, an anti-Chinese pogrom in Rock Springs, Wyoming, left twenty-eight Chinese dead.

The violence begat political action. In 1882, led by Californians, Congress choked off Chinese immigration in the Chinese Exclusion Act. There were a few loopholes. Immigrants who could pass themselves off as students were admitted. A few hundred Chinese women entered the country legally each year to become wives of Gum Shan Hok already in the country. Illegal immigration continued via Canada and Mexico (its size is impossible to determine). Otherwise, the Chinese-American community was cut off from China as well as within the United States. Chronologically, the Chinese were old immigrants; culturally and racially, they were more alien to American society than newer immigrants.

In small numbers, Japanese replaced the Chinese on the West Coast, especially as farmworkers. They began to trickle in after the Exclusion Act, often via Hawaii, where Japanese were already the backbone of the agricultural labor force. Paradoxically, Caucasians resented them not because they were docile in accepting substandard wages, but because the Japanese were ambitious to own land, and many of them prospered.

GERMANS

Today more Americans have German ancestors than have English ancestors. The immigration of Germans was constant for 200 years beginning in the early 1700s. After 1848, however, there was a political dimension to the German influx. The failure of a series of liberal revolutions in several German states—revolutions aimed at establishing American-style democracy and individual rights—forced many leading German liberals into exile. The most famous of them to come to the United States was Carl Schurz, who became a senator from Missouri, a leading liberal Republican, and a member of Rutherford B. Hayes's cabinet.

Many of the 4.4 million anonymous Germans who came to the United States in the second half of the nineteenth century, an average of about 100,000 a year, were impelled by fears that their lives were deteriorating under the German Empire, which was established in 1871. German Catholics, in particular, fled the *Kulturkampf,* the anti-Catholic campaign of the German Chancellor Otto von Bismarck.

Because many had owned land in Germany, German immigrants were generally better off than other immigrants of the period. While some settled in northeastern cities, the majority moved to the upper Midwest, where they developed farms. Wisconsin became heavily German in the late nineteenth century. By 1900 more Milwaukeeans spoke German as their first language than spoke English. Nationally, about 800 German-language newspapers were being published in 1900.

ADAPTING BY RE-CREATING

Like the Germans, Scandinavians tended to become farmers in the United States. Norwegians predominated in many counties in Wisconsin and Minnesota. Swedes were numerous in Minnesota and in the Pacific Northwest. Finns, who speak a different language than Swedes but were historically tied to them, were conspicuous in Swedish regions and elsewhere such as the logging areas of the Midwest and Northwest and in the iron mines of the Mesabi Range.

Ethnic groups that predominated over large areas found adaptation to the New World comparatively easy because they could approximate familiar Old World ways. They founded schools taught in their native languages, newspapers and other periodicals, and European-style fraternal organizations (the Germans' athletically oriented *Turnverein* and the Norwegians' musical Grieg Societies). They continued to eat familiar foods and raise their children by traditional rules. They were numerous enough to deal with the larger society from a position of strength.

The problems that these immigrants faced were common to all settlers of new lands in the West. Olë Rolvaag, a gloomy Norwegian-American writer, focused on the loneliness of life on the northern prairies, an experience shared by all pioneers; he did not write much about cultural alienation because Norwegian Americans did not feel it.

SEPHARDIC AND GERMAN JEWS

Other immigrant groups had a comparatively easy time adapting because they were few and therefore threatened no one. Sephardic Jews (Jews descended from the Jews expelled from Spain and Portugal in the 1490s) came in small numbers to the United States. Generally educated, sophisticated, and often well-fixed, they eased into middle- and even upper-class society before the Civil War, particularly in Rhode Island, New York, Charleston, and New Orleans. Considering their few numbers, they contributed a remarkable number of prominent citizens. Jefferson Davis's strongest political ally in the Confederacy was Judah P. Benjamin, a Sephardic Jew. Supreme Court Justice Benjamin Cardozo had Sephardic ancestry, as did twentieth-century financier and presidential adviser Bernard Baruch of South Carolina.

By 1880 there was a German Jewish community in the United States, perhaps 150,000 strong. Most were small-scale tradesmen or businessmen; rare was the southern town without its Jewish-owned dry goods store. Some German Jews, such as Levi Strauss, pioneered in the American ready-made clothing industry. In New York, Jews dominated the business—Germans running it, Jews from eastern Europe working in it. The Guggenheim syndicate, mostly Jewish at the top, was one of the nation's leading owners of metal mines by the turn of the century. Three of the nation's most important banks in the middle of the century were owned by German Jews; all but one, Kuhn-Loeb, were in decline by 1900, in part because of anti-Semitism in the banking establishment.

German Jews clung to their Jewish identity but quickly adopted American mores and customs. Led by Rabbi Isaac Mayer Wise of Cincinnati, German-American Jews founded Reform Judaism, which abandoned dietary laws and other observances that they regarded as archaic and that somewhat

Hold Fast!

Some immigrants may have believed that American streets were paved with gold, but not many. There is no hint that the United States offered an easy life in an immigrants' manual of 1891, although it certainly promised opportunity:

Hold fast, this is most necessary in America. Forget your past, your customs, and your ideals. Select a goal and pursue it with all your might. No matter what happens to you, hold on. You will experience a bad time, but sooner or later you will achieve your goal.

isolated them from mainstream American culture, which the German Jews embraced.

THE NEW IMMIGRATION

Adapting to America was more difficult for the new immigrants who began to arrive in large numbers after 1880. Like the Irish, unlike the Germans and British, most southern and eastern Europeans were next to penniless when they stepped off the boat. More of them were illiterate than the old immigrants had been. And their Old World experience in peasant villages and *shtetls* did not prepare them for life in the world's greatest industrial nation during its era of frenzied development.

However serious the immigrants' reasons for leaving ancestral homes, those homes were still ancestral, the rhythms of life familiar, and the customs second nature. Wherever their origins, the new immigrants were accustomed to a traditional way of life that was the antithesis of life in the United States. In the United States, they were members of a minority, one of many.

Strangest of all for people who came from traditional, preindustrial cultures where life was regulated and slowed by the seasons, the weather, and the use of hand tools, American life was regulated and rushed by the tyrannical clock and powered by the relentless churning of the dynamo. In the industrial society of the late nineteenth century, Americans were even more driven than they had been when Alexis de Tocqueville's head was set spinning by the American pace. This was particularly true in the big cities where a majority of the new immigrants settled and which, in the minds of other Americans, were intimately associated with the newcomers.

FURTHER READING

Immigration Thomas J. Archdeacon, *Becoming American*, 1983; John Bodnar, *The Transplanted: A History of Immigration*, 1985; Roger Daniels, *Coming to America: A History of Immigration and Ethnicity in American Life*, 2002; Leonard Dinnerstein and David Reimers, *Ethnic Americans: A History of Immigration and Assimilation*, 1975; Donna Gabaccia, *From the Other Side: Women, Gender, and Immigrant Life in the U.S., 1820–1990*, 1994; Matthew F. Jacobson, *Whiteness of a Different Color: European Americans and the Alchemy of Race*, 1998; David R. Roediger, *Working Toward Whiteness: How America's Immigrants Became White*, 2005.

Industrial Workers David Brody, *Workers in Industrial America*, 1979; Melvyn Dubofsky, *Industrialism and the American Worker, 1865–1920*, 1975; Foster R. Dulles and Melvyn Dubofsky, *Labor in America*, 1984; Herbert G. Gutman, *Work, Culture, and Society in Industrializing America*, 1976, and *Power and Culture: Essays on the American Working Class*, 1987; Alice Kessler-Harris, *Out to Work: A History of Wage-Earning Women in the United States*, 1982; Paul Krause, *The Battle for Homestead, 1880–1892*, 1992; Harold C. Livesay, *Samuel Gompers and the Origins of the American Federation of Labor*, 1978; David Montgomery, *The Fall of the House of Labor, 1865–1929*, 1987, and *Workers' Control in America: Studies in the History of Work, Technology, and Labor Struggle*, 1979; Daniel Nelson, *Managers and Workers: Origins of the New Factory System in the United States, 1880–1920*, 1975.

National Groups Dino Cinel, *From Italy to San Francisco: The Immigrant Experience*, 1982; Steven P. Erie, *Rainbow's End: Irish Americans and the Dilemmas of Urban Machine Politics, 1840–1945*, 1988; John Gjerde, *From Peasants to Farmers: The Migration from Norway to the Upper Middle West*, 1985; John Higham, *Send These to Me: Jews and Other Immigrants in Urban America*, 1975; Irving Howe, *World of Our Fathers: The Journey of the East European Jews to America and the Life They Made*, 1976; Thomas Kessner, *The Golden Door: Italian and Jewish Mobility in New York City, 1880–1915*, 1977; Erika Lee, *At America's Gates: Chinese Immigration During the Exclusion Era, 1882–1943*, 2003; Kerby A. Miller, *Emigrants and Exiles: Ireland and the Irish Exodus to North America*, 1985; Ronald Takaki, *Strangers from a Different Shore: A History of Asian Americans*, 1989; Donald Weber, *Haunted in the New World: Jewish-American Culture from Cahan to the Goldbergs*, 2005.

KEY TERMS

The following terms are covered in this chapter and can also be found in the list of Key Terms at the back of the book.

American Railway Union	**Homestead**	**"NINA"**	**Samuel Gompers**
crafts unions	**"new immigrants"**	**Pinkertons**	

ONLINE SOURCES GUIDE

Use this listing to find online documents, images, interactive maps, simulations, and other resources related to this chapter:

American History Resource Center
http://history.wadsworth.com/rc/us

Selected Documents
Terence Powderly's "Thirty Years of Labor"
Andrew Carnegie's essay "Wealth"
Samuel Gompers's congressional testimony regarding AFL unions

Selected Images
Terence V. Powderly of the Knights of Labor
Samuel Gompers, American Federation of Labor
Carnegie steel mill, Homestead, Pennsylvania

Interactive Time Line (with online readings)
We Who Built America: Factories and Immigrants

CHAPTER 30

Urban America

The Growth of Big Cities and Big City Problems

© Bettmann/Corbis

The mobs of great cities add just so much to the support of pure government as sores do to the strength of the human body.

Thomas Jefferson

I have an affection for a great city. I feel safe in the neighborhood of man, and enjoy the sweet security of streets.

Henry Wadsworth Longfellow

Once in the United States, the new immigrants discovered that they were exotics. Old-stock Protestants who had grown accustomed to the restrained Roman Catholic worship of the Irish and the Germans were set aback by the mysticism of the Catholic Poles and the noisy public ceremonies of the Italians. Indeed, Irish-American bishops were troubled by the "paganism" implicit in the magnificently bedecked statues of the Madonna and the gory, surrealistic depictions of the crucified Christ that peasants from Sicily and the Campania carried through the streets of "Little Italy" accompanied by the music of brass bands. The Orthodox ceremonies of the Greeks, Russians, Ukrainians, and Balkan immigrants were equally strange. The Jews and the Chinese were not even Christian and therefore were all the more alien to American traditions.

The newcomers looked different. Most of the Greeks, Armenians, Assyrians, Lebanese, and Italians were swarthy, a formidable handicap in a nation that drew a sharp color line. Polish women arrived clad in the colorful babushkas, aprons, and billowing ground-length skirts of the eastern European peasant. The Russian Jews dressed drably enough for American tastes, but the men never removed their hats. The Saturday Sabbath attracted attention not so much because the Jews disappeared from the streets but because they turned Sunday into a combination holiday and market day, offending the Sabbatarian sensibilities of some Protestants.

CITIES AS ALIEN ENCLAVES

In a novel of 1890, *A Hazard of New Fortunes,* William Dean Howells sent Basil March, a genteel middle-class American, on a ride on an elevated train in New York City. March "found the variety of people in the car as unfailingly entertaining as ever," but he also felt like a foreigner. Even the Irish, who ran the city, were outnumbered by "the people of Germanic, of Slavonic, of Pelagic [Mediterranean], of Mongolian stock. . . . The small eyes, the high cheeks, the broad noses, the puff lips, the bare, cue-filleted skulls, of Russians, Poles, Czechs, Chinese, the furtive glitter of Italians, the blonde dullness of Germans; the cold quiet of Scandinavians—fire under ice—were aspects that he identified, and that gave him abundant suggestion for the . . . reveries in which he dealt with the future economy of our heterogeneous commonwealth."

A PATCHWORK QUILT
Big cities, particularly in the Northeast and Midwest, where 80 percent of the new immigrants settled, seemed to be salients in the hands of invading armies. By 1890 one-third of the population of Boston and Chicago had been born abroad, as well as one-quarter of Philadelphia's people. When the immigrants' children, who seemed to old-stock Americans to be as stubbornly foreign as their parents, were added to this total, the anxiety of Americans like Basil March are easy to understand.

In fact, the immigrants threatened no one. Ethnic groups clustered together in **ghettos** that were exclusively their own. A map of New York, wrote journalist Jacob Riis, himself a Danish immigrant, "colored to designate nationalities, would show more stripes than the skin of a zebra and more colors than the rainbow." Jane Addams sketched a similar patchwork in the poor part of Chicago where she established Hull House—a **settlement house**, a privately funded institution providing social services to immigrants. The same was true of most large eastern and midwestern cities and of many smaller industrial towns. In Lawrence, Massachusetts, a woolens manufacturing town, more than twenty languages and probably twice that many dialects were spoken.

There were ghettos within ghettos. In New York City's Greenwich Village, an Italian community at the turn of the century, people from the region of Calabria effectively monopolized housing on some streets, immigrants from Sicily on others. On such regional blocks, Italians from a single village were sometimes the sole occupants of an "Agrigento tenement," and so on. Grocery stores and restaurants advertised themselves not as "Italian" but as purveyors of Campanian or Apulian food. Italian priests frequently ministered to the same people whom they had known back in Italy; Italian lawyers represented the same clients.

The same held true for Jewish neighborhoods, where Galician Jews (Galicia was a province of Russian Poland) looked with some wariness on Jews from Russia proper. (Each group named its "Chief Rabbi of New York.") Rumanian Jews fastidiously set up their own communities. Assimilated and well-established German Jews contributed to societies formed to help the new immigrants but remained aloof from them. Christian Germans divided on Lutheran and Catholic lines, Serbs and Croatians because the latter wrote their common language in the Latin alphabet, the Serbs in the Cyrillic (Russian) alphabet.

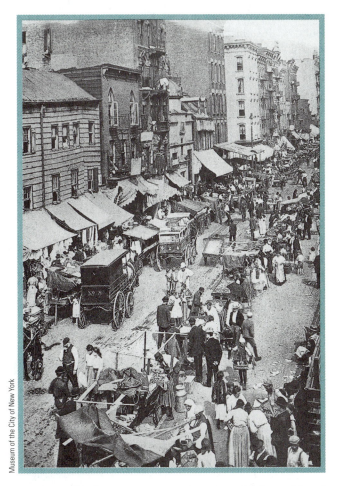

Museum of the City of New York

New York's Hester Street was a major commercial thoroughfare of New York City's largest Jewish neighborhood, the Lower East Side of Manhattan Island. The ground floor of every building was a shop; stalls lined the sidewalks, pushcarts the curbs. Similar streets, just as bustling, were found in every ethnic ghetto in all the major cities.

Protesting Progressive Education

As they do today, well-meaning middle-class Americans devised programs to help immigrants. Also like today, their plans did not always suit the people for whom they were drawn up. An Italian woman's objection, about 1920, to the permissive "child-oriented" approach to education in the public school in New York that her children attended might easily have been lodged last week by a Mexican mother in Los Angeles.

> The program of that school is suited to the children of well-to-do homes, not to our children. We send our children to school for what we cannot give them ourselves, grammar and drill. . . . We do not send children to school for group activity; they get plenty of that in the street.

Double Standard

The British writer Rudyard Kipling commented on American (and Irish-American) prejudice against immigrants when visiting San Francisco in 1889:

> The Chinaman waylays his adversary and methodically chops him to pieces with a hatchet. Then the Press roar about the brutal ferocity of the Pagan. The Italian reconstructs his friend with a long knife. The press complain of the waywardness of the alien. The Irishman and the native Californian in the hours of discontent use the revolver, not once but six times. The press records the fact and asks in the next column whether the world can parallel the progress of San Francisco.

ASSIMILATION

The desire to assimilate, to become "American," varied in intensity from group to group. Some immigrants found solace in the familiar language, customs, foods, and fellowship of "Little Italy" or "Warsaw Town." The ethnic ghetto was a buffer against the prejudices of old-stock Americans and the hostility of other ethnic groups with whom its inhabitants competed for low-level jobs. In 1920, just 25 percent of foreign-born Italians and Poles in the United States were naturalized citizens, only 17 percent of the Greeks.

Other immigrants—usually those who came to America as children—seized on American ways with enthusiasm. Nowhere was the contrast between those who clung to the old and those who embraced the new plainer than in the huge Jewish community of New York's Lower East Side. Families were often battlegrounds between those who tried to preserve *shtetl* customs in tiny apartments and sophisticated children, for whom America was the "Promised Land" and old country ways were for foolish "greenhorns."

Hard work in menial jobs was the lot of almost all immigrants at first. For some, however, economic and social advancement came quickly. Pushcart peddlers saved meager earnings and rented stores; a few who picked the right business and worked at it became well-to-do merchants. The urban political machine had room near the top for anyone who could deliver votes; it provided an avenue of advancement for those who recognized the opportunities politics provided—a considerable intellectual leap for people who came from countries where they had no say in government.

Others pursued success through careers in areas that were not quite respectable and, therefore, unattractive to members of established social groups—show business, professional sports, and organized crime (illegal business). A roster of surnames of leading entertainers, boxers, baseball players, and gangsters over the decades resembles the strata of a canyon, each layer dominated by members of a new, aspiring ethnic group. By 1920 the film industry—"Hollywood"—was dominated by foreign-born Jews, almost all of whom got started in the business by making the small investment required to open nickelodeons, the first movie houses, which were often just shops filled with folding chairs and a hand-cranked projector.

IMMIGRANT AID INSTITUTIONS

Ethnic groups established their own institutions to assist *paesani* and *landsmen*—their countrymen—in adjusting to America. Some immigrant aid societies encouraged assimilation, some clannishness. German Jewish families that were

Cities 1865–1900

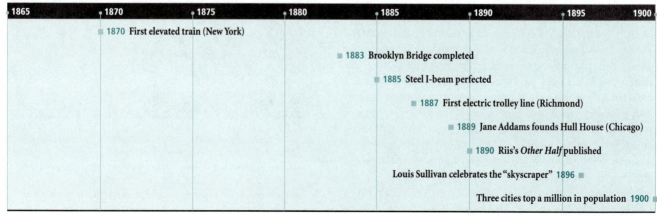

| 1865 | 1870 | 1875 | 1880 | 1885 | 1890 | 1895 | 1900 |

1870 First elevated train (New York)

1883 Brooklyn Bridge completed

1885 Steel I-beam perfected

1887 First electric trolley line (Richmond)

1889 Jane Addams founds Hull House (Chicago)

1890 Riis's *Other Half* published

Louis Sullivan celebrates the "skyscraper" 1896

Three cities top a million in population 1900

comfortably established in the United States were often dismayed by the customs of eastern European Jews, which they found disagreeable. But they nevertheless founded the Hebrew Immigrant Aid Society to minister to the needs of the poor. The Young Men's and Young Women's Hebrew Associations dated back to 1854, but they expanded in size several times over during the final decade of the century.

Among the Catholic population, which grew from 6 million in 1880 to 10 million in 1900 (making Roman Catholicism the country's largest single denomination), religious orders like the Franciscans and the Sisters of Mercy established hospitals and houses of refuge in the slums. The St. Vincent de Paul Society functioned much like the Protestant Salvation Army without the military trappings, providing food, clothing, and shelter for the desperate.

American Catholic bishops were torn between serving as an agency of assimilation and maintaining the loyalty of new immigrants who clung to their religion as part of their old country culture. The bishops, mostly Irish Americans, encouraged a "fortress" mentality among new immigrants—a defensiveness toward the dominant Protestant culture.

Reluctantly at first, the bishops approved of organizing some parishes on national lines rather than, as was traditional, geographically. In part because of the hostility of old immigrant Irish Catholics and Germans to the new immigrants (they remained in "territorial" parishes) and in part to retain the loyalty of new immigrant Catholics by providing services in their languages, two parish systems existed side by side. In one square mile around Chicago's stockyards, there were two "Irish" (territorial) Catholic churches, two Polish churches, and a Lithuanian, Italian, German, Croatian, Czech, and Slovak church.

SETTLEMENT HOUSES

Old-stock Americans created the settlement house, patterned after Toynbee Hall in a notorious London slum, to help immigrants come to terms with their new country.

During the 1880s, a number of middle-class Americans, imbued with the New England communitarian conscience that dictated concern for others, traveled to England to learn how Toynbee worked. They found that the house provided food and drink to the destitute, as traditional charities had—but also child care for employed mothers, recreational facilities, and courses of study in everything from household arts and the English language to social skills needed for advancement in society. The mostly young men and women who worked at Toynbee Hall also told the Americans that they had been morally elevated by their sacrifices and exposure to a misery they had not known in their own lives.

The first American settlement house was the Neighborhood Guild, set up in New York City in 1886. More famous, however, because of the powerful personalities of their

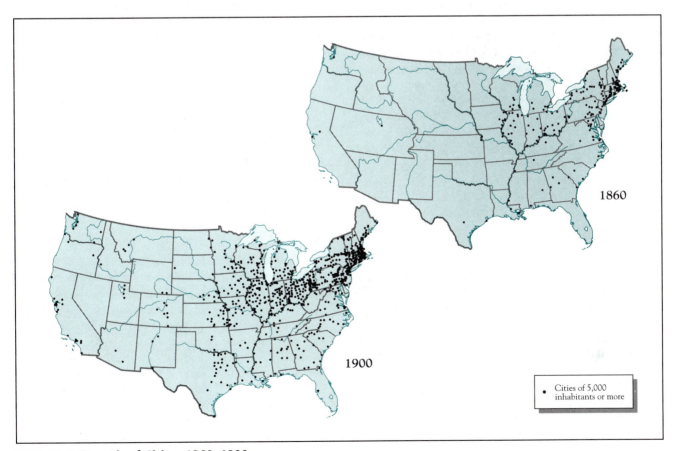

MAP 30:1 Growth of Cities, 1860–1900
In 1860 urbanization was largely a northeastern phenomenon. By 1900 the South and West were also home to many cities, several of them quite large.

founders, were Jane Addams's Hull House in Chicago (1889), Robert A. Woods's South End House in Boston (1892), and Lillian Wald's Henry Street Settlement in New York (1893). From comfortable middle-class backgrounds, well educated, and finely mannered, Addams, Woods, and Wald were exemplars of the middle class morally discomfited by the selfish materialism of their culture. Alleviating the deprivations of poor city dwellers was a way to alleviate their own spiritual unease. Hull House and several other settlements were patriotic, but also celebrated the cultural diversity the immigrants brought to the country. They promoted programs in which different ethnic groups showed off their native costumes and cookery.

OF THE GROWTH OF GREAT CITIES

Many Americans (although certainly not all) had an ingrained prejudice against cities dating back to Thomas Jefferson, who was pathological on the subject. Nevertheless, by the end of the nineteenth century, the United States was one of the world's most urbanized countries. The proportion of city dwellers in the total population, the number of cities, and the size of cities all increased faster in the United States than in any other country.

In 1790, when the first national census was taken, only 3.4 percent of Americans lived in towns of 8,000 people or more. By 1860, the eve of the Civil War, 16 percent of the population was urban, and by 1900, 33 percent. Even more striking was the increase in the number of cities. In 1790, only 6 American cities boasted populations of 8,000 or more. The largest of them, Philadelphia, was home to 42,000 people. In 1860, 141 municipalities had at least 8,000 people within their limits; by 1890, 448 did, and by 1910, 778! Fully 26 cities were larger than 100,000 in 1900, and 6 of them topped 500,000. Philadelphia counted 1.3 million people at the turn of the century and, at that, was third in size behind New York and Chicago.

FROM COUNTRY TO CITY

The immigrant flood was largely responsible for the runaway growth of cities. However, native-born Americans also moved to the cities from the country in great numbers. Chagrined at the isolation of farm life, ground down by the heavy labor, and, by the 1880s, discouraged by a slow but steady decline in farm income, they were lured by jobs for the literate and mechanically inclined that paid well. Or they visited a big city and were dazzled by the bright lights, the abundance of company, the stimulation of a world in constant motion, and the tales of the fortunes that might be made in business.

Parents, rural ministers, and editors of farm magazines begged, threatened, and cajoled in an effort to keep the children of the soil at home, but their efforts met limited success. A former farm girl told Frederick Law Olmstead, "If I were offered a deed to the best farm on condition of going back to the country to live, I would not take it. I would rather face starvation in town."

While the number of farm families increased during the late nineteenth century, the proportion of farmers in the total population declined; in some regions even the numbers of farm people dropped. During the 1880s more than half the rural townships of Iowa and Illinois declined in population while nearby Chicago underwent its fabulous growth. In New England, while the overall population of the region increased by 20 percent, three rural townships in five lost people to Boston, New York, and the dozens of mill towns that lined the region's rivers.

For the most part, the American migration from farm to city was a white migration. Only 12 percent of the 5 million blacks in the United States in 1890 lived in cities, most in the South. Nevertheless, about 500,000 blacks moved from the rural South to the urban North during the final decade of the century, foreshadowing one of the most significant population movements of the twentieth century.

METROPOLIS

Although rapid growth was the rule in cities large and small, the most dramatic phenomenon of American urbanization in the late nineteenth century was the emergence of the metropolises—the six cities of more than 500,000 people that dominated their regions like imperial capitals. Philadelphia doubled in size between 1860 and 1900. New York, with 33,000 people in 1790 and over 1 million in 1860, quadrupled its numbers until by 1900, after it combined with Brooklyn, 4.8 million lived within its five boroughs. New York was the second largest city in the world, smaller only than London.

Chicago's crazy rate of growth as the hub of the nation's railroad system amazed Americans and foreigners alike. With only a few more than 100,000 souls in 1860, Chicago increased its size twenty times in a generation, numbering 2.2 million inhabitants in 1900.

THE "WALKING" CITY

Before the 1870s, cities so populous were unimaginable. When the mass of a city's people moved around by foot or in horse-drawn conveyances, city growth was limited in area to a radius of a mile or two—the distance workers could walk to their jobs, bosses to their offices, and housekeepers to market. The well-to-do owned horses and carriages, but a working horse moved only a little faster than a pedestrian and more slowly when the streets were choked with people wending to and fro, with other horses and wagons lined up ahead.

With transportation so major a consideration in the walking city, the most desirable neighborhood was centrally located. With a twelve-hour day to work, there was little time for commuting. Lots were as narrow as twenty feet, even where the wealthy lived. Most streets were narrow; only thoroughfares were broad enough for three or four wagons to proceed side by side in two directions. Space was rarely wasted on open places; parks were few.

Except for those on the very bottom, the social classes of the walking city lived in close proximity. The wealthy needed their servants in their homes, and the businessmen who

Illustrated London News

New York City's Sixth Avenue "El" in 1884. In this splendidly drafted depiction, the locomotive is barely smoking, the station is uncrowded and surrounded by open space, and everything looks spanking clean. In fact, Els were noisy, particularly when tenements were built within a few feet of the tracks; the locomotives filled the air with coal fumes and scattered hot cinders on the street below; the iron structures were grimy within months of completion.

provided services—livery stables for their horses and vehicles, retailers of all kinds, coal and ice dealers, artisans' shops—had to be within easy reach. Small business owners lived behind or above their shops, offices, and warehouses, with their employees nearby.

The line between city and country was vividly clear. Where built-up neighborhoods, paved streets, water and gas lines, and sewers ended, farmland began. Often the edge of a large city was a belt of ramshackle shantytowns inhabited by people who had not found a role to play in the city's life, or who were discarded by a competitive society. Unlike today, when homeless people cluster in the central cores of cities, the walking city relegated the marginal to the suburbs.

Not that city center living was delightful. In fact, the congestion, pace, turmoil, noise, and dirt of urban life were such that when the opportunity to flee presented itself, the wealthy and then the middle classes were quick to seize it, leaving city centers to businesses.

GETTING AROUND

The first device making it possible for people of means to put distance between their residences and the city center was the horse car line. With charters from city hall, entrepreneurs installed light rails down major thoroughfares on which they ran horse-drawn streetcars with seats open to the public. Fares were 5 cents—too much for working people to pay twice daily. They continued to walk to their jobs, which

meant living close to the docks, warehouses, and factories. However, well-paid skilled workers, white-collar workers, and small businessmen took advantage of the quick, cheap transportation to move away from the congestion: north on the island of Manhattan, west across the easily bridged Schuylkill River in Philadelphia, north and west out of Chicago and Boston, into the hills above Cincinnati.

Making possible even more distant residential neighborhoods was the steam-powered elevated train, or **El,** which ran at high speeds above the crowded streets on ponderous (and ugly) steel scaffolding. In cities on large bodies of water, ferryboats catered to passengers. In 1870 New York completed the first El on Ninth Avenue, and the range of the trains, soon up to the northern tip of Manhattan, encouraged the middle classes to move even farther from Wall Street and the once leafy but now crowded and bawdy Bowery. In making the suburbs more accessible and desirable, the Els also began the process of pushing the residents of the shantytowns into inner-city housing abandoned by the middle classes.

The steam ferry had the same effect. As early as 1850, fast ferryboats were shuttling across the East River between Manhattan and Brooklyn every few minutes. By 1860, 100,000 people made the six-minute crossing daily. Camden, New Jersey, was Philadelphia's ferry suburb, across the Delaware River. San Francisco Bay, spacious as the great harbor is, was vexed by ferryboat traffic jams as early as 1900.

Keystone-Mast Collection, UCR/California Museum of Photography, UC Riverside

Electric trolleys on San Francisco's Market Street. They ran to every part of the city except the steepest hills, where the famous "cable cars" provided public transportation from residences to downtown. The "cow catchers" on the trolleys were designed not to save cattle but to prevent careless pedestrians from being run over.

ELECTRIC TROLLEYS

The utility of elevated trains was limited by their high construction cost. Only the richest and largest cities could shoulder the expense of the massive iron support structure. Moreover, as soon as the Els stimulated residential construction along their routes, where they descended to ground level, the noisy, dirty, dangerous locomotives roused the ire of the very people who rode on them to work and recreation.

It was the electric trolley car, pioneered in the United States by inventor–businessman Frank J. Sprague, that transformed most walking cities into sprawling conurbations. Cheap to build, faster than horse cars, easy to stop, clean, quiet, even pleasantly rhythmic in their click-clack and melodious in their bells, the trolleys were key to the growth of both metropolises and smaller cities. Richmond, Virginia, was the first to build an electric trolley system in 1887. By 1895, 850 lines crisscrossed American cities on 10,000 miles of track. They were as important to the urbanization of the United States as the railroads were to the settlement of the West.

BUILDING UP

In fostering the construction of residential neighborhoods miles from city business districts, the trolleys made it possible for many more people to congregate in city centers for work, business, and entertainment. The new moneymaking potential of real estate in town caused city center property values to soar.

The theoretical solution to the problem was obvious: multiply the square footage of midtown properties by building ever taller structures with more stories. But there were practical limits to building up. Masonry construction—piling stone on stone, laying brick on brick—meant that on the lower floors of an eight- or ten-story building, the weight-bearing walls had to be so thick as to defeat the whole purpose of building up: providing more room. Moreover, the lower levels of any building were more desirable: the more stairs a businessman (and his customers) had to climb to his office, or the hotel guest to his room, the less valuable the floor space.

New York's Flatiron Building, built in 1905, was one of the city's first skyscrapers. It was double the height of architect Louis Sullivan's pioneering Wainswright Building in St. Louis. Its unusual shape was caused by the fact that New York's Broadway (on the left), following an ancient Indian trail, cut through the city's rectangular grid street plan at an angle.

The Brooklyn Bridge shortly after it was completed in 1883. It was (and is) as stunning in its beauty as in its size. The bridge made Brooklyn, then the fourth largest city in the United States, an appendage of Manhattan. In 1898 Brooklyn was amalgamated into greater New York City as one of five boroughs.

Elisha Graves Otis's safety hoist, or elevator, solved the problem of access to upper floors. Mechanical hoists had been around since the days of the pharaohs; a steam-powered lift was put into service in England in 1835. Until Otis, however, hoisting cables and ropes snapped so often as to make a ride on an elevator a risky adventure. Beginning in 1852, Otis and his equally imaginative sons developed safety systems based on ratchets: if the hoisting cable broke, the elevator stayed where it was. No longer were the upper stories of a building the least desirable because of the effort required to reach them. They were more desirable because (in an Otis promotional brochure) "Monsieur makes the transit in half a minute of repose and quiet, and arriving there, enjoys a purity and coolness of atmosphere and an exemption from noise, dust, and exhalations." By 1878 hydraulically hoisted elevators climbed at 600–800 feet per second.

William L. Jenney solved the problem of massive weight-bearing walls. In 1885 he perfected the **I-beam girder**: a steel support with little mass that was so strong that it became possible to build towering skeletons of steel on which, in effect, builders hung decorative siding of cast iron or stone. The potential height of structural steel buildings seemed limitless; they could rise so high as to scrape the sky. Indeed,

once the method was perfected, corporations competed to erect the tallest tower as medieval cities competed to build the tallest cathedral spire.

New York was to become the most dramatic of the sky-scraper cities; but Chicago architects pioneered in the design of "tall office buildings," as Louis H. Sullivan, the most thoughtful of architects, prosaically described his graceful structures. In an article in *Lippincott's Magazine* in 1896, Sullivan explained how through the use of "proud and soaring" vertical sweeps, "a unit without a single dissenting line," the artistic form of the skyscraper reflected the essence of its construction. In the twentieth century, Sullivan's protégé, Frank Lloyd Wright, was to apply the principle of form following function to a wide variety of structures.

BUILDING OVER

Another technological innovation that contributed to the expansion of cities was the suspension bridge, which erased broad rivers as barriers to urban growth. Its pioneer was a German immigrant, John A. Roebling, who came to the United States in 1831 as a canal engineer and set up the first American factory for twisting steel wire into cable. Roebling's associates scoffed at his contention that if a bridge were hung from strong cables instead of built up on massive pillars, much broader rivers could be spanned. Obsessed with the

Sweatshops

The wealthy took their clothing wants to small shops, where tailors and milliners made fine garments by hand from fabric to suit or gown. They worked not from patterns, as someone who sews today would do, but from "fashion plates," carefully drawn, detailed pictures in magazines of people dressed in the latest styles. In the nineteenth century, Paris was considered the authority in such matters. At the beginning of the century, the middle classes depended on the women of the family for their garb. That is why needlecraft learned at a mother's knee was such an important part of a young girl's education: clothing her family would be one of the most important duties of her life as a wife and mother.

The poor made do with castoffs scavenged or purchased from merchants who bought, reconditioned, and sold used clothing. The fact that such garments had been made to fit an individual did not matter when the point was warmth and the rudiments of modesty. Only sailors, slaves, and—after 1849—miners in the West were likely to wear clothing such as nearly everyone does today, "ready-made" in quantity to standard sizes and sold "off the rack." Sailors were not in port long enough to be fitted, and they had other uses for their money than tailoring. (The first ready-made clothing stores were called "sailors' shops.") Slaves had no choice in the matter of what they put on their backs; their owners were an attractive market for tailors who abandoned the custom trade and took to producing rough, cheap garments in quantity. Miners, like sailors, were in a hurry, and they lived in an almost entirely masculine society. Their demand for sturdy,

ready-made clothing provided the impetus for the founding in 1850 of the famous Levi Strauss Company of San Francisco.

By 1900 things had changed. Nine Americans in ten were wearing ready-made togs. A "clothing revolution" had taken place as a consequence of technology with a boost from the American Civil War. The technology included inventions such as the sewing machine, patented by Elias Howe in 1846, and powered scissors that could cut through eighteen pieces of fabric at once, thus making pieces for eighteen pairs of trousers or coats of the same size. Standardized sizes were provided by the U.S. government when the Civil War made it necessary to buy uniforms for hundreds of thousands of men. The army's Quartermaster Corps measured hundreds of recruits and arrived at sets of proportions that provided a fit for almost all. It was a simple step for clothing manufacturers to do the same for women's sizes after the war ended, and ready-made clothing shops began to compete with tailors and seamstresses.

How were the new ready-made clothes manufactured? Not in factories. No outsize machinery was involved in the making of garments, nor a central source of power. (Sewing machines were treadle powered.) It made no sense to bring workers to one location as it did in textile mills. Once the garment was assembled by sewing machine, the rest was handwork such as finishing buttonholes, attaching buttons, installing linings, and prettying up a dress with ribbons and flounces. These tasks were farmed out to people working in their homes just as,

---

concept of the suspension bridge, Roebling devoted his life to perfecting a design. Before the Civil War, he had several to his credit, including an international bridge over the Niagara River near the falls.

Roebling planned his masterpiece for the East River, separating downtown New York, which was bursting at the seams, from the roomy seaport of Brooklyn on Long Island. While working on the site in 1869, he was injured, contracted a tetanus infection, and died. Without delay, his son, Washington A. Roebling, carried on the work. He too suffered serious injuries: he was crippled by "the bends," later associated with deep-sea divers, by working too long below water level on the foundations of the bridge's towers. Nevertheless, from a chair in a room overlooking the great span, now called the Brooklyn Bridge, he saw it completed in 1883, his wife carrying his instructions to the site and acting as general foreman. The Brooklyn Bridge was (and is) admired for its beauty as well as its engineering.

In providing easy access to Manhattan—33 million people crossed the bridge each year—the bridge ignited a residential

real estate boom in Brooklyn; within a few years, Brooklyn was the fourth largest city in the United States. But the bridge also spelled the end of Brooklyn's independence. A satellite of Manhattan in fact, Brooklyn was incorporated into the City of New York with Queens, Staten Island, and the Bronx by popular vote in 1898.

THE GREAT SYMBOL

The Brooklyn Bridge was dedicated with a mammoth celebration. President Chester A. Arthur proclaimed it "a monument to democracy"; sides of beef were roasted in the streets; oceans of beer and whiskey disappeared; brass bands competed in raising a din; races were run; prizes were awarded; jigs were danced; and noses were punched. A fireworks display of unprecedented splendor topped off the festivities, illuminating the fantastic silhouette from both sides of the East River. The Brooklyn Bridge was America's celebration of the city.

It was also an indictment of the city. On the morning of the gala, one dissenting newspaper editor groused that the

before the spinning jenny and power loom, cloth making had been.

The old putting-out system had involved the wives and daughters of farmers, leaving people on the land. Putting out needlework engaged poor city people, for whom the work was their entire livelihood.

The system was called "sweating," and the places in which the garment makers worked were called "sweatshops" because of the peculiarly exploitative nature of the system. A clothing manufacturer kept a small headquarters; at most, the material was cut to pattern in the shop. The pieces of garments then were handed over weekly or daily to people, usually Jewish or Italian immigrants, who took them home to their tenements. There the whole family—perhaps some boarders and neighbors too—sat down in the daylight hours to make up the garments. Some households saw a coat (called a "cloak" in the nineteenth century) or a gown through from components to completion. Others specialized in roughing the garment in, or making buttonholes, or attaching pockets, and so on.

Everyone involved was paid by the piece—so much per pocket, so much per lining. An intricate hierarchy of subcontractors and sub-subcontractors paid those below them in the chain as little as possible. The man who provided finished cloaks to the company received so much for each garment he delivered. To make a profit, he had to pay less than that to the households to which he farmed out the work. If the head of a household **sweatshop** had boarders or neighbors sewing, he had to pay them less than he was getting per piece. Everybody was "sweating" somebody else.

When a jobber's or a worker's productivity increased, the sweater above him was often inclined to cut the piece rate. Everyone down the chain got less for their work. The operator of a Chicago sweatshop explained the results to a congressional committee in 1893:

Q. In what condition do you get the garments?
A. They come here already cut and I make them up.
Q. What is the average wage of the men per week?
A. About $15 a week.
Q. How much do the women get?
A. About $6. They get paid for extra hours. . . .
Q. Are wages higher or lower than they were two years ago?
A. Lower. There are so many who want to work.
Q. How much do you get for making this garment?
A. Eighty cents.
Q. How much did you get for making it two years ago?
A. About $1.25.
Q. Is the help paid less now?
A. Yes, sir.

A cloak maker told the same panel that he had earned about $20 a week in 1885 for completing fewer garments than he had sewn in 1890, when he had made $13 to $14 a week. In 1893 he was making $11 a week for even greater productivity.

Brooklyn Bridge had "begun in fraud" and "continued in corruption." It was no secret that much of its $15 million cost had gone not into concrete, steel, and Roebling cable but into the pockets of crooked politicians.

The glories of the bridge were also tarnished by its cost in lives. At least twenty workers were killed building it, and others who just disappeared probably fell into the river unnoticed. Many more workers were maimed by the bends and badly broken bones. Then, just a few days after the dedication, a woman stumbled while descending the stairs that led from the causeway to the ground, and someone shouted, "The bridge is sinking!" In the stampede that followed, twelve people were trampled to death.

THE EVILS OF CITY LIFE

City people died at a rate not known in the United States since the seventeenth century. While the national death rate was 20 per 1,000 annually, the death rate in New York City was 25. In the slums it was 38, and for children under five years of age, 136 per 1,000. The figures were only slightly lower in other big cities, and in parts of Chicago they were higher. In one Chicago slum as late as 1900, the infant mortality rate was 200 per 1,000; one child in five died within a year of birth. By way of reference, the infant mortality rate in the United States today is less than 20 per 1,000, and the total death rate is less than 9 per 1,000 annually.

TOO MANY PEOPLE, TOO LITTLE ROOM

City people died at high rates largely because of the crowded living conditions of the poor. Philadelphia was statistically the healthiest city because, with a great deal of land on which to build, it was a city of inexpensive two-story brick "row houses." The number of residents per square foot of living space was far less than in any other metropolis. For example, in Boston and Chicago typical housing for working people was in old wooden structures that had been comfortable homes for one family; in the late nineteenth century half a dozen families, plus boarders, crowded into them.

Chicago Historical Society

■ *Frustrating traffic jams predated the automobile. Here trolleys, horse-drawn wagons, and a sea of pedestrians have created a gridlock that looks insoluble.*

In New York the narrow confines of Manhattan Island made the crowding even worse. Former single-family residences were carved into tenement houses that were homes to hundreds of people. In 1866 the Board of Health found 400,000 people living in tenements with no windows, and 20,000 living in cellars below the water table. An investigator said that cellar dwellers "exhibited the same lethargic habits as animals burrowing in the ground." At high tide their homes filled with water, and they sheltered where they could. The board closed the cellars and ordered 46,000 windows cut in airless rooms; but in 1900, people whose memories dated back to the 1860s said that they preferred conditions then.

Jacob Riis, a newspaper reporter who exposed squalid urban living conditions in an 1890 book, *How the Other Half Lives,* estimated that 330,000 people lived in a square mile of slum: almost 1,000 people per acre. New York was more than twice as congested as the London that turned Charles Dickens's stomach, and some neighborhoods were more populous than Bombay, Americans' image of hell on earth. On one tenement block in the Jewish section

of the Lower East Side, just a little larger than an acre, 2,800 people lived. In an apartment of two tiny rooms there, Riis found a married couple, their twelve children, and six adult boarders.

When architect James E. Ware designed a new kind of building to improve housing for the poor, he was accused of making the situation worse. His **"dumbbell" tenement,** named for its shape, ostensibly provided twenty-four to

Horse and Buggy Days

A dead horse was a sanitation problem in a city, but so was a horse alive. Each horse produced twenty-five pounds of manure each day. In New York City in 1900 there were about 150,000 horses. The potential litter problem, therefore, weighed between 1,300 and 1,800 tons daily, not to mention 60,000 gallons of equine urine. Most manure merely dried and crumbled where it dropped, blowing or washing away in time. Some was scooped up by the city or by private entrepreneurs and sold to farmers on Long Island or in New Jersey as fertilizer.

thirty-two apartments, all with ventilation, on a standard New York building lot of 25 by 100 feet. However, when two dumbbells were constructed side by side, the windows of two-thirds of the living units opened on an air shaft, sometimes only two feet wide, that was soon filled with garbage, creating a threat to health worse than airlessness. Nevertheless, the dumbbells met city building standards; by 1894 Manhattan had 39,000 of them, housing almost half the population.

HEALTH

Crowding led to epidemic outbreaks of serious diseases like smallpox, cholera, measles, typhus, scarlet fever, and diphtheria. In Philadelphia's row houses, it was possible to quarantine afflicted families. In other cities, quarantine did little good: where were unafflicted people to go? Even less dangerous illnesses like chicken pox, mumps, whooping cough, croup, and influenza were killers in the crowded cities. Common colds were feared as the first step to pneumonia.

In his famous book, Jacob Riis took readers on a tour of a tenement: "Be a little careful, please! The hall is dark and you might stumble. You can feel your way, if you cannot see it. Close? Yes! What would you have? All the fresh air that enters these stairs comes from the hall-door that is forever slamming." He paused at the entrance to a windowless apartment. "Listen! That short, hacking cough, that tiny, helpless wail. . . . The child is dying of measles. With half a chance it might have lived; but it had none. That dark bedroom killed it."

With New York still a city with heavy industry, the air was polluted, according to the Board of Health, by sulfur, ammonia, kerosene, acids, and phosphates—not to mention the odors of slaughterhouses and horse manure.

SANITATION

Sanitation was a serious problem in big cities. Free-roaming scavengers—chickens, hogs, dogs, and birds—handily cleaned up the garbage in small towns, and backyard latrines were adequate in disposing of human wastes. But neither worked when several hundred people lived in a building and shared a single privy. City governments collected waste; but even when they were honestly administered (which was the exception), sanitation departments simply could not keep up.

Horses compounded the problem. They deposited tons of manure on city streets daily, and special squads could not begin to keep pace. Moreover, on extremely hot and cold days, old and poorly kept horses keeled over by the hundreds; in New York the daily total could top 1,000. Although by law the owner of the dead beast was required to dispose of the carcass, at best this meant that he dumped it into the river. More often, because the task was so formidable, owners of faltering nags cut their horses out of harness and fled. In summer the corpses bloated and began to putrefy within hours.

In the poorest tenements, piped water was available only in shared sinks in the hallways, which were typically filthy.

Safe water was so heavily dosed with chemicals that it was barely palatable. The well-to-do bought bottled spring water that was trucked into the cities. Some people depended on wells in the streets that were inevitably fouled by runoff.

Tenement apartments did not have bathrooms. Children washed by romping in the water of open fire hydrants or by taking a swim in polluted waterways. If you did not come home tinged gray or brown, one survivor of New York's Lower East Side remembered, you had not washed. When a bath was necessary, adults went to public bathhouses where there was hot, clean water at a reasonable price. Many of these establishments were quite respectable. Others were known as dens of immorality.

VICE AND CRIME

As they always are, slums were breeding grounds of vice and crime. With 14,000 homeless people in New York in 1890, many of them children—"street Arabs," they were called—and work difficult to get and unsteady at the best of times, many succumbed to the temptations of sneak thievery, pocket picking, purse snatching, and, for the bolder, violent robbery. As early as the 1850s, police in New York were vying with (or taking bribes from) strong-arm gangs who were named after the neighborhoods where they held sway: the Five Points Gang, Mulberry Bend, Hell's Kitchen, Poverty Gap, the Whyo Gang.

They occasionally struck outside their areas, robbing warehouses and preying on middle- or upper-class fops who were slumming. (The best residential neighborhoods were well policed.) But the gangs' typical victims were other slum dwellers struggling to survive and escape: the workingman who paused for a beer before he took his pay envelope home, or the shopkeeper who was forced to make regular payments or risk physical violence. Whereas the homicide rate and other serious crimes declined in German and British cities as they grew larger, it tripled in American cities during the 1880s. An Italian visitor to the United States, Cesare Lombroso, exclaimed that "lawlessness is an American phenomenon with no equal in the rest of the world." The prison population of the nation doubled in the last years of the century, but plenty of thugs remained at large.

By the end of the century the more sophisticated gangs moved into vice, running illegal gambling operations, opium dens, and brothels. Prostitution flourished at every level in a society where domestic sexual activity was repressed by middle-class prudery or working-class pregnancy. There was a plentiful supply of impoverished girls and women who had no other way to survive. The lucky few set themselves up as mistresses or in fancy houses that catered to the well-to-do. More common was the wretched slattern who plied her trade on the streets, under the costly protection of a gang if she did not want to be beaten.

AN URBAN CULTURE

Yet despite all the horror stories (which no one savored more than the people who lived in the cities) and the lurid accounts of

© Bettmann/Corbis

A slum in New York City about 1900. Every big city had neighborhoods like this one: the Flats in Cleveland, Cross Keys in St. Louis, the North End of Boston, the Stockyards in Chicago.

urban life in books, newspapers, magazines, sermons, lectures, plays, and scandalized visitors' reports, a vital, exciting urban culture developed in American cities. City people compared rural "yokels" and "hayseeds" unfavorably to themselves. Once established, city people were unlikely to move to the country or even to be attracted by jobs beyond the municipal limits.

The cities continued to grow at an extraordinary rate after 1900. Indeed, had it not been for the existence of an American frontier larger than any before, it is likely that the rural population would have declined in the late nineteenth century, as it was to do in the twentieth.

FURTHER READING

The Ethnic City Thomas J. Archdeacon, *Becoming American,* 1983; Dino Cinel, *From Italy to San Francisco: The Immigrant Experience,* 1982; Roger Daniels, *Coming to America: A History of Immigration and Ethnicity in American Life,* 2002; Leonard Dinnerstein and David Reimers, *Ethnic Americans: A History of Immigration and Assimilation,* 1975; Steven P. Erie, *Rainbow's End: Irish Americans and the Dilemmas of Urban Machine Politics, 1840–1945,* 1988; Donna Gabaccia, *From the Other Side: Women, Gender, and Immigrant Life in the U.S., 1820–1990,* 1994; Irving Howe, *World of Our Fathers: The Journey of the East European Jews to America and the Life They Made,* 1976; Matthew F. Jacobson, *Whiteness of a Different Color: European Americans and the Alchemy of Race,* 1998; Thomas Kessner, *The Golden Door: Italian and Jewish Mobility in New York City, 1880–1915,* 1977; David R. Roediger, *Working Toward Whiteness: How America's Immigrants Became White,* 2005; Donald Weber, *Haunted in the New World: Jewish-American Culture from Cahan to the Goldbergs,* 2005.

Recreation Allen Guttmann, *A Whole New Ball Game: An Interpretation of American Sports,* 1988; Zane Miller and Patricia Melvin, *The Urbanization of Modern America,* 1987; David Nasaw, *Going Out: The Rise and Fall of American Amusements,* 1993; Thomas L. Philpott, *The Slum and the Ghetto,* 1978; Kathy L. Reiss, *Cheap Amusements: Working Women and Leisure in New York City, 1880–1920,* 1986; Steven A. Riess, *City Games: The Evolution of American Urban Society and the Rise of Sports,* 1989.

Urban Problems and Culture Gunther P. Barth, *City People: The Rise of Modern City Culture in Nineteenth Century America,* 1980; Edwin G. Burrows and Mike Wallace, *Gotham: A History of New York City to 1898,* 1999; Howard Chudakov, *The Evolution of American Urban Society,* 1975; William Cronon, *Nature's Metropolis: Chicago and the Great West,* 1991; Perry R. Davis, *Challenging Chicago: Coping with Everyday Life, 1837–1920,* 1998; Martin Melasi, *The Sanitary City: Urban Infrastructure in America from*

Colonial Times to the Present, 2000; Eric Monkkonen, *America Becomes Urban: The Development of U.S. Cities and Towns, 1780–1980*, 1988; Karen Sawislak, *Smoldering City: Chicagoans and* the Great Fire, 1871–1874, 1995; Stanley K. Schultz, *Constructing Urban Culture: American Cities and City Planners, 1800–1920*, 1989.

KEY TERMS

The following terms are covered in this chapter and can also be found in the list of Key Terms at the back of the book.

"dumbbell" tenement	**ghettos**	**settlement house**	**sweatshop**
El	**I-beam girder**		

ONLINE SOURCES GUIDE

Use this listing to find online documents, images, interactive maps, simulations, and other resources related to this chapter:

American History Resource Center
http://history.wadsworth.com/rc/us

Selected Documents
Jane Addams's "Twenty Years at Hull House"

Selected Images
Tenement sweatshop in New York City
Immigrants (women) sewing pants
Twelve-year-old boy in New York City sweatshop
Mulberry Street in New York City, 1900

Interactive Time Line (with online readings)
Bright Lights and Slums: The Growth of Big Cities

CHAPTER 31

The Last Frontier

Winning the Last of the West 1865–1900

Reproduced from the Collections of the Library of Congress

The frontier! There is no word in the English language more stirring, more intimate, or more beloved....It means all that America ever meant. It means the old hope of a real personal liberty, and yet a real human advance in character and achievement. To a genuine American it is the dearest word in all the world.

Emerson Hough

The conquest of the earth, which means the taking it away from those who have a different complexion and slightly flatter noses than ourselves, is not a pretty thing when you look at it too much.

Joseph Conrad

After counting the American people in 1890, the Census Bureau announced that there was no longer a frontier. No line could be drawn on the map distinguishing the part of the United States that was settled and wild lands where only Indians lived or no one at all. There were still large pockets of unsettled land, of course, but no continuous frontier.

And the Census Bureau's definition of "settled" land was not very demanding: just 2.5 people per square mile—a population density that, to us, seems appropriate to howling wilderness. And yet, even by the Bureau's standards, during the Civil War the unsettled parts of the United States comprised roughly half the nation's area. Twenty-five years later, only scattered patches of desolate desert and mountainsides were unpopulated. In a quarter of a century, Americans and immigrants plowed as much virgin land as they had during

the first 250 years after the first acre next to the cluster of huts at Jamestown was cultivated.

THE LAST FRONTIER

In 1865 the states of California and Oregon (and Washington territory) were home to 440,000 people. There were 40,000, mostly Mormons, in the Great Salt Lake Basin. Santa Fe, in New Mexico Territory, was still thriving as a trading center, and a few thousand *sassones* ("saxons," Anglo-Americans) lived among the largely Hispanic, Indian, and mixed-blood population.

Except for those population centers—none besides California very large or dense—the territory of the United States west of a north-to-south line about 150 to 200 miles

The Pony Express

The Pony Express looms larger in folklore than it does in the history of transcontinental communication. It was never intended to be more than a temporary stopgap while telegraph lines were strung from St. Joseph, Missouri, to California. It lasted only eighteen months from April 1860 to the fall of 1861. But when it was operating, it was an adventure: lone riders trotting, sometimes galloping in spurts, across half a continent carrying a few pounds of government dispatches and very expensive private letters to and from California.

Pony Express "technology" was rudimentary. It was just a string of 190 relay stations ten to fifteen miles apart. The couriers were "young, skinny, wiry fellows, not over 18," according to the company's "Help Wanted" advertisement, "expert riders willing to risk death daily . . . orphans preferred." They were based at larger stations that were 75 to 100 miles apart; they raced against a demanding schedule with mailbags. At each relay station—which was nothing more than a few wranglers, their shack, a stable, and corral—the riders changed their sweating

ponies for fresh mounts that were saddled and ready to go. The schedule allowed only minutes for essentials. The Pony Express kept some 500 horses in (from all reports) excellent condition.

The Pony Express cut twelve days off the time it had taken for Washington to communicate with Sacramento via steamships and the Isthmus of Panama. The Pony Express made 308 transcontinental runs covering 606,000 miles. It carried almost 35,000 pieces of mail. In eighteen months, only one mail pouch was lost.

---

west of the Mississippi was still, in fact, the land of the Indians. Whites and a few black settlers had barely spilled over the western boundaries of Minnesota, Iowa, Missouri, and Arkansas. Half the state of Texas was beyond the frontier.

A USELESS LAND

In 1865 most Americans were content to leave the West to the Indians so long as the army protected overland emigrants and the two transcontinental railroads that Congress had authorized. When Americans thought land, they thought agriculture. When they thought agriculture, they thought rainfall during the growing season. There were some areas of fertile, well-watered soil between eastern Nebraska and Kansas and the Sierra Nevada, but they were few and, until the railroad reached them, commercially useless. None of the three great geographical regions of the last of the American West was a Mississippi delta, a Midwest, or a Willamette Valley.

In the middle of the country rose the majestic Rocky Mountains. Their snowy peaks were known to easterners from landscape paintings by artists who had accompanied military expeditions or transcontinental wagon trains or had ventured there on their own, easel, oils, and canvases packed in wagons or on the backs of mules. The very grandeur of the Rockies, however, told Americans that the mountains could not support a population accustomed to living as people did "back east."

Between the Rockies and the Sierra Nevada lay high desert and the Great Basin, a great bowl with no outlet for rivers so that even the largest, like the Humboldt River that emigrants followed, lost heart, pooled up, and evaporated in "sinks." Most of the soil was thin and alkaline.

Thanks to the many creeks in the Wasatch Range near Salt Lake City, the Mormons had worked agricultural miracles; but as Brigham Young had calculated, no part of the West was less inviting to Americans than this genuine desert. There was no source of irrigation water for the high desert of Nevada; it grew sagebrush, creosote bush, tumbleweed (an accidental import from Europe), and a few species of pathetic grasses.

East of the Rockies were the Great Plains, a bit rainier than the Great Basin but still arid and almost treeless. Short grasses carpeted the western plains, grasses as tall as a man grew farther east, and rivers like the Missouri and the Platte meandered through them. Nevertheless, where there was not enough rain or groundwater for trees to grow, Americans believed that agriculture was impossible.

THE NATIVE PEOPLES OF THE WEST

Just after the Civil War as many as 350,000 Indians, in dozens of distinct tribes, lived traditional lives modified to varying degrees by direct or secondary contact (through other tribes) with Americans and Mexicans. Even the most forbidding parts of the Great Basin supported the Ute, Paiute, and Shoshone, who coped with the torrid, dry summers by dividing into small foraging bands and heading for higher elevations.

To the south, in the marginally more hospitable environment of present-day Arizona and New Mexico, the Pima, Zuñi, and Hopi had farmed intensively for centuries before the explorations of Francisco de Coronado in the 1530s. Their pueblos (a Spanish term the Indians adopted) were apartment complexes, some of them perched high on sheer cliffs for security, several atop mesas. Their village culture was delicately integrated. By the late 1800s, most of the Pueblo Indians had embraced Roman Catholicism or, rather, to the frustration of their priests, combined selected aspects of Catholicism with traditional religions.

The Navajo, more numerous than any other people south of the Grand Canyon (and comparative newcomers there), lived in family groups spread out over the country, not in villages. The Navajo were skilled weavers of cotton when the introduction of Spanish sheep let them raise their craft into a more durable art. Both the Navajo and the Pueblo Indians dreaded the Apache, who were also farmers and herders but, in addition, raiders who took what they could from whomever they ran across. Before the Civil War most Apache lived in Mexico, but they ranged far to the north in search of booty. Between 1862 and 1867, Apache raiders killed 400 Mexicans and Anglos in the borderlands, along with other Indians no one bothered to count.

The Indians who most fascinated post–Civil War easterners were those who seemed most determined to resist the whites and their ways: the tribes of the Great Plains. From the writings of travelers on the Plains like historian Francis Parkman and painters Karl Bodmer and George Catlin, whites learned about the Comanche, Cheyenne, and Arapaho peoples of the southern plains, and the **Mandan**, Crow, Sioux, Cheyenne, Nez Percé, Blackfoot, and other smaller tribes of the northern grasslands.

PLAINS CULTURE

The lives of the Plains Indians—their economy, social structure, religion, diet, dress—revolved around two animals: the native bison and the immigrant horse. The bison, as many as 30 million of them in 1800, provided food, bones from which tools were made, and sinews and hides that became clothing, footwear, blankets, portable shelters (the conical teepees), bowstrings, and canvases on which artists recorded heroic legends, tribal histories, and genealogies. The bison's dry manure made a tolerable fuel for cooking and warmth in a treeless land where winters were harsh.

The Plains Indians were nomadic. Except for the Mandan, they grew no crops; they trailed hundreds of miles annually after the bison herds on their horses. Long-distance trekking was not an ancient culture. Horses descended from Spanish herds in New Mexico, liberated by the thousands in an Indian revolt in 1680, multiplied, spread out, and reached the Snake River by about 1700, the central Great Plains about 1720, and the Columbia Plateau, home of the Nez Percé, about 1730. The Plains Indians learned to capture the "spirit dogs" and developed a stirrupless, saddleless, and bitless mode of horsemanship independent of Mexican example. The Comanche were widely regarded as the most skilled riders. "Almost as awkward as a monkey on the ground," painter George Catlin wrote of a Comanche warrior in 1834, "the moment he lays his hand upon a horse, his face even becomes handsome, and he gracefully flies away like a different being." (Catlin's paintings show that by 1834 some Comanche were using iron stirrups bought or stolen from Mexicans in Texas, but that was a recent development.) One Comanche band of 2,000 managed a herd of 15,000 horses.

The wanderings of the Plains tribes brought them frequently in contact with one another and with agricultural tribes to the east. They traded and could communicate with remarkable subtlety through a common sign language. Uncrowded as they were, however, and abundant as the bison were, the Plains tribes chronically battled one another. They didn't fight for territory; as nomads, they thought in terms of dominating ranges, but not of owning land. Nor, without farms, did they have much use for slaves as the Eastern Woodlands Indians had. The Plains Indians fought to steal horses and women from one another and—this they shared with the now subdued Eastern Indians—to demonstrate courage, the noblest quality of which a Great Plains male could boast.

Some tribes observed extended truces with others. But the idea that wars were unfortunate interruptions of "peace" was as foreign to their worldview as the notion that a man and woman and their children could claim exclusive ownership of 160 acres of grassland.

By 1865 every Plains tribe knew a great deal about the "palefaces" or "white-eyes." They did not even particularly dislike the wagon trains that had traversed their world for two decades. They skirmished with the white emigrants, but not much. Only 350 of 100,000 travelers to Oregon and California were killed by Indians. Mostly the outsiders were welcome so long as they kept moving. The Plains tribes traded with them, usually meat or horses in exchange for manufactures: clothing, iron tools, firearms. They collected the excess freight the wagon trains abandoned.

And they stole from the emigrants as they stole from other tribes. Poorly supervised horses were always fair pickings: on the great grasslands a tribe could never have too many horses; their upkeep was free. Kidnapping women and children was as rare as it had been common in the Eastern Woodlands. They were protected more closely than horses were, and there

The Last of the West 1860–1902

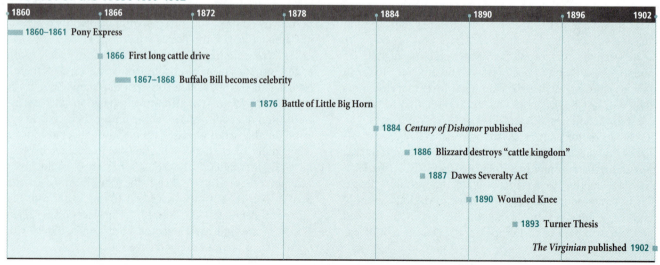

1860 — 1866 — 1872 — 1878 — 1884 — 1890 — 1896 — 1902

1860–1861 Pony Express

1866 First long cattle drive

1867–1868 Buffalo Bill becomes celebrity

1876 Battle of Little Big Horn

1884 *Century of Dishonor* published

1886 Blizzard destroys "cattle kingdom"

1887 Dawes Severalty Act

1890 Wounded Knee

1893 Turner Thesis

The Virginian published 1902

Settlers of one of the last frontiers in the lower forty-eight states: Arizona near the Verde River in 1885.

would be no trade with a wagon train from which women and children had been kidnapped; the chance of buying a musket or rifle was worth more than an unusual-looking wife. Moreover, the U.S. army, stationed in forts along the overland trail, paid little heed to Indian thievery but doggedly pursued bands accused of holding white captives.

THE DESTRUCTION OF THE BISON

This wary coexistence began to change when Congress authorized the construction of the transcontinental railroad. The men who laid the tracks of the Union Pacific and Kansas Pacific across the Plains were no more interested in staying on the Plains than the overlanders. However, their needs led, in a roundabout way, to the destruction of the bison.

To feed the construction crews, the railroads hired hunters like William F. "Buffalo Bill" Cody, an army scout and sometimes stagecoach driver, to harvest the herds. Using .50 caliber Springfield rifles, Buffalo Bill alone killed more than 4,000 bison in eighteen months in 1867–1868. That made no dent in the bison population, estimated to have been 15 million. However, when some hides were shipped back east, they caused a sensation as fashionable "buffalo robes"; and bison leather proved to be excellent material for the belts used to drive machinery. Methodical slaughter of the animals began at Dodge City, Kansas, in 1872. In three months, 700 tons of hides (43,000 animals) were shipped east from the town.

As many as 2,000 hunters were in the business at one time or another. A team of marksmen, reloaders, and skinners could down and skin a thousand bison a day. Buffalo were easy targets. They were big. Living in huge herds, they were unbothered by loud noises; they stood grazing, ignoring gunfire, as long as they did not scent or see the hunters. By 1875 the southern herd was effectively wiped out. By 1883 the northern herd was almost gone.

The railroads encouraged the slaughter because a herd of bison could damage the flimsy iron tracks merely by crossing them. Settlers on the edge of the Plains were glad for the hunters because they (correctly) linked the "Indian problem" to the abundance of bison. "So long as there are millions of buffaloes in the West," a Texan told Congress, "so long the Indians cannot be controlled." The army concurred. General Philip Sheridan, commander of western troops and an unabashed Indian hater, said that Congress should strike a medal with "a dead buffalo on one side and a discouraged Indian on the other."

To apply the finishing touches, wealthy eastern and European sportsmen chartered special trains and, sometimes without stepping to the ground, shot trophies for their mansions and clubs. Their services were not really needed and, in the case of Russian Grand Duke Alexis Alexandrovitch, not very efficient. With Buffalo Bill Cody in attendance, he fired twelve revolver shots at two buffalo and hit neither. The

Illustrated London News

THE FAR WEST.—SHOOTING BUFFALO ON THE LINE OF THE KANSAS-PACIFIC RAILROAD.

 The transcontinental railroad meant the destruction of the great herds of bison. The herds of hundreds of thousands could block the line or even damage it. Hunters shooting the animals to feed construction workers discovered that buffalo hides brought a good price in the East and killed the bison wholesale. Within a few years, 15 million were reduced to 2 or 3 million. By 1890 only a few hundred survived.

Great White Hunter then took a rifle and killed one from about ten feet.

In 1874 Congress tried to end the slaughter, prohibiting the shooting of bison except for food. President Grant, obliging his old comrade, General Sheridan, vetoed the bill. By 1889, when preservationists stepped in to save the species, fewer than a thousand American buffalo were alive. (Most of the 200,000 bison today are descended from just 77 animals.) It was probably the fastest extinction of a species in history.

THE CAVALRY

The U.S. cavalry accompanied the railroads, ostensibly to enforce the Indians' treaty rights as well as to protect the workmen. Some of these troops were captured Confederate soldiers who elected to take an oath of loyalty to the Union and serve in the West rather than languish in prisoner-of-war camps. After the war, they were joined by northern whites and by blacks in the Ninth and Tenth Cavalry Regiments, two of just four African-American units in the peacetime army.

Some officers respected the tribes and tried to deal fairly with them. General George Crook, remembered as one of the ablest of the army's Indian fighters, prided himself on dealing justly with the tribes. Others shared the values of General Sheridan, who was said to have told a Comanche chief at Fort Cobb in 1869, "The only good Indian is a dead Indian."

Overall, of course, the sympathies of the army were with the railroaders, miners, cattlemen, and eventually farmers who intruded on Indian lands. Whites assumed that because the Indians, like the Mexicans, used the land inefficiently, their claims to it were not as valid as their own. Beginning in

Moving Amidst the Hostiles

A real cavalry unit, unlike in the movies, was not just a line of men on horses. It was accompanied by long wagon trains, up to 150 vehicles! In addition to a soldier, each horse carried eighty to ninety pounds of equipment. With such loads, the animals needed frequent rests and plenty of grain.

The horses were rested without slowing the progress of a column in pursuit of an Indian band by dividing the soldiers on the march into two troops. One troop rode until it was about half a mile ahead of the wagon train. The soldiers dismounted and grazed their horses until the wagons, escorted by the second troop, were half a mile ahead. When the first troop caught up, the second troop moved ahead and the maneuver was repeated. In this way, there was always a troop, in two columns, at either side of the precious supplies. The horses had to bear their heavy load about an hour at a time with rest stops of half an hour—pretty hard work for half of a long day.

Buffalo Soldiers

The Indians called the African Americans of the Ninth and Tenth Cavalry Regiments "**Buffalo Soldiers**" because, to the Indians, the soldiers' hair resembled buffalo hide. The two black regiments' records in the West were excellent; few white regiments were in their class. The Ninth and Tenth had the lowest desertion rate and fewest court-martials of any western regiments; African-American soldiers won eighteen Congressional Medals of Honor in the Indian Wars.

Massacres

Neither Indians nor whites had a monopoly on perpetrating atrocities or suffering from them. Indians massacred other Indians—for example, in 1871 when Papagos in Arizona killed 100 Apaches. Indians massacred whites, as in New Mexico and Arizona in 1885 when Apaches murdered forty-five white civilians in one raid. Whites massacred Indians at 1863 at Bear Creek, North Dakota. Whites massacred whites in 1857 at Mountain Meadows, Utah, when Mormons slaughtered an entire wagon train of emigrants bound for California and tried to blame it on Indians.

1862, when the final wave of Indian wars began with a Sioux uprising in Minnesota, to 1890, when the last (feeble) military threat of the Sioux was shattered at Wounded Knee, South Dakota, the U.S. cavalry finished the job the buffalo hunters began: the destruction of the western tribes.

THE LAST INDIAN WARS

To the end, Indian war remained a war of few pitched battles and innumerable small skirmishes. Between 1869 and 1876, the peak years of the fighting, the army recorded 200 incidents, which did not include many Indian raids and unreported confrontations between civilians and the tribes. Still, the total casualties on the army's side (and that of the Indians) were less than in any of several Indian–white battles of the 1790s.

The army wanted to fight decisive battles. Formal battle favored the soldiers' training and superior technology. But the Indians sensibly clung to traditional hit-and-run attacks that exploited their advantage—mobility—and let them avoid fights in which, with their inferior arms and numbers, they might be wiped out. One consequence was frustration among the soldiers and a cruelty toward the enemy hardly known in the Civil War. In 1871 Commissioner of Indian Affairs Francis Walker explained that "when dealing with savage men, as with savage beasts, no question of national honor can arise. Whether to fight, to run away, or to employ a ruse, is solely a question of expediency."

"Forgive My Country"

When artist George Catlin learned of an attack by Civil War hero Philip H. Sheridan on the Cheyenne Indians, he wrote to the general:

The American journals tell me that you have . . . killed 52 warriors, and captured 400 horses and four tons of dried buffalo meat, the only and last means of their existence. Oh mercy, mercy! A small and friendly tribe when I lived amongst them, 35 years since; where are they going? What have they done? How many of them now exist, and who have got possession of their lands, their buffaloes, and wild horses? God, perhaps, may forgive my country for such cruel warfare; and oh, for my country's sake, that there could be a solvent for history, to erase such records from its pages.

By 1876, the year of the centennial, the army's final triumph seemed near. Little by little, the soldiers in their dusty blue uniforms had hemmed in the wandering tribes and whittled away at their ability to subsist. The typical state of a surrendering tribe was near starvation, with a goodly proportion of the young men already dead. But Indian resistance was not quite at an end.

CUSTER'S LAST STAND

In June 1876 a colonel of the Seventh Cavalry, George Armstrong Custer (whose fame as a Civil War hero was fading), led 265 men on what he believed would be a charge through a combined Sioux and Cheyenne encampment on Montana's Little Bighorn River. In fact, he rode into a perfectly designed and executed trap. Nearby reinforcements (Custer had foolishly divided his command) were pinned down. Several thousand Indian warriors killed every one of Custer's men.

It was a finale more than one officer had predicted for Custer. He had not been an effective Indian fighter. The **Battle of the Little Big Horn** was not the first time he neglected reconnaissance. He was peevish with other officers, impetuous, and a hog for glory. His single major victory over Indians, the battle of the Washita, was something of a fraud. His troops killed mostly women and children led by Black Kettle, the most important advocate of peace among the Plains Indians. Even then, Custer's position had been so exposed that he had to withdraw hastily, abandoning a major and eighteen men, who were killed.

But his "Last Stand" on the Little Big Horn thrilled Americans. Denied in life the advancement he believed he deserved, "Yellow Hair" (as the Sioux called him) became a romantic hero in death. A brewery commissioned an imaginative painting of the Battle of the Little Bighorn and within a few years distributed 150,000 reproductions of it.

Senior officers who had disapproved of the flamboyant Custer blamed him for the disaster, but mostly among themselves. Only in the next century would the battle be appreciated from the Indians' point of view—as a well-engineered tactical victory exploiting Custer's weaknesses, of which the Sioux and Cheyenne were well aware. The celebrations, however, were short-lived. Three large army detachments were closing in from the north, west, and east on the day of the

Smithsonian Institution, Bureau of American Ethnology

"Custer's Last Stand" so thrilled Americans that dozens of artists painted renditions of the battle. A print distributed by the Anheuser-Busch brewery was the decorative centerpiece in hundreds of salons. No white artists witnessed the battle. Red Horse, who painted this version, did; he fought in it.

battle with Custer. (Custer was supposed to have waited for them, but the chance for personal glory was too attractive.) Most of the victors were under federal control within a year; the rest were in Canada.

GOOD INTENTIONS, TRAGIC RESULTS

In 1881 a Coloradoan, Helen Hunt Jackson, published *A Century of Dishonor*, one of the decade's best sellers. In meticulous detail and with few factual errors, she traced the cynicism with which the U.S. government had dealt with the

Just Cause

By no means did all soldiers in the West think of Indians as vermin to be run into the ground. Captain Frederick Benteen, who was at the Little Bighorn (although not with Custer's doomed party), wrote of the effectiveness of the Sioux attack: "We were at their hearths and homes, their medicine was working well, and they were fighting for all the good God gives anyone to fight for." Custer himself said, "If I were an Indian, I would greatly prefer . . . the free open plains, rather than submit to the confined limits of a reservation, there to be the recipient of the blessed benefits of civilization, with its vices thrown in without stint or measure."

Indians since independence. Her list of Indian treaties was a list of broken treaties. Time and again, "Christian" whites had cheated "savage" Indians of their land, herded them onto reservations on next to worthless lands, and then chipped away at those.

By 1876 the government was no longer making formal treaties with Indians. Tribes that did not resist American control were defined as wards of the federal government; they were not citizens but were under Washington's protection and enjoyed a few privileges. After the publication of *A Century of Dishonor*, many easterners demanded that the government use this wardship in a just manner.

In 1887 Congress approved the Dawes Severalty Act. Intentions were of the best. Assuming that the traditional Indian way of life was no longer feasible, the sponsors of the Dawes Act argued that the Indian peoples must be Americanized if they were to survive. That is, they must become self-sustaining citizens through adoption of the ways of the larger culture. The Dawes Act dissolved the tribes (the "Indian Nations"), and the former treaty lands were distributed, homestead-style, 160 acres to each head of family, with an additional 80 acres for each adult member of the household. Lands left over were sold to whites. To avoid further despoliation, Indian lands could not be sold or otherwise disposed of for twenty-five years.

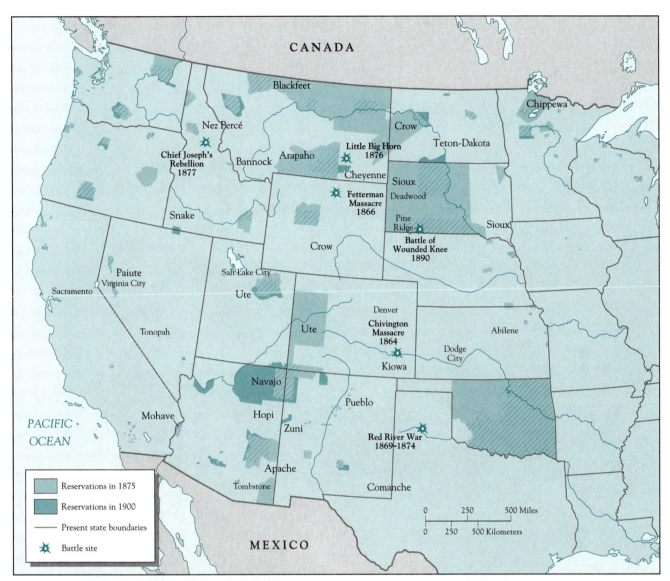

MAP 31:1 **Indian Reservations, 1875 and 1900**
Before the destruction of the bison, the Plains Indians were impeded from ranging from Canada to northern Texas only by other tribes. After 1875 they were herded onto reservations that shrank in size steadily and sharply in just twenty-five years, both by legal purchases and through white settler pressure on the federal government.

The supporters of the Dawes Act overlooked a number of important facts. First, few western Indians were farmers; traditionally they were hunters, gatherers, traders, and raiders. Second, reservation lands were rarely suited to agriculture; they were allotted to the Indians precisely because they were unattractive to white farmers. Third, tracts of a few hundred acres in the arid West were rarely enough to support efficient farmers, let alone novices at tillage and herding. Finally, the Plains Indians did not think in terms of private ownership of land. The tribe, not the nuclear family, was their basic social unit. Congress was right to recognize that nomadic hunting was impossible. It erred in relegating the tribe to the dustheap; western Indians thought in tribal terms and respected the authority of tribal leaders. The defeated Indians were confused and demoralized by the rapid disintegration of their culture, and many were debauched by idleness and alcohol.

Carlisle Indian School

Colonel Richard Henry Pratt, who had commanded African-American cavalry in the West, was an idealist who espoused the goals of the Dawes Severalty Act: assimilation of the Indians into American culture. He believed in the equality of races, but not in the equality of cultures. He founded the Carlisle Indian School in Pennsylvania to create what he hoped would be an Americanized Indian elite. "I believe in immersing the Indians in our civilization," he said, "and when we get them under, holding them there until they are thoroughly soaked."

WOUNDED KNEE

Among these desperate people appeared a religious teacher in the tradition of The Prophet. Jack Wilson, or Wovoka, was a

A Sioux village at Pine Ridge, South Dakota, in 1891. Although there were no more bison to hunt, the Sioux were still "camped" as if following a herd. In a village similar to this one, the famous Sitting Bull was shot in 1890 when, during an attempt to arrest him, a misunderstanding led to a shootout between members of his band and reservation police.

Paiute who was fascinated by the Christian doctrines of redemption and resurrection. Combining Christian ideas and native American beliefs, he preached a religion promising redemption for Indians on this earth and resurrection of the dead.

According to Wovoka, by performing a ritual dance, the Indians, who were God's chosen people, could prevail on the Great Spirit to make the white man disappear. The Ghost Dance would also bring back to life the buffalo herds and Indians who had been killed in the wars. The resurrected warriors would be led by "the Messiah who came once to live on earth with the white men but was killed by them." The old way of life, which in the 1880s adult Indians vividly remembered, would be restored. Preached throughout the West by

Wovoka's disciples, the Ghost Dance attracted tens of thousands to, at least, the hope it provided.

This kind of religion, simultaneously edifying and heartrending, is common among peoples who have seen their world turned upside down. In parts of the Southwest untouched by Wovoka's religion, defeated Indians turned to peyote, a natural hallucinogenic drug, as a way to escape a bewildering, intolerable reality at least briefly. Alcohol, long a problem among Indians, now led to widespread alcoholism.

To understand the appeal of the Ghost Dance religion, it is necessary to recall just how rapidly the culture of the Plains Indians was destroyed. The Dakota Sioux, for example, did not go to war with the whites until the end of the 1860s. Within a decade, survivors of the wars were being herded on

Geronimo

The Apache, Geronimo, who fought on after his tribe made peace with the United States was a resourceful leader. For eight years his ever-dwindling band (seventeen warriors, fourteen women, and six children at the end) evaded capture by hundreds of troops assigned to no other task but to capture him, by slipping back and forth across the Mexican border. He finally surrendered to Americans because he knew that Mexican soldiers, who were waiting for him across the border, would treat his people brutally, perhaps massacre them.

Geronimo, like Sitting Bull, became a pop culture hero during his long confinement in Florida. Dozens of journalists interviewed him. Hundreds of people paid him to pose with them for photographs.

Resourceful as he was, it is difficult to see Geronimo as a tragic hero like Sitting Bull, Crazy Horse, Chief Joseph, and dozens of other Indians who commanded wars of resistance against the whites. Geronimo rarely fought soldiers; his band lived by raiding Mexican and American farms and gratuitously killing simple Mexican farmers and Americans who neither threatened nor resisted them.

the Pine Ridge Reservation in South Dakota, where Wovoka's message was preached by Kicking Bear. There, on Wounded Knee Creek in December 1890, when soldiers guarding the Dakotas tried to take their guns away, a shoving incident led to a one-sided battle in which about 200 people, half of them women and children, were killed. For the Indians of the Great Plains, there was no escape, not even in mysticism.

THE CATTLE KINGDOM

In 1870 American forests yielded about 12.8 billion board feet of lumber. By 1900 this output had almost tripled to 36 billion. Although the increase reflects in part the development of forest industries in the southern states, the region of greatest expansion was a new one, the Pacific Northwest.

In 1870, Americans were raising 23.8 million cattle. In 1900, 67.7 million head were fattening on grasslands, mostly in the West.

Annual gold production continued at or above the fabulous levels of the gold rush era; at the end of the century, it was nearly double the totals of 1850. Annual silver production, 2.4 million troy ounces in 1870, stood at 57.7 million ounces in 1900.

THE FIRST BUCKAROOS

Measured in acreage, cattlemen won more of the West than any other kind of pioneer. They were motivated by the appetite of the burgeoning cities of the East (and Europe) for cheap beef. They were encouraged in their venture by the disinterest in the rolling grasslands of anyone save the

Erwin E. Smith Collection of the Library of Congress

Texas cowboys—the real thing! The photograph was posed. The cowboys, their sombreros, and their clothing are too clean and unrumpled (the man standing in front is in brand new clothing) for them to have met a photographer on a long drive. Probably the picture was taken after they had delivered their herd in Kansas and been paid off.

Punching Cows

It took three to four months to drive a herd of cattle from the vicinity of San Antonio to a railhead town in Kansas. To be asked to join a trail crew was something of an honor among the young men of the country. The wages were not much, only $1 a day plus board and as good a bed as the sod of the Plains provided. But because a lot of money and the life of every member of a crew depended on every other, only a cowboy who had impressed the trail boss with his skills and his reliability was invited to go.

A crew consisted of the trail boss, often the owner of the cattle; a *segundo,* his assistant; a cook (an older man); a wrangler who was in charge of the *remuda,* or small herd of horses that accompanied the expedition; and a hand for each 250 to 300 cattle. Most herds numbered 2,000 to 3,000 cattle, so a crew of ten was common. (The "cows" were mostly steers, castrated males; the name "cow-puncher" derived from the job of punching the animals with poles into corrals and loading chutes.)

A herd moved ten to fifteen miles a day, the cattle grazing when the herd was halted for that purpose or for as long as an individual steer could stop and loaf before he was told to "git along." Two of the cowboys rode "lead" or "point," carefully staying to the side of the milling steers so as to get out of the way if they stampeded. Four rode "swing" and "flank" in pairs alongside the herd; and two or three rode "drag" behind the herd, hurrying it up and riding after stragglers.

Each position had its peculiarities and was assigned with an eye to a particular cowpuncher's abilities or his standing at the moment in the trail boss's graces. If the skills of all were about equal and no one was in bad odor, the boys rotated position daily.

Riding point was the most dangerous in the event of a stampede, but it was also the most prestigious and pleasantest in terms of dust and odor. Riding drag was the safest assignment but also the least desirable job, not only because of the quality of the air, but also because there was hardly a moment when some independent-minded "dogies" were not setting off on their own. Riding swing and flank was easiest on the nerves and the ponies.

The day's drive started soon after first light and ended as late toward dusk as the trail boss was satisfied with the grass and water. But the cowboys' work was not done. After a big dinner at the chuck wagon (the cook had driven ahead of the herd and picked his spot), all hands, in pairs, "rode night" in two-hour shifts. They slowly circled the herd in opposite directions, looking out for predators and soothing the often nervous steers. The western singing tradition developed as a means of keeping a herd calm; music soothed the generally docile beasts. Night riding was detested work; not only did it cut a chunk out of a tired man's sleep, it could be dangerous. Almost all stampedes started at night, tripped by a bolt of lightning, a steer dodging a coyote, or an occasional band of Indians scattering the herd to round up a few animals for their own meals. Except for river crossings (there were four major watercourses to cross between south Texas and Kansas) the stampede was the most frequent cause of death written on the wooden markers that dotted the Shawnee, Chisholm, and Goodnight-Loving trails.

There was little singing in pouring rain. The night riders donned yellow oilskin slickers that covered them and their saddles, and cursed or slept. If a cowboy had a good night horse he could doze in the saddle; his mount knew to wake him at the end of the two-hour shift.

Cowboys on the long drive sometimes brought a horse they owned, but that was not common; the boss supplied the tough, wiry work ponies. They were geldings, about seven to ten for each hand. They were specialists. There were morning horses, afternoon horses, and night horses. Some were water horses—good swimmers that could get a cowboy across as much as a mile of strong current. The most talented mount was the cutting horse, which knew exactly how a steer would act without the rider's instructions. The best were as agile as sheepdogs.

At the end of the drive, the horses were sold along with the cattle. Few hands returned to Texas overland. After they had spent most of their money on liquor, women, and cards, cowboys climbed aboard an eastbound train, rode it to the Mississippi, and struck south by riverboat.

Indians. Their story thrills people to this day partly because the cattle kingdom was immediately romanticized, and as quickly as it rose, it was destroyed.

The cowboy rode into American legend just before the Civil War. In the late 1850s, enterprising Texans began to round up herds of wild longhorns that ranged freely in the chaparral between the Nueces River and the Rio Grande. They drove the cattle north over an old Indian trail to Sedalia, Missouri, a railroad town with connections to Chicago. Although the bosses were English-speaking, many of the actual workers were Mexicans, who called themselves *vaqueros,* "cowboys."

Vaquero itself entered American language as "buckaroo." While "Anglos" were soon the majority of this mobile workforce, former Texas slaves became cowboys too; and much of what became part of American folklore and parlance about the buckaroos was of Mexican derivation. The cowboy's distinctive costume was an adaptation of Mexican work dress. The bandana was a washcloth that, when tied over the cowboy's mouth, served as a dust screen, no small matter when a thousand cattle

Cattlemen and Sheep Men

A common theme in western folklore is conflict between cattlemen and sheepherders. Many cattlemen did indeed dislike sheep because they said they destroyed the range. While cattle strolled as they grazed, sheep ate the grass at their feet until they devoured it to the ground. That was true enough of sheep that were not moved along by a herder and dogs, but only negligent or inexperienced settlers did not tend their sheep. Many settlers preferred sheep because they could be grazed in mountain meadows and on mountainsides unsuitable for cattle. And the sheeps' labor costs were a fraction of the cattleman's. A single herder and a couple of dogs could tend several thousand sheep and, if the herder was responsible, keep them moving so the range was conserved. The fact was, neither cattlemen nor sheep men gave much thought to conserving publicly owned grasslands.

were kicking it up. The broad-brimmed hat was selected not for its picturesque qualities but because it was a sun and rain shield. Extremely durable when manufactured from beaver felt, the sombrero also doubled as a drinking pot and washbasin.

The pointed, high-heeled boots, awkward and even painful when a man was walking, were designed for riding in stirrups, where a *vaquero* spent his workday. The western saddle was an adaptation of a Spanish design and was quite unlike the English tack that easterners used. Chaps, leather leg coverings, got their name from chaparral, the woody brush against which they were designed to protect the cowboy. Spanish words adopted into English via cowboys were numerous, including *lasso, lariat, corral, cinch, bronco,* and *pronto.*

MEAT FOR MILLIONS

The Civil War and Missouri laws excluding Texas cattle (because of hoof-and-mouth disease) ended the Texas cattle drives during the war. However, in 1866, when the transcontinental railroad had reached Abilene, Kansas, a wheeler-dealer from Illinois, Joseph G. McCoy, saw the possibilities of underselling steers raised on pasture back east with Texas longhorns and mixed breeds that fattened at no cost on open range. McCoy built holding pens on the outskirts of Abilene, arranged to ship cattle he did not then have with the Kansas Pacific Railroad, and dispatched agents to Texas to induce cowboys to round up the feral animals and drive herds to Abilene on a trading route called the Chisholm Trail.

In 1867, McCoy shipped 35,000 "tall, bony, coarse-headed, flat-sided, thin-flanked" cattle to Chicago. In 1868, 75,000 of the beasts, next to worthless in Texas, passed through Abilene, and Chicago meatpackers demanded more. In 1871, 600,000 "critters" passed through the pens of several Kansas railroad towns on their way to slaughter in Chicago and then on to American dinner tables.

The profits were immense. A steer worth $5 in Texas could be driven to Kansas at the cost of a cent a mile ($5 to $8) and sold for $25, occasionally for as much as $50. The business attracted investors from back east and England. They built

"ranches" that were as comfortable as the gentlemen's clubs of New York and London. The typical cattleman at Wyoming's elegant Cheyenne Club never touched a gun, and he sat astride a horse only for a photographer so he could wow his friends back in London. His mount was a plush easy chair, his range a fine carpet; he puffed on Havana cigars when he discussed cowpunching with his fellow buckaroos.

As the railhead moved westward, so did the cowboys' destinations. Soon herds were arriving from the north as well as from the south. The citizens of cow towns like Abilene were, after two or three years, glad to see the herds penned and the cowboys catching their trains home farther west. They concluded after a few seasons that the money to be made as a cattle trading depot was not worth the damage done to their own ranches and farms by hundreds of thousands of cattle. The wild atmosphere given their towns by the rambunctious cowboys, most of them bent on a blowout after months on the trail, was not compatible with respectable civic life. As a cow town grew, its "better element" wanted churches and schools on Main Street, not saloons, casinos, and whorehouses. The stage was set for the taming of a town by "lawmen," which is the theme of so much American folklore.

Never did the cattlemen lack for a railhead town to which to take their herds. There were always newer towns to the west to welcome them and their cowboys' wages. Just in Kansas, Abilene, Ellsworth, Newton, Wichita, Dodge City, and Hays had their day as wild cow towns surrounded by holding pens and feedlots.

DISASTER

The cattle kingdom lasted only a generation. It fell abruptly thanks to a collaboration between human greed and natural disaster.

The short-term profits to be made in cattle were so great that exploiters ignored the damage that the huge herds were doing to the grasslands. Vast as the Plains were, they were overstocked and overgrazed by the mid-1880s. Unlike the bison, which had migrated constantly in search of the lushest grass, leaving the land they passed over to recover, the cattle's wanderings were limited. They permanently fouled clear-running springs that had recovered within a month from a herd of bison, trampling them into mud pits. Weeds never noticed in the West, some of them uninvited stowaways from Europe, displaced the overgrazed native grasses. Hills and buttes were scarred by cattle trails. Some species of migratory birds that had once darkened western skies twice a year simply disappeared; beefsteaks on the hoof wiped out what had been their provisions during their seasonal flights.

Then, on January 1, 1886, a great blizzard buried the eastern and southern Plains. Within three days, three feet of snow drifting into banks twenty to thirty feet high suffocated the range. Between 50 and 85 percent of the open range livestock froze or died of hunger. About 300 cowboys failed to reach shelter and died; the casualties among Indians were never counted. When spring arrived, half the American Plains reeked of death.

Drought in the summer of 1886 ruined the cattlemen who had survived the snows. Grasses that had weathered summer droughts for millennia were unable to do so after the blizzards; they withered and died. Cattle weakened by winter starved. Then, the next winter, areas that escaped the worst of the 1886 blizzard got sixteen inches of snow in sixteen hours, followed by weeks of intermittent fall.

The cattle industry recovered; the demand for beef was too great for it to die. But methodical businessmen took the business over and changed its operations. Cattle barons like Richard King of southern Texas forswore the risks of the open range. Through clever manipulation of land laws, King built a ranch that was as large as the state of Rhode Island. If no one else's success was quite so spectacular as his, others imitated King's example in Texas, Wyoming, Montana, and eastern Colorado.

The railroads that had made the long drives possible now made them obsolete. When the transcontinental lines were complete, the Northern Pacific and Union Pacific built feeder lines into Texas, the Dakotas, and Montana. The cowboy, briefly a knight-errant in popular culture, became a ranch hand, a not-so-freewheeling employee of a large commercial operation.

OH, GIVE ME A HOME

Even during the days of the long drive, the cowboy's world bore scant resemblance to the legends popular culture embraced. Despite the white complexion of the cowboys in popular literature (and in films of the twentieth century), a large proportion of cowboys were Mexican or black. In some cases, the races acted and mixed as equals. Just as often, the cowboys split along racial lines when they reached the end of the trail, frequenting segregated restaurants, barber shops, hotels, saloons, and brothels.

Black, white, or Hispanic, the cowboys were, indeed, little more than boys. Photographs they had taken in cow towns after bathing and buying new clothes, and arrest records (mostly for drunk and disorderly conduct), show a group of very young men, few older than 25. The life was too hard for anyone but youths—days in the saddle, nights sleeping on bare ground in all weather. Moreover, when a cowboy married, he could not absent himself from his own ranch or farm and wife for the months the long drives required, as an unattached young buck could on a whim.

The real buckaroos were not constantly engaged in shooting scrapes. Their skills lay in horsemanship and with a rope, not with the less-than-accurate Colt revolver that they carried chiefly as a means of signaling distant coworkers. Toting guns was forbidden in railhead towns. With a drunken binge on every cowboy's itinerary, the law officer in charge of keeping the peace could hardly tolerate shooting irons on every hip. Cowboys who did not leave their revolvers in camp checked them at the police station before they hit the saloons—or they were jailed for being armed.

THE WILD WEST IN AMERICAN CULTURE

The legend of the cowboy as a romantic, quick-drawing knight of the wide-open spaces was not a creation of a later era. The western themes familiar to everyone today were fully formed when cold reality was still alive on the Plains. Oddly, the myths of the "Wild West" were embraced not only by easterners, but by cowboys and other westerners too.

PLAY-ACTING

There were celebrity westerners before the Civil War: Daniel Boone and Davy Crockett are the best known. The most important creator of the postwar myth of the Wild West was a somewhat unsavory character named E. Z. C. Judson. A former Know-Nothing who was dishonorably discharged from the Union Army, Judson took the pen name Ned Buntline. Between 1865 and 1886 he churned out more than 400 romantic, blood-and-guts chivalric "novels" about western heroes: intrepid lawmen, brave Indian fighters, and tough, heroic women like "Calamity Jane" and "Belle Star." Some characters Buntline invented; others were real people whom Buntline thoroughly fictionalized. Calamity Jane was a real person (Martha Cannary) but a pathetic alcoholic quite unlike the fictional Jane; Belle Starr, "the Bandit Queen," was Myra Belle Shirley, a serial consort of several low-life thieves and killers. The books in which they were transformed were called "pulps" for the cheap paper on which they were printed or "**dime novels**" for their price. Judson and his many competitors aimed the mass-produced literature at adolescent boys, but they were by no means the only readers.

Buntline's mythical world enamored even those who knew better from their own lives. During the 1880s, while living as a rancher in North Dakota, future president Theodore Roosevelt helped capture two young cowboys who had robbed a grocery store. In their saddlebags, the posse found several Ned Buntline novels that, no doubt, featured outlaws who were unjustly accused of crimes. The tiny town of Palisade, Nevada, on the Central Pacific railroad won a reputation in eastern newspapers as a den of cutthroats because brawls and gunfights broke out regularly when passengers left the train for refreshment. In fact, Palisade might be thought of as a precursor of theme parks: the gunfights were staged by locals partly to twit eastern fantasies and partly because the locals were bored.

AMERICAN HEROES

In pulp fiction, and later in films, Americans learned that the bank and train robbers Jesse and Frank James were really modern-day Robin Hoods who gave the money they stole to the poor. When Jesse James was murdered, his mother Zerelda (who had lost an arm in a ruction with Pinkerton detectives) made a tourist attraction of his grave, charging admission and explaining that her son had been a Christian who read the Bible in his spare time. Jesse, according to Zerelda, closely scrutinized

Gunplay

There is more gunplay in a ninety-minute Hollywood "western" than there was in the wildest towns of the Wild West in a year. Deadwood's worst year for homicides was 1876; there were four. (Wild Bill Hickock was one of the victims.) Dodge City's worst year was 1878; there were five murders.

all train passengers and did not rob those whose hands were calloused because they, like him, were workingmen.

Billy the Kid (William Bonney), a Brooklyn-born hired gun in New Mexico, was romanticized as a tragic hero who had been forced into a life of crime by an uncaring society. James Butler "Wild Bill" Hickock, a gambler and clotheshorse who killed perhaps six people before he was shot down in Deadwood Gulch, South Dakota, in 1876, was credited with dozens of killings, all in the cause of making the West safe for women, children, and psalm books.

Hickock, Calamity Jane, and other living legends of the West personally contributed to the mythmaking by appear-

ing in Wild West shows that traveled to the East and Europe. The greatest and most successful of the shows was the creation of "Buffalo Bill" Cody, whom Buntline had made famous in his books. A decent, generous man who drank too much, Cody really had been a buffalo hunter and much-praised scout for the army. He may or may not have killed an Indian in a *mano-a-mano* "duel." He did sympathize with Indians, which worked in his favor when he recruited Sioux warriors to travel with his show. Sitting Bull, the Hunkpapa Sioux chief who had overseen the defeat of Custer, toured with Cody and thought highly of him. (Buffalo Bill was a considerate and generous employer.) Reality and myth were

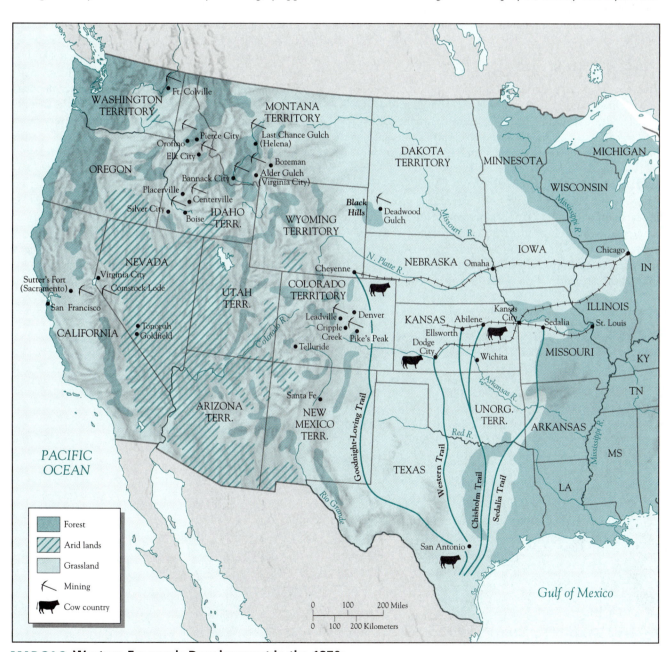

MAP 31:2 Western Economic Development in the 1870s

The cattle kingdom ran from the Canadian line to Texas between the Rockies and the farmlands in eastern Kansas and Nebraska. There were six major centers of metal mining (and many that were founded and evaporated within a year or two): California and northwestern Nevada; southern Nevada; Idaho and western Montana; the Black Hills of South Dakota centered at Deadwood; the Rockies centered around Denver; and southern Arizona. Lumbering was centered on the Washington, Oregon, and California coasts.

confused in Sitting Bull's life too, but cruelly. After a short show business career with Cody, he returned to the Rosebud Reservation, where during the Ghost Dance excitement, he was killed by Indian policemen.

Not all creators of the legendary West were frauds. Frederic Remington's paintings and bronze statues of cowboys and Indians were studiously representative and devoid of sensationalism. Owen Wister, an aristocratic easterner, was a romantic but also a talented writer. He created the finest prototype of the western knight without armor in *The Virginian,* published in 1902. If the cowboy gave you his word, Wister wrote, "he kept it; Wall Street would have found him behind the times. Nor did he talk lewdly to women; Newport would have thought him old-fashioned."

THE MINING FRONTIER

The folklore of the precious metal mining frontier is second only to the legend of the cowboy in the American imagination. Deadwood, South Dakota, for example, where Wild Bill Hickock was shot in the back and Calamity Jane spent her final years, was no cow town but a gold-mining center.

GOLD AND SILVER RUSHES

After the rich California gold fields played out, prospectors in search of "glory holes" fanned out over the mountains and deserts of the West. For more than a generation, they discovered new deposits almost annually and very rich ones every few years. In 1859 there were two great strikes. A find in the Pike's Peak area of Colorado led to a rush reminiscent of

1849. About the same time, gold miners in northern Nevada discovered that a "blue mud" that had been frustrating their operations was one of the richest silver ores ever discovered. This was the beginning of Virginia City and the **Comstock Lode.** Before the Comstock pinched out in the twentieth century, it yielded more than $400 million in silver (and quite a bit of gold too).

In 1862 Tombstone, Arizona, was founded on the site of a gold mine; in 1864 Helena, Montana, rose atop another. In 1876 rich placer deposits were discovered in the Black Hills of South Dakota. Whites were forbidden by a treaty with the Sioux from entering the Black Hills, but they went anyway, and the government defended them. (The war with the Sioux that ended Custer's career was caused by white violation of the Black Hills.) In 1877 silver was found at Leadville, Colorado, almost two miles above sea level in the Rockies.

During the 1880s the Coeur d'Alene in the Idaho panhandle drew thousands of miners, as did copper deposits across the mountains in Butte, Montana. In 1891 the Cripple Creek district in Colorado began to outproduce every other mining town. In 1898 miners rushed north to Canada's Klondike, Alaska's Yukon, and finally to Nome, where gold was mixed with sand on the beach. As late as 1901, there was an old-fashioned rush when Jim Butler, the classic grizzled old prospector in a slouch hat, "his view obscured by the rear end of a donkey," drove his pick into a desolate mountain in southern Nevada and found it "practically made of silver." From the town of Tonopah, founded on the site of Butler's discovery, prospectors discovered rich gold deposits in Goldfield, a few miles away.

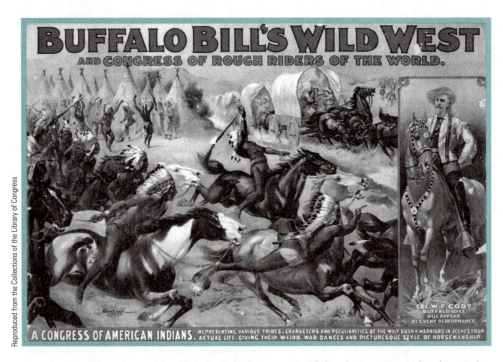

It is impossible to distinguish William F. Cody, the international show business personality, from Cody the authentic buffalo hunter and army scout. Cody was putting on shows when he was still roughriding for the Fifth Cavalry. In 1890, after he had rubbed elbows with European royalty, General Nelson Miles asked him to visit Sitting Bull to win his cooperation during the Ghost Dance excitement. Cody was on the way to speak with Sitting Bull when soldiers fired on the Ghost Dancers at Wounded Knee.

Deadwood, South Dakota, at the peak of its notoriety in 1876. The town is all bustle and movement. James Butler "Wild Bill" Hickock, a national figure, was murdered in Deadwood in 1876, but the gold camp was not really so dangerous a place. Including "Wild Bill," there were only four homicides in Deadwood in 1876, not many for a town of its size.

OF MINING CAMPS AND CITIES

Readers of the dime novels of the time and film viewers since have savored the vision of boisterous, wide-open mining towns, complete with saloons rocking with the music of tinny pianos and the shouts of bearded men. The live-for-today miner, the gambler, and the prostitute with a heart of gold are permanent inhabitants of American folklore. Nor is the picture altogether imaginary. The speculative mining economy fostered a risk-all attitude toward life and work. Even after 1900, as the case of Jim Butler and Tonopah shows, grizzled prospectors leading a burro or two excited nothing more than an indulgent smile in dozens of western towns.

However, efficient exploitation of underground (hard-rock) mining required capital and technological expertise. Consequently, the "mining camps" that were home to 5,000 to 20,000 people within a few years of their founding were also cities with a variety of urban services and a social structure more closely resembling that of eastern industrial towns than the towns of the cattleman's frontier.

In 1877, only six years after it was founded, Leadville, Colorado, boasted several miles of paved streets, gas lighting, a modern water system, thirteen schools, five churches, and three hospitals. "Camps" like Virginia City, Deadwood, and Tombstone are best remembered as tramping grounds for the likes of Wild Bill Hickock and Wyatt Earp. But they were also the sites of huge stamping mills (to crush the ores) and of miniature but busy stock exchanges, where shares in mines were traded by agents of San Francisco, New York, and London bankers as well as local miners.

In Goldfield, the last of the wide-open mining towns, one of the most important men in the camp was the urbane Wall Street financier Bernard Baruch. The Anaconda Copper Company of Butte, Montana, was one of the nation's ranking corporate giants. The Guggenheim mining syndicate was supreme in the Colorado gold fields. Rockefeller's Standard Oil was a major owner of mines in the Coeur d'Alene. If it was sometimes wild, the mining West was no mere colorful diversion for readers of dime novels, but an integral part of the national economy. In fact, the gold and silver that the hard-rock miners tore from the earth stood at the very center of a question that divided Americans more seriously than any other after the end of Reconstruction: what was to serve as the nation's money?

The miners and mine owners alone could not make a political issue of the precious metals with which coins were minted, goods bought and sold, and debts incurred and paid (or not paid). There were too few of them. However, as the century wound to a close, the money question became of great interest to a group of people who formed an important part of the American population, and who had not long before comprised a majority—the farmers on the land.

FURTHER READING

General Patricia Nelson Limerick, *Legacy of Conquest: The Unbroken Past of the American West,* 1987; Cathy Luchetti, *Men of the West: Life on the American Frontier,* 2004; Lillian Schlissel, *Black Frontiers: A History of African American Heroes in the Old West,* 1995; Richard White, *"It's Your Misfortune and None of My Own": A History of the American West,* 1991.

Plains Indians Ralph K. Andrist, *Long Death: The Last Days of the Plains Indians,* 1964; Dee Brown, *Bury My Heart at Wounded Knee,* 1970; Richard Drinnon, *Facing West: The Metaphysics of Indian Hating,* 1980; Howard L. Harrod, *Renewing the World: Plains Indians Religion and Morality,* 1987; Andrew C. Isenberg, *The Destruction of the Bison: An Environmental History, 1750–1920,* 2000; Valerie S. Mathes, *Helen Hunt Jackson and the Indian Reform Legacy,* 1990; Wilcomb E. Washburn, *The Indian in America,* 1975.

The Cattle Kingdom James H. Beckstead, *Cowboying: A Tough Job in a Hard Land,* 1991; David Dary, *Cowboy Culture: A Saga of Five Centuries,* 1981; C. L. Douglas, *Cattle Kings of Texas,* 1989; Robert R. Dykstra, *The Cattle Towns,* 1983; W. M. Elofson, *Frontier Cattle Ranching in the Land and Times of Charles Russell,* 2004; Robert F. Pace, *Frontier Texas: History of a Borderland to 1880,* 2004; J. M. Shagg, *The Cattle Trading Industry,* 1973; Richard W. Slatta, *Cowboys of the Americas,* 1990; Phyllis Zauner, *The Cowboy: An American Legend,* 1994.

The Cavalry Charles L. Kenner, *Buffalo Soldiers and Officers of the Ninth Cavalry, 1867–1898,* 1999; John P. Langellier, *Sound the Charge: The U.S. Cavalry in the American West, 1866–1916,* 1998, and *U.S. Cavalry on the Plains, 1850–1890,* 1985; William H. Leckie, *The Buffalo Soldiers: A Narrative of the Black Cavalry in the West,* 2003; TaRessa Stovall, *The Buffalo Soldiers,* 1997.

The Legendary West Robert A. Carter, *Buffalo Bill: The Man Behind the Legend,* 2000; Joy S. Kasson, *Buffalo Bill's Wild West: Celebrity, Money, and Popular History,* 2000; Larry McMurtry, *The Colonel and Little Missy: Buffalo Bill, Annie Oakley, and the Beginnings of Superstardom in America,* 2005; L. G. Moses, *Wild West Shows and the Images of American Indians, 1883–1933,* 1999; Buck Rainey, *The Reel Cowboy: Essays on the Myth in Movies and Literature,* 1996; Joseph G. Rosa, *The West of Wild Bill Hickock,* 1982, and *Wild Bill Hickock, Gunfighter: An Account of Hickock's Gunfights,* 2001.

The Mining Frontier Katherine G. Aiken, *Idaho's Bunker Hill: The Rise and Fall of a Great Mining Company, 1885–1981,* 2005; Malcolm J. Rohrbough, *Aspen: The History of a Silver Mining Town, 1879–1893,* 2000; Duane A. Smith, *Rocky Mountain Mining Camps,* 1967; William T. Stoll, *Silver Strike: The True Story of Silver Mining in the Coeur d'Alenese,* 1991; John Vernon, *All for Love: Baby Doe and Silver Dollar,* 1995; Thomas H. Watkins, *Gold and Silver in the West,* 1960; Merle W. Wells, *Gold Camps and Silver Cities: Nineteenth Century Mining in Central and Southern Idaho,* 2002.

KEY TERMS

The following terms are covered in this chapter and can also be found in the list of Key Terms at the back of the book.

A Century of Dishonor	**Buffalo Soldiers**	dime novels	Mandan
Battle of the Little Big Horn	**Comstock Lode**		

ONLINE SOURCES GUIDE

Use this listing to find online documents, images, interactive maps, simulations, and other resources related to this chapter:

American History Resource Center
http://history.wadsworth.com/rc/us

Selected Documents
The Dawes Severalty Act of 1887
Frederick Jackson Turner, The Significance of the Frontier in American History

Selected Images
Buffalo hunt, 1873
Buffalo skinner, 1874

George Armstrong Custer
Sitting Bull
Nebraska family posing in front of their sod house
A Texas longhorn steer
Cattle drive
Geronimo and his followers after his surrender, 1886

Interactive Time Line (with online readings)
The Last Frontier: Winning the Last of the West, 1865–1900

CHAPTER 32

Stressful Times Down Home

American Agriculture 1865–1896

Reproduced from the Collections of the Library of Congress

When the lawyer hangs around and the butcher cuts a pound,
Oh the farmer is the man who feeds them all.
And the preacher and the cook go a-strolling by the brook
And the farmer is the man who feeds them all.

Oh the farmer is the man, the farmer is the man,
Lives on credit 'til the fall.
Then they take him by the hand and they lead him from the land
And the middle man's the one that gets them all.

Farmers' song of the 1890s

Ever since the world's first farmer poked a hole in the ground and covered a seed with dirt, tillers of the soil have known they were at the mercy of nature, wagering a year's sustenance on the date of winter's final frost, summer's allotment of water, and early autumn storms that might destroy a crop when it was still in the fields. And then there were plant diseases, and valuable animals dropping dead, and grasshoppers—all beyond human control.

The farmer's consolation in the face of such challenges was that he or she made civilization possible. Not a single significant human achievement during the last 10,000 years would have occurred if agriculture had not been invented. Farmers have indeed fed them all. Or as William Jennings Bryan, the great hero of American farmers in the 1890s put

it, if farms were destroyed, the grass would grow in the streets of every city in the nation. But destroy the cities and leave the farms, and the cities would spring up again as if by magic.

To the farmers of the West and South who heard or read Bryan's words, the grand old truisms could ring badly off-key. To them, the big problem was not so much Mother Nature any longer, but the fact that in the America of thousand-mile-long railroads, multimillion-dollar manufacturing corporations, sinister and mighty investment banks, and a bewildering global marketplace, "artificial" forces were at work to prevent farmers from prospering even modestly. In the 1890s farmer resentments culminated in a massive and radical political movement that shook the country.

Homesteading Women

About one in five homesteaders was a woman. Some were heads of household, widows, or bold spinsters. Often several single women who intended to live together each filed for a quarter section: 160 acres. Numerous instances of three or four unmarried sisters putting substantial properties together have been documented. Legally, each quarter section remained an individual sister's property and, therefore, her dowry if she married.

Most woman homesteaders were the wives-to-be of male homesteaders. In the arid West, even 160 acres could be too little land on which to support a family except in poverty. If a woman filed before she married, she could double the size of her and her husband's property. It was easy enough for the couple to throw up a dwelling that met the government's minimal requirements on the quarter section on which they did not intend to reside. It was obvious to government agents what was going on; there were a lot of marriages between men and women with adjacent homesteads. But most officials winked at evasions of the Homestead Act's residency requirement when the "absentee" lived on the next farm.

FARMING IN A DRY LAND

Farmers rarely led the way on the final frontier. Miners and cattlemen and soldiers were the usual pioneers. Subsistence farming appealed to few nineteenth-century Americans, and commercial agriculture was feasible in the West only after the railroad arrived to connect field and corral to markets in the East. Once the railroad made its appearance, however, settlers with a plow, a couple yoke of oxen, and the right to 160 acres under the Homestead Act (or enough money to buy land from the railroads) fairly inundated the Great Plains.

SUCCESS STORY

Never in the history of the world have people put so much new land to the plow so quickly as Americans and immi-

grants did in the last three decades of the nineteenth century. Up until 1870 (260 years since the founding of Jamestown) 408 million acres of land had been brought under cultivation—an average of 1.6 million acres of new farmland a year. Between 1870 and 1900, a single generation of farmers brought 431 million acres of virgin soil into production—an average of 14.4 million acres annually.

Thanks to new agricultural machinery, crop production increased even more sharply than cultivated acreage. By 1900 American farmers were producing up to 150 percent more of the staple grains, corn and wheat, than they had in 1870. Hogs, which were a by-product of corn farming, numbered 25 million in 1870 and 63 million in 1900!

The ravenous appetites of American and foreign city dwellers fueled this amazing growth. The expansion of the railroads made it possible for crops raised by a Great Plains farmer to feed the inhabitants of Chicago and New York, even London and Warsaw.

COOL, CLEAR WATER

Farming the Plains presented Americans and immigrants from northern Europe with unfamiliar challenges. They were accustomed to climates in which summer rains nourished their crops, and wells of ten or fifteen feet were adequate sources of water for drinking and washing. Between the Atlantic seaboard and eastern Kansas, thirty-two to forty-eight inches of rain fell each year; it was wetter in the deep South. Rarely was the water table as much as ten feet below the surface.

West of about the longitude of Wichita, Kansas, however, annual precipitation declined to sixteen to thirty-two inches a year, and much of the year's rain fell during the winter in the form of snow. Farther west in the "rain shadow" of the Rocky Mountains, at about the eastern boundary of Colorado, rainfall dropped to less than sixteen inches. This was the "Great American Desert" that an early explorer called "almost totally unfit for cultivation." The central valley of California was broad and flat but rainless all summer.

Farmers under Stress 1870–1897

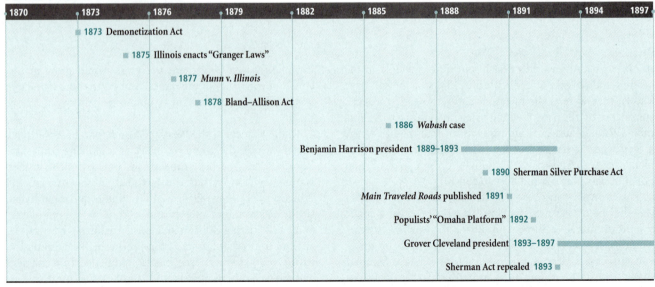

1870	1873	1876	1879	1882	1885	1888	1891	1894	1897

1873 Demonetization Act
1875 Illinois enacts "Granger Laws"
1877 *Munn v. Illinois*
1878 Bland–Allison Act
1886 *Wabash* case
Benjamin Harrison president 1889–1893
1890 Sherman Silver Purchase Act
Main Traveled Roads published 1891
Populists' "Omaha Platform" 1892
Grover Cleveland president 1893–1897
Sherman Act repealed 1893

Horses? Mules? Oxen?

Great Plains farmers used horses, mules, and oxen, but the latter were best for founding a farm on virgin land. They were cheaper to keep, subsisting on grass and hay alone; horses and mules needed grain too. Oxen were best at heavy plowing, essential for breaking sod. After the land had been tilled for several years, horses and mules had advantages. They were better for harrowing; the noisy skipping of harrows unnerved oxen. Horses and mules moved more quickly, so they were essential to exploit farm machinery. Mules were stronger than horses, less likely to sicken or spook, and "more intelligent"—easier to train. But they were more expensive, and they did not reproduce.

Californians solved their problem with large-scale collective irrigation projects. Farmers organized cooperative "ditch companies" that brought the water of the San Joaquin and Sacramento rivers, and rivers that tumbled out of the Sierra Nevada, to their fields. Their need to irrigate brought them into conflict with hydraulic miners in the foothills. Hydraulic miners literally washed down mountainsides with gravity-powered high-pressure "water cannons" to gain access to gold. The mud runoff fouled the rivers below the mines and silted up irrigation canals. Farmers were more numerous than hydraulic miners and elected legislators who shut down the mines. California water law, a hybrid of English and Spanish principles, ensured that the farmers won in the courts.

RAIN FOLLOWS THE PLOW

Cooperative ditch companies were not workable on the Great Plains. The level of even the largest rivers such as the Platte dropped too low by midsummer to be productively diverted; small streams dried up completely. Some farmers individually irrigated their fields from wells on which they mounted prefabricated windmills. The windmills were cheap, but the wells on which to mount them were not. Western

Nebraska State Historical Society Photograph Collections

◼ *A well-built sod house and stable in Custer County, Nebraska, 1887. With luck, which did not flow freely on the Great Plains in the 1890s, the family would earn the money to build a frame house within a few years. But they would use the sod house for animals or storage until, in time, the rains destroyed it.*

How to Make a Sod House

To make a sod house, pioneers on the Plains mowed an acre or two of virgin grassland in the spring when the ground was still moist. They then hitched several yoke of oxen (one account describes six to twelve oxen!) to a "grasshopper plow" that turned up the sod in strips about a foot wide and four to six inches deep. These were chopped with a spade into blocks light enough to be lifted; and, grass side down, the "Nebraska marble" was laid in overlapping courses like bricks. The walls of a sod house had to be two to three feet thick to be stable and strong enough to support the roof, which was a single layer of sod laid grass side up so that it would grow and fuse the "shingles" together. The only lumber in the house that needed to be purchased was in the rafters, ridge pole, and door. Window frames and roof boards could be made from packing crates.

aquifers were too far below the surface to be reached by digging; wells had to be drilled by professionals at a cost of $1 to $2 a foot. And every start was a roll of the dice. Plenty of drillers bragged they could tell where groundwater was accessible; none of them offered the farmer a money-back guarantee if they said 25 feet and did not hit water before 200.

To some extent, Great Plains farmers deluded themselves. The summers of the 1870s and early 1880s, when cultivators first arrived in the arid regions, were abnormally rainy. This convinced even experts like Charles Dana Wilber that "rain follows the plow." That is, Wilber said, when farmers broke the primeval sod, they altered the climate of the Plains by liberating moisture long imprisoned in the earth; it would recycle indefinitely in the form of heavier rains.

The theory was nonsense, as a devastating drought in 1887 demonstrated. However, Great Plains farmers made the most of the moisture left in the ground by winter snows by plowing more deeply than eastern farmers. The thick layer of dust that settled in furrows more than a foot deep acted as a mulch.

SOD HOUSES

Another novelty of Great Plains farming was the absence of timber that, back East, had been so abundant as to be more nuisance than resource. Except cottonwoods (a species of poplars) that grew along the shallow rivers, there were few trees on the Great Plains and, therefore, no lumber with which to build. (Cottonwoods, as their name betrays, made poor construction lumber.)

Importing lumber with which to build a frame house had to be put off until a pioneer family had harvested a few crops and squirreled away a little money. In the meantime, they lived in sod houses, which were constructed of blocks carved from the turf of the Plains—up to two feet thick in places. Sod houses were not pretty: poorly made ceilings dripped dirty drops if spring rains were heavy; and the sod houses were dusty during long, hot summers. Sod walls, however, provided better insulation than the walls of frame houses. "Soddies" were cooler in the summer and heated more cheaply in winter—the season that, on the Plains, could kill.

WIRE FENCES

The problem of fencing on the Plains was solved right at the beginning of the period when Joseph Glidden of DeKalb, Illinois, in 1873 perfected barbed wire. For a decade, dozens of inventors had been devising wires that could restrain cattle—some functional, some bizarre, but none that could be manufactured cheaply enough that a struggling farmer could fence in 160 acres. Glidden's machine mass-produced two twisted strands of cheap wire with sharp barbs every foot. (His barbed wire was nearly identical to that still used today.)

Strung on the flimsiest of scavenged fenceposts—cottonwood did nicely—farmers quickly erected a steel hedge so efficient that a starving steer would lie down and die rather than push through it. (In the great blizzard of 1886, tens of thousands of cattle fleeing ahead of the storm piled up at barbed wire fences and froze to death.)

Barbed wire was a fabulous success. The company that owned Glidden's patent produced 2.84 million pounds of it in 1876. By 1880, 80.5 million pounds had been sold. The nearly instantaneous crisscrossing of the Plains with wire fences caused clashes between homesteaders who strung it and cattlemen accustomed to grazing their herds on the government-owned open range. The fences were legal on privately owned land, but when they blocked cattle from reaching streams and water holes, cattlemen retaliated by damming streams above homesteaded land and cutting the barbed wire into shreds.

MACHINES ON THE LAND

Another invention indispensable to farming the Plains was the chilled steel plow. Invented by John Deere in 1837, it was continually perfected for slicing through ancient sod as thick

African-American Sodbusters

Benjamin "Pap" Singleton, a black carpenter in Nashville, concluded at the end of Reconstruction that African Americans could make decent lives for themselves only by doing what so many whites were doing—going west. He became known as the "Moses of the Colored Exodus" because he traveled throughout the South urging African Americans to migrate en masse to Kansas and found "colonies" of their race. For a few years his message struck a chord. By the end of 1878 more than 7,000 "Exodusters" took out homesteads in Kansas. The year 1879 saw 20,000 arrive in the state, founding several black communities, the most successful of which was Nicodemus.

White Kansans were not pleased. It was all very well that African Americans were no longer slaves, but the prospect of dozens of large all-black communities alarmed even the children of the free staters of the 1850s. While Kansas boosters continued to publicize the usual rosy lies among potential white emigrants, they responded to inquiries from southern black churches with dismaying descriptions of the hardships and risks of farming on the Plains.

as two feet by some of more than 100 improvements patented during the 1860s and 1870s. Enlarged disk harrows cultivated wide swaths with each pass, almost essential on the greater acreage of the dry country farms.

The McCormick harvester, in general use in the Midwest since the 1830s, was improved to meet the peculiar challenges of the Plains. Its manufacturer, International Harvester, and the John Deere Company competed to develop (or buy others' patents on) machines that planted seeds, shucked corn, threshed wheat, bound shocks, and shredded fodder. The value of farm machinery in use in the United States increased from $271 million in 1870 to $750 million in 1900.

Machinery made American farmers the most productive in the world. A well-equipped homesteader could cultivate six times as much land as his father had before the Civil War. Plowing and seeding wheat by hand, harvesting it with scythes, and threshing with a flail, an antebellum farmer worked fifty to sixty hours to harvest about twenty bushels of wheat per acre. With a gang plow and a horse-drawn seeder, harrow, reaper, and thresher—all in widespread use by 1890—farmers produced a much larger crop investing only eight to ten hours of work on each acre.

HARD TIMES

However, machinery cost money that was scarce among western farmers. Already short-term debtors, buying seed and provisions for the family during the growing season and settling accounts after the harvest, the farmers of the late nineteenth century were long-term debtors too. Some had purchased their land from the transcontinental railroads on credit. Homesteaders who found a 160-acre farm too small had to borrow to add to their properties. Few farmers paid for their machinery with cash. Debt up to the chin, secured by a lien on their land, was almost universal among western farmers.

Then, beginning about 1872, growers of wheat and corn and raisers of cattle and hogs watched their incomes slowly but annually sag and, after 1890, collapse. A crop that in 1872 earned a farmer $1,000 in real income (actual purchasing power) earned only $500 in 1896. A farmer 48 years of age in 1896, still actively working, had to turn out twice as many hogs or double the bushels of corn or wheat that he had produced as a young man of 24, just to enjoy the same standard of living he had known in 1872. It was at best unsettling to look back on a quarter-century of toil and to realize it had yielded little but the prospect of more struggle just to keep the bank happy.

By the 1890s, the price of corn was so low (8 cents a bushel) that some farmers stopped buying coal and burned their corn for warmth during the winter. Vernon L. Parrington, later a distinguished historian, remembered as a boy in Kansas warming himself "by the kitchen stove in which the ears were burning briskly, popping and crackling in the jolliest fashion. And if while we sat around such a fire watching the year's crop go up the chimney, the talk sometimes became bitter, who will wonder?"

Many farmers went under. Between 1889 and 1893, 11,000 Kansas farm families lost their homes when they failed to meet their mortgage payments. In several counties in western Kansas and Nebraska, nine of ten farms changed hands. The number of tenant farmers—those who did not own the land they worked—doubled from 1 to 2 million between 1880 and 1900, most of the increase coming after 1890. For every three farm families that owned their land outside the South, there was one tenant family. For them, farming was no longer the basis of proud independence and hope for the future, but grinding toil for the sake of putting meals on the table and keeping the banker from the door.

SOUTHERN FARMERS

Tenancy was even more common in the South, particularly in the cotton belt. Below the Ohio River, there were as many tenant farmers as there were families working land they owned. Among African Americans, tenants and **sharecroppers** outnumbered landowners by almost five to one.

SHARECROPPERS

Sharecropping originated in Reconstruction when, having freed blacks from bondage, the Republican party shied away from giving the freedmen the land that would have provided economic independence. The same people who had owned land in slavery times still owned it when, in 1868, the political dust of the Reconstruction debate settled.

But how, without slaves, were the crops to be got in? Even being paid for their labor, the freedmen resisted working in gangs and living collectively. They associated gangs with slavery, and they wanted a family life that had been at best imperfect in "the quarters." After Congress nullified the black codes, landowners recognized that without coercion (the blacksnake whip) the gang system was unworkable.

Moreover, in the Reconstruction South, landowners, even those who had once been proud planters, had little or no money with which to pay wages. Slaves had been their capital as well as their labor. The expensive four-year run of the Confederacy had sent what gold there was in the South abroad, mostly to Great Britain; the Confederacy's collapse destroyed the value of its paper money. As late as 1880, there was more gold in the bank vaults of the single northern state of Massachusetts than there was in all the banks of the former Confederacy.

So the land was cultivated by a no-cash arrangement that, on the face of it, was fair to both landowner and worker: sharing the crop. Landowners partitioned their acreage into family farm–size plots of ten to forty acres on which cabins were constructed. In return for the use of the dwelling and the land, *share tenants* who owned their mule, plow, and seed turned over to the landlord at harvest a quarter to a third of the crop: cotton or corn or, usually, both. *Sharecroppers* were tenants too poor to rustle up a mule, plow, and seed. The landlord provided them as well as the farm in return for half of the crop.

As a means of production, sharecropping worked quite well. Southern cotton production reached its 1860 level in 1870 and exceeded the prewar record (1859) a few years later.

■ *A sharecropper's cabin in North Carolina. Many sharecroppers were so deeply in debt to the owner of the local general store, who often owned the land they farmed, that getting free and clear was difficult to imagine. There was a kind of security in debt bondage; landlords did not evict sharecroppers who owed them. But slavery had provided that sort of security too.*

As in the West, however, greater production was accompanied by a decline in wholesale prices. The wholesale price of a pound of cotton, 18 cents in the early 1870s, fell to 6 cents by the early 1890s and, in 1894, to a nickel: $30 for a 600-pound bale!

DEBT BONDAGE

In the West, the collapse in wholesale prices caused mortgage foreclosures on farmers and their reduction to tenantry. In the South, where sharecroppers were already tenants, declining prices caused a physically and morally debilitating poverty far worse or, at least, affecting more people than in the West. Pellagra, a fatal niacin deficiency disease, was unknown in slavery times but became a problem of epidemic proportions in the South by the 1890s.

A second consequence of the agricultural depression was a widespread **debt bondage** that, according to Charles Oken in 1894, "crushed out all independence and reduced its victims to a coarse species of servile labor."

The victims were white as well as black because many white farmers of modest means before the Civil War lost their land to their creditors, usually merchants who sold seed, provisions, clothing, and other necessities on account.

The ledgers of one general merchandiser, T. G. Patrick, reveal that during one season he provided $900 worth of seed, food, and tools to a farmer named S. R. Simonton, who owned his land. When, in the fall, the price of cotton dropped well below Simonton's expectations, he was able to repay only $300, leaving Patrick with a lien against his property of $600. Simonton cut his costs drastically the following year, to just $400, but the accumulated debt of $1,000 was more than Patrick was willing to carry. He foreclosed on the farm, and Simonton became his share tenant. Tens of thousands of families had the same experience.

Tenants' and sharecroppers' debts bound them to the land like serfs. They had no alternative to buying each year's necessities on credit. If their landlord owned the general merchandise store—which was often the case—they had no choice but to buy from him with their share of the crop as collateral. With income from their share declining annually, as it did during the late 1870s and 1880s, they faced each spring with a lien on the crop they had not yet put into the ground. There was no way out; sharecroppers in debt bondage were not really free. They could not easily "quit," move, and "start fresh." In several southern states, fleeing such debts was not a matter for civil courts but a criminal offense punishable by imprisonment on a state-owned plantation or being hired out by the state, sometimes to the creditor who had put the debtor in jail.

The convict farm laborer was, of course, less free than the debt slave; he could be and usually was chained, at least at night. To be a convict in the South was a horror. Between 1877 and 1880, the Greenwood and Augusta Railroad contracted with the state of Georgia for 285 convict laborers. Almost half of them died.

HAYSEEDS

Southern black farmers needed no tutoring to know that they were not participants in American freedom. White farmers of the West as well as the South experienced a deterioration in their economic, political, social, and cultural status that was new to them. The proportion of agriculturalists in the population declined annually during the late nineteenth century. The legislators whom farmers sent to Washington and the state capitals often forgot their constituents when they made the acquaintance of back-slapping lobbyists for railroads and banks.

The urban culture of the era depicted the man of the soil in popular fiction, songs, and melodramas as a thick-skulled yokel in a tattered straw hat with a length of straw clenched between his teeth—a "hayseed" who was dumb enough to put traveling salesmen into bed with his daughters. Serious chroniclers of rural life like Hamlin Garland commiserated with struggling farmers like his father but wanted no part of the life. In *Main-Traveled Roads*, published in 1891, Garland depicted rural life as dreary and stultifying. He described what it meant to him when, one year, his father moved the family to a town—Osage, Iowa—where he had taken a job. The experience "placed the rigorous, filthy drudgery of the farmyard in sharp contrast with the carefree, companionable existence led by my friends in the village, and we longed to be of their condition."

By the tens of thousands, farmers' sons and daughters followed Garland in flight to the city. With each child who opted for urban life, farmers who clung to the Jeffersonian image of themselves as the bone and sinew of the republic became further dejected, agitated, demoralized, and embittered.

PROTEST AND ORGANIZATION

The Jeffersonian agrarian myth provided some insulation from urban ridicule of hayseeds. And farmers retaliated by condemning cities as sinks of iniquity and sin. In sturdy pillars of the older popular culture like the *McGuffey's Readers*, the ennoblement of farm life remained alive and well.

RURAL RENAISSANCE

And yet life on Great Plains farms was clearly more arduous and isolated than in the East and the Midwest, and the loneliness was worse for women, kept close to houses on 160-acre farms, than it was for the men. Aside from church and moments snatched on shopping trips to town, there was little to relieve the tedium and monotony of the farmwife. "Even my

youthful zeal" in depicting the hardships of farm life, Hamlin Garland wrote, was inadequate when he tried to describe "the lives led by the women. . . . Before the tragic futility of their suffering, my pen refused to shed its ink."

In the 1870s farm women and their husbands turned to the Patrons of Husbandry, the **Grange,** which was founded as a response to the cultural and social aridity of western life. The Grange sponsored dances, fairs, and lecturers who spoke on everything from the date of creation to the curious habits of the people of Borneo. In the 1880s new organizations—the Agricultural Wheel, the Texas State Alliance, the Southern Alliance, and the Colored Farmers' National Alliance—mushroomed all over the countryside to carry out many of the same functions. Their value was inestimable, particularly for women. A leader of the Southern Alliance, the largest of the regional organizations, declared that it "redeemed woman from her enslaved condition, and placed her in her proper sphere." Indeed, women were to play an active role in the agrarian movement at every level.

Originally the Grange and the Alliances were nonpolitical. As the agricultural depression worsened, however, gatherings of farmers inevitably asked themselves what—or who—was to blame for their difficulties. The Grangers blamed the railroads and, for a few years, successfully regulated their rates by electing sympathetic politicians to state legislatures. The Alliances and Wheels taught that the truculent individualism of the farmers in a highly organized society contributed to their distress and encouraged members to form cooperatives and other economic combinations.

CO-OPS

In consumer cooperatives, farmers pooled resources to purchase essential machinery in quantity and therefore more cheaply. Money pools sprouted all over the Midwest. Through these associations, which were capitalized by members and operated on a nonprofit basis, farmers hoped to eliminate their dependence on banks. Although some survived to serve the credit needs of members for generations as credit unions, most farmers' money pools suffered from the inexperience of their amateur administrators. Farmers too often put their own rather than professionals in charge of their co-ops; the rate of mismanagement and embezzlement was high.

Producer cooperatives aimed to counter the power of the railroads over farmers' lives after the *Wabash* case of 1886 struck down the Granger laws that had regulated charges for storing grain. Corn belt farmers pooled funds and built their own grain elevators in the expectation they could keep their crop off the market until they liked the selling price.

But co-ops could not remedy the problem that was at the root of agricultural distress: American staple farmers were too numerous and too productive for their own good. Too much land was opened to settlement by too many railroads too quickly. Improvements in farm machinery produced far more grain, livestock, and fiber than the market could absorb at prices sufficient to support farm families decently. The "free economy"—and farmers could imagine no other kind—was itself a basic cause of agrarian distress.

■ *"Mother Lease," Mary Elizabeth Lease, was one of the agrarian movement's most popular orators, and later a leading Populist. She affected "down home" manners, language, and costume; but she was, in fact, sophisticated and well educated, one of the first woman lawyers in the United States.*

SINISTER FORCES

Some agrarian leaders recognized overproduction as the heart of the farmers' woes. Canadian-born "Sockless Jerry" Simpson of Kansas called on the federal government to carve out new markets for American farm goods abroad by whatever means would turn the trick. Mary Elizabeth Lease of Kansas, one of the nation's first female lawyers and an orator of withering intensity, told farmers to "raise less corn and more hell." It was a catchy slogan but just a slogan. In a global market, an individual farmer or even 10,000 farmers could not affect wholesale prices by planting less corn or raising fewer hogs.

Moreover, many farmers refused to accept the argument that overproduction was the sole or even the chief cause of agrarian distress. Mother Lease herself pointed out that the streets of American cities teemed with hungry, ill-clad people while foodstuffs rotted in Kansas and cotton went unsold in Alabama. She and other agrarian leaders—Simpson, Ignatius Donnelly of Minnesota, William Peffer of Kansas, and Thomas Watson of Georgia—said that sinister, parasitical forces were at work like thieves in the night to enrich themselves at the expense of the men and women who actually produced wealth. Their villains included the railroaders,

politicians and judges pliantly in their employ, and most of all the "money power," a conspiracy of bankers who manipulated the value of the nation's currency.

THE MONEY QUESTION

Money has value because people agree that it represents value. It makes the exchange of goods and services workable. The value of money changes. At the time of the first European incursions in North America, the Eastern Woodlands Indians used wampum, belts of beads made of shell or stone, as a medium of exchange. Wampum was difficult and time-consuming to make; every tiny bead had to be shaped, drilled, and polished before it was strung. (The artistic merit of a belt increased or decreased its worth.) When Europeans introduced cheap glass beads into the wampum economy to buy grain, skins, or pelts from the Indians but, knowing the cheapness of the glass beads, refused to accept them as payment for iron tools and other European products, wampum was soon worthless to Indians too.

GOLD, SILVER, AND GREENBACKS

The economically sophisticated nations of the world used precious metals—gold and silver—as their medium of exchange. Gold and silver were durable and, like precontact wampum, limited in supply. There was little danger the economy would be suddenly flooded with them or that anyone would refuse to accept them as money; their value was stable. The farmer into whose hand gold coins were counted in payment for his crop knew that the suppliers of the goods his family needed would accept the gold at the same value he put on it. In the United States, gold was minted in $5 coins, $10 coins (called "eagles"), and $20 coins ("double eagles").

Coins of smaller denomination (dimes, quarters, and dollars) were silver, which was more abundant than gold and therefore less valuable by weight. In 1837, because the supply of both metals had been stable for many decades, Congress pegged the money value of silver at a ratio of sixteen ounces of silver to one ounce of gold. Silver too had intrinsic value. Large commercial transactions were carried out with paper money issued by banks that promised to redeem them in specie—gold or silver—at the face value of their notes.

During the Civil War, needing more money than it had, the Lincoln administration issued a new kind of paper money, some $433 million in bills that were called "**greenbacks**" because they were printed in green ink on the obverse. (Some banks printed the backs of their notes in a yellow—"golden"—ink.) Unlike bank notes, the greenbacks were not redeemable in gold and silver. Their value rested entirely upon the fact that the government accepted them as payment of taxes and defined the greenbacks as legal tender.

The greenbacks were never "as good as gold" (or silver). Their worth fluctuated, depending on the success or failure of the Union army or twists in federal financial policy. The more greenbacks the government printed, the less they were worth. At the end of the Civil War, a person needed $157 in greenbacks to buy what $100 in gold or silver coin would purchase.

The Cigarette Kingdom

How They Lived

If the South remained largely agricultural, said Henry W. Grady, the wisecracking editor of the section's most prestigious newspaper, the Atlanta *Constitution,* it would remain what it had been during Reconstruction: a weak, dependent appendage of the North. The "New South," he said, breaking with the principles of the defiantly agrarian South of slavery times, must industrialize.

By the end of the century, the South had wooed much of the cotton industry from the Northeast by providing a labor pool—poor whites—that would accept much lower wages than New Englanders would. Nearby coal and iron deposits made Birmingham, Alabama, the "Pittsburgh of the South," the center of a booming steel industry. By 1890 Birmingham produced more pig iron than Pittsburgh. The single most successful southern industrialist was a pioneer in a new business: the mass production, promotion, and sale of cigarettes.

Americans had long been big consumers of cigars, pipe tobacco, and plugs for chewing. (In 1890 the per capita consumption of "chaw" each year was three pounds!) Cigarettes were not unknown. Invented by a Turkish soldier in 1832, they had the advantage over chewing tobacco in that you could get your nicotine fix unobtrusively almost everywhere, and they did not create the hideous mess that chewers did with their incessant spitting. The smoke cigarettes created was less offensive to nonsmokers than cigar smoke. (In fashionable society, after dinner, the ladies left the room so that the gentlemen could enjoy their cigars.) Unlike a pipe, a cigarette could be smoked in a few minutes, always a recommendation to a people ever in a rush.

Many soldiers took to cigarettes during the Civil War. They rolled their own or they bought cigarettes that had been rolled by hand using a simple machine (they still exist) and then packaged. The fledgling industry was centered in Great Britain, but there were a number of small American companies too. Around 1880 the owner of one of them, James Buchanan "Buck" Duke of Durham, North Carolina, persuaded 125 Russian Jewish cigarette makers to settle there and hand-roll the mild "bright leaf" of the region.

But Duke's skilled labor force was soon displaced. In 1883 Buck bought the exclusive rights to a little-known cigarette-making device, the Bonsack machine. In 1884 his company churned out more "Dukes of Durham" than the entire industry had produced the previous year. Duke's production capacity was infinite—*if* he could create a big enough market for his "coffin nails." He could; Duke's skill

as a promoter was keener than his eye for technology. He enticed boys to smoke his cigarettes by printing pictures of boxers, baseball players, and actresses on the cardboards that were inserted in cigarette packs to stiffen them. In 1886 Duke began to fish for women with a "feminine" brand, "Cameos." In 1889 he spent $800,000 on advertising. Only the ready-to-eat cereal makers, Post and Kellogg, spent so much on publicizing their products. When others developed cigarette machines that did not violate Duke's patents, he proved as ruthless a competitor as John D. Rockefeller. He launched a price war that drove other cigarette makers into bankruptcy and picked up the pieces of their companies at bargain prices. A few years after the turn of the century, Duke had a near monopoly of the cigarette business; his American Tobacco Company owned or controlled 150 factories.

Cigarettes had enemies then too. The Women's Christian Temperance Union lobbied for laws against them almost as actively as they lobbied against alcohol, and they were more successful in the battle against cigarettes. In 1890 twenty-six states had some sort of anticigarette legislation on the books, mostly restricting their sale to adults. (By 1900 even North Carolina had enacted a minimum age law.) Washington, Tennessee, and several other states prohibited the sale of cigarettes to anyone. In 1898 the Tennessee Supreme Court approved that state's law by defining cigarettes as "not legitimate articles of commerce because wholly noxious and deleterious to health."

Still, the habit spread. Duke remained on the defensive but continued to sell more cigarettes each year than he had in the year previous. When, in 1904, a woman was jailed in New York for smoking in front of her children, even nonsmokers joined the attack on anticigarette zealotry. As other moralistic reforms picked up steam—the prohibition movement, the antiprostitution movement—the anticigarette movement began to fizzle. Perhaps its final celebration took place in 1912 when Topsy, an elephant at Coney Island, killed her keeper when he put a lighted cigarette in Topsy's mouth.

World War I marked an end to Buck Duke's problems. Shrewdly, he and other manufacturers gave away millions of packs of cigarettes to American soldiers. They were celebrated as patriots and created hundreds of thousands of new addicts for an expenditure that, in the long run, smokers regarded as not worth noticing. By the time the war ended, one could not legally buy a drink in the United States, but Americans, including a substantial proportion of women, were hooked on cigarettes.

INFLATION AND DEFLATION

Discounted as they were, the greenbacks nevertheless circulated. The Union survived, and the government continued to accept them. Indeed, the greenbacks had many friends because by increasing the amount of money in circulation—no matter that the greenbacks were discounted—they inflated wages and prices, including the prices at which farmers sold their crops. The Civil War was a prosperous time down on the farm. Looking back on the period from bleaker days, many farmers associated prosperity with the greenbacks. They argued that the federal government should continue to issue them to adjust the amount of money in circulation so as to accommodate the changing needs of the economy. The supply of gold and silver increased too slowly, in an explosive economy, when it increased at all.

Bankers thought otherwise. They dealt in large sums and feared having the value of their property—and the money owed to them—reduced in value by politicians interested mainly in currying favor with voters. Monetary conservatives insisted that gold (and, until 1873, silver) gave money a "natural" value. They wanted the government to "retire" the greenbacks (take them out of circulation) by not reissuing those that were paid into the treasury.

With close ties to the Republican party after the Civil War, monetary conservatives generally had their way. By February 1868, $45 million in greenbacks had been retired. The total money in circulation shrank annually; gold and silver increased in value (how much they would buy). This was deflation: wages and prices both dropped. In 1870 a dollar bought more than it had bought in 1865, and it was harder to earn.

Debtors were hurt by deflation. The $1,000 a farmer borrowed in "cheap" currency had to be repaid in deflated money. Protest was so widespread that in October 1868 Congress ordered the Treasury Department to stop retiring the greenbacks.

But the victory was short-lived. In 1875 the government ordered that for every new $100 issued by banks (money backed by gold), $80 in greenbacks be retired. In 1879 Secretary of the Treasury John Sherman ordered that all payments to the government be made in coin. This spelled the greenbacks' doom; if the government would not accept them, who would? Between 1865 and 1878, the amount of all kinds of money in circulation in the United States shrank from $1.08 billion to $773 million. Whereas in 1865 there had been $31.18 in circulation for every American, in 1878 there was but $16.25.

Southern Funeral

Henry Grady promoted southern industrialization in a speech he delivered to hundreds of southern audiences. He began with a story of a funeral he had attended in rural Georgia. "They buried him in a New York coat and a Boston pair of shoes, and a pair of breeches from Chicago and a shirt from Cincinnati." The coffin, Grady continued, was made from northern lumber and hammered together with northern-forged nails. "The South didn't furnish a thing on earth for that funeral but the corpse and the hole in the ground."

© Bettmann/Corbis

A Gold Bug cartoonist lampoons bimetallism by depicting a currency based on two standards—the value of gold and the value of silver—as a bicycle with poorly mounted wheels of different sizes on the rough country road that economists called the "business cycle."

In an attempt to stem the deflation, many farmers and some working people and small businessmen organized the Greenback Labor party, which was dedicated to the single issue of inflating the currency. Like most third parties in American history, the Greenbackers attracted few voters. In 1880 Civil War General James B. Weaver of Iowa won 308,578 votes, enough to notice. In 1884 Benjamin F. Butler won just 175,370 votes, not many more than the Prohibitionist party candidate. By 1884 inflationists had turned to another form of money for their salvation—silver coin.

SILVER TO THE FORE

Between 1837 and 1873, the price of silver in the United States was pegged to the price of gold by law at a ratio of 16:1. During the 1860s, however, American mines produced considerably less than sixteen ounces of silver for each new ounce of gold added to the money supply. Owners of silver mines ceased to sell to the U.S. mint, which paid a price fixed by law. They preferred to sell their silver to foreign buyers (or, for that matter, jewelry makers) willing to pay the equivalent of one ounce of gold for just fourteen ounces of silver, which was the actual ratio of mine production.

In 1873, with little silver being presented to the mint, Congress passed the Demonetization Act, ceasing government purchases of silver. The silver dollar was no longer coined. Rather than money with a value set by law, silver became a commodity like wheat, hogs, or lumber. Its value (in gold) was determined not by Congress but by the laws of the market: supply and demand. President Grant signed the Demonetization Act without ado or much notice. The United States was on the "gold standard"; gold alone was the basis of money. Silver dollars still in circulation were mere tokens, like a bank note.

As the ink from Grant's pen was drying, however, the relative production of silver and gold was changing dramatically. New silver strikes throughout the West and cheaper methods of smelting the ore vastly increased production. In 1861 only $2 million worth of silver had been mined in the United States compared to $43 million worth of gold. In 1873 the value of silver and gold mined was about equal, $36 million each. During the rest of the 1870s silver production increased so rapidly that its price on the private market, the only market for it, collapsed.

"THE CRIME OF '73"

Political friends of silver mining interests like Democrat Richard "Silver Dick" Bland of Missouri and Republican Senator Henry W. Teller of Colorado began to denounce the Demonetization Act as **"the Crime of '73."** They accused the government of conspiring with bankers to punish silver miners for their success. This was unalloyed nonsense. There was no crime of 1873, no wicked conspiracy. No one could have foreseen the tremendous increase in silver production when Congress passed the Demonetization Act.

Nevertheless, with silver production continuing to rise annually, monetary conservatives were relieved that the government no longer pegged its value to gold, which would have inflated the currency as the greenbacks had done. The "gold bugs," as Bland and Teller called them, looked on those who called for the remonetization of silver as a threat to the stability of the economy.

By themselves, silver mine owners and their employees did not have the political clout to influence government policy. Even after the admission of mineral-rich Colorado in 1876, mining interests had few representatives in Congress. However, inflationist congressmen from farm states—mostly southern and western Democrats but including some Republicans—seized on silver coinage as a way to get more money in circulation. In the depression year of 1878, they pushed a compromise through Congress. The Bland–Allison Bill required the secretary of the treasury to purchase between $2 million and $4 million of silver each month for minting. The silver dollar was back.

THE SHERMAN SILVER PURCHASE ACT

The silver dollar was back, but the principle of bimetallism (both gold and silver as money, the value of each pegged to the other) was not. In both Republican and Democratic administrations, the Treasury Department was safely in the hands of gold bugs dedicated to maintaining gold as the sole standard of value. The government almost invariably bought the legally mandated minimum of $2 million in silver each year. Silver dollars were still tokens; they had value only because five of them, just like 500 pennies, could be exchanged for a $5 gold piece.

Silver production continued to increase, and its market price continued to decline. By 1890 an ounce of gold bought

Populist Anti-Semitism

Populist hatred of bankers was sometimes anti-Semitic. Mother Lease called President Cleveland "the agent of Jewish bankers and British gold." Ignatius P. Donnelly's novel *Caesar's Column* blamed "Jews" for the ruination of the American farmer; but one character's explanation of why Jewish bankers exploited farmers is, perhaps, unique in the long history of anti-Semitism:

> Christianity fell upon the Jews, originally a race of agriculturists and shepherds, and forced them, for many centuries, through the most terrible ordeal of persecution the history of mankind bears record of. Only the strong of body, the cunning of brain, the long-headed, the persistent, the men with capacity to live where the dog would starve, survived the awful trial. Like breeds like; and now the Christian world is paying, in tears and blood, for the sufferings inflicted by their bigoted and ignorant ancestors upon a noble race. When the time came for liberty and fair play the Jew was master in the contest with the Gentile. . . . They were as merciless to the Christians as the Christians had been to them.

nearly twenty ounces of silver. To silver producers and agrarian inflationists, the ratio of 16:1, what it had been in 1873, took on a sacred significance.

In 1889 and 1890, the balance of power in Congress tipped to the side of the inflationists. Two states in which silver was an important commodity (Montana and Idaho) and four in which inflationist farmers and ranchers were a majority (the two Dakotas, Washington, and Wyoming) entered the Union, bringing twelve new "silver senators" to Washington.

The result was the Sherman Silver Purchase Act of 1890. It was a compromise. The Sherman law required the secretary of the treasury to purchase 4.5 million ounces of silver each month (then the nation's monthly production). However, the government purchased silver at the market price, which continued to decline—from 20:1 in 1890 to 26.5:1 in 1893. Consequently, the Sherman Act failed to relieve discontent in the mining regions.

Farmers, who wanted inflation, were also disappointed. Although President Benjamin Harrison signed the Sherman Act, he was a gold standard man. He instructed the secretary of the treasury to pay all the government's bills in gold. To distressed farmers already inclined to look for sinister forces at work in the night, the presidency itself seemed in the employ of the money power.

THE POPULISTS

In 1890 the Alliance movement was at flood tide. The Southern Alliance had 1.5 million members, the Colored Farmers Alliance a million, other groups combined about the same. Feeling their strength, the leaders of the regional organizations gathered in Ocala, Florida, in December to draw up a list of grievances and consider the possibility of organizing a third party.

Gun-toting Populists in the Kansas Legislature in January 1893. The results of the November election were disputed. These Populists chose an unorthodox means of seeing to it that their candidates were seated. Photographs like this one persuaded both Republican and Democratic conservatives that they were facing a revolution. The Populist party dominated Kansas politics in the early 1890s—by votes, not rifles and shotguns.

HESITATION

Kansas farmers were ahead of the Ocala convention. In 1890 they had organized a state People's party, calling themselves Populists after the Latin word for "the people," *populus.* They immediately won control of the state legislature. At Ocala, however, Republican and Democratic loyalties were too strong and racial anxieties too tense for the delegates to take the same leap.

Southern white farmers hesitated to form a new party because they had made inroads in the Democratic party. They feared that if they split the white southern votes between the Democratic party and a new Populist party, blacks would regain some of the political power they had held during Reconstruction. The leaders of the Colored Farmers Alliance were reluctant to give up their ties to the Republican party, which

had, however ineffectively, defended African-American civil rights.

But events were already under way that almost destroyed the old loyalties. In July 1890, the same month the Silver Purchase Act was passed, the Republican majority in the Senate failed to enact the Force Bill, a law to protect the right of southern blacks to vote. The Force Bill was the last serious effort by the Republican party on behalf of southern blacks. Some Colored Alliance leaders announced their support for a third party. Disgusted, some southern whites like Tom Watson of Georgia, a hot-tempered lawyer who had been cheated out of elective office by the Democratic party, called for an alliance between black and white tenants and small farmers. In a magazine article of 1892 he wrote, "You are kept apart that you may be separately fleeced of your earnings. You are

Discrimination
In the late nineteenth century, railroads allowed delegates to national political conventions to ride half-fare. However, this favor was not extended to delegates to the Populist party convention in Omaha. When one delegate referred to the oversight, another delegate from California delivered a diatribe that illustrated the angry antagonism of the Populists:

> The customary courtesy was denied deliberately and with insolence. I do not want this Convention to go back to the railroad company, hat in hand, and ask for any privileges whatever. The Democrats and Republicans secured half-fare, but we—not connected with railroads, but producers of the earth—have been refused equal terms. We can stand the refusal.

The Literal Truth
The religious fervor of the Omaha Populist convention would have come as no surprise to a reporter who was familiar with the **farmers' Alliances** that had organized the party. There was an element of what is today known as "fundamentalism" in them from the start. To join the Southern Farmers Alliance, for example, one had to swear belief in the divinity of Christ and "the literal truth" of the Bible. Members were forbidden to drink or gamble, which is not to say that the rules were universally obeyed or rigorously enforced.

made to hate each other because upon that hatred is rested the keystone of the arch of financial despotism which enslaves you both. You are deceived and blinded that you may not see how this race antagonism perpetuates a monetary system which beggars both."

THE OMAHA CONVENTION
In February 1892 delegates from the various Alliances and Wheels, and more than a few self-appointed spokesmen for farmers and silver miners, met in Omaha, Nebraska, to launch the new party. They adopted the name Populist from the Kansas party that had already sent several congressmen and Senator William Peffer to Washington.

To symbolize the fact that farmers of North and South had bridged the sectional chasm, the Populists nominated former Union General and Greenbacker James B. Weaver for president, and former Confederate General James G. Field for vice president. No one expected them to win, and they did not. Grover Cleveland, the Democratic candidate, won a comfortable victory in the electoral college. But Weaver ran well, winning more than a million votes and carrying Kansas. All along, the Populists at Omaha had their eyes on 1896, when they expected to restore democracy and justice to a corrupted country.

Observers of the **Omaha Convention** were taken aback by the religious fervor of the Populists, as if they were embarked not on a political campaign but on a crusade against satanic evil. "We meet on the verge of a nation brought to the verge of moral, political, and material ruin," Ignatius Donnelly of Minnesota wrote in the preamble to the party platform. "Corruption dominates the ballot box, the legislatures, the Congress, and touches even the ermine of the bench." William Peffer, looking like a biblical prophet with his waist-length beard, railed about the inequities of the land. "Conspiracy" was a word on everyone's lips—the conspiracy of the great railroads to defraud the shipper, the conspiracy of politicians to destroy democracy, the conspiracy of the money power, even the conspiracy of Jews.

"The people are at bay," Mother Lease said; "let the bloodhounds of money beware." When the Populist platform was approved, according to one unsympathetic reporter, "cheers and yells . . . rose like a tornado . . . and raged without cessation for thirty-four minutes, during which time women shrieked and wept, men embraced and kissed their neighbors, locked arms, marched back and forth, and leaped upon tables and chairs in the ecstasy of their delirium."

A FAR-REACHING PROGRAM
The atmosphere was, no doubt, unsettling for an observer. And yet the platform the Populists wrote was far from lunatic. It was a comprehensive reform program that, had it been enacted, would have transformed American development, and not necessarily for the worse.

Indeed, many of the Populists' political demands later became the law of the land. They called for the election of U.S. senators by popular vote rather than by state legislatures, a reform instituted in the Seventeenth Amendment to the Constitution in 1913. They demanded the universal use of the Australian, or secret, ballot to prevent landlords and employers from intimidating their tenants and workers into voting as they were told. By the early twentieth century, public balloting was abolished everywhere but in town meetings.

The Populists introduced the concepts of the initiative, recall, and referendum to American government. The initiative allows voters, through petition, to put measures on the ballot independent of legislatures and thus, in theory, free of manipulation by professional lobbyists. The recall allows voters, also through petition, to force a public official to stand for election before his or her term is up. The Populists said that the recall would discourage politicians from backing down on campaign pledges. The referendum allows voters to vote on laws (and recalls) directly rather than through their representatives. All three are well-established procedures in many states today.

The most controversial Populist demand was for the abolition of national banks and for government ownership of railroads and the telegraph. Their enemies pointed to this plank as evidence that the Populists were socialists. They were not; they were landowners or tenants who aspired to own land. However, they believed that natural monopolies—enterprises that could be run efficiently only under a single management—should not be in private hands. To the

The Pollock Case

The Wilson–Gorman Tariff of 1894 provided for an income tax of 2 percent on all incomes of $4,000 or more, a tiny tax on few people by our standards. Nevertheless, the tax was denounced by those who had to pay it, and in the 1895 case of *Pollock* v. *Farmers' Loan and Trust Co.*, the Supreme Court ruled that because the tax was a direct tax that did not fall on all states equally, it was unconstitutional. Only after the Sixteenth Amendment was adopted in 1913 was it constitutional to tax the wealthy at a higher rate than poorer people paid.

Populist mind, decisions that affected the interests of all should be made democratically, not by private parties.

The Populists called for a postal savings system so that ordinary people might avoid depositing their money in privately owned banks, and for a graduated income tax. In 1892 the federal income tax was 2 percent for all who earned more than $4,000 a year. The Populists were willing to see people who earned less than $4,000 pay a tax, but they wanted the wealthy taxed at a higher percentage than modestly fixed farmers and wage workers.

Finally, as one plank among many, the Populists addressed the silver question. They called for an increase in the money in circulation to $50 per capita. This inflation was to be accomplished through the free and unlimited coinage of silver, its value pegged to that of gold. In 1892 this was perhaps the mildest of the Populist demands. In a little more than a year, however, "free silver" was to become the Populists' obsession, destroying the ardor of many of them for the rest of the Omaha platform.

A MOST UNPOPULAR MAN

In February 1893 the Reading Railroad, an important eastern line, announced it was bankrupt. For two months the stock market was jittery; then it crashed. As in 1873, hundreds of banks and thousands of businesses joined the Reading in receivership. By November the country was sunk in a depression worse than that of the 1870s.

Fearing for the safety of their government bonds, American and British financiers rushed to redeem them. President Cleveland, as committed to the gold standard as Harrison, redeemed all demands made on the government in gold. By fall the government's gold reserve—the actual metal in its vaults—sank below the $100 million regarded as the minimum for maintaining the government's credit.

Cleveland blamed the crisis on the Sherman Act. "To put beyond all doubt or mistake" the commitment of the United States to the gold standard, the president called for the repeal of the Sherman Act, and a frightened Congress obliged him. That lost Cleveland the support of Democrats from the mining states. Then the news leaked that, at the height of the crisis, Cleveland had called on J. P. Morgan for help in increasing the government's gold reserve. Throughout the South and Midwest, more Democrats denounced him as Wall Street's flunky.

In 1894 Cleveland's attorney general, Richard B. Olney, crushed the Pullman strike, alienating industrial workers. When **Jacob S. Coxey**, an eccentric, idealistic millionaire from Ohio, led an almost entirely orderly march of unemployed men to Washington to ask for relief, "a petition with its boots on," Olney ridiculed the protesters by having Coxey arrested for walking on the grass.

Only a few presidents have been so unpopular as Grover Cleveland was in his second term. When his supporters, dwindling in numbers, reminded voters of the president's unquestioned integrity, William Jennings Bryan of Nebraska replied, "Cleveland may be honest, but so were the mothers who threw their children in the Ganges."

With every blow to Cleveland's reputation, the Populists celebrated. In their eyes, Cleveland's Democrats and the Republicans were indistinguishable. Both parties were the puppets of the money power. The people did indeed seem to be at bay. The word *revolution* was heard in many a gathering of "the bone and sinew of the republic."

FURTHER READING

General Edward Ayers, *The Promise of the New South, 1877–1913*, 1992, and *Southern Crossing: A History of the American South, 1877–1906*, 1995; Patricia Nelson Limerick, *Legacy of Conquest: The Unbroken Past of the American West*, 1987; Cathy Luchetti, *Men of the West: Life on the American Frontier*, 2004; Sandra Myres, *Western Women and the Frontier Experience, 1880–1915*, 1982; Nell Irvin Painter, *Standing at Armageddon: The United States, 1877–1919*, 1987; R. Hal Williams, *Years of Decision: American Politics in the 1890s*, 1993.

Agriculture Allan C. Bogue, *From Prairie to Corn Belt*, 1963; John C. Hudson, *Making the Corn Belt*, 1994; Geoff Cunfer, *On the Great Plains: Agriculture and Environment*, 2005; Gilbert C. Fite, *The Farmer's Frontier, 1865–1900*, 1966; David A. Johnson, *Founding the Far West: California, Oregon, and Nevada, 1840–1890*, 1992; Donald J. Pisani, *From the Family Farm to Agribusiness: The Irrigation Crusade in California and the West, 1858–1931*, 1984, and *To Reclaim a Divided West: Water, Law, and Power, 1848–1902*, 1992; Donald Worster, *Rivers of Empire: Water, Aridity, and the Growth of the American West*, 1986.

Farmers' Movements Mark A. Lause, *The Civil War's Last Campaign: James B. Weaver, the Greenback-Labor Party, and the Politics of Race and Section*, 2001; Donald B. Marti, *Women of the Grange: Mutuality and Sisterhood in Rural America*, 1991; Michael McGerr, *A Fierce Discontent: The Rise and Fall of the Progressive Movement in America, 1870–1920*, 2003; Darcy G. Richardson, *Others: Third Party Politics from the Nation's Founding to the Rise and Fall of the Greenback-Labor Party*, 2004; Theodore Saloutos, *Farmer Movements in the South, 1865–1933*, 1960; Irwin Unger, *The Greenback Era: A Social and Political History of American Finance, 1865–1879*, 1964; Allen Weinstein, *Prelude to Populism: Origins of the Silver Issue, 1867–1878*, 1970; Thomas A. Woods, *Knights of the Plow: Oliver H. Kelley and the Origins of the Grange in Republican Ideology*, 1991.

The Populists

Gene Clanton, *Populism: The Humane Preference in America, 1890–1900*, 1991; Lawrence Goodwyn, *Democratic Promise: The Populist Movement in America*, 1976; Steven Hahn, *The Roots of Southern Populism*, 1983; Michael Kazin, *The Populist Persuasion:* *An American History*, 1995; William A. Link, *The Paradox of Southern Progressivism, 1880–1930*, 1992; Robert C. McMath, *American Populism: A Social History, 1877–1898*, 1993; Bruce Palmer, *Men Over Money: The Populist Critique of American Capitalism*, 1980.

KEY TERMS

The following terms are covered in this chapter and can also be found in the list of Key Terms at the back of the book.

"the Crime of '73"	farmers' Alliances	greenbacks	Omaha Convention
debt bondage	Grange	Jacob S. Coxey	sharecroppers

ONLINE SOURCES GUIDE

Use this listing to find online documents, images, interactive maps, simulations, and other resources related to this chapter:

American History Resource Center
http://history.wadsworth.com/rc/us

Selected Images
Nebraska family posing in front of their sod house
Farmer turning over sod on homestead, Sun River, Montana

Mechanization on the farm
Gardiner Park County, Montana, 1887

Interactive Time Line (with online readings)
Stressful Times Down Home: Agriculture, 1865–1896

CHAPTER 33

The Days of McKinley

The United States as a World Power 1896–1903

God has not been preparing the English-speaking and Teutonic peoples for a thousand years for nothing but vain and idle self-contemplation. No. He made us the master organizers of the world to establish system where chaos reigned. He has given us the spirit of progress to overwhelm the forces of reaction throughout the earth. He has made us adept in government that we may administer government among savage and senile peoples. Were it not for such a force as this the world would relapse into barbarism and night. And of all our race, He has marked the American people as His chosen nation to finally lead in the redemption of the world.

Albert J. Beveridge

F ew presidential elections have been held amid the anxiety that swirled about the election of 1896. Like the election of 1860, which pitted North and South, the contest of 1896 seemed to pit class against class. The election was, in fact, a political watershed. When it was decided, the political era that had begun with the end of Reconstruction was dead. No one knew what the new era would be like when the campaign began. That depended on which party won the electoral college in November.

THE LANDMARK ELECTION OF 1896

The Republican convention, meeting in St. Louis in June, was an orderly affair. The party's disruptive agrarians had long since departed to sign on with the Populists. A few free silver Republicans from the metal-mining states attended. They tried to win a plank in the platform pledging the party to prop up the price of silver, but the gold bugs were in charge, and they were inflexible. The gold standard was sacred. No one was happy that silver sold so cheaply that good Republican mine owners were suffering; but silver was a commodity, like cotton or wheat. When too much was being produced, the price fell. That was the free market, which was also sacred. The silverites walked out.

MARK HANNA AND WILLIAM McKINLEY

The businesslike delegates then chose as their candidate a man who personified conservatism, prudence, respectability, and sobriety: Governor William McKinley of Ohio. Or as the

William McKinley was the personification of middle-class sobriety, integrity, and dignity. He was a perfect foil for the bombastic Bryan at a time when the middle class was increasingly conscious of its respectability. Here he is seated on the front porch of his home, from which he campaigned in 1896.

Populists and Democrats were soon saying, the Republicans sat back and allowed a beefy Cleveland industrialist, Marcus Alonzo Hanna, to choose their candidate for them.

Bald, scowling **Mark Hanna** was nearly 60 years of age in 1896, six years older than McKinley. A one-time associate of the Rockefellers, he had made a fortune in coal and iron, and he was known in business circles as a spokesman for flexibility and moderation in dealing with labor unions. Hanna feared the rising socialists as much as anyone, but he also railed against pig-headed exploitative capitalists who refused to deal with conservative labor leaders like Samuel Gompers. They were doing more than wild-eyed radicals to turn working people to the socialists.

Hanna had political ambitions for himself. For several years, however, his first priority had been to make William McKinley president. Democrats, Populists, and even some Republicans believed that McKinley was Mark Hanna's stooge. William Allen White, a Kansas Republican, described McKinley as "on the whole decent, on the whole dumb." Nobody called Mark Hanna dumb.

Actually, McKinley was not dumb either. He was the Republican party's number one expert on the tariff, a complicated issue requiring lots of study. He appeared to be dumb because of his suffocating, almost pompous dignity, which may have come naturally, or which McKinley may have cultivated while standing in front of a mirror. White wrote that "he walked among men like a bronze statue determinedly looking for a pedestal." McKinley appreciated Hanna's political labors on his behalf, and they were friends. But Hanna was not a puppeteer and McKinley was not his prop. In a way, McKinley used Hanna, who had many contacts and, unlike McKinley, was a wheeler-dealer who marched into the offices of bankers and industrialists, cigar blazing, planted a hefty haunch on the desk of the man he wanted to see, and came away with a big check for McKinley's campaign fund. McKinley may never have been president were it not for his hustling friend.

THE FRIGHTENING BOY BRYAN

Ultradignified McKinley turned out to be the perfect Republican candidate in 1896 because of the Democratic party's surprising choice. At an excited convention in July—almost as frenzied as the Populist convention of 1892—the Democrats nominated a tornado of a man who was anything but dignified. William Jennings Bryan of Nebraska, scarcely beyond the 35 years of age the Constitution requires of a president, had served two terms in Congress, where he attracted little attention.

Back home in the corn and hog belt, however, Bryan was a well-known platform orator. For four years Bryan had rushed from political rally to county fair to Grange Hall to church pulpit, speaking on behalf of the free coinage of silver. Like a vaudeville juggler aspiring to the big time, he polished and perfected his act before any audience that would have him.

Bryan's act was the "Cross of Gold" speech. A well-organized, easily understood rehash of the arguments in favor of monetizing silver and attacks on the gold bugs, Bryan's speech was, by 1896, a model of phrasing, timing, and effective theatrical gesture. Intensely religious, as were his audiences, Bryan enlisted God in the cause. The speech climaxed with the words "Having behind us the producing masses of this nation and the world, supported by the commercial interests, the laboring interests and the toilers everywhere, we will answer their demand for a gold standard by saying to them, 'You shall not press down upon the brow of labor this crown of thorns; you shall not crucify mankind upon a cross of gold.'"

Republican newspapers called Bryan blasphemous, but fundamentalist Baptist, Methodist, and Presbyterian farmers in the South and Midwest saw nothing wrong in mixing politics with biblical imagery. Bryan's speech set off an uproarious demonstration at the Democratic convention, and the next day he was nominated. Both Democrats and Republicans, distracted by Bryan's evangelical style, failed to note that on most other issues, "the boy orator of the Platte" was quite conservative. Although he said nothing at the convention about the comprehensive reform program the Populist party had put together, he had, back in Nebraska, Kansas, and the Dakotas, rejected it. The free coinage of silver would end the depression; nothing else was needed.

THE POPULISTS JOIN THE DEMOCRATS

Populist leaders did not fail to notice that Bryan was juggling with a single ball. When the party held its convention a few weeks after Bryan's nomination, they split on the meaning of the Democratic party's nomination of a free silverite. Populists committed to preserving the party's comprehensive program intact conceded that with Bryan in the race, they would lose many of the votes that, before the Democratic convention, they had counted on. They would not win the presidency in 1896. Better, however, to wait four years while gold bug Republicans discredited themselves further, and promote their program in the meantime.

Other Populists wanted to nominate Bryan. Known as "fusionists" because they wanted to merge—fuse—with the Democrats, they argued that by combining Democratic and Populist voters, victory was a cinch. Republican politicos (although not Mark Hanna) agreed with them; they believed Bryan would win if the Populists backed him.

Urban intellectual Populists like Henry Demarest Lloyd opposed fusion. They wanted to nominate a true blue Populist and accept defeat, but maintain the integrity of their program. Some southern Populists like Tom Watson of Georgia agreed. They pointed out to the convention that in the South, the enemy was not the Republican party, but the Democrats. If southern Populists fused with the Democrats, they would lose the support of black farmers with whom Watson had been trying, with some success, to form an alliance. African Americans could never vote Democratic. The Democratic party was the party of the Redeemers. Fusion meant sending African Americans back to the Republicans.

Midwestern Populists led by Jerry Simpson were unmoved by these arguments. They wanted fusion because fusion meant victory. "I care not for party names," Simpson said, "it is substance we are after, and we have it in William J. Bryan." He was backed by delegates from the mining states, some of them Republicans a month earlier. Free silver was their issue; the rest of the Populist program did not interest them. Silver mine owners were conservative businessmen; they opposed such Populist demands as government ownership of railroads and telegraph.

The fusionists had their way; the Populist party nominated Bryan. To placate the antifusionists, they nominated Tom Watson for vice president and sent a message to Bryan requesting that he drop his Democratic vice presidential candidate and name Watson as his Democratic running mate too. It was not asking much. The vice presidential nomination was not much of a prize. And Bryan's Democratic running mate was an eastern gold standard hack whose departure from the ticket would not cost the Democrats votes. But Bryan ignored the request.

THE WHIRLWIND AND THE ROCK

Before 1896 only Horace Greeley, in 1872, and James G. Blaine, in 1884, had actively campaigned by speaking all over the country. Most presidential candidates made no public appearances at all. It insulted the dignity of the office, they believed, to hustle votes as if they were running for sheriff. When, in 1866, Andrew Johnson made his "swing around the circle" on behalf of congressional candidates, his opponents said that his vulgar "speechifying" was unworthy of a president. The Republicans feigned distress when Greeley took to the stump in 1872.

After Bryan, who was inexhaustible, presidential campaigns were changed forever. He traveled 13,000 miles by train. In fourteen weeks he delivered 600 speeches in twenty-nine states—more than six speeches a day. If he was not running late after he spoke, he gobbled up potato salad, complimenting the maker on her recipe. (He was notorious as a glutton.) Reports of the enthusiasm of the crowds that greeted him in the West and South threw bankers and industrialists into a panic.

Panic was exactly what Mark Hanna wanted to see. He tapped wealthy Republicans and more than a few conservative Democrats for large contributions to McKinley's campaign. Hanna spent more on posters, buttons, rallies, picnics, advertisements, and a corps of speakers who followed Bryan around than had been spent by both parties in every election since the Civil War. The Republicans printed five pamphlets for every American voter. Hanna was so successful a fundraiser that, before election day, he began to return contributions McKinley did not need. (That does not happen today.)

Knowing that the phlegmatic McKinley could not rival Bryan on the stump, the Republicans kept their candidate at his modest home in Canton, Ohio. Republican speakers compared McKinley's self-respect with Bryan's huckstering. In fact, McKinley's campaign was as frantic as Bryan's and nearly as tiring. Delegations of party faithful streamed

The American Empire 1890–1904

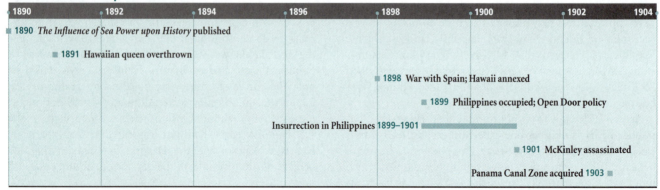

1890	1892	1894	1896	1898	1900	1902	1904

- 1890 *The Influence of Sea Power upon History* published
- 1891 Hawaiian queen overthrown
- 1898 War with Spain; Hawaii annexed
- 1899 Philippines occupied; Open Door policy
- Insurrection in Philippines 1899–1901
- 1901 McKinley assassinated
- Panama Canal Zone acquired 1903

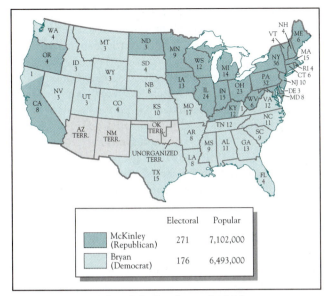

MAP 33:1 **Presidential Election of 1896**
Except for North Dakota's, California's, and Oregon's choice of McKinley, the lineup of states in the election of 1896 was sharply sectional: the agricultural states of the South and West, and the western mining states, voted for Bryan. The Northeast and Midwest voted Republican.

daily into Canton, where they walked from the depot to McKinley's home behind a marching band. McKinley emerged as if delightfully surprised to have visitors, delivered a speech from the front porch, and invited all his friends to join him for lemonade or beer. (On the walk to McKinley's house, campaign workers had tactfully determined the delegation's attitude toward alcohol.) About 750,000 people visited McKinley's home, trampling his lawn "as if a herd of buffalo had passed through." On one Saturday he made sixteen front porch speeches to 30,000 people! His "front porch campaign" was an innovation too.

THE VOTE COUNT

More people voted for Bryan, 6.5 million, than had voted for anyone ever elected president. But he lost the election. McKinley won 7 million votes and, in the electoral college, 271 to Bryan's 176. It was the first time in a quarter century that a presidential candidate had won an absolute majority. What happened? As late as September, professional election watchers believed that Bryan was well ahead.

First, although Bryan's supporters were noisy and numerous, his appeal was limited to the solid South, to hard-pressed western farmers, and to western silver miners in states with few electoral votes. McKinley swept the Northeast, including every one of the "swing states" that had been up for grabs since the Civil War. McKinley also won the largely agricultural states of Minnesota, Wisconsin, Iowa, and Michigan. Farmers there depended less on the price of a single staple crop than westerners and southerners did. (Wisconsin, for example, was already calling itself "America's dairyland.") They had not been so badly hurt by the collapse

in the prices of the staples; cows' milk was marketed in a dozen forms. The Republicans could and did win prospering farmers with the warning that "Boy Bryan" was a dangerous radical.

Nor did Bryan have much support among factory workers and city people generally. He hardly tried to win them over. Imbued with rural prejudices against big cities and the "foreigners" who lived there, he made only one visit to the 36 electoral vote swing state of New York. He was quoted as calling New York City "the enemy's country," as though the metropolis were inhabited solely by bankers and grain speculators. Fourteen of the fifteen biggest cities were controlled by Republican political machines; they delivered the urban vote to William McKinley.

A few industrialists tried to intimidate their employees into voting Republican. The Baldwin Piano Works posted notices on election eve that if Bryan won, the plant would close. But Bryan's anemic weakness in industrial areas owed nothing to such absurd threats. His single-issue free silver crusade left working people cold. Much more persuasive were the Republican arguments that the inflation Bryan advocated would hurt them by increasing prices, and that by protecting American industry, the Republicans' high tariff protected their jobs too.

Finally, shrewd Mark Hanna sensed the instincts of a new element in American politics: the growing middle class of small businessmen, professional people, salaried town dwellers, and highly skilled, well-paid workingmen— railroad engineers and firemen, factory foremen, and workers in the building trades. Conscious of their social respectability and the social gap between them and unskilled, mostly immigrant workers, they were frightened by the ragged, restive farmers who were Bryan's people. To them, the Republican party was the party of the decent, orderly, successful middle class.

THE END OF POPULISM

Just as Henry Demarest Lloyd and Tom Watson said it would, fusion with the Democrats killed the Populist party. Having sacrificed their comprehensive reform program for the chance of winning with Bryan, the Populists had nothing when Bryan lost.

In the West, the party withered away, but only partly because of fusion. In addition, slowly but perceptibly, the market prices of the staple crops rose, and along with them, so did farm income. Newly discovered gold deposits in Canada and Alaska gently inflated the currency—"naturally," the gold bugs liked to say. "Free silver!" and all the passion invested in it as a cure-all were irrelevant. Poor European harvests in the late 1890s did their part by increasing the demand for American wheat and corn.

Cotton prices lagged behind wheat and corn prices. Southern farmers and sharecroppers remained among the poorest people in the nation. Populistic politics did not die; indeed, among white southerners, they intensified. But Tom Watson's vision of interracial cooperation based on social class, if it had ever been realistic, was gone with the wind.

JIM CROW SEGREGATION

Historians differ radically about the nature of the Populists' legacy to the nation. There is, however, no questioning the fact that for black southerners—90 percent of the total African American population in 1890—the agrarian uprising was a disaster. During the 1880s, southern blacks held their own in politics. The collapse of the cotton market was colorblind: It hit white and black farmers and sharecroppers equally. In the tobacco states, blacks' economic condition actually improved.

The failure of the Force Bill in the Senate in 1890—made possible by free silver senators from the mining states—marked the end of the Republican party's serious efforts to protect the civil rights of blacks. The few idealistic old radical Republicans left, like George F. Hoar of Maine, were dying off. Young congressmen who voted for the Force Bill, like Henry Cabot Lodge of Massachusetts, lost interest in civil rights issues after 1890.

Even before 1890, populistic southern white politicians who remained in the Democratic party launched the campaign to ban African Americans from the voting booth and to draw through every southern institution an uncrossable color line that demeaned and dispirited black people. During the 1890s, at the peak of the agrarian uprising, violent mobs saw to it that "Jim Crow" segregation was enforced by adding fear to insult among African Americans. In 1896 the Supreme Court stamped its approval on what populistic southerners were doing with shotguns and rope.

BEGINNINGS OF SUPPRESSION

African-American Republicans could not hope to win control of southern state governments during the 1880s. But a substantial number of them continued to vote and run for office. In Tennessee and North Carolina, there were more African Americans holding state offices during the 1880s than there had been during Reconstruction. There were a few blacks in state office even in South Carolina, Mississippi, and Louisiana. In Virginia, North Carolina, and Kentucky, black farmers actually improved their economic lot. In Virginia in 1890, thanks in part to the insatiable hunger of Buck Duke's cigarette machines, 43 percent of black farmers owned their land, a higher percentage of landowners than among Kansas whites. In North Carolina, an African American held onto a congressional seat in a district with a white majority.

Fusion ended all that. African-American Populists could not, in 1896, vote for the candidate of the party that had been the party of the Klan and the Redeemers and was fast becoming the party of the lynch mob.

During the 1880s, Benjamin R. "Pitchfork Ben" Tillman of South Carolina (who had led a lynch mob during Reconstruction) devised the formula for political success in the New South. Representing upcountry white dirt farmers, he demanded agrarian reforms and vilified in pungent language the aristocratic "Bourbon" Redeemers who ran the "Bourbon" Democratic party. However, Tillman remained a Democrat and added vicious race baiting to his arsenal. Poor whites had two enemies: the Charleston "Bourbons" within the party and black Republicans, who were stooges for the bankers of New York as well as threats to the chastity of white women.

Tillman's formula worked. He was elected governor in 1890 and senator in 1895. And he delivered. As governor, he raised taxes on the wealthy and spent the revenue on improving public schools. All the while he laced his speeches with crude antiblack diatribes and sponsored laws to disenfranchise African Americans and segregate them from whites in public facilities such as streetcar lines.

While the Populist party disintegrated, Tillman went from success to success. He soon had imitators in other southern states. Among them, after several years of bitter withdrawal, was Tom Watson, one-time proponent of interracial cooperation. When Watson learned how to out-Tillman Pitchfork Ben in race baiting, Georgia Democrats rewarded him with a seat in the Senate.

DISENFRANCHISEMENT

Beginning in Florida and Tennessee in 1889, white supremacists experimented with laws to prevent blacks from voting. At one time or another, every southern state adopted the poll tax of one or two dollars each year as a condition of voting. In some states the poll tax was cumulative. That is, an African American whose income had improved discovered he had to pay not a dollar in order to vote but ten or twenty dollars to cover the years he had passed on election day.

The poll tax disenfranchised poor whites too. (It was originally a Bourbon law.) Populistic demagogues of the Tillman type, whose constituency was made up of poor whites, needed to exempt poor whites—their constituency—from the poll tax without colliding head-on with the Fifteenth Amendment.

One device was the "**grandfather clause**" enacted in Alabama, Louisiana, North Carolina, and Georgia. It provided that if a man's grandfather had been eligible to vote prior to radical Reconstruction, he could vote without paying the poll tax. No African American's grandfather, of course, had been eligible to vote before 1867. Grandfather clauses functioned for a few years. However, because they transparently discriminated on the basis of race, they were bound to be struck down by the Supreme Court, which they were in 1915.

Literacy and "understanding" tests, because there was no overt racial component in them, were more effective. In 1900, 50 percent of southern blacks were illiterate, but just 12 percent of whites were. Simply requiring that a voter be able to read excluded half the African-American population from the polls. Seven southern states adopted literacy tests. Others achieved the same end by introducing the secret ballot. Voters who could not read needed assistance marking their ballots; helpers were forbidden in "the sacred privacy of the voting booth."

Illiterate whites evaded the literacy requirement by opting to take an "understanding" test. Registrars read them a passage from the state constitution. If they demonstrated that they understood what it meant, they could vote. There was nothing inherently discriminatory in the laws, but there was in their application. Registrars had broad discretionary powers in administering and grading the tests. They could and did accept all explanations of the state constitution by whites, but easily found "misunderstandings" of one sort or another in African-American answers.

In Mississippi in 1888, 29 percent of black men eligible to vote voted; in 1892 only 2 percent did; in 1895 none at all. In Louisiana in 1895, 95.6 percent of black men eligible to register as voters were registered; after just two years, only 9.1 percent were. (In 1914 this figure was 1.1 percent.) There were 180,000 black registered voters in Alabama in 1900, in 1903 just 3,000.

LYNCH LAW

By the late 1890s, it took a good deal of temerity (or foolhardiness) for a black man to present himself at a rural southern courthouse to take a literacy test. The lynching of blacks suspected of having committed a violent crime against a white (most commonly rape) and even blacks who were merely "uppity" had become epidemic.

In 1890, 85 African Americans were lynched in the United States, almost all of them in the southern states. In 1892, with the agrarian revolt at white heat, 161 blacks were lynched. In only two of the years between 1890 and 1902 were fewer than 100 blacks mutilated, hanged, and incinerated by white mobs. No one feared prosecution. Law officers made themselves scarce when lynch mobs were organizing; or they aided them. Many lynchings were photographed, the faces of the people in the mob clearly recognizable. Rather than being used as evidence in court, some photos were printed on postcards and sold as souvenirs. A few lynchings were actually announced in advance. In one case in Georgia, a train was chartered to transport spectators to a hanging. In Oklahoma in 1911, a woman was lynched when she tried to protect her teenage son from a mob.

Most middle- and upper-class southern whites were disgusted by lynching; had they been in power, as they were before the populist uprising, at least some lynchings would have been investigated and mob leaders punished. The Bourbons wanted to keep the rednecks "in their place" too. But not all of the respectable classes found lynching a blot on the South. Rebecca Felton of Atlanta, a feminist and anti-alcohol crusader who lobbied for compulsory public education and

The Granger Collection, New York

Booker T. Washington built Alabama's Tuskegee Institute into one of the best African-American educational institutions in the country. His "Atlanta Compromise" of 1895 provided that blacks would live with social discrimination in return for white assistance in educating them, particularly in the "agricultural and mechanical arts," the technology needed to farm productively and get high-paying jobs in industry.

state-financed child care facilities—a true progressive—said she would be glad to see lynchings "a thousand times a week" to protect white women.

THE ATLANTA COMPROMISE

Frederick Douglass, regarded as the chief spokesman for African Americans, died in 1895. By then, another man born into slavery had risen to prominence among both blacks and whites as an educator. In 1881 Booker T. Washington took over the moribund Tuskegee Institute in Alabama and built it into one of the most respected African-American colleges in the country. Washington was a virtuoso fund-raiser. He cultivated northern millionaires sympathetic to the cause of black improvement, and they were generous.

By 1895 Washington saw the gains African Americans had won disappearing under the pressure of Jim Crow laws and poor white terrorism. He used a convention in Atlanta aimed at promoting investment in the South to propose to the wealthy and powerful southerners in attendance a compact between the two races that would benefit both blacks and whites. It was not a proposal of which Frederick Douglass would have approved. Washington accepted black disenfranchisement and a socially inferior status for blacks. "In all things … purely social," he said, "we can be as separate as the fingers, yet as one as the hand in all things essential to mutual progress." If southern state governments (and northern philanthropists) would fund mechanical, technical, and agricultural education for blacks, they—with, tacitly, Booker T. Washington guaranteeing it—would be content to remain in their place.

The southern elite, uneasy at the racial instability in the South, found Washington's proposal appealing. Many southern blacks did too. With half of the black population illiterate, few aspired to loftier places in society than their own farms or skilled work that paid well. An urbane northern African-American Ph.D. who had studied in Europe, W. E. B. DuBois, condemned Washington's "**Atlanta Compromise.**" DuBois wanted to step up the struggle for civil and social equality. He placed his hopes for the future in the creation of a black elite educated to be professionals. Washington did not oppose blacks studying medicine, law, and the liberal arts, but he was realistic: all but a few of the million southern blacks were struggling to put food on the table, and many were living in fear of lynch mobs.

Washington was less realistic about the value of the white southern elite's goodwill. The men at the Atlanta convention were Bourbons or upcoming businessmen. They had been ousted from power in some southern states and were losing influence in others as populistic demagogues took over the Democratic party. The Atlanta Compromise offered nothing to the "white trash" who took satisfaction in routinely humiliating blacks and periodically erupting murderously if an African American was accused of rape, killing a white, or simply insulting somebody they knew.

PLESSY V. FERGUSON

In 1890 Louisiana adopted a law requiring railroads to provide separate accommodations on trains and in depots for blacks and whites. (Within two years, nine states had similar laws.) An organization of New Orleans blacks formed a committee "to test the constitutionality of the separate car law." Railroad executives backed them for financial reasons: It was expensive to have "white" and "colored" cars on every train and maintain "white" and "colored" waiting rooms at every station. Homer Plessy agreed to disobey the law in order to argue in court that it violated the Thirteenth Amendment and the "equal treatment" section of the Fourteenth Amendment. He bought a train ticket, sat in a "white" car, and was arrested.

Plessy v. *Ferguson* reached the Supreme Court in 1896. By a vote of 7 to 1, the justices ruled that the Louisiana segregation law was constitutional. As long as state and city governments, public utilities, and schools provided facilities equal in quality and availability to both whites and blacks, it did not violate the Fourteenth Amendment that the facilities were separate. The doctrine of "separate but equal" legitimized the Jim Crow laws already in existence and gave the southern states the go-ahead to enact more, which they did.

The Court that sanctioned Jim Crow was not a southern court. Six of the eight justices were raised or educated in New England. The single dissenter was a southerner who, as a young man, had owned slaves. **John Marshall Harlan** wrote in his dissent that the Thirteenth Amendment forbade not only slavery but also "badges of servitude" such as the denial of access to any public facility on the basis of a person's race. "Separate" accommodations were inherently unequal. The Constitution, Harlan wrote, "is colorblind, and neither knows nor tolerates classes among citizens." (Harlan, "the last of the tobacco-chewing judges," was also the sole dissenter on the Supreme Court in 1883 when, in the civil rights cases, the Court struck down a federal law forbidding discrimination.)

AN AMERICAN EMPIRE

William McKinley hoped for a quiet presidency. He hoped to preside over the nation's retrenchment and recovery after years of depression and agitation. His confidence in the resilience of American business convinced him that prosperity was just around the corner.

McKinley got his prosperity. Even before he was inaugurated in March 1897, the economic indicators began to improve. Peace and quiet were more elusive. Little as the role suited him, President McKinley led the American people into a series of overseas adventures that transformed a nation born in an anti-imperial rebellion into an imperial power with colonies in both hemispheres.

AN INDUSTRIAL AND COMMERCIAL GIANT

In 1892 Europe's great powers upgraded their representatives in Washington from minister to ambassador in recognition of American industrial might and status in international trade. In 1890 the United States surpassed Great Britain as the world's premier industrial nation.

American ships were familiar visitors in the world's most exotic ports. As early as 1844, the United States signed a trade treaty with the Chinese Empire. In 1854 a naval squadron under Commodore Matthew Perry anchored off Yokohama, Japan, and threatened to bombard the city unless the Japanese agreed to abandon their centuries-long isolation and begin to buy American goods.

By 1870, American exports totaled $320 million, mostly agricultural produce bound for Europe. By 1890, $857 million in goods were sold abroad. American manufacturers competed with the European nations in sales of steel, textiles, and other products in Latin America and even in Europe. Standard Oil faced stiffer competition selling kerosene in the United States than it did abroad. Standard's trademark was recognized as universally as Coca-Cola's is today. Andrew Carnegie took great delight in underbidding every British steel manufacturer to land a big order for armor plate from the Royal Navy. Even the Populists' Jerry Simpson urged the government to pursue foreign markets more aggressively: "American factories are making more than the American people can consume; American soil is producing more than they can consume. . . . The trade of the world must and shall be ours."

The United States was not, however, even a third-rate military power. There were fewer than 30,000 men in the army and navy. Great Britain had ten times as many, and Britain was traditionally opposed to maintaining large professional armies in peacetime. The armed forces of Germany, France, and Russia dwarfed Great Britain's. Recently unified Italy had five times as many soldiers and sailors as the United States.

ANTI-COLONIALISM

The United States did not need much of an army. The border with Canada was unfortified by mutual agreement. Mexico was weak and compliant. The oceans were insurance against European land forces and, to the west, the rising power of Japan. (Japan's army was twice the size of America's.) Finally, unlike the nations of western Europe, which were carving up the rest of the world among themselves, the United States had no restive colonial subjects to keep under control. There was Alaska and the tiny island of Midway in the central Pacific, both acquired in 1867 (and a few tinier guano islands now completely mined), but most of the inhabitants of both had come there from the United States.

There had been serious proposals to buy Cuba from Spain. President Grant had come close to annexing the Dominican Republic. But (in addition to American military weakness) a deeply rooted conviction and a seemingly obvious fact militated against every suggestion that the United States jump into the European imperial scramble.

First, the country was founded in a rebellion against an empire, and to the end of the nineteenth century, almost all Americans looked on European imperialism as just one more of the Old World's corruptions. Second, the vastness of the American continent provided more than enough outlet for American energies; there was plenty of work to be done at home. William McKinley expressed America's anti-imperialism when he said in his inaugural address, "We must avoid the temptation of territorial expansion."

FRONTIERS, ANGLO–SAXONS, AND SHIPS

McKinley inserted this admonition into his speech because he was aware of currents that were undercutting anticolonialist traditions. One had been inspired by the Census Bureau's announcement that as of 1890, there was no longer an American frontier. For the first time in the nation's history, there was no continuous line between land that was settled (land with at least 2.5 people per square mile) and land that was "vacant" (fewer than 2.5 people per square mile). In 1893 a young historian, Frederick Jackson Turner, propounded a theory that the now extinct frontier had been the key to the vitality of democracy, social stability, and prosperity in the United States.

To this day historians discuss the "Turner Thesis." Many dozens of books embroidering on it or refuting it have been published. More important in the 1890s, Turner's ideas captivated influential men outside the universities, and they drew pessimistic lessons from them. Would the United States stagnate without the frontier, or begin to suffer the social dislocations and class conflicts of older nations? Or might economic and social and moral decline be avoided by creating new frontiers abroad?

Many intellectuals—public men as well as professors—believed that the obviously different characteristics of different nationalities were due not to geography, the culture they had inherited, or other such factors, but because they—the "races"—were inherently different, inherently superior and inferior.

In two books of 1885, historian **John Fiske** and Congregationalist minister Josiah Strong wrote that the "Anglo–Saxon" peoples (the English and Americans) had been more successful in creating free and progressive governments than other peoples because they were racially superior (Fiske) or "divinely commissioned" (Strong). It was not a betrayal of American ideals to take over the governing of others. There was a racial and religious duty to do so. A political scientist, John W. Burgess, stated flatly in 1890 that the right of self-determination did not apply to dark-skinned peoples. He wrote that "there is no human right to the status of barbarism." (It was the same argument slave owners had made when "all men are created equal" was quoted to them.)

In 1890 expansionists found yet another reason to expand the nation's power overseas in an international best seller by a naval captain, Alfred Thayer Mahan. In *The Influence of Sea Power upon History,* Mahan argued that all great nations were seafaring nations possessing powerful navies. He chided Americans for having allowed their own fleet to fall into decay. Mahan urged a massive program of ship construction, and Congress responded with the first large peacetime navy appropriations bill in the country's history.

A modern steam-powered navy needed coaling stations scattered throughout the world. That meant taking colonies, even if they were mere dots on the globe like little Midway, or building bases in friendly independent countries like Hawaii, where the United States was already dredging a harbor at the mouth of the Pearl River.

THE SPANISH–AMERICAN WAR

In 1895 Cuba, Puerto Rico, and the Philippines were all that remained of the Spanish Empire that had once claimed the entire Western Hemisphere. And that remnant was in tatters.

Rebellion was chronic in the Philippines and Cuba. An uprising in Cuba in 1895 was serious enough to rock the government in Spain. Cuban exiles living in the United States smuggled in arms from Florida, and the rebels had widespread support at home. Unintentionally, the Wilson–Gorman Tariff of 1894 aggravated the discontent by taxing Cuban sugar at rates so high that little could be sold in the American market.

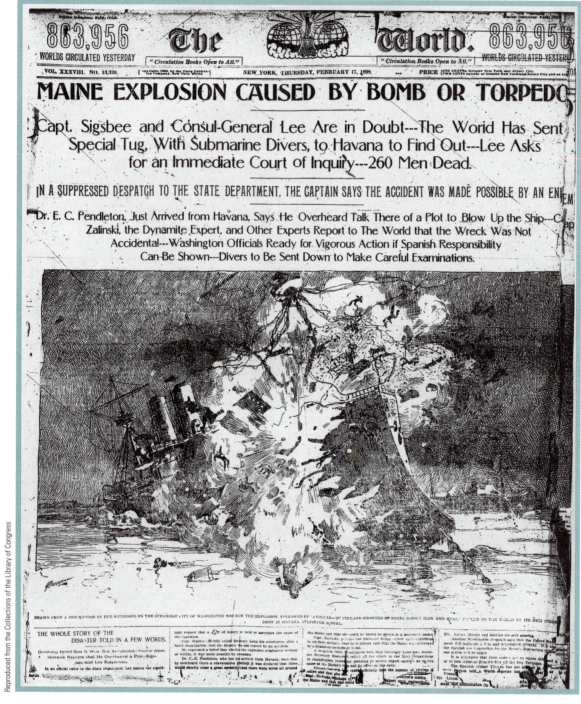

The destruction of the battleship Maine *in Havana Harbor as reported by Joseph Pulitzer's* New York World. *The disaster would have been front-page news if the* Maine *had exploded in Norfolk, Virginia. The* World *accorded it this sensational presentation because Pulitzer had been promoting war with Spain.*

The Cuban rebellion was a classic guerrilla war. The Spanish army and navy controlled the cities of Havana and Santiago and most large towns. By day, Spanish soldiers moved with little trouble amongst a peasantry that seemed peaceful and loyal. By night, however, docile field workers turned into guerrillas and skirmished with Spanish troops. As in most guerrilla wars, the combat was cruel. Both sides were guilty of atrocities, torturing and murdering captives.

Americans would have been sympathetic toward the rebels in any event. Their anger was whipped up to a frenzy when the competing newspaper chains of Joseph Pulitzer and William Randolph Hearst decided that the Cuban rebellion could be used to sell papers.

THE YELLOW PRESS

William Randolph Hearst's *New York Journal* and Joseph Pulitzer's *New York World,* and their satellite dailies in a dozen large cities, competed not only in gathering news, but by outdoing one another in exploiting sensations and contriving gimmicks with which to woo readers. The Hearst and Pulitzer chains invented the daily comic strip. The first was called *The Yellow Kid,* from which came the term *yellow press* to describe newspapers that employed such gimmicks (undignified to traditional newspapers) to increase circulation. Colorful writers squeezed the most lurid details out of celebrated murder

and sex cases and pioneered the "invented" news story. In 1889 Pulitzer's *World* sent Elizabeth S. "Nellie Bly" Cochrane around the world in an attempt to break the record of the fictional hero of Jules Verne's novel *Around the World in Eighty Days.* (She did it—in 72 days, 6 hours, and 11 minutes.)

It was no great leap from promotions like Nellie Bly to making hay out of Spanish atrocities. The yellow press dubbed the Spanish military commander in Cuba, Valeriano Weyler, "the Butcher" for his repressive policies, which included the establishment of concentration camps. Warring against a whole population, Weyler tried to stifle the uprising by herding villages into camps; everyone who was found outside the camps was defined as an enemy. This strategy was inevitably brutal, and Cubans died in the camps from malnutrition and disease.

Real suffering was not enough for Hearst and Pulitzer. They transformed innocuous incidents into horror stories and invented others. When Hearst artist Frederic Remington wired Hearst from Havana that everything was peaceful and he wanted to come home, Hearst ordered him to stay: "You furnish the pictures. I'll furnish the war." One sensational newspaper picture showed Spanish soldiers and customs officials leering at a naked American woman. It was based on a real incident—except that the woman, suspected of smuggling, had been searched quite properly in private by

Men of the Tenth Cavalry atop San Juan Hill after the battle. No one faulted the bravery of Teddy Roosevelt's Rough Riders, who fought to the right of the Tenth. However, after Roosevelt wrote a book describing the charge up the hill as if it were all Rough Riders (and mainly Theodore Roosevelt), several men who witnessed the battle said the professional Tenth was the key unit on that sector of the battle line.

female officers. In the yellow press, news that was close enough was good enough.

MCKINLEY'S DARK HOUR

McKinley wanted calm. Influential American businessmen had substantial investments in Cuba: about $50 million in railroads, mines, and sugarcane plantations. They feared the revolutionaries more than the Spanish. McKinley was their man. He hoped Spain would abandon its harshest policies and placate both Cubans and bellicose Americans by liberalizing government on the island.

The Spanish responded to American pressure. In 1898 a new government in Madrid withdrew Weyler and proposed autonomy for Cuba within the Spanish Empire. McKinley was satisfied. But the war came anyway because of two unforeseeable events.

On February 9 Hearst's *New York Journal* published a letter written by the Spanish ambassador in Washington, Enrique Dupuy de Lome. In it, Dupuy said that McKinley was "weak, a bidder for the admiration of the crowd." It was by no means an inaccurate assessment of the president. His own undersecretary of the navy, Theodore Roosevelt, said that McKinley had the backbone of a chocolate éclair. But it was insulting.

Six days later, on February 15, 1898, the USS *Maine* exploded in Havana Harbor, killing 260 sailors. To this day the cause of the disaster is debated. The explosion may have been caused by a coal fire that spread to the magazine. A bomb may have been planted by Cuban rebels who hoped to provoke the United States into declaring war on Spain. Or the tragedy may have been the work of Spanish diehards who opposed the new liberal policy in Cuba. So charged was the atmosphere that some suggested William Randolph Hearst himself planted the bomb because he needed a headline!

There were plenty of outraged headlines, and most Americans, it seemed, accepted the least credible explanation: the Spanish government, which was trying to avoid war at all costs, had destroyed the *Maine*.

McKinley vacillated for a month and a half, flooding Spain with demands for a change of policy. As late as March 26, Mark Hanna urged him to keep the peace, and on April 9 the Spanish government gave in to every demand McKinley had made. In the meantime, however, fearing that to continue resisting the war fever would cost the Republicans control of Congress in the elections of 1898, McKinley caved in. On April 11, practically ignoring the Spanish capitulation, the president asked Congress for a declaration of war and got it.

"SPLENDID LITTLE WAR"

The U.S. Army numbered 28,000 men, most of them stationed in the West. Such a force, less than half the size of the army of tiny Belgium, was not up to launching an invasion even just a short sail from Florida.

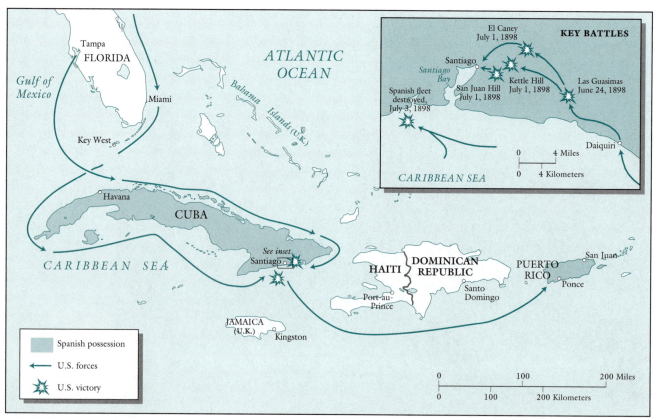

MAP 33:2 The War in Cuba

As in the Philippines, the Spanish–American War in Cuba was mainly a naval war. After the Spanish fleet was destroyed, one campaign outside Santiago in June and July 1898 was enough to force the Spanish to surrender. In part because the fighting on land was so brief, Secretary of State John Hay called the conflict "a splendid little war."

Avenging the *Maine*

William Allen White remembered the excitement in the Midwest when war was declared on Spain: "Everywhere over this good, fair land, flags were flying, . . . crowds gathered to hurrah for the soldiers and to throw hats into the air." The cry was, "Remember the *Maine;* to hell with Spain." It was all over in a few months.

But only the poor morale of the Spanish soldiers and sailors and the ineptitude of Spanish commanders made the war short and easy to bear, "a splendid little war" in the words of Secretary of State John Hay. The American army was not prepared for war. In 1898 it was only 28,000 strong. Congress authorized an increase to 65,700 men, but despite an initial rush of enlistments, the army never grew this large.

In 1898 the state militias numbered 140,000, but regular army officers were suspicious of their training and equipment. Indeed, training was inadequate in the enlarged regular army because of everyone's rush to get into action.

The problem of supply was never mastered. Companies mustered in the southern states were issued heavy woolen winter uniforms and Civil War–vintage Springfield rifles. Some of the meat provided the recruits was tainted (poisonous); it was never conclusively determined if the cause was crooked government contractors or incompetence. Sanitary conditions in the crowded training camps were such that typhoid and dysentery incapacitated recruits before they knew how to march in step. When the dead were counted at the end of 1898, 379 men were listed as killed in combat; 5,083 men died of disease.

About 274,000 served in the war; an equal number of volunteers were turned down. Among the rejects were William Jennings Bryan, who wanted a commission; Frank James, brother of the fabled train robber Jesse James; and Buffalo Bill Cody, who annoyed the War Department by writing a magazine article titled "How I Could Drive the Spaniards out of Cuba with Thirty Thousand Indian Braves." Martha A. Chute of Colorado was discouraged from her offer to raise a troop of women, as was William Randolph Hearst's suggestion of a regiment made up of professional boxers and baseball players. "Think of a regiment composed of magnificent men of this ilk," the editor of the *Journal* wrote. "They would overawe any Spanish regiment by their mere appearance."

Hearst, like Bryan, was a Democrat. McKinley did allow the formation of the Republican "Rough Riders," a name stolen from Buffalo Bill. It was a Republican collection of cowboys, athletes, and gentlemen like Undersecretary of the Navy Theodore Roosevelt. The Rough Riders were sent to Cuba, although there was no room on the ship for their horses.

In fact, few battlegrounds in Cuba or in the Philippines were suited to cavalry. Both were tropical countries, and most of the fighting was done in summer and in the jungle. The army tried to prepare for jungle warfare by authorizing the recruitment of up to 10,000 "immunes," young men who were thought to be immune to tropical diseases. However, medicine's ignorance of the nature of tropical diseases combined with racism to make the immune regiments no more serviceable than any others. Whereas the original idea had been to fill these units with men who had grown up in marshy areas of the deep South, within months recruiters were turning away white Louisianians from the bayous and accepting blacks from the upcountry South and even urban New Jersey. Blacks were believed to possess a genetic immunity to malaria, yellow fever, and other tropical afflictions. (Some Africans were genetically resistant to some forms of malaria, but by 1898 it was unlikely that much of the helpful DNA was found in many Americans.)

Blacks played a large part in both the Cuban and the Philippine campaigns. When the war broke out, there were four black regiments in the regular army: two infantry and two cavalry, the Ninth and the Tenth Horse Regiments. All four saw action. In fact, while Theodore Roosevelt was describing the capture of San Juan Hill as an accomplishment of the Rough Riders, other witnesses believed that the Rough Riders would have been wiped out had it not been for the Tenth Negro Cavalry, which was immediately to their left at the beginning of the charge and entirely integrated with the Rough Riders at the end (except for celebratory photographs). In the restrained words of the report of their commander, later to be General John J. "Black Jack" Pershing: "The Tenth Cavalry charged up the hill, scarcely firing a shot, and being nearest the Rough Riders, opened a disastrous enfilading fire upon the Spanish right, thus relieving the Rough Riders from the volleys that were being poured into them from that part of the Spanish line."

About 10,000 African Americans served in the war, 4,000 of them in the "immunes." A study of white regiments indicated that the Spanish–American War was a poor man's fight and, rather more surprising, a city man's fight. From largely rural Indiana, for example, of those volunteers who listed their occupation, only 296 were farmers. There were 322 common laborers, 413 skilled laborers, and 118 white-collar workers (clerks). Only 47 in the regiment were professional men, and 25 were merchants. The army was far less representative of the general population than were the American armies of the two world wars. In age, however, it was typical. The average age of the soldiers was 24. Their average height was 5 feet 8 inches, and their average weight was 149 pounds.

The spanking new navy was ready, however. It struck first not in Cuba but halfway around the world in Spain's last Pacific colony, the Philippines. On May 1, acting on the instructions of Undersecretary of the Navy Theodore Roosevelt (the secretary of the navy was ill), Commodore George Dewey steamed a flotilla into Manila Bay and completely surprised the Spanish garrison. He destroyed most of the Spanish ships before they could weigh anchor.

But Dewey had no soldiers with which to attack on land. For more than three months, he and his men sat outside the Manila harbor, baking in their steel ships, while Filipino rebels struggled with the Spanish garrison in the city. Finally, in August, troops arrived and took the capital. Although they did not know it, a peace treaty had been signed the previous day: shades of the Battle of New Orleans.

By that time, American troops had conquered Cuba and Puerto Rico. Secretary of State John Hay called their campaign "a splendid little war" because so few Americans died in battle. To celebrate so gaily, however, it was necessary that Hay overlook the more than 5,000 soldiers who died from typhoid, tropical diseases, and poisonous "embalmed beef"—tainted meat that was fed to the soldiers because of corruption or simple inefficiency.

Although the Spanish army in Cuba outnumbered the Americans until the last, both commanders and men were paralyzed by defeatism. Despite shortages of food, clothing, transport vehicles, medical supplies, ammunition, and horses, an American army of 17,000 landed in Cuba in June and defeated the Spanish outside Santiago at the battles of El Caney and San Juan Hill. (With 200,000 soldiers in Cuba, the Spanish had stationed only 19,000 in Santiago.)

The victory gave Americans a self-made popular hero. Theodore Roosevelt had resigned from the Navy Department to become a colonel in a volunteer cavalry unit called the **Rough Riders.** It was a highly unmilitary group, made up of cowboys from Roosevelt's North Dakota ranch, show business fops, and upper-class polo players and other athletes. The Rough Riders had to fight on foot because the army was unable to get their horses out of Tampa, Florida. They fought bravely in the hottest action on San Juan Hill but, luckily for them, were side-by-side with the Ninth and Tenth U.S. Cavalry regiments (also dismounted)—African-American units hardened by service in the West. The white Rough Riders got complete credit for a victory in which they had played only a small part.

EMPIRE CONFIRMED

When the Spanish gave up, American troops occupied not only Manila in the Philippines and much of Cuba, but also the island of Puerto Rico. But what to do with these prizes? The colonialism controversy was no longer an academic debate. It involved three far-flung island countries inhabited by millions of people who spoke Spanish or Malayan languages and adhered to traditions very different from those of Americans. The Cubans and Puerto Ricans were of familiar European and African ancestry, but the Filipinos were not.

Only a minority of the three populations wanted to become colonial subjects of the United States.

To the dismay of the imperialists, the independence of Cuba had been guaranteed before the war had begun. In order to get money from Congress to fight Spain, the administration accepted a rider drafted by Senator Henry Teller of Colorado. The Teller Amendment forbade the United States to take over the sugar island. Therefore, the great debate over imperialism centered on Puerto Rico and the Philippine Islands.

THE DEBATE

The anti-imperialists were a diverse group; their arguments were sometimes contradictory. In Congress, they included old radical Republicans like George Frisbie Hoar of Massachusetts, one-time liberal Republicans like Carl Schurz, and much of the old Mugwump wing of the party. Some Republican regulars opposed taking colonies, including the witty and dictatorial Speaker of the House of Representatives, Thomas B. Reed of Maine. A substantial part of the Democratic party, led by William Jennings Bryan, opposed annexation of any former Spanish lands. Henry Teller became a Democrat in 1900 because of his opposition to imperial expansion.

The anti-imperialists reminded Americans of their anti-colonial heritage. "We insist," declared the American Anti-Imperialist League in October 1899, "that the subjugation of any people is 'criminal aggression' and open disloyalty to the distinctive principles of our government. We hold, with Abraham Lincoln, that no man is good enough to govern another man without that man's consent."

Some of the anti-imperialists appealed to racist feelings. With many people uncomfortable with the nation's large black population, did it make sense to bring millions more nonwhite people under the flag? When Congress finally decided to take the Philippines and pay Spain $20 million in compensation, House Speaker Thomas B. Reed resigned in disgust, grumbling, "We have bought ten million Malays at two dollars a head unpicked, and nobody knows what it will cost to pick them."

However, feelings of white racial superiority worked mostly in favor of the imperialists. Shrewd propagandists like Theodore Roosevelt, who was now governor of New York; Henry Cabot Lodge; and the eloquent Albert J. Beveridge, senator from Indiana, preached that the white race had a duty and a right to govern inferior peoples. "God has not been preparing the English-speaking and Teutonic peoples for a thousand years for nothing but vain and idle self-contemplation and self-admiration," Beveridge told the Senate. He had made them "the master organizers of the world."

Well-grounded fears that if the United States evacuated the Philippines, Japan or Germany would occupy them, motivated other politicians to support annexation. But most of all, the American people were in an emotional, expansive mood. Coming at the end of the troubled, depressed, and divided 1890s, annexation of colonies seemed a way to unite the country.

Hawaii State Archives

Liliuokalani, the last monarch of Hawaii, bore no racial animosity toward the white Americans who dominated the islands economically and politically. Her husband, behind her, was Caucasian. She did, however, want to protect Hawaiian culture and language and reduce the power of the white oligarchy, then led by Sanford Dole of pineapple fame. He is seated at the left of this photograph. Dole was instrumental in deposing "Queen Lil."

HAWAII

McKinley had met less opposition in July 1898—in the midst of the Spanish–American War—when he called for the annexation of Hawaii, then an independent nation of 7 major and 1,400 minor islands in the central Pacific. (Shortly thereafter, Guam, Wake, and Baker islands were added to the new empire as coaling stations for the navy.)

The annexation of Hawaii had, in fact, been long in the making. The descendants of American missionaries in the islands had grown rich by exporting sugar and pineapples to the United States. They had the confidence of the Hawaiian king, David Kalakaua and, until 1890, they were content with the independent island paradise they virtually ran.

Then the McKinley Tariff of 1890 put a two cent per pound bounty on American-grown sugar. This encouraged American farmers to produce so much cane and sugar beets that Hawaiian imports declined sharply. Unable to affect American tariff policy from outside, the haole (white) Hawaiian oligarchy concluded that Hawaii must join the United States and benefit from the subsidy.

Their first attempt failed. In 1891 Kalakaua's sister, **Liliuokalani,** succeeded him on the throne. She was not the easy touch Kalakaua had been. She meant to preserve Hawaiian culture (and independence) by withdrawing some of the privileges the wealthy haoles enjoyed. "Hawaii for the Hawaiians," was her slogan. "Queen Lil" was popular among native Hawaiians, who not only were exploited by haole landowners but also faced the competition of immigrant Japanese plantation workers.

Alarmed, the oligarchy acted quickly with help from the American minister in Honolulu. He landed 150 marines from the USS *Boston,* who quickly took control. "The Hawaiian pear is now fully ripe . . . for the United States to pluck it," he informed Washington. The Senate had a treaty of annexation on the table when Grover Cleveland was inaugurated in March 1893. After investigating Hawaiian public opinion, Cleveland withdrew the treaty and ordered the marines to return to their ships and to the naval base at Pearl Harbor.

The haole oligarchy had gone too far to chance restoring Queen Liliuokalani. They declared Hawaii a republic. As long as Cleveland was president, they bided their time. In the excitement of the imperialist expansion of 1898, Hawaii was annexed by means of a joint resolution of the American

---

Missionary

President McKinley displayed his ignorance of the Philippines, once privately, then in a public statement. When news of Dewey's victory at Manila Bay reached him, he could not find the Philippines on a globe; he had to be shown. During the debate over acquiring the Philippines as a colony, he announced that he decided on keeping the islands after a sleepless night of anxiety and prayer. He concluded that Americans had a duty to bring Christianity to the Philippine people.

About four out of five Filipinos were Roman Catholic and had been for centuries. One in five was a Protestant. About 5 percent were Muslims.

Congress and the Hawaiian legislature, the same device under which Texas had joined the Union.

Many native Hawaiians continued to resent the takeover. Liliuokalani spent much time in the United States trying to win financial concessions for the islands' natives (and somewhat larger grants for herself). But as the white population grew and the islands attracted Japanese, Chinese, and Filipino immigrants, the native Hawaiians declined into a small minority. Like the Indians, they became foreigners in their own homeland. The islands' famous anthem, *Aloha Oe*, written by Liliuokalani, translates as "Farewell to Thee" and has more than one meaning.

THE PHILIPPINE INSURRECTION

Taking over the Philippines was neither easy nor cheap, as Thomas B. Reed had predicted. If the war with Spain had been something like splendid, the war that followed it was a great deal like hideous. The Filipinos were experienced in guerrilla warfare. Led by Emilio Aguinaldo, a well-educated patriot who was as comfortable in the jungle as he was in the library, the rebels withdrew from the American-occupied cities to the jungles and mountains and fought only when the odds favored them.

In response, the American army of occupation was expanded to 65,000 men by early 1900. Even then the troops could make little progress outside the cities. The American commanders were unable to draw the *insurrectos* into a conventional battle in which superior firepower told the tale.

The fighting was vicious. The Filipinos frequently decapitated their captives. The Americans, frustrated by their failures, the tropical heat, insects, and diseases, retaliated by slaughtering whole villages thought to support the rebels. The army never did defeat the *insurrectos*. The rebellion ended only when, in March 1901, troops under General Arthur MacArthur succeeded in capturing Aguinaldo by a clever trick. Weary of the bloodshed, Aguinaldo took an oath of allegiance to the United States and ordered his followers to do the same. (He lived to see Philippine independence in 1946.) More than 5,000 Americans died in the cause of suppressing a popular revolution, a queer twist in a conflict that began, three years earlier, in support of a popular revolution.

THE OPEN DOOR IN CHINA

The Philippines provided a superb base for Americans engaged in the China trade. On the face of it, China too was a pear ripe for plucking. The emperor had little power outside Beijing; powerful regional warlords battled one another in the provinces; and most of the imperialist nations of Europe, plus Japan, had carved out spheres of influence. There, their own troops maintained order and their own laws governed their resident citizens.

However, the most powerful of the nations in China, Great Britain, opposed partitioning China in the way Africa was being partitioned. Longer in the empire business and therefore more conscious than Japan, Russia, Germany, and Italy of the headaches and expense that attended imperial glory, the British believed that with their efficient industrial complex they could dominate the market of a weak but independent China. American businessmen believed they would win the lion's share of the prodigious purchases 160 million Chinese were capable of making. So they supported the British policy of preventing the other imperialist nations from turning their spheres of influence into full-fledged colonies.

Indeed, McKinley's secretary of state, John Hay, rushed ahead of Great Britain to circulate a series of memoranda called the **Open Door** notes. These declarations pledged the imperial powers to respect the territorial integrity of China and to grant equal trading rights in their spheres of influence to all other countries.

Anticolonialist as it was, the Open Door policy by no means established the self-determination of the Chinese people, nor did it end military intervention by outsiders. In 1900, when antiforeign rebels known as Boxers (the Chinese name of their religious movement was "Righteous

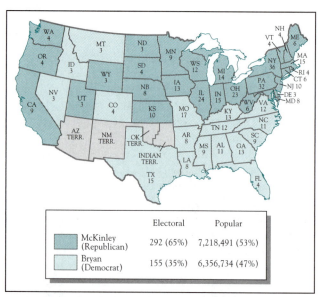

		Electoral	Popular
▨	McKinley (Republican)	292 (65%)	7,218,491 (53%)
▢	Bryan (Democrat)	155 (35%)	6,356,734 (47%)

MAP 33:3 Presidential Election of 1900
McKinley's popularity and the return of agricultural prosperity can be seen by comparing the results of his reelection in 1900 with his first victory in 1896 (see Map 33.1 on p. 542). The South and the silver-mining states were loyal to Bryan again, but he lost the western agricultural states that were his home.

Dewey's Blunder

Commodore George Dewey was a national hero after Manila Bay. He was a Democrat and might have had the party's presidential nomination in 1900. At first Dewey rebuffed the Democrats who shuddered at the thought of having Bryan again. Dewey did not think he was qualified for the office. Then he changed his mind: "Since studying the subject, I am convinced that the office of the president is not such a very difficult one to fill." His candor, which some saw as arrogance, alienated most of his supporters. One could not run for president saying that the job was a piece of cake.

Harmonious Fist") besieged 900 foreigners in the British delegation in Peking, American troops joined the soldiers of six other nations in defeating them. The victory encouraged beliefs in white superiority (despite the Japanese part in the victory) and convinced other nations that cooperation in maintaining the Open Door was the best policy in China (or so they said).

MCKINLEY MURDERED

In 1900 the Democrats again nominated William Jennings Bryan to run against McKinley. Bryan tried to make imperialism the issue, but the campaign fizzled. Americans were either happy having overseas possessions or uninterested. McKinley sidestepped the debate and emphasized prosperity; the Republican slogan was "Four More Years of the Full Dinner Pail." Dinner pails carried the day. Several states that voted Democratic–Populist in 1896 went Republican in 1900, including Bryan's own state of Nebraska and once-revolutionary Kansas.

There was a new vice president. Theodore Roosevelt had moved rapidly from his self-publicized exploits in Cuba to the governorship of New York. However, he quickly alienated the Republican party boss, Thomas C. Platt, who had looked on him as a colorful "war hero" who would do as he was told. Roosevelt refused to take orders. When he chastised several corrupt members of Platt's organization, Platt took advantage of the fact that McKinley's first vice president had died to persuade other party bosses to take Roosevelt off his hands, burying him in the impotent obscurity of the vice presidency.

Mark Hanna opposed the nomination. What would happen to the country, Hanna asked McKinley, if he died and the manic Roosevelt became president? McKinley was almost 60 and in good health. But two presidents had been assassinated within his and Hanna's memories. When he could not prevent Roosevelt's nomination, Hanna told the president, "It is your duty to your country to live another four years."

As Hanna had feared, McKinley's life was in another man's hands. On September 6, 1901, the president paid a ceremonial visit to the Pan-American Exposition in Buffalo. Greeting a long line of guests, he found himself faced by a man extending a bandaged hand. The gauze concealed a large-bore pistol with which Leon Czolgosz shot the president

point-blank in the chest and abdomen. Czolgosz was a pathetic figure, uneducated, unsophisticated, a sucker for panaceas. He told police that he was an anarchist who "didn't believe one man should have so much service and another man should have none." In fact, he had attended anarchist meetings, but that was all. He had no anarchist friends and knew little about that revolutionary philosophy; he was a sad character, a lost soul.

Eight days after the shooting, McKinley died. "Now look," Hanna shook his head at the funeral, "that damned cowboy is president."

A FLEXIBLE IMPERIALIST

Unlike the "accidental" presidents who preceded him, Teddy Roosevelt was to leave his mark on the nation. The young New Yorker (42 when he was sworn in) knew only one way to do anything: rush into the lead and stay there. Nowhere was his assertive personality more pronounced than in his foreign policy, which was almost a continuation, in striped dress trousers, of his charge up San Juan Hill.

Roosevelt's policies varied according to the part of the world with which he was dealing. With the European nations he insisted that the United States be accepted as an equal, active imperial power. Although friendship between Great Britain and the United States had long been growing, Roosevelt hastened it by responding cordially to every British request for cooperation.

Roosevelt's Asian policies were "enlightened" by comparison with the other imperial powers. He named William Howard Taft governor of the Philippines. Once the insurrection was crushed, Taft proved to be a paternalistic governor. He called the Filipinos his "little brown brothers," reflecting the nearly universal belief among whites in their own racial superiority. However, he was even-handed and accommodating in dealing with the people of the colony, something that could be said for few British and French colonial governors or for no governors in the German and Japanese colonies. Taft was committed to preparing the Philippines for eventual independence; few of the British *sahibs* in India, where independence was clearly inevitable, were so enlightened.

In China, Roosevelt supported the Open Door policy. John Hay, who authored the Open Door notes, remained secretary of state until he died in 1905. When Japan and Russia could not conclude an ugly war for preeminence in Manchuria, China's northeasternmost province, Roosevelt pressured both powers into sending delegates to Portsmouth, New Hampshire, where, under American pressure, they worked out a treaty. Roosevelt was awarded the Nobel Peace Prize for his efforts, an irony in that he was a militarist. (It would not be the last time the Nobel Committee chose absurdly in bestowing the honor.)

HIGH-HANDEDNESS IN LATIN AMERICA

Toward Latin America, Roosevelt was as arrogant and imperious as any European or Japanese imperialist. He made it clear to the other imperial nations that the United States held a preeminent position in the Western Hemisphere. In 1904, when several European nations threatened to invade the Dominican Republic to collect debts owed their citizens, Roosevelt proclaimed the "Roosevelt Corollary" to the Monroe Doctrine: when it seemed necessary to protect an American state from European intervention, the United States would itself intervene.

Marines promptly landed in the Dominican Republic and took over the collection of the nation's customs, paying European creditors out of the revenues. Between 1904 and the 1930s (and again after the 1960s), the United States repeatedly sent troops into Latin American countries even when there was no threat of European intervention. The U.S. marines became, in the words of General Smedley Butler, who commanded several interventions, "a glorified bill collecting agency."

The Roosevelt Corollary marked the beginning of Latin American resentment of *yanqui imperialismo* along with Roosevelt's means of ensuring what he considered his greatest achievement: the construction of the Panama Canal.

THE PATH BETWEEN THE SEAS

Since the early sixteenth century, when it was recognized that the Americas were not "the Indies," hundreds of explorers had looked for a water passage between the Atlantic and Pacific. The voyage around the bottom of South America was far too long. The problem became more urgent with the steam-powered ships of the nineteenth century. During the Spanish–American War, the battleship *Oregon,* stationed in San Francisco, needed sixty-seven days to get to Cuba via Cape Horn. Had there been a canal through the Isthmus of Panama, the voyage would have taken two weeks.

In the 1880s a French company had begun to dig a canal across Panama, then part of Colombia. But the project was abandoned because of engineering difficulties and the ravages of malaria and yellow fever. Three out of five French men and women in Panama died, and they were supervisors, living under the best conditions. Mortality was much higher among the laborers, mostly blacks from Jamaica. The horrors of the French experience convinced most American experts that the path between the seas should be dug not in Panama, but through healthier Nicaragua, which also provided a lower crossing than Panama did.

John Hay had a Nicaraguan canal in mind when he negotiated a treaty with Britain promising the United States full control of the project. Congress favored the Nicaragua route. Then, however, two of the most effective lobbyists of all time, an agent of the French company that held rights to the

■ *Theodore Roosevelt's means of acquiring of the Panama Canal Zone has, with justice, been faulted. The construction of the canal was a heroic triumph of engineering and organization. The greatest challenge was not excavating the canal but the gigantic task of quickly removing the blasted earth and rock. Twelve parallel railroads at this cut indicate how massive the job was.*

© Bettmann/UPI/Corbis

Panama route, Philippe Bunau-Varilla, and an American wheeler-dealer, William Nelson Cromwell, went to work in Washington's restaurants, the cloakrooms of Congress, and in the White House itself.

Their goal was to win approval of the Panama route so that they could sell the Panamanian assets of the bankrupt French company, including an American-built railroad, to the United States. There was no good reason to consider their proposal. Even if the United States opted for the Panama route that engineers said was inferior to the Nicaraguan route, the French company's rights on the isthmus were due to expire shortly, and most of its equipment was useless anyway. Nevertheless, Bunau-Varilla and Cromwell won over President Roosevelt and key members of Congress. The transaction was scandalous or absurd, one or the other.

ROOSEVELT TAKES PANAMA

Then the project stalled in Bogotá. Roosevelt offered Colombia $10 million and an annual rent of $250,000 for a zone across the isthmus. Colombia demanded $25 million. No doubt Colombian politicians were thinking of a bonanza in graft, but the higher price was not unreasonable.

Nevertheless, President Roosevelt, so accommodating with Bunau-Varilla, was suddenly indignant. Through intermediaries, he conspired with Bunau-Varilla to bypass the Colombians by instigating a parody of a rebellion in Panama. On November 2, 1903, Roosevelt sent warships to Panama. The next day, the province erupted in riots and declared its independence from Colombia. On November 6, the United States recognized the Republic of Panama. On November 18, Panama's foreign minister, none other than M. Bunau-Varilla, signed a treaty with the United States that granted perpetual use of a ten-mile-wide zone through the middle of the world's youngest nation.

Roosevelt never confirmed or denied the specifics of the byzantine events. But he boasted proudly, "I took the Canal Zone."

FURTHER READING

1896: Election and Consequences Paolo Coletta, *William Jennings Bryan*, 3 vols., 1964–1969; Robert F. Durden, *The Climax of Populism: The Election of 1896*, 1965; Steven Hahn, *The Roots of Southern Populism*, 1983; Stanley Jones, *The Presidential Election of 1896*, 1964; William L. Link, *The Paradox of Southern Progressivism, 1880–1930*, 1992; H. Wayne Morgan, *William McKinley and His America*, 1963; Francis Russell, *The President Makers: From Mark Hanna to Joseph P. Kennedy*, 1976; R. Hal Williams, *Years of Decision: American Politics in the 1890s*, 1993.

African Americans and the 1890s W. Fitzhugh Brundage, *Lynching in the New South: Georgia and Virginia, 1880–1930*, 1993; William G. Carrigan, *The Making of a Lynching Culture: Violence and Vigilantism in Central Texas*, 2004; Thomas E. Harris, *Analysis of the Clash between Booker T. Washington and W. E. B. DuBois*, 1993; Michael J. Klarman, *From Jim Crow to Civil Rights: The Supreme Court and the Struggle for Racial Equality*, 2004; Michael McGerr, *A Fierce Discontent: The Rise and Fall of the Progressive Movement in America, 1870–1920*, 2003; Dwight D. Murphey, *Lynching: History and Analysis*, 1995; Michael J. Pfeifer, *Rough Justice: Lynching and American Society, 1874–1947*, 2004; David R. Roediger, *The Wages of Whiteness: Race and the Making of the American Working Class*, 1991; Emmett J. Scott and Lyman Beecher Stowe, *Booker T. Washington: Builder of a Civilization*, 2000; John White, *Black Leadership in America: From Booker T. Washington to Jesse Jackson*, 1990.

America Abroad Helena G. Allen, *The Betrayal of Liliuokalani, Last Queen of Hawaii, 1838–1917*, 1982; H.W. Brands, *Bound to Empire: The United States and the Philippines*, 1992; Joseph Campbell, *Yellow Journalism: Puncturing the Myths, Defining the Legacies*, 2001; Kendrick A. Clements, *William Jennings Bryan: Missionary Isolationist*, 1983; Michael Dougherty, *To Steal a Kingdom*, 1992; Lloyd Gardner, Walter R. Le Feber, and Thomas McCormick, *The Creation of the American Empire*, 1973; Stanley Karnow, *In Our Image: America's Empire in the Philippines*, 1989; David McCullough, *The Path between the Seas*, 1977; Aldyth Morris, *Liliuokalani*, 1993; Thomas J. Osborne, *American Opposition to Hawaiian Annexation, 1893–1898*, 1981; John L. Offenr, *An Unwanted War: The Diplomacy of the United States and Spain over Cuba, 1895–1898*, 1992; Louis M. Perez, *The War of 1898: The United States and Cuba in History and Historiography*, 1998; Emily S. Rosenberg, *Spreading the American Dream: American Economic and Cultural Expansion, 1890–1945*, 1982; Joseph Smith, *The Spanish–American War: Conflict in the Caribbean and the Pacific 1845–1902*, 1994.

Enter Theodore Roosevelt Edmund Morris, *The Rise of Theodore Roosevelt*, 1979, and *Theodore Rex*, 2001; Eric Rauchway, *Murdering McKinley: The Making of Theodore Roosevelt's America*, 2003.

KEY TERMS

The following terms are covered in this chapter and can also be found in the list of Key Terms at the back of the book.

Atlanta Compromise	John Fiske	Mark Hanna	Rough Riders
grandfather clause	John Marshall Harlan	Open Door	
The Influence of Sea Power upon History	Liliuokalani		

ONLINE SOURCES GUIDE

Use this listing to find online documents, images, interactive maps, simulations, and other resources related to this chapter:

American History Resource Center
http://history.wadsworth.com/rc/us

Selected Documents

The Plessy v. Ferguson *decision*

W. E. B. DuBois's thoughts on Booker T. Washington

Eugene Debs's "How I Became a Socialist"

Alfred Thayer Mahan's The Influence of Sea Power upon History

Two eyewitness accounts of the American naval attack on the Spanish Fleet in Manila

Theodore Roosevelt's The Rough Riders

William Jennings Bryan's views on imperialism

Selected Images

Copper mining town outside Denver, Colorado, 1897

Farming in South Dakota, 1898

Indian children at the Carlisle school, 1900

Lynching of African Americans

Booker T. Washington at Tuskegee Institute

Advertisement for a 1901 phonograph

First Oldsmobile, 1897

Breaker boys in a coal mine, 1900

Battle of Manila Bay, 1898

Interactive Time Line (with online readings)

In the Days of McKinley: The United States as a World Power, 1896–1903

CHAPTER 34.

The World of Teddy Roosevelt

Society and Culture in Transition 1890–1917

He played all his cards—if not more.
    Oliver Wendell Holmes, Jr.

The universe seemed to be spinning round, and
Theodore was the spinner.

    Rudyard Kipling

And never did a President before so reflect the quality of his time.
    H. G. Wells

The 1890s were a time of serious economic depression, conflict between classes, widespread social upheaval, and violence. The decade began at Wounded Knee, the tragic conclusion of the Indian Wars that was more massacre than battle. In 1892 the country was paralyzed by the Pullman strike, a nationwide shutdown of railroads that began because a multimillionaire industrialist was so greedy that he cut his employees' wages but not the rents on the houses in which they were required to live. Gold and silver miners in the Rocky Mountains took potshots at strikebreakers and bosses, and union members were jailed en masse in holding pens. The federal government sent the army to crush several strikes.

Panicked wealthy conservatives believed that angry farmers in the South and West were close to armed revolution.

Even a good-natured journalist who lived among Kansas farmers, William Allen White, saw red when he was jostled on the streets of his hometown by "greasy fizzles." The federal government jailed Jacob Coxey, a mild Ohio businessman who led a peaceful march of the unemployed to Washington to present Congress with a petition. In the southern states, marginal whites—"rednecks"—routinely mobilized in mobs to torture and hang black men accused of crimes or who had merely been "insolent" with a white man or woman. During several years, there was an unpunished lynching in the United States every other day. Destitute immigrants fleeing Europe arrived in the United States at a rate of 1,000 a day (more after the turn of the century). Almost all of them got their start in the land of opportunity in congested, unhealthy slums.

Life expectancy for white people born in the United States was 45; it was lower for blacks, much lower for Indians. Infant mortality in New York City was worse than it had been in the eighteenth century. Americans were six times more likely to die of influenza than they are today, sixty times more likely to die of syphilis, and more than eighty times more likely to die of tuberculosis. Minor public health problems in the twenty-first century—typhoid, scarlet fever, strep throat, diphtheria, whooping cough, and measles—were common killers in the 1890s.

And yet, even before the decade ended with the murder of a popular president, people were speaking of "the Gay Nineties."

SYMBOL OF AN AGE

How could that be? Because the people who were articulate, who coined catch-phrases like "Gay Nineties" and "Good Old Days" for deposit in the national memory, were not impoverished immigrants, black sharecroppers, demoralized Indians, exploited factory workers, and dirt farmers unable to make a living from the land. In the United States during the 1890s, the people who shaped American culture were members of a large, economically comfortable, and educated middle class conscious of the fact that they were a distinct social class. Beginning in the 1890s, and furiously after 1900, they put their numbers to work in changing what they did not like about American society—and that included a great many things. But they liked how they lived and, in retrospect, created a vision of the 1890s and 1900s as a time when the summer sun was warmer, the hot dogs tastier, the baseball more exciting, the boys more gallant, the girls prettier, and the songs lilting and cheerful.

A RECOGNIZABLE CULTURE

The vision of the turn of the century as "the good old days" has survived because middle-class folkways and values have dominated American popular culture ever since. We need make no leap of imagination to understand the middle class

> ### Hit Tunes
>
> Two classic songs, one now international, were written in 1893. "Happy Birthday to You" began as "Good Morning to You." It was written by Patty Smith Hill, a pioneer of the kindergarten movement. Irving Berlin tried to steal it from Hill in 1921, but she sued him and won.
>
> The lyrics of "America the Beautiful" were put to the music of a hymn by Katherine Lee Bates, a professor of English at Wellesley College. Congress still receives petitions asking that it, celebrating natural grandeur, replace the militaristic (and nearly unsingable) "Star-Spangled Banner" as the national anthem.

of the 1890s and early 1900s as we must, for example, to make sense of the Puritans of Massachusetts or the slave owners of antebellum America. Middle-class people of 1900 more closely resemble us, four and five generations down the line, than they did their own parents.

The middle class of the turn of the century was a new social class. Their status and affluence were not based on the ownership of property. They were managers of the small businesses they owned or employees of big corporations. They were professional bureaucrats, engineers, and technicians, including people who dirtied their hands at work as skilled, highly trained, well-paid, and responsible workers—the "aristocracy of labor"—locomotive engineers, builders, linotype operators, the cream of the machinist's trade. They were professionals: ministers, lawyers, physicians, nurses, dentists, pharmacists, professors, schoolteachers, accountants, journalists. They were "white-collar" workers who were not all that well paid—government bureaucrats, floorwalkers in department stores—who shared the values of better-off people from whom, on the street, at church, or on holiday at the seashore, they could not be distinguished.

There were more than 5 million white-collar workers in the United States in 1900, 1.2 million professionals, 1.7 million managers, 1.3 million sales workers, and almost a million clerical workers.

Entertainment 1885–1910

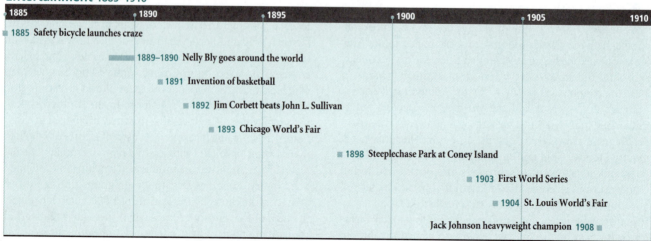

| 1885 | 1890 | 1895 | 1900 | 1905 | 1910 |

- 1885 Safety bicycle launches craze
- 1889–1890 Nelly Bly goes around the world
- 1891 Invention of basketball
- 1892 Jim Corbett beats John L. Sullivan
- 1893 Chicago World's Fair
- 1898 Steeplechase Park at Coney Island
- 1903 First World Series
- 1904 St. Louis World's Fair
- Jack Johnson heavyweight champion 1908

Theodore Roosevelt, "the bride at every wedding and the corpse at every funeral." If any other president enjoyed being president as much as Teddy Roosevelt did, none did so as boisterously. It was whispered he was constantly drunk; when Iron Age *magazine said so, Roosevelt sued for libel and won. He was, in fact, a very moderate drinker.*

The new middle class still believed in the work ethic. They took pride in the fact that they supported themselves decently and comfortably. But they also believed in "improving" themselves, and—perhaps the greatest break with the past—they believed in enjoying life. Fate and Leon Czolgosz provided them with the perfect president.

TEDDY

Vice President Theodore Roosevelt was hiking in the Adirondacks when he got the news of McKinley's death.

Old Boys

Most of Theodore Roosevelt's advisers were, like him, gentlemen of old family who assumed that they were the people intended to govern the United States. They wore their duties lightly. Cabinet meetings could seem like a gaggle of old boys joshing at the Harvard–Yale Club.

When T. R. asked Attorney General Philander C. Knox to prepare a legal justification of his actions in detaching Panama from Colombia, Knox replied, "Oh Mr. President, do not let so great an achievement suffer from any taint of legality." After a long, blustering explanation of his actions to the cabinet, T. R. asked, "Well, have I defended myself?" Secretary of War Elihu Root replied, "You certainly have, Mr. President. You have shown that you were accused of seduction, and you have conclusively proved that you were guilty of rape."

He rushed to Buffalo, paid his respects, took the oath of office, and confided to a friend, "It is a dreadful thing to come into the presidency in this way. But it would be a far worse thing to be morbid about it." Roosevelt intended to enjoy the presidency. No other chief executive before or since has had such a "bully" time living at 1600 Pennsylvania Avenue. (To Roosevelt, anything of which he approved was "bully!")

Both critics and friends of the president poked fun at his personal motto: "Walk softly and carry a big stick." They observed Roosevelt wildly waving clubs around often enough; they never knew him to walk softly. Everything Roosevelt did was accompanied by fanfares. He swaggered and strutted like an exuberant adolescent, hogging center stage and good-naturedly drowning out anyone who dared compete for the spotlight. He insisted, as one of his children put it, on being the bride at every wedding and the corpse at every funeral. "You must remember," the British ambassador said, "that the president is about six years old."

Roosevelt shattered the solemn public persona that every president had nurtured since Rutherford B. Hayes. He stormed about the country far more than any predecessor had, delivering dramatic speeches, happily mixing with crowds of all kinds, camping out, climbing mountains, and clambering astride horses and atop machines. When a motion picture photographer asked Roosevelt to move for the novel camera, he picked up an ax and furiously chopped down an unoffending tree.

THE STRENUOUS LIFE

Of an old Dutch family—a very large family by the end of the nineteenth century—Roosevelt was rich, but not nearly on a par with the Vanderbilts and Rockefellers. He was "old money," the family fortune having been earned before the industrial age, and just enough to enable its heirs to live grandly without having to earn more. Indeed, people of Roosevelt's class disdained the multimillionaires railroads, oil wells, and steel mills had created, as much because of their grasping acquisitiveness as for the fact that they were very, very rich. Teddy Roosevelt did not hesitate to give voice to his scorn. "I don't care a damn about stocks and bonds," he said. People of Roosevelt's class also looked down on politicians as vulgar men on the make. On that question, Roosevelt parted company with his kind, although he had to bear with much disapproval when he announced his intention to run for a seat in the New York State assembly in 1882.

Sickly as a boy, Roosevelt took up bodybuilding as a teenager. It seemed to release a manic energy no one had seen. He fought on the Harvard boxing team and rode with cowboys on a ranch he bought in North Dakota. As police commissioner of New York City, he accompanied patrolmen on dangerous night beats. When the war with Spain broke out, he volunteered. In dozens of articles and books—he was a prolific writer, and a pretty good one—he wrote of the glories of "the strenuous life." And all this occurred despite the fact that he suffered from angina and had to pop nitroglycerin pills.

Roosevelt liked to show off his large, handsome, and affectionate family with himself center stage, the stern but loving patriarch. He sported a modest paunch (a desirable masculine attribute in that sensible era), a close-clipped mustache, and thick pince-nez that dropped from his nose when he was excited, which was often. His teeth were odd, all seemingly incisors of the same size and about twice as many as normal. He displayed them often in a broad grin that he shed only when he took off after enemies whom middle-class Americans also found it easy to dislike: Wall Street bankers, Socialists, and impudent Latin Americans.

Unlike William McKinley, whose priggishness irked him, Roosevelt had no compunctions about smoking his cigars in public. What was the harm in a minor vice that brought a man pleasure? More than any other person, he taught Americans to believe that their president must be a good fellow and a showman.

AMERICA PERSONIFIED

Roosevelt had plenty of critics. But the vibrant new middle class thought him grand. They called him "Teddy" (they did not call McKinley "Billy") and named the cuddly animal doll they bought for their children, the teddy bear, after him. He was the first president to be routinely identified in newspapers by his initials, T. R. Even Elihu Root, a conservative gentleman who served as both secretary of war and secretary of state, waxed playful when he congratulated the president on his forty-sixth birthday in 1904. "You have made a very good start in life," Root said, "and your friends have great hopes for you when you grow up."

Kansas journalist William Allen White, the archetype of the middle-class townsman, wrote that "Roosevelt bit me and I went mad." White remained a lifelong devotee of "the Colonel," as did Finley Peter Dunne, the urbane Chicagoan who captured the salty, cynical humor of the big-city Irish in his fictional commentator on current events, Mr. Dooley. Radicals hated Roosevelt (who hated them back with interest), but they were at a loss as to how to counter his popularity. Socialists, then politically significant, stuck to the issues when they disagreed with him. There was no profit in attacking Teddy Roosevelt personally.

Although T. R. was a staunch believer in Anglo–Saxon superiority, he won the affection of African Americans when he invited Booker T. Washington to the White House and shrugged off howls of outrage from southern white supremacists. (The *Richmond Dispatch* headlined its story "Roosevelt Dines a Darkey.") Woman suffragists, gearing up for the final phase of their long battle for the vote, petitioned him respectfully. Elizabeth Cady Stanton addressed him from her deathbed in 1901 as "already celebrated for so many deeds and honorable utterances."

Much mischief was done during Theodore Roosevelt's nearly eight years in office. He committed the United States to a role as international policeman that still taints the nation's reputation. He was inclined to define his opponents in moral terms, a recurring and unfortunate characteristic of American politics since his time.

THE NEW MIDDLE CLASS

The symbiosis between the president and the middle class is one of the most striking historical facts of the years spanning the turn of the century. Like their president between 1901 and 1909, the middle class was worldly, confident, optimistic, and glad to be alive.

AN EDUCATED PEOPLE

In the late nineteenth century, for the first time, a substantial portion of the population was educated beyond "the three Rs"—"readin', 'ritin', and 'rithmetic." During the final third of the century and explosively after 1890, American education expanded and changed in character to accommodate the aspirations of the new class.

In 1860 there were only about 300 secondary schools in the United States (in a population of 31.4 million). Only about 100 of them were free. Although girls were admitted to most public elementary schools, girls of modest means rarely attended for more than a few grades, just enough to learn the basics.

There were more colleges and universities than high schools, about 560 in 1870. That number can be misleading, however. Most colleges were quite small, with a student body smaller than the menagerie that sits in a single section of a freshman survey course at a state university today. A few colleges were the exclusive preserves of the wealthy, more concerned with cementing social relationships than transmitting knowledge. Most of the remainder were run by religious denominations, serving principally young men who wanted to be ministers, or said they did.

With the exception of the polytechnic institutes, course offerings were built around the by then ancient liberal arts curriculum: Latin and Greek (and Hebrew in the schools training ministers), classical literature, philosophy, mathematics, and (largely ancient) history. No one pretended that a liberal education prepared students for careers; that was not the idea. A liberal education was part of what made a gentleman. The colleges operated by religious denominations, of course, overlay the basic curriculum with courses in correct theology. The handful of "female seminaries" and colleges that admitted women before the Civil War taught the same subjects, often watered down in consideration of female "inadequacies."

Beginning about 1880, the number of educational institutions rapidly multiplied, and the courses they offered became far more diverse. By 1900 there were 6,000 free public secondary schools in the United States; by 1915 there were 12,000 with 1.3 million pupils. Educational expenditures per pupil increased from about $9 a year in 1870 to $48 in 1920. Secondary schools no longer specialized exclusively in preparing an elite few for university; they offered courses leading to jobs in industry and business, such as the operation of the already ubiquitous typewriter.

A NEW KIND OF UNIVERSITY

The Morrill Land Grant Act of 1862 and the philanthropy of millionaires expanded opportunities for higher education.

Culver Pictures

*Commencement at Mount Holyoke in Massachusetts. It was one of the seven elite women's colleges in the Northeast (the **Seven Sisters**) equivalent to the schools of the Ivy League, then all-male institutions. All of the Sisters were "finishing schools," instilling the social graces; some had demanding curricula too.*

The Morrill Act gave federal land to states to be sold or rented to provide money for the educational needs of "the industrial classes," particularly in "such branches of learning as are related to agriculture and mechanic arts." These **land grant universities** not only fostered technical and professional education but put the liberal arts curriculum, without an overlay of religion, within the reach of all but the very poor. Many of the western state universities considered among the nation's best today owe their origins to the Morrill Act.

Gilded Age millionaires competed for esteem as patrons of learning by constructing buildings and by endowing scholarships and professorial chairs at older institutions. A few pumped so much money into struggling colleges that they were able to put their names on them. Some founded completely new universities. A story made the rounds of Harvard that when railroad magnate Leland Stanford and his wife

were touring the university looking for a site on which to erect a building in memory of their son, who had died young, President Charles W. Eliot was explaining the cost of each of the buildings they saw, and Mrs. Stanford exclaimed, "Why, Leland, we can build our own university!" And they did: Stanford University in Palo Alto, California, was founded in 1885.

Cornell (1865), Drew (1866), Johns Hopkins (1876), Vanderbilt (1872), and Carnegie Institute of Technology (1905) bear the names of the moguls who financed them. In Philadelphia, success gospel preacher Russell B. Conwell established Temple University in 1884 explicitly to educate poor boys ambitious to rise in social station. John D. Rockefeller pumped millions into the University of Chicago (1890), making it within a decade one of America's most distinguished centers of learning. George Eastman, who got his money making Kodak cameras, gave so generously to the University of Rochester that the trustees ought to have renamed it Eastman.

Midwestern and western state universities, beginning with Iowa in 1858, took the lead in admitting women to at least some programs. In the East, separate women's colleges were the rule, again thanks to wealthy benefactors. Georgia Female College (Wesleyan) and Mount Holyoke dated from before the Civil War. In the later decades of the century they were joined by Vassar (1861), Wellesley (1870), Smith (1871),

Harvard-Educated Doctors

In 1869 President Eliot of Harvard suggested to the medical school that applicants take a written examination. The medical school rejected the idea because "a majority of the students cannot write well enough." A dismayed Eliot said that anyone could walk into the building and "without further question be accepted as a medical student."

Radcliffe (1879), Bryn Mawr (1880), and Barnard (1889). Vassar's educational standards rivaled those of the best men's colleges, but it was necessary to maintain a kind of "head start" program to remedy deficiencies in the secondary education of even well-to-do girls.

STUDYING FOR CAREERS

A few institutions, most notably Yale, clung tenaciously to the liberal arts curriculum. Most American universities adopted the elective system that was pioneered by the College of William and Mary, Washington College in Virginia (now Washington & Lee), and the University of Michigan. The elective system was most effectively promoted by President Eliot of Harvard. Beginning in 1869, Eliot abandoned the rule that every student must follow the same sequence of courses. He allowed individuals to choose their field of study. "Majors" included traditional subjects but also new disciplines in the social sciences, engineering, and business administration.

From Germany, educators borrowed the concept of the professional postgraduate school. Before the 1870s, people who wanted to learn a profession usually attached themselves to an established practitioner. They were apprentices, although not bound servants. A would-be lawyer agreed with an established attorney to do routine work in his office, from sweeping floors to helping with routine deeds and wills, in return for the privilege of reading law in the office and observing and questioning his mentor. After a few years, the apprentice lawyer hung out his own shingle. Physicians and pharmacists were trained the same way. Civil and mechanical engineers learned their professions on the job. All too often, elementary school teachers received no training. Often they were unmarried young women with little more schooling than their most advanced pupils. They were miserably paid, about $200 a year in rural states, and were required to board with a local family, their behavior watched by everyone.

WOMEN, MINORITIES, AND THE NEW EDUCATION

Women dauntless enough to put up with the boorish remarks of male classmates could be found in small numbers

Tuskegee Institute in Alabama emphasized practical, vocational courses, but its famous president between 1881 and 1915, Booker T. Washington, insisted on a liberal arts curriculum so that graduates would be well-rounded. This is a class in U.S. history, which, as in white colleges, would have been highly patriotic in tone and would have avoided controversial issues.

at every level of education. By the mid-1880s, the word *coeducational* and its breezy abbreviation, "coed," had become part of the language. The first female physician in the United States, Elizabeth Blackwell, was accredited in 1849. In 1868 she established a medical school for women in New York City. By that date, the Woman's Medical College of Pennsylvania was already in operation and recognized, however grudgingly, as providing a first-class medical education.

Female lawyers were more unusual than doctors simply because women's status in the law was inferior to that of men in several particulars. In 1873 the Supreme Court approved the University of Illinois law school's refusal to admit a woman on the grounds that "the paramount mission and destiny of women are to fulfill the noble and benign offices of wife and mother." Nevertheless, by the end of the century, several dozen women were practicing law, including the Populist "Mother" Mary Lease. Antoinette Blackwell, sister-in-law of Elizabeth the physician, paved the way for the ordination of women ministers. By the turn of the century, a few liberal Protestant denominations, such as the Unitarians, had ordained women.

In small numbers, well-to-do Jews and Catholics began to take advantage of the new educational opportunities. The Sephardic and German Jews were assimilated and highly secular; they sent their sons to established institutions as prestigious as they could afford. Most Catholics, however, sent their children to the numerous sectarian colleges that various religious orders, particularly the Jesuits, had founded. The Church was hostile to much of the secular learning of non-Catholic universities and sought to insulate its young men from it. While some Catholic colleges offered excellent instruction in the traditional curriculum, it was combined with a heavy course load in Catholic doctrine, history, observance, and apologetics (defense of the religion against Protestant critics).

The most famous Catholic colleges dated from before the Civil War. Notre Dame was founded in 1842. Holy Cross (1843) and Boston College (1863) were explicitly created as foils to aristocratic Protestant Harvard, which admitted few Catholics. John Quincy Adams's dream of a "national university" was, curiously, most nearly approximated by the Catholic church with the founding in 1889 of the Catholic University of America in Washington. It is difficult to imagine Adams being quite happy about the sponsor.

On a smaller scale, educational opportunities for blacks expanded. The old colleges and universities in New England and many of the sectarian colleges of the Ohio Valley continued to admit a small number of African Americans. W. E. B. DuBois, later a founder of the National Association for the Advancement of Colored People, earned a Ph.D. at Harvard. Hamilton S. Smith earned a law degree from Boston University in 1879, the first black to do so. (He could not make a living as an attorney, however, so he enrolled at the **Howard University** School of Dentistry. Howard was a private university educating the children of the small black middle and upper class.)

In the South (also in the North), philanthropists and state governments founded institutions for blacks only. Beginning with Lincoln University in Pennsylvania (founded as the Ashmun Institute in 1854), idealistic white benefactors supported schools such as Howard in Washington (1867) and Fisk in Nashville (1866). After Booker T. Washington's Atlanta Compromise speech of 1895 and the Supreme Court's decision in *Plessy* v. *Ferguson* (1896) gave the go-ahead to segregation at all levels of education, southern state governments founded "agricultural and mechanical" schools patterned after Alabama's Tuskegee Institute (1881), at which blacks could train for manual occupations.

Rarely was state-supported African-American education financed at anything remotely resembling the funding of whites-only schools, despite the insistence of the Supreme Court that racially separate facilities be "equal" in quality. In 1915, for example, African Americans comprised 43 percent of the population of Mississippi; only 15 percent of the state's education budget went to blacks-only institutions.

Remarkably, the achievements of several of these institutions were considerable. Few scientific researchers of the period were more productive than an obscure and self-effacing Tuskegee botanist, George Washington Carver. Fisk and Howard had faculty whose achievements could not be denied (although they could be ignored.) Nevertheless, the educational level of blacks lagged so far behind that of whites that in 1910, when only 7.7 percent of the American population was illiterate (the figure includes millions of recent immigrants), one black in three above the age of 10 could neither read nor write.

A LIVELY CULTURE

Americans continued to buy the books of European authors and the works of the older generation of American poets—Emerson, Longfellow, Whitman, and Whittier. Emily Dickinson of Amherst, Massachusetts, a recluse all but unknown until after her death in 1886, was immediately recognized as a poet of rare (and sometimes bizarre) sensibility. Mostly, however, the turn of the century was a time when novelists dominated literature. A few were so popular they got rich from royalties. The best seller of the late nineteenth century was *Ben Hur: A Tale of the Christ* (1880) by former Civil War General Lew Wallace.

TWAIN AND JAMES

Samuel Langhorne Clemens, or **Mark Twain,** was a Missourian who, at the beginning of the Civil War, deserted a unit of Confederate volunteers he described as more comic than pathetic, and went west to Nevada to avoid service on either side. He brilliantly captured both the hardships and ribald humor of western life in a series of short stories and a mostly factual account of his experiences in *Roughing It* (1872). He won an international reputation with *The Adventures of Tom Sawyer* (1876), although it was intended as a book for boys, and with its sequel, *The Adventures of*

PUCKOGRAPHS—NEW SERIES, NO. I.

"MARK TWAIN,"
AMERICA'S BEST HUMORIST.

Mark Twain (the pen name of Samuel L. Clemens) was one of the most popular American writers during his lifetime. He had at least one masterpiece, The Adventures of Huckleberry Finn, *considered by many students of literature to be the greatest American novel. Although known as a humorist—he was a hilarious lecturer—Clemens had a gloomy opinion of humanity and was bitterly cynical in his old age.*

Huckleberry Finn (1885), which was by no means for juveniles only. Readers sometimes missed the profound and subtle social criticism in Twain's work—as an old man, he was melancholy and bitterly cynical—but they read him with pleasure for his wit and mastery of the American language. Twain was a showman. He made as much money from lecture tours throughout the United States and Europe as he did from his books; and he never came back from a tour without a book or two inspired by what he saw and already half-written.

The other great American novelist of the period, Henry James, settled in England because he found American culture stultifying. James set most of his novels in Europe; his characters, unlike Twain's ordinary folks, were cultivated and cosmopolitan Europeans and upper-class Americans. Like Twain, however, his subject was the American character. He dissected it by contrasting open, egalitarian, materialistic, practical, and naïve Americans with sophisticated, jaded, class-conscious, and sometimes decadent Europeans. Four of his best novels elaborating on that theme were *The American* (1877), *The Europeans* (1878), *Daisy Miller* (1879), and *The Ambassadors* (1903).

REALISM AND NATURALISM

Every literary era must have its dean. The role was filled at the turn of the century by the editor of the *Atlantic Monthly,* William Dean Howells. Like *Harper's, Forum, The Arena,* and *Scribner's,* the *Atlantic* published a mix of poetry, stories, and essays that sometimes dealt with contemporary issues. *Scribner's,* for example, published fiction by James, Sarah Orne Jewett (who wrote about New England life), and Robert Lewis Stevenson; accounts of personal experiences by Theodore Roosevelt and Henry Stanley, the explorer of Africa; and descriptions of immigrant life in New York by Jacob Riis and Abraham Cahan, the leading Jewish American writer, equally at home in English and Yiddish.

Howells himself was a realist. He had no patience with the high-flown, preposterous motives and beliefs that sentimentalist writers imputed to their characters. In *The Rise of Silas Lapham* (1885), a novel about a successful industrialist, when one sister loses a suitor to another, she does not react selflessly, nor does the sister who gets her man think seriously of sacrificing her happiness for her sister's—predictable, hackneyed themes in the popular sentimental novels by what Nathaniel Hawthorne had called a "damned mob of scribbling women." Nevertheless, neither Howells nor the *Atlantic* would have considered dealing explicitly, let alone graphically, with sexual matters or the degradation that poverty and squalor created. Because the proper upper and middle classes themselves considered such discussions unacceptable in mixed company, the writings of realists like Howells were sometimes lumped with romantic sentimentalists (who were prudes too) as a part of the "genteel tradition."

Naturalistic writers defied some of the conventions that bound even realists like Howells; a few enjoyed commercial success. In *Maggie: A Girl of the Streets* (1893), Stephen Crane depicted the poor not as noble and selfless but as miserable and helpless. In *The Red Badge of Courage* (1895), the Civil War is described as something other than glory, bugles, bravery, and flying colors. (If anything, with the GAR still numerous and influential, it was more daring a venture than Crane's book about a prostitute). In *McTeague* (1899) and *The Octopus* (1901), Frank Norris dealt with people driven almost mechanically by animalistic motives.

The most popular of the naturalists was Jack London. His *Call of the Wild* (1903) is comparable to *Huckleberry Finn* in that it is simultaneously a grand tale of adventure (about a dog) and, at a deeper level, an insightful commentary on the human condition. Theodore Dreiser broke with a moralistic literary convention by allowing characters like *Sister Carrie* (1900) to enjoy full lives despite sinful pasts. Dreiser's success was doubly remarkable because, coming from a midwestern German-speaking household, his treatment of the English language was adversarial at best, and sometimes sadistic. But he was a thinker, and he delved into corners of American society in which others feared to tread.

Nellie Bly

Elizabeth Cochran broke into journalism when she criticized an editor in Pittsburgh who said that women who did not marry were useless. Cochran told him that girls should have employment opportunities because they were "just as smart" as boys and "a great deal quicker to learn." The editor hired her.

Taking the pen name Nellie Bly from a Stephen Foster song, she wrote exposés of working and living conditions in Pittsburgh, then moved to New York to work for Joseph Pulitzer's *World*. She was a sensation after she had herself committed to an asylum for insane women and penned a blistering account of conditions there.

Then Nellie had an idea for what may have been the first "manufactured news story." She had read Jules Verne's *Around the World in Eighty Days,* in which a British dandy circled the globe with unbelievable speed. Several adventurers had tried to beat the fictional record and failed. Nellie locked herself up with train and steamship time-tables and told the *World* that she could make the trip in seventy-five days. The editors liked the idea but said only a man could do it. Nellie replied, "Very well. Start the man and I'll start the same day for some other newspaper and beat him."

She left Jersey City on November 14, 1889. After a trip that sometimes seemed leisurely as she waited for steamships to depart, she returned to her point of departure via a special transcontinental train on January 25, 1890. Her trip took seventy-two days.

A HUNGER FOR WORDS

A new type of magazine made its appearance in the 1880s and 1890s. Catering to the not so intellectual middle classes, these periodicals reflected the interaction of industrial technology, the larger reading public, and the emergence of modern advertising that was first exploited in 1883 by Cyrus H. K. Curtis and his *Ladies' Home Journal.*

Improved methods of manufacturing paper, printing, and photoengraving, as well as cheap mailing privileges established by Congress in 1879, inspired Curtis to found a magazine for women who were hungry for a world beyond the kitchen and parlor. The *Ladies' Home Journal* sold for only 10 cents (compared with the 35-cent *Atlantic* and *Harper's*) and emphasized women's interests without demanding a college education of its readers. It was not feminist by any means. Editor Edward Bok preached a domesticity that reassured homemakers that their conventional prejudices were proper. He honored the middle class as a steadying influence between "unrest among the lower classes and rottenness among the upper classes."

More daring were the new general-interest magazines of the 1890s: *McClure's, Munsey's,* and *Cosmopolitan.* They too cost a dime, putting them within reach of a mass readership. (The *Saturday Evening Post,* which Curtis bought in 1897, cost only a nickel.) While stopping short of the sensationalism of working-class publications like the infamous *Police Gazette,* they presented readers with a livelier writing style than the older journals, and they were lavish with photographs and illustrations.

McClure's and *Munsey's* pioneered the novel economics of selling their publications for less than it cost to print and mail them. They made their profit from building up subscription lists so long that they dazzled manufacturers of consumer goods wanting to reach people with advertising. Subscriptions to *McClure's* increased from 8,000 in 1893 to 250,000 in 1895. (*McClure's* collected $60,000 in advertising fees per issue.) *Munsey's* grew from 40,000 to 500,000 during the same two years. By 1900 the combined circulation of the four largest magazines totaled 2.5 million per month, more than all American magazines combined only twenty years earlier.

LIBRARIES AND LECTURES

The cultural hunger of the middle class was also expressed in the construction of free public libraries and museums. Again, rich men gave millions to build them. Enoch Pratt donated $1 million to Baltimore for its municipal library. Wealthy lawyer and presidential candidate Samuel J. Tilden gave New York City $2 million, and William Newberry founded one of the nation's great collections of rare books and valuable manuscripts in Chicago with a munificent bequest of $4 million. Beginning in 1881, steel magnate Andrew Carnegie made local libraries his principal philanthropy. Before his death in 1919, Carnegie's dollars helped found 2,800 free public libraries.

The antebellum *lyceum*—touring lecturers—was revived in 1868 by James Redpath. Large fees persuaded the "big names" of the day—statesmen, ministers, and professors—to deliver highly moral and occasionally informative addresses in auditoriums and specially erected tents in hundreds of small cities and towns.

Instead of sending lecturers out to the country, the Chautauqua movement brought people craving culture to the lecturers, plus entertainment and pleasant surroundings, for several summer months. Founded in 1874 at Lake Chautauqua in upstate New York, the original "Chautauquas" were eight-week summer training programs for Sunday school teachers. During the 1890s, cheap excursion fares on the trains made it feasible for people with no interest in teaching Sunday school to make the trip and rent a tent for the sake of the cool mountain air and relaxation. To accommodate them, the Chautauqua organizers broadened their program to include lectures on secular subjects, entertainment, and proper (no alcohol) social gatherings.

By the turn of the century, a middle-class family spending a few weeks at Lake Chautauqua could expect to hear talks by people as prominent as William Jennings Bryan and to watch "magic-lantern" (slide) shows about the Holy Land, Persia, or China presented by "professional world travelers." Distinguished professors expounded on their theories about human character, happy marriage, or child-rearing. German oompah bands, Hawaiian dancers, trained

Coney Island: Democratic Amusement

The coneys—rabbits—were just about wiped out when, in the mid-nineteenth century, Coney Island's broad beach and ocean breezes began to attract vacationers from New York, just nine miles distant. (It was not really an island; it was separated from the city of Brooklyn by a small creek.) George Cornelius Tilyou was a native son, born in 1862, who grew up, as the local argot had it, with "sand in his shoes." When he was 3, his father leased a lot on the beach for $35 a year and opened a hotel catering to Democratic political bosses from Manhattan and Brooklyn.

As a teenager, George began to look for ways to pocket vacationers' pocket change. In 1876, with the Centennial Exposition in Philadelphia attracting people from all over the nation, he filled empty medicine bottles with seawater and cigar boxes with Coney beach sand, took the train to Philadelphia, and sold them for 25 cents each. He made enough from these dubious but classic souvenirs to dabble in beachfront real estate. The township did not sell beach lots but, instead, leased it to people to whom the political machine was friendly. These favored entrepreneurs then sublet choice business locations to others, sometimes at large profits. Because of his father's contacts, Tilyou was able to open a vaudeville theater.

Then he made what appeared to be a fatal mistake. He criticized the local political boss, John Y. McKane, who protected brothels and illegal gambling

Coney Island about 1900. The photograph was made early in the morning; the vehicles, horse-drawn, are probably making deliveries. A few hours later, the amusement parks along the street will be crowded with people from Brooklyn and Manhattan. The street will be lined with two strings of trolley cars, one bringing people from the city, the other waiting to take them home.

Museum of the City of New York

dogs, Italian acrobats, and Indian fire-eaters provided lighter entertainment.

AMERICANS AT PLAY

Promoters founded more than 200 Chautauqua-type resorts in the mountains and at the seaside. By 1900 enough people could afford a long break from work or business that a vacation industry was soon flourishing. Nevertheless, resort promoters found it advisable to provide at least the appearance of usefulness for the vacations they offered. If the middle class trekked to Lake Chautauqua or Lake George in New York or to Long Beach, Atlantic City, or Cape May in New Jersey primarily for rest and relaxation, they could tell others that the wonderful cultural and educational offerings of the resort were the principal reason they went.

A similar conjunction of relaxation and constructive use of time underlay the resorts that were devoted to good health. Owners of mineral springs claimed miraculous powers for their waters. Baths in naturally heated mineral waters or in hot mud were prescribed as nostrums for dozens of af-

flictions. Hydropathy, a nineteenth-century medical fad, taught that virtually constant bathing and drinking water by the gallon improved health. For decades, the wealthy made prosperous summer resorts of places like Saratoga Springs in New York and White Sulphur Springs in Virginia. As an afterthought, Saratoga threw in horse racing and White Sulphur Springs a few golf courses.

By far the biggest health resort was not in a particularly attractive place. The "San," for Sanitorium, in Battle Creek, Michigan, was the creation of Dr. John Kellogg, who crusaded against Americans' prodigious consumption of meat and eggs and for a vegetarian diet. Providing a dozen different therapies in addition to whole-grain meals three times a day, Kellogg ran, in effect, one of the biggest hotels in the country. (His brother, W. K. Kellogg, was one of the inventors of corn flakes; C. H. Post, a patient of the San, was the other.)

WORKING-CLASS LEISURE

Working people could not afford to take a week in the mountains or at the seashore. However, leisure became a part of

dens in the district. Tilyou organized a party devoted to the idea that Coney Island's future lay in becoming a wholesome family resort. When McKane won the battle, Tilyou found himself shut out of the profitable leasing deals.

In 1893, however, McKane was jailed for stuffing ballot boxes, and Tilyou was back in business. Just in time—in the same year he went to the Chicago World's Fair and, like everyone, was awed by its centerpiece, the Ferris wheel. It was 250 feet in diameter. Suspended on the gigantic circle were thirty-six "cars," each of which held sixty people. When the fair closed, 1.5 million people had taken a whirl on it.

Tilyou contracted with George Ferris to build a wheel half its size at Coney Island, which he nevertheless advertised as "THE WORLD'S LARGEST FERRIS WHEEL!" He began to make money even before it was complete by selling concessions around the wheel to vendors. Soon Tilyou constructed other "amusements": at first simple gravity devices such as giant sliding boards and seesaws, but soon electrically powered forerunners of devices still to be found on boardwalks and at fairs today.

From another Coney Island hustler, Tilyou copied the idea of fencing in a large "amusement park" and charging a single admission fee. Coney's clientele, working-class people, could not spend extravagantly; better to commit their entire day to Steeplechase Park, where they would have to buy their food and other extras, rather than having them wander over to Tilyou's competitors, Luna Park and Dreamland.

Steeplechase Park opened in 1897. A favorite ride was a gravity-driven "horse race" imported from England. People mounted wooden horses—a beau and his belle could ride together, a big attraction—which rolled on tracks over a series of "hills" and entered the central pavilion. Upon exiting, the customers were mildly abused by a clown and costumed dwarf. The biggest hit at Steeplechase was the jet of compressed air that shot out of the floor, blowing young ladies' skirts into the air.

Innocent sexual horseplay was the idea in many of the mechanical amusements Tilyou constructed. The air jets were soon everywhere. Other amusements were designed to throw young ladies in such a position that their ankles were exposed or they landed in the laps of their escorts or, perhaps, someone whom they were interested in meeting. Tilyou's formula worked. For a time after the turn of the century, Steeplechase Park lost ground to newer amusement parks, Luna Park (featuring "a trip to the moon") and Dreamland, where visitors could stroll through the streets of an Egyptian city or among Philippine headhunters, or see the eruption of Mount Pelée, the Johnstown flood, the Galveston tidal wave, or other natural disasters.

But Tilyou was irrepressible. When Steeplechase Park burned to the ground in 1907—every wooden Coney Island attraction burned at one time or another—he hung up a sign:

I have troubles today that I didn't have yesterday.
I had troubles yesterday that I have not today.
On this site will be erected shortly a better, bigger, greater Steeplechase Park.

Admission to the Burning Ruins—10 cents.

---

their lives, too. Great urban greens, beginning with New York's magnificent Central Park, provided relief from heat and airless tenement rooms on weekends. Working people in large cities were also able to enjoy themselves at commercial amusement parks that sprang up as a means by which trolley car companies could exploit their investments to the fullest.

Traction companies made a profit only from those parts of their lines that traversed the crowded parts of cities, and then only on weekdays. However, the high cost of central city real estate required that they build their sprawling car barns (storage and repair facilities) outside the city. They were usually required to run trolleys on Saturdays and Sundays as a public service; even if they were not, they wanted to use their costly equipment on weekends.

The traction companies encouraged the construction of amusement parks at the end of the line or, in some cases, built the "playlands" themselves. The most famous was New York's Coney Island, located on the ocean in Brooklyn. The fare from downtown Manhattan was 5 cents, children riding free. Once there, for a dollar or two, a large family could ride the me-chanical amusements such as George C. Tilyou's Bounding Billows, Barrel of Love, and the Human Roulette Wheel. They could imitate Buffalo Bill at shooting galleries, visit sideshows and exotic Somali villages, or simply loll on the beach with a picnic lunch or a sausage muffled in two halves of a roll.

These homely pleasures were as exciting to working people as a trip to Saratoga was to the middle class. Coney Island, Philadelphia's Willow Grove, Boston's Paragon Park, and Chicago's Cheltenham Beach represented a well-integrated industry, manufacturing, packaging, and merchandising leisure time.

Working-class leisure was more frankly devoted to simple fun than were the middle-class Chautauquas. Nevertheless, even Coney Island's promoters said that their resort was educational and good for health. Sordid sideshows were touted with moralistic spiels. Knocking over weighted bottles for a prize of a Kewpie doll was defined as honing a valuable skill. Even suggestive dancing by "hoochie-koochie girls" like Fatima, the sensation of the Chicago World's Fair of 1893, was described as a glimpse into the culture of the Turkish

Hot Dog

The origin of the hot dog is hotly disputed. Not the origins of the mild sausage itself: it was being made commercially in Frankfurt, Germany, and Vienna, Austria, in the early nineteenth century. (Thus the names *frankfurter* and *wiener*—Vienna in German is *Wien*.) The disputed point is who first put one of the things in a soft roll and provided the classic condiments of yellow mustard, chopped onion, and sweet pickle relish.

Coney Island has a claim: hot dogs were once called "coneys" too. Some credit Anton Feuchtwanger, who sold the sausages so quickly at the St. Louis World's Fair in 1904 that he had to add the roll so his customers did not burn their fingers. Yet others say the roll was first added at a New York Giants baseball game in April 1900, where they were called "dachshund sausages." A popular cartoonist, Tad Dorgan, provided the friendlier name "hot dog."

Empire. A writer in *Harper's Weekly* approved of the trolley parks because they were "great breathing-places for millions of people in the city who get little fresh air at home."

THE FIRST FITNESS CRAZE

Good health was the rationale for a series of sporting manias that swept the United States at the turn of the century. To some extent, the concern for bodily health was introduced by German immigrants, whose *Turnvereins* (clubs devoted to calisthenics) were old-country carryovers like democratic socialism and beer gardens. However, it was obvious by the second half of the century that the urban population walked less and got less exercise generally than had its farmer forebears. In the first issue of the *Atlantic Monthly* in 1858, Thomas Wentworth Higginson asked, "Who in this community really takes exercise? Even the mechanic confines himself to one set of muscles; the blacksmith acquires strength in his right arm, and the dancing teacher in his left leg. But the professional or businessman, what muscles has he at all?" Only a society with plenty of spare time could take Higginson's question to heart.

Croquet, archery, and tennis, all imported from England, enjoyed a vogue in the 1870s. Roller skating, because it was

cheaper and sociable, was more popular. Great rinks like San Francisco's Olympian Club, with 5,000 pairs of skates to rent and a 69,000-square-foot floor, charged fees that were within reach of all but the poorest people. But no sporting fad was so widespread as bicycling.

BICYCLES

"Dandy horses" from France made an appearance in the United States during the 1860s. They were crude wooden proto-bicycles their exhibitionist owners propelled by running while straddling them. They were not big sellers. In 1876 the "bone crusher" was introduced. The front wheel was five feet in diameter; the small rear wheel was for stability. They were difficult to mount and balance and a chore to pedal. There were no sprockets and chain; the pedal crank was fixed to the big wheel, so it required one revolution of about 3 feet to move the bicycle 16 feet, a very "high gear"—indeed, climbing a hill was out of the question. They were doubly uncomfortable because the tire was solid rubber, and spills from six feet broke many bones.

Perhaps because riding one was so daring, middle-class young men took to it with a passion. In 1880 the League of American Wheelmen was founded with 44 members; by 1890, 3,500 had signed up. Ten or twenty times that number were pedaling the big wheels, and twenty-seven American companies were churning them out. With their heavy, almost ground-length skirts, few women could ride them, but enough were interested in the new sport that manufacturers made tricycles too.

In the late 1880s the "**safety bicycle**" was invented in England. In every essential, the first of them were identical to bicycles today with two wheels of equal size, pneumatic tires for a smooth ride, and sprockets and chain that made pedaling them easier. By 1900 the American Wheelmen numbered 141,500 members, and 300 different companies were making a million bikes a year.

Most important, women could and did ride safety bicycles. Bloomers enjoyed a brief revival so that women could straddle bikes modestly; the more attractive divided skirts (what would be called culottes today) were more popular. Temperance reformer Frances Willard learned to ride at the age of 53 and then proclaimed, "She who succeeds in gaining the mastery of the bicycle will gain the mastery of life"—perhaps

Cocaine

The Spanish learned of the invigorating effects of chewing the coca leaf when they conquered the Incas in the sixteenth century. Over the next three centuries, the odd European (and American) experimented with the drug; but only after 1860, when the active chemical in the plant was crystallized into "cocaine," a hundred times more powerful than the leaves, did its use spread. Parke-Davis, a drug manufacturer, called it "the

most important therapeutic discovery of the age, the benefit of which to humanity will be incalculable." The American Hay Fever Association praised it. Nor were the drug's "social benefits" neglected. In 1878 a magazine touted it as "the cure for young people afflicted with timidity in society." Cocaine was added to patent medicines and soft drinks.

By the end of the century, cocaine's addictiveness was well documented. Reformers crusaded against it, and use by the middle

class sharply declined. Cocaine came to be associated with African Americans, as a statement of the American Pharmacological Association in 1903 indicates: "The state of Indiana reports that a good many of its Negroes and a few white women are addicted to cocaine." In 1914 the police chief of Atlanta blamed 70 percent of the city's crime on cocaine. What had almost been high fashion became the vice of a despised underclass within a generation.

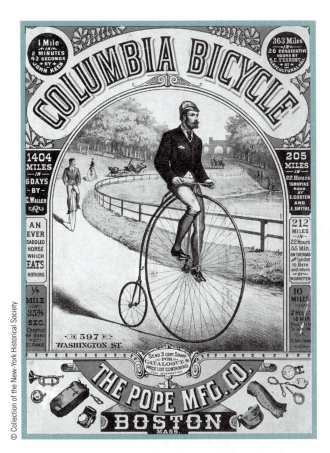

The "bone crusher" was difficult to mount and balance, and very hard to pedal. There were no sprockets and chain; it took a full revolution of the crank to turn the six-foot wheel 360 degrees: a very "high gear." A spill often meant a serious injury. And yet, even with her billowing skirts, the "new woman" of the era took to bicycles as avidly as men. The "safety bicycle," essentially the same in design as a bike today, was introduced during the "Gay Nineties."

a bit too exuberant. Founding mother of American feminism Susan B. Anthony was in her seventies and prudently passed on lessons. But she endorsed the bicycle extravagantly: "It has done more to emancipate women than anything else. I stand up and rejoice every time I see a woman ride on a wheel. It gives women a feeling of freedom and self-reliance."

She was quite right. On fair Saturdays and Sundays, the streets were full of young women in candy-striped blouses with billowing sleeves, sporty broad-brimmed hats, and flowing skirts riding through city parks. Moralists, who had not paid much attention to daring young bucks on bone crushers, found the sight of groups of female bicyclists unnerving. They might start out in proper all-girl company, but far from the oversight of chaperones, they could (and did) strike up conversations on secluded park lanes with young men. The bicycle was a step toward perdition.

THE GIBSON GIRL

The ideal young woman of the 1890s was the "**Gibson girl,**" so-called after a popular magazine illustrator, Charles Dana Gibson, whose specialty was drawings of beautiful young women, usually in humorous situations, but never themselves the object of amusement. Gibson's girls were not suffragists. They took little interest in political and social issues. The Gibson girl was, first and foremost, an object of adoration by love-struck, often ludicrous young men whom she usually "wrapped around her little finger." She was trim and fine-featured, her luxuriant hair piled atop her head. She was slyly flirtatious but never giggly; she was her own woman, as Susan B. Anthony believed bicycles would encourage.

The Gibson girl was novel in that, unlike the ideal woman of previous generations, she was no homebody, nor a delicate violet. She did not faint after the exertion of climbing a staircase. She played croquet, golf, and tennis. She rode a bicycle without chaperones. She was quite able to take care of herself, and she knew it.

Theodore Roosevelt's daughter, Alice, who became a national sweetheart when a popular waltz, "Alice Blue Gown," was named for her, was a Gibson girl. Young women imitated her style just as teenagers today dress to look like howling guitarists. And not just middle-class girls: photographs of mill workers leaving Massachusetts factories and of stenographers working in New York offices reveal an air of Gibson girl independence. Young women of the 1890s and 1900s married two to three years later than their mothers had. After marriage, they gave birth to fewer children than their mothers had.

THE CHANGING OFFICE

The telephone created jobs for women, and with the jobs a taste of independence. The typewriter did the same. Because so much handwriting was illegible, and therefore potentially costly in business, dozens of inventors had taken a stab at creating a "writing machine." The first practical typewriter was perfected in 1867 by Christopher Latham Sholes and was first marketed in 1874 by the Remington Company, a firearms manufacturer that, with the big government orders

QWERTY

The letters on the keyboard of this year's computer are arranged just as Christopher Sholes arranged them on his typewriter. The design is called "**QWERTY**" after the first six letters at the upper left. Sholes settled on the layout after many trials. For most of a century, typewriters were entirely mechanical. The typist pressed a key (hard) to raise a striker that stamped the letter on the paper. Sholes discovered that he had to space the strikers for the most frequently used letters (E, O, S, L, and so on) a distance from one another so that fast typists were not constantly jamming the machine. The arrangement of the keys followed the arrangement of the strikers.

The reasons for QWERTY no longer exist. Several inventors have designed keyboard arrangements that are much more efficient. However, as long as computers are purchased by people who already know how to type, no manufacturer is likely to pair one of these superior keyboards with a computer.

© Bettmann/Corbis

The typewriter, like the telephone, created a completely new occupation that was almost totally a feminine domain. Typists (at first they were called "typewriters," like their machine) were poorly paid; but it was clean "white-collar" work, and a young woman from a "respectable" family lost no social status by taking such a job.

of the Civil War a thing of the past, had been looking for a new product.

Before the use of the typewriter became standard in business, "secretaries" were men. They not only wrote letters for their employers in a clear hand (and made copies), but they ran various errands for the boss and represented him in minor capacities. The typewriter made it possible for businessmen to divide the job of secretary in two: assistant and typist. Men continued to hold the more responsible and better-paid job, eventually rising to the status we would describe as "junior executive." The mechanical tasks of transcribing letters and business records in type went to women.

Like telephone operators, typists did not require a level of education beyond high school. They needed to know their grammar and how to spell correctly, and maintain a neat appearance. By 1890, 15 percent of clerical workers were female; by 1900 almost 25 percent were.

SPORTS

By 1900 professional sports—competitions staged for paying customers—were a part of American life. Football, although somewhat different than the game played today, was exclu-

sively a collegiate game. It was also a moneymaker. People of all social classes avidly followed the fortunes of the nearest Ivy League team or state university. If they could afford a ticket, as middle-class people could, they attended games. Basketball had not yet made a splash. The game was invented in Springfield, Massachusetts, in 1891 by James Naismith, who was looking for a sport that his students could play

The Big Game

Football was a game for college boys, and they took it seriously: eighteen players were killed in games in 1905. Thanksgiving Day, having lost much of its religious association in the late nineteenth century, became the day of the "big game" for the nation's two most venerable colleges, Harvard and Yale. They mauled one another in neutral (and spectator-rich) New York City on Thanksgiving until Harvard's president tired of the players' off-field behavior and opted out of the rivalry. Yale had to settle for Princeton, and later Rutgers, as a Turkey Day match. In the twentieth century, other Thanksgiving rivalries developed: Penn–Cornell, Case–Western Reserve, Kansas–Missouri, Tulane–LSU, and Texas–Texas A&M.

during the long, cold, and snowy New England winter. The score of the first basketball game was 1–0: an inviting opportunity to dream of breaking the record.

The spectator sports that most captivated Americans, and therefore made the most money, were baseball and boxing. Both evolved from traditional folk recreations, but by the end of the nineteenth century, both were well-organized enterprises.

THE NATIONAL PASTIME

Baseball developed out of several ancient village games, including rounders and town ball, which were brought to the United States by English immigrants. According to Albert G. Spalding, a professional pitcher for baseball teams in Boston and Chicago, the rules of the sport were first drafted by Abner Doubleday of Cooperstown, New York, in 1839. This was poppycock. There is no evidence Doubleday invested a minute thinking about the game. Spalding circulated the tale to promote the sporting goods manufacturing company that made him a millionaire. In reality, baseball "just growed." The first recognizable baseball game to be recorded was played in New York City in 1847, but there was little agreement on even some basic rules until well after the Civil War; not until the 1890s was the game played uniformly across the nation.

Towns organized "pick-up" teams to play neighboring towns on special occasions like Independence Day. However, the professional sport emerged from upper-class baseball clubs such as the New York Knickerbockers. Soon concerned more with defeating rivals than with enjoying an afternoon of exercise with social equals, the clubs began to hire (at first surreptitiously) long-hitting and fast-pitching working-class "ringers" to wear their colors. In 1869 the first openly professional team, the Cincinnati Red Stockings, went on tour and defeated all comers.

Teams were focal points of civic pride. Important games got more attention in the newspapers than did foreign wars. After Brooklyn became a borough of New York City in 1898, its baseball team, the Trolley Dodgers, became the former city's sole symbol of an independent identity.

In its earliest years, professional baseball was open to African Americans. The catcher on an "all-star" team that toured Europe was black. In 1894, however, with lynch law at its peak in the South, white players, led by the foremost hitter of the era, Adrian "Cap" Anson (himself a northerner), demanded that professional baseball be a game for whites only. The major leagues never wrote Jim Crow into their by-laws, but the ban was rigorously enforced. When, at the turn of the century, John McGraw, manager of the New York Giants, recruited several African Americans, claiming they were Indians, he was forced to back down and send them packing.

Between 1900 and 1910, baseball became "the national pastime." The two "major leagues" had come to terms with one another and inaugurated the postseason World Series between their champions. Beginning in 1909 with Philadelphia's Shibe Park, major league teams built permanent steel and brick baseball stadiums to replace the poorly kept fields and rickety wooden bleacher seats where they had previously played.

BOXING AND SOCIETY

In 1867 the Marquis of Queensbury devised a code of rules to civilize the "manly art" of unarmed combat between two men. He had his work cut out for him. One of his civilized rules read that "all attempts to inflict injury by gouging or tearing the flesh with the fingers or nails and biting shall be deemed foul." The Marquis thought of fist-fighting as something like a duel, a "manly art" for gentlemen like Theodore Roosevelt.

But watching two strong men pummel one another was probably mankind's oldest spectator sport. In the United States, tough characters fortified with whiskey, traveling from fair to fair, offered cash prizes to any challenger who could "stay in the ring" with them for ten or fifteen minutes. The rarely won prize and the profits were paid for out of fees paid by those who wanted to watch.

Promoters soon saw better opportunities to make money by promoting and publicizing matches between two skilled professionals. The first American to win a national reputation as "champion" was a burly Boston Irishman named John L. Sullivan, who was not fit company for the Marquis of Queensbury or Teddy Roosevelt. He first offered $50, and later $1,000, to random challengers. Between 1882 and 1892 "the Boston Strong Boy" bloodied one man after another, personally collecting as much as $20,000 a fight and making much more for the entrepreneurs who organized his bouts.

Newspapers devoted column after column to important fights. Because Sullivan and his successor as heavyweight champion, Gentleman Jim Corbett, were Irish, they became objects of ethnic pride. So entangled in the culture did the sport become that when a black boxer rose to the top at the peak of populist racism, he caused a stir that reached into the halls of Congress.

JACK JOHNSON

John Arthur "Jack" Johnson of Galveston, Texas, had a national reputation by 1902, but three consecutive heavyweight champions, Jim Jeffries, Robert Fitzsimmons, and Tommy Burns, refused to fight him on racial grounds. Finally, in Australia in 1908, Burns gave in to the size of the prize that was offered; he was badly defeated. Johnson battered every

Forgotten Jack Johnsons

African-American athletes other than Jack Johnson bucked the color line and made names for themselves, if not Johnson's lasting fame. In 1875 jockey Oliver Lewis won the first Kentucky Derby; Isaac Murphy won the derby three times. Moses Walker played in baseball's National League before blacks were banned. Perhaps most extraordinary because bicycling was a middle- and upper-class recreation, in both 1899 and 1900 Marshall Taylor won the world cycling championship.

challenger, and this rankled many whites. Johnson aggravated the hostility by insulting every "great white hope" the publicists created. Tragically indiscreet, he flaunted his white mistresses at a time when southern African Americans were being strung up for ogling white women.

Southern states, which had been hospitable to prize fights (some other states banned them outright), forbade Johnson to box within their borders. Politicians raved at every Johnson victory. Congress actually passed a law that prohibited interstate shipment of a film of Johnson's victory over former champion Jim Jeffries in Reno, Nevada, in 1910. The *San Francisco Examiner* headlined its report of the bout, "Jeffries Mastered by Grinning Jeering Negro."

In 1912 Johnson was defeated not in the ring but by an indictment for transporting a woman across a state line "for immoral purposes." Johnson had taken his common-law wife from Chicago to his vacation home in Wisconsin.

Sensibly, because he was headed for a long prison term, Johnson fled to Europe. But he had trouble getting fights offering decent prizes, and he was homesick. In 1915 he fought white American boxer Jess Willard in Havana and lost. African Americans believed that Johnson threw the match as part of a deal with the Justice Department by which he could return to the United States and receive a light sentence. A famous photograph of the knockout shows Johnson on his back, looking unhurt, even relaxed, shielding his eyes from the Caribbean sun. In fact, Johnson was probably beaten; he was aging, out of shape, stale, and depressed. It was another

five years before he returned to the United States, now much too old to humiliate white boxers in the ring. He was imprisoned for eight months. It would be thirty years before another African-American prizefighter would be allowed to fight a white champion. The color line extended far beyond the southern states.

MORAL REFORM

One spectator sport declined during the sports-crazy "good old days": horse racing. There were 314 commercial racetracks in the United States in 1897 but only 25 in 1908.

The collapse had nothing to do with the horses. Then, as now, people usually attended horse races to gamble on the outcome rather than to admire the strength, speed, and grace of the animals. Among the vices the new middle class assailed, and the only one they came close to abolishing (or pushing underground), was gambling. State after state responded to moralistic middle-class demands and banned gambling during the first years of the twentieth century. In 1912, virtually as a condition of admission to the Union as states, Arizona and New Mexico had to prohibit gambling in their constitutions. Poker games survived, and illegal bookmakers appeared out of the air to take bets on prizefights and baseball games. But there was no concealing gambling at a racetrack. The "sport of kings" almost went extinct. And the "progressives," as middle-class reformers soon called themselves, had plenty of other fish to fry, and a progressive president to lead them.

FURTHER READING

General John W. Chambers, *The Tyranny of Change: America in the Progressive Era*, 1980; Alan Dawley, *Struggles for Justice: Social Responsibility and the Liberal State*, 1991; Michael McGerr, *A Fierce Discontent: The Rise and Fall of the Progressive Movement in America, 1870–1920*, 2003; Nell Irvin Painter, *Standing at Armageddon: The United States, 1877–1919*, 1987.

Education and Leisure Burton J. Bledstein, *The Culture of Professionalism*, 1976; David Bloch, *Baseball before We Knew It: A Search for the Roots of the Game*, 2005; Frank Deford, *The Old Ball Game: How John McGraw, Christy Mathewson, and the New York Giants Created Modern Baseball*, 2005; Lynn Gordon, *Gender and Higher Education in the Progressive Era*, 1990; Bob Mee, *Bare Fists: The History of Bare-Knuckle Prize-Fighting*, 2005; David Nasaw, *Going Out: The Rise and Fall of Public Amusements*, 1993; Kathy Peiss, *Cheap Amusements: Working Women and Leisure in Turn-of-the-Century New York*, 1986; Steven A. Reiss, *Touching Base: Professional Baseball and American Culture in the Progressive Era*, 1980; Robert W. Rydell, *All the World's a Fair: Visions of Empire at American International Expositions, 1876–1916*, 1984.

Gender and Race Carl M. Degler, *At Odds: Women in the Family in America from the Revolution to the Present*, 1980; Ann Douglas, *The Feminization of American Culture*, 1977; Thomas E. Harris, *Analysis of the Clash between Booker T. Washington and W. E. B. DuBois*, 1993; David Leverine Lewis, *W. E. B. DuBois*, 2 vols., 1993, 2000;

Elaine May, *Great Expectations: Marriage and Divorce in Post-Victorian America*, 1980; Steven Mintz, *A Prison of Expectations: The Family in Victorian Culture*, 1983; David R. Roediger, *The Wages of Whiteness: Race and the Making of the American Working Class*, 1991; Rosalind Rosenberg, *Beyond Separate Spheres*, 1982; Carolyn Smith-Rosenberg, *Disorderly Conduct: Visions of Gender in Victorian America*, 1985; John White, *Black Leadership in America: From Booker T. Washington to Jesse Jackson*, 1990.

The New Middle Class Burton Bledtsein and Robert D. Johnston, eds., *The Middling Sorts: Explorations in the History of the American Middle Class*, 2001; Stuart M. Blumin, *The Emergence of the Middle Class: Social Experience in the American City, 1700–1900*, 1989; Richard W. Fox and T. Jackson Lear, *The Culture of Consumption: Critical Essays in American History, 1880–1980*, 1983; William Keach, *Land of Desire: Merchants, Power, and the Rise of a New American Culture*, 1993; Lewis D. Saum, *The Popular Mood of America, 1860–1890*, 1990; Thomas J. Schlereth, *Victorian America: Transformations in Everyday Life, 1876–1915*, 1999; Warren J. Sussman, *Culture as History: The Transformation of American Society in the Twentieth Century*, 1984.

Theodore Roosevelt David McCullough, *Mornings on Horseback: The Story of an Extraordinary Family*, 1982; Nathan Miller, *Theodore Roosevelt: A Life*, 1992; Edmund Morris, *The Rise of Theodore Roosevelt*, 1979, and *Theodore Rex*, 2001.

KEY TERMS

The following terms are covered in this chapter and can also be found in the list of Key Terms at the back of the book.

Gibson girl	**land grant universities**	**"QWERTY"**	**Seven Sisters**
Howard University	**Mark Twain**	**safety bicycle**	

 ## ONLINE SOURCES GUIDE

Use this listing to find online documents, images, interactive maps, simulations, and other resources related to this chapter:

American History Resource Center
http://history.wadsworth.com/rc/us

Selected Documents
Booker T. Washington's Atlanta Exposition Address (1895)
Belle Linder Israel's "The Way of the Girl" (1909)

Selected Images
Faculty council of Tuskegee Institute, including
   Booker T. Washington, 1902

Tenement sweatshop in New York City
Suffragist marching, 1912
Woman suffrage headquarters, Cleveland, Ohio, 1912
W. E. B. DuBois

Interactive Time Line (with online readings)
Teddy Roosevelt and the Good Old Days: American Society in Transition, 1890–1917

CHAPTER 35

Age of Reform

The Progressives

Reproduced from the Collections of the Library of Congress

'Tis not too late to build our young land right, Cleaner than Holland, courtlier than Japan, Devout like early Rome with hearths like hers, Hearths that will recreate the breed called man.

Vachel Lindsay

A man that'd expect to thrain lobsters to fly in a year is called a loonytic; but a man that thinks men can be tu-rrned into angels be an illiction is called a rayformer an' remains at large.

Finley Peter Dunne

In 1787 Thomas Jefferson wrote to a friend, "A little rebellion, now and then, is a good thing, as necessary in the political world as storms in the physical." In another letter he wrote, "The tree of liberty must be refreshed from time to time with the blood of patriots and tyrants."

Many people have agreed with Jefferson that political progress, even holding the line in defense of freedom, is possible only by taking up arms. The enemies of progress and liberty—"tyrants"—must be crushed by force or intimidated by a show of force.

But that does not seem to have been the case in the United States. During more than two centuries that, worldwide, have been wracked by social convulsions and bloody carnage, the United States has been an island of stability if not necessarily of (to borrow a phrase from the Constitution) "domestic tranquility." Only once has the country suffered a bloody rebellion: when the southern states seceded in 1861.

But it is difficult to describe a rebellion dedicated to protecting slavery as irrigating the tree of liberty. However imperfect the results, Americans have confronted political and social evils and accommodated changed conditions with reforms and a minimum of violent upheaval.

THE PROGRESSIVES

Continual adjustment of laws is the essence of representative government. Vital institutions evolve constantly. However, momentous reform movements have come to the United States in waves; when they have receded, the country has been significantly changed.

The first great wave of reform was the rise of the evangelicals during the age of Andrew Jackson. It began as a religious movement—individuals seeking salvation—but became political when evangelicals concluded that they had a

Upper and Lower

In Edward Bellamy's *Looking Backward,* a book of 1888 that started many middle-class people on the road to progressivism, Dr. Lecte, the guide to the enlightened world of the future, described the anxiety of being in the middle in turn-of-the-century America: "In your day, riches debauched one class with idleness of mind and body, while poverty sapped the vitality of the masses by overwork, bad food, and pestilent homes."

God-ordained duty to improve society and raise the morals of Americans. The wave of reform that rose at the end of the nineteenth century and crested after 1900 had religious aspects and was profoundly concerned with personal morals. But the new reform was not inspired by a religious revival; it was a secular movement. And the reformers were as likely to call for political, economic, and social change as for moral improvement.

They were a diverse lot. The aspirations of some conflicted head-on with the programs of others. But few objected when they were labeled "progressives."

IN THE MIDDLE

Most progressives, both leaders whose names made headlines and the envelope-stuffing rank and file, were middle class and WASP—white Anglo–Saxon Protestants with roots in America three, four, or more generations deep. There were exceptions. Alfred E. Smith of New York was Irish Catholic and working class; he still spoke in the accent of the Lower East Side when he was governor of the state. Lillian Wald, one of the pioneers of the settlement house movement, and Louis D. Brandeis, a Louisville lawyer who battled monopolistic corporations, were from German Jewish families. W. E. B. DuBois, the archenemy of Booker T. Washington who helped to found the National Association for the Advancement of Colored People, was African American. Many "blue-stockings," upper-class women who found the whirl of high society boring, were prominent in a welter of progressive organizations.

Women were conspicuous in every wing of the reform movement except in government. In 1900 only five states permitted women to vote and hold elective office. Women dominated in some progressive reforms: settlement houses, temperance, movements to suppress prostitution, and, of course, the woman suffrage movement.

Progressives were acutely aware of the fact that they were "in between." They felt that they (and what was good about America) were threatened from above by the plutocrats industrialization had created: the obscenely wealthy, powerful, and often arrogant heads of the great corporations and banks. John D. Rockefeller (the country's richest person) and J. P. Morgan were their personifications of unacceptable power, but they had plenty of others on whom to fasten.

And they felt that their world was threatened by the numbers and morals of the industrial working class, and particularly the immigrants clustered in the large cities. Progressives

A cartoon illustrating progressive fears of what the power of big business meant for the country. "Monopoly" was not welcome in Theodore Roosevelt's White House, of course, or so most progressives believed.

worried that Italians, Jews, Poles, Greeks—a dozen other ethnic groups—seemed to resist becoming Americans, assimilating American culture, and the middle-class values and moral codes of the progressives. They were as unnerved by the socialist politics of some immigrants as they were by the plutocrats' strangulation of ordinary people's economic opportunity. Edward Bok bemoaned lower-class "unrest" and upper-class "rottenness." A progressive physician, James Weir, called the rich "effeminate, weak" and warned of the "savage inclinations" of the working class.

Almost every progressive reform was aimed at bridling and regulating concentrations of wealth and power or uplifting the working classes. Philosopher William James was not just getting off a sarcastic quip when he observed that the progressives wanted to transform the whole world into "a middle-class paradise."

Formidable as their enemies were, progressives were optimists. They believed they would prevail. "Our shamelessness is superficial," wrote progressive journalist Lincoln Steffens; "beneath it lies a pride which, being real, may save us yet."

Some were insufferably self-righteous. Robert M. LaFollette of Wisconsin, a reform governor and then a senator, was humorless. To "Fighting Bob," life was one long crusade for what was right. California's Hiram Johnson irked even his devoted aides with his clenched-teeth sanctimony. Thomas B. Reed, a decidedly unprogressive Speaker of the House, told Teddy Roosevelt, "If there is one thing for which I admire you more than anything else, Theodore, it is your original discovery of the Ten Commandments." When a Democratic party delegation arrived at New Jersey Governor Woodrow Wilson's home to inform him he had been nominated to run for president, Wilson told them, "Before we proceed, I wish it clearly understood that I owe you nothing; God ordained that I should be the next president of the United States."

GOVERNMENT THE ANSWER

Almost all progressives believed that an active government was the key to reform—both the bridling of the corporations and the uplift of the masses. In their faith in the state, they differed from earlier reformers, who were apt to consider government a part of the problem. Jane Addams, whose career as a reformer began as a worker among the poor immigrants of Chicago, had herself been suspicious of city and state government because it was so often in the hands of corrupt political machines. But she concluded that private efforts like her Hull House were "today inadequate to deal with the vast numbers of the city's disinherited."

As for the corporations that dominated the economy, progressives concluded that a powerful state in the right hands was the only agency that could bring them to heel. The goals were still Jeffersonian, Herbert Croly wrote in *The Promise of American Life,* published in 1909: the welfare of the many as opposed to the interests of the few. To Croly and most progressives, however, the sacred Jeffersonian principle of "the less government the better" had been rendered obsolete by the magnitude of twentieth-century social problems and the power of the plutocrats. Croly would have Jeffersonian ends achieved through the use of Hamiltonian means: the power of the state. His most important convert, Theodore Roosevelt, said in 1910, "The betterment which we seek must be accomplished, I believe, mainly through the national government."

COAT OF MANY COLORS

Beyond a commitment to government action, progressivism was variety, a frame of mind—by no means a single, coherent, coordinated movement. There were Democratic

Brownsville

The limitations of progressives in matters involving race were displayed by the federal government's actions after black soldiers of the Twenty-Fifth Infantry Regiment were accused of shooting up Brownsville, Texas, in August 1906. Although no individual was found guilty of the crime or even tried for it, progressive President Theodore Roosevelt dishonorably discharged all 167 black soldiers stationed at the fort, including six winners of the Medal of Honor.

Circumstantial evidence indicated that a few of the men were guilty of the shooting; other evidence exonerated the others. But Roosevelt was more interested in calming the tempers of whites who assumed the worst of blacks than in seeking justice. The only prominent white politician to take up the cause of the victimized African-American soldiers was a rock-ribbed Republican conservative, Senator Joseph B. Foraker of Ohio.

progressives and Republican progressives. In 1912 unhappy Republicans formed their own party, the Progressive party. Some progressives considered socialists as their kin (as long as they rejected violent revolution).

On some specific issues, progressives differed among themselves as radically as they differed from the "old guard" with whom they all battled. Thus, although most progressives believed that labor unions had the right to fight for the betterment of their members, others opposed unions on the same grounds they disliked powerful corporations. Both were organized special interest groups at odds with the good of the whole. On one occasion, leaders of the National American Woman Suffrage Association said that women should be strikebreakers if by so doing they could win jobs from which men (and unions) excluded them.

Progressives even disagreed about laws regulating child labor. By 1907 about two-thirds of the states governed or influenced by progressives forbade the employment of children under 14 years of age. However, when progressives in Congress passed a federal child labor law in 1916, the progressive

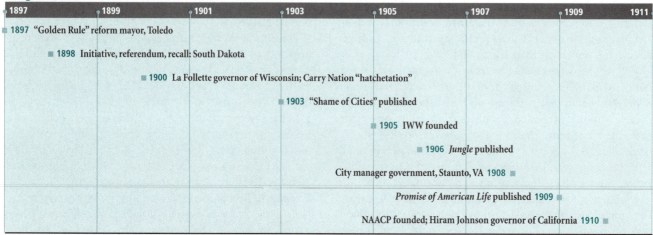

Progressives 1897–1911

| 1897 | 1899 | 1901 | 1903 | 1905 | 1907 | 1909 | 1911 |

1897 "Golden Rule" reform mayor, Toledo

1898 Initiative, referendum, recall: South Dakota

1900 La Follette governor of Wisconsin; Carry Nation "hatchetation"

1903 "Shame of Cities" published

1905 IWW founded

1906 *Jungle* published

City manager government, Staunto, VA 1908

Promise of American Life published 1909

NAACP founded; Hiram Johnson governor of California 1910

DINNER GIVEN AT THE WHITE HOUSE BY PRESIDENT ROOSEVELT TO BOOKER T. WASHINGTON, OCTOBER 17th, 1901

There were no photographers present when President Roosevelt entertained Booker T. Washington at the White House. This composite was created by an African American to express black pride in Washington's stature. Despite Washington's acquiescence in the color line and the exclusion of blacks from politics in the South, Roosevelt's invitation caused howls of protest all over the section.

President Woodrow Wilson expressed grave doubts before he signed it for political reasons. Wilson worried that to forbid children to work infringed on their rights as citizens. This was essentially the same reasoning stated by the very conservative Supreme Court in *Hammer* v. *Dagenhart* (1918), which struck down the federal child labor law.

Some progressives were ultranationalists. Others subscribed to a humanism that embraced all people of all countries. Some were jingo imperialists. Senator Albert J. Beveridge of Indiana saw no conflict in calling for broadening democracy at home while the United States ruled colonies without regard to the will of their inhabitants. Other progressives were anti-imperialists; some were isolationists who looked on Europe as a fount of corruption to be dealt with as little as necessary.

RACE

Many, probably most, progressives could not imagine blacks as citizens equal to whites, participating fully and actively in American society. Some were frank racists, especially the southern progressives such as Governor James K. Vardaman of Mississippi, Governor Jeff Davis of Arkansas, and Senator Benjamin "Pitchfork Ben" Tillman of South Carolina (who had led a lynch mob during Reconstruction). As president of Princeton University, Woodrow Wilson approved of Jim Crow practices in the town. As president, he approved the introduction of Jim Crow in the federal government. Other progressives tolerated discrimination against blacks out of habit or because they feared the consequences of racial equality with 45 percent of the African-American population illiterate.

Other progressives ranked racial prejudice and discrimination among the worst evils afflicting America. Journalist **Ray Stannard Baker** wrote a scathing exposé of racial segregation in a series of magazine articles titled "Following the Color Line." In 1910 white progressives, including Jane Addams, joined with the African American Niagara Movement to form the National Association for the Advancement of Colored People. Except for his color, W. E. B. DuBois, the guiding spirit of the Niagara Movement, was the progressive *par excellence.* Genteel, middle-class, university-educated, he was devoted to the idea that an intellectual elite should guide government, and that the "talented tenth" of the black population would lead the race to civil equality in the United States.

FOREBEARS

So diverse a movement had a mixed ancestry. From the Populists' Omaha Platform the progressives took a good deal. Progressive William Allen White, who had opposed the Populists, had the grace to acknowledge that the progressives "caught the Populists in swimming and stole all of their clothing except the frayed underdrawers of free silver." (Everything, in other words, that William Jennings Bryan had repudiated in 1896.) Like the Populists, progressives called for the direct election of senators and a graduated income tax that hit the wealthy with a higher rate than the middle class. Both reforms were enacted by constitutional amendment in 1913. Progressives favored the **initiative, referendum,** and **recall,** also Populist proposals. Some progressives wanted to nationalize the railways and banks. Others, who disliked the idea of federal government ownership of anything, believed that local public utilities—water, gas, and electric companies, and sometimes trolley car lines—being natural monopolies and not competitive, should be city owned.

The progressives also harkened back to the "good government" idealism of the liberal Republicans of the 1870s and 1880s. All were opposed to urban political machines that mobilized lower-class ethnic voters with small favors and jobs and provided lots of graft for the bosses, as well as city and state machines (Pennsylvania's was the classic example) that did the bidding of big business.

In exalting expertise and efficiency as the keys to bringing order to the often chaotic and wasteful economic competition of the late nineteenth century, the progressives owed a debt to some unlikely forebears. Mark Hanna (who died in 1904) was no progressive, but he had called on capital and organized labor to cooperate rather than, through bitter strikes, open the door to class conflict. Frederick W. Taylor, the father of "scientific management," took little interest in politics. Nevertheless, in his conviction that the engineer's approach to solving problems could be fruitfully applied to human behavior, he was a forebear of the progressive movement. The progressives believed that society could be engineered as readily as Taylor engineered the shape of the shovel a workingman used to perform his job.

PROGRESSIVISM DOWN HOME

Progressivism originated in the cities. During the 1890s, capitalizing on widespread disgust with corrupt political machines, a number of reform mayors swept into office and won national reputations. Most called for little more than mere honesty in public officials. But unlike the "Goo-Goos" of the 1870s and 1880s, they were not easily ousted after a year or two.

GOOD GOVERNMENT

One of the first city reformers was Hazen S. Pingree, a shoe manufacturer who was elected mayor of Detroit in 1890. Pingree spent seven years battling the corrupt alliance between the owners of the city's public utilities and Detroit city councilmen. In nearby Toledo, Ohio, another small businessman, Samuel M. Jones, ran for mayor as a reformer in 1897. Professional politicians mocked him as an addleheaded eccentric because he plastered the walls of his factory with the Golden Rule and other homilies. But his employees, whom Jones treated fairly by sharing profits with them, were devoted to him, and workers in other companies envied their jobs. As "Golden Rule" Jones, he took control of Toledo and proved to be a no-nonsense administrator. Within two years, he rid Toledo's city hall of graft.

Another progressive mayor was Cleveland's Thomas L. Johnson, elected in 1901. Not only did he clean up a dirty government, but he actively supported woman suffrage, reformed the juvenile courts, took over public utilities from avaricious owners, and put democracy to work by presiding over open town meetings at which citizens could air their grievances and suggestions.

Lincoln Steffens, a staff writer for *McClure's* magazine, called Cleveland "the best-governed city in the United States." Steffens was an expert. In 1903 he authored a sensational series of articles for *McClure's* called "The Shame of the Cities." Researching his subject carefully in the country's major cities, he named the grafters (this meant a libel suit if he was reckless), exposed corrupt connections between elected officials and businessmen, and demonstrated how ordinary people suffered daily from corrupt government.

Steffens's exposés accelerated the movement for municipal reform. Joseph W. Folk of St. Louis, whose tips put Steffens on his city's story, was able to indict more than thirty politicians and prominent Missouri businessmen for bribery and perjury as a result of the outcry that greeted "The Shame of the Cities." Hundreds of reform mayors elected after 1904 owed their success to the solemn, bearded journalist.

THE MUCKRAKERS

The chief medium through which the gospel of progressivism was spread was the mass-circulation magazines. Well established by the turn of the century thanks to their cheap price and lively style, periodicals like *McClure's*, the *Arena*, *Collier's*, *Cosmopolitan*, and *Everybody's* became even more successful when their editors discovered the popular appetite for the journalism of exposure.

The discovery was almost accidental. Samuel S. McClure himself had no particular interest in reform. Selling magazines and advertising in them was his business, hobby, and obsession. When he hired Ida M. Tarbell and Lincoln Steffens at generous salaries, he did so because they wrote well, not because they were reformers. Indeed, Tarbell began the "History of the Standard Oil Company," exposing John D. Rockefeller's dubious business practices, because of a personal grudge: Rockefeller had ruined her father, himself a

Ida M. Tarbell, one of the most conscientious researchers and best writers among the muckrakers. Her most famous work was a highly critical study of John D. Rockefeller and the Standard Oil Trust.

© UPI/Bettmann/Corbis

pioneer oil man. Steffens was looking for a story, any story, when he stumbled upon "The Shame of the Cities."

But when Tarbell's and Steffens's sensational exposés caused circulation to soar, McClure and other editors were hooked. The mass-circulation magazines soon brimmed with sensational revelations about corruption in government, chicanery in business, social evils like child labor and prostitution, and other subjects that lent themselves to indignant, excited treatment. In addition to his series on racial segregation, Ray Stannard Baker dissected the operations of the great railroads. John Spargo, an English-born socialist, discussed child labor in "The Bitter Cry of the Children." David Graham Phillips, later a successful novelist, described the U.S. Senate, then elected by state legislatures, as a millionaires' club.

President Roosevelt called the journalists "**muckrakers**" after an unattractive character in John Bunyan's religious classic of 1678—still well known among Protestants—*Pilgrim's Progress.* The writers were so busy raking through the muck of American society, he said, that they failed to look up and see the glories in the stars. He had a point, especially when, after a few years of muckraking, the quality of the journalism of exposure deteriorated into sloppy research and wild, ill-founded accusations made for the sake of filling pages with type and attracting attention. A contemporary parallel would be programming on cable television. During

the first decade of the century, no fewer than 2,000 articles and books of exposure were published. Inevitably, like so many other crusaders, the muckrakers ran out of worthy enemies. Muckraking became the province of hacks and sensation-mongers.

But the dirt could be real enough, and the early reform journalists were as determined to stick to the facts as to arouse their readers' indignation. Their work served to disseminate the reform impulse from one end of the country to the other. The ten leading muckraking journals had a combined circulation of 3 million. Because the magazines were also read in public libraries and barbershops, and just passed around, the actual readership was many times larger.

IN THE JUNGLE WITH UPTON SINCLAIR

Upton Sinclair was the most influential muckraker of all. In 1906 he had finished his novel *The Jungle.* His subject was a Lithuanian immigrant in Chicago whose dreams were destroyed by ethnic prejudice and exploitation. Sinclair was a socialist; *The Jungle* ends with the protagonist vowing to smash the capitalist system that had destroyed his life. It was not a theme apt to appeal to many readers. None of the mass-circulation magazines would serialize it. (Serial publication in periodicals was a key to a successful book.) Sinclair had to turn to a Socialist party weekly, the *Appeal to Reason.* The *Appeal* was far from obscure; one special issue sold over a million copies. *The Jungle* issues also sold briskly, and as a book, it sold 100,000 copies. One copy reached the desk of President Roosevelt.

Sinclair's book converted neither T. R. nor many other people to socialist revolution. Indeed, its literary qualities collapse in the final chapters, when the protagonist takes up the red flag. However, millions of people were disturbed by the passages of the book in which Sinclair luridly described the conditions under which meat was processed in Chicago slaughterhouses. *The Jungle* publicized documented tales of rats ground up into sausage, workers with tuberculosis coughing on the meat they packed, and a production line that was filthy from cattleman to butcher shop.

"I aimed at the nation's heart," Sinclair later said, "and hit it in the stomach." He meant that within months of the publication of *The Jungle,* a federal meat-inspection bill that had been languishing in Congress was rushed through under public pressure and promptly signed by President Roosevelt. It, and a second Pure Food and Drug Act, which forbade food processors to use dangerous adulterants (the pet project of a chemist in the Agriculture Department, Dr. Harvey W. Wiley), expanded the power of government in a way that was inconceivable a few years earlier.

EFFICIENCY AND DEMOCRACY

In 1908 Staunton, Virginia introduced the city manager system of government. The office of mayor was abolished. Voters elected a city council, which then hired a nonpolitical, professionally trained administrator to manage the city's affairs. Proponents of the city manager system reasoned that democracy was protected by the people's control of the

White Primary

Mississippi instituted a primary in 1902, the same year as Oregon's, usually considered the nation's first. Mississippi's primary was designed not only to take the nomination of candidates for office away from party bosses but also to insulate politics more effectively from African Americans.

Mississippi was effectively a one-party state. The only Republicans in the deep South were the few blacks who held onto the right to vote. They were so few that Democratic candidates were assured of winning general elections. If, however, two or three Democrats ran against one another in the general election, black voters could determine who won, which opened the possibility of Democrats fishing for African-American votes.

To avoid this possibility, Democrats in Mississippi and other states devised the white primary. It was a private election, open only to registered Democrats. To prevent blacks from voting, Democratic primaries were "whites only." The success of the device depended on all Democrats accepting the winner of the primary as the only Democrat in the general election. The demands of white supremacy ensured that few Democrats ever violated the rule.

council to which the city manager answered. However, because the daily operations of the city were supervised by an executive who did not depend on votes (and the machines that delivered them), they would be carried out without regard to special interests. By 1915 over 400 mostly medium-sized cities followed Staunton's example.

The "Oregon system" was the brainchild of one of the first progressives to make an impact at the state level. William S. U'ren believed that the remedy for corruption in government was simple: more democracy. Efficient, well-organized, and wealthy special interests were able to thwart the good intentions of the people. Time after time, U'ren pointed out, elected officials forgot their campaign promises and worked closely with the big corporations to enact legislation favorable to big business no matter what the voters wanted.

Between 1902 and 1904, U'ren persuaded the Oregon legislature to adopt reforms pioneered in South Dakota in 1898: the initiative, recall, and referendum. The initiative enabled citizens to bypass the legislature by proposing a law by petition. The recall enabled them, again by petition, to force an elected official to face voters before the end of his term. The referendum was an election in which bills proposed by initiative were enacted or rejected, and at which recalled officials were ousted or given a vote of confidence. The Oregon system also included the first primary law. It took the power to nominate candidates for public office away from party bosses and gave it to the voters. U'ren also led the national movement for a constitutional amendment providing that U.S. senators be elected by popular vote rather than in the state legislatures. Few people before or since William S. U'ren have had such faith in majority vote and the people's wisdom and sense of responsibility. U'ren lived to the ripe old age of 90, long enough to see twenty states adopt the initiative and thirty the referendum, but none that managed to construct heaven on earth.

FIGHTING BOB AND THE WISCONSIN IDEA

The career of Wisconsin's Robert M. "Fighting Bob" La Follette is a history of progressivism in itself. Born in 1855, he studied law and served three terms in Congress as a party-line Republican during the 1880s. As a young man, he showed few signs of the crusader's itch. Then a senator offered him a bribe to fix the verdict in a trial. La Follette flew into a rage at the shameless audacity of the proposition, and he never quite calmed down for the rest of his life.

In 1900 he ran for governor in defiance of the Republican organization. He attacked the railroad and lumber interests that dominated Wisconsin through the Republican party. He promised to devote the resources of the state government to the service of the people, and his timing was perfect: La Follette was elected. As governor, he pushed through a comprehensive system of regulatory laws that required businesses touching the public interest to conform to clear-cut rules and submit to close inspection of their operations.

La Follette did not stop with the negative regulatory powers of government. He created agencies that provided positive services for ordinary people. La Follette's "**Wisconsin idea**" held that in the complex modern world, legislators needed experts to assist them. A railroad baron could not be kept on a leash unless the government could draw on the knowledge of specialists who knew as much about railroad operations as the men who owned the railroads. Insurance premiums could not be held at reasonable levels unless the state was able to determine when the insurance company's profit was reasonable and when it was rapacious. The government could not determine which side was right in a labor dispute unless it had the counsel of economists.

La Follette formed a close and mutually beneficial relationship between the state government and the University of Wisconsin. The Wisconsin legislature funded the university more generously than any other state institution in the country enjoyed. For decades Wisconsin had the best public

Attempted Murder?

In late May 1908, Robert La Follette led a filibuster in the Senate. He spoke for nearly seventeen hours before giving up. Through much of this time, La Follette sipped a tonic of milk and raw eggs prepared in the Senate dining room. After he took violently ill on the floor, it was discovered that there was enough ptomaine in the mixture to kill a man. Because no one else suffered from eating in the Senate dining room that day, many assumed that La Follette's enemies had tried to kill him.

university in the United States. In return, the state government had the counsel of distinguished economists like Richard Ely, Selig Perlman, and John Rogers Commons, who were attracted to Wisconsin's prestige and high salaries. The Wisconsin law school helped build up the first legislative reference library in the United States so that assemblymen no longer had to rely on lobbyists for the data necessary to draft laws on complex subjects.

The university's agriculture school not only taught up-to-date methods to future farmers, it sent experts across the state to "consult" in Wisconsin's fields and barns. La Follette even made use of the university football team. When he heard that political enemies planned to cause trouble at a rally, he showed up in the company of burly linemen, who folded their arms and surrounded the platform. La Follette applied other machine methods to the cause of reform. His political organization was as finely integrated as Tammany Hall's. Party workers in every precinct got out the vote, and if they were honest, they were rewarded with patronage.

In 1906 La Follette took his crusade to Washington as a U.S. senator; he held his seat until his death in 1925. He was much loved in Wisconsin and elsewhere. He was "Fighting Bob," incorruptible and unyielding in what he regarded as right. La Follette's mane of brown hair, combed straight back, which turned snow white ("overnight," it was said, when enemies poisoned him), waved wildly during his passionate speeches.

PROGRESSIVE LEADERS

In New York State, Charles Evans Hughes came to prominence as a result of his investigation into public utilities and insurance companies. Tall, erect, and dignified, with a smartly trimmed beard that was going out of fashion, he lacked the personal dash of La Follette and Teddy Roosevelt, who called him "a cold-blooded creature" and later "the bearded lady." Nevertheless, he had a large following in New York.

George Norris of Nebraska, a Republican, was elected to Congress in 1902 and to the Senate in 1912. He was an unrelenting critic of big business, one of the few progressives who did not slow down during the conservative 1920s. Another was Hiram Johnson of California. He came to progressivism by much the same path as La Follette. A prim, humorless trial lawyer from Sacramento, Johnson began the prosecution of the political boss of San Francisco, Abe Ruef, as just another job. Ruef held no office; he collected payoffs from brothels, gambling dens, thieves, and just about everyone who needed a city charter or license to do business in the city. Well-educated and sophisticated (as no other big city bosses were), Ruef held his office hours in the evenings in private rooms at San Francisco's best restaurants. He kept one quarter of the boodle he collected as his commission, gave one quarter to Mayor Eugene E. Schmitz, and divided the rest among cooperative city aldermen. On one occasion, $250,000 changed hands over dinner. In return, Ruef's gang ran a famously wide-open city.

This was all garden-variety graft. However, as Johnson's prosecutors dug more deeply, they discovered that Ruef and Schmitz also had ties to the most powerful corporation in California, the Southern Pacific Railroad. The fact that the state's most distinguished (and pretentious) businessmen were linked, however indirectly, to vice and straight out bribery transformed Hiram Johnson into "a volcano in perpetual eruption, belching fire and smoke." In 1910 he was elected governor on the slogan "Kick the Southern Pacific out of politics."

William E. Borah of Idaho could spout rectitude as eloquently as La Follette and Johnson, and his supporters were equally devoted to him; he held his Senate seat from 1907 until 1940. But he did not come to Washington as a progressive; he had a long and cozy relationship with Idaho's mining and ranching interests. In the Senate he usually voted with the progressives but—as was discovered only decades after his death—secretly accepted cash gifts from special interests throughout his career, a latter-day Daniel Webster.

MAKING PEOPLE BETTER

Progressives were as concerned with the masses below them as they were with big businessmen on high. Plutocratic monopolies and corporation control of politics mocked democracy and threatened the middle class's opportunities. The industrial working class was susceptible to revolutionary socialism. The urban hordes of immigrants from southern and eastern Europe seemed to resist assimilation, to refuse to become good Americans embracing the values and morality of the middle class. The immigrants could at least be educated. Most northern progressives, however (there were exceptions), had given up on African Americans. Only a few of them raised their voices against the Jim Crow segregation and discrimination that southern progressives were institutionalizing in the South.

SEXUAL MORALITY

The crusade against sexual immorality, among the middle classes as well as the masses, began decades before reformers called themselves progressives. In the 1870s, supported by a New York State law he had sponsored, a young employee of the Young Men's Christian Association in New York, **Anthony Comstock,** began a single-minded crusade against obscenity. Comstock's target was pornography, which photography had made more readily available; but he also called for the prohibition of advertisements with sexual allusions and books that so much as mentioned sexual activity.

In 1873 Congress enacted a law empowering postmasters to examine the mail for obscene material and to destroy it. Comstock doubled as a postal inspector and head of the New York Society for the Prosecution of Vice. Although the courts occasionally rejected his definition of obscenity, politicians feared crossing him and gave him his head. In his final report in 1914 (he died the next year) Comstock boasted that he had been responsible for 3,697 arraignments under the obscenity laws, with 2,740 defendants pleading guilty or convicted. Some prosecuted books are now considered literary classics and are routinely assigned to high school students. Comstock

Bindlestiffs, Tramps, and Bums   *How They Lived*

Today we associate "the homeless" with big cities. The penniless, derelicts, and the mentally ill congregate in cities because it is there they find social services, police protection, and the society of people like themselves.

From about 1880, homelessness was associated with young males, almost all white, who crisscrossed the country on empty railroad cars or walked the roads and highways. When they congregated, it was in "hobo jungles": camps along railroad tracks or in the run-down "tenderloin" sections or "skid roads" of small cities like Spokane, Washington; Fresno, California; and Helena, Montana; as well as in New York, Chicago, and Seattle. (The term "skid road" originated in Seattle; it was a street where logs had been skidded downhill to the waterfront.)

Migrant casual workers were essential to the economy of the wheat belt (from the Dakotas to eastern Oregon and Washington) and in the vegetable- and fruit-growing regions of the Pacific states (from Washington's apple country south through the entire length of California's Central Valley), and even to potato growers on Long Island and in Maine. All were crops that required comparatively little labor until the harvest. Then for a few weeks—different weeks according to the crop or latitude—many workers laboring hard all day every day were needed before rains ruined the wheat or fruits and vegetables rotted. Small family farms made do with local teenagers. Big commercial operations, and there was hardly any other kind in the wheat belt where expensive machinery required a grower to be well capitalized, needed armies of hundreds of workers to descend on them. And, when the crop was in, to disappear, because there was nothing for the pickers and harvest hands to do and even less local interest in having large numbers of jobless, unattached young men in the vicinity.

The wheat and fruit and vegetable belts could not have existed without migrant workers. But the workers were scorned. They were typically dirty, unshaven, and dressed in rough work clothing. Riding the rails or tramping the roads, their only baggage was a bindle, a bedroll with very little wrapped inside. They were often rambunctious when not working, and inevitably, many of them were unsavory sorts who were a source of crime. Mostly the crime was theft, and it was opportunistic rather than methodical: picking up something salable they stumbled across. There were also assaults, armed robberies, and rape. But crimes against people (except against one another) were not common. Still, the occasional lurid incident was enough to arouse wariness, fear, and hostility toward every hobo who walked into town for a meal or knocked at a kitchen door offering to chop firewood in return for a night's shelter in the barn.

Casual workers insisted that they did not steal, and in general, they were telling the truth. There was a hierarchy among the homeless men of the progressive era. The bindlestiffs (their name for themselves) were at the top of the pyramid. They prided themselves on being working-men who earned their living honestly. They differed from factory workers, they said, only in that they had no homes and families and moved constantly from one short-term job to another. They thought of themselves as free and independent—good old American values—because, if a boss offended them, they did not grovel; they rolled up their blankets and moved on.

The tramps, as the bindlestiffs called them, were homeless too; they too rode the rails and camped in hobo jungles. But they did not work. They survived by panhandling, stealing, and sometimes more serious crimes. The working hobos looked down on them as parasites.

There was a class of homeless men even lower than the tramps, the "home guard." They were bums who neither worked nor traveled. They lived more or less permanently in the tenderloins and skid roads. The bindlestiffs came to these districts when they were looking for work at employment agencies and to spend the winter. Lodging, meals, and drink were cheap on skid road. The home guard, with whom bindlestiffs rubbed elbows and said they despised, were more pathetic than sinister: people reduced to bare survival by alcoholism and mental deficiency.

Such distinctions were lost on the farmers and townspeople for whom dusty, wandering men were almost a daily sight. When, beginning about 1908, the IWW began to have some success organizing bindlestiffs, conventional people began to see the masses of homeless men as part of a dangerous conspiracy. Unexplained fires and damaged machinery were blamed on them as, a few centuries earlier, they were blamed on witches. There was a myth that mysterious markings on gateposts and buildings were a code with which hobos informed one another that the police were brutal in the town or that a particular woman was a soft touch for a sandwich.

After World War I, the age of the hobo came to an end. Tramps still wandered, but there were fewer working bindlestiffs. The increasing hostility of the railroads to unpaying passengers on freight trains played a part in their disappearance. Cheap secondhand automobiles, abundant by 1920, made it possible for four or five bindlestiffs to migrate from job to job inconspicuously and more safely. In time, cheap cars meant that families, including children, replaced single men as the agricultural workforce.

cast a large net. Publishers took to printing "banned in Boston" on the dust jackets of their books to boost sales. Boston's "Watch and Ward" society, another of Comstock's organizations, was the nation's most industrious.

The American Society of Sanitary and Moral Prophylaxis aimed its betterment campaign at men, Protestant middle class more than working class, who were not likely to read its pamphlets or attend its lectures in middle-class churches and halls. The society's message was traditional, the strict sexual morality of the churches: no sexual activity outside marriage. The "purity movement" also reached out to young women— separately. It was the first respectable, mainstream effort to discuss sex openly and frankly with middle-class girls.

PROSTITUTION

Some "purity movement" organizations rescued prostitutes, feeding and housing while preaching morality to them and finding them "honest employment." But the war against prostitution was another of those campaigns that, progressives recognized early on, was too big for private, voluntary action. Not many people believed that prostitution was a positive good; but many accepted it as an inevitable evil—the "world's oldest profession." At best, they thought, it could be kept out of sight of decent people by restricting it to the

A prostitute in a Colorado mining town. In such largely male enclaves, brothels were openly tolerated even when illegal; many whores married and lived conventional lives. On the streets of cities, prostitutes could look forward to little more than venereal disease and poverty.

Providence Public Library

fringes of towns and cities. Although most states had laws criminalizing prostitution before 1900, they were enforced (and then spasmodically) only against streetwalking "hookers" who were a public nuisance. Discreetly operated "houses of ill repute" were tolerated in most cities with or without payoffs to police. Even quite small towns had women on the wrong side of the tracks who would entertain gentlemen callers (or teenage boys) bold enough to knock on the door.

In cities, prostitution ran the gamut from lushly furnished and expensive brothels for high-society swells, such as Sally Stanford's in San Francisco, to "the cribs," tiny cubicles rented by whores who serviced workingmen for a dollar. Because their pay was so low, thousands of working women moonlighted as prostitutes part time.

The progressives, spearheaded by women's organizations, were determined to wipe out the institution because it corrupted young women simply because they were poor, because it spread venereal disease, and because patronization of prostitutes destroyed the sanctity of even middle-class marriages. During the first decade of the twentieth century, states enacted stricter laws against prostitution and, prodded by progressive organizations, enforced them rigorously. In 1917, prodded by the army when it established a big training camp nearby, even New Orleans's wide-open Storyville, the birthplace of jazz, was officially closed. By 1920, all but a few states had antiprostitution laws on the books. Only Nevada, with its mining camp attitudes and next to no moral progressives, continued to tolerate the institution within the law.

CRUSADE AGAINST ALCOHOL

The anti-alcohol crusade that began with the evangelicals never died. The Methodist and Baptist churches, with uneven success, forbade drinking as a condition of membership. At one time or another, dozens of states enacted prohibition of alcohol sales, some compromising with "local option" laws that permitted counties or towns to forbid the sale and even the consumption of beer, wine, and liquor. Rarely was enforcement taken seriously for more than a year or two, and states repealed prohibition laws as quickly as others enacted them.

The Prohibition party began running presidential candidates in 1872; it peaked in strength in 1892 when General John Bidwell won 270,000 votes. In 1879 the Women's Christian Temperance Union elected the able and energetic Frances E. Willard president. She crisscrossed the country espousing at a minimum individual abstinence; but the WCTU also introduced the idea of a constitutional amendment prohibiting, on a national level, the manufacture and sale of intoxicating beverages.

Women of the WCTU often publicized their cause by entering both fancy hotel bars and sleazy saloons, kneeling and praying. Willard died in 1898. Two years later, in Wichita, Kansas, an avid anti-alcohol crusader vitalized the prohibition movement by entering an illegal but wide-open saloon not with a Bible but with a hatchet. While the bartender and tipplers looked on dumbfounded, hid under tables, or fled, Carry Nation smashed the bottles and glasses, the mirror

Votes for Women? Who Cares?

Not everyone answered the question with an emphatic yes or no. Socialist Helen Keller said that woman suffrage was a nonissue; it was not important:

> You ask for votes for women. What good can votes do when ten-elevenths of the land in Great Britain belongs to 200,000 and only one-eleventh to the rest of the 40,000,000 population? Have your men with their millions of votes freed themselves from this injustice?

Theodore Roosevelt came to a similar conclusion—it did not matter much if women voted:

> I do not regard it as a very important matter. I am unable to see that there has been any special improvement in the position of women in those states in the West that have adopted woman's suffrage, as compared to those states adjoining them that have not adopted it. I do not think that giving the women suffrage will produce any marked improvement in the condition of women. I do not believe that it will produce any of the evils feared.

behind the bar, and much of the furniture. For six months she repeated her forays across Kansas and was arrested thirty times.

Middle-class progressives disapproved of Carry Nation's "hatchetations," but the one-woman demolition squad gave the movement new life. Again, women headed the prohibition campaign, emphasizing social and political arguments more than their moral distaste for drinking. They pointed out that in big cities, saloons were the local headquarters of political machines. Close the saloons, and the bosses would be crippled. Progressive prohibitionists argued that much of the misery of the working classes was the consequence of husbands and fathers spending their wages on demon rum and John Barleycorn. Because the public bar was an all-male institution, the temperance movement formed a close alliance with suffragists.

The prohibition movement was not exclusively a progressive phenomenon. Ministers interested in no other reforms also supported it. Except in big cities in the Northeast and Midwest, however, progressive politicians, even those who enjoyed a beer or a drop of the creature, became sympathizers, for the prohibitionists' votes if not because of their arguments.

Big-city progressives like Alfred E. Smith and Robert Wagner of New York opposed the prohibitionists. The large Roman Catholic and Jewish populations of the cities had no religious tradition against alcohol; on the contrary, they used wine as a part of religious observance. But they were in the minority, and in time, they lost the battle.

FEMINISM AND PROGRESSIVISM

The woman suffrage movement was almost as old as prohibitionism, and in 1900 it seemed as far from its goal—a

constitutional amendment guaranteeing women the vote—as the anti-alcohol forces were. Despite fifty years of labor by the now elderly leaders of the suffragists, Elizabeth Cady Stanton and Susan B. Anthony, the victories were few. In their twilight years at the beginning of the Progressive Era, Stanton and Anthony could look back on liberalized divorce laws, women voters in six western states, a movement unified for the moment in the National American Woman Suffrage Association, and the initiation of a new generation of leaders including Carrie Chapman Catt and Anna Howard Shaw, a British-born physician.

But the coveted prize was as remote as it had been at Seneca Falls in 1848. Most articulate Americans, women as well as men, continued to believe that women's finer moral sense made it best that they remain in a domestic sphere separate from men's public sphere. If women participated in public life, they would be sullied as men were and would lose their moral influence in the home.

In fact, when Anthony died in 1906, success was less than fifteen years away. The democratic inclinations of the progressives made it increasingly difficult for them to deny the franchise to half the American people. Even progressive leaders who had no personal enthusiasm for the idea of female voters publicly supported the cause.

CHANGING STRATEGIES

The key to the victory of the women's suffrage movement was a fundamental shift in its strategy. Under the leadership of Carrie Chapman Catt, the National American Woman Suffrage Association came to terms with popular prejudices

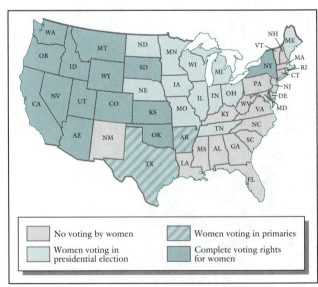

MAP 35:1 Woman's Suffrage before the Nineteenth Amendment
Women's suffrage became part of the Constitution in 1919. By that date, however, as this map indicates, hard-core and absolute opposition to women voting was restricted largely to white males in New England and the South—strange bedfellows, indeed. Elsewhere women voted in at least some elections before the Amendment was ratified.

Under Carrie Chapman Catt, the National American Women Suffrage Association shunned the confrontational tactics of British suffragists. The Americans emphasized their respectability, femininity, and even domesticity, as in this parade.

as Stanton and Anthony never quite could. Catt's movement quietly shelved the comprehensive critique of women's status in American society that earlier feminists developed, including, sometimes, doubts about the institution of marriage. The new suffragists downplayed, even jettisoned, the argument that women should have the right to vote because they were equal to men—like men—in every way.

A few "social feminists" clung to the old verities. Charlotte Perkins Gilman, an independently minded New Englander, argued in *Women and Economics* (1898) that marriage was itself the cause of women's inequality. Alice Paul, a Quaker like many feminists before her, insisted that the suffrage alone was not enough to resolve "the woman question."

But most middle-class suffragists argued that women should have the right to vote precisely because they were not like men; they were more moral, just as traditionalists said. Their votes would purge society of its evils. Not only did the suffragists ingeniously turn the most compelling antisuffrage argument in their favor—the belief that women were the morally superior sex—but they told progressives that in allowing women to vote they would be gaining huge numbers of supporters. Among the enemies of progressivism that women voters would counterbalance were ignorant, easily corrupted new immigrants and socialists, whose numbers were growing in the first decade of the twentieth century.

LEFT OF PROGRESSIVISM

Many progressives advocated municipal ownership of public utilities, but they were not socialists. Roosevelt, La Follette, Johnson, and others warned that if the reforms they proposed were not enacted, socialism would grow in the United States as it had in Europe. They could point as a threat to the astonishing growth, in just a few years, of the Socialist party of America. Founded in 1900, the Socialists nominated the leader of the Pullman strike, Eugene V. Debs, for president; he won 94,768 votes. In 1904 Debs threw a scare into progressives and conservatives alike by polling 402,460 votes. The Socialist party came close to establishing itself as a permanent fixture in American politics. Debs was a nationally known and respected figure; he ran for president five times.

DEBS AND BERGER

In some ways Debs resembled progressive politicians. He was a fiery, flamboyant orator, a master of the theatrical and gymnastic style of public speaking still in favor. He was more a moralist than an intellectual or, certainly, an ideologue. Debs freely admitted that he had little patience with the endless doctrinal hairsplitting with which other socialists were enamored. He was an exhorter, most at home in the company of ordinary working people; he shared their prejudices

The "Red Special." In 1908 the Socialists were so confident presidential candidate Eugene V. Debs would make a strong showing ("socialism is coming like a prairie fire and nothing can stop it," crowed the Appeal to Reason) that the party strained its resources to charter a train so Debs could make a nationwide whistle-stop tour.

and foibles and their lack of pretension. Unsurprisingly, Debs's followers worshiped him as progressives worshiped La Follette, Borah, and Roosevelt.

But Debs was not a progressive under a different name. He did not dread class conflict; he encouraged it, and he told working people they should take charge. He was a Marxist to the extent that he believed that the class that produced wealth should decide how that wealth was to be distributed.

Victor Berger of Milwaukee, the second most important Socialist in the United States, did link socialism and progressivism. An Austrian immigrant, middle-class in background, and the practical politician that Debs was not, Berger forged an alliance of Milwaukee's large German-speaking population, the city's labor movement, and many reform-minded middle-class people. His Social Democratic party (a semiautonomous part of the Socialist party) forbade revolutionary rhetoric, which Berger believed frightened voters away from the party. Without denying them, Berger soft-pedaled socialism's ultimate goals. He promised Milwaukee honest government and efficient city-owned public utilities. On one occasion, when he and Debs were being interviewed by a journalist, Debs said that capitalists would not be compensated when their factories were taken from them: their property was stolen from working people, and theft would not be

rewarded. Berger interrupted: no, capitalists would be compensated for their losses. Property might very well be theft; but Berger would not alienate his middle-class supporters with talk of confiscation.

To the radical members of the party, Berger's "sewer socialism" (a reference to his emphasis on city ownership of utilities) was nothing more than progressivism. Berger thought otherwise. He insisted that by demonstrating to the American people the Socialists' ability to govern a large city, the Socialist party would win their attention to the revolutionary part of its program. In 1910 he got what seemed his chance to do just that. Berger was elected to the House of Representatives, and Socialist candidates for mayor and city council were swept into power in Milwaukee.

LABOR'S QUEST FOR RESPECTABILITY

Berger also hoped to advance the fortunes of socialism by capturing the American Federation of Labor. Socialists were a large minority in the AFL. They were probably a majority among union members who were not Roman Catholic. At the federation's annual conventions, the socialists challenged the antisocialist leadership of Samuel Gompers and several times came close to ousting him from the presidency.

In the end they failed. Presenting a moderate face to the American people was central to Gompers's strategy for establishing the legitimacy of the labor movement, and his version of moderation included support of progressive capitalism. His willingness to cooperate with employers won him many friends among progressives (and some conservatives such as Mark Hanna). In 1905 President Theodore Roosevelt intervened in a coal miners' strike in such a way as to appear as if he was favorable to the miners. During the William Howard Taft administration (1909–1913) progressives established a Commission on Industrial Violence with a membership that was skewed in a pro-union direction. Progressive Democratic President Woodrow Wilson named Samuel Gompers to several prestigious government posts and appointed a former leader of the AFL's United Mine Workers, William B. Wilson, to be the first secretary of labor.

The union movement grew in the favorable climate of the Progressive Era. Membership in the AFL rose from about 500,000 in 1900 to 1.5 million in 1910, with some 500,000 workers holding cards in independent organizations. Still, this was a pittance in a nonagricultural labor force of almost 20 million.

Wobblies

Members of the IWW were called Wobblies. There are several explanations of the origin of their name. According to one, the IWWs were so strike-prone that they were "wobbly" workers. The story the IWW favored told of a Chinese restaurant operator in the Pacific Northwest who gave credit only to Wobblies because he could depend on them to pay. When someone asked for a meal on credit, the restaurant owner, unable to pronounce the name of the letter W, asked "I-Wobbly-Wobbly?"

Tamiment Library, New York University

THE "WOBBLIES"

The most important unions outside the AFL were the conservative Railway Brotherhoods of Locomotive Engineers, Firemen, Conductors, and Brakemen. (The Brotherhood of Pullman Car Porters, the members of which were African Americans, was not founded until 1925.) Then there was the revolutionary Industrial Workers of the World or, as members were called, "the Wobblies."

Founded in 1905 by radical socialists and labor leaders disgusted by Gompers's conservatism and his refusal to organize unskilled workers, the IWW found some friends among progressives. In the West progressives supported the Wobblies when, between 1909 and 1913, they mounted a series of free speech fights to protect their campaign to recruit migrant farm workers. IWW strategy was to plead their case where the casual workers—"hoboes" or "bindlestiffs"—congregated in the tenderloin districts of western cities like Spokane, Washington, and Fresno, California. Much like preachers, they spoke from soapboxes set up on street corners.

When municipal authorities tried to crush the campaigns by arresting the soapboxers, the Wobblies responded by reading publicly from the Declaration of Independence and the Constitution. It was brilliant public relations. Middle-class progressives with no love for Wobbly revolutionism were infuriated at the suppression of free speech.

In 1912 progressive organizations in the East, particularly women's clubs, helped the IWW win its greatest strike victory among immigrant textile mill workers in Lawrence, Massachusetts. They publicized the horrendous living conditions in Lawrence, lobbied congressmen, and took the children of strikers into their homes, a masterful public relations ploy.

More often, however, mere mention of the Wobblies sent chills down progressives' spines. The IWW was frankly revolutionary and, unlike the Socialist party, did not categorically rule out violence. In advocating sabotage, IWW leaders

Birth Control

Margaret Sanger was a nurse in New York City. She ministered to poor women giving birth to children they could not afford to support, and to girls and women who came to the hospital after botched abortions. In 1912 she devoted herself to publicizing and providing women with condoms, diaphragms, and spermicidal ointments. Two years later she coined the term *birth control*, mainly as a means to avoid offending middle-class progressive women she recruited to support her cause. Despite the euphemism, she was jailed when she opened a birth control clinic in 1916. Her enemies equated the advocacy of birth control with promoting sexual promiscuity.

Nevertheless, Sanger's insistence that "a woman's body belongs to herself alone" and that women "cannot be on an equal footing with men until they have full and complete control over their reproductive function" appealed to many progressives. Ironically, although Sanger's concern was poor women, her American Birth Control League (later Planned Parenthood) had its greatest influence on educated middle-class women.

insisted that it was a passive, nonviolent tactic: "striking on the jobs," working inefficiently. But individual members of the union spoke of driving spikes into logs bound for sawmills and throwing hammers into the works of harvesters, threshers, and balers.

Moreover, the IWW recruited among the very social groups that progressives regarded as the threat from below: unassimilated immigrants in eastern cities and the wandering, homeless casual workers of the grain belt and Pacific Coast states. A lasting alliance such as Victor Berger formed with progressives in Milwaukee was out of the question. Indeed, Berger led a movement within the Socialist party to remove Wobbly leader William D. "Big Bill" Haywood from the party's National Executive Committee.

FURTHER READING

General John W. Chambers, *The Tyranny of Change: America in the Progressive Era,* 1980; John M. Cooper, *The Pivotal Decades: The United States 1900–1920,* 1990; Alan Dawley, *Struggles for Justice: Social Responsibility and the Liberal State,* 1991; Steven J. Diner, *A Very Different Age: Americans of the Progressive Era,* 1998; Michael McGerr, *A Fierce Discontent: The Rise and Fall of the Progressive Movement in America, 1870–1920,* 2003; William L. O'Neill, *The Progressive Years: America Comes of Age,* 1975; Nell Irvin Painter, *Standing at Armageddon: The United States, 1877–1919,* 1987.

Moral Reform Anna L. Bates, *Weeder in the Garden of the Lord: Anthony Comstock's Life and Career,* 1995; Edward Behr, *Prohibition: Thirteen Years That Changed America,* 1996; Paul Boyer, *Urban Masses and Moral Order in America, 1820–1920,* 1978; Norman Clark, *Deliver Us from Evil,* 1976; Arthur Ekirch, *Progressivism in Practice,* 1974; Martin E. Marty, *Modern American Religion: The Irony of It all, 1893–1919,* 1986; Elaine May, *Great Expectations: Marriage and Divorce in Post-Victorian America,* 1980;

J. T. Patterson, *America's Struggle against Poverty,* 1981; James M. Timberlake, *Prohibition and the Progressive Movement,* 1963.
Progressives Mina Carson, *Settlement Folk: Social Thought and the American Settlement Movement, 1815–1930,* 1990; Ellen Chesler, *Woman of Valor: Margaret Sanger and the Birth Cintrol Movement in America,* 1997; Robert M. Crumden, *Ministers of Reform: The Progressive Achievement in American Civilization, 1880–1930,* 1983; Glenda E. Gilmore, ed., *Who Were the Progressives?,* 2002; Dewey W. Grantham, *Southern Progressivism,* 1983; Char Miller, *Gifford Pinchot and the Making of Modern Environmentalism,* 2001; Nathan Miller, *Theodore Roosevelt: A Life,* 1992; Edmund Morris, *Theodore Rex,* 2001; Nancy Unger, *Fighting Bob La Follette: The Righteous Reformer,* 2000.

Women, Feminism, Suffrage Mari Jo Buhle, *Women and American Socialism, 1877–1920,* 1981; Nancy Cott, *The Grounding of American Feminism,* 1987; Carl M. Degler, *At Odds: Women in the Family in America from the Revolution to the Present,* 1980; Robyn

Munly, *Creating a Female Dominion, in American Reform, 1890–1935*, 1991; William L. O'Neill, *Everyone Was Brave: The Rise* and Fall of Feminism, 1969; Rosalind Rosenberg, *Beyond Separate Spheres*, 1982.

KEY TERMS

The following terms are covered in this chapter and can also be found in the list of Key Terms at the back of the book.

Anthony Comstock	muckrakers	recall	Wisconsin idea
initiative	Ray Stannard Baker	referendum	

 ## ONLINE SOURCES GUIDE

Use this listing to find online documents, images, interactive maps, simulations, and other resources related to this chapter:

American History Resource Center
http://history.wadsworth.com/rc/us

Selected Documents
Jane Addams's "Twenty Years at Hull House" (1911)
Herbert Croly's "The Promise of American Life" (1909)
Ida M. Tarbell's "The History of the Standard Oil Company"
The Niagara Movement's "Declaration of Principles" (1905)

Selected Images
Ida Tarbell
Antisaloon league
Eugene V. Debs
Women suffragists emphasizing their respectability
Mary Church Terrell, one of the founding members of the NAACP
Walter F. White, an officer of the NAACP

Interactive Time Line (with online readings)
Age of Reform: The progressives

CHAPTER 36

The Progressive Presidents

Roosevelt, Taft, and Wilson 1901–1916

Reproduced from the Collections of the Library of Congress

Big business is not dangerous because it is big, but because its bigness is an unwholesome inflation created by privileges and exemptions which it ought not to enjoy.

Woodrow Wilson

We demand that big business give the people a square deal; in return we must insist that when anyone engaged in big business endeavors to do right he shall himself be given a square deal.

Theodore Roosevelt

By 1904 some congressmen of both political parties were describing themselves as "progressive." President Roosevelt did not object when the label was fixed to him, although privately he found it amusing. He was, after all, from a well-established aristocratic family who socialized with the richest people in the country. Roosevelt wrote to the decidedly non-progressive Senator Chauncey Depew with mock weariness: "How I wish I wasn't a reformer, Oh Senator! But I suppose I must live up to my part, like the Negro minstrel who blackened himself all over!"

Was T. R. mocking his own sincerity? Perhaps in part; then again, his family's status and fortune were (unlike railroader Depew's) preindustrial; he was not one of those capitalists he called "malefactors of great wealth." He had seen old families like his elbowed aside by the industrial *nouveaux riches* of the late nineteenth century. Mrs. Astor reacted to the slight by creating "The Four Hundred," a short list of *anciens riches*

New Yorkers acceptable in her ballroom. Theodore Roosevelt reacted by going into politics and refusing, like most of his peers, to play the flunky for big business and its henchmen, the Republican party bosses.

No, the sigh of resignation in his letter to Depew was feigned. Teddy Roosevelt loved, most of all, to be in the thick of things. When an assassin put him into the White House, it was already obvious that progressive reform was where the action was. One wonders if the conservative McKinley's great personal popularity would have survived the Progressive Era that was unfolding as he prepared to shake hands in Buffalo.

T. R. TAKES OVER

At first, the accidental president moved cautiously. He knew that the Republican old guard distrusted him as a "damned cowboy." Mark Hanna was openly discussing challenging

Church and State

Beginning in 1864, the motto "In God We Trust" (from *The Star-Spangled Banner*) was inscribed on most American coins. In 1907 President Roosevelt ordered the motto removed. He said that it was at best an unseemly entanglement of religion and government.

After rare popular criticism of the beloved president, Congress reversed his order. Roosevelt let the issue die.

In 1955 "In God We Trust" was added to paper currency. During the 1970s, a series of protests similar to Roosevelt's took the motto to the Supreme Court. In 1983 Justice William Brennan, who generally approved of sentiments fashionable among self-styled "liberals," allowed its use to continue on the grounds that the words "have lost any true religious significance."

Roosevelt for the 1904 Republican presidential nomination with party bosses Tom Platt of New York and Matthew Quay of Pennsylvania. T. R. was well aware of their power within the party.

In the end, no one was to contest T. R.'s leadership in 1904. Mark Hanna died unexpectedly in February that year, Matt Quay a little later. Had they been hale and hearty at the Republican convention, they would not have dared to contest the nomination. In just three years, the "cowboy" had built up a personal following in the country far more enthusiastic than McKinley's had ever been. Roosevelt moved slowly. At the top, he quietly replaced the conservative hacks McKinley had appointed to the cabinet. He won the loyalty of the competent conservatives he inherited from McKinley by giving them an autonomy in their departments they had not previously enjoyed.

Roosevelt did not fear talent. The men from McKinley's cabinet he retained were able: Secretary of State John Hay, Secretary of War Elihu Root (who succeeded Hay in the State Department in 1905), and Attorney General Philander C. Knox.

BUSTING TABOOS AND TRUSTS

In April 1902 T. R. directed Attorney General Knox, a former corporation lawyer, to have a go at the country's most powerful corporate organizers. His target, the Northern Securities Company, was designed by J. P. Morgan and railroaders Edward H. Harriman and James J. Hill to put an end to destructive railroad competition in the northwestern quarter of the country. Funded by the nation's two richest banks, Northern Securities was a holding company patterned after Morgan's United States Steel Corporation.

Morgan was stunned. McKinley had allowed the Sherman Antitrust Act to languish, almost unused. In a revealing moment, Morgan wrote to the president, "If we have done anything wrong, send your man to my man and we can fix it up." That was, indeed, how things had been done during the McKinley and Cleveland administrations. And that was why Roosevelt chose to do things differently. He remembered very well that cartoonists had drawn President Cleveland sitting in Morgan's waiting room, holding his hat.

In 1904 Knox won the case. The Supreme Court agreed that the Northern Securities Company "restrained trade" and ordered it to dissolve. Progressives cheered. When Roosevelt, who relished applause, instituted several more antitrust suits, forty in all (twenty-five were won), progressives nicknamed him the "trustbuster."

Roosevelt continued to socialize comfortably with the big businessmen Knox was suing. Indeed, in 1907, whether or not his man actually met with Morgan's man, he allowed United States Steel to gobble up a regional competitor, Tennessee Coal and Iron, without comment. The trustbuster's criteria for why one business combination was acceptable and another not were vague. To some extent, Roosevelt's trust-busting was political grandstanding that could pay dividends in popularity only when it was a novelty. Having

National Reforms 1900–1914

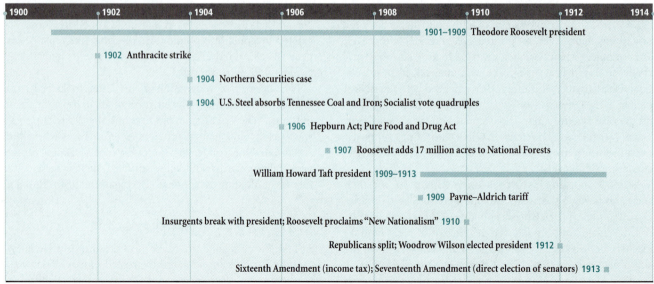

| 1900 | 1902 | 1904 | 1906 | 1908 | 1910 | 1912 | 1914 |

1901–1909 Theodore Roosevelt president

1902 Anthracite strike

1904 Northern Securities case

1904 U.S. Steel absorbs Tennessee Coal and Iron; Socialist vote quadruples

1906 Hepburn Act; Pure Food and Drug Act

1907 Roosevelt adds 17 million acres to National Forests

William Howard Taft president 1909–1913

1909 Payne–Aldrich tariff

Insurgents break with president; Roosevelt proclaims "New Nationalism" 1910

Republicans split; Woodrow Wilson elected president 1912

Sixteenth Amendment (income tax); Seventeenth Amendment (direct election of senators) 1913

North Wind Picture Archives

■ *By the end of the miner's strike of 1902, coal was so scarce and expensive that people scavenged to cook their meals. Here a newspaper artist depicts men dredging the bottom near docks where coal barges were moored. T. R. rightfully anticipated a serious crisis if the strike continued into the winter.*

demonstrated to big business that he was not its flunky and won the approval of voters in the election of 1904, Roosevelt lost interest. He did not, as events were soon to show, regard bigness itself as criminal.

THE GREAT COAL STRIKE

Roosevelt became president at a time of disturbing and increasing conflict between employers and workers. There were 1,098 strikes in 1898, 1,839 in 1900, and 3,012 in 1901—almost 60 a week on average! In May 1902 a strike that augured to touch almost everyone in the country erupted in Pennsylvania. About 140,000 anthracite miners and helpers walked off the job, demanding an eight-hour day, a 20 percent pay hike, guarantees against cheating in weighing the coal they mined, and official recognition of the United Mineworkers Union as their bargaining agent.

Demand for coal was not high in May, so the dozens of mine owners—coal was not a consolidated industry like oil or steel—agreed to hold the line on every issue. To universal surprise, the ethnically fragmented miners also held firm all summer. By the fall, orders for coal that the operators could not meet began to pour in. In the Northeast, the retail price of a ton of anthracite climbed from $5–6 to $15–20. Coal-burning factories began to shut down. Worse, winter was coming. Most city homes were heated by coal furnaces.

Practically for the first time in a big strike, public opinion was with the workers. The miners were well disciplined; there was virtually no violence. Coal mine workers were wretchedly paid, particularly given the fact that their jobs were dangerous; mine explosions and cave-ins were common. Moreover, the president of the United Mine Workers, **John Mitchell,** appeared to be an attractive, reasonable man, whereas the spokesman for the mine operators, George Baer, was a public relations disaster.

Had the public (had the miners!) known more about Mitchell, he would not have been so popular. He was a drunk; he took bribes from mine owners to settle local disputes; and he was contemptuous of the miners. "They remind me very much of a drove of cattle, ready to stampede," he said in private. Baer, however, was a fool in public, given to defending the mine owners with his unique interpretation of the Bible. "Strikes began with Genesis," he said, not privately. "Cain was the first striker, and he killed Abel because Abel was the more prosperous fellow." Even more disastrous was his statement to a reporter that the welfare of the miners would be looked after "by the Christian men to whom God in His infinite wisdom has given the control of the property interests of this country."

Roosevelt knew whose side to appear to be on and where to look for help in ending the strike before cold weather. He announced that if the strike continued, he would send in the army to run the mines. Quietly, he asked J. P. Morgan to tell Baer and the other operators to sit down and talk. The likes of George Baer did not defy J. P. Morgan. He and his colleagues went to Washington. Roosevelt's men shuttled between two rooms (the operators would not meet face-to-face with Mitchell), and the strike was ended.

It was a compromise: pay was increased by 10 percent; the workday was reduced to nine hours; the mine owners did not recognize the UMW. In an industry in which employers had rarely made any concessions, however, the miners believed they had won. People did not freeze to death in their homes that winter. And just about everyone but the mine operators heaped praise on Theodore Roosevelt.

TEDDY'S GREAT VICTORY

Roosevelt was riding high in 1904. He was unanimously nominated for reelection and presented with a large campaign chest. The Democrats, hoping to capitalize on the grumbling of big-business Republicans, did an about-face from the party's populist agrarianism of 1896 and 1900. They nominated a Wall Street lawyer and judge with a record of sympathy for labor, Alton B. Parker. Urbane but colorless, Parker was the antithesis of William Jennings Bryan and, Democratic bosses hoped, a foil to the histrionic Roosevelt.

The second most colorful politician in the country would have looked like a cardboard cutout next to T. R. In the end, few of Parker's Wall Street friends seem to have voted for him. J. P. Morgan, although recently stung in the **Northern Securities case,** donated $150,000 to Roosevelt's campaign. Morgan recognized that for all his bombast, Roosevelt hewed to an anti-inflationary money policy and did not molest the high tariff. Morgan calculated—correctly—that Roosevelt would ease off on his trust-busting. Morgan had not reached the pinnacle of American finance by letting personal grudges dictate business decisions.

Roosevelt won a lopsided 57.4 percent of the vote. His 336–140 electoral sweep was the largest since Grant's in 1872. The only unwelcome election news was the fact that Eugene V. Debs, the Socialist party candidate, won 400,000 votes. That was only 3 percent of the total. Nevertheless, it was a fourfold increase over Debs's vote in 1900.

ROOSEVELT'S REFORMS

Theodore Roosevelt lost few opportunities to denounce socialists. When, in 1905, two socialist leaders of the Western Federation of Miners were arrested in Colorado and transported without an extradition hearing across state lines to be put on trial in Idaho, Roosevelt shrugged it off. It did not matter because the two, Charles Moyer and William D. Haywood, were "undesirable citizens." The two were accused of engineering the bombing murder of a former governor of Idaho.

Their lawyer, Clarence Darrow, then at the outset of a distinguished career as "attorney for the damned," complained (justifiably enough) that the president's statement had rendered a fair trial difficult, if not impossible. Nevertheless,

> ### American Essence
> William Allen White called Coca-Cola "the sublimated essence of all that America stands for." The soda pop began as a kind of health food. An Atlanta druggist concocted it in 1886 as an alternative to alcohol. Within a year, a pious Methodist named Asa G. Candler purchased all rights to "Coke" for $2,300 and promoted it, because of its "kick," as a "brain tonic." Indeed, coca leaves—also the source of cocaine—were one of the ingredients until 1902, when caffeine quietly replaced them as "kick." Before that year, it may have been slightly addictive. For decades, southerners called Coca-Cola "dope."

Darrow won the case. The prosecution's star witness was the actual bomber and easy to discredit.

REGULATING THE RAILROADS

As they had been for thirty years, the great railroads were a focus of popular resentment. The arrogance of their directors and the vital role of transportation in the national economy preoccupied progressives at every level of government. Prodded by Wisconsin Senator La Follette and others, Roosevelt supported passage of the Hepburn Act in 1906. It authorized the Interstate Commerce Commission to set maximum rates that railroads could charge their customers and forbade them to pay rebates to big shippers.

Rebates were already illegal, but the prohibition had not been effectively enforced. The Hepburn Act gave the ICC some teeth. Even more than the Northern Securities prosecution, the Hepburn Act represented a reversal of the federal government's deferential treatment of the railroads. Also in 1906, Congress passed a law holding railroad companies liable to employees who suffered injuries on the job. By Western European standards, it was a mild compensation law; but in the United States it marked a sharp break with precedent, which held employees responsible for most of their injuries.

PURER FOOD

Roosevelt also signed the Pure Food and Drug Act and the Meat Inspection Act in 1906. The former forbade adulteration of foods by large processors engaged in interstate commerce, enforced stringent sanitary standards on them, and put the lid on the patent medicine business, a freewheeling industry of hucksters who marketed sometimes addictive drugs as "feel-good" nostrums. Mrs. Winslow's Soothing Syrup and Lydia Pinkham's Vegetable Compound, touted as relief for "female complaints," were alcoholic elixirs laced liberally with opiates. Even Coca-Cola, already the all-American soft drink, had originally been fortified with a coca derivative, although not cocaine, and the company had abandoned it by 1906.

By providing hefty penalties for violators, the Pure Food and Drug Act eliminated sometimes toxic preservatives and fillers from canned and bottled foodstuffs, which were increasingly part of the American diet. The Meat Inspection Act mandated federal inspection of meatpacking plants to eliminate the abuses that Upton Sinclair detailed gruesomely in *The Jungle.*

Big meatpackers like Armour, Swift, Wilson, and Cudahy grumbled about the federal inspectors, notebooks in hand, puttering about their plants. However, the Meat Inspection Act worked in their favor in their competition with smaller, local slaughterhouses. With their greater resources, the big meatpackers found compliance with federal standards little more than a nuisance. Smaller companies were able to stay in business only by slashing costs at every turn, which sometimes meant paying little attention to sanitation. The big packers made advertising hay of the inspection stamps on their half-sides of beef and legs of pork: the government endorsed them, they said. Small companies unable to meet federal standards closed their doors or restricted their sales to the states in which they were located. Like all such federal programs, meat inspection applied only to firms involved in interstate commerce.

PRESERVING NATURE

Theodore Roosevelt and his progressive allies were not always farseeing. Many of their reforms were the fruit of passionate impulse or of playing to the whims of their constituents. In their campaign to conserve natural resources, however—an issue of particular interest to the president—

President Roosevelt and America's leading preservationist, John Muir, in Yosemite National Park. Roosevelt was not hostile to Muir's campaign to preserve national wonders for their own sake; he was an enthusiastic outdoorsman. However, Roosevelt was primarily a conservationist; his chief purpose was to reserve valuable resources—timber, minerals, oil, and watersheds—for future generations.

Reproduced from the Collections of the Library of Congress

Progressive Legacy

Progressive opposition to unmonitored, unregulated exploitation of natural resources bore immeasurable fruits. In 1900 Virginia or white-tailed deer numbered about 500,000; in 1992 that number was 18.5 million. About 650,000 wild turkeys survived in 1900; in 1992 there were 4 million. In 1907 the government counted some 41,000 elk in the United States; the species was at risk of extinction. In 1992 there were 772,000, enough to be pests in some regions.

they looked to the distant future and created monuments for which they are rightfully honored.

Roosevelt was the first American president born in a big city. Still, he had been a passionate outdoorsman most of his life, long before it was fashionable. He loved camping, riding, hiking, climbing, and hunting. As a historian, he was more sensitive than most of his contemporaries to the role of the wilderness in forging the American character. He actively courted and gained the friendship of **John Muir,** a sometimes mystical Californian who founded the Sierra Club in 1892. Muir's interest in nature was aesthetic, cultural, and spiritual. "God has cared for these trees," (California's redwoods), Muir said, "saved them from drought, disease, avalanches, and a thousand straining, leveling tempests and floods; but He cannot save them from fools." Muir lobbied to protect from exploitation natural wonders like the redwoods and Yosemite Valley, which he helped to establish as a national park in 1890.

RESOURCES IN JEOPARDY

Roosevelt shared Muir's sentiments to some extent. As president, he created a number of national parks and national monuments. But Muir was, properly described, a preservationist. His supporters in Congress ran into powerful opposition with his projects. "Not a cent for scenery," the crusty, reactionary Speaker of the House, Joseph G. Cannon of Illinois, snapped at them.

Roosevelt found the programs of conservationists like his tennis partner, America's first professionally trained forester, Gifford Pinchot, more feasible politically. Pinchot had little gut sympathy for Muir's campaign to preserve unblemished nature for its own sake. (Had Pinchot known the term, he would have called Muir a "tree hugger." He did say that "wilderness is a waste.") Pinchot's concern was protecting forests from rapacious exploiters interested only in short-term profits. He wanted to ensure that future generations would have access to enough timber and nonrenewable natural resources such as minerals, coal, and oil to maintain a decent life. In December 1907 T. R. told Congress,

> To waste, to destroy our natural resources, to skin and exhaust the land instead of using it so as to increase its usefulness, will result in undermining in the days of our children the very prosperity which we ought by right to hand down to them amplified and developed.

Pinchot and Roosevelt had good reason to be concerned. Lumbermen in the Great Lakes states had already mowed down forests that had been thought inexhaustible, leaving behind ugly and valueless scrub. Western ranchers put too many cattle on grasslands, destroying valuable forage and transforming the land into weed lots and desert. Coal and phosphate mining companies and drillers for oil thought in terms of next year's profits; the fact that, in a century, the United States might run out of these resources never crossed their minds.

Americans as a people had been reckless with the land since Jamestown Colony. What Pinchot and Roosevelt understood was that there was a big difference between what frontiersmen could do with axes and oxen-drawn plows and the destruction wreaked by greedy corporations.

THE NATIONAL FORESTS

The National Forest Reserves were established in 1891 when Congress authorized the president to withhold forests in the public domain from private ownership. Unlike National Parks (there was just one in 1891), the Forest Reserves could be exploited. The Interior Department was entrusted with licensing and monitoring loggers. Presidents Harrison, Cleveland, and McKinley declared 46 million acres of woodland as Reserves. However, when Roosevelt became president, it was clear that cut-and-run loggers and cattlemen had ignored government authority in many of the Reserves.

In 1905 Roosevelt renamed the Reserves the National Forests and named Pinchot to head the Forest Service. He also transferred authority over National Forests to the Agriculture Department. In part this was because the Interior Department had been complicit in abuse of the Reserves. In part the transfer also reflected the basic goals of the forestry profession: looking on trees as a crop and monitoring how much timber was harvested so that a forest replenished, by growth, the lumber that was removed—"sustained yield."

In two years Roosevelt added 125 million acres to the National Forests, tripling their size. He also reserved for future use 68 million acres of coal deposits, almost 5 million acres of phosphate beds (vital to production of munitions), several known oil fields, and 2,565 sites suitable for the construction of dams for irrigation and generation of electrical power.

Roosevelt's National Forests represented the best kind of the progressives' hopes for government. The system promised an indefinite supply of forest products for the nation and put the government in the business of flood control and development of hydroelectric power. The National Forests also provided recreational opportunities by constructing cabins, campgrounds, and trails.

Most of the big logging companies were happy with the system. It took them out of the land-owning business—a big savings—and Pinchot was no John Muir; he wanted timber cut if it was cut responsibly.

In the western states there was angry opposition to Roosevelt's policies. Cattlemen, clear-cut loggers, and private power companies banded together to fight the

> ### Taft on the Presidency
> "The major part of the work of a President is to increase the gate receipts of expositions and fairs and bring tourists to town."

conservationists. In 1907, with support from knee-jerk reactionaries like Joseph Cannon, western congressmen attached a rider to the Agriculture Department's annual appropriation forbidding the creation of National Forests in six western states. Roosevelt had no choice but to sign the bill. But he had one last swipe at what he called the "predatory interests." Before he signed, he reserved 17 million acres of forest land in the interdicted states.

THE REFORMER RETIRES

In 1908 Roosevelt asked Congress to provide for federal investigation of major labor disputes and close regulation of the stock market. Antiprogressive "Old Guard" politicians ignored him; Roosevelt was a "lame duck." The year 1908 saw a presidential election, and four years earlier, celebrating the victory of 1904—no one has ever explained an act so totally out of Teddy's character—Roosevelt declared that "a wise custom which limits the President to two terms regards the substance and not the form, and under no circumstances will I be a candidate for or accept another nomination."

Having served three and a half years of McKinley's term, Roosevelt defined himself as a two-term president. In 1908 he probably regretted his pledge. Theodore Roosevelt took great personal pleasure in being president. Unlike Calvin Coolidge and Ronald Reagan, who enjoyed the honor of the presidency as a personal homage, Roosevelt was a worker too. He was not yet 50 years of age in 1908, and he was as popular as ever. He would have won reelection easily had he set aside his pledge not to run. Only his enemies would have reminded him of it.

But he kept his word and settled for handpicking his successor, which no president had been able to do since Andrew Jackson. Secretary of War **William Howard Taft** was not a particularly well-known figure. Roosevelt's glow was so bright that no one close to him was. But he had been a more loyal and valuable aide to T. R. than anyone else: a superb governor and a troubleshooter in the difficult Philippines, and a trusted supervisor of construction of the Panama Canal. "I think that it is very rare," Roosevelt said, "that two public men have ever been so much as one in all the essentials of their public beliefs."

A CONSERVATIVE PRESIDENT IN A PROGRESSIVE ERA

Taft did not want to be president. He was a superb administrator, efficient and tactful. But he wanted to be a judge and regretfully passed up two opportunities to be a Supreme Court justice because Roosevelt needed him. He abhorred

"No tendency is quite so strong in human nature," William Howard Taft observed, "as the desire to lay down rules of conduct for other people." He may have been thinking of those progressives who believed that government could eliminate undesirable behavior by passing laws against it. Prohibitionists were a diverse lot, but in the end, they all desired that no one be able to sit down and have a drink.

The "purity movement" was contemporary with the prohibition movement. Its targeted evil was sexual immorality. Like prohibitionism, its origins were religious and suasionist. Purity societies combated illicit sex, from fornication to prostitution, by brother's keeper persuasion of sinners (and potential sinners) that they should live cleanly. They condemned the "double standard" that held women to strict chastity while overlooking (within limits) illicit male sexual activity. Some purity organizations rescued and reformed prostitutes, whom they saw as the principal, because so accessible, sexual outlet for immoral men.

When they were discouraged by the meager dividends of persuasion, purity crusaders, like the temperance movement, turned to legislation. Fornication and adultery were not the business of the federal government. Nor was prostitution, but spotty local enforcement of antiprostitution laws turned the purity movement to look for a national solution to the problem. They found grounds from which to strike at prostitution nationally in the Constitution's interstate commerce clause. The **Mann Act,** or White Slave Traffic Act of 1911, made it a federal crime to "transport, or cause to be transported, or aid or assist in obtaining transportation for, . . . in interstate or foreign commerce, . . . any woman or girl for the purpose of prostitution or debauchery, or for any other immoral purpose."

The bill sailed through Congress, partly because it was skin off no congressman's nose, and partly because in 1911 the country was in the midst of one of its periodic hysterias over "white slavery." White slaves were girls and women who were unwittingly lured into prostitution by being seduced or raped while drunk or drugged (and therefore "ruined"), whence they were effectively "enslaved" in whorehouses by their corrupters. No doubt such things happened. By 1910, however, some muckrakers and politicians had created a white slavery monster; it was a pervasive, even organized nationwide phenomenon. Dozens of "white slave narratives," patterned on nineteenth-century slave and captive nun narratives, were published. At least six movies of the era had white slavery as a theme. In four years after 1910, the *Reader's Guide* listed 156 magazine articles on the subject compared to 36 during the twenty years preceding 1910. A U.S. attorney wrote that "the white slave traffic is a system operated by a syndicate . . . with 'clearing houses' or 'distributing centers' in nearly all the big cities."

This was nonsense, of course, and when no syndicate could be found, federal authorities began using the Mann Act to arrest men who had crossed a state line with willing women, their "girlfriends," and who were having illicit but clearly noncommercial sexual relations. In *Caminetti* v. *the U.S.* (1917), the Supreme Court approved the prosecution of interstate noncommercial sex because the Mann Act had criminalized not just prostitution but also crossing a state line for "other immoral purposes." The Prohibition Era was a boom time for convictions and imprisonment of men caught taking the train with their sexual partners from Philadelphia to Atlantic City for the weekend.

If the Mann Act was not about white slavery or even, in its application, about prostitution, what was it about?

It was a reflection of the same social anxieties that gave the country Prohibition, the Red Scare, immigration restriction, and the anti-Catholic, anti-Semitic Ku Klux Klan: the perception that undesirable new immigrants and big cities were destroying old American verities. There was a powerful anti-immigrant, particularly anti-Semitic component in the white slavery scare. Although ignorant immigrant girls were the slavers' major targets, they also made captives of once-decent young American women who were working and living in the cities without parental supervision. Living an "unnatural" life, they were susceptible to ruination, which led to prostitution. Jane Addams wrote, "Many a working girl at the end of a day is so hysterical and overwrought that her mental balance is plainly disturbed." Girls gone to the city "dated" rather than "courted," with chaperones, as they would have done back home. "The danger begins," wrote Florence Dedrick in 1909, "the moment a girl leaves the protection of Home and Mother."

Progressive Era Americans believed that an unmarried girl's casual sex was a step toward prostitution, just as a glass of beer was a step toward drunkenness. In fact, the definition of prostitution as the sale of sexual services ("promiscuous inchastity for gain" in the language of the day) was not universal. Iowa defined a prostitute as a woman who "indiscriminately" practiced sexual intercourse that she "invites or solicits by word or act"—what we might call flirtation. Alabama defined a prostitute as "a woman given to indiscriminate lewdness." A widely used Webster's dictionary defined *prostitution* as "the act or practice of offering the body to an indiscriminate intercourse with men."

The common thread in these definitions was not money changing hands but the fact that a woman's sexual activity was casual. A "loose" or "easy" woman was a prostitute. (Women we would call prostitutes were specified as "professional prostitutes.") Slang for a working girl who went out to dinner or a few drinks with a date and had sex was "charity girl," a prostitute who was free. The Mann Act boyfriend–girlfriend prosecutions of the 1910s and 1920s were yet another reflection of values in flux and the anxieties the changes caused.

electioneering; only once in his 50 years—he was the same age as Roosevelt—had he run for office, a judgeship. Regularly in his correspondence he dashed off the exclamation "I hate politics!" He might have turned down the offer of the nomination had not his wife relished the prospect of being first lady and turned the heat up at home.

To a people who delighted in Roosevelt's gymnastic style, Taft's very body militated against his success. He weighed more than 300 pounds. He slept a lot, once in an open car in a motorcade in his honor. His single form of exercise, golf, was considered a sissy's game in 1908, or a plutocrat's: the best-known American golfer was John D. Rockefeller.

Taft was no crony of plutocrats, but neither was he their enemy. Roosevelt seems to have overlooked the fact that Taft, as an administrator, had taken no interest in progressive reforms, either for or against. By disposition, Taft was conservative.

THE ELECTION OF 1908

The election was an anticlimax. The Democrats returned to William Jennings Bryan as their candidate—a sacrificial lamb, really. The thrill was gone, and without the thrill,

The Smithsonian Institution

William Howard Taft. Taft did not want to be president; he hated politics. He agreed to run for the office in 1908 because Theodore Roosevelt, to whom he was devoted, told him that he was indispensable. (Taft's wife wanted him to take the job too.)

Taft detested being president. He may have agreed to run for reelection in 1912 only because his falling-out with Roosevelt had been so bitter that he wanted revenge on his former boss.

Winston Churchill on the Old Guard Republicans

About the time of the Payne–Aldrich tariff, Winston Churchill in Britain was arguing against a proposal by his Conservative party to enact a protective tariff. He warned that such an innovation would betray the party's ideals. It would transform the Conservatives into a different party, "perhaps like the Republican party in the United States . . . , rigid, materialist, and secular whose opinions . . . turn on tariffs and . . . cause the lobbies to be crowded with the touts of protected industries."

It would take another seventy years, but with the ascendancy of Margaret Thatcher in Great Britain in 1979, the traditionalist and paternalistic Conservative party of Winston Churchill was re-created in the commercialistic image of the American Republicans.

Bryan did not amount to much. The Boy Orator of the Platte was jowly and was rapidly losing his hair.

Moreover, his once worshipful followers, the staple farmers of the Midwest, were no longer struggling to survive. They were prospering, beginning to dress as well as the townsmen they had jostled in 1896 and to build substantial homes.

Even Bryan's 1900 issue, imperialism, was moribund thanks in large part to Taft, who, as American governor of the Philippines, could claim credit for having transformed the rebellious Filipinos, whom he called his "little brown brothers," into an apparently content colonial population. Puerto Rico was quieter. Hawaiians did the hula for increasing numbers of American tourists. Central America simmered, but the specter of American power kept the lid on. Thousands of West Indians were digging their way across Panama under American direction.

Bryan won a smaller percentage of the popular vote than in either of his two previous tries. The Socialist party was also disappointed. Bubbling with optimism at the start of the campaign, they chartered a private train, the "Red Special," on which candidate Debs crisscrossed the country. Debs's crowds were big and enthusiastic. He won only 16,000 more votes than he had in 1904. People came out to listen to him; his personality was appealing and he gave a good speech; but they did not vote for him.

TAFT VERSUS THE INSURGENTS

Taft continued to prosecute monopolies. His administration initiated ninety antitrust suits in four years, twice as many as Roosevelt in almost eight years. But nobody called him "trustbuster." That was in large part due to the fact that Taft ran afoul of the progressives in Congress almost immediately after taking office when he stumbled over an issue that Roosevelt had dodged: the tariff.

In 1909 import duties were high: an average of 46.5 percent of the imports' value. Progressives in both parties wanted them reduced. American industry no longer needed protection to survive. American industry was the most efficient in the world; half the streetcars in Great Britain and all the government telephones and typewriters in London were American made. Most American products undersold other nations' everywhere in the world. Progressives argued—they were right—that high tariffs subsidized corporate profits by adding to the prices at which American consumers bought them.

Taft was sympathetic. In 1909 he called Congress into special session for the purpose of revising the Dingley Tariff of 1897. The House drafted a moderate reduction of duties in the Payne Bill. In the Senate, however, Nelson Aldrich of Rhode Island, an unreserved spokesman for industrialists, attached no fewer than 800 amendments to the bill that utterly transformed it into a high-tariff bill, the Payne–Aldrich Tariff Act. On most important commodities, the Payne–Aldrich tariff was higher than the Dingley Tariff it was supposed to have reformed.

Taft was in a bind. He had called for lower duties, but he was more comfortable with Aldrich and the five corporation lawyers in his cabinet than he was with low-tariff Democrats and high-voltage Republican progressives like La Follette and Jonathan Dolliver of Iowa. After equivocating, Taft worked out what he thought would be an acceptable compromise. The Old Guard got their high tariff but accepted a 2 percent corporate income tax and a proposed constitutional amendment that legalized personal income taxes. (It was ratified in 1913 as the Sixteenth Amendment.) Instead of emphasizing the progressive aspects of the deal, as T. R. would have done, Taft described the Payne–Aldrich Act as "the best tariff that the Republican party ever passed."

The progressive Republicans were angry, but they broke openly with Taft only when he sided with House Speaker Cannon against them. Moralistic, even priggish as many of them were, they detested Cannon for his tobacco chewing, frequent public drunkenness, and foul mouth. Worse, Cannon used his power as Speaker to keep progressive Republican representatives off important committees. In a vote on rules that was usually on strict party lines, Republican "**Insurgents**" voted with the Democrats to strip Cannon of his powers.

Taft found Cannon's company as repellent as the Insurgents did. But he was a party man. In 1910 he denied the Insurgents access to party campaign funds.

Putting Rockefeller in His Place

John D. Rockefeller was informed that the Justice Department had busted the Standard Oil trust when he was playing golf with a Catholic priest. He advised the priest to put any savings he had into Standard stock. It was good advice. The breakup of the trust multiplied Rockefeller's fortune, already the biggest in the nation, several times. Between January and October 1912, shares in the companies carved out of the trust rose from 360 to 595 (Standard of New Jersey, now Exxon); 260 to 580 (Standard of New York, now Mobil), and 3,500 to 9,500 (Standard of Indiana, now Amoco).

TEDDY RETURNS

Former president Roosevelt was abroad during Taft's troubles. Shortly after Taft's inauguration, to give his successor an opportunity to function outside his aura, Roosevelt had gone to east Africa, where he shot a bloody swath through the abundant big game of Kenya and Tanganyika (Tanzania). He bagged over 3,000 animals, some of which he had stuffed to give his home at Oyster Bay, Long Island, that certain something. He then went to Europe to bask in an adulation that was scarcely less fierce than he enjoyed at home. He hobnobbed with aristocrats and politicians who thought of him as the ultimate American, a twentieth-century Ben Franklin. Roosevelt topped off his long junket by representing Taft at the funeral of Britain's King Edward VII, strutting and shining even amidst the largest collection of royalty ever assembled in one place.

In Italy, Roosevelt was visited by a fuming Gifford Pinchot. As Chief Forester, Pinchot had protested to Taft when Secretary of the Interior Richard Ballinger released to private developers several hydroelectric sites Roosevelt had reserved. Taft backed him, but when Pinchot leaked the story to *Collier's* magazine, which was still in the muckraking business, Taft fired him. When Roosevelt returned to the United States in June 1910, he exchanged only the curtest greetings with the president. He gave speeches on behalf of Republican congressional candidates, at first playing down the split between Old Guard and Insurgents. Then, at Osawatomie, Kansas, in September 1910, Roosevelt proclaimed what he called the **New Nationalism,** a comprehensive program for further reform.

Roosevelt called for woman suffrage, a federal minimum wage for female workers, abolition of child labor, strict limitations on the power of courts to issue injunctions in labor disputes, and a national social insurance scheme much like the Social Security system today. Simply proposing a national program as if he were the president addressing Congress was an insult to Taft. Roosevelt went further when he demanded that a commission set tariff rates "scientifically," a direct attack on the president. Roosevelt hinted that he was interested in running for the presidency again.

CHALLENGING TAFT

Roosevelt's presidential ambitions were disturbing news to Robert La Follette. He was himself preparing to challenge Taft for the Republican nomination in 1912. La Follette sent mutual friends to ask Roosevelt his intentions, implying that he would drop out if T. R. was running. Roosevelt responded that he was not interested in the White House. In January 1912 La Follette organized the Progressive Republican League to promote his candidacy.

Most progressive Republicans supported La Follette, including Roosevelt backers who not so secretly hoped that their real hero would change his mind. In fact, Roosevelt was itching to run. When, in March 1912, La Follette collapsed from exhaustion while making a speech, Roosevelt announced with unseemly haste, "My hat is in the ring."

The Granger Collection, New York

The "trustbuster" when he was president, Roosevelt never really believed that businesses that were big were intrinsically undesirable (as Woodrow Wilson did). When he ran against Wilson and Taft in 1912, Roosevelt clearly distinguished between "good trusts" that accepted regulation and "bad trusts" that he still intended to "bust." The cartoonist's great white hunter was based on Roosevelt's well-publicized gunning expedition in east Africa, where he shot just about every living thing except bears and human beings.

La Follette was not seriously ill, and he never forgave T. R. for having, as he believed, used him as a stalking-horse. But Fighting Bob was no match for the old master when it came to stirring up party activists, and his campaign fell apart. Roosevelt swept most of the thirteen state primary elections, winning 278 convention delegates to Taft's 48 and La Follette's 36. If La Follette was beaten, however, the suddenly aroused Taft was not, and he had a powerful weapon in his arsenal.

Taft controlled the party organization. As president, he appointed people to thousands of government jobs, wedding their careers to his own success. In the Republican party, the power of the patronage was particularly important in the southern states. In the deep South, the Republican party consisted of little more than professional officeholders, including African Americans, who made decent livings as postmasters, customs collectors, agricultural agents, and the like. Although the Republicans won congressional seats in the South rarely and next to no electoral votes, the southern states sent a substantial bloc of delegates to Republican conventions. They were in Taft's pocket. Along with northern

and western party regulars, they outnumbered the delegates Roosevelt won in the primaries.

When the convention awarded 235 of 254 disputed votes to Taft, Roosevelt's supporters shouted "Fraud!" and walked out. They organized the Progressive party, or, because it was nicknamed for the battle with the Republican elephant and the Democratic donkey, the Bull Moose party. (In a backhanded reference to La Follette's allegedly poor health and Taft's obesity, Roosevelt had said that he was "as strong as a bull moose.")

DEMOCRATIC PARTY PROGRESSIVISM

In one piece, the Republican party was clearly the nation's majority party. Split into two, however, the GOP was vulnerable. The Democrats smelled victory. When their convention assembled in Baltimore, there was an abundance of would-be nominees.

Because the southern states delivered all their electoral votes to the Democratic candidate, whoever he was, the South had a virtual veto on the nomination. A candidate needed to win not a simple majority but two-thirds of the delegates. No one solidly opposed by the southern Democrats could be nominated.

In 1912 several Democratic hopefuls were southerners, so the delegates were divided. Half a dozen candidates divided the delegates among them through forty-five ballots. William Jennings Bryan, rather pathetically, hoped that the Democrats would turn to him as a compromise candidate. As a three-time loser, however, Bryan was not very attractive. When he faced that fact, he used what influence he had left to turn the convention to the southern-born governor of New Jersey, Woodrow Wilson.

A MORAL, UNBENDING MAN

Woodrow Wilson's rise in politics really was meteoric. He was a college professor who in 1902 was named president of Princeton University, the first nonminister to hold that post at the Presbyterian school.

Actually, Wilson had a lot of the Presbyterian clergyman in him. His father and both grandfathers had been ministers. So was his wife's father. He was raised to observe an unbending

Horseplay

Stern and ministerial in his public persona, the private Woodrow Wilson was rather playful. On the morning after marrying his second wife in 1915, he was seen in a White House corridor doing a dance and singing, "Oh, you beautiful doll." His daughters (by his first wife) gave no evidence that they had suffered moralistic browbeating. One of their amusements in the White House was to join tourists being shown around by guides and to make loud remarks about the homeliness and vulgarity of the president's daughters.

Calvinist morality and to be acutely sensitive to the struggle between good and evil in the world. Wilson had his light side. He was an affectionate father, an avid baseball fan, and—more unusual, because the movies were then a working-class entertainment—a film fan. In public, though, he was formal, sometimes icy.

As late as 1910, Wilson was merely an author and educator, albeit an honored one. He had transformed Princeton from an intellectually lazy finishing school for rich young men into an institution that commanded respect. But Wilson's willfulness caught up with him in the most trivial of matters. He tried to shut down Princeton's eating clubs, which were exclusive student associations much like fraternities, and clashed with the university's trustees and alumni, "old boys" ever dedicated to preserving alma mater as they remembered her.

With his academic career a disappointment, it was a godsend when New Jersey's Democratic party, then under attack for corruption, asked him, because of his upright public image, to run for governor. To everyone's surprise except Wilson's, who attributed election victories to God, he won. The upset victory made him a national figure overnight. He was less a social reformer than a good (honest) government progressive, and he set about cleaning up both the state bureaucracy and the Democratic party. Like Teddy Roosevelt in New York a decade earlier, Wilson was soon at odds with the party's bosses. They were delighted when he decided to seek the presidency. Ironically, in terms of what was to follow, he offered himself to the Democratic convention as a safe and sane middle-of-the road alternative.

THE CAMPAIGN OF 1912

Wilson's New Freedom was a decidedly less ambitious blueprint for reform than Roosevelt's New Nationalism. Wilson emphasized states' rights to the extent that he opposed the Progressive party's program as strongly as Taft did. He said that Roosevelt's proposals would mean a dangerous expansion of federal powers.

The two men differed sharply on the question of the trusts. Roosevelt had concluded that consolidation, even monopoly, was inevitable in a modern industrial society. Therefore, the federal government should supervise and even direct the operations of the big corporations in the public interest. Wilson condemned this vision as "a partnership between the government and the trusts." He believed that competition in business was still possible and desirable. The progressive government's task was to ensure free market competition by breaking up the trusts.

Taft, having exacted revenge on his former boss and hating electioneering as much as ever, practically dropped out of the campaign. More Republicans supported Roosevelt than supported the president. It would have been difficult for Wilson to lose the election. Nevertheless, he campaigned tirelessly and skillfully. Articulate, as a college professor is supposed to be, Wilson was also exciting as not all professors are. Lifelong dreams of winning public office flowered in eloquent speeches that left no doubt that the schoolmaster was a leader.

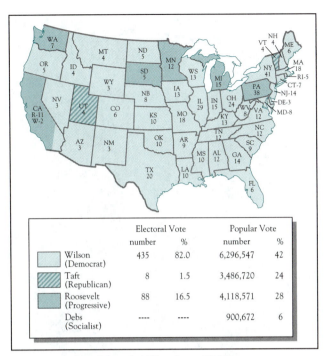

	Electoral Vote		Popular Vote	
	number	%	number	%
Wilson (Democrat)	435	82.0	6,296,547	42
Taft (Republican)	8	1.5	3,486,720	24
Roosevelt (Progressive)	88	16.5	4,118,571	28
Debs (Socialist)	----	----	900,672	6

MAP 36:1 Presidential Election, 1912
Woodrow Wilson won only 42 percent of the popular vote in 1912. Only in the four-candidate elections of 1824 and 1860 was a president elected with a smaller share. The Republican party was still the majority party it had been since 1896. By splitting in two, however, the Republicans handed the election to the minority Democrats.

Wilson won only 41.9 percent of the popular vote but a landslide in the electoral college, 435 votes to Roosevelt's 88 and Taft's 8. Eugene V. Debs, making his fourth race as the Socialist party nominee, won 900,000 votes, 6 percent of the total. The big jump after four years of a conservative president lent credence to the progressive claim that only a reformer president could stifle the socialist challenge.

TARIFFS, TAXES, AND TRUSTS

Wilson was an Anglophile. As president of Princeton, he vacationed in Great Britain almost every summer. He admired the British and Canadian parliamentary system in which the head of government, the prime minister, is a member of Parliament. He could not alter America's constitutional separation of powers, but he did the next best thing. For the first time in a century, a president addressed Congress in person.

Wilson's brief address was aimed less at persuading congressmen than at inspiring their constituents to put the heat on them, and it worked. A number of Democratic senators who were dragging their feet on tariff revision fell into line. The Underwood–Simmons Tariff reduced the Payne–Aldrich rates by 15 percent and put iron, steel, woolens, and farm machinery on the free list.

A lower tariff meant reduced revenue. To make up the loss, Wilson sponsored both a corporate and a personal income tax. The personal tax was not high by present standards. People who earned less than $4,000 a year (a good middle-class

Culver Pictures

When Woodrow Wilson ran for president in 1912, his "New Freedom" was not so coherent or systematic as Theodore Roosevelt's "New Freedom." He was, in fact, an anticorruption "good government" progressive, as this admiring cartoonist seems to have understood. The righteous civilian behind patrolman Wilson is William Jennings Bryan, who tipped the 1912 nomination to Wilson.

income) paid nothing. On annual incomes between $4,000 and $20,000, a tidy sum in 1913, the rate was only 1 percent. People in the highest bracket, $500,000 and up, paid only 7 percent.

In 1914 Congress enacted antitrust legislation that was half New Freedom, half New Nationalism. The Clayton Antitrust Act fined corporations for business practices that stifled competition. It forbade interlocking directorates (the same men sitting on the boards of competing companies and coordinating policies) and declared that officers of corporations would be held personally responsible for offenses committed by their companies. Congress also created the Federal Trade Commission to supervise the activities of the trusts.

THE FEDERAL RESERVE SYSTEM

The Federal Reserve Act of 1913 was designed to hobble the power of Wall Street by giving the federal government a say in banking. The law established twelve regional Federal Reserve Banks, which dealt not directly with people but with other banks. The **Federal Reserve System** was owned by private bankers, who were required to deposit 6 percent of their capital in it. However, the president appointed the majority of the directors, who sat in Washington, theoretically putting the government in control of the money supply.

The greatest power of the Federal Reserve System was its control of the discount rate: the level of interest at which money is lent to other banks for lending to private investors and buyers. By lowering the discount rate, the Federal Reserve Board could stimulate investment and economic expansion in slow times. By raising the rate, the Federal Reserve could cool down an overactive economy that threatened to blow up in inflation and financial panic.

The Federal Reserve System did more systematically and openly what the notorious J. P. Morgan had done in several dramatic incidents. (Morgan died in 1913.) But it did not hobble powerful banks like the House of Morgan. Representatives of the big private New York banks sat on the Federal Reserve Board. Nevertheless, the system, still in place today, held the great banks accountable. There would never again be a J. P. Morgan, a single man with such immense financial power that the government had to go to him to put the lid on crises.

WILSON CHANGES DIRECTION

The Democrats retained majorities in House and Senate after the congressional elections of 1914, but many Bull Moosers who had lost their seats in the House in the Republican party split in 1912 regained them as Republicans. It was obvious to the president and Democratic strategists that if the president was to survive the election of 1916 against a reunited Republican party, the Democrats had to woo progressives who had voted for Teddy Roosevelt in 1912.

To do so, Wilson backed New Nationalist social legislation that he had warned against in 1912 and, in fact, as late as 1914. He did not like laws that favored special interest groups, farmers any more than bankers. However, to win support in the Midwest, where progressive Republicans were strongest, he agreed to the Federal Farm Loan Act of 1916, which provided low-cost credit to farmers. Early in his administration, Wilson had opposed a child labor law on constitutional grounds. In 1916 he signed the Keating–Owen Act, which severely restricted the employment of children in most jobs.

The Adamson Act required that railroads put their workers on an eight-hour day with no reduction in pay. Wilson even moderated his approval of Jim Crow legislation, although, during his first years as president, Washington took on the racial character of a southern city that it had not had during the long era of Republican supremacy. Despite his lifelong opposition to woman suffrage, the president began to encourage the states to enfranchise women; he hinted that he would support a constitutional amendment that would guarantee that right nationwide.

Wilson, anticipating that Theodore Roosevelt might well win the 1916 Republican nomination with no Republican incumbent able to use patronage against him, had co-opted much of T. R.'s New Nationalism. It is impossible to say how effective his change of direction would have been in 1916 because, by the summer of that year, domestic reform was no longer the issue on voters' minds. Simultaneously with the enactment of Wilson's reforms, the great powers of Europe had tumbled into the bloodiest war in history. Theodore Roosevelt was still Wilson's great rival—the two men despised one another personally—but T. R. was a war hawk while Wilson, reluctantly in 1916, was the candidate pledged to keeping the United States out of the conflict.

FURTHER READING

General John W. Chambers, *The Tyranny of Change: America in the Progressive Era*, 1980; John M. Cooper, *The Pivotal Decades: The United States 1900–1920*, 1990; Robert M. Crumden, *Ministers of Reform: The Progressive Achievement in American Civilization, 1880–1930*, 1983; Alan Dawley, *Struggles for Justice: Social Responsibility and the Liberal State*, 1991; Steven J. Diner, *A Very Different Age: Americans of the Progressive Era*, 1998; Michael McGerr, *A Fierce Discontent: The Rise and Fall of the Progressive Movement in America, 1870–1920*, 2003; Nell Irvin Painter, *Standing at Armageddon: The United States, 1877–1919*, 1987.

Reforms James T. Kloppenberg, *Uncertain Victory: Social Democracy and Progressivism in European and American Thought, 1870–1920*, 1986; James Harvey Young, *Pure Food: Securing the Federal Food and Drugs Act of 1906*, 1989; Oliver Zunz, *Making America Corporate, 1870–1980*, 1990.

Republicans D. F. Anderson, *William Howard Taft: A Conservative's Conception of the Presidency*, 1973; Paolo E. Coletta, *The Presidency of William Howard Taft*, 1973; Char Miller, *Gifford Pinchot and the Making of Modern Environmentalism*, 2001; Nathan Miller, *Theodore Roosevelt: A Life*, 1992; Edmund Morris, *Theodore Rex*, 2001; Nancy Unger, *Fighting Bob La Follette: The Righteous Reformer*, 2000.

Woodrow Wilson Lloyd E. Ambrosius, *Woodrow Wilson and Wilsonian Statecraft*, 1991; Klement L. Clements, *The Presidency of Woodrow Wilson*, 1992; Ronald M. Saunders, *In Search of Woodrow Wilson: Beliefs and Behavior*, 1998.

KEY TERMS

The following terms are covered in this chapter and can also be found in the list of Key Terms at the back of the book.

Federal Reserve System	**John Mitchell**	**Mann Act**	**Northern Securities Case**
Insurgents	**John Muir**	**New Nationalism**	**William Howard Taft**

ONLINE SOURCES GUIDE

Use this listing to find online documents, images, interactive maps, simulations, and other resources related to this chapter:

American History Resource Center
http://history.wadsworth.com/rc/us

Selected Documents
Woodrow Wilson's "The New Freedom"

Selected Images
Disassembly line, Chicago meatpacking plant
William Howard Taft on horseback
Woodrow Wilson, 1912

Interactive Time Line (with online readings)
Standing at Armageddon: The Progressives in Power
1901–1916

CHAPTER 37

Over There

The United States and the First World War 1914–1918

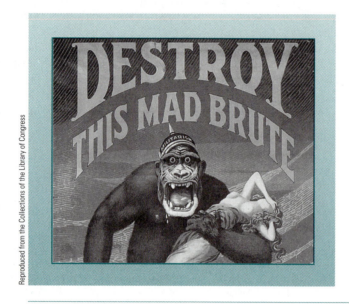

Good Lord! You're not going to send soldiers over there, are you?
Senator Thomas S. Martin

The world must be made safe for democracy. Its peace must be planted upon the tested foundations of political liberty. We have no selfish ends to serve. We desire no conquest, no dominion. We seek no indemnities for ourselves, no material compensation for the sacrifices we shall freely make.

President Woodrow Wilson

A few days before Wilson's inauguration in 1913, an aide reminded him of some difficulties in relations with Mexico. Wilson remarked, "It would be the irony of fate if my administration had to deal chiefly with foreign affairs."

Wilson did not fear the challenge of foreign policy. His self-confidence was sturdy enough to cover it and a great deal more. He once said, "I am sorry for those who disagree with me, because I know they are wrong." But his academic and political interests had been domestic; he had never paid much attention to the snarls of international relations. When the Woodrow Wilson of 1913 thought about the rest of the world, he did so in the context of his personal assumptions and sentiments, not as an expert after long study.

WILSON, THE WORLD, AND MEXICO

Like most Americans, the president was proud that in population and industrial might, the United States ranked with a handful of countries as a great nation. Also like others, he believed that the United States was unique: Insulated by broad oceans, the United States needed no large standing army. Spared that expense, America expended its wealth in constructive ways. Founded on an idea rather than because of an accidental inheritance of a common culture and territory, the United States could act toward other countries in accordance with principles rather than out of narrow self-interest.

MORAL DIPLOMACY

Wilson had criticized Teddy Roosevelt's gunboat diplomacy as bullying. He pointedly announced that his administration would deal with the weak and turbulent Latin American countries "upon terms of equality and honor." As a progressive who was suspicious of Wall Street, Wilson disapproved of Taft's dollar diplomacy. Shortly after taking office, Wilson canceled government backing of an investment scheme in China because it implied that the United States had an obligation to intervene if the investors' money was threatened. If Wall Street wanted to risk money in China, fine; but Wall Street would have to risk it without expecting the government to insure it against losses.

Wilson was influenced by the same inclinations to Christian pacifism to which Secretary of State Bryan was strongly committed. Bryan believed that war was justified only in self-defense; if nations seriously discussed their conflicts, they could avoid spilling blood. With Wilson's approval, Bryan negotiated conciliation treaties with thirty nations. The signatories pledged that in the event of a dispute, they would talk for one year before considering war. Bryan believed that during such a "cooling-off" period, virtually every conflict between nations could be resolved without turning to force.

THE MISSIONARY

Once in the cockpit, Wilson found that applying high ideals was more difficult than flying the recently invented airplane. In part, this was because of the eternal untidiness of reality. It was also because Wilson was the creature of assumptions and prejudices that conflicted with his moral and political principles.

A southerner, Wilson reflexively assumed that the white race was superior to others. He was no redneck apt to join a lynch mob. Wilson was of the southern social class that abominated the brutalities of "white trash." Wilson's attitudes toward African Americans were kindly but patronizing; he was confident that social segregation and the exclusion of blacks from government were the only ways of maintaining racial peace. The academic world in which he had spent his adult life was permeated with pseudoscience that taught Caucasian superiority. As president, Wilson found it easy to be courteous with racially mixed Latin American nations, but difficult to think of them as his equals.

His commitment to diplomacy by good example was complicated by a missionary's impulse to prescribe proper behavior. When weaker nations did not willingly emulate American ways of doing things, Wilson could wax arrogant. If other people did not recognize what was best for them,

MAP 37:1 The Mexican Expedition

Both the navy's attempted occupation of Vera Cruz in 1914 and the army's search for Pancho Villa in northern Mexico in 1916 ended in failure and frustration.

teacher could reach for the hickory stick. He was not so vulgar as T. R. about chastising naughtiness, but he was not so different from him as both men believed. In 1915 Wilson ordered the marines into black Haiti when chaotic conditions erupted there. The next year, he sent troops to the Dominican Republic.

¡VIVA MADERO! ¡VIVA HUERTA! ¡VIVA CARRANZA!

In 1911 the Mexican dictator for thirty-five years, Porfirio Díaz, was overthrown. British and American investors, whom Díaz had favored, were worried. The leader of the revolution, Francisco Madero, had spoken of returning control of Mexican resources to Mexicans. Americans owned $2 billion in property in Mexico: most of the country's railroads, 60 percent of the oil wells, and more mines than Mexicans owned. About 50,000 Americans lived more or less permanently in Mexico.

Madero and Wilson might have been able to talk. Both were well-educated classic nineteenth-century liberals. They never had the chance. Quietly encouraged by American diplomats appointed by Taft, a group of generals led by the hard-drinking, no-nonsense Victoriano Huerta staged a coup shortly before Wilson was inaugurated. Madero was murdered.

Wilson announced that he would not deal with "a government of butchers" and successfully persuaded Britain to withdraw its hasty recognition of the Huerta regime. When peasants rebelled in several parts of Mexico and a Constitutionalist army took shape behind a somber, long-bearded aristocrat, Venustiano Carranza, Wilson openly approved.

Then, in April 1914, the United States intervened directly in Mexico's civil war. Seven American sailors on shore leave in Tampico were arrested by one of Huerta's colonels. He freed them almost immediately—Huerta, an old Díaz man, wanted no trouble with the gringos—but he refused the rather excessive demand of Admiral Henry T. Mayo that he apologize by means of a twenty-one-gun salute. Claiming that American honor had been insulted (and in order to head off a German ship carrying arms to Huerta), Wilson sent troops into the Gulf port of Vera Cruz.

Pancho in Retirement

In 1920, no more able to capture Pancho Villa than Pershing had been, the Mexican government made peace with him. Villa and about 400 of his soldiers and their families were promised they would not be molested if they remained on several haciendas at La Purísima Concepción de El Canutillo in Chihuahua.

Villa was ready for such a retirement; he was too rich to be hiding in the desert. The villistas mechanized their farms and founded schools. Pancho himself became something of a health nut; he jogged. The villistas still worshipped him, but many Mexicans on whom he had preyed did not. He dared not leave the hacienda without an armed escort of fifty men. But he was assassinated just a few years after he retired.

To Wilson's surprise, hundreds of Mexican civilians joined with Huerta's soldiers to resist the Americans; 400 were killed. Wilson had failed to understand that while Huerta was not beloved, the humiliation of the Mexican War was fresh in the Mexican memory. Even Carranza, in far-off northeastern Mexico, condemned the American landing. Alarmed by the fix into which he had gotten himself, Wilson quickly agreed to an offer by Argentina, Brazil, and Chile to mediate the crisis.

¡VIVA VILLA!

Before anything could be resolved, Carranza ousted Huerta. However, there was no breather for Mexico. Carranza quarreled with one of his generals, a bizarre, charismatic character who was born Doroteo Arango but was universally known as **Pancho Villa.** Alternately jovial and sadistic, part-time bandit and part-time social revolutionary, Villa was romanticized in the American press by a young journalist, John Reed, as "The Robin Hood of Mexico." Villa relished the celebrity and played for American approval. For a time, Wilson believed that Villa represented democracy in Mexico.

Nonetheless, Wilson opted for stability. When Carranza's army marched into Mexico City in October 1915, Wilson recognized his de facto control of the government. This

Neutrality and War 1910–1919

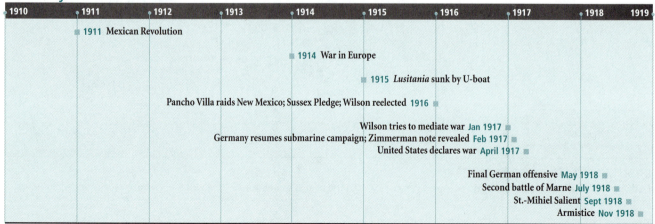

1910	1911	1912	1913	1914	1915	1916	1917	1918	1919

1911 Mexican Revolution

1914 War in Europe

1915 *Lusitania* sunk by U-boat

Pancho Villa raids New Mexico; Sussex Pledge; Wilson reelected 1916

Wilson tries to mediate war Jan 1917

Germany resumes submarine campaign; Zimmerman note revealed Feb 1917

United States declares war April 1917

Final German offensive May 1918

Second battle of Marne July 1918

St.-Mihiel Salient Sept 1918

Armistice Nov 1918

© Bettmann/Corbis

Pancho Villa (Doroteo Arango), center, was charismatic and a superb guerrilla commander. His numerous villistas were devoted to him, and he was popular in Chihuahua—not with everyone, however, because Villa preyed on Mexican villagers. His murder of American engineers and raid on Columbus, New Mexico, led to a futile intervention in Mexico by American troops.

stung Villa, and he displayed his seamier side. Calculating that American intervention would cause chaos in Mexico, thus creating an opportunity for him to seize power, Villa stopped a train carrying American engineers who had been invited by Carranza to reopen abandoned mines. He summarily shot all but one of them. Early in 1916 he dispatched raiders across the border into the dusty little desert town of Columbus, New Mexico, where, in a surrealistic shoot-'em-up, they killed seventeen people.

Carranza wanted to run Villa down, both to placate the United States and because Villa pretty much controlled the large state of Chihuahua. Instead of giving him a chance, Wilson ordered General John J. Pershing and 6,000 troops, including the African-American Tenth Cavalry, to capture the bandit general. As in Vera Cruz, the intervention was humiliating. Villa was at home in the arid mountains of northern Mexico. Ordinary Mexicans adored him or feared him; they shrugged when Pershing's officers asked them for information. Villa easily evaded the expedition, leading the American soldiers 300 miles over a zigzag route. They never caught sight of Villa's army. They did, however, aggravate the situation by exchanging fire with Carranza's troops on several occasions. In one skirmish forty were killed. Partly out of ignorance and partly out of arrogance, Wilson had alienated every political faction in Mexico.

In January 1917 he called "Black Jack" Pershing home, not so much because of his failure in Mexico, but because the United States was now facing a showdown with a more formidable enemy than Pancho Villa, the German Empire.

THE GREAT WAR

By 1917 Europe had been at war for two and a half years. In June 1914 a Serbian nationalist had assassinated Archduke Franz Ferdinand, the heir to the Emperor of Austria–Hungary. The issue (Serbia and Austria–Hungary had been at odds for thirty years) was Bosnia–Herzegovina, mostly Serbian in population but incorporated into Austria–Hungary a few years earlier.

At first it appeared that the incident would pass with expressions of grief and wrath. Franz Ferdinand's murder was not the first act of terrorism by a Serbian, and there was no conclusive proof that the Serbian government had sponsored the killer. Moreover, Europe had seen an epidemic of sensational assassinations during the previous decades; they were almost routine. At worst, European diplomats thought (or hoped) there would be another localized Balkan war—yet another familiar phenomenon—between little Serbia and Austria–Hungary, which was a plenty big country but a second-rate military power.

Those hopes were dashed because of a web of mutual obligations that the great powers of Europe had written into secret treaties with one another; the pathetically weak character of the Russian czar, Nicholas II; the irresponsibility of the German Kaiser, Wilhelm II; and a frenzied arms race in which Russia, Germany, and France had been engaged for a generation.

Slavic Serbia looked to the greatest Slavic country, Russia, as its protector, and the czar backed Serbia in its defiance of

What's in a Name?

The British called it the European War. Americans were inclined to use that name until the United States intervened in April 1917. Then a few elegant but awkward tags were floated: War for the Freedom of Europe, War for the Overthrow of Militarism, War for Civilization, and, best known, Wilson's War to Make the World Safe for Democracy. Only after it was over did Great War and World War become standard—until 1939, when the outbreak of another worldwide war made it World War I.

Austria. A decaying Austria–Hungary looked to Germany for support; instead of urging restraint, the Kaiser permitted Austria to present Serbia with an ultimatum that Serbia could not possibly accept short of giving up part of its sovereignty. The czar, who regarded himself as the "little father" of all Slavs, assured Serbia that it would not stand alone. France, all its political parties sworn to avenge the country's defeat by Germany in 1871, was drawn into what was shaping up to be a major war by secret agreements promising support to Russia in the event of war against Germany. Even Britain, traditionally aloof from European entanglements, had been so frightened by Germany's construction of a worldwide navy—second in size only to Britain's—that the nation had signed agreements with both France and Russia.

Bulgaria and Turkey were associated with the "**Central Powers**" (Germany, Austria–Hungary, and Italy), and the "Allies" (England, France, Russia, and eventually Italy, which switched sides) had ties with Rumania as well as Serbia. By August 1914 much of Europe was at war. Eventually thirty-three nations would be involved.

AMERICANS REACT

Americans reacted to the explosion with a mixture of disbelief and disgust. "This dreadful conflict of the nations came to most of us as lightning out of a clear day," a congressman said. For a generation, Americans had paid little attention to European saber rattling; their own Teddy Roosevelt was himself a blusterer with a military strut. But T. R. had, in a pinch, understood the difference between a bully display and actions that led to catastrophe. Until 1914, so had the Europeans. Even Kaiser Wilhelm, a widely ridiculed figure because of the extravagant uniforms he fancied, his gleaming spiked helmets embellished with gold and silver, and a comic-opera waxed mustache, had pulled back from war on several occasions. It was not unreasonable to assume, as Americans did, that constant threats of war without going to war would continue indefinitely. They did not believe that powerful, civilized countries would apply the twentieth century's technology to slaughtering one another by the millions.

Once the Allies and Central Powers began to do just that, Americans consoled themselves that the United States, at least, was above such savagery. They blamed Europe's tragedy on Old World corruptions, kings and princes, nationalistic hysteria, and insane stockpiling of armaments that were superfluous if they were not used and suicidal if they were.

Never did American political and social institutions look so superior. Never had Americans been more grateful to have an ocean between themselves and Europe. As reports of hideous carnage on the battlefield began to hum over the Atlantic cables, Americans shuddered and recounted their blessings. No prominent person lodged an objection when President Wilson proclaimed America's absolute neutrality. When, however, the president also called on Americans to be "neutral in fact as well as in name, . . . impartial in thought as well as in action," he was, as he was wont to do, demanding too much of human nature, even the human nature of what Wilson called "this great peaceful people."

SYMPATHY FOR THE ALLIES

For many Americans, Great Britain was their ancestral motherland. For others, their English linguistic and cultural legacy uniquely tied the United States to Britain. Wilson was an unblushing Anglophile. He wrote a book in which he praised the British parliamentary form of government. In his first year in office he resolved the last outstanding points of conflict with Great Britain: a minor border dispute in British Columbia, a quarrel between Canadian and American fishermen off Newfoundland, and British objections to discriminatory tolls on the Panama Canal.

Hardly noticed at first, the American and British financial establishments were intimately interwoven. The House of Morgan, the most powerful investment bank in the United States, had begun as a British bank; despite Wilson's open disapproval, the Morgan bank acted as the agent for British war bond sales in America. By the middle of 1915 Edward Stettinius, a Morgan partner, purchased up to $10 million worth of American goods ranging from weapons to wheat for the British government each day. By 1917 Great Britain owed Americans $2.3 billion. By comparison, the Germans had managed to borrow only a meager $27 million in the United States. Wall Street had good reason to want a British victory or, at least, to pale at the thought of a British defeat.

Some Americans felt ties to France. Francophilia had been fashionable among the wealthy in the late nineteenth century. The historically minded still called France America's "oldest friend," the indispensable ally of the Revolution. And France was, except for the United States, the only republic among the world's major powers.

SYMPATHY FOR THE CENTRAL POWERS

In 1914 one American in three was foreign-born or the child of immigrants. Many had sentimental attachments to the "old country" that made them sympathetic to Germany or Austria–Hungary or unfriendly toward Britain or Russia. Millions of Americans traced their roots to Germany; a good many of them still spoke German or preserved other aspects of German culture. Millions more had personal memories of life in the Austro–Hungarian Empire. Serbs excepted, their memories were often positive. Hungarians, Czechs, Slovaks, Slovenes, and even Jews from the German-speaking parts of Austria came to the United States for economic reasons, not because they were persecuted at home. Very few expected or

THE ROAD TO WAR SUMMER 1914

① **June 28**
Assassination at Sarajevo

② **July 28**
Austria–Hungary declares war on Serbia

③ **July 30**
Russia begins mobilization

④ **August 1**
Germany declares war on Russia

⑤ **August 3**
Germany declares war on France

⑥ **August 4**
Great Britain declares war on Germany

⑦ **August 6**
Russia and Austria–Hungary at war

⑧ **August 12**
Great Britain declares war on Austria–Hungary

Legend:
- Allied Powers and possessions, 1916
- Central Powers, 1916
- Neutral countries
- British naval blockade
- Trench line, western front, 1915
- Eastern front, 1915

MAP 37:2 The Central Powers and the Allies
Italy was tied to the Central Powers in 1914, but its obligations applied only to defensive wars. The Italian government said that Austria–Hungary and Germany were the aggressors and remained neutral. Later Italy entered the war on the Allied side.

suggested that America side with their motherland. But Anglo–American cultural attachments meant nothing to them. The National German League, with 3 million members, sponsored an active propaganda campaign touting the virtues of German culture.

Some German Americans joined with Irish Americans in the German–Irish Legislative Committee for the Furtherance of United States Neutrality. Many—by no means all—of the nation's 4.5 million people of Irish ancestry still fondly nursed their ancestral hatred of Great Britain. When the

British crushed a rebellion in Ireland in 1916, a few prominent Irish Americans declared for the German cause.

Similarly, Russian and Polish Jews had been discriminated against by the czars and, for thirty years, had suffered from brutal mob violence abetted by the authorities. Their "old country" was not beloved. Indeed, Jews from the Russian Empire often looked positively on Germany and Austria, where Jews had been granted civil equality with Christians. Socialists, a large minority in the German American community and among Jews from Eastern Europe, hated Russia above all other countries because of the viciousness of the czar's secret police.

With such a tangle of conflicting loyalties, Wilson's insistence on neutrality made sense politically. In the industrial states and the large cities, the Democratic party depended on the support of ethnic voters.

DEADLY STALEMATE

Both Allies and Central Powers expected a quick victory. Nations rushing into war always do. For German military strategists, however, facing powerful enemies in both the east and the west as Germany did, a quick decisive victory had long been thought essential. The "**Schlieffen Plan,**" developed in 1905 and repeatedly updated since, was designed to resolve the problem of waging war on two fronts—two wars, in effect. Germany had defeated France easily in 1871, but German generals respected the French army of 1914. France's weaponry was modern; the army was efficient and prepared to launch a massive attack quickly; and the French had built daunting fortifications the length of the Franco–German border.

Russia's army was huge—by far the biggest in the world—but the Germans were contemptuous of Russian officers; Russian reserves were poorly trained and often armed with out-of-date weapons. Because of the size of the country, it took many more weeks to mobilize the Russian army than it took the French. So the premise of the Schlieffen Plan was to defeat France quickly with a massive, lightning attack that (as in 1870–1871) would surround or even capture Paris, then move the victorious German troops rapidly east to meet the oncoming Russians. In the meantime, weak German forces on the eastern front would take their losses; their assignment was to delay the Russian advance, not defeat them. The fighting would take place in territory inhabited by Poles, not by

Germans. (Poland did not exist as a nation; most of the country was ruled by Russia.)

The greatest difficulty in the way of a quick defeat of France was the French fortifications. The Schlieffen Plan's solution was to invade France through neutral Belgium. Germany had signed agreements to respect Belgian neutrality, but the generals reasoned that when the existence of the German nation was at risk, treaties were "scraps of paper."

The Schlieffen Plan failed. Instead of providing an avenue into France, the Belgians mounted a resistance that stunned the German army. Just capturing the city of Liége took the Germans twelve days, longer than they expected to be fighting in Belgium. The frustrated invaders treated captured Belgian soldiers ferociously and civilians scarcely better. At the very start of the war, German soldiers earned a reputation as savage "Huns." The image influenced American public opinion profoundly.

During the fighting in Belgium, the Russians advanced deeply into German territory. That was anticipated, but the German General Staff lost its nerve. At a critical moment, the army on the western front was weakened to divert troops eastward to stop the Russians.

The Germans stopped them—dramatically. At the Battle of Tannenberg, they captured a million Russian soldiers! On the western front, however, the French stopped the German advance. The war bogged down in a stalemate that neither side had foreseen. The opposing armies dug entrenchments and heaped up earthworks on lines stretching 475 miles. Between the German and Anglo–French trenches was a "no man's land" of moonscape craters, spools of barbed wire, and the smell of death. During the nineteenth century, most European conflicts had been wars of rapid movement, quickly concluded. Stalemate was something new. Periodically for three years men on both sides hurled themselves "over the top" and died by the tens of thousands to advance their trench line a few miles.

THE NEW TECHNOLOGY OF KILLING

A revolution in military technology (and the slowness with which the generals comprehended it) made the war unspeakably bloody. Although airplanes, their pilots, and their "dogfights" captured the popular imagination, the war in the air was little more than a show. (Soldiers in the trenches considered pilots playboys, but the life expectancy of British

British Hero

Had Americans merged into the British army, they would have been commanded by General Douglas Haig. It is a wonder that Haig rose so high—he had been a one-man disaster in the Boer War—and incomprehensible that he remained in charge. Haig called the machine gun "a much overrated weapon" even after the Germans mowed down his soldiers by the tens of thousands per hour in the catastrophic offensives he ordered on the Somme in 1916 and at Ypres in 1917.

"The role of the cavalry on the battlefield," Haig said, "will always go on increasing." The horses knew better even if they did not understand Haig when he said, "Bullets have little stopping power against a horse." (Seven thousand horses—draft horses, not chargers—were killed at

Ypres.) How Haig reconciled his absurdity with the fact that there was not a single major cavalry action in World War I is a mystery.

Great Britain honored General Haig for his wisdom and brilliant offensives by ennobling him as an earl and erecting a statue of him in Whitehall. Had Americans served under Haig, the United States could have had statues of him too.

pilots at the front was two weeks, and not much longer for French and German airmen.)

Nor was poison gas, another new weapon, decisive. Its victims suffered horribly. When the Germans bombarded three miles of Allied trenches at Ypres in Belgium in April 1915, 5,000 soldiers were killed, and another 10,000 suffered permanently damaged lungs. But gas was an unreliable weapon; a shift in the wind blew the toxic fumes back on the army that had loosed the attack. Moreover, effective gas masks were soon issued to troops on both sides. At the end of the war, it was calculated that gas was responsible for 1.3 million casualties, but at the expense of firing 66 million shells.

The **machine gun,** by way of contrast, became the symbol of the war. It made the nineteenth-century infantry assault an exercise in mass suicide. When soldiers went "over the top," they were mowed down by hurricanes of lead from enemy machine gun nests. A two-man machine gun crew had the firepower of a hundred men with rifles. On the first day of the Battle of the Somme in July 1916, 60,000 British soldiers were killed or wounded, a majority of them during the battle's first half hour. By the time the Somme campaign sputtered to an end, with nothing gained, British losses were 400,000, French losses 200,000. The Germans lost 500,000 men. The machine gun, more than any other factor, made the war a static, defensive stalemate.

The British developed the tank to neutralize German machine guns. The armored vehicles, on treads to cross land pocked with deep craters, could be driven unharmed directly at machine gun emplacements. But the British generals rarely used their edge to full advantage. They attached tanks to infantry units, which slowed them to a walk; and until the tanks destroyed enemy machine guns, the advancing infantry suffered the usual horrendous losses. Only late in the war was it recognized that tanks were most effective when they advanced ahead of foot soldiers, in groups. Only after the war did military tacticians develop effective techniques of tank warfare.

THE WAR AT SEA

The casualty lists sickened Americans, but it was the war at sea that touched national interests. As always, naval warfare was economic warfare, aimed at destroying the enemy's commerce and thereby the enemy's capacity to carry on the fight. The British, with naval superiority, immediately proclaimed a blockade of Germany.

According to the rules of war, enemy merchant ships were fair game, although tradition required that the crews of sinking ships be rescued. The ships of neutral nations had the right to trade with any nation so long as they did not carry contraband (defined at the start of the war as munitions).

The rules of blockade were more complicated, and the British introduced several new wrinkles. In addition to warships patrolling trade routes leading to Germany, the Royal Navy mined parts of the North Sea. Ships, including neutral ships, risked destruction by entering mine fields. Britain also redefined contraband to include almost all trade goods, including some foodstuffs. When neutral Holland, Denmark, and Sweden began to import goods for secret resale to Germany (pastoral Denmark, which had never purchased American lard, imported 11,000 tons of it in the first months of the war), the British slapped strict regulations on trade with those countries.

American objections were mild. The German market was never important to the United States, let alone the Danish market. Wartime sales to Britain and France rose so sharply that few exporters needed to do business with Germany, particularly if it meant sending ships into minefields. American trade with the Allies climbed from $825 million in 1914 to $3.2 billion in 1916, a fourfold increase in two years.

So long as quick victory on land was on the table, Germany was indifferent to the British blockade. Its agricultural base was adequate for the army's and the country's basic needs. When the war stalemated, however, the General Staff recognized the necessity of throttling Britain's economy, which was vitally dependent on imports, including much of the food needed to keep the population from starving. Germany's tool was another recent creation of military technology: the Unterseeboot (undersea boat, or U-boat)—the submarine.

SUBMARINE WARFARE

The modern submarine was the invention of an American, John P. Holland. (All four of the developers of the machine gun were American.) When the U.S. Navy rejected his device, Holland took it to Germany. The Germans recognized the submarine's potential to destroy merchant ships; but emphasizing their land forces, they had only twenty-five submarines ready at the start of the war. By February 1915, however, Germany's flotilla of U-boats, each armed with nineteen torpedoes, was large enough that the waters

Code Breaking

Another technology new to war was radio. Its usefulness as a means of communication was limited by the fact that radioed messages could be heard by the enemy too. This was a disadvantage to the Germans on the western front because they relied heavily on radio. The French and British had good communications by telegraph. When the French retreated in 1914, they destroyed the telegraph lines in the territory the Germans were occupying.

German radio messages were coded, but the French were masters in deciphering them. The British had broken the German diplomatic code when, in early 1917, they intercepted the Zimmerman telegram that invited Mexico to attack the United States as a German ally. The message was sent from Sweden on a cable that touched land on Great Britain and was tapped. The Zimmerman telegram also passed through Washington, where, at the German embassy, a few changes were made. There the British intercepted it a second time. They gave Wilson the version that was altered in Washington so the Germans would not know the British were reading their diplomatic dispatches in Europe.

© Bettmann-UPI/Corbis

U-Boat 15, *a first-generation German submarine. When the fleet numbered a hundred at the end of 1916, the German General Staff believed that submarines could starve Britain out of the war before the United States could send enough soldiers to Europe to make a difference.*

surrounding the British Isles could be proclaimed a war zone. All enemy merchant ships within those waters were to be sunk, and the safety of neutral ships could not be absolutely guaranteed. Within days, several British vessels went to the bottom. President Wilson warned the Kaiser that he would hold Germany to "strict accountability" for American lives and property lost to U-boats.

Some Britons and Americans criticized submarine warfare as peculiarly inhumane because U-boats did not save the crews of the ships they sank. This was true enough. On the surface, submarines were helpless. A light six-inch gun mounted on the bow of a freighter was enough to sink one. The first generation of submarines were slow in diving; British merchant vessels could ram them. Therefore, German submarine commanders had no choice but to strike without warning, giving crew and passengers of target vessels no opportunity to evacuate the ship, as an enemy warship could do. Since submarines were tiny, their crews cramped, there was no room to take aboard people who abandoned a ship when it began to sink. Survivors of torpedoed vessels were on their own in the midst of the ocean.

Many Americans grumbled that if the British blockade was illegal, the German submarine campaign was immoral. The British were thieves, but the Germans were murderers,

drowning seamen by the hundreds—and not only seamen. On May 7, 1915, the English luxury liner *Lusitania* was torpedoed off the coast of Ireland; 1,198 people of the 1,959 passengers aboard were killed, including 139 Americans. What kind of war was this, Americans asked, that killed innocent travelers? *The New York Times* described the Germans as "savages drenched with blood."

WILSON WINS A VICTORY

The Germans replied that they had warned Americans specifically against traveling on the *Lusitania* in advertisements in New York and Washington newspapers. They pointed out that the ship was carrying 4,200 cases of small arms purchased in the United States and some high explosives—contraband. So many people were lost because the *Lusitania* went down in a mere eighteen minutes, blown wide open not by the torpedo but by a secondary explosion. The British, the Germans said, were hiding war materiel behind a shield of innocent passengers.

Wilson sent Germany several strongly worded memoranda. The second was so antagonistic that the pacifistic Bryan feared it would mean war. He resigned rather than sign it. Wilson replaced him in the State Department with Robert Lansing, an international lawyer.

George Stephenson put the first locomotive on rails because running on a road required more power than his steam engine could generate; more powerful engines were so heavy that they would tip over a carriage because of the potholes that marked the best macadam highways. It was not long, however, before tinkerers were experimenting with self-propelled vehicles that could run on roads. In 1867 an American, Richard Dudgeon, built a steam carriage to move people around cities. But it was dirty, noisy, and hot; it had no future competing with horse car lines.

One problem facing the automobile (self-moving vehicle) dozens of inventors imagined was the roughness of roads and even many city streets. The "ride" on rigid wagon wheels was too rough for complex engines, whether they were powered by steam or the experimental internal combustion engine that ran on gasoline. The bicycle mania of the 1880s and 1890s partially solved the problem. Bicyclists successfully lobbied to have city streets and many country roads paved with concrete or "blacktop." In 1888 an Irishman invented the pneumatic (inflated) rubber tire, which gave bikes a safer, more comfortable ride

From the Collections of Henry Ford Museum & Greenfield Village

and created the possibility of mounting an engine on a "horseless carriage." Rather good steam-powered cars were developed and sold by the Locomobile and Stanley companies. After the perfection of the storage battery in 1892, electric cars hit the streets. Both steam and electric cars were produced into the 1920s, but they never really competed with automobiles powered by internal combustion engines fueled by gasoline.

In 1900 thirty competing American companies manufactured 8,000 cars. They were quite expensive; only the wealthy and fanatics willing to spend more than they could afford bought them and made nuisances of themselves racing around, running down dogs, and frightening horses. Carmakers competed for attention in races on tracks and endurance drives over hundreds of miles, happily reported by newspapers hungry for colorful stories.

Henry Ford, a self-taught engineer who worked for Thomas Edison in Detroit, was the major figure in transforming the automobile from a plaything of the rich and an instrument of entertainment into convenience (eventually a near-necessity) that all but the poor could afford to buy. Ford built his first automobile in 1896. A mechanical genius, he constantly improved his designs and moved into manufacturing. From early on, it was Ford's idea to

"build a car for the great multitude," a starkly basic, easy-to-drive vehicle assembled by mass production techniques in quantities so large that the selling price would be within the reach of almost everyone. That car was the Model T, which made its debut in 1908. It had a four-cylinder, twenty-horsepower engine and a two-speed (plus reverse) planetary transmission operated by pedals (so there was no gear grinding), and it sat high off the ground on wheels three feet in diameter. It cleared obstacles that brought other cars to a halt with a dismaying metallic crunch.

The first Model T Ford cost $825. That was not peanuts in 1908, but it was less than every other carmaker charged. Ford sold 10,000 Model Ts the first year. The Model T was dubbed the "tin lizzie" and the "flivver" because it looked flimsy. In fact, it was the toughest car in the country. Its body was made of a vanadium–steel alloy with a tensile strength of 170,000 pounds compared to the 60,000 pound strength of the steel in other American cars. (It took other manufacturers five years to adopt Ford's alloy.) In 1909, in a New York to Seattle race, only two cars finished, both Model T's.

Ford made comparatively few changes in the Model T each year. However, with his eye on increasing production and lowering the price, he perfected the assembly line on which the cars were made, reducing each of the hundreds of operations required to build so complex a machine to simple, repetitive tasks performed quickly by workers standing in one place. The parts each man attached were brought to them by a finely orchestrated conveyor operation. In 1910 Ford made and sold 19,000 Model Ts; in 1912 that figure was 78,440. The year 1914 saw 260,720 Model Ts roll off the assembly line—half of all the cars made in the United States that year. There was a new Model T every couple of minutes. The price of the car dropped almost annually, bottoming out at $290, which was peanuts. When, after nineteen years, the Model T was discontinued (only the Volkswagen Beetle had a longer run), 15 million had been built.

Ford was not only very rich; he was deservedly a folk hero. As he said he would do, he "democratized" the automobile. If not "everybody" could afford a Model T, tens of millions of ordinary people could. Not many technological devices so profoundly changed how people lived in so short a time. Perhaps only television and the home computer are in a class with the tin lizzie.

While making no formal promises, the Germans stopped attacking passenger vessels, and the *Lusitania* uproar faded. Then, early in 1916, the Allies announced that they were arming all merchant ships, and Germany responded that the U-boats would sink all enemy vessels without warning: it was **"unrestricted submarine warfare."** On March 24, 1916, a sitting duck, the *Sussex*, a French channel steamer on a scheduled run between Dieppe and Folkestone, went down with an American among the casualties. Wilson threatened to break diplomatic relations with Germany, then considered a prelude to a declaration of war, if unrestricted submarine warfare were continued.

The German General Staff did not want the United States in the war. Plans for a major offensive were afoot, and the German navy did not have enough U-boats to sustain a full-scale attack on British shipping. In the Sussex Pledge of May 4, 1916, the Germans promised to observe the rules of visit and search before attacking enemy ships. This meant abandoning the submarine's effectiveness, but it kept the United States at home, which at the time was the whole idea.

AMERICA GOES TO WAR

Wilson had won a spectacular diplomatic victory at the beginning of his campaign for reelection. He was enthusiastically renominated at the Democratic convention, and his campaign was given a theme that did not entirely please him. The keynote speaker, New York Governor Martin Glynn, built his speech around the slogan "He Kept Us Out of War." Wilson did not like the slogan because, as he confided to an aide, "I can't keep the country out of war. Any little German lieutenant can put us into war at any time by some calculated outrage." He meant that a submarine commander, acting quite on his own, could bark out the order that would torpedo the Sussex Pledge. Like many national leaders before and since, Wilson had trapped himself in a position where control of a momentous decision was out of his hands.

Wilson had begun to prepare for the possibility of war as early as November 1915, when he asked Congress to beef up the army to 400,000 men and to fund a huge expansion of the navy. To some extent, he was pushed into "preparedness" by his political enemy, Theodore Roosevelt. T. R. jabbed and poked at the fact that the army totaled 108,000 men, ranking it seventeenth in the world; that the Quartermaster Corps (supply) had only recently begun using trucks; and that at one point in 1915 the American artillery had enough ammunition for only two days' fighting—with cannons that were obsolete.

On the other side, Wilson had to contend with pacifists. Henry Ford chartered a ship to sail to Europe to seek peace. Feminists Jane Addams, Carrie Chapman Catt, and Charlotte Perkins Gilman formed the Women's Peace Party and attended a pacifist conference in the Netherlands. There were dozens of similar groups.

Much more worrying was an antipreparedness faction in Congress led by Representative Claude Kitchin of North Carolina. With widespread backing among western progressives, on whom Wilson generally depended for support, Kitchin pointed out that it had been Europe's preparedness that plunged the continent into war in the first place. If the United States had the means to fight in the war, it was all the more likely that the United States would enter the war. Wilson had to settle for a compromise: less of a military buildup than the interventionists wanted, but more than Kitchin and his supporters liked.

THE ELECTION OF 1916

The Progressive party nominated Teddy Roosevelt, but, his enthusiasm of 1912 having passed, he wanted the Republican nomination too. When he realized that Republican conservatives wanted nothing to do with him, he insulted the Bull Moosers by supporting his personal friend, Senator Henry Cabot Lodge of Massachusetts, for the Republican and Progressive nominations. Lodge was warlike enough, but he was virtually a reactionary on economic and social questions. Even the Republican conservatives knew better than to nominate Lodge. They settled on Supreme Court Justice Charles Evans Hughes. He had been a moderately progressive governor of New York, but he was not a loose cannon like T. R. Roosevelt dropped out of the race. William Allen White wrote that the Progressives were "all dressed up with nowhere to go." In fact, Progressive voters were to go to both the Republicans and the Democrats, depending on their position on intervention.

Hughes's integrity was unimpeachable. In dignity and bearing, he was Wilson's match. He was not so eloquent as the president, but he spoke in high-sounding phrases. Hughes's weakness as a candidate was the fact that his views on the war differed little from Wilson's. Like the president, he wanted to keep the United States out of it but recognized that a change in German submarine policy (or the "little German lieutenant") could drag the country into the conflict. If Hughes was personally a "me too" candidate, Theodore Roosevelt, who stormed about the country on Hughes's behalf, represented the judge as the war candidate; he described Wilson, the president who "kept us out of war," as a weakling.

These perceptions of the candidates probably cost Hughes the presidency. It was a very close race. Hughes carried every northeastern state but New Hampshire and every midwestern state but Ohio. He went to bed on election night, a Tuesday, believing he was president. Then, in the wee hours of Wednesday morning, one antiwar western state after another turned in majorities for Wilson. His electoral vote count grew in three- and four-point increments, whittling away at Hughes's lead. Not until Friday was it known for certain that Wilson had carried California by a paper-thin margin and was reelected by 277 electoral votes to Hughes's 254.

UNRESTRICTED SUBMARINE WARFARE

Elated, Wilson tried to mediate between the Allies and Central Powers. He had concluded that only by ending the war could he keep the United States out of it. During the winter of 1916–1917 he seemed to be making progress, at

The American *announces the news to New York City. Every newspaper in the country reported the declaration in banner headlines.*

least with the Germans. For a short time Wilson considered the British the major obstacle to peace.

On January 22, 1917, Wilson presented his mediation plan to Congress. Only a "peace without victory," a "peace among equals" with neither winners nor losers, could end the slaughter. But Wilson had more than a cessation of hostilities

in mind. He also meant to pledge the belligerents to the principles of national self-determination and absolute freedom of the seas and to establish an international mechanism to prevent wars in the future. It was all illusion. Wilson and the American people were in for a rude awakening. The president's proposal was only half-digested when a week later the

German ambassador informed the president that, as of February 1, Germany would resume unrestricted submarine warfare.

What happened? First, 1916 had been devastating for both the Allies and the Central Powers. A German offensive against the fortress city of Verdun cost each side more than 300,000 men. (The Germans intended the battle to be a slaughter so as to demoralize the Allies into suing for peace.) A British offensive along the River Somme killed more than a million soldiers. The German General Staff faced the fact that Germany could not win the war on the ground. However, the navy believed that its submarines could take Britain out of the war in just a few months.

The submarine fleet was up to a hundred vessels, with more under construction. With an all-out assault on British shipping, the German admirals (and generals) calculated that the British could literally be starved into capitulation. Abandoning the Sussex Pledge meant American intervention, of course. However, because the United States was far from ready for action, the Germans believed the war would be over before more than a token American army could be landed in Europe. "They will not even come," the Navy Minister informed the General Staff, "because our submarines will sink them. Thus, America from a military point of view means nothing, and again nothing, and for a third time nothing."

FAILING TO KEEP THE PEACE

Wilson broke diplomatic relations with Germany and asked Congress for authority to arm American merchant ships. When progressive Republicans La Follette, Norris, and Borah filibustered against the bill, Wilson denounced them as "a little group of willful men, representing no opinion but their own."

The president, not Theodore Roosevelt, was now the leader of the "war party." On the evening of April 2, after submarines sent three American freighters to the bottom, a solemn Wilson asked Congress for a formal declaration of war. "The right is more precious than peace," he said, "and we shall fight for the things which we have always carried nearest our hearts."

For four days a bitter debate shook the Capitol. Six senators and about fifty representatives held out against war to the end. They blamed Wilson for failing to be truly neutral; some claimed that the United States was going to spill its young men's blood in order to bail out Wall Street's loans to England and to enrich the munitions manufacturers, the "merchants of death." In the most eloquent antiwar speech, Senator George Norris of Nebraska said, "We are going into war upon the command of gold. . . . We are about to put the dollar sign on the American flag."

WHY AMERICA WENT TO WAR

In years to come, historians known as **revisionists** said that Norris had been right. With varying emphases, they agreed that special interests wanted into the war and methodically maneuvered the United States into it. To the extent that Wall

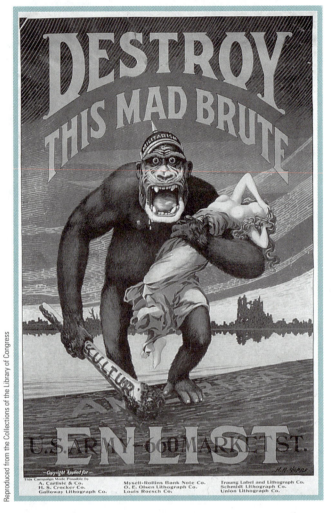

The Hun! This poster is aimed at recruiting enlistees after the United States declared war on Germany. Pro-intervention propaganda groups had been disseminating the same subhuman image of Germans for more than a year.

Street favored a British victory for the sake of its investments and that munitions makers profit from war, they were correct.

But to say that certain interest groups wanted war is not to say that they had their way with Woodrow Wilson and Congress. Wilson was as unlikely to take a cue from Wall Street and the Dupont munitions works as he was to seek Theodore Roosevelt's opinion on a point of theology. To Wilson, freedom of the seas was sacred, a right on which Americans had insisted since the 1790s. Moreover, the president shared in the profound shift in public sentiment from 1914, when virtually no American dreamed of going to war, to the spring of 1917, when the majority favored entering the conflict. The reasons for the about-face lay in the growing belief that imperial Germany represented an evil force in the world.

THE HUN AND HIS *KULTUR*

The image of Germans as barbaric Huns driven by a diabolical **Kultur** (merely the German word for "culture" but—that K!—having a sinister ring in American ears) had origins in the German violation of Belgian neutrality. Figuratively at

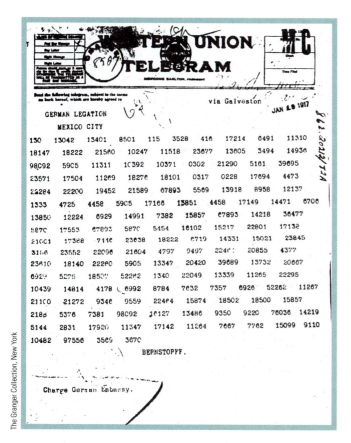

The Zimmerman telegram. It was transmitted, in code, through the same channels ordinary telegrams were sent.

first, the British and French called the invasion "the rape of Belgium" and soon discovered the propaganda value of that ugly word. In fact, the German occupation of Belgium was high-handed and harsh, although harsher than British controls in Ireland more in degree than substance. Nonetheless, wall posters depicting the broken body of an adolescent girl being dragged away by a bloated, beastlike German soldier in a spiked helmet aroused the revulsion it was designed for.

German insistence that their troops observed proprieties toward Belgian civilians was undermined in October 1915 when the occupation forces executed Edith Cavell, the British head of the Berkendael Medical Institute in Brussels. Cavell was, in fact, guilty of acts defined in international law as espionage; she helped British prisoners of war escape. But hanging a nurse was profoundly stupid in an era when women were only rarely executed for committing murder.

German saboteurs were probably not so active in the United States as prowar propagandists claimed. Nevertheless, several German diplomats were caught red-handed in 1915 when a bumbling agent left incriminating papers on a train; and in 1916 the huge Black Tom munitions stores in New Jersey were completely destroyed in a suspicious explosion.

The anti-German propaganda blockbuster was a telegram. On February 25, 1917, the British gave Wilson a message that the German foreign minister, Arthur Zimmerman, had telegraphed to the Mexican government. The telegram said

that in the event that the United States declared war on Germany, Germany would finance a Mexican attack on the United States (which, it was calculated, would keep the American army home). When Germany won the war, Mexico would be rewarded with the return of the "lost provinces" of New Mexico and Arizona, taken by the United States after the Mexican War seventy years earlier.

It was an ill-advised, even foolish proposal. Mexico was still wracked by civil turmoil, in no condition to make war on Guatemala, let alone the United States. Still, with American dander already up, the **Zimmerman telegram** persuaded many people that the Huns were indeed a worldwide threat.

THE AMERICAN CONTRIBUTION

The German provocation of the United States was a gamble. The bet was that the massive U-boat assault on British shipping would starve Britain out of the war before American troops could affect the outcome. For three months, it appeared the Germans would win the bet. In February and March 1917, submarines sank 570,000 tons of shipping around Great Britain. In April the total ran to almost 900,000 tons. A quarter of the British merchant fleet lay at the bottom of the sea. (Altogether, 203 U-boats sank 5,408 ships during the war.) At one point in April 1917, Britain had enough food on hand to feed the nation for only three weeks.

But the German wager was lost. At the insistence of American Admiral William S. Sims, freighters ceased to travel alone. Guarded by warships, particularly the small, fast destroyers, designed as antisubmarine weapons, ships crossed the Atlantic in convoys. Over the objections of the Royal Navy (but with the support of Prime Minister David Lloyd George), Sims built a "bridge of ships." In May 1917 U-boat kills dropped sharply to a level far below German projections. By July the American navy had taken sole responsibility for battling submarines in the Western Hemisphere and sent thirty-four destroyers to Queenstown in Ireland (now Cobh) to assist the British. So successful was the convoy system that of the 2 million American soldiers sent to France in 1917 and 1918, only 200 drowned because of submarines. In the meantime, by commandeering more than a hundred German ships that were in American ports (including the huge *Vaterland*, renamed the *Leviathan*) and by launching a

The Doughboys

Sergeant York (he was actually a corporal when he performed his amazing feat) was simple and uneducated—a hillbilly—and all the more lionized because he was so ordinary. Excepting his extraordinary bravery and marksmanship (and luck), he was representative of the men of the American Expeditionary Force.

The majority of the doughboys had less than seven years schooling; one in four was illiterate. According to primitive IQ tests administered to all recruits (which need not be taken with a great deal of seriousness), half fell into the category of "moron." Ten percent of the soldiers were African American. Almost one doughboy in five was an immigrant.

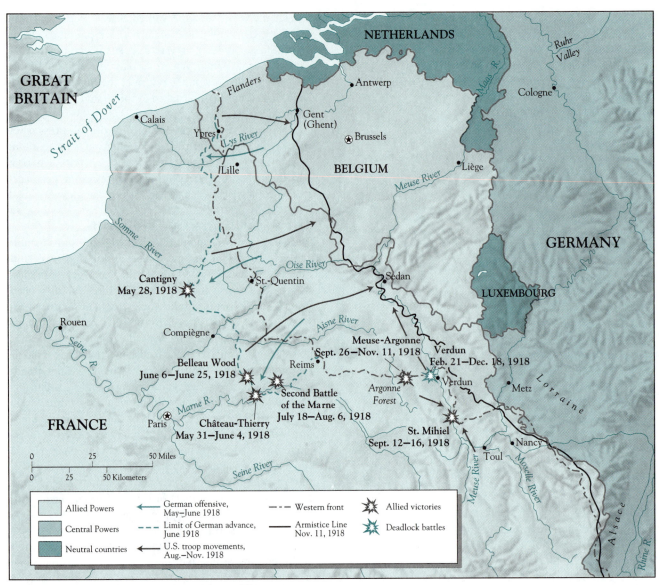

MAP 37:3   American Operations in World War I

1918 was the year of war for American troops. Most of the significant American battles with the Germans were fought on the Allies' southern flank.

massive shipbuilding program, the Americans were soon producing two ships for every one that the Germans sank.

THE FIGHTING OVER THERE

As soon as the United States declared war, the British asked Wilson to send them 500,000 raw recruits whom they would train and incorporate into the British Expeditionary Force. Wilson refused; the Americans would be trained at home and go "over there," in the words of a popular song, under American command. General Pershing arrived in Paris in July 1917 with the first units of the American Expeditionary Force, the First Infantry Division. This was only a symbolic gesture. Pershing refused to send his inadequately trained men to the front. The first Americans to see action, near Verdun in October, were used only to beef up French, British, and Canadian units decimated by the fighting the previous year.

The autumn of 1917 went poorly for the Allies. The Germans and Austrians defeated the Italian army in Italy and, in November, knocked Russia out of the war. A liberal democratic government that had deposed the czar in March 1917 proved unable to keep the mutinous Russian army supplied, and revolutionary Communists, the Bolsheviks, led by Vladimir Ilyich Lenin, seized power promising "peace and bread." The Treaty of Brest-Litovsk, which the Germans

Never Such a War

At the end of the war, the trenches on the western front ran from the English Channel to the border of Switzerland. There were so many soldiers massed along and behind this line that there was one man for every four inches of front.

World War I Casualties	Total Mobilized Forces	Killed or Died	Wounded	Prisoners & Missing	Total Casualties
United States	4,791,000	117,000	204,000	5,000	326,000
Russia	12,000,000	1,700,000	4,950,000	2,500,000	9,150,000
France	8,410,000	1,358,000	4,266,000	537,000	6,161,000
British Commonwealth	8,904,000	908,000	2,090,000	192,000	3,190,000
Italy	5,615,000	650,000	947,000	600,000	2,197,000
Germany	11,000,000	1,774,000	4,216,000	1,153,000	7,143,000
Austria–Hungary	7,800,000	1,200,000	3,620,000	2,220,000	7,020,000
Total	58,520,000	7,707,000	20,293,000	7,187,000	35,187,000

forced on Russia, was yet another diplomatic blunder. Its terms were so vindictive and harsh that yet more Americans were convinced that imperial Germany was beyond the pale of civilization. By shutting down the eastern front, however, the Germans were able to reinforce their army in France.

In May 1918 Germany launched a do-or-die offensive. The Allies fell back to the Marne River, close enough to Paris that the shelling could be heard on the Champs Elysées. But there were now 250,000 American troops in France; 27,000 fought at Château-Thierry near the hottest part of the fighting. By the middle of July, when the Germans ventured one last drive toward Paris, about 85,000 Americans helped hurl them back at Belleau Wood.

By the summer of 1918 the Americans in France represented the margin of victory over the Germans. The best of the German generals, Erich von Ludendorff, attributed the crash in German morale to "the sheer number of Americans arriving daily at the front." In July Americans took on the attack on a bulge in the German lines called the St.-Mihiel Salient and succeeded in clearing it out. The final American battle was along a twenty-four-mile line in the Argonne Forest, a rugged country just short of the border between France and Germany. It had been transformed into a ghostly wasteland by four years of digging and shelling. Over a million "doughboys" were sitting in that position when, on November 11, 1918, the Germans capitulated.

ARMISTICE

In the trenches and back home, Americans celebrated deliriously. Millions of people gathered in city centers throughout the country, dancing and whooping. The Yanks had won the war! Had not the Germans stalemated the French and British until our boys went "over there"? Just a year after the Americans began to fight, it was all over. Pershing was a hero. An even greater hero was "Sergeant York," Alvin C. York, a Tennessee mountain boy who, a few weeks before the armistice, attacked a German machine gun nest alone, killed seventeen men with seventeen bullets, and single-handedly marched 132 prisoners and thirty-five machine guns back to American lines.

The American intervention was the key to the Allied victory. But the joy in the United States was possible only because the American sacrifice was comparatively minor. Over 100,000 American soldiers died, more than half of them from disease. By comparison, 1.4 million French and almost a million British soldiers died. Three-quarters of all the Frenchmen who served in the war were casualties. France and Britain were badly maimed. Germany and Russia were maimed and defeated. If it was not entirely true that the United States "won the war," it was quite true that the United States was the only belligerent nation where people could feel like victors.

FURTHER READING

General John W. Chambers, *The Tyranny of Change: America in the Progressive Era, 1890–1920,* 2000; John M. Cooper, *Pivotal Decades: The United States, 1900–1920,* 1990; Steven J. Diner, *A Very Different Age: Americans of the Progressive Era,* 1998; Michael McGerr, *A Fierce Discontent: The Rise and Fall of the Progressive Movement in America, 1870–1920,* 2003; Nell Irvin Painter, *Standing at Armageddon: The United States, 1877–1919,* 1987.

Intervention in Mexico John S. D. Eisenhower, *Intervention: The United States and the Mexican Revolution, 1913–1917,* 1993; Michael J. Gonzales, *The Mexican Revolution, 1910–1940,* 2002; Friedrich Katz, *The Secret War in Mexico: Europe, the United States, and the Mexican Revolution,* 1981; F. J. McLinn, *Villa and Zapata: A Biography,* 2000; Robert L. Scheina, *Villa: Soldier of the Mexican Revolution,* 2004.

The League of Nations John M. Cooper, *Breaking the Heart of the World: Woodrow Wilson and the Fight for the League of Nations,* 2001; Donald E. Davis and Eugene P. Trani, *The First Cold War The Legacy of World War I in U.S.–Soviet Relations,* 2002; Lloyd M. Gardner, *Safe for Democracy: The Anglo–American Response to Revolution, 1913–1923,* 1984; Thomas J. Knock, *To End All Wars: World War I and the Quest for a New World Order,* 1992; William C. Widenor, *Henry Cabot Lodge and the Search for an American Foreign Policy,* 1980.

The War Arthur Barbeau and Florette Henri, *Unknown Soldiers: Black American Troops in World War I,* 1974; John H. Chambers, *To Raise an Army: The Draft Comes to Modern America,* 1987; Edward Coffman, *The War to End All Wars: The American Exprience in World War I,* 1987; Martin Gilbert, *The First World War: A Complete History,* 1994; John Keegan, *The First World War,* 1999; Paul Kennedy, *The Rise and Fall of the Great Powers: Economic Change and Military Conflict from 1500 to 2000,* 1987.

Woodrow Wilson Lloyd E. Ambrosius, *Woodrow Wilson and Wilsonian Statecraft,* 1991; Klement L. Clements, *Woodrow Wilson: World Statesman,* 1987, and *The Presidency of Woodrow Wilson,* 1992; Robert H. Ferrell, *Woodrow Wilson and World War I, 1917–1921,* 1985; Gerald Horne, *Black and Brown: African Americans in the Mexican Revolution, 1910–1920,* 2005; Phyllis L. Levin, *Edith and Woodrow: The Wilson White House,* 2001; Ronald M. Saunders, *In Search of Woodrow Wilson: Beliefs and Behavior,* 1998.

KEY TERMS

The following terms are covered in this chapter and can also be found in the list of Key Terms at the back of the book.

Central Powers	machine gun	Schlieffen Plan	Zimmerman telegram
Kultur	Pancho Villa	"unrestricted submarine warfare"	
Lusitania	revisionists		

 ## ONLINE SOURCES GUIDE

Use this listing to find online documents, images, interactive maps, simulations, and other resources related to this chapter:

American History Resource Center
http://history.wadsworth.com/rc/us

Selected Documents
A sample of a war propaganda pamphlet

Selected Images
Francisco "Pancho" Villa
Lusitania in New York, 1907

General John J. Pershing
Troops leaving for camp, 1917
U.S. troops wearing gas masks
American soldiers firing machine guns in France, 1918
Henry Cabot Lodge

Interactive Time Line (with online readings)
Over There: The United States and the First World War, 1914–1918

CHAPTER 38

Over Here

World War I at Home 1917–1920

The National Archives

Once lead this people into war, and they'll forget there ever was such a thing as tolerance. To fight you must be ruthless and brutal, and the spirit of ruthless brutality will enter into the very fiber of our national life.

Woodrow Wilson

When I think of the many voices that were heard before the war and are still heard, interpreting America from a class or sectional or selfish standpoint, I am not sure that, if the war had to come, it did not come at the right time for the preservation and reinterpretation of American ideals.

George Creel

Woodrow Wilson called the Great War "a war to make the world safe for democracy." He sent the doughboys to Europe and threw the industrial might of the United States behind the Allies in the belief there would be no victors in the traditional sense of the word. Instead, the peacemakers would create a new world order dedicated to settling disputes between nations justly and peaceably. Wilson also called the war "a war to end all wars."

THE PROGRESSIVE WAR

The First World War was simultaneously the apogee of progressivism, when reformers turned their ideas into policy, and the undoing of the progressive movement. For two years,

progressive moralists and social planners had free rein in Washington. Within a few years of the armistice, however, there was no progressive movement—only a few voices crying in the wilderness in Congress and hearing only echoes.

SPLIT

The question of intervention split the progressives. A few itched to fight from the start, most notably Theodore Roosevelt. When the United States declared war, he asked for a command in Europe. Wilson ignored him. Other Republican progressives, mostly westerners like Robert La Follette of Wisconsin, George Norris of Nebraska, William E. Borah of Idaho, and Hiram Johnson of California, fought the declaration of war. When they lost, they moderated their antiwar rhetoric but not their opinion that intervention was foisted

Profiteering

Woodrow Wilson was America's most prominent movie fan; producers sent him prints of whatever films he requested—free. But there were others. As well as any statistic, the earnings history of Mary Pickford, "America's Sweetheart," the nation's favorite leading lady, tells how quickly and overwhelmingly movies captured the hearts of Americans who had to pay to see them. A minor Broadway actress before 1910, Mary Pickford made $25 a week. In 1910 moviemaker Carl Laemmle lured her into movies with the astronomical weekly salary of $175. In 1914 Adolph Zukor of Famous Players paid Pickford $20,000, then $52,000 a year. In 1915 she demanded and got $104,000 per movie plus half of the profits it earned. In June 1916 her price per movie was $1 million guaranteed against half the profits.

on the country by munitions makers and bankers. The "willful men" prolonged the debate on the Conscription Act of 1917 for six weeks until Congress exempted boys under 21 from the draft. Any affinity the isolationist progressives had felt with Wilson before April 1917 dissipated thereafter.

Democratic party progressives wholeheartedly supported the war. Like Wilson, they came to believe that Germany was a serious threat to free institutions everywhere. Moreover, in the task of mobilizing resources to fight the war, and in the wave of patriotic commitment that swept the country, progressives saw a golden opportunity to put their ideas for economic and social reform to work.

They were right on one count. It was impossible to wage a modern war while clinging to the idea of a free, unregulated economy. Armies numbering millions of men could not be supplied with food, clothing, shelter, medicine, and arms by competing private companies free to do entirely as their owners chose to do. France and Britain had clamped tight controls on their factories and farms in 1914. Germany already had them. When America went to war, progressives knew that their government had to do the same, and they were delighted. At the core of their beliefs was the assumption that the power of the state, in the right hands, was a force for good. Now the whole country, caught up by patriotism, would be behind them.

They were not disappointed—for the duration. Proposals for regulation of businesses that were rejected as radical in peacetime proved, in the urgency of wartime, to be less than was necessary. The federal government virtually took over the direction of the economy.

PLANNED ECONOMY

And the government grew like a mushroom. Government spending increased tenfold. The federal bureaucracy doubled in size. Employees of the executive branch, 400,000 in 1916, numbered 950,000 in 1918.

All kinds of new agencies were set up during the twenty months that the United States was at war. Some were useless and wasteful, established without thought; they served little purpose beyond providing desks, chairs, inkwells, and salaries for the functionaries who ran them. A few agencies were plain failures. The Aircraft Production Board was commissioned to construct 22,000 airplanes in a year. The figure was unrealistic, but the 1,200 craft that the board actually delivered were far fewer than a hustler with a bank loan could have supplied.

Some agencies were quite successful. The Shipping Board, founded in 1916 before the declaration of war, produced vessels twice as fast as German submarines could sink them. Privately run shipbuilding companies, loaded with deadwood in management, were not up to that achievement.

The United States Railway Administration, headed by Wilson's son-in-law and Secretary of the Treasury William G. McAdoo, was created early in 1918 when moving the volume of freight the war created proved to be beyond the capabilities of the men who ran the nation's railroads. The government paid the stockholders a rent equal to their earnings in the prewar years and simply took over. McAdoo untangled a colossal snafu in management within a few weeks; he reorganized the railroads into an efficient system such as the nation had never known. About 150,000 freight cars short of the number needed to do the job in 1917, American railroads had a surplus of 300,000 cars by the end of the war.

The war production boards were coordinated by a superagency, the **War Industries Board,** headed by Wall Street financier Bernard Baruch. His presence at the top of the planning pyramid indicated that the progressives had not won their campaign for a directed economy without paying a price. American industry and agriculture were regulated as

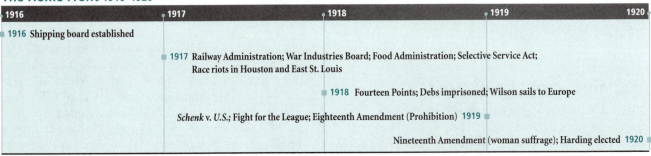

The Home Front 1916–1920

1916 — 1916 Shipping board established

1917 — 1917 Railway Administration; War Industries Board; Food Administration; Selective Service Act; Race riots in Houston and East St. Louis

1918 — 1918 Fourteen Points; Debs imprisoned; Wilson sails to Europe

Schenk v. U.S.; Fight for the League; Eighteenth Amendment (Prohibition) **1919**

Nineteenth Amendment (woman suffrage); Harding elected **1920**

Hooverizing

Herbert Hoover encouraged city dwellers to plant "victory gardens" in their tiny yards. Every tomato that was raised at home, he said, freed commercially produced food for the front. He promoted classes for homemakers in economizing in the kitchen and distributed cookbooks on how to prepare leftovers. The impact of his programs was so great that, half-seriously, Americans coined the verb *hooverize* to mean "economize," and they used it. Chicago proudly reported that the city's housekeepers had hooverized the monthly output of garbage down by a third.

never before. But elected officials and public-spirited experts with no stake in the profits were not always in the driver's seat.

HERBERT HOOVER

Food Administrator Herbert C. Hoover's task was as difficult as McAdoo's, and it kept him in the public eye. Hoover's job was to organize food production, distribution, and consumption so that America's farms fed the army and the American people, met some of the needs of the Allied armies, and made up Great Britain's eternal shortfall.

Only 43 years old when he took the job, Hoover was known as the "boy wonder." An orphan, Hoover grew up in California with relatives. He worked his way through Stanford University, graduated as a mining engineer, and decided to work abroad on new strikes, where he could share in the profits, rather than for a salary in the United States. He had his share of adventures; Hoover and his wife were besieged in China during the Boxer Rebellion. Mostly he developed mines, made shrewd personal investments, and was so soon a millionaire that he was bored with moneymaking when still a young man.

Hoover's ambitions were in public service. He believed that able, wealthy men like himself had responsibilities to society. He got his chance to start out in a high-profile position when he happened to be in London at the outbreak of the war. He was asked to take over the problem of getting food to the people of devastated Belgium, and he jumped at the challenge. Hoover liquidated his business interests, mastered the complex and ticklish task of feeding people in a war zone, and saved hundreds of thousands of lives.

He did it without charm or personal flash. Hoover was serious, intense, and, to appearances, humorless. He shared the progressive faith in the application of scientific and engineering principles to social problems. It tells us that progressivism was alive and well in 1917 that Hoover became a war hero in the same rank as General Pershing, Sergeant York, and America's ace airplane pilot, Captain Eddie Rickenbacker.

THE BUREAUCRAT AS WAR HERO

In one important way, Hoover differed from most progressives, and it helps to explain his popularity. Even undertakings as massive as organizing food production, distribution,

and consumption, Hoover believed, did not require the state's coercive powers. It could be done by voluntary cooperation.

Unlike the Railway Administration, which took control of the nation's railroads on its own terms, Hoover did not force anything on anyone. Food was not rationed in the United States as it was in every other country in the war. Instead, Hoover designed colorful publicity campaigns urging Americans, in the spirit of patriotism and "pulling together," to observe Wheatless Mondays, Meatless Tuesdays, Porkless Thursdays, and so on. The program worked because compliance was easy, yet psychologically gratifying. Making do without a commodity vital to the war effort one day a week was painless, but it allowed civilians to feel that they were part of the fighting machine. It was shrewd psychology and it was not just hype. When tens of millions of people observed a Meatless Tuesday, the additional tonnage of meat available for export in just one week was enormous.

Hoover increased farm production through a combination of patriotic boosting and cash incentives. Acreage planted in wheat increased from 45 million in 1917 to 75 million in 1919. American shipments of foodstuffs to the Allies tripled over prewar levels that were already high. Hoover added "Miracle Man" to his list of flattering nicknames. Another young Washington administrator, Undersecretary of the Navy Franklin D. Roosevelt, wanted the Democratic party to nominate Hoover for president in 1920.

MANAGING PEOPLE

People were mobilized along with railway cars and potatoes—workers and housewives as well as soldiers. In May 1917 Congress passed the Selective Service Act, the first draft law since the Civil War. Registration was compulsory for all men between the ages of 21 and 45. (In 1918 the minimum age was lowered to 18.) From the 10 million who registered within a month of passage (24 million by the end of the war), local draft boards selected able-bodied recruits according to quotas assigned by the federal government.

Some occupational groups were deferred as vital to the war effort, but no one was allowed to buy his way out as had occurred (and had been bitterly resented) during the Civil War. Indeed, authority to make final selections was given to local draft boards to silence critics who said that conscription had no place in a democracy. The draft contributed about 3 million young men to the armed forces in addition to 2 million who volunteered.

About 21,000 draftees claimed to be conscientious objectors on religious grounds, although, in the end, only 4,000 insisted on assignment to noncombatant duty, as medics or in the Quartermaster Corps. Approximately 500 men refused to cooperate with the military in any way, some for political rather than religious reasons. They were imprisoned and, in general, treated poorly. Camp Leonard Wood in Missouri had an especially bad reputation. In Washington State, a man who claimed that Jesus had forbidden him to take up arms was sentenced to death. He was not executed, but the last conscientious objector was not freed from prison until 1933,

The National Archives

Members of the 369th Infantry. The army was segregated by race; the 369th was entirely African American except for senior officers. Although General Pershing refused British demands that American soldiers be merged into depleted British units, he "loaned" the 369th to the French. They were so effective, the entire unit was awarded the French Croix de Guerre. Note the medal each soldier is wearing.

long after most Americans had come to agree with him that the war had been a mistake.

SOCIAL CHANGES

War is a revolutionary, or, at least, a revolutionary agitator. The changes impressed on American society from the top in the interests of victory inevitably affected social relationships. Some groups consciously took advantage of the government's wants, needs, and preoccupations to achieve old goals. Others were merely caught up by the different rhythms of a society at war.

LABOR TAKES A SEAT

In order to keep factories humming, Wilson made concessions to the labor movement that would have been unthinkable a few years earlier. He appointed Samuel Gompers, the patriotic president of the American Federation of Labor, to Baruch's War Industries Board. The Postmaster General refused to deliver an issue of a socialist magazine in which

Gompers was criticized. In return for recognition and favors, Gompers pledged the AFL unions to a no-strike policy for the duration of the conflict.

Because wages rose during the war, there were comparatively few work stoppages. Business boomed, and employers dizzy with bonanza profits did not jeopardize them by resisting moderate demands by their employees. Most important, the National War Labor Board, on which five AFL men sat, mediated many industrial disputes before they disrupted production.

The quiet incorporation of organized labor into the federal decision-making process made the AFL respectable as it never had been before—Samuel Gompers's dream come true. From 2.7 million members in 1914, the union movement (including independent unions) grew to 4.2 million in 1919.

BLACKS IN WARTIME

Booker T. Washington died in 1915. When America went to war two years later, there was no African American of his stature to act as a "spokesman for the race." The president of the National Association for the Advancement of Colored People was white. Moreover, most of its members were middle-class northerners. Founded only in 1910, the organization had little prestige among the masses of African Americans, who were poor and uneducated and lived in the South. Probably most blacks had never heard of the organization.

W. E. B. DuBois, the scholar–editor of the NAACP journal, the *Crisis,* said, as Frederick Douglass had during the Civil War, that the willingness of young black men to serve in the army should be rewarded by the government's support of African-American civil rights. DuBois was not naïve about the possibilities. He was well aware that President Wilson was a southerner who approved (if quietly) of the South's Jim Crow segregation laws. In an open letter to Wilson, he was content to pressure the president on the lynching epidemic in the South. He pointed out the irony of fighting against the savagery of "the Hun" in Europe while ignoring the savagery of American lynch mobs. Wilson issued a stronger antilynching statement than he ever had previously, but he said nothing about the federal antilynching act that was one of the NAACP's goals. Lynching incidents declined to thirty-eight

in 1917; the annual average for the five prewar years was fifty-nine. But 1917 was a fluke. There were sixty-four lynchings in 1918 and eighty-three in 1919, the highest total since the bloody 1890s.

About 400,000 African Americans served in the armed forces. They were strictly segregated in "Negro units." All but a few black sailors were assigned to the galleys as cooks, dishwashers, cafeteria line workers, and waiters at officers' messes. Few enlisted in the interests of their race. Black doughboys joined up for the same reasons whites did: the chance for adventure (they were young men), a clean, warm bed and three good meals a day (like white enlistees, most blacks had dirt-poor backgrounds), or because they were drafted. Except for those assigned to the three well-trained black units in the regular army, few African-American enlistees and draftees were in combat units. Most dug trenches or loaded trucks behind the lines. Only a small minority were taught skills that would be useful to them after the war.

Segregation in the military paid one dividend to black leaders like W. E. B. DuBois, who regarded the creation of an educated African-American elite as a high-priority goal.

Photographs and Prints Division, Schomburg Center for Research in Black Culture, New York Public Library, Astor, Lenox and Tilden Foundations

Three generations of a family from the deep South arrive in a Chicago railway station. They appear to be as apprehensive as immigrants from Italy or Poland at Ellis Island—as indeed they ought to have been. Moving from the rural South to big, bustling, noisy industrial cities like Chicago, Detroit, and Philadelphia was as culturally shocking as moving from Sicily to New York. African-American migrants had the advantage of speaking the language, but they faced a racial prejudice far harsher than the discrimination immigrants experienced.

Unlike in the Civil War, when black soldiers were commanded by whites, the army trained and commissioned 1,200 African-American officers. Only a handful rose higher in rank than captain, but the fact that black officers existed was a point of pride in African-American communities.

MIGRATION: FROM JIM CROW TO RACE RIOT

World War I was a landmark in African-American history because the war years were the beginning of the massive emigration of blacks from the rural South to northern industrial cities. Each year before 1914, about 10,000 blacks drifted from the South to Philadelphia, New York, Detroit, Chicago, and other cities. After 1914, just when American factories needed new workers to fill orders from Europe, the risks of ocean travel choked off immigration. More than 1.2 million immigrants entered the United States in 1914, but only 326,000 in 1915. In 1918 only 111,000 immigrants were recorded, the fewest in a year since the Civil War and, except for two Civil War years, the fewest since 1844.

Industry could not afford to observe the informal color line that had kept African Americans out of factory jobs that paid good wages. Lured by the abundant jobs and the chance to escape rigid racial segregation, 100,000 blacks moved north each year, usually by train. It was not so great a leap in miles as the European immigration, but just as wrenching socially and culturally. Plowing the Mississippi delta one week and working on an assembly line in Detroit the next, and moving from an isolated sharecropper's cabin to an apartment in a congested city, was an elemental psychological upheaval.

Most of the African Americans who moved north were young—not yet conditioned, like their parents, to tolerate the daily humiliations of Jim Crow. This was particularly true of veterans who had found in France not a colorblind culture, as many blacks described it in letters home, but one in which race counted for little. However, the epidemic of race riots that began during the war owed not to the insolence of the odd "uppity Negro," as newspapers usually reported, but to the rapid growth of the black population in northern cities and, consequently, the expansion of African-American communities into neighborhoods white people thought of as their own.

Between 1910 and 1920, Detroit's African-American population rose from 5,700 to 41,000, Cleveland's from 8,400 to 34,000. Chicago's black population, already substantial in 1910 at 44,000, more than doubled to 109,000. Philadelphia, with the nation's largest black population in 1910 (84,000), was home to 134,000 African Americans in 1920.

There was a frightening race riot in industrial East St. Louis, Illinois, in 1917. At least forty and possibly three times that many people were killed. In 1918 there were race riots in Philadelphia and nearby Chester, Pennsylvania. The first postwar year, 1919, was worse, possibly because demobilized white veterans were competing with blacks for jobs as well as places to live. More than twenty cities experienced race-based violence. Chicago was a racial battleground for five days; thirty-eight deaths were recorded. At least

The National Archives

A woman welding in a wartime factory. Women in such industrial jobs were not as common as they would be during the Second World War. But World War I women filled a good many jobs outside factories from which they were barred before the war.

forty people were killed in a riot in Washington. The war was not the window of opportunity that DuBois believed or, at least, hoped it would be.

VOTING AT LAST

Personally, President Wilson did not like the idea of women voting (although his only children were daughters). But the suffrage movement was too long in the field and, by 1917, too large to be denied. Wilson announced his support of a constitutional amendment guaranteeing the vote to women, and Congress sent the Nineteenth Amendment to the states in June 1919, six months after the armistice. In August 1920 ratification by Tennessee added it to the Constitution. The right of citizens to vote, it read, "shall not be denied or abridged by the United States or by any State on account of sex." Carrie Chapman Catt, head of the National American Woman Suffrage Association, had no doubt about what put the long-sought reform over. It was the war, the one-time pacifist said, that enfranchised American women.

Catt was a progressive on social and economic issues, but a conservative feminist; the suffrage was her goal. She sold woman suffrage to progressive politicians by assuring them that responsible middle-class white women would provide the votes to counterbalance the political power of immigrant radicals and corrupt political machines.

Alice Paul was the leader of the radical wing of the suffrage movement. She and her followers had employed showy, militant tactics in the campaign to win the vote. They chained themselves to the fence around the White House, and Paul burned a copy of Wilson's Fourteen Points to dramatize what she saw as his hypocrisy. (Carrie Chapman Catt shuddered.) The radical feminists—they adopted the name after the Nineteenth Amendment was enacted—believed that the woman vote, because women thought differently than men did, would change American society, particularly women's social and economic status, in far more fundamental ways than the progressive movement proposed.

During the wartime labor shortage, women took jobs that had been considered entirely unsuitable for them. Working-class women took factory jobs. Women operated trolley cars, drove delivery trucks, cleaned streets, and directed traffic. But it was a temporary phenomenon. The belief that men and women had different "spheres" was still powerful. When the veterans returned home, most women in nontraditional occupations quit and made way for the men.

THE MORAL WAR

One of the reforms suffragists said that women voters would push over the top was in place before the Nineteenth Amendment. The prohibition movement appeared to be stalled before the war. In 1914 only one state in four had some sort of prohibition law on the books, and many were casually enforced. By the end of 1917, when a constitutional amendment providing for nationwide prohibition was proposed, only thirteen states were completely "dry." And yet within a year and a half, prohibition was the law of the land.

The war added several new arguments to the anti-alcohol armory. Distilleries consumed a great deal of grain that the Food Administration was urging Americans to conserve. It was hard to defend whiskey guzzling when people were told to eat less bread. Shortly after declaring war, Congress passed the Lever Act forbidding the sale of grain to distilleries.

Brewers, who had distanced themselves from distillers, contrasting the wholesome beer garden with the disreputable saloon, found themselves vulnerable because most breweries were run by German Americans, their Teutonic names proudly emblazoned on bottle, keg, and delivery wagon. They were easy targets for prohibitionists waving flags: beer was the beverage of the hated Hun. Congress approved the **Eighteenth Amendment,** prohibiting "the manufacture, sale, or transportation of intoxicating liquors"—wine as well as beer and spirits—in 1917. The war was over before it was ratified.

THE CAMPAIGN AGAINST PROSTITUTION

Modern wars have usually meant a relaxation of sexual morality because military service removes so many young men (and more than a few young women) from the social restraints of family and community. So it was in World War I. The doughboys in France discovered that, with the war two years old, brothels were everywhere, even in tiny French villages.

Moral progressives in the Wilson administration joined forces with army doctors to try to control the inclinations of the young recruits. They were warned of the dangers of venereal disease—"A German bullet is cleaner than a French whore"—with disagreeable photographs of syphilitic chancres and victims of the disease whose faces had been disfigured. Physicians drummed the symptoms of gonorrhea into soldiers' heads. In France, the army obliged both doctors and moral progressives by forbidding soldiers on leave to take their holiday in wide-open Paris. (The order was ineffective; soldiers on leave took their chances rather than miss the chance to see "Gay Paree"; deserters invariably headed for Paris where they could lose themselves in the city's seamier quarters.)

Josephus Daniels, the deeply religious secretary of the navy, actually believed that having authority over so many young men provided him an opportunity to improve their sex morals. With amazing obliviousness to reality, he called navy ships "floating universities" of moral reform. Daniels gave orders to the navy to clear out the red-light districts that had been a fixture in every port. The army did the same in towns near its training camps—most famously Storyville, across the river from New Orleans.

Prostitution no more disappeared than people stopped drinking alcohol. But the flush of excitement in the reformers' short-term victories confirmed their belief that, among its horrors, the war had transformed society into a laboratory where it could be reshaped for the better.

CONFORMITY AND REPRESSION

As Wilson had privately predicted, the white-hot patriotism of wartime scorched political expression. "Free speech" was not defined as broadly as it is today, but it was generally accepted that all political opinion short of advocating violence was protected by the First Amendment. Once the United States was at war, however, federal, state, and local governments harassed and even jailed those who vociferously criticized the war and winked at vigilante actions against people who did not conform to patriotic demands.

THE CAMPAIGN AGAINST THE SOCIALISTS

The Socialist party of America was the most important national organization to oppose the declaration of war and, once the United States was in, to criticize the intervention. In April 1917, as war was being declared in Washington, the party held an emergency convention in St. Louis and proclaimed "unalterable opposition" to a conflict that killed working people while paying dividends to capitalists. The party's stance did not hurt it at the polls. The Socialist vote increased during the war; voting Socialist was the only way non-Socialists who opposed the war could register their disapproval.

Governments moved promptly to squelch the possibility of a Socialist-led antiwar bandwagon. The legislature of New York expelled seven Socialist assemblymen simply because they opposed the war. Not until after the war did courts rule the expulsion unconstitutional. Socialist Victor Berger was elected to Congress from Milwaukee but was denied his seat by the House. When, in the special election to fill the vacancy, he defeated an opponent supported by both the Democratic and Republican parties, Congress again refused to seat him. Berger's district remained unrepresented until 1923, when he was finally allowed the place he had been elected to fill five years earlier. In the meantime, Postmaster General Albert S. Burleson denied the Milwaukee Socialists' *Social Democratic Herald* and other Socialist newspapers cheap mailing privileges. Most of them never recovered from the blow. The golden age of the American socialist press was over.

The most celebrated attack on the Socialists was the indictment and trial of the party's longtime and much beloved leader, Eugene V. Debs, for a speech in which he advocated resistance to the draft. In sending Debs to an Atlanta penitentiary, the Wilson administration was taking a chance. The four-time presidential candidate was admired by many non-Socialists. At his trial in September 1918, Debs was at his most eloquent. "While there is a lower class I am in it; while there is a criminal element I am of it; while there is a soul in prison, I am not free," he told the jury. But in jailing him and a few other prominent Socialists such as Kate Richards O'Hare, the government made it clear that dissent on the issue would not be tolerated.

THE DESTRUCTION OF THE IWW

The suppression of the IWW, the **Industrial Workers of the World,** was heavier-handed than the government's harassment of the socialists. There was an apparent irony in this: while the IWW, like the Socialist party, officially opposed the war, the head of the union, Secretary–Treasurer William D. "Big Bill" Haywood, tried to soft-pedal the war issue. The IWW was enrolling new members by the thousands every month. Haywood, a union man before anything else, hoped to ride out the patriotic hysteria and emerge from the war with the IWW a powerful labor organization.

However, the federal government set out to emasculate the IWW less because of its opposition to the war than because it was an increasingly large and effective labor organization. By 1917 IWW membership was concentrated in three sectors of the economy that were vital to the war effort: among the migrant harvest hands who brought in the nation's wheat; among loggers in the Pacific Northwest (Sitka spruce lumber was essential to aircraft manufacture); and among copper miners in Globe and Bisbee, Arizona, and Butte, Montana. Unlike the American Federation of Labor, Wobbly unions refused to pledge not to strike during the war.

The IWW was also a tempting target for repression because it represented workers on the very bottom and preached revolution. In contrast, most Socialist party leaders were middle-class and moderate people, and the party's program was no more radical than the programs espoused by many progressives. The socialists had friends, the IWW not many.

The IWW was crushed by a combination of vigilante terrorism and government prosecution. In July 1917, 1,000 "deputies" wearing white armbands to recognize one another rounded up 1,200 Wobbly strikers in Bisbee, put them aboard a chartered train, and dumped them in the Hermanas desert of New Mexico, where they were without food for thirty-six hours. The next month, IWW organizer Frank Little was lynched in Butte, possibly by police officers in disguise. In neither case was there any serious attempt to identify the vigilantes.

In the grain belt, sheriffs and farmers had a free hand in dealing with suspected Wobblies. In the Sitka spruce forests of Washington and Oregon, the army organized the Loyal Legion of Loggers and Lumbermen to counter the popularity of the IWW. There, at least, working conditions were improved as the union was repressed, but Loyal Legion attacks on the IWW were frequently vicious. Local police and federal agents ignored the obvious violations of civil rights and violence.

CIVIL LIBERTIES SUSPENDED

The fatal blow on the IWW fell in the fall of 1917. The Justice Department raided IWW headquarters in several cities, rounded up the union's leaders, and indicted about 200 under the Espionage Act of 1917. Later enhanced by the Sedition Act of 1918, the Espionage Act not only outlawed overt treasonable acts but made it a crime to "utter, print, write, or publish any disloyal, profane, scurrilous, or abusive language" about the government, the flag, or the uniform of a soldier or sailor. A casual snide remark was enough to warrant bringing charges; a few cases were based on little more than wisecracks.

In *Schenck* v. *the United States* (1919), the Supreme Court unanimously upheld this broad, vague legislation. As if to leave no doubt about the Court's resolve, Oliver Wendell Holmes, Jr., the most liberal justice on the Court, was assigned to write the opinion, which established the principle that when "a clear and present danger" existed, such as the war, Congress had the power to pass laws that would not be acceptable in normal times.

Even at that, the prosecutors never proved that either IWW leaders or the organization itself was guilty of sedition. In effect, the individuals who were sentenced to up to twenty years in prison were punished because of their membership in an organization the government wanted dead. Some liberals who had no taste for IWW doctrine were shocked at the government's cynicism and fought the prosecutions. In 1920, led by Roger Baldwin, they organized the American Civil Liberties Union to guard against a repetition of the repressions of the Great War.

MANIPULATING PUBLIC OPINION

The attack on the Socialists and the Wobblies was not the only reflection of the spirit of ruthless intolerance that Wilson feared the war would loose. Many otherwise ordinary people were stirred by patriotism to believe that they were part of a holy crusade against a foe with the wiles and powers of the devil.

There were many violent acts against individual German Americans. Most incidents were spontaneous; for example, a midwestern mob dragged a German-American shopkeeper from his home, threw him to his knees, forced him to kiss the

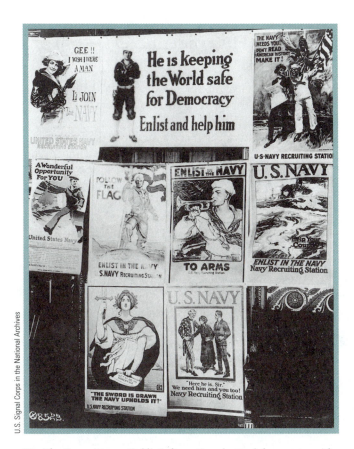

U.S. Signal Corps in the National Archives

■ *The Committee on Public Information plastered the country with patriotic posters in the first intensive government propaganda program in American history. Poster art reached an unprecedented level of effectiveness during World War I. Artistically, poster art has never been as good since.*

American flag, and made him spend his savings on war bonds. But intolerance and even vigilante activity were also abetted and even instigated by the national government.

The **Committee on Public Information** was entrusted with the task of mobilizing public opinion behind the government. Headed by George Creel, a progressive newspaperman who had devoted his career to fighting the very sort of intolerance he now encouraged, Creel's job was twofold. First, to avoid discouragement, the CPI censored news from the front. CPI dispatches emphasized victories and suppressed or played down stories of setbacks and accounts of the misery of life in the trenches. With most editors and publishers solidly behind the war, Creel had no difficulty persuading them to censor their own correspondents.

Second, the CPI attempted to mold public opinion so that even minor deviations from full support of the war were branded as disloyal. Obviously, not all German Americans could be condemned as disloyal. (Only 6,300 Germans were actually interned, compared with 45,000 of Great Britain's much smaller German-born community.) However, the CPI could and did launch a massive propaganda campaign that depicted German *Kultur* as intrinsically evil.

The CPI issued 60 million pamphlets, sent prewritten editorials to pliant (or merely lazy) newspaper editors, and subsidized the design and printing of posters conveying the impression that a network of German spies was ubiquitous in the United States. With money to be made in exploiting the theme, the infant film industry centered in Hollywood, California, rushed to oblige. A typical title of 1917 was *The Barbarous Hun*. In May 1917 a movie producer, Robert Goldstein, was arrested and convicted under the Espionage Act for making a film about the American Revolution, *The Spirit of '76*. One scene showed a redcoat impaling an American baby on his bayonet. Goldstein's crime was to have aided the enemy by disparaging America's British ally.

At movie theaters during intermissions, some 75,000 "Four-Minute Men," all volunteers, delivered patriotic speeches of that duration, 7.5 million messages in all. Film stars like action hero Douglas Fairbanks, comedian Charlie Chaplin, and "America's Sweetheart," Mary Pickford, appeared at Liberty Bond rallies and spoke anti-German lines written by the CPI.

LIBERTY HOUNDS AND BOY SPIES

The anti-German hysteria sometimes took laughable form—laughable today. Restaurants revised their menus so that sauerkraut became "liberty cabbage," hamburgers were called "Salisbury steak" (after a British lord), and frankfurters and wiener sausages, named after German and Austrian cities, became universally known as "hot dogs."

The real dog, the dachshund, had to be rebred into a "liberty hound." Towns with names of German origin voted to choose more patriotic designations. Berlin, Iowa, became Lincoln; Germantown, Nebraska, became Garland. German measles, a common childhood disease, were "patriotic measles." Hundreds of schools and some colleges dropped the German language from the curriculum. Dozens of symphony orchestras refused to play the works of German composers, leaving conspicuous holes in the repertoire. Prominent German Americans who wished to save their careers found it advisable to imitate opera singer Ernestine Schumann-Heinck. She was a fixture at patriotic rallies, her ample Wagnerian figure draped with a large American flag and her magnificent voice singing "The Star-Spangled Banner" and "America the Beautiful."

But the firing of Germans from their jobs, discrimination against German farmers, burning of German books, and beating up of German Americans were not so humorous. Nor was the treatment of other people designated as less than fully patriotic by organizations of self-appointed guardians of the national interest with names like "Sedition Slammers," "Terrible Threateners," and "Boy Spies of America." Members stopped young men on the streets and demanded to see their draft cards. It was not an atrocity, although perhaps more than an obnoxious annoyance. But the assumption that one citizen had the right to police another was indicative of an unhealthy social mood. The largest of the self-anointed enforcers of patriotism was the American Protective League. At one time it numbered 250,000 members, although many people probably signed up merely to avoid being themselves harassed.

"They Dropped Like Flies": The Great Flu Epidemic

About 8 million soldiers died in Europe between 1914 and 1918. But the war was an amateur killer compared with the "Spanish flu." During only four months late in 1918 and early in 1919, a flu pandemic—an epidemic over a large geographical area, worldwide in the case of this flu—killed 21 million. The American army in Europe lost 49,000 men in battle and 64,000 to disease, the majority to the flu. At home 548,452 American civilians died, ten times as many as soldiers felled in battle.

The disease first appeared in the United States in March 1918 at Fort Riley, Kansas. After a dust storm, 107 soldiers checked into the infirmary complaining of headaches, fever and chills, difficulty breathing, and aches and pains. The illness had hit them in an instant; one moment they were feeling fine, the next they could barely stand. Within a week, Fort Riley had 522 cases, and in a little more than a month, when the disease abruptly disappeared, 8,000 cases. About fifty of the men died. That was not particularly disturbing in an era when a number of common contagious diseases were deadly.

A policeman directing traffic during the flu epidemic of 1918. Several cities fined people who did not wear masks when outdoors.

"Obey the laws
And wear the gauze.
Protect your jaws
From septic paws."

National Archives

Some doctors noted, however, the curiosity that the victims were in the prime of life and, after basic training, in excellent physical condition.

The soldiers from Fort Riley were shipped to Europe in May. The flu made a brief appearance in the cities of the eastern seaboard, but it did not rival any of several American flu epidemics of the past, including a serious one in 1889 and 1890. In Europe in 1918, the disease was more deadly. In neutral Switzerland alone, 58,000 died of it in July. Deaths from the flu in the trenches were so numerous that German General Erich von Ludendorff curtailed a major campaign. By June the flu was sweeping Africa and India, where the mortality was "without parallel in the history of disease." The catastrophe in India could be attributed to the wretched poverty of the subcontinent. But what of Western Samoa, where 7,500 of the island's 38,000 people died?

The totals had not yet been calculated when the flu began a second world tour. The war had created ideal conditions for a pandemic. People moved about in unprecedented numbers; 200,000 to 300,000 crossed the Atlantic to Europe each month, and almost as many crowded westbound steamships. The war also crowded people together on land. Conditions were perfect for both the spread and the successful mutation of viruses. With so many hosts handy, the emergence of new viral strains was all the more likely.

WILSON AND THE LEAGUE OF NATIONS

Why did Woodrow Wilson tolerate and even encourage these activities? The answer lies in the fact that the president's dream of building a new world order after the war became an obsession. Before the war there was an easygoing quality to Wilson. He worked only three or four hours a day and never on Saturday and Sunday. He was a regular at Washington

Senators baseball games. When the war came, he hardly ever stopped toiling.

Like no president before him (but like several since), Wilson lost interest in domestic affairs except as they affected his all-consuming foreign concerns. The one-time enemy of big government presided over its extraordinary expansion. Repression of dissenters, even unjust and illegal repression, appeared to hasten the defeat of the Kaiser, so Wilson suppressed liberal values that had guided his life.

That is apparently what happened in August, either in western Africa, France, or Spain (which got the blame; Americans called the disease the "Spanish flu"). A deadlier mutation swept the world. This time the effects in the United States were cataclysmic.

In Boston, where the Spanish flu first struck, doubtless carried there by returning soldiers, 202 people died on October 1, 1918. New York City reported 3,100 cases in one day; 300 died. Later in the month, 851 New Yorkers died in one day, the record for an American city. Philadelphia lost 289 people on October 6; within one week, 5,270 were dead. The city's death rate for the month was 700 times the usual. Similar figures came in from every large city in the country. Just as worrisome, the flu found its way to the most isolated corners of the United States. A winter logging camp in Michigan, cut off from the rest of humanity, was afflicted. Oregon officials reported finding lone sheepherders dead by their flocks.

Most public officials responded as well as could be expected to a catastrophe that no one understood. Congress, many of its members laid low, appropriated money to hire physicians and nurses to set up clinics. Many cities closed theaters, schools, and churches and prohibited public gatherings such as parades and sporting events. Several cities required people to wear gauze masks and punished violators with fines of up to $100. Others, notably Kansas City, where the political boss said frankly that the economy was more important, carried on as usual and were no harder hit than cities that took extreme precautions.

Nationwide and worldwide, about one-fifth of the population caught the Spanish flu; the death rate was 3 percent. Philadelphia gathered its dead in carts, as had been done during the bubonic plague epidemics of the Middle Ages. The A. F. Brill Company, a manufacturer of trolley cars, turned over its wood shop to coffin makers. Authorities in Washington, D.C., seized a trainload of coffins headed for Pittsburgh.

Then, once again, the disease disappeared. There was a less lethal wave (perhaps another mutation) in the spring of 1919, with President Wilson one of the victims. But the worst was over about the time that the First World War ended, allowing physicians to reflect on the character of the disease and to wonder what they could do if it recurred.

There were some oddities upon which to reflect. The first has already been noted: the Spanish flu struck very suddenly, giving individuals no way to fight it except to lie down and hope. Second, the disease went relatively easy on those people who are usually most vulnerable to respiratory diseases, the elderly, and it was hardest on those who usually shook off such afflictions, young people. In the United States the usual death rate for white males between the ages of 25 and 34 was, during the 1910s, about 80 per 100,000. During the flu epidemic it was 2,000 per 100,000. In a San Francisco maternity ward in October, nineteen out of forty-two women died of flu. In Washington, a college student telephoned a clinic to report that two of her three roommates were dead in bed and the third was seriously ill. The report of the police officer who was sent to investigate was "Four girls dead in apartment." Old people died of the flu, of course, but the death rate among the elderly did not rise a single point during the epidemic. Finally, people who had grown up in poor big-city neighborhoods were less likely to get the disease and, if they got it, less likely to die of it than were people who had grown up in more healthful rural environments.

These facts eventually led scientists to conclude that the Spanish flu was a mutation of a common virus that caused a milder form of flu. It was postulated, although never proven, that the deadly germ was the issue of an unholy liaison between a virus that affected humans and another that affected hogs. Spanish flu became known as "swine flu."

If the theory was true, it explained why poor city people, who were more likely to suffer a plethora of minor diseases, had developed an immunity to the virus that farm people had not. Moreover, city people had no contact with swine, as many farm folks did. Because old people were spared in 1918 and 1919, it may be that swine flu was related to the less fatal virus that had caused the epidemic of 1889 to 1890. Having been exposed to that "bug," the elderly were immune to its descendant during the Great War.

THE PRESIDENT'S OBSESSION

In January 1918 Wilson presented Congress with his blueprint for the postwar world. It consisted of Fourteen Points, which, Wilson said, were to be incorporated into the treaty that ended the war. Most of Wilson's points dealt with specific European territorial problems, but five general principles wove through the plan.

First, defeated Germany must be treated fairly and generously to avoid festering resentments that would lead to another war. Wilson was well aware that for more than forty years before World War I, French politicians had demanded revenge for Germany's defeat of France in 1870. In practical terms, Wilson meant that Germany must not be stripped of territory populated by Germans, and the nation must not be saddled with huge reparations payments such as Germany had forced on France.

Second, Wilson said, the boundaries of all European countries must conform to nationality as defined by language.

National Self-Determination

President Wilson thought "national self-determination" was central to avoiding future wars. If boundaries defining states were drawn on national lines, there would be no nationalistic resentments such as those that produced the Serbian terrorist who assassinated Archduke Franz Ferdinand.

But Wilson was well aware, long before he drafted the Fourteen Points, that southeastern Europe—the Austro–Hungarian empire—could not be carved up into states in which all nationalities would have "the freest opportunity of autonomous development." Drawing lines around language groups in southeastern Europe would create a thousand tiny principalities, not nation–states.

Wilson's secretary of state, Robert Lansing, was flabbergasted by the consequences that would flow from the principle of national self-determination, not only in Europe, but in the French and British empires. "The phrase is simply loaded with dynamite.," Lansing said. "It will raise hopes which can never be realized. It will, I fear, cost thousands of lives."

To date it has cost millions, and we are still counting.

Wilson believed that the aspirations of people to govern themselves was a major cause of the war. He avoided mention of the nonwhite people in Britain's and France's colonies, but he did call for Germany's colonies to be disposed of on some basis other than as spoils of war.

Third, Wilson demanded "absolute freedom upon the seas, . . . alike in peace and in war." This was a reference to the German submarine campaign that Wilson blamed for American involvement, but it also hearkened to Britain's historical inclination to use British primacy on the oceans to interfere with American shipping.

Fourth, Wilson demanded disarmament. It was obvious to all parties that the arms race of the two decades preceding the war had been a major cause of the tragedy.

Finally, and most important to Wilson, he called for the establishment of "a general assembly of nations," a congress of countries, to replace the alliances and secret treaties that contributed to the debacle of 1914. More than any other aspect of his program, the **League of Nations** came to obsess the president.

WILSON FOOLS HIMSELF

When an Allied breakthrough in the summer of 1918 put victory within view, Wilson turned nearly all his energies to planning for the peace conference to be held in Paris. He announced that he would personally head the American delegation.

The enormity of World War I justified his decision, but Wilson paid too little attention to a clear shift in the mood of the electorate. In the midterm election of 1918, just a week before the armistice, the voters returned Republican majorities of 240 to 190 to the House of Representatives and of 49 to 47 to the Senate. Not only was Congress Republican, but it had a decidedly nonidealistic tinge. The machine bosses and

professional politicians who had resisted reform for a decade were coming back to Washington.

They were not all reactionaries, nor Wilson-haters; they were the kind of men who were willing to deal. It was Wilson who was uncooperative. He did not recognize that the election of so many Republican regulars might reflect a weariness with the endless exhortations of his administration. The president did not even include a prominent Republican among the delegates he took with him to Europe on December 4, although any treaty had to be ratified by the Republican Senate.

Wilson also misinterpreted his reception in England, France, and Italy. Everywhere he went he was cheered and buried in flowers by crowds of tens of thousands. It had to have been a heady experience for a man who, ten years earlier, was content to be a university president hosting garden parties. Wilson believed that the people of Europe had risen to greatness along with him. They were voicing their support for a peace without victors and a postwar world organized on principles of justice.

THE PEACE CONFERENCE

He was mistaken. The crowds were not welcoming the author of **the Fourteen Points;** they were cheering Wilson the conqueror, the leader of the nation that had ended four years of stalemate. The leaders of the Allies, the men with whom Wilson sat down in Paris, understood this. They knew that after four years of savagery and sacrifice on an unprecedented scale, the people of the victorious nations wanted to taste the fruits of victory. The other three members of the "Big Four"—Georges Clemenceau of France, Lloyd George of Great Britain, and Vittorio Orlando of Italy—paid lip service to Wilson's idealism. But once behind the closed doors of the conference room, they put their national and political interests first.

Georges Clemenceau was the most candid. "God gave us the Ten Commandments and we broke them," he said; "Wilson gives us the Fourteen Points. We shall see." Clemenceau was a shrewd, tough, and nasty infighter who had been turned into a cynic by a lifetime in French politics. He blamed Germany for the war, and he wanted Germany to pay for the death and destruction. Belgium and France had been the battlefields, not Germany. Germany was physically untouched. (The Allies had crossed the German border at only one point at the time of the armistice.) Wilson might speak of a peace without reparations; the entire northeast of France was a ruin. Germany had to pay for that.

Prestige

John Maynard Keynes, of the British delegation at the Versailles Conference, wrote that Woodrow Wilson enjoyed a prestige and a moral influence unequaled in history: "His bold and measured words carried to the peoples of Europe above and beyond the voices of their own politicians. The enemy peoples trusted him to carry out the compact he had made with them; and the Allied peoples acknowledged him not as a victor only but almost as a prophet."

The "Big Four" at the Versailles Peace Conference: Vittorio Orlando of Italy; David Lloyd George of Great Britain; Georges Clemenceau of France; and President Woodrow Wilson. None had the international prestige Wilson enjoyed. But the leaders of all three of the other victorious powers had national and political interests that conflicted with Wilson's idealistic plans for the postwar world. Being experienced, even cynical, realists, they knew how to win concessions from the idealistic Wilson.

British Prime Minister David Lloyd George was personally cordial to Wilson, and there was no ravaged earth in Britain. But Lloyd George was no idealist, and his constituents had suffered the loss of almost a million sons, husbands, and fathers with a million more men maimed. There were billions in pensions to be paid to them and to the widows of the dead soldiers. But the British economy was shattered. Lloyd George too held Germany liable for the suffering and damage.

Vittorio Orlando of Italy went to Versailles to ensure that Italy was rewarded with Austrian territory, particularly the South Tyrol and the Dalmatian port of Fiume. The Tyrol's 200,000 people were German-speaking Austrians; Fiume's population was largely Croatian. That Italy should have them was a blatant violation of Wilson's principle of "national self-determination."

The Japanese delegate, Count Nobuaki Makino, meant to retain the German colonies in the Pacific that Japan had seized. So much for Point Five.

SO MUCH FOR THE FOURTEEN POINTS

Bit by bit, the Versailles Conference redrew Wilson's blueprint until the president's chaste Greek temple looked like a farmhouse to which rooms, dormers, and lean-tos had been added over a century. Three of the Fourteen Points survived intact; six were completely scuttled; five were compromised almost beyond recognition.

Wilson had little choice but to give in. Clemenceau pointed out that Germany had extracted large reparations from France after the Franco–Prussian war, although France had been the aggressor only technically and that war too had been fought in France, not in Germany. In creating the new nations of Poland and Czechoslovakia, large regions populated by Germans had to be included within their borders. Otherwise, Poland would have no seaport (which Wilson himself had promised), and Czechoslovakia, without the mountains of the Sudetenland, would be defenseless. Indeed, if all Germans living contiguously had been incorporated into Germany, the nation would have had a larger German population than it had in 1914. Victors do not write treaties that enlarge the power of the vanquished.

In the Balkans, Wilson's national self-determination— ethnically homogeneous nations—was impossible. The region was a crazy quilt of Hungarian, Rumanian, German, Croatian, Serbian, Slovenian, Bulgarian, and Albanian counties, towns, and villages. Rumanian communities sat cheek by jowl with Hungarian communities. Every city was home to several ethnic groups. The only alternative to Balkan nations with large ethnic minorities nursing ancient resentments was a forced relocation of millions of people. Italy's demand for the South Tyrol was unjustified. Even the Italian army said that the province was not essential to Italian defense. But Orlando wanted it to show Italian voters their

Round Robin

A *round robin* is a petition or statement that is signed by several people with no one of them identified as the leader or instigator. All sign around the text of the document to disguise the order of signing. The intent of the round robin is precisely the opposite of what John Hancock did when he signed his name so prominently to the Declaration of Independence.

sacrifices had been rewarded, and he got his prize (although not Fiume).

Cruel realities exposed the Fourteen Points as the ivory-tower doodlings of an idealist. Wilson faced up to this, although he never openly admitted it. Staking all on the League of Nations, believing that it would resolve the injustices in the Treaty of Versailles, Wilson gave in.

ARTICLE 10

Shelving the Fourteen Points did not much bother the senators who would ratify or reject the treaty, particularly the twelve of the forty-nine Republican senators, mostly westerners, who announced that they were "irreconcilable" in their opposition to ratifying it. To them, entering the war had been a mistake. They meant to isolate the United States from Europe's corruptions and squabbles—not, in a League of Nations, involve Americans in every one of them.

In March 1919 the other thirty-seven Republican senators signed a **round robin** stating they would vote to ratify the treaty if Wilson agreed to certain reservations, which varied from senator to senator. The reservations that counted revolved about Article 10 of the Covenant of the League of Nations. It pledged all member states to "preserve against external aggression the territorial integrity and . . . political independence of all members." Article 10, the reservationists said, committed the United States to go to war if any other League member was attacked. Bulgaria? Uruguay? That was a surrender of national sovereignty, the reservationists said, America's independence of action.

Wilson replied that Article 10 was nothing more than a moral obligation; the United States was not surrendering its independence of action. This was cant. If the obligation was merely moral, it was meaningless, which Wilson, who wrote it, did not believe. Nevertheless, although he had given in to the Allies on dozens of points, he refused to change a word of Article 10 to win the backing of enough Republican senators—not many were needed—to get the treaty ratified. In his righteous recalcitrance, he created an opening for the chairman of the Senate Foreign Relations Committee, Henry Cabot Lodge of Massachusetts (who openly admitted he "hated" Wilson), to humiliate the president.

THE FIGHT FOR THE LEAGUE

Lodge was an unlikely giant-killer. He was not especially popular with his colleagues in the Senate. As determined to have his way as Wilson was, Lodge lacked the greatness to which Wilson could rise. In the battle over the League, however,

Lodge proved an infinitely better politician. Perceiving that Wilson grew less flexible as the debate developed, Lodge became open and cooperative with the mild reservationists, Republicans who wanted to vote for the League with a few adjustments of wording. Understanding that the longer the debate dragged on, the less the American people would be interested in it, Lodge played for time. He read the entire 264 pages of the treaty into the record of his committee's hearings, even though it had been printed and placed on every senator's desk.

Lodge's calculations were dead right. While a majority of Americans probably favored American participation in the League during the first months of 1919, their interest waned slowly but perceptibly in the summer.

The climax came in September. With the treaty about to come before the Senate, Wilson announced an exhausting 8,000-mile speaking tour that his doctors, worried about his extremely high blood pressure, begged him not to undertake. He believed that by rallying the people behind him, he could pressure the reservationist senators to vote for the treaty as it stood. By September 25, when his train moved into Colorado, the crowds seemed to be with him. At Pueblo, however, his speech was slurred, and he openly wept. Wilson had suffered a mild stroke or was on the verge of a nervous breakdown due to exhaustion. His physician canceled the tour and rushed him back to Washington. A few days later, Wilson crumpled to the floor of his bedroom, felled by a cerebral thrombosis, a blood clot in the brain.

THE INVISIBLE PRESIDENT

No one knows how seriously Wilson was disabled in 1919. For six weeks, his protective, strong-willed wife isolated him from everyone but physicians. She screened every document brought to him and returned them with shaky signatures at the bottom. When suspicious and concerned officials insisted on seeing the president, they discovered that his left side was paralyzed and his speech was halting. However, he appeared to be in complete control of his wits. To a senator

A Gentleman to the End

During his final two years as president, Woodrow Wilson was a different man than he had been before the war. His inflexibility on the ratification issue was self-destructive. His refusal to pardon Eugene V. Debs and other imprisoned critics of the war after the armistice was vindictive. But he was a gentleman to the end. In 1920 his personal secretary, Joseph Tumulty, showed him evidence that seemed to confirm the decades-old whispers in Ohio that "Negro blood" flowed in Warren G. Harding's veins. He suggested that it would help the Democrats in the election if the information was released. Wilson replied, "We cannot go into a man's genealogy; we must base our campaign on principle, not backstairs gossip." In fact (though there is no evidence Wilson personally authorized it), the San Francisco post office destroyed 250,000 copies of a pamphlet smearing Harding because of his "mixed blood."

who told him, "We've all been praying for you," he replied, "Which way, Senator?"

Wilson did not meet officially with his cabinet for six months, and photographs of that occasion show a haggard old man with an anxiety in his eyes that cannot be found in any earlier picture. Even if the clarity of his thinking was not affected, his removal from the scene probably had little effect on the outcome of the battle. In the pink of health, Wilson had refused to entertain a compromise.

The outcome was defeat. In November, on Wilson's instructions, the Democratic senators voted with the irreconcilables to kill the treaty with the Lodge reservations by a vote of 55 to 39. When the treaty was introduced without the reservations, the reservationists and the irreconcilables defeated it against the Democrats. In March, over Wilson's protest, twenty-one Democrats worked out a compromise with the reservationist Republicans and again voted on the treaty. The twenty-three Democrats who went along with Wilson's insistence that he get the original treaty or no treaty at all made the difference. They and the irreconcilables defeated it.

THE ELECTION OF 1920

Incredibly, Wilson believed that he could win the League of Nations in the presidential election of 1920. He wanted to be the Democratic party's nominee. That was too much for even the most loyal Wilsonians. They ignored Wilson's hints and chose Governor James M. Cox of Ohio, a party regular who looked like a traveling salesman. For vice president the Democrats nominated a staunch young Wilsonian with

a magical name: Undersecretary of the Navy Franklin D. Roosevelt. The Democrats were pessimistic. But maybe the Roosevelt name on the Democratic ticket would win enough progressive votes to put the party across.

The Republicans had better reason to expect victory. They knew they were still the majority party. Wilson's victory in 1912 had been possible only because of the split of the Republican vote. He won reelection in 1916 by a hair because western voters believed that Wilson would keep the country out of the war. The Republican victory in the congressional elections of 1918, even with the war still raging, confirmed their majority.

As often happens when a party's candidate looks like a shoo-in, there was a catfight for the nomination. General Leonard Wood, an old comrade of Theodore Roosevelt (but no progressive) battled Illinois Governor Frank O. Lowden, who had a reputation as an innovative scientific farmer. Both arrived in Chicago with large blocs of votes, but thanks to a cadre of favorite son candidates, neither had a majority.

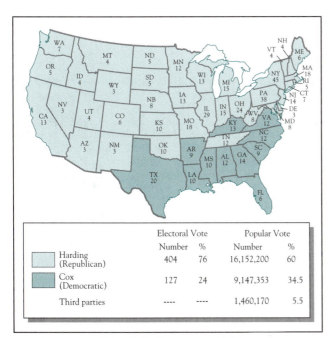

		Electoral Vote		Popular Vote	
		Number	%	Number	%
	Harding (Republican)	404	76	16,152,200	60
	Cox (Democratic)	127	24	9,147,353	34.5
	Third parties	----	----	1,460,170	5.5

MAP 38:1 Presidential Election, 1920

Harding's election restored the Republican party's "natural" supremacy in national elections. Indeed, he enhanced it. He swept the entire Northeast and West where the Democratic party had been strong. He even cracked the "Solid South," winning majorities in West Virginia and Tennessee.

Brown Brothers

Warren G. Harding spoke all over the country during the campaign of 1920. However, he also gave several speeches from the porch of his home in Marion, Ohio. He intended to remind voters of William McKinley's "front porch campaign" in 1896. McKinley had been the epitome of dignity, propriety, and safe and sane conservatism—of "normalcy." That was exactly the image Harding meant to convey.

Early in the proceedings, reporters cornered a wheeler-dealer from Ohio named Harry M. Daugherty. They asked him whom he thought would be nominated. Daugherty replied genially, "Well boys, I'll tell you what I think. The convention will be deadlocked. After the other candidates have failed, we'll get together in some hotel room, oh, about 2:11 in the morning, and some fifteen men, bleary-eyed with lack of sleep, will sit down around a big table, and when that time comes Senator Harding will be selected."

Warren G. Harding of Ohio, a handsome, likable man, was considered one of the least competent members of the Senate. Journalists and fellow senators joked about him. Perhaps because of that, he was acceptable to all Republicans but the now marginal progressives.

THE GREAT BLOVIATOR

Candidate Harding waffled on the treaty, sometimes appearing to favor it with reservations, other times hinting he would let the whole thing die. The theme of his campaign was the need for the country to cool off after two decades of experimental reform and wartime crusading. This strategy allowed Harding to make use of a technique he called "bloviation." Bloviating, as Harding was happy to explain, was "the art of speaking for as long as the occasion warrants, and saying nothing." In Boston Harding declared that "America's need is not heroism but healing, not nostrums but normalcy, not agitation but adjustment, not surgery but serenity, not the dramatic but the dispassionate, not experiment but equipoise, not submergence in internationality but sustainment in triumphant nationality."

The acerbic journalist H. L. Mencken said that Harding's speech reminded him of "stale bean soup, of college yells, of dogs barking idiotically through endless nights." But he added that "it is so bad that a sort of grandeur creeps through it." A Democratic politician remarked that the **normalcy** speech "left the impression of an army of pompous phrases moving over the landscape in search of an idea."

But Harding did have an idea. The great bloviator sensed that no issue, including the League of Nations, was as important to the American people in 1920 as getting back to "normalcy." He was right. He won 61 percent of the vote, more than any candidate who preceded him in the White House since popular votes were recorded.

Wilson lived quietly in Washington until 1924. His wit returning after his retirement, he said, "I am going to try to teach ex-presidents how to behave." He set a good example. A semi-invalid specter out of the past, he took drives almost daily in the elegant Pierce-Arrow automobile that was his pride and joy, attended vaudeville performances and baseball games, and watched movies, of which he was an avid fan, at home.

Unlike Harding (whose funeral he lived to attend), he was a giant who loomed over an age. His intelligence, dignity, steadfastness, and sense of rectitude overshadowed even the boisterous Theodore Roosevelt, something T. R. himself must have sensed: like Lodge, he "hated" Wilson. Wilson's end was therefore more tragic than that of any other president, including those who were assassinated. Wilson, like the tragic heroes of great drama, was murdered not by his enemies or by his weaknesses, but by his virtues.

FURTHER READING

General John W. Chambers, *The Tyranny of Change: America in the Progressive Era, 1890–1920*, 2000; John M. Cooper, *Pivotal Decades: The United States, 1900–1920*, 1990; Steven J. Diner, *A Very Different Age: Americans of the Progressive Era*, 1998; Michael McGerr, *A Fierce Discontent: The Rise and Fall of the Progressive Movement in America, 1870–1920*, 2003; Nell Irvin Painter, *Standing at Armageddon: The United States, 1877–1919*, 1987.

African Americans Arthur Barbeau and Florette Henri, *Unknown Soldiers: Black American Troops in World War I*, 1974; Alfred R. Brophy and Randalll Kennedy, *Reconstructing the Dreamland: The Tulsa Race Riot of 1921*, 2002; Gary Gerstle, *American Crucible: Race and Nation in the Twentieth Century*, 2001; Joe W. Trotter, *The Great Migration in Historical Perspective*, 1991; William Tuttle Jr., *Race Riot: Chicago in the Red Summer of 1919*, 1970.

Conformity and Repression Kathleen Kennedy, *Disloyal Mothers and Scurrilous Citizens: Women and Subversion during World War I*, 1999; Frederick C. Luebke, *Bonds of Loyalty: German-Americans and World War I*, 1974; Paul L. Murray, *World War I and the Origin of Civil Liberties in the United States*, 1979; Richard Polenberg, *Fighting Faiths: The Abrams Case, the Supreme Court, and Free Speech*, 1987; Nick Salvatore, *Eugene V. Debs: Socialist and Citizen*, 1980; Harry M. Scheiber, *The Wilson Administration and Civil Liberties, 1917–1920*, 1960; Stephen Vaughan, *Holding Fast the Inner Lines: Democracy, Nationalism, and the Committee of Public Information*, 1980.

The Home Front Alfred W. Crosby, *America's Forgotten Pandemic: The Influenza of 1918*, 1989; Edward Coffman, *The War to End All Wars: The American Experience in World War I*, 1987; John W. Chambers, *To Raise an Army: The Draft Comes to Modern America*, 1987; Alan Dawley, *Struggle for Justice: Social Responsibility and the Liberal State*, 1991; David Kennedy, *Over Here: The First World War and American Society*, 1980; A. McCartin, *Labor's Great War: The Struggle for American Democracy and the Origins of Modern Labor Relations, 1912–1921*, 1997; Daniel T. Rodgers, *Atlantic Crossings: Social Politics in a Progressive Age*, 1998; Ronald Schaffer, *America in the Great War: The Rise of the War Welfare State*, 1991.

Wilson and the League Lloyd E. Ambrosius, *Woodrow Wilson and Wilsonian Statecraft*, 1991; Klement L. Clements, *Woodrow Wilson: World Statesman*, 1987, and *The Presidency of Woodrow Wilson*, 1992; John M. Cooper, *Breaking the Heart of the World: Woodrow Wilson and the Fight for the League of Nations*, 2001; Robert H. Ferrell, *Woodrow Wilson and World War I, 1917–1921*, 1985; Thomas J. Knock, *To End All Wars: World War I and the Quest for a New World Order*, 1992; Ralph Stone, *The Irreconcilables: The Fight against the League of Nations*, 1970; William C. Widenor, *Henry Cabot Lodge and the Search for an American Foreign Policy*, 1980.

Women and the Vote Sarah Evans, *Born for Liberty: A History of Women in America,* 1989; Sally H. Graham, *Woman Suffrage and the New Democracy,* 1996; Maurine W. Greenwald, *Women, War, and Work,* 1980; Louise M. Newman, *White Woman's Rights: The Racial Origins of Feminism in the United States,* 1993.

KEY TERMS

The following terms are covered in this chapter and can also be found in the list of Key Terms at the back of the book.

Committee on Public Information

Eighteenth Amendment

hooverizing

Industrial Workers of the World

League of Nations

normalcy

round robin

the Fourteen Points

W. E. B. DuBois

War Industries Board

 ## ONLINE SOURCES GUIDE

Use this listing to find online documents, images, interactive maps, simulations, and other resources related to this chapter:

American History Resource Center
http://history.wadsworth.com/rc/us

Selected Documents
A sample of a war propaganda pamphlet
President Woodrow Wilson's Fourteen Points

Selected Images
Ford Motor Company assembly line
U.S. Food Administration poster stressing conservation
New jobs for women
Women workers in Puget Sound Navy Yard, 1919
Women aircraft workers, 1919
Navy recruiting poster

Interactive Time Line (with online readings)
Over Here: World War I at Home, 1917–1920

CHAPTER 39

Troubled Years

America after the Great War 1919–1923

© UPI/Bettmann/Corbis

My candle burneth at both ends; It will not last the night. But, ah, my foes, and, oh, my friends—It gives a lovely light.
Edna St. Vincent Millay

Grown up, and that is a terribly hard thing to do. It is much easier to skip it and go from one childhood to another.
F. Scott Fitzgerald

The decade of the 1920s—the Roaring Twenties—is the most popular of "historical eras." In popular culture, thanks to dozens of novels, pictorial histories, and movies, the 1920s are remembered as the years when Americans, weary of the reforming fervor of the progressives and disillusioned by the war that was supposed to save humanity but only killed off young men by the millions, decided to have a little fun and ended up having a lot.

The Twenties of lore were a time of upscale speakeasies supplied by crude but lovable bootleggers; college boys with big capital letters on their sweaters and flapper girls dancing the Charleston and talking flippantly about sex; sweating, smiling black musicians playing "Dixieland" jazz; the worship of sports heroes—Babe Ruth, Harold "Red" Grange, Jack Dempsey, Gertrude Ederle—and movie stars: Charlie Chaplin, Rudolph Valentino, Mary Pickford, Clara Bow. The 1920s were the automobile's glamour age: every other car on the road was still a Model T Ford, but the Twenties brought sleek Cadillacs and Packards too.

The list could go on, but at any length it would be a misrepresentation. Red Grange did score four touchdowns in twelve minutes, and Gertrude Ederle did swim the English channel two hours faster than the few men who had managed the crossing before her. But only the urban upper and middle classes had the time and leisure to talk much about such things.

The rich got richer during the 1920s. The wealthiest 20 percent of families increased their share of national income by 10 percent; the poorest 60 percent saw their share reduced by 13 percent. Factory workers still put in long days for enough money to get by. Coal miners, a major occupational group then, continued to suffer layoffs that seasonally reduced them to bare survival. Southern, midwestern, and western farmers were mired in a depression that began with the end of World War I. Few rural families had electricity in their homes; even at the end of the decade, a third of American homes were without it.

Even the sensations and glitter enjoyed by a few characterized not a decade but about five years. The "Roaring Twenties" began about 1923. Between 1919, the first postwar year, and 1923, the American middle class was preoccupied not with the Charleston, but by labor unrest and racial conflict, bolshevism and immigrants. Even after the hedonism and glitter hit the newspapers, social tensions and fears swirled about in undercurrents.

"THE WORST PRESIDENT"

Warren Gamaliel Harding presided over the decade's troubled years. Harding had been a journalist, the owner of a small town newspaper. He worked his way up in Ohio politics with a ready smile, a firm handshake, and editorial support of the Republican party line in the Marion *Star*. He was a Rotarian, a label that was used with pride by "boosters" like himself but with contempt by cynical writers like H. L. Mencken and Sinclair Lewis. Ohio's Republican bosses particularly liked Harding because whenever they asked him for a favor, Harding said yes. Harding himself said that if he had been born a woman, he would have been forever "in the family way." He was incapable of saying no.

Ohio sent him to the Senate in 1914; for Harding he may as well have gone to heaven. Being senator meant making speeches; the "bloviater" was a master orator. Being just one senator among ninety-six, however, and a lifelong party regular, Harding was not expected to take the lead in anything. That was fine with him and with the Republican organization: the Senate always has a surplus of prima donnas, so a passive, obliging fellow like Harding was a treasure. No one objected that Harding helped old cronies find government jobs they were unfit to perform. And the affable Ohioan had plenty of time to enjoy the all-night poker, bourbon, and cigar parties that were his second-favorite recreation.

As for his favorite, newspaper reporters were far more restrained in dealing with the private lives of high public officials than they are today. They criticized Harding as the least effective senator—there are no indications this bothered him—but they steered clear of rumored adultery with Washington courtesans. Only after Harding's death did one of his lady friends, Nan Britton, go public with the story that Harding had fathered her illegitimate daughter.

A DECENT MAN

It is not difficult to feel sympathy for Harding. He was a weak man, but he lacked cant, a rare quality in a politician. He had no illusions about his intelligence and capacity for leadership; he freely admitted that he could not hope to be "the best president," but that he would try to be "the best liked." Personally, Harding was kind and decent. After eight years of the brilliant but self-righteous Wilson, Americans did not find an ordinary mind and a self-effacing personality unattractive.

Harding displayed his human side at Christmas 1921 when he pardoned Eugene V. Debs and other socialists who had opposed the war. (Wilson commuted the sentences of a hundred small fish convicted under the dubious Espionage Act, but he was vindictive toward Debs to the end.) Harding urged the directors of United States Steel Corporation to reduce the workday in their mills to eight hours—not because he thought the employees' workday was anyone's business but the owners', but because he was appalled at the idea of anyone working twelve-hour days.

Most striking was Harding's response when political enemies whispered that African blood ran in his veins. In a time when white racism was virtually universal, that kind of talk could ruin a career. Other politicians would have responded to such an accusation with a lawsuit or even uglier countersmears. Harding shrugged; he told a friend, How did he know whether one of his forebears "had jumped the fence"?

SMART GEEKS: HOOVER, HUGHES, MELLON

Some of Harding's cabinet appointments were dictated by party politics. As usual, the Republicans' "elder statesman," 1916 candidate Charles Evans Hughes, was secretary of state. Eastern money got the Treasury Department; Harding named a Pittsburgh banker, Andrew Mellon, as secretary of

Inventor of the Backyard Barbecue

Henry Ford invented the charcoal briquette. He devised the process for making them in order not to waste the mountains of wood scraps produced by the manufacture of dashboards and other wooden parts for the Model T. He and Thomas Edison built the first briquette factory and turned it over to a partner, Charles Kingsford, to operate.

the treasury. When the Republicans, to their delight, discovered that the popular Herbert Hoover was not a Wilsonian Democrat but a Republican, they put him in Harding's cabinet as secretary of commerce. All-business, all-efficiency Hoover made Harding uncomfortable. Harding called him "the smartest geek I know" but admitted to friends he was always glad to see Hoover leave the room.

As during the war, Hoover was a tireless worker. He wanted to be president, but he did not conspicuously promote himself. He believed that achievements would take care of his career. Harding was not the only old guard Republican to be uneasy with his activism. But Hoover mollified conservatives by shunning the state interventionism of the Wilson administration. He tried to bring order to industry by forming voluntary associations. He hoped they would eliminate waste, develop uniform standards of production, and end "destructive competition." This was fine with the heads of the great corporations. Hoover's associations let them make entirely legal arrangements with competitors, but there was no federal official ready to prosecute if they stepped over the line.

The United States had not ratified the Treaty of Versailles. Therefore, the country was, legally, still at war with Germany. Secretary of State Hughes eliminated that technicality by having Congress "resolve" that the war was over and recognize the new German republic. Hughes then pulled off a coup in international relations that caught the world's naval powers by surprise. He invited representatives of the naval powers to Washington to discuss disarmament. The delegates, expecting the usual drone of platitudes and round of dinners and receptions (without any drinks: Prohibition was in force), were stunned when Hughes opened the conference with a detailed

plan for reducing the size of the world's navies. The five nations with the largest navies were to destroy some capital ships (battleships and battle cruisers) and to cancel construction already under way or planned.

Everyone agreed that the arms race was a contributing cause of the Great War. The delegates at the Washington conference had little choice but to listen. Hughes reminded them that by reducing the size of their navies, their governments would save millions: the construction of a single capital ship was a major line item in a national budget.

In the **Treaty of Washington** of 1921, the five major naval powers agreed to limit their fleets according to a ratio that reflected their interests and defensive needs. For each five tons that Great Britain and the United States kept afloat in capital ships, Japan would have three, and France and Italy somewhat smaller fleets.

Each nation gave up ships, but each benefited, too. Great Britain maintained equality on the high seas with the United States, a primacy that American plans for ship construction would have destroyed. (The United States scrapped thirty battleships and cruisers that were under construction or on the drawing boards.) The American government slashed its expenditures, a high priority for the Harding administration. Japan, which needed only a Pacific navy while Britain and the United States had worldwide interests, got parity (even superiority) in the Pacific. Italy and France were spared the strain of an arms race that might bankrupt them, but they remained dominant in the Mediterranean.

THE HARDING SCANDALS

Naval disarmament was the chief accomplishment of the Harding administration. Most of the president's appointees were either servants of special interests or crooks. Secretary of the Treasury Andrew Mellon pursued tax policies that extravagantly favored the rich. More dismaying were the cronies to whom Harding gave government jobs for old times' sake. As soon as they settled in their Washington offices, they set about filling their pockets and ruining their generous friend in the White House.

Attorney General Harry Daugherty winked at violations of the law by political allies. Probably with Daugherty's

Postwar Instability 1919–1929

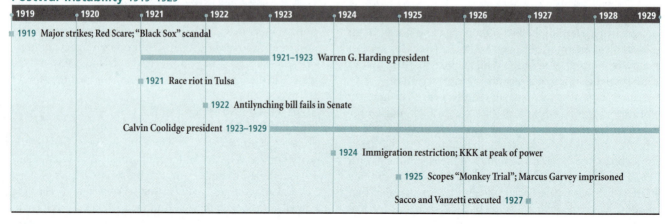

1919 Major strikes; Red Scare; "Black Sox" scandal

1921–1923 Warren G. Harding president

1921 Race riot in Tulsa

1922 Antilynching bill fails in Senate

Calvin Coolidge president 1923–1929

1924 Immigration restriction; KKK at peak of power

1925 Scopes "Monkey Trial"; Marcus Garvey imprisoned

Sacco and Vanzetti executed 1927

knowledge, Jesse L. Smith, a personal friend of the president, sold favorable decisions and public offices for cash. Charles R. Forbes, the head of the Veterans Administration, pocketed money intended for hospital construction. The grandest thief of all, Secretary of the Interior Albert B. Fall, leased the navy's petroleum reserves at Teapot Dome, Wyoming, and Elk Hills, California, to two freewheeling oil men, Harry Sinclair and Edward L. Doheny. In return, Fall accepted "loans" of about $300,000. Fall tarred Harding with his corruption because he had earlier persuaded the president to transfer the oil reserves from the authority of the navy to Fall's Department of the Interior.

By the summer of 1923, Harding knew that his administration was shot through with thievery. When he set out on a vacation trip to Alaska, he knew that it was only a matter of time before the scandals hit the newspapers. His health was suffering; his famous handsome face is haggard in the last photographs. Nevertheless, he remained loyal to his treacherous pals. He allowed Forbes to flee abroad, and he took no action against the others.

Jesse Smith eventually killed himself. Mercifully, because he was personally innocent of wrongdoing, Harding died shortly after disembarking from his Alaskan cruise at San Francisco. Only later did the nation learn of the thievery in his administration and the irregularities in the president's personal life. So tangled were Harding's affairs that scandalmongers suggested that Harding's wife poisoned him to spare him the disgrace that was coming, and they were widely believed. Actually the president suffered massive heart failure.

Library & Archives Division, Historical Society of Western Pennsylvania, Pittsburg, Pa.

A handbill announcing the end of the steel strike of 1919 in eight languages. Many steelworkers were immigrants, particularly from Slavic eastern Europe.

POSTWAR TENSIONS: LABOR, REDS, IMMIGRANTS

The nation's social tensions strained and snapped even before Harding moved into the White House. Had the president been a pillar of moral strength and probity, the postwar years and the short era of "normalcy" would have been no less troubled by labor unrest, a fear of communism that bordered on the hysterical, hostility to new immigrants, racial conflict, and religious reaction.

1919: YEAR OF CONFLICT

During the war, the American Federation of Labor seemed to be part of the federal power structure. In return for recognition of their respectability, most unions did not strike during the hostilities. Unfortunately, while wages rose slowly during 1917 and 1918, the prices of consumer goods rose quickly. Then they soared during runaway postwar inflation. The war's end also meant the cancellation of huge government contracts. Tens of thousands of people in war-related jobs were thrown out of work, leading to the inevitable: 3,600 strikes in 1919 involving 4 million workers.

The strikers' grievances were generally valid, but few Americans outside the labor movement were sympathetic. When employers described the strikes of 1919 as the work of

revolutionaries aimed at destroying middle-class decency, much of America agreed. In Seattle, a dispute that began on the docks of the busy Pacific port turned into a general strike involving almost all of the city's 60,000 working people. Most of the strikers were interested in nothing more than better pay. However, the concept of the general strike was associated with class war and revolution. Seattle Mayor Ole Hansen depicted the dispute as an uprising sponsored and led by dangerous foreign Bolsheviks. With the help of U.S. Marines, Hansen crushed the strike.

STEELWORKERS AND POLICE

The magnates of the steel industry employed similar methods to fight a walkout in September 1919 by 350,000 workers, mostly in the Great Lakes region. The men had good reason to strike. Many of them worked a twelve-hour day and a seven-day week. It was not unusual for individuals to put in thirty-six hours at a stretch. That is, if a man's relief failed to show, he might be told to stay on for another twelve-hour shift or lose his job. When the extra shift ended, his own began again.

Steelworkers took home subsistence wages. For some unmarried Slavic immigrants, home was not even a bed to themselves. They contracted with a boardinghouse to rent a bed half the day. After their shift and a quick meal, they rolled under blankets still warm and damp from the body of a fellow worker who had just trudged off to the mill.

These wretched conditions were well known. Yet the heads of the industry, Elbert Gary of United States Steel and Charles Schwab of Bethlehem Steel, persuaded the public that the strike of 1919 was the work of revolutionary agitators like William Z. Foster. Although Foster's leadership was in the AFL's bread-and-butter tradition, he had been a Wobbly in the past (and he would become the head of the American Communist party), so the company's line was plausible. Moreover, many steelworkers were immigrants from eastern Europe, the nursery of bolshevism. The strike failed.

The Boston police strike of 1919 frightened Americans most of all. While the shutdown of even a basic industry like steel did not jar the rhythms of daily life, the absence of police officers on the streets caused a jump in crime in Boston as professional hoodlums, lowlifes, and the desperately poor took advantage of the situation.

Boston's policemen, mostly of Irish background, were underpaid. They earned 1916 wages, not enough to support their families decently in a city where prices had tripled during the war. Nevertheless, they commanded little public support when they walked out. When Massachusetts Governor Calvin Coolidge ordered the National Guard into Boston to take over police functions and break the strike, the public applauded. When Samuel Gompers asked Coolidge to restore the beaten workers to their jobs, the governor replied, "There is no right to strike against the public safety by anybody, anywhere, anytime." It made Coolidge a national hero and won him the Republican vice presidential nomination in 1920.

RED SCARE

Public reaction to the strikes of 1919 revealed a widespread hostility toward recent immigrants. This xenophobia took its most virulent form in the Red Scare of 1919. Even before the armistice, a new stereotype had replaced the "Hun" as the villain Americans loved to hate: the seedy, lousy, bearded, and wild-eyed Bolshevik—the "Red."

The atrocities during the civil war following the Russian Revolution of 1917 were real, lurid, and numerous. Nevertheless, American newspapers exaggerated them and even invented tales of mass executions, torture, children being turned against their parents, and women being proclaimed the common sexual property of all men. Americans were ready to believe the worst about a part of the world from which so many recent immigrants had come.

Many believed that foreign-born communists were a major threat to the security of the United States. In March 1919 the Soviets organized the Third International, or Comintern, an organization explicitly dedicated to fomenting revolution worldwide. So it seemed no accident when, in April, the post office discovered thirty-eight bombs addressed to prominent capitalists and government officials. In June a few bombs reached their targets. One bomber who was identified (he blew himself up) was an Italian. In Chicago, in September 1919, two American Communist

© UPI/Bettmann/Corbis

Bartolomeo Vanzetti and Nicola Sacco became the center of a worldwide protest when they were tried and convicted for an armed robbery that resulted in a murder. Ballistics tests done late in the twentieth century indicate that Sacco was probably involved, but the evidence against the two in the 1920s was scanty and, in part, contrived. The widespread belief at the time that they were railroaded because they were Italians and anarchists was justified.

parties were founded. The press emphasized the immigrant element in the membership.

Only a tiny minority of American immigrants were radicals. The most prominent Communists boasted a WASP ancestry as impeccable as Henry Cabot Lodge's. Max Eastman, the editor of the radical magazine *The Masses,* was of old New England stock. John Reed, whose *Ten Days That Shook the World* was the classic sympathetic account of the Russian Revolution, was a bright-eyed Harvard boy from Portland, Oregon. William Z. Foster had no ethnic ties. William D. Haywood, who fled to the Soviet Union rather than go to prison, said he could trace his ancestry "to the Puritan bigots."

But dread of a ghost can be as compelling as fear of a grizzly bear. Americans were uneasy in 1919; the temptation to exploit the anxiety was too much for President Wilson's attorney general, **A. Mitchell Palmer.** He hoped he might be able to ride the Red Scare into a presidential nomination by ordering a series of well-publicized raids on Communist offices.

Only 39 of the hundreds of people Palmer arrested could legally be deported. Nevertheless, the attorney general put 249 people on a steamship bound for Russia that was dubbed "the Soviet Ark." On New Year's Day 1920, Palmer's agents again swooped down on hundreds of locations, arresting 6,000 people. Some of them, such as a Western Union delivery boy, merely had the bad luck to be in the wrong place at the wrong time. Others were arrested while peering into the windows of communist storefronts. All were jailed at least briefly.

Radical Eloquence

Murderer or victim of injustice, Bartolomeo Vanzetti was a man of rare eloquence. The mistakes he made in his adopted language added poignancy to his statements. Shortly before his execution, he wrote with some foresight,

> If it had not been for these thing, I might have live out my life talking at street corners to scorning men. I might have die, unmarked, unknown, a failure. Now we are not a failure. This is our career and our triumph. Never in our full life could we hope to do such work for tolerance, for joostice, for man's understanding of men as now we do by accident. Our words—our lives—our pains—nothing! The taking of our lives—lives of a good shoemaker and a poor fish peddler—all! That last moment belongs to us—that agony is our triumph.

Bartolomeo Vanzetti and Nicola Sacco were executed after a long international debate about the fairness of their trial. For half a century, communists, socialists, and liberals remembered them as martyrs.

Palmer's celebrity fizzled when he predicted mass demonstrations on May Day 1920, the socialist and communist holiday, and nothing happened. By midsummer the great Red Scare was over. Antiforeigner sentiment, however, continued to shape government policy and public opinion.

SACCO AND VANZETTI

The most celebrated victims of the marriage of antiradicalism to xenophobia were Nicola Sacco and Bartolomeo Vanzetti. In 1920 the two Italian immigrants were arrested for an armed robbery in South Braintree, Massachusetts, during which a guard and a paymaster were killed. They were found guilty of murder and were sentenced to die in the electric chair.

Before they were executed, the recently founded American Civil Liberties Union and several Italian-American societies learned that hard evidence against **Sacco and Vanzetti** was scanty; some, in fact, appeared to have been invented by the prosecution. (It was.) The judge at the trial, Webster Thayer, had been openly prejudiced against the defendants; he was overheard speaking of them as "those damned dagos." The ACLU, Italian-American associations (and the Italian government), and distinguished lawyers like Felix Frankfurter of Harvard University concluded that the men were innocent; they had been sentenced to death because they were Italian and, worse, they were known anarchists.

Sacco and Vanzetti won admiration by acting with dignity in prison. They insisted on their innocence of the murders while refusing to compromise their political beliefs and their right to have them. "I am suffering," Vanzetti said, "because I am a radical and indeed I am a radical; I have suffered because I was an Italian, and indeed I am an Italian . . . but I am so convinced to be right that if you could execute me two

times, and if I could be reborn two other times, I would live again to do what I have done already."

The movement to save Sacco and Vanzetti was international. Massachusetts granted several stays of execution; several of the irregularities of the trial were conceded. Nevertheless, the two were electrocuted in 1927. By that time, their guilt or innocence had ceased to be relevant. Sacco and Vanzetti's defenders could see nothing in the case against them except ethnic and political prejudice. The state of Massachusetts was not going to admit the possibility it was executing innocent men.

IMMIGRATION RESTRICTED

In 1883 Emma Lazarus had written, "Send these, the homeless, tempest-tost to me, I lift my lamp beside the golden door." As if they had heard her, European immigrants poured into the United States at up to a million people per year until 1915, when naval warfare made Atlantic crossings risky. By 1918 annual immigration had declined to 110,000.

Most of the new immigrants were from eastern and southern Europe. Disturbed that the new immigrants huddled together, apparently uninterested in becoming Americans, xenophobic old-stock Americans organized the Immigration Restriction League in 1894. Henry Cabot Lodge was a member, as were distinguished historians such as Albert Bushnell Hart, John Fiske, and Herbert Baxter Adams and the presidents of Harvard and Stanford University. The league was influential: several times Congress enacted a "literacy test" for would-be immigrants, requiring that adults must prove their ability to read in order to be admitted. (Most new immigrants could not read.) But three presidents (Cleveland, Taft, and Wilson) vetoed the bills.

Originally, opposition to immigration was cultural (the newcomers' cultures were alien to American values) and economic (they drove down wages.) However—perhaps inevitable in the era of Jim Crow—it took on a racial character. In 1899 William Z. Ripley published *Races of Europe*, which categorized Europeans into three subraces: the Teutonic, the Alpine, and the Mediterranean. Although all had positive traits (Ripley credited the Mediterranean Italians with a finely developed artistic sense), there was no question that Teutons—Britons, Germans, and northern Europeans, generally—were the people with an intrinsic commitment to liberty and democracy.

In 1916 an esteemed natural scientist, Madison Grant, took up where Ripley left off. In *The Passing of the Great Race* Grant maintained that through intermarriage with old-stock Americans, the new immigrants were literally destroying, through dilution, the nation's prized genetic heritage. The book was immensely successful, running through several editions. (During the war, Grant demoted the Germans out of the great race.) When immigration rose to 800,000 in 1921, the time for action had come. This time Congress's criterion was not literacy, but would-be immigrants' country of origin.

The Immigration Restriction Act of 1921 limited admissions to 350,000 people a year except for Latin Americans, who were freely admitted. Asians were completely excluded. Each European nation was entitled to send a number of immigrants equal to 3 percent of the number of people of that nationality who were residents of the United States in 1910. An amendment to the law in 1924 reduced the number of European immigrants to 150,000 and the national quota to 2 percent, and changed the base year to 1890. Most southern and eastern Europeans had come to the United States after 1890, so the quotas for Poland, Czechoslovakia, Hungary, Rumania, Yugoslavia, Bulgaria, Russia, Greece, and Italy were quite low. Only 5,802 Italians were admitted each year, 6,524 Poles, and 2,784 Russians. Those quotas were filled each year before the end of January. The quotas for the prosperous countries of northern and western Europe were generous and rarely filled. The annual quota for Great Britain under the 1924 law was 75,000. The quota was never filled; during the 1930s, only 2,500 Britons emigrated to the United States each year.

RACIAL TENSIONS

During the war W. E. B. DuBois, editor of the NAACP's newspaper, *The Crisis,* had urged African Americans to enlist in the army rather than wait to be drafted. DuBois hoped that by demonstrating their patriotism, blacks' claims to social equality would, after the armistice, be heard. Among African Americans, DuBois was heard. *The Crisis,* read mostly by educated blacks and white sympathizers before the war, increased its subscription list to 100,000 in 1918. But hopes for changes after the war were dashed immediately.

Lynching of African Americans declined during the 1920s, but it was still common in the South. Lynch mobs had so little fear of punishment that they rarely interfered with photographers. This murder of five was the worst single instance since the lynching of blacks became a major problem during the 1890s.

The Granger Collection, New York

The More Things Change . . .

Showboat, a Broadway musical of 1927, introduced the classic lament "Ol' Man River." The original lyrics began,

> Niggers all work on the Mississippi,
> Niggers all work while the white folks play

In a movie made a few years later, the line was changed to

> Darkies all work on the Mississippi. . . .

African-American operatic singer Paul Robeson found this offensive too. When he sang the song, it began

> There's an old man called the Mississippi. . . .

In a Broadway revival of *Showboat* in 1946:

> Colored folks work. . . .

In a 1951 movie:

> Here we all work. . . .

In a 1993 revival on stage, it was back to

> Niggers all work on the Mississippi. . . .

RACE RIOTS AND LYNCHINGS

Shortly after the armistice there was a race riot in Elaine, Arkansas, in which several hundred blacks and whites were arrested. Twelve were sentenced to death. (The Supreme Court later freed them.) In 1919 much of Chicago exploded. A black teenager swimming in Lake Michigan drifted into "whites only" waters. He was battered with rocks thrown from the beach and drowned. Whites and blacks battled one another in the streets, sometimes with guns, for five days; 38 people were killed, 500 injured. The death toll in other race riots that summer was 120. In 1921 a citywide race riot in Tulsa left at least 100 people dead and 1,000 homes and shops in the once-prosperous African-American business district destroyed.

In the first year after the war, seventy-six blacks were lynched, more than in any year since 1904. Ten of them were veterans, several still in uniform. In both 1920 and 1921, lynchings exceeded fifty, and the House of Representatives enacted the Dyer Bill, which provided for federal prosecution of sheriffs and other police officials who cooperated with or ignored lynch mobs. The bill died in the Senate when southerners filibustered against it.

Nevertheless, lynchings decreased in 1923 and never again reached 1919 levels. To some extent, southern police authorities got the message of the unsuccessful Dyer Bill: if they did not act on their own to stop lynchings, they risked federal intervention. More important, middle-class white southerners and southern newspapers had had their fill of the savagery and what it meant for the South's reputation. Southern sheriffs willing to shrug off northerners' criticisms were not willing to risk the opposition of influential southern whites.

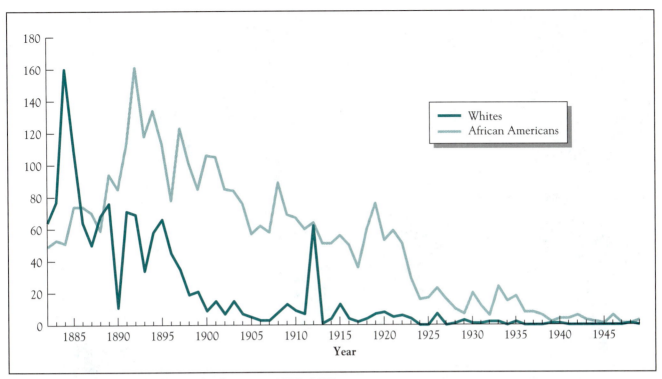

CHART 39:1 Lynchings in the United States, 1875–1950
Before the rise of southern populism during the 1890s, lynching was common in the United States, but blacks were not singled out as victims. By 1900 (except in 1912), lynchings of whites virtually ceased. By the 1920s, middle-class social pressures on southern sheriffs (who previously had often been accomplices to lynchings) resulted in a steady decline in mob murders of blacks. Not until World War II, however, were the numbers of lynching victims reduced to two or three per year.

THE KU KLUX KLAN

The increase in lynchings in the early 1920s paralleled the rise of a revived Ku Klux Klan. The Klan was founded in 1915 by a Methodist minister, William Simmons, after he viewed *The Birth of a Nation,* a film that glorified the suppression of blacks after the Civil War. Under Hiram Wesley Evans, the second KKK gave local units and officials exotic names such as Klavern, Kleagle, Grand Dragon, and Exalted Cyclops. Evans was as much businessman as ideologue. The Klan had a monopoly of "official" regalia that all members were required to buy. Local organizers were given cash incentives to sign up recruits and sell the costumes; they kept a percentage of all the money that they collected. By 1923 Klan membership may have been as high as 4.5 million.

In the South the KKK was, as always, an antiblack organization. Elsewhere KKK leaders exploited whatever hatreds, fears, and resentments were most likely to keep the costume orders rolling in. In the Northeast, where Catholics and Jews were numerous, Klan leaders inveighed against them. In the Owens Valley of California, a region of small farmers whose irrigation water was drained southward to feed the growth of Los Angeles, the big city was the enemy. In the Midwest, some Klaverns concentrated their attacks on saloonkeepers who ignored Prohibition and "lovers' lanes" where teenagers in automobiles flaunted traditional morality the old-fashioned way. The brief heyday of the Klan reflected the fear of poor, Protestant, small-town people that the America they had known (or idealized) was being destroyed by immigrants, big cities, and an immorality they associated with cities and immigrants.

By 1924 numerous state legislators and congressmen, a few senators, and the governors of Oregon, Ohio, Tennessee, and Texas were Klansmen or openly sympathetic with the Klan. In Indiana, Grand Dragon David Stephenson was the state's political boss. At the Democratic national convention of 1924, the Klan was strong enough to prevent the party from adopting a plank critical of its bigotry and to veto the nomination of a Catholic, Governor Alfred E. Smith of New York, to run for president.

That was, however, the KKK's last hurrah. In 1925 David Stephenson was found guilty of second-degree murder in the death of a young woman whom he had taken to Chicago for a tryst. In an attempt to win a light sentence, Stephenson turned over evidence showing that virtually the whole administration of the Klan was involved in thievery and that Indiana's Klan politicians were thoroughly corrupt. By 1930 the KKK dwindled to 10,000 members.

MARCUS GARVEY AND THE CALL OF AFRICA

At its peak, the Klan was endorsed from an unlikely quarter, by the founder of the United Negro Improvement Association, **Marcus Garvey.** Jamaica born and based in New York's Harlem, Garvey, like the Klan, preached separation of the

Ku Kluxers praying around a cross in a park. To signal their presence to blacks, Catholics, Jews, or others the KKK considered undesirable, they soaked crosses in kerosene and burned them by night: small crosses in front of the homes of people they were warning off, crosses twenty to thirty feet high on hilltops at major gatherings.

races. In his widely circulated newspaper, *Negro World,* he hammered on the theme that Africans had once had a civilization far superior to that of whites. "When Europe was inhabited by a race of cannibals, a race of savages, naked men, heathens, and pagans," Garvey told cheering crowds, "Africa was peopled by a race of cultured black men who were masters in art, science, and literature." To seek the acceptance of whites was humiliating and self-destructive. African Americans (and black West Indians) should, among themselves, pool resources and work toward the day when they would return to Africa and build a great nation.

How seriously Garvey took his ultimate goal is impossible to say. After the disillusionments of 1919, however, tens of thousands of blacks living in northern cities joined the UNIA. Many who did not join approved of Garvey. On one occasion, Garvey claimed a million followers, on another 4 million. The *Negro World* had a circulation of 200,000, more than the NAACP's *The Crisis.* Garvey was a canny showman. He founded paramilitary orders with exotic names like "The Dukes of the Niger" and the "Black Eagle Flying Corps," which he dressed in gaudy costumes. In

parades in Harlem, Philadelphia, Detroit, and other cities with large African-American populations, he rode in parades in a ceremonial uniform as the "president of Africa."

Garvey was not all show. He encouraged blacks to found businesses in Harlem and other cities' African-American neighborhoods and urged blacks to patronize them rather than businesses owned by whites. Indeed, he owned or was a partner in a number of enterprises. His most ambitious, the Black Star steamship line (which would carry black Americans to Africa), was his undoing. Black Star was capitalized at $750,000 raised by sales of stock to 35,000 investors. With classic 1920s hoopla, Garvey touted shares in the company as an "opportunity to climb the great ladder of industrial and commercial progress."

Black Star was a disaster, soon bankrupt with virtually no assets. Utterly ignorant of the shipping business, Garvey purchased three old ships that needed expensive repairs before they could be moved. A fourth ship on the books did not exist. When the federal government prosecuted Garvey for mail fraud, he claimed he had paid for the fourth ship but it was not delivered. The paperwork showing that he had been

Baseball has medieval roots, but it took shape in more or less modern form in New York in the 1840s. At first it was a gentleman amateurs' game; but after the Civil War it was popular enough that professional teams were formed. The first professionals were barnstormers, touring the country and picking up games with all comers willing to pay the fees they charged for showing off how well the game could be played. By the turn of the twentieth century, sixteen teams were organized into two major leagues. The champions of the American and National Leagues met each fall in a World Series.

Baseball was a business—risky, but potentially very profitable for the owners of the clubs. By 1910 most major league teams had built permanent, sometimes imposing closed playing fields. To see a game, fans had to buy a ticket; there was no more watching from outside an open field ringed only with ropes or low wooden fences.

In theory, winning teams attracted the most spectators and were, therefore, the most profitable. But it did not always work that way. Cornelius McGillicuddy (Connie Mack, the owner of the Philadelphia Athletics) said that the ideal season was one in which the A's contended for the pennant (the league championship) until the last days of the season, then lost to some other team. If the A's won, Mack's players wanted more pay the next year.

To prevent disappointed players from jumping to another team, club owners devised the "reserve clause," which was in every player's contract. It was based on the proposition that a baseball player was a professional like a physician or lawyer, not an employee. Unlike factory workers who (as their employers never tired of saying) were free to quit when they did not like their pay, a professional baseball player worked under contract. The reserve clause contracted a player not to play for another team without the club owner's consent. His services were *reserved* unless his contract was sold—he was "traded"—to another club owner. Clubs could not bid against one another for the best players.

Business techniques varied from team to team. Connie Mack's A's were one of the dominant teams in the American League before World War I. They won six pennants and three World Series. Twice Mack sold off his star players for cash he could pocket. (In 1931, when the A's were the best team in baseball, he did it again.)

Charles A. Comiskey, owner of the Chicago White Sox, had another way of lining his pockets. He was content with mediocre players earning the poorest pay in the major leagues. Chicago was big enough that the White Sox sold plenty of tickets to fans who wanted to see the visiting teams play. Then, during the war, the White Sox jelled behind a hard-hitting outfielder, Joseph "Shoeless Joe" Jackson; a superb third baseman, George "Buck" Weaver; second baseman Eddie Collins (sold to Comiskey by Connie Mack); and several excellent pitchers. In 1919 the White Sox won the American League pennant despite the fact that the club payroll and the players' expense accounts were the lowest in the league. The team's two leading pitchers, who won fifty games between them, were paid a combined salary of only $8,600.

The White Sox were regarded as unbeatable against the Cincinnati Reds in the World Series. Unable to attract many bets on the Reds, bookmakers increased the payoff. Even before the Series began, it was rumored that a notorious gambler, Arnold Rothstein, had arranged for the White Sox to throw the series and that he had bet a lot of money on the Reds. The Reds won. The inevitable investigation revealed that eight White Sox, including Jackson, had taken money from Rothstein. Jackson admitted it, but said he had played his best to win. Buck Weaver insisted he had turned the gamblers down, which the other accused players confirmed. (The gamblers never contacted Eddie Collins, who knew nothing of the scheme.)

The eight accused "Black Sox" were acquitted in criminal court. But they were banned from organized baseball for life by a newly installed commissioner, Judge Kenesaw Mountain Landis. Fearing the whole baseball business would be ruined if fans suspected a "fix" whenever there was an upset in a game, Landis was merciless. Buck Weaver proved he had accepted no bribes; but he was banned too because he had not revealed that Rothstein had approached him.

Still, it was not Landis who saved the baseball business but an ugly, pot-bellied, spindly legged, and vulgar player from Baltimore who was changing the nature of the game and earning huge salaries from his club, the New York Yankees. George Herman "Babe" Ruth had been an excellent pitcher for the Boston Red Sox. In 1919, playing outfield on days he did not pitch, Ruth hit twenty-nine home runs, double that of any previous player. Baseball "before Ruth" was a game of tactics played by lithe, swift men who eked out runs one at a time with scratch hits and gritty base running. Now, with a single swing, the "Sultan of Swat" could put up to four runs on the scoreboard. The fans loved it. Purchased from the Red Sox by the Yankees for $100,000, Ruth hit fifty-nine home runs in 1921. Rather than haggle endlessly with their golden goose, the Yankee ownership paid him annually higher salaries. By the end of the decade, when his pay was higher than that of the president of the United States, Ruth said nonchalantly, "I had a better year than he did."

Ruth made the Yankees the richest team in baseball. In 1923 New York opened the largest baseball ground of the era, Yankee Stadium, which was nicknamed "the house that Ruth built." Club owners and Commissioner Landis took notice too. If home runs sold tickets, they would have more home runs. They denied that the baseball itself was retooled into a livelier "rabbit ball"; however, they began to put new balls in play after they were hit a few times and began to soften. The "slugger" became the star of the game. Hack Wilson of the Chicago Cubs hit fifty-six home runs in 1930; Jimmy Foxx of the Athletics threatened to eclipse Ruth when he hit fifty-eight in 1932 and was promptly sold by Connie Mack, who had not abandoned his old business plan.

Bottoms Up

One argument wets marshaled against Prohibition was that it actually increased drinking and drunkenness. The statistics, while fragmentary, do not support them. Between 1906 and 1910, per capita alcohol consumption in the United States was 2.6 gallons per year. In 1934, the first year after the Prohibition Amendment was repealed, consumption stood at 1.2 gallons. Not until 1971, a generation after Prohibition, did consumption of alcohol reach pre–World War I levels.

The death rate from chronic alcoholism peaked in the United States in 1907 at 7.3 per 100,000. By 1932, the last full year of Prohibition, the rate had declined to 2.5 per 100,000.

Prohibition did cause accidental self-poisonings. About 1,000 people died annually from drinking adulterated moonshine during Prohibition's first years. By 1933 about 50,000 "jake walkers" roamed the streets, sometimes suffering cruel taunts. "Jake walkers" suffered from a nervous disorder caused by drinking methyl or wood alcohol ("jake") over an extended period. They lost muscular control so that they walked in jerky steps, their toes touching the ground before their heels.

the victim of fraud was not convincing. Insisting to the end that he had not defrauded investors, Garvey was convicted and sentenced to five years' imprisonment. His sentence was commuted after two years, after which he was immediately deported to Jamaica.

By that time, without Garvey on the scene, the UNIA had collapsed. However, the attraction of Africa did not die. African-American fraternal lodges took African names. Baptist and Methodist churches added "Abyssinian" or "Ethiopian" to their names. In Detroit a mysterious figure named W. D. Fard (or Wali Farad) founded the Nation of Islam, claiming that Christianity was the white man's religion. Even W. E. B. DuBois wrote that "the spell of Africa is upon me. The ancient witchery of her medicine is burning in my drowsy, dreamy blood."

PROHIBITION AND FUNDAMENTALISM

Progressive reformers (and the Great War) were instrumental in making Prohibition part of the Constitution. By the time the Eighteenth Amendment went into effect in 1920, however, only a small minority of congressmen still called themselves progressives, and even fewer state governors still espoused reform. One of the few, the popular Alfred E. Smith of New York, elected four times during the 1920s, was and always had been a "wet," opposed to Prohibition and unembarrassed to break the law. Although a moderate drinker himself, he kept liquor in his office so he could offer visitors a drink.

WETS, DRYS, AND BOOTLEGGERS

President Harding, never a progressive and on the record as supporting Prohibition, enjoyed a finger or two of bourbon with his cronies. Except for politically expedient "drys"

like Harding, however, the cleavage between supporters and enemies of Prohibition during the 1920s had nothing to do with where people stood on reform, or even whether they were Democrats or Republicans, and little to do with whether they drank.

Overwhelming majorities of people who lived in big cities were "wets" and, therefore, majorities in states in which there were big cities. In 1923 New York's legislature repealed the law it had enacted to enforce the Eighteenth Amendment. The rural South and rural counties in the Midwest were dry. Catholics and, therefore, the states where they were numerous, like Massachusetts, Connecticut, and Rhode Island, were wet. Protestants who called themselves "fundamentalists" (they believed in the literal truth of the Bible—Baptists, Methodists, Pentecostals) were dry. The "Bible Belt," from the deep South extending west to the Rocky Mountains, was the citadel of Prohibition's defenders. California was split: the central part of the state, dominated by cosmopolitan San Francisco, was wet, whereas southern California, dominated by Los Angeles, a city of midwesterners, was dry.

Violation was nationwide. The mountain South had a tradition of moonshining (illegal distilling) and now had a market for raw "white lightning" that extended far beyond a select circle of local tipplers. Bootleggers from midwestern cities contracted for truckloads of moonshine weekly. Canada relaxed restriction on its distillers, which sold more humane whiskey and gin to brokers who, in turn, sold it to Americans with speedboats that could dodge or even outrun Coast Guard and Treasury Department vessels on the Great Lakes. Rum production in the sugar islands of the West Indies quadrupled. The rum, along with British Scotch and gin picked up in Bermuda, was sold from freighters anchored outside American territorial waters to Americans in small, fast boats who ferried it into small fishing ports or even to beaches. Residents of northeastern cities knew that they could buy a bottle or two of "dago red" in Italian neighborhoods. Shops sold kits for making wine or "bathtub gin" with instructions warning buyers what not to do lest they unwittingly manufacture an alcoholic beverage. "Prohibition," commented Will Rogers, the nation's favorite humorist, "is better than no liquor at all."

Congress, after passing the Volstead Act to enforce the Eighteenth Amendment, provided only a fraction of the funds needed to counter such widespread violation. When states like New York and Illinois refused to assist in enforcement, the result was open mockery of federal law—indeed, of the Constitution. Democratic Mayor James J. Walker of New York openly frequented fashionable speakeasies. Republican William "Big Bill" Thompson ran for mayor of Chicago in 1927 on a "wide-open-town" platform and won. Illinois Governor Len Small pardoned bootleggers as quickly as they were convicted, violent gangsters included.

AL CAPONE: THE GANGSTER AS BUSINESSMAN

Alphonse "Al" Capone built up a finely tuned organization on the south side of Chicago that, at its peak, supplied 10,000 speakeasies, employed 700 people, and grossed $60 million in one year—and he did not have a monopoly of the city's bootleg business. Capone needed the administrative acumen of a corporation executive and dependable friends in government. Capone bristled when he was called a gangster. "What's Al Capone done?" he told a reporter. "He's supplied a legitimate demand.... Some call it racketeering. I call it a business. They say I violate the Prohibition law. Who doesn't?"

Some of Capone's business methods were unorthodox. With so much money at stake, he had plenty of competition. Between 1920 and 1929, Chicago gangsters shot down 450 to 550 rivals in their homes, in restaurants and speakeasies, and on the streets. (In Detroit, the major port of entry for the products of the Seagram and Canadian Club distilleries, the "Purple Gang," according to city historians, was bloodier.)

Few innocent bystanders were killed in these frays. As conscious of their image as other businessmen supplying the public, Capone and bootleg bosses in other cities kept their competitive techniques on a professional level. Oddly, given that Chicago had experienced about fifty fatal gang shootings a year, public opinion in Chicago soured on Capone only when in the St. **Valentine's Day Massacre** of 1929, his gunmen, disguised as policemen, killed seven members of rival Bugsy Moran's gang in a warehouse.

Capone was Italian, as were his predecessors in the Chicago organization, Johnny Torrio and "Big Jim" Colosimo. But as a group, the country's big-city bootleg bosses were a multicultural coalition. Moran and his predecessor, Dion O'Bannion, along with Owney Madden of New York, were Irish. Arthur "Dutch Schultz" Flegensheimer of New York was of German ancestry. Joseph Saltis, another Chicago bootlegger, was Polish ("Polack Joe"). Maxie Hoff of Philadelphia, Solly Weissman of Kansas City, "Little Hymie" Weiss, and the bosses of the "Purple Gang" were Jewish.

Illegal business attracted members of ethnic groups on the bottom of the social ladder because success required no social status or family connections, no education, and, to get started, little money. With less to lose than the respectable and socially established people who looked down on them (but patronized their speakeasies), immigrants and ethnics with a crooked bent were less likely to be discouraged by high risk. But the majority of Americans were not inclined to take a sociological view of the matter. To them, organized crime was violent, and "foreigners," especially Italians, were the source of it.

HOLLYWOOD

Jews were perceived as "the problem with the movies." The film industry was dominated by Jewish immigrants or the sons of immigrants. Seven of the eight major studios, centered in Hollywood, California, by the 1920s, had been founded by Jews such as former scrap iron dealer Louis B. Mayer of MGM and former furrier Adolph Zukor of Paramount. Most had gotten into the business by investing in nickelodeons—tiny theaters showing a sequence of very short films of anything that moved for a ticket costing five cents. Nickelodeons were respectable enough, but they were decidedly low-class. Most were located in storefronts in immigrant neighborhoods; immigrants and working people generally were their chief audience. It was for that reason that Jews with money to invest—"pariah capitalists" as the sociologist Max Weber called them—had the business to themselves. And the nickelodeon operators soon learned that there was a great deal more money to be made in distributing and producing films.

Hollywood was booming by 1919, turning out 700 films a year. Some of them inspired complaints by Protestant ministers that nudity in films and the loose morality associated with actors and actresses was due to the "non-Christian" nature of the movie business. In 1922 three sex and murder scandals in Hollywood panicked the movie "moguls." A few city governments had already established censorship boards. If censorship spread, the business would be crippled. Sensitive to the anti-Semitism underlying much of the protest, the big studios hired Will Hays, Harding's Postmaster General, as the industry's spokesman. Hays was the epitome of the Midwestern Protestant old stock and ably fought all attempts at government censorship of films. By the end of the decade he persuaded the moguls to adopt their own voluntary censorship. The "Hays Code" forbade films in which

---

Hooray for Hollywood

The first moviemakers set up shop wherever they happened to be when they got into the business. Most worked around New York City. By the 1920s filmmaking was centered in Hollywood, one of the small towns that grew together to form Los Angeles. The usual explanation of the choice of location was the weather: early filmmakers depended on natural light, and southern California is one of the sunniest parts of the nation. There was, however, another reason for choosing Hollywood. Early movie studios were constantly involved in lawsuits over patents, copyrights, and contracts. Hollywood was only a hundred miles from Mexico. If a legal wrangle began to look bad, filmmakers could make a quick dash for the border.

Anti-Semitism

For a time during the 1920s, Henry Ford financed a newspaper, the *Dearborn Independent,* that claimed there was a Jewish "international conspiracy" to destroy Christian civilization. The most curious aspect of this kind of anti-Semitism was that it posited an alliance between rich Jewish bankers like the Rothschild family of Europe and Jewish socialists and communists.

Few Americans took the allegations seriously. However, anti-Semitism was acceptable and even respectable when it took the form of keeping Jews out of some businesses (banking, ironically) and social clubs. Several Ivy League universities adopted Jewish quotas as part of their admissions policies (Jews were admitted, but only up to a certain percentage of each class), but the protest was so great that in official policy, at least, the schools quickly backed down.

Celebrated defense attorney Clarence Darrow and three-time presidential candidate Williams Jennings Bryan were personally hostile to one another by the end of the Scopes "Monkey Trial" in Dayton, Tennessee. Darrow had set out to make a fool of Bryan by putting him on the witness stand, and Bryan played into his hands. However, the two adversaries agreed, obviously not happily, to pose together for a photographer.

adultery was unpunished and divorce was portrayed sympathetically. Hays discouraged films in which married couples slept in the same bed. Independent filmmakers sometimes ignored the Hays Code, but not the major studios. When a Hays Code censor told Walt Disney to remove the udders from his cartoon cows, he did.

THE EVOLUTION CONTROVERSY

The clash between fundamentalist Protestantism and the secular values of 1920s America reached a climax in a controversy over Charles Darwin's theory of the evolution of species. Indeed, the word *fundamentalist* was coined just before World War I by a religious journal condemning Darwinism as evil because it denied the biblical account of creation. Revivalists like Billy Sunday and even William Jennings Bryan, who became a militant fundamentalist when he re-

tired from politics, urged people to prohibit the teaching of evolution in public schools. Tennessee enacted a law to that effect, which set the scene for a dramatic confrontation of country versus city, dry versus wet, old-fashioned Protestant America versus cosmopolitan America in the little Appalachian town of Dayton.

In the spring of 1925 a group of men who had been arguing about evolution over coffee decided to test the new state law in the courts. One of them, a high school biology teacher named John Scopes, agreed to violate the law in front of adult witnesses. Scopes would explain Darwin's theory; the witnesses would have him arrested; and the law would be tested in a trial.

The men's motives were mixed. The earnest young Scopes hoped that the law would be struck down by the courts as unconstitutional. Some of his friends wanted to see it confirmed. Several Dayton businessmen did not particularly care either way. They looked on a sensational trial as a way to put their town on the map—and as a way to make money when curiosity seekers, cause pleaders, and newspaper reporters, the more the merrier—flocked to Dayton and needed lodging, meals, and other services.

THE "MONKEY TRIAL"

They succeeded beyond their dreams. The **"Monkey Trial,"** so called because evolution was popularly interpreted as meaning that human beings were descended from apes, attracted broadcasters and reporters by the hundreds; among them was the nation's leading iconoclast, Henry L. Mencken, who came to poke fun at the "rubes" of the Bible Belt.

The number-one rube was Bryan, aged now (he died shortly after the trial), who agreed to come to Dayton to advise the prosecution. Bryan wanted to fight the case on the strictly legal principle that in a democracy, the people of a community had the right to dictate what could be taught in tax- supported schools. His advice was ignored. Their heads spinning from the carnival atmosphere in the town, even the prosecuting attorneys wanted the trial to be a debate between religion and science.

The defense, funded by the American Civil Liberties Union, was game. Like Bryan, they doubted they could win the case on its legal merits. Scopes freely admitted he had violated state law. The ACLU's intention, articulated by a distinguished libertarian lawyer, Arthur Garfield Hays, was to argue that the biblical account of creation was a religious doctrine that could not take precedence over science in schools because of the constitutional separation of church and state. Scopes's defense also maintained that freedom of intellectual inquiry, including a teacher's right to speak his or her mind in the classroom, was essential to the health of a democracy.

Hays was assisted by the era's most famous criminal lawyer, Clarence Darrow, who loved publicity and drama more than he loved legal niceties. Darrow looked on the trial as an opportunity to discredit fundamentalists by making Bryan look like a superstitious old fool. Bryan played into Darrow's hands. He consented to take the stand as an expert witness on the Bible. Under the trees—the judge feared that the floor of the tiny courthouse would collapse under the weight of the crowd—Darrow and Bryan talked religion and science. Was the world created in six days of twenty-four hours each? Was Jonah literally swallowed by a whale?

Darrow's supporters rested content that Bryan turned out looking like a monkey. Hays and the ACLU were disappointed that the points they had hoped to make were lost in the uproar over Darrow's grilling of Bryan. Fundamentalists were crestfallen when Bryan admitted that some parts of the Bible may have been meant figuratively. John Scopes was found guilty and had to pay a fine. The only winners in the Monkey Trial were Dayton's businessmen, who raked in outside dollars for almost a month, and H. L. Mencken, who wrote a dozen articles mocking Bryan and the hicks of the Bible Belt.

FURTHER READING

General Lynn Dumenil, *The Modern Temper: American Culture and Society in the 1920s*, 1995; David Goldberg, *Discontented America: The United States in the 1920s*, 1999; Nathan A. Miller, *A New World Coming: The 1920s and the Making of Modern America*, 2003; Michael E. Parrish, *America in Prosperity and Depression*, 1992.

Harding Administration John W. Dean, *Warren G. Harding*, 2004; Robert H. Ferrell, *The Strange Death of President Harding*, 1996; Kendrick A. Klements, *Hoover, Conservation, and Consumerism: Engineering the Good Life*, 2000.

Immigrants and Nativists Matthew F. Jacobson, *Whiteness of a Different Color: European Immigrants and the Alchemy of Race*, 1998; Desmond S. King, *Making Americans: Immigration, Race, and the Origins of the Diverse Democracy*, 2000; David R. Roediger, *The Wages of Whiteness: Race and the Making of the American Working Class*, 1991.

Prohibition Edward Behr, *Prohibition: Thirteen Years That Changed America*, 1996; Douglas Bukowski, *Big Bill Thompson and the Politics of Image*, 1998; Norman M. Clark, *Deliver Us from Evil*, 1976; Stanley Coben, *Rebellion against Victorianism: The Impetus for Cultural Change in 1920s America*, 1991; John D'Emilio and Estelle B. Freedman, *Intimate Matters: A History of Sexuality in America*, 1988; Lawrence M. Friedman, *Crime and Punishment in American History*, 1993; Humbert S. Nelli, *The Business of Crime*, 1976; Andrew Sinclair, *Prohibition: The Era of Excess*, 1962.

Racial, Ethnic, and Religious Tensions D. M. Chalmers, *Hooded Americanism*, 1981; Neal Gabler, *An Empire of Their Own: How the Jews Invented Hollywood*, 1988; Kenneth T. Jackson, *The Ku Klux Klan in the Cities, 1915–1930*, 1967; Edward J. Larson, *Summer for the Gods: The Scopes Trial and America's Continuing Debate over Science and Religion*, 1997; Lawrence Levine, *Defender of the Faith: William Jennings Bryan, The Last Decade, 1915–1925*, 1987; Nancy MacLean, *Behind the Mask of Chivalry: The Making of the Second Ku Klux Klan*, 1994; George M. Marsden, *Fundamentalism and American Culture*, 1980; Robert Sklar, *Movie-Made America*, 1975; Kathleen Slee, *Women of the Klan: Racism and Gender in the 1920s*, 1991; Judith Stein, *The World of Marcus Garvey*, 1986; Ferenc M. Szasz, *The Divided Mind of Protestant America, 1880–1930*, 1982; William Tuttle Jr., *Race Riot: Chicago and the Red Summer of 1919*, 1970; Mark A. Viera, *Sin in Soft Focus: Pre-Code Hollywood*, 1999; John White, *Black Leadership in America: From Booker T. Washington to Jesse Jackson*, 1990; Garry Wills, *Under God: Religion and American Politics*, 1990.

KEY TERMS

The following terms are covered in this chapter and can also be found in the list of Key Terms at the back of the book.

A. Mitchell Palmer   **Sacco and Vanzetti**   **Treaty of Washington**   **"wets"**

Marcus Garvey   **"Monkey Trial"**   **Valentine's Day Massacre**

 ## ONLINE SOURCES GUIDE

Use this listing to find online documents, images, interactive maps, simulations, and other resources related to this chapter:

American History Resource Center
http://history.wadsworth.com/rc/us

Selected Documents
H. L. Mencken's "Star-Spangled Men"
Transcripts from the Scopes trial
Babe Ruth children's story, "The Home-Run King"

Selected Images
Women's fashions, 1920
Children listening to radio, 1923
Harding showing his speaking style
Harding recording his voice, 1920
Ku Klux Klan leaders
African-American musicians in a pool hall

Interactive Time Line (with online readings)
The Days of Harding: Troubled Years, 1919–1923

CHAPTER 40

Calvin Coolidge and the New Era

When America Was Business 1923–1929

Courtesy of Sears, Roebuck & Company

Civilization and profits go hand in hand.... The business of America is business.
Calvin Coolidge

Perhaps the most revolting character that the United States ever produced was the Christian businessman.
H. L. Mencken

Vice President Calvin Coolidge was visiting his father in tiny Plymouth Notch, Vermont, when he got the news of Harding's death. Instead of rushing to Washington to be sworn in ceremoniously, Coolidge walked downstairs to the farmhouse parlor, where his father, a justice of the peace, administered the presidential oath by the light of a kerosene lamp. To the very pinnacle of his political career, Coolidge was the epitome of unpretentious rectitude. Or, some have suggested, he had a sure eye for showmanship.

THE COOLIDGE YEARS

Coolidge was not a bit like his predecessor. Far from handsome, his facial features were pinched just short of comically. When he smiled, he seemed to say he wished he were somewhere else. Alice Roosevelt Longworth, the acidulous daughter of Teddy Roosevelt, said that Coolidge looked as though he had been weaned on a pickle.

Harding's private life was tawdry; Coolidge was impeccably proper. Indeed, his personal habits were dreary; his idea of a good time was a nap. He spent twelve to fourteen hours out of twenty-four in bed except on slow days, when he was able to sneak in a few extra winks. When in 1933 writer Dorothy Parker was told that Coolidge had died, she asked, "How could they tell?"

A QUIET CLEVER MAN

Coolidge might have cracked his subtle smile had he heard that. He was known as "Silent Cal," but when he spoke he was often witty. Attempting to break the ice at a banquet, a woman seated next to Coolidge remarked pleasantly that a friend had bet her that the president would not say three words to her all evening. "You lose," Coolidge replied, and returned to his plate. "I found out early in life," the successful politician noted, "that you don't have to explain something you haven't said."

Brown Brothers

Calvin Coolidge enjoyed outdoor recreation, including fishing. But this photograph is just one of the dozens of costume poses he was always willing to strike for photographers. Anglers did not wear a boater (the flat-topped sporty summer hat) or the tight, starched collar, necktie, and three-piece suit in which Coolidge is dressed. (In another photo, showing him bringing in freshly cut hay, Coolidge was in patent leather shoes that could be ruined by a small scuff.)

He was clever. At a meeting of American heads of state in the West Indies, Coolidge was sitting in a semicircle with his colleagues when a waiter began to walk down the line serving drinks. It was Prohibition; if Coolidge took a drink while out of the country, it would make juicy front-page news. If Coolidge righteously waved the waiter away, he might insult his host and fellow guests, all enjoying their daiquiris. For Coolidge, it was no problem. As the waiter was about to present his tray to the president, Coolidge bent over to tie his shoe, and he remained hunched over until the waiter got the point and moved on.

Coolidge was not nearly so laconic as the legends say. In 1917, the year the United States went to war, Woodrow Wilson gave seventeen speeches. In 1925, when nothing much happened, President Coolidge gave twenty-eight. It was small talk and chitchat in which he had no interest. However, he liked to play the clown in silent poses. (It was the age of the silent movies!) He posed for photographers in costumes that were ludicrous on him: a ten-gallon hat and a Sioux war bonnet. He strapped himself into skis on the White House lawn and dressed as a farmer working at the hay—in patent leather shoes with a Pierce Arrow, waiting for him, in the background. The photos were Coolidge's way of saying that he was at one with the American people of the 1920s in enjoying novelties and pranks. When he was asked about one of the costumes, he said that "the American public wants a solemn ass as president and I think I'll go along with them."

He was surely at one with the American people in abdicating political and cultural leadership to the business community. If Coolidge had a religion, it was the worship of financial success; if he had a philosophy, it was that millionaires knew what was best for the country. "The man who builds a factory builds a temple," he said, a strange piety for a man who devoted not a day of his life to business or building.

KEEPING COOL WITH COOLIDGE

Coolidge quietly dismissed the political hacks and personal cronies to whom Harding had given high positions. He probably knew of the scandals that were soon to be revealed. He retained the businessmen Harding had appointed to his cabinet, notably Herbert Hoover (although Coolidge was as

The Roaring Twenties 1920–1930

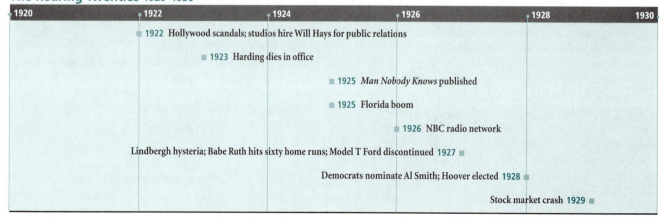

1920	1922	1924	1926	1928	1930

■ 1922 Hollywood scandals; studios hire Will Hays for public relations

■ 1923 Harding dies in office

■ 1925 *Man Nobody Knows* published

■ 1925 Florida boom

■ 1926 NBC radio network

Lindbergh hysteria; Babe Ruth hits sixty home runs; Model T Ford discontinued 1927 ■

Democrats nominate Al Smith; Hoover elected 1928 ■

Stock market crash 1929 ■

uncomfortable with him as Harding had been) and Secretary of the Treasury Mellon. Then he sat back to preside over a "don't rock the boat" administration such as he had headed as governor of Massachusetts. Coolidge was a reactive, not a proactive, chief executive like Wilson and Theodore Roosevelt.

Within a year of his takeover, the erratic postwar economic slump had run its course. Thanks to Coolidge's squeaky-clean record, neither he nor the Republican party suffered a voter backlash when the Harding scandals hit the headlines. By early 1924, an election year, Republicans were able to drown out Democratic criticism by crowing about "Coolidge prosperity."

The Democrats tore themselves apart. The convention, held in New York, pitted the state's popular governor, Alfred E. Smith, against William G. McAdoo, a Californian whose support came mostly from the South and the West. Smith, an urban machine politician (although a personally uncorrupt one) and a Roman Catholic, was backed by delegates from northeastern and midwestern industrial states, where the party depended on white ethnic, mostly Catholic voters. Neither could win the two-thirds vote Democratic party rules required. After more than a hundred ballots, the weary delegates compromised on a dark horse candidate, John W. Davis.

The party's choice was significant. The Republicans had already repudiated their progressives when they nominated Harding and Coolidge. Both McAdoo and Smith had progressive credentials. McAdoo had been a Wilsonian, Smith a reform governor. John W. Davis was a conservative Wall Street lawyer; he would have been at home in Coolidge's cabinet.

Davis did not have to neglect his lucrative law practice for long: he won only 29 percent of the popular vote. The stragglers of the once-dominant progressive movement (17 percent of the total vote) cast their ballots for an aged Robert LaFollette. Clearly, most of LaFollette's supporters were Democrats: Coolidge won a decisive 54 percent of the popular vote.

For four more years, Calvin Coolidge napped through good times. He was retired for eight months when, in October 1929, "Coolidge Prosperity" and what businessmen called the **"New Era"** came crashing to an end.

MELLON'S TAX POLICIES

The keystone of New Era government was the tax policy of the secretary of the treasury, Andrew Mellon of Pittsburgh. Mellon looked less like a cartoonist's bloated moneybags than like a sporting duke, but a moneybags he was. With his chiseled features and trim physique, dressed in deftly tailored suits and tiny pointed shoes, Mellon was one of the half dozen richest men in the country. He was a banker with close ties to the steel industry.

Believing that prosperity depended on the extent to which his fellow capitalists reinvested their profits in economic growth, Mellon favored the rich by slashing the taxes that fell most heavily on them. He reduced the personal income tax on people who made more than $60,000 a year; by 1929 the treasury was actually shoveling tax refunds back to large corporations. United States Steel received a check for $15 million. To make up the loss in revenue, Mellon pressured other departments to cut expenditures.

Essential spending was paid for in two ways. The Republican Congress raised the tariff; the Fordney–McCumber Tariff of 1922 hoisted import duties to levels not seen for a generation. Second, Mellon increased regressive taxes—that is, taxes that fell disproportionately on the middle and lower classes. The costs of some kinds of postal services increased. The excise tax was raised, and a federal tax was imposed on automobiles. Both were paid mostly by ordinary consumers. To those who complained that these measures penalized the middle classes and to some extent the poor, Mellon replied that the burden on each individual was small, and that, overall, his scheme helped ordinary people as well as the rich.

Mellon contended that when businessmen reinvested their government-sponsored windfalls, they created jobs and, therefore, the means to a better standard of living for all. The share of the middle and lower classes in Coolidge prosperity would **"trickle down"** to them because of continued reinvestment. Moreover, the inducement to get rich, encouraged by business culture, would reinvigorate the spirit of enterprise among all Americans.

For six years, from late 1923 to late 1929, it appeared as if Mellon was right. He was toasted as "the greatest secretary of the treasury since Alexander Hamilton." Just how much damage his policies did to the national economy would not be appreciated until after the collapse of the New Era. As early as 1924, however, Mellon's dedication to the immediate interests of big business and banking drew criticism that he was helping to make a shambles of the international economy.

A FOREIGN POLICY FOR BANKERS

The Treaty of Versailles required Germany to pay Belgium, France, and Great Britain $33 billion in reparations. Almost from the beginning, Germany's democratic government fell behind in its payments. Wartime expenditures—more in four years than Germany had spent in the preceding forty years—had left the country on the brink of bankruptcy.

Racy Reading

In 1919 publisher Emanuel Haldeman-Julius sensed that there was a mass market for books if they could be priced cheaply and marketed correctly. His "Little Blue Books" were printed in a small format. Haldeman-Julius eventually published 2,000 titles and sold 500 million copies of them. Many were racy for the times or, at least, had racy come-ons.

Haldeman-Julius preferred to republish older books that were no longer under copyright. No royalties had to be paid, and they could be retitled to boost sales. When he renamed Théophile Gautier's *Golden Fleece* as *The Quest for a Blond Mistress,* annual sales jumped from 600 to 50,000. Haldeman-Julius had similar results when he retitled Victor Hugo's *The King Amuses Himself* as *The Lustful King Enjoys Himself.*

However, France and Britain refused German requests to reduce the reparations. Their economies were at least as shaky as Germany's, and both countries had huge debts to American banks, which they had to pay.

When Germany fell so far behind that it was obvious some adjustments had to be made in Germany's obligations (in the end, only $4.5 billion of the $33 billion Germany owed was actually paid), the British and French asked the Coolidge administration to persuade their American creditors to forgive some of their debts for the sake of international financial stability. Coolidge refused. When asked to explain his reasons, he replied, "They hired the money, didn't they?"

In fact, American bankers, including the secretary of the treasury, were delighted with the international flow of money. British and French debts payments flowed into the United States. American banks made loans to Germany so that it could make reparations payments to Britain and France. Every major European power was paying interest to American bankers. The argument that bleeding western Europe of its wealth might destabilize the continent politically (as, indeed, it contributed to the Nazi takeover in Germany) and lead to another great war made no impression on the tunnel-visioned Coolidge and Mellon.

Nor did an increasingly isolationist Congress take heed. Congress refused to reduce the extremely high Fordney–McCumber import duties so that Germany, France, and Britain could sell more products in the United States.

ISOLATION FROM EUROPE, INTERVENTION IN LATIN AMERICA

After the Treaty of Washington, the Harding and Coolidge administrations resisted making cooperative cause with other nations. Instead of Wilson's dream of a democratic Europe, each year saw another country slip or, in some cases, plunge into dictatorship: all the Balkan countries, Italy, and Poland. Increasing numbers of Americans became convinced that the midwestern isolationists who had fought against intervening in the Great War had been right. The United States should have stayed out. Europe was a mess and always would be.

In 1928 Coolidge's secretary of state, Frank B. Kellogg, joined with the French foreign minister, Aristide Briand, to write a treaty that "outlawed" war as an ""instrument of national policy." More than sixty nations signed the Kellogg–Briand Pact, itself an indication that it was a meaningless statement of a pious sentiment. And pious sentiments were as far as the United States would go.

In Latin America the Harding and Coolidge administrations were positively aggressive—when American investments were at risk. There were a good many such investments, $5.4 billion by 1929. Thanks to the war, the United States had replaced Great Britain as the major financial power in Latin America, particularly in the Caribbean.

Regarding Europe, American banks and other investors cared for little but their financial interests, and they had the unconditional backing of the government. If investment could be protected only by supporting military dictators, the world's greatest democracy backed them. If protecting investment meant military intervention, the Harding and Coolidge administrations (like the progressive Wilson and Roosevelt administrations) "sent in the marines." At one time or another during the 1920s, marines occupied Nicaragua, Honduras, Cuba, Haiti, and the Dominican Republic, departing only when the money was flowing smoothly to American banks and an amenable president was in power.

PROSPERITY AND BUSINESS CULTURE

Today, with many years of hindsight, it is easy to see the damage the Coolidge administration did. But Coolidge was popular to the end of his presidency, and the pro-business Republican party had comfortable majorities in the House of Representatives (narrower majorities in the Senate) in every Congress between 1919 and 1931. Only in the South, some lightly populated western states, and in a few big cities could the Democrats count on winning elections.

THE PREDESTINED ELECTION OF 1928

In 1928 the 54 percent of the popular vote that Coolidge had won in 1924 rose to 58 percent. The victorious Republican candidate was Herbert Hoover, the secretary of commerce for eight years.

National Archives

Al Smith, a successful and popular Democratic governor of New York (he was elected to four terms), deluded himself that he could win a national election in 1928, the height of "Republican prosperity." Smith carried only half the states of the "Solid South," due at least in part to southern suspicion of his Catholic religion.

Hoover's opponent, Alfred E. Smith of New York, had spent four years mending fences with southern and western Democrats who had denied him the nomination in 1924. In the general election, however, Smith was unable to win over western and southern voters. For the first time since Reconstruction, some prominent southern whites, including Methodist Bishop James Cannon, urged voters to vote Republican because a Roman Catholic could not be trusted with presidential power. Anti-Catholicism was a potent force in the South.

Smith also aroused the dislike of southern and western voters with his nasal New York City accent. Heard over the radio—or "raddio" as Smith called it—his voice conjured up all the unsavory images traditionally associated with New York City. And Smith was vocal in his opposition to Prohibition. His position did not hurt him in the Northeast or in cities in the industrial Midwest. But fundamentalists in the West and South—mostly Democrats—religiously opposed drinking.

Hoover refused to have anything to do with the Catholicism issue. Personally (privately) he was dubious about Prohibition, unhappy with many of its consequences. But in 1928, playing his politics by the Republican book, he called Prohibition "a great social and economic experiment, noble in motive and far-reaching in purpose."

Had **Al Smith** been a Kansas Baptist who drank nothing stronger than Dr. Pepper, he would have lost in 1928. It is a mystery why he wanted so badly to run for president. When the country is as prosperous as it was in 1928, the party in power does not lose elections. The Republicans added thirty

Let's Have a Look under the Hood

Americans and Britons speak a different language when they talk about cars. What Americans call the *hood*, the British call the *bonnet*. Some other differences:

American English	British English
clunker or junker	banger
gas	petrol
generator	dynamo
headlight	headlamp
muffler	silencer
station wagon	estate wagon
trunk	boot
windshield	windscreen

The differences are a case study in how languages develop. The automobile roared into history long after the United States and Great Britain had gone separate political and cultural ways, but before instantaneous electronic communication made words coined on one side of the Atlantic immediately familiar on the other.

The early automobile was largely a French development, which is why many automotive terms were taken from the French language: *automobile* itself, *cabriolet* (later shortened to *cab*), *chassis*, *chauffeur*, *coupe*, *garage*, *limousine*, and *sedan*.

congressmen and seven senators to already large majorities. Herbert Hoover—and the business culture of the New Era—had a resounding mandate.

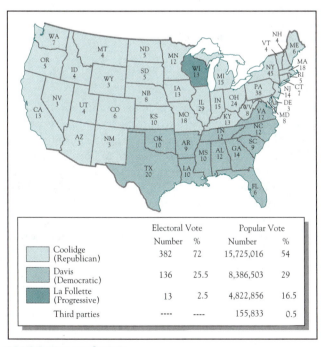

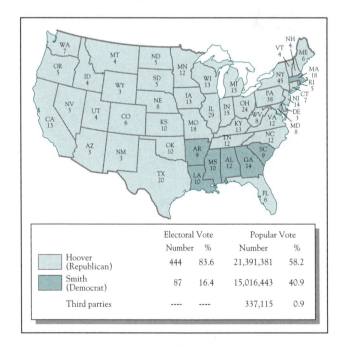

MAPS 40:1 and 40:2

John W. Davis, Democratic presidential candidate in 1924, was trounced by Republican Calvin Coolidge. He won electoral votes only in the "Solid South." The 1928 candidate, Alfred E. Smith, carried only six southern states, unheard of for a Democrat since 1876. One reason was Smith's religion: he was a Catholic, and anti-Catholicism was a powerful force in the South. Smith's religion did win him heavily Catholic but usually Republican Massachusetts and Rhode Island.

Culver Pictures, Inc.

Automobile ownership was within the reach of all but the very poor by the mid-1920s. Even struggling farmers had their Model T Fords. Middle-class people in cities and towns who wanted cars that were more comfortable and a few notches upscale had two or three dozen "makes" from which to choose. The abundance of used cars for sale put cars better than the Model T within reach of decently paid working people. One consequence was the Sunday traffic jam such as in this photograph.

THE SHAPE OF PROSPERITY

Industrial and agricultural productivity soared during the 1920s, even though there was not much increase in the size of the industrial workforce, and the number of agricultural workers actually declined. Wages did not, however, keep up with the contribution that more efficient workers were making to the economy. While dividends on stocks rose 65 percent between 1920 and 1929, wages increased only 24 percent.

Nevertheless, the increase in wages was enough to satisfy the working people who enjoyed them. Consumer goods were cheap, and business promoted an alluring new way for families to live beyond their means—consumer credit.

BUY NOW, PAY LATER

Before the 1920s, ordinary people commonly bought their groceries on account, settling up weekly. Borrowing large sums was something businessmen did to expand and farmers did to get a crop. Banks lent money for productive enterprises that would themselves (so everyone hoped) earn the means

of repayment. People borrowed to buy homes, which did not generate income but which were the borrower's security that the bank could seize if payments were not forthcoming.

During the 1920s, Americans began to borrow for a new purpose—so they could live more pleasantly. They went into debt neither to increase their income nor to provide their families a home, but to consume.

The chief medium of consumer borrowing was the installment plan. A refrigerator priced at $87.50 could be ensconced in a corner of the kitchen for a down payment of $5 and monthly payments of $10. Even a comparatively low-cost item like a vacuum cleaner ($28.95) could be taken home for $2 down and "E-Z payments" of $4 a month. During the New Era, 60 percent of automobiles were bought on time; 70 percent of household furnishings; 80 percent of refrigerators, radios, and vacuum cleaners; and 90 percent of pianos, sewing machines, and washing machines. With 13.8 million people owning radios by 1930 (up from next to none in 1920), the Americans who were basking in the glow of Coolidge prosperity were also up to their necks in hock.

The incomparable Super-Heterodyne in a *custom-built* model

RADIOLA 30A
Custom-built,
Complete
with Radiotrons
$495

—simplified socket-power operation

Radio engineers all recognize the Super-Heterodyne as the finest achievement in radio receiver design.

In response to the demand for de luxe models of the RCA Super-Heterodyne—with the convenience and efficiency of operation from the electric light socket (without batteries or liquid-containing devices)—RCA offers the new custom-built Radiola 30A. This cabinet receiver, because of its extreme selectivity, is ideally adapted for use in the congested broadcasting areas.

Each instrument (with the self-contained RCA Loudspeaker) has been hand-built and individually tested.

R A D I O   C O R P O R A T I O N   O F   A M E R I C A
New York   Chicago   San Francisco

Authorized
Dealer
RCA

Buy with confidence where you see this sign

RCA Radiola
MADE BY THE MAKERS OF THE RADIOTRON

Radio rivaled automobiles as the boom consumer industry of the 1920s. RCA (Radio Corporation of America) dominated the business. The sale of cheap, no-frills receivers made the company one of the country's biggest in less than a decade. There were expensive models, gussied up to be parlor furniture, for those who wanted to display the fact that they could afford them. This "custom-built" Radiola was no mere appliance.

Traditional moralists warned that borrowing to consume was a sharp break with American ideals of frugality and the axioms of Benjamin Franklin. But others spoke more loudly and in more congenial tones. They were the advertisers, members of a new profession dedicated to creating desires in people—advertising men called them "needs"—that people had never particularly felt before they were told about them.

BUY, BUY, BUY

Traditionally, advertisements had been simple announcements. In the nineteenth century merchants placed tiny notices in newspapers—the size of "classifieds" today—describing what they had for sale. During the 1870s Robert Bonner, the editor of the *Ledger*, a literary magazine, accidentally learned the curious effect on the human brain of repetition. He placed his customary one-line ad in a daily newspaper—"Read Mrs. Southworth's New Story in the *Ledger*." The compositor misread his specification of "one line" as "one page." The line ran over and over, down every

column. To Bonner's surprise, the bill for his blunder did not bankrupt him; his magazine sold out in an afternoon.

The lesson was unmistakable: people were sheep who needed only guidance to trot this way and that. During the 1890s C. W. Post, with scarcely a cent to his name, borrowed money to plaster a city with the name of his new breakfast cereal, Post Toasties. He was a millionaire within a month. Bombarded by the name of the novel ready-to-eat breakfast in newspapers and painted on the sides of buildings, along with the command to eat it, people bought the stuff. By the 1920s advertisers had moved on to making preposterous claims and telling outright lies in newspapers and magazines, on billboards along highways (a new advertising medium created by the automobile), and on the radio. Advertisers discovered the effectiveness of sexual titillation. Pictures of suggestive young ladies were the centerpieces of advertisements for such utterly asexual products as soda pop, tickets on railroads, razor blades, and luxury automobiles.

Advertising became a "profession," and the pros considered themselves practical psychologists. They sold goods by exploiting anxieties and, in the words of Thorstein Veblen, "administering shock effects" and "trading on the range of human infirmities which blossom in devout observances, and bear fruit in the psychopathic wards." In the Coolidge era the makers of Listerine Antiseptic, a mouthwash, invented the disease "halitosis," of which the symptoms included nothing more than a curter than usual greeting from a friend: "Even your best friend won't tell you" (that you have "BAD BREATH"). Listerine made millions. A picture of a

Anxiety Ad

The text that follows is from a magazine advertisement of the 1920s for Listerine Antiseptic, a mouthwash. It accompanied an illustration showing an attractive elderly and poignantly sad woman sitting in a darkened parlor (with a photograph of Calvin Coolidge on the wall) poring over old letters and a photograph album.

> Sometimes, when lights are low, they come back to comfort and at the same time sadden her—those memories of long ago, when she was a slip of a girl in love with a dark-eyed Nashville boy. They were the happiest moments of her life—those days of courtship. Though she had never married, no one could take from her the knowledge that she had been loved passionately, devotedly; those frayed and yellowed letters of his still told her so. How happy and ambitious they had been for their future together. And then, like a stab, came their parting . . . the broken engagement . . . the sorrow and the shock of it. She could find no explanation for it then, and now, in the soft twilight of life when she can think calmly, it is still a mystery to her.

Listerine went on so as to leave no doubt that "halitosis"—bad breath—was the source of the woman's life-destroying tragedy. You never know.

wealthy fop on a yacht conversing with a beautiful young woman was captioned: "You'd like to be in this man's shoes...yet he has 'ATHLETE'S FOOT'!" Fleischmann's yeast, losing its market as people bought bread rather than baking it at home, advertised its product as just the thing to cure constipation and eradicate adolescent pimples. The success of anxiety advertising made underarm deodorants, without which humanity had functioned for millennia, a necessity.

CHAIN STORES

Manufacturers of low-priced commodities like mouthwash advertised nationally. If they succeeded in creating a demand for their brand, they were able to get higher wholesale prices for Chef Boy-Ar-Dee Spaghetti or tubes of Ipana toothpaste than unadvertised brands of competing products. Wholesalers charged "Mom and Pop" grocery stores and sundries shops a premium because their orders were small. A centrally managed chain of stores, however, bought the same goods by the hundreds of cases and paid a lower per-unit price, enabling it to retail at a lower price the products that had to be the best because the ads said they were. The 1920s marked the beginning of the steady decline of the small, locally owned retail shop.

By 1928, 860 chain stores competed for the dollars of a population that was eating more expensively. Among the biggest success stories between 1920 and 1929 were the first supermarkets: Piggly-Wiggly (from 515 to 2,500 stores), Safeway (from 766 to 2,660 stores), and A & P (Atlantic and Pacific Tea Company, from 4,621 to 15,418 stores). Chains came to dominate the sundries and clothing trades (F. W. Woolworth, from 1,111 outlets in 1920 to 1,825 in 1929, and JC Penney, 312 to 1,395); auto parts (Western Auto, 5 to 54); tobacco (United Cigar, 2,000 shops to 3,700); and, of course, the retailing of gasoline. Standard Oil of New Jersey owned twelve gas stations in 1920, a thousand in 1929.

THE LIMITS OF COOLIDGE PROSPERITY

A few economists joined moralists to criticize mindless consumption. They pointed out that the day would dawn when everyone who could afford a car, a washing machine, and other consumer durables would have them. They would no longer be buying, and consumer industries would be in serious trouble.

Another weakness of the Coolidge economy was that significant numbers of Americans did not share in the good times and were, therefore, shut out of the buying spree. The 700,000

Courtesy of Sears, Roebuck & Company

Sears Roebuck was already the country's mail-order giant at the beginning of the 1920s, the farmer's department store in a catalog. Under Julius Rosenwald, Sears branched out into chain stores, earning a reputation for selling quality goods at low prices. The Sears formula worked so well that it maintained the company as a leading retailer for fifty years.

to 800,000 coal miners and 400,000 textile workers and their dependents suffered depressed conditions and wages throughout the decade; they did not buy their share of cars, vacuum cleaners, and canned spaghetti. Staple farmers were once again struggling after the good years of 1900–1920. Even farmers who were doing well lived where there was no electricity; they bought no appliances that had to be plugged in. The southern states lagged far behind the rest of the country in income and standard of living. Rural blacks, Indians, and Hispanics tasted Coolidge prosperity only in occasional bites.

BUSINESS CULTURE

But economically deprived groups are rarely politically articulate when mainstream society is at ease in its world. In the 1920s, mainstream America was quite at ease, and businessmen took the credit for their comfort.

Locally, small businessmen's clubs like Rotary, Kiwanis, Lions, and Junior Chambers of Commerce seized community leadership and preached boosterism: "If you can't boost, don't knock." Successful manufacturers like Henry Ford were looked to for wisdom on every imaginable question. Any man who made $25,000 a day, as Ford did during most of the 1920s, must be an oracle. Even the man once the most hated

I Hear a Melody

Sales of sheet music and rolls for player pianos declined by a third during the 1920s. With the advent of radio and phonograph ownership, the pop music business became almost synonymous with the sale of records. As early as 1921, the record industry sold 100 million "platters" in the United States. With the stock market crash, the business collapsed as quickly as it had grown. In 1932 only 6 million records were sold.

in America, John D. Rockefeller, now in his eighties and retired in Florida much of the year, became an object of respect and affection, thanks to Coolidge prosperity, the skillful image building of public relations expert Ivy Lee, and Rockefeller's extraordinary philanthropy.

The career of an advertising man, Bruce Barton, showed just how thoroughly the business culture dominated the way Americans thought. In 1925 Barton published **The Man Nobody Knows.** It depicted Jesus not primarily as the son of God, the Messiah, or even a brooding moral teacher with a beard, but as a businessman, hale fellow well-met, a good sport, an entrepreneur, a hustler, and an advertising genius who founded a successful company. Instead of finding Barton blasphemous, Americans bought *The Man Nobody Knows* by the hundreds of thousands. It was a best seller for two years.

John Jacob Raskob of General Motors promoted the worship of business in popular magazines such as the *Saturday Evening Post*. Because the value of most kinds of property was rising throughout the 1920s under the stewardship of business, Raskob said that it was a simple matter for workingmen to save money and invest it, thus becoming capitalists themselves. Middle-class Americans with a nest egg in the bank believed him. They plunged their savings into one get-rich-quick scheme after another, feeding but at the same time dooming the speculative economy.

GET RICH QUICK
The most colorful get-rich-quick craze centered on Florida—an isolated, thinly populated agricultural state in the nineteenth century. When Henry Flagler, after retiring from

Standard Oil, built a railroad the length of the state, the Atlantic shore became a popular winter resort for the wealthy. Train connections with eastern and midwestern cities, and retirement to Florida by celebrities like Rockefeller and William Jennings Bryan, put middle-class people on notice of the Sunshine State's possibilities as a vacation destination and retirement paradise for ordinary folks.

THE FLORIDA LAND BOOM
The development of places like Fort Lauderdale and Miami Beach would take time, of course. In the meantime, Florida boosters argued, money could be made by buying orange groves and sandy wasteland at bargain prices and holding them until the developers of resort hotels and retirement homes showed up, willing to pay much more for choice sites. One need not even wait for the developers to pocket a profit. Another investor, thinking the land was worth more than the price at which it was bought from the orange grower, might get off the train next week.

The price of Florida land rose not because new residents were pouring in, but because speculators bought land to sell as soon as possible to other speculators. Money (or rather, down payments and obligations to pay monthly installments) changed hands in a whirl. Lots in Miami Beach on which no one was dreaming of building anything changed hands a dozen times within a few months, the price climbing with every sale. Some speculators never had to make a mortgage payment. At the height of the craze, a Miami newspaper printed 500 pages of advertisements of land for sale. There were over 2,000 real estate offices in the little city.

Because the price of every acre in Florida seemed to be skyrocketing, northerners were willing to buy sight unseen, and fraud was inevitable. More than a few snowbound dreamers in Chicago and Minneapolis purchased tracts of alligator-infested swamp from fast-talking salesmen who assured them that they were purchasing a site that Piggly-Wiggly was looking at. Others bought beachfront lots that were closer to the ocean than they counted on—underneath

Fads, Sensations, and Ballyhoo

Fads (fashions wildly popular for a short period), sensations (events or people of intense popular interest), and ballyhoo (a deliberate clamor promoting a fad, a sensation, or a new toilet disinfectant) were not new in the 1920s. And they are so much a part of twenty-first-century life that we are inured to them.

They were virtually the theme of popular culture in the 1920s, and people had not yet developed the immunities that enable us to survive them without serious emotional scars.

Some 1920s fads were commercial, briefly paying bonanza profits for those who jumped in early enough to exploit them. A mania for crossword puzzles was launched by a new publisher, Simon and Schuster, and financed the company for years. Yo-yos made money for their manufacturers. Mah-Jongg, a Chinese gambling game with such inscrutable rules that it is possible no American ever played it correctly, was introduced in 1922. The next year, although they were expensive, Chinese-made Mah-Jongg sets outsold radios. The game became an obsession of middle- and upper-class women, some of whom played all day every day for months. When Chinese manufacturers ran out of the shin bones of calves from which Mah-Jongg tiles were made, they were supplied by Chicago slaughterhouses.

Other fads made little or no money for anyone: Contract Bridge, an enthusiasm that rivaled Mah Jongg, and college boys swallowing live goldfish. Exhibitionists had no reward beyond seeing their names in the newspaper: "Clarence Tillman, 17, local high school student, put forty sticks of chewing gum in his mouth at one time, sang 'Home, Sweet Home,' and between verses of the song, drank a gallon of milk."

Barnstormers, daredevils who walked on or hung from a plane's wing, could not charge admission for an exhibition in plain sight for miles around. They counted on fees from county fairs, which barely covered expenses. One barnstormer said that the greatest personal danger he faced during the short-lived fad was starvation. Flagpole sitting—balancing for days atop a flagpole—was less dangerous but equally unremunerative. For reasons the best historians have been unable to determine, Baltimore was the storm center of the fad with as many as twenty flagpole sitters at one time. The mayor crowed with pride in his citizenry's achievement.

Newspapers ballyhooed innocuous events to increase sales: the visits of the Prince of Wales in 1924 and Queen Marie of Romania in 1926; the death of movie sex symbol Rudolph Valentino at age 31; the 655-mile trek across Alaska by the dog, Balto, to bring diphtheria serum to a sick Eskimo in Nome. The prince, the queen, and Valentino's funeral were mobbed by thousands of people who, mercifully, were not asked to reflect on why they were there. Statues of Balto were erected. Charles Lindbergh, who made the first nonstop flight across the Atlantic, created hysteria wherever he went. Gertrude Ederle was only marginally less lionized when she swam the English Channel. In 1927 Nan Britton's *The President's Daughter,* about the child she bore by Warren G. Harding, sold 50,000 copies.

Publishing was the storm center of sensationalism. Newspapers nationwide covered in detail stories like the

six feet of salt water at high tide. But the fuel of the mania was not fraud. It was a foolishness inherent in the human species brought out by a culture that exalted money-making as the purpose of life.

THE FLORIDA LAND BUST

As with all speculative manias, the day arrived when there were no more buyers betting on higher prices in the future. After a few months of making mortgage payments on land that no one wanted, would-be Florida land barons decided, as herdlike as they had bought it, to get out of Florida real estate. The market was flooded with properties at ever-declining prices. Speculators caught holding overpriced land saw their paper fortunes evaporate; banks that had lent them money to speculate failed; people who trusted those banks with their savings lost their accounts.

The final collapse was triggered by a hurricane that demonstrated, as one observer unimprovably phrased it, what a soothing tropical breeze could do to Florida when it got a running start from the West Indies. The price of Florida land plunged to dollars per acre. Citrus growers who had cursed themselves a thousand times for selling their groves so cheaply at the beginning of the boom discovered that, thanks to a chain of defaults, they were back in possession of their orchards only a little worse for the wear of speculators tromping through them. Wilson Mizner, a ballyhoo expert who lost more than $1 million in a month, was (like few others) good-humored about the debacle. "Always be pleasant to the people you meet on the way up," he said, "because they are always the very same people you meet on the way down."

BUYING ON MARGIN

Even before Florida busted, money-bedazzled middle-class Americans were fueling another speculative mania, driving up the prices of shares on the New York Stock Exchange.

Speculation in stocks had been a game for the rich. However, the prosperity of the 1920s blessed hundreds of

eighteen-day entrapment in a Kentucky cave of Floyd Collins, dying slowly of exposure. (His neighbors sold hamburgers to the crowds at the entrance to the cave.) When evangelist Aimee Semple McPherson disappeared for thirty-seven days in 1926, then emerged from the Arizona desert claiming she had been kidnapped, she recreated her abduction for photographers. Reporters prolonged the story by revealing that Aimee had actually been holed up in a "love nest."

Sex sold. The trial of movie comedian Roscoe "Fatty" Arbuckle for the death of a young woman at an orgiastic party was national news in 1922, along with the unsolved murder of movie bigwig William Desmond Taylor because he was said to have been "involved" with stars Mabel Normand and Mary Miles Minter. (Taylor was homosexual; Normand and Minter really were "just good friends.") Luckily, a sensational murder case came along annually, the greatest of them the trial of Chicago rich boys Nathan Leopold and Richard Loeb for the "thrill" killing of a fourteen-year-old neighbor.

The New York *Mirror* successfully pressured the police to reopen a murder case on which they had given up. An Episcopal minister, Edward Hall, and his lover, Mrs. James Mills, had been found shot on an isolated farm. The *Mirror* produced an eccentric neighbor who raised hogs, immediately dubbed "the pig woman," who claimed that Reverend Hall's widow and several of her relatives had killed the paramours. (They were acquitted and successfully sued the *Mirror*.)

The *Mirror* was a tabloid. These new dailies (the first, in 1919, was the New York *Daily News*) were half the size of traditional newspapers and opened like a book. The format was a brilliant idea. The size and easy-turning pages appealed to people who rode crowded subways and trolley cars. But the **tabloids** were more than convenient: they virtually ignored traditional news and, lavishly plastering their pages with large photographs, reported sex scandals and violent crimes in breathless, suggestive prose. Their popularity was instantaneous. Within five years, the *Daily News* had the largest circulation in the nation. Its biggest scoop was a front-page photograph of the electrocution of Ruth Snyder, who had murdered her husband. The picture was taken illegally with a hidden camera.

Even apologists for the tabloids were appalled by the *Evening Graphic,* which they called the "Pornographic." It was published by Bernarr MacFadden, the "father of physical culture," who had been having trouble with obscenity laws for decades, mostly for displaying his well-sculpted body while wearing little clothing. MacFadden solved the problem of how to illustrate a story when there were no photographs. The "composograph" was put together by pasting photos of the celebrities of the moment on cartoons of titillating scenes. One showed Enrico Caruso welcoming Valentino to Italian heaven.

MacFadden also published the immensely popular women's magazine, *True Story,* containing tear-jerking love stories as sexy as the law allowed "told" by ordinary women "just like" the readers. Founded in 1926, it was soon selling 2 million copies of each issue. MacFadden followed with *True Romances, True Detective,* and others, all of them actually written by employees in cubicles in MacFadden's offices.

---

thousands of less than wealthy people with savings accounts. To tap their capital, New York stock brokerage houses opened offices nationwide and offered would-be Jim Fisks and Hetty Greens an installment plan in which, it could seem, there were only a few installments to pay—or none at all.

That is, investors with a few hundred or thousands of dollars with which to "play the market" were urged to buy stocks "on margin." They bought shares of RCA, the New York Central, or Illinois Widget by putting down as little as 10 percent of the price of those companies' shares. They were able to hold title to ten times as many shares as they could buy if they paid cash. The broker lent them the balance of the stocks' price with the stocks serving as collateral. When the shares were sold—at a big profit, of course—the loans were paid off, and the speculators pocketed ten times what they would have made had they been so foolish as to have bought the stocks with cash. At least that was how the 1.5 million Americans playing the market in 1926 understood margin buying to work.

THE BULL MARKET

Beginning in 1927, that was how it did work. Prices of shares climbed almost every day as more and more people rushed to buy stock. All through 1928 and into the summer of 1929, values went crazy. American Telephone and Telegraph climbed from $209 a share to $303; General Motors went from $268 to $452 on September 3, 1929. Some obscure issues enjoyed even more dizzying rises. And with each tale of a fortune made overnight, related breathlessly at country club, lodge hall, or community dance, or on the porch of the church on Sunday, more people were hooked, carrying their savings to stockbrokers. In 1928 and 1929, 600 local brokerages were opened, an 80 percent increase in access to the market.

Ideally, the value of a share in a corporation represents the earning capacity of the company; the money a corporation realizes by selling shares is used to improve the company's plant, equipment, or marketing capacity or in other productive ways. Thus when the price of stock in General Motors or RCA

Lucky Lindy

The photo shows Charles A. Lindbergh, with the *Spirit of St. Louis,* the plane designed and built for one purpose: to make Lindbergh the first person to fly the Atlantic solo. There was a prize of $25,000 waiting for the pilot who did it. Several men, including French World War I ace René Fonck and polar explorer Admiral Richard A. Byrd, had crossed the ocean with copilots in huge trimotor biplanes, but neither had done it alone.

Lindbergh, an unknown airmail pilot, believed that big, fuel-hungry planes were the wrong approach to the challenge. His plane was starkly simple and light. Except for the cockpit and wing, the *Spirit* was a gas tank. It was by no means a reckless experiment, but that was how the press played it, depicting Lindbergh as an innocent, daring, all-American boy. Staying awake for two and a half days was Lindbergh's toughest problem, but he managed it. At Le Bourget Field outside Paris, he was greeted by a screaming crowd of 100,000. Back in the United States, hysterical celebrations of Lindbergh's achievement went on for months.

Lindbergh was not nearly as simple and innocent as publicists depicted him. He hoped to parlay his feat into getting rich in commercial aviation, and he did. But he was shy, as his discomfort in this photograph shows. He was a businessman; he did not like putting himself on display as Calvin Coolidge did.

From the Collections of the Library of Congress

rose, it represented—in theory—the expansion of the automobile and radio companies.

During the Coolidge bull market, however, the prices of shares represented little more than the willingness of people to pay higher prices for them because, as in Florida, they expected someone else to buy the shares from them at yet higher prices. It was immaterial that the companies in which they had put their money did not pay dividends or use their capital to improve productive capacity. The rising prices of stocks fed on themselves. It became more profitable for companies to put their increasing capital into speculation—making loans to margin buyers, for example—rather than into production. The face value of shares bore little relationship to the health of the American economy. In fact, by October 1929, $16 billion of the value of shares on the New York Stock Exchange (18 percent of all capitalization) was in loans on the margin.

Politicians, unable to understand what was happening or afraid to appear pessimistic amidst the buoyant optimism, reassured their constituents that there was nothing wrong. When a few economists warned that the bull market was a bubble that had to burst with possibly calamitous consequences, other economists scolded them. President Coolidge told the country that he reckoned that stock prices were cheap, thus encouraging more people to rush to the broker. Even the Federal Reserve System fueled the irrationality by lowering its interest rates to a record low in 1927—making it easier to buy stocks on borrowed money.

THE INEVITABLE

Joseph P. Kennedy, a Boston millionaire (and father of President John F. Kennedy), said in later years that he sold all of his stocks during the summer of 1929 when the man who shined his shoes mentioned that he was playing the market. Kennedy reasoned that if a man who worked for a quarter and tips was buying stock, there was no one left out there to bid prices higher. The crash was coming soon.

Kennedy was right. On September 3, 1929, the average price of shares on the New York Stock Exchange peaked in the morning and then dipped sharply. For a month, prices spurted up and down—another sign that some people (but not all) thought it was time to cash in and hide the cash under a mattress. On "Black Thursday," October 24, a record 13 million shares changed hands, and values collapsed. General Electric fell $47\frac{1}{2}$ points in one day; other major issues dropped almost as much.

It's a Woman's Market

During the 1920s, women possessed 40 percent of the nation's wealth and made 35 percent of all stock market transactions, revealing that they were slightly more conservative speculators than men. Women owned well over half of A.T. & T. and the Pennsylvania Railroad.

In the spring of 1929, Eunice Fuller Barnard opened a brokerage house for women only. *The North American Review,* obviously not a feminist magazine, reported,

Day in and day out through a long five hours, aggressive and guttural dowagers, gum-chewing blondes, shrinking spinsters who looked as if they belonged in a missionary society meeting, watch, pencils in hand, from the opening of the market till the belated ticker drones its last in the middle of the afternoon.

Wall Street on Black Friday, October 1929. Many of the people milling about aimlessly were speculators stunned by the money they had lost in just a few hours. Others, no doubt, were in the crowd as spectators and, human nature being what it is, quietly enjoying the comeuppance the others had suffered.

On Tuesday, October 29, the wreckage was worse. In a panic now, speculators dumped 16 million shares. Clerical workers on Wall Street had to work all night just to sort out the avalanche of paperwork. When the dust settled, more than $30 billion in paper value had been wiped out.

It had been phony value, representing the irrational belief that prices for pieces of paper would rise indefinitely. Nevertheless, it was value people believed was in their pockets. Its sudden obliteration shattered business confidence and popular faith in business culture. The Great Crash eventually contributed to the hardship of millions of people who could not have distinguished a share in Seaboard Air Lines from the label on a bottle of cognac.

CRASH AND DEPRESSION

The Great Crash of 1929 did not cause the Great Depression of the 1930s. That was the result of fundamental weaknesses in the economy that had little to do with the mania for speculation. But the crash accelerated the collapse of the American economy that was quietly before October 1929.

Middle-class families that had played the market lost their savings. Banks that had lent money to speculators went belly-up. When they closed their doors, they wiped out the savings accounts of simple, frugal people who thought a bank was a vault where their money was protected from burglars and fires.

Myth

The Union Cigar Company was no industrial giant, but the collapse of its stock in the Great Crash of 1929 nevertheless made history. When the price of Union shares dropped from $113.50 to $4 in one day, the president of the company jumped to his death from a hotel room. The incident helped fuel a legend that rich men shouting "Ruined!" were hurling themselves by the dozen from high buildings during late 1929 and early 1930. Cartoonists in newspapers and magazines had a field day with the theme. But it was wishful thinking; the suicide rate was actually higher in the months just preceding the crash than it was after it.

Corporations whose cash assets were decimated curtailed production or shut down, throwing people out of work or cutting their wages. Unemployed workers who had taken out mortgages were unable to meet payments and lost their homes. Farmers lost the means by which they made a living. The defaults caused additional bank failures.

Virtually everyone but the very rich had to reduce consumer purchases, and there were not enough very rich people to sustain five-and-dimes and vacuum cleaner manufacturers, forcing yet other businesses and factories to close their doors. And so it went—from buy, buy, buy to down, down, down.

FURTHER READING

General Lynn Dumenil, *The Modern Temper: American Culture and Society in the 1920s*, 1995; David Goldberg, *Discontented America: The United States in the 1920s*, 1999; Gerald Leinhard, *1927: High Tide of the Twenties*, 2001; Nathan A. Miller, *A New World Coming: The 1920s and the Making of Modern America*, 2003; Michael E. Parrish, *America in Prosperity and Depression*, 1992.

Business and the Crash Bernard C. Beaudreau, *Mass Production, the Stock Market Crash, and the Great Depression*, 1996; William Frazer and John Guhrie, *The Florida Land Boom: Speculation, Money, and the Banks*, 1995; Morton Keller, *Regulating a New Economy: Public Policy and Economic Change in America, 1900–1933*, 1990; Maury Klein, *Rainbow's End: The Crash of 1929*, 2001; Anthony J. Mayo, *In Their Time: The Greatest Business Leaders of the Twentieth Century*, 2005; Charles Perrow, *Organizing America: Wealth, Power, and the Origins of Corporate America*, 2002; Barre A. Wigmore, *The Crash and Its Aftermath: A History of Securities Markets in the United States, 1929–1933*, 1985.

Coolidge and Hoover Hendrik Booraem, *The Provincial: Calvin Coolidge and His World, 1885–1895*, 1994; Robert H. Ferrell, *The Presidency of Calvin Coolidge*, 1998; Kendrick A. Klements, *Hoover, Conservation, and Consumerism: Engineering the Good Life*, 2000; George H. Nash, *The Life of Herbert Hoover*, 1988; Thomas B. Silver, *Coolidge and the Historians*, 1982; Joan Hoff Wilson, *Herbert Hoover: Forgotten Progressive*, 1975.

Popular Culture Loren Baritz, *The Culture of the Twenties*, 1969; Stanley Coben, *Rebellion against Victorianism: The Impetus for Cultural Change in 1920s America*, 1991; Richard W. Fox and T. Jackson Lears, *The Culture of Consumption: Critical Essays in American History, 1880–1980*, 1983; Jackson Lenes, *Fables of Abundance: A Cultural History of Advertising in America*, 1994; Roland Marchand, *Advertising and the American Dream*, 1985; Warren J. Susman, *Culture as History: The Transformation of American Society in the Twentieth Century*, 1984.

KEY TERMS

The following terms are covered in this chapter and can also be found in the list of Key Terms at the back of the book.

Al Smith	**"New Era"**	**tabloids**	**"trickle down"**
Florida land boom	***Spirit of St. Louis***	***The Man Nobody Knows***	

 ## ONLINE SOURCES GUIDE

Use this listing to find online documents, images, interactive maps, simulations, and other resources related to this chapter:

American History Resource Center
http://history.wadsworth.com/rc/us

Selected Images
Ford Motor Company showroom, 1925
Children listening to radio, 1923

Advertisement for new hairstyles for women, 1920s
New electrical appliances, 1920s
Coolidge throwing out first baseball, June 1924

Interactive Time Line (with online readings)
Calvin Coolidge and the New Era: When America Was Business, 1923–1929

CHAPTER 41

Hard Times

The Great Depression 1930–1933

From the Collections of the Library of Congress

What our country needs is a good big laugh. If someone could get off a good joke every ten days, I think our troubles would be over.

Herbert Hoover

Prosperity is just around the corner.
Herbert Hoover

The stock market crash made headlines. The Great Depression quietly descended like an evening mist, experienced by individuals one by one. By the end of 1930, however, the gloom had engulfed the nation and was far more serious than the collapse of the value of securities. There had been depressions before. What made this one "Great" was the fact that it got worse and bigger and went on and on without relief or signs of an end. The economy would not fully recover until 1938, when the approach of another great war jolted industry into full production of goods for which there were suddenly plenty of anxious buyers.

Except for the Civil War, the Depression of the 1930s shook the nation more than any other shared experience. Adults who suffered deprivation during the Thirties would be haunted by the experience until they died. Depression children would tell tales they only half understood to their children. Not until the late 1960s did a generation come of age for which the Great Depression was "ancient history" and therefore not very interesting.

THE FACE OF THE CREATURE

Not every Depression story was a tale of woe. Families took pride in the fact that when times were toughest, they stuck together and carried on with vitality or at least made do. Whether the memories were sweet or sour, however, the Depression generation was the last to date for which values and political behavior were forged in an era of prolonged economic anxieties.

DISMAYING NUMBERS

During the first year after the crash, 4 million workers lost their jobs. Still in 1931, 100,000 people were laid off weekly.

The Ongoing Crash

Like the Depression it triggered, the stock market crash of 1929 was not an episode quickly done with. People who still owned stocks after the bust (every share sold at a loss was purchased by someone) watched their bargain-basement investments dwindle for three years. In 1930 stocks had half the value they had in October 1929. Through the end of 1932 they declined another 30 percent. One had to be sufficiently well off to put stocks away and forget them to make money from investment. The stock market did not reach 1929 levels until World War II.

An unemployed worker with style. His wit may not have gotten him a job, but it told the world he had not been shattered.

By 1932 a quarter of the workforce was unemployed: 13 million people with 30 million dependents. (The population of the United States was about 125 million.) In heavily industrialized areas the numbers were worse. In Chicago 40 percent of people who wanted work did not have it. For a year in Toledo, Ohio, 80 percent were unemployed. In some coal-mining towns like Donora, Pennsylvania, virtually no one had a job. African Americans, "the last hired and the first fired," had it worse than whites: nationally, 35 percent were unemployed.

Those who held onto their jobs took pay cuts—gladly, given the alternative. Between 1929 and 1933 the average weekly earnings of manufacturing workers fell from $25 to less than $17. Farmers' income, already low in 1929, plummeted. By the winter of 1932–33 some corn growers were burning their crop to heat their homes (shades of the 1890s!) because they could not sell it. Wheat farmers had to sell five bushels to earn enough to buy a pair of shoes. The wholesale price of cotton dropped to 5 cents a pound: $30 for a 600-pound bale.

With no money coming in, hundreds of thousands could not pay rent or the monthly mortgage. They lost their homes. One farm family in four was pushed off the land by 1933, mainly in the cotton, grain, and pork belts of the South and Midwest. In one day, a fourth of the farms in Mississippi went on the auction block.

The Great Depression 1929–1945

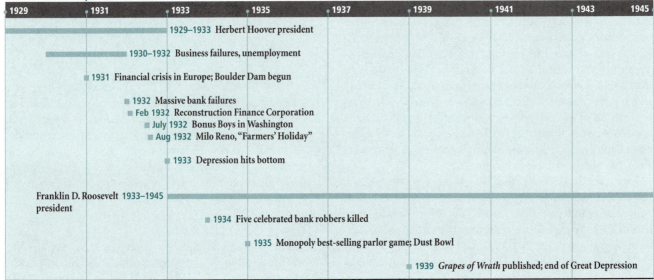

1929	1931	1933	1935	1937	1939	1941	1943	1945

1929–1933 Herbert Hoover president

1930–1932 Business failures, unemployment

1931 Financial crisis in Europe; Boulder Dam begun

1932 Massive bank failures
Feb 1932 Reconstruction Finance Corporation
July 1932 Bonus Boys in Washington
Aug 1932 Milo Reno, "Farmers' Holiday"

1933 Depression hits bottom

Franklin D. Roosevelt 1933–1945 president

1934 Five celebrated bank robbers killed

1935 Monopoly best-selling parlor game; Dust Bowl

1939 *Grapes of Wrath* published; end of Great Depression

People who could not pay the rent did not go shopping. More than 100,000 small businesses went bankrupt, 32,000 just in 1932 (88 a day). Doctors and lawyers reported big drops in income. When county and city property tax collections dwindled, even schools—pretty much everyone's first priority—were hit. In several midwestern cities like Dayton, Ohio, children went on a three-day week for lack of money to pay their teachers' salaries. Chicago's teachers worked without pay for months; some were not compensated for years; others never were. In January 1933, 1,000 schools in Georgia did not reopen after Christmas vacation.

Banks failed at a rate of 200 a month during 1932. Savings accounts of $3.2 billion simply evaporated. When New York's big Bank of the United States went under in December 1930, 400,000 people lost their deposits. Most of the accounts were small, hard-earned money that working-class families had squirreled away as a hedge against personal misfortune.

WHAT DEPRESSION LOOKED LIKE

Not everyone was hit, of course; but just about everyone was reminded of the Depression at every turning and newspaper delivery. Each week, more than 5,000 men lined up at a New York employment agency to apply for 500 low-level jobs. When the city of Birmingham, Alabama, called for 800 workers to put in an eleven-hour day for $2, there were 12,000 applicants. In 1931 a Soviet agency, Amtorg, announced openings in Russia for 6,000 skilled technicians; 100,000 Americans said they would go. Once-prosperous skilled workers and small businessmen sold apples or set up shoeshine stands on street corners.

Charitable organizations were paralyzed by the scope of demand. Philadelphia's social workers managed to reach only one-fifth of the city's unemployed and could provide each of those families only $4.23 for a week, not enough to

Men line up for a free meal at a "soup kitchen" in New York City. They had hit rock bottom, but practically everyone is wearing a hat or cap. Men in hats are rarely seen today, but during the 1930s to be in public without one was as improper as being shirtless. An employer with a menial job to fill would feel uneasy enough about a hatless man to pass him over. Notice how orderly the queue is. Only two relaxed policemen can be seen.

buy the cheapest food they needed. "Soup kitchens"—free meals mostly set up by churches—offered little more than a slice of bread and a bowl of stew, but for three years many ran at capacity. A journalist described the crowd at the Municipal Lodging House in New York City in 1930: "There is a line of men, three or sometimes four abreast, a block long, and wedged tightly together—so tightly that no passer-by can break through. For this compactness there is a reason: those at the head of the gray-black human snake will eat tonight; those farther back probably won't."

On the outskirts of cities (and in the middle of New York's Central Park), homeless men and women built shantytowns out of scavenged lumber, scraps of sheet metal, and cardboard boxes. The number of people who wandered the country—a new generation of tramps, this one including women—brought the scale of the catastrophe to rural America. Railroads gave up trying to keep tramps off freights; there were too many of them. The Missouri Pacific railroad had counted 14,000 people hopping its freights in 1928; in 1931 they estimated they had 186,000 "passengers." In 1931 some 1.5 million people were moving about the country in search of work.

In a broad belt running north and south from the Dakotas into Texas, a severe annual drought beginning in 1931 piled natural catastrophe on top of manmade depression. Only farmers with deep artesian wells produced crops until rainfall levels rose in 1939. By 1935 fields plowed for a generation were so powdery that the topsoil blew away. Hardest and most dramatically hit was the "**Dust Bowl**": northern Texas, southern Kansas, southeastern Colorado, and the epicenter: western Oklahoma. Dust storms blew dirt through crevices in homes and blacked out the sun for days at a time. Some Oklahoma counties saw 90 percent of the population on the dole and then, beginning in 1935, lost half their population. The "**Okies**" (originally a derogatory term) gave up, abandoned even farms they owned, and—most of them—headed west on "Route 66" to California.

THE FAILURE OF THE OLD ORDER

Will Rogers, the nation's most popular humorist, quipped that the United States would be the first country to drive to the poorhouse in an automobile. He was trying to infuse a sense of proportion into the way people thought about the Depression. President Hoover made the same point, rather more clumsily. "No one is starving," he said.

They were right. The Depression was not a pandemic or plague laying the continent waste. The United States was as rich in material blessings as ever. There was plenty of food. The capacity of American factories to produce goods ranging from pins and trousers to vacuum cleaners to airplanes was the same in 1932 as it had been in 1929.

Indeed, the fact that so many were deprived in the mouth of a cornucopia was what bewildered many and embittered others. An elderly California physician, Francis E. Townshend, was transformed into an angry crusader when, one morning, he looked out his window to see old women picking through the garbage pails of a grocery store that was heaped high with foodstuffs. "Ten men in our country could buy the whole world," Will Rogers cracked, not humorously this time, "and 10 million can't buy enough to eat."

In fact, it was abundance—superabundance—too much food, too many goods—combined with the greed of New Era businessmen and the Coolidge administration's dereliction of its responsibilities that caused the disaster.

NOT ENOUGH CUSTOMERS

During the 1920s, the American economy churned out things to sell in ever-increasing plenty, but the people who ran the country did not spread around the money to buy them to enough of the population. The president and Congress, partly because of obsolete principles they assumed were eternal, partly in obeisance to big business, ignored signs that the combination of overproduction and underconsumption was a dangerous mix—such signs were obvious even before 1929—and clung to policies that worsened the situation.

Federal tax policies favored the wealthy, who pumped their modestly taxed income into speculation to produce more. Some of their investment inflated the price of stocks to the bursting point; some of it increased the production of goods that were already too abundant. Andrew Mellon said that the wealth capitalists invested and reinvested would trickle down as prosperity to working people in the form of wages and to farmers in sales of their crops.

But wages in general lagged far behind the growth of the wealth concentrated at the top. Consumers were never able to consume the nation's agricultural produce at a price that made farmers into consumers too, and by 1928 it was obvious to the few economists who looked at the figures that people were not buying all the pins, trousers, and vacuum cleaners that manufacturers were churning out. Too many of the "big ticket" commodities such as cars and refrigerators (and even vacuum cleaners) were purchased on installment plans—with money, in other words, that the buyers did not have.

Large and visible sectors of the population were so impoverished that they were unable to buy much of anything, even on credit. Coal miners, not a very important occupational group today, were just that during the Twenties: more than 600,000 men were mine workers. Their low wages—frozen since 1920 at just enough to pay the rent and feed the family—meant that miners and their families never did buy many of the consumer goods on which Coolidge Prosperity was based.

For farmers who produced the staples—corn, wheat, pork, cotton—the Depression began not in 1930 but in the aftermath of World War I. American farms were so productive that the prices at which they sold their crops dropped steadily; years in which farmers broke even were "good years." (Thanks to Prohibition, even the country's booze was distilled from Canadian grain.) Electricity reached only one American farm in ten. The other nine were buying nothing that had to be plugged in, including lamps and lightbulbs.

The South, still largely rural, was a glaringly obvious "pocket" of nonconsumers. Per capita income in the deep South—rural Georgia, Alabama, Mississippi, and Louisiana—was about half the per capita income of the rest of the country. Sharecroppers might not see $20 in cash in a year. They bought their seed and food on credit and hoped that their share, when the crop was sold, would cover the previous year's expenditures. Nothing was trickling down to them.

African Americans who fled the South to northern and midwestern cities were part of the money economy but—as a group—were not buying much more than necessities. The black middle class was growing, but most urban African Americans had low-paying menial jobs. They could not consume much.

American foreign policy contributed to the problem of an inadequate domestic market by making it difficult for Europeans to buy American products. Foreign policy was designed to serve American finance virtually to the point of ignoring other American economic interests. Banks were encouraged to make huge loans to Germany on the assumption that the Germans would use much of the money to make reparations payments to the British and French, who would then repay their debts to the United States. Bankers made lots of money from the transactions.

But American factories and farmers did not. The Republican party's high tariffs—when American industry needed no "protection"—made it difficult for Europeans to sell their produce in the United States to pay for American goods ranging from big-profit American machinery (which was coveted) to dirt-cheap American foodstuffs. Congress was so obstinately blind to the obvious that in 1930, in the depths of the Depression, the new Hawley–Smoot Tariff raised the average duty on European imports from 40 percent to 60 percent!

HERBERT HOOVER, SCAPEGOAT

Herbert Hoover was justly proud when he was elected president. Except for the military heroes (Washington, Taylor, and Grant), he was the only president who was not a professional politician. Unfortunately for him, the singular nature of the American presidency is such that if things go badly during a president's watch, he takes the fall, no matter how innocent of blame he is.

Hoover was not responsible for the Great Depression. He had been in office less than eight months when the sky fell.

One of dozens of "Hoovervilles" quickly erected in empty space (there was one in New York's Central Park) by people who lost their homes. Some survived for years, left alone by authorities as long as they were orderly. Most were. Others, unsurprisingly, were nests of drunkenness, altercations, sickness, and crime.

© Bettmann/Corbis

He had not indicated in any way that he planned to depart from Coolidge's practice of passively presiding. Still, he was infinitely more perceptive than Coolidge and had never been passive; he was the one member of Coolidge's cabinet who was not an obliging flunkey of the banks and corporations. He had been considered a "progressive"; he made Coolidge nervous.

No matter: he got the blame from the start. The shantytowns where the homeless dwelled were called "**Hoovervilles.**" Men sleeping on park benches called the newspapers they wrapped around themselves for warmth "Hoover blankets." An empty pocket turned inside out was a "Hoover flag"; a boxcar was a "Hoover Pullman."

When the president visited hard-hit Detroit, riding in a motorcade, the people on the sidewalk stared at him, silently. Wisely, he cut personal appearances to a minimum, but his disappearance from view contributed to the popular belief that he was doing nothing or was paralyzed by the enormity of the crisis. He could not take a brief vacation without arousing scorn. "Look here, Mr. Hoover, see what you've done," an Appalachian song had it, "You went a-fishing, let the country go to ruin." The "Great Humanitarian" who saved the Belgian people from famine during the war was now callously indifferent to the sufferings of Americans.

HOOVER'S PROGRAM

In truth, Hoover was stunned by the Depression, personally depressed, subdued, and withdrawn. An adviser later said that talking with him in his office was like sitting in a bath of ink. But he was not unmoved by the suffering in the country. He gave a big chunk of his annual income to charities helping the stricken. No other president has been half as generous.

Nor was Hoover paralyzed. He worked more steadily and harder over four years than any president but James K. Polk and, in his second term, Woodrow Wilson. Polk's exhaustion contributed to his death at age 54 just months after leaving office. Defying his doctor's orders, Wilson pushed himself into a disabling stroke midway through his term.

© UPI-Bettmann/Corbis

Boulder Dam, *now called Hoover Dam, the first great public works program of the Great Depression. It was a miracle of engineering that made possible, with the cheap electricity the dam generated, another kind of miracle: the bizarre, superilluminated city of Las Vegas, Nevada.*

Hoover had a program to fight the Depression that would have been beyond Coolidge. He recognized that Andrew Mellon's regressive taxes had contributed to the Depression by reducing consumers' buying power, so he abandoned some of them. He persuaded Congress to commit $500 million a year to public works, building or improving government properties so as to put people to work. The greatest of his projects was great, indeed: a 700 foot high, 1,200 foot wide wall of concrete spanning the Colorado River southeast of Las Vegas that, seventy years after its completion, is still among the world's greatest feats of engineering. Hoover's Reconstruction Finance Corporation (RFC), established in 1932, was a federal agency that funneled money to banks, railroads, and other vital businesses teetering on the edge of collapse.

Such an attempt by the federal government to kick-start and manipulate the economy (and the public works expenditures) had been anathema to the Republican party establishment for a decade. Whatever Hoover's plans when he was sworn into office in March 1929, his administration was activist.

But everything he did was too late, was too little, or increased his unpopularity. Reducing taxes on consumers did nothing for the millions who were unemployed and earning nothing. Public works projects did nothing for anyone but those who were employed by them. Boulder City, Nevada, thrown up overnight to house workers on the dam, was a

---

No One Has Starved

No one starved, but some came close, as *The New York Times* reported:

Middletown, New York, December 24, 1931—Attracted by smoke from the chimney of a supposedly abandoned summer cottage near Anwana Lake in Sullivan County, Constable Simon Glaser found a young couple starving. Three days without food, the wife, who is 23 years old, was hardly able to walk.

Danbury, Connecticut, September 6, 1932—Found starving under a rude canvas shelter in a patch of woods on Flatboard Ridge, where they had lived for five days on wild berries and apples, a woman and her 16-year-old daughter were fed and clothed today by the police and placed in the city almshouse.

Weeknights at Eight

How They Lived

Commercial radio broadcasting began in 1920; the first nationwide radio network, the National Broadcasting Company, was founded in 1926. By the time of the Great Depression, radio moguls had developed a programming formula that hooked Americans. In addition to news, sporting events, and music, the networks (NBC, the Columbia Broadcasting System, Mutual, and, after 1935, the American Broadcasting Company) broadcast "soap operas" during the day for housewives; serialized stories—mostly adventures—for children in the afternoons when school was out; and, in the evening, comedy, dramatic, and mystery series "for the entire family."

Radio receivers were cheap during the Thirties; a pretty good one could be bought for $10–20. So there was no cheaper form of commercial entertainment. Radio was one of the few growth industries of the Depression decade. Receivers were ensconced in about 12 million American households in 1930, 28 million in 1940.

With so huge an audience, makers of low-priced consumer necessities (canned soup) and seminecessities (underarm deodorants) devoted the largest chunks of their advertising budgets to radio. In 1935, with operating expenses of about $80 million, the networks and local stations took in $113 million from advertisers. In 1940 expenses were up to $114 million, but advertising revenues had almost doubled to $216 million.

The manufacturers of Pepsodent toothpaste stumbled on the best bargain on the airwaves. In 1928 they contracted with two white minstrel show performers who were doing a program in southern black dialect in Chicago: *Sam 'n' Henry*. When the show went national with Pepsodent, Freeman Gosden and Charles Correll chose two new names: Amos and Andy. The show was a hit from the start, and its popularity never flagged until external pressures crushed it.

Amos 'n' Andy was a situation comedy based on minstrel show humor set in Harlem, which, by the Thirties, was the undisputed capital of black America. Gosden, who was from Richmond, said that the character of Amos Jones was based on an African-American friend from his boyhood. Amos was the honest, hardworking proprietor and sole driver of the Fresh Air Taxi Company. (His cab had no windshield.) The "nice guy" who patiently tried to talk sense to the comic characters, Amos became a comparatively minor figure. The characters the audience wanted to hear were Amos's broadly comic friends in a fraternal lodge, the Mystic Knights of the Sea.

The central (and most popular) character was George Stevens, the "Kingfish" of the lodge, a fast-talking con man who dependably bungled his swindles and ended up outsmarting himself. The Kingfish's inevitable mark, Andrew H. Brown (Andy), was infinitely gullible, so simpleminded that even the inept Kingfish could bilk him. They were the end men of the minstrel shows: the city slicker and the yokel.

Everyone in America, it seemed, listened to the program, which ran on weeknights at eight o'clock. Few needed to be told what Amos, Andy, the Kingfish, and the minor characters were like. Lightnin' swept up the men's lodge; Algonquin J. Calhoun was a shyster lawyer; Ruby Jones was as sensible and decent as her husband Amos; and Sapphire Stevens was a shrew who made life as miserable for her husband George as he made it for Andy.

In November 1951, *Amos 'n' Andy* went from radio to television in a weekly half-hour format with African-American actors who mimicked the voices Gosden and Correll had created. Although African Americans had listened to the radio show as avidly as whites for thirty-two years, middle-class black organizations like the NAACP and African-American newspapers denounced the show's stereotypes as "a gross libel on the Negro." Gosden had a point when he replied that the show "helped characterize Negroes as interesting and dignified human beings." There was nothing offensive about Amos and Ruby Jones, and white humor depended on stereotypes for laughs as much as *Amos 'n' Andy* did.

But times had changed. With the Civil Rights movement and African-American militancy approaching their flood, institutions like the TV networks were becoming hypersensitive to criticism. The televised *Amos 'n' Andy* remained popular among whites—less so among blacks—and ran through a hundred episodes. Then it disappeared.

---

hive of working-class prosperity. It was also a speck in the desert. The RFC shored up several important banks and railroads that might otherwise have gone under. But with one in four workers without a job, it looked like a welfare program for multimillionaires.

HOOVER'S LIMITATIONS

Most urgently needed was relief for those who had been earning decent livings one day and through no fault of their own were impoverished, some of them homeless, the next. Hoover would not hear of proposals that the federal government shoulder any such responsibility. Relieving misery was a matter for private charities or, Hoover conceded, municipal and state governments. But charities' resources were reduced to little more than operating expenses during the Depression's first year, as were most city and state governments.

In approving state but opposing federal relief measures, Hoover was expressing an obsolete nineteenth-century

Monopoly

The parlor game Monopoly was invented during the Depression by an out-of-work engineer, Charles Darrow; 200 million Monopoly sets were sold between 1935 and 2000.

Monopoly was a fight-the-Depression fantasy that revived the fantasies of 1920s speculators. Players purchased real estate on streets of varying desirability in Atlantic City, New Jersey. They built houses and hotels on them and charged other players rent if a toss of the dice made them tenants.

The winner was the player who reduced other players to destitution and won a monopoly of streets, houses, and hotels. But there was then not a soul in Atlantic City who could afford to rent a house or check into a hotel.

Interestingly, Darrow patterned his game on The Landlord's Game, an obscure board game patented by Elizabeth Magie in 1904. Magie was a "Single-Taxer." She was trying to demonstrate the evils of land ownership.

distinction between state and federal powers. (He was not alone in clinging to the principle.) He was also inconsistent because his philosophical reason for opposing government relief of distress by handouts logically applied to state relief programs too. That is, Hoover believed that the virtue of the American character was its "rugged individualism." Americans were independent and self-reliant; they "stood on their own two feet," took personal responsibility for their welfare, and made their own way. This self-reliance was not in their genes, but in their culture. To give Americans money for doing nothing would eviscerate them morally.

Hoover was a "self-made man." He did not rise from the dregs of society (his father was a blacksmith), but neither did he have an inheritance. Orphaned as a boy, he had largely made his own way: earning a university education as a mining engineer and, working on salary in Australia and China, investing his savings in failing mines he recognized were potentially rich but mismanaged, reorganizing them. Before Hoover was 40, he was a millionaire.

What he failed to recognize was the role of his extraordinary personal talents in his success and the role of luck—it had not been all hard work and self-reliance. He failed or refused to admit that had he been a penniless 21-year-old mining engineer just out of college in 1930 who lost his job when the mine shut down, he would have faced a bleak future. There was no room in the incantation of "rugged individualism" for social and economic forces beyond the most rugged individual's control. Hoover was reduced to other incantations. "Prosperity," he said too often for his crumbling popularity, was "just around the corner."

Then, in 1931, Hoover's prediction briefly seemed to be coming true. What we call economic indicators made modest gains. Hoover brightened: the country was turning the corner. But in May one of Europe's most powerful banks failed. The Kreditanstalt of Vienna had been shaky for years. Europe's other great banks had propped it up, so when the Kreditanstalt collapsed, other banks followed it. In September Great Britain abandoned the gold standard as the only alternative to the collapse of the Bank of England. (The bank ceased to redeem its paper money in gold coin.) Worried that the paper dollar—with the British pound the chief international currency—would lose its value, foreign and American investors withdrew $1.5 billion in gold from American banks, launching a new wave of business failures.

RESPONSES TO HARD TIMES

If Americans blamed Hoover, few blamed capitalism. This was not for a lack of trying by the nation's two anticapitalist political parties, the Socialist Party of America and the Communist party. Leaders of both concluded (reasonably enough) that if ever there was a real opportunity to move from the political fringe and become authentic political alternatives to the capitalist parties, the Depression had provided it. There was something basically wrong, socialist and communist newspapers and recruiters argued, when people were willing and able to work and produce plenty of everything for everyone, but millions of workers had lost their jobs and millions of farmers had been forced off the land. The enemy was not the hapless Hoover; the enemy was the system.

THE NOT-SO-RED DECADE

After polling 49,000 votes in prosperous 1928, Communist party presidential candidate William Z. Foster doubled his count in 1932 to 103,000. Socialist candidate Norman Thomas did better. He won 267,000 votes in 1928 and 882,000 in 1932.

Still, both were disappointed, and with good reason. The combined anticapitalist vote of less than a million was paltry next to the discredited Hoover's 16 million votes. And Hoover was buried in a landslide by the Democratic party candidate, Franklin D. Roosevelt of New York. Indeed, the combined socialist and communist vote was less than the Socialist party presidential candidate had won twenty years earlier from an electorate that was half the size of the electorate of 1932.

And 1932 was the high-water mark. Although Roosevelt's reform program was hardly socialistic, the Socialist party, which advocated peaceful, piecemeal, democratically supported evolution toward socialism, was largely co-opted. In 1936 Norman Thomas won only 187,000 votes.

The communists made some converts among intellectuals. Novelists Theodore Dreiser, Mary McCarthy, Sherwood Anderson, and John Dos Passos; detective story writer Dashiell Hammett and playwright Lillian Hellman; and critics Edmund Wilson and Granville Hicks either joined "the party" or espoused communism as a desirable alternative to the system that had brought economic disaster to the

United States. The famous journalist Lincoln Steffens returned from a trip to the Soviet Union and said, "I have seen the future, and it works." Even F. Scott Fitzgerald, the celebrator of the flappers and "flaming youth" of the 1920s, flirted with Marxist ideas that he never quite understood.

But the intellectuals' entrance into the party was a revolving door that never stopped turning. Few—well-known writers and obscure college professors alike—remained communists for long. While intellectuals who can be told what to think are not rare, silent obeisance to a "party line" does not go with the way of life. Independent thought and even mild reservations were not tolerated in the Communist party. There was a large exodus of party members in 1938 when the Soviet dictator Joseph Stalin tried many leading communists for treason in "show trials" at which many confessed to crimes that they clearly had never committed. Stalin had already had every admiral in the Soviet navy and seven generals shot. Half the officers in the army were executed or imprisoned. Treason on such a scale was obviously absurd. Staying on top by murdering potential rivals was too much for many idealistic American communists to swallow.

On the face of it, the party was successful in penetrating a number of labor unions, including one of the labor movement's two umbrella organizations, the Congress of Industrial Organizations. Wyndham Mortimer of the United Automobile Workers, CIO journalist Len De Caux, and CIO lawyer Lee Pressman were just three communists in high-ranking positions. Communists headed the United Electrical Workers, the Mine Mill and Smelter Workers, and several smaller unions. Dozens of hard-working communist organizers were instrumental, even essential, to the rapid growth of the steelworkers, automobile workers, and longshoremen unions.

But communist influence among the rank and file was negligible. Most of the party members in leadership positions concealed or denied their communist affiliation. They were Leninists. They did not believe ordinary workers were capable of making a revolution. For their own good, they had to be manipulated by the "militant minority" organized in secret, small cells.

Similarly, the party had little success in enlisting African Americans despite the fact that party activists, often courageously, led successful rent strikes in the black neighborhoods in northern cities. Others spearheaded attempts to organize sharecroppers in the South (whites as well as blacks); and with only belated support from liberals, communists led a campaign to save the lives of the "Scottsboro Boys," nine young black men convicted of rape in Alabama in 1931 on tainted evidence. Had the communists not made the fight, the hapless Scottsboro Boys would have been executed.

A CURIOUS RESPONSE

Americans—whites and blacks, unskilled workers and Ph.D.s—did not see the Depression as evidence that capitalism had failed. Herbert Hoover was not alone in attributing success and failure to individuals. Psychologists and sociologists marveled that the most common initial response to the Depression was self-blame. They reported that homeless hitchhikers apologized for their shabby clothing. A walk through big-city parks revealed scores of unsuccessful job seekers slumped on benches, heads in hands, elbows on knees, collars drawn up, wondering where they had failed.

Gillette, a manufacturer of razor blades, exploited the feeling of personal failure with an advertisement showing a husband ashamedly telling his wife that he still had not found a job. The message was that employers had turned him down not because there were no jobs for anybody, but because he cut a poor appearance with his poorly shaved whiskers. A maker of underwear put the responsibility for the unemployment of a bedridden man squarely on his own shoulders. He was out of work not because 13 million others were, but because he wore an inferior brand of undershirt and had caught a cold.

EPISODES OF VIOLENCE

There was violence, most of it spontaneous: food riots in St. Paul and other cities, people storming groceries and clearing the shelves. Wisconsin dairy farmers stopped milk trucks and dumped the milk into ditches, partly in anger at the low prices paid by processors and partly to dramatize their need for help. In Iowa, the National Farmers' Holiday Association told hog raisers to withhold their products from the market—to take a holiday—and attracted attention by blockading highways. Eat your own products, Holiday Association leader Milo Reno told the Iowans, and let the money men eat their gold.

But such incidents were few. For the most part, Americans coped with the Depression peacefully. In fact, the most violent episode of the early Depression was launched not by stricken people but by the authorities: the attack on the "Bonus Expeditionary Force" in Washington in the summer of 1932.

In 1924 Congress had voted to reward World War I veterans with a "bonus" of $1,000 to be paid in 1945. When the Depression threw thousands of old soldiers out of work, they asked for payment of half the bonus immediately. Congress obliged, but Hoover vetoed the bill; it was "relief," he said. Congress passed the bill over his veto, and Democrats, knowing that it gave them the popular side of an issue in a presidential election year, called for paying veterans the entire bonus immediately. In support, 20,000 veterans (and some wives) massed in Washington. When Congress adjourned in July without taking action, all but about 2,000 of the demonstrators left the capital. Those who remained squatted in empty government office buildings or moved to a "**Bonus Boys**" Hooverville on Anacostia Flats—wasteland on the outskirts of the city. There were some fistfights and drunkenness, but the camp was, on the whole, remarkably peaceful. The Bonus Boys policed themselves and cooperated with authorities.

Hoover persuaded himself that the Bonus Boys were led by communist agitators. (They were not; the most influential organization among them was the anticommunist American Legion.) The president sent General Douglas MacArthur

"Bonus Boys" preparing to join the demonstration in Washington. Hoover's decision to evict squatters from government buildings was justified. General MacArthur's destruction of the Bonus Boy shanty town, which Hoover did not authorize, ruined what was left of the president's reputation.

with troops to clear out the Bonus Boys who were living in government buildings. He said nothing about Anacostia Flats. MacArthur, a brave and talented soldier who unfortunately already had a reputation for making up his own orders, assembled armored vehicles and tear gas and, when the shacks were clear, moved into the Bonus Boy camp and razed it. Hoover let MacArthur's insubordination pass, and blame for the spectacle of young soldiers driving old soldiers off at bayonet point was heaped on him.

MIDWESTERN ROBIN HOODS

Americans expressed their disenchantment with values they had accepted during the Twenties in some curious ways. Businessmen, lionized just a few years earlier, became objects of ridicule in films, on radio programs, and in the columns and comic strips of daily newspapers. Ordinary people, especially in the heartland between the Appalachians and the Rockies, lavished tacit approval on a new kind of criminal: the heavily armed midwestern bank robber who exploited the sleepiness of small towns and the effectiveness of automobiles for making "getaways" on little-traveled rural roads to elude capture—for a time.

Gangsters like **John Dillinger,** "Pretty Boy" Floyd, and "Machine Gun" Kelly were not looked at askance as the urban, ethnic bootleggers of Prohibition had been. Some small-town newspapers portrayed them romantically, as free spirits who injured only the rich (who had injured the country).

The bank robbers reveled in the publicity. Bonnie Parker and Clyde Barrow, who headed a small gang, took photographs of one another clowning with guns; Bonnie Parker wrote a rhyming account of their adventures more or less in the form of a chivalric ballad with an inevitably tragic conclusion: "It's curtains for Bonnie and Clyde." It was printed in hundreds of papers. Reporters had no trouble finding waitresses to whom John Dillinger had given $20 tips.

It was all nonsense. Unlike the Prohibition's businessmen, gangsters like Al Capone, Depression bank robbers were small-time operators who botched as many holdups as they pulled off. Detroit's Purple Gang and other bootleg rings had killed gangster competitors but not "civilians," who were their customers. The midwestern bank robbers were reckless with their guns, killing bank guards and even bystanders when, leaving a bank, they opened fire to create a smokescreen of confusion covering their getaway.

Nor did they enjoy the garish luxury of the Al Capones. Their faces well known because of the publicity, they could spend the money they stole only by holing up in dingy hideouts and dining on canned soup and beans until the treasury was depleted. Nevertheless, because their targets were the hated banks that foreclosed on farms, and because most of them had a rural or small-town WASP background (there were no Italians or Jews in the bank robbing game), they had plenty of admirers. John Dillinger (who killed ten men) made it a point to be personally generous. "Pretty Boy" Floyd, who operated chiefly in Oklahoma, never had trouble finding folks who would hide him. When he was buried in

Salisaw, Oklahoma, in 1934 (after being gunned down), 20,000 people attended the funeral.

THE MOVIES: THE DEPRESSION-PROOF BUSINESS

Hollywood, particularly Warner Brothers studios, exploited the gangster phenomenon by making movies slyly glamorizing lawbreakers while carefully ending the films with a moralistic law-and-order message. Like the adulterous woman in nineteenth-century novels, who had to be killed off no matter how she had been manipulated by others, movie gangsters paid for their crimes "in a hail of bullets" or seated in an electric chair. But the message was clear: criminals played by George Raft, Edward G. Robinson, and former dancer James Cagney had been pushed into their careers by poverty and social injustice, and most had redeeming personal qualities.

The film industry's depression was serious—several studios went in receivership—but it lasted only a year or so. Movies flourished during the worst years of the Thirties, occupying the central position in American entertainment that they would hold until the coming of television. In the middle of the decade, nineteen of the twenty-five highest salaries in the United States, and forty of the highest sixty-three, were paid to motion picture executives. Star actors and actresses raked it in.

Why? First, tickets were cheap: 25 cents—10 cents for children—at neighborhood theaters. Theater owners sweetened the pot by inventing the double feature for evenings when business was slowest. A quarter bought two "B" movies (cheaply made formula comedies or westerns that the studios rented for a flat fee rather than a percentage), a newsreel, a travelogue, and, to keep the kids coming back every Saturday afternoon, cliff-hanger serials.

Each week, 85 million people watched Marie Dressler, Janet Gaynor, Shirley Temple, Mickey Rooney, Jean Harlow, and Clark Gable in a dizzying array of adventures and fantasies. The favorite themes were escapist. During the mid-1930s, Shirley Temple, an angelic little blonde girl who sang and danced, led the list of moneymakers. Her annual salary was $300,000, and her films made $5 million a year for Fox Pictures. Royalties from Shirley Temple dolls and other paraphernalia made her a multimillionaire before she reached puberty (which ended her film career). Choreographer Busby Berkeley made millions for Warner Brothers by staging plotless dance tableaux featuring dozens of beautiful starlets (transformed by mirrors and camera tricks into hundreds).

MUSIC, MUSIC, MUSIC

The recorded music business, by way of contrast, did not recover from the Depression until the 1940s. Sales of 78 rpm records, usually priced at 35 cents, had risen to $50 million a year during the 1920s; in 1932 sales were $2.5 million. The chief casualties were "hillbilly" groups and African-American blues and jazz musicians, whose markets were two of the hardest-hit social groups in the country. Columbia, Decca,

Straight Shooters

Network radio's late afternoons and early evenings were given over to juvenile programs featuring young adventurers like Little Orphan Annie and Jack Armstrong, the "All-American Boy"; aviators and space explorers; and cowboys like the Lone Ranger and Tom Mix (who was a real person).

They combined strident morality and patriotism with cliff-hanging conclusions to most fifteen-minute broadcasts, thus ensuring that listeners would let nothing get in the way of tuning in, "same time, same station," the next day. Sponsors promoted their products by offering premiums (like secret decoder rings) for the cost of a quarter—plus a box top or two proving purchase of the product. They also organized "clubs" for devotees. Tom Mix's club was called the Straight Shooters and required members to swear a pledge:

I promise to shoot straight with my parents by obeying my father and mother.

I promise to shoot straight with my friends by telling the truth always, by being fair and square at work and at play.

I promise to shoot straight with myself by striving always to be my best, by keeping my mind alert and my body strong and healthy.

I promise to shoot straight with Tom Mix by regularly eating good old Hot Ralston, the official Straight Shooter cereal, because I know Hot Ralston is just the kind of cereal that will help build a stronger America.

and RCA discontinued their "race record" division, which had targeted an African-American market. Only a few black performers like blues singer Bessie Smith and cornet player Louis Armstrong continued to sell enough records to stay in the business.

The jukebox, playing a record for a nickel in cafes and bars, slowly improved business. By 1939, 225,000 jukeboxes were scratching up 13 million "platters" a year. Sales of records increased from 10 million in 1933 to 33 million in 1938 (and then soared, with war and the return of prosperity, to 127 million in 1941).

The chief beneficiaries were the "big bands" that promoted their records by touring and playing swing, an intricately harmonized orchestral jazz music designed for dancing. For 50 cents people could dress up and dance for three hours to the music of Benny Goodman, Harry James, and other groups. It was not an every-evening diversion. The big bands had to rush from city to city on a series of one-night stands. Even the most popular orchestras might play in thirty different ballrooms in as many nights.

But they were popular. In the Palladium Ballroom in Hollywood, California, Harry James once drew 8,000 dancers in a single night, 35,000 in a week. At other capitals of swing, like the Glen Island Casino in New Rochelle, New York, big bands earned extra revenue by playing on the radio too. Because a good radio could be ensconced in the parlor for $10 or $20 and operated for the cost of electricity, this was Depression-era America's favorite distraction.

THE ELECTION OF 1932

Nostalgia for the Thirties of people who were young then—memories of a favorite radio program, of going to a ballroom or to a movie palace decorated like a Turkish seraglio—fixed on the middle and later years of the Depression decade. In the summer of 1932, when the economy hit bottom, the country's mood was somber.

A ROOSEVELT FOR THE DEMOCRATS

Senator Joseph I. France of Maryland challenged Hoover for the Republican presidential nomination. He won primaries in New Jersey, Pennsylvania, Illinois, and Oregon. Had presidential nominations been determined by primaries as they are today, Hoover would have been rejected by his own party. But primary elections were few in 1932; in most states, professional politicos still made the decisions, and they could not abandon an incumbent president even though they knew that Hoover and the party were doomed in November.

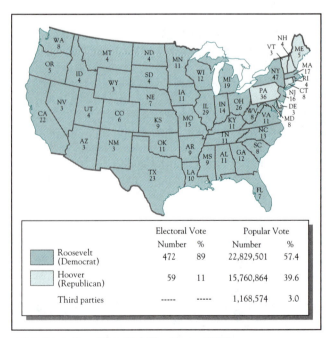

		Electoral Vote		Popular Vote	
		Number	%	Number	%
	Roosevelt (Democrat)	472	89	22,829,501	57.4
	Hoover (Republican)	59	11	15,760,864	39.6
	Third parties	-----	-----	1,168,574	3.0

MAP 41:1 Presidential Election, 1932
Few electoral college maps looked like the map of Roosevelt's victory in 1932. Only in New England, and in Pennsylvania, where the old Republican machine still ran the show, did the Republicans carry any states.

From the Collections of the Library of Congress

Franklin D. Roosevelt said nothing in his campaign to lead voters to believe he would launch a massive reform program. In effect, he ran by contrasting his ebullient, confident personality to Hoover's glumness.

Democratic hopefuls, confident that their party's nomination was a ticket to the White House, had a catfight. The chief contenders were John Nance Garner of Texas, who had inherited the McAdoo Democrats of the South and West; Al Smith, the party's standard-bearer in 1928, who believed he deserved a second go; and Smith's successor as governor of New York, Franklin Delano Roosevelt.

When the beginnings of a convention deadlock brought back memories of the bitterly divided party of 1924, some Garner delegates switched to Roosevelt and gave him the nomination. FDR—newspapers already called him by his initials in headlines—then presented the nation with the first indication of his flair for the dramatic and his willingness to break with tradition. Rather than wait quietly at home to be officially notified of his nomination, Roosevelt rushed to a plane, flew to the Chicago convention through nasty weather, and personally told the cheering Democrats that he meant to provide a "**New Deal**" for the American people. Roosevelt simultaneously slapped at the discredited Republican "New Era" and reminded voters of both parties—the older ones, anyway—that he was a distant cousin of the energetic president of the Square Deal, Theodore Roosevelt.

THE CAMPAIGN

Hoover's campaign was dispirited; it could not have been otherwise. He was in the impossible position of having to defend policies that had failed. Roosevelt, like any candidate for public office who expects to win easily, avoided taking any stand apt to be controversial. When so many people are voting against a known quantity, any strong statement—any specifics—can only lose the challenger votes.

The one obvious difference between FDR and the president was their personalities: Roosevelt's buoyant charm, good humor, and self-confidence, which came naturally to him, versus Hoover's gloominess. The campaign was all image. Roosevelt smiled constantly. He conveyed to his audiences that he was a man who knew how to take charge. His theme song, blared by brass bands at every rally, was the upbeat "Happy Days Are Here Again." It was enough. FDR's victory was lopsided: 472 electoral votes to Hoover's 59.

In 1933 Inauguration Day was a full four months after the election. The interregnum—when the presidency was to change hands—was six weeks longer than it is today. In a time of crisis like 1933, four months was too long; it meant one more long winter of depression and Hoover's failure. Powerless and a bit hysterical about what Roosevelt might do, Hoover grasped a straw; he asked Roosevelt, in the interests of dampening anxieties, to endorse several of his policies.

Roosevelt did not bite. He avoided making any commitments either in support of Hoover or criticizing him. He disappeared from the public eye on what was, in fact, a hardworking vacation. Roosevelt met for long hours several days a week with experts on agriculture, industry, banking, and relief. His "brains trust," as reporters called it (people decided they preferred "brain trust") was organized by Raymond Moley, a professor at Columbia University. Most of the men invited to FDR's estate at Hyde Park to present their ideas were professors at Ivy League universities. Whatever Roosevelt had in mind—and he relished the suspense he was creating—there was going to be an entirely new crowd in Washington. The businessmen who had set the capital's tone under Coolidge and Hoover turned over their D.C. apartments and sold their suburban homes in Virginia and Maryland to intellectuals, men (and—this was quite new—a few women) from universities and state social agencies.

FURTHER READING

General Michael Bernstein, *The Great Depression: Delayed Recovery and Economic Change in America, 1929–1939,* 1987; David M. Kennedy, *Freedom from Fear: The American People in Depression and War,* 1990; Charles Kindleberger, *The World in Depression,* 1973; Robert McElvaine, *The Great Depression,* 1984, and *Down and Out in the Great Depression,* 1983 (a collection of letters describing personal experiences); James McGovern, *And a Time for Hope: Americans in the Great Depression,* 2000.

Hoover George H. Nash, *The Life of Herbert Hoover,* 1988; Arthur M. Schlesinger Jr., *The Crisis of the Old Order,* 1957; Joan Hoff Wilson, *Herbert Hoover: Forgotten Progressive,* 1975.

Other Topics Roger Daniels, *The Bonus March,* 1971; James N. Gregory, *American Exodus: The Dust Bowl Migration and Okie* *Culture in California,* 1989; Bruce Schumann, *From Cotton Belt to Sunbelt,* 1990; Robert Sklar, *Movie-Made America,* 1975; Raymond Walters, *Negroes and the Great Depression.*

KEY TERMS

The following terms are covered in this chapter and can also be found in the list of Key Terms at the back of the book.

Bonus Boys	**Dust Bowl**	**John Dillinger**	**Okies**
Boulder Dam	**Hoovervilles**	**New Deal**	**Will Rogers**

 ## ONLINE SOURCES GUIDE

Use this listing to find online documents, images, interactive maps, simulations, and other resources related to this chapter:

American History Resource Center
http://history.wadsworth.com/rc/us

Selected Documents
Franklin D. Roosevelt's first inaugural address (1933)
Roosevelt's first fireside chat (March 12, 1933)

Selected Images
A soup kitchen, 1931
Republican cartoon showing Hoover trying to solve the country's problems
Bonus Army camp, 1932
Caricature of Herbert Hoover, 1932

Interactive Time Line (with online readings)
National Trauma: The Great Depression, 1930–1933

CHAPTER 42

Rearranging America

FDR and the New Deal 1933–1938

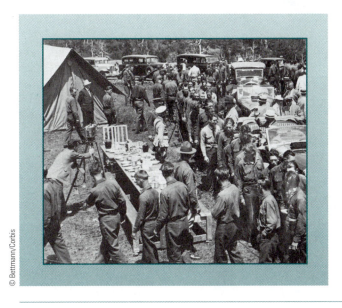

This generation of Americans has a rendezvous with destiny.
Franklin D. Roosevelt

A few days before his inauguration in 1933, Franklin D. Roosevelt visited Miami. From the crowd surging around him, a jobless worker named Joe Zangara, later found to be mentally unbalanced, emptied a revolver at Roosevelt's party, which included Anton Cermak, the mayor of Chicago. Cermak died from his wounds. The president-elect escaped without a scratch.

Americans learned from the episode that they had a leader who was cool in a crisis. Roosevelt barely flinched during the chaos. Just what the president-elect intended to do about the Great Depression, however, few people knew. In fact, Roosevelt had no "plan." He was not a man of ideology or blueprints. He was the quintessential pragmatist, the legendary American mechanic who said, "Well, let's start it up and see why it doesn't run. And then fix it."

THE PLEASANT MAN WHO CHANGED AMERICA

Henry Cabot Lodge had called Roosevelt "a well-meaning, nice young fellow, but light." Edith Galt Wilson said that he was "more charming than able." In 1932 Walter Lippmann,

dean of political columnists, called Roosevelt "a pleasant man who, without any important qualifications, would very much like to be president." Many people wondered if someone who had enjoyed the pampered and sheltered life Roosevelt had enjoyed was capable of appreciating the hardship that had befallen millions of Americans.

SILVER SPOON

The new president was born into an old and rich New York family that had slipped just a bit in recent generations. Still, FDR's boyhood vacations were spent in Europe and at yachting resorts in Maine and Nova Scotia. He attended the most exclusive private schools and was adored and sheltered to the point of suffocation by his mother. When Roosevelt went to Harvard, Sara Roosevelt packed up and rented a house near the university so she could keep an eye on her boy. FDR's wife, Eleanor Roosevelt, was from the same tiny, exclusive social set. She was the president's distant cousin; they shared the same last name. Even the immense charm with which Roosevelt ran his campaign—a jaunty air, toothy smile, and cheery small talk that came easily—was the charm of a socialite.

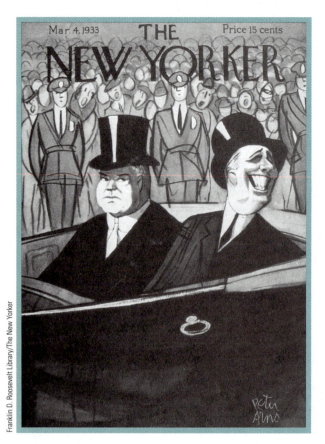

Mar. 4, 1933 **THE NEW YORKER** Price 15 cents

Franklin D. Roosevelt Library/The New Yorker

peter Arno

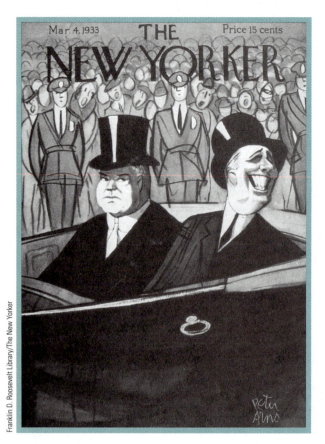

> Illustrator Peter Arno had to prepare this magazine cover weeks before Roosevelt's inauguration in 1933. Uncannily, he got the scene just right, FDR exuding cheerful confidence, Hoover immersed in gloom.

Mother, May I Have My Allowance?
Unless holding public office counts, FDR was never gainfully employed. He paid his bills from an allowance given him in cash in a plain envelope each month by his mother, Sara Roosevelt, until she died in 1941. FDR was almost 60 and president of the United States for two full terms before he supported himself—on his inheritance.

the sun through—it was obvious that he was a natural leader. From his first day as president, Roosevelt dominated center stage as his cousin Theodore had done thirty years earlier, and without TR's bluster. He held eighty-three press conferences in 1933, ninety-six in 1940. (Recent presidents have had four or five a year.) Roosevelt had no fear of reporters; he used them. They did not catch him in dubious dealings.

Whereas Teddy had been liked and hated, Franklin Roosevelt was loved and hated. Poor white and black sharecroppers and African Americans living in big cities tacked his photograph to the wall next to cheap prints of Christ in Gethsemane, and they named their children for him.

Few other presidents, however, have been so passionately hated. It was said that some of the nation's wealthiest people could not bear to pronounce his name; they referred to him through clenched teeth as "that man in the White House" and as a "traitor to his class."

ROOSEVELT'S CONTRIBUTION
Roosevelt's self-confidence reflected a less attractive facet of his personality. He was the center of the universe in which he lived. "He was the coldest man I ever met," said his successor as president, Harry S Truman. "He didn't give a damn personally for me or you or anyone else in the world." But FDR's public persona was bubbling, buoyant, and ingratiating, and that in itself was a contribution to the battle against the

For all Mother Roosevelt's efforts, however, she had not created the "aristosissy" novelist Gore Vidal called FDR. From the moment he delivered his ringing inaugural address—the clouds over Washington parting on cue to let

The New Deal 1933–1945

1933	1935	1937	1939	1941	1943	1945

1933–1945 Franklin D. Roosevelt president

Mar–June 1933 The Hundred Days
Bank holiday
CCC
AAA
TVA
NRA
Nov 1933 CWA

Apr 1935 WPA
May 1935 REA
NRA unconstitutional
July 1935 Wagner Act
Aug 1935 Social Security
Sept 1935 Huey Long murdered

1936 FDR landslide reelection

1937 Supreme Court fight; CIO breaks with AFL

Blueblood

Roosevelt's bloodline was as aristocratic as they came in the United States. The first Roosevelts were Dutch, not patroons, but the proprietors of a lot of prime Hudson Valley land and, later, successful merchants. Generation after generation, they rarely married outside their social class. FDR was descended from or related by marriage to eleven previous presidents. (Only one of them, Martin Van Buren, was a Democrat.)

Franklin and Eleanor were utterly indifferent to the trappings of wealth. Having plenty of money and the entitlements it provided were as natural a part of life as eggs for breakfast. One rang a bell if one wanted a car; what else did people do when they were going out? FDR's personal staff during the Depression was smaller than that of Hillary Clinton when she was First Lady, no official position at all, sixty years later. Even during World War II, his staff was smaller than that of Albert Gore, vice president during the 1990s.

So oblivious to personal comforts were the Roosevelts that the White House deteriorated during their occupancy so that, in one visitor's words, it resembled a "dingy residential hotel." In fact, by 1945, the building was in danger of collapsing. FDR's successor, Harry Truman, had to move out of the White House so structural repairs could be made.

Depression. His optimism was infectious. The mood in Washington changed overnight in March 1933. Roosevelt shrewdly exploited his charisma by launching a series of "Fireside Chats" on the radio. Informally, as if he were seated in each of the nation's living rooms, he explained what he was trying to accomplish and what he expected of his hosts.

Roosevelt was more than a charmer. He was not afraid to make decisions. And although he preferred to blame his enemies when things went wrong or have his aides take the blame for them—he was, after all, a professional politician—when there was no other way, he accepted responsibility for his mistakes.

He was decisive. A day after he was sworn in, he called Congress into special session to enact crisis legislation, and he declared a bank holiday. Calling on emergency presidential powers, he ordered all banks to close their doors temporarily to forestall additional failures. Although the bank holiday tied up people's savings, the drama of his action won wide approval.

In 1933 Justice Oliver Wendell Holmes Jr. said privately that the president had "a second-class intellect." It was true enough that Roosevelt was no intellectual. He never fully understood the complex economic and social processes with which his administration had to grapple. However, and rightly, he did not think it necessary that he should. He had professors at his command, the "brains trust," and he was open to suggestions from all quarters.

But no one ever cowed him. No one in his administration was so foolish as to try. He was the boss of his stable of headstrong, bickering intellectuals. He stroked their vanities when it suited his purposes, played one brains truster

against another as only a supreme egotist would, and yet (at first) he retained the loyalty of all, including those whose advice he ignored. Roosevelt never lacked talented advisers because he did not fear talent.

In the end, Roosevelt's greatest strength was his flexibility. "The country needs bold, persistent experimentation," he said. "It is common sense to take a method and try it. If it fails, admit it frankly and try another." Roosevelt's pragmatism suited the American temperament far better than Hoover's religious attachment to a tattered ideology.

AN ACTIVE FIRST LADY

One of FDR's greatest political assets was his remarkable wife, Eleanor. No First Lady before her had an active public life of her own. Decades later, in the age of anything-goes journalism, it was revealed that her marriage to FDR had been shattered when she learned that her husband was having an affair with her own social secretary, Lucy Mercer. Eleanor offered Franklin a divorce. He begged off: a divorced man had no political future. Eleanor agreed on the condition that Lucy had to go, and she did, or so Eleanor believed.

Eleanor's upbringing was as privileged as FDR's, but unlike his, it was emotionally painful. She was unattractive and awkward with an unpleasantly shrill voice; and she was painfully aware that she was an ugly duckling merely tolerated by her aristocratic social set. It caused something of a sensation among the New York gentility when she and handsome, outgoing Franklin were married in 1905. FDR's mother tried so hard to quash the match that she and Eleanor were never more than civil with one another.

Perhaps in part because her personal life had been scarred in childhood, Eleanor (who had five children in 1933) threw herself into the social and political causes that, in the twentieth century, were acceptable avocations for well-to-do women. Her political interests were a godsend to Franklin when, in 1921, a year after running for the vice presidency, he was paralyzed from the waist down by polio. He never walked again, except for a few steps for the sake of appearances in heavy, painful leg braces, with an aide or one of his sons at his side poised to save him from falling.

Eleanor urged Franklin not to give up his political ambitions, and she became his legs. She was a locomotive, tirelessly traveling, schmoozing with politicians, and filling in for her husband at less important political functions. She kept her political campaigning low-key when FDR ran for governor of New York in 1928 and for president in 1932. Not everyone was as tolerant of activist women as upper-class New Yorkers. Indeed, FDR's political enemies were as vile in

Pragmatist

In a conversation with Secretary of Commerce Daniel Roper, Roosevelt made his pragmatism explicit: "Let's concentrate upon one thing. Save the people and the nation, and if we have to change our minds twice a day to accomplish that end, we should do it."

AP/Wide World Photos

Eleanor Roosevelt was probably in her thirties before she thought of poor or struggling people as other than servants or charity cases. As First Lady, remarkably, she sat down, unaffected, as an equal with grimy coal miners, illiterate African-American sharecroppers, and—here—a destitute woman collecting a basket of free food for her family. Mrs. Roosevelt's compassion was profound but never took the form of condescending pity.

attacking her as they were in their personal assaults on the president.

THE LIBERAL ROOSEVELT

Eleanor provided FDR with more than a mobile alter ego. Where the president was indeed detached, even cold as Harry Truman observed, Eleanor was compassionate, genuinely moved by the misery and injustices suffered by the "forgotten" people on the bottom of society. She interceded with her husband—nagged him—to appoint women to high government positions. She supported organized labor when FDR tried to straddle the sensitive issue of unions. She made the grievances of African Americans a particular interest, persuading FDR to name blacks like educator **Mary McLeod Bethune** to government posts. Much of the devotion of African Americans that redounded to FDR in the form of votes was earned not by him—FDR was much more concerned with placating white racist southern Democrats—but by "that woman in the White House." In 1932, 70 percent of black voters voted against Roosevelt; in 1936, 75 percent voted

for him. This revolutionary change in voting behavior owed to a number of things, but one of them was Mrs. Roosevelt.

THE HUNDRED DAYS

Never before or since has the United States experienced such an avalanche of legislation as Congress enacted in the spring of 1933. By nature deliberate, Congress had been jolted by the economic crisis and Roosevelt's landslide election victory—which included big Democratic majorities in both Senate and House. Roosevelt's legislative demands, new ones delivered to the Capitol almost daily, were enacted without serious debate. Some bills were passed without being read. During what became known as **The Hundred Days,** FDR might as well have been a dictator and Congress a rubber stamp Reichstag. Conservative congressmen simply shut up, cowed by their own failure and the decisiveness of the New Deal Democrats.

SAVING BANKS AND FARMS

The most pressing problems were the imminent collapse of the nation's financial system, foreclosures on farm and home mortgages, and the distress of the millions of unemployed workers.

Passed during the bank holiday, the Emergency Banking Act eliminated weak banks merely by identifying them. Well-managed banks in danger of folding were saved when the Federal Reserve System issued loans to them. When the government permitted banks to reopen, people concluded that they were safe. They ceased to withdraw their deposits and returned money that they had hidden in the cellar. Roosevelt halted the drain on the nation's gold reserve by forbidding the export of gold and, in April 1933, by taking the nation off the gold standard. No longer could paper money be redeemed in gold coin. Instead, the value of money was based on the government's word, and the price of gold was frozen by law at $35 an ounce. ("Well, that's the end of Western civilization," a particularly idiotic Wall Street financier said.)

Keynes

New Deal economics is often described as "Keynesian" after the British economist John Maynard Keynes. When Keynes and FDR met, however, Roosevelt could not comprehend what Keynes was saying, and Keynes later called the president an economic illiterate.

The New Deal did, nevertheless, reflect some of Keynes's principles. For example, Keynes argued that consumption, not investment, was the key to prosperity in a modern economy. Therefore, in times of depression, massive deficit spending by the government (spending borrowed money) should be designed to stimulate consumption. Private investment would go to where the profits were. Although far from consistently (and perhaps inadequately understood by the president), this is what the New Deal did.

The New Deal attempted to halt the dispossession of farmers by establishing the Farm Credit Administration. The FCA refinanced mortgages for farmers who had missed payments. Another agency, the Home Owners' Loan Corporation, provided money for town and city dwellers who were in danger of losing their homes.

HELP FOR THE HELPLESS

Nothing better illustrated the contrast between Hoover's paralysis and Roosevelt's flexibility than the establishment of the Federal Emergency Relief Administration. Whereas Hoover had resisted federal relief measures on ideological grounds, the FERA quickly distributed $500 million to states so they could save or revive their exhausted programs for helping the desperately poor. The agency was headed by Harry Hopkins, an Iowan turned New York social worker with a cigarette dangling from his lip and a fedora pushed back on his head.

Hopkins disliked handouts as much as Hoover did. He believed that people who were capable of working should be required to work in return for government assistance. It did not matter to him that their jobs were not particularly useful. His point was that government-funded jobs should not only get money into the hands of those who needed it to get by; the jobs should also give relief workers a sense of personal worth.

Nevertheless, Hopkins soon recognized that the crisis had become so severe that money had to be distributed around the country more quickly than jobs could be invented. Shelving his belief in work for pay, he and FERA put up with extensive boondoggling and bureaucratic waste. FDR was pleased. He worried less about economic and moral principles than he did about politics. FERA created hope where there had been despair and increased the popularity of the president and the New Deal. Hopkins was so efficient Roosevelt soon made him one of his closest advisers. In time, he would choose the former social worker to represent him in secret discussions with world leaders.

ALPHABET SOUP: THE CCC

New federal bureaucracies (and speaking in initials) were the order of the day. With an initial appropriation of $500 million, the **Civilian Conservation Corps (CCC)** employed 274,375 young men between the ages of 17 and 25 in 1,300 camps. In 1935 CCC workers numbered 502,000 in 2,514 camps. Eventually some 2.9 million people served in the corps, about 10 percent of them African American.

© Bettmann/Corbis

No one but dyed-in-the-wool New Deal haters had a bad word for the Civilian Conservation Corps. The CCC provided decently paid jobs for young men who, without them, could have idled on street corners or worse; and the jobs were "in the woods"—in the fresh air in national parks and forests—a treat in itself for city boys. CCC workers were required to send most of their paychecks to their families: their wives or more often (these were young men's jobs) their parents. Although some but not all CCC crews were segregated by race, blacks, Mexican Americans, and Indians were actively recruited and paid the same as white workers.

Signed on for six-month terms and organized into crews, they reforested land that had been raped by cut-and-run lumbermen and undertook other conservation projects in national parks and forests. The CCC built 46,854 bridges, 318,076 check dams, 3,116 fire lookouts, 87,500 miles of fence, and 33,087 miles of terracing to resist erosion. Workers were paid $30 a month, of which they were required to send $22–25 home to their families. The CCC provided bed and board; the idea was that their paychecks would provide relief for the workers' families and a tonic for the consumer economy, not go into workers' savings accounts.

The CCC was one of the New Deal's most popular programs both because of its achievements—visitors to national forests and parks today still hike on CCC-built trails—and because it got city boys into the fresh air of the woods and mountains.

ALPHABET SOUP: CWA AND WPA

Critics of the CCC sniped at its quasimilitary discipline (the army ran the program), but the idea of relief through jobs rather than charity remained a mainstay of the New Deal. The Civil Works Administration (CWA), which Harry Hopkins headed after November 1933, put 4 million unemployed people to work within a few months. The CWA built roads, constructed public buildings—many post offices, city halls, and recreational facilities still in use today—and taught in bankrupt school systems.

When the CWA spent more than $1 billion in five months, FDR shuddered and called a halt to the program. But private investors would not or could not take up the slack, and unemployment threatened to rise once again. In May 1935 the president turned back to Congress to establish the **Works Progress Administration (WPA)** and asked Harry Hopkins to run it.

The WPA broadened the CWA's program. In addition to basic construction and repair, the agency hired artists to paint murals in public buildings and organized actors into troupes that brought theater to people who never had seen a play. Photographers created a treasury of Americana, taking 77,000 pictures. The Writers' Program, with John Cheever as editor and other soon-to-be-distinguished contributors such as Saul Bellow, Ralph Ellison, and Richard Wright, as well as hundreds of writers of no fame who nevertheless liked to eat, wrote guidebooks to each of the forty-eight states, several of which are still seen as models of the genre (if no longer of much use to travelers). In the South, the WPA sent out workers to collect the reminiscences of old folks who remembered having been slaves. There were not many still alive, but ten years down the line there would have been none. The *Slave Narratives* were and are a precious treasure. By 1943, when the WPA was liquidated, it had spent more than $11 billion and employed 8.5 million people. The National Youth Administration, part of the WPA, provided jobs for 2 million high school and college students.

REPEAL

The Twenty-First Amendment, the repeal of Prohibition, might be listed as one of the New Deal's relief measures. On March 13, 1933, FDR called for the legalization of weak beer, and when the amendment was ratified in December, most states legalized more potent beverages.

Certainly many people looked on the privilege of buying drink legally as relief. An Appalachian song praising Roosevelt pointed to repeal of Prohibition as his most important act: "Since Roosevelt's been elected, moonshine liquor's been corrected. We've got legal wine, whiskey, beer, and gin." Breweries and distilleries were up and running as if they had been closed for no more than a week. Winemakers, most of whom had torn out their vines and planted orchards, needed several years to recover.

THE NRA

The New Deal's relief programs were successful. Direct benefits reached only a fraction of the country's hardship cases, but they were usually the worst off. Moreover, the government's mere willingness to act was a morale booster.

To the New Dealers, however, relief was just a stopgap. Fermenting with ideas, dozens of men (only two women, Eleanor Roosevelt and Secretary of Labor Frances Perkins, had access to FDR) wanted to put the government to work stimulating economic recovery. In this, they were less effective.

The National Recovery Administration (NRA) was a bold and controversial attempt to bring order and prosperity to the shattered economy. It was headed by General Hugh Johnson, something of a blowhard but also an inexhaustible organizer and cheerleader. A one-time Bull Moose Progressive, he believed zealously that the economy should be ordered.

Johnson supervised the preparation of codes for each basic industry and, before long, some less-than-basic industries, too. NRA codes set minimum standards of quality for products and services, fair prices at which they were to be sold, and the wages, hours, and conditions under which employees worked. **Section 7(a)** of the act creating the NRA was pathbreaking in the area of labor relations: it required a company that agreed to the codes that benefited it in numerous ways to bargain collectively with its workers through labor unions selected by a majority of the company's employees.

The NRA was designed to eliminate waste, inefficiency, and, most of all, destructive competition—the goal of industrial consolidators since John D. Rockefeller. In making the federal government the referee among competing companies and between employers and employees, the NRA was the legatee of Theodore Roosevelt's New Nationalism and the

© Bettmann/Corbis

For a year, popular enthusiasm for the NRA seemed to border on hysteria. NRA "happenings" like this one—the "bathing beauties" (a phrase of the era) are being stenciled with the NRA's Blue Eagle, the idea being that when they tanned in the sun, they would have a pale eagle to show off—were obviously staged. NRA head Hugh Johnson was a promoter without equal. But there was genuine popular enthusiasm too: the NRA seemed like a panacea that would put an end to "Old Man Depression."

mobilization of the economy during the First World War, including a younger Herbert Hoover's work as Food Administrator. The difference was that the NRA codes were compulsory and intended to be permanent. A business was bound to its industry's code not by the moral suasion in which Hoover placed so much faith but by the force of law. Noncompliance meant prosecution.

BLUE EAGLE MANIA

Critics of the NRA, including some within the New Deal, likened it to the Fascist system that had been set up in Italy by Benito Mussolini after 1922, and even to the Nazi economy in Germany that Hitler was setting up in 1933. The criticism was not unfounded, but it was unfair. Mussolini and Hitler suppressed free labor unions; the NRA gave them a role in making industrial policy.

More to the point was the criticism that **Blue Eagle** functionaries (the NRA's symbol was a stylized blue eagle) sometimes went ridiculously far in their codes. Hugh Johnson was code-crazy; he wanted to regiment peripheral and even trivial businesses. There was a code for the burlesque "industry" that specified how many strippers were to undress per performance, what vestments they were to discard, and the quality of tassels and G-strings. Had prostitution been legal in the United States, Johnson would have risen to even greater heights.

Such extremes were made possible by the enthusiasm, almost a frenzy, with which Americans at first took to the NRA. Rooted on by the bombastic Johnson, 200,000 people marched in an NRA parade in New York carrying banners emblazoned with the NRA motto, "We Do Our Part." The Blue Eagle was painted on factory walls, pasted on shop windows, and adopted as a motif by university marching bands.

Briefly, Hugh Johnson seemed as popular as Roosevelt himself. He was certainly more conspicuous. Johnson stormed noisily about the country, publicly castigating as "chiselers" any businessmen who did not meekly fall into line. Apparently he inherited his extraordinary style from his mother. At an NRA rally in Tulsa, she said that "people had better obey the NRA because my son will enforce it like lightning, and you can never tell when lightning will strike."

NEW DEAL—FAILURES AND SUCCESSES

The New Deal suffered a serious setback in the Supreme Court. The Court was quite conservative: seven of the nine justices had been appointed by the Republican presidents Taft, Harding, Coolidge, and Hoover. The **"nine old men,"** as FDR was to denounce them, had no sympathy for the

New Deal's fundamental reforms of the relationship between government and the economy. They declared a law regulating railroad finances and the NRA unconstitutional in 1935 and the Agricultural Adjustment Act—the foundation of FDR's farm policy—invalid in 1936.

DEATH OF THE BLUE EAGLE

The NRA was killed by a suit brought by a small company that slaughtered chickens for the kosher kitchens of observant Jews. The Schechter brothers, owners of the company, argued that the sanitary standards mandated by the NRA were incompatible with the ritual requirements of kosher slaughter and that the code represented unjustifiable federal interference in intrastate commerce. (Their business was almost entirely within New York State.) In 1935 the Supreme Court ruled unanimously that the Schechters were right: the NRA was unconstitutional.

There was little fuss. Popular enthusiasm for the NRA had cooled. Although he did not say so publicly, FDR was glad to see the Blue Eagle and Hugh Johnson go. Many NRA codes were so nit-picking as to be ridiculous, even impediments to recovery. And Congress moved promptly after the Court's decision to salvage the one provision of the codes that still had widespread support, Section 7(a). In the Wagner Labor Relations Act of 1935, the New Dealers reinstated the requirement that employers recognize and negotiate with labor unions that had the support of a majority of the companies' employees. In fact, the Wagner Act went further by setting up the National Labor Relations Board to investigate unfair labor practices and to issue cease and desist orders to employers found guilty of them.

FARM POLICY

Another salvage operation preserved parts of the Agricultural Adjustment Act. Enacted during the Hundred Days, the Agricultural Adjustment Act established the Agricultural Adjustment Administration (AAA) to enforce the principle of parity, for which farmers' organizations had agitated throughout the 1920s.

Parity meant increasing farm income from the depths it had plumbed to the ratio that farm income had borne to the prices of nonfarm products during the prosperous years of 1909 to 1914. The AAA accomplished this by restricting farm

> ### The Regulated Society
> Regulatory agencies act as watchdogs over specific aspects of American life. For example, the Interstate Commerce Commission (ICC) regulates the movement of goods and people across state lines, assigning rights over certain routes to trucking companies, setting rates, settling disputes, and so on. The Federal Communications Commission (FCC) keeps an eye on radio and television broadcasters. Today fifty-five major regulatory commissions in the U.S. government turn out 77,000 pages of decisions and rules each year.

production. Growers of wheat, corn, cotton, tobacco, rice, and hogs were paid government subsidies to keep some of their land out of production. The costs of this expensive program ($100 million was paid to cotton farmers in one year) were paid by a tax on processors—millers, refiners, butchers, and packagers—which was, of course, passed on to consumers in higher food, clothing, and tobacco prices.

Because the 1933 crop was already in the ground when the AAA was enacted, it was necessary to destroy some of it. "Kill every third pig and plow every third row under," ordered Secretary of Agriculture Henry A. Wallace. Some people were repelled by the slaughter of 6 million hogs and 220,000 pregnant sows. Others wondered why food was being destroyed when millions were hungry. (Actually, 100 million pounds of the prematurely harvested pork was diverted to relief agencies, and inedible waste was used as fertilizer.) Economically, however, the AAA worked; the income of hog farmers began to rise immediately.

Fully a quarter of the 1933 cotton crop was plowed under, and the fields were left fallow. Unfortunately, because cotton farmers tended the fields still under cultivation more intensely, production actually rose in 1933. It took two years for cotton (and wheat and corn) prices to rise by 50 percent.

A less desirable consequence of the AAA was to throw people off the land. Landlords dispossessed tenant farmers to collect the subsidies fallow land would earn without the headaches of actual farming. Between 1932 and 1935, 3 million American farmers lost their livelihood. Most of them were dirt-poor black and white tenants in the South.

ELECTRICITY

New Dealers were devoted to the AAA. Its rejection by the Supreme Court was a far more serious blow than the loss of the Blue Eagle. The Democrats in Congress salvaged what they could. In the Soil Conservation and Domestic Allotment Act (1936), parity and limitation of production were restored under the guise of conserving soil.

More worrying was the fear that, piece by piece, the Supreme Court would dismantle the entire New Deal. Roosevelt's supporters were particularly worried about the Tennessee Valley Authority (TVA), created in 1933, and the Rural Electrification Administration (REA) of 1935. Old Bull Moose Progressives, inspired by the New Nationalism of FDR's cousin, Theodore Roosevelt, twenty years earlier, had long dreamed—they could do little but dream during the conservative Republican 1920s—of these exercises in government planning that would bring benefits to impoverished people whom private enterprise ignored.

Cities and towns were electrified by 1933, but much of the countryside was not. Power companies that could reach tens of thousands of customers by stringing a mile of wire in urban areas could not afford the same fixed costs in rural areas where there might be a dozen houses (or none at all) on a mile of road. The REA lent the entire cost of electrifying the countryside to power companies (favoring publicly owned companies over private companies when there was a choice) at just 3 percent interest payable over twenty years. At such

Not Feeling Sorry for the Rich

How They Lived

Very rich Americans lost plenty of paper wealth in the stock market crash of 1929, but most remained rich. During the first years of the New Deal, "high society" was less conspicuous than it had been during the 1920s. By 1935, however, a new kind of social whirl had emerged.

Unlike the "flaming youth" of the 1920s, flaunting their sexuality and slumming at African-American jazz joints, the "café society" of the Depression years centered around posh former speakeasies that had come aboveground as restaurants and nightclubs. There one sat, chatted, and danced, seeing and being seen. In New York City, the capital of café society, the chic clubs were El Morocco, the Stork Club, and "21."

Ordinary Americans were intrigued by the "rich, young, and beautiful" café set. Whom Alfred Gwynne Vanderbilt was dating was breathlessly reported in nationally syndicated "society columns" by hangers-on like Walter Winchell and "Cholly Knickerbocker," welcome in café society because they were its publicists. It was news if the heiress of a widget fortune dropped in at El Morocco several times a week to dance the rhumba with her "agile husband." Naughtier items made reference to agile hubbies dancing the rhumba with willowy beauties not their wives.

Debutantes (or debs), young women who were "coming out" when in fact they had been lounging around nightclubs since they were 15 or 16, were the queens of café society. The leading deb of 1937 was Gloria "Mimi" Baker, whose mother replied to someone who called her a decadent aristocrat, "Why, Mimi is the most democratic person, bar none, I've ever known." In fact, café society was "democratic" in ways that previous high societies had not been. Because status was based partly on beauty, on what passed as wit, and simply on being well known, the café set admitted movie stars, athletes, and musicians of modest antecedents.

International "playboys" jumped at the opportunity to do more than be photographed at nightclubs they could not afford, and therein lay a great morality play of the 1930s. Barbara Hutton, who had to endure painful diets to keep her weight down to glamour level, was sole heiress to $45 million made in very small increments in the five-and-tens of F. W. Woolworth. In 1933 she married Alexis Mdivani, who claimed to be a dispossessed Russian prince. Almost immediately after the marriage, the debonair Mdivani began to make Barbara miserable, railing at her weight problem. Drawing on the $1 million that Barbara's father had given him as a wedding present, the prince spent much of his time with other women. In 1935 Barbara won Mdivani's consent to an unmessy divorce by paying him $2 million more.

Almost immediately she married a Danish count, Kurt von Haugwitz-Reventlow. Hutton showered the playboy with gifts, including a $4.5 million mansion in London. They were divorced in 1937. The same photographers who snapped pictures of laughing, dancing debutantes at the Stork Club rushed to get shots of tearful Barbara Hutton, the "poor little rich girl."

Some of the people who pored over the pathetic pictures pretended sympathy. "She's made mistakes," wrote columnist Adela Rogers St. Johns, "been a silly, wild, foolish girl, given in to temptations—but she's still our own . . . an American girl fighting alone across the sea." Others openly took pleasure in her self-inflicted misery. "Why do they hate me?" Barbara asked. "There are other girls as rich, richer, almost as rich."

---

rates, even twelve households paying electric bills along a mile of wire meant a profit.

The REA was a nationwide program. Farms in rural New England were no more likely to be electrified in 1933 than ranches in Wyoming. (When Calvin Coolidge was sworn in as president at his father's home in Plymouth Notch, Vermont, in 1923, it was by the light of a kerosene lantern.) The TVA was regional, limited to the shores of the Tennessee River that arises in Virginia, loops through Tennessee and northern Alabama, and flows into the Ohio River in Kentucky. But it involved far more than electric lights. It promised a systematic, comprehensive, far-reaching economic reconstruction of many of the poorest regions in America: electrification, jobs in a massive construction project, flood control (the Tennessee was a killer river), manufacturing where there was none, and social planning.

TVA

The TVA was the nearly lifelong darling not of a southerner but of a Nebraskan Republican senator (he became an Independent in 1936), George Norris. Norris fastened on southern Appalachia as a laboratory for an unprecedented experiment in economic and social development. The Tennessee River valley was so poor for much of its length that it would be impossible for the government to make things worse than they were.

The TVA would construct a series of dams both to control the annual floods and to generate electricity. Appalachia's "hillbillies," plagued by poor health and ignorance, would begin to enjoy the comforts of the twentieth century. The electricity would also power factories, especially for the manufacture of fertilizers, which would provide jobs for people who had lived literally hand to mouth. Although not much was made of this during the 1930s (people wanted jobs; they were not thinking about their vacations), the lakes behind the dams on the river would be recreational centers.

Norris also pointed out that by generating electricity itself, the government would be able to determine the fairness of the prices private companies elsewhere in the country charged their customers. Until the 1930s, the actual cost of generating electrical power was a mystery outside the industry.

During the 1920s, Henry Ford tried to buy key sites on the Tennessee River from the government, notably Muscle Shoals, a tumultuous rapids, to build a privately owned power plant. Norris fought Ford off in Congress, arguing that the Tennessee valley provided too good a testing ground for regional planning to give it to one of the country's richest men so he could get richer. Had the government giveaway of its oil reserves at Teapot Dome not been exposed as scandalous during the debate over the Tennessee valley, frightening Republican congressmen, Ford would likely have gotten Muscle Shoals. But although Norris and his allies kept Muscle Shoals in government hands, they were unable to implement government development of the region until Roosevelt's election.

"CREEPING SOCIALISM"

Fiscal conservatives were appalled by the astronomical expenditures of the New Deal. With a good-humored wit he should have exhibited when he was president, Herbert Hoover spoke of the decimal point in the government's debts "wandering around among the regimented ciphers trying to find some of the old places it used to know."

Conservatives—southern Democrats as well as Republicans—assailed the REA and the TVA as socialistic. Big business, which had been happy enough with FDR's banking reforms and the NRA, funded a political offensive against New Deal programs that put the government into the production and distribution of electrical power. As early as 1934, bankers and big businessmen founded the American Liberty League, accusing Roosevelt of trying to destroy free enterprise and set up a socialist dictatorship.

Most Liberty Leaguers were Coolidge–Mellon Republicans, but they were joined by some prominent Democrats, including two of the party's presidential nominees, John W. Davis and Alfred E. Smith. Davis was a corporation lawyer; he found Liberty League company familiar. Smith, however, who had tapped FDR to be his successor as governor of New York, had himself been friendly to bold reforms during the 1910s and 1920s. Bitter that his defeat in the presidential election of 1928 and Roosevelt's nomination in 1932 ended his political career before he was 60, he had fallen in with the bankers and businessmen he once denounced.

Countering the Liberty Leaguers was like swatting flies for Roosevelt. Ordinary Americans generally remained wary of big businessmen, even bitter toward them, throughout the 1930s. FDR labeled the Liberty Leaguers "economic royalists." They never had much of a following.

The Supreme Court was another matter; it seemed to be a major threat to the New Deal. Making one of his rare political miscalculations, Roosevelt proposed saving the New Deal by adding to the Court justices who would endorse his reforms. The reaction to the "court packing" plan was almost universally hostile. The New Deal remained popular, but Roosevelt's scheme smelled of tampering with the Constitution to win a political contest. Roosevelt quickly retreated. The crisis passed when the Court approved several New Deal reforms that had been thought vulnerable. Then time lent a hand: beginning in 1937, retirements and deaths enabled FDR to manufacture a pro–New Deal majority without changing the size of the Court. When Roosevelt died in 1945, eight of the nine justices were his appointees.

POPULIST SPELLBINDERS

FDR made his court-packing proposal in 1937. Perhaps he was overconfident because he won reelection so easily in 1936, carrying every state except Maine and Vermont.

Oddly enough, none of his political strategists, including the canny Postmaster General James A. Farley, anticipated a landslide until well along in the election year. They were worried that FDR might lose.

The problem was not the Republican party as such but a trio of charismatic critics of the president who came out of nowhere to build up large personal followings among the ordinary people on whose votes FDR counted. If the three joined forces—and the possibility was discussed—the third party they formed would not itself win the election, but it might hand the election to the Republicans.

FATHER COUGHLIN

Charles E. Coughlin, a Catholic priest in suburban Detroit, had broadcast a weekly religious radio program since 1926. With a mellow baritone voice and a hint of Scots in his accent (Father Coughlin was born and raised in Canada), he had a large Catholic audience even before the Depression turned his interests toward politics. He condemned Hoover and endorsed FDR in the 1932 election. The next year he told his listeners that "the New Deal is Christ's deal."

Within a year, however, Coughlin had soured on New Deal financial policy. Like many populists before and since, Father Coughlin believed that the manipulation of the money supply by sinister "international bankers" underlay the economic suffering of the common people and a good deal more that was wrong with the world. The argument has always been so technical that it can attract a mass following only because, implicitly or explicitly, it has drawn on a deeply rooted prejudice: anti-Semitism. "International bankers" meant the Rothschild family, which was code for "the Jews." By the end of 1934, inveighing against the Federal Reserve System, Coughlin had an estimated weekly audience of 10 million.

What worried Democratic party vote counter Jim Farley, himself a Catholic, was that most of Coughlin's devotees were big-city Catholics in the northeastern and midwestern industrial states with big blocs of electoral votes. The Democrats needed to win those states.

DR. TOWNSEND

Like Father Coughlin, Dr. Francis E. Townsend of California stumbled on a panacea—a cure-all—that attracted the interests of millions of people. Townsend had been a rather mild retired physician, a different type than the high-voltage Coughlin, and his following was drawn from entirely different social groups. The core of Townsend's support—1.5 million members of 7,000 Townsend Clubs by 1936—were elderly people, mostly Protestant and middle class.

The Townsend Plan, on which the doctor expounded tirelessly at rallies and on radio, was an old age pension plan that, Townsend argued, would quickly end the Depression and then sustain prosperity. Unlike Coughlin's convoluted vision of reality, the Townsend Plan was stunningly simple. The federal government would pay a monthly pension of $200—a great deal of money in the 1930s— to every person over 60 years of age, with two conditions attached.

First, the pensioners would be forbidden to hold jobs. Second, they were obligated to spend every cent of their $200 within the month they received it. Thus, Townsend said, his plan would not only provide security for the elderly, it would reinvigorate the economy, creating jobs for young men and women making the things and performing the services that the old folks were buying.

Economists shook their heads. The Townsend Plan was not financially plausible; it could not be funded, and it would not work if it could. When FDR ignored Townsend, the doctor retaliated. He condemned the president and began discussing the possibility of a third party with disciples of Father Coughlin and aides of a spellbinder who was already a political power among yet another group: poor and modestly fixed white southerners.

THE KINGFISH

Huey P. Long rose from among the poor white farmers of northern Louisiana to educate himself as a lawyer. He clawed his way up in state politics as a colorful, populistic sweating stump orator baiting the railroad and oil industry elites that ran the state. Unlike most southern demagogues—and most remarkably, for Long used plenty of cheap tricks in other areas—he avoided race-baiting. He never questioned segregation laws (to have done so in the South was political death), but he refused to fall back on "nigger baiting" to win votes. Indeed, Long won the votes of many Louisiana blacks (mostly in New Orleans) who had held onto the right to vote because, unlike most southern populists, he improved social services for African Americans too.

As governor of Louisiana between 1928 and 1932, Long built roads and hospitals and provided free textbooks and lunches for schoolchildren—benefits almost unknown elsewhere in the South and not universal elsewhere. Long was a clown; he called himself "the Kingfish" after a ridiculous

character on the popular radio program *Amos 'n' Andy*. Picking up a megaphone, he led cheers at Louisiana State University football games (and personally fired the football coach when LSU lost a game Long thought should have been won).

He was ruthless. He bribed and even strong-armed state legislators who threatened to vote against him. He was boorish, a drunk who ate off other people's plates at restaurants and summoned his aides at four o'clock in the morning. He was neurotic: he recoiled violently when people touched him without warning, and he spent most nights in hotels well guarded by the state police, changing his address often and suddenly. (It would be going too far to say he was paranoid: his enemies called openly for his assassination and organized a kind of SWAT team, complete with machine guns, and spoke of storming the state capitol.)

He was also very popular throughout the South and Midwest. He intended to run against FDR in 1936 on a platform called "Share the Wealth" or "Every Man a King." Long said he would confiscate, through taxation, every dollar in excess of $1 million of individual annual incomes. To people buying food on credit, it was an appealing program.

FDR had good reason to fear Long's presidential candidacy. He would likely carry at least half a dozen southern states that the Democrats assumed were in their column. If Townsend and Coughlin supported him, which they were likely to do, he would win over enough Democratic voters outside the South to give many votes to the Republicans.

CO-OPTATION AND A MURDER

Roosevelt's response to the spellbinders' political threat was to try to co-opt them. He undercut Coughlin's money monomania by making moderate monetary reforms. To steal Townsend's thunder, he sponsored the Social Security Act of 1935. The pensions it paid the elderly were peanuts compared to the $200 per month that dazzled the Townsendites. But the monthly **Social Security** checks that were in the mail before the election were real, whereas, when all but the most zealous Townsendites calmed down, the doctor's promises seemed as unlikely as the promise of winning a fortune with a lottery ticket. Thanks to FDR and the New Deal, for the first time the U.S. government assumed responsibility for helping people too old to work.

Well-Funded

In 1934 radical novelist Upton Sinclair won the Democratic party's nomination for governor of California by proposing a comprehensive social welfare program known as EPIC, "End Poverty in California." FDR was less than delighted by the emergence of another spellbinder in the party; he sat out the campaign. The Republicans spent $4 million in the successful effort to defeat Sinclair. In 1932 the Republicans had spent only $3 million nationally in the campaign to reelect President Hoover. Sinclair was defeated.

In 1935, to co-opt Huey Long's Share the Wealth program, Roosevelt and Congress revised the income tax law. The rates paid by the well-to-do were radically increased, up to a much-publicized 90 percent for those with the highest incomes. The 90 percent rate was largely a sham from the start: loopholes in the complex tax law meant that only a handful of people ever paid anything near that percentage, but it sounded as confiscatory as Long's proposal.

And yet it may have been an accident of history that ensured FDR's landslide victory in 1936. In September 1935 Huey Long was shot down in the Louisiana Capitol building by a young man not for political but for personal reasons. Long, with his arrogance, had ruined the career of a member of his family. (The assassin died immediately; half a dozen Long bodyguards emptied their revolvers into his body.)

The Republican candidate in 1936 was Governor **Alfred M. Landon** of Kansas. He was no Liberty Leaguer but a moderately progressive and likable midwesterner. His assignment, to defeat FDR, was impossible. Straining to come up with an issue on which to differ with the president, Landon unwisely settled on Social Security pensions, calling them "unjust, unworkable, and a cruel hoax." Social Security was popular. Support for the Townsend Plan had evaporated. Father Coughlin continued to have a following, although it declined. He became increasingly and more openly anti-Semitic, praising Adolf Hitler and the Nazis. When World War II began, his bishop (who had previously encouraged Coughlin) took him off the radio.

THE LEGACY OF THE NEW DEAL

Even before 1936, the character of the New Deal underwent a significant change. In 1933 FDR thought of the New Deal as a new deal for everyone. He believed, with some justification, that the Hundred Days legislation saved American capitalism. He felt betrayed when big business, instead of recognizing his services, vilified him.

In 1935, threatened by the populist rabble-rousers and encouraged by Eleanor, Roosevelt accepted his role as being the president of the people on the bottom. In his break with "the classes" and embrace of "the masses," FDR made the New Deal era a period of American history ranking in significance with the age of the War for Independence and the era of the Civil War.

BLACKS BECOME DEMOCRATS

If Roosevelt emphasized the problems of the disadvantaged after 1936, he deftly avoided taking up the unique disadvantages African Americans suffered because of the color line. This was a conscious political decision. FDR was a lifelong Democrat. In national elections the Democratic party depended on the "Solid South," the former slave states that, with rare exceptions, sent solidly Democratic delegations to Congress and delivered all their electoral votes to the Democratic party. Even with the Solid South, the Democratic party

African Americans in the northern states found there were no legal obstacles to exercising the right to vote (or violent reprisals). During the 1930s blacks not only converted from the Republican to the Democratic party, they voted in annually increasing numbers.

was the minority party between 1896 and 1932; during those forty-two years there was a Democratic president for only eight years.

The southern Democratic party was racist, unabashedly committed to white supremacy and Jim Crow segregation. Even though many southern congressmen abandoned the New Deal after 1936, Roosevelt concluded that he dare not criticize racial discrimination. He refused even to endorse a federal antilynching bill, and he accepted segregation by race in work gangs on federal building projects like the TVA and even outside the South. Roosevelt did, however, resist southern Democratic demands that African-American government employees be paid less than whites doing the same jobs.

He was pleasant enough with lobbyists from the NAACP (Roosevelt was always pleasant), and Eleanor Roosevelt saw to it that he listened to individual black leaders like Mary McLeod Bethune.

Nevertheless, New Deal programs benefited African Americans simply because a large majority of them were poor. Black people moved into more than a third of new housing units constructed by the federal government, and they shared proportionately in relief and public works projects. As a result, there was a revolution in African-American voting patterns. In 1932 about 75 percent of black voters were loyal Republicans. They still thought of the GOP as the party of Lincoln and emancipation and of Republican congressmen as the chief supporters of antilynching bills. The only African-American congressman in 1932 was a Republican, Oscar De Priest of Chicago.

By 1936 more than 75 percent of African-American voters were Democrats. Even De Priest was defeated by a black New Dealer—and the trend continued for forty years until blacks were more than 90 percent Democratic.

THE GROWTH OF THE UNIONS

In the first years of the New Deal, Roosevelt was wary of organized labor. Left to his personal predilections, he would have stayed neutral in labor disputes. However, when militant unionists like John L. Lewis of the coal miners (a lifelong Republican) and Sidney Hillman and David Dubinsky of the large needle-trades unions made it clear they would throw their influence behind the president only in return for administration support, Roosevelt gave in. Lewis raised $1 million for the president's 1936 election campaign, insisting that Roosevelt be photographed accepting the check from him. Within a month, the photograph was reproduced on thousands of posters with the message "The President Wants You to Join the Union."

FDR disliked Lewis—a lot of people did—but he gave Sidney Hillman unlimited access. He valued Hillman's advice and counted on him to keep organized labor friendly. FDR's stock answer to questions of policy in which the unions had an interest was "Clear it with Sidney."

Lewis, Dubinsky, and Hillman were leaders of the Committee on Industrial Organization, which, after the Wagner Act of 1935 guaranteed employees the right to be represented by unions, launched massive organizing campaigns in basic industries: coal, steel, rubber, electricity, automobiles. At first a faction within the American Federation of Labor, the CIO left the AFL in 1937, renaming itself the Congress of Industrial Organizations.

The CIO's organizational campaigns won members in astonishing numbers. The parent organization of the United Steel Workers was founded in 1936. By May 1937 it had 325,000 members. The United States Steel Corporation, the nerve center of antiunionism in the industry, recognized the union as bargaining agent without a strike.

The United Automobile Workers enlisted 370,000 members in a little more than a year. The story was similar among workers in rubber, glass, lumber, aluminum, electrical products, coal mining, needle trades, and even textiles. "The Union" came to have a mystical significance in the lives of many workers. Workers fought for the right to wear union buttons on the job. The union card became a certificate of honor. Old hymns were reworded to promote the cause. Professional singers like Woody Guthrie, Pete Seeger, and Burl Ives lent their talents to organizing campaigns. In 1933, fewer than 3 million American workers belonged to a union. In 1940, 8.5 million did; in 1941, 10.5 million.

LABOR WARS

Not every employer responded as sensibly to its unionized employees as United States Steel did. Tom Girdler of Republic Steel called the CIO "irresponsible, racketeering, violent, communistic" and threatened to crush the union with armed force. In this heated atmosphere occurred the "Memorial Day Massacre" of 1937, so called because Chicago police attacked a crowd of union members, killing ten and seriously injuring about a hundred.

Although there was no personal violence and little destruction of property, labor's "sit-down" strikes worried even pro-union politicians because they involved the seizure of

© Bettmann/UPI/Corbis

Sit-down strikers, workers who shut down factories but remained in them, "occupation forces," celebrate a victory. New Deal Democrats intervened to settle sit-down strikes in workers' favor but they were uncomfortable with the strikes because they were illegal appropriations of property.

The Indian New Deal

Roosevelt's commissioner of the Bureau of Indian Affairs was John Collier. A determined man who had worked with Pueblo Indians, Collier administered the "Indian New Deal," an upending of fifty years of American Indian policy as fundamental as Roosevelt's reforms.

Since the Dawes Act of 1884, American policy had been to "Americanize" Indians living on reservations—that is, to urge them to give up old ways of life and assimilate into American culture. Reservation lands were allotted to individuals as private property in the hope they would farm them; government Indian schools trained children to adopt white culture; pupils wore American clothing and were punished if they were heard speaking tribal languages. The campaign against Indian traditions actually intensified during the 1920s. The BIA outlawed traditional Indian religions and banned polygamy; some BIA agents forcibly cropped boys' hair.

John Collier reversed BIA policy. The Indian Reorganization Act of 1934, which Collier wrote, allowed tribal corporations to take over the Dawes Act allotments and vest ownership of the entire reservation in the tribe. Traditional religions and crafts were encouraged; management of Indian schools was turned over to the tribes.

Most tribes (181 of 258) agreed to reorganization; 77 did not. Among the latter were the Navajo, the largest tribe in the nation. More prosperous than most other Indians, the Navajo denounced Collier's policies as "back to the blanket" patronization, designed to keep Indians quaint and marginal.

The well-meaning Dawes Act helped few Indians. Most of the 130 million acres allotted to individuals in small parcels could not be farmed, and few western Indians knew how to farm. About 49 million acres had been sold to whites by 1934. The well-meaning **Indian Reorganization Act** also had deleterious consequences. Many tribal corporations were taken over by conniving elites who were, ironically, quite comfortable with the political and legal devices of mainstream America. They used their control of reservation lands to enrich themselves, securing the acquiescence of the "back to the blanket" traditionalists by turning education and cultural affairs over to them. Many traditionalist schools neglected even grade school basics in favor of indoctrinating Indian children in traditions their grandparents had abandoned half a century earlier; these were as alien to school-age Indians as farming had been to Indians given Dawes Act allotments.

It has been observed that when a wise and humane Indian policy would have promoted tribal authority and traditional culture—the late nineteenth century, when the old ways were still vital—the United States called on Indians to leave them behind; but when the old ways were dead and Indians needed programs to help them prosper in the larger society, American Indian policy sent them "back to the blanket."

---

property. The first took place in January 1937 during a strike by 150,000 General Motors employees. Most of the United Automobile Workers walked out as usual. At GM's plant in Flint, Michigan, however, they stayed in the factory; they "sat down." Family members and sympathizers brought food and clothing. The workers policed themselves. No doubt remembering what the attack on the Bonus Boys did to Herbert Hoover's reputation, FDR, through Michigan Governor Frank Murphy, mediated the dispute. After forty-four days the sit-down strikers emerged from the factory happy with the settlement.

Henry Ford eventually came to terms with the United Automobile Workers, but at first he vowed, like Girdler, to fight unionization with force. He employed a small army of toughs from the Detroit underworld and fortified his factories with tear gas, machine guns, and grenades. At the "Battle of the Overpass" in Detroit, Ford "goons" (as anti-union strong-arms were called) severely beat organizer Walter Reuther and other UAW officials. Violence, including numerous murders, was so common in the coalfields of Harlan County, Kentucky, that the area became known in the press as "Bloody Harlan."

THE BOTTOM LINE

The greatest achievement of the New Deal was to ease the economic hardships suffered by millions of Americans and, in doing so, to preserve their confidence in American institutions. In its relief measures, particularly the agencies that put jobless people to work, Roosevelt's administration was a resounding success.

As a formula for economic recovery, the New Deal failed. When unemployment dropped to 7.5 million early in 1937 and other economic indicators looked bright, Roosevelt began to dismantle many New Deal programs. The result was renewed collapse, a depression within a depression. Conditions in 1937 never sank to the levels of 1930–1933. But the recession of 1937 was painful evidence that for all their flexibility, experimentation, and spending, the New Dealers had not unlocked the secret of maintaining prosperity during peacetime. Only when preparations for another world war led to massive purchases of American goods from abroad (and to rearmament at home) did the Great Depression end. By 1939 the economy was on the upswing. By 1940, with Europe at war, the Great Depression was history.

Through such programs as support for agricultural prices, rural electrification, Social Security, insurance of bank deposits, protection of labor unions, and strict controls over the economy, the federal government came to play a part in people's daily lives that had been inconceivable before 1933. In the TVA, the government became a producer of electrical power and commodities such as fertilizers. It was not socialism, as conservative critics of the New Deal cried, but in an American context it was something of a revolution.

Although unavoidable, the most dubious side effect of the new system was the extraordinary growth in the size of government. Extensive government programs required huge bureaucracies to carry them out. The number of federal employees rose from 600,000 in 1930 to a million in 1940. In that bureaucracies are ultimately concerned with their own well-being and inevitably divert funds meant for their mission to pay benefits to bureaucrats (not to mention the aggravations of dealing with bureaucracies), the New Deal contributed to American life, along with its many blessings, a phenomenon that has at one time or another driven every American to near distraction.

A POLITICAL REVOLUTION

Between 1896 and 1933, the Republican party was the nation's majority party. The Great Depression and New Deal changed that. FDR and Jim Farley forged a new majority— an alliance of southern whites, northern and western liberals, blue-collar workers (particularly union members and urban white ethnics), and African Americans in the North, with substantial support from western farmers. The New Deal alliance was not without problems. Beginning in 1937, some southern Democrats, who disapproved of even the New Deal's minimal concessions to blacks and the prominence in Washington of "Yankee liberals," often voted with Republicans against New Deal measures.

Still, grassroots support for the New Deal among southern whites prevented the crack from becoming a split during FDR's presidency. The Democratic majority forged during the 1930s lasted for half a century. Between 1930 and 1980, a Republican lived in the White House for only eighteen years. During the same fifty years, Republicans had a majority in the Senate for only six years and in the House of Representatives for only four. Between 1930 and 1997, two-thirds of a century, the Republican party simultaneously controlled the presidency, Senate, and House for just two years: 1953 to 1955.

FURTHER READING

Aides and Opposition Alan Brinkley, *Voices of Protest: Huey Long, Father Coughlin and the Great Depression*, 1982; Steven Fraser, *Labor Will Rule: Sidney Hillman and the Rise of American Labor*, 1991; William Ivy Hair, *The Kingfish and His Realm: The Life and Times of Huey P. Long*, 1991; Abraham Holtzman, *The Townsend Movement*, 1963; Paul A. Kurzman, *Harry Hopkins and the New Deal*, 1974; William Leuchtenburg, *The Supreme Court Reborn: The Constitutional Revolution in the Age of Roosevelt*, 1995; Donald Lisio, *The President and Protest*, 1974; T. H. Watkins, *Righteous Pilgrim: The Life and Times of Harold L. Ickes*, 1990.

The New Deal Andrew Achenbaum, *Social Security: Visions and Revisions*, 1986; Anthony J. Badger, *The New Deal: The Depression Years 1933–1940*, 1989; Edward D. Berkowitz, *America's Welfare State: From Roosevelt to Reagan*, 1991; Alan Brinkley, *The End of Reform: New Deal Liberalism in Recession and War*, 1995; Steve Fraser and Gary Gerstle, *The Rise and Fall of the New Deal Order, 1930–1980*, 1989; Irwin E. Hargrove, *Prisoners of Myth: The Leadership of the Tennessee Valley Authority, 1933–1990*, 1994; David M. Kennedy, *Freedom from Fear: The American People in Peace and War,* 1999; Harvard Sitkoff, *A New Deal for Blacks*, 1978; T. H. Watkins, *The Great Depression in the 1930s*, 1993.

Politics and Labor Michael Denning, *The Cultural Front: The Laboring of American Culture in the Twentieth Century*, 1990; Paul Kleppner, *Who Voted?: The Dynamics of Electoral Turnout, 1870–1980*, 1982; Greg Mitchel, *The Campaign of the Century: Upton Sinclair's Race for Governor of California*, 1992; Nancy J. Weiss, *Farewell to the Party of Lincoln: Black Politics in the Age of FDR*, 1983; Robert H. Zieger, *American Workers, American Unions, 1920–1985*, 1986.

The Roosevelts Blanche Wiesen Cook, *Eleanor Roosevelt: A Life*, 1992; Kenneth S. Davis, *FDR*, 4 vols., 1972–1993; Frank Freidel, *Franklin D. Roosevelt: Rendezvous with Destiny*, 1990; Joseph P. Lash, *Eleanor and Franklin*, 1971; Lawrence W. Levine and Cornelia R. Levine, *The People and the President: America's Conversation with FDR*, 2002; Lois Scharf, *Eleanor Roosevelt: First Lady of American Liberalism*, 1987.

KEY TERMS

The following terms are covered in this chapter and can also be found in the list of Key Terms at the back of the book.

Alfred M. Landon	Indian Reorganization Act	Section 7(a)	Works Progress Administration (WPA)
Blue Eagle	Mary McLeod Bethune	Social Security	
Civilian Conservation Corps (CCC)	"nine old men"	The Hundred Days	

ONLINE SOURCES GUIDE

Use this listing to find online documents, images, interactive maps, simulations, and other resources related to this chapter:

American History Resource Center
http://history.wadsworth.com/rc/us

Selected Documents
Franklin D. Roosevelt's first inaugural address (1933)
Francis Perkins's "People at Work" (1934)
Excerpt from Supreme Court decision in Schechter Poultry Corp. *v.* United States *(1935)*
Luisa Moreno's "Caravans of Sorrow"

Selected Images
Depositors gathering outside a bank, April 1933
Franklin Delano Roosevelt

Eleanor Roosevelt, 1933
A&P grocery store advertisement, 1933
National Recovery Administration poster
President Roosevelt visits a Civilian Conservation Corps camp in 1933
Working a farm near Tupelo, MS, 1936
Dust storm, Elkhart, KS, 1937
Dorthea Lang photograph titled "Cover Wagon Again," 1935

Interactive Time Line (with online readings)
Rearranging America: FDR and the New Deal, 1933–1938

CHAPTER 43

The Second Great War

America and the World 1933–1942

Reproduced from the Collections of the Library of Congress

I ask that the Congress declare that since the unprovoked and dastardly attack by Japan on Sunday, December seventh, a state of war has existed between the United States and the Japanese Empire.

Franklin D. Roosevelt

In 1933, the same year Franklin D. Roosevelt became president, Adolf Hitler of the extreme right-wing National Socialist, or Nazi, party, was named chancellor in Germany. The character and values of the two new national leaders could hardly have been more different. The patrician Roosevelt was a liberal, dedicated to democracy. Hitler, lower middle class and with few social graces, was contemptuous of democracy and individual freedoms.

Both, however, were virtuosos in the use of modern mass communications. Roosevelt was at his best as a soothing voice on the radio. In "Fireside Chats," and later in special addresses, he reassured Americans that by reform they could preserve what was of value in their way of life. Hitler's métier was in person before rallies of tens of thousands of supporters and through loudspeakers the Nazis hung from buildings in the centers of large cities, exhorting Germans to blame the Versailles Treaty for their troubles and to hate those whom he defined as enemies within, particularly Communists and Jews.

Both men knew they must inevitably clash; but the United States was not high on Hitler's list of the countries he meant

to deal with, and FDR experimented with a foreign policy designed to avoid entanglement in another great war.

NEW DEAL FOREIGN POLICY

When he took office, Roosevelt seemed as uninterested in foreign policy as Woodrow Wilson had been. Like Wilson, he passed over professional diplomats in picking a secretary of state. He made a political appointment—a senator from Tennessee, Cordell Hull, whose courtly bearing belied his log cabin origins.

Hull and Roosevelt were generally content to follow the guidelines charted by Hoover and his distinguished secretary of state, Henry L. Stimson. Where they departed from precedent, their purpose was to further the New Deal's program for economic recovery at home.

THE GOOD NEIGHBOR

Roosevelt and Hull even embraced Hoover's phrase "good neighbor" to describe the changed role the United States meant to play in Latin America. No more would the United

States intervene militarily in the Caribbean and Central America, or even apply strong-arm financial pressure to protect the interests of American capitalists, as five previous presidents had done. Roosevelt withdrew U.S. marines from Nicaragua, the Dominican Republic, and Haiti. Like Hoover, he refused to intervene in Cuba despite the chronic civil conflict on the island and America's self-bestowed right in the Platt Amendment to send troops in times of trouble.

In 1934, when peace was restored to Cuba under a pro-American president who later made himself dictator, Fulgencio Batista, Hull formally renounced the Platt Amendment. No longer would the "Colossus of the North" use its might to have its way in the island country. Even in 1938, when Mexico seized the properties of American oil companies and offered little compensation, Roosevelt was conciliatory. A few years later American diplomats worked out a fair settlement with Mexico that was acceptable to all but the greediest oilmen.

The **Good Neighbor policy** paid dividends that Roosevelt could not have imagined in 1933: despite strenuous German efforts to secure a foothold in the Western Hemisphere, most Latin American nations resisted. The few South American countries that were cozy with Hitler were very cautious. During World War II every Latin American country except Argentina declared war on Germany. Only Brazil sent troops to Europe, but that was not the point. Had even one South American country, even distant Argentina, let Germany establish bases, it would have inhibited the American contribution to the war effort in Europe and in the Pacific.

THE STIMSON DOCTRINE

Roosevelt's Asian policy also followed paths staked out during the Hoover administration. The challenge in east Asia was to maintain Chinese independence and territorial integrity and access to the China trade—the Open Door Policy—in the face of an increasingly aggressive and expansion-minded Japan. The problem was complicated by the fact that China's Nationalist government, headed by Generalissimo Chiang Kai-shek, was ignored in much of the country, inefficient, and riddled with corruption.

Late in 1931, exploiting Chinese weakness, the Japanese army detached the province of Manchuria from China and set up a puppet state called Manchukuo. Hoover considered but rejected Stimson's proposal that the United States retaliate by imposing severe economic sanctions, denying Japan raw materials, particularly oil and iron, that were vital to Japanese industry and its navy. Instead, Hoover announced that the United States would not recognize the legality of any territorial changes resulting from the use of force. Curiously, this policy became known as the **Stimson Doctrine.**

The Stimson Doctrine was little more than a rap on the knuckles, no more substantial than the Kellogg–Briand pact. Japanese militarists, driven by a compelling and even fanatical sense of national destiny, shrugged it off. In 1932 they attacked Shanghai, the center of Chinese commerce. In 1937 the Japanese bombed the city; it was the first massive aerial bombing of a civilian population. Nevertheless, Roosevelt went no further than Hoover had in 1932. He (and the tottering League of Nations) responded with a scolding. With the Depression hanging on stubbornly at home, FDR had no intention of risking a conflict with Japan that American public opinion would not have tolerated and in which he had little interest.

RECOGNITION OF THE SOVIET UNION

When Roosevelt parted ways with Hoover's foreign policy, the impetus was his determination to defeat the Depression. Thus in May 1933 he scuttled an international conference in London that Hoover had endorsed for the purpose of stabilizing world currencies. Delegates of sixty-four nations had already gathered when Roosevelt announced that he would not agree to any decisions that ran contrary to his domestic

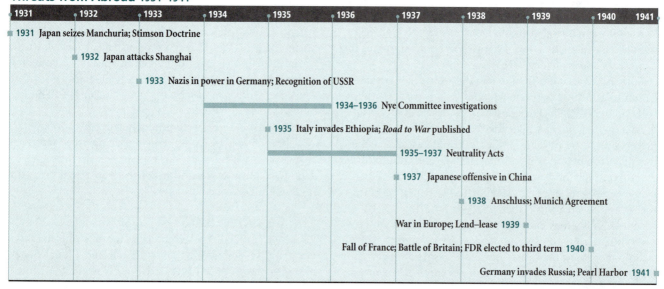

Threats from Abroad 1931–1941

1931	1932	1933	1934	1935	1936	1937	1938	1939	1940	1941

- 1931 Japan seizes Manchuria; Stimson Doctrine
- 1932 Japan attacks Shanghai
- 1933 Nazis in power in Germany; Recognition of USSR
- 1934–1936 Nye Committee investigations
- 1935 Italy invades Ethiopia; *Road to War* published
- 1935–1937 Neutrality Acts
- 1937 Japanese offensive in China
- 1938 Anschluss; Munich Agreement
- War in Europe; Lend–lease 1939
- Fall of France; Battle of Britain; FDR elected to third term 1940
- Germany invades Russia; Pearl Harbor 1941

recovery program. He meant to take the United States off the gold standard, which the conference hoped to restore internationally. The conference collapsed.

In November 1933 Roosevelt formally recognized the Communist regime in the Soviet Union, which four presidents had refused to do. In part he was facing reality. Only a few years earlier the permanence of Communist party rule had been uncertain; but by 1933 the dictatorship of Joseph Stalin was firmly in control of the country. Roosevelt had another reason for recognition (although it proved illusory). He was persuaded that the economically backward Soviet Union would be a large market for ailing American manufacturers.

INTERNATIONALISM

Increasing trade was also the motive behind Secretary of State Hull's strategy of reducing tariff barriers through reciprocity. With a southern Democrat's distaste for high tariffs, Hull negotiated reciprocal trade agreements with twenty-nine countries. The high Republican rates of the 1920s were slashed by as much as half on the goods of countries that agreed to reduce their duties on American products.

Better Public Relations through Chemistry

As the nation's biggest munitions manufacturer, E. I. Du Pont de Nemours and Company had a serious public relations problem during the 1930s. The Nye Committee investigations into American intervention in World War I often centered on the Du Ponts as "merchants of death." The coming of World War II and the nation's renewed need for munitions redeemed the Du Ponts. Even earlier, however, Du Pont's creation of nylon, the first completely synthetic textile and a miracle fabric in its versatility, helped created a benign image for the company.

Roosevelt would probably have liked to have played a more active role in world affairs. He admired his cousin Theodore's forcefulness, although by no means all the specifics of his foreign policy. More important, both he and Hull were Wilsonian internationalists. FDR had enthusiastically supported the League of Nations when Wilson was fighting his ill-destined battle to lead the United States into it. While FDR was recovering from polio and house-bound, he studied and wrote about foreign policy.

U.S. Army Photograph

Adolf Hitler entertains Spain's Francisco Franco. Massive German and Italian aid made Franco's victory in the vicious Spanish Civil War possible. When World War II began, Franco hoped for an Axis victory but remained neutral. His shrewdness and luck in doing so enabled him to remain in power after the war.

ISOLATIONISM

But FDR was a politician who counted votes. He was no crusader willing to destroy himself fighting for righteous causes. Never in his public statements did he wander far from the popular mood, and a public opinion poll taken in 1935 said that 95 percent of Americans were isolationists. They believed that the United States had no vital interests in either Europe or Asia, and they were dead-set against a repetition of what they regarded as the big mistake of intervening in the World War in 1917.

Isolationist sentiments intensified between 1934 and 1936 when Senator Gerald Nye of North Dakota began a series of investigations into the political machinations of the munitions industry. Nye claimed that the United States had been manipulated into war by "merchants of death" led by the giant Du Pont Corporation. They were only too willing to see young men of all nationalities slaughtered for the sake of sales. Big corporations generally were still in bad repute when a persuasive writer, Walter Millis, in 1935 published *The Road to War,* which popularized the "merchants of death" explanation of World War I.

NEUTRALITY POLICY

In a series of Neutrality Acts passed between 1935 and 1937, Congress said "never again" with an exclamation point. Taken together, the three laws warned American citizens against traveling on ships flying the flags of nations at war (no *Lusitanias* this time) and required that nations at war pay cash for all American products they bought and carry their purchases in their own ships. There would be no American ships torpedoed even by accident, and no American property would be destroyed because of a war among Europeans. Finally, belligerent nations were forbidden to buy arms in the United States and to borrow money from American banks. This law was Congress's rebuke of munitions makers and greedy bankers. There would be no powerful lobbies in Washington representing parties with a vested interest in the victory of one side or another as, isolationists said, had been the case in 1917.

Critics of the Neutrality Acts argued that they worked to the disadvantage of countries that were the victims of aggression. Those nations would be unprepared for war, whereas aggressor nations would equip themselves from their own or even American factories before declaring war. This, the critics said, was the message of fascist Italy's invasion of Ethiopia in 1935 and the Spanish civil war that began in 1936. The fascist rebels led by a reactionary general, Francisco Franco, were swamped with armaments and even troops from Italy and Germany. Neutrality policy denied the legitimate republican government of Spain access to armaments in the United States.

THE WORLD GOES TO WAR

Each year of the 1930s brought new evidence that the world was drifting into another bloodbath. In 1934 Hitler began rearming Germany. In 1935 he introduced universal military training, and Italy invaded Ethiopia. In 1936 Franco launched the Spanish civil war, which Italy and Germany used as an opportunity to test their weapons and military tactics.

In July 1937 Japan sent land forces from Manchukuo into China proper and occupied Beijing, then called Peiping, and most of the coastal provinces. In March 1938 Hitler forced the political union or *Anschluss* of Austria and Germany, increasing the resources of what he called the Third Reich, or empire. In September, claiming that he wanted only to unite all Germans under one flag, Hitler demanded that Czechoslovakia surrender the Sudetenland to him.

The Sudetenland had never been a part of Germany, although it was populated largely by people of German language and culture. But it was Czechoslovakia's mountainous natural defenses in the west. Czechoslovakia was the only democratic state in central Europe; France and Britain had guaranteed its borders. The generals of the German army did not want a general war in 1938. They told Hitler the army was not prepared. Hitler dismissed their advice, saying that France and Britain would back down. In fact, he hoped France would declare war over the Sudetenland. When the British prime minister, Neville Chamberlain, gave in to every one of Hitler's demands, even when he increased them, Hitler was (in private) disappointed. But he took the Sudetenland and, in March 1939, seized the Czech half of Czechoslovakia and set up a puppet regime in the Slovak east.

THE THREE AGGRESSOR NATIONS

In some respects, the three aggressor nations of the 1930s were very different. At bottom, Japan expanded into China for economic reasons. Although a modern industrial nation, Japan itself was poor in the natural resources essential to an industrial economy: coal, iron, and petroleum. China had plenty of coal and iron. Japan could trade for them, offering its own manufactures in exchange. But China's political instability made trade as unreliable as it made aggression and imperial domination inviting.

Moreover, beginning in the 1920s and accelerating after 1930, ultranationalistic army officers, infused with the premodern tradition of the samurai—the fighting man—began to cow the constitutional civilian government by assassinating antimilitarist ministers and terrorizing those they did not kill.

Many high-ranking naval officers still fumed with anger against the United States because of the Treaty of Washington, which limited the size of the Japanese navy to three-fifths the size of the American fleet. When others pointed out that the limitations benefited Japan because, in a naval arms race, the United States could afford to build fifty warships to every three Japan built, the irrationality of supernationalism closed the officers' ears. Until the summer of 1941, the militarists in the army and navy were restrained only by the fact that the United States provided much of the oil the country imported as well as copper, cotton, and cheap scrap iron. (Japan was America's third biggest customer.)

Japan and the United States were at odds over China. Fascist Italy under dictator Benito Mussolini directly

© UPI-Bettmann/Corbis

Benito Mussolini, il duce, "the leader"; Hitler adopted the same word in German, Führer, *in imitation of the Italian dictator (as did Franco,* el caudillo, *in Spain). To many Americans, Mussolini was a comical figure; he strutted and struck operatic poses. But he ruled Italy ruthlessly and, in 1935, launched the wave of aggression that was to lead to another European war when Italy invaded Ethiopia.*

threatened no American interests. Indeed, Italy's industry was backward and inefficient. Except for a few elite units, the Italian military commanded little respect. The army suffered significant setbacks during the conquest of Ethiopia at the hands of undisciplined irregulars sometimes armed with muskets European nations had abandoned sixty years earlier.

And it was easy not to take Mussolini seriously, despite the fact that he was ruthless in imprisoning and even murdering political opponents. He strutted and affected the poses of a character in an opera. Much of his regime was a show. The Italian army maintained a string of tanks made of sheet metal because they passed muster in parades.

Aside from his Charlie Chaplin mustache, there was nothing comical about Adolf Hitler: by 1935 his control of the most populous and most industrialized nation of Europe was absolute. Moreover, he was far more cunning than Mussolini, and unlike *il duce,* he had a master plan not merely for territorial expansion. Hitler planned to extend German rule over the entire European continent, making junior partners of racially pure peoples and slaves of Slavic peoples, whom Hitler despised, and ridding Europe entirely of Jews.

AND THE WAR CAME

In the summer of 1939, Germany and the Soviet Union announced that they had signed a nonaggression treaty. Hitler's interest in Russian neutrality was obvious. He had been demanding that Poland turn over to Germany a region largely populated by ethnic Germans known as the "Polish Corridor" because it provided Poland with its only access to the sea.

Britain and France had guaranteed Poland's borders, and after the lesson of Czechoslovakia, they made it clear that a German invasion of Poland meant war. Hitler wanted the war, but not a war on two fronts as in 1914–1918. The Nazi–Soviet pact guaranteed that Russia would not contest the German conquest of Poland. (Indeed, secret provisions of the treaty gave eastern Poland to the Soviets as well as three small states on the Baltic Sea: Lithuania, Latvia, and Estonia.)

Stalin's motives in agreeing to the treaty are cloudier or, at least, more complex. He had sought an anti-German alliance with Britain and France, but both nations dragged their feet long enough to unnerve him. He suspected (and he was not entirely mistaken) that Britain and France wanted to see the

MAP 43:1 German and Italian Aggression, 1934–1939

Italy's invasion of Ethiopia in 1935 was the first of a series of territorial aggressions by the fascist powers that culminated in World War II. Only when Nazi Germany invaded Poland in September 1939 did France and England respond with a declaration of war.

huge armies faced one another without moving. The French and British expected a defensive war like World War I. Their armies huddled behind the Maginot Line, an awesome line of modern fortifications to which the French had dedicated vast resources.

They were still fighting World War I—the static war of attrition that they had won. The Germans had other plans—a war of rapid movement and maneuver. Appreciating what motor vehicles and airpower meant to armed conflict, they were preparing for *Blitzkrieg* (lightning war): sudden, massive, fast-moving, precisely coordinated land, sea, and air attacks on Denmark, Norway, the Netherlands, Luxembourg, and Belgium, where the Maginot Line was weakest. Except for northern Norway, every country targeted by the Germans collapsed in days, including, in June 1940, France. The British managed to evacuate their troops and some French and Polish units from the port of Dunkirk only by mobilizing virtually every ship and boat capable of crossing the English Channel. The motley fleet returned nearly 340,000 men to England to await a German invasion.

THE INVASION OF RUSSIA

"We shall fight on the beaches, we shall fight on the landing grounds, we shall fight in the fields and in the streets, we shall fight in the hills; we shall never surrender," said the new British prime minister, Winston Churchill. His eloquence inspired many Americans as well as Britons. But after Germany's easy defeat of France, few Americans (and not all Britons) were confident that the British could repel a German invasion.

Hitler did not invade Great Britain, in part because the Germans did not have the naval edge that would guarantee the success of a massive amphibious operation, and in part because Hitler admired the British and hoped to negotiate a peace and alliance with them. He believed that with Germany's overwhelming superiority in the air, he could bomb Great Britain into accepting his terms.

The almost daily and nightly air attacks of the Battle of Britain—only bad weather provided a respite—savaged the

Nazis and Communists fight a war that would exhaust them both. Stalin preferred a scenario in which Germany would fight a long, mutually destructive war with Britain and France.

Almost two years later, when Hitler launched a massive attack on the Soviet Union, Stalin's defenders said that the dictator knew it was coming and had signed the Nazi–Soviet pact to win time in which to prepare. But the evidence indicates otherwise. The Soviets were unprepared by the German invasion of June 1941. Stalin really had believed that the Soviets would be spectators at a war in western Europe and pick up the pieces when it was concluded.

The Poles resisted heroically. But their obsoletely equipped and trained army was no match for the German *Wehrmacht* while the Soviets attacked from the rear. Several Polish divisions managed to evacuate to Great Britain and France.

THE FALL OF FRANCE, THE BATTLE OF BRITAIN

There they were to taste another stunning defeat, but only after months of no fighting at all during the winter of 1939–1940. Journalists wrote of the "phony war" as the two

The Party Line

A week before Germany invaded the Soviet Union, the Almanac Singers, loosely associated with the Communist party, released a record, *Songs for John Doe*, which included the antiwar lyric "I hate war, and so does Eleanor, and we won't be safe until everybody's dead."

After Russia was invaded, the American Communist party was instructed to work for American intervention in the war. *Songs for John Doe* was quickly withdrawn from the market, and people who had already purchased it were asked to return it. It is a rare collector's item today.

The Communist party newspaper, the *Daily Worker*, was so confused by the overnight change in the party line that it ran antiwar and prowar articles on the same page.

country's factories and cities. But almost miraculously, the fighter pilots of the Royal Air Force, although outnumbered, destroyed so many German planes that they gained the edge, although never domination, in the skies.

What the outcome might have been had the Battle of Britain continued cannot be known. Hitler wanted to conserve the *Lüftwaffe* (the German air force) for a campaign much more important to him: the conquest of the Soviet Union. In May 1941 British intelligence warned the Soviets of the exact date the Germans would launch their attack. German companies under contract to the Soviet Union ceased to make shipments. Stalin ignored the signs. The Soviet armies were stunned and disintegrated. Three million Soviet troops were put out of commission before fall when, finally, the Red Army held. The fighting was barbaric on both sides. Hitler lost 750,000 men in the first year in Russia, more than in the entire war to that point. Still, he expected victory the next year. His *Wehrmacht* nearly surrounded Leningrad in the north and was close to Moscow. In 1942 the Germans advanced in the south to Stalingrad.

THE UNITED STATES AND THE WAR

The sudden fall of France changed American public opinion about neutrality. In March 1940, during the "phony war," only 43 percent of Americans believed that a German military victory in Europe would threaten the United States. They were probably voicing their disbelief in the possibility of a German victory because in July, when Germany did dominate western Europe, four of five Americans were worried.

Winston Churchill's eloquence and the phlegmatic but heroic resistance of the English during the constant German bombing aroused an unprecedented sympathy for Great Britain. This was deftly encouraged by an unabashed Anglophile radio news reporter based in London, Edward R. Murrow. In nightly broadcasts—"live" was new in 1940—Murrow tacitly encouraged American support for Great Britain with his low-key but shrewdly worded descriptions of life during the "Blitz," sometimes with exploding German bombs providing the sound effects: "You will have no dawn raids, as we shall probably have if the weather is right. You may walk the night in the light. Your families are not scattered by the winds of war. You may drive your high-powered car as far as time and money will permit."

ROOSEVELT LEADS THE WAY, CAUTIOUSLY

President Roosevelt played no small part in nudging public opinion in the direction of intervention. As early as 1938, when few Americans could conceive of getting involved in a European war (the French and British governments were still appeasing Hitler), Roosevelt had concluded that only force—or a convincing show of it—would stop Hitler.

But he knew not to get too far ahead of the country; he studiously avoided using the word "preparedness." FDR's technique was to float trial balloons by delivering militant

anti-Nazi speeches. If the popular reaction was hostile or just uneasy, he backed off; if it was supportive, he pushed a bit further.

In 1939, at FDR's behest, Congress amended neutrality policy so that war materials could be sold on a cash-and-carry basis. (American ships were still banned from the trade.) In 1940, with the war under way and a majority of Americans worried about how a Nazi victory would affect them, FDR announced that he was "lending" Britain fifty aging destroyers the navy had in mothballs. In return, the British gave the United States permission to establish eight naval bases in Bermuda, Newfoundland, and the West Indies. Because the deal was a trade rather than a giveaway, Roosevelt could describe it as an American defensive measure: the United States was securing the Western Hemisphere. It was, in fact, defensive; but it was primarily a British aid package. The Royal Navy got many sorely needed antisubmarine weapons and, by leaving the defense of the western Atlantic to the United States, freed British vessels for transfer to European waters.

National defense was also the justification for the Burke–Wadsworth Act of September 1940, which appropriated $37 billion to build up the navy and army air corps and instituted the first peacetime draft law in American history. The draft was a lottery. More than 16 million young men were registered; each was assigned a number between 1 and 8,500, about 2,000 men per number. Henry L. Stimson (now FDR's secretary of war) picked the first number (#158), and the other 8,499 were drawn and listed in order. So a potential draftee knew whether he was likely to be called soon, later, or not at all. The first draftees were in uniform in November 1940; 900,000 would be called up under the law for one-year terms of service.

FDR had little difficulty winning support for these measures. Even the draft had the approval of two-thirds of the population. Nevertheless, when Roosevelt decided to break with tradition and run for a third term as president in 1940, he found it advisable to assure the electorate that "your boys are not going to be sent into any foreign wars," which he could not have fully believed.

THE THIRD TERM

Despite the favorable shift in public opinion, Roosevelt was worried that a Republican nominee who staked out a less aggressive position on the war (which Wilson, not the Republicans, had done in 1916) might win the election. He was being practical, not arrogant, when he concluded that he had a better chance to win the election than any other Democrat who wanted to run.

Vice president John Nance Garner was a tobacco-chewing provincial with little appeal outside the South. Jim Farley, the postmaster general, was a political strategist, but winning elections, not running a government, was his specialty. (FDR was perhaps a bit arrogant in thinking that only he could lead the country through yet another grave crisis.) Besides, Farley was a Catholic; it was only twelve years since Al Smith had lost half the southern states because of the religion issue. All Democrats, not just FDR, had good reason to shy away

© UPI–Bettmann/Corbis

Wendell Willkie and Madame Chiang Kai-shek in China, 1943.

from nominating a Catholic. Joseph P. Kennedy, a rich businessman of dubious ethics who was ambassador to Britain, was also Catholic and, much worse, a defeatist; he was sure that Great Britain was doomed.

So FDR blithely ignored the two-term tradition, and his decision proved wise because the Republicans chose a surprisingly attractive nominee. Utilities magnate Wendell Willkie had been a Democrat, and even a New Dealer. He was keenly intelligent, outgoing, and personable without the toadying so common among politicians today; he was a good speaker and, like FDR, no ideologue.

Had Willkie not emphasized the fact that he had few objections to Roosevelt's policy toward the war, he might have run a better race, even won the election. Instead he ran on domestic issues. He denounced FDR for concentrating too much power in the presidency. He made much of the terrific waste of money by the careless or incompetent administration of many New Deal programs. He claimed he was a better bet than FDR to keep the United States out of the war. But it was a "me too" campaign. Willkie did not propose to undo the changes the New Deal had made in the country,

and he intended to continue helping Great Britain resist the Nazis.

Willkie won more popular votes than any losing candidate before him. Roosevelt's popularity was not what it had been. But it had peaked so high in 1936 that he still had a comfortable cushion. He won almost 55 percent of the popular vote, more than Calvin Coolidge had won in 1924.

THE UNDECLARED WAR

Shortly after the election, Roosevelt responded to Churchill's plea for additional aid by sending the Lend–Lease Bill to Congress. As enacted, lend–lease provided that the United States would serve as the "arsenal of democracy," turning out arms of all sorts to be "loaned" to Britain. Eventually, when lend–lease was extended to the Soviet Union, aid under the act totaled $54 billion.

To help the British defend their shipping against "wolf packs" of German submarines, Roosevelt proclaimed a neutral zone that extended from North American waters to Iceland. He sent troops to Greenland, a possession of conquered Denmark, and ordered American destroyers to patrol the sea lanes, warning British ships of enemies beneath the waves. This permitted the British to concentrate their navy in home waters.

This put the United States at war with Germany in everything but name. In August 1941, like two allies, Roosevelt and Churchill met on two ships, the British *Prince of Wales* and the American cruiser *Augusta,* off the coast of Newfoundland. They adopted what amounted to war aims redolent of the general provisions of the Fourteen Points. The Atlantic Charter called for self-determination of nations after the war; free trade and freedom of the seas; the disarmament of

Lend–Lease

Britain could not afford to pay for the armaments Winston Churchill asked President Roosevelt for in 1940. Britain had already spent $4.5 billion in the United States for arms; in December 1940 its reserve was only $2 billion. Roosevelt explained the "loan" of destroyers and other arms to Britain to the American people with a parable:

> Suppose my neighbor's house catches fire, and I have a length of garden hose. If he can take my garden hose and connect it up with his hydrant, it may help him to put out the fire.
>
> Now what do I do? I don't say to him before that operation, "Neighbor, my garden hose cost me $15; you have to pay me $15 for it." [But] I don't want $15—I want my garden hose back after the fire is over.

Neither Churchill nor FDR (nor anyone with sense) believed the old destroyers would be "returned" at the end of the war or that the United States would want those that were still afloat. Because lend–lease was, in Churchill's words, "a decided unneutral act," he and Roosevelt thought it possible (both men hoped) that it would provoke Hitler into declaring war on the United States.

Two Different Worlds

In December 1940 Adolf Hitler told Germans that there could be no reconciliation between Germany on one side and Great Britain and the United States on the other. They were "different worlds."

The next month FDR accepted Hitler's dichotomy. He said that after the war the world would be consecrated to Four Freedoms: "freedom of speech and expression, freedom of worship, freedom from want, freedom from fear." Harry Hopkins remarked, "That covers an awful lot of territory, Mr. President. I don't know how interested Americans are going to be in the people of Java." Indeed, when Norman Rockwell illustrated the "Four Freedoms," they were idealizations of American life.

aggressor nations; and some new means of collective world security that would evolve into the United Nations.

It was only a matter of time before guns were fired. After a few ambivalent incidents involving German submarines and American destroyers, the USS *Reuben James* was sunk in October 1941 with a loss of 100 sailors.

AMERICA FIRST

Still, Roosevelt did not ask Congress for a formal declaration of war. He hoped, without a great deal of confidence, that Britain and the Soviet Union might defeat Germany without the further expenditure of American lives. More important, Roosevelt did not want to go into an all-out war without a unified people behind him. By the fall of 1941 he had a majority in support of war. Most Americans had concluded, grimly rather than with enthusiasm, that Hitler had to be defeated. Even the Communist party, which had loudly opposed American aid to Britain until Hitler invaded the Soviet Union, had moved literally overnight into the prowar camp. Big business had concluded that Hitler represented a threat to American commercial primacy as well as to democracy.

Still, Wilson had had a majority behind him. FDR wanted the virtual unanimity that Wilson never had. In 1941 there was an antiwar movement as vocal and influential as had fought Wilson to the bitter end. The pro-Nazi German-American Bund and William Pelley's Silver Shirts did not worry the president—they were small, unpopular organizations. Nor were Father Coughlin, still on the radio and still sympathetic to Hitler, or pacifists led by socialist Norman Thomas, of much concern. Neither had a numerically significant following.

However, isolationists had organized and abundantly funded the active **America First Committee,** persuasive in many circles because of the prestige of some of its supporters. Former president Hoover, ex-New Dealer Hugh Johnson, and progressive intellectuals like Charles A. Beard despised Hitlerism. They were, however, also Anglophobic and even more hostile to the Soviet Union. Going to war, they thought, would entrench the Communists in Moscow and save the British Empire, unworthy and undesirable goals. The America Firsters hammered on the theme that going to war in 1917

was a mistake. Let the British pull their own chestnuts out of the fire this time. The America Firsters decorated rally platforms with celebrities. Aviators Charles Lindbergh and Eddie Rickenbacker, film actress Lillian Gish, and Alice Roosevelt Longworth, Teddy's daughter (and FDR's cousin) gave speeches or just stood up and waved.

The Committee's case was weakened because most members agreed that the United States should arm for defense. Roosevelt and the rival Committee to Defend America by Aiding the Allies carefully characterized every contribution to the British cause in just such terms. Nevertheless, Roosevelt stood pat. He confided to Churchill that he would not ask for a declaration of war until some dramatic incident—an attack bigger than the sinking of the *Reuben James*—silenced the America Firsters.

As it turned out, both sides of the debate missed the point. Everyone's eyes were on Europe and the Atlantic Ocean. The incident that put the United States into the war was plenty dramatic, but it happened in the Pacific.

AMERICA GOES TO WAR

When France fell, the Japanese moved into the French colonies of Indochina. The "peace party" in the Japanese cabinet, headed by Prince Fumimaro Konoye, continued to negotiate with the United States, hoping for American concessions that would enable Japan to break the stalemate into which the war in China had bogged down. By October 1941 it was clear there would be no concessions, and General Hideki Tojo, head of the "war party" that thought war with the United States was essential and could be won, became premier. Tojo ordered preparations for an American war to begin.

PEARL HARBOR

Curiously, the Japanese and American governments both concluded on the same day that they were unlikely to resolve their differences without war. Although talks continued—empty formalities on both sides—Secretary of State Hull handed responsibility for Japanese affairs over to the War Department. Within hours, halfway around the world, Admiral Isoroku Yamamoto was instructed to prepare for the surprise attack on Pearl Harbor, the American naval base in Hawaii, for which he had drawn up the plans.

Yamamoto had consistently opposed a war with the United States. He had told the cabinet, "If I am told to fight regardless of the consequences, I shall run wild for the first six months or a year, but I have utterly no confidence for the

Line-Ups

Surprise was essential at Pearl Harbor. Had the United States had just half a day's warning, Admiral Yamamoto's flotilla would have been in grave danger. He had six aircraft carriers, two battleships, two heavy cruisers, one light cruiser, nine destroyers, three submarines, and 432 planes. Several aircraft carriers were on maneuvers in nearby waters. The Japanese attack was a gamble.

AP/Wide World Photos

The major consequence of the devastation the Japanese wreaked on American warships and airplanes at Pearl Harbor in December 1941 was the fact that, in an instant, it mobilized public opinion in favor of war. Even the military defeat was not as bad as it looked. Fortuitously, the Pacific Fleet's aircraft carriers were not at Pearl Harbor, and of the battleships bombed, only the Arizona was destroyed. Two of the crippled battleships were towed to California for repairs before the end of the month.

second or third year." He believed that destroying the American fleet at Pearl Harbor was essential to even a year of running wild.

Not every Japanese strategist agreed. Admiral Takijiro Onishi wanted to attack the Dutch East Indies (Indonesia) and British Singapore. Indonesia was rich in oil to replace the American oil that was no longer available. Moreover, if the United States was not attacked, perhaps the country would not go to war. Then Japan would have a stronger position from which to negotiate a favorable settlement. Hitting Pearl Harbor, Onishi said, no matter how successful tactically, would only unite Americans behind an all-out war. He agreed with Yamamoto that winning a war against a mobilized United States was, at best, unlikely.

Yamamoto carried the day, and on December 7, 1941, his fleet launched an attack that was perfectly executed. Japanese planes sank or badly damaged eight battleships, seven other vessels, and 188 airplanes, and killed or wounded 3,435 servicemen.

But Yamamoto's heart was not in his officers' giddy celebrations. Three American aircraft carriers he believed would be anchored at Pearl Harbor were at sea. Carrier-borne aircraft were the key to war in the broad Pacific. Pearl Harbor was the proof of that; no Japanese ship even approached Hawaii. And the United States had not lost one aircraft carrier. "I fear we have only awakened a sleeping giant," he told his officers, "and his reaction will be terrible."

THE REACTION

The giant awakened with a start. Pearl Harbor was attacked on Sunday. The next day, Roosevelt went before Congress and described December 7, 1941, as "a day that will live in infamy."

Old Pals

Kichisaburo Nomura, the Japanese ambassador to the United States in 1941, had known President Roosevelt personally for twenty-five years. Nomura had been naval attaché at the Japanese embassy during the First World War when Roosevelt was undersecretary of the navy.

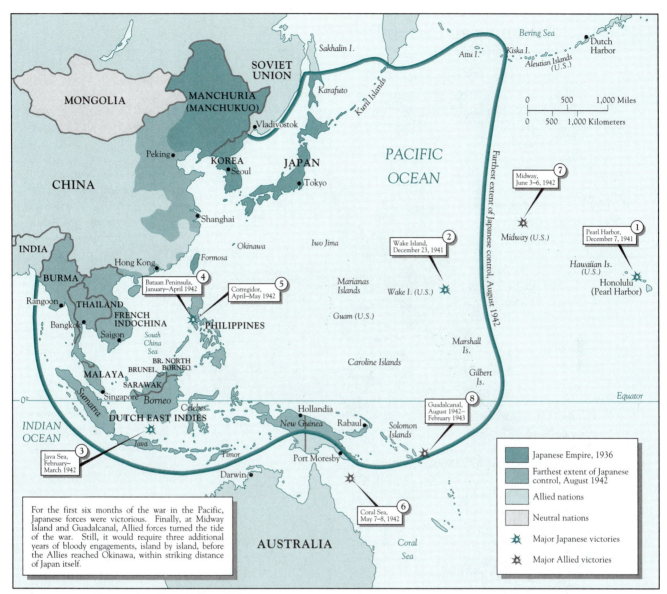

MAP 43:2 Japanese Empire, 1931–1942
As distant from Japan as the outer defensive perimeter of August 1942 was, it was not as far as Admiral Yamamoto and other strategists believed necessary to force the United States to negotiate a peace rather than fight a costly war. The Japanese military had hoped to occupy and fortify Midway Island (for regular air strikes against Hawaii), all of New Guinea, the Solomon Islands, and at least northern Australia—and to control the sea lanes to Australia—to deny the United States a base from which to launch a counterattack.

He got his unanimous vote, or very nearly so. In both houses of Congress, only Representative Jeannette Rankin of Montana, a pacifist who had also voted against entry into the First World War, refused to vote for the declaration of war.

In every city in the nation for weeks, the army's and navy's recruitment offices were jammed with young men. Pearl Harbor was so traumatic an event in the lives of Americans that practically every individual who lived through it would remember exactly what he or she was doing when news of the attack was announced.

Quietly at the time, openly later, Roosevelt's enemies accused him and other top officials of having plotted to keep Pearl Harbor and nearby Hickham Field, an airfield, unprepared for the attack. It was said that Washington knew the

assault was coming but withheld vital intelligence from Hawaii, sacrificing American lives for the political purpose of getting the United States into the war.

In fact, the lack of preparation at Pearl Harbor was inexcusable. As early as 1924, air power advocate General Billy Mitchell pointed out that Pearl Harbor was vulnerable to air attack. In 1932 Admiral Harry Yarnell snuck two aircraft carriers and four cruisers to within bombing range of Oahu before he was detected. Had his force been hostile, an attack like that of December 7, 1941, would have ensued. In early December 1941, numerous indications that something was brewing were either ignored or reached the appropriate commanders only after unjustifiable delays. At Hickham Field, fighter planes were drawn up wing tip to wing tip so

Rationing and Scrap Drives

German submarines set four-man sabotage teams ashore in Florida and on Long Island (they were captured immediately) and, in June 1942, sunk two ships within view of vacationers at Virginia Beach, Virginia. Japanese subs ran a few torpedoes up on California beaches; and several paper bombs, explosives held aloft by balloons pushed by the wind, detonated over Oregon, causing a forest fire. Otherwise the continental United States was physically untouched by the war. People on the home front experienced the war only through the loss of their friends and family members and in the form of shortages of consumer goods.

Reproduced from the Collections of the Library of Congress

Because the Japanese controlled 97 percent of the world's rubber-tree plantations in Malaya, automobile tires were the first goods taken off the market. Washington froze the sale of new tires and forbade recapping early in 1942; the armed forces badly needed tires, and the national stockpile of rubber was only 660,000 tons, about what civilians consumed in a year. Huge quantities of rubber were collected in scrap drives. A Seattle shoemaker contributed six tons of worn rubber heels that, for some reason, he had saved. People cleared closets of old overshoes, and the secretary of the interior took to picking up rubber doormats in federal office buildings. Reclaimed rubber was not suitable for tire manufacture, but it was used to make other products.

It was the fear of a rubber shortage, not of a gasoline shortage, that underlay the first controls on driving automobiles. FDR proclaimed a nationwide speed limit of 35 miles per hour; pleasure driving was banned. (Zealous officials of the Office of Price Administration jotted down license numbers at picnics, racetracks, concert halls, and athletic events.) The miles a car could be driven was determined by the sticker issued to each car owner. Ordinary people received "A" stickers, which entitled them to four gallons of gasoline a week, later three, and for a short time two. A "B" added a few gallons; they were issued to workers in defense plants for whom no public transportation was available. Physicians and others whose driving was essential got "C" cards and a few more gallons. Truckers ("T") got unlimited gas, as did some others, including political bigwigs whose "X" cards were a point of angry resentment. Counterfeiting of gas cards (usually "C" category) was common, and stickers were stolen from federal offices. The OPA discovered

they could be protected against sabotage on the ground. This simplified their destruction from the air, and when the attack began, few fighters were able to get into the air.

But there was no conspiracy to set Pearl Harbor up for a devastating defeat. The blunders of officials in Washington and the military in Hawaii were just another example of bureaucratic incompetence. The keys to the Japanese victory were its planning, its execution, and more than a little luck in pulling off total surprise. Nevertheless, there is little doubt that Pearl Harbor was not completely unwelcome news to President Roosevelt. He was relieved to get officially into the war with the whole country behind him.

GETTING THE JOB DONE

Of all the nations that went to war, only Japan, whose participation in the First World War was nominal, celebrated at its start. In Europe and the United States there was little of the exuberance with which Europeans greeted the first days of World War I. In the United States the attitude was and remained that there was a job to be done.

Popular songs of the era, "I'll Be Seeing You" and "I'll Never Smile Again," were melancholy, about the separation of lovers and their longing to be together again. There was little of the foot-stomping patriotism of George M. Cohan's anthem of World War I, "Over There." Seven times during the war, popular illustrator Norman Rockwell painted covers for the *Saturday Evening Post* showing an American soldier coming home.

ORGANIZING FOR VICTORY

Mobilization of the military had begun before Pearl Harbor. By December 1941 more than 1.5 million Americans were in

that 20 million gallons worth of cards were missing just in Washington.

Surplus gasoline could not be collected, but just about every other commodity vital to the war effort could be and was. Organizations like the Boy Scouts sponsored scrap drives through 1942 and 1943, collecting iron, steel, brass, bronze, tin, old nylon stockings (for powder bags), and bacon grease (for munitions manufacture). Many scrap campaigns were more trouble than they were worth, but not those that collected iron, steel, tin, and paper. Scrap iron and steel made a significant contribution to manufacturing, and about half of the country's tin and paper products originated not in mines and forests but in neighborhood drives. The Boy Scouts' first scrap paper drive was so productive that in June 1942 the government had to call a temporary halt to it.

The tin shortage was responsible for the rationing of canned foods. To buy a can of corn or sardines, as well as coffee, butter, cheese, meat, and some other food items, a consumer had to hand the grocer ration stamps as well as money. Books of stamps were issued regularly and served as a second, parallel currency. To buy a pound of hamburger, a shopper needed meat stamps worth seven "points" as well as the purchase price. A pound of butter cost sixteen points; a pound of cheese, eight points; and so on. The tiny stamps—which were color-coded red (meat, butter), blue (processed food), green, and brown—were a bother. More than 3.5 billion of them changed hands every month. To restock shelves, a grocer had to turn in stamps collected from customers to a wholesaler who, in turn, had to deposit them with a bank to make additional purchases.

Except for butter, rations were not stringent. The weekly sugar ration was eight ounces a person, about as much as

a dentist would wish on a patient in the best of times. In 1943, despite rationing, the American standard of living was 16 percent higher than it had been in 1939. By 1945 Americans were eating more food and spending more money on it than ever before. Only butter consumption dropped appreciably, from seventeen to eleven pounds per capita per year.

The OPA noticed curious facts about coffee and cigarette consumption. Coffee was rationed because few ships were available to carry it from South America. When rationing began in November 1942 (one pound per person every five weeks), people began to hoard it. At restaurants, diners traded their dessert for an extra cup. When coffee rationing was discontinued in July 1943, coffee sales dropped! Then, in the fall, when a coffee stamp was mistakenly included in the ration books, Americans stripped market shelves bare. When the OPA announced that there was no coffee ration, sales dropped again. Cigarettes were rationed because 30 percent of the industry's production was reserved for 10 percent of the population that was in the armed forces. Among civilians, the principle that rationing defined a commodity as desirable may have caused an increase in smoking.

A more salutary consequence of wartime shortages was the popularity of gardening. There was no shortage of fresh vegetables, and they were never rationed. But canned vegetables were, and space on trucks and trains was at a premium. So the government encouraged "**victory gardens.**" Some 20.5 million families planted them; by 1945 Americans were raising between 30 and 40 percent of the vegetables grown in the United States in small gardens. When the war was over, however, Americans quickly shed their good taste. By 1950 they had returned to canned and frozen vegetables.

uniform. By the end of the war, the total number of soldiers, sailors, and airmen, and women in auxiliary corps, climbed to 15 million.

The draft accounted for the majority of "**G.I.s,**" the soldiers' self-adopted name that referred to the "government-issue" designation of uniforms and other equipment. Draft boards made up of local civic leaders worked efficiently and with remarkably few irregularities to fill the armed forces' demands. The "Friends and Neighbors" who informed young men of their fate with the salutation "Greetings" exempted only the physically disabled and those with jobs designated as essential to the war effort, including farmers and agricultural workers. (One draftee in three was rejected for physical reasons.)

With time, another category of exemption was added: "sole surviving sons," who were men of draft age whose brothers had all been killed in action. In the windows of

homes that lost a soldier were hung small red, white, and blue banners, with stars enumerating the house's losses. The woman of the house was called a "Gold Star Mother."

Money was mobilized, too. When the war began, the government was spending $2 billion a month on the military. During the first half of 1942 its expenditure rose to $15 billion monthly. By the time Japan surrendered in August 1945, the costs of the war totaled more than $300 billion. In less than four years, the American government spent more money than it had spent during the previous 150 years of the nation's existence. The national debt, already high in 1941 at $48 billion, doubled and redoubled to $247 billion.

BIG BUSINESS

A few businessmen resisted the government's wartime restrictions, particularly the labor laws. The least graceful was

Sewell L. Avery, head of the retail chain Montgomery Ward. The New Deal had saved his company from bankruptcy, and during the war, full employment meant bonanza profits for Ward's. But Avery had to be carried bodily to jail for refusing to obey a law that guaranteed his employees the right to join a union.

He was not typical. Most big businessmen, including former opponents of the administration, accepted unionization and rushed to Washington to join the government. They were responding to the call for national unity. But corporation executives also recognized that the government's astronomical wartime expenditures meant prosperity. General Motors collected 8 percent of all federal expenditures between 1941 and 1945, $1 of every $12.50 that the government spent.

General Motors President William S. Knudsen was therefore delighted to be a "dollar-a-year man," a business executive who worked for Roosevelt for that sum, as if he was patriotically sacrificing big money. Knudsen headed the War Resources Board (WRB), established in August 1939 to plan for the conversion of factories to military production. For all the cynical patriotic palaver about dollar-a-year men, the country did need their organizational know-how.

NEW ALPHABET AGENCIES

After the congressional elections of 1942, which brought many conservative Republicans to Washington, Roosevelt announced that "Dr. New Deal" had been dismissed from the country's case and "Dr. Win-the-War" was now engaged. He explained that because there was now full employment, social programs were no longer necessary.

However, the establishment of new government agencies of different kinds continued apace. In addition to Knudsen's WRB, the Supplies Priorities and Allocation Board (SPAB), under Donald M. Nelson of Sears Roebuck and Company, was commissioned to ensure that raw materials, particularly scarce and critical ones, were diverted to military industries. The Office of Price Administration (OPA) had the task of controlling consumer prices so that the combination of high wages and scarce goods did not cause runaway inflation.

After Pearl Harbor, a National War Labor Board (NWLB) was set up to mediate industrial disputes. Its purpose was to guarantee that production was not interrupted and that wage increases were kept within government-defined limits. This irked many of Roosevelt's former supporters in the labor movement, none more important than John L. Lewis of the United Mine Workers, who returned to the Republican party. But the NWLB also worked to ensure that employees were not gouged by avaricious employers. The board was reasonably successful. There were strikes, including a serious one led by Lewis in 1943; but labor relations were generally good, and union membership continued to rise.

The Office of War Mobilization (OWM) was the most important of the new alphabet agencies. Theoretically it oversaw all aspects of the mobilized economy, as Bernard Baruch had

Kaiser Graphic Arts

Liberty Ships

Maximum mass production means making something no better than it has to be in order to function. What counts is the number of the commodity produced, whether it is chewing gum or an automatic dishwasher.

World War II's "liberty ships" may be the most amazing application of the principles of mass production in the history of the concept. Liberty ships were "no frills" boxcars of the seas: 441 feet long and 57 feet across the beam, with a rudimentary engine. Some 800 of them were lost during the war, most to enemy action, but more than a few in storms. Because they were welded rather than riveted together, liberty ships were not the sturdiest of vessels.

But they were as good as they had to be. Welding made it possible for American shipyards employing men and women with no experience in shipbuilding to finish a liberty ship in as few as forty days after the keel was laid. Some 2,700 of them were built between 1941 and 1944. By the end of the war, several new ones rolled down the ways each day. Liberty ships were so cheap that when one completed a single voyage (carrying freight enough to fill 300 railroad cars), it paid for itself. Their design was such a masterpiece of simplicity that with just a few old salts aboard, inexperienced crews of forty-five (plus thirty-five navy gunners and signalmen) could sail one.

done during the First World War. It was considered important enough that James F. Byrnes of South Carolina resigned from the Supreme Court to head it as a kind of assistant president.

SUCCESS

The size of the federal government swelled at a dizzying rate—from 1.1 million civilian employees in 1940 to 3.3 million in 1945. (State governments grew at almost the same rate.) Inevitably there were waste (agencies doing the same thing), inefficiency (agencies fighting with one another), and corruption (lots of people doing nothing but collecting paychecks). But with national unity and military victory constantly touted as essential, the few critics of the problems, such as Republican Senator Robert A. Taft of Ohio, were unable to have much effect. Taft was a thoughtful man but also a knee-jerk carper. The most effective check on waste, inefficiency, and corruption was the Senate War Investigating Committee, which was headed by a New Deal Democrat, Senator Harry S Truman of Missouri.

The lessons learned during the First World War and the administrative skills of dollar-a-year businessmen worked wonders in production. New factories and those formerly devoted to the manufacture of America's automobiles canceled civilian production and churned out trucks, tanks, the famous jeeps, and amphibious vehicles in incredible numbers. In 1944 alone, 96,000 airplanes (260 per day) rolled out of American factories. Industrialist Henry J. Kaiser perfected an assembly line for producing simple and cheap but serviceable freighters—the **liberty ships.** American shipbuilders sent 10 million tons of shipping down the ways between 1941 and 1945. The Ford Motor Company alone produced more war materiel than all of Italy.

THE WORKERS

Unemployment vanished. Factories running at capacity had difficulty finding people to fill jobs. There was a significant shift of population to the West Coast as the demands of the Pacific war led to the growth of defense industries in Seattle, Oakland, San Diego, and Long Beach. Among the new Californians

Women Pilots

Women numbering 350,000 volunteered for military service during World War II. A few of them were pilots, which inspired the idea of training other women to fly. The thousand who served in the Women's Airforce Service Pilots did not fly in combat, but by testing aircraft, towing targets at artillery training bases, and ferrying planes from factories to seaports for shipment to the war zones, they freed a thousand male pilots for combat duty.

WASP pilots were better in one way than army air corps and navy pilots: they were more versatile. Combat pilots specialized in the particular aircraft to which they were assigned. The WASP pilots who ferried planes flew them all. When the B-29 was introduced, many air corps pilots disliked them, saying the plane was too difficult to fly. They were told, "If girls can fly them, ..."

A Jim Crow Military

African Americans served in every branch of the armed forces, but in racially segregated units. As in World War I, most were assigned to undesirable noncombatant duty. A notable exception was the Ninety-Ninth Air Force Fighter Squadron, the "Tuskegee Airmen," who fought in Europe.

Black nurses were subjected to an indignity they bitterly resented. When not caring for wounded African-American soldiers, they were assigned to German prisoners of war rather than to hospitals for white American soldiers.

A black soldier traveling in the South in April 1944 told of being unable to get coffee at diners and restaurants. Finally the men in his group were given cups at a railroad station lunchroom, but they had to stand outside: "About a dozen German prisoners of war, with two American guards, came to the station. They entered the lunchroom, sat at the tables, had their meals served, talked, smoked, in fact had quite a swell time. I stood on the outside looking in, and I could not help but ask myself why are they treated better than we are?"

(the population of the Golden State rose from 6.9 million in 1940 to 10.5 million in 1950) were hundreds of thousands of African Americans. Finding well-paid factory jobs previously closed to them, blacks also won a sense of security unknown to earlier generations because of the colorblind policies of the CIO unions and FDR's executive order in 1941 that war contractors observe fair practices in employing blacks.

Women, including many of middle age who had never worked for wages, entered the labor force in large numbers. The symbol of the woman performing "unladylike" jobs was "Rosie the Riveter," forearms like a boxer's, assembling airplanes and tanks with heavy riveting guns. Women performed just about every kind of job in the industrial economy. Rosie dressed in slacks, tied up her hair in a bandanna, and left her children with her mother. But off the job she remained reassuringly feminine by the standards of the time. By the end of the war, 16.5 million women were working; they were more than a third of the civilian labor force.

Few of these genuinely independent women were feminists. Rosie after Rosie told newspaper reporters that they looked forward to the end of the war, when they could quit their jobs and return to the home as wives and mothers. They were the perfect wartime workforce: intelligent, educated, energetic, patriotic, and, most of them, uninterested in competing with the soldiers who eventually would come back and take their jobs.

PROSPERITY

The Office of Price Administration was remarkably successful in its difficult assignment. Coveted consumer goods—coffee, butter, sugar, some canned foods, meat, shoes, liquor, silk, rayon, and nylon—were scarce because of rationing, but high wages gave workers the money to spend on what was available. (Real wages rose 50 percent during the war.) The black market (illegal sale of rationed goods) never got out of control, and prices rose only moderately between 1942 and 1945. Instead of consuming wholesale, Americans pumped their wages into savings accounts, including $15 billion in loans to the government in the form of war bonds. It became a point of patriotic pride with some women to paint the seams of nylon stockings on their calves (although a pair of stockings was still coveted).

There was an element of good-humored innocence in the way Americans fought the Second World War. If they did not believe that a problem-free world would follow victory (which no one doubted they would win), Americans were confident that they and their allies were in the right. By the time the fighting was over, 290,000 Americans were dead. Shocking as that figure is, American losses were negligible compared to the losses of other belligerents. Winston Churchill had described the year 1940, when the British stood alone against Nazism, as "their finest hour." The years America was at war were our finest day.

FURTHER READING

American Neutrality　Wayne S. Cole, *Charles A. Lindbergh and the Battle against Intervention in World War II*, 1974, and *Roosevelt and the Isolationists, 1932–1945*, 1983; Kenneth S. Davis, *Franklin D. Roosevelt: Into the Storm, 1937–1940*, 1993; Thomas Guinsburg, *The Pursuit of Isolationism in the United States Senate from Versailles to Pearl Harbor*, 1982; Waldo H. Heinrichs, *Threshold of War: Franklin D. Roosevelt and American Entry into World War II*, 1988; Douglass Little, *Malevolent Neutrality: The United States, Great Britain, and the Origins of the Spanish Civil War*, 1985; Donald C. Witt, *How War Came: The Immediate Origins of the Second World War, 1938–1939*, 1989.

Conflict with Japan　Robert J. Burtow, *Tojo and the Coming of War*, 1961; Warren Cohen, *America's Response to China*, 1971; Roger Dingman, *Power in the Pacific*, 1976; John W. Dower, *War without Mercy: Race and Power in the Pacific War*, 1986; Ronald H. Spector, *Eagle Against the Sun: The American War with Japan*, 1985; Gerhard L. Weinberg, *A World at Arms: A Global History of World War II*, 1994; H. P. Willmott, *The Great Crusade: A New Complete History of the Second World War*, 1990.

New Deal Foreign Policy　Selig Adler, *Uncertain Giant: American Foreign Policy between the Wars*, 1966; Robert Dallek, *Franklin D. Roosevelt and American Foreign Policy, 1932–1945*, 1979; Lloyd C. Gardner, *Economic Aspects of New Deal Diplomacy*, 1964; Irwin F. Gellman, *Good Neighbor Diplomacy*, 1979; Akira Iriye, *The Globalizing of America, 1913–1945*, 1990; John E. Wiltz, *From Isolationism to War, 1931–1941*, 1968.

Pearl Harbor　Charles R. Anderson, *Day of Lightning, Years of Storm: Walter C. Short and the Attack on Pearl Harbor*, 2005; Edwin P. Hoyt, *Yamamoto: The Man Who Planned Pearl Harbor*, 1996; Daniel Madsden, *Resurrection: Salvaging the Battle Fleet at Pearl Harbor*, 2003; Gordon W. Prange, *At Dawn We Slept: The Untold Story of Pearl Harbor*, 1981, and *December 7, 1941: The Day the Japanese Attacked Pearl Harbor*, 1988; Michael Slackman, *Target: Pearl Harbor*, 1990.

KEY TERMS

The following terms are covered in this chapter and can also be found in the list of Key Terms at the back of the book.

America First Committee　　Good Neighbor policy　　　　Stimson Doctrine　　　victory gardens

G.I.s　　　　　　　　　　　　liberty ships

 ## ONLINE SOURCES GUIDE

Use this listing to find online documents, images, interactive maps, simulations, and other resources related to this chapter:

American History Resource Center
http://history.wadsworth.com/rc/us

Selected Documents
Roosevelt's war message to Congress, December 8, 1941
Roosevelt's "Four Freedoms" address
"The Atlantic Charter" 1941

Selected Images
Aftermath of the attack on Pearl Harbor
Navajo Signal Corp

Interactive Time Line (with online readings)
Another Great War: America and the World, 1933–1942

CHAPTER 44

World War II

The Pinnacle of Power 1942–1945

U.S. Navy Photo in the National Archives

We are now in this war. We are all in it—all the way. Every single man, woman, and child is a partner in the most tremendous undertaking of our American history.

Franklin D. Roosevelt

Nazi Germany was defeated by British pluck, Russian blood, and American industrial might.

By holding out alone against Hitler in 1940 and 1941, Britain prevented the Nazis from establishing an impregnable "Fortress Europe." In saving their island, the British saved the base that made an invasion of continental Europe possible.

The Soviet Union sapped the might of the German *Wehrmacht,* killing 4.9 million German soldiers and wounding 5.8 million—four times as many casualties as the Americans and British inflicted.

The United States, with an economy double the size of Germany's, Italy's, and Japan's combined, kept both Britain and Russia afloat with its incredible industrial output both before and after entering the war. American strategists (to the chagrin of the British military) designed the formula that defeated Germany in the West.

Without the American army and navy, Britain and the Soviet Union might have fought Germany to exhaustion, toppled Hitler, and signed an advantageous treaty. But they could not have won the total victory with which the war

ended had the United States not been a full participant. The war maimed Great Britain; even in victory, Britain was no longer a major world power. The war bled the Soviet Union worse than it bled Germany: 6.1 million soldiers dead compared to 3.2 million German troops, plus 20 million civilians killed.

The Pacific war against imperial Japan was largely an American show. The Australians fought bravely in New Guinea and the British in Burma; the Chinese tied down a million Japanese soldiers (without fighting them much). But the United States provided the numbers of fighting men and the greatest navy ever assembled. World War II was America's "Great War," the victory perhaps America's greatest contribution to Western civilization.

STOPPING JAPAN

Americans knew that they were in a fight between December 1941 and August 1945. Adults remembered the day Pearl Harbor was attacked, D-Day when the invasion of Europe

Prisoners of War

The Americans who surrendered on Wake Island in the Philippines were prisoners of war for more than three years. About 35 percent died in Japanese camps, and that was not the war's worst prisoner of war statistic. Two-thirds of the Russians taken prisoner by the Germans died in camps. As many as 80 percent of the Germans captured by the Russians died. Only 1 percent of Germans in American POW camps died, and the figure was lower for Americans in German *Stalags*. The vicious SS operated most German prisoner of war camps, but the *Luftwaffe* insisted on guarding captured American and British airmen and strictly observed the Geneva Convention on the treatment of POWs. Until the Battle of the Bulge in December 1944, almost all American soldiers in German hands were airmen.

began, the day Franklin D. Roosevelt died, and V-E Day and V-J Day, when Germany and Japan surrendered. The memories ended up sweet, sustaining a generation with the knowledge that their lives had had some meaning. But the war began with defeat.

HUMILIATION AND ANGER

The first months after Pearl Harbor brought nothing but bad news. After Admiral Yamamoto paralyzed the American Pacific fleet, the Japanese army advanced easily into Malaya, Hong Kong, the Philippines, Java, and Guam. Within a few weeks, the dramatic Japanese battle flag, rays emanating from the rising sun, snapped in the breezes of British Singapore, Malaya, Burma, and the Dutch East Indies (present-day Indonesia).

There was heroism in the disaster. On Wake Island in the central Pacific, a mere 450 marines held off a Japanese onslaught for two weeks, killing 3,000 before they surrendered. On Luzon in the Philippines, 20,000 G.I.s under General Douglas MacArthur and a larger force of Filipinos fought valiantly to hold back far greater numbers of Japanese on the Bataan Peninsula and, at the end, the rocky fortress island of Corregidor in Manila Bay. At first the men thought they would be relieved. Slowly the sickening truth sank in: They were the "battling bastards of Bataan," quite alone, an ocean away from a crippled navy. Nevertheless, they grimly carried out the hopeless task of delaying and punishing the Japanese.

General MacArthur did not stay. Once Roosevelt realized that the Philippines must fall, he ordered the nation's best-known general to flee to Australia. FDR must have been tempted to let MacArthur fall into Japanese hands. (MacArthur was prepared to surrender.) With good reason, he disliked and distrusted the general. Indeed, aside from a coterie of devoted aides, MacArthur had alienated most of the military's top brass. He was an egomaniac and a insufferable posturer in Mussolini's league. He had orchestrated the cultivation of an image complete with trademark props—sunglasses and corncob pipe. "I studied dramatics under MacArthur," General Dwight D. Eisenhower waspishly remarked. MacArthur also had a history of ignoring orders or interpreting them to suit himself.

For all that, his military genius and personal bravery could not be denied. FDR believed that MacArthur was, if not essential to winning the war with Japan, vital. The general's connection with the Philippines was lifelong and mutually affectionate. When MacArthur left the islands, he promoted his mystique and inspired the Philippine resistance (the most effective resistance in Asia or Europe) with a radio message that concluded, "I shall return."

On May 6, 1942, the last ragged, starving, and sick defenders of Corregidor surrendered. American dismay at their defeat gave way to livid anger when reports trickled back to the United States of Japanese cruelty toward their prisoners on the infamous **Bataan Death March.** Of 10,000 men forced to walk to a prison camp in the interior, 1,000 died on the way. (Another 5,000 died in camp.)

World War II 1942–1945

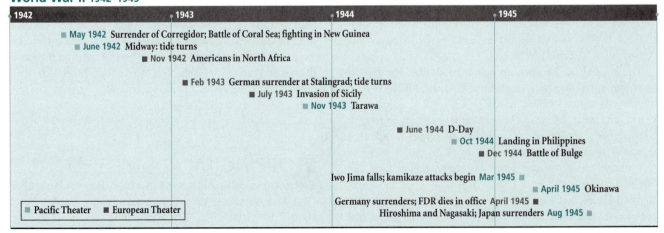

1942	1943	1944	1945

- May 1942 Surrender of Corregidor; Battle of Coral Sea; fighting in New Guinea
- June 1942 Midway: tide turns
- Nov 1942 Americans in North Africa
- Feb 1943 German surrender at Stalingrad; tide turns
- July 1943 Invasion of Sicily
- Nov 1943 Tarawa
- June 1944 D-Day
- Oct 1944 Landing in Philippines
- Dec 1944 Battle of Bulge
- Iwo Jima falls; kamikaze attacks begin Mar 1945
- April 1945 Okinawa
- Germany surrenders; FDR dies in office April 1945
- Hiroshima and Nagasaki; Japan surrenders Aug 1945

■ Pacific Theater   ■ European Theater

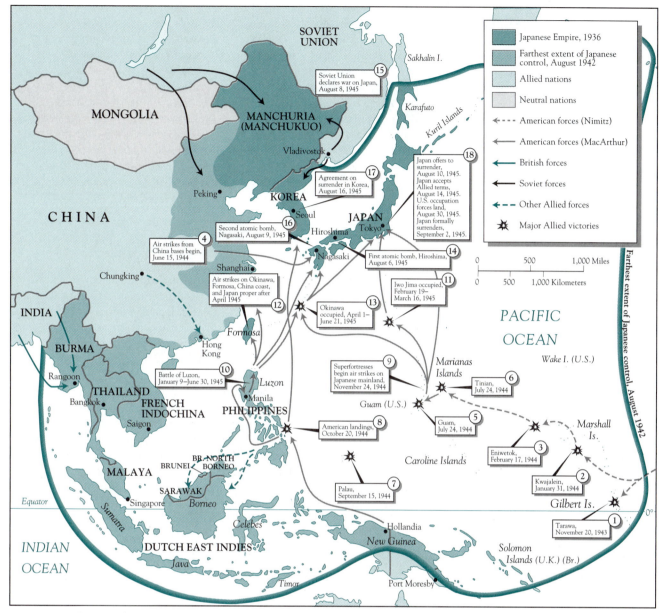

MAP 44:1 The Pacific Theater

The Japanese empire faced enemies on four fronts. British and colonial troops attacked Burma from India; Chinese Nationalists and Communists faced the Japanese in China on a static front; General MacArthur's soldiers and marines, with naval support, drove through New Guinea to the Philippines; and Admiral Chester Nimitz's forces "island-hopped" through the central Pacific to Iwo Jima and Okinawa, dearly won positions from which land-based American planes could bomb Japan with little opposition. By the summer, Japanese air power consisted of little more than suicide kamikaze planes that wreaked havoc on American ships but meant nothing to American bombers.

THE JAPANESE PLAN

During the siege of Corregidor, the Japanese piled up victories in south Asia and Oceania. British and imperial forces in the East—not many after two years of war in Europe—were captured or retreated to India and New Guinea. Japanese strategy was to establish a defensive perimeter of invulnerably fortified islands far enough from Japan that the Americans, after they recuperated from Pearl Harbor, could not bomb the home islands. Then, the Japanese believed, they could

negotiate a treaty that recognized Japanese imperial domination in China, south Asia, and the eastern Pacific. No Japanese ever entertained the fantasy of conquering the United States or even inflicting a crushing military defeat.

By early May the first phase of the Japanese plan—establishment of an **outer perimeter**—seemed near completion. Japanese soldiers occupied the Solomon Islands and most of New Guinea. At Port Moresby in New Guinea, however, Australian and American forces halted the advance,

MacArthur and The Joint Chiefs

General MacArthur's campaign was of tertiary importance to the Joint Chiefs of Staff. Only 15 percent of American resources were assigned to his front. His army had only five tons of supplies per soldier compared to fifteen tons per soldier in North Africa.

The reason for the inequity was that there was no urgency to MacArthur's assignment. His job was to slog it out with the Japanese on the large landmasses of New Guinea and the Philippines. Higher priorities were the European front and Admiral Nimitz's island-hopping campaign in the central Pacific, aimed at securing airbases close enough to Japan that big land-based bombers could pummel the country. There were compelling reasons for defeating Germany and bombing the Japanese homeland as soon as possible.

No explanation mollified MacArthur. He blamed his shortages on the personal jealousy and malice of Chief of Staff George Marshall, whom he despised. Marshall did not much like MacArthur either; but he repeatedly went out of his way to accommodate MacArthur's demands, and he argued that several incidents of insubordination (a MacArthur specialty) should be ignored.

However, even paranoids have real enemies. Admiral Ernest J. King of the Joint Chiefs so loathed MacArthur that he reacted to everything the general said or did with knee-jerk condemnation. Had MacArthur sent him a birthday cake, King would have stomped it underfoot.

---

preventing a serious assault on Australia. Yamamoto moved his fleet, as yet unscarred, to the **Coral Sea** off Australia's northeastern coast. His object was to cut the supply line between Hawaii and Australia, thus choking off the resistance in New Guinea and making a landing in Australia possible.

THE CORAL SEA AND MIDWAY

On May 6 and 7, 1942, the Japanese and American fleets fought to a standoff. The battle of the Coral Sea was a new kind of naval encounter in that the ships of the opposing forces never caught sight of one another. Carrier-based aircraft did the fighting, against one another and against enemy vessels. The Japanese sustained lighter losses than the Americans—early in the war, Japanese pilots were more skilled than American pilots, and their fighter planes, the "Zeros," were superior to American aircraft—but the battle was a strategic defeat for Japan. Admiral Yamamoto was forced to abandon his plan to cut the southern shipping lanes. He had "run wild" not for a year or even six months, but for only five months.

Yamamoto turned to the central Pacific, where Japanese supply lines were more dependable. His goal was the American naval and air base on the island of Midway, about a thousand miles northwest of Hawaii. There, between June 3 and June 6, 1942, the Japanese suffered a resounding defeat. The American fleet under Admirals Raymond A. Spruance and Frank Fletcher lost the carrier *Yorktown* to Japanese dive-bombers and torpedoes, but American planes destroyed four Japanese carriers.

© Corbis

Navy torpedo planes attack the Japanese aircraft carrier Shoho at the Battle of the Coral Sea. (One is below the bow, one silhouetted against the smoke.) This is how most World War II naval battles were fought, planes against ships. Only occasionally were enemy ships close enough to fire at one another with their big guns. Battleships had to have carrier protection. Their chief use was shelling Japanese targets on land.

It was worse than a one-for-four trade. Japan lacked the wealth and industrial capacity to replace fabulously expensive aircraft carriers as easily as the United States could. The United States had twice the population of Japan and seventeen times the national income. During the war Japan commissioned 14 new carriers, the United States 104. The loss of a carrier was a serious blow to the American navy; plans had to be revised when one went down. But when the Japanese lost a carrier, the country's war-making capacity was significantly reduced.

With the defeat at Midway, Japan's offensive capacity was ended. By holding Midway, the Americans controlled the central Pacific just seven months after Pearl Harbor. Much earlier than he had planned, Yamamoto had to shift to defending what the Japanese had won.

Yamamoto did not live to see the disastrous end of the war that he feared was inevitable. By 1943 the Americans had cracked the Japanese navy's radio code; they read Japanese communiqués only minutes after the commanders to whom they were addressed digested them. They learned that Yamamoto would be flying over Bougainville in the Solomon Islands, and they shot down his plane and killed him. By remaining silent until the Japanese announced Yamamoto's death, they nurtured the Japanese illusion that the American attack had been routine and not aimed specifically at Yamamoto. Had the Japanese known that, they would have realized their code had been deciphered.

ANTI-JAPANESE HYSTERIA

About 200,000 Japanese immigrants (called *Issei*) and Japanese Americans (*Nisei*) lived in Hawaii, and 120,000 lived in the continental United States, all but a few in the Pacific states. For fifty years California politicians had exploited racist feelings by railing against them as the "yellow peril." Newspapers owned by William Randolph Hearst had been particularly ugly. (Hearst, convinced in his vanity that he was Japan's number one target after Pearl Harbor, hurriedly moved out of his palace, San Simeon, which overlooked the Pacific and could easily have been shelled from a submarine had the Japanese taken him seriously.)

He was not the only hysteric in the wake of Pearl Harbor. For a few days parts of Los Angeles were near panic because of a rumor the Japanese were invading. Coastal communities in California organized networks of civilian lookouts, training binoculars on the horizon. In Hawaii several high-ranking army officers panicked and called on Washington to evacuate the *Issei* and *Nisei*. They were sent back to other concerns when they were reminded that Japanese Americans represented between a third and a half of the Hawaiian population. They were 90 percent of the carpenters and transportation workers in the islands. Evacuate them, and the Hawaiian economy would cease to exist. Moreover, there was no indication that more than a handful of Japanese Americans harbored sympathies for the enemy. A mere 1,400 of the 200,000 Hawaiian Japanese were interned as suspects; many of them were guilty only of big talk.

In California, Japanese Americans were just 1 percent of the population. There, however, popular hysteria threatened to develop into social disorder. Chinese and Koreans wore buttons that read "I am not Japanese" so as not to be roughed up as many *Issei* and *Nisei* were. The Justice Department announced that very few Japanese, all known to the Federal Bureau of Investigation, were disloyal. (Two thousand suspects were arrested; most were quickly exonerated of wrongdoing.) Indeed, Japan's consul in Los Angeles had advised Tokyo that, in the event of war, no help whatsoever would be forthcoming from the Japanese-American community. He never bothered to plan a program to recruit saboteurs.

INTERNMENT CAMPS

But California's attorney general, Earl Warren, and the commanding general at San Francisco's Presidio, John W. DeWitt, joined the anti-Japanese clamor. DeWitt argued, in a triumph of logic, that "the very fact that no sabotage has taken place to date is a disturbing and confirming indication that such action will be taken." FDR gave in. Executive Order 9066 forbade "Japanese," including American-born citizens, to reside in a broad "coastal zone." About 9,000 *Issei* and *Nisei* responded by heading east by train and automobile. Service stations would not sell them gasoline; some were illegally turned back at the Nevada line. So early in 1942 the federal government forcibly removed 110,000 Japanese Americans from their homes and interned them in hurriedly constructed camps in seven states, from inland California to Arkansas.

Many federal officials were appalled by the idea of American concentration camps. Because the criteria for relocation were ancestry and race, and many internees were native-born citizens, the federal government itself was flouting the Fourteenth Amendment. When any reply to complaints was forthcoming, it was "Don't you know there's a war on?" In June 1943, Governor Earl Warren said that if the internment camps were closed, "No one will be able to tell a saboteur from any other Jap." In *Korematsu* v. *the United States* (1944) the Supreme Court voted 6 to 3 to uphold an action that cost 110,000 people their freedom for several years and about $350 million in lost property. The internment of Japanese Americans was by far the least justifiable federal violation of civil liberties in the history of the United States. However, the internment camps should not be equated with Nazi, Japanese, and Soviet camps.

Life in the camps was humiliating; but there was no cruelty, brutality, or forced labor, let alone murder. On the contrary, many camp supervisors were disgusted by the internment. They helped internees find employment outside the fences, provided recreational and educational programs in the camps, helped internees protect property they had been forced to abandon, and nagged Washington to end internment. Some 17,000 *Nisei*, the majority from Hawaii, enlisted in the army. Some served as translators and interrogators in the Pacific; most were combat soldiers in Europe.

About 1,700 pro-Nazi Caucasians were arrested; 10,000 German alien residents and a few Italians were interned.

The Germans were, in fact, released as much as a year after the Japanese internment was ended. Most Japanese internees were home or, at least, released in 1944, the last of them early in 1945. By then no one high in the government was justifying the program; most officials regarded it as a bad policy best not mentioned. Interestingly, ex-internees did not like to discuss their experiences. They regarded internment as a personal humiliation they pretended never happened.

DEFEATING GERMANY FIRST

Even before Midway ended Japan's offensive capacities, President Roosevelt and his advisers concluded that, in the words of George Marshall, the head of the Joint Chiefs of Staff, "Germany is still the prime enemy and her defeat is the key to victory. Once Germany is defeated, the collapse of Italy and the defeat of Japan must follow." The reasoning was sound. Japan could not conceivably win its war. Nazi Germany, if entrenched in Fortress Europe, could. Japan did not threaten the Western Hemisphere. The Nazis had ideological bedmates in several South American dictators, and there were large German populations in Brazil, Uruguay, and Argentina. Except for a few months early in 1942, most resources were devoted to the European theater of operations; just 15 percent (later 30 percent) of men and materiel went to the Pacific.

FRICTION AMONG THE ALLIES

Roosevelt and British Prime Minister Churchill sometimes disagreed, but the two men were bound together by affection, admiration, and wary trust. Their relations with Soviet premier Stalin, however, were limited by suspicions that, on Stalin's part, had foundations but could brim over into paranoia. Churchill had been a staunch anti-Communist throughout his long career and did not pretend that the Russian alliance was anything but a matter of expediency. He said that if Satan declared war on Germany, he would manage to say a kind word about the devil in Parliament.

Roosevelt, however, had never considered Communist rule in Russia as an American concern. Personally, he had a soft spot for Stalin. He believed he could allay the Russian's

The Comic Book War
Comic book superheroes, the greatest of whom was Superman, joined in the war against the Germans and Japanese. Among the patriotic volunteers were Captain Aeor, Batman, Green Mantle, Ajax, Captain America, Tarzan, and The Fighting Yank, whose motto was "No American can be forced into evil." It was never explained why, with such warriors battling away in every issue, particularly Superman, who was capable of reversing the rotation of the earth, the war was not concluded in the spring of 1942.

The Sherman Tank
By 1943 most American weapons were superior to their German and Japanese equivalents. One exception was the Sherman tank. It was slower than the German Tiger tank, its cannon had considerably less range, and its armor was inferior. Nevertheless, Sherman tanks won most of their battles. The difference was numbers. Germany was able to build 8,000 tanks during the war, the United States 50,000. The Sherman's relative weaknesses were known before it went into production. The army opted for mass production rather than better and more expensive tanks that took longer to build.

suspicions that he and Churchill wanted to sit out the ground war while Germany and the Soviet Union destroyed one another.

To hinder the German onslaught in Russia, the U.S. Army Air Corps (the forerunner of the Air Force) joined the British in nearly constant day and night bombing raids over Germany. Eventually 2.7 million tons of bombs would level German cities. On an impulse explicable only by Roosevelt's sensitivity to Stalin's fears—because it was utterly out of the question—FDR told Stalin that before 1942 was out, the British and Americans would open a second front in the west, easing the pressure on the Soviets. The best the two western Allies could do to honor his pledge was an attack on German and Italian forces in North Africa. It was not a front that meant enough to Hitler to weaken his army in Russia.

THE AFRICAN CAMPAIGN AND STALINGRAD

The British and Anzacs (Australians and New Zealanders) had been fighting a seesaw stalemate in Libya and Egypt with Italian troops and German Field Marshal Erwin Rommel's *Afrika Korps* since the beginning of the war. In mid-1942 the Germans and Italians had the upper hand, holding a line not far from Alexandria and thus threatening the Suez Canal, Britain's link with India.

In October, under the command of British General Bernard Montgomery, their arsenal beefed up by Sherman tanks from the United States, the British launched a counterattack at El Alamein. Montgomery sent the Germans reeling, and in November 1942, as Montgomery advanced from the east, Americans commanded by General Dwight D. Eisenhower landed far to the west in French North Africa.

Making a deal with French generals bound by treaty to do Hitler's bidding, Eisenhower moved eastward. At Kasserine Pass in February 1943, American tank forces fought their first major land battle in the European theater. It was a stinging defeat, humiliating Eisenhower; but it only delayed the Americans, and they were soon reinforced. When Hitler recalled Rommel, Germany's best field commander, to Germany, the *Afrika Korps* crumbled before the better-supplied American and British troops.

Almost simultaneously, deep within the Soviet Union, the Russians won one of the war's two pivotal Allied victories. At Stalingrad (now Volgograd) they had stopped a German army assigned to seize oil fields in the Caucasus. Hitler made his worst military decision of the war when, overruling his generals, he ordered them to take and hold Stalingrad at all costs. Instead, the Germans were surrounded and unable to break out. At least 60,000 German soldiers had been killed when, reduced to 110,000 men in two small pockets with no airfield, General Friedrich Paulus, ignoring Hitler's orders to fight to the last man, surrendered. (In the last days, Hitler had promoted Paulus to field marshal, reminding him that no German field marshal had ever surrendered.) Only 5,000 of the 110,000 German prisoners survived Russian prisoner of war camps.

The battle of Stalingrad marked the end of Germany's offensive power on the eastern front. It was the turning point of the war. The disaster could have been avoided and the war with Russia at least prolonged had Hitler listened to his generals.

THE INVASION OF ITALY

In July 1943 an American, British, and Anzac force opened what they hoped would be a meaningful second front by invading Sicily. They overran the island in six weeks, and Americans got a colorful hero to crow about: the commander of the Third Army, General **George W. Patton,** who won the race across the island. Patton was a throwback, a warrior. He was a spit-and-polish commander; in Italy he ordered his men at the front to shave daily, wear neckties, and wash their jeeps. Oddly, his soldiers liked him because of his personal bravery and the coarse "blood and guts" language in which he rallied them (and because he was a winner—a superb commander of tanks).

When the Allied troops moved from Sicily into Italy proper, knocking the Italian army out of the war, Americans also got a dud general—perhaps the worst American field commander of the war (although somehow he survived a series of blunders that ended the rapid Allied advance and transformed the Italian front into a static front that sapped the morale of the troops). Mark Clark, commander of the Fifth Army, was a pretty good desk man but a disaster on the battlefield. He ordered the leveling, by bombardment, of an ancient mountain monastery, Monte Cassino, where German forces were holed up; the rubble he created improved their defenses. After a dramatically successful amphibious landing at Anzio north of Monte Cassino led by

Preserving a Virile Race
General Patton was always a little loony. On occasion his eccentricity left the charts. In the final months of the war he ordered all Medal of Honor and Distinguished Service Cross winners under his command to the rear. He feared they would try to outdo themselves and be killed: "In order to produce a virile race, such men should be kept alive."

G.I. Racketeers
In Naples, where supplies for American forces in Italy were landed, a third of the total, ranging from cigarettes and chocolate bars to trucks and tanks, was stolen by G.I. rings that sold the goods on the Italian black market and even in North Africa. One entire train vanished.

a subordinate, a cautious Clark kept the men within the beachhead; the Germans counterattacked and came close to capturing them. They held on, but another offensive opportunity had fizzled because of Clark. In June 1944, when the Germans abandoned Rome, Clark ignored orders to forget the city and engage the Germans while they were on the run; instead he staged a victory parade into Rome. Meanwhile, the Germans regrouped on the "Gothic Line," which held to the end of the war, grinding up Clark's men.

Oddly, General Eisenhower, now supreme commander in Europe, tolerated Clark's failures and appalling vanity. But when the valuable but not quite balanced Patton, visiting a hospital, slapped a shell-shocked G.I. and accused him of cowardice, Eisenhower relieved him of his command of the Seventh Army.

IKE

Eisenhower had no intention of losing Patton's services for the duration of the war, but the uproar at home was too great to ignore. The affable, smiling Ike was a politician and a diplomat, sensitive to public opinion and a master at smoothing over differences among headstrong associates and subordinates. George C. Marshall had recognized his talents when, in June 1942, he picked Eisenhower over 366 officers senior to him to take command of all Allied forces in Britain and oversee the planning and mobilization of men and resources for the invasion of Europe. (Eisenhower was a lowly major in 1941, a major general in 1942, lieutenant general two months later, and a full general in 1943!)

"**Operation Overlord**" was to be by far the greatest amphibious invasion in world history. Ike oversaw the assembling of 4,000 vessels, 11,000 aircraft, tens of thousands of motor vehicles and weapons of all sorts, and the training and billeting of 2 million soldiers. He supervised the complex plans. And possibly most difficult, he maintained superb relations with the British, who needed to be treated like equal partners and (less successfully—it was impossible) managed the head of the Free French forces, Charles De Gaulle. Eisenhower even had a working relationship with Soviet Marshal Georgi Zhukov, better than Roosevelt's with Stalin.

Eisenhower used the suspended Patton to deceive the Germans as to where the Allies would invade. He named him commander of an army stationed in southeastern England (far from the real jumping-off points of the D-Day forces) that did not exist except as mock-ups, visible from the air, of barracks, tanks, trucks, planes, and other components of an invasion force. The ruse worked; the Germans were better

Ike's Contingency Report

Knowing that he would have little free time on D-Day, on the evening before the assault, General Eisenhower scribbled out the following note to be dispatched to Washington in the event that the invasion of Normandy was a failure:

> Our landings in the Cherbourg-Havre area have failed to gain a satisfactory foothold and I have withdrawn the troops. My decision to attack at this time and place was based upon the best information available. The troops, the air corps and the navy did all that bravery and devotion to duty could do. If any blame or fault attaches to the attempt it is mine alone.

"Replacement"

British and German policy was to withdraw divisions that were drastically reduced by casualties, replacing them at the front with entirely new or refreshed divisions. The American army kept decimated divisions on the front line and replaced lost men with fresh recruits. Divisions that fought all the way from Normandy to Germany had a 100 percent replacement rate. Four divisions had a 200 percent replacement.

prepared for the invaders around Calais, where the English Channel is narrowest, than they were in Normandy. For the real fighting, Patton was given command of the genuine Third Army.

POLITICS AND STRATEGY

There were uneasy hours, but D-Day was a colossal success. In one day 175,000 soldiers were put ashore. By the end of June, there were 450,000 American, British, Canadian, Free French, and Polish troops in France, and 71,000 vehicles. The army charged across France and into Paris on August 25. By September they were in Belgium and across the German border. In three months the Allies had taken more territory than,

from a much closer base, the Allies of World War I had taken in more than three years.

The British and Americans disagreed about how to finish off the enemy. Field Marshall Montgomery wanted to concentrate Allied forces in a single mighty thrust into the heart of Germany. The plan had much to recommend it. However, Eisenhower tactfully rejected it for military and diplomatic reasons. He feared that a rapid Blitzkrieg advance on a narrow front would expose the Allies' flank and even its long supply line to a German counteroffensive that might surround the army. Ike preferred to exploit the Allies' overwhelming superiority in men and armaments by advancing slowly on a broad front extending from the North Sea to the border of Switzerland.

Also arguing against a rapid thrust into Germany was the fact that, now that he at last had a second front, Stalin was worried that the Allies planned to negotiate a separate peace with Germany from deep within the country and join

D-Day, the "Longest Day" of the war and by far the most important day for the Allies on the western front. Had the Germans repelled the invasion of Fortress Europe in 1944, it would have been at least a year before another landing anywhere on half the scale of D-Day could be attempted. The massive scale of the invasion— it remains the greatest amphibious attack in world history—is captured by this astounding photograph of just a few hundred yards of coastline, taken shortly after the landing.

Did FDR Prolong the War?

To reassure the pathologically suspicious Stalin that the United States would not betray him, President Roosevelt said that "unconditional surrender" was the only term on which he would end the war with Germany. Few of his military advisers approved of his position. Churchill tried to talk FDR out of making the statement. They argued that when the German military knew the war was lost, they would kill Hitler, suppress the Nazis, and negotiate a peace, saving hundreds of thousands of lives. If Roosevelt insisted on Germany's unconditional surrender, the German generals would have nothing to gain by seizing power. Roosevelt was forcing them to fight to the bitter end for a regime many top generals detested.

Ironically, Stalin was more than willing to betray Roosevelt and Churchill by negotiating a separate peace with Germany.

In July 1943 he had high-ranking German officers the Russians had captured broadcast to Germany that the Soviet Union did not wish to destroy Germany, only Hitler and the Nazis. This is what some German generals and admirals wanted to hear from FDR, but they neither trusted nor wanted to deal with the Communists. Stalin's attempt to inspire a military coup in Germany fell flat.

German troops in attacking the Red Army. A broad, slow advance would put Stalin's suspicions to rest. Eisenhower was himself concerned that unless an orderly rendezvous of Allied and Russian troops was arranged—which could be done only when German resistance had ended—there might be spontaneous fighting between the two armies.

As always, however, Eisenhower aimed to please. He consented to Montgomery's proposal that he command a miniversion of his strategy by making a dash into the Netherlands to capture the mouth of the Rhine River. Montgomery was defeated, less because his plan was faulty than because, atypical for him, he executed it poorly.

THE BATTLE OF THE BULGE AND THE END

Some historians suggest that Eisenhower gave Montgomery the go-ahead because he hoped the British general would fall on his face. (Neither man much liked the other.) If so, Eisenhower sustained his own setback and near-disaster in December 1944. Paused in their broad, slow advance and expecting no real action until spring, the American army in Belgium was hit with a German offensive far more powerful than Eisenhower believed the Germans were capable of.

The German goal was to split the broad front in two, surround the troops in the north, and capture the Belgian port of Antwerp, through which the Allies were receiving most of their supplies. The **Battle of the Bulge,** so-called because of the huge bulge the Germans pushed into American lines, came disturbingly close to succeeding. Snow and overcast prevented the Allies from bringing their control of the air into play. An entire division under General Anthony McAuliffe was surrounded at Bastogne. McAuliffe won his entry in quotation books by replying "Nuts!" when the Germans demanded he surrender. (An anonymous medic was the author

of a cleverer remark: "They've got us surrounded, the poor bastards.")

During two anxious weeks, Patton led the Third Army in a race from the south, whence he attacked the German flank. Then the weather cleared, permitting the planes to fly, and one by one, but regularly, German defenses collapsed.

The Soviets closed in on Berlin, and a Hitler close to a breakdown withdrew to a bunker under the Chancery in Berlin, where he presided over the disintegration of his "Thousand-Year Empire." To the end, he clung to the perverse Nazi romanticism. It was *Götterdämmerung*, the final battle of the Norse gods. The German people deserved their misery, he said, for letting their *Führer* down. On April 30, 1945, Hitler committed suicide after naming Admiral Karl Doenitz his successor as *Führer*. A few days later, Doenitz surrendered.

THE YALTA CONFERENCE

Eisenhower's sensitivity to Russian suspicions reflected President Roosevelt's policy. He had insisted on "unconditional surrender" because he thought it would reassure Stalin that the United States would fight to the end. At a meeting with Stalin at Teheran in Iran late in 1943, and again at Yalta in the Crimea in February 1945, FDR did his best to assuage the Russian dictator's fears by not unambivalently rejecting Stalin's suggestions about the organization of postwar Europe.

A few years later, when the Soviet Union was the Cold War enemy and Americans lamented Russian domination of Eastern Europe, Yalta became a byword for diplomatic blunder—even, to many, for a treasonous sellout to Communism. It was at Yalta that Roosevelt did not press Stalin for specifics when Stalin said that the Soviet Union had "special interests" in Eastern Europe.

Right-wing extremists said that FDR handed the Poles, Czechs, Hungarians, Rumanians, and Bulgarians over to Stalin because he was himself a Communist sympathizer. Rational critics of American diplomacy said that the president's weariness and illness, obvious in his haggard face and sagging jaw, affected his mental powers when he dealt with the coolly calculating Stalin. At the Yalta conference, quite privately, a British air marshall had remarked, "His brain is

And Have You Heard the One About . . . ?

In the final days of the war, with tens of millions dead and Germany in ruins, an army officer accompanying Hitler joked about the sound of Russian artillery in the suburbs of Berlin that soon it would be possible to travel from the eastern front to the western front by trolley car. Hitler chuckled.

GERMAN OCCUPATION ZONES AT WAR'S END

BRITISH ZONE
Berlin
SOVIET ZONE
FRENCH ZONE
AMERICAN ZONE

0 200 400 Miles
0 200 400 Kilometers

ICELAND

NORWAY
Oslo
SWEDEN
Stockholm
FINLAND
Helsinki
Leningrad

North Sea

DENMARK
See Inset
Copenhagen

Baltic Sea

Dublin
IRELAND
UNITED KINGDOM
London

NETH.
Amsterdam
GERMANY
Berlin

13 German surrender Reims, May 7, 1945

BELGIUM
Brussels
LUX.
Reims
Paris
FRANCE

Invasion of Normandy, June 6, 1944 — 7

ATLANTIC OCEAN

Western front, June 1944 — 8

Berlin fell, May 2, 1945 — 12
Dresden
Prague

Battle of the Bulge, Dec. 1944–Jan. 1945 — 9
Berne
Vienna
VICHY FRANCE
SWITZ.

Western front, February 1945 — 10
Nice
ITALY
Marseilles

PORTUGAL
Lisbon
SPAIN
Madrid

GIBRALTAR (U.K.)

SP. MOROCCO
Port Lyautey
Oran
Algiers
ALGERIA

FR. MOROCCO

Surrender in Tunisia of Axis armies in Northern Africa, May 13, 1943 — 4

TUNISIA
Tunis
Sardinia
Corsica
Rome
Sicily

Italian front, February 1945 — 6
Naples
Salerno

Adriatic Sea

CROATIA
SERBIA
MONT.
ALBANIA
Tirana
GREECE
Athens

Aegean Sea

FRENCH NORTH AFRICA (Vichy France) Joined Allies November 1942

Tripoli

Mediterranean Sea

LIBYA (It.)

Malta (U.K.)
Crete (Gr.)
Rhodes (It.)
Cyprus (U.K.)

EGYPT
Cairo

Red Sea

UNION OF SOVIET SOCIALIST REPUBLICS

Tallinn
Riga
Kaunas
Moscow

Russian front, December 1941 — 1

Smolensk
Tula
Minsk
Pinsk

Russian front, February 1945 — 11

Battle of Stalingrad, August 1942–January 1943 — 3

Russian front, Spring 1944 — 5

Warsaw
GOV'T. GEN. OF POLAND
Kiev

Stalingrad

Russian front, November 1942 — 2

SLOVAKIA
Budapest
HUNGARY

ROMANIA
Bucharest

Yalta

Black Sea

BULGARIA
Sofia

TURKEY
Ankara

SYRIA

LEBANON
Beirut
Damascus

PALESTINE (BR. MANDATE)
Jerusalem
Amman
TRANS-JORDAN (BR. MANDATE)

Legend:
- Axis powers and satellites
- Farthest extent of Axis control
- Allied and Allied-controlled nations
- Neutral nations
- Advancing Western fronts
- Advancing Eastern fronts
- ✸ Major battles

MAP 44:2 Allied Advances in Europe and Africa

The destruction of a 500,000-man German army at Stalingrad and the successful American, British, and Canadian invasion of Normandy were the battles that determined the defeat of Nazi Germany. With the exception of a setback at the Battle of the Bulge, an unanticipated German counteroffensive late in 1944, the war against Germany after Stalingrad and Normandy was a war of slow but steady attrition and advance.

Churchill, Roosevelt, and Stalin at the Yalta Conference. Stalin was older than FDR, Churchill eight years older. That anyone who saw the age, weariness, and illness in Roosevelt's face should have been shocked when, two months later, he was dead—least of all those who met with him regularly—is a lesson in the infinite human capacity for wishful thinking.

obviously not what it was . . . [he] is completely unable to think hard about anything."

Plausible as that may have been, Roosevelt at his best could not have done much at Yalta to affect Stalin's intentions. He did not give Stalin anything that he did not already have. By February 1945 the Red Army occupied the Eastern European countries that Stalin insisted must have governments "friendly" to the Soviet Union. No doubt Churchill and FDR expected Poland and other Eastern Europe countries to have greater independence than they were to have. Historians still disagree as to whether Stalin was set on completely dominating the region in 1945 or made the decision

to eliminate all opposition to Russian rule only two years later, when the Cold War was well under way.

THE TWILIGHT OF JAPAN, THE NUCLEAR DAWN

Also on Roosevelt's mind at Yalta was his desire to enlist the Soviet Union in the war against Japan in order to save American lives in the final battles. While agreeing that the Red Army would attack Japanese forces in China, Stalin insisted on delaying any action until August 1945.

Amphibious Landing

"Tarawa was not a very big battle, as battles go," wrote G. D. Lillibridge, who was a second lieutenant there in November 1943, "and it was all over in seventy-two hours." The casualties were only 3,300 marines, about the same number of Japanese soldiers, and 2,000 Japanese and Korean laborers who doubled as soldiers.

"Bloody Tarawa" was nevertheless a pivotal battle. If the totals were small by World War II standards, the incidence of casualties was shocking. Lillibridge's 39-man platoon lost 26; 323 of 500 drivers of landing craft died; overall, more than a third of the Americans involved were killed or wounded. The figures stunned the admirals who planned the battle. Tarawa was their introduction to the fanaticism of the Japanese soldier. Only seventeen Japanese on the tiny atoll of Betio were captured, most because they were too seriously wounded to commit suicide.

This willingness to die for a code of honor incomprehensible to Americans was not something that could be taught in a training film. It was bred into Japan's young men from infancy. In his reflections on the battle, Lillibridge remembered a Japanese his platoon had trapped. Another Japanese marine was moaning in agony from his wounds. The defender would reassure his dying friend, then hurl challenges and insults at Lillibridge's platoon, then comfort his buddy again.

Betio was two miles long and 800 yards wide—half the size of New York's Central Park. The Japanese airstrip there was the chief objective of the American assault. Japanese planes based in Tarawa had been harassing American

supply lines between Hawaii and Australia. Tarawa was also an experiment. Admirals Chester W. Nimitz and Raymond Spruance wanted to test their theories of amphibious assault on a small, lightly manned island before what they knew would be far more difficult fighting in the Marshall Islands. "There had to be a Tarawa, a first assault on a strongly defended coral atoll," an American officer explained.

Amphibious assault against an entrenched enemy was a new kind of fighting for the American military. Still, they thought that Tarawa would be easy. They had no illusions about the fierceness of Japanese soldiers, but they not had much time to dig in. The American assault force was overwhelming, covering eight square miles of Pacific. The naval bombardment itself would "obliterate the defenses." Lieutenant Lillibridge told his platoon that "there was no need to worry, no necessity for anyone to get killed, although possibly someone might get slightly wounded."

The predawn bombardment did destroy Rear Admiral Keiji Shibasaki's communications. However, the network of concrete blockhouses, coconut-log pillboxes, and underwater barricades was hardly touched by the big guns and bombs. Nature was a Japanese ally. The tide was lower than expected, so the larger American landing crafts could not clear the reef that fringed Betio. All but the first wave of marines had to wade, breast deep, 800 yards to shore.

This was an element of amphibious attack in the Pacific that was painfully tested at Tarawa. Could men

PACIFIC STRATEGY

After Midway in June 1942, the United States aided the Chinese by flying supplies from British India "over the hump" of the Himalayas. The Kuomintang troops under Chiang Kai-shek and Communist soldiers commanded by Mao Zedong tied down a million strong Japanese army. But they were more hostile toward one another than toward their common enemy. The Japanese, Chiang Kai-shek said, were "a disease of the skin"; the Chinese Communists were a "disease of the heart."

The American forces in the Pacific were divided into two distinct commands. After the conquest of the Solomon Islands, which were vital to Australia's security, troops under Douglas MacArthur pushed toward Japan via New Guinea and the Philippines. MacArthur was a bizarre man who often acted as if he were the immortal he posed as being. He exposed himself foolishly to Japanese fire until his aides physically restrained him. He ordered his men to take antimalaria drugs but refused to take them himself. But he was a superb commander. He planned and executed eighty-seven amphibious landings, all successful. Few generals worked so hard to minimize their men's casualties as he did.

The second American advance on Japan, through the central Pacific, was commanded by Admiral Chester W. Nimitz. MacArthur's goal was personal: he wanted to liberate the Philippines to redeem his promise of 1942, regardless of the fact that his superiors had concluded (sensibly) that the Philippines should be bypassed. Nimitz's goal was to island-hop near enough to Japan that big American bombers, which had to be based on land, could bomb the country into submission.

ISLAND WARFARE

To soldiers slogging through the mud and cold of Europe, the troops in the Pacific were on a holiday, basking in a balmy climate and only after long intervals of relaxation meeting the enemy in battle. Life behind the lines in the Pacific could be pleasant, but it could be miserable, too. "Our war was waiting," novelist James Michener wrote. "You rotted on New Caledonia waiting for Guadalcanal. Then you sweated twenty pounds away in Guadal waiting for Bougainville. . . . And pretty soon you hated the man next to you, and you dreaded the look of a coconut tree."

with no more armor than "a khaki shirt" and no way to defend themselves even get to the beach, let alone establish enough of a base from which to displace an enemy who, during these same critical minutes, freely wreaked havoc?

Wading to the beach was the first horror that would haunt the survivors of Tarawa and subsequent Pacific landings for the rest of their lives. Men remembered it as a "nightmarish turtle race" run in slow motion. It was "like being completely suspended, like being under a strong anesthetic." "I could have sworn that I could have reached out and touched a hundred bullets." "The water never seemed clear of tiny men." They had to push through the floating corpses of their comrades and hundreds of thousands of fish dead from the bombardment. The still lagoon remained red with blood all day.

The second nightmare waited on the beach. Shibasaki had constructed a sea wall of coconut logs, three to five feet high. To the Americans, it looked like shelter. In fact, Japanese mortars had been registered and tested to batter the long thin line precisely. To peek above the log palisades was to draw the fire of 200 well-positioned Japanese machine guns. Marines remembered that they were capable of moving beyond the sea wall only because to remain there meant certain death. About half the American casualties were suffered in the water, most of the rest on the beach.

One by one, almost always at close quarters, the blockhouses and pillboxes were destroyed, but it took three days to secure the tiny island. The aftermath was almost as devastating to morale as the unexpected difficulties of the battle. The vegetation that had covered the island was almost entirely gone. Thousands of corpses floating in the surf and festering in the blockhouses bloated and rotted in the intense heat. The triumphant marines looked like anything but victors. They sat staring, exhausted. "I passed boys who . . . looked older than their fathers," General Holland Smith said. "It had chilled their souls. They found it hard to believe they were actually alive."

Smith and the other commanders learned from the "training exercise" at Tarawa that one did not gamble on tides over coral reefs. Not until the last months of the Pacific war, when the close approach to the Japanese homeland made much larger forces of Japanese defenders even fiercer in their resistance, would the extremity of Tarawa's terror be repeated.

The Pacific commanders also learned that while the vast American superiority of armament and firepower was essential and ultimately decisive, taking a Pacific island was a much more personal and human effort than twentieth-century military men had assumed. With a grace rare in a modern officer, General Julian Smith frankly asserted, "There was one thing that won this battle . . . and that was the supreme courage of the Marines. The [Japanese] prisoners tell us that what broke their morale was not the bombing, not the naval gunfire, but the sight of Marines who kept coming ashore."

But in Nimitz's theater of operations, capturing islands that were specks on the map meant battles more vicious than any in Europe: "a blinding flash . . . a day of horror . . . an evening of terror." Japanese soldiers were more frightening enemies than Germans. They were indoctrinated with the belief that it was a betrayal of national and personal honor to surrender under any circumstances.

A TERRIFYING ENEMY

To an astonishing extent, they did fight to the death, taking American marines and soldiers with them long after it was obvious the battle was won. It took the Americans six months to win control of microscopic Guadalcanal in the Solomons,

Language Lessons

Much fighting in the Pacific was at close quarters. So Japanese soldiers were taught a little English so they could shout at the Americans. Two of the language lessons were "Surrender, all is resistless" and "FDR eat shit."

even though the defenders did not have time to complete their fortifications. At Tarawa in the Gilbert Islands, only 17 of 5,000 Japanese were captured alive. In the Marshall Islands 79 of 5,000 survived the battle. Of 35,000 Japanese on Saipan, including civilians, all but 1,000 fought to the death or committed suicide. On the Alaskan island of Attu, which the Japanese occupied much of the war, only 27 soldiers were captured; 2,700 committed suicide when they could fight no more.

The deadliness of fighting Japanese led to American brutalities that were rare in Italy and France, where soldiers surrendered when their situation was hopeless in the Pacific. And American public opinion was indifferent to reports of American atrocities. Eisenhower had to cashier Patton because of the uproar when he slapped a soldier. Newspaper editors applauded reports of American sailors machine-gunning Japanese sailors treading water in the ocean after their ship had been sunk.

American atrocities in the Pacific war are commonly attributed to racism. Evidence indicates that it was largely cultural in motivation, the consequence of a Japanese view of the soldier's duty that was incomprehensible to Americans and

U.S. Navy Photo in the National Archives

Soldiers who made it to the beach in an amphibious landing on a Pacific island. Many were killed in the surf, but the worst was not behind these men. Japanese fortifications were designed so that their maximum firepower could be trained on the beaches, and few Japanese soldiers surrendered. Many of their defensive positions had to be taken in costly face-to-face fighting.

the cause of many casualties American troops saw as unnecessary. Vicious treatment of the Japanese became common only after several years of fighting soldiers who fought on and killed until they were killed. After the war, when American troops occupied Japan, their behavior was generally exemplary, and many soldiers quickly became quite fond of the Japanese.

FIGHTING TO THE LAST MAN

By the spring of 1945, Japan's situation was hopeless. America's war with Germany was over. When the fall of Saipan in November 1944 provided a base from which bombers could reach Japan, the country's wooden cities burned up like tinder when hit by incendiary bombs. A single raid on Tokyo on March 9, 1945, killed 85,000 people and destroyed 250,000 buildings.

After the huge Battle of Leyte Gulf in October 1944 (which involved 282 warships, more than at the Battle of Jutland in World War I), the Japanese navy, for practical purposes, ceased to exist while the Americans cruised the seas with 4,000 vessels,

shelling the Japanese coast at will. U.S. submarines destroyed half of Japan's merchant fleet within a few months.

When the United States invaded Okinawa in April 1945, Japanese air power was reduced to little more than kamikaze suicide pilots flying slapped-together planes packed with high explosives. They did terrific damage. At

Glorious Victory

Just before the American invasion of the Philippines, Japanese Admiral Shigeru Fukudane, whose task force was in fact devastated, reported to Tokyo that he had sunk eleven American carriers, two battleships, and various other warships. Emperor Hirohito declared a national holiday.

In fact, the U.S. navy lost no ships to Fukudane. Admiral William "Bull" Halsey released a statement: "The Third Fleet's sunken and damaged ships have been salvaged and are retiring at high speed toward the enemy."

Navajo Code Talkers

About 400 Navajo Indians served with the marines in the Pacific in a unique capacity. In combat, the "code talkers" handled radio communications between units by speaking in a code in the Navajo language. Navajo was an unwritten language with unique linguistic rules and subtle inflections essential to correct understanding. The code talkers confounded the Japanese who intercepted the messages. They correctly deduced that they were dealing with a Native American language, but they did not come close to cracking the code. It was widely believed, but probably not true, that each code talker was assigned a non-Navajo buddy whose orders were to shoot him if they were in danger of being captured. Other Native American tribes performed the same function in Europe.

Okinawa they sunk 36 ships (more than were sunk at Pearl Harbor) and damaged 300. The Japanese turned the biggest battleship in the world, the *Yamato,* into a kamikaze. With 2,300 sailors aboard, the *Yamato* steamed for Okinawa on April 6, 1945, with just enough fuel for a one-way trip. It never got there. Attacked by 400 carrier-based planes, the great ship was hit by at least ten torpedoes and twenty-one bombs and sank.

And yet, the closer the Americans got to the Japanese homeland, the more fanatically the Japanese fought. Taking Iwo Jima, a volcanic island wanted for a landing strip, cost 28,000 American lives. In almost three months on Okinawa, 80,000 Americans were killed or wounded. More than 100,000 Japanese were killed; only 8,000 surrendered. (Around 100,000 civilians may have committed suicide.)

The military estimated that the invasion of Japan, scheduled for November 1, 1945, would cost 1 million casualties, as many as the United States had suffered in more than three years in both Europe and the Pacific. The Japanese still had 5 million men under arms.

A DEATH AND A BIRTH

This chilling prospect put the atomic bomb, conceived as a weapon to be used against now-defeated Nazi Germany, on the table in the Pacific theater. The **Manhattan Project,** code name for the program that secretly developed the first nuclear weapon, dated to 1939 when Albert Einstein, a refugee from Naziism, wrote in longhand to President Roosevelt that it was possible to unleash inconceivable amounts of energy

U.S. Army Photo

Hiroshima: what a single bomb did.

Was the Bomb Necessary?

At first there was only wonder that two bombs could destroy two cities. Within a year, however, when novelist John Hersey detailed the horrors the people of Hiroshima suffered, some Americans began openly to question if dropping the atomic bombs had been necessary, as President Truman insisted, to avoid a million American casualties (and several million Japanese casualties) that the planned invasion of Japan would mean.

Could not the Japanese have been persuaded to surrender, critics asked, by demonstrating the power of the bomb on an uninhabited island as Secretary of War Stimson had proposed to the president? Truman's defenders replied that no one was sure that the bombs would work. An announced demonstration that fizzled would have encouraged Japanese diehards, who were numerous and influential, to hold on.

Decades later, historians (known as *revisionists*) said that "Little Boy" and "Fat Man" were dropped not primarily to end the war with Japan but to inaugurate the Cold War with the Soviet Union. Truman cynically slaughtered the people of Nagasaki and Hiroshima to put the Russians on notice that the United States held the trump card in any armed conflict between the wartime allies. Critics argued that there was no hard evidence that Truman's anti-Soviet sentiments, which were strong enough, had anything to do with his decision to use the atomic bombs. The simplest explanation of the event—he did it to end the war quickly—was the correct explanation.

The debate has not ended.

by nuclear fission, splitting an atom. Einstein was a pacifist, but he was aware that German scientists were interested in and capable of producing a nuclear bomb. Such a device in Hitler's hands first was an appalling prospect.

Einstein was too prestigious to ignore, and the government secretly allotted $2 billion to the Manhattan Project. Under the direction of J. Robert Oppenheimer, scientists worked on Long Island, underneath a football stadium in Chicago, and at isolated Los Alamos, New Mexico. In April 1945 they told Washington that they were four months away from testing a bomb. At one point the Manhattan Project was consuming one-seventh of the electricity generated in the United States.

The decision of whether to use the bomb against Japan did not fall to President Roosevelt. Reelected to a fourth term in 1944 over Governor Thomas E. Dewey of New York, Roosevelt died of a stroke on April 12, 1945. He was at Warm Springs, Georgia, sitting for a portrait painter when he said, "I have a terrific headache," and slumped in his chair.

The outpouring of grief that swept the nation at the loss of the man who was in office longer than any other president was real and profound. Silent crowds lined the tracks to watch the train that brought FDR back to Washington for the last time. People wept in the streets. But in Washington the sorrow was overshadowed by apprehension that his successor, Harry S Truman, was not up to his job.

TRUMAN, "LITTLE BOY," AND "FAT MAN"

Truman was an honest politico who rose as a dependable, hard worker in the not-so-honest Kansas City Democratic machine. He proved his abilities as chairman of an important Senate committee during the war, but impressed few as the caliber of person to head a nation. Unprepossessing in appearance, bespectacled, a dandy (he once operated a haberdashery), and given to salty language, Truman was nominated as vice president in 1944 as a compromise candidate. Democratic conservatives wanted the left-liberal vice president, Henry A. Wallace, out of the number two spot, but they could not force southerner James J. Byrnes on the party's liberal wing. Harry Truman was a compromise candidate.

Although FDR was obviously in bad health, Truman was shocked to learn he was president. "I don't know whether you fellows ever had a load of hay or a bull fall on you," he told reporters on his first day in office, "but last night the moon, the stars, and all the planets fell on me." If he too was unsure of his abilities, Truman did not shy from difficult decisions and never doubted his responsibility. A plaque on his desk read "The Buck Stops Here"; as president, he could not "pass the buck" to anyone else.

When advisers informed him that the alternative to using the atomic bomb was a million American casualties, he did not hesitate to give the order to use it. On August 6, a bomb nicknamed "Little Boy" was dropped on Hiroshima, killing 100,000 people in an instant and dooming another 100,000 to death from injury and radiation poisoning. Two days later, a bomb of different design, "Fat Man," was exploded over Nagasaki with the same results.

Incredibly, some in the Japanese high command wanted to fight on. Had they known that the Americans had no more atomic bombs in their arsenal, they might have carried the debate. But Emperor Hirohito stepped in and agreed to surrender on August 15, 1945, if he could remain emperor. The United States agreed. The war ended officially on the decks of the battleship *Missouri* on September 2.

FURTHER READING

General Michael C. Adams, *The Best War Ever: America and World War II*, 1994; William L. O'Neill, *A Democracy at War: Americans Fight at Home and Abroad in World War II*, 1993; Ronald Takaki, *A Multicultural History of America in World War II*, 2000; Gerhard L. Weinberg, *A World at Arms: A Global History of World War II*, 1994; H. P. Willmott, *The Great Crusade: A New Complete History of the Second World War*, 1990.

The Atomic Bomb Gar Alperovitz, *The Decision to Use the Atomic Bomb*, 1995; Paul Boyer, *By the Bomb's Early Light*, 1985; John H.

Dower, *Embracing Defeat: Japan in the Wake of World War II*, 1990; Greg Herken, *The Winning Weapon*, 1980; Richard Rhodes, *The Making of the Atomic Bomb*, 1986; Martin Sherwin, *A World Destroyed*, 1975; J. Samuel Walker, *Prompt and Utter Destruction: Truman and the Use of the Atomic Bomb against Japan*, 1997.

Battles and Soldiers Stephen Ambrose, *D-Day: June 6, 1944: The Climactic Battle of World War II*, 1994, and *Band of Brothers: E Company, 506th Regiment, 101st Airborne from Normandy to Hitler's Eagle's Nest*, 2001; Tom Brokaw, *The Greatest Generation*, 2001; Don Davis, *Lightning Strike: The Secret Mission to Kill Admiral Yamamoto and Avenge Pearl Harbor*, 2005; John Dower, *War without Mercy: Race and Power in the Pacific War*, 1986; Kennett Lee, *G.I.: The American Soldier in World War II*, 1997; Gerald F. Linderman, *The World within War: America's Combat Experience in World War II*, 1997; Studs Terkel, *The Good War*, 1984; John Toland, *The Rising Sun: The Decline and Fall of the Japanese Empire*, 1970; Russell F. Weigley, *The American Way of War: A History of United States Military Strategy and Policy*, 1973, and *Eisenhower's Lieutenants: The Campaigns in France and Germany, 1944–1945*, 1981.

Commanders Stephen Ambrose, *The Supreme Commander: The War Years of General Dwight D. Eisenhower*, 1970; Michael Beschloss, *The Conquerors: Roosevelt, Truman, and the Destruction of Hitler's Germany, 1941–1945*, 2002; James MacGregor Burns, *Roosevelt: The Soldier of Freedom*, 1970; Ed Cray, *General of the Army: George L. Marshall, Soldier and Statesman*, 1990; David Eisenhower, *Eisenhower at War, 1943–1945*, 1986; Eric Larrabee, *Commander-in-Chief: Franklin Delano Roosevelt, His Lieutenants, and Their War*, 1987; William Manchester, *American Caesar: Douglas MacArthur*,

1880–1960, 1978; Gerhard L. Weinberg, *Visions of Victory: The Hopes of Eight World War II Leaders*, 2005.

Diplomacy and Politics Robert Beitzell, *The Uneasy Alliance: America, Britain, and Russia, 1941–1943*, 1972; Warren Cohen, *America's Response to China: A History of Sino–American Relations*, 2000; Robert Dallek, *Franklin D. Roosevelt and American Foreign Policy, 1932–1945*, 1979; Thomas Fleming, *The New Dealers War: FDR and the War within World War II*, 2001; Joseph P. Lash, *Roosevelt and Churchill*, 1976; Nelson Lichtenstein, *Labor's War at Home: The CIO in World War II*, 1983; Richard W. Steele, *Free Speech and the Good War*, 1999; Harold G. Vatter, *The U.S. Economy in World War II*, 1985.

The War at Home John M. Blum, *V for Victory: Politics and American Culture during World War II*, 1976; Stephanie Coontz, *The Way We Never Were: American Families and the Nostalgia Trap*, 1992; Roger Daniels, *Concentration Camps USA*, 1971, and *Prisoners without Trial*, 1993; Thomas P. Dougherty, *Projections of War: Hollywood, American Culture, and World War II*, 1993; Doris Kearns Goodwin, *No Ordinary Time*, 1994; Susan N. Hartmann, *The Home Front and Beyond: American Women in the 1940s*, 1982; Peter Irons, *Justice at War: The Story of the Japanese-American Internment Cases*, 1983; John W. Jeffries, *Wartime America: The World War II Home Front*, 1996; Clayton R. Koppoes and Gregory Black, *Hollywood Goes to War: How Politics, Profits, and Propaganda Shaped World War II Movies*, 1990; Robert R. Lingeman, *Don't You Know There's a War On?: The American Home Front, 1941–1945*, 1970; Gregg Robinson, *By Order of the President: FDR and the Internment of Japanese Americans*, 2001; William Tuttle, *Daddy's Gone to War*, 1993; Michi Weglyn, *Years of Infamy: The Untold Story of America's Concentration Camps*, 1976.

KEY TERMS

The following terms are covered in this chapter and can also be found in the list of Key Terms at the back of the book.

Bataan Death March	**Coral Sea**	**Manhattan Project**	**outer perimeter**
Battle of the Bulge	**George W. Patton**	**Operation Overlord**	

ONLINE SOURCES GUIDE

Use this listing to find online documents, images, interactive maps, simulations, and other resources related to this chapter:

American History Resource Center
http://history.wadsworth.com/rc/us

Selected Documents
Statement by the president of the United States, August 6, 1945

Selected Images
American troops wading ashore at Butaritari, November 1943
General Dwight Eisenhower meets with paratroopers before D-Day
D-Day invasion

Interactive Time Line (with online readings)
Fighting World War II: At the Pinnacle of Power, 1942–1945

CHAPTER 45

Cold War

The United States and the Nuclear Age 1946–1952

© Bettmann/Corbis

The release of atomic energy constitutes a new force too revolutionary to consider in the framework of old ideas.

Harry S Truman

Science has brought forth this danger, but the real problem is in the minds and hearts of men.

Albert Einstein

The world has achieved brilliance without wisdom, power without conscience. Ours is a world of nuclear giants and ethical infants.

Omar Bradley

Few wars have ended so abruptly as the war with Japan. On August 6, Emperor Hirohito was willing to have his ministers exhort his subjects to fight the Americans village to village, to be slaughtered by the hundreds of thousands and, perhaps, to kill themselves for him by the millions. On August 14, with some of his ministers still urging resistance, he commanded the Japanese to surrender.

And never was a new historical era so unmistakably proclaimed as by the fireballs over Hiroshima and Nagasaki. In 1945 the world had undergone a major passage and knew it.

THE SHADOW OF COLD WAR

The world had not left the past behind. History is legacy. The consequences of actions past live on whether or not people recognize the fact. Three legacies of the Second World War were so profound that they shaped the United States and the world for half a century, and are still with us.

LEGACIES

The first legacy of the Second World War was the powerful weapon that ended it. Nuclear bombs meant that it was

Margaret Bourke-White. LIFE Magazine © Time, Inc./Getty Images.

Nazi concentration camp inmates awaiting release by Allied troops in 1945. These men were slave laborers—the lucky ones because their lives had some value to the Nazis.

technologically possible for humanity to shatter civilization, perhaps even the natural balance of the earth.

A second legacy of the war was the recognition that human beings were morally capable of "pushing the button." This is not to say that President Truman's decision to use atomic bombs against Japan was reprehensible. Neither Truman nor his advisers understood the implications of human mastery of nuclear fission—to where Little Boy and Fat Man might lead. What revealed the depravity of which human beings are capable was the discovery of the Nazi death camps in the spring of 1945. Reliable evidence that the Nazis were systematically killing Jews and others had been in Allied hands for two years. But no one was prepared to learn that between 6 million and 7 million people were industrially murdered, their bodies industrially disposed of; nor to be confronted by the photographs of the walking skeletons of Auschwitz, and Buchenwald and the others, themselves not quite human anymore; nor for the photographs of the human garbage dumps, arms and legs protruding obscenely from hillocks of corpses that the Nazis had not had time to incinerate. These spectacles mocked every delusion before, during, and since that, at heart, people are good.

The third legacy of the war was that only two nations emerged genuine victors—the United States and the Soviet Union—and that, once the Nazis were defeated, they had little in common. For two years after the war, Russian and American leaders seemed to be trying to preserve the cooperation that had brought Germany down. Sixty years later, no one has definitively proved the sincerity or the deviousness of the motives and acts of the key leaders in either country in 1945, 1946, and 1947. No one has persuasively apportioned *blame* for starting the "Cold War." Almost the only thing about the postwar whirl of events that can be stated as historical fact is that by the end of 1947, the world's only two great military powers glowered at one another belligerently, stopping short only of World War III.

The great majority of Americans (although not all) believed that the ungrateful, treacherous, atheistic Russian Communists, bent on ruling the world, started the Cold War. Until September 1949 it was enough to be angry. The United States held the trump card: "the bomb." Then, in September 1949, years before American scientists said controlled nuclear fission was within the competence of Soviet science, Russia exploded an atomic bomb. The catastrophe for which the species had demonstrated its capacity was no longer in only American hands. In a nuclear war, Americans would be victims as well as executioners.

ROOTS OF ANIMOSITY

Perhaps Hitler should be blamed for the Cold War. American principles and revolutionary Communist ideology had never been compatible and never could be. The United States and the Soviet Union could never be "friends." American electoral democracy and dedication to individual liberty could not be reconciled with the "dictatorship of the proletariat" in Russia (the Communist party in practice) or with the subordination of individual freedoms to (depending on who was choosing the words) the good of the people as a whole or the power of the Communist party. The Communist commitment to fomenting revolution throughout the world was incompatible with the American belief that the world must embrace democracy and capitalism.

But the incompatibility of American and Soviet ideology did not necessarily mean inflexible hostility. Until Stalin seized control in the Soviet Union in the late 1920s, it was by no means certain that the Communist party would retain control of the ailing Soviet Union. The United States could wait, more or less passively, hoping the regime would crumble on its own. By 1933, when it was clear that Stalin's government was stable, the United States acknowledged the reality by extending diplomatic recognition to the Soviet Union

so that two of the most populous countries in the world could communicate with one another. Throughout the 1930s, despite Stalin's ruthless attempts to modernize the Soviet economy, Russia remained a backward country that did not threaten the United States in any way.

Hitler's invasion of the Soviet Union in 1941 created the conditions that made the Cold War possible. It energized the Soviet people in what Russians called the "Great Patriotic War." Soviet industrialization and massive American material aid transformed a country that had been a second-class "player" in international affairs into an industrial and military juggernaut second in might only to the United States. Hitler's war demoted Germany, Great Britain, and France—previously more than capable of restraining Russian ambitions in Europe—to ailing, impoverished nations struggling against further decline.

Hitler's war created the dangerous bipolar confrontation of great powers committed to incompatible ideologies.

IT STARTED IN EASTERN EUROPE

Exactly what Stalin had in mind in 1945 for postwar Europe cannot be known. He had, in the interests of the alliance, proclaimed an end to international revolution. His public statements and diplomatic demands late in the war (and after) were often uncongenial to the United States but, taken at face value, not beyond negotiation. President Roosevelt was confident he could continue to "work with" Stalin.

Just what Roosevelt believed was to be the status of the nations of Eastern Europe liberated from the Nazis is unknown. As a Wilsonian, he was committed to national self-determination and democratic governments in Poland, Czechoslovakia, Austria, Hungary, Rumania, Bulgaria, and Yugoslavia—nations World War I had revived or created. But he was aware that, except in Czechoslovakia, the democratic governments in every one of those countries had fallen to

Cold War 1945–1953

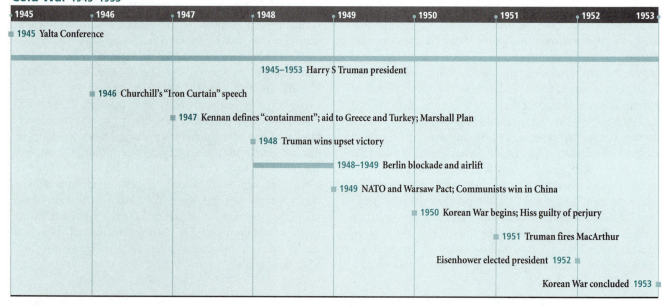

1945	1946	1947	1948	1949	1950	1951	1952	1953

1945 Yalta Conference

1945–1953 Harry S Truman president

1946 Churchill's "Iron Curtain" speech

1947 Kennan defines "containment"; aid to Greece and Turkey; Marshall Plan

1948 Truman wins upset victory

1948–1949 Berlin blockade and airlift

1949 NATO and Warsaw Pact; Communists win in China

1950 Korean War begins; Hiss guilty of perjury

1951 Truman fires MacArthur

Eisenhower elected president 1952

Korean War concluded 1953

more or less ruthless dictatorships quite on their own. It is less clear whether he appreciated that democracy and individual freedoms, as defined in the Atlantic Charter, were alien to Eastern European history and culture.

Certainly anyone as devious and manipulative as FDR understood that when Stalin said at Yalta that the nations bordering the Soviet Union must be "friendly," Stalin was not talking pieties. But how could a democratic Poland be "friendly" to Russia? The Nazis ruled Poland for 5 years; Russia had ruled the country, and not gently, for almost 150 years. Historically, Poles looked on Russia more than on Germany as the national enemy. The notion that the war against the Nazis had ushered in a new era in Russo–Polish relations was resoundingly discredited in 1943 when the Germans released evidence that the Red Army had massacred 5,000 Polish army officers at Katyn in 1940. Late in the war, with Russian troops advancing rapidly toward Warsaw, the Polish government-in-exile in London called for an uprising behind German lines. As soon as it started, Stalin abruptly halted the Russian advance so that the Germans could butcher the Polish partisans.

A democratic Poland could not be "friendly" to Russia. A Poland friendly to the Soviet Union would not be a democratic Poland. To a lesser degree, the same was true of Rumania, Hungary, and Czechoslovakia. And in 1945 the whole of Eastern Europe was occupied by the Red Army.

TRUMAN DRAWS A LINE

Whatever Roosevelt may have had in mind, it died with him. And Harry Truman was not the sly manipulator Roosevelt had been. As a man and as president, in Dean Acheson's words, Truman was "straightforward, decisive, simple, entirely honest." He neither liked nor trusted the Soviets, and he did not hide it. Even before he met Stalin at Potsdam, he summoned Soviet Ambassador V. M. Molotov to the White House and scolded him so harshly for beginning to set up puppet governments in Eastern Europe that Molotov exclaimed, "I have never been talked to like that in my life!" For a man who was close to the brutal, bullying Stalin, this was surely not the truth, but that Molotov said it indicates how hard-nosed Truman had been.

By 1946 it was obvious that the Russians were not going to permit free elections in Poland. Although Truman was

The G.I. Bill
The government was generous with the veterans of World War II. The "G.I. Bill of Rights" provided unprecedented educational opportunities. Of 14 million men and women eligible to attend college free under the G.I. Bill, 2.2 million actually did. Colleges and universities swelled. The University of Wisconsin had 9,000 students in 1945, 18,000 in 1946. Elite Stanford University went from 3,000 to 7,000 in the same year.

The G.I. Bill educated 22,000 dentists, 67,000 physicians, 91,000 scientists, 238,000 teachers, 240,000 accountants, and 450,000 engineers.

The 52–20 Club
Members of the 52–20 Club of 1945 and 1946 were demobilized soldiers and sailors who were allowed $20 a week for 52 weeks or until they found jobs. Although many were accused of avoiding work because of this payment, the average length of membership in the club was only three months.

restrained in official pronouncements, he applauded a speech by Winston Churchill in Fulton, Missouri, in March 1946, which Truman had read in advance. An "Iron Curtain" had descended across Europe, the former prime minister said, and it was time for the Western democracies to confront the Soviet Union. In September Truman himself signaled that, if a Cold War had not begun, the wartime alliance was dead. He dismissed Secretary of Commerce and former vice president Henry A. Wallace, the only member of his cabinet who called for the United States to be more accommodating with the Soviets.

CONTAINMENT AND THE TRUMAN DOCTRINE

In 1947 Truman's policy evolved beyond "getting tough with the Russians." In a long memorandum later published anonymously in the influential journal *Foreign Affairs*, a Soviet expert in the State Department, George F. Kennan, argued that Russian actions in Eastern Europe should not be understood in terms of Communist revolutionary zeal alone. Long before Communism, Russia had been pushing its frontiers—or trying to push them—to the west. The new wrinkle in Stalin's expansion was the Soviet conviction that the capitalist states of Western Europe were determined to destroy Communism.

It was impossible to come to a dependable accommodation with the Soviet Union as long as its leaders clung to this conviction. Only time, probably a long time, would alter the premises of Soviet foreign policy.

However, Kennan argued, Soviet territorial expansion could be halted without a war. The United States must make it unmistakably clear at what point Soviet expansion would not be tolerated: just where the Iron Curtain hung in 1947. The Russians, he predicted, would "test" American resolve to hold this line by limited aggression not sufficient to merit all-out war. Now that the Soviets had secure borders, however, if the United States responded in kind to Soviet probes, the Russians would back off. Soviet expansionism, in other words, could be "contained" without going to war.

Containment policy did not yet have its name—Kennan's essay had not yet been published—when Truman put it to work. The Soviet Union had stepped up its aid to Communist guerrillas in Greece and Turkey. On March 12 Truman asked Congress to appropriate $400 million in military assistance to the pro-Western governments of Greece and Turkey. It was more than enough for them to crush the

Learning from Past Mistakes

In a number of ways, FDR and Harry S Truman pointedly departed from American policy toward Europe after the First World War. In sponsoring the United Nations, the United States departed radically from the American boycott of the League of Nations. Unlike Woodrow Wilson, who named no prominent Republican to his peace commission at Versailles, thus contributing to American opposition to the League, Roosevelt made Republican Senator Arthur H. Vandenberg, a former isolationist, a member of the American delegation that wrote the Charter of the United Nations.

With the Marshall Plan, President Truman recognized the folly of the Coolidge administration of the 1920s in refusing to aid Europe economically by arranging for a significant modification of the flow of reparations from Germany and debt payments by Britain and France.

rebels, whom the Soviets, as Kennan predicted, promptly abandoned. Truman's policy of decisively supporting governments threatened by Communist rebels came to be known as the **Truman Doctrine.**

THE MARSHALL PLAN

The United States regarded France and Italy as at risk of Communist takeover too. The threat in those countries was not an armed revolutionary movement but Communist political parties with widespread popular support. In parliamentary elections, the Italian Communist party dependably won about 25 percent of the vote, the French party less.

Truman's advisers persuaded him that the French and Italian Communists were flourishing because they offered a plausible response to the widespread unemployment and poverty due to the war's destruction of the economies of the two countries and all of Europe. The remedy was to redistribute the dangerously disproportionate share of the world's wealth in American hands.

On June 5, 1947, Secretary of State George C. Marshall proposed that the United States spend huge sums to reconstruct Europe's national economies. Not only were former Allies and victims of German aggression invited to apply for assistance, but also defeated Germany (then divided into British, French, American, and Soviet zones of occupation), nations

Marshall's Plan

"The truth of the matter is that Europe's requirements for the next three or four years of foreign food and other essential products—principally from America—are so much greater than her present ability to pay that she must have substantial additional help, or face economic, social, and political deterioration of a very grave character."

neutral during the war such as Sweden and Switzerland, and even the Soviet Union and the nations behind Churchill's Iron Curtain.

Marshall and Truman calculated that Russia and the satellite states would reject the offer as a plot to destroy socialism. Stalin had made it clear as early as mid-1946 that the Soviet Union would tolerate no Western interference in its internal affairs (which, by mid-1947, meant the affairs of the Russian satellite nations too). He had turned down an international proposal by Bernard Baruch to outlaw nuclear weapons because the plan involved enforcement on the scene by the United Nations, which had been formed in 1945.

As anticipated, the Soviets condemned the **Marshall Plan,** and the Communist regimes in Eastern Europe, now including Czechoslovakia, did the same. The massive American financial and technical aid went to sixteen nations, both those with strong Communist political parties and countries where Communism was weak: Switzerland, the Netherlands, Ireland, Norway. Winston Churchill called the Marshall Plan "the most unsordid act in history." In fact, it was in American interests that Western Europe should prosper; but the Marshall Plan was, indeed, unique in its generosity.

FREEZING THE LINES

Containment worked. The Russian sphere of influence froze where it was when the Marshall Plan was introduced. But the Russians continued to test American resolve to hold the line. In June 1948, with a trumped-up explanation, Stalin blockaded the city of West Berlin, which was deep within Communist East Germany. Unable to provision the city of 2 million by train and truck, the United States seemed to have two options: give up West Berlin or invade East Germany.

Instead, a massive airlift was organized. For a year, huge C-47s and C-54s flew in the necessities and a few of the luxuries that the West Berliners needed to hold out. Day and night, planes flew into West Berlin, unloaded, and returned for a new load. It was an extraordinary operation that many experts thought was bound to fail. More than 250,000 flights carried 2 million tons of everything from candy bars to coal. The immensity of the operation and American tenacity in maintaining it made it clear to the Soviets that the United States did not want war, but the limits of Soviet expansion had been drawn. West Berlin was outside of them. The Soviets responded as Kennan predicted. Instead of shooting down the planes—an act of war—they watched. In May 1949 they lifted the blockade.

By then the Cold War had entered a new phase. In April 1949 the United States, Canada, and nine western European nations formed the North Atlantic Treaty Organization, a military alliance (the first, during peacetime, in American history). In September the Soviet Union responded with the Warsaw Pact, an alliance of the nations of Eastern Europe. In September 1949 the Soviet Union exploded its first atomic bomb, and soon thereafter the United States perfected the hydrogen bomb, a much more destructive weapon. The nuclear arms race was under way.

Berlin schoolchildren watch a C-54 landing the food they would eat and the clothes they would wear. The Berlin Airlift was a massive, finely integrated operation. Air Force mechanics changed 60,000 spark plugs on airlift planes every month.

© Bettmann/Corbis

DOMESTIC POLITICS UNDER TRUMAN

President Truman's foreign policy was decisive and, in Europe, successful. But he struggled with postwar domestic problems: rapid inflation, a serious housing shortage, and a series of bitter industrial disputes. At first he seemed to founder. He could not "command" Congress, as FDR had done for eight years. Indeed, led by the conservative senator from Ohio Robert A. Taft (son of President Taft), Congress began to defy the president.

1946: REPUBLICAN COMEBACK

The Republicans ran their 1946 congressional election campaign on an effective two-word slogan: "Had Enough?" The results seemed to say that voters had. They sent Republican majorities to both houses of Congress for the first time since 1928. A freshman Democratic senator who survived the landslide, J. William Fulbright of Arkansas, was so crestfallen he suggested that in the interests of a functional government, Truman resign in favor of a Republican successor. Truman

did not take the proposal well, and the Republicans did not take it seriously. They were, however, understandably confident that they would elect their nominee in 1948—Taft assumed it would be himself—and in the meantime they set out to dismantle as much of the New Deal as they could.

Their most striking success was the Taft–Hartley Labor–Management Relations Act of 1947. Enacted over Truman's veto, it repealed the government's tacit backing of the labor union movement. Taft–Hartley emphasized the rights of workers to refuse to join unions by abolishing the "closed shop." Under the Wagner Act of 1935, when a majority of a company's employees chose a union as their bargaining agent, all the company's employees were required to belong to that union as a condition of employment. Taft–Hartley made it illegal to dismiss employees who refused to join the union or to pay a fee equivalent to union dues.

Taft–Hartley was far from the "slave labor" law Truman called it. Nor did it cripple the union movement as some Republicans hoped. Its chief effect was to arouse organized labor, now more than 10 million strong, to rally behind Truman. This unexpected support (as a senator Truman had not been particularly friendly to organized labor) presented the president with an effective way of battling a Congress determined to embarrass him: embarrass Congress before the voters. He vetoed eighty anti–New Deal bills, converting himself into a crusading liberal. When Republican critics mocked his homey manners and common appearance, he denounced his enemies in Congress as stooges of the rich and privileged.

He coined his own two-word slogan: the "Fair Deal." He sent proposal after proposal expanding social services to Capitol Hill. Among his programs was a national health insurance plan such as most European nations had adopted. They were all rejected, of course, but Truman had cut a bumper crop of political hay. He stole the initiative from Taft and the big Republican majorities in Congress. He denounced the "no-good do-nothing Congress" that denied Americans sensible programs designed to improve their lives.

CIVIL RIGHTS

Truman, although a southerner by conviction, also took on the Democratic southern segregationists who voted with Republican conservatives more often than they voted with liberal northern and western Democrats. He sent Congress an antilynching bill that embarrassed Taft, who had never abandoned an old-fashioned Republican sympathy for African Americans but was now courting southern Democrats. The bill failed. Truman asked Congress to declare the poll tax illegal and to enact legislation to protect blacks who had gotten good factory jobs during the war. The Republican–southern Democrat coalition defeated both. To show he meant business—and that he, unlike Congress, was doing his job—he issued an executive order banning racial discrimination in the armed

forces, in the civil service, and in companies that did business with the government.

Truman did not attack Jim Crow segregation laws in the southern states. (Personally, he approved of them.) But he went much further in attacking the civil inequality of African Americans than Roosevelt had even entertained.

FOUR CANDIDATES

In the spring of 1948, Truman's popularity was on the upswing. His attacks on the "do-nothing" Congress swung many people to his side. Americans were getting accustomed to the president's hard-hitting style. Still, no political expert gave Truman a chance to survive the presidential election in November. The Democrats had been in power sixteen years, longer than any party since the Virginia dynasty of Jefferson, Madison, and Monroe. The inefficiency of many New Deal bureaucracies was blatant, and rumors of corruption were persistent.

Then, to turn worse into impossible, the Democratic party split three ways. Henry A. Wallace led left-wing liberals into the newly formed Progressive party. He claimed to be FDR's true heir and insisted that there was no reason to abandon the nation's wartime friendship with the Soviet Union. Democrats from the deep South, angry at Truman's civil rights bills and criticism of racial discrimination in the party platform written by the liberal mayor of Minneapolis, Hubert H. Humphrey, formed the States' Rights or "Dixiecrat" party. They named Strom Thurmond of South Carolina as their candidate. Thurmond was no Bilbo-like redneck; he condemned lynchings and had urged prosecution of white yahoos who attacked blacks violently. But he was an aggressive proponent of Jim Crow segregation.

Thurmond had no illusions that he could win the election. (Wallace, who had a mystical streak and the eternal left liberal delusion that Americans were progressive at heart, may have thought he could.) Thurmond hoped the electoral votes he won would be the ones that would have elected Truman, thus impressing on northern Democrats the necessity of acquiescing in the South's racial policies.

Presented with what looked like sure victory, the Republicans passed over their leading conservative, Senator Robert A. Taft of Ohio. Taft worried Republican moderates. His blanket opposition to New Deal reforms made him look like a man who wanted to turn the clock back to 1932 (or even 1913, when his father left the White House). His personality was peevish. Republican professionals calculated that if any candidate would send swing voters back to the Democrats, it was Taft. They nominated the colorless but safe Thomas E. Dewey, the party's candidate in 1944.

GIVE 'EM HELL, HARRY

Dewey's campaign strategy was to run a low-key, noncommittal campaign. Every poll showed him winning with ease. Therefore, as other sure winners had done since 1840, when William Henry Harrison's advisers told him to say nothing about anything, Dewey took no strong stands. A misstep

© UPI-Bettmann/Corbis

Harry S Truman displays the premature edition of the Chicago Tribune *announcing the results of the 1948 presidential election.*

could only alienate voters who were voting more against Truman than for Dewey.

Truman, facing defeat, did what candidates in his position must do—the opposite of Dewey. He pulled out the stops and campaigned hard, hoping that one or another of his Fair Deal proposals would touch a nerve or that his rambunctious style would excite voters. "Give 'em hell, Harry," a supporter shouted at a rally, and Truman did. In the spring he traveled 9,500 miles by train, delivering seventy-three speeches in eighteen states. During the summer of 1948 he called Congress into special session, and a corps of assistants led by Clark Clifford sent bill after bill to the Republican Congress. As the Republicans voted down his proposals, Truman went back on tour, totaling up 32,000 miles and 356 speeches. Did Americans want four years of such negativism under Thomas E. Dewey?

On election night, when only the states in the Eastern time zone had reported, Dewey had swept the Northeast, and partial returns showed him winning the entire Midwest. The editor of the passionately anti-Democratic Chicago *Tribune* decided to scoop the competition by declaring Dewey president in a banner headline. The next day Truman took

uncontained delight in posing for photographers with the newspaper. He had won. He squeaked out majorities in Illinois and Ohio, big states thought to be in Dewey's pocket,

Panpan Asobi

The American occupation forces in Japan tried 6,000 Japanese, mostly army and navy officers, for war crimes—primarily abuse of prisoners of war, toward whom Japanese soldiers were in fact vicious. Some 900 Japanese were executed. (The Soviets, who were at war with Japan for a week, may have executed 3,000.) But American soldiers, accustomed to Japanese combat soldiers fighting to the death and civilians on Okinawa choosing to jump from cliffs rather than fall into American hands, were astonished from their first days ashore by the deference and politeness and, in time, the affection of the Japanese people—not to mention their affection for the Japanese. During the war, a common children's game was kamikaze: boys put on headbands and pretended to crash planes into American ships. By the end of 1945 they were playing yamiichi gokko ("black market") and panpan asobi ("prostitute and customer").

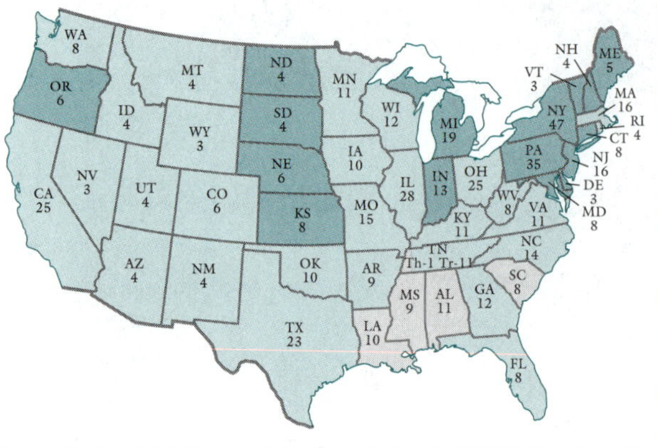

		Electoral Vote		Popular Vote	
		Number	%	Number	%
	Truman (Democrat)	303	57	24,105,812	49.9
	Dewey (Republican)	189	36	21,970,065	45.3
	Thurmond (States' Rights)	39	7	1,169,021	2.4
	Wallace (Progressive)	----	----	1,157,172	2.4

MAP 45:1 Presidential Election, 1948

Dewey's sweep of the Northeast and favorable early returns from the Midwest are why Republicans went to bed on election night believing they had won. By noon the next day, the final counts in Ohio and Illinois, which had looked to be Dewey states, gave Truman a swing of 100 electoral votes. And the late-reporting West was solidly Democratic. The election of 1948 was one of the greatest surprise upsets in the history of American presidential elections.

and swept the western states. The Dixiecrats were as stunned as the Republicans. Thurmond carried only four southern states, Truman the rest.

SUCCESS IN JAPAN, CONFLICT WITH CHINA

The Democrats won both houses of Congress too, but little more was heard of the Fair Deal. Like Wilson and FDR, Truman found his administration diverted from domestic concerns by a crisis abroad—not in Europe but in Asia.

In Asia only the Philippines and Japan were firm American allies. Granted independence in 1946, the Philippines were still beholden to American financial aid and responded with pliant friendship. In Japan a capitalist democracy was emerging slowly under an enlightened American military occupation and Marshall Plan–level financial aid. Douglas MacArthur, commanding the occupation forces, understood Japanese culture. He assumed the role of a *shogun*. (*Shoguns* were figures who, for much of Japanese history, were the real rulers of the country, while never molesting the sacred persons of the emperors.) He was as remote as Hirohito had been before the war. According to his logs, in five years he

spoke more than twice with only sixteen Japanese ministers. He did not socialize with Japanese; he whiled away his evenings watching Hollywood movies.

REJECTED OPTION

China was another story. Chiang Kai-shek's Nationalists and Mao Zedong's Communists remained at odds, and their armies fought sporadic battles. China hands in the State Department were at a loss as to what, if anything, the United States should do. They had been since early in the Second World War. The United States recognized Chiang's Nationalist regime as China's legitimate government, but until the Cold War, many high-ranking Americans denounced the Nationalists as at best ineffective, at worst hopelessly corrupt. General Joseph "Vinegar Joe" Stilwell had peppered Washington denunciations of Chiang's refusal to launch a meaningful attack on the Japanese. He advocated improving contacts with Mao's Communist forces, which, he said, were not hard-line Reds but peasants who had been exploited by Chiang's government.

After the war, as a special envoy to China, George C. Marshall concluded that Chinese Communist leaders were, indeed, Communists but not tools of the Soviet Union. He believed they could be encouraged to chart a course independent of Russia. Implicitly, in other words, containment policy should not be applied to China. Mao and Chou En-lai were not Russian agents. Other China experts advised the State Department that the Chinese Communists were amenable to cooperation with the United States.

THE CHINA LOBBY

The intensification of the Cold War in Europe helped damp any American inclinations to seek a rapprochement with the Chinese Communists. Kennan defined the conflict with the Soviet in terms of power politics. However, it was portrayed in movies and by most politicians as a struggle of ideologies. Although the Communist dictator of Yugoslavia, Josef Broz Tito, was as hostile to the Soviet Union as any nation, popular anti-Communism made improving relations with Yugoslavia impossible. Americans believed that all Communists were set on destroying their way of life.

Moreover, Chiang Kai-shek had powerful American friends, the **"China Lobby,"** organized and rallied by his brilliant and articulate wife, "Madame Chiang," who spent much of her time in the United States. The China Lobby was a network of conservative congressmen; influential religious leaders like the Catholic archbishop of New York, Francis Cardinal Spellman; the editors of many important newspapers; and one of the nation's most powerful molders of public opinion, Henry Luce, the publisher of *Time* and *Life* magazines (and the son of missionaries in China).

Through 1949, the China Lobby bombarded Americans with propaganda, most of it skewed, some of it false: most Chinese loved Chiang; Chiang was defeating Mao's forces on the battlefield; Mao followed Russian orders. The campaign was so effective that Americans were profoundly shocked at the end of the year when newspapers reported, out of the blue, that Chiang and what was left of his army had fled mainland China to the island province of Taiwan (then better known by its Portuguese/Japanese name, Formosa). How could this have happened to the Generalissimo? The China Lobby responded that the Chinese people had not repudiated Chiang. They and he had been betrayed by inadequate American support. The lobby demanded that aid be increased and that Chiang be "unleashed" for an assault on the mainland.

Truman and his new secretary of state, Dean Acheson, knew better than to unleash Chiang Kai-shek. He had proved his ineptitude in dealing with the Communists for twenty years. He needed massive American aid just to govern and defend Taiwan. To allow him to attack the Communist regime would involve the United States in a war on the Asian mainland that every American military strategist, most notably Douglas MacArthur, had said would be catastrophic.

AN UNEXPECTED WAR

Truman and Acheson applied the principle of containment to Red China despite the fact that Kennan had based his strategy on Russian history. But what were China's legitimate limits? Taiwan had been Chinese since antiquity. Chiang's Nationalists insisted that Taiwan was China, not an independent state. The United States had little choice but to support Chiang on the island, but to do so itself showed the irrelevance of containment policy in Asia. Historically, Tibet was a Chinese province, although the impoverished and isolated country had become effectively independent during the Chinese civil wars. Should the United States guarantee Tibet's borders? And what of Quemoy and Matsu, two tiny islands a few miles off the coast of China that were occupied by Chiang's Nationalists? What of the Republic of Korea, set up by the United States in the southern half of the Korean peninsula? A regime established by the Russians governed in the North. Koreans were ethnically distinct from the Chinese, and the country had been a Japanese colony for more than fifty years. But traditionally Korea had been subject to China, a tributary state. Was South Korea equivalent to the nations of Western Europe, off-limits to China as the Netherlands were off-limits to Russia?

Soldiers in Korea. They were America's "forgotten soldiers" even during the conflict. The object given them—simply to hold the line—was less than exhilarating. After the initial retreat, advance, and pullback, the war bogged down into a stalemate in rugged mountains.

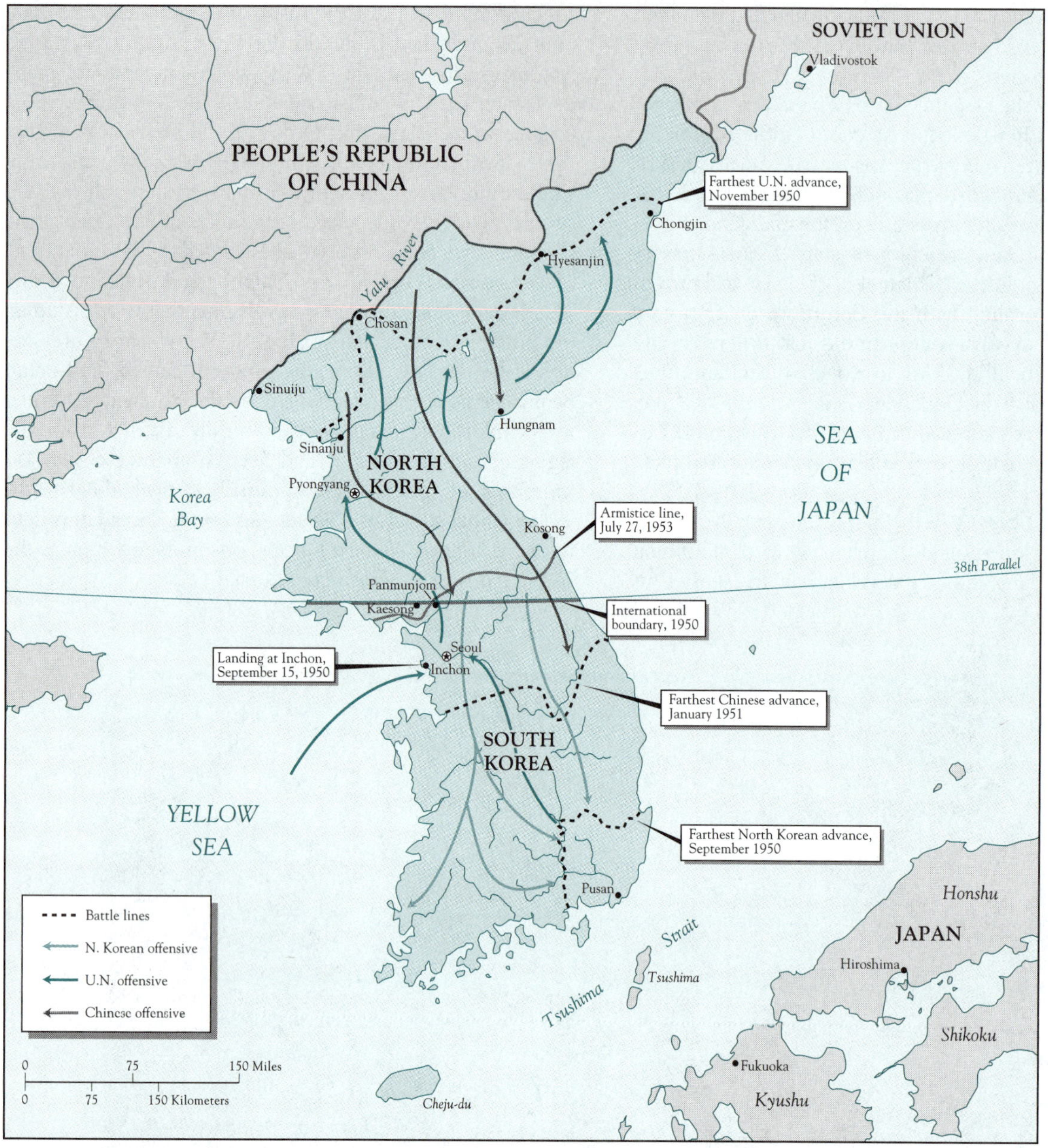

MAP 45:2 The Korean War
During the frantic last half of 1950 until 1953, newspapers regularly, sometimes daily, ran front-page maps of Korea to show the rapidly changing front line. Then the war bogged down in a stalemate.

The Korean question ceased to be academic in June 1950 when a North Korean army poured across the thirty-eighth parallel, which had been the line dividing the Russian and American occupation zones after World War II but was not recognized as a national boundary. The Russians were gone from North Korea in 1950, but they had trained and equipped the large North Korean military. The North Koreans rapidly drove the South Korean army and the American Eighth Army, still based in the country, to the toe of the peninsula.

THE KOREAN CONFLICT

There was an American fleet in Korean waters, so Truman could respond immediately. Because the Soviet delegate to the United Nations was absent, the United States was able to win UN approval of a "police action" to expel the North Korean troops from the South. With the United States providing almost all of the "police," General MacArthur took command.

The old soldier was to have one last day of glory. MacArthur engineered a daring amphibious landing at Inchon, deep behind North Korean lines. American troops cut off and captured 100,000 North Koreans. MacArthur took back all of South Korea in just two weeks.

The Americans and ROKs (soldiers of the Republic of Korea) surged northward, crossing the thirty-eighth parallel in September 1950. By October 26 they had occupied virtually the entire peninsula. One forward unit reached the banks of the Yalu River, the boundary between Korea and Chinese Manchuria.

MacArthur had instructions not to approach the Yalu lest the Chinese feel threatened; but his advance was so rapid that Truman had little time to reflect on MacArthur's confident assurance that the Chinese would not intervene. MacArthur was dead wrong. Perhaps confusing China Lobby propaganda with official American policy, the Chinese feared that the ease of the victory in Korea meant an advance into Manchuria was on the way. Twice before, Manchuria had been the avenue through which China had been invaded. Mao Zedong threw 200,000 "volunteers"—battle-tested regular army soldiers, actually—into the conflict, and by the end of 1950 they pushed MacArthur's army back to a line that zigzagged across the thirty-eighth parallel.

There, whether because the Chinese were willing to settle for a draw—a containment policy of their own—or because American troops found their footing and dug in, the war bogged down into a stalemate. For two years the Americans, ROKs, and token delegations of troops from other United Nations countries fought the North Koreans and Chinese over forlorn hills and ridges that did not even have names, only numbers given them by the military. Even after armistice talks began in a truce zone at Panmunjom, the war dragged on, meaninglessly chewing up lives.

The Chinese had protected their borders, and the Americans had ensured the independence of the Republic of Korea. But in the Cold War, with ideology taking on a religious significance on both sides, neither side knew quite how to end the war. Some days at Panmunjom, the negotiators simply sat at the table all day, saying nothing.

MACARTHUR'S COMEUPPANCE

With good reason, Americans were frustrated. Not five years after the Second World War, the Korean War put 5.7 million young men in uniform, killed 37,000 of them, and wounded 100,000. Defense expenditures soared from $40 billion in 1950 to $71 billion in 1952. Truman and Acheson said that the goal was containment; but having contained, they were unable to conclude hostilities. What was wrong?

Early in 1951 General MacArthur gave his explanation. Forgetting his own warning against a war with the Chinese on the Asian mainland, he told reporters that the only reason he had not won the war was that Truman would not permit him to bomb the enemy's supply depots in Manchuria. Later

© Bettmann/Corbis

New York City's traditional ticker tape parade for General MacArthur after his dismissal and retirement. For a month he was a national hero. Then he was forgotten.

MacArthur went further; he sent a letter to Republican Congressman Joseph W. Martin in which he wrote that "there is no substitute for victory" and assailed the commander-in-chief for accepting the stalemate. In April Martin went public with the letter.

Not even George McClellan had so blatantly challenged the president's constitutional authority as commander-in-chief. Truman's military advisers were appalled, and on April 11, with the support of the Joint Chiefs of Staff, the president fired MacArthur. Americans—what seemed a large majority of them—were shocked. They knew MacArthur the brilliant commander of the war against Japan. They knew little of MacArthur's history of insubordination; his superiors, from Herbert Hoover to George C. Marshall, had let every incident pass. They did not know that twice between 1945 and 1951, Truman had effectively ordered MacArthur to come to the United States for discussions (and honors) and MacArthur refused. It was easy to reckon that the great general knew better how to fight the Chinese than Harry Truman did. Returning home a retiree, the general was feted with ticker tape parades and cheered by Congress (a Democratic Congress) after a speech heard on the radio by more people than had tuned in to Truman's inaugural address in 1949.

MacArthur concluded his speech by quoting a line from an old barracks song: "Old soldiers never die; they just fade away." He had no intention of fading. Establishing his residence and command center at New York's Waldorf–Astoria Hotel,

Bureaucratic Misrepresentation

Before 2000, the official death count for the Korean War was 52,246. That number was carved on the Korea Memorial. In June 2000 it was revealed that the bureaucracy had included all deaths in the military during those years, from all causes and no matter where they occurred, in the total. Of 20,617 deaths of military personnel off the battlefield, only 3,275 occurred in Korea. The corrected total of Korean War deaths is 36,940.

The Negro Leagues

"Organized baseball"—the major and most minor leagues—never had a rule on the books that banned African-American players, which makes its whites-only policy the most successful and longest-lived "gentleman's agreement" in American business history. The color line was instigated by players during the 1890s, the bleakest decade for blacks since slavery times. The taboo was not broken until 1947, when Jack Roosevelt "Jackie" Robinson took the field for the Brooklyn Dodgers.

It is impossible to say if players or management were the bulwark of baseball segregation for fifty years. No major league team was located in a southern city (unless one counts St. Louis as southern), but many major league players were lower-class southerners for whom Jim Crow was sacrosanct.

Then again, the greatest of the redneck players, Ty Cobb of Georgia, told light-skinned African American Larry Brown, with whom Cobb played in a winter league in Cuba, that he would pay for Brown to take Spanish lessons so he could join Cobb's Detroit Tigers masquerading as a white Cuban. Babe Ruth, from quasi-southern Baltimore, played against African-American teams during off-seasons and several times told reporters that the best players in the Negro leagues would be the best players in the major leagues too. But even Ruth, who rarely hesitated to speak his mind, never openly advocated desegregating baseball. The fears that if whites and blacks played on the same teams, racial brawls would be chronic—a version of the old proslavery argument that freeing the slaves would cause social turmoil—pretty much precluded open discussion of the subject.

On several occasions, team owners discussed desegregation privately. In 1931, when the Depression cut sharply into attendance, several owners discussed making up their losses by fielding African-American stars, thus attracting black fans to their stadiums. But the suggestion came to nothing. Blacks were hit harder financially by the Depression than whites, and black attendance at major league games was already high. At a World Series game in New York in 1932, one paying customer in five was black. When the Chicago White Sox played at home on the same day the Chicago American Giants of the Negro American League were playing, the White Sox almost always attracted more African Americans than the Giants did. Dan Burley, an African-American sportswriter, said that if you asked a black baseball fan "practically anything . . . about the white majors, he can quote you records by the dozens as glibly and as accurately as a hired publicity man." But the same fan was likely not to know how many teams there were in the Negro leagues.

In 1942 the executives of the white National League acted decisively to keep black players out. The Philadelphia Phillies, after finishing last for five years, were for sale cheap. Bill Veeck, a colorful promoter, was trying to put together a syndicate to buy the team. He approached several owners of Negro league teams and told them confidentially that he would have open tryouts in 1943 and hire blacks "if they could beat out the white players the Phillies had." Because the Phillies players were so bad, that would have meant a largely African-American team. One of the Negro League owners, possibly Etta Manley of the Newark Eagles, knowing that the end of the color line in the major leagues meant the end of the Negro leagues, leaked Veeck's plan to the National League. In a panic, the league bought the Phillies to keep the team out of Veeck's hands.

By the end of World War II, the Negro American League and the Negro National League were prospering. In September 1944, 46,000 people attended an interleague all-star game. It had been a struggle to get there, and in some ways the short history of the Negro leagues paralleled the early history of the white majors with a time lag of about

---

MacArthur issued a series of political proclamations. He wanted the Republican presidential nomination in 1952.

But MacArthur was a poor politician. Half his life he had lived abroad; he assumed that the people would come to him. They did not. As the very good politician Harry S Truman predicted when he dismissed the general, the enthusiasm for MacArthur dissipated within months. Meanwhile, the Korean conflict dragged on, dissipating Truman's popularity too.

YEARS OF TENSION

Periodically in American history, during times of great political or social stress, many people have turned to conspiracy theories to account for their frustrations. The era of the Korean War was such a time. Large numbers of Americans came to believe that their failure to enjoy a sense of security after the victory in the Second World War was the work of sinister forces at work within the United States.

"TWENTY YEARS OF TREASON"

The view that, at Yalta, President Roosevelt sold out Eastern Europe to Stalin was an early expression of the belief that betrayal explained the Communist menace. In March 1947 President Truman inadvertently fueled anxieties by ordering all government employees to sign loyalty oaths: statements that they did not belong to the Communist party or to other disloyal groups. Thirty states followed the federal example, requiring a loyalty oath even of menial employees

three decades. Thus many early club owners, white and black, were shady characters—heads of city numbers rackets in the case of the Negro leagues. Respectable blacks with capital were no more interested in investing in semi-respectable baseball than genteel whites had been.

Chronic brawling and attacks on umpires had been a problem in the white leagues in the 1890s because they scared potential ticket buyers away from games. The owners were able to crack down with tough punishments and did. In a Negro league championship game as late as 1934, one player shoved an umpire and two players punched him. None was ejected from the game. League bosses knew that if they were, their teammates would have walked off the field too.

The Negro leagues never got control of teams or players. Each team was an independent enterprise with headstrong owners. If a league decision displeased an owner, the team left the league. There was as much money to be made—sometimes more—barnstorming with independent black and white teams and popular gimmick-costumed teams like the House of David, the Jewish Clowns, Jim Thorpe's Indians, and the Zulu Cannibal Giants. In 1934 the fifth game of the Negro National League championship series had to be postponed for ten days when the Philadelphia Stars unexpectedly lined up several games that were more lucrative than playing for the pennant.

Star players were uncontrollable. The Negro leagues adopted the "reserve clause" by which white major league teams, ironically, held their players in a kind of bondage. The best players—the ones who attracted the fans—ignored it. In 1937 Dominican dictator Rafael Trujillo decided to make the club he owned the best in the world. He hired eighteen of the best African-American players (nine from the Pittsburgh Crawfords), including Leroy "Satchel" Paige (possibly the best pitcher of all time), Josh Gibson

(who, Babe Ruth said, would lead the white majors in home runs), and James "Cool Papa" Bell. They played only one season for the Ciudad Trujillo team, complaining that between games owner Trujillo virtually imprisoned them. They had no trouble finding jobs in the Negro leagues despite having jumped their contracts. If their old team did not take them back, another team would. They were too valuable in selling tickets for the owners to form the solid front that the owners in the white majors had.

Only about half the Negro league teams had enough capital to have their own home fields. The Homestead Grays (Pittsburgh) owned a good stadium. The Philadelphia Stars' Passon Field was better than the Phillies' Baker Bowl and better located than the Athletics' Shibe Park. But they were the exceptions. Other Negro league teams had to arrange their schedules when white major and minor league teams were on the road so that they could rent their stadiums. St. Louis and Detroit, with large African-American populations, did not have Negro league teams because the owners of Sportsman's Park and Briggs Stadium refused to rent to blacks.

Jackie Robinson's success doomed the Negro leagues. Branch Rickey of the Dodgers, usually depicted as a hero because he broke the color line, did not compensate the Kansas City Monarchs, Robinson's Negro league team, for taking him, nor the Newark Eagles when Rickey signed pitcher Don Newcombe, nor the Baltimore Elite Giants when he signed catcher Roy Campanella.

"We are built on segregation," a Negro league owner said. "If there was no segregation . . . we'd all probably be out of business." And so they were. Newark Eagles home attendance was 120,000 in 1946, 60,000 in 1947, 35,000 in 1948. By 1953 there were only four teams left in the Negro American League. By the end of the decade, the most successful African-American big business was dead.

who waxed the floors of the state university's basketball courts.

Truman also contributed to the belief that there was treason within the federal government by allowing his supporters to "red-bait" Henry Wallace in the 1948 presidential

Political Cleansing

During World War II about 100 federal employees were fired, and another 30 resigned because of investigations into their background. Between 1947 and 1956 there were 2,700 dismissals and 12,000 resignations described as "security-related."

campaign. Wallace was eccentric, even wacky; his analysis of Soviet intentions in 1948 and the possibility of reviving good relations was almost certainly mistaken. The tiny American Communist party supported his candidacy in 1948, which did not help his reputation, but he was no Communist stooge. In calling him one, as many Truman Democrats did, they created a political tactic that, in the end, could only work against their party. If there were traitors in high places, the Democratic party was responsible; as of 1952, Democrats had been running the country for twenty years.

Before 1952, frustrated right-wing Republicans like John Bricker of Ohio and William F. Knowland of California raised the specter of "twenty years of treason." But the

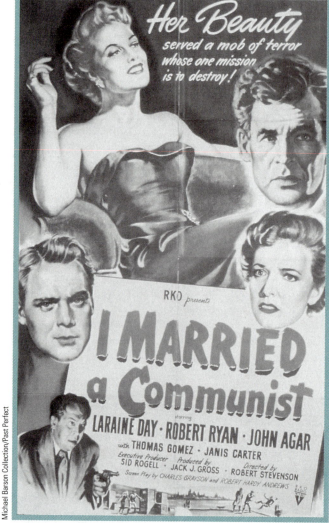

Michael Barson Collection/Past Perfect

Hollywood was a center of the Communist scare. Screenwriters accused of Communist sympathies were blacklisted, and the studios rushed into production films encouraging the belief in widespread subversion. Ads for I Married a Communist did not forget sex, but complicated its appeal with the horrors of cohabitation with a Communist.

two chief beneficiaries of the second **Red Scare** were Richard M. Nixon, a young first-term congressman from southern California, and Joseph McCarthy, the junior senator from Wisconsin.

ALGER HISS AND RICHARD NIXON

Richard M. Nixon built his career on the ashes of the career of a former New Deal bureaucrat named Alger Hiss. A bright young Ivy Leaguer in the 1930s when he went to Washington to work in the Agriculture Department, Hiss had risen to be a middle-level aide to Roosevelt at the Yalta Conference. He was aloof and fastidious in manner, rather a snob, and he was a militant liberal.

In 1948 a journalist, Whittaker Chambers, who admitted to having been a Communist during the 1930s, accused

Hiss of having helped him funnel classified American documents to the Soviets. At first Chambers aroused little fuss. Chambers had a reputation for erratic behavior and for making wild claims; his accusations of Hiss seemed like an irresponsible smear. And because of the statute of limitations, none of the crimes of which he accused Hiss could be prosecuted. Moreover, Hiss was no longer working for the government.

Hiss could have ignored Chambers. Instead he forced the issue for what seemed at the time his personal honor but which, in retrospect, probably reflected his arrogance and snobbery. Indignantly, he swore under oath that Chambers's claims were lies. He said he did not even know Chambers.

To liberals, Hiss, with his exemplary record of public service, was telling the truth. The seedy Chambers was a liar. But many ordinary Americans, especially working-class ethnics and citizens of western farming states, were not so sure. With his aristocratic accent and expensive tailored clothing, Hiss personified the eastern intellectual establishment, traditionally an object of suspicion west of the Appalachians.

Congressman Nixon shared these feelings. On little more than a hunch, he pursued the Hiss case when other Republicans had lost interest. Nixon persuaded Chambers to produce microfilms that seemed to show that Hiss had in fact retyped classified documents on his own typewriter, which was in Nixon's possession. Questioning Hiss at a congressional hearing, he poked holes in Hiss's testimony. Largely because of Nixon's doggedness, Hiss was convicted of perjury, lying under oath. Suddenly it was plausible to wonder how many other New Dealers had been spies. Republicans pointed out that Hiss was a personal friend of Secretary of State Dean Acheson.

SENATOR JOE MCCARTHY

Joseph McCarthy of Wisconsin was an unlikely character to play a major role in the government of a nation. Socially awkward and furtive, he was also a bully who had won election to the Senate in 1944 by posing as a combat marine, which he was not. McCarthy was facing an election in 1952 that he seemed likely to lose; his record in the Senate was undistinguished. He needed a big issue but turned down as dull a proposal that he champion the building of the St. Lawrence Seaway (which would benefit Wisconsin economically). Almost by accident, he decided to try out the question of Communist subversion of the government, in which he had taken little interest.

In 1950 McCarthy told a Republican audience in Wheeling, West Virginia, that he had a list of 205 Communists who were working in the State Department with the full knowledge of Secretary Acheson. McCarthy had no list. Just two days later he could not remember if he had said the names on it totaled 205 or 57. He never released the name of a State Department Communist or of a Communist anywhere in the government. But in his reckless quest for publicity, McCarthy had stumbled on the effectiveness of the "big lie"—making fabulous accusations so forcefully and repetitively that many people concluded, "It must be true."

When a few senators denounced his irresponsibility, McCarthy discovered just how sensitive the nerve he had touched was. Senator Millard Tydings of Maryland was a conservative whose distinguished family name gave him practically a proprietary interest in a Senate seat in his state. In 1950, after Tydings denounced him, McCarthy threw his support behind Tydings's opponent. He fabricated a photograph—like a tabloid composograph without the jokes—showing Tydings shaking hands with American Communist leader Earl Browder. Tydings was defeated.

McCARTHYISM

Other senators who were disturbed by McCarthy got the point. If McCarthy could retire a senator with as safe a seat as Tydings had, why risk their own careers by alienating him? By 1952 McCarthy was so powerful that when Republican presidential candidate Dwight D. Eisenhower was campaigning in Wisconsin and, with him on the platform, McCarthy denounced George Marshall as disloyal, Eisenhower said nothing. It was the worst blot on Eisenhower's career; Marshall had lifted him from obscurity to put him in command of the war in Europe.

Even liberal Democrats in Congress rushed to prove their loyalty and escape McCarthy's wrath by voting for reckless laws like the McCarran Internal Security Act, which defined dozens of liberal lobby groups as "Communist fronts." The McCarran Act also provided for the establishment of concentration camps for disloyal citizens in the event of a national emergency. The Supreme Court fell into line in *Dennis et al.* v. *United States* (1951). By a vote of 6 to 2, the Court agreed that membership in the Communist party was sufficient evidence in itself to convict a person of advocating the forcible overthrow of the U.S. government, a serious crime. (It was on this principle that, in 1919, several hundred members of the IWW were imprisoned despite the fact that the government had no evidence that any of them had performed seditious acts or made seditious statements.)

At the peak of McCarthy's power, only a very few universities (including the University of Wisconsin) and journalists like cartoonist Herbert Block and television commentator

Eisenhower ("Ike") campaigning in Iowa in the fall of 1952. His smiling, fatherly image was what the country wanted.

AP/Wide World Photos

Edward R. Murrow refused to be intimidated. Not until 1954, however, did McCarthy's career come to an end. Failing to get preferential treatment from the army for a friend of his aide, Roy Cohn, McCarthy retaliated by accusing the army of tolerating infiltration by Communists. He had stepped over the line. The Senate was emboldened to move against him; he was censured in December 1954 by a vote of 72 to 22. It was only the third time in American history that the nation's most exclusive club turned on one of its own members.

THE MAKING OF A POLITICIAN

Nixon and McCarthy built their careers on exploiting and aggravating anxieties. But the staid leader of the conservative Republicans, Senator Taft of Ohio, encouraged them as a way of chipping away at the hated Democrats.

The Republican Party turned neither to Taft nor to a mover and shaker to guide them through the 1950s. Instead they chose a man with no background in party politics, whose strength was a warm personality and whose talent was a knack for smoothing over conflict.

After World War II, General Dwight David Eisenhower wrote his memoirs of the war, *Crusade in Europe,* and early in 1948 he accepted the presidency of Columbia University. Leaders of both parties approached him with offers to nominate him as president. Truman told Ike that if he would accept the Democratic nomination, Truman would gladly step aside.

Eisenhower was not interested. He was a career military man who, unlike MacArthur, believed that soldiers should stay out of politics. It is not certain that Eisenhower ever bothered to vote before 1948. But academic life did not suit him either. Ike's intellectual interests ran to pulp western novels. After a lifetime accustomed to military order and expecting his instructions to be carried out, he found the chaos of shepherding academics intolerable.

As one of New York City's most eminent citizens, Eisenhower drifted into close professional and personal association with the wealthy eastern businessmen who dominated the moderate wing of the Republican party. They showered him with gifts such as had turned General Grant's head, as well as investment advice that was inevitably sound. As an administrator himself, something of a businessman in uniform, Eisenhower found it easy to assimilate their politics.

In 1950 Ike took a leave of absence from Columbia to command NATO troops in Europe. There, because the Korean War dragged on and because of MacArthur's insubordination (which he found deplorable), Ike grew more receptive to the blandishments of his Republican friends that he seek the presidential nomination. Eisenhower had no illusions, as Taft did, that everything the New Deal had done could be dismantled. He opposed all radical programs. He was convinced to run by evidence of corruption in the Truman administration and the belief that it was unhealthy for one party to be in power as long as the Democrats had.

THE CAMPAIGN OF 1952

Some conservative Republicans who admired Taft (like Congressman Richard Nixon) wanted Eisenhower to run. Winning the election was more important than honoring their veteran leader. The Eisenhower moderates convinced them that Taft's uncompromising principles would alienate voters who had benefited from the New Deal and knew it, but who were otherwise weary of the long Democratic era.

Eisenhower's opponent was the governor of Illinois, Adlai E. Stevenson. He was a New Deal liberal, but not associated with the increasingly unpopular Truman administration. Stevenson was an effective campaigner; he was personable, witty, and as attractively modest in bearing as Eisenhower. For a few weeks late in the summer of 1952, there were hints that Stevenson was catching up with Ike; but they probably amounted to nothing more than the fact that reporters assigned to cover Stevenson were charmed and captivated by his articulate speeches.

Eisenhower had too much going for him, and Eisenhower's campaign managers shrewdly turned Stevenson's intelligence and wit against him. They pointed out that "eggheads" like Stevenson (intellectuals) were the people who were responsible for "the mess in Washington." Despite Eisenhower's resistance to what he considered the tawdriness of it, they applied the techniques of television commercials to "selling" Eisenhower, filming a series of short TV "spots" in which an ordinary person asked a simple question and Eisenhower answered in a few "hard-hitting" words. Ike administered the *coup de grace* to the Stevenson campaign when he promised that, when he was elected, he would personally go to Korea and end the aimless war. Stevenson had no choice but to defend the principles of limited conflict on which the frustrating war was based.

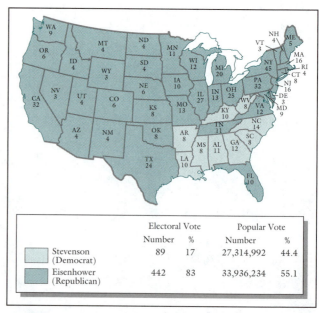

		Electoral Vote		Popular Vote	
		Number	%	Number	%
	Stevenson (Democrat)	89	17	27,314,992	44.4
	Eisenhower (Republican)	442	83	33,936,234	55.1

MAP 45:3 Presidential Election, 1952
Eisenhower's victory in the election of 1952 was a true landslide. He even carried four southern states.

LANDSLIDE

Stevenson won nine southern states. Although he supported civil rights for African Americans, he brought the Dixiecrats back into the Democratic party by naming as his running mate a southern moderate, Senator John Sparkman of Alabama. Otherwise, Eisenhower swept the country, winning 56 percent of the popular vote.

In December, before he was inaugurated, Eisenhower kept his promise to go to Korea. He donned military gear and was filmed sipping coffee with soldiers on the front lines. He had long recognized that prolonging the stalemate was senseless. Without blustering, which would have defeated his purpose, he suggested that using the atomic bomb might be the only way to end the war. It was a bluff; Eisenhower had said in private that it had not been necessary to use the bomb to defeat Japan. But it worked: whether or not the new "collective leadership" in the Soviet Union applied pressure to the Chinese (Stalin died in March 1953), the Chinese agreed to end the hostilities in July 1953. It was an auspicious beginning for President Dwight David Eisenhower.

FURTHER READING

General Paul Boyer, *Promises to Keep: The United States since World War II,* 1995; William H. Chafe, *The Unfinished Journey: America since World War II,* 1986; John P. Diggins, *The Proud Decades: America in War and Peace, 1941–1960,* 1988; James Gilbert, *Another Chance,* 1984; William L. O'Neill, *A Better World,* 1982, and *American High: The Years of Confidence, 1945–1960,* 1987; James T. Patterson, *Grand Expectations: The United States 1945–1974,* 1996; David Reynolds, *One World Divisible: A Global History since 1945,* 2001; Michael S. Sherry, *In the Shadow of War: The United States since the 1930s,* 1995.

The Cold War Paul Boyer, *By the Bomb's Early Light,* 1985; John L. Gaddis, *Strategies of Containment,* 1982, and *We Now Know: Rethinking Cold War History,* 1997; Andrew Grossman, *Neither Dead nor Red,* 2001; Gregg Herken, *The Winning Weapon: The Atomic Bomb in the Cold War, 1945–1950,* 1980; Walter La Feber, *America, Russia, and the Cold War, 1945–1980,* 1981; Melvyn Leffler, *A Preponderance of Power: National Security, the Truman Administration, and the Cold War,* 1992, and *The Specter of Communism,* 1994; Thomas J. McCormick, *America's Half-Century: U.S. Foreign Policy in the Cold War,* 1989; Alan Nadel, *Containment Culture: American Narrative, Postmodernism, and the Nuclear Age,* 1995; Arnold A. Offner, *Another Such Victory: President Truman and the Cold War,* 2002; Thomas G. Paterson, *Cold War Critics: Alternatives to American Foreign Policy in the Truman Years,* 1972; Ronald W. Powaksi, *The Cold War, 1917–1971,* 1998; Stephen Whitfield, *The Culture of the Cold War,* 1996.

Espionage and Red Scare Virginia Carmichael, *Framing History: The Rosenberg Story and the Cold War,* 1993; David Caute, *The Great Fear: The Anti-Communist Purge under Truman and Eisenhower,* 1978; Richard Fried, *Nightmare in Red,* 1990; M. J. Heale, *American Anti-Communism: Combating the Enemy Within, 1880–1970,* 1990; Stanley Kutler, *The American Inquisition,* 1982; Victor Navasky, *Naming Names,* 1980; David M. Oshinsky, *A Conspiracy So Immense: The World of Joe McCarthy,* 1983; Richard G. Powers, *Not without Honor: The History of American Anti-Communism,* 1995; Thomas C. Reeves, *The Life and Times of Joe McCarthy,* 1982; Ellen Schrecker, *The Age of McCarthyism,* 2001; Sam Tanenhaus, *Whittaker Chambers,* 1997; Allen Weinstein, *Perjury!: The Hiss–Chambers Case,* 1997, and *The Hiss–Chambers Conflict,* 1978; Allen Weinstein, Ronald Radosh, and Joyce Milton, *The Rosenberg File: A Search for the Truth,* 1983; Allen Weinstein and Alexander Vassiliev, *The Haunted Wood: Soviet Espionage in America, the Stalin Era,* 1999.

Korea Bruce Cumings and Jon Holliday, *Korea: The Unknown War,* 1988; R. F. Haynes, *The Awesome Power: Harry S. Truman as Commander in Chief,* 1973; Callum A. MacDonald, *Korea, the War before Vietnam,* 1986; William Manchester, *American Caesar: Douglas MacArthur,* 1978; David Rees, *Korea: The Limited War,* 1964; William Stueck, *The Korean War: An International History,* 1995.

The Negro Leagues Neil Lanctot, *Negro League Baseball: The Rise and Ruin of a Black Institution,* 2004; Jules Tygiel, *Baseball's Great Experiment,* 1983; Ernest C. Withers and Daniel Wolff, *Negro League Baseball,* 2004.

The Truman Presidency Stephen Ambrose, *Eisenhower,* 1983–1984; William C. Berman, *The Politics of Civil Rights in the Truman Administration,* 1970; Robert H. Ferrell, *Harry S. Truman and the Modern American Presidency,* 1994; Alonzo L. Hamby, *Man of the People: A Life of Harry S. Truman,* 1995; Susan Hartmann, *Truman and the Eightieth Congress,* 1971; Norman D. Markowitz, *Rise and Fall of the People's Century: Henry A. Wallace and American Liberalism, 1941–1948,* 1974; David McCullough, *Truman,* 1992; James T. Patterson, *Mr. Republican: A Biography of Robert A. Taft,* 1975; Allen Yarnell, *Democrats and Progressives: The 1948 Election as a Test of Postwar Liberalism,* 1974.

KEY TERMS

The following terms are covered in this chapter and can also be found in the list of Key Terms at the back of the book.

"China Lobby"	Marshall Plan	Red Scare	Truman Doctrine
containment	McCarthyism		

ONLINE SOURCES GUIDE

Use this listing to find online documents, images, interactive maps, simulations, and other resources related to this chapter:

American History Resource Center
http://history.wadsworth.com/rc/us

Selected Documents
George Orwell, 1946 newspaper column on negotiations in the United Nations
George Kennan, "Long Telegram"
Excerpts from NSC-68

The Truman Doctrine
Lillian Hellman defies HUAC
Joseph McCarthy, speech warning of the Communist threat

Selected Images
MacArthur visits the front in the Korean War
American troops advancing in Korean War
Jackie Robinson
Dwight Eisenhower

Interactive Time Line (with online readings)
Cold War: The United States and the Nuclear Age

CHAPTER 46

"Happy Days"

Popular Culture in the Fifties 1947–1963

A multitude of uniform, unidentifiable houses, lined up inflexibly, at uniform distances on uniform roads, in a treeless waste, inhabited by people of the same class, the same incomes, the same age group, witnessing the same television performances, eating the same tasteless prefabricated foods, from the same freezers, conforming in every outward and inward respect to a common mold manufactured in the same central metropolis.

Lewis Mumford

The voters of 1952 chose a Republican president for the first time in twenty-four years. No one called the election a political "revolution." Voters wanted a change of pace, that was all. They would live with the Cold War; they had no choice. But they wanted out of Korea, where soldiers were dying daily for reasons the Democrats did not persuasively explain. Most Americans remained grateful for the New Deal's reforms; they did not want a return to the days of Hoover and Coolidge. But FDR himself had proclaimed the New Deal at an end; liberal Democratic proposals to revive the spirit of reform fell flat. Ordinary people were weary of reformers' moral demands and the sacrifices the war had required. They wanted to enjoy the fruits of living in the world's richest nation. In fact, they were already enjoying them when they elected Dwight David Eisenhower to the White House.

LET THE GOOD TIMES ROLL

The grinning, amiable Ike was reassuring. He promised peace in Korea. He replaced the political pros, do-gooder intellectuals, and apparatchik liberal planners of the Roosevelt–Truman era with administrators like himself and with the stolid businessmen who had swarmed around him since 1945.

Ike's advisers were not colorful. "Eight millionaires and a plumber," a Democrat sniffed when Eisenhower announced his cabinet. (The plumber, the secretary of labor, resigned within a year to be replaced by another millionaire.) When Congress created the Department of Health, Education, and Welfare, Eisenhower's pick to head it was not a social worker, briefcase bulging with new programs, but a military bureaucrat like himself: Oveta Culp Hobby, the head of the Women's Army Corps.

The Long Decade

As an era with a distinct personality, the years 1950–1959 mean little. Many historians date the beginning of "The Fifties" to 1947. The armed forces had been demobilized; the Cold War with the Soviet Union had taken shape; people were beginning to spend freely on new homes, cars, and consumer goods; television was becoming a player in people's lives.

Did the decade end in 1960 with the election of a president quite unlike Eisenhower, John F. Kennedy? Culturally, no. Kennedy brought changes in both policy and style, but his presidency was too short to be significant. Popular culture remained pretty much what it had been until Kennedy was assassinated in November 1963. Only then were events and upheavals unmistakably "Sixties" in character.

IKE'S STYLE AND ITS CRITICS

Eisenhower was soothing. Rather than leaping into political catfights with claws flashing—Truman's style—Ike sidled away when the caterwauling started, leaving the dirty work to his subordinates. Vice President Nixon was one hatchet man. (Ike never had anything else for him to do.) Eisenhower's special assistant, New Hampshire Governor Sherman Adams, screened everyone who wanted to see the president. He turned back those who might ruffle Ike, entangle him in a controversy, or trick him into making an embarrassing statement. Adams vetted every document that was to cross the president's desk. He weeded out the ones he thought trivial and summarized the others. Eisenhower wanted it that way: no more than a page or two on any subject—"briefs" such as he had dealt with as a general.

Democratic critics claimed that Adams was too powerful, that he made many presidential-level decisions himself. He did. Eisenhower was no micromanager; he delegated authority to trusted aides and soon appreciated the flinty New Englander's services. In 1958, when it was revealed that Adams had rigged some government decisions to favor an old friend and then accepted a gift from him—not much, a vicuña wool overcoat—he had to resign. Eisenhower let Adams go, but he bitterly resented losing him.

The president also gave the members of his cabinet a loose rein. They were to study the issues and report their findings briefly; if they disagreed among themselves, they debated—briefly—while Ike listened. Eisenhower, who never shirked ultimate responsibility, made the decision. He preferred compromise to backing one adviser over another. That was how he had handled generals at one another's throats during the war.

Intellectuals poked fun at what seemed to be Eisenhower's losing battle with the English language. Ike had never been comfortable speaking to large audiences. His preferred playing fields were the closed conference and the morale-boosting "public appearance" when he could beam, wave, lead cheers, and shake the hands of sixty people a minute. At presidential press conferences, when faced with a contentious reporter, he sometimes lapsed into gobbledygook. When asked what he was doing about an economic downturn, he replied,

> This economy of ours is not so simple that it obeys to the opinion or bias or pronouncements of any particular individual, even to the president. This is an economy that is made up of 173 million people and it reflects their desires: they're ready to buy, they're ready to spend, it is a thing that is too complex and too big to be affected adversely or advantageously just by a few words or any particular—say a little this and that, or even a panacea so alleged.

In some cases, at least, Eisenhower knew exactly what he was doing. When an aide warned him he would be asked a question better not answered, he said, "Don't worry. I'll just confuse them." Eisenhower was, in fact, quite a good writer; his prose was simple, direct, economical, and clear.

WE'RE IN THE MONEY

Critics mocked Eisenhower's unconcealed love of leisure. The nation was drifting, they said, while Ike relaxed on his gentleman's farm on the battlefield at Gettysburg (a gift of

Fifties Culture 1946–1960

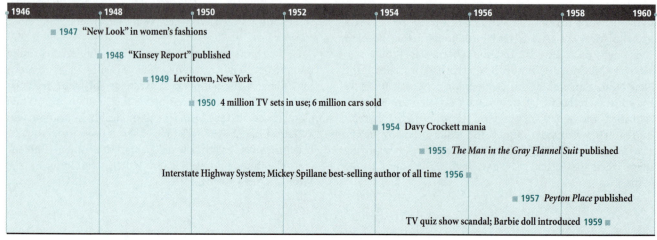

1946	1948	1950	1952	1954	1956	1958	1960

- 1947 "New Look" in women's fashions
- 1948 "Kinsey Report" published
- 1949 Levittown, New York
- 1950 4 million TV sets in use; 6 million cars sold
- 1954 Davy Crockett mania
- 1955 *The Man in the Gray Flannel Suit* published
- Interstate Highway System; Mickey Spillane best-selling author of all time 1956
- 1957 *Peyton Place* published
- TV quiz show scandal; Barbie doll introduced 1959

wealthy businessmen) and took too many vacations in places where the golf courses were always green, the sun warm, the clubhouses air-conditioned, and the martinis dry. But the mockers found an audience only among themselves. The majority of Americans did not object to a president who liked to take it easy. In 1956, when Ike ran for reelection against Adlai Stevenson shortly after suffering a serious heart attack and undergoing major surgery, voters reelected him by a greater margin than in 1952. Better Ike recuperating on a fairway than a healthy Stevenson telling them to roll up their sleeves and get to work making America better.

For a large majority of white Americans, the 1950s were good times. This was not because the New Deal and World War had spread the nation's wealth around more equitably. People defined as living in poverty were about as numerous as they had been in the 1920s. The lowest-paid fifth of the population earned the same 3 to 4 percent of national income that they had earned during the Coolidge era. The wealthiest fifth of the population continued to enjoy 44 to 45 percent of earnings. The remaining 60 percent, therefore—the American middle class (households with an annual income of $3,000–10,000, about $22,000–75,000 in today's money)—was proportionately no better off than before the New Deal.

The difference in the 1950s was the size of the pie from which the slices were cut. Never in history had the world's richest nation been so much richer than all the others. Two-thirds of the world's gold reserves were in the United States, half the world's manufacturing. Each year Americans consumed a third of the world's goods. Energy, notably gasoline, was dirt cheap thanks to the wartime increase in refining capacity. In 1950 **discretionary income** (income not needed to pay for necessities) totaled $100 billion compared with $40 billion in 1940.

Traditional values—thrift and frugality—dictated that such money be saved or invested: it was capital. After the Great Depression, however, when so many had pinched pennies just to get by, and after the deprivations of the war years, middle-class Americans, both white collar and blue collar, itched to spend on goods and services that made life more comfortable, varied, and stimulating. Consumer-oriented businesses obliged them.

FADS

In late 1954 and early 1955, Hollywood's Walt Disney telecast three programs about a half-forgotten frontiersman and politician, Davy Crockett of Tennessee. Disney's Davy wore a

Actor Fess Parker in full Davy Crockett regalia with three children pleased to be the owners of what appear to be top-of-the-line coonskin caps. Walt Disney Studios was the first movie-maker to exploit a film by licensing an avalanche of merchandise tied to it. Some Davy Crockett memorabilia can be purchased to this day in the tasting room of Fess Parker's winery near Santa Barbara, California.

Sweating Less, Eating Better

Air-conditioning was slow to catch on. Willis Carrier applied refrigeration to cooling air as early as 1902, but his "refrigerated mountain ozone" was put into few homes before World War II. Even people who could afford air-conditioning thought there was something perverse about it. President Roosevelt, too good a politician to issue pronouncements based on his personal tastes, vilified it. Carrier and his competitors survived only because factories in which temperature was vital (printing plants, spinning mills) installed air-conditioning. During the 1930s movie theaters adopted the device as a way to increase ticket sales during the summer. It worked, but in 1950 only 1 percent of American homes was air-conditioned. Then the industry took off, first in the Southwest, then nationwide. By 1980 half the homes in the country were air-conditioned (by 2000 that figure was 80 percent).

Clarence Birdseye was another inventor who could not sell cold. During the 1920s he perfected a method of freezing fish, vegetables, and fruit so that, unlike canned foods, they tasted approximately like fresh food when they were thawed. Birdseye's icy blocks were expensive, however; his company barely survived the Depression. In the Fifties, with more money to spend, middle-class diets changed. People ate less of the cheap, starchy, filling staples like potatoes that had sustained their parents. Meat, vegetable, and fruit consumption increased. Frozen food meant strawberries in January and peas all year around.

---

coonskin cap with a hooped tail hanging down his neck—headgear, historians rushed to point out, that the real Crockett did not. Who cared? There was a mania for the caps. The price of coonskins soared from 25 cents to $6 per pound, and most of the 10 million Crockett hats sold were made from rabbit or cat skins or synthetic fur. Schoolchildren's lunch boxes were decorated with pictures of Davy shooting bears. After the bell they played with plastic long rifles and Bowie knives reasonably safe for use in backyard Alamos. (Crockett was killed in the Mexican army's assault on the Alamo in 1836.) Within a year, Americans spent $100 million on some 3,000 different Crockett items, from fringed pseudo-buckskin shirts to wading pools, on which the magic name and image were embossed. In the summer of 1955, several large department stores reported that 10 percent of their sales were in Davy Crockett paraphernalia.

In 1958 Wham-O, a toy manufacturer, brought out a plastic version of an Australian exercise device, a simple hoop that one twirled about the hips by means of hulalike gyrations. Almost overnight 30 million "hula hoops" were sold for $1.98, 100 million within six months. Simple as the toy was to make, four Wham-O factories could not keep up with demand. Like the Crockett mania, the hula hoop craze lasted less than a year; then one could be had for 50 cents.

Chlorophyll, a long-known chemical compound found in most plants, became a rage when manufacturers of more than ninety products, ranging from chewing gum to dog food, proclaimed that the green stuff improved the odor of those who chewed it, shampooed with it, and rubbed it into their armpits. Americans spent $135 million on chlorophyll products. The boom may have ended when scientists pointed out that goats, famously hard on the nose,

---

New Institutions

Two products of the 1950s that looked like fads proved to be sturdy institutions. In 1947 Earl Tupper patented a polyethylene container for storing leftovers in the refrigerator. His innovation was a lid that hermetically sealed the container. "Tupperware" was ingenious and useful, but it sold poorly. Browsers in hardware and "five-and-dime" stores could not figure out what it was good for.

In 1951 a marketing whiz, Brownie Wise, persuaded Tupper to yank his products from stores and sell them directly by demonstrating their usefulness to the people who would be using them: housewives. She recruited a huge sales force, almost all women, who, in turn, found women who would invite fifteen or twenty acquaintances to afternoon "Tupperware Parties." After a bit of socializing, the saleswoman demonstrated Tupperware and took orders. Usually she identified another hostess or two as well. In return for tidying up the house and putting out refreshments, hostesses made $10–25 depending on how many items their guests purchased. Wise's marketing technique was a roaring success.

Equally remarkable was the success of a doll that was neither a baby nor a stuffed animal. "Barbie" was an 11½-inch-tall teenager of proportions so voluptuous and feet so tiny that, had she been flesh and blood, she could not have walked without frequent spills. But the Mattel Corporation gambled that, for the Christmas shopping season of 1959, Barbie would sell big. And as a fashion model, Barbie needed dozens of skirts, dresses, and accessories, which Mattel thoughtfully offered.

The Barbie doll was a paper doll (a cardboard cutout with paper changes of costume attached by foldover tabs) in three dimensions. A dime would buy a paper doll and a queenly wardrobe. Barbie and her clothing cost rather more than a dime, and her owners' appetites for fashions were voracious. Within a few years Mattel was the nation's fourth largest manufacturer of "women's clothing." Barbie loved animals; Mattel provided twelve horses, seventeen dogs, and five cats as pets. Barbie soon had a little sister the age of her owners and a steady date, Ken; they were both dressy too. Barbie made new friends every Christmas, including, in 1980, Hispanic and African-American girls. In forty years Barbie pursued eighty careers, all requiring equipment. In 1992 "Army Barbie" went to war in Iraq. In 1997 "Wheelchair Barbie" coped with a handicap. As of 2006 Mattel had sold a billion Barbies.

consumed chlorophyll constantly. Or like all crazes, it just ran its course.

Some investors who dreamed up surefire fads did not fare so well. Trampolines, for example, were extensively promoted but were too big, were too expensive, and broke too many kids' bones. Some fads profited only the newspapers and magazines that reported them, such as college students competing to see how many of them could squeeze into a telephone booth.

THE BOOB TUBE

The most significant new consumer bauble of the decade was the home television receiver. TV was introduced as a broadcast medium in 1939. However, "radio with a picture" remained a toy of electronics hobbyists until after the war. In 1946 there were just six commercial TV stations in the United States and 8,000 privately owned receivers, one per 18,000 people.

Gambling that middle-class Americans would spend money on yet another kind of entertainment, the radio networks sidled into television, at first offering several hours of programming each evening. Furniture stores left TV sets in their display windows turned on, and sure enough, knots of people gathered to watch. Manufacturers of sets like Dumont peddled their product as a healthful social innovation:

"There is great happiness in the home where the family is held together by this new common bond!"

By 1950 almost 4 million sets had been sold, one for every thirty-two people; by 1952 that figure was 18 million. In 1956 some 442 stations (now called "channels") were on the air. By 1970 more households would be equipped with a TV set than with refrigerators, bathtubs, or indoor toilets.

A few high-minded network executives hoped that television would be an agent of education and cultural uplift. They telecast serious plays, both classics and original dramas, on the "small screen." But no one deluded himself as Herbert Hoover did during the 1920s when he said that radio should be free of commercial advertising. From TV's first days, "sponsors" peddling consumer goods interrupted programs every fifteen minutes with their spiels. The first commercial blockbusters were variety shows, one hosted by Milton Berle, a manic burlesque clown; another, *Toast of the Town* on Sunday evenings, was hosted by Ed Sullivan, a stiff, awkward gossip columnist.

COWBOYS AND QUIZ SHOWS

In 1955 the networks found another moneymaker in a venerable American genre, the western. Within two years they launched more than forty programs set in the "Wild West." By 1957 one-third of "prime time" (the evening hours

In a film of 1955, The Man in the Gray Flannel Suit, *actor Gregory Peck, portraying Tom Rath, a rising young executive unhappy with his work, comes home to be ignored by his children, who have something better to do than to greet Daddy—watch TV! Rath commuted from his suburban home to downtown New York by train each day where, in his gray flannel uniform, he was indistinguishable from thousands of others. It was on his commutes that his mind dwelled on the "rat race" he was running.*

between supper and bedtime) was given over to horses, sheriffs, bad men, and the occasional "saloon girl" with a heart of gold. In Los Angeles it was possible to watch sixty-four hours of westerns each week.

One of the first westerns, *Gunsmoke,* ran through 635 episodes. A quarter of the world's population saw at least one episode in which Marshall Matt Dillon made Dodge City, Kansas, safe for decent law-abiding citizens. *Death Valley Days* revived the career of actor Ronald Reagan. As the host who introduced stories with different characters each week, he was able to "play himself" before millions of viewers. His self was likable; the program set Reagan onto a trail of celebrity that eventually led to the White House.

Quiz shows offering huge prizes caught the popular imagination. The first was *The $64,000 Question.* (The name was a clever play on an old radio quiz show in which the ultimate challenge was "the $64 question.") Millions sat entranced as secretaries, postal clerks, and idiot savants rattled off the names of Polish kings, flyweight boxers of the 1920s, and lines from Shakespeare's plays. Then, in 1959, a government investigator revealed that a popular contestant on a show called *21,* a young university instructor named Charles Van Doren, had been fed answers. So had others who had appealing personalities, while unattractive contestants were instructed to take a dive.

The exposé was sensational because Van Doren had grimaced with agony when he pretended to struggle to retrieve some obscure morsel of knowledge from deep within his mind, gasping for air to avoid fainting when he came up with the answer. Academics said they were shocked by Van Doren's betrayal of their profession's integrity. The producers of the quiz shows said that they were entertainers, not intelligence testers: it was a show, for goodness sake. Ordinary folks just changed the channel. *Gunsmoke* was still going strong, although its writers admitted stress coming up with fresh

I Like Ike, but . . .

On January 20, 1953, 29 million Americans watched the inauguration of President Dwight D. Eisenhower on television. However, the previous evening, 44 million watched *I Love Lucy.*

stories. "We've used up De Maupassant," said one, referring to a prolific author of short stories, "and we're halfway through Maugham" (another).

ECONOMIC AND CULTURAL FALLOUT

Television's expropriation of so many leisure hours virtually destroyed social dancing and transformed radio and movies. The big bands that had toured the country playing at ballrooms could not compete with TV. The high costs of moving thirty or more musicians and several tons of equipment between one-night stands meant that bands needed to play to full houses to survive. The competition of free entertainment at home was too much for them.

The major radio networks—NBC, CBS, and ABC (and, for a few years, Dumont)—became the major TV networks. They retooled their most popular radio shows for television and, in the Sixties, abandoned radio broadcasting in the evening. Who listened to *Gunsmoke* or *Amos 'n' Andy* when they could watch them? In the evenings, the networks provided little more to locally owned affiliates than hourly news and sports reports, the odd half hour of commentary, and special events. Local stations filled the vacated hours with their own disk jockeys who played recorded music and prattled moronically between "numbers." Local radio reported weather and traffic conditions, broadcast local sporting events, and reminded listeners who were working or driving of the time. The character of the medium was entirely changed in just a few years.

Each week in 1946, 82 million Americans had gone to the movies. Ten years later that figure was cut in half. The biggest Hollywood studios (MGM, Paramount, Warner Brothers, RKO, 20th Century Fox) responded by experimenting with themes taboo on TV, particularly sex (what else?) and with spectacular films ("with a cast of thousands!") that could not be "experienced" on TV's small screen: in 1952, for example, *Quo Vadis?* (ancient Rome) and *The Greatest Show on Earth* (the circus).

Indeed, Hollywood made its "big screen" bigger—wider, actually—with technological innovations such as Cinemascope. There were experiments with **"3-D"** (three-dimensional) movies: wearing special cardboard spectacles smudged with greasy thumbprints (buttered popcorn), moviegoers shrieked as they dodged spears and anything else that an actor could hurl at the camera. That novelty wore off quickly.

Neighborhood theaters, especially in cities, did not fare as well as the Hollywood studios. They depended on repeat patronage, locals who could walk to the movies for the sake of an evening out. Small theaters could not afford the high rental fees charged for new films, let alone install Cinemascope at a cost of $12,000–25,000. Instead they ran three different programs each week, at least one of them a double feature. Their staples were old films and "B" movies, cheaply made formula films that rented at a small fixed price.

By 1950 "B" movies were supplied by studios on Hollywood's "poverty row" such as Republic and Monogram. The trouble was that, in effect, TV was showing several half-hour

Republic Films

Republic Pictures was the classiest "B" movie studio. Its facilities and technology were as good as MGM's, and its stars—John Wayne, Gene Autry, Roy Rogers, and Judy Canova—were very popular. While the major studios made, at most, thirty films a year—fewer during the 1950s—Republic churned out a hundred strictly budgeted films and serials annually between 1935 and 1950. Republic's annual earnings ranked near the top in Hollywood.

Republic was brilliantly managed by Herbert J. Yates until, faced with TV's challenge, he did everything wrong. Yates did not recognize (as other "B" studios did) that Republic was perfectly set up for TV production: formula films made quickly were what Republic was already doing. Then, hungry for cash, Yates sold several hundred old Republic films, mostly westerns, to TV.

Neighborhood theater owners, Republic's market, were enraged. They were in a life-and-death competition with television, and

Yates was arming the enemy. Several of their regional associations boycotted Republic films.

This was Hollywood, so there had to be a salacious angle to Republic's collapse. Yates had been notorious for firing actors if just two of their films failed to turn a profit. But when his wife, actress Vera Hruba Ralston, failed to catch on with moviegoers, Yates continued to star her in movie after movie—twenty-six of them; only two broke even. Republic ceased production in 1956 and dissolved in 1960.

"B" movies each evening for free. Theaters that had been neighborhood social centers closed: 55 in New York City just in 1951, 134 in Los Angeles. By 1963 half the movie houses in business in 1947 were boarded up.

TV AND READING

The "one-eyed monster" did not much affect the circulation of highbrow magazines like the *Atlantic* and *Harper's,* an indication that more educated people were less likely to be hooked on TV. However, general-interest magazines that had been middlebrow stalwarts like the *Saturday Evening Post, Collier's, Look,* and even *Life,* a picture magazine, saw their readership drop. In time they all folded. By way of contrast, new sex and scandal lowbrow magazines such as *Confidential* and *Hush Hush,* which trafficked in material TV would not touch, boomed. In 1955 *Confidential* sold more than 4 million copies a month.

Sales of new hardcover books remained steady. Cheap paperback editions of classics and last year's best sellers boomed—another sign that educated readers were less smitten with television. However, less educated people were reading too. They made a publishing phenomenon of **Mickey Spillane,** who created a crude, even sadistic, detective, Mike Hammer, for whom, every twenty or thirty pages, women dropped their clothing. Hammer shot one such woman in the belly. Spillane's first book, *I, the Jury,* sold 3 million copies in a 25-cent paperback. By 1956 Spillane had published seven books; every one was on a list of the ten best-selling books of fiction in American history.

What Americans cut out in order to watch TV was socializing. Instead of chatting with neighbors or with relatives by phone or getting together in the evening at dances and clubs, people barricaded themselves in their homes, resenting interruptions. Food processing companies invented the "TV dinner," a complete meal in an aluminum foil tray that could be put in and taken out of the oven during commercials and eaten in silence from a "TV table," a metal tray on folding legs, one for each member of the family. Not even suppertime conversation, the central moment of American family life, had to get between viewers and their favorite shows.

SUBURBIA

Social critics said that the TV-addicted family, staring dumbly at the flickering tube during the few hours all were together, had abandoned the personal interactions that alone gave the modern nuclear family meaning. If so, television provided substitutes. In 1954 a group of psychologists

© Bettmann/Corbis

The Nelsons (Ozzie, Harriet, Ricky, and David), one of the most popular of television's many happy suburban families during the 1950s. The Nelsons were unique in that they played themselves; they really were a family. The show was the first of the "reality TV" programs, forty years ahead of its time.

Fifties Nostalgia

Unlike westerns and quiz shows, TV programs revolving around families never lost their appeal. Television kept them going by tweaking the formula. For example, the parents could have eight young children packing the house but still be about 30 by killing off their first spouses, marrying the widow and widower, and combining two sets of kids. Or the kids could organize a wholesome rock and roll band.

In 1974 *Happy Days* made its debut. The show was set in the Fifties (nostalgia for the golden age after less than twenty years). The parents were ten years older than couples in Fifties family programs, and their children were teenagers. It was a big success.

described the most popular morning program (housewives were the audience), *The Arthur Godfrey Show*, as shrewdly creating an "illusion of the family structure" but without conflicts. Godfrey was the most amiable of husbands and fathers, but there was on the program no wife or mother figure. Viewers vicariously filled those roles.

In the evenings, television provided affectionate, happy families to watch. In *Ozzie and Harriet* (first aired in 1952), *Make Room for Daddy* (1953), *Father Knows Best* (1954), and *Leave It to Beaver* (1957), the adults were young, healthy, handsome, even-tempered, middle-class, and, of course, white. Father, the breadwinner, might be wise or a lovable bumbler. Mother, a homemaker, worshiped him or, at least, was formally submissive even when she, the kids, and viewers knew that she was the one who held everything together. The children—two or three—were great friends with one another, often mischievous but never nasty, and ultimately obedient and respectful. TV families were utterly without ethnic identification; they were vaguely mainstream Protestant but never dealt with religion or anything controversial. Mom, Dad, and the kids did not watch TV at dinnertime: they interacted with one another.

TV's idealized families (except *Make Room for Daddy*) lived in the suburbs (and Daddy moved his family there after a year or two) because the suburbs were where the white middle class of the Fifties watched TV.

WHITE FLIGHT

One TV family had an African-American maid who functioned—almost—as one of the family. However, hers was just about the only black face ever seen in television's portrait of suburban America. In fact, the massive movement of population from cities to suburbs after World War II owed in part to white people's racial anxieties. During the war, African-American neighborhoods in big cities expanded rapidly as southern blacks migrated north and west to take high-paying factory jobs open to them for the first time. When African Americans pushed into white neighborhoods, the result was "white flight."

Another cause of the flight to suburbia was a severe urban housing shortage. Construction of new homes had been virtually suspended during the war. Suddenly, in 1945 and 1946, millions of returning veterans and their wives, and often an infant—a four years' backlog of young families—needed places in which to live. The demand for apartments and houses in the cities pushed prices and rents far beyond their means.

Municipal housing authorities backed by federal money began to demolish old neighborhoods to build multistoried apartment buildings. That aggravated the housing shortage in the short run. And in some cities, "fair housing" laws meant that public housing was open to blacks. Whites shunned the new "developments." Young white couples squeezed into single rooms or, even less comfortable for many, moved in with parents. What was to be done?

ASSEMBLY-LINE HOMES

The answer was entirely new "bedroom communities" on cheap land outside cities but still accessible to the factories and offices where people worked. Such land was plentiful because, before universal ownership of automobiles, American cities were compact; they ended where the trolley lines ended. About 10,000 acres within the city limits of Philadelphia were still being farmed at the end of World War II. Of the million housing starts in 1946 (compared with 142,000 in 1944), most were in the suburbs.

Most suburban houses were built, five a year on average, by small contractors. William Levitt, who had mass-produced barracks for the army early in the war and had then been in the Seabees, the navy's construction unit that turned captured Pacific islands into airfields and bases, saw that the massive demand for housing could be met (with massive profits) by producing affordable homes quickly using assembly-line methods.

On 1,000 acres of potato farm on Long Island, twenty-five miles from New York City but close to a commuter railroad, Levitt unleashed a panzer division of excavating machines that graded a hundred acres a day while, in their dust, surveyors drove color-coded stakes into the ground, laying out gently curving streets. With the earth movers advancing to the next tract, ditchers opened trenches that were instantly occupied by water, gas, sewer, and electrical lines. Every sixty feet, cement trucks poured slabs (no cellars or foundations—a

The Goldbergs: Exception to the Rule

The first TV family, *The Goldbergs*, had been fixtures on radio for twenty years when they were first televised in 1949. Except for the characters' lovability, the program was a model for what not to do to have a successful program during the Fifties. The principal characters were well along in middle age; they lived in the city; they were lower middle class at best; they were very ethnic—Molly Goldberg's friend, Mrs. Bloom, had a thick Yiddish accent—and now and then the program addressed controversial political and social themes. In 1954 the Goldbergs moved to the suburbs, but it did not help.

© Archive Photos/Lambert

Levittown, New York. The houses were all the same but not really, as a satirical song had it, "made of ticky-tacky." Ordinary people could not afford granite chateaus in the best of taste. When the Levitts perfected their mass production techniques in Levittown, Pennsylvania, they had a house ready for occupancy every sixteen minutes.

kind of construction new in the East). When the slabs were dry, carpenters erected partially prebuilt frames of identical one-story "Cape Cod" two-bedroom homes. Next, closely coordinated, one crew on the heels of another, came roofers, floor layers, plumbers, electricians, and painters. One man did nothing but bolt washing machines to floors, trotting from one house to another.

There were missteps. When cement trucks bogged down in mud, Levitt learned that streets had to be paved before house construction began. Eventually he reduced his operation to twenty-seven steps and had thirty-six homes ready for occupancy each day. In March 1949 he set a date when sales would begin at **Levittown,** New York. People were in line a week in advance; they camped at the sales office. On the first day open, Levitt signed papers (with whites only) for 1,400 houses at $7,900 each. Levitt's profit was $1,000 per home. Within two years Levittown, New York, was a community of 17,000 homes. Fixed-rate mortgages payable over twenty years, hard to get before World War II, put a Levitt home within reach of any young (white) family with a steady income. Factory workers made $2,500 to $3,500 a year.

Construction of Levittown, Pennsylvania, outside Philadelphia, began in the fall of 1951. Crews there finished a house every sixteen minutes! There were also Levittowns in New Jersey and Florida (Levitt built 140,000 homes),

and developments constructed by others using Levitt's methods fringed every large American city. By 1960 as many Americans lived in suburbs as in cities. It was a demographic revolution.

CONFORMISTS OR INNOVATORS?

Suburbanites were as homogeneous as what critics called their "cookie-cutter" houses. The adult population of the new communities was 95 percent Caucasian, 20 to 35 years of age, and recently married with young children—most families living on roughly the same income from skilled occupations and white-collar jobs.

Suburbanites were staunch supporters of the Eisenhower equilibrium, and they swelled the membership of churches and synagogues to far beyond prewar levels. But they insisted their clergymen not disturb them with hard-hitting moral prescriptions, let alone fire and brimstone. Rabbi Joshua Liebman, Catholic Bishop Fulton J. Sheen, and Protestant Reverend Norman Vincent Peale became national figures by solacing people. Even that most unnerving of American religious phenomena, revivalism, was gussied up by a slick Baptist preacher from North Carolina, Billy Graham, who restricted conversion hysteria to a little gentle sobbing.

A survey of Christians showed that while 80 percent said that the Bible was the revealed word of God, only 35 percent could name the authors of the four gospels (50 percent could not name one of them). Jewish suburbanites organized Reform congregations that did not follow the dietary laws and observance of the Sabbath that would have set them apart from their Christian neighbors.

Critics of suburbia, like Lewis Mumford, called its culture dull, superficial, bland, and stultifyingly conformist. And yet the stark newness of the suburban communities required the first inhabitants to devise new ways of doing things from scratch. Lacking established social services and governments, they formed an intricate network of voluntary associations entirely supported by private funds and energies. There were the new churches and synagogues, thousands of new chapters of political parties, garden clubs, literary societies, and bowling leagues. With small children so numerous, school districts had to be created and developed quickly. Extrascholastic programs revolving around children—dancing schools, Cub Scouts and Brownies, little leagues, community swimming pools—had few precedents in cities.

With everyone a stranger in town, the informal cocktail party and backyard barbecue were effective ways by which people could introduce themselves to one another. Unlike at a formal dinner, guests milled around at the stand-up socials, finding compatible friends efficiently. Alcohol lubricated conversation; statisticians noticed that suburbia effected a significant alteration of American drinking habits. Consumption of neutral spirits like gin and vodka, which could be disguised in sweet soda and fruit juices for people who did not particularly like the taste of liquor, soared. Whiskey, with its decidedly "acquired taste," declined in popularity. In 1954 the Lipton Company created a foodstuff that was soon virtually a requirement at suburban socials: "Festival California Dip." It could be made in thirty seconds by mixing a dehydrated onion soup powder with sour cream and opening a bag of potato chips.

AUTOMOBILES

The new suburbs would not have been possible had automobiles not been accessible to everyone with a decent job. Consumer (short-term) credit was easier than it had been before the war. This meant debt: suburbanites were typically saddled with monthly payments. Between 1946 and 1970,

Chevrolet, Ford, and Plymouth were the lowest-priced American cars and the best sellers. All three were big, and advertisements made them look even bigger. With only one child, unusual in 1958 (the date of the ad), this couple, Mom a Marilyn Monroe lookalike, could impress the neighbors with their sportiness.

short-term loans increased from $8 billion to $27 billion. But they put a car in every suburban garage.

As suburbia expanded to land far from commuter railroads, the car became the only way between home and work. Automobile factories, devoted entirely to military production during the war, were astonishingly quick to reconvert to cars and fill the demand. Even in 1945, the year the war

The Burrowing Beetle

"American automobiles are not reliable machines for reasonable men," wrote social critic John Keats in 1958, "but illusory symbols of sex, speed, wealth, and power for day-dreaming nitwits." Already, however, an imported German car that was the antithesis of the huge, over-chromed, high-powered American cars of the 1950s was a familiar sight on American roads. The Volkswagen was tiny, unadorned, and

cheap—$1,280 until the end of the decade. Its design remained the same every year, whereas American cars were annually made over. It was called the "Beetle"—derisively at first—because of its sloping silhouette. Henry Ford III called it "a little shit box."

Introduced in the United States in 1949, in 1954 only 8,000 Beetles were sold. The next year sales swelled to 32,000. A rebellion against American gas guzzlers was under way. Sales of the VW peaked in 1968 at

423,000 and remained well over 300,000 annually into the 1970s.

American automakers resisted responding to the Beetle with a small car until 1959, when General Motors unveiled the Chevrolet Corvair. It was small and more stylish than the VW, but GM ignored serious safety problems its own engineers had pointed out. The Beetle was dethroned only by equally utilitarian but more comfortable Japanese imports in the 1970s.

ended, almost 70,000 new cars were sold. In 1950 sales of new cars reached 6.7 million, in 1955 8 million. Used car sales increased in proportion. During the Eisenhower decade, car registrations leapt from 49 million to 74 million.

Indeed, the new suburbs created the phenomenon of the modestly fixed "two-car family." While father drove to work, mother daily clocked dozens of miles shuttling among markets and shops (suburban developments were built without them) and chauffeuring children from school to doctor and dentist and from Little League to ballet lessons to, in the suburban sea of children, an interminable series of birthday parties. By 1960 one suburban family in five owned two vehicles. In Philadelphia there were 67 cars for every 100 people; in the Philadelphia suburbs, the ratio was 120:100.

Cars have always been status symbols. The street-watcher of 1925 knew what it said about income that one driver owned a Model T, another a Stutz Bearcat. In the postwar suburbs, with houses much the same, the automobile became the major means by which people displayed the fact that they had moved up an economic notch (or were pretending they had). Paychecks and bank accounts did not show; the family car did. Automobile manufacturers provided a finely tuned social scale beginning with "the low-priced three"—Chevrolet, Ford, and Plymouth—up to Pontiac, Mercury, and Dodge, with Cadillac, Lincoln, and Chrysler at the pinnacle of achievement.

Automobiles were never gaudier, before or since. One disapproving designer called the cars of the Fifties "jukeboxes on wheels." The talisman of car design was the "tail fin," a muted version of which first appeared on the 1948 Cadillac. At first, when designers grafted the entirely nonfunctional fins onto their cars, the response was ridicule, and in 1953 most cars dropped them. Sales drooped! Tail fins were almost universally restored. Even the cheapest cars were festooned with chrome. According to the head of styling for Chrysler Corporation in 1959, his designers did not like it. "But people have demanded it. . . . Every attempt that I know of to strip a car, to take off the chrome, has met with failure."

THE AUTOMOBILE ECONOMY

Automobiles demanded roads. States and counties paid the bills for roads providing access to suburban developments that had been constructed without concern for it. In 1956 Congress passed the **Interstate Highway Act,** which pumped $1 billion a year into highway construction. (By 1960 expenditures rose to $2.9 billion annually.) Most of the limited-access interstates ran cross-country (justifying them as integral to national defense), but 5,000 miles of them connected suburbs to big cities.

Not only did highways encourage further suburban sprawl, but they made the cities even less livable for all but the rich. Already sapped of their middle classes, once-vital urban neighborhoods were carved into isolated residential ghettos walled off by the massive concrete abutments of the freeways. Suburbanites' cars roared in on them daily, raising noise levels and fouling the air. Only the poor, who had no choice, would live in the road-walled neighborhoods, which were soon

run-down. The progressively poorer (and blacker) cities deteriorated physically. During the 1960s, further reducing urban tax bases, department stores, offices, and light industries closed their doors in city centers and moved to the suburbs.

Universal car ownership in the suburbs stimulated the growth of businesses devoted to or dependent on automobiles. Service stations (gasoline consumption doubled during the 1950s), parts and accessories stores, car washes, and drive-in restaurants blossomed in the suburbs. The first drive-in theater dated to 1933, but few were built when car ownership was limited and gasoline was rationed. For the new suburbanites with multiple restless and noisy children, however, drive-ins were places where they could watch a movie without worrying about the tots disturbing others. By 1958 there were more than 4,000 drive-in movie theaters in the United States.

Suburban "shopping malls" or "plazas" grew at a more dizzying rate. In 1945 America had just eight automobile-oriented retail centers: large department stores and a dozen or more specialty shops surrounded by twenty-acre parking lots. In 1960 there were almost 4,000.

Motels, most commonly "tourist cabins" before World War II, had a reputation (like that of the drive-in theater as a "passion pit") for the "hot sheet trade." They were revolutionized by the automobile economy. Motel chains like Holiday Inn trumpeted the cleanliness of their rooms and diversions for children, especially swimming pools. Traveling families came to prefer them to downtown hotels. Women said that they prized the informality of motels because they did not know how to dress at a "good hotel." More important, as at the drive-in, children could be allowed to run at motels. Excluding Las Vegas and Miami Beach—special cases—only eight new downtown hotels were built between 1945 and 1963. Motels, especially along the interstate highways, were built by the thousands.

MAP 46:1 Interstate Highway System

Following a system first established by the National Highway Act of 1925, east–west highways ended in an even number. Thus, in the West, I-40 paralleled and eventually replaced historic "Route 66." North–south highways ended in an odd number. On the West Coast I-5 provided a faster alternative to U.S. 101. On the East Coast I-5 retired U.S. 1 to handling local traffic.

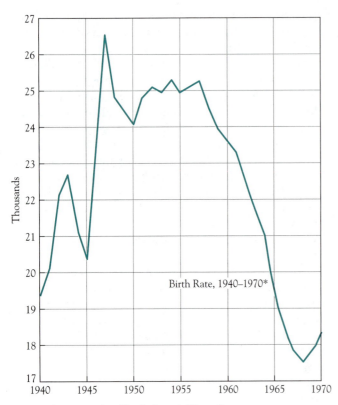

CHART 46:1 The Baby Boom: The Fuel of Fifties Prosperity

During the 1920s, the American birthrate declined—slowly. During the Great Depression, it dropped more steeply. World War II saw an increase; the drop in 1945 reflects the fact that so many American men were overseas. Then came the boom when separated couples were reunited.

Experts said the increase would be short-lived; the birthrate would return to prewar levels. They were wrong. From 1950 to 1964, the number of births increased almost annually, dropping dramatically only in the 1960s. Not until the 1970s did the birthrate return to what demographers called "normal."

Birth Rate, 1940–1970

*Based on estimated total live births per 1,000 population.

BABY BOOM

During the 1930s about 2.5 million babies were born in the United States each year. In 1946 the total was 3.4 million. The jump surprised no one. The war had separated millions of couples. However, demographers said, after a few years of couples making up for lost time, the lower birthrate typical of the first half of the century would reassert itself. They were wrong. Annual births continued to increase until 1961 (4.2 million), and they did not drop to pre–"**baby boom**" levels until the 1970s.

Although all races and social groups participated in the baby boom, children were most noticeable in suburbia because almost all suburban adults were young. Proportionately, children were more numerous there than in city or country. In Philadelphia there were 65,000 births during the 1950s. In the Philadelphia suburbs there were 332,000.

Beginning about 1952, when the first baby boomers started school, massive efforts were required to provide educational and recreational facilities for them. As the boomers matured, they attracted attention to the needs of each age group they swelled. By the end of the 1950s, economists observed that middle-class teenagers were a significant consumer group in their own right. They had $10 billion to spend each year, every cent of it discretionary because necessities were provided by their parents.

Young people's magazines appeared: *Seventeen* (clothing and cosmetics for girls) and *Hot Rod* (automobiles for boys). Film studios made movies about adolescent problems; the most famous, *Rebel Without a Cause*, was about affluent, white, suburban teenagers. Adolescents claimed a new kind of popular music as peculiarly their own. Rock and roll was derived from African-American rhythm and blues but sanitized for white juveniles and usually performed by whites.

Rock and roll could be seen as rebellious—always attractive to adolescents. Elvis Presley, a truck driver from Memphis, might have been ignored had his career depended on his superb baritone. But he titillated teenagers and scandalized their parents with an act that included suggestive hip movements. However, rebellion was just part of the phenomenon. Rock and roll songs exploited juvenile themes: senior proms, double-dating, and teenage lovers lost tragically to the world while racing to beat the Twentieth Century Limited to the crossing. A new kind of record, the nearly unbreakable 45 rpm disk that sold for only 89 cents, competed well for teenagers' dollars.

And not only teenagers' dollars: during the 1950s many adults adopted adolescent fashions and idols. By the end of the decade, television's most popular afternoon program was *American Bandstand*, on which adolescents just out of school danced to popular rock and roll records and expressed their opinions of just-released songs and recently discovered singers. It was scheduled just after school hours for a teenage audience. Advertisers soon discovered, however, that a large proportion of *American Bandstand*'s audience consisted of housewives watching alongside their sons and daughters or even alone at their ironing boards.

DISSENTERS

In 1960 sociologist Daniel Bell wrote in *The End of Ideology* that the anticapitalist critique of American society was dead. The ideologies of socialism and communism were exhausted, "the old passions spent." Socialists and communists had assailed capitalism for its material failures—the exploitation and impoverishment of working people while the rich grew richer. However, Bell argued, modern capitalists, unlike the greedy moneybags of yore, recognized that corporations had social responsibilities alongside their economic purposes, and that workers with enough money to be consumers were more profitable than workers whose wages were an expense to be kept at a minimum.

CRITICS OF ABUNDANCE

In fact, the Socialist and Communist parties withered away during the 1950s. Socialist party membership declined to

The World of Fashion

How They Lived

In 1840 the British consul in Boston wrote that Americans did not observe social proprieties in dressing. They did not wear clothing appropriate to their social station as Britons did. Instead, Americans of all classes dressed more or less alike. Even servant girls were "strongly infected with the national bad taste for being over-dressed; they are, when walking the streets, scarcely to be distinguished from their employers."

By the 1950s, the democratization of fashion was complete. The wealthy had a monopoly of "the latest" from Paris only for as long as it took the American garment makers to copy the designs and mass-produce cheap versions of expensive "originals." Indeed, middle-class women's insistence on being fashionable shortened the natural life cycle of styles. The only way wealthy women could display their immunity to spending restraints was to jump rapidly, even annually, from one "look" to another. For a few months, anyway, they were ahead of the power shears and sewing machines of New York's garment district. By the end of the 1950s, clothing manufacture was (by some criteria) the third largest industry in the United States.

During the Second World War, fashion was a product of the shutdown of dress designers in German-occupied Paris; the shortage of textiles; the prominence of the military in daily life; and the entry of millions of women into professions and jobs previously closed to them.

Because American designers were accustomed to imitating Paris couturiers, they were disoriented by the fall of France and could come up with only variations on prewar styles. Not only did the government buy up all the silk and nylon available, it restricted the amount of other fabrics that could go into clothing. Skirts could be no larger than seventy-two inches around at the hem. Belts wider than two inches and more than one patch pocket were forbidden, as were frills, fringes, and flounces. The result was a severe look in women's dress. It was accentuated by the fact that with so many uniforms on the streets, civilian clothing took on a military cast. The silhouette of women's clothing was straight and angular with padded shoulders—"masculine."

In 1947 Christian Dior, a Paris designer, reestablished French primacy in the fashion world. His "New Look," he explained, celebrated the end of wartime shortages with long, full, and flowing skirts. Dior proclaimed a new femininity in fashion. An American fashion editor wrote, "Your bosoms, your shoulders and hips are round, your waist is tiny, your skirt's bulk suggests fragile feminine legs." Dior blouses were unbuttoned at the top; formal bodices were cut in a deep V or slung low to expose shoulders.

Dior was either very lucky or a shrewd psychologist. In the United States, the chief market for fashion in the postwar years, women were opting in droves for the home over the office, factory, and public life. But the domesticity of the 1950s did not mean long hours of tedious housework. Thanks to labor-saving home appliances and the money to buy them, a yen for recreation and "partying" after the austere years of rationing, and the slow but steady relaxation of moral codes, the 1950s housewife was able to be "fashionable" in Dior's "New Look."

Another phenomenon affecting postwar fashion was the baby boom. Just as the numerical dominance of children and then adolescents led to juvenile themes in films and popular music, the two-thirds of the female population that was under 30 influenced the way all women dressed. "For the first time in fashion," wrote Jane Dormer, "clothes that had originally been intended for children climbed up the ladder into the adult wardrobe." While Dior decreed what was worn on dressy occasions, American teenagers set the standards for casual wear—for women of all but advanced ages. The most conspicuous of these styles was that of the ingénue. "Childlike circular skirts," crinolines, hoop skirts, and frilled petticoats were seen not only at high school proms but at cocktail parties on mothers of five. Women of 40 wore their hair "down" or in ponytails, both styles associated with juveniles and considered inappropriate for mature women.

Hollywood responded to and encouraged the fashion by coming up with actresses such as Audrey Hepburn, Debbie Reynolds, and Sandra Dee, who specialized in playing naïve, girlish parts. Well into their thirties, they (and their emulators) clung to what clothing historian Anne Fogarty called the "paper doll look." Not until the 1960s, when women adopted new values and styles, would the ingénue look, like all fashions to a later age, be ridiculed.

2,000–3,000. The Communists had about 5,000 members, but (it was revealed decades later) 1,500 of them were FBI informants.

There were still dissenters, and the commercial success of their books showed that they had a large audience. But the social critics of the Fifties did not make capitalist greed the villain; their targets were the moral, social, and cultural consequences of abundance. They tacitly conceded that capitalism was meeting the material needs of the masses of people.

In 1950 David Riesman suggested in *The Lonely Crowd* that comfortable Americans were "other-directed." That is, they did not, as their forebears had, take their values from their heritage and upbringing, from what they were; they thought and acted according to what was acceptable to those around them. In *White Collar* (1951) C. Wright Mills made a similar point. In return for generous paychecks, corporations insisted that their middle-class employees conform supinely to corporation ideals. Curiously (Mills was considered a radical of the

Rebel Without a Cause *was aimed at teenagers. Adults, depicted as boorish or insensitive (quite unlike teenagers), were not likely to find it appealing. Entertainment aimed at the young was nothing new; a movie sympathetic to rebellion against parents was.*

left), he unfavorably contrasted dull suburbanites in white collars with the energetic and individualistic (and exploitative) entrepreneurs of the past. William H. Whyte made points similar to Mills's in *The Organization Man* (1956): jobs in corporations and government bureaucracies placed a premium on anonymity, lack of enterprise, and suppression of imagination. Lewis Mumford execrated the suburbs as the hotbed of conformism.

Other best sellers (in paperback) elaborated on these themes: John Keats's *Insolent Chariots* (1958), the tyranny of the automobile; Vance Packard's *Hidden Persuaders* (1957), advertising; and Packard's *Status Seekers* (1961), getting a symbolic leg up on others.

The most widely heard voice in this choir was that of novelist Sloan Wilson in **The Man in the Gray Flannel Suit** (1955). Its principal characters were a suburban couple who were far better off than they had imagined ever being when the war ended. They had an active social life, but found it unsatisfying. They needed a new car and new furniture but were already struggling with debt. The husband commuted to work by train anonymously in a sea of men in white collars, neckties, and gray flannel suits. Grimly, he daydreamed nostalgically of his years as a soldier in Europe during World War II.

BEATNIKS AND SQUARES

C. Wright Mills displayed his rebellion not only in books but in his personal life. A professor, he refused to wear the uniform of his profession: tweed jacket, starched shirt, bow tie. Even at prestigious Columbia University, he dressed in rumpled khaki trousers and plaid flannel shirts without a necktie (unknowingly pioneering the uniform of professors today).

Except for the fact that he drew a salary from a large institution, he was a "beatnik," a gently mocking nickname given to young bohemians who shunned the rat race of regular jobs, family life, consumption, debt, and conformity. (The word *beatnik* was derived from *Beat*, a term the beatniks applied to themselves which, they said, was short for "beatific": they were "the blessed.")

The two best-known beatniks (both out of Columbia University) were writers. Allen Ginsberg's long poem *Howl* (1956) was praised by established poets as notable as William Carlos Williams. Jack Kerouac's *On the Road* (1957), a novel about young men wandering in an old car around the country, was a best seller.

Most large cities had beatnik colonies, the men dressing in khakis and T-shirts, the women shunning cosmetics and the "perms" of the "squares," their name for conformists. They romanticized African Americans for the "naturalness" of their lives, particularly jazz musicians, from whom they adopted marijuana. They rejected conventional sexual morality: men and women lived together without marrying—a practice still offensive in "respectable society." Some were homosexuals. Their gathering places in beatnik centers like Greenwich Village in New York, Venice in Los Angeles, and North Beach in San Francisco were coffeehouses, and the chief activity there was listening to other beatniks read poetry.

Like other bohemian movements before and since, Beat was mostly style so that anyone could dabble in it. No sooner did newspaper reporters write articles about the beatnik scene in Greenwich Village or North Beach than, on weekends, the coffeehouses were crowded with squares who had swapped their gray flannel suits and their wives their billowing dresses for beatnik accoutrements.

FIFTIES WOMEN

A more significant rebellion against the popular culture of the Fifties was not recognized when it was first expressed. In 1956 a housewife named Grace Metalious published a novel, *Peyton Place,* that was promoted as lifting "the lid off a small New England town." The book was a melodramatic tale of greed, petty animosities, revenge-taking, and illicit sex in a town that, on the surface, was idyllic and harmonious. Its theme was hypocrisy. *Peyton Place* was sensationally successful because of its explicit sex scenes. (Actually they were few, brief, and chastely tame by contemporary standards.)

However, as feminists would point out more than a decade later, *Peyton Place* made a profound point that was overlooked during the Fifties. Its three principal characters, a woman and two quite mature teenage girls, were strong characters who tried, mostly succeeding, to take charge of their lives—not just their sex lives—on their own terms. They were the antithesis of the ideal Fifties woman, the deferential housewife of TV's suburban families.

In 1957, the year *Peyton Place* sold its millions of copies, another woman began to write an explicit critique of what she called the "feminine mystique." **Betty Friedan** was an intelligent, well-educated woman who had given up a career to become a wife and mother in the accepted "other-directed" mode. In 1957 she attended a reunion of her alma mater, Smith College, with a commission to write an article about her generation for *McCall's* magazine.

McCall's expected a piece on the theme of "togetherness," the ideal of suburban domesticity, wife happily supporting husband, that the magazine promoted. Instead Friedan wrote of her middle-aged classmates' unhappiness with their lives. *McCall's* rejected the article; Friedan expanded it into a book published in 1963, *The Feminine Mystique*. The new mystique made the housewife–mothers, who never had a chance to do anything else, the model for all women; it presupposed that history had reached a final and glorious end, as far as women were concerned. Friedan claimed that many women no longer accepted the role society prescribed for them. They wanted careers and independence, the same opportunities society offered to men.

Before the book was released, Friedan's publisher sent an advance copy to a paperback company, offering to sell the

> **Predicting the Future**
> *Cosmopolitan* and *Better Homes and Gardens* magazines both had a go at predicting what the home of the 1980s would be like. They hit a couple of bull's-eyes—the video recorder and the microwave oven (a very fast oven, actually); some near misses—robotic vacuum cleaners that would putter around the floor without attendance, avoiding furniture and cocktail party guests; and some faux pas—an "ultrasonic closet" that would clean clothing overnight and a kitchen appliance that would fabricate disposable dishes before each meal. In 1957 Disneyland opened the "House of the Future." It was so far off base that ten years later, it was quietly torn down overnight.

rights to the paperback edition. The head of the company was out of town. When he returned, every woman in the office had read it. They told him, "This is the book we've been waiting for. You've got to buy it." Friedan had tapped into a cauldron of dissent and resentment. In 1966 she founded the National Organization for Women, which was inspired by her book. The NOW was to lead the powerful revival of American feminism in the final decades of the twentieth century, a social movement second in importance, perhaps, only to the Civil Rights movement.

FURTHER READING

General Stephen Ambrose, *Eisenhower the President*, 1984; William H. Chafe, *The Unfinished Journey: America since World War II*, 1986; John P. Diggins, *The Proud Decades: America in War and Peace 1941–1960*, 1988; Fred I. Greenstein, *The Hidden Hand Presidency: Eisenhower as Leader*, 1994; Chester Pach and Elmo Richards, *The Presidency of Dwight D. Eisenhower*, 1991; James Patterson, *Grand Expectations*, 1996.

Dissenters Winifred Breines, *Young, White, and Miserable: Growing Up Female in the Fifties*, 1994; Bruce Cook, *The Beat Generation*, 1971; Betty Friedan, *The Feminine Mystique*, 1963; John Kenneth Galbraith, *The Affluent Society*, 1958; John Keats, *Insolent Chariots*, 1958; C. Wright Mills, *The Power Elite*, 1956; Vance Packard, *The Hidden Persuaders*, 1957; Richard H. Pells, *The Liberal Mind in a Conservative Age*, 1985; David Riesman and Nathan Glazer, *The Lonely Crowd: A Study of the Changing American Character*, 1950; William H. Whyte, *The Organization Man*, 1956.

Social and Cultural History Stephanie Coontz, *The Way We Never Were*, 1992, and *Marriage: A History*, 2005; Richard W. Fox and T. J. Jackson Lears, *The Culture of Consumption: The Transformation*

of American Society 1880–1980, 1983; David Halberstam, *The Fifties*, 1993; Eugenia Kaledin, *Mothers and More: American Women in the 1950s*, 1984; David Marc, *Demographic Vistas: Television in American Culture*, 1984; Elaine T. May, *Homeward Bound: American Families in the Cold War Era*, 1988; Larry May, ed., *Recasting America: Culture and Politics in the Age of the Cold War*, 1989; William L. O'Neill, *American High: The Years of Confidence, 1945–1960*, 1987; Mark Silk, *Spiritual Politics: Religion and America Since World War II*, 1988; Lynn Spigel, *Make Room for TV: Television and the Family Ideal in Postwar America*, 1992; Warren J. Susman, *Culture as History: The Transformation of American Society in the Twentieth Century*, 1984; Stephen J. Whitfield, *The Culture of the Cold War*, 1991.

Suburbia and Automobiles Michael Furman, *Automobiles of the Chrome Age*, 2004; Kenneth T. Jackson, *Crabgrass Frontier: The Suburbanization of the United States*, 1985; Landon Y. Jones, *Great Expectations: America and the Baby Boom Generation*, 1980; Tom Lewis, *Divided Highways: The Interstate Highway System and the Transformation of American Life*, 1997; Dan McNichol, *The Roads that Built America*, 2003; Zane Miller, *Suburb*, 1981; Robert C. Woods, *Suburbia*, 1959.

KEY TERMS

The following terms are covered in this chapter and can also be found in the list of Key Terms at the back of the book.

"3-D"	discretionary income	Levittown	*The Man in the Gray Flannel Suit*
baby boom	*Gunsmoke*	**Mickey Spillane**	
Betty Friedan	**Interstate Highway Act**		

ONLINE SOURCES GUIDE

Use this listing to find online documents, images, inter-active maps, simulations, and other resources related to this chapter:

American History Resource Center
http://history.wadsworth.com/rc/us

Selected Documents
John Clellon Holmes, "This Is the Beat Generation"
John Kenneth Galbraith, "The Affluent Society" (1958)

Selected Images
Women's fashions, 1954
Elvis Presley

Interactive Time Line (with online readings)
Eisenhower Country: American Life in the 1950s

CHAPTER 47

Cold War and Civil Rights

The Eisenhower and Kennedy Years 1953–1963

© UPI-Bettmann/Corbis

I have a dream.
Martin Luther King Jr.

The middle of the road is all of the usable surface. The extremes, right and left, are in the gutters.
Dwight D. Eisenhower

We stand today on the edge of a new frontier—the frontier of the 1960s—a frontier of unknown opportunities and perils—a frontier of unfulfilled hopes and threats.

John F. Kennedy

Except for their aversion to political extremes, Dwight D. Eisenhower and John F. Kennedy had little in common. They could not have carried on an unguarded conversation, or even have been comfortable making small talk. They were of different generations; Ike was 27 the year Kennedy was born. Ike's family was modestly fixed but rigidly proper; until he was 50, he and his wife scraped by on a peacetime major's salary—not much. Kennedy's parents were quite rich, but neither his father nor his grandfathers were known for personal integrity. Ike's charm was homey; Kennedy's was sophisticated; he was a wit.

Nevertheless, the decade these two different men occupied the White House was an era of more continuity than either they or their supporters would have admitted. America was prosperous; economic downturns between 1953 and 1963 were mild and brief. Ike's and Kennedy's domestic policies differed more in rhetoric than substance. Their foreign policies—defined by the Cold War and nuclear standoff—differed in tactics but were founded on the same principles. Most important of all, the decade of their presidencies was given historical unity by the final push, actually the first determined push, of African Americans for civil equality since Reconstruction.

THE MIDDLE OF THE ROAD

Before World War II Dwight D. Eisenhower was a provincial. As a career soldier, he had lived on army bases and mixed only with other officers. It was a narrow universe insulated from the profound social upheavals of the twentieth century.

Political Hucksters

In the final weeks of the 1952 Eisenhower presidential campaign, America was introduced to television advertising techniques applied to politics and (although the term was not coined until decades later) the "sound bite." Political parties had used radio and television before October 1952. They paid to have speeches broadcast and for short "commercials" that, like a poster on a telephone pole, were admonitions: "Vote Democratic," "Wendell Willkie for President."

Then as now, however, people changed stations or channels when a half hour speech was scheduled. By 1952 they had long since developed immunities to baritones instructing them to "Buy this!" or "Try that!"

Eisenhower's campaign managers came up with the idea of flooding TV with twenty-second ads too suddenly and briefly on the screen to be turned off and catchy enough to make an impression. An unseen announcer said, "Eisenhower answers the nation." An ordinary-looking man or woman asked a very brief question: "What about the high prices of groceries?" or "Can anything be done about the corruption in Washington?" Cut to Ike, who, in a firm, decisive voice, answered just as succinctly—he had only ten or twelve seconds—with a meaningless homily, often involving his wife Mamie.

Eisenhower hated doing them. He complained between every take that the ads made him look like a cheap huckster. Today candidates and officials already elected prepare their sure-to-be-aired ten-second insights in advance with the verbal precision of poets. Short-attention-span Americans will not have their leaders any other way.

Unlike General MacArthur, under whom he served for several years, Eisenhower was an apolitical officer. He may never have voted when he was in uniform. As late as 1950, few people knew for certain if he was a Democrat or a Republican. He was, in fact, a moderate Republican by then. He was comfortable in the company of the wealthy businessmen who befriended him after the war. He did not, like Senator Taft, want to raze the New Deal and bury the rubble. But the size of the federal bureaucracy and the mountain of national debt disturbed him; the government had to be scaled back. Trying to come up with a label for what was little more than a pragmatic point of view, Ike (or a speechwriter) called his program "**dynamic conservatism**"—not very catchy, and it never caught on.

DYNAMIC CONSERVATISM

Ike's secretary of agriculture, Ezra Taft Benson of Utah, was an unabashed reactionary in his hostility to government regulation and social welfare programs. Given his head, Benson would have rampaged through the federal bureaucracies like an avenging angel. When Dr. Jonas Salk developed a vaccine that promised to wipe out polio, a scourge of children, Secretary of Health, Education, and Welfare Oveta Culp Hobby said the federal government would not fund a "socialistic" immunization program. Secretary of Defense Charles Wilson (formerly the head of General Motors) sounded like a ghost from the Coolidge era when he said, "What is good for the country is good for General Motors and vice versa." Eisenhower's businessman advisers urged him to favor a corporation, Dixon-Yates (free enterprise), over the Tennessee Valley Authority ("creeping socialism") as the builder and operator of a generating facility for the Atomic Energy Commission.

In every issue, Eisenhower backed off. Benson's Agriculture Department continued to subsidize farmers. The Soil Bank Act of 1956 authorized the payment of money to landowners for every acre they took out of cultivation. Within ten years, $1 of every $6 that farmers and agricultural corporations pocketed came not from produce sales but from the federal government for crops never planted.

When the parents of the baby boomers protested Hobby's refusal to pay for Salk vaccinations, Ike approved a federal immunization program. He took no instructions from General Motors. Indeed, in his farewell address in 1960,

Civil Rights 1947–1963

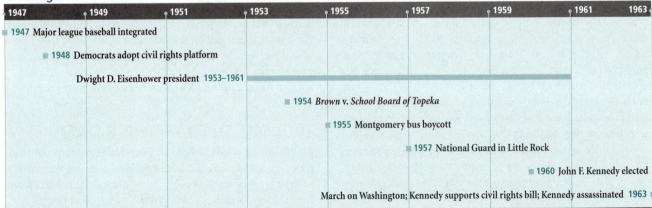

1947	1949	1951	1953	1955	1957	1959	1961	1963

■ 1947 Major league baseball integrated

■ 1948 Democrats adopt civil rights platform

Dwight D. Eisenhower president 1953–1961

■ 1954 *Brown v. School Board of Topeka*

■ 1955 Montgomery bus boycott

■ 1957 National Guard in Little Rock

■ 1960 John F. Kennedy elected

March on Washington; Kennedy supports civil rights bill; Kennedy assassinated 1963

Eisenhower warned of the power of the "military industrial complex": high-ranking army and navy officers shoveling federal money to defense contractors in return for high-paying sinecures when they retired from the service. When Eisenhower discovered that Dixon-Yates was knee-deep in collusion with AEC officials to influence him, he awarded the coveted construction project to neither Dixon-Yates nor the TVA, but to an authority in the public sector.

Ike did hope to balance the federal budget. But when he slashed federal spending, his biggest cuts were in military expenditures, not in social programs. More than 10 million names were added to the list of Social Security pensioners during Eisenhower's presidency. Secretary of the Treasury George Humphrey provided the president with a rationale for reducing military spending in what was called **"more bang for a buck"**—reduced appropriations for the conventional army and navy in favor of building up America's nuclear arsenal and the planes and missiles capable of delivering them, which was considerably cheaper.

CAUTIOUS COLD WARRIOR

In foreign policy, Eisenhower found himself holding back his advisers just as he had to restrain Ezra Taft Benson's impulse to dismantle the federal bureaucracy. Eisenhower wanted to be remembered as a man of peace as well as a victorious general; the Cold War he inherited in 1953 was frigid. He ended the Korean War in July. The death of Joseph Stalin three months earlier gave the administration a breather as half a dozen Russian leaders schemed to inherit Stalin's power.

Nevertheless, the Soviet Union had been a nuclear power for four years when, shortly after Stalin's death, Eisenhower was given a lengthy report that concluded that America's large nuclear arsenal did not provide the United States and its European allies with a military edge on the Soviets. Striking at the Warsaw Pact's huge armies with atom bombs would not destroy their capacity to roll over the much smaller NATO forces in western Europe because the Soviet troops were dispersed and mobile. Atomic bombs and hydrogen bombs were not effective weapons against armed forces. Their destructive power was meaningful only when used against cities, which meant making war on civilians.

Despite the popular assumption that America would be laid waste, the United States would not, in 1953, have been hard-hit in a nuclear exchange. The Soviets had planes capable of reaching North America, but most Russian bombs would be dropped on the more accessible cities of western Europe. American bombers based in Europe would level Russian cities. The death and destruction on both sides of the Iron Curtain would be devastating. What would be left on the continent was the Red Army.

In a word, nuclear war was unthinkable. Nuclear capability was a deterrent, but neither side in the Cold War could risk attacking with its bombs and, if attacked, could only finish up the European doomsday the enemy had begun.

Eisenhower understood this. Unfortunately, Republican party politics had saddled him with advisers who did not grasp the fact that the United States and the Soviet Union were in a standoff. Containment policy provided a way of working within the standoff: limited responses to limited provocations. But saving money was not Treasury Secretary George Humphrey's only justification of his "more bang for a buck" policy. He growled that the United States had "no business getting into little wars," which containment could mean. "Let's intervene decisively with all we have got," Humphrey said, "or stay out." Secretary of State John Foster Dulles's views were also at odds with Eisenhower's inherent caution.

DULL, DULLER, DULLES

On the basis of credentials, Dulles should have been a masterful foreign minister. Diplomacy was his life. It was in his blood; he was related to two secretaries of state. His career in foreign relations stretched back fifty years. When the Democrats were in power, he practiced international law. But Dulles was handicapped by a personality that was unfit for the talky world of diplomacy ("Dull, Duller, Dulles," the Democrats gibed), and his worldview was outdated and counterproductive.

Dulles was a Calvinist; he believed that Communism was a satanic evil. He was unable to respond when Nikita Khrushchev, who emerged as top dog in the Soviet power struggle that followed Stalin's death, hinted that he wanted to

America Underground

For several years during the Fifties, fear of a Soviet nuclear attack was so intense it spawned a building boom in "fallout shelters." These were covered pits in suburban backyards to which, upon hearing the sirens announcing the approach of Soviet bombers, families would repair and survive the atomic bomb that was sure to fall on their community. *Popular Science* and *Popular Mechanics* magazines published plans for do-it-yourself models. A

professionally built shelter, carpeted and painted beige, the signature wall paint color of the decade, cost $3,000, more than all but luxury cars. A Los Angeles woman told a newspaper that even if her family was not bombed, their backyard shelter "will make a wonderful place for the children to play in." Others observed that fallout shelters were useful storage areas. In religious journals, ministers and priests argued whether, when the bombs fell, a person was morally justified in shooting neighbors

who had not been so prudent as to dig their own and were trying to horn in. Neither side of the question ever definitively won the debate.

One manufacturer in Texas was called "The Peace O' Mind Shelter Company." Another firm, in a pamphlet called "How to Survive an Atomic Bomb," advised, "Things are probably going to look different when you get outside. If the bomb hit within a mile and a half of where you are, things are going to look very different."

ease tensions. In 1955 the Soviets agreed with the Western powers to withdraw all troops from Austria and allow the creation of a non-Communist, neutral democracy in the country. That should have convinced Dulles that the Soviets were not monomaniacal in their determination to expand Communism, but it did not.

Dulles's inflexibility made him unpopular not only in neutral countries but with allies. To make matters worse, he insisted on representing the United States in person. He flew 500,000 miles on the job, demoralizing American ambassadors by turning them into ceremonial figures who greeted his plane and then disappeared. Dulles's unbending moralism—and fifty years of European empires that kept the lid on their colonies and Latin American republics as deferential to the United States as if they were colonies—had left him incapable of adjusting to the realities of the 1950s.

The old empires were falling apart; new Asian and African republics were founded almost annually. Committed at least in word to social and economic reform, usually socialistic, the leaders of the new nations were rarely pro-Soviet, and they wanted American financial aid. But Dulles demanded unqualified support of the United States in the Cold War. In Latin America, reformers of necessity had to reduce or regulate the American economic interests in their countries. Dulles's career as a diplomat and lawyer had been dedicated to maintaining those interests intact. By writing off as an enemy every government that had differences with the United States—dividing the world into "us" and "them"—Dulles alienated foreign governments that sought friendship. He was midwife to the birth of violent, anti-American revolutionaries around the world.

PICKING THE WRONG FRIENDS

In cooperation with his brother, Allen Dulles, who headed the covert Central Intelligence Agency (CIA), the secretary of state used American influence and power to support reactionary regimes because they were anti-Communist. Some were headed by brutal dictators: in Portugal, Nicaragua, the Dominican Republic, and Cuba.

In 1953 the United States helped the Shah of Iran oust a reform-minded prime minister, Mohammed Mossadegh, despite the fact that, sharing a long border with the Soviet Union, no Iranian government could afford to cozy up to Russia. In 1954 the CIA played a major role in overthrowing the democratically selected prime minister of Guatemala, Jacobo Arbenz Guzmán, because he intended to nationalize banana plantations owned by an American company.

Also in 1954, Dulles refused to sign the Geneva Accords, an agreement ending a long war between Vietnamese nationalists and France. The leader of the nationalists, Ho Chih Minh, was a Communist but also independent-minded. He had courted American friendship and financial aid; the Vietnamese were traditionally hostile to China. But Dulles rebuffed him as one of "them." As soon as the French evacuated Vietnam, Allen Dulles and the CIA began secretly to prevent the democratic elections provided for in the Geneva agreement. By 1956 the Dulleses had aligned the United States

with another unpopular reactionary in South Vietnam, Ngo Dinh Diem.

BRINKMANSHIP: THEORY AND PRACTICE

Eisenhower deferred to Dulles in these policies. Dulles was the expert. As supreme commander during World War II, Ike had allowed his subordinates a great deal of latitude to make decisions with good results. He did not object when Dulles preached "**brinkmanship,**" which Dulles defined as "the ability to get to the verge without getting into war" in order to affect American policy. However, when Dulles said it was his intention not merely to contain Soviet expansion, but to encourage people living under Communism to overthrow their oppressors, brinkmanship became too hot a potato for the cautious Eisenhower.

The United States' official radio network in Europe, the Voice of America, and the CIA-funded Radio Free Europe broadly implied to Eastern Europeans that the United States would assist them if they rebelled against Soviet domination. To what extent the message influenced events in the summer of 1956 is difficult to say. However, when thousands of Poles rioted in favor of Wadyslaw Gomulka, a Communist who had criticized Russian domination of the country, the Soviets quickly relented and allowed Gomulka to assume power.

Then the Hungarians rose up in favor of an even more strident critic of the Soviets, Imre Nagy. It appeared Russia would again compromise. Within days the riots evolved into widespread rebellion, and the rebels appealed to the United States to send troops or, at least, assistance. Eisenhower was silent, and on Eisenhower's insistence Dulles was too. Going to the brink was one thing, but intervening in Hungary was leaping over it. The Soviets invaded Hungary and harshly suppressed the rebels. Hundreds of thousands of Hungarians fled the country. They hated the Soviet Union but were disillusioned with John Foster Dulles.

Also in 1956, when Egypt seized the Suez Canal, Eisenhower and Dulles first appeared to encourage Britain, France, and Israel to invade Egypt. However, after their troops had landed and Khrushchev threatened to send Russian "volunteers" to assist the Egyptians, Eisenhower denounced the invasion and forced the three allies into a humiliating withdrawal. Brinkmanship sounded good until one was standing on the edge of the chasm. In the nuclear age, there was no margin of error.

PEACEFUL COEXISTENCE

While Dulles rattled his saber, Eisenhower cautiously responded to the peaceful overture of the rotund, homely, and clever Ukrainian who, after a period of "collective leadership" in the Soviet Union, emerged as Stalin's successor. Nikita Khrushchev bewildered American Kremlinologists (experts on the Soviet Union), which was no doubt one of his intentions. At times he was a coarse buffoon who drank too much vodka in public and showed it. At the United Nations in New York, he stunned the General Assembly when, to protest a disagreeable speech, he took off his shoe

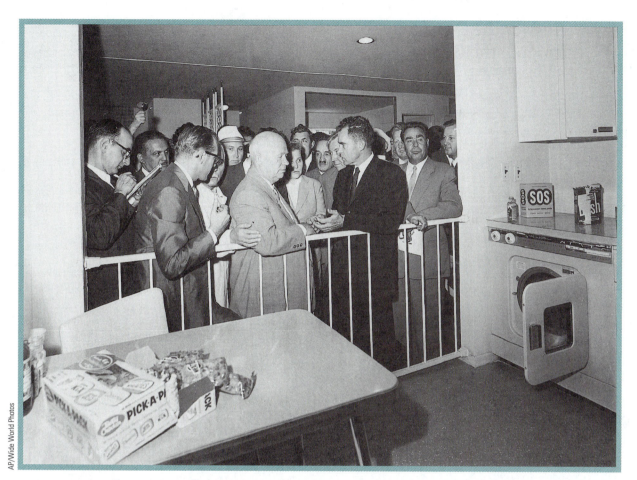

Vice President Nixon's "kitchen debate" with Nikita Khrushchev, about American abundance and the drabness of Soviet daily life, was well planned—by Nixon. Photographers were positioned to catch just such shots as this: a stunned Khrushchev unable to respond.

and banged it on the desk in front of him. On other occasions Khrushchev was witty, charming, ingratiatingly slick.

In 1956 Khrushchev denounced Stalin, his totalitarian regime, and the crimes he had committed. Statues of Stalin were removed almost everywhere in the Soviet Union; his corpse was removed from Lenin's tomb, and Stalingrad became Volgograd. The premier denounced the United States, then turned around and called for "peaceful coexistence" with American capitalism. The Cold War would be resolved, Khrushchev said, not by war, but by "historical forces." When he said "We will bury you" to American capitalists, he made it clear that he meant that the world would peacefully choose the Soviet way of life.

DEBATE IN THE KITCHEN

The contrast between the American and Soviet ways of life mocked Khrushchev's boasts. Stalin's government by terror was no more, but Soviet citizens remained under tight political controls. The secret police were more selective in their depredations but remained intact, well-funded, and capable of ruthlessness. When, in 1958, Russian writer Boris Pasternak was awarded the Nobel Prize for a novel, *Dr. Zhivago*, that was

critical of Communism (it was published abroad)—Stalin would have had him killed—Khrushchev's regime ordered Pasternak to decline the prize and live under virtual house arrest.

The American and Soviet standards of living were not comparable. With the U.S.S.R. matching the infinitely richer United States in defense expenditures, little wealth and industry were dedicated to producing consumer goods. Long lines of poorly dressed women waiting hours daily at shops to buy not only modest luxuries but basic foodstuffs were common sights in Soviet cities.

In 1959, on a goodwill visit to Russia, Vice President Nixon shrewdly exploited the drama of the contrast. At an exposition he snookered Khrushchev into a capitalism-versus-communism discussion in front of a mockup of an appliance-filled American kitchen. American newspaper photographers had been carefully positioned to capture Nixon's easy victory in what was dubbed the "**kitchen debate.**"

It was a setup, but there was nothing contrived about the yawning gulf between material life in the two nuclear powers, and Khrushchev knew it. He wanted a rapprochement with the United States—peaceful coexistence—so he could

Answer the Door, Somebody's Ring the Bell

How They Lived

During the 1950s and 1960s most Americans were introduced to the Jehovah's Witnesses for the first time. Rather than preaching from street corners, Witnesses knocked on the doors of grand houses, middle-class tract homes still smelling of fresh paint, and urban apartments, and they drove up long dusty driveways to farmhouses out in the country. Neatly dressed, usually in pairs (often racially mixed, highly unusual at that time), they clutched Bibles and handbags stuffed with copies of two monthly magazines printed on cheap paper, *The Watchtower* and *Awake!* The people at the door were not selling something; their magazines were free, although they accepted donations. They were rarely smiling, and they were never jolly or backslapping like salespeople or in the time-honored evangelical tradition. They were solemn, even grim. Their ice-breaking question was cheerless: did the householder think that all was well with the world?

The Jehovah's Witnesses were not a new religious sect. The denomination was close to a century old in the 1960s. But the Witnesses had only recently become numerous enough to bring their message in person to what seemed to be almost everybody. Their numbers counted because their religion obligated all believers to witness their faith—to proclaim it—as the early Christians had, and to accept—to welcome—the consequences. In the Roman Empire the consequences had often been martyrdom. In the United States in the 1950s it often meant a door slammed in the Witnesses' faces, orders to get the hell off the property, a snarling dog let loose, and occasionally, in the country, a shotgun fired over their heads. That was all right with devoted Witnesses too. Witnessing was as important to them as making converts.

The Jehovah's Witnesses took shape during the 1870s in Allegheny City, Pennsylvania. The founder of the sect, Charles Taze Russell, had been a Presbyterian and an Adventist who discovered that he himself was "God's Mouthpiece." The Witnesses were (and are) fundamentalists in that they believed that the Bible was "inspired and historically accurate." Indeed, they considered the Bible a reliable guide to coping with even the fine details of daily life such as, in practice, few other fundamentalists did. They were far nimbler than other fundamentalists in finding the appropriate biblical citation for an occasion or to answer a question asked by the more hospitable people on whom they called. The best could have the right page in the Good Book within five seconds.

The Witnesses differed from other fundamentalist denominations in that they earnestly believed that "the end of the world" was right around the corner. In 1876 Russell predicted that Armageddon—the final battle between good and evil—would occur in 1914. When the First World War, with its unprecedented horrors, erupted in that year, Witness membership jumped. Russell's successor named 1918 as the date. Others set it at 1925, 1941, 1975, and 1984. In anxious times like the Cold War during the Eisenhower and Kennedy presidencies, the warning at the front door that Armageddon could happen any minute was not preposterous. Thousands of people without religious inclinations were building fallout shelters. The Witnesses made most of their converts among the poor and uneducated.

The Witnesses also differed from other fundamentalists in being utterly free of racial prejudice and in their refusal to cooperate with the military in any way. Their rejection of racism resulted in a disproportionate number of converts among African Americans (and, during the 1970s and 1980s, in black Africa). Their refusal to serve in the armed forces was not pacifistic. They were not pacifists; they looked forward zestfully to Armageddon, when they would themselves take up arms for Jehovah and exterminate those who had rejected their message. Thousands of Witnesses were imprisoned during World War II and the Korean conflict as conscientious objectors who would not consider even serving as medics or performing other alternative service. All human governments were evil; the United States was no less diabolical an institution than the Soviet Union.

The Jehovah's Witnesses did not believe in hell. When Jehovah's kingdom began (Witness "churches" were called Kingdom Halls), the "instruments of Satan" would simply cease to exist. Only 144,000 elect would reside in heaven with the Lord God Jehovah. The rest of the Witnesses, more than 600,000 in the United States by the 1970s, 2 million worldwide, would live under Jehovah's rule on earth.

The mark of Fifties and Sixties America can be seen in the Witnesses' vision of Jehovah's earthly kingdom. Pictorial representations of the future life in *Awake!* and *The Watchtower* in the twenty-first century are drawn in a distinctively 1950s style. They show lions lying down with lambs (a biblical image) on a broad, seemingly endless and weedless lawn mowed as closely as a golf green surrounding a sprawling "ranch-type" house such as was the ideal for Americans of the era. The occasion, repeated over and over in the magazines, is a suburban barbecue. Paradise is a consumer paradise but with no hint that its comforts require working overtime to make time payments. The illustrations could be advertisements for the latest in charcoal grills except for the fact that the smiling hosts and guests at the party are black, brown, and Asian as well as white suburbanites.

safely divert some of Russia's arms race expenditures to improving Soviet agricultural production and creating consumer industries.

THE U-2

When Dulles resigned a month before he died of cancer in 1959, Eisenhower personally took charge of foreign policy. Nixon's trip to Russia was just the first in what was to be a series of goodwill visits. Eisenhower lavishly feted Khruschev on a grand tour of the United States that Khruschev turned to his advantage with his common touch. Expecting a Communist monster, Americans found the Soviet leader a good-humored, unpretentious guest with an unaffected interest in everyday things. Khrushchev drew laughter nationwide when, having been refused admission to Disneyland, he explained that the amusement park was a cover for rocket installations.

Eisenhower was scheduled to visit Russia in May 1960. He had every reason to expect to be as great a success personally as Khruschev had been. Ike had been portrayed as a hero in the Soviet Union during the war, and he had remained cordial with Marshall Georgyi Zhukov, a general who had been unafraid to contradict Stalin. Then, on May 5, Khrushchev announced that the Russians had shot down an American plane in their airspace. It was a U-2, a top-secret high-altitude craft designed for spying. Assuming that the pilot had been killed in the crash (or had committed suicide, as U-2 pilots were given the means to do), Eisenhower said that it was a weather-monitoring plane that had wandered off course.

Khrushchev pounced. The pilot was alive and had confessed to being a spy. Probably in an attempt to save Eisenhower's visit, Khrushchev implied that the flight might have been ordered by subordinates without Eisenhower's approval. Ike refused to shirk responsibility. Democrats had been criticizing him for allowing the reckless Dulles to determine foreign policy. The president acknowledged that he had personally approved the U-2 flight. Khrushchev had no choice but to condemn Eisenhower as a warmonger and cancel his tour. The Cold War was quite chilly again.

1960: CHANGING OF THE GUARD

The chill in the Cold War suited the political strategy of a contender for the 1960 Democratic presidential nomination, John Fitzgerald Kennedy. A 42-year-old senator from Massachusetts, Kennedy claimed that the Eisenhower administration had, with its cuts in military spending, allowed the Russians to open a dangerous "**missile gap**": a gross disparity between the number of intercontinental ballistic missiles the Soviets had available to strike the United States, and the number of missiles in the American arsenal. This was irresponsible nonsense. It was nonsense because Eisenhower's "more bang for a buck" policy had favored spending on missiles and nuclear warheads at the expense of conventional forces. It was

irresponsible because Kennedy ignored the obvious fact that after an exchange of nuclear weapons, there would no winner.

THE CANDIDATES

Kennedy won the Democratic nomination by a handful of votes on the first ballot. He then offered the vice presidential spot to his rival at the convention, Lyndon B. Johnson of Texas. Neither Kennedy nor his chief adviser, his brother Robert F. Kennedy, expected Johnson to accept. Johnson was a powerful man as majority leader of the Senate. The vice presidency was, as another Texan, John Nance Garner, had called it, "not worth a pitcher of warm piss." But Kennedy was weak in the South. He hoped that the courtesy invitation to Johnson, a southerner, would prompt him to campaign actively for Kennedy in the South—and just as important, persuade southern politicians, unhappy about the northern party's support of integration, that President Kennedy would listen to them.

When Johnson accepted, the Kennedy brothers were shocked. They should not have been. Their offer was a win–win opportunity for Johnson. Texas law permitted him to run for both vice president and reelection to the Senate. If the Republicans won the presidential election, he would still be majority leader—the Democrats had an overwhelming 64–34 majority—and the front-runner for the 1964 Democratic nomination by virtue of helping Kennedy in 1960. If Kennedy won, Johnson calculated, he would be credited for the victory because southern state electoral votes were essential to a Democratic victory. Texas, which Johnson knew he could carry, had voted Republican in 1952 and 1956.

The Republican nominee, Vice President Richard Nixon, had a touchy assignment. Although Eisenhower had never liked him, he had to defend Eisenhower's administration but, at the same time, offer something new so as to appeal to a mania for change, youth, and "vigor" that Kennedy's success in primary elections had revealed. ("Vigor" was Kennedy's favorite buzzword.) Nixon was only five years older than Kennedy, although he never overcame the popular perception that Kennedy was the youth candidate. Nixon emphasized his experience, eight years in the executive branch of

Not Maine, Missouri

Politicos used to say, "As Maine goes, so goes the nation." Maine was the bellwether in presidential elections because Maine voters chose state and local officers more than a month before national elections, and until 1932 Maine had a pretty good record for picking the winner in presidential races.

Since 1932, however, Maine has picked wrong as often as right. Missouri has a much better record. In the twentieth century, Missourians have voted for every winning presidential candidate except once, in 1956. Republicans who believe in such indicators and want to retire early on election night should focus on Ohio. No Republican presidential candidate has won an election unless he carried Ohio.

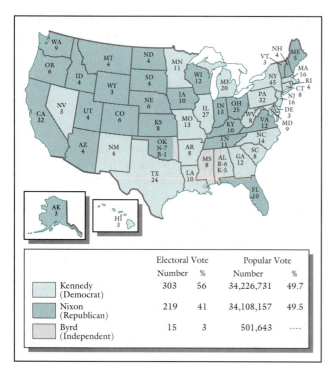

	Electoral Vote		Popular Vote	
	Number	%	Number	%
Kennedy (Democrat)	303	56	34,226,731	49.7
Nixon (Republican)	219	41	34,108,157	49.5
Byrd (Independent)	15	3	501,643	----

MAP 47:1 The Election of 1960

The only "geographical feature" of the electoral college lineup in 1960 was Nixon's near sweep of the West. Within a great many states, however, the vote was very close. Kennedy narrowly defeated Nixon in Illinois. He defeated the third party segregationist candidate narrowly in several southern states.

the government. It was a good arguing point, although Eisenhower thoughtlessly embarrassed Nixon by saying he could not recall a major decision to which Nixon had contributed.

The Democrats revived the "Tricky Dicky" theme that had dogged Nixon since he entered politics. He could not be trusted: "Would you buy a used car from this man?" was a favorite Democratic joke. But mostly they ran a superbly efficient campaign. Drawing on Kennedy's father's millions, the campaign was well-funded. Kennedy had put to rest the dictum that a Catholic could not be elected president during the primaries by winning in West Virginia, a Bible Belt state. His religion was a positive in the northeastern and industrial midwestern states, where Catholics were numerous. Labor unions mobilized to get their members out on election day. Johnson crisscrossed the South as tirelessly as if he were the presidential candidate.

A CLOSE ELECTION

The popular vote was closer than in any election since 1888. Kennedy won by a wafer-thin margin of 118,574 votes out of almost 70 million cast. (An unreconstructed Dixiecrat won 500,000 votes and 15 electoral votes in the South.) Kennedy's 303 to 219 electoral vote margin, decisive on its face, concealed very close scrapes in several large states. Kennedy may well have carried Illinois (27 electoral votes) because of

extensive ballot box fraud in Chicago, governed by the last of the old-time city bosses, Mayor Richard E. Daley.

Some pundits said that Kennedy won because his young high-society wife, Jacquelyn, was more glamorous than Pat Nixon, who was plain and abhorred public life, or because the Massachusetts senator looked better in the first of four televised debates with Nixon. Nixon was, in fact, extremely nervous at the debate. Beads of perspiration collected on his upper lip, and ineptly applied makeup failed to cover his heavy five-o'clock shadow.

But such explanations were fatuous. Nixon looked fine and performed well in the other three debates. Enfranchised Americans have often voted foolishly, but it is difficult to believe that several hundred thousand people in four closely run states chose Jackie over Pat as First Lady. It was just a very close election; they happen. The country was prosperous. Had Eisenhower been able (and willing) to run, he would have won in a walk. (He was forbidden a third term by the Twenty-Second Amendment, pushed through by Republicans as a posthumous slap at FDR.) But Nixon was no Eisenhower, and Kennedy touched a nerve with the not yet hackneyed theme that it was "time to get this country moving again."

John F. and Jacquelyn Kennedy, young, attractive, and stylish. They cut a figure that could hardly have differed more from the elderly dignity of the 70-year-old Eisenhowers and even the unglamorous Nixons. The "classiness" Kennedy brought to Washington appealed to city people and upwardly mobile suburbanites but was not so popular in the South.

CAMELOT

As president, Kennedy was a master at projecting an attractive and novel image of what a president should be. He was no more an intellectual than Eisenhower (his favorite writer was Ian Fleming, creator of the British super spy James Bond); but he won the hearts of the intelligentsia by inviting venerable poet Robert Frost to read a verse at his inauguration and cellist Pablo Casals to perform at the White House. Jacquelyn Kennedy, although a callow 32 years old and with neither the inclination nor the training to live in the spotlight, proved to be a trouper, fashionable without snobbery, and articulate on TV in discussing cultural matters and her personal project of recovering the lost history of the White House by assembling and refurbishing artifacts of past presidents.

Kennedy himself was a wit. He charmed (and thereby co-opted) a majority of the White House press corps with humorous quips, some carefully prepared in advance, some extemporaneous. He even preempted effective criticism of his appointment of his brother Robert as attorney general by stating that "Bobby" needed to have some experience before he practiced law. Kennedy's popularity with reporters won him a more favorable press than even FDR had enjoyed. All the intellectuals and reporters in the country did not add up to enough numbers to carry the state of Wyoming, but they shaped public opinion.

The Kennedy family was large, athletic, and competitive. Kennedy appealed to young suburbanites by releasing films and photographs of his brothers, sisters, and in-laws playing rough-and-tumble touch football on the beach at the Kennedy family vacation compound in Hyannisport on Cape Cod—but few pictures of the homes that would have drawn attention to the Kennedy wealth and privilege. He and Jacquelyn were the parents of two small, photogenic children, an ingratiating asset absent in the White House since the days of the only president who was younger than Kennedy, Teddy Roosevelt.

There were plenty of Kennedy haters; but in the glow of "Camelot," as Kennedy lovers called his brief presidency, they sounded sour and carping. *Camelot* was a blockbuster musical of the early 1960s, based on the idyllic, mythical reign of King Arthur in ancient Britain. Adultery destroyed Arthur's Camelot. Kennedy did not cease his adulteries when he was elected president. He would be brought down before he was in office three years, by an assassin.

KENNEDY FOREIGN POLICY

Kennedy was an unapologetic Cold Warrior. Neither John Foster Dulles nor, twenty years later, President Ronald Reagan exceeded the belligerence of Kennedy's statement that "Freedom and Communism are in deadly embrace; the world cannot exist half-slave and half-free." The "missile gap" was nonsense, but Kennedy sincerely believed that Ike had neglected the nation's security. He lavished money on research programs designed to improve the rockets with which, in a war with Russia, nuclear weapons would be delivered.

FLEXIBLE RESPONSE AND THE THIRD WORLD

However, Kennedy's foreign policy advisers, mostly from universities and "think tanks," disdained Dulles's brinkmanship and frequent threats of "massive retaliation." Secretary of State Dean Rusk, Walt W. Rostow, and McGeorge Bundy revived and updated containment with their policy of "**flexible response.**" The United States would respond to Soviet and Chinese actions in proportion to their seriousness.

If the Soviets or Chinese were suspected of actively aiding guerrilla movements fighting regimes friendly to the United States, the United States would fund the military forces of those regimes and send specialists to advise them; it was the Truman Doctrine plus on-site counselors. If the Soviets were suspected of subverting elections in the Third World, the United States would launch its own covert manipulative operations. Kennedy sponsored the development of elite anti-guerrilla units in the army, notably the special forces called "**Green Berets**" after their distinctive headgear. He increased funding of the Central Intelligence Agency, which had 15,000 agents around the world.

Truman and Eisenhower had thought in traditional terms: Wealthy Europe and Japan were the places that counted in the Cold War competition. Kennedy stated that "the great battleground for the defense and expansion of freedom today is the whole southern half of the globe—Asia, Latin America, Africa, and the Middle East—the lands of the rising peoples."

He preferred to back the democratic reform movements in the developing countries to which Dulles was usually hostile; he was willing to work with democratic socialists, as Dulles had not been. Kennedy took the initiative in organizing the Alliance for Progress in the Western Hemisphere, a program that promised economic aid to Latin American nations in the hope that they would adopt free institutions. However, the choice in undeveloped countries was rarely between liberal reformers and Communists. Envy of American riches; resentment of the economic power and profiteering of American investors in their countries; the fact that the United States supported exploitative dictators so long as they were anticommunist; Soviet opportunism; and the romantic zaniness that is common among revolutionaries all meant that Third World liberation movements were inclined to be suspicious of American intentions and willing to overlook the less than exemplary Russian record in Eastern Europe because the Soviets talked a good revolutionary game. Consequently, Kennedy and his successors often found their only friends among reactionaries that Dulles had supported reflexively.

THE BAY OF PIGS

"Flexible response" proved to be a disaster in Cuba. Once a compliant American dependency, since 1959 Cuba had been governed by a revolutionary regime headed by Fidel Castro. In 1960, baiting the United States in interminable but effective speeches to huge crowds, Castro began to expropriate American-owned properties before negotiating compensation. Eisenhower approved a secret CIA project to arm and train 2,000 anti-Castro Cubans in Florida and Central America. They were not ready to move until after Kennedy was in office. He had his misgivings, but the CIA assured him that Castro was unpopular. At the sound of the first gunfire,

the CIA assured him, anti-Castro rebellions would break out all over the island. The prospect of a major triumph at the beginning of his presidency was attractive; dismissing the anti-Castro Cubans would have provided ammunition to Republicans ever ready to accuse Democrats of being too easy on Communists.

On April 17, 1961, the invaders waded ashore at the Bahía de Cochinos, the Bay of Pigs, on Cuba's southern coast. Everything went wrong. There was no uprising. Castro's soldiers, seasoned by years of guerrilla warfare, made short work of the outnumbered liberators. Instead of ousting an anti-American but possibly still flexible regime, Kennedy pushed Castro, who feared another invasion, into the arms of the Soviets.

Kennedy's Bay of Pigs fiasco heartened Nikita Khrushchev to take a harder line with the United States. When he met with Khruschev in Vienna in June, Kennedy found himself outwitted and upstaged. The Ukrainian tongue-tied him in private and, when they appeared together before reporters and cameras, patronized him as a nice boy who only needed experience. Kennedy returned home seething with anger. Khrushchev went back to Moscow encouraged to act aggressively. The Soviets resumed nuclear testing in the atmosphere and ordered the sealing of the border between East and West Berlin.

THE BERLIN WALL

The Communist regime of East Germany had been plagued by defections, most painfully by trained technologists who could double and triple their incomes in West Germany's booming economy. The "brain drain" was crippling East German industry, and Western propagandists made hay of the East Germans defectors who were "voting with their feet." To put an end to the problem, Khrushchev built a wall around West Berlin that was as ugly in appearance as it was symbolically.

Republicans urged Kennedy to bulldoze the wall. Kennedy let it stand. The wall was on East German soil; to knock it down meant trespassing, "invading" as the Soviets would certainly call it, and they might respond militarily. Moreover, the wall did not threaten either the United States or West Berlin, and he reasoned—correctly—that it was a self-inflicted propaganda disaster for the Soviets. It was, particularly when East Germans continued to flee by crashing gates, scaling the wall, or tunneling under it. East German border guards were ordered to shoot, and they did.

THE MISSILE CRISIS

In October 1962 a U-2 flight over Cuba revealed that the Soviets were constructing missile installations. Such a threat a hundred miles from the United States was intolerable. Before he informed the public, however, Kennedy assembled his most trusted advisers. He rejected a proposal by Dean Acheson that the sites be bombed, and another that American troops invade the island. Although Kennedy did not know it at the time, he had decided correctly. The CIA (wrong again, as it would be repeatedly up to the Iraq War of 2003) had told him

The Cuban missile crisis did not rivet Americans to their television sets as Kennedy's assassination would. The deliberations were top-secret and known to only a handful of people in Washington and the Soviet Union. But few people changed channels when President Kennedy explained how close to nuclear war the nation was.

that only a handful of Russians were in Cuba; in fact 40,000 Russian troops were there. The CIA also grossly underestimated the size of the Cuban army, which numbered 270,000 men and women.

After hours of agonizing discussion, Kennedy adopted his brother's moderate and flexible approach to the crisis. Announcing the discovery of the missile sites on television, he proclaimed a naval blockade of Cuba and demanded that the Soviets dismantle the installations and remove all nuclear devices. Castro panicked. He fled to a bunker beneath the Soviet Embassy and demanded a Russian nuclear strike on the United States. Because Kennedy had made it clear he wanted to talk, Castro's hysteria gave Khrushchev pause. He too believed in flexible response. Now he wondered about his Cuban ally's reliability.

For four days construction work on the sites continued, and Soviet ships carrying twenty missiles continued on their way to Cuba. (Twenty missiles were already there; forty would represent fully a third of the Russian arsenal.) Americans gathered solemnly around their television sets, apprehensive that the nuclear holocaust would begin any minute. Secretary of State Dean Rusk summed it up when he said, "We're eyeball to eyeball."

Rusk was able to add, "I think the other fellow just blinked." The Cuba-bound Russian freighters stopped in midocean. After several hours, shadowed by American planes, they turned around. On October 26 Khrushchev sent a long conciliatory letter to Kennedy in which he said he would remove the missiles from Cuba if the United States pledged never to invade Cuba. The next day he sent a second message that the Soviets would remove the nuclear weapons from Cuba if the United States removed its missiles from Turkey, which bordered the Soviet Union.

Kennedy could have accepted Khruschev's second offer as happily as the first. Before the missile crisis began, he had been considering dismantling the nonessential Turkish missile sites as a conciliatory gesture. However, reasoning from the difference between the two Soviet notes that there were division and indecision in the Kremlin, he saw the chance for some diplomatic one-upmanship that might strengthen Khruschev's more accommodating advisers. He ignored Khruschev's second note, as if it had been lost in the mail, and accepted the terms of the first letter. On October 28 Khrushchev accepted the bargain as if he had never mentioned Turkey.

CIVIL RIGHTS: THE BATTLE IN THE COURTS

In his inaugural address Kennedy promised an idealistic moral reinvigoration in America. "The torch has been passed to a new generation of Americans," he said, admonishing the younger generation, "Ask not what your country can do for you; ask what you can do for your country." He sent Congress a pile of innovative legislation that he called the "New Frontier": a Peace Corps of Americans working in undeveloped nations for little more than expenses; federal aid to education including low-interest loans for students; special assistance to chronically depressed Appalachia and decaying center cities. In 1962 Kennedy proposed a massive space research and development program as an assertion of national pride. The goal was to put an American on the moon by 1970.

The space program passed Congress, as did a few other Kennedy proposals like the Peace Corps. Despite big Democratic majorities in both houses, however, most New Frontier legislation died because southern Democrats voted with Republicans to kill it. (They supported the space program because it meant jobs in the South, the Peace Corps because it was cheap.) The reason was Kennedy's frequent statements in favor of civil rights for African Americans. Until 1963 they were all rhetoric, but segregationist southern congressmen wanted the president's awareness of their political muscle to be painful.

EISENHOWER, KENNEDY, AND RACE

Dwight D. Eisenhower went to West Point when he was 20. His entire adult life was lived in the military. The civilian remnant of his mind remained in the small towns of Texas and Kansas where he grew up in the horse, buggy, and kerosene lamp days.

The few African Americans in Abilene, Kansas, and Denison, Texas, in the early twentieth century lived entirely apart from whites. Eisenhower's proper, churchgoing sort of people bore blacks no animosity. They were the kind of people who were disgusted when they heard of lynchings. But it did not occur to them that there was anything amiss about the color line that decreed an inferior civil and social status for blacks. In the army African Americans were strictly segregated in a few units reserved for them. If a white officer did not command black troops as Eisenhower never did—there were very few black officers in the peacetime army, most of them chaplains—he never gave African Americans a thought.

Kennedy too had lived in an all-white world. Boston had the smallest African-American population of any big city. Even politicians there, like Kennedy's father and maternal grandfather, did not concern themselves with "the Negro vote," as politicians in other northern cities did. In JFK's rarefied world of private schools, Harvard, Cape Cod, and upper-class London (his father was FDR's ambassador to Great Britain), the only blacks were servants. Kennedy was a naval officer during World War II; in the navy African Americans were cooks, dishwashers, and waiters.

BEING BLACK IN AMERICA IN 1953

In 1953 Jim Crow segregation was as thoroughgoing in the southern states as it had been in 1910, and discriminatory laws of one sort or another remained in many states outside the South. Only sixteen of forty-eight states, all but one of them northeastern, had no state laws discriminating against African Americans. Except in small towns where only a handful of blacks lived, and in states like North Dakota that

The "colored" waiting room at a train depot. By law, such public accommodations had to be "equal" in quality. They rarely were. Often there was no "colored" facility. African Americans waited outside whatever the weather, or walked into a field to relieve themselves. If there was no "colored" shower room in a bus terminal, black people did not shower.

© Bern Keating, Southern Media Archive, Special Collections, University of Mississippi Libraries

had fewer than a hundred African Americans, informal residential segregation was universal.

Several northern states, where blacks could legally attend any state teacher's college, maintained one that was all black so as to discourage would-be African-American teachers from attending the others. In Philadelphia and other cities, by a custom as inviolable as law, public swimming pools were open to blacks only one or two days a week, when whites did not use them. In Wildwood, New Jersey, a major summer resort with five miles of ocean beach, African Americans knew to picnic and bathe on only one short stretch, much of which was made dank by a large pier. Blacks promenaded on the amusement-lined boardwalk only one evening each week.

In the former Confederate states, schools, hospitals, buses and trolleys and trains, waiting rooms, movie theaters, grandstands, rest rooms, parks, libraries, and even sometimes telephone booths were labeled "white" and "colored." Churches were segregated. Blacks were not allowed to stay in "whites only" hotels or to eat in "whites only" restaurants, which is to say almost all of them. Washington, D.C., was a Jim Crow town. Many federal agencies would not hire blacks except as janitors and cafeteria workers.

Prejudice

African-American contralto Marian Anderson on racial prejudice: "Sometimes, it's like a hair across your cheek. You can't see it, you can't find it with your fingers, but you keep brushing at it because the feel of it is irritating."

Author James Baldwin: "It is a great shock at the age of 5 or 6 to find that in a world of Gary Coopers you are the Indian."

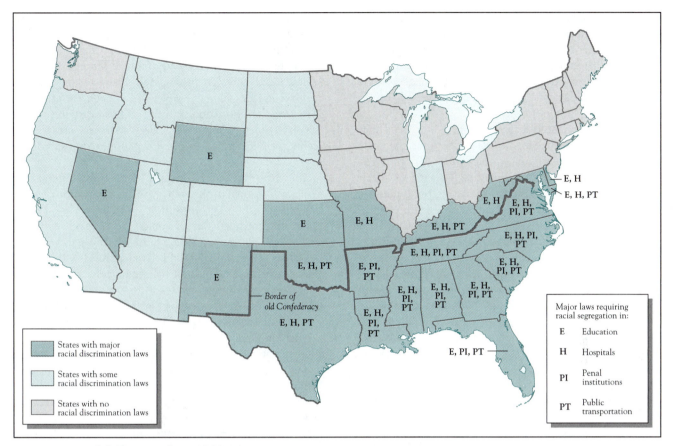

MAP 47:2 Racial Segregation, 1949

State laws drew a "color line" through public institutions and most public accommodations in all the states where, a century earlier, slavery had been legal. More than ten states that had never known slavery had laws that discriminated against African Americans in one way or another. Even states with no discriminatory legislation on the books unofficially approved it. In Pennsylvania, for example, while blacks could attend any one of the state-supported teacher's colleges; one of them, Cheyney State, was all black. Rather than deal daily with prejudice, almost all African Americans who wanted to be teachers enrolled there.

A black family making a long trip by car faced daunting logistical planning, identifying before they left exactly where they could stop for meals or a room, even for gasoline, without facing humiliation or running out of supplies.

WINDS OF CHANGE

But signs of change were in the air. During World War II revulsion of the Nazis' racial laws caused some states to repeal old laws prohibiting interracial marriages. Except in the deep South, long-established devices to keep blacks from voting were crumbling. In 1940 only 3 percent of southern blacks eligible to vote were registered; by 1953, 20 percent were. In 1947 a star player for the Kansas City Monarchs in the American Negro League cracked the most conspicuous segregated institution outside the South, major league baseball, when he joined the Brooklyn Dodgers. By the end of the season several teams had signed black players. By 1953 only a few major league teams still refused to sign blacks.

In 1948 President Truman ordered an end to segregation in the armed forces. Generals and admirals dodged the order until the Korean War, when military necessity ended segregation by unit. The high casualties reduced both black and white regiments by half and more, rendering them tactically useless. It was not feasible to wait for new recruits. So the weakened black and white regiments were combined to form operational units.

Lynchings, after a brief spike in numbers in 1946, when six African Americans were lynched in the South for acting "uppity," were rare. Southern governors who were militant "no compromise" supporters of Jim Crow, like Strom Thurmond of South Carolina, made it clear they would pursue participants in lynchings and prosecute them for murder. When a lynching occurred, it was national news. In 1955 a Chicago boy, Emmett Till, who was visiting relatives in rural Mississippi, was tortured and murdered after he showed off to his country cousins by flirting with a white woman. His murderers were acquitted and were soon boasting of the crime. What was new about the death of Emmett Till was the outrage expressed throughout white America.

VICTORIES IN THE COURTS

The National Association for the Advancement of Colored People (NAACP) had decided in the 1930s to fight an unrelenting campaign against segregation laws, with an emphasis on laws discriminating against African Americans in education. The legal foundation of segregation in schools and colleges was *Plessy* v. *Ferguson,* a Supreme Court ruling in 1896. *Plessy* held that so long as states provided public facilities for blacks that were equal in quality to those provided for whites, it was constitutional that the facilities for the two races be separate.

In fact, state-financed facilities in the South were rarely equal in quality. Well into the 1930s, the Jim Crow states offered few if any postgraduate programs for African Americans. Missouri met the requirement that citizens receive "equal treatment" before the law by paying the tuition—at out-of-state law schools and medical schools—for qualified blacks. Confident that this formula did not meet the *Plessy* test, the NAACP pursued to the Supreme Court the cause of a black man who wanted to attend the University of Missouri law school. In the *Gaines* case of 1938, the Court ruled that the "equal treatment" clause of the Fourteenth Amendment entitled qualified African Americans to be admitted to the "white" law school if a state did not have a law school for blacks.

The segregationist response to *Gaines* demonstrated how tough the NAACP's fight was. Most southern states ignored the decision; several that had provided no postgraduate opportunities for African Americans began to pay their tuition out of state—exactly what the Court had found unconstitutional. The segregationists knew that the NAACP had trouble finding plaintiffs. Southern blacks who wanted to be lawyers or doctors just wanted to attend school somewhere, not sacrifice their careers to a cause that would eat up years of their lives. Only in 1948, when Truman's attorney general began to file *amicus curiae* (friend of the court) briefs in support of the NAACP, did the Court rule that a state must either provide a law school for blacks or admit black applicants to its whites-only school. (Oklahoma chose to open a black law school.)

In 1950 the NAACP's chief counsel, Thurgood Marshall, won two major cases on the same day. Oklahoma had admitted an African American to its graduate program in education but segregated him within the school: he was forced to sit at a desk outside the doors of classrooms. Unanimously in *McLaurin* v. *Oklahoma* the Court forbade this discrimination.

Texas maintained two law schools. In *Sweatt* v. *Painter* the Court held, again unanimously, that the black law school was not the "equal" of the white law school because a degree from the black school was not as prestigious as one from the white school and because blacks training to be lawyers were denied the opportunity to meet and interact with the whites who would be their professional colleagues.

McLaurin and *Sweatt* had results. Within six months about 1,000 African Americans were admitted to formerly all-white graduate schools in Arkansas, Kentucky, Maryland, and Oklahoma. Delaware desegregated all of its graduate schools. NAACP optimists believed that the way was now clear to end segregation in elementary and secondary education.

Brown v. School Board of Topeka

Thurgood Marshall and NAACP president Roy Wilkins were not so confident. They knew that graduate education was an easier nut to crack because uneducated, lower-class southern whites—the political backbone of Jim Crow—took little interest in it. (Among African Americans, only a small elite took an interest in graduate school.) Ordinary whites were, however, passionately interested in primary and secondary schools, which their children attended. Desegregation of schools would almost certainly mean massive, violent protest. The Court, Marshall and Wilkins feared, would hesitate to provide a pretext for social upheaval in the midst of the Cold War.

They read the Court correctly. In 1952 only one justice, William O. Douglass, favored, with no reservations, ruling school segregation unconstitutional. The liberal Hugo Black saw distinctions between "reasonable segregation" and "unreasonable segregation," although he leaned toward outlawing school segregation. So did Felix Frankfurter, although he hesitated because he did not believe judges should impress their personal values on the law. A one-vote majority of the Court, led by Chief Justice Fred Vinson, said they saw nothing unconstitutional in segregated primary and high schools.

Then, in September 1953, an apparently healthy Vinson suddenly died. To succeed him President Eisenhower named former California Governor Earl Warren. Informally—at a White House social—Eisenhower let Warren know that he hoped to avoid the uproar that an antisegregation decision would mean. Warren was annoyed at Ike's meddling, and his presence on the Court meant that in the key case, **Brown v. School Board of Topeka,** a majority of justices favored ending segregation. But Warren wanted a unanimous vote and a single opinion to make it clear to segregationists that there was no wiggle room. It seemed an impossible task, but Warren pulled it off. Even a firmly prosegregation southern justice was convinced by Warren's case for the importance of unanimity and signed Warren's opinion.

WHITE RESISTANCE

There was grumbling everywhere. In the cities and larger towns of the upper South, however, where fewer whites were virulent bigots, schools desegregated peacefully. In Mississippi and Alabama politicians said they would never comply with *Brown.* It took six years of litigation for a young woman, Autherine Lucy, to be allowed to register at the University of Alabama, and then there was a riot on campus. In 1959, when an African American tried to enroll at the University of Mississippi, he was arrested on a lunacy warrant and committed to an asylum for a psychiatric examination. When he was released, he prudently left the state: the "cause" was one thing; his life was another.

In Arkansas, where trouble was not expected, the schools crisis exploded. In Little Rock in September 1957 a mob of white adults greeted the first black pupils at Central High School with shouts, curses, and rocks. Claiming that he was keeping the peace, Governor Orval Faubus called out the Arkansas National Guard to prevent the black children from enrolling.

Eisenhower was furious, but he was angrier at Earl Warren than at Faubus. He said that naming Warren as chief justice

© UPI-Bettmann/Corbis

Arkansas Governor Orval Faubus mobilized the National Guard to prevent black students from attending Central High School in Little Rock on the grounds they were the cause of a riot. President Eisenhower federalized the Guard and assigned them to protect the African-American students. It was a unique incident in the history of the National Guard.

was the biggest mistake of his presidency. But Governor Faubus was defying the federal government, which the president would not tolerate. Eisenhower took control of the Arkansas National Guard and ordered it to enforce integration at Central High.

CIVIL RIGHTS: FROM THE COURTS TO THE STREETS

In the meantime, the civil rights movement entered a new phase: direct action by hundreds of thousands of African Americans. The leader of the upheaval was Martin Luther King Jr., a young Baptist preacher in Montgomery, Alabama, who won fame as the leader of a battle against racial segregation on the city's buses.

MARTIN LUTHER KING JR.

In Montgomery, like almost everywhere in the South, blacks were required by law to sit in several rows of seats in the back of buses. In Montgomery when the whites-only section was full, seated blacks had to stand, a row at a time, to make room for whites who boarded. In 1955 Rosa Parks, a seamstress, refused to give up her seat to a white passenger and was arrested. Led by the city's black ministers, Montgomery's African Americans retaliated by boycotting the bus system.

They walked or carpooled to work with such unanimity that the city bus system faced bankruptcy.

Journalists and television reporters flocked to Montgomery to report on the extraordinary protest. King emerged as the boycott's spokesman in part because of his eloquence and the prestige of his church but also because, as a newcomer, he had less to lose than better-established ministers.

Or so he thought. He was repeatedly arrested and roughed up by police. His home was bombed. Nevertheless, King pleaded with blacks to remain nonviolent. Nonviolent civil disobedience, King explained, meant refusing to obey morally reprehensible laws such as those that sustained segregation, but without violence. When arrested, protesters should not resist. Not only was this the "Christian way," he said, but it was also politically effective. When decent white people were confronted on their television sets with police officers brutalizing peaceful blacks and their white supporters simply because they demanded their rights as citizens, they would, King believed, force politicians to change the laws.

King's technique worked. Some labor leaders such as Walter Reuther of the United Automobile Workers marched with the young minister and helped finance the Southern Christian Leadership Conference (SCLC), which King founded. After 1960, when SCLC's youth organization, the Student Nonviolent Coordinating Committee (SNCC), peacefully violated laws that prohibited blacks from eating at lunch counters in

© UPI-Bettmann/Corbis

Martin Luther King Jr. was already de facto spokesman for African Americans when, in August 1963, he led the 200,000-strong "March on Washington" in support of civil rights legislation despite President Kennedy's pleas to call it off. Kennedy was still looking for a formula by which he could win the support of both blacks and southern segregationists. King forced the president to choose sides, and Kennedy chose civil rights.

the South, white university students in the North picketed branches of the offending chain stores in their hometowns. When white mobs burned a bus on which white and black "freedom riders" sponsored by CORE, the Congress on Racial Equality, were peaceably defying segregation in public transportation, the federal government sent marshals south to prosecute violent racists.

KENNEDY AND THE MOVEMENT

President Kennedy too was impressed, even moved, by King and the determination of the civil rights demonstrators. Sensitive to the importance of black voters to the Democratic party in the North, he repeatedly condemned southern white violence and praised the nonviolence of the civil rights movement. But he was torn. The political importance of the southern Democrats to the party's success had been demonstrated in his election. Had three or four more southern states voted for the segregationist candidate, the election

would have gone to the House of Representatives. Had, in addition, Nixon carried Texas, Kennedy might have lost. And he still hoped to win over southern congressional representatives to the New Frontier by steering a middle course between white segregationists and the civil rights movement.

When two southern governors, Ross Barnett of Mississippi and George Wallace of Alabama, said they would personally prevent the integration of their state universities, Kennedy and his brother, the attorney general, tried to cut a deal with them by phone. When Barnett would not budge, however, an unhappy Kennedy sent 400 marshals and 300 soldiers to the University of Mississippi. It cost $4 million to ensure James Meredith his right to attend a state university. In Alabama Governor Wallace physically blocked the door to the registration hall long enough to be photographed, but not so long as to risk indictment for resisting the federal government. In April 1963 Medgar Evers, the moderate leader of the NAACP in Mississippi, was shot to death in the driveway of his home.

THE MARCH ON WASHINGTON

The Kennedys were wedded to the civil rights movement, however, only by a massive rally, the March on Washington, in August 1963. Martin Luther King Jr. called for the demonstration hoping that so dramatic a statement would force decisive federal action against all racial discrimination. The Kennedys personally pleaded with King to call it off lest there be a riot, leading to social turmoil all over the country. They promised, in return, to send a civil rights bill to Congress. They pointed out that during World War II FDR had rewarded labor leader A. Philip Randolph with an antidiscriminatory presidential order when Randolph agreed to cancel an African-American march on Washington he was organizing.

King faltered briefly: could he defy the president and attorney general? But he told the Kennedys no. He was not asking for a presidential order, which Kennedy could deliver, but an act of Congress that, it was clear by 1963, the president could not guarantee. The March was aimed not at the Kennedys but at Congress and the nation.

About 200,000 people followed King through the streets of Washington to the Lincoln Memorial, where he delivered his greatest sermon and what is considered among the greatest orations in American history. "I have a dream today," he began:

> I have a dream today that one day . . . little black boys and black girls will be able to join hands with little white boys and white girls and walk together as sisters and brothers. . . . When we let freedom ring, when we let it ring from every village and every hamlet, from every state and every city, we will be able to speed up that day when all of God's children, black men and white men, Jews and Gentiles, Protestants and Catholics, will be able to join hands and sing, in the words of that old Negro spiritual, "Free at last! Free at last! Thank God Almighty, we are free at last!"

President and Mrs. Kennedy in their open limousine in Dallas minutes before the president was assassinated. He was in high spirits. A year before the election of 1964, his popularity was increasing. His apprehensions that Texans would be cool or even hostile—Lyndon Johnson had to nag him into making the trip—had been allayed. He had been warmly applauded everywhere.

Kennedy announced his endorsement of a sweeping civil rights bill to be debated in Congress in 1964.

ASSASSINATION

By the fall of 1963 Kennedy had regained the confidence he exuded in 1960. His triumph in the Cuban missile crisis made him less uncomfortable about his alienation of southern white segregationists. Public opinion polls showed his popularity up well above the 50 percent mark in California and other western and midwestern states that Nixon had carried in 1960. Their electoral votes would more than compensate for southern states lost because of his support of civil rights legislation. Vice president Johnson assured him that more white southerners than Kennedy realized were moderate on racial questions. With African Americans successfully registering to vote everywhere but in the hard-nosed states of the deep South, the Democrats would, as in 1960, run strongly in the South.

Johnson invited Kennedy to make a goodwill tour of Texas with him. Kennedy hesitated. He feared he would be booed and jeered. But Johnson persevered and Kennedy agreed.

They were met in San Antonio with cheering crowds, and Kennedy was reassured. Then, as the motorcade passed through a broad open space called Dealey Plaza in downtown Dallas, the president's head was blown to bits by rifle fire. Within hours Dallas police arrested Lee Harvey Oswald, a ne'er-do-well former marine and hanger-on of pro-Castro groups who worked in a textbook clearinghouse overlooking Dealey Plaza.

Kennedy's death unleashed a storm of anxieties and conspiracy theories. Because right-wing political organizations like the John Birch Society were active in Dallas, some liberals were inclined to blame right-wing "kooks" for the assassination. They circulated stories of Dallas schoolchildren cheering when they heard Kennedy had been killed. (The rumors were false.) Oswald's own political associations were, in fact, entirely with organizations of the left. He had lived for a time in the Soviet Union and tried to renounce his American citizenship. Many right-wingers believed that Communist agents were responsible.

Lee Harvey Oswald did not clear things up. Two days after his arrest he was shot to death in the basement of the Dallas police headquarters by a nightclub operator named Jack Ruby. Ruby said he was distressed to the point of distraction by the death of the president whom he idolized. Ruby was a somewhat sleazy character with underworld connections. His appearance added to the story the theory that the Mafia had killed Kennedy.

A NATIONAL TRAGEDY

A commission headed by Chief Justice Earl Warren found that Oswald was not part of a conspiracy. He acted alone. He was a misfit like Charles Guiteau and Leon Czolgosz. He

Modern Communications

When George Washington died in Virginia in 1799, it took a week for the news to reach New York City, almost another week to reach Boston. Within half an hour of John F. Kennedy's death, 68 percent of the American people knew about it.

wanted to do "a great thing." But sloppiness in gathering evidence and soft spots in several of the Warren Commission's conclusions only intensified belief in conspiracies and multiplied the number of theories. Although several independent investigations confirmed the commission's findings (while faulting much of its work), suspicions never died. In 1988 a large majority of Americans said that they did not accept the official account of the murder. In 1991 a Hollywood film implicating government agencies in the killing, all allegedly coordinated by an aesthete from New Orleans, was a huge commercial success.

John F. Kennedy was not a major president, not even a "near great," an unfortunate term some historians have used. He accomplished little domestically, and in foreign policy his success in the missile crisis was to pale in significance set beside Kennedy's then barely noticed military intervention in Vietnam, an involvement that was to escalate out of control and poison American life.

Still, the assassination was truly a national tragedy, like Lincoln's murder, much more so than Garfield's and McKinley's. Kennedy had aroused an idealism and patriotic selflessness that, after his death, was to dissipate into disillusionment, cynicism, and mindless political and social mischief. Daniel Moynihan, an official in his administration who was to become a prominent senator from New York, summed it up pretty well for a generation when he told of a conversation at Kennedy's funeral: journalist "Mary McGrory said to me that we'll never laugh again. And I said, 'Heavens, Mary. We'll laugh again. It's just that we'll never be young again.'"

FURTHER READING

General P. A. Carter, *Another Part of the Fifties*, 1983; William H. Chafe, *The Unfinished Journey: America since World War II*, 1986; John P. Diggins, *The Proud Decades: America in War and Peace 1941–1960*, 1988; James Gilbert, *Another Chance: America since 1945*, 1984; David Halberstam, *The Fifties*, 1993; Godfrey Hodgson, *America in Our Time: From World War II to Nixon*, 1976; William L. O'Neill, *American High: The Years of Confidence, 1945–1960*, 1987; James Patterson, *Grand Expectations*, 1996.

Civil Rights Taylor Branch, *Parting the Waters: America in the King Years, 1954–1963*, 1988; David L. Chappell, *A Stone of Hope: Prophetic Religion and the Death of Jim Crow*, 2004; Mary Dudziak, *Cold War, Civil Rights*, 2000; David Garrow, *Bearing of the Cross: Martin Luther King Jr. and the Southern Christian Leadership Conference*, 1986; Gerald Horne, *Fire This Time*, 1995; Michael J. Klarman, *From Jim Crow to Civil Rights: The Supreme Court and the Struggle for Racial Equality*, 2004; Stephen B. Oates, *Let the Trumpet Sound, The Life of Martin Luther King Jr.*, 1982; James Patterson, *Brown v. Board of Education: A Civil Rights Milestone and Its Troubled Legacy*, 2001; Harvard Sitkoff, *The Struggle for Black Equality, 1954–1992*, 1993; John White, *Black Leadership in America from Booker T. Washington to Jesse Jackson*, 1990.

Eisenhower's Presidency C. C. Alexander, *Holding the Line: The Eisenhower Era, 1952–1961*, 1975; Stephen Ambrose, *Eisenhower the President*, 1984; B. W. Cook, *The Declassified Eisenhower*, 1981; Robert A. Divine, *Eisenhower and the Cold War*, 1981; Fred I. Greenstein, *The Hidden Hand Presidency: Eisenhower as Leader*, 1994; Chester Pach and Elmo Richardson, *The Presidency of Dwight D. Eisenhower*, 1991; Elmo Richardson, *The Presidency of Dwight D. Eisenhower*, 1979.

Foreign Policy Robert R. Bowie and Richard H. Immerman, *Waging Peace: How Eisenhower Shaped an Enduring Cold War Strategy*, 2000; Lawrence Freedman, *Kennedy's Wars: Berlin, Cuba, Laos, and Vietnam*, 2000; Walter L. Hixson, *Parting the Curtain: Propaganda, Culture, and the Cold War, 1945–1961*, 1997; T. Hoopes, *The Devil and John Foster Dulles*, 1973; Zachary Karabell, *Architects of Intervention: The United States, the Third World, and the Cold War, 1946–1962*, 1999; John Prados, *Presidents' Secret Wars: CIA and Pentagon Covert Operations from World War II through the Persian Gulf*, 1996.

John F. Kennedy Robert Dallek, *An Unfinished Life: John F. Kennedy, 1917–1963*, 2003; Seymour Hirsch, *The Dark Side of Camelot*, 1997; Bruce Miroff, *Pragmatic Illusions: The Presidential Politics of John F. Kennedy*, 1976; L. G. Paper, *The Promise and the Performance: The Leadership of John F. Kennedy*, 1975; Herbert Parrnet, *Jack: The Struggle of John Fitzgerald Kennedy*, 1980, and *JFK: The Presidency of John Fitzgerald Kennedy*, 1983; Richard Reeves, *President Kennedy: Profile of Power*, 1994.

The Kennedy Assassination Gerald D. McKnight, *Breach of Trust: How the Warren Commission Failed the Nation and Why*, 2005; Gerald L. Posner, *Case Closed: Lee Harvey Oswald and the Assassination of JFK*, 1993; Art Simon, *Dangerous Knowledge: The JFK Assassination in Art and Film*, 1996; David R. Wrone, *The Zapruder Film: Reframing JFK's Assassination*, 2003; Barbie Zelizer, *Covering the Body: The Kennedy Assassination, the Media, and the Shaping of Collective Memory*, 1992.

KEY TERMS

The following terms are covered in this chapter and can also be found in the list of Key Terms at the back of the book.

brinkmanship	dynamic conservatism	Green Berets	missile gap
Brown v. *School Board of Topeka*	flexible response	kitchen debate	"more bang for a buck"

ONLINE SOURCES GUIDE

Use this listing to find online documents, images, interactive maps, simulations, and other resources related to this chapter:

American History Resource Center
http://history.wadsworth.com/rc/us

Selected Documents
Eisenhower's response to the Little Rock crisis (September 24, 1957)
Martin Luther King Jr. statement on ending the Montgomery bus boycott
Eisenhower's farewell speech on the "military–industrial" complex

Selected Images
North Carolina school refusing to admit African Americans, 1956
Martin Luther King Jr.

Interactive Time Line (with online readings)
Ike and Camelot: Politics under Eisenhower and Kennedy, 1953–1963

CHAPTER 48

Johnson's Great Society

Reform and Conflict 1961–1968

Gino Beghe

We have a problem in making our power credible, and Vietnam is the place.
John F. Kennedy

The battle against Communism must be joined in Southeast Asia with strength and determination.
Lyndon B. Johnson

In classical tragedy, the protagonist overcomes great obstacles to rise to lofty heights. Then, at the pinnacle of glory, he is destroyed, not so much by his enemies (although they are there to pick up the pieces) but by defects in the tragic hero's character.

Lyndon Baines Johnson and Richard Milhous Nixon, the presidents between 1963 and 1974, were tragic heroes. Both shook off political handicaps to win their nation's highest office by overwhelming majorities in 1964 and 1972. Both savored the exercise of power unhindered by introspection. Both were great successes within the spheres in which they had prepared to labor: Johnson as a domestic reformer completing the work of his idol, Franklin D. Roosevelt; Nixon as an arranger of affairs among nations, which he regarded as the twentieth-century American president's principal responsibility.

And both saw their careers end in ashes: Johnson because he clung to a war that was both lost and discredited, Nixon because of an act that was not only criminal but entirely

unnecessary, a two-bit burglary that, had it not been exposed to disgrace him, would have accomplished nothing for him.

LBJ

As a style, Kennedy's white-tie Camelot was a sharp break with Eisenhower's bureaucratic, low-gloss Washington. Lyndon Johnson, never comfortable among the glib intellectuals and Ivy Leaguers who surrounded Kennedy, ran a just-folks, nitty-gritty White House, informal just so everyone knew who the king was. He enjoyed watching the Kennedy holdovers in his administration try to fit in.

Kennedy had grown up rich, privileged, and self-confident. He attended prestigious private schools and Harvard; he had only to make phone calls to publish his senior thesis as a book; and he was a playboy.

Johnson's family was not poor, as he sometimes pretended. But the Johnsons were unpretentious provincials,

Lyndon B. Johnson. Political pundits of the time and since have observed that had it not been for the war in Vietnam, Johnson would have ranked behind only his idol, Franklin D. Roosevelt, as the greatest president of the century. Instead Johnson was forced to retire from the presidency in 1969, four years earlier than he planned, and lived in an obscurity that must have been painful for him. He died in 1973.

for Sam Rayburn, now Speaker of the House. By 1955 Johnson was majority leader.

THE "JOHNSON TREATMENT"

LBJ, as he liked to be called, was as deft a herder of Democrats (and Republicans) as Rayburn, although not as quiet about it. In turns he put together majorities in the Senate by administering large doses of syrupy Texas charm and cutting deals with senators who had pet projects to bring money to their states; when necessary, he knew how to twist a politician's arm without breaking it. The scuttlebutt was that, like FBI Director J. Edgar Hoover, Johnson "had something" on almost everyone in the Senate—enough that he could tacitly, with a smile, blackmail those whose votes he needed for a bill and who were resisting.

The vice presidency declawed Johnson. Outside the Senate, Johnson had no goodies to dangle in front of southern senators to persuade them to support the New Frontier. President Kennedy rarely asked his advice. Robert F. Kennedy did little to disguise his dislike for him; sometimes he ignored his presence.

As the president of a grief-stricken nation, however, Johnson was able to force several of Kennedy's proposals on some of the senators and congressmen who had stalled them. The Economic Opportunity Act of 1964 created VISTA, a domestic Peace Corps, and funded "Head Start" programs to remedy educational deficiencies among children of poor families. The Wilderness Preservation Act set aside 9.1 million acres of federally owned land as wilderness closed to economic exploitation and even intensive recreational development.

Johnson's greatest achievement before he stood for election in his own right was the Civil Rights Act, which Kennedy had to be pulled and pushed into endorsing and for which he could not have rounded up the votes in Congress.

A SOUTHERNER ENDS SEGREGATION

Between 1955 and 1964, when civil rights activists were fighting racial segregation in the South, a few voices suggested that when the Jim Crow laws were finally gone, white and black southerners would have healthier relationships than black and white northerners. The reasoning was that while segregation by law was a southern institution, interactions between southern blacks and whites on a personal level were "human," sometimes intimate, and often affectionate and respectful. In the North, by way of contrast, while African Americans suffered no legal disabilities, residential segregation precluded all but formal interactions; white racism was muted but intense; black resentments and hostility to whites were rarely voiced openly, but were more common than white people imagined.

So long as southern policemen were using fire hoses and attack dogs on civil rights demonstrators, such speculations found no audience. But Lyndon Johnson, on record as endorsing Jim Crow segregation as late as 1960 (obligatory in Texas), had long been disgusted by the system. He had said

ranching people from the hill country of central Texas for whom getting ahead meant finding a line of work that did not require sweating all day. Johnson went to a teacher's college and taught school for a year; but he was already attracted to the tumult and machinations of Texas politics. In 1931 (the Depression) he went to Washington as a congressman's aide and became a devotee of the New Deal. His faith in the federal government's power and duty to shape society for the better never wavered.

Johnson got lucky when fellow Texan Sam Rayburn, a major power in the House after more than twenty years as a member, took a shine to him. With Rayburn's help, Johnson was elected to Congress in 1936. Except for a brief stint in the navy, he remained there until in 1948 he won a Senate seat by so narrow a margin of controversial votes that Texans called him "Landslide Lyndon." Texas politicians had been called worse; Johnson shrugged and became the voice in the Senate

privately, "I'll tell you what's at the bottom of [segregation]. If you can convince the lowest white man he's better than the best colored man, he won't notice you're picking his pocket. Hell, give him somebody to look down on, and he'll empty his pockets for you." LBJ had never courted African-American voters in Texas, but he was popular among Mexican Americans, also a submerged people, because he had been open to their grievances.

By 1964, like the Kennedys, Johnson realized that the Democratic party's future in the big cities of the North and Midwest depended on retaining the overwhelming support black voters gave it, and increasing the number of African Americans who were registered. In the South, Johnson anticipated that die-hard white racists would bolt the party (although not, perhaps, their move en masse to the Republican party). The southern Democratic party could continue to win elections by putting together an alliance of blacks and progressive southern whites without strong racial antipathies. The Civil Rights Act of 1964 was not only just and overdue in Johnson's view, it was politically sensible.

The Civil Rights Act decisively ended segregation in public schools and pulled down the "white" and "colored" signs on public accommodations that had been a part of everyday southern life for more than half a century. It created a Fair Employment Practices Commission to end a yawning gap in joblessness between whites and blacks in the North as well as the South. It was the first federal legislation directed against racial discrimination since the end of Reconstruction.

THE GREAT SOCIETY

In 1964 the Democrats held their nominating convention in Atlantic City, New Jersey, an unusual location for such an event. The Democrats selected Atlantic City because it was a badly decayed former resort with large slums. Meeting there was a statement of the party's determination to attack the problem of poverty in America, the surprising extent of which had been revealed in *The Other America* by socialist Michael Harrington in 1962.

The convention promised to be uneventful. Johnson would be nominated unanimously. The only question of interest was whom he would pick to be vice president. However, yawning newspaper and television reporters were rewarded with two unanticipated and colorful incidents to break the monotony—one apparently comic relief, one quite serious. Both, in fact, pointed toward the party's future.

WOMEN'S LIBBERS AND FREEDOM DEMOCRATS

Atlantic City's last handhold on its past glories was the fact that the annual Miss America Pageant was still held in the convention hall where the Democrats were meeting. On the boardwalk outside the hall, a small group of women, calling themselves the Women's Liberation Movement, built a small bonfire, removed their brassieres from under their blouses, and ceremonially burned them. Brassieres, they explained, like Miss America, were symbols of the reduction of women to the status of "sex objects." That was it for the moment; newspapers printed titillating photos, and TV anchormen chortled about the "bra burners." But in retrospect less than ten years later, this was the unlikely beginning of "women's lib"—an uprising of generally educated middle-class women that, in a remarkably short time, would transform every major American institution, most dramatically the Democratic party.

Inside the convention, an African-American woman, Fannie Lou Hamer of Mississippi, challenged the credentials of the official Mississippi delegates who had been sent to Atlantic City by a state party that had adopted "White Supremacy" as its motto. Hamer represented delegates from the mostly black Freedom Democratic party; she claimed that they represented the Democratic party of the Civil Rights Act.

To avoid an ugly floor fight that would mar his moment of glory, Johnson proposed a compromise: splitting Mississippi's votes between the official white party and the Freedom

Escalation and Frustration in Vietnam 1963–1969

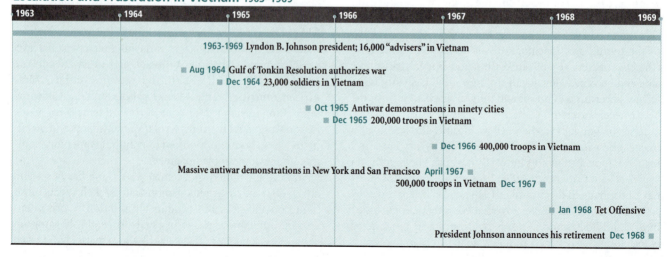

| 1963 | 1964 | 1965 | 1966 | 1967 | 1968 | 1969 |

1963-1969 Lyndon B. Johnson president; 16,000 "advisers" in Vietnam

Aug 1964 Gulf of Tonkin Resolution authorizes war
Dec 1964 23,000 soldiers in Vietnam

Oct 1965 Antiwar demonstrations in ninety cities
Dec 1965 200,000 troops in Vietnam

Dec 1966 400,000 troops in Vietnam

Massive antiwar demonstrations in New York and San Francisco April 1967
500,000 troops in Vietnam Dec 1967

Jan 1968 Tet Offensive

President Johnson announces his retirement Dec 1968

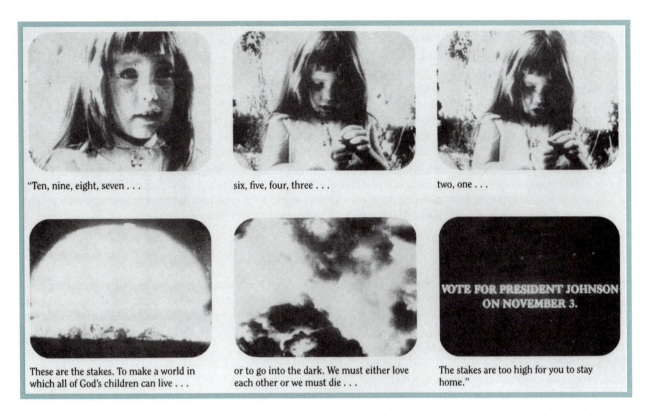

"Ten, nine, eight, seven . . .   six, five, four, three . . .   two, one . . .

These are the stakes. To make a world in which all of God's children can live . . .   or to go into the dark. We must either love each other or we must die . . .   The stakes are too high for you to stay home."

VOTE FOR PRESIDENT JOHNSON ON NOVEMBER 3.

This Democratic party television "spot" of 1964, showing a little girl counting down while plucking petals from a daisy, and then obliterated by a nuclear explosion, so enraged Republicans that the Democrats withdrew it. Its brief run and the continuing discussion of it served the Democratic party's purpose, tarring Republican candidate Barry Goldwater as trigger-happy and unfit to be entrusted with nuclear weapons.

Democrats. His point man with Hamer's group was Senator Hubert Humphrey of Minnesota, whom Johnson had picked for the vice presidential spot and who had fought longer and more actively for African-American rights than any other prominent politician.

Hamer wanted a floor fight to dramatize her cause, but it was too difficult to turn a friend like Humphrey down. The Freedom Democrats accepted the deal. The white supremacy Democrats did not want a floor fight they would almost certainly lose; they wanted fellow southerner Lyndon Johnson to seat them. Furious, they rejected the compromise and walked out of the convention, announcing that Mississippi's whites would vote Republican in November.

Like the brassiere burning on the boardwalk, the episode was of no great moment in the short run. Johnson did not expect to carry Mississippi anyway. But the white walk into the Republican party, rather than into a third "Dixiecrat" party as segregationists had done in the past, augured a revolution in partisan loyalties in which the Democrats were to be the losers.

THE ELECTION OF 1964

The Republican convention made for better news. Senator Barry Goldwater of Arizona, a conservative reincarnation of Robert Taft—anti–New Deal, Fair Deal, and New Frontier— had locked up the nomination. Personally, Goldwater was temperate and unbigoted. But he won the nomination because of the tireless work of right-wing extremists who remembered Senator McCarthy as a persecuted hero.

Many were members of the **John Birch Society,** which operated reading rooms throughout the country where, with the zeal of evangelical missionaries, they worked to convert others to their belief that the United States and much of the rest of the world was under the control of a Communist conspiracy far more vast and successful than anything Joe McCarthy had imagined. The founder and major financial supporter of the "Birchers," candy manufacturer Robert Welch, had said that Dwight D. Eisenhower and John Foster Dulles were active agents of the conspiracy.

Many Birchers were racists and anti-Semites (ironic because one of Goldwater's grandfathers was Jewish). That such people should set the tone of a major party convention, if not dominate it, was an extraordinary event. But they did; when liberal Republican Nelson Rockefeller of New York tried to address the convention, he was drowned out and forced to leave the podium.

Rockefeller and others asked Goldwater to repudiate the John Birch Society and other extremists. He refused. Instead, in his acceptance address, he told the convention that "extremism in the pursuit of liberty is no vice." Goldwater's chances of defeating Johnson were nil from that moment, and probably before. The nation had not fully recovered from the

The World Turned Upside Down

Before 1965 African Americans were an insignificant force in politics everywhere in the United States except in large cities, where they were 20 to 30 percent of the population. Even in those cities, few black Democratic politicians were nominated for high office except in solidly African-American congressional districts.

The Voting Rights Act changed that. Atlanta, New Orleans, Newark, Gary, and Detroit elected black mayors during the 1970s. By 1984 three of the nation's ten largest cities—Chicago, Los Angeles, and Philadelphia—had black mayors. Tom Bradley of Los Angeles, a former policeman, narrowly missed winning the governorship of California in 1982.

Rather more astonishing, in Alabama's gubernatorial election in 1982 George Wallace, the symbol of resistance to black equality in the 1960s, and who ran for president on a thinly veiled anti-black platform in 1968, courted black voters, and—when the totals were in and analyzed—discovered that he owed his election victory to African Americans. (Alabama's blacks found Wallace's Republican opponent by far a worse choice.) Even southern Republicans, whose support base was southern whites unreconciled to black equality, ceased to make appeals for votes based on race. In 1982 Strom Thurmond of South Carolina was addressing black audiences, fishing for votes.

Kennedy assassination, and Goldwater had frequently mused casually about using nuclear weapons against Communist enemies. Democratic propaganda easily depicted him as a man who would rush to push the red button in a crisis.

Johnson won 61 percent of the popular vote and majorities in all but six states, five of them southern. His landslide swept Democrats into Congress from districts that had voted Republican for twenty years. The Democrats had a majority in the Senate of 68–32 and, in the House, of 295–140: the greatest imbalance since the heights of the New Deal.

THE VOTING RIGHTS ACT OF 1965

The loss of five southern states where few blacks were registered to vote confirmed Johnson's belief that African-American votes were essential to the party's future. In the Voting Rights Act of 1965, enacted easily with such large Democratic majorities, the federal government put its power behind the rights of African Americans to vote. Protected in this right for the first time since Reconstruction, southern blacks rushed to register. Just ten years after Martin Luther King Jr.'s Montgomery bus boycott, the institutional obstacles to racial equality were gone. Before long, southern white politicians who had built their careers on race baiting were showing up at black gatherings—beaming, shaking hands, kissing babies, and lamenting past misunderstandings.

A black former civil rights activist, Julian Bond, was elected to the Georgia state assembly. He was amused that businessmen who had denounced him as a dangerous radical not long before now took him out to lunch to lobby for their legislative needs. By the early 1970s all southern Democrats were courting African-American voters. But that was possible only because hard-nosed white segregationists began, one by one, to abandon the Democratic party.

JOHNSON'S DOMESTIC PROGRAM

LBJ idolized FDR. He hoped that history would remember him as the president who completed the social reform of the United States that the New Deal had started. He promised a **Great Society** in which "no child will go unfed and no youngster will go unschooled; where every child has a good teacher and every teacher has good pay, and both have good classrooms; where every human being has dignity and every worker has a job; where education is blind to color and employment is unaware of race; where decency appeals and courage abounds."

Johnson's "War on Poverty," begun in 1964 with VISTA and the "Job Corps," two new programs directed by the Office of Economic Opportunity, was augmented in 1965 with Medicare: health insurance for people over 65 years of age.

Medicare also benefited working-class and middle-class families, some of whom lost their health insurance when they retired. By generously funding schools, colleges, and universities and providing cheap student loans, the Great Society made higher education available to hundreds of thousands of young people from working families who otherwise could not have afforded it.

College professors, always poorly paid, some working nights and summers to support families, within two years found themselves pocketing salaries that boosted them into the upper middle class. Johnson also appealed to the intellectuals of the liberal Democratic coalition with the National Arts and Humanities Act of 1965. This established the National Endowment for the Arts, which made large grants to museums as well as to individual artists and musicians, enabling them to devote themselves entirely to their art, usually for a year. The National Endowment for the Humanities provided similar grants to scholars.

So many new bureaucracies created so suddenly inevitably meant inefficiency and waste (a great deal: there were not enough competent professional administrators to go around) and corruption (not much and mostly petty: college professors scratching each other's backs to get grants). Even administered competently and with integrity, the Great Society would have been expensive. But it was affordable. In 1964, before initiating the whirlwind of new social programs, Johnson and Congress were able to cut income tax revenues by $10 billion. It was not excessive expenditures on domestic programs that were to destroy Johnson. Nor were the groups that were the big beneficiaries of the Great Society to stand by him when things went badly; indeed, they were the first to denounce him.

A New Immigration Policy

The Immigration and Nationality Act of 1965 aroused little controversy when it was enacted. In repealing the discriminatory national quotas that had been the basis of immigration law since the 1920s, the act seemed more a peripheral, even just symbolic repudiation, blow at racial and ethnic discrimination than a reform that

would have significant consequences. In 1965 few Italians, Poles, Rumanians, and other eastern Europeans—against whom the quota system had been aimed—were clamoring to emigrate to the United States.

However, exclusion of Chinese and other Asian would-be immigrants (policies that dated to the 1880s) was also repealed. Discrimination against the large "overseas

Chinese" population in many southeast Asian countries, and the horrors of the wars in Indochina that were escalated after 1965, were to combine with impoverishment in Latin America and the Caribbean to create a massive influx of immigrants of nationalities hardly known in the United States in 1965. The Immigration and Nationality Act made this major social phenomenon possible.

VIETNAM! VIETNAM!

"Were there no outside world," president watcher Theodore H. White wrote in 1969, "Lyndon Johnson might conceivably have gone down as the greatest of twentieth-century presidents." Clearly White had written off that possibility only five years after LBJ's landslide victory. So had many of the president's devotees. By 1967 no one was saying, as LBJ's aide, Jack Valenti had said, "I sleep each night a little better . . . because Lyndon Johnson is my president." More typical was the remark of Senator Eugene McCarthy, a liberal Democrat: "We've got a wild man in the White House, and we are going to have to treat him as such."

What happened? Vietnam happened. President Johnson enmeshed the United States in a war in a southeast Asian country that, before 1964, most Americans could not have found on a globe. American involvement in Vietnam began with covert CIA operations during the Eisenhower administration. Kennedy sent combat soldiers to Vietnam (11,000 the day he was killed) to prop up the pro-American regime in South Vietnam. But it was Johnson who turned the American intervention in Vietnam into a major war that poisoned American society.

A LONG WAY FROM THE LBJ RANCH

Indochina—Vietnam, Laos, and Cambodia—had been a French colony. There, as in Africa, the French fostered the development of a native elite that embraced French culture and, for the most part, Roman Catholicism. This Indochinese elite prospered and played a major role in governing the colony. Even peasants who were Catholic (a large minority) enjoyed small preferences over the Buddhist majority.

There were, as in most colonies, nationalistic anti-imperialists determined to drive the French out. During the 1920s Ho Chih Minh, who lived abroad, emerged as the leader of the small and scattered but growing nationalist movement. Ho was a Communist; in fact, he was one of the founders of the French Communist party in 1920. Ho lived in Russia and China until World War II, when he returned to Vietnam to organize a guerrilla army, the Viet Minh, to fight the Japanese who had occupied the country.

Ho thought he had a friend in President Roosevelt. FDR detested imperialism; the alliance with the British required FDR to say little about the British Empire, but France was occupied and Roosevelt disliked and distrusted Free French

leader Charles de Gaulle. He made it clear on several occasions that when Japan was driven out of Indochina, he did not want the colony restored to France. In 1945, with many supporters who were not Communists, Ho Chih Minh proclaimed the Republic of Vietnam, patterning the proclamation on the American Declaration of Independence. However deep or shallow his commitment to Communist ideology was at the time—scholars differ—Ho was clearly courting the United States. He was even amenable to cooperation with France. When French troops returned to Vietnam shortly after the war, Ho proposed keeping Vietnam within the French imperial community as a self-governing commonwealth like Canada and Australia in the British empire.

The French refused and set up a puppet regime. Ho and the Viet Minh returned to the jungles and rice paddies and resumed the guerrilla war they had fought against the Japanese. For the United States, the fatal year was 1950. The Cold War was at its hottest; the Korean War was at its height. The ideology that defined all Communists as part of a unified international conspiracy was fixed in the popular mind and in national policy. Defining Ho Chi Minh as a Soviet stooge, the United States began to funnel aid to the French. After a decisive defeat in 1954, the French gave up and went home.

The **Geneva Accords** of that year divided an independent Vietnam at the seventeenth parallel into two transitional zones. Ho's Viet Minh would administer the northern half of the country from Hanoi; non-Communist nationalists would administer the south from the city of Saigon. In nationwide democratic elections in 1956, the Vietnamese would choose a permanent government. The United States participated in drawing up the Geneva Accords; then–Secretary of State Dulles refused to sign them, quickly adding that the United States would respect the agreement. Dulles can only have had covert subversion of the Geneva Accords in mind.

AN AMERICAN SHOW

Between 1954 and 1956 about a million Vietnamese, most of them Catholics, fled from the north to the south. The Eisenhower administration helped a Vietnamese exile then living in the United States, Ngo Dinh Diem, return to Saigon, where he took control of the ostensibly transitional government. Touted in the United States as Vietnam's George Washington, Diem received $320 million in American aid just in 1955. His regime stabilized South Vietnam, but it was clear

AP/Wide World Photos

Ho Chi Minh, the evil nemesis for those who believed victory in Vietnam was essential in the global battle with Communism. To many who opposed the war, Ho was an enlightened and moderate national leader who had sought American friendship and who could have been productively dealt with peacefully had not the United States adopted the stance that everyone who was a Communist was a diabolical enemy. Ho may have been little more than a symbol by the 1960s when the conflict in Vietnam escalated into a full-blown war. He was in his seventies and rarely appeared in public.

that his backers would lose to the Viet Minh in the 1956 elections. Diem's anti-French credentials were good enough, but he did not have Ho Chi Minh's following. With Washington's approval, Diem canceled the election and proclaimed South Vietnam's independence.

Another anti-Communist Vietnamese might have pulled it off. Plenty of South Vietnamese favored Ho, but a majority did not; they preferred independence from the North. Diem, however, blinded by his privileged past and the large American subsidy, was surrounded by corrupt relatives and cronies. He squandered aid that could have developed the country's economy and won friends. He increased taxes, jailed critics, and favored Catholics to an extent the French never had. In 1960 opposition groups, including Communists, formed the National Liberation Front (NLF) and began attacking isolated patrols of Diem's army, murdering village officials loyal to

Diem and terrorizing uncooperative peasants. In parts of the country their guerrillas controlled, the NLF set up local governments, collecting taxes and enforcing the law.

Diem called the NLF the Viet Cong—Vietnamese Communists—although there non-Communists in the NLF leadership in the 1950s and many non-Communists in the guerrilla army. But *Communist* was the magic word to use in Washington, where Diem's beautiful and articulate sister, "Madame Nhu," was as effective a lobbyist as Madame Chiang had been. Both the Eisenhower and Kennedy administrations pumped millions into his regime.

KENNEDY'S UNCERTAINTY

Kennedy's foreign policy advisers urged him to send troops as well as money, telling him that the Viet Cong were weak and could be easily defeated. He hesitated. Kennedy had been stung by bad CIA advice at the Bay of Pigs and wondered why Diem's 250,000-strong ARVN (Army of the Republic of Vietnam) could not handle 15,000 poorly equipped, mostly part-time peasant guerrillas. Finally he sent 3,000 Green Berets, specialists in counterinsurgency, to advise and train the ARVN. When the situation worsened, the Viet Cong expanding its territorial base and launching effective raids deep within areas Diem controlled, Kennedy sent troops to defend the Green Beret bases and other American facilities. By November 1963, when Kennedy was murdered, 16,000 American soldiers were in South Vietnam.

Kennedy had, however, soured on Diem several months earlier. He had learned of the corruption in Diem's regime, and Diem's military ineffectiveness was obvious. When the military asked for an increase in American forces in the country, he replied that the intervention in Vietnam was like "taking a drink. The effect wears off, and you have to take another."

In the meantime, anti-Diem protests in Saigon and Hue led by Buddhist monks threatened social chaos. (Several monks set themselves aflame with gasoline in city intersections). Several ARVN generals approached American diplomats. They were prepared, they said, to oust the unpopular president if the United States approved. Kennedy gave the go-ahead and readied a plane to bring Diem and his family to exile in the United States. But the generals brutally murdered Diem, his relatives, and close associates. A month later, Kennedy was dead. As Americans coped with the assassination, the rebel generals began to squabble among themselves, coming close to fighting a civil war within the civil war.

MR. JOHNSON'S WAR

Johnson agreed to the modest increase in the American military presence that Kennedy had rejected. But he, like Kennedy, seemed to want out of the mess. Through intermediaries, he offered economic aid to North Vietnam in return for opening peace talks. The North Vietnamese replied that they could not speak for the NLF, which was partially true. In 1964 the NLF depended on aid from North Vietnam but was still a largely South Vietnamese operation. The NLF refused to negotiate until American troops were withdrawn. In early 1964 the NLF was riding high, and the South Vietnamese government was in danger of collapsing. The NLF's intransigence was a decision that, within a few years, all parties involved would regret.

DOMINOS AND THE GULF OF TONKIN RESOLUTION

Johnson refused to withdraw before talking. Never expert in foreign policy, he shared the assumption that Communism was a monolithic international movement. He thought in containment terms: the United States had drawn a line at the seventeenth parallel and had to hold it.

With better justification, he believed that if he withdrew the American soldiers, the ARVN would collapse, the NLF and North Vietnam would overrun South Vietnam, and there would be no peace talks. Johnson also accepted the domino theory of Communist expansion awkwardly propounded by President Eisenhower: "You knock over the first one, and what will happen to the last one is the certainty that it will go over very quickly."

When Johnson looked at Asia, he saw a line of fallen dominos stretching from Russia through China to North Korea and North Vietnam, and a line of standing dominos in South Vietnam, Laos, Cambodia, Indonesia, Malaysia, the Philippines, and even Japan. In 1961, when he was vice president, he said, "We must decide whether to help these countries to the best of our ability or throw in the towel in the area and pull back our defenses to San Francisco." As president, he vowed that he was "not going to be the president who saw southeast Asia go the way China went."

In August 1964 LBJ was informed that North Vietnamese patrol boats had attacked American destroyers in the Gulf of Tonkin. It is not certain if the incident actually occurred, but its authenticity was as irrelevant to Johnson as the authenticity of the Mexican aggression that James K. Polk used as grounds for war with Mexico in 1846. Johnson had already prepared what came to be called the **Gulf of Tonkin Resolution.** He asked Congress for authority "to take all necessary measures to repel any armed attack against the forces of the United States and to prevent future aggression."

Only two senators voted no: Wayne Morse of Oregon, a lifelong maverick, and Ernest Gruening of Alaska. Gruening said that he would not vote for "a predated declaration of war." In fact, Johnson was to use the Gulf of Tonkin Resolution to turn the Vietnam conflict into a major war. By the end of 1964 the American military contingent in South Vietnam increased to 23,000 men, still described as advisers.

ESCALATION

In February 1965 the Viet Cong attacked an American base near Pleiku. Citing the Gulf of Tonkin Resolution, Johnson sent in 3,500 marines, the first official combat troops. In April 20,000 more troops arrived, and then more and more. By the end of 1965 there were 200,000 American soldiers in South Vietnam—a huge army. This number doubled by the end of 1966 and reached 500,000 by the end of 1967.

Between 1965 and 1968 the Air Force bombed North Vietnam. To deprive the Viet Cong of cover in the jungle that covered much of South Vietnam, planes sprayed defoliants over tens of thousands of acres, killing trees, underbrush, and crops. American soldiers were then able to move in on search-and-destroy missions against Viet Cong who were no longer concealed.

Johnson's policy of step-by-step increases in the size of the war was known as "escalation." The object was to demonstrate to the enemy that every aggression would be met by an increase in technologically superior American military power. Resistance was hopeless. Twice, in 1965 and 1967, LBJ calculated that the Viet Cong had gotten the point; he stopped bombing and offered peace talks.

Both proposals were rejected. North Vietnam was now deeply involved in the war. Ho's government (Ho was quite

© Bettmann/Corbis

What the war looked like to American combat troops: a platoon pinned down in a rice paddy by unseen enemies. American technological superiority meant little against an enemy that refused to be drawn into the decisive large-scale battle for which the American army and marines were trained and equipped. When the Viet Cong and North Vietnamese risked such a battle, as in the "Tet Offensive" of 1968, they were defeated. By 1968, however, Americans were too puzzled by years of military ineffectiveness and disgusted by the high casualties even to believe that "Tet" was a victory.

old; it is not clear how many decisions were his) met each American escalation with an escalation of its own. By 1966, by American count, 100,000 North Vietnamese soldiers were in the fight. China and the Soviet Union both escalated their contributions to the war, supplying North Vietnam with ground-to-air missiles and other sophisticated weapons.

THE TET OFFENSIVE

At the beginning of 1968, the American commander, General William Westmoreland, announced that victory was within reach. His timing could not have been worse. Within days, during celebrations of Tet, Vietnam's lunar New Year, 70,000 Viet Cong and North Vietnamese launched simultaneous attacks on thirty South Vietnamese cities. It was the first major conventional military battle of the war since the French defeat in 1954. For several days the NLF and Viet Cong controlled much of the city of Hue. In Saigon commandos attacked the American embassy. The Viet Cong took back jungle areas the search-and-destroy missions had cleared.

The American forces regrouped. When the Tet Offensive was over, the Viet Cong and North Vietnamese had suffered horrendous casualties. By military definitions, the battle was an American victory. In May North Vietnam agreed to begin

peace talks in Paris. However, the American people's confidence in the war was shaken by the initial defeat and the increasing number of American boys dead and wounded, reported each evening on the television news like a football score. In 1965, 26 Americans died each week; in 1966, 96 a week; and in 1967, 180. In 1968, during the Tet Offensive, more than 280 Americans were killed in Vietnam each week. The cost of the war had risen to $25 billion a year—nearly $70,000,000 a day!

Despite this tremendous effort and loss of life, victory seemed as distant as ever. A few weeks after the Tet Offensive, public approval of Johnson's handling of the war dropped from 40 percent to 26 percent. LBJ was stunned. Years later, two top aides confessed they were sufficiently worried about his state of mind that they secretly consulted psychiatrists.

TROUBLED YEARS

Johnson craved consensus. He used the word in speeches as often as Kennedy had used the word *vigor*. When he made his plea for the Civil Rights Act, he quoted the book of Isaiah— "let us come together"—and the title of a song King's non-violent protesters sang, "We Shall Overcome." He earnestly hoped, and may have believed, that all Americans would rise above the blight of racial hatred and discrimination. His overwhelming election victory in 1964 persuaded him that consensus—a near unity of Americans on basic political principles—was a realistic possibility. He wanted a consensus behind his war in Vietnam too. What he got was a people more bitterly divided than Americans had been since the Civil War. The cleavage has not yet been closed.

HAWKS AND DOVES

Until 1965 the chief critics of Johnson's Vietnam policy were conservative Republicans like Goldwater, a few retired generals, and right-wing extremists like the John Birchers. They said that in moving so cautiously Johnson was making the same mistake President Truman had made in Korea. He was fighting a war for strictly limited goals—which, indeed, was the principle of containment policy—rather than for total victory. He was encouraging the enemy by repeatedly saying that he wanted negotiations; in the two world wars, Americans demanded unconditional surrender. Known as "hawks" (aggressive birds in the popular mind), they wanted to use the whole of American military might to obliterate the Viet Cong and North Vietnam. Former Air Force Chief of Staff Curtis LeMay called for bombing North Vietnam "back into the Stone Age." Former film actor Ronald Reagan said, "We should declare war on North Vietnam. We could pave the whole place over by noon and be home by dinner."

As LBJ escalated the war to something like the totality of American military might, minus only nuclear weapons, most hawks eventually fell in behind him. Then his chief critics were "doves," who called for a unilateral end to the fighting or, at least, more earnest efforts to negotiate a peace. Personally, Johnson was mystified by their attacks; twice he had halted aerial bombing and curtailed ground operations while inviting the enemy to peace talks.

As the war dragged on and the casualty lists mounted, the antiwar forces grew. Most doves were liberal Democrats—warm supporters and beneficiaries of the Great Society: congressional representatives, university professors and schoolteachers, ministers, priests and nuns, middle-class professionals, African-American civil rights leaders, and even a few retired generals. College students, more than a few sustained by Great Society–underwritten loans and exemption from the draft, provided the numbers that made the dove protests conspicuous.

Mass demonstrations made good television news and put the antiwar movement at the center of public attention. In October 1965, 100,000 people attended demonstrations in ninety cities. In April 1967, about 300,000 Americans marched in opposition to the war in New York and San Francisco. Some young men burned their draft cards and went to jail rather than into the army. About 40,000 went into exile to avoid the draft—most to Canada and Sweden, which refused to extradite them. More than 500,000 soldiers deserted (almost all briefly) during the Vietnam years, and there were some 250,000 "bad

Gino Beghe

A pacifist wall poster of the Vietnam era. It and dozens conveying the same message decorated tens of thousands of college students' rooms and apartments in the late 1960s. Pacifists, who opposed all war, often on religious grounds, were an important component of the antiwar movement. Some protesters regarded the Vietnam War as a bad war in a bad cause; others were pro–Viet Cong and pro–North Vietnam; yet others said the war should be ended simply because it could not be won.

discharges," uncooperative soldiers the army preferred to get rid of rather than imprison, as would have occurred during a popular war.

Draft dodgers with influential social and political connections flocked to the National Guard to escape the draft and assignment to Vietnam. Later president George W. Bush, to be elected in 2000 and 2004, pulled strings to win safety in the Guard; his predecessor, William Clinton, was trying to do so when he found a better way to avoid service. As president, Clinton sent soldiers to several wars; Bush and his vice president, Dick Cheney, another Vietnam era draft dodger (he said he had "other priorities" at the time), took the United States into a war in Iraq that reminded many of Vietnam.

The Drug Culture   *How They Lived*

Two "mind-bending" drugs were at the heart of the "counterculture" of the 1960s: cannabis and LSD. Cannabis is hemp, a plant cultivated in America for its fiber since colonial times. George Washington grew it at Mount Vernon; in Kentucky it became a commercial crop second only to tobacco; Henry Clay's plantation raised mainly hemp.

Some Indian tribes smoked the dried leaves of the plant with tobacco to dull pain. Several southern planters noticed that their slaves smoked or chewed the leaves, but took little interest. Before the Civil War, only a few people observed that inhaling the smoke from burning hemp leaves was good for a "high," including physicians who prescribed cannabis in a tincture (cannabis dissolved in alcohol) to treat pain, poor appetite, hysteria, and depression.

Its use as a "recreational drug" in the United States has two origins. In midcentury a brief vogue for things Turkish among swells in eastern cities led to the founding of hashish clubs, where they enjoyed the euphoria they had read about in the books of French novelists Alexandre Dumas and Honoré de Balzac. About the same time, settlers in Texas and New Mexico noticed Mexicans smoking hemp for its intoxicating effects. (The first antimarijuana law was enacted in El Paso, Texas.) The practice spread to New Orleans, where patrons of the city's high-class brothels picked it up at the end of the century from African-American musicians who were in the process of inventing jazz.

During the 1920s white musicians, attracted to jazz as it spread north to Kansas City, St. Louis, and Chicago, adopted "weed," "reefers," and "pot." Among whites, smoking marijuana remained pretty much a musicians' practice until, in the 1950s, beatniks picked up on it in the jazz clubs they frequented. The hippies of the 1960s inherited marijuana from the beat generation and created a mass market for it among the millions of young people who imitated their fashions.

LSD—lysergic acid diethylamide—is a synthetic drug with a shorter and simpler history. It was created in 1938 by a Swiss researcher, Albert Hoffman, who was looking for a new headache medication to compete with aspirin. He concocted LSD but set it aside as a dead end. In 1943 Hoffman ingested a larger dose than he had previously and reported that he fell into "a kind of drunkenness which was not unpleasant and which was characterized by extreme activity of imagination, . . . an uninterrupted stream of fantastic images of extraordinary plasticity and vividness and accompanied by an intense, kaleidoscope-like play of colors."

In the late 1950s the cerebral British writer Aldous Huxley, who had experimented with mescaline, a natural hallucinogenic drug, as a way to enhance his intellectual perceptions, "dropped acid" and wrote glowingly of its potential to inspire artistic creativity. LSD was not then an illegal substance. (Marijuana was, under federal laws of 1936, 1951, and 1956.) A young psychologist at Harvard, Timothy Leary, began ex-perimenting with the drug. He soon abandoned science for the joy of his mystical experiences during LSD "trips." When he began to preach its use, Harvard fired him. In 1966, just in time for San Francisco's Summer of Love, when the country first learned about the flower children, Leary founded the League for Spiritual Discovery. He toured the country with sound and light shows to spread the gospel of LSD.

Jolyon West, a researcher who examined regular LSD users (and administered the drug to an elephant, which died, and Siamese fighting fish, which swam up and down instead of forward and backward), concluded that the drug was dangerous. He said that one young man he interviewed "reminds me of teenagers I've examined who've had frontal lobotomies. . . . This boy likes himself better. You have to realize that lobotomies make people happy. They attenuate those inner struggles and conflicts that are characteristics of the human condition."

Such warnings did not influence hippies. Their purpose, however poorly they articulated it, was, in Leary's words, to "tune in, turn on, and drop out," ostensibly from the materialistic mass culture of America, but also from the internal unhappiness that reality has been known to cause. LSD and marijuana did the trick in the short run; few adolescents and young adults of any era have thought about the long run.

The beatniks looked on marijuana as recreational, "fun," relaxing. Leary and the hippies transformed pot and LSD into sacraments. Some New Leftists who wanted to span the gap between the political "movement" and the apolitical "counterculture" said that using drugs was a revolutionary act: "Drug consciousness is the key to it." Abbie Hoffman, a charter member of the Student Nonviolent Coordinating Committee (SNCC) who had worked hard to register African-American voters in Mississippi and was a prominent leader of the antiwar movement, found a new cause in drugs. He told of a girl who approached him: "We got to talking about civil rights, the South, and so on. She asked about drugs. I asked if she had ever taken LSD. When she responded that she hadn't, I threw her a white capsule."

The New Left's revolution never occurred. The personal revolutions of the 1960s and 1970s numbered in the millions. LSD did not, however, make the transition into the frankly materialistic hedonism of the 1970s. The evidence piled up that Jolyon West had understood the drug better than Timothy Leary had. Marijuana use, shorn of its 1960s religious significance, spread rapidly across the length and breadth of American society. In 1969 a country and western singer sold millions of copies of a record called "Okie from Muskogee." It was a superpatriotic, anti-hippie song about salt-of-the-earth Oklahomans that began "We don't smoke marijuana in Muskogee." A newspaper reporter wondered about that. He drove to Muskogee and bought an ounce of weed within half an hour of parking his car.

THE ARGUMENTS

The antiwar movement never spoke with one voice; the reasons different doves gave for their opposition to the war were incompatible with the motivations of some of their fellow demonstrators. A very few protestors were members of radical groups like the Progressive Labor party, a tiny sect that admired Mao Zedong. They were not "doves" at all, but openly hoped for a military defeat of the "imperialist capitalist" United States. Youthful romantics, who knew little about Communism and were many times more numerous than the Marxists, were enchanted by the spectacle of the outnumbered Viet Cong resisting American power.

Other doves, like the famous pediatrician, Dr. Benjamin Spock, were anti-Communists. However, they believed that the United States was fighting against the wishes of a majority of the Vietnamese people and, therefore, was in the wrong. They disapproved of the fact that their powerful nation was showering terrible destruction on a small country.

Religious pacifists such as Quakers opposed the war because they opposed all wars. Other morally concerned people, who believed that some wars were justified, felt that the war in Vietnam was not. They objected to the fact that with no clear battle lines, American troops unavoidably made war on civilians as well as on enemy soldiers. Bombs and defoliants took many innocent lives. And there were, as in most wars, atrocities. The most publicized occurred at the village of My Lai in March 1968 when American troops killed 347 unarmed men, women, and children. The Viet Cong were guilty of similar crimes, but that, some doves said, did not justify Americans stooping to the same level. (Others dodged the issue.)

Some critics of the war were concerned not with moral issues but with international relations and military policy. They pointed out that the United States was exhausting itself fighting in a small, unimportant country while the power of China and the Soviet Union was untouched. Diplomat George Kennan and Senator William Fulbright of Arkansas argued that the United States was neglecting its commitments elsewhere in the world. Senators Gaylord Nelson of Wisconsin and Wayne Morse of Oregon pointed out that the American war effort was alienating other small "Third World" (neutral) nations and even America's allies.

BLACK SEPARATISM

Complicating the destruction of Johnson's consensus by the antiwar protests were attacks on the Great Society by many young African Americans, more direct beneficiaries of Johnson's policies than college professors and students. Martin Luther King Jr., although a pacifist, tried at first not to speak about the war; he appreciated the significance of the Civil Rights and Voting Rights Acts. By 1968, however, he too had called for greater efforts to end the conflict.

King found his own leadership of American blacks under fire. The attack came from an organization his philosophy of civil disobedience had inspired, the Student Nonviolent Coordinating Committee or SNCC (pronounced "snick").

SNCC had sponsored boycotts of national chain stores that tolerated Jim Crow discrimination in southern branches, which inspired many northern whites to become civil rights activists. SNCC also had promoted the "Freedom Summer" in Mississippi, a campaign to register black voters that produced the Freedom Democratic Party of 1964 and helped ensure passage of the Voting Rights Act.

Without warning, newly elected leaders of SNCC like Stokely Carmichael and Hubert "H. Rap" Brown expelled all white members (many of whom had risked their lives during the Freedom Summer; two were murdered), condemned racial integration as an unworthy goal, and called for "Black Power!" **"Black power"** was instantaneously a catchword in the television age, but it meant different things to the people who adopted it. To civil rights campaigner Jesse Jackson and some intellectuals like sociologist Charles Hamilton, black power meant pressure politics in the time-honored tradition of American ethnic groups: African Americans demanding concessions on race issues as the price of the votes they could deliver or withhold.

To black nationalists in the tradition of Marcus Garvey, black power was a demand for a geographical separation of the races: a part of the United States should be set apart as a black nation (one group specified Georgia, Alabama, and Mississippi). No one took this program seriously.

In San Francisco, African-American teenagers and college students formed the Black Panther party, which ran candidates in elections and sponsored Garvey-like self-help programs, the most publicized of which was a lunch program for black schoolchildren. Black Panther leaders Huey P. Newton, Bobby Seale, and Eldridge Cleaver believed that by carrying legal firearms—shotguns and hunting rifles—they would display their earnestness. On one occasion they tried to enter the California state legislature with their guns. The consequence of their ill-advised tough guy pose was, of course, the successful determination of police in Oakland, the Black Panther base, to destroy the organization. The chief Black Panther legacy was the adoption of the most refined combat weapons by African-American drug dealers against one another and unlucky black bystanders.

To the great majority of African Americans who embraced black power, it meant dressing in dashikis, wearing hairstyles called "Afros," and—much more significant—resisting friendships and social relationships with whites. Just as Marcus Garvey found in the 1920s that he shared a common ground with the Ku Klux Klan, black power social separatists were proponents of the racial division that segregationists said was necessary.

MALCOLM X AND VIOLENCE

The most formidable spokesman for black separatism was Malcolm Little, a one-time petty criminal who called himself Malcolm X because, he said, white slave owners had destroyed the memory of his African name and saddled his ancestors with "Little." An adherent of a religious sect known as the Nation of Islam, or Black Muslims (Christianity was the "white man's religion"), Malcolm could be a spellbinding

AP/Wide World Photos

Malcolm X appealed mostly to African Americans who were disillusioned with the civil rights movement led by Martin Luther King Jr., despite its success in forcing the passage of the Civil Rights Act of 1964 and the Voting Rights Act of 1965. Malcolm X's defiant posture and refusal to rule out violence enamored some black adolescents and young adults and many white college professors. He was a superb orator. When he broke with the Black Muslims because of the hypocrisy of their leader whom he had worshiped, he probably ensured that he would be murdered by them, which he was in 1965.

orator. He rejected King's call for blacks to integrate into American society. Instead, Malcolm said, blacks should separate from whites and glory in their negritude (their "blackness"). Many young African Americans, almost all northerners, were captivated by his gospel of pride and defiance. One of Malcolm's converts (although not to Islam) was SNCC's Stokely Carmichael, who said in 1966, "If we are to proceed toward true liberation, we must cut ourselves off from white people."

Malcolm X did not categorically rule out the use of violence. His sometimes careless words on the subject appealed to former civil rights workers who had been beaten by police and, even more, to teenagers in the urban ghettos already drifting into the gang culture that was to become a fixture of life in African-American neighborhoods. H. Rap Brown proclaimed as his motto "Burn, Baby, Burn." When Martin

Luther King Jr. was shot and killed by a white man in 1968, another wave of African-American riots swept the country, and the Black Muslims increased in numbers.

But Malcolm knew that violence, except in self-defense, was suicide. Rehabilitated from his criminal past by the Black Muslims, he insisted that African Americans face the fact that they were themselves responsible for many of their woes, including the violent crime in black neighborhoods. His strict moral code led to his downfall. On learning that the head of the Nation of Islam, whom he had idolized, was a racketeer and a womanizer, Malcolm left the sect and became an orthodox Muslim, which meant rejecting racism. He was gunned down by Black Muslim assassins in 1965.

THE STUDENT MOVEMENT

Not all discontent among university students was directed into the antiwar movement. By 1963 it was clear that the baby boomers were not apolitical as the youth of the 1950s had been. Students demonstrated against capital punishment, protested against violations of civil liberties by the House Un-American Activities Committee, and worked in the civil rights movement. In 1963 Students for a Democratic Society (SDS) issued the Port Huron Statement, a comprehensive critique of American society largely written by a graduate of the University of Michigan, Tom Hayden. SDS called for young people to take the lead in drafting a program by which the United States could be made genuinely democratic and a force for peace and justice.

The New Left, or "the Movement," as SDS and similar groups were collectively labeled, was not so much a political phenomenon as an expression of anger and frustration. Hayden and a few others tried to channel student energies into concrete concerns like the problems of the poor and the power of large corporations. But most of the campus riots of the late 1960s were unfocused, aimed at the war but also reflecting trivial local grievances such as student participation in setting university rules.

Marketing Malcolm

In 1991 filmmaker Spike Lee guessed that the story of Malcolm X, unknown to the generation of young African Americans (and whites) who had been born after his assassination, would have popular appeal. He was right. His biographical film depicting Malcolm as a hero was a huge commercial success. Like producers of animated children's movies who have a line of dolls and figurines of their characters ready for sale when the film opens, Lee and others were ready with Malcolm X baseball hats, X T-shirts, X coffee mugs, X brand potato chips ("We dedicate this product to the concept of X, the suppressed African heritage of American blacks"), even X air fresheners for cars ("this is the lowest-priced item for Afro-Americans to show their support"). Warner Brothers, which distributed Lee's film, responded to complaints that Malcolm X was being cheapened: "The last thing we want is a poor product dragging down the image of Malcolm X."

The era of massive campus protests began at the University of California at Berkeley with the founding of the Free Speech Movement in 1964. By 1968 the demonstrations took a violent turn when students at Columbia University seized several buildings and refused to budge until their inchoate and ever-shifting demands were met. (They were forcibly removed by police.)

THE COUNTERCULTURE

For many young people the New Left was a way station, a place where they killed some time on the way to personal rebellion. In the Haight–Ashbury district of San Francisco and in New York's "East Village" in 1967, thousands of teenagers congregated to establish what they called a "counterculture," a new way of living based on "love," a word of unnumbered meanings. Love, to the "flower children" or "hippies," as they called themselves, added up to promiscuous sex, drugs, and extravagant colorful fashions that, like adolescent fashions since the 1920s, were designed to identify their wearers as a distinct group and to disturb those outside the group, "everyone over 30."

Conventional Americans were alternately disturbed by the apparent laziness and immorality of the "long-haired kids" and amused by them. "Far more interesting than the hippies themselves," sociologist Bennett Berger observed, "is America's inability to leave them alone." In New York and San Francisco, tour buses took curiosity seekers through hippie neighborhoods as if they were exotic foreign countries. Entrepreneurs, compelled to find a way to make money out of everything, found that commercializing the counterculture was easy. Advertisers used hippie themes to

sell their clients' wares. Musical groups created "acid rock," a sound created by amplified musical instruments that hippies embraced.

Some flower children retreated from the cities to communes that friendly intellectuals compared to the utopian communities of nineteenth-century America. However, individual self-gratification was the central principle of hippiedom, and drugs played a large part in the counterculture. Few communal ventures lasted much beyond the visits of journalists and photographers recording the first moments of the brave new world. "Do your own thing" was a hippie mantra; taking out the garbage and disinfecting the commune commode were few hippies' "thing."

THE ELECTION OF 1968

Lyndon Johnson, able to shout gleefully while striding through an airplane in 1964, "I am the king! I am the king!" discovered in 1968 that not even a reigning monarch can survive a serious social, cultural, and moral crisis. He did not even try. Early in 1968, the Great Society in tatters, he announced that he would not run for reelection. The man who brought LBJ to this humiliating pass was a previously quiet senator from Minnesota, Eugene McCarthy.

EUGENE McCARTHY

Eugene McCarthy was a tall man with a gray solemnity about him. His record as a liberal workhorse was solid, but no one thought of him as a mover and shaker. When he was elected to the Senate, Minnesota already had its walking earthquake of energy and exuberance in Hubert Humphrey. But McCarthy was anguished by the issue that Humphrey, vice president after 1965, had no choice but to dodge the war in Vietnam. Late in 1967 McCarthy announced that he would challenge President Johnson for the Democratic presidential nomination the next year.

Pundits admired McCarthy's dignity and principle. Some were taken with his diffidence, a quality rare in politicians. McCarthy seemed sincerely to believe that a public servant should serve. But the experts gave him little chance to beat Johnson in the primaries. McCarthy's only power base was the antiwar movement. Professional politicians wanted nothing to do with him. Labor unions, vital to Democratic success at the polls, begrudged him several votes he had cast against their legislative programs. McCarthy had no support among blacks or white ethnics, bulwarks of the party in the North or in the South. He was the candidate, or so it seemed, of just a small segment of the educated white middle class—those who opposed the war in Vietnam.

JOHNSON RETIRES

Time would prove the experts right. In early 1968, however, antiwar activists were so aroused that, like Barry Goldwater's right-wing Republican shock troops in 1964, they were able to turn the Democratic party upside down. Thousands of university students dropped their studies and rushed to

Robert F. Kennedy celebrating his victory in the important Democratic primary election in California. His win by no means guaranteed he would gain the party's nomination, but it put him in a strong position to compete for delegates with front-runner Hubert Humphrey, who was handicapped by his support of the unpopular Vietnam War. None of this mattered just minutes after this photograph was taken when, in a hotel kitchen, Kennedy was shot point-blank in the head and died.

New Hampshire, site of the first presidential primary. They got "clean for Gene," shearing their long hair, shaving their beards, and donning neckties and jumpers so as not to distract the people of the culturally conservative state from the issue at hand—the war. Sleeping on the floors of the McCarthy campaign's storefront headquarters, they rang doorbells, handed out pamphlets at supermarkets, and stuffed envelopes.

President Johnson kept his name off the ballot; the governor of New Hampshire ran as his stand-in. The vote between him and McCarthy was evenly split, but in a traditionally cautious state, that amounted to a rebuke of an incumbent president. McCarthy's supporters had good reason to look forward to primary victories elsewhere, and Johnson knew it. He announced he would retire when his term expired.

THE DEMOCRATS: WHO WILL END THE WAR?

The announcement caught everyone by surprise, including Vice President Humphrey, who was in Mexico on a goodwill tour. He rushed back to Washington to throw his hat in the ring. He had an edge on McCarthy because of his long-standing ties with organized labor, African Americans, big-city political machines, party professionals, and big money contributors.

But McCarthy's people believed they could beat Humphrey. To them, the sole issue was the war, and as vice president, Humphrey was part of the prowar camp. What neither Humphrey nor McCarthy foresaw was that in the wake of Johnson's retirement, Robert F. Kennedy, now a senator from New York, announced his candidacy.

Kennedy was a threat to both McCarthy and Humphrey. Johnson had eased him out of his cabinet, so he was not identified with the war. His connections with minorities were as strong as Humphrey's—much stronger than McCarthy's. He was a personal friend of Cesar Chavez, leader of the mostly Hispanic farmworkers' union in California and the Southwest. Even with blacks, on whose behalf Humphrey had labored since the 1940s, Kennedy was personally popular. When Martin Luther King Jr. was assassinated in April 1968, Bobby's response seemed more sincere than the respects any other Democrat paid. RFK had maintained his connections with the party pros and labor leaders. Among Democrats, his political realism and opportunism made him anathema only to the moralists who supported McCarthy. Even some antiwar militants, who had backed McCarthy as a means of making a statement, switched to Kennedy because they believed he, unlike McCarthy, could win in the general election.

Martin Luther King Jr.'s funeral in Atlanta. Although he was the educated middle-class son of a prominent African-American preacher, his casket was pulled on a farmer's wagon by mules to the cemetery to symbolize the esteem in which he was held by rural black southerners. Only Frederick Douglass and Booker T. Washington commanded the love and respect of American blacks that King did. No African American since his death in 1968 has attained his stature.

Kennedy ran well in the primaries, although not without setbacks. McCarthy won the next-to-last primary in Oregon. Then, on the night Kennedy won the final primary in California, he was assassinated, shot point-blank in the head by Sirhan B. Sirhan, a Jordanian who disliked Kennedy's support for the Jewish state of Israel.

The fourth murder of a prominent political leader in five years demoralized the antiwar Democrats and contributed to weeklong riots in Chicago during the Democratic national convention. Most of Kennedy's supporters refused to unite behind McCarthy; they backed Senator George McGovern of South Dakota as their antiwar candidate. With a divided opposition, Humphrey won the Democratic nomination on the first ballot.

NIXON AND WALLACE

Richard M. Nixon easily won the Republican nomination at a placid convention in Miami. Although the former vice president had retired from politics in 1962 after failing in an attempt to become governor of California, he had doggedly rebuilt his position within the GOP. He firmed up his support among eastern moderate Republicans and won over Republican conservatives by working hard for Goldwater in 1964. After 1964 Nixon attended every local Republican function to which he was invited, no matter how small the town, insignificant the occasion, or dubious the candidate he was to endorse. By making himself available to the party's grassroots workers, Nixon built up active cadres of supporters.

The Democrats remained divided. Many in the antiwar wing of the party announced that they would vote for the pacifist pediatrician Benjamin Spock. Humphrey tried to woo them back by hinting that he would end the war, but as Johnson's vice president, he could not repudiate LBJ's policy. Humphrey's ambiguity enabled Nixon to waffle on the war issue. He espoused a hawkish military policy while reminding voters that a Republican president, Dwight D. Eisenhower, had ended the war in Korea.

The chief threat to a Nixon victory seemed to be the **American Independent party,** founded by Governor George Wallace when he concluded he had no chance to win the Democratic nomination. A diminutive, combative man—reporters called him a bantam fighting cock—Wallace barnstormed the country and attempted to forge a coalition of southern segregationists, right-wing extremists, and blue-collar working people who felt that the Democratic party had forgotten them in its rush to appeal to blacks. The "white backlash" appeared to grow after Robert Kennedy was killed.

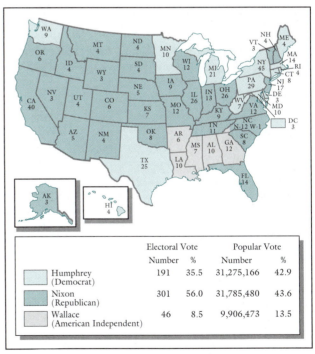

	Electoral Vote		Popular Vote	
	Number	%	Number	%
Humphrey (Democrat)	191	35.5	31,275,166	42.9
Nixon (Republican)	301	56.0	31,785,480	43.6
Wallace (American Independent)	46	8.5	9,906,473	13.5

MAP 48:1 Presidential Election, 1968

George Wallace's strategy was to deny both Nixon and Humphrey a majority in the electoral college. Had he carried one more southern state and one of the big midwestern industrial states where he campaigned hard—Illinois, Indiana, Ohio—he would have succeeded.

The Prophet of '68

The most astute analyst of the election of 1968 (before election day) was Kevin Phillips, then a Republican party strategist. Phillips foresaw that the Republicans would dominate national elections for decades because the Democrats had abandoned their working-class base to embrace sentiments that appealed to articulate and active educated liberals but few other groups. "Sure," he said, Hubert Humphrey would carry Riverside Drive in November, referring to a New York City neighborhood fashionable among intellectuals and well-to-do liberals. "La-de-dah. What will he do in Oklahoma?" among frustrated working people. Even George Wallace's spoiler campaign would help the Republicans in the long run: "We'll get two-thirds to three-fourths of the Wallace vote in 1972. I'd hate to be the opponent in that race. When Hubie [Humphrey] loses, [Eugene] McCarthy and [liberal Congressman Allard] Lowenstein backers are going to take the party so far to the left they'll just become irrelevant. They'll do to it what our economic royalists did to us in 1936."

Phillips's prophecy proved amazingly on target. He and other conservatives had their day of glory on election day in 1980 when Ronald Reagan won the presidency in a landslide. But Phillips soon soured on the Reagan administration and attacked it because, as he saw it, Reagan became the stooge of a new generation of "economic royalists," betraying the working-class base that Phillips had hoped to build.

Many blue-collar white ethnics who had liked Kennedy found Wallace more to their taste than civil rights pioneer Hubert Humphrey.

A CLOSE CALL

Wallace knew he could not win the election. His purpose was to win enough electoral votes that neither Humphrey nor Nixon had a majority. Then the House of Representatives would elect the next president. Because each state casts one vote when the House selects the president, anti-integration southern state delegations—at least twelve of them—could make a deal with Nixon: a reversal of Democratic party civil rights policies in return for their votes.

Fearing this possibility, Humphrey called on Nixon to pledge jointly with him that neither would deal with Wallace and his thinly veiled appeal to racism. Humphrey proposed that he and Nixon agree that in case neither won in the electoral college, the candidate with fewer electoral votes would direct his supporters in the House to vote for the electoral vote leader. This would render the Wallace campaign irrelevant.

Believing that Wallace would take more votes from Humphrey than from him, Nixon evaded the challenge. In the end it did not matter. Although Wallace did better than any third-party candidate since 1924, winning 13.5 percent of the popular vote and forty-six electoral votes, Nixon eked out a plurality of 500,000 votes and a majority in the electoral college. It was close. A rush of blue-collar workers back to Humphrey during the final week of the campaign indicated to some pollsters that Humphrey might have won had the election been held a week or two later. Some Democratic strategists blamed the loss on Johnson, who, peevish now even toward his loyal vice president, did little to help Humphrey.

FURTHER READING

General James Baughman, *The Republic of Mass Culture*, 1992; Ronald Berman, *America in the Sixties*, 1968; John M. Blum, *Years of Discord*, 1991; Howard Brink, *Age of Contradiction*, 1998; William Chafe, *The Unfinished Journey*, 1986; David Farber, *Age of Great Dreams*, 1994; James Gilbert, *Another Chance: America since 1945*, 1984; Jim F. Heath, *Decade of Disillusion: The Kennedy–Johnson Years*, 1975; James T. Patterson, *Grand Expectations: The United States, 1945–1974*, 1996.

Civil Rights and Black Anger Clayborne Carson, *In Struggle: SNCC and the Black Awakening of the 1960s*, 1981; David Garrow, *Bearing of the Cross: Martin Luther King Jr. and the Southern Christian Leadership Conference*, 1986; David J. Garrow, Taylor Branch, *Pillar of Fire: America in the King Years, 1963–1965*, 1998; Gerald Horne, *Fire This Time*, 1995; Michael J. Klarman, *From Jim Crow to Civil Rights: The Supreme Court and the Struggle for Racial Equality*, 2004; Sam A. Levitan, et al., *Still a Dream: The Changing Status of Blacks since 1960*, 1975; Stephen B. Oates, *Let the Trumpet Sound, The Life of Martin Luther King Jr.*, 1982; H. Sitkoff, *The Struggle for Black Equality*, 1981; Harvard Sitkoff, *The Struggle for Black Equality, 1954–1992*, 1993; Thomas Sugrue, *Origins of the Urban Crisis*, 1996; William

L. Van Deburg, *New Day in Babylon: The Black Power Movement and American Culture, 1965–1975*, 1992; John White, *Black Leadership in America from Booker T. Washington to Jesse Jackson*, 1990.

Critics on the Right William C. Berman, *America's Right Turn: From Nixon to Bush*, 1994; Mary Brennan, *Turning Right in the Sixties*, 1995; Dan Carter, *The Politics of Rage: George Wallace and the Origins of the New Conservatism*, 1995; Robert A. Goldberg, *Barry Goldwater*, 1995; Lisa McGirr, *Suburban Warriors: The Origins of the New American Right*, 2001; Richard Perlstein, *Barry Goldwater and the Undoing of the American Consensus*, 2001.

Johnson and the Great Society Irving Bernstein, *Guns or Butter: The Presidency of Lyndon Johnson*, 1996; Robert Caro, *The Years of Lyndon Johnson: The Path to Power*, 1982, and *Means of Ascent*, 1990; Robert J. Dallek, *Lone Star Rising: Lyndon Johnson and His Times, 1908–1960*, and *Flawed Giant: Lyndon Johnson and His Times, 1961–1973*, 1998; Doris Kearns, *Lyndon Johnson and the American Dream*, 1976; Allen J. Matusow, *The Unraveling of America: A History of Liberalism in the 1960s*, 1984; Merle Miller, *Lyndon: An Oral Biography*, 1980; James T. Patterson, *America's Struggle against Poverty,*

1900–1980, 1981; Bruce L. Schulman, *Lyndon B. Johnson and American Liberalism,* 1994.

"The Movement" Jerry Anderson, *The Movement of the Sixties,* 1995; Joseph R. Conlin, *The Troubles: A Jaundiced Glance back at the Movement of the 1960s,* 1982; Sara Evans, *Personal Politics: The Roots of Women's Liberation in the Civil Rights Movement and the New Left,* 1979; Todd Gitlin, *The Whole World Is Watching: Mass Media and the Making and Unmaking of the New Left,* 1980, and *The Sixties: Years of Hope, Days of Rage,* 1987; Maurice Isserman and Michael Kazin, *America Divided: The Civil War of the 1960s,* 1999; James Miller, *"Democracy Is in the Streets": From Port Huron to the Sea of Chicago,* 1987; Kirkpatrick Sale, *SDS,* 1973.

Vietnam Christian Appy, *Working-Class War,* 1993; George Q. Flynn, *The Draft: 1940–1973,* 1993; Stanley Karnow, *Vietnam,* 1983; Lloyd C. Gardner, *Pay Any Price: Lyndon Johnson and the Wars for Vietnam,* 1995; George Herring, *America's Longest War: The United States and Vietnam, 1950–1975,* 1986; G. M. Kahn, *Intervention: How America Became Involved in Vietnam,* 1986; David Kaiser, *American Tragedy: Kennedy, Johnson, and the Origins of the Vietnam War,* 2001; Gabriel Kolko, *Anatomy of a War,* 1985; David W. Levy, *The Debate over Vietnam,* 1995; Frederick Logevall, *The Origins of the Vietnam War,* 2001; Robert D. Schulzinger, *A Time for War: The United States and Vietnam, 1941–1975,* 1997; Tom Wells, *The War Within: America's Battle over Vietnam,* 1994; Marilyn B. Young, *The Vietnam–American Wars,* 1991.

KEY TERMS

The following terms are covered in this chapter and can also be found in the list of Key Terms at the back of the book.

American Independent party	**Geneva Accords**	**Gulf of Tonkin Resolution**	**John Birch Society**
black power	**Great Society**		

 ## ONLINE SOURCES GUIDE

Use this listing to find online documents, images, interactive maps, simulations, and other resources related to this chapter:

American History Resource Center
http://history.wadsworth.com/rc/us

Selected Documents
The "Port Huron Statement" of the Students for a Democratic Society (1962)
Betty Friedan's The Feminine Mystique
Lyndon B. Johnson's "Great Society" speech
Martin Luther King Jr.'s "I Have a Dream" speech
Excerpts from the Civil Rights Act of 1964
The Tonkin Gulf Incident and President Johnson's message to Congress (1964)

Stokely Carmichael and Charles V. Hamilton's "Black Power: The Politics of Liberation in America"

Selected Images
Lyndon Johnson
Civil rights march, Alabama, 1965
B-52 bomber taking off from Marianas Islands
Helicopter deploying American troops in the Vietnam War
University of California–Berkeley student during free speech sit-in, 1964

Interactive Time Line (with online readings)
Johnson's Great Society: Reform and Conflict, 1961–1968

CHAPTER 49

The Presidency in Crisis

The Nixon, Ford, and Carter Administrations 1968–1980

Official White House Photo

In a country where there is no hereditary throne or hereditary aristocracy, an office raised far above all other offices offers too great a stimulus to ambition. This glittering prize, always dangling before the eyes of prominent statesmen, has a power stronger than any dignity under a European crown to lure them from the path of straightforward consistency.

James Lord Bryce

Americans expect their presidents to do what no monarch by Divine Right could ever do—resolve for them all the contradictions and complexities of life.

Robert T. Hartmann

The heroes of Greek myth were constantly pursuing Proteus, the herdsman of the seas, because he could foresee the future and, if captured, had no choice but to reveal what he knew. Proteus was rarely caught. He also had the power to assume the shape of any creature, a trick that enabled him to wriggle out of the gods' clutches.

Richard Milhous Nixon's political enemies said that they were never quite able to get a handle on him because he was always changing his shape. Liberal Democrats called him "Tricky Dicky." At several turns of Nixon's career, even his Republican supporters found it necessary to assure voters that the "Old Nixon" was no more; the Nixon that deserved their votes was a "New Nixon."

John F. Kennedy, who defeated Nixon in the presidential election of 1960, said that Nixon pretended to be so many different things that he had himself forgotten who he was. Barry Goldwater, Republican presidential candidate in 1964, said that Richard Nixon was "the most complete loner I've ever known." Robert Dole, Republican presidential candidate in 1996, was nasty. When he saw former presidents Jimmy Carter, Gerald Ford, and Nixon standing together at a ceremonial function, he said, "There they are: see no evil, hear no evil, and evil."

THE NIXON PRESIDENCY

No one except his daughters loved Nixon. It may be that no one liked him. He lacked the personal qualities essential to success in late twentieth-century politics: he was not physically attractive; he lacked social graces, wit, "charisma."

He was shy; when he was not holding a pose, his manner was furtive. He could disguise his discomfort in front of a crowd only by a mighty act of will. He had little "going for him" but his will. That is why he is a compelling historical figure.

ODD DUCK

The liberals' dislike of Nixon had the intensity of a hatred; Republicans who were appalled by the fuzzy-headedness of the liberals accepted Nixon as their leader only when there was no alternative—or because "Tricky Dicky" tricked them too. In 1952 Dwight D. Eisenhower wanted to dump Nixon as his vice presidential running mate. But in a brilliantly conceived and executed half-hour television address that sidestepped the question of political graft that had put him on the hot seat, Nixon put Eisenhower in a position in which he would alienate more voters by dropping Nixon from the ticket than he would pick up. Nixon had good reason to distrust Eisenhower. When Nixon was running for president in 1960, emphasizing his experience—eight years serving Ike as vice president—Eisenhower humiliated him by saying he could not recall an instance in which Nixon had contributed to an administrative decision.

Conservative Republicans whom Nixon served for two decades distrusted him. When Nixon faced impeachment in 1973 and 1974, aides who owed their careers to him trampled one another in their haste to betray him. All was forgiven at his funeral in 1994: eulogists focused on his achievements, which were numerous, one momentous. Except for his daughters, however, no one at the memorial service spoke of him with affection.

Richard Nixon clawed his way to the top from a drab middle-class background in Whittier, California. Although he overstated it in his midcareer autobiography, *Six Crises,* he overcame formidable obstacles. Nixon was not a Horatio Alger hero because he was all pluck and little luck. Whatever else historians may say of Richard Nixon, he earned everything he got.

POLITICAL SAVVY

President Nixon had little interest in domestic issues. He believed that "the country could run itself domestically without a president." He left all but the most important decisions to two young White House aides, H. R. Haldeman and John Ehrlichman. With a cultivated arrogance in which they

President Nixon in the Oval Office with his widely disliked young aides, H. R. Haldeman (foreground) and John Ehrlichman (seated, rear). Nixon secretly recorded conversations in the office. His decision to do so was curious if for no other reason than because the tapes revealed him to be a foul-mouth. In the end, proof on the recordings of his implication in criminal activities destroyed him.

delighted, Haldeman and Ehrlichman insulated Nixon from Congress and sometimes from his cabinet. They were themselves unpopular. Like Nixon, they would have few friends when the roof collapsed. Because he did not want to be distracted by fights on domestic issues, Nixon's record was moderate—not at all what his right-wing supporters expected. Indeed, it was during his administration that "affirmative action," a program sacred to liberals in the 1980s and 1990s, first became federal policy.

Politicking, which Nixon had never enjoyed, he left to Vice President Spiro T. Agnew, a former governor of Maryland whom Nixon named to the ticket to attract the blue-collar and ethnic voters whom third-party candidate George Wallace was trying to seduce. (Agnew's ancestry was Greek.) Agnew relished his role as Nixon's hit man. He stormed about the country delighting Republican conservatives by flailing antiwar students and the weak-willed, overpaid educators who indulged their disruptive activities. He excoriated liberal Supreme Court justices and the "liberal" news media. Agnew was fond of alliteration and could push it too far. His masterpiece was "nattering nabobs of negativism"—that is, journalists.

Agnew's liberal baiting gave Nixon a superb smokescreen: despite his many denunciations of big-spending liberal government, the president did not intend to dismantle the ponderous bureaucracies the Great Society had created. His only major modification of Lyndon Johnson's welfare state was the "**New Federalism**": turning federal revenues over to the states so that they, rather than the federal government, could run social programs. The New Federalism actually increased the total size of government bureaucracies in the United States. Nixon (and later genuine right-wing presidents like Ronald Reagan and George W. Bush) found that the numerous

agencies that liberals created justified high-paying, do-nothing jobs for political hacks in the Republican party too. Barry Goldwater may have been the last prominent sincere believer in "small government" in the nation's history.

On some fronts Nixon might as well have been a Democrat. He sponsored a scheme for welfare reform, the Family Assistance Plan, that was to provide a flat annual payment to poor households if their breadwinners registered with employment agencies. (It failed in Congress.) When, in 1971, Nixon worried that a jump in inflation might threaten his reelection the following year, he slapped on wage and price controls—a Republican anathema since World War II.

Nixon understood that the people who ran the Republican party wanted little more of government than that it be business-friendly. As for the party's grassroots "conservatives," Nixon knew that while they caterwauled angrily about New Deal–Great Society spending, they were motivated into voting and activism by their aversion to the social and cultural causes that liberals embraced in the 1970s. The conservatives were upset by what they considered kid-gloves favoritism toward African Americans; assaults on traditional morality by feminists and "gay rights" activists; the anti-Americanism endemic in the antiwar movement; and Supreme Court decisions, praised by liberal lawyers and academics, that "coddled criminals" and hobbled police. Agnew's speeches kept them happy.

THE WARREN COURT

Fourteen associate justices served on the Supreme Court between 1953 and 1969 when Earl Warren was Chief Justice, many of them pulling in different directions than Warren. Nevertheless, critics of the Court's general direction during the 1950s and 1960s (and continuing into the 1970s) spoke

Revolution and Reaction in Foreign Policy 1969–1981

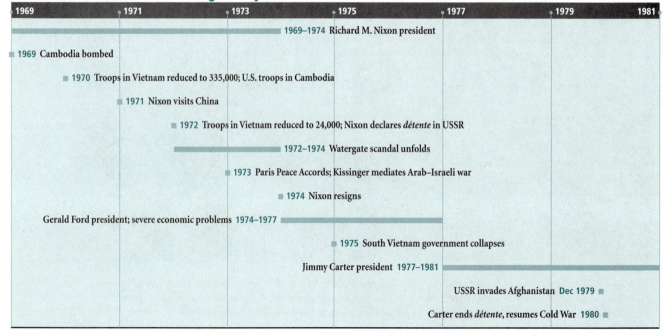

| 1969 | 1971 | 1973 | 1975 | 1977 | 1979 | 1981 |

1969–1974 Richard M. Nixon president

1969 Cambodia bombed

1970 Troops in Vietnam reduced to 335,000; U.S. troops in Cambodia

1971 Nixon visits China

1972 Troops in Vietnam reduced to 24,000; Nixon declares *détente* in USSR

1972–1974 Watergate scandal unfolds

1973 Paris Peace Accords; Kissinger mediates Arab–Israeli war

1974 Nixon resigns

Gerald Ford president; severe economic problems 1974–1977

1975 South Vietnam government collapses

Jimmy Carter president 1977–1981

USSR invades Afghanistan Dec 1979

Carter ends *détente*, resumes Cold War 1980

Affirmative Action

Originally, as Lyndon Johnson defined it, "affirmative action" was an admonition to employers and universities to aggressively recruit members of racial minorities and women as a way of righting past wrongs done to those groups. By the 1980s affirmative action had come to mean giving preference in employment and admission to educational institutions to women, African Americans, Hispanics, Indians, and Pacific Islanders. As such, by 1990 it was a defining position of the "politically correct," especially academics and university administrators. They were so determined to preserve preferences in admissions policies that when courts and referenda struck down affirmative action programs, they contrived methods to preserve racial preferences while adhering to the letter of the law. (By 2000 the numbers of white women in virtually all educational programs made them casualties rather than beneficiaries of affirmative action.)

Preferential affirmative action never had majority support. Public opinion polls revealed that a majority of members of both groups discriminated against (whites, Asian Americans, males) and groups that benefited (African Americans, Hispanics, women) opposed race- or gender-based preferences. Because Democratic candidates for public office could not afford to oppose affirmative action vigorously (they needed "P.C." voters), the party's stand contributed to the decline of Democratic voters at the end of the century.

Ironically, Republicans, not Democrats, were responsible for the reinterpretation of affirmative action to mean preferential treatment. Arthur Fletcher, an official in the Nixon administration, developed policies to favor businesses owned by members of minority groups when doling out federal contracts. Nixon approved. Republican strategists understood that in helping to create more African-American and Hispanic businessmen and women, they were creating Republican voters and campaign contributors. The percentage of African Americans voting Republican was still tiny in the 1980s but grew annually as the numbers of wealthy and middle-class black people increased. Affirmative action did not affect voting patterns among women: women remained almost evenly divided between the two major parties—the Democrats holding a slim edge—as they had been since the 1930s.

with hostility and even bitter anger of the "Warren Court." They condemned the Supreme Court for "judicial activism," which was defined as making law and distorting the Constitution to further a "liberal" political agenda rather than judging according to law and the Constitution.

Strident and often shrill denunciations of the Supreme Court began with Warren's first major case, *Brown* v. *Board of Education of Topeka* (1954). Because the Court drew on sociological and psychological evidence to argue that separating white and black pupils in schools was inherently unequal treatment of the races, critics—defenders of racial segregation—claimed that the Court had stepped beyond its judicial function. Some constitutional scholars, who abhorred segregation and were glad to see the Court rule against it, agreed that in *Brown* the Court had indeed made (or repealed) law. This was hardly the first time the Court had done so. What was new was that the Warren Court was applauded by liberals for its progressivism. In the past—during the New Deal of the 1930s and, in 1905, when a conservative Court struck down an anti–child labor law—liberals had been the critics accusing the justices of advancing a political agenda.

During the 1960s several Court decisions dealing with the rights of accused criminals angered many northern city dwellers, blacks and whites. In *Escobedo* v. *Illinois* (1964) the court ruled that a petty criminal against whom there was considerable evidence must be freed because, when he asked to see a lawyer, the police delayed until they had extracted a confession. Popular criticism of the decision had nothing to do with "judicial activism"; the constitutional issue in *Escobedo* was straightforward. People were angry because the obviously guilty criminal was released on "a technicality." Much more controversial was *Miranda* v. *Arizona* (1968), in which the Court ruled that the defendant's confession could not be used against him in his trial because the police had not informed him of his right to see a lawyer. Critics of the Court said that the constitutional right to counsel surely did

Griswold and *Roe*

Griswold v. *Connecticut* (1965) was a Warren Court ruling that aroused little immediate fuss because the law it negated was, in the words of one justice, "silly." It was an old, widely ignored, and unenforced Connecticut law forbidding the sale of contraceptive devices—condoms. Few people anywhere approved of the law.

However, the Court's rationale in declaring the law unconstitutional was as grotesque, in a different way, as Chief Justice Taney's infamous 1857 opinion for the Court in the *Dred Scott* case. The Court found that the Bill of Rights included, in its "penumbra," or shadow, a "right to privacy" that the Connecticut law violated. In another context Justice William Brennan, who concurred in the *Griswold* decision, actually wrote that some words that appear in the Constitution were not to be taken literally.

In 1973, four years after Warren retired, the Court drew on *Griswold* (and other precedents) to rule that state legislatures could not deny a woman her "right" to have an abortion. Ironically, the opinion in *Roe* v. *Wade* was written by a justice Nixon had appointed to bring judicial restraint to the Court, Harry Blackmun. Chief Justice Warren Burger, whom Nixon named to replace Earl Warren, concurred in *Roe*.

not include the right to know that right existed. The Court was rewriting the Constitution. Other rulings threw out evidence collected in police searches if the evidence in question had not been specifically described in a search warrant or if it was not in a defendant's immediate proximity.

To people troubled by crime, petty and violent, the Court was "soft on criminals." To some legal scholars, the problem was that the Court's decisions were based on the nonjudicial questions "Is it fair?" and "Does it protect the individual?" rather than "Does the Constitution explicitly forbid it?"

A well-organized and well-funded "Impeach Earl Warren" movement made no progress, although the chief justice was vilified by most Republican politicians. Warren had, in fact, become an active liberal on the bench. In 1968, worried that Richard Nixon would be elected president in November, Warren told President Johnson to appoint his successor immediately; when the new chief justice was confirmed, Warren would resign. Johnson promoted a Texas crony already on the Court, Abe Fortas, to the chief justiceship. Republicans immediately discredited Fortas by revealing that he had improperly accepted fees for making public appearances. Republicans were thrice rewarded. Warren was humiliated when he had to administer Nixon's presidential oath. Nixon got to appoint his successor and another justice when the discredited Fortas also resigned from the court.

NIXON AND VIETNAM

Nixon had watched the Vietnam War abruptly terminate Lyndon Johnson's political career. "The damned fool" had, in the words of a protest song of the time, mired the country "hip deep in the Big Muddy" and could do nothing but tell the nation to "push on." Nixon had bigger fish to fry, and he wanted out of the war. But how? The North Vietnamese refused to negotiate. Simply to pull out—surrender—violated Nixon's lifelong gospel of hanging tough with Communists.

VIETNAMIZATION

As Nixon saw it, public opinion had turned against the war because it was indeed unwinnable; why, then, continue to send American boys to the slaughter? To isolate hard-core antiwar protesters (pacifists, leftists sympathetic to the enemy, excitable college students) from the majority of the population, Nixon assigned Spiro Agnew the job of smearing the militants as anti-American. Simultaneously he reduced the long weekly casualty lists, which had alienated working people whose sons were the young men drafted, by turning

> ### Cleanup
> In 1912 the Chicago Sanitation Department cleared the streets of the carcasses of 10,000 dead horses. In 1968 the Chicago Police Department cleared the streets of 24,500 carcasses of dead automobiles.

the war (and the casualties) over to the ARVN, the South Vietnamese army.

The United States would "participate in the defense and development of allies and friends," he said, but Americans would no longer "undertake all the defense of the free nations of the world. . . . In the previous administration, we Americanized the war in Vietnam. In this administration we are Vietnamizing the search for peace."

The large but unreliable ARVN was retrained to replace Americans on the front lines. As South Vietnamese units were deemed ready for combat, American troops came home. At about the same rate that LBJ had escalated the American presence, Nixon deescalated it. From a high of 541,000 American soldiers in South Vietnam when Nixon took office, the American force declined to 335,000 in 1970 and 24,000 in 1972.

Nixon returned the American role in the war to where it had been in 1964. The difference was that in 1964 there were few well-trained North Vietnamese troops in South Vietnam. By 1970 the North Vietnamese army had absorbed the Viet Cong. As Nixon hoped, the influence of the student antiwar movement declined. What he did not anticipate was that another less theatrical but far more formidable opposition emerged. Mainstream Democrats who had dutifully supported Johnson's war now demanded that the Republican Nixon make more serious efforts to end it.

EXPANDING THE WAR

Even a conservative but disgusted Republican Senator George Aiken suggested that the United States simply declare victory in Vietnam and pull out. Nixon could not do that. He owed his election to hawks who believed that Johnson failed in Vietnam because he had not been tough enough. Nixon reassured them: "We will not be humiliated. We will not be defeated." Much as he and his foreign policy guru, Henry A. Kissinger, wanted done with the war, they believed they had to salvage the independence of South Vietnam to save face.

So Nixon tried to bludgeon North Vietnam into negotiations by expanding the scope of the war with low-casualty air attacks. In the spring of 1969 he sent bombers over neutral Cambodia to destroy sanctuaries where about 50,000 North Vietnamese troops rested between battles. For a year the American people knew nothing of this new war. Then, in 1970, Nixon sent ground forces into Cambodia, an offensive that could not be concealed.

The result was renewed uproar. Critics condemned the president for attacking a neutral nation. Several hundred university presidents closed their campuses for fear of student violence. Events at two colleges proved their wisdom. At Kent State University in Ohio, the National Guard opened fire on demonstrators, killing four and wounding eleven. Ten days later, two students demonstrating at Jackson State College in Mississippi were killed by police.

A now hostile Congress reacted to the widening of the war by repealing the Gulf of Tonkin Resolution. Nixon responded that repeal was immaterial. As commander in chief, he had the right to take whatever military action he believed necessary. Nonetheless, when the war expanded further into Laos in February 1971, he made sure that ARVN troops carried the burden of the fighting.

FALLING DOMINOS

Vietnamization did not work. Without American troops by their side, the ARVN was humiliated in Laos. The Communist organization in that country, the Pathet Lao, grew in strength until, in 1975, it seized control of the small, backward, and traditionally peaceful country. Tens of thousands of refugees fled.

In Cambodia the consequences were worse. Many young Cambodians were so angered by the American bombing and invasion that they flocked to join the Khmer Rouge, which increased in size from 3,000 in 1970 to 30,000 in a few years. In 1976 its commander, Pol Pot, came to power with a regime as criminal as the Nazi government of Germany. In three years Pol Pot's fanatical followers murdered 3 million people in a population of 7.2 million!

Eisenhower's Asian dominoes had fallen not because the United States was weak in the face of a military threat, but because the United States had expanded a war that in 1963 was not much more than a brawl. In the process, Indochinese neutrals like Cambodia's Prince Sihanouk were undercut. By the mid-1970s North Vietnam was dominated by an army, Laos by a small Communist organization, and Cambodia by a monster.

In South Vietnam the fighting dragged on until the fall of 1972, when after suffering twelve days of earth-shaking bombing, the North Vietnamese finally agreed to meet with Kissinger and arrange a cease-fire. The Paris Accords they signed went into effect in January 1973. The treaty required the United States to withdraw all its troops from Vietnam within sixty days and the North Vietnamese to release the prisoners of war they held. Until free elections were held, North Vietnamese troops would remain in South Vietnam.

South Vietnamese president Nguyen Van Thieu believed he had been sold out. Nixon had left him facing a massive enemy force. For two years the country simmered. In April 1975 the ARVN collapsed, and the North Vietnamese moved on a virtually undefended Saigon. North and South Vietnam were united, Saigon renamed Ho Chi Minh City. Ironically, Cambodia's nightmare ended only when the North Vietnamese invaded the country, overthrew Pol Pot, and installed a puppet regime that, if dictatorial, was something less than evil.

THE BOTTOM LINE

America's longest war ravaged a prosperous country. Once an exporter of rice, Vietnam was short of food through the 1980s. Approximately a million ARVN soldiers lost their

Vietnamese refugees fleeing Hue during the final victory of the Viet Cong and North Vietnamese in 1975. Ten percent of the population eventually fled the country. The United States admitted 600,000 refugees.

AP/Wide World Photos

lives, the Viet Cong and North Vietnamese about the same number. Estimates of civilian dead ran as high as 3.5 million. About 5.2 million acres of jungle and farmland were ruined by defoliation. American bombing also destroyed hundreds of towns, bridges, and highways. The Air Force dropped more bombs on Vietnam than had fallen on Europe during World War II.

The vengeance of the victors (and Pol Pot) caused a massive flight of refugees. About 10 percent of the people of southeast Asia fled after the war. Some spent everything they owned to bribe crooked North Vietnamese officials to let them go. Others piled into leaky boats and cast off into open waters, unknown numbers to drown. To the credit of the United States, some 600,000 Vietnamese, Laotians, Cambodians, and ethnic minorities like the Hmong and Mien (whom every government in southeast Asia mistreated) were admitted to the United States.

The war cost the United States $150 billion—more than any other American conflict except World War II. Some 2.7 million American men and women served in the conflict; 57,000 of them were killed and 300,000 were wounded. Many were disabled for life. Some lost limbs; others were poisoned by Agent Orange, the toxic defoliant the army used to clear jungle. Yet others were addicted to drugs or alcohol. Mental disturbances and violent crime were inordinately common among Vietnam veterans.

And yet for ten years Vietnam veterans were ignored and shunned. Politicians—not only liberals who opposed the war, but also the superpatriotic hawks who wanted the troops to fight on indefinitely—neglected to vote money for government programs to help them. Only in 1982, almost a decade after the war ended, was a monument to the soldiers erected in Washington, D.C.

NIXON–KISSINGER FOREIGN POLICY

Nixon called the Vietnam war a sideshow. Henry A. Kissinger said that it was a mere footnote to history. Both men wanted to bring the conflict to an end so they could bring about a reordering of relations among the world's great powers.

THE LONG CRUSADE

For more than twenty years before the Nixon presidency, virtually all American policy makers divided the world into two hostile camps and a "Third World" of unaligned, mostly undeveloped states. Nuclear weapons made all-out conflict between the United States and the Soviet Union unthinkable. Incompatible ideologies made mistrust inevitable and antagonism almost inevitable. The only prospect for a change in the dangerous standoff was—or so it had seemed—the internal collapse of one of the two superpowers.

Before he was elected president, Nixon said nothing to indicate that he imagined another possibility. But when he was presented with the opportunity for a revolution in American foreign policy—and the state of the world—he seized it.

THE PREMISES OF DÉTENTE

For all his public repetitions of Cold War orthodoxy, Nixon recognized even before 1968 that the world had changed significantly since the 1950s. The old bipolar view of geopolitics did not make sense with underdeveloped countries claiming an identity as a neutral "Third World"; with Japan the world's third largest economic power; with the nations of Western Europe groping their way toward an economic, political, and military role independent of the United States; and with the People's Republic of China clearly not a pawn of the Soviet Union. Reports had reached the West of Sino–Soviet battles on their 2,000 mile border.

Nixon intended to win his niche in history by effecting a diplomatic reshuffling after which *five* centers of power would balance one another and, therefore, deal with one another rationally. In 1971 he said, "It will be a safer world and a better world, if we have a strong and healthy United States, Europe, Soviet Union, China, Japan—each balancing the other, not playing one against the other, an even balance."

There was no idealism in Nixon's goal of *détente* (relaxation of tensions without illusions of friendship). He prided himself on being a hard-headed realist and chose a similar man as his in-house adviser on foreign policy (who probably introduced the president to the French word that he attached to his policy).

Henry Kissinger was witty, urbane, brilliant, and cheerfully conceited. He was a refugee from Naziism who, after living in the United States for thirty years, still spoke in so thick and guttural an accent that his critics thought it an affectation. As a scholar he was an unashamed proponent of *Realpolitik,* the diplomacy of the realist—an amoral, opportunistic approach to international relations associated with two of Kissinger's historical idols, Austrian Chancellor Metternich and German Chancellor Otto von Bismarck. The

AP/Wide World Photos

President and Mrs. Nixon at the Great Wall of China. Americans were astonished (although, within a few years, thousands of American tourists would have their photos snapped in the same place). Hard-line Republican Cold Warriors were flabbergasted. For more than a quarter century Americans had been told by their leaders, Richard Nixon prominent among them, that Communist China was an outlaw nation. Longtime advocates of diplomatic relations with China, liberals who were longtime political enemies of Nixon (who thought of him as an outlaw!) were benumbed.

Soviet Union and the United States adhered to two sets of principles that they could not compromise, Kissinger argued. Rather than risking the unthinkable war, however, the "superpowers" had to recognize that, "for the sake of peace, stability based on an equilibrium of forces was at least conceivable." Friendship was out of the question, but tranquility through **détente** was not.

In 1971 Nixon and Kissinger were presented, rather dramatically, with evidence that the leaders of China had come to the same conclusion.

RAPPROCHEMENT WITH CHINA

Since the Korean War, the only contacts between China and the United States had been mutual imprecations. Then in 1971 an American table tennis team touring Japan received an invitation from the People's Republic to fly on over and play a few games in China before returning home. Thus were diplomatic signals conveyed in the mysterious East.

Kissinger virtually commanded the Ping-Pong players to go. (They were trounced; the Chinese could not have been expected to invite an American basketball team to play before the home fans.) And he opened top-secret talks with Chinese diplomats, flying to Beijing where he arranged for a goodwill tour of China by Nixon himself. Only then was the astonishing news released: the lifelong scourge of Communism would tour the Forbidden City, view the Great Wall, and sit down with chopsticks at a Mandarin banquet with Mao Zedong and Zhou Enlai, drinking toasts to Sino–American amity with fiery Chinese spirits.

Nixon's meeting with Mao was ceremonial; the chairman was senile. Zhou, however, who had long advocated better relations with the United States, was active and alert. The cordiality of his protégés, Hua Guofeng (who would succeed Mao in 1976) and Deng Xiaoping (whom Mao had jailed), reassured Nixon that he had calculated correctly in coming to China.

Nixon invited Chinese students to study at American universities, and China opened its doors to American tourists, who came by the tens of thousands, clambering up the Great Wall and buying red-ribboned trinkets by the ton. American businesspeople involved in everything from oil exploration to the bottling of soft drinks flew to China, anxious to sell

American technology and consumer goods in the market that had long symbolized the traveling sales representative's ultimate territory. The United States dropped its veto of Communist China's claim to a seat in the United Nations (always an absurd position) and established a legation in Beijing. In 1979 the two countries established full diplomatic relations.

SOVIET POLICY

The "China market" did not prove as great a bonanza as it had been in American business dreams for a century. Japan grabbed the market in electronic consumer baubles. (Japan already owned the "America market"!) And before long the Chinese were cutting into American sales elsewhere of films and recordings by making unauthorized "bootleg" copies of them. While Chinese leaders, particularly Deng Xiaoping and his coterie, had big plans for economic development, their chief motive in courting the United States was China's tense relations with the Soviet Union. The Chinese were "playing the America card."

That was all right with Nixon and Kissinger. They were "playing the China card," showing the Soviet Union, the one country in the world capable of wreaking destruction on the United States, the possibility of a cozy Sino–American relationship. The gambit worked. In June 1972, just months after his China trip, Nixon flew to Moscow and signed an agreement to open what came to be called the Strategic Arms Limitation Talks (SALT)—the first significant step toward slowing down the arms race since the Kennedy administration.

At home, the photos of Nixon clinking champagne flutes with Mao and hugging Brezhnev bewildered right-wing Republicans and flummoxed Nixon's liberal critics. In fact, as Nixon understood, only a Republican like him with impeccable Cold Warrior credentials could have accomplished what he did.

SHUTTLE DIPLOMACY

Nixon was grateful to Kissinger and, in 1973, named him secretary of state. For a year Kissinger's diplomatic successes piled up. His greatest triumph came in the Middle East after the Yom Kippur War of 1973, in which Egypt and Syria attacked Israel and, for the first time in the long Arab–Israeli conflict, fought the Israelis to a draw.

Knowing that the Israelis were not inclined to accept less than victory, and fearing the consequences of a prolonged war in the oil-rich Middle East, Kissinger shuttled frantically among Damascus, Cairo, and Tel Aviv, carrying proposals and counterproposals in his briefcase. Unlike John Foster Dulles, who had also represented American interests on the fly, Kissinger was a sly, flexible, realistic, and ingratiating diplomat. He ended the war, winning the gratitude of Egyptian President Anwar Sadat while not alienating the Israelis.

After 1974 Kissinger was less successful, in part because of revived world tensions that were not his doing. Soviet Premier Leonid Brezhnev may have wanted to reduce the chance of a direct conflict between Russia and the United States. However, he was enough of an old Bolshevik to continue aiding guerrilla movements in Africa and Latin America that, in Kissinger's view of détente, he should have terminated. Cuba's Fidel Castro, with a large army he needed to keep in trim, sent combat troops to help out in several countries, notably Angola in southwestern Africa.

Nixon and Kissinger had little choice but to respond by aiding anti-Soviet and anti-Cuban Angolans. Right-wing Republicans opposed to détente vilified Kissinger as something akin to a traitor while, in Angola and elsewhere, he was pursuing the confrontational policies they advocated. Liberal Democrats, haunted by what the United States had done in Vietnam and never able to commend Nixon and Kissinger for détente, denounced the intervention in Angola.

They found better reason to attack Kissinger in 1974 when it was revealed that, covertly the previous year, the United States had aided and may have instigated a military coup in Chile that deposed and murdered President Salvador Allende. Allende was a bungler, but he was also Chile's democratically elected president; and his American-sponsored successor, Agostín Pinochet, instituted a brutal regime in which opponents were tortured and murdered by the thousands. Kissinger replied to critics that "covert action should not be confounded with missionary work." That left-liberal critics of American foreign policy were often soft-headed, as Kissinger implied, was undeniable; but underwriting Nazi-like murderers was stretching hard-headed *Realpolitik* into the realm of criminality.

WATERGATE AND GERALD FORD

When news of the Pinochet connection broke in the United States, Kissinger was no longer serving Richard Nixon. The crisis of the presidency that began when Lyndon Johnson was repudiated became graver when Nixon was forced to resign in disgrace. The debacle had its beginnings in the election campaign of 1972 in which, thanks to the Democratic party's self-transformation, victory was in Nixon's pocket from the start.

REDEFINING LIBERALISM

Between 1968 and 1972 many middle-class Democrats, educated and affluent members of what a conservative judge and scholar, Robert Bork, called "the New Class"—teachers, professors, lawyers, social workers, and other government-employed professionals—acquired an influence in the party out of proportion to their numbers. They had little interest in the economic issues that, during the New Deal, had bound working people, white and black, to the party of Franklin D. Roosevelt. They were sympathetic to, even patronizing of, African Americans. Indeed, New Class liberals sympathized with the anti-integration turn black militants had taken with the "black power" movement and the death of Martin Luther King Jr.

Otherwise they were motivated by demands that often seemed more psychological—self-therapeutic—than political. The sympathy with victims of discrimination and repression

The Persistent Ones

When Nixon ran for reelection in 1972, he became the seventh person to run for president three times as the nominee of a major party. The seven and the dates of their nominations, with years they won in boldface, were

Thomas Jefferson: 1796, **1800**, **1804**
Andrew Jackson: 1824, **1828**, **1832**
Henry Clay: 1824, 1832, 1844

Grover Cleveland: **1884**, 1888, **1892**
William Jennings Bryan: 1896, 1900, 1908
Franklin D. Roosevelt: **1932**, **1936**, **1940**, **1944**
Richard M. Nixon: 1960, **1968**, **1972**

Technically, John Adams, like FDR, ran for president four times. That is, although it was intended that he be George Washington's vice president in 1788 and 1792, constitutionally, he was, like Washington, a candidate for president. Before 1804 there were no vice presidential candidates; the presidential candidate who finished second in the electoral college became vice president.

Eugene V. Debs was the Socialist party's presidential candidate five times: 1900, 1904, 1908, 1912, and 1920. Norman Thomas was the Socialist candidate six times: 1928, 1932, 1936, 1940, 1944, and 1948.

(an important component of white support of the civil rights movement) they extended to some other racial and ethnic minorities and to themselves, middle-class women, and homosexuals.

In 1972, new Democratic party rules designed to take the party away from professional politicians and labor leaders and make it more representative of the American population (African Americans, Latinos, women in state delegations proportionate to their numbers in the population) put New Class liberals almost in control of the party's nominating convention in Miami. Old-time party stalwarts who had been delegates at every convention because they got out the vote—big-city political machine stalwarts, union leaders, southern "good old boys" who had not already gone Republican—found themselves at home watching the convention on television because of the McGovern Rules, named after the liberal, antiwar senator from South Dakota, George McGovern.

THE ELECTION OF 1972

The Democratic convention of 1972 was the youngest political convention ever. There were far more women, blacks, Hispanics, and Indians on the floor than ever before, and most were militantly antiwar. They nominated Senator McGovern and adopted a platform calling for a negotiated end to the southeast Asian war (then Vietnamized but expanded), and they supported the demands of feminist organizations that abortions be made available to women who wanted them.

A decent man profoundly grieved by the war, McGovern tried to distance himself from his supporters' most extreme proposals, notably the demand that homosexuality be accepted as an alternative lifestyle. McGovern was not hostile to homosexuals, but he understood politics: the "gay" plank was unlikely to win the favor of blue-collar workers who traditionally voted Democratic. He arranged that the convention's "gay rights" debate be scheduled late at night when few were watching the convention on television—and the issue quietly buried before dawn. McGovern emphasized his pledge to bring peace to Vietnam and to sponsor tax reforms benefiting middle- and lower-income people, and his record of integrity as contrasted with Nixon's reputation for deviousness.

He never had a chance. Vietnamization had reduced the antiwar movement's cause to pleas for moral national behavior. There were no more long casualty lists to anger working people. Virtually no labor unions supported McGovern, and most of the Democratic pros sat on their hands. McGovern had moderated the demands of the lifestyle liberals, but he could not repudiate them any more than Goldwater could have repudiated the John Birch Society in 1964. The cold fact was that the platform of the Miami convention represented the sentiments of a rather small segment of the upper middle class.

Nixon won 60.8 percent of the popular vote, a swing of 20 million votes in eight years. He carried every state but Massachusetts (and the District of Columbia). The fact that he was a shoo-in from the beginning of the campaign makes the surreptitious activities of his Committee to Reelect the President (an unwisely selected name—it abbreviated as **CREEP**), and Nixon's approval of them, impossible to explain except as a reflection of an abnormal psychology.

COVERING UP A BURGLARY

On June 17, 1972, early in the presidential campaign, Washington police arrested five men who were trying to plant electronic eavesdropping devices in Democratic party headquarters in an upscale apartment and office complex called the **Watergate**. Three of the suspects were on CREEP's payroll. McGovern tried to exploit the incident, but he got nowhere when Nixon and his campaign manager, Attorney General John Mitchell, denied any knowledge of the incident and described the burglars as common criminals.

Nixon may not have known in advance about the break-in. However, he learned shortly thereafter that the burglars had acted on orders from his aides. He never considered reporting or disciplining his men. Instead he instructed his staff to find money to keep the men in jail quiet. Two of them, however, James E. McCord and Howard Hunt, refused to take the fall. They informed Judge John Sirica that they had taken orders from highly placed administration officials.

Rumors flew. Two reporters for the *Washington Post*, Robert Woodward and Carl Bernstein, made contact with an anonymous informant identified as "Deep Throat" (the title

Sex: From No-No to Everybody's Doing It

What Americans of the 1970s called "traditional sexual morality" was an amalgam of the ancient Judeo–Christian sexual code and the middle-class propriety of the nineteenth century—Victorianism. With occasional aberrations, Judaism and Christianity defined masturbation, fornication, adultery, and oral and anal intercourse as sins. Homosexuality was "the sin that dare not speak its name." Bestiality was equally abominable. Through most of history, the latter two sins and sometimes adultery were punishable by death. The Victorian age prohibited sexual topics in literature and decent conversation—as improprieties. In the nineteenth century bowdlerizers published editions of Shakespeare and even the Bible from which all "indecencies" had been removed.

The Victorian "gag rule" resulted in shocking surprises on their wedding nights for some middle-class brides. One bride-to-be taken aside by her sister and informed of what the honeymoon held in store wrote that she thought her sister was having fun with her. Men were expected to know. Although no moralist approved of males enjoying an active sexual life, the "double standard" winked at men who had sexual intercourse before marriage.

Prudery reached its apex in the United States during the last three decades of the nineteenth century and the first decade of the twentieth century. Anthony Comstock, who headed the New York Society for the Suppression of Vice, promoted a federal law and several state laws that made it a serious criminal offense to send "indecent and obscene materials" through the mails or otherwise to publish and distribute them. Comstock's target was pornography, but also medical discussions of sexual intercourse, anatomy, and birth control.

The code of silence no more reflected actual practice than laws forbidding theft meant there was no embezzlement, robbery, or burglary. Some daughters of the middle class had illegitimate babies, although when they announced their pregnancy, families able to do so kept it a dark secret, spiriting the daughter off on an extended visit to an aunt and either putting the infant up for adoption or introducing it after a few months as an orphaned relation. It is impossible to know how widespread adultery was. It made the newspapers only when an irate husband killed the man who had cuckolded him, the lovers did away with the superfluous husband, or adultery was cited as grounds in a celebrated divorce case.

The code began to totter at the turn of the twentieth century when jobs and bright lights attracted respectable young women to the big city. Away from their families' supervision, they "dated" rather than "courted"—no chaperones. Those for whom the sex drive was more powerful than the pull of traditional sexual morality experimented. American women born after 1900 (coming of age during the "Roaring Twenties") indulged in premarital sex far more often than their mothers had. The only remaining powerful deterrent to enjoying a "liberated" sex life was the fear of pregnancy and venereal disease. Margaret Sanger, a nurse who devoted her life to disseminating information about birth control and prophylactic devices, was harassed not so much because she wanted to spare married women the constant pregnancies that impoverished them and ruined their health, but because of the (justified) belief that knowledge of contraception encouraged unmarried women and girls to tread where they should not.

If the 1920s marked the first "sexual revolution," the second began in 1960 when G. D. Searle Pharmaceuticals marketed an oral contraceptive and medicine had apparently conquered sexually transmitted diseases. The flower children, determined to transcend (or defy) their parents' values, defined the "love" on which the counterculture was based as promiscuous sex: sexual intercourse on a whim

---

of a pornographic movie) who fed them inside information. A special Senate investigating committee headed by Sam Ervin of North Carolina picked away at the tangle from yet another direction, tracing not only the Watergate break-in and cover-up but other illegal acts and "dirty tricks" to the White House.

THE IMPERIAL PRESIDENCY

Each month brought new, dismaying insights into the inner workings of the Nixon presidency. On Nixon's personal command, an "enemies list" had been compiled. On it were journalists, politicians, intellectuals, and even movie stars who criticized the president. One Donald Segretti was put in charge of spreading half-truths and lies to discredit Nixon's

critics. G. Gordon Liddy, who was involved in the Watergate break-in, proposed fantastic schemes involving yachts and prostitutes to entrap Democrats in career-ending scandals. The dirty-tricks campaign grew so foul that not even J. Edgar Hoover, the unsqueamish head of the FBI, would touch it.

Watergate was just one of the administration's several illegal break-ins. Nixon's aides engineered the burglary of a Los Angeles psychiatrist's office to secure medical information about a patient, Daniel Ellsberg, a Defense Department employee who published confidential information about the prosecution of the war in Vietnam.

Observers spoke of an "imperial presidency." Nixon and his coterie had become so arrogant in the possession of

with anyone because it was pleasurable and *natural,* which were the things that counted. The hippies tried to shock "people over 30" by talking about sex—endlessly. In fact, the Victorian gag rule had already been repealed. A series of Supreme Court decisions in the 1950s allowed the publication of books that had long been banned because of episodes of explicit sex. In 1959 D. H. Lawrence's long-suppressed *Lady Chatterley's Lover* was cleared for sale in the United States. In 1966 the Supreme Court approved publication of an eighteenth-century pornographic classic, *Fanny Hill.* In 1969 the Court said that because of the right of privacy, it was not illegal to possess obscene or pornographic material.

During the 1970s casual sex and pornography went big-time. Languishing movie theaters ran pornographic films and tried, with some success, to attract women as dates or in groups. "Singles bars," explicitly advertised as places where one could meet a sexual partner for a "one-night stand," were fixtures in nearly every town. "Adult motels" suspended mirrors on ceilings and pumped pornographic movies to TV sets in perfumed rooms. Apartment complexes were retooled to accommodate "swinging singles" with party rooms, saunas, and hot tubs. Marriage practices could hardly remain unaffected. The divorce rate soared from 2.5 divorces per 1,000 marriages in 1965 to 5.3 per 1,000 in 1979. The illegitimate birthrate tripled during the 1960s and 1970s, and the number of abortions increased at the same rate.

Homosexuals benefited from the new openness and relaxation of sexual attitudes. They began "coming out of the closet," proclaiming that their sexuality was an important part of their individual identity and nothing of which to be ashamed. Hundreds of gay and lesbian groups took to the streets in colorful parades. They formed lobbies, soon supported by "politically correct" liberals, to push for laws prohibiting discrimination against homosexuals in housing and employment. The din was such that someone remarked, "The sin that dare not speak its name cannot sit down and shut up."

"Swinging" proved to be a fad among heterosexuals. Singles bars and singles apartments lost their panache. Pornographic movie theaters closed by the hundreds, in part because, except for aficionados of the genre, the films were boring ("when you've seen one, you've seen them all"), but mostly because the Internet brought porn into homes.

During the 1980s venereal disease caused a decline in casual sex from the frenzy of the 1970s. A penicillin-resistant strain of gonorrhea made the rounds among "swingers"; chlamydia and herpes were epidemic. More serious was a new affliction, Acquired Immune Deficiency Syndrome—AIDS—which slowly and agonizingly killed most of its victims. In developed countries like the United States (although not in the Third World) AIDS was largely a disease of homosexuals, hemophiliacs, and intravenous drug users. (It is transmitted only through exchange of bodily fluids and contact with the bloodstream.) By the 1990s, however, public health authorities no longer described it as a threat to only homosexuals and junkies, in part because it was not politically correct to do so and in part because researchers would have had great difficulty getting funds to research a disease thought to be the exclusive problem of groups on which conventional Americans looked with distaste.

It is difficult to imagine a reversal of the "sexual revolution" short of a totalitarian government next to which Afghanistan's Taliban look like a crowd of Dutch uncles. The sex drive is powerful—something that Victorian moralists understood clearly in the zeal with which they attempted to repress it.

power that they believed they were above the law. Indeed, several years later Nixon told an interviewer on television, "When the president does it, that means it is not illegal."

If imperial in their pretensions, however, "all the president's men" were singularly lacking in a sense of nobility. One by one Nixon's aides deserted, each convinced that he was being set up as the fall guy for his colleagues. The deserters described their roles in the Watergate cover-up and dirty-tricks campaign and named others higher up who told them what to do.

In the midst of the scandal, Vice President Spiro Agnew pleaded no contest to income tax evasion and charges that he accepted bribes when he was governor of Maryland. Agnew was forced to resign in October 1973. He was replaced under the Twenty-Fifth Amendment by Congressman Gerald Ford of Michigan.

RESIGNATION

Then came Nixon's turn. He had recorded conversations in the Oval Office that clearly proved his active role in the Watergate cover-up. After long legal wrangles, the president was ordered to surrender the tapes to the courts.

Why Nixon did not destroy the tapes early in the crisis, before destruction became a criminal offense, is difficult to understand. Some insiders said he intended to profit by selling them after he retired. Others said that, like Lyndon Johnson, his mind cracked. Nixon had for some years been medicating himself with illegally acquired Dilantin, a drug that alleviates

Gerald Ford, the "accidental president" who won widespread affection by not pretending to be anything but the plainspoken and hardworking public servant he had been in Congress. He drew criticism when he pardoned former president Nixon in advance of any crimes of which he might be accused. Nevertheless, and despite serious economic problems he was helpless to address, he was defeated only narrowly in 1976 when he ran for reelection in the only national campaign of his long career. There were two attempts to assassinate him in California by disturbed women of no particular political convictions.

anxiety, and began to overuse the pills. Secretary of State Kissinger was startled when Nixon asked him to kneel with him and pray. (Neither was religious.) Secretary of Defense Schlesinger quietly informed the Joint Chiefs of Staff not to carry out any orders from the White House until they were cleared with him or Kissinger.

After the House of Representatives Judiciary Committee recommended impeaching Nixon, he threw in the towel. On August 9, 1974, on national television, he resigned the presidency and flew to his home in San Clemente, California.

A FORD, NOT A LINCOLN

Gerald Ford had held a safe seat in the House from Michigan; he rose to be minority leader on the basis of seniority and his

reliable party loyalty. His ambition, before events made him vice president and, quickly, president, was to be Speaker of the House before he retired.

Ford attracted ridicule. He was not particularly bright. Lyndon Johnson told reporters that Ford's problem dated from the days when he played center on the University of Michigan football team without a helmet. Others quipped that he could not walk and chew gum at the same time. Newspaper photographers lay in wait to snap shots of him bumping his head on door frames, tumbling down the slopes of the Rockies on everything but his skis, and slicing golf balls into crowds of spectators.

But Ford's simplicity and forthrightness were a relief after Nixon's squirming and deceptions. He told the American people that fate had given them "a Ford, not a Lincoln." Democrats howled "deal" when Ford pardoned Nixon of all crimes he may have committed, but Ford's explanation, that the American people needed to put Watergate behind them, was plausible and in character. Two assassination attempts by deranged women in California helped to win sympathy for the first president who had not been elected to any national office.

Despite his unusual route to the White House, Gerald Ford had no more intention of being a caretaker president than John Tyler when he became the first president to succeed to the office by reason of death. But it was Ford's misfortune, as it had been Tyler's, to face serious problems without the support of an important segment of his party. The Republican party's right wing, now led by former California Governor Ronald Reagan, did not like détente or Nixon's (now Ford's) refusal to launch a frontal attack on government regulation and the liberal welfare state.

RUNNING ON HALF-EMPTY

The most serious of the woes facing Ford struck at one of the basic assumptions of twentieth-century American life: that cheap energy was available in unlimited quantities to fuel the economy and support the freewheeling lifestyle of the middle class.

Constitutional Contradiction?

Gerald Ford was named vice president under the provisions of the Twenty-Fifth Amendment, which was ratified in 1967. It stipulates that "whenever there is a vacancy in the office of the Vice President, the President shall nominate a Vice President. . . ." When Ford succeeded to the presidency, he appointed Nelson A. Rockefeller to the vice presidency. Neither the president nor the vice president held office by virtue of election. However, as some constitutional experts were quick to point out, Article II, Section 1, of the Constitution provides that the president and vice president are to "be elected."

The contradiction was there before 1967. Between 1886 and 1947, had a president died or resigned and there was no vice president, he would have been succeeded by the secretary of state, who was not an elected official. It never happened.

Several times during the 1970s, gasoline was in such short supply that across the nation, Americans had to wait in lines for hours to fill up—when filling stations did not run dry first. There was no gasoline for sale in some cities for days at a time. The entire state of Hawaii, to which all gasoline came by ship, was brought nearly to a halt awaiting tankers from California.

By the mid-1970s, 90 percent of the American economy was run by the burning of fossil fuels: coal, natural gas, and especially petroleum. Fossil fuels are nonrenewable sources of energy. Unlike food crops, lumber, and water—or, for that matter, a horse and a pair of sturdy legs—they cannot be called on again once they have been used. The supply of them is finite. Although experts disagreed about the extent of the world's reserves of coal, gas, and oil, no one challenged the obvious fact that one day they would be gone.

The United States was by far the world's biggest user of nonrenewable sources of energy. In 1975, while comprising about 6 percent of the world's population, Americans consumed a third of the world's annual production of oil. Much of it was burned to less than basic ends. Americans overheated and overcooled their offices and houses. They pumped gasoline into a dizzying variety of purely recreational vehicles, some of which brought the roar of the freeway to the wilderness and devastated fragile land. Their worship of the private automobile meant that little tax money was spent on public mass transit. Consumer goods were overpackaged in throwaway containers of glass, metal, paper, and petroleum-based plastics; supermarkets wrapped lemons individually in transparent plastic, and fast-food cheeseburgers were cradled in Styrofoam caskets that were

discarded within seconds of being handed over the counter. The bill of indictment, drawn up by environmentalists, went on; but resisting criticism and satire alike, Americans increased their consumption.

OPEC AND THE ENERGY CRISIS

About 60 percent of the oil that Americans consumed in the 1970s was produced at home, and large reserves remained under native ground. But the nation also imported huge quantities of crude. In October 1973 Americans discovered just how little control they had over the 39 percent of their oil that came from abroad.

In that month the Organization of Petroleum Exporting Countries (**OPEC**) temporarily halted oil shipments and announced the first of a series of big jumps in the price of their product. One of their justifications was that the irresponsible consumption habits of the advanced Western nations, particularly the United States, jeopardized their future. If countries like Saudi Arabia and Nigeria continued to supply oil cheaply, consuming nations would continue to burn it profligately, thus hastening the day when the wells ran dry. On that day, if the oil-exporting nations had not laid the groundwork for another kind of economy, they would be destitute. Particularly in the Middle East, there were few alternative resources to support fast-growing populations. By raising prices, OPEC said, the oil-producing nations would earn capital with which to build for a future without petroleum, while encouraging the consuming nations to conserve, thus lengthening the era when oil would be available.

From a geopolitical perspective there was much to be said for this argument; but few ordinary Americans (and few greedy dissolutes in the OPEC countries) thought geopolitically. Arab sheiks and Nigerian generals grew rich, and American motorists were stunned when they had to wait in long lines to pay unprecedented prices for gasoline. In some big cities and Hawaii, gasoline for private cars was virtually unavailable for several weeks.

The price of gasoline never climbed to Japanese or European levels, but it was shock enough for people who were accustomed to buying "two dollars worth" to discover that $2 bought little more than enough to get them home. Moreover, the prices of goods that required oil in their production climbed too. Inflation, already 9 percent during Nixon's last year, rose to 12 percent a year when Ford was president.

WHIP INFLATION NOW!

Opposed to wage and price controls such as Nixon employed, Ford launched a campaign called WIN! for "Whip Inflation Now!" He urged Americans to deter inflation by refusing to buy exorbitantly priced goods and by ceasing to demand higher wages. The campaign was ridiculed from the start, and within a few weeks Ford quietly retired the WIN! button he wore on his lapel. He had seen few others in his travels about the country and had begun to feel like a man in a funny hat.

Instead, Ford tightened the money supply to slow down the economy, which resulted in the most serious recession since 1937, with unemployment climbing to 9 percent. Ford was stymied by a vicious circle: slowing inflation meant throwing people out of work; fighting unemployment meant inflation; trying to steer a middle course meant **stagflation**—mild recession plus inflation.

Early in 1976, polls showed Ford losing to most of the likely Democratic candidates. Capitalizing on the news, California Governor Ronald Reagan, the post-Goldwater sweetheart of right-wing Republicans, launched a well-financed campaign to replace Ford as the party's candidate. Using his control of the party organization, Ford beat Reagan at the convention; but the economic travails of his two years in office took their toll. His pardon of Nixon may have hurt him with voters. In November 1976 he lost narrowly to an unlikely Democratic candidate, James Earl Carter of Georgia, who called himself "Jimmy." The Democrats were back, but the decline in the prestige of the presidency continued.

QUIET CRISIS

Since Eisenhower, every president had been identified closely with Congress. The day of the governor candidate seemed to have ended with FDR. Governors did not get the national publicity that senators did. Then Jimmy Carter came out of nowhere to win the Democratic nomination in 1976. His political career consisted of one term in the Georgia assembly and one term as governor.

It was Carter's lack of association with the federal government that helped him win the nomination and, by a slim margin, the presidency. Without an animus for Gerald Ford, voters were attracted to the idea of an "outsider," which is how Carter presented himself. "Hello, my name is Jimmy Carter and I'm running for president," he told thousands of people face-to-face in his softly musical Georgia accent. Once he started winning primaries, the media did the rest. When television commentators say that a bandwagon is rolling, American voters know they have an obligation to get aboard.

Inauguration Day, when Carter and his shrewd but uningratiating wife Rosalyn walked the length of Pennsylvania Avenue, was very nearly the last entirely satisfactory day of the Carter presidency. Whether the perspective of time will attribute his failure as chief executive to his unsuitability to the office, or to the massiveness of the problems he faced, it is difficult to imagine historians of the future looking at the Carter era other than dolefully.

PEACEMAKING

Carter had some successes. He defused an explosive situation in Central America where Panamanians were protesting American sovereignty in the Panama Canal Zone. The narrow strip of U.S. territory bisected the small republic and seemed insulting in an age when nationalist sensibilities in small countries were as touchy as boils.

Most policy makers saw no need to hold the canal zone in the face of the protests. The United States would be able to occupy the canal within hours in a crisis. Why antagonize the Panamanians? In 1978 the Senate narrowly ratified an agreement with Panama to guarantee the permanent neutrality of the canal itself while gradually transferring sovereignty to Panama, culminating on December 31, 1999. Ronald Reagan, who began to campaign for the presidency as soon as Carter was inaugurated, denounced the treaty; Panama, he insisted, was as much a part of the United States as Santa Barbara County, California.

Carter's greatest achievement was to save the rapprochement between Israel and Egypt that began to take shape in November 1977 when Egyptian President Anwar Sadat risked the enmity of the Arab world by calling for peace in

Carter and the Segregationists

Jimmy Carter had an unusual record for a white southerner of his era on racial questions. In the 1950s, as a successful businessman in Plains, Georgia, he was invited to join the racist White Citizens' Council. Annual dues were a modest $5. Carter replied, "I've got $5 but I'd flush it down the toilet before I'd give it to you."

Jimmy Carter's finest day as president. In 1978 he persuaded Egyptian president Anwar Sadat (left) to sign the Camp David Accords, establishing a process leading to peace between Egypt and Israel. He had to threaten Israeli prime minister Menachem Begin (right) to sign; Begin had no intention of making peace at the conference. The fact that Carter was not awarded the Nobel Peace Prize for his astonishing diplomacy while the Nobel Committee regularly awarded it to revolutionaries who advocated violence exposed the political character of the committee. (Carter won the prize in 2002 for his humanitarian work after leaving the presidency.)

the Middle East before the Israeli parliament. Rather than cooperate with Sadat, Israeli Prime Minister Menachem Begin, a former terrorist, refused to make concessions commensurate with the Egyptian president's high-stakes gamble.

In 1978 Carter brought Sadat and Begin to Camp David, the presidential retreat in the Maryland woods outside Washington. Sadat grew so angry with Begin's refusal to compromise that he actually packed his suitcases. Although Carter was unable to persuade Begin to agree that the West Bank of the Jordan River, which Israel had occupied in 1967, must eventually be returned to Arab rule, he did bring the two men together. In March 1979 Israel and Egypt signed a treaty.

THE END OF DÉTENTE

While Carter advanced the cause of peace in the Middle East, he shattered the détente that Nixon, Kissinger, and Ford had nurtured. Like Nixon, Carter virtually ignored his first secretary of state and looked for advice to a White House assistant, Zbigniew Brzezinski.

Kissinger was a flexible, even cynical opportunist. Brzezinski was a true believer, an anti-Soviet ideologue and unrepentant Cold Warrior. A Polish refugee from Communism, Brzezinski's hatred of the Soviet Union blinded him to opportunities to improve relations between the nuclear superpowers. Moreover, where Kissinger had been smooth and a charmer, Brzezinski was tactless and crude in a world in which protocol and manners could be as important as substance. The foreign ministers of several of America's allies discreetly informed the State Department that they would not deal with him.

Carter's hostility toward the Soviet Union had other origins. A deeply religious man, moralistic to the point of sanctimony, he denounced the Soviet Union for trampling on human rights. In March 1977 Carter interrupted and set back the Strategic Arms Limitation Talks with completely new proposals. Eventually a new SALT II treaty was negotiated and signed, but Carter withdrew it from Senate consideration in December 1979 when the Soviet Union invaded Afghanistan to prop up a client government. He refused to allow American athletes to compete in the Olympics when they were held in Moscow. Détente was dead. Glowering confrontation was back.

PLUS C'EST LA MÊME CHOSE

Inflation worsened under Carter, rising to almost 20 percent in 1980. By the end of the year, $1 was worth 15 cents in 1940 money. That is, on average, it took $1 in 1980 to purchase what in 1940 had cost 15 cents. The dollar had suffered fully half of this loss of value during the 1970s.

Carter could not be faulted for the energy crisis. After the crunch of 1974, Americans became more energy conscious, replacing their big "gas guzzlers" with more efficient smaller cars. Even this sensible turn contributed to the nation's economic woes, however. American automobile manufacturers had repeatedly refused to develop small energy-efficient cars. For a time during the 1960s, after the success of the German-made Volkswagen "Beetle," Ford, General Motors, and Chrysler made compact cars. But within a few years compact models had miraculously grown nearly as large as the road monsters of the 1950s. In the energy crunch of the 1970s American automakers had nothing to compete with a flood of Japanese imports: Toyotas, Datsuns, and Hondas. The automobile buyers' dollars sailed across the Pacific.

Even then, by 1979, oil consumption was higher than ever, and a higher proportion of it was imported than in 1976. American oil refiners actually cut back on domestic production, which led many people to wonder if the crisis was genuine or just a cover while the refiners reaped windfall profits. They did: as prices soared, the oil companies paid dividends the industry had never known.

The price of electricity rose by 200 percent. Utility companies called for the construction of more nuclear power plants in anticipation of even higher rate increases. But Americans had become apprehensive about nuclear energy following an accident and near-catastrophe at the Three Mile Island nuclear plant near Harrisburg, Pennsylvania, and the release, at about the same time, of *The China Syndrome*, a film that portrayed a disconcertingly similar accident. Then it was revealed that a big California reactor about to go online was riddled with construction flaws and built over a major earthquake fault. Was anything in America going right?

MALAISE

Carter was repeatedly embarrassed by his aides and family, and he himself had a talent for pulling boners. Suspicious of the Washington establishment, he surrounded himself with cronies from Georgia who did not or would not understand the capital's etiquette and ritual. Banker Bert Lance, whom Carter wanted as budget director, was tainted by irregular loan scams, petty but unacceptable. Ambassador to the United Nations Andrew Young stupidly met secretly with leaders of the terrorist Palestine Liberation Organization, which the United States did not recognize. Carter had to fire him.

The national press, stimulated by the role journalists had played in exposing the Watergate scandal, leapt on every trivial incident—a Carter aide tipsy in a cocktail lounge; the president's "down-home" brother Billy's ignorant opinions—to embarrass the president. The religious Carter foolishly told an interviewer for *Playboy* magazine, as if he were confessing at a revival, "I've looked on a lot of women with lust. I've committed adultery in my heart many times." In 1980, when Carter's presidency was on the line, his mother told a reporter, "Sometimes when I look at all my children, I say to myself, 'Lillian, you should have stayed a virgin.'"

The Carter administration lacked direction. "Carter believes fifty things," one of his aides said, "but no one thing. He holds explicit, thorough positions on every issue under the sun, but he has no large view of relations between them." Carter was not unlike most Americans in his engineer mentality. As a problem arises, he believed, face it and solve it.

Such pragmatism had worked for Franklin D. Roosevelt. It did not work for Jimmy Carter. With him at the helm, government resembled a ship without a rudder, drifting aimlessly. Carter was sensitive to what journalists called a national malaise, but he only embarrassed himself when he tried to address the amorphous problem. He called 130 prominent men and women from every sector of American life to Washington; having listened to them, he was able to announce only that there was "a crisis of the American spirit," right back where he started from.

FURTHER READING

General Howard Brink, *Age of Contradiction*, 1998; James Baughman, *The Republic of Mass Culture*, 1992; John M. Blum, *Years of Discord*, 1991; Peter Caroll, *It Seemed Like Nothing Happened in the 1970s*, 1982; Richard W. Fox and T. Jackson Lears, *The Culture of Consumption: Critical Essays in American History*, 1983; David Frum, *How We Got Here: The 70s, the Decade That Brought You Modern Life*, 2000; James Gilbert, *Another Chance: America since 1945*, 1984; Godfrey Hodgson, *America in Our Time*, 1976; James T. Patterson, *Grand Expectations: The United States, 1945–1974*, 1996; Bruce J. Schulman, *The Seventies: The Great Shift in American Culture*, 2001; Warren J. Sussman, *Culture as History: The Transformation of American Society in the Twentieth Century*, 1984.

Aftermath W. Carl Biven, *Jimmy Carter's Economy: Policy in an Age of Limits*, 2001; John Dambrell, *The Carter Presidency*, 1993; Burton J. Kaufman, *The Presidency of James Earl Carter*, 1993; Clark Mollenhoff, *The Man Who Pardoned Nixon*, 1976, and *The President Who Failed*, 1980; Richard Reeves, *A Ford, Not a Lincoln*, 1975.

Foreign Policy R. L. Garthoff, *Détente and Confrontation*, 1985; Walter Isaacson, *Kissinger*, 1992; Richard A. Melanson, *American Foreign Policy since the Vietnam War: The Search for Consensus from Nixon to Clinton*, 2001; Robert Morris, *Uncertain Greatness: Henry Kissinger and American Foreign Policy*, 1977; W. B. Quandt, *Decade of Decision: American Foreign Policy toward the Arab–Israeli Conflict,*

1978; Robert D. Schultzinger, *Henry Kissinger: Doctor of Diplomacy,* 1989; G. Sick, *All Fall Down: America's Tragic Encounter with Iran,* 1985; Gaddis Smith, *Morality, Reason, and Power,* 1986.

Nixon and His Administration Stephen E. Ambrose, *Nixon,* 3 vols., 1987, 1989, 1991; Sam Ervin, *The Whole Truth: The Water-gate Conspiracy,* 1980; Stanley Kutler, *Abuse of Power: The New Nixon Tapes,* 1997, and *The Wars of Watergate: The Last Crisis of Richard Nixon,* 1992; Allen J. Matusow, *Nixon's Economy: Booms, Busts, Dollars, and Votes,* 1998; Kim McQuaid, *The Anxious Years: America in the Vietnam–Watergate Era,* 1989; David Rudenstine, *The Day the Presses Stopped: A History of the Pentagon Papers Case,* 1996; Jonathan Schell, *The Time of Illusion,* 1976; Melvin Small, *The Presidency of Richard M. Nixon,* 1999; Gary Wills, *Nixon Agonistes: The Crisis of the Self-Made Man,* 1970.

Nixon's Vietnam Christian Appy, *Working-Class War,* 1993; George Q. Flynn, *The Draft: 1940–1973,* 1993; A. E. Goodman, *The Lost Peace: America's Search for a Negotiated Settlement of the Vietnam War,* 1978; George Herring, *America's Longest War: The United States and Vietnam, 1950–1975,* 1986; Stanley Karnow, *Vietnam,* 1983; Jeffrey Kimball, *Nixon's Vietnam War,* 1998; Gabriel

Kolko, *Anatomy of a War,* 1985; David W. Levy, *The Debate over Vietnam,* 1995; Robert D. Schulzinger, *A Time for War: The United States and Vietnam, 1941–1975,* 1997; Tom Wells, *The War Within: America's Battle over Vietnam,* 1994; Marilyn B. Young, *The Vietnam-American Wars,* 1991.

Politics William C. Berman, *America's Right Turn: From Nixon to Bush,* 1994; Dan Carter, *The Politics of Rage: George Wallace and the Origins of the New Conservatism,* 1995; John R. Greene, *The Limits of Power,* 1992; Lisa McGirr, *Suburban Warriors: The Origins of the New American Right,* 2001; A. J. Reichley, *Conservatives in an Age of Change: The Nixon and Ford Administrations,* 1981.

Social and Cultural Divisions Lydia Chavez, *The Color Bind,* 1998; Stephanie Coontz, *The Way We Never Were: American Families and the Nostalgia Trap,* 1992; Alice Echols, *Daring to Be Bad: Radical Feminism in America, 1967–1975,* 1990; Peter Hoffer, *Roe v. Wade,* 2001; Thomas Sowell, *Affirmative Action around the World: An Empirical Study,* 2004; David Marl, *Democratic Vistas: Television in American Culture,* 1984; Arthur M. Schlesinger Jr., *The Disuniting of America: Reflections on a Multi-Cultural Society,* 1992; Winifred Wandersee, *On the Move: American Women in the 1970s,* 1988.

KEY TERMS

The following terms are covered in this chapter and can also be found in the list of Key Terms at the back of the book.

CREEP	**New Federalism**	**stagflation**	**Watergate**
détente	**OPEC**	**Vietnamization**	

 ## ONLINE SOURCES GUIDE

Use this listing to find online documents, images, inter-active maps, simulations, and other resources related to this chapter:

American History Resource Center
http://history.wadsworth.com/rc/us

Selected Documents
A denunciation of antiwar protestors by Vice President Spiro Agnew
An account of the Tet Offensive from the Defense Department's Pentagon Papers (1971)
Paris Peace Accord (1973)
Roe v. Wade (1973)
Jimmy Carter, 1980 state of the union speech

Selected Images
Richard Nixon answering media questions during Watergate
Spiro T. Agnew
Gerald Ford taking oath of office
Liftoff of *Apollo 11,* July 1969
First man on moon, July 1969
James Earl ("Jimmy") Carter

Interactive Time Line (with online readings)
Presidency in Crisis: The Nixon, Ford and Carter Administrations, 1968–1980

CHAPTER 50

Morning in America

The Age of Reagan 1980–1993

The White House/David Hume Kennerly

I have long believed there was a divine plan that placed this land here to be found by people of a special kind, that we have a rendezvous with destiny. Yes, there is a spirit moving in this land and a hunger in the people for a spiritual revival. If the task I seek should be given to me, I would pray only that I could perform it in a way that would serve God.

Ronald Reagan

Republicans were planning for the presidential election of 1980 even before Inauguration Day 1977. Democrat Jimmy Carter was president by a very slim margin. He won the election of 1976 only because, as a southerner, he carried southern states that had been drifting into the Republican column since the 1960s. His popularity, always tentative, began to decline immediately when the "stagflation" that had helped him defeat Gerald Ford refused to retire with Ford. Then came disaster in Iran.

THE AYATOLLAH AND THE ACTOR

Iran was not high on Americans' list of concerns. Thanks to magazine articles and television portraits—the Shah of Iran had long been an "item" with personality journalists— Americans assumed that he was an effective and popular ruler in the little-known country. With Iran's Westernized middle class (and the rich), the Shah was popular. His secular modernization policies had created and enriched them. Perhaps because he knew only of such up-to-date urban Iranians, Jimmy Carter described Iran as an "island of stability" in the chaotic Middle East.

The Shah had, however, ignored the plight of Iranian peasants who, as backward farmers usually are, had been impoverished by Iran's modernization. Even oil industry workers, on whose labor the country's wealth was based, were paid inadequately and poorly treated while upper-level foreign employees, many of them Americans, lived in luxury. Labor union leaders and even middle-class liberals feared and hated the Shah's SAVAK, or secret police, who never achieved the exquisite efficiency of the Gestapo but were nasty enough. Worst of all, it turned out, the attempt to reduce the influence of Islam, which the Shah regarded as an obstacle to modernization, by emphasizing Iran's ancient pre-Muslim Persian past offended the powerful mullahs (Muslim religious teachers), for whom nothing that was not Islamic was acceptable

© UPI-Bettmann/Corbis

Diplomats and embassy employees held hostage by revolutionary students in Teheran. They were separated, moved from place to place, lived sometimes in filth, and were mistreated for a year for no reason other than their captors' desire to humiliate the United States. They succeeded in destroying Jimmy Carter's presidency. Americans were frustrated by Carter's apparent inability to free them.

to God. In Turkey in the 1920s and 1930s, Kemal Ataturk had successfully neutralized the power of Islam's reactionary leaders. The Shah only angered them, and the ignorant peasantry looked to them, not the Shah, for guidance.

THE IRANIAN TRAGEDY

Muslim clerics backed by peasants and workers took control of much of Iran. The Ayatollah Khomeini, who envisioned a pure Islamic state patterned after the early, premedieval caliphates, returned from his exile in France to assume leadership of a rival Iranian government. The Shah concluded that his day was over. Fortunately he had hidden a large fortune abroad, much of it in American banks. In October President Carter admitted him to the United States. Had the Shah asked for political asylum, Carter would have refused. He hoped to establish a working relationship with the new Iranian regime. But the Shah asked only for a temporary visa to receive medical treatment for his terminal cancer. Carter's personal sense of decency trumped his political instincts. Reluctantly, he let the Shah in.

Retaliating, Iranian students, for whom personal decency was an incomprehensible concept, seized the American embassy in Teheran, taking fifty Americans hostage. For more than a year they languished in confinement as Carter tried to apply reason and diplomacy in a conflict with people in the grip of religious and anti-American fanaticism. There was no point to holding the hostages except to defy and discomfit the world's greatest power. But not until January 20, 1981,

the day he handed the presidency over to Ronald Reagan—whom the Iranians feared might drop nuclear bombs on the country—were the hostages released.

There was little sympathy for the Ayatollah in the United States, even among knee-jerk "Blame-America-Firsters" in the universities. His Islamic regime executed not only political opponents but "moral offenders," including ordinary people who owned videotapes of Hollywood films. Next to the Ayatollah, the Shah looked like Good King Wenceslaus.

THE ELECTION OF 1980

Carter easily beat back a challenge for the Democratic presidential nomination by Massachusetts Senator Edward Kennedy. Ronald Reagan defeated middle-of-the-road Republicans

The Ayatollah

Khomeini, who was not politically naïve, probably did not want to prolong the hostage crisis as long as it lasted; but he did not control the students who held the Americans. Khomeini was, however, a religious fanatic such as it is difficult to imagine coming to power in traditionally Christian countries. His fanaticism helped to prolong an eight-year war with Iraq that killed 200,000 Iranians, including boys dispatched on suicide missions. In 1989 he issued a *fatwah*, a proclamation promising salvation (and money) to any Muslim who murdered a British author, Salmon Rushdie, for writing an offensive book.

The Year of Silver

In 1980 Nelson Bunker Hunt and William Herbert Hunt, sons of a right-wing extremist billionaire, hatched an audacious scheme to corner the nation's silver supply. They bought up so much silver bullion and silver futures that, they hoped, scarcity would drive the price of the metal to astronomical heights, when they would dump their cache at incredible profits. They actually cornered 200 million ounces of silver, half the world's deliverable supply. The price of silver climbed from less than $5 an ounce to more than $50. Americans (and others) rushed their silver wedding gifts to dealers to be melted down: so much for dear Aunt Lulu's thoughtfulness and good taste.

The cornering attempt failed. The Federal Reserve and other major holders of silver flooded the market, and the price collapsed to $10 in a few weeks. The Hunts had failed, but to the relief of the nation, they did not have to go on welfare.

George H. W. Bush and Congressman John Anderson in the primary elections. When Anderson announced he would run as an independent, Reagan placated some Republican moderates by naming Bush as his running mate.

Rather than attack Carter's handling of the hostage crisis head-on, Reagan criticized his foreign policy in generalities. He hammered on America's low prestige abroad, attributing it to Carter's "softness." A massive military buildup and the will to use force, Reagan said, were needed to end the slide of American influence, prestige, and pride. Domestically, Reagan had a ready-made issue in the weak economy. He said he would strengthen it by reducing regulation of business, which he said had destroyed initiative. He would end inflation, increase employment, cut government spending (except on the military), and balance the federal budget by 1984. It was an incompatible combination of goals, but it appeared to be a *program*, which Carter had never had.

Fundamentalist preachers turned politicians, like the Reverend Jerry Falwell and Pat Robertson, created a loosely organized political machine for Reagan, a legion of "ward heelers" to get out the vote and PACs (political action committees) to raise money. They assailed the liberal social and cultural policies that they blamed for a decline in morality. Falwell's PAC, the "**Moral Majority,**" blamed the Democrats for everything from the high divorce rate to the increase of violent crime in big cities.

THE MANDATE

The experts predicted a close election. Many believed the winner would be determined in California, the last big state to report returns. In fact, the election of 1980 was over two hours before the polls closed on the West Coast. Reagan won an electoral college landslide, 489 votes to just 49 for Carter. He won 43.9 million popular votes to Carter's 35.5 million, with 5.7 million going to John Anderson. Apparently many voters simply lied to the pollsters, perhaps embarrassed to admit they were going to vote for an old movie star.

The half-century-old Democratic party coalition was dead. The Irish-American and Italian-American vote, always dependably Democratic, went to Reagan. In all but three states, Slavic Americans voted Republican. Jews, once 80 percent Democratic, split evenly, as did labor union members. Reagan won 60 percent of the elderly, who—conventional wisdom had it—voted to protect their Social Security, which meant voting Democratic. Young people, indulged and lionized by liberal intellectuals since the 1960s, cast 60 percent of their votes for the aged Republican candidate.

The Moral Majority's PACs defeated the half dozen liberal Democratic senators they had targeted, including 1972 presidential nominee George McGovern. For the first time in nearly thirty years the Republicans had a majority in the Senate. The Democrats still held the House. However, several conservative Democrats, stunned by the results of the election, announced that they would support the president's program. A new era had begun.

Conservative Zenith 1979–1993

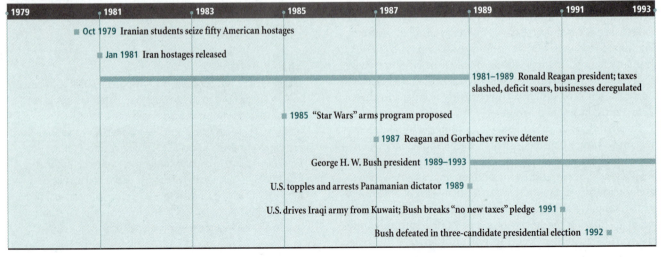

1979 — 1981 — 1983 — 1985 — 1987 — 1989 — 1991 — 1993

Oct 1979 Iranian students seize fifty American hostages

Jan 1981 Iran hostages released

1981–1989 Ronald Reagan president; taxes slashed, deficit soars, businesses deregulated

1985 "Star Wars" arms program proposed

1987 Reagan and Gorbachev revive détente

George H. W. Bush president 1989–1993

U.S. topples and arrests Panamanian dictator 1989

U.S. drives Iraqi army from Kuwait; Bush breaks "no new taxes" pledge 1991

Bush defeated in three-candidate presidential election 1992

THE REAGAN REVOLUTION

Reagan turned 78 before he left the White House in 1989, making him the oldest person ever to hold the post. A few years after retiring he was struck down by Alzheimer's disease. And yet this elderly actor stamped his personality and values on the 1980s as indelibly as Franklin D. Roosevelt had impressed his on the 1930s.

MAN OF THE DECADE

"He has no dark side," an aide said of Reagan. "What you see is what you get." Americans had seen a lot of Ronald Reagan for more than forty years. He appeared in fifty-four films in the 1930s and 1940s, often as the lead. During the 1950s he hosted a popular television show. Always political—a New Deal liberal as a young man—Reagan became a tireless and eloquent campaigner for conservative causes. He was governor of California between 1967 and 1975.

Few people who knew Reagan personally disliked him. He may have been a zealot—his mind was not subtle—but his manner was avuncular and good-natured. He was a master of the homey, morale-building sound bite: "The difference

between an American and any other person is that the American lives in anticipation of the future because he knows what a great place it will be." He was a cheerful raconteur, a walking *People* magazine with a treasury of show business stories. He conveyed his good nature to both large audiences and small groups gathered in a parlor. He won the affection of even his critics when, shortly after his inauguration, shot in the chest by an unbalanced young man, he cracked jokes on the operating table. Reagan was called the **"Great Communicator"** for his ability to sell himself and his policies. He was also called "the Teflon president." He was so well liked that nothing messy stuck to him—neither his own poor decisions, nor an administration that brimmed with scandal, nor the ridicule of former aides.

The criticisms that did not stick to Reagan were legion. After a lifetime at home in the Babylon of Hollywood evincing no interest in religion, he presented himself as a born-again Christian to accommodate fundamentalist voters. More than a hundred officials in his administration were accused of misconduct; most resigned, and some went to jail. Reagan's popularity rating remained steady. Liberal pundit Garry Wills threw up his hands in exasperation: Reagan had "bedazzled" the nation.

Sandra Day O'Connor, the first woman to sit on the Supreme Court, with President Reagan and Chief Justice Warren Burger. O'Connor was expected to be a dependable conservative justice. She usually was, but sometimes surprised Court watchers. She was neither a mischievous nor a creative jurist; her historical significance was that she shattered the last "gender line" in the federal government.

AP/Wide World Photos

Bonzo

Liberals made fun of Ronald Reagan's movie career, particularly a low-budget film in which he costarred with a chimpanzee, *Bedtime for Bonzo*. They got nowhere. The president had been a competent actor, loved Hollywood, never apologized for being a movie star, and even had the last laugh about *Bedtime for Bonzo*. When a reporter asked him to autograph a publicity photo of him and the chimpanzee, he wrote underneath his signature, "I'm the one with the watch."

SOCIAL POLICIES

Reagan believed that the liberal Supreme Court had betrayed its function by becoming result-oriented, legislating a political agenda in its judicial decisions. Among the consequences Reagan saw were social ills such as the "coddling" of lawbreakers.

During his eight years in office, a series of Supreme Court vacancies allowed him to continue the transformation of the Court that Richard Nixon had begun. (Ford and Carter appointed no justices.) Reagan's first appointee was **Sandra Day O'Connor** of Arizona, a protégée of Nixon's most conservative appointee, William Rehnquist. By naming her, the first woman on the Court, Reagan snookered feminists, all of them Democrats: they had no choice but to applaud while he added a generally dependable conservative vote. In 1986 Reagan made Rehnquist chief justice and added Antonin Scalia, a brilliant arch-conservative with a biting writing style, to the Court. Only in 1988, at the end of his term, did a Reagan nomination fail. The Senate found Robert Bork, a talented jurist and superior constitutional scholar, too political in his judgments. A second nominee, a conservative mediocrity, was dumped for the trivial reason that he had smoked marijuana while in law school.

Given that the liberals' hero on the Court was William Brennan, who was many times more "political" than Bork, and that liberals were inclined to favor the legalization of marijuana, the Democratic senators' principal motivation in rejecting Reagan's nominees was probably to win a rare victory in a fight with the president.

REAGANOMICS

Reagan's popularity owed partly to good luck. Some of the problems that had hobbled Ford and Carter resolved themselves after 1980. A vicious eight-year war between Iran and Iraq prevented the Ayatollah from vexing the United States. The senility of the corrupt and unresponsive Soviet leader Leonid Brezhnev and, after his death in 1982, three years of geriatric caretaker leadership left the Cold War adversary with little direction until 1985. OPEC, which had dictated world energy prices during the 1970s, fell apart, and the retail cost of gasoline declined.

But the keystone of Reagan's popularity was the fact that his presidency was a time of steadily increasing prosperity.

The good times, Reagan believed, were due to his economic policy, which critics called "Reaganomics."

Reaganomics was based on the **"supply-side"** theories of Arthur Laffer, who emphasized increasing the nation's supply of goods and services while allowing the distribution of wealth—each person's share—to take care of itself. In essence, this meant cutting the taxes in the upper income brackets. Whereas modestly fixed people would spend tax savings on consumer goods, supply-siders argued, the affluent already had all the extras. They would invest their tax savings, thus providing the economy with capital. The economic growth that resulted would mean jobs for people on the bottom. The formerly unemployed would no longer need public assistance (enabling government to reduce spending on social programs) and would begin to pay taxes. Greater revenues would allow Reagan to balance the budget, as he had promised he would do.

PROSPERITY IN PRACTICE

Democrats who had paid attention in their history classes pointed out that Reaganomics closely resembled the "trickle-down" economics of the Coolidge era, which had contributed to the Great Depression. Reagan was not impressed. At his behest, Congress reduced taxes by 25 percent over three years. The drop, for those with good incomes, was considerable. An upper-middle-class family making $75,000 a year paid federal income taxes of 52.9 percent during the 1950s and 39.3 percent during the 1970s. By 1985, after the Reagan tax cut, such a family was taxed only 29.6 percent of its income. The rich did even better. The average tax bill on an annual income of $500,000–$1 million in 1981 was $301,072. By the time Reagan left office it was $166,066, proportionately less than a waiter in Western Europe paid.

Government revenues dropped by $131 billion, which Reagan said he would make up by slashing expenditures on bureaucracy and social programs. He cut 37,000 jobs from the federal payroll and reduced spending on education, medical research, food stamps, and other programs instituted during the 1960s to aid the poor. Federal spending on low-income housing dropped from $32 billion in 1980 to $7 billion in 1988.

THE DEFICIT MUSHROOMS

But Reaganomics did not work as Arthur Laffer had predicted. Much of the tax break for the upper middle class and the wealthy went not into investment but into consumption

Priorities in the 1980s

In 1983 the United States spent 57 cents per capita on public broadcasting, as compared to $10 per capita in Japan, $18 in Great Britain, and $22 in Canada. In the private sector, the cost of making one episode of a cops-and-robbers program, *Miami Vice*, was $1.5 million. The annual budget of the real vice squad in the city of Miami, a major clearinghouse for imported drugs, was $1.1 million.

Urban Decay

In New York City every day between 1977 and 1980, 600 to 2,100 subway cars were out of service because of age, mistreatment, and vandalism. Between 80 and 300 trains had to be canceled each day. There were 2,200 to 5,000 fires in the New York subway system each year. A subway trip that had taken ten minutes in 1910 took forty minutes in 1980.

of ever more expensive luxury goods. By 1986 investment in manufacturing was only 1 percent higher than it had been in the recession year of 1982. However, sales of high-priced homes boomed. Expensive imports like Jaguar and Mercedes-Benz automobiles soared. Americans imported better wines and, for a few years, even their drinking water: Perrier, a bottled French mineral water, became a mania. The image of a ship crossing the Atlantic with a cargo of water burning tons of unrenewable fossil fuels was mind-boggling, although there is no evidence it intruded on the minds of many.

Money to feed the consumption binge also came from abroad. West German, Japanese, and Arab investors pumped money into the United States, buying real estate, corporations, banks, stocks, and U.S. Treasury bonds in huge blocks. From being the world's leading creditor nation when Reagan took office, the United States became the world's biggest debtor. In 1981 foreigners owed Americans $2,500 for each American family of four. By 1989 the United States owed foreigners $7,000 for each family of four. Again, people were more interested in their tax savings.

The federal deficit—the government's annual debt—grew worse each year Reagan was in office. The costs of Social Security, pensions, and especially Reagan's military buildup were immense. The president did not miss a step. He regularly called for a constitutional amendment mandating a balanced budget while his administration spent and borrowed at levels that smashed all records. In 1981 the federal government owed $738 billion, about 26 cents on each dollar produced and earned in the United States that year. In 1989 the debt was $2.1 trillion, about 43 cents on each dollar produced and earned. The president who criticized Jimmy Carter's borrowing borrowed more money in eight years than thirty-nine previous presidents had borrowed in two centuries. That he continued to charm a large majority of Americans hints at aspects of human nature that historians can gratefully refer to other university departments or, in sectarian institutions, to the chaplain.

DEREGULATION

Since the New Deal, the federal government had regulated most important aspects of national economic life. This regulation, Reagan said, discouraged the spirit of enterprise. As president, he weakened the regulatory apparatus by abolishing some agencies and cutting the budgets of others. To head some offices, Reagan appointed officials who deliberately neglected to do what their jobs mandated. Airlines, trucking companies, banks, and stockbrokers found there were fewer

federal watchdogs dropping in, and those who did were apt to be friendly.

Profits increased. Airlines closed down routes where profits had been slim and raised fares on crowded air lanes. In 1981 a person could fly from San Francisco to Los Angeles for $36. In 1989 the same ticket cost $148. Getting from big cities to small ones by air became extremely expensive, when it was possible. By the hundreds, small towns that had boasted regularly scheduled flights lost them. Consumer advocates claimed that the deregulated airlines sent unsafe planes and unqualified pilots aloft. Similar criticisms were made of the condition of trucks and the qualifications required of truck drivers. In fact, serious accidents involving big "semi" trucks increased during the decade.

Several of Reagan's appointees to environmental agencies despised the people they called "tree huggers"—conservation and environmentalist activists. The head of the Environmental Protection Agency, Ann Burford, was forced to resign in 1983 when it was revealed she had actively interfered with enforcement of the EPA's regulations. Reagan's secretary of the interior, James Watt of Colorado, tried to open protected scenic coastlines to offshore oil drillers.

Environmental groups grew rapidly. The Wilderness Society had 48,000 members in 1981, 240,000 in 1989. The Natural Resources Defense Council increased its membership from 85,000 to 170,000. The World Wildlife Fund had 60,000 members in 1982, 1 million in 1990. The Sierra Club and Audubon Society made similar gains. Reagan was nonplussed. He even vetoed a Clean Water Act aimed at stopping the dumping of toxic industrial wastes.

FINANCIAL FRAUD

Deregulation of financial institutions led to irresponsible and sometimes corrupt practices in banks and savings and loan associations. In 1988 alone, 135 savings and loans had to be bailed out or closed by the Federal Savings and Loan Insurance Corporation (FSLIC).

This agency, like the Federal Deposit Insurance Corporation (FDIC) for banks, insured savings accounts. Before the Reagan deregulation, however, the FSLIC and FDIC also enforced strict management standards on financial institutions. During the Reagan years, supervision was virtually nil and shoddy practices multiplied. George W. Bush, the son of the vice president, was the beneficiary of transactions that would not have been allowed before deregulation. An energy

Who's Got What?

In 1929, the year of the Great Crash, the richest 1 percent of Americans owned 44 percent of the nation's net household wealth. This lopsided distribution of wealth was believed to have been a major cause of the economic crisis of the 1930s.

By 1976, the richest 1 percent's share of the nation's wealth had been reduced to 20 percent. By 1989, the year Ronald Reagan left office, the top 1 percent owned 48 percent of the nation's net wealth—more than in 1929.

company paid him $120,000 during a year in which the company was losing $12 million. The company also lent him $180,000 at low interest to buy stock in the company. Then, one week before huge losses were announced and the price of the company's stock dropped by 60 percent, Bush sold his shares for $850,000.

The champion wheeler-dealer of the 1980s was probably Michael Milken, who sold deregulated savings and loans billions of dollars in "junk bonds"—loans that promised to pay high interest precisely because conservative investors (and regulated banks) would not touch them; before deregulation, savings and loans were prohibited from making such investments. Milken collected $550 million in commissions and eventually went to jail. So did several prominent figures on Wall Street. Freed of close supervision by the Securities and Exchange Commission (SEC), stockbrokers turned to fraud. By paying bribes to executives in large corporations, they learned before the general public of important decisions that affected the price of stocks. Using this insider information, they bought and sold shares at immense profits.

The Reagan administration continued to approve corporate mergers and takeovers that did little but enrich a few individuals. In 1970 there were 10 corporate reshufflings paying fees of $1 million or more to those who arranged them. In 1980 there were 94, and in 1986, 346. In 1988 the government approved a deal between tobacco giant R. J. Reynolds and the Nabisco Company despite the fact that even the principals admitted the only consequences would be higher prices for consumers, fewer jobs, and personal profits of $10 million for a handful of top shareholders.

THE ELECTION OF 1984

In 1984 Walter Mondale of Minnesota, vice president under Jimmy Carter, won the Democratic party presidential nomination by beating back challenges from Senator Gary Hart of Colorado and Reverend Jesse Jackson, a civil rights activist who, a few years later, was to coin the term *African American*. Jackson was an orator in the tradition of the black churches from which he had emerged an ordained minister. Hart was popular among educated, generally young and affluent Democrats who thought more in terms of attitudes and lifestyle than concrete issues.

Mondale, an old-line New Dealer and party regular, hoped that labor union and African-American support and the "sleaze factor," the corruption in the Reagan administration, would be enough to help him overcome the president's personal popularity. But he was unable to bring back the traditionally Democratic voters who had gone for Reagan in 1980. The Republicans depicted Mondale as a pork-barrel politician, promising something to every constituent group. His play to win over Hart's supporters by naming a congresswoman, Geraldine Ferraro, as his running mate made little political sense. Feminists were not apt to vote Republican under any circumstances, and Republican women were not moved by Mondale's clumsy appeal to "sisterhood."

Reagan's popularity was at flood tide in 1984. He won by a landslide, carrying 59 percent of the vote and every state except Mondale's Minnesota and the District of Columbia. He announced that the theme of his second term was "Morning in America."

FOREIGN POLICY IN THE EIGHTIES

Reagan was a hard-line Cold Warrior. In 1982 he called Russia an "evil empire . . . the focus of evil in the world." In 1985 he promulgated the Reagan Doctrine—pretty much warmed-over John Foster Dulles—that the United States would support anti-Communist struggles everywhere in the world. Before he left office in 1989, however, Reagan scored a major breakthrough in nuclear arms reduction and set the stage for a historic rapprochement between the United States and the Soviet Union. His policies toward other parts of the world were also sometimes surprising.

SOUTH AFRICA AND THE MIDDLE EAST

Reagan criticized South Africa's policy of apartheid (strict segregation of races), but he resisted calls for economic sanctions some said would force the South African regime to change. He continued to support rebels in Angola who were fighting a Soviet-backed government defended by Cuban troops.

Reagan continued Jimmy Carter's policy of aiding anti-Russian rebels in Afghanistan despite the fact that they were Muslim fundamentalists like those who had swept Khomeini to power in Iran. In 1983 he sent marines to Lebanon, which was torn by a multisided civil war. When a suicide bomber driving an explosive-laden truck killed 241 sleeping marines, he withdrew the force. His Teflon worked as ever. Reagan was not widely criticized either for sending the marines into Lebanon or for withdrawing them in failure.

In 1986 Reagan won applause by bombing Libya. The Libyan leader, Muammar Qadaffi, had long been suspected of financing terrorists. When American intelligence claimed to have evidence of a direct link between Qadaffi and terrorists in West Germany, American bombers raided several Libyan cities. Public opinion was favorable.

CENTRAL AMERICA

In October 1983 Reagan ordered a surprise occupation of **Grenada,** a tiny Caribbean island nation of 110,000 people. Grenada was in chaos after the assassination of a Marxist president. Grenada was so small that the invasion had a comic-opera flavor, but it was popular in the United States.

Reagan's policy in Central America was more controversial. Liberals opposed American support of a repressive government in El Salvador and the administration's opposition to the revolutionary Sandinista government of Nicaragua. When, in 1983, El Salvador elected a moderate president over an extreme rightist, criticism of Reagan's policy in that country faded too.

However, many congressional representatives continued to oppose American subsidy of the Nicaraguan *contras,* guerrillas fighting the Sandinista government. Some said that the United

States was causing turmoil and misery in a long-misgoverned country by keeping it at war. Others said that the contras were reactionary and antidemocratic. Still others feared that the United States would become involved in another quagmire like Vietnam. Beginning in October 1984, a worried Congress attached the Boland Amendments to several bills providing money for foreign aid. These prohibited the government from directly aiding the Nicaraguan contras.

THE IRAN–CONTRA AFFAIR

Reagan had no intention of abandoning the *contras*. He told his aides "to figure out a way to take action." They embarked on a bizarre adventure that mocked the president's depiction of world politics as a competition between good and evil. Two national security advisers, Robert McFarlane and John Poindexter, and a marine colonel, Oliver North, secretly sold eighteen Hawk missiles to the Ayatollah Khomeini's Iran. Some of the profits from the deal simply disappeared into someone's pocket. The balance was given to the *contras*.

The roles of Defense Secretary Weinberger and the president in the affair were never clearly determined. Weinberger was indicted for withholding information, and Reagan changed the story of his involvement several times. Either he had sanctioned violation of the Boland law—an impeachable crime—or he did not know what was going on in his administration.

Liberals screamed. But Ronald Reagan was no ordinary political target. Times were good; stocks and real estate values were rising; football players were better than ever; and television entertainers brought tears and laughter nightly into American living rooms. To the bewilderment of Democrats, the public took little interest in the issue. Colonel North, convicted in 1989 of three criminal acts, went on in 1994 to miss, by a narrow margin, election to the Senate from Virginia.

CHANGING POLICIES

Even before the **Iran–Contra affair** made the news, Reagan's foreign policy underwent significant changes. Rather than defend an anti-Communist dictator in Haiti in 1986, American

Reproduced from the Collections of the Library of Congress

Nancy Reagan, vulnerable to mockery because of her love of the trappings of wealth and belief in astrology, was devoted to her husband and his legacy. Some of President Reagan's aides said that her influence was the key to the president's sudden abandonment of warlike confrontation with the Soviet Union. Mrs. Reagan understood that presidents who made peace were remembered more favorably than warmongers.

agents played an important role in persuading him to go into exile. The United States also played a central role in the ouster of the pro-American but abysmally corrupt president of the Philippines, Ferdinand Marcos. When Marcos declared himself the victor in a disputed election, riots broke out throughout the country. Fearing a civil war, the United States supported his opponent, Corazon Aquino. Marcos was given asylum in Hawaii to get him out of the Philippines.

Reagan was unsuccessful in his attempt to ease out Manuel Noriega, the military dictator of Panama. Evidence indicated that Noriega was involved in smuggling cocaine and other drugs to the United States. He was indicted in the United States, and Reagan cut off the flow of American dollars to Panama. However, Noriega's hold on the Panamanian army was strong, and he rallied public support by baiting the United States—always a crowd-pleaser in Latin America.

WEAPONS BUILDUP

The most important of Reagan's foreign policy shifts was in his view of the Soviet Union. Calling the SALT II treaty a "one-way street" with Americans making all the concessions

---

Doublespeak

Aided by journalists, spokesmen for the armed forces during the Gulf War purveyed a jargon that, had the context not been a war, would have been ludicrous. The resistance to plain English, from the Joint Chiefs of Staff to associate deans at community colleges, cannot speak well of the health of the culture.

Armed situation	= Battle
To visit a site	= To bomb
Hard targets	= Buildings
Soft targets	= People
Service the target, degrade, attrit, neutralize, eliminate, cleanse, sanitize, impact	= What bombs do to hard targets and soft targets

Cutthroat Competition

In 1984 it was revealed that the Defense Department paid General Dynamics $7,417 for an alignment pin that cost 3 cents at a hardware store, McDonnell–Douglas $2,043 for a nut anyone could buy for 13 cents, Pratt and Whitney $118 for 22-cent plastic stool leg covers, and Hughes Aircraft $2,543 for a $3.64 circuit breaker. A congressman went to a hardware store and purchased the twenty-two tools in a standard-issue military repair kit. He paid $92.44; for the same kit the federal government paid a patriotic defense contractor $10,186.56.

to the Soviets, he refused to submit it to the Senate for ratification. In 1986 Reagan announced that the United States would no longer be bound by SALT I.

In the meantime the president had sponsored the greatest peacetime military buildup in the nation's history, spending $2 trillion on both old and new weapons systems. Battleships were taken out of mothballs and put to sea despite the fact that one could be sunk by one cheap missile in the armories of a dozen nations. Reagan revived the MX missile, which he renamed the Peacekeeper. When it was announced that the Peacekeepers were to be installed in old Minuteman missile silos, critics said if Reagan was not just pumping money into the treasuries of defense contractors, he was planning a first strike against the Soviets. It was well known that the Russians had the Minuteman sites targeted. The Peacekeepers were useless unless they were fired in a surprise attack.

In 1983 Pershing II missiles were installed in West Germany from where they could hit Soviet targets in five minutes. The Russians responded by increasing their striking capability. A new arms race was under way. By 1985 the two superpowers had more than 50,000 nuclear warheads between them.

The most controversial of Reagan's weapons proposals was SDI, the Strategic Defense Initiative, known as "Star Wars" after the popular movie. In theory, SDI was a system by which satellites orbiting the earth would be equipped with lasers fired at missiles by computer. Reagan claimed that the system would create an umbrella preventing a successful missile attack on the United States.

Criticism of Star Wars took several forms. Some scientists said that SDI simply would not work, pointing out that low-flying missiles and planes would be unaffected by lasers from space. Bankers worried that the astronomical costs of the project would bankrupt the United States. Antiwar groups said that SDI was an offensive, not a defensive, weapon. By making the United States safer from nuclear attack, it would encourage a first-strike attack on the Soviet Union. Others said that the Soviets would simply develop countermeasures, which had always been the case in military technology, and the insanity would continue.

TURNING TOWARD DISARMAMENT

Still, it was not criticism that led President Reagan to reverse direction in defense policies. During Reagan's second term the hawkish Casper Weinberger resigned as secretary of defense, and the more statesmanlike secretary of state, George Schultz, the dove of the Reagan administration, increased his influence over the president.

White House insiders said that Nancy Reagan played a major part in persuading the president to turn toward

Five presidents gather to dedicate the Ronald Reagan Presidential Library in 1993. From left to right: George H. W. Bush, Ronald Reagan, Jimmy Carter, Gerald Ford, Richard M. Nixon.

Weapons

Ronald Reagan said that his predecessor, Jimmy Carter, had neglected the military, and he increased Carter's defense budgets by 28 percent. However, the weapons systems developed during the Carter administration—the Tomahawk Cruise Missile, the F-117 Stealth Fighter, and the HARM antiradar missile—were critical in the easy victory in the 1991 Gulf War, whereas Reagan-era innovations had dubious histories. His "Star Wars" would have been fabulously expensive and, many experts believed, would not have worked. The battleships Reagan recommissioned at great expense were back in mothballs within a few years. (The battleship's obsolescence was clear even in the 1940s; during the 1970s Falklands War, a dirt-cheap, widely available Argentinean missile sank a British cruiser.) Reagan's B-1 bomber was a $30 billion flop: The ninety-seven planes built were cursed by engine failure and icing on wings.

Critics who said Reagan was less interested in an effective military than in enriching defense contractors had grounds for their suspicions.

disarmament. Devoted to her husband, she was concerned about his place in history, and she knew that presidents who worked for peace had higher historical reputations than those who seemed to be warmongers.

The concerns of allies in Europe also influenced the president. Chancellor Helmut Kohl of West Germany, President François Mitterand of France, and Prime Minister Margaret Thatcher of Great Britain remained loyal to the NATO alliance. However, all made it clear that they were unnerved by some of Reagan's more reckless speeches. Most important, the Soviet Union underwent profound changes during the 1980s.

MIKHAIL GORBACHEV

In 1985 Mikhail Gorbachev emerged as head of both the Soviet government and Communist party. At home Gorbachev tried to institute far-reaching economic and political reforms. The policy of *perestroika* (restructuring) was designed to revive the Soviet economy, which had been moribund under strict government control. *Glasnost* (opening) promised political and intellectual freedoms unheard of in the Soviet Union.

If his reforms were to succeed, Gorbachev needed to divert Soviet resources from the military to the domestic economy. Doing that depended on American cooperation. At first Reagan resisted Gorbachev's proposals to end the arms race. Then, in Washington in December 1987, the two men, all smiles and handshakes, signed a treaty eliminating many short-range and medium-range missiles. The Soviets destroyed 1,752 missiles and the Americans 867. These represented only 4 percent of the nuclear missiles in existence. Nevertheless, nuclear power 32,000 times the force of the Hiroshima bomb was wiped out.

THE BUSH PRESIDENCY

The Democrats approached the presidential campaign of 1988 with high hopes. They believed that the Reagan presidency was an aberration, the personal triumph of a fabulously popular individual. A majority of governors were Democrats. The Democratic party enjoyed a comfortable majority in the House and had regained control of the Senate in 1986. Why should the Democrats not regain the presidency, too?

1988: DUKAKIS VERSUS BUSH

In 1988 the Democratic party was swamped with would-be presidential candidates. The early front-runner was Gary Hart, the former senator from Colorado who had opposed Mondale in the 1976 primaries. But in a bizarre sequence of events, including publication of a photo showing the married Hart with a beautiful young model on his lap aboard a yacht called the *Monkey Business,* political analysts suggested that the candidate's judgment was perhaps a little less than what was called for by the presidency.

When Hart withdrew from the race, the remaining candidates were ridiculed as "the seven dwarfs" for their deficiency of presidential stature. In fact, several of the dwarfs were able men, and Jesse Jackson remained, as he had been in 1976, one of the nation's most exciting speakers. Because he was black, however, party professionals considered him unelectable. They hoped that Senator Sam Nunn of Georgia, a respected expert on national defense, would jump into the thirty-five primary election races; or that Governor Mario Cuomo of New York, another inspiring orator whose thoughtful humanism was tempered by hard-headed political realism, would run.

But neither did, and the nomination went to Governor Michael Dukakis of Massachusetts. The son of Greek immigrants, Dukakis was a successful governor, balancing budgets while the Reagan administration spent and borrowed. During his administration a state with serious economic difficulties became a prosperous center of finance and high-tech industry. For vice president, Dukakis chose the courtly Senator Lloyd Bentsen of Texas, reminding voters of the Massachusetts–Texas combination that had won the election of 1960.

The Republican nominee was Vice President George Bush, who handily defeated Senator Robert Dole of Kansas in the primaries. Bush was a wealthy oilman who had held a number of appointive positions in government before becoming vice president under Reagan. He became the administration's chief cheerleader and established ties with Republican conservatives who earlier had looked on him as a liberal.

As his running mate, Bush chose Senator Dan Quayle of Indiana, all of whose achievements since first tying his shoes seemed to owe to his father's wealth and influence. Quayle admitted he had "majored in golf" at college. There was evidence that he had dodged military service during the Vietnam War when his father's friends created a place for him in the National Guard. Quayle's political career was built on his movie star good looks and careful programming by political handlers. During the campaign of 1988 they made sure that he spoke mostly to screened groups of the party faithful and to elementary school pupils.

THE CAMPAIGN

Dukakis attacked Bush's judgment for picking Quayle, but Dukakis's public persona was mechanical and dull. Pundits joked about "Zorba the Clerk." By way of contrast, winning the Republican nomination seemed to liberate Bush. As Dukakis grew drabber and grayer, Bush exuded confidence and authority, promising both to continue the policies of the "Reagan–Bush administration" and to usher in "a kinder, gentler America."

While Bush took the high road, Republican strategists smeared Dukakis because a murderer paroled in Massachusetts during his governorship killed again. They hammered on the fact that Dukakis was a member of the American Civil Liberties Union, which had become a citadel of New Age wackiness, defending elementary school pupils who wore to classes T-shirts bearing obscene messages as their sacred right of free speech. Dukakis, put on the defensive, was forced to point out that he had not been the author of Massachusetts parole policies but was mandated to observe them when he was governor. He said he disagreed with many of the positions the ACLU had adopted since the 1970s. But he had lost the initiative—deadly when challenging an entrenched administration. Bush led throughout the campaign and won 54 percent of the vote.

DUBIOUS LEGACY

A few months before Bush's election, Ronald Reagan told a joke to a Republican audience. Two fellows, he said, were out hiking in the woods when a grizzly bear came trotting toward them. One of the men pulled a pair of sneakers out of his pack and began putting them on. The other said, "You don't think you can outrun that bear, do you?" The first one said, "I don't have to outrun the bear. I just have to outrun you."

Ronald Reagan outran George H. W. Bush. When he retired to his California ranch in January 1989, it still appeared to be morning in America. In fact, Bush inherited a host of problems Reagan had created and then had outrun.

THE COLLAPSE OF COMMUNISM

In May 1989 thousands of student demonstrators gathered in Tiananmen Square, a huge plaza in the center of the Chinese capital. Soviet Premier Gorbachev was visiting Beijing; the students used the occasion to demand *glasnost*-like reforms in China. Within two days there were a million people in the square. The drama was played out "live" on American television because two television news bureaus were in China to cover the Gorbachev visit. They found they had stumbled on a much bigger story. Americans even caught some glimpses of the brutal suppression of the

The demolition of the Berlin Wall, begun by demonstrators brick by brick and later finished by bulldozers, was the dramatic symbol of the final fall of the Iron Curtain and the end of the Soviet empire in Eastern Europe.

rebellion, which resulted in at least 500 and, according to some sources, 7,000 deaths.

Communist hard-liners were shaken by Tiananmen Square, but the army remained loyal, and they held onto power. In Eastern Europe, however, the countries that had been satellites of the Soviet Union since World War II exploited Gorbachev's relaxation of controls to oust their Communist rulers. Poland elected a non-Communist government in mid-1989. By the end of the year, Czechoslovakia did the same. In October Erich Honecker, the Communist chief of East Germany, resigned, and the next month a festive crowd breached the Berlin Wall. In December the hated dictator of Rumania, Nicolae Ceausescu, was murdered by rebels. In April 1990 Hungary elected an anti-Communist government. In a few astonishing months a European order almost half a century old was overturned.

Communist party control of the Soviet Union also dissipated. *Glasnost* had opened up Soviet society, but *perestroika* had not revitalized the Soviet economy. Food shortages in cities led to protests. On May Day, 1990, Communism's holiday, Gorbachev and his colleagues were roundly jeered as they reviewed the traditional parade. A few days later Boris Yeltsin, a critic of Gorbachev, was elected president of the Russian Republic, the largest constituent of the Soviet Union. For the next year and a half Yeltsin increased his following at Gorbachev's expense by calling for a free market economy and supporting claims to independence in many of the other fourteen Soviet republics. At the end of 1991 the Soviet Union was formally dissolved.

SUCCESSES IN LATIN AMERICA

President Bush could crow that Republican policies had won the Cold War. Reagan's get-tough rhetoric and the fabulously expensive arms race had laid bare the weaknesses of the

MAP 50:1 The Soviet Bloc, 1947–1989 (top); Eastern Europe, 2003 (bottom)
The map of Central and Eastern Europe was changed as radically in the early 1990s as it had been altered by the Treaty of Versailles following World War I. *The Times* of London had the bad luck to publish a splendid new edition of its definitive *World Atlas* just as the breakup of the old Soviet Union and Yugoslavia gave birth to a dozen new nations. In a sporting effort to sell the obsolete books, the *Times* advertised it as an atlas of the "old world order."

Communist states. More important, with the leaders of the Soviet Union preoccupied by the chaos at home, Bush and his secretary of state, James Baker, were able to win a series of victories both in the corridors of diplomacy and on the battlefield.

In December 1989 Bush succeeded in toppling Manuel Noriega from power in Panama. After an American military officer was shot in Panama City, Bush unleashed 24,000 troops. Within a few days, with little loss of American lives, Noriega was out of power and under arrest, and a client government was installed in Panama City.

In February 1990, as Soviet and Cuban aid to Nicaragua dried up, the Sandinistas were voted out of power by a political alliance backed by the United States. A less desirable right-wing party took control of El Salvador but, thanks to American prodding, moderated its policies and signed an armistice and agreement with leftist rebels, ending the long war in that country. World affairs were going well for the president.

CRISIS IN THE MIDDLE EAST

Bush's greatest success abroad was in the Middle East. It was precipitated in August 1990 by Iraq's occupation of Kuwait, a small sheikdom floating on oil. Fearing that Iraqi president Saddam Hussein would next invade Saudi Arabia, the Bush administration secured a unanimous vote in the United Nations Security Council calling for a boycott of all foreign trade with Iraq. Although rich in oil, Iraq needed to import most of the materials to support a modern economy.

Bush and Secretary of State Baker did not believe economic sanctions would resolve the problem. They feared, with plenty of precedents to back them up, that as time went on, the boycott would disintegrate. That fear, and apprehensions for the security of Saudi Arabia, prompted Bush to send a token American military force to Saudi Arabia on August 7. Far from flinching, Saddam Hussein grew more defiant, annexing Kuwait to Iraq. Bush then sent more than 400,000 troops to Arabia. Other nations, particularly Britain and France, sent large contingents.

THE HUNDRED HOURS WAR

In January, after Saddam Hussein ignored a United Nations ultimatum that he evacuate Kuwait, the American-led force launched a withering air attack that, in little more than a week, totaled 12,000 sorties. With an American television reporter in Baghdad, the world was presented with the phenomenon of watching a war from both sides.

In the face of the onslaught, Hussein sent most of his air force to neighboring Iran, leaving the skies to American planes. Probably, like some Americans, he believed that his huge army, dug in behind formidable defenses, could turn back any ground assault. He was wrong. His army was large, but most Iraqi soldiers were poorly trained and mistreated by their officers. The air war was chillingly effective, not only devastating Iraqi communications and the transportation system, but terrifying front-line Iraqi troops. When the ground attack came on February 23, 1992, most

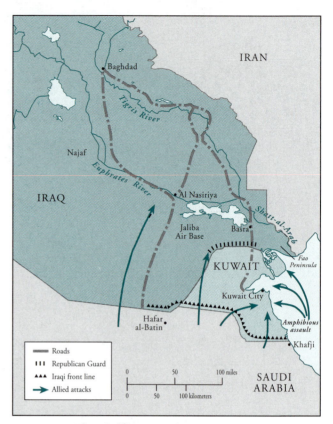

MAP 50:2 The Gulf War, 1991
After weeks of bombardment that destroyed Iraqi communications and demoralized the highly touted Iraqi army, American and allied troops advanced through Kuwait and Iraq, surrounding, crushing, or forcing into a disorderly retreat almost all Iraqi forces. Confident that Iraqis would depose the discredited Saddam Hussein, President Bush allowed the best Iraqi units to escape unscathed. They rallied behind Saddam and kept him in power.

surrendered without resistance. In just a few days the Iraqi army was routed by a flanking action designed by General Norman Schwarzkopf. Believing that Saddam could not survive the humiliating defeat—that his generals would oust him—Bush ordered a halt to the ground war when it was 100 hours old, leaving the Iraqi army's best units intact.

MIXED RESULTS

A few months later, Bush's sudden termination of the advance looked like a blunder. Saddam Hussein remained in power, rebuilt his military force, and brutally suppressed rebellions among Kurds in northern Iraq and Shi'ite Muslims in the south. Only a decade later, when Bush's son President George W. Bush invaded and tried to occupy Iraq, did it become clear that his father had good reasons (or good luck) in halting the American advance after liberating Kuwait.

For the briefest of moments, the United Nations' decisiveness in chastising a petty dictator seemed to give the

AP/Wide World Photos

The Iraqi army collapsed within days of the beginning of George H. W. Bush's "100 Hours War" in 1991. Unfortunately, a fragment of the army, permitted to escape on the assumption it would be needed to ensure stability under a new Iraqi government, remained loyal to dictator Saddam Hussein. Bush's wisdom in not attempting to occupy Baghdad, however, was demonstrated ten years later when his son, President George W. Bush, took the city and subjected American troops and Iraqi civilians to almost daily attacks by Muslim suicide bombers.

organization the prestige it was designed to have decades earlier and never did. Then, however, when a vicious multisided ethnic war broke out in Yugoslavia, neither the UN, NATO, nor the European Community took decisive action. For three years, while the United States and the nations of Western Europe issued empty threats, Bosnian Serbs, Croatians, and Muslims battled one another with tribal savagery.

Nor did victory in the Gulf War preserve George Bush's presidency, as he believed it would. He proclaimed that under his leadership, Americans had put the "Vietnam Syndrome," a demoralized army, and defeatism at home behind them. The president's ratings in public opinion polls soared in early 1991. In the excitement of watching a miraculously successful war on television, Americans seemed to forget their serious economic problems at home. But it was only for a season. By 1992, a presidential election year, a stubborn recession virtually relegated the **Hundred Hours War** to the realm of ancient history. American public affairs had become—the name of a television comedy show—a "short attention span theater."

PRIMARY ELECTIONS, 1992

Bush was challenged in the Republican primaries by a right-wing television commentator, Patrick Buchanan, who had vociferously opposed the Gulf War. Buchanan won no early primaries, but by taking almost 40 percent of the Republican

votes in some states, he signaled that Bush was in trouble in his own party.

The Democratic party's primary campaign proved to be unlike any other in recent history. Instead of one candidate in the field pulling ahead early and coasting to the nomination, several would-be nominees won the convention delegates of at least one state. Senator Thomas Harkin of Iowa, a liberal with a populist tinge, won his own state. Paul Tsongas of Massachusetts won New Hampshire and Maryland. Senator Robert Kerry of Nebraska won South Dakota. Most surprising of all, former California Governor Jerry Brown, despite a nagging reputation for bizarre beliefs (he was sometimes called "Governor Moonbeam") won most of the delegates from Colorado.

Then, however, young Governor William Clinton of Arkansas rushed to the head of what humorist Russell Baker called "the march of the Millard Fillmores." He rode out a past as a Vietnam War draft dodger, accusations of adultery, and claims that he was too slick to be trusted. He sewed up the convention before it met. Clinton's strategy was to woo the New Age liberals who had supported Gary Hart by speaking for liberal lifestyle issues (he was pro-abortion and pro–affirmative action, and he called for an end to discrimination against homosexuals) while appealing to moderates with an economic policy that emphasized growth.

THE ELECTION OF 1992

Some populist conservatives who had never liked the aristocratic Bush swarmed to the independent candidacy of H. Ross Perot, a self-made Texas billionaire. Although Perot offered little in the way of a program, hundreds of thousands of uneasy Americans formed local "Perot for President" organizations. The candidate himself pledged to spend millions of his own money in the cause. By July, polls showed him leading both Bush and Clinton.

On the day Clinton was to accept the Democratic nomination, Perot was on the ballot in twenty-four states. Then he suddenly quit the race, claiming that he and his daughter had been threatened by assassins. Many of Perot's supporters condemned him; but others continued to gather signatures on petitions. Perot jumped back into the contest and outclassed both Bush and Clinton in the first of the candidates' televised debates. His 19 percent showing in the general election was more than any third-party presidential candidate had won since Theodore Roosevelt in 1912.

Perot's candidacy helped Bill Clinton carry several mountain states that had not gone Democratic since 1964. Clinton also won California. In electoral votes, the entire Northeast and several southern states also went Democratic. Although Clinton won only 43 percent of the popular vote—one of the lowest proportions for a winning candidate—he had 370 electoral votes to Bush's 168.

FURTHER READING

Author's Note: 1980 is a quarter of a century ago. The events discussed in this chapter happened "only yesterday," all of them within the memories of people still in their thirties. It is debatable that any book about events so recent should be called history (not to mention chapters of textbooks heavily reliant on those books). Whatever other attributes an honest historian must possess, a personal detachment only the elapse of many years makes possible is one of them. However honest, earnest, and unpolemical a book about "only yesterday" may be, it is not, indisputably, history. I have not listed books by participants in the events of this era; they are, at least in part, self-justifying and therefore suspect. I have listed very few books that were written in the midst of the events that are their subjects.

General Richard J. Barnet and John Cavanaugh, *Global Dreams: Imperial Corporations and the New World Order*, 1994; Paul Boyer, *Promises to Keep: The United States since World War II*, 1995; Theodore Draper, *The Enemy We Knew: Americans and the Cold War*, 1993; Barbara Eherenreich, *The Worst Years of Our Lives: Irreverent Notes from a Decade of Greed*, 1990; Haynes Johnson, *Sleepwalking through History: America in the Reagan Years*, 1997, and *Divided We Fall: Gambling with History in the Nineties*, 1994; Garry Wills, *Reagan's America: Innocents at Home*, 1987.

Carter and the Hostage Crisis James Bill, *The Eagle and the Lion: The Tragedy of Americans' Iranian Relations*, 1987; Burton Kaufman, *The Carter Presidency*, 1993; Michael Ledeen and William Lewis, *Debacle: The American Failure in Iran*, 1981; Clark R. Mollenhoff, *The President Who Failed: Carter Out of Control*, 1980; Gaddis Smith, *Morality, Reason, and Power*, 1986.

The First George Bush John R. Greene, *The Presidency of George Bush*, 2000; David Mervin, *George Bush and the Guardianship Presidency*, 1998; Herbert Parmet, *George Bush: The Life of a Lone Star Yankee*, 1997.

Fundamentalism and Conservatism Scott Appleby, *The Glory and the Power: The Fundamentalist Challenge to the Modern World*, 1992; S. Blumenthal, *The Rise of the Counter-Establishment*, 1986; John Ehrman, *The Rise of Neoconservatism: Intellectuals and Foreign Affairs, 1945–1994*, 1995; William Martin, *With God on Our Side: The Rise of the Religious Right in America*, 1996; Martin E. Marty and R. Lisa McGirr, *Suburban Warriors: The Origins of the New American Right*, 2001; John Schoenwald, *A Time for Choosing: The Rise of Modern American Conservatism*, 2001; Peter Steinfels, *The Neoconservatives*, 1979; Garry Wills, *Under God: Religion and American Politics*, 1990.

Issues of the 1980s Theodore Draper, *A Very Thin Line: The Iran–Contra Affair*, 1991; Frances Fitzgerald, *Way Out There in the Blue: Reagan, Star Wars, and the End of the Cold War*, 2000; R. L. Garthoff, *Détente and Confrontation: American–Soviet Relations from Nixon to Reagan*, 1985; Doyle McManus, *Landslide: The Unmaking of the President, 1984–1988*, 1989; Richard A. Melanson, *American Foreign Policy since the Vietnam War: The Search for Consensus from Nixon to Clinton*, 2001; Robert L. Pacelle, *The Transformation of the Supreme Court's Agenda from the New Deal to the Reagan Administration*, 1991; Kevin Phillips, *The Politics of Rich and Poor: Wealth and the American Electorate in the Reagan Aftermath*, 1995; John W. Sloan, *The Reagan Effect: Economics and Presidential Leadership*, 2000; G. F. Treverton, *Covert Action*, 1987; Bob Woodward, *Veil: The Secret Wars of the C.I.A., 1981–1987*, 1987.

Ronald Reagan Lou Cannon, *President Reagan: The Role of a Lifetime*, 1991; A. Edwards, *Early Reagan: The Rise to Power*, 1987; Fred Greenstein, *The Reagan Presidency*, 1993; Edmund Morris, *Dutch: A Memoir of Ronald Reagan*, 1999; William E. Pemberton, *Exit with Honor: The Life and Presidency of Ronald Reagan*, 1997; Michael Schaller, *Reckoning with Reagan*, 1992; John W. Sloan, *The Reagan Effect: Economics and Presidential Leadership*, 1999.

KEY TERMS

The following terms are covered in this chapter and can also be found in the list of Key Terms at the back of the book.

"Great Communicator"	Hundred Hours War	Moral Majority	supply-side
Grenada	Iran–Contra affair	Sandra Day O'Connor	

ONLINE SOURCES GUIDE

Use this listing to find online documents, images, interactive maps, simulations, and other resources related to this chapter:

American History Resource Center
http://history.wadsworth.com/rc/us

Selected Documents
Ronald Reagan's "Evil Empire" address (March 8, 1983)
Ronald Reagan's "Star Wars" speech (March 23, 1983)
George Bush's "New World Order" speech (March 6, 1991)

Selected Images
Ronald Reagan
Nancy Reagan
Gorbachev and Bush signing the START Treaty in
    June 1990

Interactive Time Line (with online readings)
Morning in America: The Age of Reagan, 1980–1993

CHAPTER 51

The Millennium Years

Decadence? Renewal? 1993–2006

© Reuters NewMedia Inc./Corbis

History never looks like history when you are living through it. It always looks confusing and messy, and it always feels uncomfortable.

John W. Gardner

When people accept futility and the absurd as normal, the culture is decadent.

Jacques Barzun

In 1930 two recent university graduates published *1066 and All That*. It was a satire of what students "retained" from a course in English history. Written like a "C" essay on an exam, the book was a series of hilarious snap student historical judgments based on fuzzy recollections of lectures and readings: this king was "a good king," an English defeat on the battlefield was "a bad thing," and so on. *1066* concluded with World War I, which in fact marked the end of Britain's reign as the world's most powerful nation. The final sentence of *1066* is "America was thus clearly top nation, and History came to a." (In England the period that ends a sentence is called a "stop.")

America has been "top nation" ever since, and history has not come to a stop. The twentieth century was, however, as much an era of trial for Americans as of glory: world wars, the Great Depression, the long nuclear standoff with the Soviet Union, assassinations, Vietnam, Watergate. Three of the century's last seven presidents broke the law. The "American century" culminated in two decades characterized by popularly approved greed.

Futurology: 1900

In 1900 the *Ladies Home Journal* told its readers that in the year 2000, the letters C, X, and Q would have been dropped from the alphabet; the second most widely spoken language in the United States would be Russian; Nicaragua and Mexico would be states; everyone except "weaklings" would walk ten miles each day; fruits would be huge, raspberries the size of baseballs.

The *Journal* had some things right: automobiles have replaced horses; central heating is ubiquitous; there are submarines and airplanes; and pictures are transmitted from space.

Rev. Sun Myung Moon joins several thousand "Moonies" in holy matrimony. This was just one of several well-publicized mass marriages of members of the cult. The matches were arranged by Moon. In most cases bride and groom had never met until moments before the ceremony; they trusted Moon (who claimed divinity) with all personal decisions.

CULTURAL DISSONANCE

Americans celebrated January 1, 2000, as the beginning of a new millennium. The big party was festive, but not everyone put on a paper hat. Many thoughtful men and women were apprehensive that the United States was rotting culturally, socially, morally, and politically. A respected scholar in his nineties, Jacques Barzun, wrote that civilization was decadent. Curiously, he employed the same image with which *1066 and All That* concluded. Decadence, Barzun wrote, is not history coming to a stop. Decadence is "a very active time, full of deep concerns, but peculiarly restless, for it sees no clear lines of advance. . . . Institutions function painfully. Repetition and frustration are the intolerable result. Boredom and fatigue are great historical forces."

Barzun pointed to "the open confessions of malaise" in America, "the search in all directions for a new faith or faiths, dozens of cults . . . , the impulse to primitivism," and endless political bickering. "Most of what government sets out to do for the public good is resisted as soon as it is proposed. Not two, but three or four groups, organized or impromptu, are ready with contrary reasons as sensible as those behind the project. The upshot is a floating hostility to things as they are."

CULTS

Many cults of the late twentieth century were rackets. A few targeted adults who had good jobs or owned small businesses. Gurus promised, in return for large fees (sometimes everything the suckers owned), to reveal the mystical secret to greater financial success. Other cults promised lots of sex. In rural Oregon in 1981 the Baghwan Shree Rajneesh collected several thousand followers in his well-guarded ashram by promising regular orgies. Most of the era's cults recruited emotionally discombobulated teenagers and young adults with little experience of life and less appreciation for their inherited culture. The most successful were Transcendental Meditation (TM) and the Moon Unification Church.

In the 1960s TM, the brainchild of the Maharishi Mahesh Yogi, promised inner peace. The Maharishi sold training courses in meditation, awarding graduates with unique mantras—syllables on which they were to concentrate when transcending. When some movie stars and rock and roll idols endorsed TM, the Maharishi was swamped by seekers clutching wads of dollars. For a few years Transcendental Meditation did a pretty good business with hippies. When the baby boom generation turned from saving the world to

The Comic and the Pathetic

The "John Coltrane Consciousness" cult taught that the source of spiritual power was a jazz saxophonist who had died in 1967 but, somehow, continued to wail for those who would hear.

The Heaven's Gate cult was not so amusing. In March 1997 in Rancho Santa Fe, California, thirty-nine members committed ritual suicide. They expected to be picked up and revived by a spaceship that was hiding in the tail of the then-visible Hale-Bopp comet.

consumerism in the 1970s, the Maharishi advertised that TM was also the way to increase one's income and personal collection of consumer durables.

Sun Myung Moon, a Korean, preached a theology that boiled down to the doctrine that he, Moon, was God. Thousands of young Americans (tens of thousands worldwide) placed their lives in his hands. The Moonies (as scoffers dubbed the faithful) cut off all contact with family and friends. Moon made their personal decisions, even selecting each Moonie's spouse. He simultaneously married thousands of just-introduced couples at massive ceremonies.

The Unification Church amassed capital a dime at a time. At airports and other busy public places, Moonies, smiling robotically as if they had been drugged, cornered hurrying travelers and shoppers and asked for donations. They offered a flower, thrust into the prospect's face, as a premium. The impatient were rude. The intimidated and the kindly contributed. Few accepted the flower, helpfully cutting Moonie operating expenses.

With the take Moon purchased farms, food processing plants, even a newspaper. Menial jobs at his enterprises were performed by Moonies whose pay consisted of bed, board,

close supervision, and ongoing indoctrination. Distraught parents called it "brainwashing." Some hired professional "deprogrammers" to seize their Moonie children physically and shock them out of their trances.

NEW AGE

Cloistered cultists like the Moonies were few compared to the hordes of Americans who embraced one or another manifestation of "New Age," which did not require withdrawal into a fortified ashram. New Age was a "New Global Movement toward Spiritual Development, Health and Healing, Higher Consciousness, and Related Subjects." With roots in "hippie" culture, its influence peaked in the 1980s and 1990s. New Age books were published by the hundreds of titles annually. New Age art (sunsets, misty mountains) adorned calendars and teacups; New Age music (twanging sitars, not much melody) replaced Muzak in small shops selling the books and recordings along with Sixties drug paraphernalia, tarot cards, distilled scents, divination bones, and crystals possessing who knew what powers.

The market was huge: mainstream bookstores and record shops added New Age departments next to the paperback Westerns and the "rap" records. Sedona, a wealthy community in the red rock country of Arizona, was a New Age pilgrimage destination because of the concentration there, among the many golf courses, of spiritually energizing "vortexes." Marfa, Texas, offered dancing lights in the nocturnal sky.

ALTERNATIVE LIFESTYLE

New Age promised a "transformative experience." It was emphatically "spiritual," not religious. Western religion—Christianity and Judaism—were "traditional," "conventional," "old." New Age rejected convention and tradition—history!—and as much of mainstream American lifestyle as

"Our Times" 1993–2005

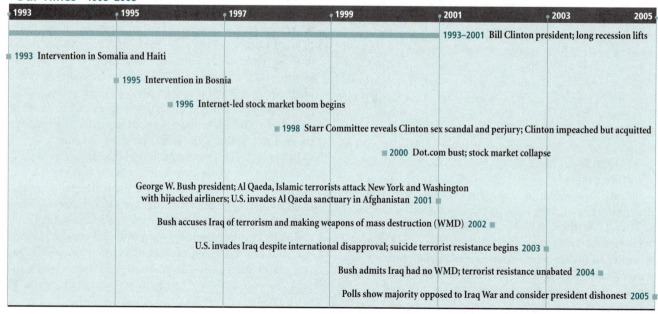

| 1993 | 1995 | 1997 | 1999 | 2001 | 2003 | 2005 |

1993–2001 Bill Clinton president; long recession lifts

1993 Intervention in Somalia and Haiti

1995 Intervention in Bosnia

1996 Internet-led stock market boom begins

1998 Starr Committee reveals Clinton sex scandal and perjury; Clinton impeached but acquitted

2000 Dot.com bust; stock market collapse

George W. Bush president; Al Qaeda, Islamic terrorists attack New York and Washington with hijacked airliners; U.S. invades Al Qaeda sanctuary in Afghanistan 2001

Bush accuses Iraq of terrorism and making weapons of mass destruction (WMD) 2002

U.S. invades Iraq despite international disapproval; suicide terrorist resistance begins 2003

Bush admits Iraq had no WMD; terrorist resistance unabated 2004

Polls show majority opposed to Iraq War and consider president dishonest 2005

New Agers found it convenient to discard. New Age embraced the novel, the non-American, the non-Western, the primitive—whatever could be defined as "alternative."

Rather than take a throbbing toe to a physician, New Agers sought out holistic practitioners, Vedantic healers, counselors at vegetarian groceries, a dozen schools of massage, acupuncturists, aroma therapists, herbalists. They pored over fantasies that had been written for children such as J. R. Tolkien's *Lord of the Rings.* They were fascinated by (non-biblical) prophets such as the sixteenth-century Michel de Nostradamus and the twentieth-century American Edgar Cayce. They subscribed to supernatural or extraterrestrial explanations of plane crashes, puzzling noises in the cellar, and dreams of being tucked into bed with Marie Antoinette. New Age needed no publicity department. With the spread of cable television, armies of television reporters, assigned to fill the endless hours of airtime with cheaply produced stories, sought out New Agers for interviews and "a day in the life of" documentaries. In the 1990s the Internet provided New Age retailers a fishery richer than Newfoundland's Grand Banks had ever been.

New Age was not political. However, because it could be dabbled in by people who had jobs, lived within society, mated (in "new egalitarian relationships"), and raised children (with a "new openness"), the mentality it encouraged shaped American culture as the cults did not. The "political correctness" that rattled American education in the final decades of the century had other origins—a "postmodernist" intellectual movement that rejected objective truths—but it also reflected New Age in its scorn for Western culture; patronization of groups the mainstream society had marginalized; practices that discomfited conventional Americans; contempt for ordinary workaday white people; and intolerance of dissenters.

PARTY LINE UNIVERSITIES

When intolerance took the form of a vegetarian disdaining cheeseburger eaters, it was harmless. When college students and professors were bullied for opposing the dictates of "political correctness," PC's demand for intellectual conformity undercut the ideal of freedom of inquiry on which American higher education had been based for a century. Feminists and proponents of racial and ethnic (but not intellectual) diversity in colleges, and censors of language defined as "insensitive," demanded that university administrators require students and faculty to participate in "sensitivity training" programs staffed by the politically correct.

Sincere believers in PC were probably never numerous. However, the few were able to set the tone in many universities because being labeled a racist, sexist, or homophobe (as the McCarthyites of the 1950s labeled their critics "Communists") was enough to ruin an academic career. Silent acquiescence in PC's dictates was enough to win toleration; only open dissent was dangerous. Students learned which instructors would lower their grades if they voiced an unacceptable opinion. Junior faculty knew what shibboleths to approve in order to win favorable reports from the committees that handed out tenure and promotions. For academic administrators PC was a bonanza: the apparatus needed to enforce political correctness meant more high-paying nonteaching university jobs, the purpose of their lives.

Examples of PC's powers of intimidation provided conservative journalists with plenty of copy. Thus in 1998, when 3,000 copies of an anti-PC publication at Georgetown University were destroyed, one campus newspaper ignored the incident; a second applauded the theft; the university president said nothing. When feminists at Ohio State destroyed a student newspaper because it had published a cartoon that offended them, the university stated, "The big thing was the cartoon, not the missing papers." In 2000 an anthropology professor at Bowling Green University in Ohio was forbidden to teach a course called "Political Correctness" because, in the words of the curriculum committee, "We forbid any course that says we restrict free speech."

THE OCCULT RIGHT

PC was rarely violent against persons. That was not the case with its mirror image on the far right of the political spectrum. Bewildered by cultural and moral upheavals, some Christian fundamentalists hatched visions of a great conspiracy of New Agers, intellectuals, liberals, feminists, gay rights activists—and eventually all Democratic politicians who

A Pejorative Label

The term "politically correct" originated with 1930s and 1940s Communists. They said, quite frankly, that if obvious facts, intellectual honesty, and common sense were at odds with the party line, party members must nonetheless support the party line: it was *politically* correct.

There are only the flimsiest links between the American Communist party, which was dead by 1970, and the political correctness of the century's final decades.

The author recalls, from the mid-1970s, a former party member who was in the process of embracing extreme feminism calling his new views "politically correct." In 1971 Angela Davis, an academic who had run for office as a Communist candidate and who later embraced PC causes, proclaimed that there was no "opposing argument to an issue which has only one correct side."

The head of the National Organization of Women in 1975 silenced members who opposed her program by stating that her position was "politically correct," but she may well have never met a real Communist. In its bullying of critics, PC was more the heir of anti-Communist McCarthyism than of the American Communist party. The term itself was exclusively pejorative. Only PC's critics used it as a term of ridicule. PC college professors never did.

supported their causes including, after 1993, the Clinton administration. They were working together to destroy Christianity and American values.

The occult right's medium was "talk radio," a phenomenon that emerged in the 1980s when A.M. radio stations lost the music broadcasting business to F.M. stations. To survive, they needed an equally cheap format to fill their airtime and sell advertising. Their salvation was pioneered in 1983 by a former disk jockey named Rush Limbaugh. Limbaugh harangued for hours against affirmative action, abortion on demand, illegal immigrants, homosexuals, gun control, New Age looniness, and other manifestations of the era's cultural dissonance.

Limbaugh was often well prepared, witty, and good-humored. His hundreds of imitators were appallingly ignorant boors. They survived, even prospered, by shouting and by nudging listeners who phoned in to advocate violence against the enemy such as by law, they had to avoid. The audience for these ravings was huge. By 2000 Limbaugh's daily three-hour program was broadcast on 660 stations. His annual income exceeded $10 million. Nor did the talk radio audience consist exclusively of the "angry white working-class males" whom liberals found it easy to dismiss. A fifth of talk radio listeners were African American (almost double the proportion of blacks in the population), almost half were women, a third were middle-class, and about 20 percent were Democrats.

CLINTON AND THE WORLD

The Democratic president who replaced George Bush in 1992 and was soon a favorite talk radio villain, William Jefferson Clinton, was no sinister ideologue out to destroy anything. Clinton was a principle-free political opportunist whose sights had been set on the presidency since he was a teenager in Hot Springs, Arkansas. He advanced himself in politics on a quick intelligence, personal charm, and long-term calculation. A Southern Baptist by birth (his claim on southern voters), he attended the Roman Catholic elite's Georgetown University, familiarizing himself with the workings of an urban, northern subculture as exotic to Southern Baptists as the world of the Laplanders. He was a Rhodes Scholar, making the acquaintance of Americans earmarked as political, professional, and business leaders. He won admission to the prestigious law school at Yale University, no big deal for sons of Yale alumni like Clinton's predecessor and successor, George H. W. Bush and George W. Bush, but ingress into a tiny elite such as few men of Clinton's background could imagine.

A MASTERFUL POLITICIAN

At Yale Clinton met his wife, the equally intelligent and ambitious Hillary Rodham. She had been a Republican but had drifted away. Bill Clinton had been a liberal Democrat since he was a teenager. He idolized John F. Kennedy, supported the Great Society, and—while well modulated—opposed the

Janet Reno

AP/Wide World Photos

Janet Reno was the first woman to be attorney general, one of the four top cabinet positions. President Clinton also named the first woman secretary of state, Madeleine Albright.

More noteworthy, perhaps, Reno was the only attorney general in American history to serve eight years, a two-term president's entire tenure. William Wirt was attorney general for twelve consecutive years under two presidents—just missing, by weeks, serving a full eight years under James Monroe.

Four members of Clinton's cabinet served eight years; the others were Bruce Babbit, Interior; Donna Shalala, Health and Human Services; and Richard W. Riley, Education. During the two-term presidencies of Reagan and Eisenhower, only one cabinet member stayed in office from beginning to end. The record for longevity in the cabinet is held by Harold Ickes, who was secretary of the interior under two presidents from 1933 to 1946, inching out William Wirt.

Vietnam War. He dodged the draft but knew better than to jeopardize his political career by burning his draft card. He hedged his bets by seeking a place in the Arkansas National Guard, an expedient usually identified with well-to-do Republicans like Dan Quayle and George W. Bush.

In 1978, just 32, Clinton was elected governor of Arkansas. He started with a bang, sponsoring a state-level Great Society; but when taxes to finance his program rose, he was defeated in 1980. Clinton got the message: regulating big business and advancing the interests of the less privileged was not a ticket to political advancement during the Age of Reagan.

Clinton dropped the label "liberal" and styled himself a **"New Democrat"**—that is, a Democrat liberal on racial questions and lifestyle issues, but fiscally responsible and friendly to business. Beginning in 1982, he won four successive gubernatorial elections. His energy was boundless; he loved to campaign; he savored the 1980s equivalent of kissing babies—schmoozing to the wee hours at fund-raising parties. His success at the polls and his golden touch as a fund-raiser made him a national figure. By 1992 Clinton had everything going for him but a problematic sex drive, which exposed him to a career-ending scandal. Clinton's sexual escapades, probably exaggerated, were common gossip in Little Rock; but the governor was lucky or, as his frustrated Republican opponents said, "slick."

FOREIGN POLICY: INTERVENTION AND PAYOFFS

Clinton entered the White House lacking a coherent foreign policy. This was inevitable with the Cold War ended. During the era of bipolar nuclear standoff, the essence of every

© Mathew Mendelsohn/Corbis

President and Mrs. Clinton. Bill Clinton's campaign statement "You get two for the price of one" backfired when Republicans said that Hillary Clinton was a "co-president." Mrs. Clinton was unpopular at first after making her own gaffes disdaining housewives and marital fidelity. She gained popularity during the Monica Lewinsky scandal when she behaved with impeccable dignity.

president's foreign policy was given to him: he had one big problem—the Soviet Union. Clinton was immediately beset by a series of little problems. He responded haltingly, reluctantly ordered military interventions, and had successes and failures.

Resource-poor Somalia was plunged into a vicious, clan-based civil war when the end of the Cold War ended the superpower subsidies that had kept the country more or less functioning. The capital of Mogadishu was in shambles. Water supply, power, telephones, police—all virtually vanished. Teenage thugs with sophisticated weapons, left behind by the U.S.S.R. and Americans, terrorized the streets. The arid countryside starved.

With United Nations approval, Clinton sent troops. As a relief mission, the intervention was successful. Somalia's famine was ended. However, when American soldiers tried to capture the most venal of the Somali warlords, the civil war resumed with American troops in the middle. One patrol of peacekeepers was literally torn to pieces by a Mogadishu mob. Clinton had to negotiate just to get American soldiers out of the country without further casualties.

Haiti was on the verge of a Somalian chaos. The country's proximity to the United States gave its agony an urgency beyond unpleasant videotape on the evening news. Thousands of refugees fled the country in boats incapable of making a landfall. Their desperate hope was to be picked up by the U.S. Coast Guard so they could petition for political asylum in the United States.

Americans were already uneasy about the massive immigration of uneducated, impoverished people from other Caribbean and Central American countries. Pressured by a "Haitian lobby" of liberals and the deposed president of Haiti, Jean-Bertrand Aristide, Clinton sent a warship to Port-au-Prince in October 1993. When a few hundred rowdies shouted at the vessel from the docks, Clinton ordered the ship to turn around. He assembled a blue ribbon diplomatic team headed by former president Jimmy Carter and popular General Colin Powell. They persuaded Haiti's military dictators to go into exile, possibly sweetening the pot with personal financial aid. In September 1994, 3,000 American troops landed, returning Aristide to the presidency. They trained the police and army the country needed to function minimally (and to stem the flight of refugees to America). Clinton also persuaded North Korea to suspend its program to build nuclear weapons by providing a cash incentive.

Somalia and Haiti were nations: countries with clear-cut borders and populations sharing common languages, religions, and ways of life. Bosnia–Herzegovina in the Balkans was multicultural. Three hostile ethnic populations had lived in peace only when forced to do so by authoritarian regimes: the Turks, the Austrians, and after 1945 the Yugoslavian Communists. When Yugoslavia disintegrated, Bosnian Serbs attacked Bosnian Croatians and Bosnian Muslims, who also battled one another. The Croatians and Serbs were well-armed by independent Croatia and Serbia (officially still called Yugoslavia). The Muslims, ignored even by the richest Islamic countries, suffered the most.

Some Americans called for intervention. Others said the western European nations should stabilize what was, after all, a European country. A third group opposed any action, arguing that nothing that happened in Bosnia affected American interests, and that intense ethnic hatreds were as intrinsic to Balkan life as lamb stew. Indeed, every truce Clinton, Russia, the United Nations, and NATO engineered fell apart in weeks, even days. Finally, by the end of 1995, a combination of American air strikes and economic pressure on Serbia to rein in the Bosnian Serbs established enough of a peace to permit American and European soldiers to move in as peacekeepers.

MEXICO AND NAFTA

Clinton pushed **NAFTA** (the North American Fair Trade Area Treaty) through Congress against a potent but oddly assorted opposition: the declining labor movement to which Democrats had traditionally deferred; the flaky billionaire

What's Imported?

It was difficult in the 1990s to say what was a domestic product and what was imported. The Ford Crown Victoria was assembled in Canada; the Mercury Grand Marquis included parts made in six different countries. Forty percent of all "Japanese cars" sold in America were manufactured in the United States. Television sets bearing the American trademark Zenith were, in fact, Mexican products. Mitsubishi TVs were manufactured in Santa Ana, California.

politician **Ross Perot** and his Reform party; and isolationists like television commentator Pat Buchanan.

NAFTA provided for the elimination, over fifteen years, of trade barriers among Canada, the United States, and Mexico. It was an emulation of the European Community, which had been an economic boon for western Europe.

Mexico quickly became, after Canada, the nation's second biggest trading partner. Each day during the 1990s, a million barrels of crude oil, 432 tons of peppers, 250,000 lightbulbs, 100–200 Volkswagens, and $51 million in automobile parts crossed the border into the United States. On both sides of the Rio Grande in Texas and northeastern Mexico, a bilingual culture neither American nor Mexican, but bound together by mutually rewarding economic interests, emerged almost overnight.

Clinton hoped that greater prosperity in Mexico would stem the massive illegal Mexican immigration into the United States. However, NAFTA significantly helped only the Mexican states of Nuevo Leon and Coahuila. Impoverished Mexicans from farther south continued to sneak across the border in astonishing numbers.

NEWCOMERS

Between 1924 and 1965 immigration had been a minor facet of American life. The southern and eastern Europeans who were the mainstay of the "new immigration" of 1880–1924 were effectively excluded. Until 1943 Chinese could not legally enter the United States except in miniscule numbers.

Ethnic discrimination was eliminated from immigration law in 1965. The change meant little to eastern Europeans and Chinese living under Communist regimes. However, the gigantic refugee problem created by the Vietnam War, and an act of 1980 making admission easier for political refugees, opened the gates to Vietnamese, Laotians, Indochinese tribal peoples like the Hmong, and Chinese living in southeast Asia. During the century's final decades, the Asian American population doubled to 11 million. About 800,000 Cubans emigrated during the same period. Most settled in Florida, especially Miami, where they were so numerous that half the city was called "Little Havana."

There were Russian Jewish, Haitian, Dominican, Arab and other Muslim, and Nigerian immigrants. But by far the greatest influx was from Mexico, augmented by Central Americans with similar cultures. Almost 4 million Mexicans entered the United States legally and many more illegally. Like the "new immigrants," they had been impoverished by a modernization at home that rendered them economically superfluous.

The reception accorded the immigrants was much like that the "new immigrants" experienced eighty years earlier: anxiety that they were unassimilable. In fact, although the newcomers gathered in ethnic enclaves, they appeared to be more amenable to "Americanization" than the first generation of "new immigrants" had been. Asian Americans, particularly, embraced America's "get ahead" culture. The

John Ledgard/The Economist

Election day in southern California. The large numbers of Mexicans in the southwest (José displaced Michael as the most common name given baby boys in both Texas and California) worried some Americans. Would the borderlands be Mexicanized? These all-American "Vote for . . ." posters imply the Americanization of Hispanic Americans, as did the insistence of some Mexican immigrants that their children be educated in the English language, not in the bilingual classes well-meaning educators tried to encourage.

frequency with which Asian immigrant children won national spelling bees and science fairs became a national joke. Most Asian-American organizations opposed affirmative action because Asians won admission to colleges and professional schools on their merits in larger proportions than Caucasian applicants did.

The issue that caused the greatest anxiety was language. By 2003 Spanish was the first language of 18 million Americans, many of whom spoke no English. Because 90 percent of Mexican Americans lived in the southwestern corner of the country—adjacent to Spanish-speaking Mexico—many Americans worried about the future of the culturally and politically unifying role of the English language. During the 1970s and 1980s, French linguistic nationalism in Quebec had come close to breaking up the Dominion of Canada.

A lobby called "**U.S. English**" worked to make English the official national language by constitutional amendment, and the exclusive language of state governments by statute or referendum. Most liberal Democrats fought these proposals. The education lobby insisted that Spanish-speaking children be schooled at least partly in their native tongue. The state of California published its official documents in Spanish (and a dozen other languages). U.S. English publicized polls showing that a majority of Spanish-speaking and Asian immigrants wanted their children educated exclusively in English, but won few decisive victories.

CLINTONIAN AMERICA

Clinton's domestic policies reprised the formula that had been successful in Arkansas. Fiscally he was conservative as Reagan and the Bushes were not. Reagan, in particular, prattled endlessly about balancing the federal budget while spending and borrowing at astronomical levels. Clinton ran the most frugal administration since Calvin Coolidge. He reduced the number of federal employees and the deficit. In several years his budgets resulted in a surplus, the first since the 1950s.

Clinton was a liberal in promoting the amalgamation of African Americans into the political and social mainstream. Clinton's goodwill toward African Americans was real. He also tried to reform the nation's health care, something that had been on the liberal agenda since the 1940s. In that, partly because of his own blunders, he failed.

HEALTH CARE

Americans with medical insurance enjoyed excellent health care, although at greater cost than in any other nation. The annual per capita expenditure on medical care was $3,700; in Switzerland, the second most expensive country, costs were $2,644. Americans paid several times what people of other nations paid for prescription drugs, including drugs manufactured in the United States. Moreover, in 1993, 39 million Americans had no insurance. Consequently, by virtually every index of public health (infant mortality, death of women in childbirth, and so on) the United States ranked lower than every other developed nation and some poor countries—thirty-seventh in the world overall. Only Haiti and Bolivia had lower immunization rates than the United States.

Why? In large part because of unalloyed greed in business, liberated by the Reagan administration. Pharmaceutical companies took profits of 1,000 percent, in some cases more. Surveys revealed that medical students were interested more in the money and leisure the profession provided than in health care. Most aspired to be specialists who worked fewer hours than general practitioners and had several times a family doctor's income. In Britain and Germany, 70 percent of physicians were primary care doctors, in Canada 51 percent. In the United States, just 13 percent of physicians were. The health care bureaucracy, like administrators in government, education, and corporations, was grotesquely bloated. The number of American physicians increased by 50 percent between 1983 and 1998. The number of "health care managers" increased 683 percent.

HILLARY CLINTON'S PROJECT

Harry S Truman and Lyndon Johnson tried and failed to enact comprehensive federal health care programs. The American Medical Association (the doctors' lobby) and the drug and medical insurance companies teamed up with Republicans to tar their programs as "socialistic." Clinton faced the same opposition, so he rejected a reform proposal patterned on culturally similar Canada's "single payer" health insurance. (Everyone paid premiums; a consortium of insurance companies paid medical bills according to a scale of fees set by the government.)

Instead Clinton tried to appease the insurance companies by leaving them (and their profitability) intact. In return for accepting federal regulation of fees and premiums, insurers would be subvented by government payment of the expenses of the 39 million uninsured Americans.

Actually, Clinton's scheme was much more complicated—too complicated. No one, including the voluble president, ever explained clearly how it would work. This played into the hands of Republicans and some Democrats in Congress who wanted no reform. They saddled Clinton's semicoherent bill with so many amendments that they transformed it into gibberish.

Clinton blundered by appointing his wife to head the campaign to win political support for the reform. Hillary Clinton was able, but she was out of her depth contending with Republican politicos and powerful lobbies. Moreover, she got off to a bad start as first lady. During the 1992 campaign Clinton had hinted at a kind of "co-presidency" with Mrs. Clinton: "You get two for the price of one." But the "co-president" almost immediately presented herself as a spoiled rich girl when she told a TV interviewer that she was not the kind of woman who stayed home and baked chocolate chip cookies; and she sneered at a country-and-western lyric that called on women to "stand by your man." That sort of thing went over well enough at feminist luncheons but was insulting to women who baked cookies and believed in spousal loyalty.

President Clinton addresses Congress in 1995. Vice President Gore (left) was a loyal and industrious vice president who would win a plurality of popular votes in his run for the presidency in 2000, but lose in the electoral college. Speaker of the House Newt Gingrich (right) tried to topple Clinton with his congressional muscle, and wrecked his own career in the process.

Mrs. Clinton good-humoredly did penance for her gaffes by whipping up batches of cookies for groups visiting the White House; but so far as health care reform was concerned, the damage was done. In the summer of 1994 the president abandoned his proposal.

MIDTERM SETBACK

In the congressional election of 1994, the Republicans won control of both Senate and House. The new Speaker of the House, a pugnacious right-winger, Newt Gingrich, called it a "revolution." Within a year, 137 Democratic officeholders, including several congressional representatives, switched to the Republican party. Among them was the Democrats' Native American trophy senator from Colorado, Ben Nighthorse Campbell.

The election of 1994 was less a personal setback for Clinton (as he would soon demonstrate) than it was another milestone in the drift of the electorate from the Democratic majority of 1932–1968 to a Republican ascendancy that continued into the next century. The generation of Americans whose lives had been enhanced by the New Deal was gone or going. Beginning in 1968, working and middle-class white voters, in ever-increasing numbers, came to see the Democratic party as the party of minorities and causes they considered outlandish like feminism, abortion on demand, and gay rights.

A Republican strategist, Kevin Phillips, had recognized this discomfiture with the changing Democratic party when it was still nascent. As early as the 1960s, he had urged the Republicans to tap the unease by abandoning their lapdog subservience to big business and becoming a fiscally responsible populist party, defending the traditional moral values of ordinary working people. Phillips was delighted with the results of his insight until the 1980s, when Ronald Reagan showed that Republicans could exploit conventional Americans' cultural and moral discomfort as a smokescreen while they pandered to the interests of the rich. A bitter Phillips denounced the Reagan Republicans for remaining the "party of the plutocrats."

Clinton indulged big business and catered to the wealthy as lavishly as Reagan had. That too had been part of his successful formula in Arkansas. His Securities and Exchange Commission brought not a single action for fraudulent manipulation of stock prices during a decade when American business practices plumbed depths of corruption deeper than in the 1980s. During his presidency, while the earnings of the poorest fifth of the population rose 1 percent, the income of the richest fifth climbed by 15 percent. On his last day in office Clinton issued 170 pardons, absolving among others billionaire Marc Rich, a fugitive in Switzerland for seventeen years because of a $50 million tax swindle, and four men who had bilked federal education and housing agencies of $40 million.

But Clinton, unlike Reagan, could not attract Americans of conventional moral views. Indeed, he alienated them when he ordered the military to enlist and commission open homosexuals. The uproar was so great that he had to retreat to a policy of "don't ask, don't tell," which had been unwritten army and navy policy since George Washington was a colonel. He burned his fingers when he appointed to high offices lifestyle liberals with whom he and Hillary had socialized. A woman he named to the Justice Department was revealed to have proposed multiple votes on election day for African Americans as compensation for injustices suffered by their ancestors, about as absurd a suggestion as a satirist could devise. His surgeon general said in a speech that public schools should teach children how to masturbate.

These were Clinton's contributions to the Republican victory in 1994. Fortunately for Clinton, however, when it came to blundering, he was not in Newt Gingrich's league.

1996: A PERSONAL VICTORY

Gingrich was a Reaganite without Reagan's ingratiating personality. The victory in the election of 1994, which made him Speaker of the House, went to his head. He believed his own press releases that said his power equaled Clinton's.

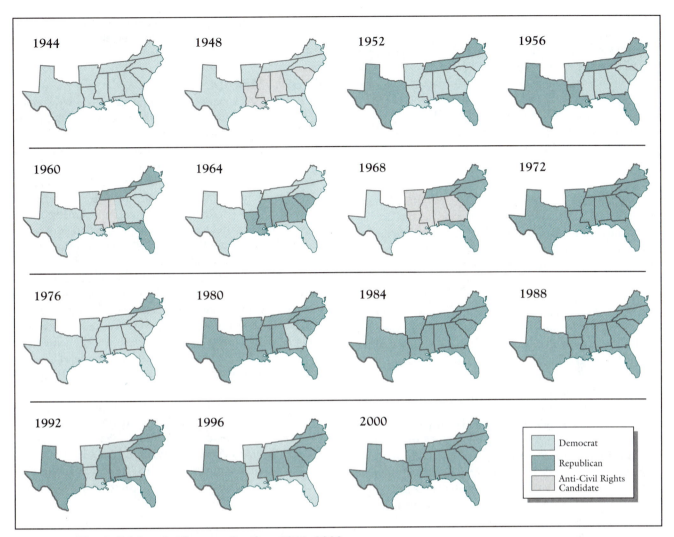

MAP 51:1 The Solid South Changes Parties, 1944–2000

Between 1880 and 1944 the former Confederate states (the "Solid South") voted Democratic. Only a few black southerners, who were Republican, were enfranchised; the electorate was white. Except in Tennessee, a large majority of white southerners voted Democratic because it was the party of "white supremacy." Almost all electoral college maps for elections between 1880 and 1940 were identical to the 1944 map shown here.

Race was the reason the South was solidly Democratic. Race was the reason why, in fits and starts beginning in 1948, the former Confederate states moved from the Democratic to the Republican column.

By 1948 most African-American voters in the North were Democrats. In that year Democratic liberals included a call for civil rights for blacks in the party platform. In protest, four southern states voted "Dixiecrat." Between 1952 and 1968 the South was no more solid in its voting patterns than the rest of the country. Race played a role in the third party successes in 1960 and 1968, but the Republican victories in the South in 1952 and 1956 were probably due to Dwight D. Eisenhower's personal popularity as a victorious general. Unease in the "Bible Belt" about John F. Kennedy's Catholicism explains the Republican victories in the South in 1960.

After the Democratic party's Voting Rights Act of 1965, black southerners voted in increasing numbers as Democrats. Offended white southerners now voted Republican because the national GOP was at best indifferent to African-American causes. (Nationally, fewer than 10 percent of blacks voted Republican.) After 1968 the Democrats were able to win enough white votes in the South to combine with their black political base and carry southern states only when the party nominated a southerner to run for president: Jimmy Carter of Georgia in 1976 (but not in 1980!) and Bill Clinton in 1992 and 1996.

In 2000, when both presidential candidates were southerners, the former Confederate states voted solidly Republican. The electoral votes of the "Solid South" put George W. Bush in the White House; he lost the popular vote. A partisan revolution was complete.

Overlooking the fact that Clinton had reduced the deficit, Gingrich spoke of cutting Medicare and Social Security costs as economy measures. This was a mistake Reagan never made. It was one thing to cut expenditures on programs helping the impoverished. Poor people did not vote in large numbers. It was quite another thing to arouse the elderly, who, mobilized by the powerful American Association of Retired Persons, were politically alert and active. Gingrich handed the political center, which had given the Republicans their victory in 1994, back to the president.

Then, late in 1995, the Gingrich Congress refused to approve the administration's operating expenses, an act unprecedented in irresponsibility. Clinton had no choice but to lay off tens of thousands of federal workers, shut down some federal offices completely, and close the national parks. Gingrich capitulated. Clinton greeted 1996, his reelection year, with his popularity rising.

The Republican candidate was a witty quintessential midwesterner, Senator Robert Dole of Kansas. A sturdy party regular for almost half a century and majority leader of the Senate, Dole was presidential caliber. His handicaps were his age (72), a loathing for the humiliations of political campaigning that he refused to conceal, and a self-deprecating honesty in responding to questions.

Dole revived the Whitewater scandal that had played a minor role in the campaign of 1992. In 1978 the Clintons had invested borrowed money in a vacation home development in Arkansas called Whitewater. The project flopped, and (according to Clinton's accusers) the governor steered state money to Hillary Clinton's law firm that was used to help bankers recoup their Whitewater losses. Under their guidance, Mrs. Clinton turned a small personal investment in commodities into a remarkably large profit.

In the spring of 1996 two of the Clintons' Whitewater associates were convicted of fraud. Republicans thirsted for Clinton blood, but they could not convert their suspicions into allegations that would stick. The Whitewater issue fizzled. Republican revelations that the Democratic party had sold "sleep-overs" in the White House to big campaign contributors revealed Clinton's tawdriness, but that was not news. The issue did not catch on. In November Clinton again failed to win half the popular vote (Ross Perot was in the race

A Day in the Life . . .

On a given day in 1996,

- 6,000 Americans died.
- 11,000 babies were born (31 percent of the mothers were not married).
- 7,000 people married.
- 3,000 people were divorced.
- 170,000 people were injured.
- The post office handled 495 million pieces of mail.
- Banks processed 27 million ATM transactions.

again), but he easily carried the electoral college, 379 to 159. It was a personal but not a party victory. The Democrats failed to gain control of Congress.

CYBERAMERICA

By 1996 the stock market was beginning a 1920s style boom. "Clinton prosperity" was based on computers, just as Coolidge prosperity had been built on the "high-tech" industries of the New Era: automobiles and radio. Computers changed Americans' daily routines as profoundly as automobiles had, and much more so than radio did. During the 1960s government, educational bureaucracies, and big business had computerized their operations. At first many people were troubled by the new experience of blacking out boxes on **IBM cards** to apply for jobs, collect government checks, and enroll in courses at school; then carrying machine-punched cards of which they could make no sense from one clerk who could make no sense of them to yet another. Were the machines that alone could read the cards running everything? Science fiction writers churned out tales of societies tyrannized by computers. The masterpiece of the genre was a 1968 film, *2001: A Space Odyssey,* in which the villain was HAL, a computer that spoke in a voice both soothing and sinister.

Despite *2001* (and the declaration of the president of Digital Equipment Corporation that "there is no reason anyone would want a computer in their home"), Americans began to adopt little HALs during the 1970s. By 1977 IBM had sold 25,000 "personal computers." By 1981 there were 2 million of them in American homes and offices, and the mania was just starting.

THE INTERNET BUBBLE

The Internet—instantaneous linkage of computers over telephone lines—was, like the computer, developed for the military. However, it was turned over to the National Science Foundation for civilian use in 1990: fortuitous timing for Bill Clinton. With the growth of the World Wide Web, anyone who was "online" could, by typing a "search" word, gain access to a world of research tools. The Web also opened up what seemed to be infinite commercial possibilities.

People could book airline tickets and hotel rooms or buy just about anything sold anywhere in the world from home. Internet companies, called "**dot.coms**" for the suffix on most Web sites (.com), popped up like daffodils, their owners sanguine they would take over retailing from shops and mail-order catalog companies. More than 300 dot.coms issued stock in 1998 and 1999. Web sites that provided services or information free told investors they would reap huge dividends from the advertising the sites flashed on computer screens.

Nine percent of American households were on the Internet in 1996, 20 percent in 1998, 50 percent by 2001. How could an investor lose? Capital swarmed to any enterprise connected with the Web. "Breathe the word 'Internet' around a stock, and anything can happen." In 1996 the value of stock in Yahoo, a "search engine," rose 153 percent in one day. Other "start-up" companies had similarly giddy experiences.

All stocks, including shares in "old economy" companies, followed the uphill trek at slower but steady rates.

In so heady an atmosphere, it was no more acceptable to mention 1929 than it was to discuss venereal disease at a college beer party. Bill Gates, whom computer software made the world's richest person, wrote in 1995, "Gold rushes . . . encourage impetuous investments. A few will pay off, but when the frenzy is behind us, we will look back incredulously at the wreckage of failed ventures and wonder, 'Who founded these companies? What was going on in their minds?'"

There was, for example, www.doodoo.com, which delivered a box of horse manure to any house in America for $19.95. Others less ridiculous would, nevertheless, seem to have been doomed to anyone thinking about them for five minutes: dot.coms making restaurant reservations (why not the phone?) and taking orders for the week's milk, eggs, and Cheez-Its (easier than a ten-minute stop at the supermarket?). And as in the 1920s, there were too many heavily financed dot.coms competing in markets that were palpably limited: travel agencies, medical advisers, wine and cigar dealers, chinaware discounters.

Inevitably in a soaring stock market, there was fraud. But the Clinton luck held, just as in the boom of the 1920s Calvin Coolidge's luck had. From a Dow Jones Industrial Average value of 2,365 in 1990, the stock market peaked at more than 11,000 (a rise of 400 percent) in 2000, Clinton's final year as president.

PRETTY WOMAN

Clinton was also lucky, but barely, when he committed perjury during a sex scandal of his own making. The Republicans first turned to the president's libido in 1996 when Whitewater fizzled as a campaign issue. A right-wing foundation promoted a lawsuit by Paula Jones, an Arkansas state employee when Clinton was governor. Jones said that Clinton had invited her to his hotel room, exposed himself, and asked for sex. Another Arkansas woman said the then-governor had physically assaulted her, leaving her with a visible injury on her lip.

A commission investigating Whitewater headed by Republican lawyer Kenneth Starr then discovered Monica Lewinsky, who at age 22 in 1995 had been an unpaid intern at the White House. She had told friends of ongoing sexual play with Clinton. When White House aides became aware of the hanky-panky, they fired Lewinsky. Clinton sent her to his friend, Vernon Jordan, who found her a job in New York City. Her generous salary looked very much like hush money.

When Lewinsky first testified before the Starr Commission, she denied any sexual contact. Alas for her, one of her confidantes had recorded their phone conversations. Starr advised Lewinsky that she would be prosecuted for perjury unless she cooperated. She told all. Clinton stonewalled and waxed indignant, swearing under oath that he had had no sexual relationship with "that woman." Starr sprung his trap: he had physical evidence, one of Lewinsky's dresses stained with the president's semen. Clinton admitted to "inappropriate sexual contact" with Lewinsky.

IMPEACHMENT

The **Starr Report,** released in September 1998, described the Clinton–Lewinsky encounters in lurid detail. Clinton's supporters denounced it as pornography. Starr, they said, should have listed the dates and circumstances of the encounters—period. They had a point. But the pro-Clinton forces were just as cynical. Feminists who had run a Republican senator from Oregon out of office in 1994 for sexually harassing women called Paula Jones "trailer park trash" and Lewinski a disloyal tool of the Starr Commission. Intellectuals wrote essays in prestigious journals explaining that the president had not perjured himself because fellatio—Clinton's and Lewinsky's specialty—was not sex in the sense vaginal intercourse was.

On December 19, 1998, the House of Representatives impeached the president on several counts of perjury and obstruction of justice—based on Lewinsky's claim that Clinton had instructed her to lie to Starr. The debate in the Senate (the jury in federal impeachment trials) centered on the value of the uncorroborated part of Lewinsky's testimony and whether Clinton's perjury amounted to the "high crimes and misdemeanors" the Constitution states as warranting conviction. The debate was immaterial. It was a Republican versus Democrat contest, and in the evenly divided Senate, the prosecution had nowhere near the two-thirds majority needed to convict. Clinton was acquitted.

THE ELECTION OF 2000

The only reputation to emerge enhanced from the mess was Hillary Rodham Clinton's. Never widely liked, she won admiration by weathering the humiliating scandal with quiet dignity. Ironically, she became a sympathetic public figure when she "stood by her man." In 2000 she was elected as a senator from New York State.

Vice President Albert Gore, who laid low during the scandal, was the Democratic nominee. Arizona Senator John McCain, an independent-minded moderate Republican, won primaries in New England; but Texas Governor George W. Bush, son of the former president and funded with $60 million in mostly corporate contributions, won the nomination.

Gore's personal morality was as clean as Clinton's was squalid. His public presence, however, was wooden. He espoused traditional liberal proposals to appeal to working people; paid lip service to PC causes as Clinton had done; but otherwise, also like Clinton, Gore tried to occupy the political center, depicting Bush as a stooge for big business.

George W. Bush played the Texas good old boy with an easy manner and boyish smile. The Democrats tried to exploit Bush's prodigal youth, but with their sitting president a wayward middle-aged man, made little headway. Bush appeased the religious fundamentalists of the Republican right, but not much was required. With Perot's Reform party in a shambles, they had nowhere else to go.

Bush's vulnerability was that he appeared to be "not very bright." In fact, Bush's college entrance exam scores had been higher than Clinton's; he was not stupid but ignorant. An interviewer sandbagged him with an easy quiz of general knowledge that Bush failed miserably. He said Nigeria was a continent and Africa a country. His self-embarrassments ran on for pages, lovingly compiled by the Democrats: "One of the great things about books is sometimes there are some fantastic pictures"; "It isn't pollution that's harming the environment. It's the impurities in our air and water."

AP/Wide World Photos

George W. Bush had been considered the family clown as a young man. No one expected much of him. After a prolonged adolescence, he pulled himself together and exploited his father's connections to own a baseball team and become a popular governor of Texas. Critics said he was stupid, but he was smart enough. However, he was ignorant about many questions presidents necessarily face and depended on a small group of advisers to tell him what to say and do.

Bush's handlers drilled him in sticking to prepared remarks and responses. Republicans implied that President Bush would be surrounded by experienced advisers and that vice presidential nominee Richard "Dick" Cheney, a former secretary of defense who was clearly no dummy, would be something of a co-president.

The election was more than close. Gore had a 500,000 popular vote plurality, but neither candidate had a majority in the electoral college. Florida's returns were contested, and the situation was knottier than in the "stolen election" of 1876. It involved irregularly counted absentee ballots, unreliable voting machines, punch-out ballots to which the "**chads**" (the paper punch-outs) were still clinging, and sloppy erasures on pencil-marked ballots. The dispute took a month to resolve. On December 9, by a 5–4 vote, the Supreme Court effectively gave the election to Bush; the four dissenters assailed the majority for making a political rather than a judicial ruling.

Did Bush really win Florida? It is impossible to say. From the day after the election to the day after the Supreme Court's decision, everyone involved in untying the tangle looked not for facts but for a formula that would put their candidate in the White House. Both sides altered their "principled" arguments during the controversy. A political scientist discovered that had the Republicans' initial proposal to resolve the dispute been adopted, Gore would have won Florida by 3 votes. Had the Democratic party's first formula been implemented, Bush would have won the state by 1,665 votes.

CATASTROPHE, RENEWAL, WAR

The new president's situation was unenviable. More Americans had preferred his opponent. If he had not "stolen" Florida's electoral votes, neither had he won them on election day. Like Rutherford B. Hayes in 1877, Bush's legitimacy as president was shaky. Doubts of his competence revived when, during the administration's first months, Vice President Cheney made as many presidential-level announcements as Bush did.

9/11

On September 11, 2001, suicide terrorists hijacked four airliners. They crashed one into the Pentagon and two into the twin towers of New York's World Trade Center. When (by cellular phone) the news reached passengers on a fourth hijacked plane, men knowing they were dead anyway heroically stormed the cockpit, sacrificing their lives so that another target, probably the White House, would be spared. The plane crashed in rural Pennsylvania.

The total destruction of the World Trade Center was videotaped from start to finish. The world witnessed a horror previously associated only with special effects in Hollywood disaster films. In New York 2,801 people died, including 343 firemen and 75 policemen who were in the buildings within minutes of the first attack. The nation's anguish was greater than on Pearl Harbor Day. For months dazed Americans watched telecasts of the crumbling skyscrapers, the search for bodies, and burials, day after day, of dead office workers, plane passengers, and firemen.

The perpetrators were agents of Al Qaeda, a fanatical Islamic terrorist organization headed by a Saudi millionaire, Osama bin Laden. Bin Laden operated from Afghanistan,

© Reuters NewMedia Inc./Corbis

The unthinkable horror that brought America together as a people—briefly—and won Americans a sympathy worldwide they had not known since 1945. New York's World Trade Center was completely destroyed. In Washington, the Pentagon was badly damaged. A fourth hijacked plane was heading toward Washington, probably to attack the White House or Capitol, when heroic passengers rushed the suicide terrorists. The plane crashed in the Pennsylvania countryside.

then governed by the Taliban, which the United States had helped bring to power by arming fundamentalist Muslims against the Soviet Union in the 1970s. The Taliban had transformed a functional, even prosperous country into a hellhole. They had ended education for girls, required women in public to cover themselves head to toe, destroyed pre-Muslim antiquities that were world treasures, and preached hatred of non-Muslims.

At first 9/11 looked like the master stroke of a diabolically efficient organization. Within a few months, however, it was revealed that the conspirators had been amateurish, dropping clues to their intentions that American authorities ignored. Pilot training schools had reported to intelligence agencies that surly young Arabs were paying cash to learn how to fly airliners but were uninterested in lessons in taking off and landing—pretty obvious stuff. One of the suicide

Good Taste

In August 2002, as the first anniversary of the horrors of September 11 approached, the Hallmark company released a line of 9/11 greeting cards Americans could send one another. "9/11" T-shirts and baseball caps had been on the market for months.

bombers virtually spelled out the plan out to an Agriculture Department employee in Florida when he applied for a government grant to learn how to fly crop duster aircraft. Crop dusting had long been red-flagged; it was well known to be the means by which terrorists would disperse chemical or biological toxins. But the incident was not reported until after September 11. A suspected terrorist who was probably assigned to one of the suicide teams was in custody for weeks before the attack; authorities refused to examine information in his personal computer out of respect for his "constitutional right to privacy."

A PEOPLE UNITED

Rarely has a people responded to so devastating an enemy blow with the decency and restraint of Americans after 9/11. A few Arab Americans were manhandled; there were insults and graffiti, but that was all. Publishers rushed dozens of books about Islam into print. Their common preachment was that acts like the September attacks were not intrinsic to the Muslim religion. Respected scholars writing about the beauties of the Koran, the Muslim holy book, failed to mention passages that minimized the rights of nonbelievers. Few authors noted that most of the resentments that festered in Muslim countries were the fruit of their own oppressive and exploitative social systems and had nothing to do with the United States. Media pundits played down the fact that 9/11 was widely celebrated in Muslim countries. President Bush made a point of honoring Islam in every statement in which he condemned the terrorists.

The president rose to the occasion that had been thrust on him with dignity, compassion, temperance, and eloquence. The minority president's "approval rating" reached unprecedented levels. Bush secured the cooperation of Afghanistan's neighbors and rushed military aid to the country's "Northern Alliance," which was already fighting the Taliban. A well-planned attack destroyed or captured all large Taliban and Al Qaeda units within weeks, but the remnants escaped into the mountains on the Pakistan border, from which they immediately began to launch guerrilla attacks. Bush and his advisers ignored the lesson in the problems of occupying a country in which a large proportion of the population was hostile to their presence.

WAR ON TERROR AND IN IRAQ

Bush exploited his popularity at home and sympathy abroad to proclaim a "War on Terror." Al Qaeda leaders captured in Afghanistan were imprisoned at Guantanamo Bay in Cuba so they could be questioned without the legal snarls their lawyers would engineer in American courts. The highest-level captives were held in undisclosed locations. Hundreds of suspected Muslim terrorists in the United States were rounded up. Every European country exploited the mood of outrage to arrest Muslim extremists they had been watching. American airport security, exposed as slapdash (the terrorists all carried razor knives), became as stringent as Israel's. Attorney General John Ashcroft proposed far-reaching suspensions of civil liberties but retreated to more modest innovations in the face of protest. A Homeland Security Act gave the federal government broad powers in dealing with perceived terrorist threats.

Even before Afghanistan was stabilized, Bush and Secretary of Defense Donald Rumsfeld focused the War on Terror on Saddam Hussein's regime in Iraq. Many people were puzzled. For ten years Saddam's only provocations had been blowhard threats to kill George H. Bush. There was no evidence of an Iraq–Al Qaeda connection; all indications were that Saddam and bin Laden were hostile to one another. Nevertheless, Bush proclaimed that if future World Trade Center tragedies were to be averted, Saddam's regime and his **WMD,** "weapons of mass destruction" (chemical and biological weapons and missiles to deliver them), had to be destroyed.

Bush's characterization of Saddam as a monster was unanswerable: his regime had murdered thousands. Twice he had invaded neighboring countries. His secret police ensured that the common people were docile. Saddam Hussein had used poison gas against Iran and his own people. But there was no evidence he possessed anything resembling WMD. After a year, Secretary of State Powell was able to produce as evidence two photographs of a government installation in the desert that had been reordered in the weeks before United Nations weapons inspectors arrived. The pictures proved nothing.

PAINTED IN A CORNER

Germany opposed invading Iraq because of the lack of evidence the country was a threat. More important, because they held vetoes in the United Nations Security Council, so did France, Russia, and China. While the United States, Great Britain, and Australia prepared an assault force in Kuwait, Saudi Arabia, and the Persian Gulf, American diplomats tried to find a formula for a U.N. resolution that would approve an invasion.

The worldwide sympathy for the United States that followed 9/11 dissipated everywhere. By the end of 2002 European public opinion, even in Great Britain, denounced Bush as a "warmonger." There were massive protests in every large world city, including in the United States. Pacifists opposed the war, of course. Muslim countries defended Iraq, although rarely Saddam Hussein. Some opponents of the war demanded proof that Iraq was a serious terrorist threat and called for bridling Saddam Hussein by means short of war. Albert Gore said that by fixating on Iraq, the United States was forgetting the fact that Al Qaeda, an enemy that had actually struck a blow, was far from neutralized. North Korea, already in possession of missiles capable of hitting South Korean and Japanese cities, exploited Bush's Iraq fixation by announcing that it was resuming its program to construct nuclear warheads. Early in 2003, always reliable Turkey voted against allowing Bush's coalition to invade Iraq from the north.

THE SECOND IRAQ WAR

Nevertheless, on March 19, 2003, the "coalition of the willing" invaded. The assault was astonishingly swift and, for the coalition, low in casualties. During two weeks of withering air and missile assaults, British marines surrounded Basra, Iraq's second largest city, while American soldiers and marines sped in three columns to the outskirts of Baghdad. Television generals warned that the Americans faced a block-by-block bloodbath in Baghdad.

But it was not to be. The defenders of Baghdad (and Basra) collapsed or, rather, evaporated. On April 9, American tanks rolled unopposed into the heart of the city. Crowds of Iraqi men celebrated hysterically. Mobs looted government buildings in both major cities. The antiwar protesters, hundreds of thousands strong three weeks earlier, evaporated too. France, Germany, and the United Nations, surprised at the ease of the conquest, stated that they should have important roles in the reconstruction of Iraq without explicitly mentioning the oil that would pay for their services. President Bush, in a theatrical display he would soon regret, appeared before soldiers and sailors on an aircraft carrier and proclaimed the war at an end.

The conventional war was over. Within a few months, however, suicide terrorists were driving cars and trucks packed with high explosives into American military installations and even marketplaces crowded with Iraqi shoppers. Soldiers and foreign civilians were kidnapped and beheaded on videotape. Iraqi officials who cooperated with the Americans were assassinated. Not even a six-mile freeway

between Baghdad and its airport was safe. Concealed guerrillas with handheld rockets destroyed army trucks, paralyzing convoys. In some weeks the attacks occurred daily; on several days there were half a dozen attacks the breadth of the country. When there were three- or four-day lulls, generals or Bush administration functionaries announced they had everything under control. Immediately new attacks killed more American soldiers.

No weapons of mass destruction were found. After a year President Bush admitted that his information had been faulty. In fact, no American intelligence agency had provided any hard evidence of WMD in Iraq. The CIA told the president what he made it clear he wanted to hear. Military intelligence had told him Saddam Hussein almost certainly did not have WMD. There were questions.

Nevertheless, Bush was a wartime president and was reelected in 2004, but narrowly in the electoral college. His opponent, Senator John Kerry of Massachusetts, was a strong candidate. He was a twice-decorated Vietnam War veteran who had criticized the war when he returned to the United States. Republican propagandists (whose candidate was a Vietnam War draft dodger!) smeared Kerry as a coward who did not deserve his medals.

It is impossible to say if the dirty campaign, which Bush would not repudiate, affected the election. Bush's margin in

The American and British armies steamrolled into Iraq. Superior weaponry and better-trained soldiers won the conventional battles and even the dreaded urban war with ease. But there was no effective response to fanatics willing to die driving cars and trucks packed with explosives into groups of soldiers or, more commonly, sites crowded with Iraqis trying to go about their daily business. The military's fear of such a campaign was one reason President Bush's father had not tried to occupy Baghdad. The passage of time and opening of documents may reveal why George W. Bush saddled the army with the task of combating suicide terrorists in a country where the Americans were the foreigners.

In his comic strip Doonesbury, *Garry Trudeau brilliantly mocked just about every American social, cultural, and political foible for three decades. He was able to extract a wry laugh from the bursting of the Internet bubble, which launched the stock market collapse that began in 2000. The cartoonist poked fun at the fact that in the 1990s there was no penalty in the upper echelons of business just for being incompetent.*

the electoral college was 286–252. He won Florida easily, but the vote in Ohio was close with reports of irregularities. If Kerry had actually carried Ohio, he would have won the election. But the Democrats did not call for a Florida-style review of the Ohio returns.

Bush's opinion poll ratings were declining even before the election. His "approval rating" dropped below 50 percent within months of his second inauguration, mostly because of the war. He boasted of the formation of a government in Iraq. But its future was dubious to even those who followed the news casually. The Iraqi army and police were ineffective. Three bitterly inimical groups in the country each had a geographical base: Shi'te Muslims in the South, aided militarily from Iran; Sunni Muslims in the center of Iraq, who had enjoyed privileges under Saddam Hussein; and Kurds in the north, Sunni Muslims but ethnically distinct from the majority Arabs and long the victims of persecution. In November 2005 Americans discovered a Shi'ite-operated jail where Sunni prisoners were tortured and starved.

Al Qaeda suicide bombings of American soldiers and Iraqi civilians—many by non-Iraqi Arabs—continued. The Bush administration's assurances that the resistance would soon be destroyed were increasingly reminiscent of Johnson's assurances about the Vietnam War. Bush's boyish persona had worn thin as the casualty count mounted. It was revealed that when a diplomat had reported to Bush and then gone public that Saddam Hussein had not, as Bush had claimed, tried to buy materials for nuclear weapons in Niger, the administration retaliated by exposing the fact that the diplomat's wife was a CIA agent. The administration had "blown the cover" of its own secret agent!

By the end of 2005, public opinion polls showed that a majority of Americans doubted the president's honesty as well as his competence. A majority also regarded the invasion of Iraq as a mistake and called for withdrawal.

AND ON THE HOME FRONT . . .

Like Reagan and Clinton, Bush was not faulted for his pro–big business, pro-wealthy domestic policies. The administration had wiped out the Clinton surpluses by the end of 2001. The national debt resumed its annual increase before the Reagan debt had been barely touched. Bush raised farm subsidies that Clinton had reduced. He increased logging in national forests that had not recovered from Reagan's "cut and run" permissiveness. He withdrew the United States from the Kyoto Global Warming Treaty and eased pollution controls on industry. He scrapped limits on dumping coal mining wastes in streams and rejected automobile fuel efficiency standards presented to him after a long study. The fines the Environmental Protection Agency was authorized to impose were reduced by 60 percent.

THE HI-TECH BUBBLE BUSTS

The stock market peaked in March 2000, then collapsed. The crash was triggered by the bursting of the hi-tech bubble. Dot.coms folded by the hundreds, some because they were absurd enterprises from their inception and others because their directors squandered capital on advertising and their own salaries. The Internet advertising bonanza did not materialize. "Web surfers," who had known to go to the bathroom during television commercials for fifty years, had no trouble ignoring the ads on their computer monitors.

Shrewd Investment
In 2002 Wall Streeters with a sense of humor circulated the following stock analysis: If, a year earlier, an investor bought $1,000 in Nortel Networks stock, the portfolio was now worth $42. If, instead, the investor had spent $1,000 on beer, at a nickel a can deposit, his portfolio was worth $91.

New Orleans under water after Hurricane Katrina in 2005. Three days before the hurricane hit, a meteorologist on the evening national network news described, with uncanny precision, what would happen if Katrina hit New Orleans head-on, even stating accurately how many feet of water would deluge various neighborhoods. The Bush administration made no preparations for the disaster whatsoever, prompting critics to ask if officials even watched TV news, let alone listened to government scientists' warnings. Public confidence in the president's competence, already low because of the Iraq war, plunged in the wake of Katrina.

Greed in the Universities

Academic administrators who embraced political correctness paid themselves well. The annual salary of Mark G. Yudoff, head of the University of Texas, was $787,000. John W. Shumaker of the University of Tennessee earned $735,000 a year. This was small potatoes compared to the rape of company assets by corporation executives, but it too reflected the culture's greed.

Educational moguls also prepared for their golden years, building up the estates they would bequeath their heirs. In 1992 David Gardner retired as president of the University of California at age 59. He was supposed to collect a pension of $60,000 a year. However, in the months just before his departure, a university official whose job was to design retirement packages for fellow administrators arranged with the state to present Gardner with a severance check for $797,000 and annual payments of $126,000.

Gardner explained that he was retiring so young because his wife had recently died and the grieving educator could not carry on without her. Fortunately, with only $345 in pension coming in each day, he found a job with an $825 million foundation for which the late Mrs. Gardner's support was not vital.

Capitalized at $135 million, AllAdvantage.com had assured advertisers their spiels would be seen because AllAdvantage would *pay* Internet users 50 cents an hour to allow ads to stream across their screens. Two million people signed up. In three months advertisers paid AllAdvantage $10 million; AllAdvantage paid its members $40 million.

The predicted Internet domination of retailing proved illusory. In 2000 less than 1 percent of American retail sales were made online. In early 2001 the shares of a third of dot.coms devoted to huckstering were valued at less than $10. An Internet wine merchant, capitalized at $200 million, dismissed 235 of 310 employees in January 2001 and was foreclosed in April. Internet use continued to increase, but perhaps dismaying to those who had envisioned a nobler new cyber-America, the category of web site getting the most "hits" was pornography.

A ballyhooed telecommunications boom also busted. Executives overbuilt and bled their capital reserves to enrich themselves personally, destroying billions in investment and throwing tens of thousands of employees out of work.

For example, the century-old Montana Power Company had monopolized electricity sales in the state in return for submitting to close regulation by the Montana legislature. Its power was as cheap as anywhere in the nation, and the company, without fail, had paid annual dividends of 7 percent. Rather than taking pride in running a model corporation providing an essential public service, in 1997 Montana Power and the Wall Street brokerage house Goldman Sachs convinced the Montana legislature to deregulate the state's electrical power industry. This enabled Montana Power to sell its mines, dams, and power lines for $2.7 billion. The company got out of the power business entirely, renamed itself TouchAmerica, and pumped its capital into telecommunications, burying fiber optic cables all over the thinly populated state. There were, of course, few customers. Hundreds of workers lost their jobs and pension savings; the price of electricity in Montana soared, briefly by 800 percent; shares in TouchAmerica dropped from $30 to 33 cents. There was a bright side: Goldman Sachs pocketed a fee of $20 million, and TouchAmerica's top executives divided up a tenth of the company's capital among themselves.

COUNTRY CLUB CROOKS

The collapse of several corporations exposed fraud and outright thievery among the big business elite. The directors and executives of Enron, an energy broker, abetted by their auditor, Arthur Andersen, stole or destroyed $67 billion of its stockholders' investments. WorldCom (telecommunications) lost $9 billion to theft and $140 billion in stock value, all covered up by accountants for five years so that the company could woo investors. Webvan squandered $1.2 billion in start-up capital, much of it going into the pockets of the company's organizers. Two weeks before Webvan declared bankruptcy, its founder sold his shares at a personal profit of $2.7 million. About 17,000 people lost their jobs.

In the corporate world of the Clinton–Bush years, there was no penalty for being a failure. In April 2001, hours before filing for bankruptcy, the Pacific Gas and Electric Company paid its top executives bonuses. Coca-Cola's CEO, after supervising the loss of $4 billion in capital, was given a severance check for $18 million. American Telephone and Telegraph fired CEO John Walther after nine months because he "lacked intellectual leadership." Nevertheless AT&T wrote him a check for $26 million. Under Jill Barron, toy manufacturer Mattel lost $2.5 billion. Barron went back on the job market with $40 million in severance pay and bonuses in her purse.

Jacques Barzun did not include cynical, conscienceless greed as a sign of a society's decadence. Edward Gibbon, whose *Decline and Fall of the Roman Empire* appeared in 1776, the year the United States declared its independence, did.

FURTHER READING

Author's note: The books listed here are, necessarily, books authored by men and women writing about people and issues of their own time. It is impossible that they could aspire to the objectivity a biographer of

Martin Van Buren enjoys or be as detached from their subject as a historian of women's legal status in the eighteenth century. Students should, of course, read Van Buren biographies and books about eighteenth-century law critically. In reading the books listed here (and the textbook chapter just concluded), students should have their critical faculties on red alert.

Cultural Crisis David G. Barker, *Rushed to Judgment: Talk Radio, Persuasion, and American Political Behavior,* 2002; Robert Hughes, *Culture of Complaint: The Fraying of America,* 1993; Haynes Johnson, *The Best of Times: America in the Clinton Years,* 2001; Richard Pells, *Not Like Us: How Europeans Have Loved, Hated, and Transformed American Culture since World War II,* 1997; William Martin, *With God on Our Side: The Rise of the Religious Right in America,* 1996; Martin E. Marty and R. Scott Appleby, *The Glory and the Power: The Fundamentalist Challenge to the Modern World,* 1992; Lisa McGirr, *Suburban Warriors: The Origins of the New American Right,* 2001; Ruth Rosen, *The World Split Open: How the Modern Women's Movement Changed America,* 2000; Gini Scott, *Can We Talk?: The Power and Influence of Talk Shows,* 1996; Garry Wills, *Under God: Religion and American Politics,* 1990.

George W. Bush Bill Minutaglio, *First Son: George W. Bush and the Bush Family Dynasty,* 1999; Bob Woodward, *Bush at War,* 2002.

Investigation and Impeachment Joe Conason and Gene Lyons, *The Hunting of the President,* 2000; Allan M. Dershowitz, *Sexual McCarthyism: The Clinton Scandal and the Emerging Constitutional Crisis,* 1998; Marvin L. Kalb, *One Scandalous Story: Clinton, Lewinski, and Thirteen Days That Tarnished American Journalism,* 2001; Richard Posner, *An Affair of State: The Investigation, Impeachment, and Trial of President Clinton,* 1999.

Islamic Terrorism Benjamin R. Barber, *Jihad vs. McWorld: How the Planet Is Both Falling Apart and Coming Together and What This Means for Democracy,* 1995; Benjamin Daniel, *The Age of Sacred Terror,* 2002; Fred H. Halliday, *Two Hours That Shook the World: September 11, 2001: Causes and Consequences,* 2002.

Party Politics: 1990s Thomas Byrne and Mary D. Edsall, *Chain Reaction,* 1992; Jack W. Germond and Jules Witcover, *Mad as Hell: Revolt at the Ballot Box,* 1993; Stephan Gillon, *The Democrats' Dilemma,* 1992; William Greider, *Who Will Tell the People?,* 1992; Kathleen Hall Jamieson, *Packaging the Presidency,* 1992; Kevin Phillips, *Boiling Point: Democrats, Republicans, and the Decline of Middle-Class Prosperity,* 1993, and *Wealth and Democracy: A Political History of the American Rich,* 2003.

Party Politics: 2000s Kenneth Baer, *Reinventing Democrats,* 2000; Alan M. Dershowitz, *Supreme Injustice: How the High Court Hijacked Election 2000,* 2001; Charles Lewis, *The Buying of the President,* 2000; Richard A. Posner, *Breaking the Deadlock: The 2000 Election, the Constitution, and the Courts,* 2001; Jeffrey Toobin, *Too Close to Call: The Thirty-Six Day Battle to Decide the 2000 Election,* 2001.

The Clinton Years William C. Berman, *From the Center to the Edge: The Politics and Policies of the Clinton Presidency,* 2001; James M. Burns and Georgia J. Sorenson, *Dead Center: Clinton–Gore Leadership and the Perils of Moderation,* 1999; Elizabeth Drew, *The Struggle between the Gingrich Congress and the Clinton White House,* 1996; David Halberstam, *War in a Time of Peace: Bush, Clinton, and the Generals,* 2001; Thomas H. Henricksen, *Clinton's Foreign Policy in Somalia, Bosnia, Haiti, and North Korea,* 1996; John Hohenberg, *Reelecting Bill Clinton: Why American Chose a "New" Democrat,* 1997; David Maraniss, *First in His Class: A Biography of Bill Clinton,* 1995; Bob Woodward, *The Agenda: Inside the Clinton White House,* 1994.

KEY TERMS

The following terms are covered in this chapter and can also be found in the list of Key Terms at the back of the book.

chads	**NAFTA**	**Starr Report**	**WMD**
dot.coms	**"New Democrat"**	**U.S. English**	
IBM cards	**Ross Perot**		

 ## ONLINE SOURCES GUIDE

Use this listing to find online documents, images, interactive maps, simulations, and other resources related to this chapter:

American History Resource Center
http://history.wadsworth.com/rc/us

Selected Documents
Clinton's speech at the 1996 Democratic Convention
An account of the lives of undocumented immigrants in Texas, 1994
Excerpts from the Starr Report

Selected Images
Presidents Bush, Reagan, Carter, Ford, and Nixon gather for historic shot
Bill Clinton
Hillary Rodham Clinton

Interactive Time Line (with online readings)
The Millennium Years: Decadence? Renewal?

Appendix

THE DECLARATION OF INDEPENDENCE
The Unanimous Declaration of the Thirteen United States of America

When in the Course of human events it becomes necessary for one people to dissolve the political bands which have connected them with another, and to assume among the Powers of the earth, the separate and equal station to which the Laws of Nature and of Nature's God entitle them, a decent respect to the opinions of mankind requires that they should declare the causes which impel them to the separation.

We hold these truths to be self-evident, that all men are created equal, that they are endowed by their Creator with certain unalienable Rights, that among these are Life, Liberty and the pursuit of Happiness. That to secure these rights, Governments are instituted among Men, deriving their just Powers from the consent of the governed. That whenever any Form of Government becomes destructive of these ends, it is the Right of the People to alter or to abolish it, and to institute new Government, laying its foundation on such principles and organizing its Powers in such form, as to them shall seem most likely to effect their Safety and Happiness. Prudence, indeed, will dictate that Governments long established should not be changed for light and transient causes; and accordingly all experience hath shewn, that mankind are more disposed to suffer, while evils are sufferable, than to right themselves by abolishing the forms to which they are accustomed. But when a long train of abuses and usurpations, pursuing invariably the same Object evinces a design to reduce them under absolute Despotism, it is their right, it is their duty, to throw off such Government, and to provide new Guards for their future security. Such has been the patient sufferance of these Colonies; and such is now the necessity which constrains them to alter their former Systems of Government. The history of the present King of Great Britain is a history of repeated injuries and usurpations, all having in direct object the establishment of an absolute Tyranny over these States. To prove this, let Facts be submitted to a candid world.

He has refused his Assent to Laws, the most wholesome and necessary for the public good.

He has forbidden his Governors to pass Laws of immediate and pressing importance, unless suspended in their operation till his Assent should be obtained; and when so suspended, he has utterly neglected to attend to them.

He has refused to pass other Laws for the accommodation of large districts of people, unless those people would relinquish the right of Representation in the Legislature, a right inestimable to them and formidable to tyrants only.

He has called together legislative bodies at places unusual, uncomfortable, and distant from the depository of their Public Records, for the sole Purpose of fatiguing them into compliance with his measures.

He has dissolved Representative Houses repeatedly, for opposing with manly firmness his invasions on the rights of the People.

He has refused for a long time, after such dissolutions, to cause others to be elected; whereby the Legislative Powers, incapable of Annihilation, have returned to the People at large for their exercise; the State remaining in the mean time exposed to all the dangers of invasion from without, and convulsions within.

He has endeavoured to prevent the Population of these States; for that purpose obstructing the Laws for Naturalization of Foreigners; refusing to pass others to encourage their migrations hither, and raising the conditions of new Appropriations of Lands.

He has obstructed the Administration of Justice, by refusing his Assent to Laws for establishing Judiciary Powers.

He has made Judges dependent on his Will alone, for the tenure of their offices, and the amount and payment of their salaries.

He has erected a multitude of New Offices, and sent hither swarms of Officers to harass our People, and eat out their substance.

He has kept among us, in times of peace, Standing Armies without the Consent of our legislatures.

He has affected to render the Military independent of and superior to the Civil Power.

He has combined with others to subject us to a jurisdiction foreign to our constitution, and unacknowledged by our laws; giving his Assent to their Acts of pretended Legislation:

For Quartering large bodies of armed troops among us:

For protecting them, by a mock Trial, from Punishment for any Murders which they should commit on the Inhabitants of these States:

For cutting off our Trade with all parts of the world:

For imposing Taxes on us without our Consent:

For depriving us in many cases, of the benefits of Trial by Jury:

For transporting us beyond Seas to be tried for pretended offences:

For abolishing the free System of English Laws in a neighbouring Province, establishing therein an Arbitrary government, and enlarging its Boundaries so as to render it at once an example and fit instrument for introducing the same absolute rule into these Colonies:

For taking away our Charters, abolishing our most valuable Laws, and altering fundamentally the Forms of our Governments:

Text is reprinted from the facsimile of the engrossed copy in the National Archives. The original spelling, capitalization, and punctuation have been retained. Paragraphing has been added.

For suspending our own Legislatures, and declaring themselves invested with Power to legislate for us in all cases whatsoever.

He has abdicated Government here, by declaring us out of his Protection, and waging War against us.

He has plundered our seas, ravaged our Coasts, burnt our towns, and destroyed the lives of our people.

He is at this time transporting large Armies of foreign Mercenaries to compleat the works of death, desolation and tyranny, already begun with circumstances of Cruelty and perfidy scarcely paralleled in the most barbarous ages, and totally unworthy the Head of a civilized nation.

He has constrained our fellow Citizens taken Captive on the high Seas to bear Arms against their Country, to become the executioners of their friends and Brethren, or to fall themselves by their Hands.

He has excited domestic insurrections amongst us, and has endeavoured to bring on the inhabitants of our frontiers, the merciless Indian Savages, whose known rule of warfare, is an undistinguished destruction of all ages, sexes and conditions.

In every stage of these Oppressions We have Petitioned for Redress in the most humble terms: Our repeated Petitions have been answered only by repeated injury. A Prince, whose character is thus marked by every act which may define a Tyrant, is unfit to be the ruler of a free People.

Nor have We been wanting in attentions to our British brethren. We have warned them from time to time of attempts by their legislature to extend an unwarrantable jurisdiction over us. We have reminded them of the circumstances of our emigration and settlement here. We have appealed to their native justice and magnanimity, and we have conjured them by the ties of our common kindred to disavow thee usurpations, which, would inevitably interrupt our connections and correspondence. They too have been deaf to the voice of justice and of consanguinity. We must, therefore, acquiesce in the necessity, which denounces our Separation, and hold them, as we hold the rest of mankind, Enemies in War, in Peace Friends.

WE, THEREFORE, the Representatives of the UNITED STATES OF AMERICA, in General Congress, Assembled, appealing to the Supreme Judge of the world for the rectitude of our intentions, do, in the Name, and by Authority of the good People of these Colonies, solemnly publish and declare, That these United Colonies are, and of Right ought to be FREE AND INDEPENDENT STATES; that they are Absolved from all Allegiance to the British Crown, and that all political connection between them and the State of Great Britain, is and ought to be totally dissolved; and that, as Free and Independent States, they have full Power to levy War, conclude Peace, contract Alliances, establish Commerce, and to do all other Acts and Things which Independent States may of right do. And for the support of this Declaration, with a firm reliance on the protection of divine Providence, we mutually pledge to each other our Lives, our Fortunes and our sacred Honor.

THE CONSTITUTION OF THE UNITED STATES OF AMERICA

We the People of the United States, in Order to form a more perfect Union, establish Justice, insure domestic Tranquility, provide for the common defence, promote the general Welfare, and secure the Blessings of Liberty to ourselves and our Posterity, do ordain and establish this Constitution for the United States of America.

Article. I.

SECTION. 1. All legislative Powers herein granted shall be vested in a Congress of the United States, which shall consist of a Senate and House of Representatives.

SECTION. 2. The House of Representatives shall be composed of Members chosen every second Year by the People of the several States, and the Electors in each State shall have the Qualifications requisite for Electors of the most numerous Branch of the State Legislature.

No Person shall be a Representative who shall not have attained to the Age of twenty five Years, and been seven Years a Citizen of the United States, and who shall not, when elected, be an Inhabitant of that State in which he shall be chosen.

Representatives and direct Taxes[1] shall be apportioned among the several States which may be included within this Union, according to their respective Numbers, which shall be determined by adding to the whole Number of free Persons, including those bound to Service for a Term of Years, and excluding Indians not taxed, three fifths of all other Persons.[2] The actual Enumeration shall be made within three Years after the first Meeting of the Congress of the United States, and within every subsequent Term of ten Years, in such Manner as they shall by Law direct. The Number of Representatives shall not exceed one for every thirty Thousand, but each State shall have at Least one Representative; and until such enumeration shall be made, the State of New Hampshire shall be entitled to chuse three; Massachusetts eight; Rhode Island and Providence Plantations one; Connecticut five; New York six; New Jersey four; Pennsylvania eight; Delaware one; Maryland six; Virginia ten; North Carolina five; South Carolina five; and Georgia three.

When vacancies happen in the Representation from any State, the Executive Authority thereof shall issue Writs of Election to fill such Vacancies.

The House of Representatives shall chuse their Speaker and other Officers; and shall have the sole Power of Impeachment.

SECTION. 3. The Senate of the United States shall be composed of two Senators from each State, chosen by the Legislature thereof, for six Years; and each Senator shall have one Vote.[3]

Immediately after they shall be assembled in Consequence of the first Election, they shall be divided as equally as may be into three Classes. The Seats of the Senators of the first Class shall be vacated at the Expiration of the second Year, of the second Class at the Expiration of the fourth Year, and of the third Class at the Expiration of the sixth Year, so that one third may be chosen every second Year; and if Vacancies happen by Resignation, or otherwise, during the Recess of the Legislature of any State, the Executive thereof may make temporary Appointments until the next Meeting of the Legislature, which shall then fill such Vacancies.[4]

No Person shall be a Senator who shall not have attained to the Age of thirty Years, and been nine Years a Citizen of the United States, and who shall not, when elected, be an Inhabitant of that State for which he shall be chosen.

The Vice President of the United States shall be President of the Senate, but shall have no Vote, unless they be equally divided.

The Senate shall chuse their other Officers, and also a President pro tempore, in the Absence of the Vice President, or when he shall exercise the Office of President of the United States.

The Senate shall have the sole Power to try all Impeachments. When sitting for that Purpose, they shall be on Oath or Affirmation. When the President of the United States is tried, the Chief Justice shall preside: And no Person shall be convicted without the Concurrence of two thirds of the Members present.

Judgment in Cases of Impeachment shall not extend further than to removal from Office, and disqualification to hold and enjoy any Office of honor, Trust or Profit under the United States: but the Party convicted shall nevertheless be liable and subject to Indictment, Trial, Judgment and Punishment, according to Law.

SECTION. 4. The Times, Places and Manner of holding Elections for Senators and Representatives, shall be prescribed in each State by the Legislature thereof, but the Congress may at any time by Law make or alter such Regulation, except as to the Places of chusing Senators.

The Congress shall assemble at least once in every Year, and such Meeting shall be on the first Monday in December, unless they shall by Law appoint a different Day.[5]

SECTION. 5. Each House shall be the Judge of the Elections, Returns and Qualifications of its own Members, and a

---

Text is from the engrossed copy in the National Archives. Original spelling, capitalization, and punctuation have been retained.

[1]Modified by the Sixteenth Amendment.

[2]Replaced by the Fourteenth Amendment.

[3]Superseded by the Seventeenth Amendment.

[4]Modified by the Seventeenth Amendment.

[5]Superseded by the Twentieth Amendment.

Majority of each shall constitute a Quorum to do Business; but a smaller Number may adjourn from day to day, and may be authorized to compel the Attendance of absent Members, in such Manner, and under such Penalties as each House may provide.

Each House may determine the Rules of its Proceedings, punish its Members for disorderly Behaviour, and, with the Concurrence of two thirds, expel a Member.

Each House shall keep a Journal of its Proceedings, and from time to time publish the same, excepting such Parts as may in their Judgment require Secrecy; and the Yeas and Nays of the Members of either House on any question shall, at the Desire of one fifth of those Present, be entered on the Journal.

Neither House, during the Session of Congress, shall, without the Consent of the other, adjourn for more than three days, nor to any other Place than that in which the two Houses shall be sitting.

SECTION. 6. The Senators and Representatives shall receive a Compensation for their Services, to be ascertained by Law, and paid out of the Treasury of the United States. They shall in all Cases, except Treason, Felony and Breach of the Peace, be privileged from Arrest during their Attendance at the Session of their respective Houses, and in going to and returning from the same; and for any Speech or Debate in either House, they shall not be questioned in any other Place.

No Senator or Representative shall, during the Time for which he was elected, be appointed to any civil Office under the Authority of the United States, which shall have been created, or the Emoluments whereof shall have been encreased during such time; and no Person holding any Office under the United States, shall be a Member of either House during his Continuance in Office.

SECTION. 7. All Bills for raising Revenue shall originate in the House of Representatives; but the Senate may propose or concur with Amendments as on other Bills.

Every Bill which shall have passed the House of Representatives and the Senate shall, before it become a Law, be presented to the President of the United States; If he approve he shall sign it, but if not he shall return it, with his Objections to that House in which it shall have originated, who shall enter the Objections at large on their Journal, and proceed to reconsider it. If after such Reconsideration two thirds of that House shall agree to pass the Bill, it shall be sent, together with the Objections, to the other House, by which it shall likewise be reconsidered, and if approved by two thirds of that House, it shall become a Law. But in all such Cases the Votes of both Houses shall be determined by yeas and Nays, and the Names of the Persons voting for and against the Bill shall be entered on the Journal of each House respectively. If any Bill shall not be returned by the President within ten Days (Sundays excepted) after it shall have been presented to him, the Same shall be a Law, in like Manner as if he had signed it, unless the Congress by their Adjournment prevent its Return, in which Case it shall not be a Law.

Every Order, Resolution, or Vote to which the Concurrence of the Senate and House of Representatives may be necessary (except on a question of Adjournment) shall be presented to the President of the United States; and before the Same shall take Effect, shall be approved by him, or being disapproved by him shall be repassed by two thirds of the Senate and House of Representatives, according to the Rules and Limitations prescribed in the Case of a Bill.

SECTION. 8. The Congress shall have power To lay and collect Taxes, Duties, Imposts and Excises, to pay the Debts and provide for the common Defence and general Welfare of the United States; but all Duties, Imposts and Excises shall be uniform throughout the United States;

To borrow Money on the credit of the United States;

To regulate Commerce with foreign Nations, and among the several States, and with the Indian Tribes;

To establish an uniform Rule of Naturalization, and uniform Laws on the subject of Bankruptcies throughout the United States;

To coin Money, regulate the Value thereof, and of foreign Coin, and fix the Standard of Weights and Measures;

To provide for the Punishment of counterfeiting the Securities and current Coin of the United States;

To establish Post Offices and post Roads;

To promote the Progress of Science and useful Arts, by securing for limited Times to Authors and Inventors the exclusive Right to their respective Writings and Discoveries;

To constitute Tribunals inferior to the Supreme Court;

To define and punish Piracies and Felonies committed on the high Seas, and Offences against the Law of Nations;

To declare War, grant Letters of Marque and Reprisal, and make Rules concerning Captures on Land and Water;

To raise and support Armies, but no Appropriation of Money to that Use shall be for a longer Term than two Years;

To provide and maintain a Navy;

To make Rules for the Government and Regulation of the land and naval Forces;

To provide for calling forth the Militia to execute the Laws of the Union, suppress Insurrections and repel Invasions;

To provide for organizing, arming, and disciplining, the Militia, and for governing such Part of them as may be employed in the Service of the United States, reserving to the States respectively, the Appointment of the Officers, and the Authority of training the Militia according to the discipline prescribed by Congress;

To exercise exclusive Legislation in all Cases whatsoever, over such District (not exceeding ten Miles square) as may, by Cession of particular States, and the Acceptance of Congress, become the Seat of the Government of the United States, and to exercise like Authority over all Places purchased by the Consent of the Legislature of the State in which the Same shall be, for the Erection of Forts, Magazines, Arsenals, dock-Yards, and other needful Buildings;—And

To make all Laws which shall be necessary and proper for carrying into Execution the foregoing Powers, and all other Powers vested by this Constitution in the Government of the United States, or in any Department or Officer thereof.

SECTION. 9. The Migration or Importation of such Persons as any of the States now existing shall think proper to admit, shall not be prohibited by the Congress prior to the Year one thousand eight hundred and eight, but a Tax or duty may be imposed on such Importation, not exceeding ten dollars for each Person.

The Privilege of the Writ of Habeas Corpus shall not be suspended, unless when in Cases of Rebellion or Invasion the public Safety may require it.

No Bill of Attainder or ex post facto Law shall be passed.

No Capitation, or other direct, Tax shall be laid, unless in Proportion to the Census or Enumeration herein before directed to be taken.

No Tax or Duty shall be laid on Articles exported from any State.

No Preference shall be given by any Regulation of Commerce or Revenue to the Ports of one State over those of another: nor shall Vessels bound to, or from, one State, be obliged to enter, clear, or pay Duties in another.

No Money shall be drawn from the Treasury, but in Consequence of Appropriations made by Law, and a regular Statement and Account of the Receipts and Expenditures of all public Money shall be published from time to time.

No Title of Nobility shall be granted by the United States: And no Person holding any Office of Profit or Trust under them, shall, without the Consent of the Congress, accept of any present, Emolument, Office, or Title, of any kind whatever, from any King, Prince, or foreign State.

SECTION. 10. No State shall enter into any Treaty, Alliance, or Confederation; grant Letters of Marque and Reprisal; coin Money; emit Bills of Credit; make any Thing but gold and silver Coin a Tender in Payment of Debts; pass any Bill of Attainder, ex post facto Law, or Law impairing the Obligation of Contracts, or grant any Title of Nobility.

No State shall, without the Consent of the Congress, lay any Imposts or Duties on Imports or Exports, except what may be absolutely necessary for executing its inspection Laws: and the net Produce of all Duties and Imposts, laid by any State on Imports or Exports, shall be for the Use of the Treasury of the United States; and all such Laws shall be subject to the Revision and Controul of the Congress.

No State shall, without the Consent of Congress, lay any Duty of Tonnage, keep Troops, or Ships of War in time of Peace, enter into any Agreement or Compact with another State, or with a foreign Power, or engage in War, unless actually invaded, or in such imminent Danger as will not admit of delay.

Article. II.

SECTION. 1. The executive Power shall be vested in a President of the United States of America. He shall hold his Office during the Term of four Years, and, together with the Vice President, chosen for the same Term, be elected, as follows:

Each State shall appoint, in such Manner as the Legislature thereof may direct, a Number of Electors, equal to the whole Number of Senators and Representatives to which the State may be entitled in the Congress: but no Senator or Representative, or Person holding an Office of Trust or Profit under the United States, shall be appointed an Elector.

The Electors shall meet in their respective States, and vote by Ballot for two Persons, of whom one at least shall not be an Inhabitant of the same State with themselves. And they shall make a List of all the Persons voted for, and of the Number of Votes for each; which List they shall sign and certify, and transmit sealed to the Seat of the Government of the United States, directed to the President of the Senate. The President of the Senate shall, in the Presence of the Senate and House of Representatives, open all the Certificates, and the Votes shall then be counted. The Person having the greatest Number of Votes shall be the President, if such Number be a Majority of the whole Number of Electors appointed; and if there be more than one who have such Majority, and have an equal Number of Votes, then the House of Representatives shall immediately chuse by Ballot one of them for President; and if no Person have a Majority, then from the five highest on the List the said House shall in like Manner chuse the President. But in chusing the President, the Votes shall be taken by States, the Representation from each State having one Vote; A quorum for this Purpose shall consist of a Member or Members from two thirds of the States, and a Majority of all the States shall be necessary to a Choice. In every Case, after the Choice of the President, the Person having the greatest Number of Votes of the Electors shall be the Vice President. But if there should remain two or more who have equal Votes, the Senate shall chuse from them by Ballot the Vice President.[6]

The Congress may determine the Time of chusing the Electors, and the Day on which they shall give their Votes; which Day shall be the same throughout the United States.

No Person except a natural born Citizen, or a Citizen of the United States, at the time of the Adoption of this Constitution, shall be eligible to the Office of President, neither shall any Person be eligible to that Office who shall not have attained to the Age of thirty five Years, and been fourteen Years a Resident within the United States.

In Case of the Removal of the President from Office, or of his Death, Resignation, or Inability to discharge the Powers and Duties of the said Office, the Same shall devolve on the Vice President, and the Congress may by Law provide for the Case of Removal, Death, Resignation or Inability, both of the President and Vice President, declaring what Officer shall then act as President, and such Officer shall act accordingly, until the Disability be removed, or a President shall be elected.[7]

The President shall, at stated Times, receive for his Services, a Compensation, which shall neither be encreased nor diminished during the Period for which he shall have been elected, and he shall not receive within that Period any other Emolument from the United States, or any of them.

Before he enter on the Execution of his Office, he shall take the following Oath or Affirmation:—"I do solemnly swear (or affirm) that I will faithfully execute the Office of President of the United States, and will to the best of my Ability, preserve, protect and defend the Constitution of the United States."

---

[6]Superseded by the Twelfth Amendment.
[7]Modified by the Twenty-fifth Amendment.

SECTION. 2. The President shall be Commander in Chief of the Army and Navy of the United States, and of the Militia of the several States, when called into the actual Service of the United States; he may require the Opinion, in writing, of the principal Officer in each of the executive Departments, upon any Subject relating to the Duties of their respective Offices, and he shall have Power to grant Reprieves and Pardons for Offences against the United States, except in Cases of Impeachment.

He shall have Power, by and with the Advice and Consent of the Senate, to make Treaties, provided two thirds of the Senators present concur; and he shall nominate, and by and with the Advice and Consent of the Senate, shall appoint Ambassadors, other public Ministers and Consuls, Judges of the supreme Court, and all other Officers of the United States, whose Appointments are not herein otherwise provided for, and which shall be established by Law; but the Congress may by Law vest the Appointment of such inferior Officers, as they think proper, in the President alone, in the Courts of Law, or in the Heads of Departments.

The President shall have Power to fill up all Vacancies that may happen during the Recess of the Senate, by granting Commissions which shall expire at the End of their next Session.

SECTION. 3. He shall from time to time give the Congress Information of the State of the Union, and recommend to their Consideration such Measures as he shall judge necessary and expedient; he may, on extraordinary Occasions, convene both Houses, or either of them, and in Case of Disagreement between them, with Respect to the Time of Adjournment, he may adjourn them to such Time as he shall think proper; he shall receive Ambassadors and other public Ministers; he shall take Care that the Laws be faithfully executed, and shall Commission all the Officers of the United States.

SECTION. 4. The President, Vice President and all civil Officers of the United States, shall be removed from Office on Impeachment for, and Conviction of, Treason, Bribery, or other high Crimes and Misdemeanors.

Article. III.

SECTION. 1. The judicial Power of the United States, shall be vested in one supreme Court, and in such inferior Courts as the Congress may from time to time ordain and establish. The Judges, both of the supreme and inferior Courts, shall hold their Offices during good Behaviour, and shall, at stated Times, receive for their Services, a Compensation, which shall not be diminished during their Continuance in Office.

SECTION. 2. The judicial Power shall extend to all Cases, in Law and Equity, arising under this Constitution, the Laws of the United States, and Treaties made, or which shall be made, under their Authority;—to all Cases affecting Ambassadors, other public Ministers and Consuls;—to all Cases of admiralty and maritime Jurisdiction;—to Controversies to which the United States shall be a Party;—to Controversies between two or more States;—between a State and Citizens of another State;[8]—between Citizens of different States,—between Citizens of the same State claiming Lands under Grants of different States, and between a State, or the Citizens thereof, and foreign States, Citizens or Subjects.

In all Cases affecting Ambassadors, other public Ministers and Consuls, and those in which a State shall be Party, the supreme Court shall have original Jurisdiction. In all the other Cases before mentioned, the supreme Court shall have appellate Jurisdiction, both as to Law and Fact, with such Exceptions, and under such Regulations as the Congress shall make.

The Trial of all Crimes, except in Cases of Impeachment, shall be by Jury; and such Trial shall be held in the State where the said Crimes shall have been committed; but when not committed within any State, the Trial shall be at such Place or Places as the Congress may by Law have directed.

SECTION. 3. Treason against the United States, shall consist only in levying War against them, or in adhering to their Enemies, giving them Aid and Comfort. No Person shall be convicted of Treason unless on the Testimony of two Witnesses to the same overt Act, or on Confession in open Court.

The Congress shall have Power to declare the Punishment of Treason, but no Attainder of Treason shall work Corruption of Blood, or Forfeiture except during the Life of the Person attainted.

Article. IV.

SECTION. 1. Full Faith and Credit shall be given in each State to the public Acts, Records, and judicial Proceedings of every other State. And the Congress may by general Laws prescribe the Manner in which such Acts, Records and Proceedings shall be proved, and the Effect thereof.

SECTION. 2. The Citizens of each State shall be entitled to all Privileges and Immunities of Citizens in the several States.

A Person charged in any State with Treason, Felony, or other Crime, who shall flee from Justice, and be found in another State, shall on Demand of the executive Authority of the State from which he fled, be delivered up, to be removed to the State having Jurisdiction of the Crime.

No Person held to Service or Labour in one State, under the Laws thereof, escaping into another, shall, in Consequence of any Law or Regulation therein, be discharged from such Service or Labour, but shall be delivered up on Claim of the Party to whom such Service or Labour may be due.

SECTION. 3. New States may be admitted by the Congress into this Union; but no new State shall be formed or erected within the Jurisdiction of any other State, nor any State be formed by the Junction of two or more States, or Parts of States, without the Consent of the Legislatures of the States concerned as well as of the Congress.

The Congress shall have Power to dispose of and make all needful Rules and Regulations respecting the Territory or other Property belonging to the United States; and nothing in this Constitution shall be so construed as to Prejudice any Claims of the United States, or of any particular State.

---

[8]Modified by the Eleventh Amendment.

SECTION. 4. The United States shall guarantee to every State in this Union a Republican Form of Government, and shall protect each of them against Invasion; and on Application of the Legislature, or of the Executive (when the Legislature cannot be convened) against domestic Violence.

Article. V.

The Congress, whenever two thirds of both Houses shall deem it necessary, shall propose Amendments to this Constitution, or, on the Application of the Legislatures of two thirds of the several States, shall call a Convention for proposing Amendments, which, in either Case, shall be valid to all Intents and Purposes, as Part of this Constitution, when ratified by the Legislatures of three fourths of the several States, or by Conventions in three fourths thereof, as the one or the other Mode of Ratification may be proposed by the Congress; Provided that no Amendment which may be made prior to the Year One thousand eight hundred and eight shall in any Manner affect the first and fourth Clauses in the Ninth Section of the first Article; and that no State, without its Consent, shall be deprived of its equal Suffrage in the Senate.

Article. VI.

All Debts contracted and Engagements entered into, before the Adoption of this Constitution, shall be as valid against the United States under this Constitution, as under the Confederation.

This Constitution, and the Laws of the United States which shall be made in Pursuance thereof; and all Treaties made, or which shall be made, under the Authority of the United States, shall be the supreme Law of the Land; and the Judges in every State shall be bound thereby, any Thing in the Constitution or Laws of any State to the Contrary notwithstanding.

The Senators and Representatives before mentioned, and the Members of the several State Legislatures, and all executive and judicial Officers, both of the United States and of the several States, shall be bound by Oath or Affirmation, to support this Constitution; but no religious Test shall ever be required as a Qualification to any Office or public Trust under the United States.

Article. VII.

The Ratification of the Conventions of nine States, shall be sufficient for the Establishment of this Constitution between the States so ratifying the Same.

Done in Convention by the Unanimous Consent of the States present the Seventeenth Day of September in the Year of our Lord one thousand seven hundred and Eighty seven and of the Independence of the United States of America the Twelfth. **In witness** whereof We have hereunto subscribed our Names,

Articles in Addition to, and Amendment of, the Constitution of the United States of America, Proposed by Congress, and Ratified by the Legislatures of the Several States, Pursuant to the Fifth Article of the Original Constitution.

Amendment I[9]

Congress shall make no law respecting an establishment of religion, or prohibiting the free exercise thereof; or abridging the freedom of speech, or of the press; or the right of the people peaceably to assemble, and to petition the Government for a redress of grievances.

Amendment II

A well regulated Militia, being necessary to the security of a free State, the right of the people to keep and bear Arms shall not be infringed.

Amendment III

No Soldier shall, in time of peace, be quartered in any house, without the consent of the Owner, nor in time of war, but in a manner to be prescribed by law.

Amendment IV

The right of the people to be secure in their persons, houses, papers, and effects, against unreasonable searches and seizures, shall not be violated, and no Warrants shall issue, but upon probable cause, supported by Oath or affirmation, and particularly describing the place to be searched, and the persons or things to be seized.

Amendment V

No person shall be held to answer for a capital or otherwise infamous crime, unless on a presentment or indictment of a Grand Jury, except in cases arising in the land or naval forces, or in the Militia, when in actual service in time of War or public danger; nor shall any person be subject for the same offence to be twice put in jeopardy of life or limb; nor shall be compelled in any criminal case to be a witness against himself, nor be deprived of life, liberty, or property, without due process of law; nor shall private property be taken for public use, without just compensation.

Amendment VI

In all criminal prosecutions, the accused shall enjoy the right to a speedy and public trial, by an impartial jury of the State and district wherein the crime shall have been committed, which district shall have been previously ascertained by law, and to be informed of the nature and cause of the accusation; to be confronted with the witnesses against him; to have compulsory process for obtaining witnesses in his favor, and to have the Assistance of Counsel for his defence.

Amendment VII

In suits at common law, where the value in controversy shall exceed twenty dollars, the right of trial by jury shall be preserved, and no fact tried by a jury, shall be otherwise reexamined in any Court of the United States, than according to the rules of the common law.

---

[9]The first ten amendments were passed by Congress September 25, 1789. They were ratified by three-fourths of the states December 15, 1791.

Amendment VIII

Excessive bail shall not be required, nor excessive fines imposed, nor cruel and unusual punishments inflicted.

Amendment IX

The enumeration in the Constitution, of certain rights, shall not be construed to deny or disparage others retained by the people.

Amendment X

The powers not delegated to the United States by the Constitution; nor prohibited by it to the States, are reserved to the States respectively, or to the people.

Amendment XI[10]

The Judicial power of the United States shall not be construed to extend to any suit in law or equity, commenced or prosecuted against one of the United States by Citizens of another State, or by Citizens or Subjects of any Foreign State.

Amendment XII[11]

The Electors shall meet in their respective States and vote by ballot for President and Vice-President, one of whom, at least, shall not be an inhabitant of the same State with themselves; they shall name in their ballots the person voted for as President, and in distinct ballots the person voted for as Vice-President, and they shall make distinct lists of all persons voted for as President, and of all persons voted for as Vice-President, and of the number of votes for each, which lists they shall sign and certify, and transmit sealed to the seat of the government of the United States, directed to the President of the Senate;—The President of the Senate shall, in the presence of the Senate and House of Representatives, open all the certificates and the votes shall then be counted;—The person having the greatest number of votes for President, shall be the President, if such number be a majority of the whole number of Electors appointed; and if no person have such majority, then from the persons having the highest numbers not exceeding three on the list of those voted for as President, the House of Representatives shall choose immediately, by ballot, the President. But in choosing the President, the votes shall be taken by states, the representation from each state having one vote; a quorum for this purpose shall consist of a member or members from two-thirds of the states, and a majority of all the states shall be necessary to a choice. And if the House of Representatives shall not choose a President whenever the right of choice shall devolve upon them, before the fourth day of March next following, then the Vice-President shall act as President, as in the case of the death or other constitutional disability of the President.— The person having the greatest number of votes as Vice-President, shall be the Vice-President, if such number be a majority of the whole number of Electors appointed, and if no person have a majority, then from the two highest numbers on the list, the Senate shall choose the Vice-President; a quorum for the purpose shall consist of two-thirds of the whole number of Senators, and a majority of the whole number shall be necessary to a choice. But no person constitutionally ineligible to the office of President shall be eligible to that of Vice-President of the United States.

Amendment XIII[12]

SECTION. 1. Neither slavery nor involuntary servitude, except as a punishment for crime whereof the party shall have been duly convicted, shall exist within the United States, or any place subject to their jurisdiction.

SECTION. 2. Congress shall have power to enforce this article by appropriate legislation.

Amendment XIV[13]

SECTION. 1. All persons born or naturalized in the United States, and subject to the jurisdiction thereof, are citizens of the United States and of the State wherein they reside. No State shall make or enforce any law which shall abridge the privileges or immunities of citizens of the United States; nor shall any State deprive any person of life, liberty, or property, without due process of law; nor deny to any person within its jurisdiction the equal protection of the laws.

SECTION. 2. Representatives shall be apportioned among the several States according to their respective numbers, counting the whole number of persons in each State, excluding Indians not taxed. But when the right to vote at any election for the choice of electors for President and Vice-President of the United States, Representatives in Congress, the Executive and Judicial officers of a State, or the members of the Legislature thereof, is denied to any of the male inhabitants of such State, being twenty-one years of age, and citizens of the United States, or in any way abridged, except for participation in rebellion, or other crime, the basis of representation therein shall be reduced in the proportion which the number of such male citizens shall bear to the whole number of male citizens twenty-one years of age in such State.

SECTION. 3. No person shall be a Senator or Representative in Congress, or elector of President and Vice-President, or hold any office, civil or military, under the United States, or under any State, who, having previously taken an oath, as a member of Congress, or as an officer of the United States, or as a member of any State legislature, or as an executive or judicial officer of any State, to support the Constitution of the United States, shall have engaged in insurrection or rebellion against the same, or given aid or comfort to the enemies thereof. But Congress may by a vote of two-thirds of each House, remove such disability.

SECTION. 4. The validity of the public debt of the United States, authorized by law, including debts incurred for

---

[10]Passed March 4, 1794. Ratified January 23, 1795.

[11]Passed December 9, 1803. Ratified June 15, 1804.

[12]Passed January 31, 1865. Ratified December 6, 1865.

[13]Passed June 13, 1866. Ratified July 9, 1868.

payment of pensions and bounties for services in suppressing insurrection or rebellion, shall not be questioned. But neither the United States nor any State shall assume or pay any debt or obligation incurred in aid of insurrection or rebellion against the United States, or any claim for the loss or emancipation of any slave; but all such debts, obligations, and claims shall be held illegal and void.

SECTION. 5. The Congress shall have the power to enforce, by appropriate legislation, the provisions of this article.

Amendment XV[14]

SECTION. 1. The right of citizens of the United States to vote shall not be denied or abridged by the United States or by any State on account of race, color, or previous conditions of servitude—

SECTION. 2. The Congress shall have power to enforce this article by appropriate legislation.

Amendment XVI

The Congress shall have power to lay and collect taxes on incomes, from whatever source derived, without apportionment among the several States, and without regard to any census or enumeration.

Amendment XVII[15]

The Senate of the United States shall be composed of two Senators from each State, elected by the people thereof, for six years; and each Senator shall have one vote. The electors in each State shall have the qualifications requisite for electors of the most numerous branch of the State legislatures.

When vacancies happen in the representation of any State in the Senate, the executive authority of such State shall issue writs of election to fill such vacancies: Provided, That the legislature of any State may empower the executive thereof to make temporary appointments until the people fill the vacancies by election as the legislature may direct.

This amendment shall not be so construed as to affect the election or term of any Senator chosen before it becomes valid as part of the Constitution.

Amendment XVIII[16]

SECTION. 1. After one year from the ratification of this article the manufacture, sale, or transportation of intoxicating liquors within, the importation thereof into, or the exportation thereof from the United States and all territory subject to the jurisdiction thereof for beverage purposes is hereby prohibited.

SECTION. 2. The Congress and the several States shall have concurrent power to enforce this article by appropriate legislation.

SECTION. 3. This article shall be inoperative unless it shall have been ratified as an amendment to the Constitution by the legislatures of the several States, as provided in the Constitution, within seven years from the date of the submission hereof to the States by the Congress.

Amendment XIX[17]

The right of citizens of the United States to vote shall not be denied or abridged by the United States or by any State on account of sex.

Congress shall have power to enforce this article by appropriate legislation.

Amendment XX[18]

SECTION. 1. The terms of the President and Vice-President shall end at noon on the 20th day of January, and the terms of Senators and Representatives at noon on the 3d day of January, of the years in which such terms would have ended if this article had not been ratified; and the terms of their successors shall then begin.

SECTION. 2. The Congress shall assemble at least once in every year, and such meeting shall begin at noon on the 3d day of January, unless they shall by law appoint a different day.

SECTION. 3. If, at the time fixed for the beginning of the term of the President, the President elect shall have died the Vice-President elect shall become President. If a President shall not have been chosen before the time fixed for the beginning of his term, or if the President elect shall have failed to qualify, then the Vice-President elect shall act as President until a President shall have qualified; and the Congress may by law provide for the case wherein neither a President elect nor a Vice-President elect shall have qualified, declaring who shall then act as President, or the manner in which one who is to act shall be selected, and such person shall act accordingly until a President or Vice-President shall have qualified.

SECTION. 4. The Congress may by law provide for the case of the death of any of the persons from whom the House of Representatives may choose a President whenever the right of choice shall have devolved upon them, and for the case of the death of any of the persons from whom the Senate may choose a Vice-President whenever the right of choice shall have devolved upon them.

SECTION. 5. Sections 1 and 2 shall take effect on the 15th day of October following the ratification of this article.

SECTION. 6. This article shall be inoperative unless it shall have been ratified as an amendment to the Constitution by the legislatures of three-fourths of the several States within seven years from the date of its submission.

Amendment XXI[19]

SECTION. 1. The eighteenth article of amendment to the Constitution of the United States is hereby repealed.

SECTION. 2. The transportation or importation into any State, Territory, or possession of the United States for delivery or use therein of intoxicating liquors, in violation of the laws thereof, is hereby prohibited.

---

[14]Passed February 26, 1869. Ratified February 2, 1870.

[15]Passed May 13, 1912. Ratified April 8, 1913.

[16]Passed December 18, 1917. Ratified January 16, 1919.

[17]Passed June 4, 1919. Ratified August 18, 1920.

[18]Passed March 2, 1932. Ratified January 23, 1933.

[19]Passed February 20, 1933. Ratified December 5, 1933.

SECTION. 3. This article shall be inoperative unless it shall have been ratified as an amendment to the Constitution by conventions in the several States, as provided in the Constitution, within seven years from the date of the submission hereof to the States by the Congress.

Amendment XXII[20]

No person shall be elected to the office of the President more than twice, and no person who has held the office of President, or acted as President, for more than two years of a term to which some other person was elected President shall be elected to the office of the President more than once.

But this Article shall not apply to any person holding the office of President when this Article was proposed by the Congress, and shall not prevent any person who may be holding the office of President, or acting as President, during the term within which this Article becomes operative from holding the office of President or acting as President during the remainder of such term.

Amendment XXIII[21]

SECTION. 1. The District constituting the seat of Government of the United States shall appoint in such manner as the Congress may direct:

A number of electors of President and Vice President equal to the whole number of Senators and Representatives in Congress to which the District would be entitled if it were a State, but in no event more than the least populous State; they shall be in addition to those appointed by the States, but they shall be considered, for the purposes of the election of President and Vice President, to be electors appointed by the State; and they shall meet in the District and perform such duties as provided by the twelfth article of amendment.

SECTION. 2. The Congress shall have power to enforce this article by appropriate legislation.

Amendment XXIV[22]

SECTION. 1. The right of citizens of the United States to vote in any primary or other election for President or Vice President, or for Senator or Representative in Congress, shall not be denied or abridged by the United States or any State by reason of failure to pay any poll tax or other tax.

SECTION. 2. The Congress shall have power to enforce this article by appropriate legislation.

Amendment XXV[23]

SECTION. 1. In case of the removal of the President from office or of his death or resignation, the Vice President shall become President.

SECTION. 2. Whenever there is a vacancy in the office of the Vice President, the President shall nominate a Vice President who shall take office upon confirmation by a majority vote of both Houses of Congress.

SECTION. 3. Whenever the President transmits to the President pro tempore of the Senate and the Speaker of the House of Representatives his written declaration that he is unable to discharge the powers and duties of his office, and until he transmits them a written declaration to the contrary, such powers and duties shall be discharged by the Vice President as Acting President.

SECTION. 4. Whenever the Vice President and a majority of either the principal officers of the executive department or of such other body as Congress may by law provide, transmit to the President pro tempore of the Senate and the Speaker of the House of Representatives their written declaration that the President is unable to discharge the powers and duties of his office, the Vice President shall immediately assume the powers and duties of the office of Acting President.

Thereafter, when the President transmits to the President pro tempore of the Senate and the Speaker of the House of Representatives his written declaration that no inability exists, he shall resume the powers and duties of his office unless the Vice President and a majority of either the principal officers of the executive department or of such other body as Congress may by law provide, transmit within four days to the President pro tempore of the Senate and the Speaker of the House of Representatives their written declaration that the President is unable to discharge the powers and duties of his office. Thereupon Congress shall decide the issue, assembling within forty-eight hours for that purpose if not in session. If the Congress, within twenty-one days after receipt of the latter written declaration, or, if Congress is not in session, within twenty-one days after Congress is required to assemble, determines by two-thirds vote of both Houses that the President is unable to discharge the powers and duties of his office, the Vice President shall continue to discharge the same as Acting President; otherwise, the President shall resume the powers and duties of his office.

Amendment XXVI[24]

SECTION. 1. The right of citizens of the United States, who are eighteen years of age or older, to vote shall not be denied or abridged by the United States or by any State on account of age.

SECTION. 2. The Congress shall have power to enforce this article by appropriate legislation.

Amendment XXVII[25]

No law, varying the compensation for the service of the Senators and Representatives, shall take effect, until an election of Representatives shall have intervened.

---

[20]Passed March 12, 1947. Ratified March 1, 1951.

[21]Passed June 16, 1960. Ratified April 3, 1961.

[22]Passed August 27, 1962. Ratified January 23, 1964.

[23]Passed July 6, 1965. Ratified February 11, 1967.

---

[24]Passed March 23, 1971. Ratified July 5, 1971.

[25]Passed September 25, 1989. Ratified May 7, 1992.

Admission of States

Order of admission	State	Date of admission	Order of admission	State	Date of admission
1	Delaware	December 7, 1787	26	Michigan	January 26, 1837
2	Pennsylvania	December 12, 1787	27	Florida	March 3, 1845
3	New Jersey	December 18, 1787	28	Texas	December 29, 1845
4	Georgia	January 2, 1788	29	Iowa	December 28, 1846
5	Connecticut	January 9, 1788	30	Wisconsin	May 29, 1848
6	Massachusetts	February 6, 1788	31	California	September 9, 1850
7	Maryland	April 28, 1788	32	Minnesota	May 11, 1858
8	South Carolina	May 23, 1788	33	Oregon	February 14, 1859
9	New Hampshire	June 21, 1788	34	Kansas	January 29, 1861
10	Virginia	June 25, 1788	35	West Virginia	June 20, 1863
11	New York	July 26, 1788	36	Nevada	October 31, 1864
12	North Carolina	November 21, 1789	37	Nebraska	March 1, 1867
13	Rhode Island	May 29, 1790	38	Colorado	August 1, 1876
14	Vermont	March 4, 1791	39	North Dakota	November 2, 1889
15	Kentucky	June 1, 1792	40	South Dakota	November 2, 1889
16	Tennessee	June 1, 1796	41	Montana	November 8, 1889
17	Ohio	March 1, 1803	42	Washington	November 11, 1889
18	Louisiana	April 30, 1812	43	Idaho	July 3, 1890
19	Indiana	December 11, 1816	44	Wyoming	July 10, 1890
20	Mississippi	December 10, 1817	45	Utah	January 4, 1896
21	Illinois	December 3, 1818	46	Oklahoma	November 16, 1907
22	Alabama	December 14, 1819	47	New Mexico	January 6, 1912
23	Maine	March 15, 1820	48	Arizona	February 14, 1912
24	Missouri	August 10, 1821	49	Alaska	January 3, 1959
25	Arkansas	June 15, 1836	50	Hawaii	August 21, 1959

Population of the United States
(1790–2005)

Year	Total population (in thousands)	Number per square mile of land area (continental United States)	Year	Total population (in thousands)	Number per square mile of land area (continental United States)
1790	3,929	4.5	1829	12,565	
1791	4,056		1830	12,901	7.4
1792	4,194		1831	13,321	
1793	4,332		1832	13,742	
1794	4,469		1833	14,162	
1795	4,607		1834	14,582	
1796	4,745		1835	15,003	
1797	4,883		1836	15,423	
1798	5,021		1837	15,843	
1799	5,159		1838	16,264	
1800	5,297	6.1	1839	16,684	
1801	5,486		1840	17,120	9.8
1802	5,679		1841	17,733	
1803	5,872		1842	18,345	
1804	5,065		1843	18,957	
1805	6,258		1844	19,569	
1806	6,451		1845	20,182	
1807	6,644		1846	20,794	
1808	6,838		1847	21,406	
1809	7,031		1848	22,018	
1810	7,224	4.3	1849	22,631	
1811	7,460		1850	23,261	7.9
1812	7,700		1851	24,086	
1813	7,939		1852	24,911	
1814	8,179		1853	25,736	
1815	8,419		1854	26,561	
1816	8,659		1855	27,386	
1817	8,899		1856	28,212	
1818	9,139		1857	29,037	
1819	9,379		1858	29,862	
1820	9,618	5.6	1859	30,687	
1821	9,939		1860	31,513	10.6
1822	10,268		1861	32,351	
1823	10,596		1862	33,188	
1824	10,924		1863	34,026	
1825	11,252		1864	34,863	
1826	11,580		1865	35,701	
1827	11,909		1866	36,538	
1828	12,237		1867	37,376	

Figures are from *Historical Statistics of the United States, Colonial Times to 1957* (1961), pp. 7, 8; *Statistical Abstract of the United States* (1974), p. 5, Census Bureau for 1974 and 1975; and *Statistical Abstract of the United States* (1988), p. 7.

(continued)

Population of the United States *(continued)* (1790–2005)

Year	Total population (in thousands)	Number per square mile of land area (continental United States)	Year	Total population (in thousands)[1]	Number per square mile of land area (continental United States)
1868	38,213		1907	87,000	
1869	39,051		1908	88,709	
1870	39,905	13.4	1909	90,492	
1871	40,938		1910	92,407	31.0
1872	41,972		1911	93,868	
1873	43,006		1912	95,331	
1874	44,040		1913	97,227	
1875	45,073		1914	99,118	
1876	46,107		1915	100,549	
1877	47,141		1916	101,966	
1878	48,174		1917	103,414	
1879	49,208		1918	104,550	
1880	50,262	16.9	1919	105,063	
1881	51,542		1920	106,466	35.6
1882	52,821		1921	108,541	
1883	54,100		1922	110,055	
1884	55,379		1923	111,950	
1885	56,658		1924	114,113	
1886	57,938		1925	115,832	
1887	59,217		1926	117,399	
1888	60,496		1927	119,038	
1889	61,775		1928	120,501	
1890	63,056	21.2	1929	121,700	
1891	64,361		1930	122,775	41.2
1892	65,666		1931	124,040	
1893	66,970		1932	124,840	
1894	68,275		1933	125,579	
1895	69,580		1934	126,374	
1896	70,885		1935	127,250	
1897	72,189		1936	128,053	
1898	73,494		1937	128,825	
1899	74,799		1938	129,825	
1900	76,094	25.6	1939	130,880	
1901	77,585		1940	131,669	44.2
1902	79,160		1941	133,894	
1903	80,632		1942	135,361	
1904	82,165		1943	137,250	
1905	83,820		1944	138,916	
1906	85,437		1945	140,468	

[1]Figures after 1940 represent total population including armed forces abroad, except in official census years.

(continued)

Population of the United States *(continued)*
(1790–2005)

Year	Total population (in thousands)	Number per square mile of land area (continental United States)	Year	Total population (in thousands)[1]	Number per square mile of land area (continental United States)
1946	141,936		1976	218,035	
1947	144,698		1977	220,239	
1948	147,208		1978	222,585	
1949	149,767		1979	225,055	
1950	150,697	50.7	1980	227,225	64.0
1951	154,878		1981	229,466	
1952	157,553		1982	232,520	
1953	160,184		1983	234,799	
1954	163,026		1984	237,001	
1955	165,931		1985	239,283	
1956	168,903		1986	241,596	
1957	171,984		1987	234,773	
1958	174,882		1988	245,051	
1959	177,830[2]		1989	247,350	
1960	180,671	60.1	1990	250,122	70.3
1961	186,538		1991	254,521	
1962	189,242		1992	245,908	
1963	189,197		1993	257,908	
1964	191,889		1994	261,875	
1965	194,303		1995	263,434	
1966	196,560		1996	266,096	
1967	198,712		1997	267,744	
1968	200,706		1998	270,299	
1969	202,677		1999	274,114	
1970	205,052	57.52	2000	281,400	
1971	207,661		2001	286,909	
1972	209,896		2002	289,947	
1973	211,909		2003	290,850	
1974	213,854		2004	293,656	
1975	215,973		2005	296,410	

[1]Figures after 1940 represent total population including armed forces abroad, except in official census years.

[2]Figures after 1959 include Alaska and Hawaii.

Presidential Elections
(1789–1832)

Year	Number of states	Candidates[1]	Parties	Popular vote	Electoral vote	Percentage of popular vote[2]
1789	11	**George Washington***	**No party designations**		69	
		John Adams			34	
		Minor Candidates			35	
1792	15	**George Washington**	**No party designations**		132	
		John Adams			77	
		George Clinton			50	
		Minor Candidates			5	
1796	16	**John Adams**	**Federalist**		71	
		Thomas Jefferson	Democratic-Republican		68	
		Thomas Pinckney	Federalist		59	
		Aaron Burr	Democratic-Republican		30	
		Minor Candidates			48	
1800	16	**Thomas Jefferson**	**Democratic-Republican**		73	
		Aaron Burr	Democratic-Republican		73	
		John Adams	Federalist		65	
		Charles C. Pinckney	Federalist		64	
		John Jay	Federalist		1	
1804	17	**Thomas Jefferson**	**Democratic-Republican**		162	
		Charles C. Pinckney	Federalist		14	
1808	17	**James Madison**	**Democratic-Republican**		122	
		Charles C. Pinckney	Federalist		47	
		George Clinton	Democratic-Republican		6	
1812	18	**James Madison**	**Democratic-Republican**		128	
		DeWitt Clinton	Federalist		89	
1816	19	**James Monroe**	**Democratic-Republican**		183	
		Rufus King	Federalist		34	
1820	24	**James Monroe**	**Democratic-Republican**		231	
		John Quincy Adams	Independent Republican		1	
1824	24	**John Quincy Adams**	**Democratic-Republican**	**108,740**	**84**	**30.5**
		Andrew Jackson	Democratic-Republican	153,544	99	43.1
		William H. Crawford	Democratic-Republican	46,618	41	13.1
		Henry Clay	Democratic-Republican	47,136	37	13.2
1828	24	**Andrew Jackson**	**Democratic**	**647,286**	**178**	**56.0**
		John Quincy Adams	National Republican	508,064	83	44.0
1832	24	**Andrew Jackson**	**Democratic**	**687,502**	**219**	**55.0**
		Henry Clay	National Republican	530,189	49	42.4
		William Wirt	Anti-Masonic	}	7	
		John Floyd	National Republican }	33,108	11	2.6

[1]Before the passage of the Twelfth Amendment in 1804, the Electoral College voted for two presidential candidates; the runner-up became vice president. Figures are from *Historical Statistics of the United States, Colonial Times to 1957* (1961), pp. 682–83; and the U.S. Department of Justice.

[2]Candidates receiving less than 1 percent of the popular vote have been omitted. For that reason the percentage of popular vote given for any election year may not total 100 percent.

*Note: Boldface indicates the winner of each election.

Presidential Elections
(1836–1888)

Year	Number of states	Candidates	Parties	Popular vote	Electoral vote	Percentage of popular vote[1]
1836	26	**Martin Van Buren**	**Democratic**	**765,483**	**170**	**50.9**
		William H. Harrison	Whig		73	
		Hugh L. White	Whig		26	
		Daniel Webster	Whig	739,795	14	
		W. P. Mangum	Independent		11	
1840	26	**William H. Harrison**	**Whig**	**1,274,624**	**234**	**53.1**
		Martin Van Buren	Democratic	1,127,781	60	46.9
1844	26	**James K. Polk**	**Democratic**	**1,338,464**	**170**	**49.6**
		Henry Clay	Whig	1,300,097	105	48.1
		James G. Birney	Liberty	62,300		2.3
1848	30	**Zachary Taylor**	**Whig**	**1,360,967**	**163**	**47.4**
		Lewis Cass	Democratic	1,222,342	127	42.5
		Martin Van Buren	Free Soil	291,263		10.1
1852	31	**Franklin Pierce**	**Democratic**	**1,601,117**	**254**	**50.9**
		Winfield Scott	Whig	1,385,453	42	44.1
		John P. Hale	Free Soil	155,825		5.0
1856	31	**James Buchanan**	**Democratic**	**1,832,955**	**174**	**45.3**
		John C. Frémont	Republican	1,339,932	114	33.1
		Millard Fillmore	American	871,731	8	21.6
1860	33	**Abraham Lincoln**	**Republican**	**1,865,593**	**180**	**39.8**
		Stephen A. Douglas	Democratic	1,382,713	12	29.5
		John C. Breckinridge	Democratic	848,356	72	18.1
		John Bell	Constitutional Union	592,906	39	12.6
1864	36	**Abraham Lincoln**	**Republican**	**2,206,938**	**212**	**55.0**
		George B. McClellan	Democratic	1,803,787	21	45.0
1868	37	**Ulysses S. Grant**	**Republican**	**3,013,421**	**214**	**52.7**
		Horatio Seymour	Democratic	2,706,829	80	47.3
1872	37	**Ulysses S. Grant**	**Republican**	**3,596,745**	**286**	**55.6**
		Horace Greeley	Democratic	2,843,446	[2]	43.9
1876	38	**Rutherford B. Hayes**	**Republican**	**4,036,572**	**185**	**48.0**
		Samuel J. Tilden	Democratic	4,284,020	184	51.0
1880	38	**James A. Garfield**	**Republican**	**4,453,295**	**214**	**48.5**
		Winfield S. Hancock	Democratic	4,414,082	155	48.1
		James B. Weaver	Greenback-Labor	308,578		3.4
1884	38	**Grover Cleveland**	**Democratic**	**4,879,507**	**219**	**48.5**
		James G. Blaine	Republican	4,850,293	182	48.2
		Benjamin F. Butler	Greenback-Labor	175,370		1.8
		John P. St. John	Prohibition	150,369		1.5
1888	38	**Benjamin Harrison**	**Republican**	**5,477,129**	**233**	**47.9**
		Grover Cleveland	Democratic	5,537,857	168	48.6
		Clinton B. Fisk	Prohibition	249,506		2.2
		Anson J. Streeter	Union Labor	146,935		1.3

[1]Candidates receiving less than 1 percent of the popular vote have been omitted. For that reason the percentage of popular vote given for any election year may not total 100 percent.

[2]Greeley died shortly after the election; the electors supporting him then divided their votes among minor candidates.

Presidential Elections
(1892–1932)

Year	Number of states	Candidates	Parties	Popular vote	Electoral vote	Percentage of popular vote[1]
1892	44	**Grover Cleveland**	**Democratic**	**5,555,426**	**277**	**46.1**
		Benjamin Harrison	Republican	5,182,690	145	43.0
		James B. Weaver	People's	1,029,846	22	8.5
		John Bidwell	Prohibition	264,133		2.2
1896	45	**William McKinley**	**Republican**	**7,102,246**	**271**	**51.1**
		William J. Bryan	Democratic	6,492,559	176	47.7
1900	45	**William McKinley**	**Republican**	**7,218,491**	**292**	**51.7**
		William J. Bryan	Democratic; Populist	6,356,734	155	45.5
		John C. Wooley	Prohibition	208,914		1.5
1904	45	**Theodore Roosevelt**	**Republican**	**7,628,461**	**336**	**57.4**
		Alton B. Parker	Democratic	5,084,223	140	37.6
		Eugene V. Debs	Socialist	402,283		3.0
		Silas C. Swallow	Prohibition	258,536		1.9
1908	46	**William H. Taft**	**Republican**	**7,675,320**	**321**	**51.6**
		William J. Bryan	Democratic	6,412,294	162	43.1
		Eugene V. Debs	Socialist	420,793		2.8
		Eugene W. Chafin	Prohibition	253,840		1.7
1912	48	**Woodrow Wilson**	**Democratic**	**6,296,547**	**435**	**41.9**
		Theodore Roosevelt	Progressive	4,118,571	88	27.4
		William H. Taft	Republican	3,486,720	8	23.2
		Eugene V. Debs	Socialist	900,672		6.0
		Eugene W. Chafin	Prohibition	206,275		1.4
1916	48	**Woodrow Wilson**	**Democratic**	**9,127,695**	**277**	**49.4**
		Charles E. Hughes	Republican	8,533,507	254	46.2
		A. L. Benson	Socialist	585,113		3.2
		J. Frank Hanly	Prohibition	220,506		1.2
1920	48	**Warren G. Harding**	**Republican**	**16,143,407**	**404**	**60.4**
		James N. Cox	Democratic	9,130,328	127	34.2
		Eugene V. Debs	Socialist	919,799		3.4
		P. P. Christensen	Farmer-Labor	265,411		1.0
1924	48	**Calvin Coolidge**	**Republican**	**15,718,211**	**382**	**54.0**
		John W. Davis	Democratic	8,385,283	136	28.8
		Robert M. La Follette	Progressive	4,831,289	13	16.6
1928	48	**Herbert C. Hoover**	**Republican**	**21,391,993**	**444**	**58.2**
		Alfred E. Smith	Democratic	15,016,169	87	40.9
1932	48	**Franklin D. Roosevelt**	**Democratic**	**22,809,638**	**472**	**57.4**
		Herbert C. Hoover	Republican	15,758,901	59	39.7
		Norman Thomas	Socialist	881,951		2.2

[1]Candidates receiving less than 1 percent of the popular vote have been omitted. For that reason the percentage of popular vote given for any election year may not total 100 percent.

Presidential Elections
(1936–2004)

Year	Number of states	Candidates	Parties	Popular vote	Electoral vote	Percentage of popular vote[1]
1936	**48**	**Franklin D. Roosevelt**	**Democratic**	**27,752,869**	**523**	**60.8**
		Alfred M. Landon	Republican	16,674,665	8	36.5
		William Lemke	Union	882,479		1.9
1940	**48**	**Franklin D. Roosevelt**	**Democratic**	**27,307,819**	**449**	**54.8**
		Wendell L. Willkie	Republican	22,321,018	82	44.8
1944	**48**	**Franklin D. Roosevelt**	**Democratic**	**25,606,585**	**432**	**53.5**
		Thomas E. Dewey	Republican	22,014,745	99	46.0
1948	**48**	**Harry S Truman**	**Democratic**	**24,105,812**	**303**	**49.5**
		Thomas E. Dewey	Republican	21,970,065	189	45.1
		J. Strom Thurmond	States' Rights	1,169,063	39	2.4
		Henry A. Wallace	Progressive	1,157,172		2.4
1952	**48**	**Dwight D. Eisenhower**	**Republican**	**33,936,234**	**442**	**55.1**
		Adlai E. Stevenson	Democratic	27,314,992	89	44.4
1956	**48**	**Dwight D. Eisenhower**	**Republican**	**35,590,472**	**457**	**57.6**
		Adlai E. Stevenson	Democratic	26,022,752	73	42.1
1960	**50**	**John F. Kennedy**	**Democratic**	**34,227,096**	**303**	**49.9**
		Richard M. Nixon	Republican	34,108,546	219	49.6
1964	**50**	**Lyndon B. Johnson**	**Democratic**	**43,126,506**	**486**	**61.1**
		Barry M. Goldwater	Republican	27,176,799	52	38.5
1968	**50**	**Richard M. Nixon**	**Republican**	**31,785,480**	**301**	**43.4**
		Hubert H. Humphrey	Democratic	31,275,165	191	42.7
		George C. Wallace	American Independent	9,906,473	46	13.5
1972	**50**	**Richard M. Nixon**	**Republican**	**47,169,911**	**520**	**60.7**
		George S. McGovern	Democratic	29,170,383	17	37.5
1976	**50**	**Jimmy Carter**	**Democratic**	**40,827,394**	**297**	**50.0**
		Gerald R. Ford	Republican	39,145,977	240	47.9
1980	**50**	**Ronald W. Reagan**	**Republican**	**43,899,248**	**489**	**50.8**
		Jimmy Carter	Democratic	35,481,435	49	41.0
		John B. Anderson	Independent	5,719,437		6.6
		Ed Clark	Libertarian	920,859		1.0
1984	**50**	**Ronald W. Reagan**	**Republican**	**54,281,858**	**525**	**59.2**
		Walter F. Mondale	Democratic	37,457,215	13	40.8
1988	**50**	**George H. Bush**	**Republican**	**47,917,341**	**426**	**54**
		Michael Dukakis	Democratic	41,013,030	112	46
1992	**50**	**William Clinton**	**Democratic**	**44,908,254**	**370**	**43.0**
		George H. Bush	Republican	39,102,343	168	37.4
		H. Ross Perot	Independent	19,741,065		18.9
1996	**50**	**William Clinton**	**Democratic**	**47,402,357**	**379**	**49**
		Robert J. Dole	Republican	39,198,755	159	41
		H. Ross Perot	Reform	8,085,402		8
2000	**50**	**George W. Bush**	**Republican**	**50,456,062**	**271**	**47.9**
		Albert Gore	Democratic	50,996,582	266	48.4
		Ralph Nader	Green	2,858,843		2.7
2004	**50**	**George W. Bush**	**Republican**	**60,693,281**	**286**	**52**
		John F. Kerry	Democratic	57,355,978	251	47
		Ralph Nader	Green	240,896		

[1]Candidates receiving less than 1 percent of the popular vote have been omitted. For that reason the percentage of popular vote given for any election year may not total 100 percent.

Justices of the U.S. Supreme Court

Chief Justices appear in bold type

	Term of Service	Years of Service	Appointed by
John Jay	1789–1795	5	Washington
John Rutledge	1789–1791	1	Washington
William Cushing	1789–1810	20	Washington
James Wilson	1789–1798	8	Washington
John Blair	1789–1796	6	Washington
Robert H. Harrison	1789–1790	—	Washington
James Iredell	1790–1799	9	Washington
Thomas Johnson	1791–1793	1	Washington
William Paterson	1793–1806	13	Washington
John Rutledge[1]	1795	—	Washington
Samuel Chase	1796–1811	15	Washington
Oliver Ellsworth	1796–1800	4	Washington
Bushrod Washington	1798–1829	31	J. Adams
Alfred Moore	1799–1804	4	J. Adams
John Marshall	1801–1835	34	J. Adams
William Johnson	1804–1834	30	Jefferson
H. Brockholst Livingston	1806–1823	16	Jefferson
Thomas Todd	1807–1826	18	Jefferson
Joseph Story	1811–1845	33	Madison
Gabriel Duval	1811–1835	24	Madison
Smith Thompson	1823–1843	20	Monroe
Robert Trimble	1826–1828	2	J. Q. Adams
John McLean	1829–1861	32	Jackson
Henry Baldwin	1830–1844	14	Jackson
James M. Wayne	1835–1867	32	Jackson
Roger B. Taney	1836–1864	28	Jackson
Philip P. Barbour	1836–1841	4	Jackson
John Catron	1837–1865	28	Van Buren
John McKinley	1837–1852	15	Van Buren
Peter V. Daniel	1841–1860	19	Van Buren
Samuel Nelson	1845–1872	27	Tyler
Levi Woodbury	1845–1851	5	Polk
Robert C. Grier	1846–1870	23	Polk
Benjamin R. Curtis	1851–1857	6	Fillmore
John A. Campbell	1853–1861	8	Pierce
Nathan Clifford	1858–1881	23	Buchanan
Noah H. Swayne	1862–1881	18	Lincoln
Samuel F. Miller	1862–1890	28	Lincoln
David Davis	1862–1877	14	Lincoln
Stephen J. Field	1863–1897	34	Lincoln
Salmon P. Chase	1864–1873	8	Lincoln
William Strong	1870–1880	10	Grant
Joseph P. Bradley	1870–1892	22	Grant
Ward Hunt	1873–1882	9	Grant

[1]Acting Chief Justice; Senate refused to confirm appointment.

(continued)

Justices of the U.S. Supreme Court (continued)

Chief Justices appear in bold type

	Term of Service	Years of Service	Appointed by
Morrison R. Waite	1874–1888	14	Grant
John M. Harlan	1877–1911	34	Hayes
William B. Woods	1880–1887	7	Hayes
Stanley Matthews	1881–1889	7	Garfield
Horace Gray	1882–1902	20	Arthur
Samuel Blatchford	1882–1893	11	Arthur
Lucius Q. C. Lamar	1888–1893	5	Cleveland
Melville W. Fuller	1888–1910	21	Cleveland
David J. Brewer	1890–1910	20	B. Harrison
Henry B. Brown	1890–1906	16	B. Harrison
George Shiras, Jr.	1892–1903	10	B. Harrison
Howell E. Jackson	1893–1895	2	B. Harrison
Edward D. White	1894–1910	16	Cleveland
Rufus W. Peckham	1895–1909	14	Cleveland
Joseph McKenna	1898–1925	26	McKinley
Oliver W. Holmes, Jr.	1902–1932	30	T. Roosevelt
William R. Day	1903–1922	19	T. Roosevelt
William H. Moody	1906–1910	3	T. Roosevelt
Horace H. Lurton	1910–1914	4	Taft
Charles E. Hughes	1910–1916	5	Taft
Willis Van Devanter	1911–1937	26	Taft
Joseph R. Lamar	1911–1916	5	Taft
Edward D. White	1910–1921	11	Taft
Mahlon Pitney	1912–1922	10	Taft
James C. McReynolds	1914–1941	26	Wilson
Louis D. Brandeis	1916–1939	22	Wilson
John H. Clarke	1916–1922	6	Wilson
William H. Taft	1921–1930	8	Harding
George Sutherland	1922–1938	15	Harding
Pierce Butler	1922–1939	16	Harding
Edward T. Sanford	1923–1930	7	Harding
Harlan F. Stone	1925–1941	16	Coolidge
Charles E. Hughes	1930–1941	11	Hoover
Owen J. Roberts	1930–1945	15	Hoover
Benjamin N. Cardozo	1932–1938	6	Hoover
Hugo L. Black	1937–1971	34	F. Roosevelt
Stanley F. Reed	1938–1957	19	F. Roosevelt
Felix Frankfurter	1939–1962	23	F. Roosevelt
William O. Douglas	1939–1975	36	F. Roosevelt
Frank Murphy	1940–1949	9	F. Roosevelt
Harlan F. Stone	1941–1946	5	F. Roosevelt
James F. Byrnes	1941–1942	1	F. Roosevelt
Robert H. Jackson	1941–1954	13	F. Roosevelt
Wiley B. Rutledge	1943–1949	6	F. Roosevelt

(continued)

Justices of the U.S. Supreme Court *(continued)*

Chief Justices appear in bold type

	Term of Service	Years of Service	Appointed by
Harold H. Burton	1945–1958	13	Truman
Fred M. Vinson	1946–1953	7	Truman
Tom C. Clark	1949–1967	18	Truman
Sherman Minton	1949–1956	7	Truman
Earl Warren	1953–1969	16	Eisenhower
John Marshall Harlan	1955–1971	16	Eisenhower
William J. Brennan, Jr.	1956–1990	34	Eisenhower
Charles E. Whittaker	1957–1962	5	Eisenhower
Potter Stewart	1958–1981	23	Eisenhower
Byron R. White	1962–1993	31	Kennedy
Arthur J. Goldberg	1962–1965	3	Kennedy
Abe Fortas	1965–1969	4	Johnson
Thurgood Marshall	1967–1994	24	Johnson
Warren E. Burger	1969–1986	18	Nixon
Harry A. Blackmun	1970–1994	24	Nixon
Lewis F. Powell, Jr.	1971–1987	15	Nixon
William H. Rehnquist[2]	1971–2005	34	Nixon
John P. Stevens III	1975–	—	Ford
Sandra Day O'Connor	1981–	—	Reagan
Antonin Scalia	1986–	—	Reagan
Anthony M. Kennedy	1988–	—	Reagan
David Souter	1990–	—	G. H. Bush
Clarence Thomas	1991–	—	G. H. Bush
Ruth Bader Ginsburg	1993–	—	Clinton
Stephen G. Breyer	1994–	—	Clinton
John G. Roberts, Jr.	2005–	—	G. W. Bush

[2]Chief Justice from 1986 (Reagan administration).

KEY TERMS

3-D
Short for three-dimensional movies, colloquial reference to one of the gimmicks with which the movie industry responded when television viewing cut sharply into movie attendance. Using two cameras and providing special plastic and cardboard "glasses" to customers, the studios produced a three-dimensional effect much like the stereopticon viewers of the late nineteenth century.

A Century of Dishonor
Influential book published in 1881 by Helen Hunt Jackson. It traced the history of United States treatment of Indians as a series of treaties repeatedly violated not by the tribes but by the U.S. government. Jackson's book contributed to a groundswell of sympathy for Indians in the East that led directly to the Dawes Severalty Act of 1887.

abolition
Declaration of slavery's illegality by the government, as opposed to manumission, which refers to the freeing of individual slaves. In the years after the Revolution, all of the northern states abolished slavery.

Adams, Samuel (1722–1803)
Protest leader in Boston who may have been instrumental in escalating resentment of British policies to full-blown rebellion. He failed to arouse the city after the Boston Massacre but conceived of and organized the Boston Tea Party that led directly to open warfare.

Adams-Oñis Treaty (1819)
A diplomatic triumph for Secretary of State John Quincy Adams. Spain sold Florida to the United States for $5 million. Adams's only concession to Spain was to agree to the Spanish version of the border between Spanish Texas and Louisiana.

Alamo
The name given to an old, largely abandoned mission compound in San Antonio, Texas. (Alamo means "cottonwood tree.") It became the symbol of Texan independence when, in March 1836, Mexican president Santa Anna defeated a handful of defenders there and executed the survivors. Less than two weeks later, Santa Anna massacred other Texas rebels at Goliad, but somehow they are not so well remembered.

Algonkian
Linguists' names to the three major language families of the Eastern Woodlands Indians. There was also a distinct tribe in Canada the French called Algonquin.

America First Committee
Influential organization opposing American intervention in World War II. Motivated by hostility to the Soviet Union, Anglophobia, or the belief that Britain was doomed to lose the war, the Committee opposed President Roosevelt's massive aid to Great Britain until the Japanese attack of Pearl Harbor ended the debate.

American Colonization Society
Founded in 1817 to help free blacks emigrate to West Africa. The society hoped that by answering slave owners' fears of a large free black population in the United States, they would be encouraged to free their slaves. Presidents Madison and Monroe supported it, as did other prominent southerners like John Marshall and Henry Clay.

American Independent party
Third party organized by Alabama Governor George Wallace to contest the 1968 election. Wallace hoped to unite southern whites disturbed by civil rights legislation and northern working-class whites resentful of what they considered special privileges extended to minorities.

American Railway Union
Apparently successful union of railroad workers led by Eugene V. Debs (later the head of the Socialist Party of America). The ARU was destroyed by federal intervention when its members supported strikers at the Pullman Palace Car Company in 1894.

"American style," the
A term used by British military officers, often disdainfully, for the adoption by colonials of Indian methods of making war: concealment, ambush, raids, and undisciplined individual action in battle.

American System
The name Henry Clay gave to his comprehensive Federalist-like program to reconcile the sometimes conflicting economic interests of Northeast, West, and South. Clay's "system" included federally financed internal improvements on a massive scale, a somewhat liberalized federal land policy, a high protective tariff to subsidize the development of manufacturing, and the Second Bank of the United States to moderate the nation's financial institutions.

Amherst, Jeffery (1717–1797)
British general, the commander of troops in North America in the French and Indian War who turned the tide of the war in Britain's favor. Later he refused to command British troops against Americans in the War for Independence.

Anaconda Plan
Name given to the blockade of the Confederacy General Winfield Scott proposed in 1861. Ridiculed at first, the blockade was adopted after the Union defeat at Bull Run. By the end of the war, the blockade had, like the constrictor snake, asphyxiated the southern economy.

annulment
Declaration by a religious or civil authority that an apparent marriage between a man and a woman was, in fact, never a valid marriage, as opposed to a divorce, which dissolves a valid marriage. Roman Catholics were (and are) not permitted to divorce; their marriages can be annulled for one of several specified reasons.

Anti-Masonic party
Founded in 1826 after the murder of a man who had published a book about the Masonic Order's secret rituals, it was a single-issue party aimed at destroying what seemed like the pervasive power of a sinister conspiracy. Briefly, the party had astonishing success, peaking in 1832 when it elected more than fifty congressmen. Most Anti-Masons became Whigs when that party was organized.

Arnold, Benedict (1741–1801)
One of the few well-trained, professional soldiers in the colonies at the outbreak of the Revolution. In 1775, in uneasy cooperation with Vermont militia leader Ethan Allen, he captured Fort Ticonderoga and several other frontier forts from the British. In 1776 he led a poorly planned, provisioned, and executed attack on Montreal and Quebec. A hero of the Battle of Saratoga in 1777, he believed he had been passed over for promotion and attempted to betray West Point to the British. His name became synonymous with "traitor."

assumption
The second part of Secretary of the Treasury Alexander Hamilton's financial (and political) program, the assumption of all state debts by the federal government. Hamilton overcame the opposition of Virginians James Madison and Thomas Jefferson by offering to use his influence to locate the permanent national capital on the Potomac River.

Atlanta Compromise
A "compact" between southern whites and blacks proposed by African-American educator Booker T. Washington in 1895. Blacks would accept social discrimination if they were provided opportunities to improve their economic lot by learning technical skills. Most southern blacks and

middle- and upper-class whites supported the Atlanta Compromise. It had no effect on lower-class whites' often violent racism.

baby boom
Term coined to describe the soaring birthrate that began in 1946 when young couples separated by World War II were reunited. Demographers expected the spike in the birthrate to be brief, but births remained high until 1964.

Baker, Ray Stannard (1870–1946)
One of the most responsible investigators (and best writers) among the muckraking journalists, Baker was critical of the Jim Crow segregation laws that were being enacted across the South at the turn of the century with progressive support. He became a devoted protégé of Woodrow Wilson and wrote an admiring biography of him.

Barbary Pirates
Commerce raiders sanctioned by the rulers of the Barbary States of North Africa (Morocco, Algiers, Tunis, Tripoli). They seized merchants of countries that did not pay an annual tribute. The United States sometimes paid the tribute but several times attempted to end the Barbary Pirate menace by bombarding and raiding their bases.

Bataan Death March
Forced march in 1942 of 10,000 American and Filipino prisoners of the Japanese up the Bataan Peninsula in the Philippines to prison camps in the interior. Japanese contempt for soldiers who surrendered resulted in deliberate starvation, beating, and even murder of the men. About 1,000 men died on the march. Another 5,000 died in the camps before the end of the war. The survivors were living skeletons, like the inmates of Nazi concentration camps.

Battle of Saratoga
On October 17, 1777, after several weeks of battling, British General John Burgoyne surrendered his entire army of redcoats and Hessians to General Horatio Gates near what is now the resort town of Saratoga, New York. Armies did not often surrender in the eighteenth century; they retreated to fight another day. Partly because of his own bad luck and partly because he was not reinforced as he expected, Burgoyne was trapped in the wilderness. The American victory was so momentous it brought France into the war.

Battle of the Bulge
Completely unforeseen German counteroffensive in Belgium in December 1944 aimed at splitting the Allied forces and capturing Antwerp, which was the key port in the Allies' supply line. The attack was initially successful, driving a large "bulge" in Allied lines.

Battle of the Little Big Horn
Greatest single victory by Plains Indians during the wars with the U.S. Cavalry. In June 1876 Colonel George Armstrong Custer led 250 men into a trap set by several thousand Sioux and Cheyenne warriors, who killed every soldier.

Battle of Yorktown
Only the second time during the War of Independence that a British army surrendered. General Charles Cornwallis was trapped on the Yorktown peninsula because three columns of American and French troops moved quickly to cut off any escape by land and a French fleet from the West Indies arrived to prevent British ships from evacuating Cornwallis by sea. The British surrendered in October 1781.

Benton, Thomas Hart (1782–1858)
Senator from Missouri between 1820 and 1851. He was a tireless spokesman on behalf of small family farmers. A personal enemy of Andrew Jackson (they were involved in a gunfight), he reconciled with Jackson when Jackson was elected president in 1828, and was one of his most valuable supporters in Congress.

Beringia
Scientific name (after Danish explorer Vitus Bering) for the "land bridge" between Siberia and Alaska during the last Ice Age over which human beings first crossed to the Americas.

Berkeley, Sir William (1606–1677)
Royal governor of Virginia (1642–1652, 1660–1677), he promoted emigration, particularly among Anglican gentry, and governed Virginia autocratically with the support of the wealthiest planters. Forced to flee a rebellion led by Nathaniel Bacon in 1676, he returned and hanged so many of Bacon's followers that King Charles II removed him from office.

Bessemer process
Technique of making steel from iron cheaply by blasting molten iron so that impurities (except for a precise quantity of carbon) were oxidized. It was developed simultaneously in the 1850s by Henry Bessemer in England and William Kelly in the United States. Although it was universally called the "Bessemer process," the U.S. Patent Office recognized Kelly as the earlier inventor.

Bethune, Mary McLeod (1875–1955)
African-American educator, the daughter of former slaves, she and Eleanor Roosevelt became close personal friends. As head of the Negro Affairs Division of the National Youth Administration, Bethune was the highest-ranking African American in the Roosevelt administration.

Biddle, Nicholas (1786–1844)
President of the Second Bank of the United States between 1823 and 1836. Biddle was a conservative and responsible banker who transformed the B.U.S., after poor beginnings, into a valuable regulatory institution. As a politician, however, Biddle was inept. He boasted not only of his power, but of the mischief he could cause if he chose to act irresponsibly. His arrogance played into the hands of the anti-Bank Jacksonians, who argued that, in a democracy, no private institution should have such power.

black codes
Laws enacted in 1865 by former Confederate states considered by President Johnson to be restored to the Union. Although they varied in details from state to state, all of the black codes reduced African Americans to a social and civil status inferior to that of whites. Northern anger over the black codes contributed to the defeat of Johnson's Reconstruction policies.

Black Friday
September 24, 1869. The price of gold plunged in hours from $162 an ounce to $135 when President Grant dumped $4 million in government gold on the market. Businesses were wiped out by the thousands. Tens of thousands of working people lost their jobs. The panic was brief but serious.

black power
Rallying cry coined by Stokely Carmichael, militant head of the Student Nonviolent Coordinating Committee during the mid-1960s. The slogan was used by diverse groups and individuals and meant many things ranging from black separatism to bloc voting.

Bleeding Kansas
Antislavery northerners' political reference to the violence in Kansas Territory between free-state and slave-state settlers that began in the wake of the Kansas–Nebraska Act of 1854.

bloody shirt
Republican party political appeal to voters of the Civil War generation. When orators "waved the bloody shirt," they reminded voters of the deaths and maimings in the war that was caused by the South, and that the Democratic party was the party of the South.

Blue Eagle
The symbol of the National Recovery Administration (NRA). For a year, during popular enthusiasm for the NRA's close regulation of businesses large and small, the Blue Eagle was ubiquitous in the United States.

blue laws
Laws regulating moral behavior such as activities forbidden on the Lord's Day, Sunday. Every American colony enacted them. The Puritan colonies of Massachusetts and Connecticut had the most comprehensive codes and were most rigorous in enforcing the laws.

Bonus Boys
World War I veterans who, in the summer of 1932, came by the thousands to Washington in an attempt to pressure Congress and the president to give them immediately as a Depression relief measure a bonus of $1,000 due them by law for their military service in 1945. President Hoover ordered General Douglas MacArthur to evict them from government buildings. MacArthur exceeded his instructions and attacked the Bonus Boys' Hooverville. The incident destroyed what was left of Hoover's reputation.

Booth, John Wilkes (1838–1865)
Well-known actor, a fanatical pro-Confederate, Booth organized a conspiracy to kill the leading members of the Lincoln administration after the fall of Richmond. Only he succeeded—in killing President Lincoln.

border ruffians
Name given by abolitionists and Free Soilers to western Missourians who regularly crossed the border into Kansas Territory to vote in territorial elections and bully free-state settlers.

Boulder Dam (Hoover Dam)
Colossal concrete dam on the Colorado River between Arizona and Nevada that is still one of the civil engineering wonders of the century. It is 700 feet high and spans 1,200 feet. The water in Lake Meade behind the dam irrigates farms in three states and Mexico. The power generated by the dam made possible the growth of Las Vegas, Nevada.

"bounty jumpers"
Professional deserters, more a problem in the Union than in the Confederacy. They enlisted in units that paid recruits a cash bounty, quickly deserted, and enlisted, for another bounty, in another unit.

Bourbons
Name given to the Democratic party political bosses of the southern states during the late nineteenth century; "Bourbon" was a reference to the family name of the kings of old-regime France, whose rule was synonymous with extreme conservatism. The Bourbons were displaced in some states in the 1890s by populistic Democrats, who assailed them for neglecting the needs of poor white southerners.

Bradley Martin ball
Extravagant high-society costume ball in New York in January 1897 during the depths of a serious depression, it was denounced as callous by moralists and as foolish by some business leaders, notably the great banker J. P. Morgan.

Brant, Joseph (1742–1807)
A Mohawk (his Iroquois name was Thayendanegea) who was an Anglican and related by marriage to a British official, he convinced most of his tribe to ally with the British against the Revolutionaries. He was the joint commander of a force that was defeated at Fort Stanwix when it tried to join Burgoyne's army at Saratoga.

brinkmanship
"The ability to get to the verge without getting into war" to further American foreign policy goals in the words of its chief exponent, 1950s Secretary of State John Foster Dulles. In the Cold War nuclear standoff the practice of brinkmanship did not allow much margin for miscalculation.

broad construction
A term applied later to Alexander Hamilton's contention that any action not explicitly forbidden to the federal government by the Constitution was constitutional. It became a unifying principle of the Federalist Party. Opposition to broad construction contributed to the emergence of the Jefferson Republican party.

Brown v. School Board of Topeka
Historic unanimous Court decision of 1954 that ruled racially segregated "separate but equal" schools, and by implication other racially discriminatory public institutions, to violate the constitutional rights of African Americans.

Buffalo Soldiers
Plains Indians' name for the African-American soldiers of the Ninth and Tenth Cavalry Regiments. Although other explanations of the name have been suggested, it almost certainly reflected the fact that the soldiers' nappy hair reminded straight-haired Indians of a bison's coat.

burned-over district
The name given to a swath of land across western New York that experienced one religious excitement after another in the 1820s, 1830s, and 1840s. It was a hotbed of religious mania and experimentation. Among the notable people who lived in the "district" were Charles Grandison Finney, William Miller, the Fox sisters, and Joseph Smith.

Calvert, George (1550?–1632)
and Cecilus Calvert (1605?–1675), father and son, the First and Second Lords Baltimore. Favorites at the court, they were Roman Catholic and envisioned their Maryland colony as a refuge for English Catholics, who were persecuted at home. All Christian worship was tolerated in Maryland under the Calverts.

carpetbaggers and scalawags
Derisive terms applied by southern Democrats to northerners who came to the South after the war to loot the defeated states (carpetbaggers) and southerners who betrayed the South and the white race to control the state governments by manipulating black voters (scalawags).

caucus
An Algonkian word adopted by Americans to mean a meeting of like-minded people to plan strategy for a common goal. Between 1804 and 1824 the Republican party named its presidential nominees in a caucus of the party's senators and representatives. (Until 1820 the Federalists did likewise.)

cavaliers
The name assumed by those who supported King Charles I in the English Civil War, it is an Anglicization of the French word for "knight." When they were defeated in the Civil War, many cavaliers of middling rank emigrated to Virginia to form the core of the Tidewater aristocracy.

Centennial Exposition
One of the earliest world's fairs, and the first in the United States, it was held in Philadelphia in 1876 to commemorate 100 years of independence. It is best known because its theme was American industry and technology. The telephone was first demonstrated at this exposition.

Central Powers
The name of the alliance of Germany, Austria–Hungary, and Italy in 1914. (Bulgaria was an associated nation.) The combination was opposed by the Allied Powers of Russia, France, and Britain. Many historians regard the existence of two hostile alliances of powerful countries as an important cause of World War I.

chads
A word known to few people before November 2000 when "chads" became central to determining the winner of the presidential election in Florida and, with Florida, the electoral college. A chad was the tiny piece of perforated paper popped out of punch card ballots used in some Florida election districts. Republicans claimed that if the chad was still clinging to the ballot, the ballot was invalid.

Channing, William Ellery (1780–1842)
Prominent Boston clergyman who, in 1819, denounced the Calvinist (Congregationalist) doctrine of predestination. He was instrumental in the founding of the American Unitarian Association in 1825 and became a moderate advocate of the abolition of slavery.

"China Lobby"
Name given (by its critics) to the not formally organized but active and influential network of prominent Americans who promoted Chiang Kai-shek as a great democratic leader who deserved massive American support in his civil war with the Chinese Communists. The "Lobby" included such people as Joseph Cardinal Spellman, Catholic archbishop of New York, and the publisher of *Time* and *Life* magazines, Henry Luce.

Citizen Genêt (1763–1834)
Edmond Charles Genêt, minister of France during the months President Washington was trying to keep the United States neutral in the war between France and Britain. Genêt commissioned Americans as French privateers, whose capture of British merchant ships caused Washington to order him to leave the country.

"Civil War Amendment"
Between 1804 and 1865, there were no amendments to the Constitution. Three amendments were rapidly ratified in the wake of the Civil War. The Thirteenth (1865) abolished slavery. The Fourteenth (1868) required the states to treat all citizens equally. The Fifteenth (1870) forbade denying the vote to any person on the basis of race, religion, or "previous condition of servitude"—that is, because citizens had been slaves.

Civilian Conservation Corps (CCC)
Created in 1933, the CCC provided jobs in national parks, national forests, and other federally owned lands. After initial anxieties, it was an extremely popular program. By the time it was disbanded in 1942, 500,000 men between the ages of 18 and 25 had passed through it.

civilized tribes," "the
A term applied to the Cherokee, Creek, Choctaw, and Chickasaw peoples of Georgia, Alabama, and Mississippi because they, unlike other tribes, were sedentary, farmed the land, and adopted other aspects of white American culture, including, in the case of the Cherokee, a comprehensive school system and newspapers. Although the civilized tribes disproved the rationale for removal—the incompatibility of white and Indian cultures—they too were forced off their lands.

Clinton, DeWitt (1769–1828)
Nephew of Jefferson's second vice president, Clinton was elected governor of New York in 1817. During the preceding decade he had been the chief promoter of a plan to join the Hudson River and Lake Erie with a canal more than 300 hundred miles long. After twice failing to win federal financial backing, he persuaded the New York legislature to fund "Clinton's Folly," the Erie Canal. The Erie Canal guaranteed that New York City would become—as it has remained—the nation's great metropolis.

Columbian Exchange
Term coined in the late twentieth century to describe the exchange, beginning in 1492, between the "Old World" (Europe, Africa, and Asia) and the "New World" of plants, animals, and micro-organisms previously known to only one of the "worlds."

Columbus, Christopher (1451?–1506)
Italian-born navigator who, in the employ of the queen of Castille (Spain), made a landfall in the Americas in 1492 while searching for a direct sea route to east Asia. He was the discoverer of America who "counted"; the European absorption of the Americas began with his voyage.

Committee on Public Information
Wartime agency headed by a progressive journalist, George Creel, the CPI censored war news in the interests of morale and also emphasized, through propaganda, the importance of universal patriotism, encouraging the suppression of dissent.

Common Sense
Pamphlet written by Thomas Paine and published in January 1776. In splendid prose, Paine vilified George III as a tyrant and condemned the institution of monarchy. It is generally agreed that the pamphlet was the single most persuasive propaganda in the debates of the Revolutionary era. Paine would write several more important works during the late 1700s.

Comstock, Anthony (1844–1915)
Anti-obscenity crusader who sponsored and wrote anti-obscenity laws in New York, Boston, and other cities, and even a federal law forbidding the use of the mails for distributing obscene materials. As a postal inspector, Comstock claimed to have destroyed 160 tons of obscene publications. His definition of obscenity included pamphlets explaining birth control methods. British playwright George Bernard Shaw coined the term "Comstockery" to describe excessive prudery.

Comstock Lode
The richest silver deposit in the United States, discovered—or rather recognized as silver—by gold miners in 1859. The principal town on the Comstock Lode was Virginia City, about midway between Reno and Carson City, Nevada. Virginia City produced silver well into the twentieth century.

conquistadores
Spanish for "conquerors." Beginning with the soldiers of Hernán Cortés, it was the name adopted by the men who won Mexico and Peru for Spain, as well as Spanish explorers who found no great kingdoms to conquer such as Francisco Coronado in the American Southwest.

containment
Name given to American policy toward the Soviet Union inspired by a memorandum by State Department officer George Kennan. Its purpose was to avoid war by measured responses to Soviet actions "containing" further Russian expansion.

copperheads
Strictly speaking, pro-Confederate northerners. However, Republicans used the term loosely to apply to Democrats who favored negotiation with the Confederacy or otherwise criticized Lincoln's policy so as to taint all critics with disloyalty.

Coral Sea
Site, off Australia, of the first great Japanese–American naval battle of World War II in early May 1942. The Japanese won a tactical victory, losing a light carrier but sinking an American fleet carrier. However, Coral Sea was a strategic defeat. Admiral Isoroku Yamamoto had not, as he hoped, cut the American supply line to Australia to force American and Australian troops to abandon Port Moresby in New Guinea.

corporate colony
A colony with a royal charter vesting governing powers in the shareholders of a commercial company. When landowners in corporate colonies became, in effect, the shareholders, corporate colonies were self-governing. Plymouth, Massachusetts Bay, Rhode Island, and Connecticut were such commonwealths for much of their history.

"corrupt bargain"
The charge hurled by Jacksonians at President John Quincy Adams and his secretary of state, Henry Clay, when the House of Representatives chose Adams over General Jackson in the skewed election of 1824. Jacksonians believed or, at least said, that in return for being named secretary of state, Clay used his influence in the House to have Adams chosen over Jackson.

Cortés, Hernán (1485–1547)
Spanish conqueror of Mexico, a bold soldier who combined the military

superiority of his soldiers, shrewd diplomacy, and manipulation of the Aztec emperor Moctezuma to conquer the empire for Spain.

cotton diplomacy
Confederate president Jefferson Davis's attempt in 1861 to bring Great Britain into the war on the southern side by creating a shortage of raw cotton on which the British textile industry depended. Davis kept the 1860 crop off the market. The strategy failed.

"cotton Whigs" and "conscience Whigs"
Terms applied during the 1850s to northern Whig politicians who were abolitionists (conscience Whigs) and those who hoped to downplay slavery and the sectional split as political issues because of the importance of southern cotton to northern industry—and because they hoped to avoid the split of the Whig party along sectional lines.

coverture
The English legal principle defining the status, in the law, of married women. When a woman married, her legal person was subsumed into her husband's. She was obligated to obey him; he controlled (although he did not legally own) any property she had held before the marriage.

Coxey, Jacob S. (1854–1951)
Wealthy businessman of Massillon, Ohio, who in 1894 led a march of the unemployed to Washington to petition for inflation of the nation's money supply and a massive public works program to create jobs. Although the march was well publicized for six weeks, Congress and the president ignored Coxey. He was arrested in the capital for a trivial offense.

crafts unions
Labor organizations comprising exclusively skilled workers such as locomotive engineers, carpenters, plumbers, iron molders, and so on. Crafts unions were generally successful in forcing employers to negotiate wages, hours, and job conditions.

Crawford, William F. (1772–1834)
Georgia politician; secretary of the treasury in 1824; considered the Virginia Dynasty candidate when the Republican caucus nominated him to stand for the presidency. His support was mostly restricted to the southern states.

CREEP
Phonetic acronym of the Committee to Reelect the President, President Nixon's campaign organization in 1972. The men caught burglarizing the Democratic party's national headquarters were CREEP employees, a revelation that eventually led to the president's downfall.

Crime of '73," "the
Name given to the Demonetization Act of 1873 by advocates of bimetallism, money redeemable in either gold or silver coin. The Demonetization Act, which terminated silver coinage, was motivated by the fact that national silver production was low in 1873 and the market price of the metal so high that few producers were presenting it to the U.S. mint at the government's submarket buying price. It was called a "crime" only several years later, when silver production had soared and the price of silver had declined.

dark horse candidate
A major party's candidate for the presidency who had not been considered a possible nominee, but who was selected by the party when it was unable to agree on serious contenders. In 1844 James K. Polk of Tennessee was the Democratic party's dark horse candidate when delegates who favored the annexation of Texas refused to accept Martin Van Buren, the party's most prominent leader. In 1883 the Republicans chose a dark horse candidate, James A. Garfield, when the convention deadlocked among three nominees who were bitterly opposed to one another.

de Champlain, Samuel (1570?–1635)
Founder of Quebec and, thereby, of the French empire in North America. He was the first governor of New France (Canada).

de Gardoqui, Diego
A Spanish diplomat who tried to divide the commercial northern states from the agricultural states by proposing to the Confederation Congress that Spain would open her colonies to American merchants if the United States gave up its treaty rights to navigate the Mississippi River. Northerners wanted to accept the offer; southerners and westerners threatened to break up the Confederation if the deal was made. The Mississippi was vital to them.

debt bondage
The plight of many southern tenant farmers, both black and white, in the final decades of the nineteenth century and well into the twentieth. Because of declining cotton and corn prices, tenants found themselves in debt to merchants (who were often their landlords) even after selling the year's crop, and therefore unable to terminate their tenancies. Debt put them in bondage.

Declaratory Act
Enacted by Parliament in March 1766, on the same day the Stamp Act was repealed, it stated Parliament's constitutional right to tax colonials. It was both a face-saving action and an assertion of a principle on which a large majority of members of Parliament agreed.

Democratic-Republicans
(and National-Republicans)
In 1828 there was just one political party, the Republicans. There were, however, two factions. Andrew Jackson's backers, with John C. Calhoun and Martin Van Buren, Jackson's southern and northern lieutenants, called themselves Democratic-Republicans. They were, by their own definition, the party of democracy. John Quincy Adams's supporters—his chief lieutenant was Henry Clay—called themselves National-Republicans to emphasize both Adams's and Clay's commitment to energetic national government. The Democratic-Republicans became the Democratic Party. The National-Republicans later became Whigs.

détente
The Nixon–Kissinger policy toward the Soviet Union and China: a realistic recognition that maintaining Cold War hostility indefinitely meant risking nuclear war and, in the meantime, involved the great powers in expensive, self-destructive limited wars, like the war in Vietnam. Détente did not end the Cold War as Nixon and Kissinger had hoped. Soviet leader Leonid Breszhnev and presidents Jimmy Carter and Ronald Reagan scuttled it.

Dillinger, John (1903–1934)
One of several midwestern bank robbers of the Great Depression who became something of a popular hero, in part because he cultivated a Robin Hood image, "robbing the rich and giving to the poor."

dime novels
Brief, cheaply produced, sensationalistic adventure books of the late nineteenth century often about western heroes, sometimes real people like James B. "Wild Bill" Hickok and William F. "Buffalo Bill" Cody. They were aimed at adolescent boys but were read by a great many adults and, certainly, adolescent girls too.

discretionary income
An individual's or household's income in excess of what is needed for necessities— "spending money." Traditional American culture prescribed that such money be saved or invested. In the 1920s people were encouraged to spend it on consumer goods. A considerable rise in discretionary income during and after World War II was the key to the consumption that has driven the American economy since.

dot.coms
Colloquial term for Internet companies that attracted billions in investment during a speculative mania in the late 1990s. A majority of them collapsed, many disappearing completely, in 2000–2001, wiping out the money invested in them.

"doughface"
Contemptuous name applied by antislavery northerners to northern Democrats who supported the South in sectional issues: "a northern man with southern principles." The implication was that they kneaded their faces, like dough, to appear to be one thing before northerners and another before southerners. Presidents Pierce and Buchanan were doughfaces; the greatest of the doughfaces was Stephen A. Douglas, and his attempt to mollify sectionalists in North and South was his undoing.

Douglas, Stephen A. (1813–1861)
Perhaps the most capable Democratic politician of the 1850s, he would certainly have been a more constructive president than either Franklin Pierce or James Buchanan, both of whom the party chose in preference to him. Determined to soothe sectional animosities, Douglas aggravated them so badly with his Kansas–Nebraska Act of 1854 that, even in 1860, when he might well have won the presidential election, southern Democrats rejected him and split the party.

Drake, Francis (1540?–1596)
English adventurer, commander of the second voyage around the world, the greatest of the "sea dogs." His seizures of Spanish ships and raids of Spanish seaports were so bold and damaging that the Spanish invested him with diabolical powers. He was a major figure in organizing England's defense against the Spanish Armada.

DuBois, W. E. B. (1868–1963)
African-American scholar and civil rights activist, he opposed Booker T. Washington's "Atlanta Compromise," instead urging blacks to demand full civil rights. DuBois believed that the future of African Americans depended on the creation of an educated elite, "the talented tenth." He was for many years editor of the *Crisis,* the journal of the National Association for the Advancement of Colored People.

"dumbbell" tenement
Winning design in a competition to find a healthful apartment building affordable by the poor. James E. Ware's dumbbell, so-called because of its shape from above, provided a window for every apartment. Unfortunately, when dumbbell tenements were constructed next to one another, the ventilation shaft between them was so narrow as to defeat the purpose of the design.

durante vita
Latin, a legal term meaning "throughout life." In Maryland and Virginia during the 1650s and 1660s, it was applied to Africans in servitude, explicitly defining them, on the basis of their race, as slaves.

Dust Bowl
A broad belt in the heart of the country extending from the Dakotas to Texas where, in 1935, after a prolonged drought, winds whipped the powdery topsoil into the air, where it was so dense that visibility in the worst-hit areas was reduced to ten feet for days at a time. The worst part of the Dust Bowl was in northern Texas and western Oklahoma.

dynamic conservatism
Dwight D. Eisenhower's "philosophy" of government in 1953. The words had little meaning; Eisenhower was a pragmatic president without an ideology who meant only to scale back the size of the government the New Deal and World War II had created.

East India Company
Trading corporation organized in 1600 much like the Virginia and Plymouth companies that founded the first English colonies in North America. Unlike them, the East India Company succeeded and, by 1773, was governing much of the Indian subcontinent. Parliament's Tea Act, which led to rebellion in the American colonies, was enacted to help the East India Company out of serious financial difficulties.

Eaton, Peggy (O'Neill)
The wife of Jackson's Secretary of War, John Eaton, whose reputation for sexual license caused her social ostracism by the wives of the members of Jackson's cabinet. The tempest in Washington society virtually immobilized the administration and threatened to shatter the recently built Democratic party coalition. In providing Jackson with a way out of the mess that offended no one, Martin Van Buren won the president's favor and, in time, Jackson's selection of him as his successor.

Eighteenth Amendment
The Prohibition amendment that forbade the manufacture, sale, transportation, and importation of intoxicating liquors in the United States.

El
Short for "elevated," or elevated railway; a solution to rapid, long-distance transportation in big cities. Pulled by steam locomotives in the nineteenth century, the passenger trains ran on iron and steel structures along principal streets, leaving the roadways below to pedestrians and horses and wagons. They were too expensive for all but the largest cities such as New York, Chicago, and Philadelphia.

Elizabeth (1533–1603, reigned 1558–1603)
Queen of England during the era in which England, previously a nation of secondary importance in Europe, began its rise to the rank of the world's great powers. The first

English attempts to found colonies in North America occurred during the "Elizabethan Age."

Emancipation Proclamation
Presidential order of September 22, 1862, stating that all slaves in territory controlled by rebels as of January 1, 1863, were henceforth free under American law. Lincoln hoped the proclamation might induce Confederates to make peace before 1863 as their best chance to retain their slaves.

enclosure movement
The practice of landowners in England from the sixteenth through the eighteenth centuries of enclosing with hedges fields previously devoted to crops, thus converting them into pasture for sheep. Farmers were thrown off the land that once supported them and formed a large impoverished class from which many settlers of the colonies were drawn.

Enlightenment
Term applied to the emergence of rationalism among educated Europeans and colonials in the late seventeenth and eighteenth centuries, and the decline of traditional nonrational religious beliefs among them.

enumerated articles
Colonial exports that could be shipped only to England even if their ultimate destinations were elsewhere. They were the colonies' most valuable and most easily sold produce: tobacco, cotton, sugar.

factory system
Manufacturing goods by machinery in watermill-powered (later steam-powered) factories by employees working full-time for wages. It replaced the "putting out system," hand manufacture at home, usually part-time as a supplement to farming and paid for by the "piece," the amount produced. The invention of powered machinery that replaced dozens, even hundreds of home workers made "cottage industry" obsolete in most kinds of manufacture.

farmers' Alliances
Farmers organizations of the 1880s, originally nonpolitical but, by 1890, active proponents of several reforms. There were three Alliances with more than a million members each: a "Colored Farmers" Alliance and a white organization in the South, and a white Alliance in the West.

favorite son
Candidate for a party's presidential nomination who is not a serious contender but who is nominated by a state as a personal honor or as a compromise possibility in a convention that deadlocks between two (or more) serious candidates. A favorite son candidate differs from a

dark horse candidate in that the former's name is put into nomination from the start of a convention. Franklin Pierce was a favorite son candidate to whom the Democrats turned in 1852.

Federal Reserve System
Created in 1913, it was a network of regional Federal Reserve Banks governed by a board of directors, most of whom were named by the president, with the power to regulate the money supply by setting the interest rates at which state banks borrowed money. The Federal Reserve was designed to give the government a say in banking decisions previously in the hands of the great New York private banks like J. P. Morgan. The Federal Reserve was a partial return to what Hamilton had envisioned in the Bank of the United States.

Field, Cyrus (1819–1892)
Successful self-made businessman (a paper manufacturer) who became obsessed with the idea of telegraphically linking the United States and Europe by means of a transatlantic cable. He sank his fortune and other large investments into several attempts between 1857 and 1866, succeeding in the latter year.

"Fifty-Four Forty or Fight!"
A popular slogan in 1845, this referred to the northern boundary of the Oregon Country (the southern boundary of Russian Alaska) at 54° 40' north latitude. If Great Britain did not yield the whole of Oregon, the United States would go to war. President Polk used the patriotic hysteria behind the slogan but had no intention of going to war with Britain in an attempt to win the northern part of Oregon (now British Columbia), where there was no American presence worth mentioning. He persuaded the British to divide the Oregon Country at the Webster–Ashburton line, 49° north latitude, which is the present Canadian–American border.

fire-eaters
A name applied to young southern politicians of the 1850s for whom the defense of slavery and the denunciation of antislavery northerners (in inflammatory words) was the heart of their politics. Commonly, they threatened secession from the Union when they believed slavery was threatened or the honor of white southerners insulted.

Fiske, John (1842–1901)
A Harvard historian who was the leading exponent of social Darwinism, the philosophy of Herbert Spencer, in the United States. Spencer's interest was in relationships within a society. He coined the phrase *survival of the fittest*, justifying as natural the fact that some grew extremely wealthy while masses

languished in poverty. Fiske applied this harsh principle to relations among the peoples—the "races"—of the world. That the white race dominated other races, he said, was not unjust or immoral, but the natural outcome of white superiority.

Fitzhugh, George (1806–1881)
Southern lawyer whose books combined praise of slavery as a benign institution and condemnation of the materialism of the North with its exploitation of free wage workers. He was a major proponent of the "positive good" proslavery argument.

Five Nations
Another name for the Iroquois Confederation of New York; the nations were the Mohawk, Senecas, Onandagas, Oneidas, and Cayugas. During the seventeenth century they were invaluable allies of the English colonies against the French.

flexible response
The Kennedy administration's alternative to the Eisenhower–Dulles Soviet policy of brinkmanship and "massive retaliation." The United States would respond to Soviet (or Chinese) provocations not with empty threats of all-out war but in proportion to the seriousness of the provocations, openly or covertly.

Florida land boom
Runaway speculation of the mid-1920s in land on Florida's Atlantic shore, especially in Miami Beach. Land prices reached absurd levels and then collapsed suddenly, wiping out millions of dollars. Despite the hard-hitting lesson in the inevitable consequences of irrational speculation, hundreds of thousands of Americans immediately began to speculate in stocks.

Fort Ross
Russian stockade and village built on the Pacific Ocean deep within Spanish Alta California in 1812. Russian expansion far to the south of Alaska worried John Quincy Adams. Fort Ross was a major reason for the proclamation of the Monroe Doctrine. The Russians hoped to supply Alaska with foodstuffs produced at Fort Ross. In 1839 they found another source of supply and abandoned the fort.

Foster, Stephen Collins (1826–1864)
The first writer of popular songs to be recognized as an individual. Despite the fact that he endlessly polished his lyrics before publishing his songs, Foster was a prolific musician and writer. He wrote many kinds of music, including genteel "parlor songs" for middle-class families. However, he was best known for songs, some in dialect, written for minstrel shows, which he insisted should not be called

"Ethiopian songs," which he regarded as demeaning. Foster meant to humanize African-American slaves and their relationships.

Fourteen Points, the
President Woodrow Wilson's list of American goals in the treaties that would end World War I. Most points were specific but expressed Wilson's ideals of national self-determination, freedom of the seas, and an organization of nations that would prevent future wars.

freedmen
Former slaves who were freed by the Emancipation Proclamation and the Thirteenth Amendment. The term referred to all former slaves—children and women as well as men.

Freedmen's Bureau
Federal agency administered by the army, established in March 1865. Its purpose was to provide food, clothing, and medical treatment to former slaves and white refugees and to supervise the distribution of small farms carved out of abandoned and confiscated lands. President Johnson's July 1866 veto of a bill extending the life of the Freedmen's Bureau transformed the tension between the president and congressional Republicans into open political conflict.

Freeman, Elizabeth
A slave in Massachusetts called "Mumber" or "Mumbet" who sued her master for her freedom on the grounds that the state constitution declared that "all men are born free and equal." She won her case; the judges freed all slaves in Massachusetts.

Freeport Doctrine
Propounded by Stephen A. Douglas in a debate with Abraham Lincoln at Freeport, Illinois. Although the *Dred Scott* decision said that territorial legislatures could not prohibit slavery, Douglas argued that a territory could keep slave owners out by failing to enact laws protecting property rights in slaves.

Friedan, Betty (1921–)
Author of *The Feminine Mystique*, published in 1963. It was scathingly critical of the social and cultural role assigned to middle-class women in the 1950s: lively housewife–mother and sexually attractive helpmate to her husband. Friedan became famous overnight and in 1966 was one of the founders of the National Organization of Women, which spearheaded the new feminism of the later twentieth century.

Fugitive Slave Act
One of the provisions of the North–South Compromise of 1850, it was designed to foil the underground railroad by which

1,000 to 1,500 slaves were escaping their masters each year. Antislavery northern state judges who had frustrated attempts to return runaway slaves were bypassed by the creation of federal commissioners who ruled on the claims of slave owners and slave catchers and assisted them. Northerners who aided runaway slaves were fined and jailed. The Fugitive Slave Act of 1850 meant that it was not enough for runaway slaves to escape to a free state; they had to get beyond the reach of American law, to Canada.

funding
The foundation of Hamilton's financial plan for the new government: the federal government would establish its credit by repaying the Confederation debt in full at face value. Speaker of the House James Madison opposed rewarding speculators by paying them on a par with payments to patriots who had lent the government money during the Revolution. But Hamilton won in Congress.

G.I.s
The name for themselves adopted by World War II soldiers. It referred to "government issue," the bureaucratic term for uniforms and other equipment handed out to recruits. It was the equivalent of the World War I term "doughboy."

"gag rule"
Derogatory term for a rule adopted by the House of Representatives in 1836 to table—that is, not to consider—abolitionist petitions presented to Congress. Congressman John Quincy Adams, while finding the abolitionists disruptive, insisted they had a right to be heard and eloquently fought against the gag rule.

Gage, General Thomas (1721–1787)
Commander of the British army in America named royal governor of Massachusetts in 1774 in the wake of the Boston Tea Party and the Coercive (Intolerable) Acts. Tragically for Gage, who was married to an American woman and sympathetic to Americans (he had lived in the colonies since 1763), it fell to him to administer policies that led to rebellion. His troops called him "Tommy the Old Woman" because of his reluctance to take aggressive action against the rebels, which was a reflection of his hopes that the dispute could be resolved without war.

GAR
The Grand Army of the Republic, a Union veterans' association (the equivalent of the Veterans of Foreign Wars today), founded in 1866, was a social organization and officially nonpolitical. In fact, it was a Republican party auxiliary, promoting pensions for veterans, a Republican issue. Its membership peaked in 1900 at 400,000.

Garvey, Marcus (1887–1940)
A Jamaica-born journalist who opened the United Negro Improvement Association (UNIA) in New York in 1916. He called for separation of the black and white races and a black "return" to Africa. Garvey was quite popular among African Americans in New York and other northern cities; but in 1923 the federal government imprisoned him for mail fraud, and the UNIA fell apart.

Gaspée
A royal schooner stationed in Narraganset Bay to collect customs and catch smugglers. When chasing suspected smugglers in 1772, the *Gaspée* ran aground. At night, it was boarded by colonials and burned, an act of rebellion. An intensive investigation failed to turn up a single witness willing to incriminate any of the arsonists.

Geneva Accords
International agreement of 1954 on the future of newly independent Vietnam. For two years the Communist-dominated Viet Minh would administer the northern half of the country, anti-Communist nationalists the south. In 1956 a democratic election would establish the nation's permanent government. The elections were never held when, with American backing, South Vietnam refused to participate.

ghettos
In its most common American usage, urban ethnic neighborhoods inhabited largely by members of a single national, cultural, or linguistic group. The original ghetto, in Venice, Italy, was the part of the city in which Jews were required to reside.

Gibson girl
The "ideal woman" of the 1890s, both in the fashions she wore and in her active lifestyle. The confident, glamorous Gibson girl was named after an illustrator, Charles Dana Gibson, who drew her in various situations for virtually all the prestigious magazines of the period. The most famous real Gibson girl was President Theodore Roosevelt's daughter, Alice.

gold standard
A currency in which paper money is redeemable on demand for gold coin or bullion. The value of gold standard money is stable because the amount of gold in existence does not decrease and rarely increases quickly. The United States went "on the gold standard" in 1873 when money ceased to be based on silver as well as gold. American money ceased being redeemable in gold in 1933.

Good Neighbor policy
American diplomatic policy in Latin America, instituted by President Hoover and adopted by Franklin D. Roosevelt, that reversed thirty years of gunboat diplomacy (military intervention) and dollar diplomacy (financial bullying). Hoover and FDR respected the sovereignty of the Latin American republics and dealt with them as equal states.

graduation
A reform of federal land law associated with Senator Thomas Hart Benton of Missouri, graduation provided that federal land unsold after auction be offered at half the minimum per acre price and, later, at one-quarter of the minimum. It was designed to make federal land affordable to a larger number of people.

grandfather clause
A device employed by several southern states to ensure that race-neutral disqualifications from the right to vote such as literacy tests applied only to African Americans. If a man's grandfather had voted before 1867, he was exempt from the obligation to prove his literacy. Because the laws clearly disqualified blacks, none of whose grandfathers could vote before 1867, the Supreme Court ruled grandfather clauses unconstitutional in 1915.

Grange
Popular reference to the Patrons of Husbandry, a farmer's organization founded after the Civil War to provide social and cultural diversions to farm families. (Local lodges of the patrons were called "granges," an old word for farmhouse.) During the 1870s, the Grange was politically active in a campaign to regulate railroad freight and storage rates.

Great Awakening
A widespread revival of religious piety in the colonies during the mid-eighteenth century. It split old denominations like the Congregationalists, Presbyterians, and Anglicans and promoted new ones, the Methodists and Baptists.

"Great Communicator"
Nickname attached to Ronald Reagan, president from 1981 to 1989, for his skill, honed by a career as a film actor, of persuading Americans to support him. The nickname was a play on Henry Clay's the "Great Compromiser." Reagan's critics called him the "Teflon president" because none of the many scandals of his administration "stuck" to him.

"Great Disappointment"
On March 21, 1844, thousands or hundreds of William Miller's followers—reports vary widely—gathered on hilltops or in churches in upstate New York to await the Second Coming of Christ, which Miller had predicted would occur on that day. When it did not occur, the Millerites called the day the "Great Disappointment." There was a second disappointment in October.

Great Society
President Lyndon B. Johnson's name for the reform legislation he pushed through Congress before and especially after his landslide victory in the election of 1964. Many of its social programs failed to accomplish Johnson's hopes. The Great Society was expensive, although it was the addition to them of the costs of the war in Vietnam that caused the government's fiscal crisis of the 1970s.

Greeley, Horace (1811–1872)
Founder of the *New York Tribune,* Greeley promoted free public education, temperance, and abolition. He was a founder of the Republican party, and during the last years of the Civil War, he was a radical who criticized Lincoln. By 1872 he had lost faith in radical Reconstruction and ran for president as the Liberal Republican and Democratic parties' candidate.

Green Berets
Officially known as "Special Forces," they were members of elite units in the U.S. Army specially trained in anti-guerrilla warfare in the Third World. The Green Berets were a favored project of President John F. Kennedy, who placed great importance on countering Soviet-inspired insurrections in undeveloped nations.

Green Mountain Boys
Informal militia in "Vermont," mountainous forestland claimed by the colonies of Massachusetts, New Hampshire, and New York. The leader of the militia, Ethan Allen, insisted that Vermont was independent of all. In 1775, along with militia from Massachusetts, the Green Mountain Boys forced the surrender of the British garrison at Fort Ticonderoga.

greenbacks
Colloquial term for paper money issued by the federal government during the Civil War; the backs of the bills were printed in green ink. Greenbacks were not redeemable in gold and fluctuated in value. During the 1860s and 1870s, their continuance divided gold standard conservatives and inflationists, especially farmers, who wanted to keep the greenbacks in circulation.

Grenada
Tiny Caribbean island republic occupied by American troops in 1983 when its Cuban-backed "Marxist" government collapsed. President Reagan justified the invasion because of the presence of Cuban troops, who turned out to be construction workers too old for military service.

Grenville, George (1712–1770)
First Lord of the Treasury who sponsored the Sugar Act of 1764 and the Stamp Act of 1765, taxes on the colonies that resulted in the first protests that led to the American Declaration of Independence.

Grimké, Sarah and Angelina (1792–1873) and (1805–1879)
Daughters of a distinguished and wealthy South Carolina planter and slave owner. They became abolitionists, and then, despite their social standing, they were harassed violently, so they moved to the North. Both were active members of the American Anti-Slavery Society. Angelina married abolitionist orator Theodore Dwight Weld.

Gulf of Tonkin Resolution
Legal basis for the American war in Vietnam, it gave the president authority to take whatever measures he thought necessary to defend against attacks on American armed forces. It was named for an incident in the Gulf of Tonkin in August 1964 when North Vietnamese patrol boats were said to have fired on American destroyers.

Gunsmoke
The most popular and longest-lasting of the more than forty "westerns" introduced by the television networks during the mid-1950s. At the peak of the mania, a third of television time in the evening was dedicated to shows set in the "Wild West." *Gunsmoke* had 635 half-hour episodes, a record for television production that lasted until the late 1990s.

"Half-Breeds" ("Stalwarts")
Two bitterly opposed factions of the Republican party during the 1870s and early 1880s. The Stalwarts, led by Senator Roscoe Conkling of New York, unabashedly defended the spoils system; "stalwart" workers for the party should be rewarded with government jobs. The Half-Breeds, led by Senator James B. Blaine of Maine, flirted with the civil service reform movement but, in reality, used the patronage as cynically as the Stalwarts did.

Hanna, Mark (1837–1904)
Cleveland industrial and an associate of John D. Rockefeller, he was, as early as the 1880s, impressed by William McKinley and determined to make him president. McKinley's lack of intellectual luster and his close relationship with Hanna persuaded many that Hanna manipulated McKinley as if he were a puppet. In fact, the two men seem to have had a friendship of equals.

Harlan, John Marshall (1833–1911)
Long-serving justice of the Supreme Court who was the sole dissenter in *Plessy* v. *Ferguson* (1896), which approved "separate but equal" public accommodations for blacks and whites: segregation. In an eloquent dissent, Harlan, a southerner who had owned slaves as a young man, wrote that separate facilities for blacks were inherently equal because they were "badges" of inferiority.

headright system
Device meant to encourage emigration to Virginia. An emigrant was granted fifty acres of land for every person (per head) whose costs of transportation to Virginia he paid: himself, members of his family, other free people, and servants.

Henry the Navigator (1394–1460)
Portuguese prince who devoted his life to organizing expeditions of discovery into the Atlantic and to the south of Portugal along the western coast of Africa. He also encouraged improvements in ship design and navigational instruments.

Henry, Patrick (1736–1799)
Virginia lawyer who rose to prominence as a protestor in the 1760s and 1770s as a fiery anti-British orator. Henry remained in politics after independence but lost his following due in part to his inconsistency.

Hiawatha (1520?–?)
Poet Henry Wadsworth Longfellow's spelling of the name of a sixteenth-century Iroquois who devoted his life—successfully—to eliminating war among the five Iroquois tribes of New York and establishing a confederacy for the resolution of intertribal disputes.

hidalgo
Spanish for low-ranking noble. Many Spaniards who were not of noble blood claimed to be hidalgos, demanded the rights accorded nobility, and affected aristocratic manners and pretensions.

Homestead
The largest factory in the world when it was constructed in the 1870s outside Pittsburgh, Pennsylvania. Homestead was the centerpiece of Andrew Carnegie's steel manufacturing empire and the site of a violent strike in 1892.

Homestead Act
Adopted by Congress in May 1862, it gave 160 acres of federal land free to any citizen or immigrant intending to become a citizen who agreed to build a dwelling, live on the land, and cultivate it.

Hooverizing
Slang term during World War I (and for some years thereafter) meaning economizing. Herbert C. Hoover, wartime Food Administrator, issued one voluntary program after another for economizing on food production.

Hoovervilles
The humorous but bitter name—a dig at President Herbert Hoover—given to ramshackle shantytowns built on vacant lots in cities during the early Depression by unemployed people who lost their homes. In New York City a huge,

sprawling Hooverville was built in Central Park.

Howard University
Founded in 1867 and named for the white general who headed the Freedman's Bureau, O. O. Howard, this was the most prestigious and probably the best African-American university in the country. No longer a blacks-only institution, it remains reputed for excellence.

Huguenots
French Protestants similar to the English Puritans; their religious beliefs were similar to those of England's Puritans. They were a minority in France troublesome to the Crown until one of them became king as Henri IV. He became a Catholic but, in 1598, issued an edict giving the Huguenots limited toleration and political rights. When toleration was revoked in 1685, most of them left France.

Hundred Hours War
President George H. W. Bush's name for the astonishingly rapid destruction of the much-vaunted Iraqi army in 1991 when the United States expelled Iraq from oil-rich Kuwait. The president was disappointed in the aftermath of the brilliant military campaign. He expected the obviously discredited Saddam Hussein to be overthrown by Iraqis, but he was not.

Hutchinson, Anne (1591–1643)
Extraordinary Massachusetts woman who confounded the governors of the colony by challenging orthodox religious teachings and the seventeenth-century assumption that religious doctrine was for women to accept and not to ponder. She was banished to Rhode Island but relocated in New Netherlands, where she was killed by Indians.

I-beam girder
Steel girder, so-called because it was shaped like an "I" in cross-section. Perfected by William L. Jenney in 1885, it made possible the construction of skyscrapers because the weight of the tall buildings was borne by a riveted internal skeleton rather than thick stone foundations and walls.

IBM cards
Properly known as "Hollerith cards" after their inventor, they were most Americans' introduction to the computer. Data were fed into early computers on the cards (slightly larger than a dollar bill) in which clerks punched holes representing names, addresses, and courses in which students wished to register; or, a step forward, students and applicants and examinees for a job blacked in "machine-readable" boxes on the cards. The computer did the rest.

impressment
The eighteenth- and nineteenth-century term for what we would call conscription or the draft. Impressment was forced military service. During the 1790s and early 1800s, British impressment of seamen on American ships into the Royal Navy (the British claimed they were British subjects and therefore subject to impressment) contributed to the growth of demands that the United States go to war to defend the country's honor and independence.

indentured servants
The principal source of labor in the colonies during the seventeenth century, and a major source in the northern colonies during the eighteenth century. In return for passage to America and some other compensation, poor men and women, mostly English during the 1600s, bound themselves to work for a master for three to seven years. Their contract was called an "Indenture."

Indian Reorganization Act
Law of 1934 allowing Indian tribes to form corporations that could take control of lands previously allotted to individual Indians, a system that had resulted in the loss of much of the land reserved for Indians in 1884. The Reorganization Act encouraged traditional Indian religions, crafts, and customs.

Industrial Workers of the World
Revolutionary labor union founded in 1905, it opposed the American Federation of Labor's insistence on admitting only skilled workers. Instead the IWW admitted all workers and organized them in "industrial unions" that included all workers in an industry. Members were known as "Wobblies," a name they accepted.

initiative
A progressive political reform at the state or municipal level. A means by which voters can bypass elected legislators who fail to enact a popularly supported law, it provides that if a specified number of signatures on a petition are certified, the measure on the petition will be presented to voters in a referendum. If it wins a majority, the measure becomes law regardless of the legislature's or governor's inaction.

Insurgents
The name given to progressive Republican congressmen, mostly from the Midwest, who angered President Taft by voting with Democrats in the House of Representatives to reduce the powers of the reactionary House Speaker, Joseph Cannon. Taft denied campaign funds to the Insurgents in the midterm election of 1910. Two years later, the Insurgents deserted the Republican party to support Progressive party candidate Theodore Roosevelt in the presidential election.

Inter Caetera
A papal bull (proclamation by the pope binding on Catholics) of 1493 in which Pope Alexander VI divided all the world's land not in the possession of a Christian ruler between Spain and Portugal.

interchangeable parts
Mass-produced castings of small metal parts so nearly identical that they could be used interchangeably: one of the foundations of the industrial economy. Eli Whitney demonstrated gun locks made of interchangeable parts before Congress. He was awarded a contract for 10,000 muskets. His process proved to be not up to the job, but the technology was perfected by others.

internal improvements
What today would be called "public works." Internal improvements were government-financed (sometimes government-owned) construction projects designed to boost the economy. They included harbor improvements, dredging rivers for navigation, and roads. The greatest and most famous federally financed internal improvement of the early nineteenth century was the National Road.

Interstate Commerce Commission (ICC)
The first permanent federal regulatory commission, established by Congress in 1887 in response to demands for the regulation of railroads. The ICC was ineffective in its early years not because of lack of authority but because most commissioners were closely tied to the nation's great railroad companies.

Interstate Highway Act
Congressional act of 1956 appropriating $1 billion a year—by 1960 $2.9 billion—to construct limited-access, fast highways connecting major cities and, eventually, ringing cities. The act was justified by fiscal conservatives as essential to national defense.

Iran–Contra affair
Secret arrangement engineered by top officials in the Reagan administration to aid pro-American rebels in Nicaragua (the "contras") in violation of the Boland Act. Missiles were sold to the Khomeini government in Iran, which had abetted the long captivity of American hostages with some of the profits given to the contras. If President Reagan was aware of the transaction, he was guilty of a federal crime. If he was not, high-ranking members of his administration were making policy without his knowledge.

Iroquois
Linguists' names to the three major language families of the Eastern Woodlands Indians. There was also a distinct tribe in Canada the French called Algonquin.

Jay Cooke and Company
The largest and most prestigious investment bank in the United States during the 1860s and early 1870s, it was the federal government's borrowing agency during the Civil War. When the bank failed in 1873, it caused a panic that led to a serious depression.

jayhawkers
Armed free-state irregulars in eastern Kansas in the middle and late 1850s, the equivalent of the proslavery border ruffians from Missouri.

Jesuits
Priests belonging to the Society of Jesus, a well-educated, disciplined, militant, flexible order devoted to missionary work. Jesuits were the most important religious order in New France. They were extremely successful in winning Indians to Roman Catholicism.

John Birch Society
Right-wing extremist organization founded by candy manufacturer Robert Welch. Members believed an international Communist conspiracy had infiltrated and controlled American education, churches, and the federal government. It was influential in the Republican party during the mid-1960s.

John Brown's Raid
Seizure of the federal arsenal at Harper's Ferry, Virginia, by a small band of men led by abolitionist John Brown in the fall of 1989. Brown's tiny army was killed or captured within a few days, but the threat of a slave rebellion Brown intended to start convinced many southerners that abolitionists, abetted by the Republican party, threatened their personal safety.

"Johnny Reb" (and "Billy Yank")
The name Union soldiers chose to personalize Confederate soldiers, the equivalent of Johnny Reb's "Billy Yank."

joint occupation
After Spain and Russia abandoned their claims to the Oregon Country (the present states of Oregon and Washington, the Idaho panhandle, and the Canadian province of British Columbia), the United States and Great Britain agreed to a "joint occupation" of the area. This put other nations on notice that their claims in Oregon would be resisted. However, by granting the few transient British and American nationals there equal rights and protection, joint occupation avoided an Anglo–American conflict. By the mid-1840s, a large American population in the south part of the Oregon Country made the unusual device obsolete.

Jomini, Antoine-Henri (1779–1869)
Swiss general whose treatise on battlefield tactics, *The Art of War,* was translated into English and adapted into a book widely read at West Point. To some extent, every Union and Confederate officer with formal military training had been educated in Jomini's school.

judicial review
The Supreme Court's power, now accepted without question, to declare an act of Congress signed by the president unconstitutional, therefore invalidating it. There is no mention of such a power in the Constitution, although the principle was well known. The Supreme Court asserted its right to invalidate acts of Congress in *Marbury* v. *Madison,* 1803.

King Caucus
The term coined in 1824 to denigrate the caucus or meeting of Republican senators and representatives to select the party's presidential candidate. 1824 was the final year the caucus met.

King George III (1738–1820, reigned 1760–1820)
King of Great Britain during the crisis that led to the American War of Independence and the Revolution itself. He was somewhat unfairly made the scapegoat of American grievances. His reign was longer than that of any other British monarch except Queen Victoria, although he was helplessly insane during the final decades of his life.

king's friends," "the
The name given the Parliamentary faction bound by patronage to George III. Unlike his predecessors, George I and George II, who favored the "Whigs" who had put them on the throne, George III favored the "Tories" who supported greater royal participation in government.

kitchen debate
Propaganda stunt well-planned and executed by Vice President Nixon on a visit to the Soviet Union in 1959. At an exposition, in front of a mockup of a well-equipped modern American kitchen, Nixon engaged Soviet Premier Khruschev in a comparison of the American and Russian standards of living that Nixon could not lose.

"Know-Nothing" party
Derisive name for the American party of the 1850s, an anti-immigration and anti-Catholic movement that won control of several states between 1852 and 1854, electing forty-three members of Congress.

Kultur
The German word for "culture." German nationalists spoke much of the virtues, even the superiority, of German culture. Anti-German propagandists exploited popular revulsion toward the harsh German occupation of Belgium and what seemed to some the immorality of submarine warfare to describe *Kultur,* using the alien and vaguely menacing German spelling and pronunciation, as meaning brutality and savagery.

land grant universities
The Morrill Act of 1862 gave state governments federal lands—30,000 acres for each member of Congress—which were to be used to finance public universities. They were required to have agricultural and mechanical courses of study and military science, but were permitted to add other programs that the states chose. The sixty-nine schools eventually founded under the Morrill Act are known as land grant universities. Eventually 17 million acres were distributed to the states in aid of education.

Landon, Alfred M. (1887–1987)
Governor of Kansas and the Republican presidential nominee in 1936. Landon was a former Bull Moose Progressive and considered himself a liberal. The Republican party chose him to dodge the label "economic royalists" that FDR had pinned on them. Landon won the electoral votes of only two states.

League of Nations
The international organization founded in the Treaty of Versailles that would, President Wilson hoped, avert future wars by providing a permanent assembly in which differences between nations would be peacefully resolved. Opposition to the League was widespread in the United States, which was never a member.

Lecompton Constitution
Proposed Kansas state constitution, making Kansas a slave state, submitted to Congress in the fall of 1857. Congress rejected the Lecompton Constitution because Stephen A. Douglas and other northern Democrats joined Republicans in insisting that it be ratified by a territorywide referendum.

Levittown
Name of several American cities built after World War II by William Levitt in response to the severe housing shortage.

liberty ships
Freight-carrying vessels mass-produced during World War II. They were fragile but quickly and cheaply made. About 2,700 of them were built between 1941 and 1945. At the end of the war, several new ones were finished every day.

Liliuokalani (Lydia Kamekeha, 1838–1917)
During the long reign as king of Hawaii by her pro-American brother, David Kalakaua, Liliuokalani, like him, was an ally of the small white American oligarchy that dominated the islands. However, when she became queen in 1891, she revoked

the constitution that gave the Hawaiian Americans their power and proclaimed that only native Hawaiians could vote. She was immediately overthrown, and seven years later, the United States annexed Hawaii.

Looking Backward

A novel by Edward Bellamy published in 1888, it depicted twenty-first century America as a utopia made possible by democratic socialism, which Bellamy called "Nationalism." The novel inspired the creation of mostly middle-class "Nationalist Clubs." Bellamy himself joined the Populist party, founded in 1892, but was disillusioned when, four years later, the Populists abandoned their reform program.

Louisbourg

A French fortress on Cape Breton Island (northern Nova Scotia). The French were the masters of fortification architecture, and they considered Louisbourg impregnable. It was a haven for French privateers who harassed New England fishermen and merchant ships. An army of New Englanders captured the fortress at a great cost in lives in 1745. British peacemakers returned it to France, causing considerable resentment in New England.

Lusitania

A British transatlantic liner torpedoed and sunk by a German submarine off the coast of Ireland in May 1915. Some 1,200 of 2,000 people aboard were killed, 139 Americans among them. A wave of anti-German anger swept the United States because the ship ostensibly carried only passengers. (In fact, there were munitions aboard.)

machine gun

The most significant of many weapons first used on a massive scale between European powers during World War I. The machine gun, at relatively little cost, increased a soldier's firepower from 50 to 100 times. Its impact ended the era of the infantry (and cavalry) charge.

Mainline Canal, the

The most ambitious of the canals built in imitation of the Erie Canal's astonishing success, Pennsylvania's Mainline Canal was specifically designed to restore Philadelphia as a legitimate competitor of New York City as an exporter of western produce and a supplier of manufactures to the West. It was longer than the Erie and traversed far more difficult terrain, which was its undoing. There were 174 locks on the Mainline Canal compared to the Erie's 84.

Mandan

Unique Plains Indian tribe in that, in addition to hunting bison, Mandan were also farmers and lived in substantial dwellings in fixed villages. They had been hospitable to whites since they provided winter quarters for the Lewis and Clark expedition. The Mandan were destroyed as a tribe by smallpox and by the enmity of the Sioux, who repeatedly attacked them.

Manhattan Project

Code name for the huge, expensive, secret development of the first atomic bomb. It began in three locations in 1939 with hundreds of scientists, few of whom knew the purpose of the specialized research to which each was assigned. The bomb was intended for Germany, which, President Roosevelt feared, might be first to develop an atomic bomb. Germany was defeated before the bomb was finished, but the only two in existence (one was exploded in a test) were dropped on Japan, ending the war.

"Manifest Destiny"

Clearly obvious destiny, a phrase coined by Democratic party journalist John L. O'Sullivan in a newspaper article favoring the annexation of Texas in 1845. It was, he wrote, America's "manifest destiny to overspread the continent." The phrase caught on as a slogan during the Mexican War and became part of American political language.

Mann Act (1911)

Federal law making it a crime to transport a woman across state lines for prostitution or "other immoral purposes." Ostensibly aimed at organized "white slavery," entrapment of girls into unchasteness and, therefore, prostitution by seduction or rape, most Mann Act defendants were men who crossed a state line accompanied by women with whom they had consensual sexual relations with no money changing hands.

manumission

The legal freeing of a slave by an owner, a synonym for *emancipation,* manumission was a legal procedure regulated by states. During the 1780s and for several decades thereafter, with slavery in widespread disrepute, southern states made manumission easy.

Marquette, Jacques (1637–1675) and Louis Joliet, sometimes Jolliet (1645–1700)

A Jesuit priest and trapper who found the portage connecting the Great Lakes and the Mississippi River system, descended the Mississippi to the mouth of the Arkansas River, and concluded that the Mississippi emptied into the Gulf of Mexico, not the Pacific. Their discoveries laid the groundwork for the expansion of the French Empire.

Marshall Plan

American program, announced in 1947, for financial aid to European nations where World War II had so destroyed the economy that rapid recovery was impossible without outside assistance. It was designed to head off the social turmoil that might bring Communists to power.

McCarthyism

Named for Senator Joseph McCarthy of Wisconsin who, in the early 1950s, used the effective technique, the term refers to the silencing of critics and the intimidation of potential critics by accusing all opponents of being secret Communists, "fellow travelers"(non-Communists who backed the party lines), or "comsymps" (Communist sympathizers). McCarthy included even General George C. Marshall in this category.

mercantilism

The name later given to the philosophy that dominated English economic policy beginning in the seventeenth century. Mercantilists held that the government should closely regulate a nation's economic activity, particularly in encouraging trade, to increase the flow of wealth, in the form of gold and silver coin, into the nation.

mercenary

Soldier who fights for whoever will pay him rather than for king, country, religion, or any other such cause. Armies of the sixteenth century (and through the eighteenth) were comprised largely of mercenary soldiers.

merchants-adventurers companies

Enterprises involved in foreign trade owned not by an individual but by several, sometimes numerous shareholders, who shared the costs of investment, the risk, and any profits. They were chartered by the king and given special privileges to encourage investment. The companies that founded the earliest English colonies were patterned on the merchants-adventurers companies.

Merrimack

The world's first ironclad warship, a ram, introduced by the Confederate navy in March 1862 to break the blockade of the Chesapeake Bay by wooden vessels. The *Merrimack* was effective but was immediately neutralized by a Union ironclad, the *Monitor,* which fought her to a draw.

Mesoamerica

Mexico and Central America, the land mass between North and South America. (In Greek *meso* means "between.") It was the home of one of the two advanced civilizations that originated in the Western Hemisphere.

Metacomet (?–1676)

Wampanoag chief known to New Englanders as "King Philip." In 1675 he formed the first pan-Indian anti-white alliance in American history, winning the cooperation of tribes that were ancestral enemies. Briefly successful, King Philip's rebellion was crushed; he was killed, his head impaled on a stake in Boston.

metes and bounds

Legal description of property lines that refers to other properties and roads and to natural features of the land such as watercourses, outcroppings of rock, even trees. Of European origin, the metes and bounds system was adopted by the colonies and even used in lands sold in Kentucky during the 1780s after the system had been abandoned in the Northwest Territory.

Millerites

Followers of William Miller, who preached that the end of the world—the Second Coming of Christ—would come in 1843 or 1844. When his prophecy proved faulty, remnants of the Millerites regrouped as the Seventh Day Adventists.

minié balls

Despite the word *ball*, conical bullets favored by both northern and southern infantry during the Civil War because of the more disabling wound they produced.

minstrel show

Minstrel is a medieval word meaning a traveling musician. In the United States beginning in the 1840s, the word was applied specifically to a formulaic stage show featuring white performers in "blackface" makeup pretending to be plantation slaves who sang, danced, parried humorously with one another, and performed comic skits. Minstrel shows remained popular throughout the nineteenth century.

missile gap

Disparity between the number of intercontinental ballistic missiles in the American and Russian nuclear arsenals unfavorable to the United States. It was a theme of John F. Kennedy's campaign for the presidency in 1960. The "gap" did not exist, but President Eisenhower could not respond without revealing how many missiles the United States had and how many American intelligence believed the Soviets possessed.

Missouri Compromise (1820)

Engineered by Henry Clay to end an angry North–South sectional split over the application for statehood, with slavery, of Missouri Territory. Missouri was admitted as a slave state, Maine as a free state so that the numbers of slave and free states remained equal. The compromise forbade future slave states in territory north of 36° 30′ north latitude, placating antislavery northerners.

Mitchell, John (1870–1919)

A coal miner at the age of 12, he was president of the United Mineworkers Union before he was 30, increasing its membership from 40,000 to 200,000. He became extremely popular as the moderate head of the union during the bitter anthracite miners' strike of 1902, which ended in a victory for the workers. Later he became a vice president of the American Federation of Labor. Mitchell was not the stainless hero many believed him to be. Late in his career he was beset by well-founded rumors that he took payoffs from mine owners to settle disputes.

Moctezuma II, sometimes Montezuma (1480?–1520, reigned 1503–1520)

Emperor of the Aztecs. His bewilderment at the appearance of Cortés with his army and his indecisiveness were key elements in the extraordinary Spanish conquest of Mexico.

"Monkey Trial"

Trial in Dayton, Tennessee, in 1925. John Scopes was prosecuted for violating a state law prohibiting the teaching of Darwin's theory of evolution in public schools. The trial was sensational news nationally because of the participation of celebrities such as William Jennings Bryan and attorney Clarence Darrow.

Monroe Doctrine

Proclaimed by President Monroe in 1823 (although he did not use that name), its significant provision was that the United States declared the Western Hemisphere closed to further colonization and restoration of imperial authority. In diplomatic but unambivalent language, Monroe stated that any such European actions would be regarded as an act of war against the United States.

Moral Majority

Political action committee organized in 1980 by the Rev. Jerry Falwell to work for the presidential campaign of Republican nominee Ronald Reagan. Falwell blamed liberal Democratic politicians and courts for the decay of traditional moral standards and an increasing crime rate.

"moral suasionists"

The temperance movement of the early nineteenth century split early on how to fight the evil of drunkenness. Moral suasionists said that drinking, in moderation or at all, was the individual's moral decision. Their program was to encourage people to drink moderately or preferably to swear off drinking "T-totally." Legal suasionists insisted on removing the possibility of drinking by forbidding the manufacture and sale of alcoholic beverages.

"more bang for a buck"

Flippant description of President Eisenhower's policy of sharply reducing federal expenditures on the traditional army and navy in favor of spending on the production of nuclear weapons and the planes and missiles to deliver them, a less expensive defense program.

muckrakers

Journalists specializing in exposés of corruption in business and politics or examining social evils such as racial discrimination or child labor practices. They were given the name by President Theodore Roosevelt because they "raked muck" looking for stories. The term was taken from a well-known religious book of the Reformation period, John Bunyan's *Pilgrim's Progress.*

mugwumps

Derogatory name given to Republican reformers, mostly genteel New Yorkers, who supported Democratic presidential candidate Grover Cleveland in 1884 because of his honest record. "*Mugwump*" was said to be an Algonkian Indian word meaning "big shot."

Muir, John (1838–1914)

Born in Scotland, raised in Wisconsin, Muir suffered an accident that injured his eyesight but sent him on a 1,000-mile hiking trip when he became enamored of wilderness. Success as a fruit grower and marriage to a well-to-do woman allowed Muir to devote himself full-time to exploration of the Sierra Nevada and remote parts of Alaska. He was instrumental in protecting California's Yosemite Valley as the second national park in 1890. Two years later he founded the Sierra Club, still the nation's largest and most influential preservationist organization.

Muskogean

Linguists' names to the three major language families of the Eastern Woodlands Indians. There was also a distinct tribe in Canada the French called Algonquin.

NAFTA

The North American Free Trade Area Treaty, signed by Canada, the United States, and Mexico in 1994. Patterned on the European Common Market, which had been an economic boon for western Europe, NAFTA provided for the elimination of trade barriers among the three North American countries over a period of fifteen years.

National Road

Also called the Cumberland Road after its eastern terminus, Cumberland, Maryland, the head of navigation on the Potomac River. Originally it ran to Wheeling (then in Virginia, now West Virginia) on the Ohio River. Henry Clay of Kentucky promoted its extension to Vandalia, Illinois, which provided cross-country transportation to parts of Ohio, Indiana, and Illinois that did not have easy access to the Ohio River. Eventually the road continued to the Mississippi opposite St. Louis.

Nauvoo
City in western Illinois that, during several years in the 1840s as the home of Joseph Smith and the Mormons, was the largest city in the state. Nauvoo prospered, but after Joseph Smith was murdered by a mob in 1844, Brigham Young led the Mormons to the Great Salt Lake basin.

Navigation Acts
Parliamentary acts (1660–1663) regulating colonial trade so that it benefited the mother country. For example, all trade had to be carried in English or colonial-owned ships manned by English or colonial sailors.

New Deal
The slogan of the Democratic party's presidential campaign coined by candidate Franklin D. Roosevelt when he dramatically flew to Chicago after his nomination to address the nominating convention. He pledged himself to a "New Deal for the American people."

"New Democrat"
Designation adopted by a number of rising young Democratic politicians after the Reagan–Republican election sweep of 1980. With the label of "liberal" in bad odor, the New Democrats supported black civil rights and liberal positions such as abortion on demand but appealed to tax-conscious voters by promising responsible, frugal spending policies. The most successful of the New Democrats was Bill Clinton of Arkansas.

"New Era"
Slogan coined by apologists for the Coolidge years, 1923–1929, when (they said) business culture, endorsed and abetted by the federal government, had ushered in permanent and ever-increasing prosperity. The New Era ended with the stock market crash of October 1929.

New Federalism
Nixon's slogan (which never caught on) for his policy of distributing to the states federal money to finance Great Society programs. It was a meaningless sop to anti–Great Society Republicans. It did not reduce Lyndon Johnson's welfare state legislation and actually increased the size of government bureaucracies.

new immigrants
A term coined during the 1890s to distinguish the immigrants of that period, mostly from southern and eastern Europe, from the "old immigrants" of the years preceding 1880, most of whom were British, Irish, and German. Many Americans believed that the new immigrants could not be assimilated.

New Nationalism
The name Theodore Roosevelt gave to the far-reaching program of progressive reform he outlined at Osawatomie, Kansas in 1910. Roosevelt revived the program and the name in his Bull Moose party candidacy for the presidency in 1912. His Democratic opponent in the election (and the victor), Woodrow Wilson, called his much less ambitious program the New Freedom.

"NINA"
Abbreviation found in "help wanted" advertisements in newspapers, on shop windows, and at factory gates during the later nineteenth century. It meant "no Irish need apply," reflecting hostility toward Irish Americans during the period.

"nine old men"
President Franklin D. Roosevelt's ill-advised term in 1937 for the nine justices of the Supreme Court after they invalidated, by narrow margins, several key New Deal laws. Roosevelt wanted to add justices to the Court to ensure a pro–New Deal majority. For the first time in his presidency, public opinion was against him, and he backed off.

normalcy
Word popularized during the presidential campaign of 1920 by Republican candidate Warren G. Harding. Harding used the term instead of *normality* in the speechwriter's text because, to him, *normality* implied mental health. The word was widely ridiculed.

Northern Securities Case (1904)
The Northern Securities Company was a holding company designed by banker J. P. Morgan. Its purpose was to end ruinous competition of three major northwestern railroads. Theodore Roosevelt earned the nickname the "trustbuster" when his administration convinced the Supreme Court that the company was a monopoly illegally in restraint of trade. The company was dismantled.

Northwest Ordinances
A series of laws enacted by the Confederation Congress between 1784 and 1787 that provided for the creation of future states in the Northwest Territory: lands west of Pennsylvania and north of the Ohio River. Slavery was forbidden in the Northwest Territory so as to reserve the land for family farmers.

O'Connor, Sandra Day (1930–)
First woman to sit on the Supreme Court. She was appointed by President Reagan in 1981 because he expected her to be a solid conservative vote on the Court and, no doubt, to annoy feminists, most of whom were Democrats. O'Connor was an undistinguished justice; her conservatism was cautious, never shrill like some other Republican-named justices of the era. She retired, pending appointment of a replacement, in 2005.

Okies
Name given to the thousands of Dust Bowl refugees (not all from Oklahoma) who migrated west to California, mostly by automobile, along U.S. Highway 66. Originally the term was derogatory, signifying dirt-poor, ignorant yokels; but after a few years, the "Okies" themselves, taking pride in overcoming disaster, adopted it fondly.

Omaha Convention
1892 convention of the newly founded Populist party in Omaha, Nebraska. Its platform called for comprehensive political, economic, and social reforms.

Omnibus Bill
Henry Clay's name for the law he drafted to resolve the sectional crisis of 1850 with compromise between militantly proslavery southern congressmen and antislavery northerners, both abolitionists and Free Soilers. In this context omnibus means "including all"; Clay's bill addressed all differences between proslavery and antislavery Americans and required each side to make concessions. In the end, all of Clay's proposals were adopted, but not as a single act of Congress. Zealots of both sides voted against the Omnibus Bill because they refused to concede some questions for the sake of a compromise.

OPEC
Acronym for Organization of Petroleum Exporting Nations, a cartel formed behind Saudi Arabian leadership in 1960 but not effective until the 1970s. OPEC's mostly undeveloped countries had large oil reserves and cooperated in reducing production, thereby raising the price of oil. During the early 1970s OPEC's production cuts caused severe gasoline shortages in the United States.

Open Door
The name given to an international China policy defined in a series of "Open Door notes" that Secretary of State John Hay circulated among the imperial powers to sign. The Open Door policy guaranteed that China would not be carved into colonies and that all nations would have the right to trade everywhere in the country. The British, who had devised the policy to avoid an imperialist scramble such as the one that carved up Africa, gladly signed Hay's notes. Germany and Japan disliked the policy but were pressured to sign.

Operation Overlord
Name of the project—unprecedented in scale—of assembling the massive force of soldiers, weaponry, and a transport fleet for the invasion of western Europe in World War II. Overlord culminated in D-Day, June 6, 1944, on the beaches of Normandy. It was headed from its inception in June 1942 by Dwight D. Eisenhower, whose command of the complex secret operation and conciliatory management of difficult subordinates was masterful.

Orphan Boy
A Mississippi steamboat, undistinguished among the hundreds of paddle-wheelers on the river when it was built in 1841 except that, with 40 tons of cargo aboard, it floated in water just two feet deep. That was the record. Most designers settled for a draft of four feet and much more tonnage in cargo.

Ostend Manifesto
Declaration signed in Ostend, Belgium in 1854 by the American ministers to Spain, France, and Britain. It recommended to President Pierce that the United States should offer to buy Cuba from Spain for $120 million and, if Spain should refuse, take Cuba by force.

outer perimeter
First Japanese strategic object in World War II, to establish a ring of strong defensive positions from the mid-Pacific south and west to New Guinea (even northern Australia) and in southeast Asia, thus preventing the United States from attacking closer to Japan than 2,000–3,000 miles.

Pacific Railway Act
Congressional legislation of 1862 authorizing the first transcontinental railroad, it set the pattern for western railway construction by subsidizing (with land grants, loans, and other financial guarantees) private companies to build and own the lines.

paddyrollers
Southern dialect for patrollers: armed and mounted bands of white men, sometimes volunteers, sometimes hired by the county, who rode the roads and plantations of the South by night looking for slaves who were abroad. With broad legal powers, the usually rough men were known for their brutality, feared, and hated.

Paleo-Indians
literally "old Indians" (*paleo* is Greek for "old"); anthropologists' term for the ancestors of the native Americans whom Europeans called "Indians."

Palmer, A. Mitchell (1872–1936)
Attorney General under Woodrow Wilson who, during Wilson's convalescence in 1919, tried to win support for his presidential ambitions by launching a series of raids on radical and, particularly, communist offices and meeting places.

Patton, George W. (1885–1945)
Commander of the Seventh and later the Third Army in Europe in World War II, he was probably the best American battlefield commander. He understood as early as World War I that the tank and mobility held the key to future wars. He was killed in an automobile accident shortly after the war ended. There was no role for him in Cold War America except that of shrill dissident.

"peculiar institution"
Term by which white southerners referred to slavery. It was a euphemistic alternative to saying the word *slavery*, just as eighteenth-century slave owners had called their slaves "servants" and nineteenth-century planters often called their slaves "my people." However, it was also a pointed reference to the fact that although slavery was not unique to the South by the fourth decade of the century, it was almost unique, distinct and particular to the American South.

Pendleton Act
Federal law of 1883, enacted in the wake of Garfield's assassination, it established the Civil Service Commission, which administered examinations to applicants for some government jobs so that appointments were made on the basis of merit rather than party affiliation. By 1900 almost half of all government employees were protected from dismissal for political reasons.

Penn, William (1644–1718)
Heir of a wealthy English family who became the leading member of the Society of Friends (Quakers) and consecrated his land grant in America (Pennsylvania) to Quaker principles, including religious toleration.

Pennsylvania System
An early but quickly abandoned prison reform: all inmates lived in solitary confinement in individual cells. The hope was that long meditation on their crimes would result in individual reform; it was a method of punishing crime rooted in the evangelical belief in personal redemption. However, the Pennsylvania System was expensive, and mental breakdowns among convicts were frequent. More successful was the Auburn System, in which convicts were together for work and meals (although rarely permitted to converse).

Perot, Ross (1930–)
Erratic, self-made Texas millionaire and philanthropist who declared himself an independent candidate for president in 1992 during a television interview. His announcement caused a groundswell of support among people, mostly described as conservatives, who put him on the ballot in almost all fifty states. Perot drew 19 percent of the popular vote and would probably have drawn more had he not briefly withdrawn from the campaign alleging personal attacks on his daughter.

Perry, Oliver Hazard (1785–1819)
American naval officer who, with a fleet of ten vessels, hurriedly and poorly built on the banks of Lake Erie, and defeated and captured a superior British fleet in the Battle of Lake Erie. By eliminating further British threats on the lake, Perry's victory compensated for serious American setbacks on land, restoring the war on the Canadian border to a deadlock.

pet banks
The Whigs' name for the state banks in which, after they lost the Bank War with Jackson, the president deposited government revenues. Many of the pet banks proved irresponsible when sums of money previously unimaginable were given to them. Their freewheeling "wildcat" loans contributed to a repeat of the Panic of 1819 and, after Van Buren's inauguration in 1837, a serious depression.

petite guerre
French for "little war," roughly the equivalent of the English term "American style." Petite guerre consisted of sudden surprise attacks on outlying New England villages and towns, destruction of them, and quick withdrawal. Attacks were usually supervised by French officers but carried out by Indians.

Pickett's Charge
The Confederate frontal assault on the Union center across open country on the third day of the Battle of Gettysburg in July 1863. It was a blunder. Lee attacked the Union army at its strongest point.

pig iron
The form in which manufacturers of steel and finished iron goods purchased iron from iron smelters. The ingots were called "pigs" because of their rounded shape, like a pig at rest.

Pike, Zebulon (1779–1813)
Army officer who, on orders from Louisiana Governor James Wilkinson in 1806, explored the southern part of the Louisiana Purchase and into Spanish Mexico. Pike's party traveled 4,000 miles; but the expedition was not as celebrated as Lewis and Clark's, probably because, in part, President Jefferson suspected Pike was involved in the "Burr Conspiracy." He was not.

Pilgrims
Term applied to the small sect of Separatist Puritans by one of their leaders, William

Bradford. They were Calvinists but insisted on separating from the Church of England; they were the dominant people in the Plymouth colony, founded in 1620.

Pinkertons
Employees of the Pinkerton Detective Agency. Originally a company that provided bodyguards and criminal investigators, the agency was best known in the late nineteenth century for helping employers destroy labor unions among their workers.

Pitt, William the elder (1708–1778)
Energetic and effective head of the British government during the French and Indian War. Pitt designed the policy of concentrating British military might in North America.

placer mining
The method of mining employed by the men who flocked to California in the great gold rush of 1949 and for several years thereafter. Placer gold was pure gold mixed with sand, earth, and gravel of river beds. Extracting it was an entirely mechanical process—washing it from the worthless dirt called "tailings"; no chemicals or expensive heavy machines were necessary. The Forty-Niners shoveled the gravel into a wooden box or trough with riffles at the bottom to catch the heavy gold while a constant stream of water floated the lighter sand and clay away. As long as the placer deposits held out, a poor man was at no disadvantage. Anyone willing to work could mine placer gold.

Plymouth Company (and London Company)
Commercial companies—early corporations—chartered by the Crown in 1606 and granted land in North America where they were authorized to found colonies. The London Company founded Jamestown, Virginia, in 1607, the Plymouth Company Plymouth Plantation in Massachusetts in 1620.

pocket veto
Article 1, Section 7, of the Constitution provides that a bill approved by Congress becomes a law ten days after the president receives it (or sooner if he signs it) unless he vetoes the bill, explaining his objections to it. However, if Congress "prevents" the president's return of an unsigned bill by adjourning within ten days of sending it to the president, the bill fails to become law, and the president is not required to write a veto message. This is called a "pocket veto."

Pontiac (1720?–1769)
Chief of the Ottawas, a loyal ally of the French during the French and Indian War. Like King Philip before him and Tecumseh after him, he led a multitribal uprising against the British in 1763 aimed at driving them out of what is now Ohio, Indiana, Michigan, and Illinois. His warriors

captured ten of twelve British forts; they were defeated at the battle of Bushy Run.

popular sovereignty
Strictly defined, rule by the majority of people. In politics after 1854, the term referred to the principle of the Kansas–Nebraska Act that a majority of the settlers of Kansas (and other territories) would decide by majority vote whether they would enter the Union as slave states or as free states.

"positive good"
Catchword applied to the aggressive defense of slavery that was a response to the abolitionist movement during the 1830s. Most white southerners had considered slavery at best a necessary evil saddled on the South by history. After 1830, proslavery Americans ceased to be defensive and maintained that slavery was a positive good for both whites and blacks.

preemption
Sometimes called "squatter's rights," it was a proposed reform of federal land law that allowed squatters, people who had improved federal land before it was offered for sale, to buy what were their homes at the minimum per acre price. Preemption was designed to prevent speculators from outbidding actual settlers for land they had improved.

Proclamation of 1763
Shaken by the unforeseen Indian uprising led by Pontiac, the king and Parliament forbade colonials to settle west of the Appalachian ridge that separates the watersheds of streams flowing into the Atlantic and those emptying into the Ohio and Mississippi rivers. It was intended to allow a cooling-off of relations with the Indians, most of whom had been allies of the French.

proprietary colony
A colony owned by a man or group of men who were given large American land grants and the right to govern them by the king. Most of the colonies were, at least briefly, proprietary colonies. The two most successful were Maryland, owned by the Calvert family, and Pennsylvania, owned by the Penns.

Puritans
The name given to and accepted by English Calvinist Protestants; the word referred to their determination to purify the Church of England of Roman Catholic rituals and practices. Puritan emigrants peopled much of New England.

Quebec Act
Parliamentary act of 1774 regarded by some colonists as one of the Coercive (Intolerable) Acts designed to punish Massachusetts. It gave official status to the French language and Roman Catholic religion in Quebec and extended the boundaries of the province to the Ohio

River, which incorporated into the province the country over which Britain and the colonies had fought France in the French and Indian War.

Queen Isabella (1451–1504, reigned 1475–1504)
Queen of Castille (Spain), known as "Isabella the Catholic" for her piety; she sponsored and partly financed Christopher Columbus's historic explorations.

"QWERTY"
The arrangement of keys on the keyboard of the first successful typewriter, it remains the arrangement of computers today. The configuration of letters was dictated by the fact that the strikers on manual typewriters were mechanically operated. To avoid jamming, Sholes kept the strikers of the most frequently used letters at a distance from one another.

recall
A progressive political reform at the state or municipal level, often coupled with the initiative. The recall enables voters to remove an elected official from office before his or her term has expired. As soon as a sufficient number of signatures on a petition to recall an official are certified, the question is put to voters in a referendum. If a majority votes to recall, the official is removed from office.

rectangular survey
The innovative system of land survey adopted by the Confederation Congress for the Northwest Territory. It impressed a gridiron pattern on the Territory before opening the land to sales. The rectangular survey was later adopted to other territories acquired by the United States from France and Mexico.

Red Scare
Term first applied to the post–World War I era when Attorney General A. Mitchell Palmer encouraged widespread fear that Communists seriously threatened American institutions and stability. The second Red Scare was during the Korean War, when Republicans, particularly Senator Joseph McCarthy of Wisconsin, convinced many Americans that the federal government was honeycombed with Communist subversives.

referendum
A popular election not to choose among candidates for a public office but to approve or disapprove a measure such as legislation put on the ballot by initiative, an official up for recall, or an amendment to a state constitutional or municipal charter.

Regulators
Back country farmers in the Carolinas who resented the neglect of their interests by the North and South Carolina colonial

governments. They created their own illegal county governments and collected taxes, which they refused to send to the colonial capitals. The Regulators were defeated in the Battle of Alamance in 1771.

removal
The Indian policy of the federal government and most western state governments between the 1810s and the 1840s. Because Indian communal culture, based largely on hunting, was incompatible with American individualism and agriculture, Congress, the presidents, and state legislatures signed treaties, one by one, with the eastern tribes in which the Indians agreed to remove to west of the Mississippi, usually to Indian Territory (present-day Oklahoma), giving up their claims to land east of the river.

Revere, Paul (1735–1818)
Boston silversmith and leader of the city's Sons of Liberty. His engraving of the Boston Massacre of 1770 misrepresented the British soldiers as aggressively attacking Bostonians. In 1774, on horseback, Revere rushed the militant Suffolk Resolves from Boston to Philadelphia where the First Continental Congress was meeting. The next spring, he made the shorter but more famous "Midnight Ride of Paul Revere," dashing into the Massachusetts countryside to warn rebellious farmers that British troops were marching to Concord to seize colonial arms stored there.

revisionists
Historians of World War I who claimed that underlying the stated reasons for American intervention in World War I was the fact that American financiers and munitions makers had so great a stake in a British victory that they maneuvered the United States into the war.

rider
Legislator's term for a (usually unrelated) clause that is attached to a bill already under consideration in Congress or in a state assembly. The proponent of the rider avoids the risk of having a committee prevent it from reaching the floor. By attaching it as an "amendment" to a bill that Congress cannot easily vote down, such as an appropriations bill, those who dislike the rider will—it is hoped—have to hold their noses and vote for it.

"Rock of Chickamauga"
Nickname given to Civil War General George H. Thomas for preventing a rout of Union troops at Chickamauga by holding his line like a "rock." Thomas was a Virginian but refused to join the Confederacy.

Rogers, Will (1879–1935)
The most popular humorist of the 1920s and early 1930s. Originally a rope trick performer in vaudeville, Rogers's running patter, sharply witty but delivered in a folksy Oklahoma drawl, and his engaging smile made him a national favorite on the stage, on radio, and in films. Part Cherokee, Rogers boasted of his Indian heritage. He was highly political and actively praised President Roosevelt.

Rough Riders
The informal name given to a volunteer cavalry unit of the Spanish–American War associated with future president Theodore Roosevelt (although he was actually second in command). The name was stolen from Buffalo Bill's *Wild West* show. Many of the Rough Riders were showpeople, athletes, and cowboys. By exaggerating the Rough Riders' role in capturing San Juan Hill outside Santiago de Cuba, Roosevelt made his name a household word.

round robin
A petition on which signers wrote their names not below the text of their demands, but in the margins around the text. The message was that there was no single instigator or leader of the movement, but that all signed it as equals.

royal colony
A colony administered by the Crown. No colonies were founded as royal colonies. However, all were "royalized," taken over by the monarch, before the War for Independence except Rhode Island, Connecticut, Maryland, and Pennsylvania.

Sacco and Vanzetti
Italian immigrant anarchists arrested for armed robbery and murder in 1920, convicted for the crime, and sentenced to death. They became the focus of an international protest movement based on the belief that they were innocent and were being railroaded because they were Italian immigrants and political radicals. Sacco and Vanzetti were electrocuted in 1927.

safety bicycle
Invented late in the 1880s (by whom is disputed), it replaced the dangerous big-wheel "bone crusher" and in the 1890s made bicycling, already a popular recreation among young men, a national mania. In essentials, the design of the safety bicycle is identical to bicycles today. Its most important social consequence was its attractiveness to women, who defied the convention that women should be physically inactive; young women became as avid bicyclists as young men.

salutary neglect
Salutary means "healthy," "wholesome." The term refers to the colonial policy of British Prime Minister Robert Walpole: so long as the colonies were profitable to British manufacturers and merchants, it would be folly to antagonize colonials by close political control and even strict enforcement of trade laws the colonials violated.

Samuel Gompers (1850–1924)
Principal founder of the American Federation of Labor and its annually elected president from 1886 to 1924. Gompers believed in organizing only skilled workers and in working for "bread and butter" goals: high wages and shorter hours. He opposed ultimate utopian goals.

Santa Fe Trail
Trail between Independence, Missouri and Santa Fe in Mexico (now New Mexico) blazed by William Becknell, a trader, in 1821. For fourteen years, wagon convoys of increasing size carried American goods over the trail, exchanging them for furs, silver, and gold. The Santa Fe Trail tied Santa Fe more closely economically to the United States than to Mexico.

Schlieffen Plan
Secret German military plan to resolve Germany's problem in facing powerful enemies in both the east (Russia) and the west (France). First proposed in 1905 and often amended, the plan called for an all-out attack on France, forcing France (and possibly Britain) out of the war before Germans moved east to fight Russia.

Scotch-Irish
Protestant Irish from Northern Ireland (Ulster) whose ancestors were lowlands Scots settled in Ireland on lands confiscated from Catholic Irish. They had been a combative people in Scotland and Ireland; they remained so in North America, where they were the largest single immigrant group in the eighteenth century. Most settled on the frontier and were the vanguard of expansion into Indian lands.

sea dogs
The name adopted by intensely Spain-hating English seafarers, mostly from Devonshire in the southwest, who, during Elizabeth I's reign, raided and looted Spanish ships and ports when, officially, England and Spain were at peace.

Second American Party System
Between the mid-1790s and about 1816, the Federalists and the Jefferson Republicans competed for power in the United States. The Federalists disintegrated after the War of 1812 and, until 1824, the Republicans were effectively the only American party. In 1824 the Republicans shattered. Beginning in 1828 the Democratic-Republicans, later the Democratic party, cohered under the leadership of Andrew Jackson. In 1834 the Whig party was organized in opposition to the Democrats. This second party system survived until the 1850s, when the Whig party fell apart. The emergence of a new

Republican party, which included former Whigs, marked the beginning of the third party system that survives today.

Second Continental Congress

Meeting of delegates from the thirteen colonies, convened in 1775, which dispatched George Washington to take command of rebellious militiamen in Massachusetts and, in July 1776, adopted the Declaration of Independence. The Congress was the governing body of the "United States" throughout the War for Independence.

Section 7(a)

The section of the National Industrial Recovery Act of 1933 that obligated employers to bargain with labor unions approved by a majority of employees. When the Supreme Court declared the NRA unconstitutional, Congress reenacted Section 7(a) as the Wagner Act of 1935.

Serra, Junípero (1713–1784)

A Franciscan missionary in Mexico who, between 1769 and 1784, founded nine missions in California between San Diego and San Francisco. The missions were self-sufficient Indian communities governed by priests like Serra. Eventually, missions were built within a (long) day's walk of one another so that travelers along the *camino real* never had to sleep outdoors.

settlement house

An immigrant aid institutions, founded in immigrant neighborhoods during the final decades of the nineteenth century, that provided charity but also educational and recreational programs. The most famous one was Hull House, founded by Jane Addams in Chicago.

Seven Sisters

Seven elite women's colleges in the Northeast, most founded in the late nineteenth century. Named after the Pleiades, seven sisters of Greek mythology—and a constellation—they were the social equivalent and, at the turn of the century, probably the educational equals of the Ivy League colleges. Four of the Sisters were in Massachusetts (Mount Holyoke, Radcliffe, Smith, and Wellesley); two were in New York (Barnard and Vassar); and one was in Pennsylvania (Bryn Mawr).

sharecroppers

Tenant farmers who, in return for use of the land, a cabin, a mule and plow, and seed, gave the proceeds from the sale of (usually) half of the crop to the owner of the land. Sharecropping developed in the South in response to the fact that landowners needed people to work the land and former slaves needed a means of making a living and a place to live.

Shays' Rebellion

Armed uprising of several thousand farmers in western Massachusetts led by Daniel Shays. They resented the state's taxation policies, which favored mercantile interests in Boston, and Boston's political domination of the state. The rebellion was easily suppressed; but the fact that it started at all sufficiently alarmed conservatives that they welcomed the proposal to meet and strengthen United States government.

Sherman Antitrust Act

Congressional legislation of 1890, it forbade business combinations (monopolies and near-monopolies) "in restraint of trade"—that is, combinations designed to eliminate competition. It was ineffective during the 1890s because the attorneys general of the decade were unsympathetic with its purposes and the courts hostile.

Sherman bow ties

The name given by General Sherman's soldiers in Georgia to sections of rail that they heated over fires of railroad ties and bent into the shape of bow ties around telegraph poles. "Sherman bow ties" symbolized of the totality of the destruction the army wreaked in Georgia.

siglo de oro

Spanish for "golden century." It refers to the 1500s when American gold and silver made Spain by far the richest, most powerful, and most feared country in Europe.

"single tax"

The brainchild and rallying cry of a movement inspired by Henry George's book, *Progress and Poverty*, published in 1879. George's proposed "single tax" was to be levied on "unearned increment"—income from mere ownership of property, such as rents, which owed nothing to enterprise or ingenuity.

slave driver

Term applied to a supervisor of slaves—an overseer—who was himself a slave. In African-American folklore after the Civil War, slave drivers were more brutal than white overseers or masters. Frederick Douglass said as much in his autobiography. The personal exemption from heavy labor being a slave driver entailed, and other privileges, were apt to encourage such behavior.

"slavocracy"

A word contrived by antislavery Republicans as an equivalent of *democracy* or *aristocracy*, meaning rule by the "slave power."

Smith, Al (Alfred E. Smith, 1873–1944)

Popular and successful reform governor of New York through most of the 1920s,

he was the Democratic presidential candidate in 1928. Smith lost, mainly because it was a time of prosperity. But because of anti-Catholicism he also failed to carry eight southern states that were dependably Democratic: Smith was a Roman Catholic.

social Darwinism

Philosophy or "ideology" of the late nineteenth century that justified great wealth, even when made by ruthless and unethical means, by defining economic life in terms associated with the Darwinian theory of evolution: "survival of the fittest" and "law of the jungle."

Social Security

The name given to the federal program that, beginning in 1935, provided pensions for the elderly. Federal old age pensions were not in the New Deal's original plans; the Democratic party established Social Security because of the popularity of an unrealistic pension plan advocated by Dr. Francis Townsend of California.

Specie Circular

President Jackson's 1836 directive to the Treasury Department to accept only specie (gold and silver coin) in payment for federal lands. Jackson's purpose was to halt a runaway inflation in paper money issued by state banks, a crisis for which he was in part responsible. With only about one gold dollar for every ten paper dollars in circulation, the Specie Circular caused a rash of bank failures and, a year later, a serious depression.

Spillane, Mickey (1918–)

Author of the "Mike Hammer" crime novels popular during the 1950s; by 1956 all seven of Spillane's books were on the list of the ten best-selling books of all time. Private detective Mike Hammer was brutal, in fact murderous; Spillane also pushed laws proscribing the description of sexual activities to the era's limits.

Spirit of St. Louis

Name of the plane specifically designed by Charles A. Lindbergh and others for a single flight: the first solo crossing of the Atlantic by air, which Lindbergh completed in 1927 in the greatest occasion of popular hysteria in a decade in which there were many.

"spoils system"

The view that government jobs should be used by the party in control to reward those who supported the party and worked for its success in elections. Government jobs were the "spoils" of political war. A Jackson supporter, William Marcy, put it bluntly in 1829: "To the victor belongs the spoils." In introducing the spoils system to the federal government in 1829, Jackson broke with the tradition—an ideal rather than, necessarily, the reality—that the people best qualified to do a government job should be appointed to it.

stagflation

Term coined during the presidency of Gerald Ford to describe an unprecedented economic phenomenon: simultaneous inflation and recession (stagnation). Previously inflation had characterized an overheated economy, and prices had fallen during recessions.

"Stalwarts" (and "Half-Breeds")

Two bitterly opposed factions of the Republican party during the 1870s and early 1880s. The Stalwarts, led by Senator Roscoe Conkling of New York, unabashedly defended the spoils system; "stalwart" workers for the party should be rewarded with government jobs. The Half-Breeds, led by Senator James B. Blaine of Maine, flirted with the civil service reform movement but, in reality, used the patronage as cynically as the Stalwarts did.

Stamp Act of 1765

Second attempt by Parliament to tax the colonies. It was met with violent protest and the Stamp Act Congress, a concerted action by delegates from nine colonies. The Stamp Act was repealed before it went into effect.

Stanton, Elizabeth Cady (1815–1902)

One of the founders of American feminism, she resented the disabilities she suffered because of her sex from girlhood. In 1840, on her wedding trip to Europe, she and several other women were denied the right to sit on the floor of an antislavery convention. From then on, while raising seven children, Stanton devoted her life to winning the vote and professional opportunities for women and reforming divorce laws.

Starr Report

Report of a committee chaired by Kenneth Starr ostensibly investigating the Clintons' involvement in dubious finances in Arkansas. Finding nothing incriminating, the committee investigated Clinton's sexual relationship with a young White House intern, Monica Lewinski. Starr tricked Clinton into lying under oath, then presented physical evidence proving his perjury. The Starr Report led directly to Clinton's impeachment in 1998.

Stimson Doctrine

American proclamation in 1931 (erroneously attributed to Secretary of State Henry L. Stimson; it was President Hoover's decision) that the United States would recognize no territorial changes accomplished by armed aggression. It was a response to the Japanese detachment of Manchuria from China.

Stono

A plantation in South Carolina that was the center of a slave rebellion in 1739. The slaves, some of them Roman Catholics from the Congo, hoped to escape to Spanish Florida, where, outside St. Augustine, there was a fortified village of runaway black slaves.

strict construction

The counterpart to "broad construction" argued in Washington's cabinet by Secretary of State Thomas Jefferson. Jefferson said that the Bank of the United States Hamilton proposed was unconstitutional because the Constitution did not specifically allow Congress to create such an institution. Jefferson's strict construction of the Constitution was a foundation of his commitment to small, weak government.

subtreasury system

After the demise of the Second Bank of the United States in 1836 and President Jackson's unsuccessful experiment depositing federal funds in state banks, the "pet banks," President Martin Van Buren in 1837 attempted to disassociate the government from banking by establishing "subtreasuries," essentially government vaults in which all federal monies would be stored. The system was never really functional because the government ran a deficit each year of Van Buren's presidency.

Suffolk Resolves

A series of resolutions drafted in Boston (Suffolk County, Massachusetts) in 1774 and carried to the First Continental Congress in Philadelphia where they were adopted. The Suffolk Resolves were assertive without being rebellious in their opposition to the Intolerable Acts; they helped to steer the colonial protest movement toward defiance of the king and Parliament.

Sugar Act (1764)

Parliamentary legislation that lowered the duty on molasses imported from outside the empire but also provided for enforcement by vice-admiralty courts, which were without juries. It was the first attempt to tax the colonies that was roundly protested.

supply-side (economics)

Name given to a federal economic policy formulated by Arthur Laffer and adopted by the Reagan administration. Cutting taxes the wealthy paid would increase the nation's supply of goods and services; unemployment would be reduced by the growing economy; the distribution of wealth—each person's share—would take care of itself. "Reaganomics," as critics called the president's policy, was an updating of the "trickle down" theories of Andrew Mellon, secretary of the treasury during the 1920s.

sweatshop

Name applied to hand manufacturing in private apartments, it was the bulwark of the needle trades (finishing men's and women's garments with buttonholes and the like). The sweatshop was the urban equivalent of the traditional "putting-out" system.

swing states

States in which the Democratic and Republican parties were about equal in strength during the late nineteenth century and that could, therefore, "swing" either way in presidential elections. The most important swing state was New York, with 35–36 electoral votes. Only in 1876 did the victorious presidential candidate fail to carry New York, and that contest is known as the "stolen election."

tabloids

Strictly speaking, newspapers printed in a new format introduced during the 1920s. Their pages were half the size of traditional newspapers and turned like the pages of a book rather than unfolding. They were convenient for urban readers who commuted in crowded trolleys and subways. In practice, tabloids emphasized sensational scandals over conventional news.

Taft, William Howard (1857–1930)

The twenty-seventh president of the United States, he was unfairly maligned as a reactionary (and has been since by some historians). In fact, Taft was an able functionary with a phlegmatic judicial temperament—which he knew. He did not want to be president and hated being president. He wanted to be a judge, and fortune smiled on him. In 1921 the Chief Justice of the Supreme Court died just a few months after his successor would have been named by the Democratic Wilson. But a Republican was president, and he gave Taft the job that he had wanted for fifteen years.

Tammany Hall

A social club that became the Democratic party's political machine in New York City. Into the 1920s, Tammany Hall ran New York City except for brief interludes when reformers won elections by protesting Tammany's corruption.

Tenochtitlán

Capital of the Aztec empire, a large, sophisticated, and well-defended city surrounded by Lake Texcoco in the valley of Mexico, the site of present-day Mexico City. The Aztecs called themselves the Mexica.

Tenskwatawa (1770?–1834?)

Also known as "The Prophet," a Shawnee visionary, brother to the great chief Tecumseh, who, with great success, preached a revival of traditional Indian ways to the Indians of the Northwest Territory. He founded "Orphet's Town," or Tippecanoe, in northern Indiana. In 1811, ignoring the instructions of the absent Tecumseh, he ordered an attack on a force led by William Henry Harrison that ended in a devastating defeat for the Indians and the destruction of Tippecanoe. The Prophet moved to Missouri and Kansas and continued to preach his message with less success.

The Burr Conspiracy
In 1805 and 1806 Aaron Burr, his political career ruined, traveled down the Mississippi with an Irish adventurer from Ohio, meeting confidentially with several prominent westerners, including Andrew Jackson of Tennessee and, in New Orleans, the governor of the Louisiana Territory, James Wilkinson. Most historians suspect he planned to establish a new country in Mexican Texas, possibly including parts of Louisiana. Wilkinson accused him of treason; Burr was tried but acquitted.

The Hundred Days
Term coined in the summer of 1933 for the first three and a half months of the Roosevelt administration, when FDR deluged Congress with bills to relieve those hit hardest by the Depression, to stimulate economic recovery, and to reform the abuses the New Dealers believed caused the Great Depression.

The Influence of Sea Power upon History
A book by American navy captain (later admiral) Alfred T. Mahan, published in 1890. Mahan wrote that no nation could be great unless it had an industrious foreign trade protected by a powerful navy. His persuasiveness made the book a best seller and influential for many years on European leaders like the emperor of Germany and Winston Churchill of Great Britain as well as on Americans. Mahan's theories convinced Congress to build a modern navy; the need of steam-powered ships for coaling stations throughout the world contributed to the American turn to imperialism during the 1890s.

The Man in the Gray Flannel Suit
Novel of 1955 by Sloan Wilson that, despite its critique of suburban life and middle-class ambition to accumulate material goods, was a best seller among people like the characters of the novel. Its popularity indicated to some social critics that apparently placid Americans were discontented with their lot.

The Man Nobody Knows
Best-selling book by advertising company executive Bruce Barton, published in 1925. It depicted Jesus as a business executive (and advertising man). Rather than being condemned as blasphemous, Barton's bizarre portrayal of Jesus was accepted in the business culture of the Coolidge era.

The Wilderness
Heavily wooded country west of Chancellorsville, Virginia, where General Grant began his assault on Richmond in early May 1864; 30,000 soldiers were killed, wounded, or captured in two days, 18,000 of them Union troops.

three-fifths compromise
The most artificially contrived provision of the Constitution of 1787, it averted a northern state–southern state split by providing that slaves (numerous only in the South) be counted as three-fifths of a person in the apportionment of each state's tax burden and representation in Congress.

Tidewater
Land bordering the broad, slow-moving tidal rivers of the Chesapeake Bay; the most valuable land in Virginia and Maryland because at high tide seagoing ships could tie up directly at plantations. The "Tidewater aristocracy" became Virginia's ruling class.

time zones
A part of everyone's life today, the four times zones of the contiguous United States were proposed in 1870 and adopted by the federal government in 1883. Previously, time was a local concern, set by town and city governments. Unsurprisingly, even in adjacent cities, "the right time" was different. Once railroads, which ran "by the clock," extended 1,000 miles and more, efficiency and safety demanded uniform time nationally.

"Tippecanoe and Tyler Too"
The Whigs' euphonious campaign slogan in 1840. Tippecanoe referred to William Henry Harrison's victory over the Indians of the Old Northwest almost thirty years previously. The Whigs unembarrassingly imitated the Democrats' celebration of Jackson as the "hero of New Orleans." Vice presidential candidate John Tyler had little following outside Virginia, but "Tyler Too" rhymed nicely. (Tippecanoe and Tyler Too did not carry Virginia.)

Townshend Duties
Parliamentary taxes on various colonial luxury imports. All were abolished after an effective colonial boycott except the duty on tea.

Treaty of Ghent (1814)
Anglo–American treaty ending the War of 1812, negotiated in Ghent (now Belgium) by John Quincy Adams, Albert Gallatin, Henry Clay, and several other commissioners. The talks dragged on because the British insisted on establishing an Indian buffer state between the United States and Canada. In the end, both sides agreed to end the war on the status quo antebellum—that is, with nothing changed from what it had been before the war.

Treaty of San Lorenzo (Pinckney's Treaty)
Treaty with Spain in 1795. Spain gave up claims to disputed territory (most of present-day Alabama and Mississippi) and, more important at the time, agreed to allow Americans in the West to export their crops through New Orleans, then a Spanish city.

Treaty of Washington (1921)
Post–World War I naval disarmament treaty engineered by Secretary of State Charles Evans Hughes. The United States, Great Britain, Japan, France, and Italy agreed to limit the size of their navies in proportion to their defensive needs.

trickle down
Phrase coined by Andrew Mellon, secretary of the treasury during the 1920s, to justify cutting taxes for the rich and increasing the tax burden on the middle and working classes. When the wealthy invested their windfalls, Mellon argued, prosperity would "trickle down" to all.

Truman Doctrine
The government's policy to resist Soviet-backed attempts to overthrow anti-Communist governments with massive financial and military aid.

Twain, Mark (Samuel Langhorne Clemens, 1835–1910)
Probably the single most popular American writer of the late nineteenth century, best known for The Adventures of Huckleberry Finn, simultaneously a boy's adventure story, a critique of racism, and a satire of antebellum southerners. Twain was a prolific writer for newspapers and magazines as well as in books; he was also a successful and hilarious lecturer in great demand in Europe as well as at home.

Twelfth Amendment (1804)
After the original method of electing the president and vice president resulted in a president and vice president of different political parties in 1796, and, in 1800, a tie that gave the choice of president to the defeated political party, it was clear that the Constitution needed to be amended. The Twelfth Amendment provided that presidential electors separately designate their choice for president and their choice for vice president, a system that is still in effect.

U.S. English
A propaganda organization and political lobby of the 1990s dedicated to winning a constitutional amendment stating that English was the official language of the United States. Members of the

organization feared that the concentration of Spanish-speaking immigrants in the Southwest would result in the loss of the politically and culturally unifying power of a single national language.

Uncle Tom's Cabin
Novel by Harriet Beecher Stowe, published in 1852. It was undoubtedly the most effective antislavery propaganda ever published. "Uncle Tom" is a kindly, religious slave who, in being passed from owner to owner, experiences both the worst and the best of southern slave owners. Stowe based his experiences on actual events she gleaned from newspapers. When assailed by southerners for distorting reality, she published a "key" to her novel, containing references documenting every significant event in the book.

underground railroad
Informal term for networks of white and black abolitionists in the northern states who helped fugitive slaves win their freedom by hiding them from authorities; providing food, shelter, and money; and passing them on to the next "conductor" on the line. Few conductors were able to stay on the job for many years because once they were identified, they were harassed by officials and professional slave catchers.

"unrestricted submarine warfare"
Name given to Germany's total exploitation of the U-boat, a weapon on which it held a monopoly. It meant attacking, without warning, all ships of every type engaged in trade with Great Britain. Because it violated the American principle of complete freedom of the seas for neutral vessels, Germany's resumption of the policy as of February 1, 1916, ensured American intervention on the side of the Allies.

Valentine's Day Massacre
The February 1929 murder of seven rival gang members by gunmen employed by Chicago bootlegger Al Capone. Although there had been hundreds of "gangland murders" in Chicago, the massacre aroused so much anger that authorities became much more serious in their attempts to bring Capone down.

vertical integration
A means of dominating an industry, used most famously by steelmaker Andrew Carnegie; it involved getting control of sufficient sources of raw materials to provide for a company's needs (in Carnegie's case, iron and coal mines) and transportation (Great Lakes ore boats and a railroad from Lake Erie to the Carnegie mill near Pittsburgh). Through cost cutting at every step of the business, Carnegie's selling price was far lower than that of

competitors who dealt with independent mines and railroads.

Vesey, Denmark (1767?–1822)
A free black carpenter and Methodist preacher in Charleston, Vesey organized an abortive slave rebellion in 1822. He had been a seaman as a boy and intended for the rebel slaves to seize ships and sail for Haiti. An informer betrayed the conspiracy, and Vesey and other ringleaders were hanged.

Vespucci, Amerigo (1451–1512)
Italian explorer who made two of the earliest European voyages to the Western Hemisphere (possibly several more). He was first to recognize that the lands Columbus discovered were not "the Indies" but were a "New World," previously unknown to Europe. A German mapmaker mistakenly believed Vespucci had discovered this New World and named it "America," the Latin form of his name.

vice-admiralty courts
Courts originally restricted to special litigations in which decisions were rendered by judges without juries. George Grenville tried to transfer the cases of accused violators of the Sugar Act and Stamp Act to these courts because colonial juries, especially in smuggling cases in New England, frequently ignored overwhelming evidence of guilt and acquitted their neighbors.

victory gardens
Small family gardens, dubbed "victory gardens" when the federal government promoted them as a contribution to the war effort during World War II. By 1945, 20.5 million families were tending them; in that year between 30 and 40 percent of the nation's vegetable production was home-grown.

Vietnamization
President Nixon's policy of replacing American combat troops in Vietnam with South Vietnamese troops. In part, his program was designed to halt the increasing opposition to the war among working people who were sustaining the high casualties of the war.

Villa, Pancho (1877–1923)
The name under which Doroteo Arango, a Mexican revolutionary soldier and sometimes bandit, was first romanticized, then execrated in the United States. Villa's calculated murder of American engineers and raid of Columbus, New Mexico, a border town, prompted Woodrow Wilson to send the U.S. Army to find and capture him in 1916. Villa eluded the expedition.

Virginia Dynasty
Four of the first five presidents were Virginians; thus, sometimes sarcastically,

politicians alluded to a dynastic succession in the presidency. Even in 1824 two of the four candidates for the presidency, Crawford and Clay, were Virginia-born.

virtual representation
British constitutional principle that members of the House of Commons represented not only the people of the district from which they were elected, but all British subjects.

Wade, Benjamin F. (1800–1878)
Republican senator from Ohio; he was one of the leaders of the radical Republicans who demanded that southern rebels be harshly punished at war's end.

Wade–Davis Bill
Reconstruction plan enacted by Congress in July 1864 to counter Lincoln's proclamation setting terms by which the former Confederate states would be readmitted to the Union. It differed from Lincoln's plan in requiring 50 percent rather than 10 percent of a state's voters to take an oath of loyalty to the Union; and Congress, not the president, would direct the Reconstruction process.

"War Hawks"
Ultranationalistic members of the Congress, mostly westerners and southerners, all under 40 and Jefferson Republicans, many just elected to Congress for the first time, whose calls for war against Britain to defend American honor pressured President Madison in 1812 into asking for a declaration of war that he had worked to avoid.

War Industries Board
World War I superagency headed by financier Bernard Baruch and entrusted with coordinating production of industries vital to the war effort.

Watergate
Name of a luxury apartment and office complex in Washington where, in 1972, the Democratic party had its headquarters. When burglars in the office were arrested, a long, complex sequence of revelations tied the crime and an attempt to cover it up to President Nixon. The "Watergate scandal" was the cause of his disgrace and resignation in 1974.

Wayne, "Mad Anthony" (1745–1796)
Got his nickname because of his reckless bravery during the Revolution when he fought at Quebec, Brandywine—he captured Stony Point on the Hudson River, a major victory over the British—and in the South against Cornwallis. In 1794 he defeated the twice victorious Indians of the Northwest Territory at the Battle of Fallen Timbers.

Webster, Daniel (1782–1852)
Massachusetts Whig politician, usually considered the greatest orator in an age of

great orators. In a Senate debate with Robert Hayne over the doctrine of nullification in 1830, Webster made an eloquent plea for the Union against state sovereignty as the wellspring of American liberty.

"wets"
The name applied during the 1920s to people who opposed Prohibition and called for its repeal. Supporters of Prohibition were known as "drys."

Whiskey Rebellion
Uprising of farmers in western Pennsylvania protesting the federal excise tax of 7 cents on a gallon of whiskey, practically their only export to the East. Determined to demonstrate the authority of the federal government, Washington led a large army toward the rebellious area to suppress the rebels. The rebellion fell apart before force was necessary.

Whitman, Marcus and Narcissa
(1802–1847) and (1808–1847)
Presbyterian missionaries in the Oregon Country; along with another couple, the Whitmans went overland to the Oregon Country in 1836. (The two wives were the first women to cross the North American continent since Sacajawea with the Lewis and Clark party.) The Whitmans' mission at Walla Walla was spectacularly unsuccessful, in part because of the couple's disdainful attitude toward the Indian culture. When a measles epidemic devastated the local Indians in 1847, they murdered the Whitmans and twelve other whites.

Williams, Roger (1603?–1683)
A learned, cantankerous minister, an early emigrant to Massachusetts Bay who quarreled with the governors of the colony, was banished, and founded the town of Providence, which became the core of the Rhode Island colony. Williams insisted that religious belief was an individual choice and responsibility; Rhode Island tolerated all forms of worship.

Wilmot Proviso
A rider attached to an army appropriations bill in 1846, at the beginning of the war with Mexico, by Congressman David Wilmot, providing that "neither slavery nor involuntary servitude shall ever exist" in any lands taken from Mexico. The House of Representatives approved it and attached the Wilmot Proviso to fifty bills during and after the war. Each time, the proviso was removed in the Senate. The Wilmot Proviso inspired the formation of the Free Soil party.

Winthrop, John (1588–1649)
Prominent English Puritan who elected to emigrate to America rather than live in a country he believed sinful and a target of divine wrath. He was governor of the Massachusetts Bay colony ten of the colony's first twenty years and a major force in shaping the colony's character.

Wirt, William (1772–1834)
One of the best lawyers of his era, he argued 174 cases before the Supreme Court. Attorney general between 1817 and 1829, he strengthened the office. His patriotic and adulatory biography of Patrick Henry, published in 1817, made a Revolutionary War hero of the orator.

Wisconsin idea
The name given to the close partnership between the state government and state university in Wisconsin, initiated by the progressive Republican governor Robert M. La Follette early in the twentieth century. For example, the university's agricultural school not only educated future farmers but provided agents to visit farmers and advise them on agricultural problems.

WMD
Weapons of mass destruction. George W. Bush's claim that Saddam Hussein possessed chemical, biological, and possibly nuclear weapons with which he planned to launch a massive terrorist war was his chief justification for invading Iraq. No WMD were found after a year of searching. The revelation of the poor intelligence on which the president acted (or his outright lie) contributed to the sharp drop in his popularity in mid-2005.

Wolfe, General James (1727–1759)
British general who commanded the successful capture of Quebec in 1759. He was killed in the battle.

Worcester* v. *Georgia (1832)
When the state of Georgia arrested a Congregationalist minister for living among the Cherokee Indians without a state license to do so, the minister sued on the grounds that Georgia laws did not apply to Cherokee treaty lands. By a 5–1 vote, the Supreme Court found in Worcester's favor: the Cherokee nation's treaty with the United States took precedence over state laws. Georgia ignored the decision, and President Jackson refused to enforce the Court's decision.

Works Progress Administration (WPA)
The New Deal's broadest jobs program. The WPA not only provided money for construction projects but hired unemployed writers, scholars, actors, painters, and sculptors. Popular with the intelligentsia, the WPA was vilified by conservatives because many of its productions had a leftist political slant.

X, Y, Z Affair, the
X, Y, and Z were code names for three French diplomats who told Americans seeking to negotiate a treaty that talks could begin only after the United States made a loan to France and paid a large bribe to the French foreign minister. Indignation in the United States made President Adams briefly popular as he prepared to defend the nation's honor in a war with the French.

Zimmerman telegram
Diplomatic note wired to Mexico by German Foreign Minister Arthur Zimmerman, proposing that if the United States declared war on Germany, Mexico should attack the United States to keep the American army home. At the end of the war, Mexico would be rewarded by the return of the "lost provinces" of New Mexico and Arizona. The telegram was intercepted by the British and divulged to the United States to encourage American intervention in the war.

Photo Credits

Chapter 25

National Archives, 408; National Archives, 409; North Wind Picture Archives, 412; The Valentine Museum, 414; North Wind Picture Archives, 415; The Granger Collection, New York, 419; Culver Pictures, Inc., 421.

Chapter 26

University of Hartford Collection, 424; Harcourt Picture Collection, 425; © Bettmann/Corbis, 428; The Smithsonian Institution, Negative #46685D, 429; Culver Pictures, Inc., 434; University of Hartford Collection, 435; © Bettmann/Corbis, 436; Culver Pictures, Inc., 439.

Chapter 27

Southern Pacific Transporation Company. #X462, 442; University of Oregon Library. #CN312, 445; U.S. Dept. of the Interior, National Park Service, Edison National Historic Site. Photo taken by Matthew Brady, 1878, 446; The Granger Collection, New York, 449; Southern Pacific Transporation Company. #X462, 454; From the Collections of the Library of Congress, 455; The Granger Collection, New York, 458.

Chapter 28

Courtesy of The New-York Historical Society, New York City, 461; Courtesy of The New-York Historical Society, New York City, 463; North Wind Picture Archives, 464; © Corbis, 467; The Granger Collection, New York, 469; Keystone-Mast Collection, UCR/California Museum of Photography. University of California, Riverside, 470; Photograph by Byron. The Byron Collction, Museum of the City of New York, 471; The Granger Collection, New York, 472.

Chapter 29

Reproduced from the Collections of the Library of Congress, 475; Culver Pictures, Inc., 476; Museum of the City of New York., #RiisEE, photograph by Lewis Hine. The Jacob A. Riis Collections, 478; Culver Pictures, Inc., 479; Reproduced from the Collections of the Library of Congress, 481; AP/Wide World Photos, 486; From the collections of the Kam Wah Chung Museum, Oregon Parks & Recreation Department, 488.

Chapter 30

© Bettmann/Corbis, 492; Museum of the City of New York, 493; Illustrated London News, 497; Keystone-Mast Collection, UCR/California Museum of Photography. University of California, Riverside, 498; Reproduced from the Collections of the Library of Congress, 499 L; Reproduced from the Collections of the Library of

Congress, 499 R; Chicago Historical Society, 502; © Bettmann/ Corbis, 504.

Chapter 31

Reproduced from the Collections of the Library of Congress, 506; Courtesy of the American Museum of Natural History, New York. neg #127375, 509; Smithsonian Institution, Bureau of American Ethnology, 512; Reproduced from the Collections of the Library of Congress, 514; Erwin E. Smith Collection of the Library of Congress on deposit at the Amon Carter Museum, Fort Worth, 515; © Bettmann/Corbis, 521; Reproduced from the Collections of the Library of Congress, 520.

Chapter 32

Reproduced from the Collections of the Library of Congress, 523; Nebraska State Historical Society Photograph Collections, 526; Reproduced from the Collections of the Library of Congress, 529; The Granger Collection, New York, 531; © Bettmann/ Corbis, 533; The Kansas State Historical Society Topeka, Kansas/FK2.2 H1893*23, 535.

Chapter 33

Reproduced from the Collections of the Library of Congress, 539; Reproduced from the Collections of the Library of Congress, 540; The Granger Collection, New York, 544; Reproduced from the Collections of the Library of Congress, 547; The Granger Collection, New York, 548; Hawaii State Archives, 552; © Bettmann/UPI/Corbis, 555.

Chapter 34

Reproduced from the Collections of the Library of Congress, 558; Reproduced from the Collections of the Library of Congress, 559; Culver Pictures, 562; Reproduced from the Collections of the Library of Congress, 563; Reproduced from the Collections of the Library of Congress, 565; © Collection of The New-York Historical Society, 570; © Bettmann/ Corbis, 571; Museum of the City of New York, 568.

Chapter 35

Reproduced from the Collections of the Library of Congress, 575; The Granger Collection, New York, 577; The Smithsonian Institution, Neg. #73628, 578; © UPI/Bettmann/Corbis, 580; Providence Public Library, 583; Reproduced from the Collections of the Library of Congress, 586; #2730C75, Tamiment Library, New York University, 587.

Chapter 36

Reproduced from the Collections of the Library of Congress, 590; North Wind

Picture Archives, 592; Reproduced from the Collections of the Library of Congress, 594; The Smithsonian Institution, 597; The Granger Collection, New York, 599; Culver Pictures, 601.

Chapter 37

Reproduced from the Collections of the Library of Congress, 602; © Bettmann/ Corbis, 605; © Bettmann-UPI/Corbis, 610; The New York Public Library, 613; Reproduced from the Collections of the Library of Congress, 614; The Granger Collection, New York, 615; From the Collections of Henry Ford Museum & Greenfield Village, 611.

Chapter 38

The National Archives, #11-SC-35757, 619; The National Archives. #165-WW-127-8, 622; Photographs and Prints Division, Schomburg Center for Research in Black Culture, New York Public Library, Astor, Lenox and Tilden Foundations, 623; The National Archives, #11-SC-35757, 624; U.S. Signal Corps photo #111-SC8523 in the National Archives, 627; U.S. Army Photo, #158964, 631; Brown Brothers, 633; National Archives #165-WW-269.c-7, 628.

Chapter 39

© UPI/Bettmann/Corbis, 638; Library & Archives Division, Historical Society of Western Pennsylvania, Pittsburg, Pa, 639; © UPI/Bettmann/Corbis, 640; The Granger Collection, New York, 642; © UPI/ Bettmann/Corbis, 644; AP/Wide World Photos, 648.

Chapter 40

Courtesy of Sears, Roebuck & Company, 651; Brown Brothers, 652; National Archives, 654; Culver Pictures, Inc., 656; Courtesy of Sears, Roebuck & Company, 658; From the Collections of the Library of Congress, 662; © UPI/Bettmann/ Corbis, 663.

Chapter 41

Reproduced from the Collections of the Library of Congress, 665; © Radio Times Hulton Picture Library, London. Liaison Agency, Inc./Getty Images, 666; © UPI-Bettmann/Corbis, 667; © Bettmann/ Corbis, 669; © UPI-Bettmann/Corbis, 670; © Brown Brothers, 674; Reproduced from the Collections of the Library of Congress, 677.

Chapter 42

© Bettmann/Corbis, 679; Franklin D. Roosevelt Library/The New Yorker, 680; AP/Wide World Photos, 682; © Bettmann/ Corbis, 683; © Bettmann/Corbis, 685;

Index